4/17 261 - 88
4/22 788 - 818
4/24 823 - 40, 845 - 54

Land Use Controls

Land Use Controls

Cases and Materials

Third Edition

Robert C. Ellickson
Walter E. Meyer Professor
of Property and Urban Law
Yale University

Vicki L. Been
Elihu Root Professor of Law
New York University

PUBLISHERS

111 Eighth Avenue, New York, NY 10011
www.aspenpublishers.com

© 2005 Aspen Publishers, Inc.
a Wolters Kluwer business
www.aspenpublishers.com

Printed in the United States of America.

2 3 4 5 6 7 8 9 0

ISBN 0-7355-3996-0

Library of Congress Cataloging-in-Publication Data

Ellickson, Robert C.
    Land use controls : cases and materials / Robert C. Ellickson,
Vicki L. Been. — 3rd ed.
        p. cm.
    Includes index.
    ISBN 0-7355-3996-0 (hardcover : alk. paper)   1. Land use—Law and
legislation—United States—Cases.   I. Been, Vicki L., 1956- II. Title.

    KF5698.A4E4 2005
    346.7304'5–dc22   2005017994

About Aspen Publishers

Aspen Publishers, headquartered in New York City, is a leading information provider for attorneys, business professionals, and law students. Written by preeminent authorities, our products consist of analytical and practical information covering both U.S. and international topics. We publish in the full range of formats, including updated manuals, books, periodicals, CDs, and online products.

Our proprietary content is complemented by 2,500 legal databases, containing over 11 million documents, available through our Loislaw division. Aspen Publishers also offers a wide range of topical legal and business databases linked to Loislaw's primary material. Our mission is to provide accurate, timely, and authoritative content in easily accessible formats, supported by unmatched customer care.

To order any Aspen Publishers title, go to *www.aspenpublishers.com* or call 1-800-638-8437.

To reinstate your manual update service, call 1-800-638-8437.

For more information on Loislaw products, go to *www.loislaw.com* or call 1-800-364-2512.

For Customer Care issues, e-mail *CustomerCare@aspenpublishers.com*; call 1-800-234-1660; or fax 1-800-901-9075.

Aspen Publishers
a Wolters Kluwer business

Summary of Contents

Table of Contents   *xiii*
Preface   *xxix*
Acknowledgments   *xxxi*

Chapter One

The Land Development Process   1

A.   The Setting   1
B.   The Land Development Industry   16
C.   The Product   24
D.   The Regulators: Local Governments   29

Chapter Two

Markets and Planners: An Initial Look at Relative
Institutional Competence   31

A.   Economic Analysis of Land Use Conflicts   32
B.   Competing Conceptions of Local Politics   46
C.   Planning, Planners, Plans   50

Chapter Three

Zoning and the Rights of Landowners and Developers   73

A.   The Evolution of Zoning   74
B.   Landowners' and Developers' Constitutional Rights As Constraints
       on Inefficient Zoning Measures   94

C. Landowners' and Developers' Constitutional Rights as Constraints
    on Zoning Measures That Impose Unfair Burdens   125
D. Constraints on Zoning Measures That Threaten Civil Liberties   209
E. Procedural and Remedial Aspects of Landowners' and Developers'
    Constitutional Rights   233
F. Legislative Initiatives to Increase Landowners' and Developers' Rights   274

Chapter Four

Zoning Changes and the Rights of Neighbors   283

A. Constraints on Zoning Changes by Administrative Bodies   286
B. Constraints on Zoning Changes by Legislative Bodies   302
C. The Procedural Rights of Developers and Their Neighbors   352
D. Constraints on Land Use Decisions by Neighbors   393

Chapter Five

Subdivision Regulations, Building Codes, Aesthetic Controls   411

A. Subdivision Regulations   411
B. Assuring the Quality of Construction: Building Codes   444
C. Aesthetic Regulation   469
D. Streamlining the Regulatory Process   505

Chapter Six

Alternatives to Public Regulation: Nuisance Law, Fees
and Rewards, Covenants   511

A. The Common Law Rights of Neighbors: Nuisance Law   511
B. Beneficence Law (the Converse of Nuisance Law)   539
C. Covenants Among Neighbors   550
D. Residential Community Associations   582
E. Land Use in the Absence of Zoning   607

Chapter Seven

Financing the Urban Infrastructure   615

A. Special Assessments   619
B. Development Exactions   634
C. Municipal Duties to Provide Services   679
D. Easing the Fiscal Pressure on Municipalities   689

Chapter Eight

Discriminatory Land Use Controls   691

A. Discrimination Against Racial and Ethnic Minorities   692
B. Discrimination Against the Poor   709

C.   Discrimination Against Unconventional Households   710
D.   Discrimination Against People with Disabilities   716

Chapter Nine

The Regional Obligations of Municipalities   731

A.   Obligations to Consider the Negative Spillover Effects of Uses
       Located Near Municipal Borders   733
B.   Obligations to Consider Regional Needs for Locally Undesirable
       Land Uses   740
C.   Obligations to Allow (or Provide) Low- and Moderate-Income Housing   760
D.   Municipal Obligations to Accommodate Pressures for Regional Growth   788

Chapter Ten

Government as Landowner, Developer, and Financier   819

A.   Government as Landowner   820
B.   Government as Land Assembler: Eminent Domain   823
C.   Government as Developer   861
D.   Government as Financier   868

Table of Cases   893
Author Index   905
Subject Index   917

Table of Contents

Preface   *xxix*
Acknowledgments   *xxxi*

Chapter One

The Land Development Process   1

A.   The Setting   1
   1.   Population Trends   1
       a.   National Population Growth   1
       b.   Migration Between Regions   2
            Edward L. Glaeser & Jesse M. Shapiro, City Growth   2
       c.   Suburbanization   5
            Peter Mieszkowski & Edwin S. Mills, The Causes of
               Metropolitan Suburbanization   6
            Note on Population Movement Within Metropolitan Areas   9
            Sheryll D. Cashin, Middle-Class Black Suburbs and the
               State of Integration   11
            Note on Housing Segregation   12
   2.   The Supply of Land   13
            William A. Fischel, The Economics of Zoning Laws   13
            Note on Land and Landowners   14
B.   The Land Development Industry   16
            President's Committee on Urban Housing, A Decent Home   16
            Note on Developers and Homebuilders   18
            Sherman J. Maisel, Real Estate Finance   20
            Note on Financing Land Development   23
C.   The Product   24
   1.   Housing and Other Structures   24
       a.   The Housing Stock   24

        b. The Pace of New Construction   26
        c. Housing Prices   27
D. The Regulators: Local Governments   29

Chapter Two

Markets and Planners: An Initial Look at Relative
Institutional Competence   **31**

A. Economic Analysis of Land Use Conflicts   32
    1. The Potential of Decentralized Decisionmaking   32
            Charles E. Lindblom, The Intelligence of Democracy   32
            Note on Coordination from Below   34
    2. The Possibility of Coasian Bargaining   34
            Neil K. Komesar, Housing, Zoning, and the Public Interest 34
            Note on the Coase Theorem and Bargaining Among Neighbors 38
            Note on Possible Economic Rationales for Zoning   40
    3. Evidence of Externalities   41
            William A. Fischel, The Economics of Zoning Laws   41
            Note on Research on Externalities   43
B. Competing Conceptions of Local Politics   46
            William A. Fischel, The Homevoter Hypothesis   46
            Frank I. Michelman, Political Markets and Community
                Self-Determination   47
            Note on Conceptions of Local Government   48
C. Planning, Planners, Plans   50
    1. The Planning Process   51
        a. Planning Theory   52
            American Planning Association, Policies and Commentary 53
            Note on Planning Theory   55
        b. The Planning Profession   55
            Anthony J. Catanese & W. Paul Farmer, Personality,
                Politics, and Planning   55
            Note on the Planning Profession   57
    2. The Comprehensive Plan   58
        a. State Statutes That Require a Local Government to Adopt a Plan 58
        b. State Regulation of the Elements of a Municipality's Plan 59
            Florida Stat. ch. 163.3177   60
            South Carolina Code Ann. §6-29-510   61
        c. Sample Plans   62
            American Law Institute, Model Land Development Code   62
            Edward J. Kaiser & David R. Godschalk, Twentieth Century
                Land Use Planning   63
            Note on the Contents of Comprehensive Plans   63
    3. Criticisms of Comprehensive Planning   65
        a. Can Planners Gather and Process the Pertinent Information? 65
            Lon L. Fuller, Freedom—A Suggested Analysis   65
            John Rahenkamp, Land Use Management   66
            Charles E. Lindblom, The Science of "Muddling Through" 67

		Friedrich A. Hayek, *The Road to Serfdom*	68
		Note on Planners' Weighty Informational Requirements and Limited Cognitive Capacities	68
	b.	Do Planners Have Appropriate Incentives?	69
	c.	Can Planning Be Reconciled with Democracy?	69
		American Law Institute, *Model Land Development Code*	69
		James C. Scott, *Seeing Like a State*	70
		Note on Planning and Democracy	70

Chapter Three

Zoning and the Rights of Landowners and Developers   73

A.	The Evolution of Zoning	74
	1. Zoning Before *Euclid*	74
	a. Early Regulatory Efforts	74
	2. The *Euclid* Decision	76
	Village of Euclid v. Ambler Realty Co.	76
	Note on *Euclid*	81
	3. The Modern Zoning Ordinance	86
	Introductory Note on Post-Euclidean Zoning Techniques	86
	Note on Sanctions Imposed on Violators of Local Land Use Regulations	92
B.	Landowners' and Developers' Constitutional Rights As Constraints on Inefficient Zoning Measures	94
	1. The Substantive Due Process Challenge: Judicial Review of the "Reasonableness" of Legislative Line-Drawing Through Cost/Benefit Analysis	95
	a. The Nature of the Substantive Due Process Inquiry	96
	Nectow v. City of Cambridge	96
	b. The Role of Federal Courts in Land Use Cases	98
	Coniston Corp. v. Village of Hoffman Estates	99
	Note on Substantive Due Process Challenges in the Federal Courts	102
	c. The Role of State Courts in Land Use Cases	104
	Twigg v. County of Will	104
	Cormier v. County of San Luis Obispo	107
	Note on State Court Review of the Reasonableness of Zoning Restrictions	110
	2. Constraints on the Use of Zoning to Limit Competition	112
	a. The Substantive Due Process Challenge	112
	Sprenger, Grubb & Associates, Inc. v. City of Hailey	112
	Note on Legitimate Purposes for the Exercise of Zoning Power	114
	Note on Determining Legislative Motivation	115
	Note on Zoning Techniques That Raise a Red Flag About Anticompetitive Purposes	117
	b. Challenges Under the Federal Antitrust Laws	119
	City of Columbia v. Omni Outdoor Advertising, Inc.	119
	Note on the Application of Antitrust Laws to Zoning	123

C. Landowners' and Developers' Constitutional Rights as Constraints on
    Zoning Measures That Impose Unfair Burdens   125
    1. Discriminatory Line Drawing   126
            Layne v. Zoning Board of Adjustment   126
            Note on Equal Protection   128
    2. Discrimination Against a Particular Landowner   129
            Village of Willowbrook v. Olech   129
            Note on *Olech* and "Class of One" Challenges   130
    3. Arbitrary Wealth Redistributions: Zoning for Purely Fiscal Purposes   133
            Note on Zoning for Fiscal Purposes   133
    4. Confiscatory Zoning Classifications (The Takings Issue)   134
        a. The Original Focus on Physical Takings   134
                William Michael Treanor, The Original Understanding of
                    the Takings Clause and the Political Process   134
                Mugler v. Kansas   136
                Note on the Original Focus of the Takings Clause   137
        b. Going Too Far   140
                Pennsylvania Coal Co. v. Mahon   140
                Note on *Pennsylvania Coal*   142
        c. Justifications for the Compensation Requirement   145
                Frank I. Michelman, Property, Utility, and Fairness   146
                Note on Utilitarian Theories of Compensation   147
                Note on Compensation as Cost Internalization   149
                Lawrence Blume & Daniel L. Rubinfeld,
                    Compensation for Takings   151
                Note on Using Compensation to Reduce Risk   152
                William Michael Treanor, The Original Understanding
                    of the Takings Clause and the Political Process   154
                Note on Political Process Failure Theories   156
        d. The Ad Hoc Balancing Test   158
                Penn Central Transportation Co. v. City of New York   158
                Note on *Penn Central*   163
                Note on Transferable Development Rights   165
        e. Per Se Takings — Exceptions to *Penn Central*   167
                Note on the Per Se Rule Against Permanent Physical
                    Occupations   168
                Lucas v. South Carolina Coastal Council   169
                Note on *Lucas*   177
        f. Tensions Between *Penn Central* and the Per Se Rules of
                Loretto and *Lucas*   180
                Palazzolo v. Rhode Island   180
                Note on the Notice Question   184
                *Tahoe-Sierra Preservation Council, Inc. v. Tahoe Regional
                    Planning Agency*   185
                Note on the Denominator Problem   192
                Lingle v. Chevron U.S.A. Inc.   193
                Note on the Relationship Between the Takings Clause and
                    the Due Process Clause   196
        g. The Special Problem of Nonconforming Uses and Vested Rights   197
                Village of Valatie v. Smith   197

	Note on Nonconforming Uses	199
	Valley View Industrial Park v. City of Redmond	202
	Note on Vested Rights	206
D.	Constraints on Zoning Measures That Threaten Civil Liberties	209
	1. Freedom of Religion	209
	Congregation Kol Ami v. Abington Township	210
	Note on the Free Exercise of Religion	218
	2. Freedom of Speech	220
	City of Renton v. Playtime Theatres, Inc.	220
	City of Los Angeles v. Alameda Books, Inc.	222
	Note on Adult Entertainment	227
	3. Other Fundamental Rights	231
E.	Procedural and Remedial Aspects of Landowners' and Developers' Constitutional Rights	233
	1. Jurisdiction	233
	2. Ripeness	234
	Williamson County Regional Planning Commission v. Hamilton Bank	234
	Note on When the Ripeness Requirements Apply	239
	Note on the "Final Determination" Requirement	240
	Note on the "State Remedies" Requirement	244
	San Remo Hotel, L.P. v. City & County of San Francisco	245
	Note on *Williamson County* and Issue or Claim Preclusion	250
	3. Abstention	251
	Sinclair Oil Corp. v. County of Santa Barbara	251
	Note on Abstention	253
	4. Remedies	256
	Introductory Note on the "Compensation" Question	256
	First English Evangelical Lutheran Church of Glendale v. County of Los Angeles	258
	Note on *First English*	264
	Wheeler v. City of Pleasant Grove (Wheeler III)	267
	Note on Determining Compensation for Temporary Regulatory Takings	269
F.	Legislative Initiatives to Increase Landowners' and Developers' Rights	274
	Bert J. Harris, Jr., Private Property Rights Protection Act	276
	Oregon Initiative Measure No. 37	278
	Note on Takings Statutes	279

Chapter Four

Zoning Changes and the Rights of Neighbors	**283**

	Background Note on Government Structures	284
	Note on Problems Posed by Overlapping Government Structures	285
A.	Constraints on Zoning Changes by Administrative Bodies	286
	1. Variances	286
	Matthew v. Smith	286
	Note on Variances	289

			Note on the "Steady Leak"	294
			Eric H. Steele, Participation and Rules — The Functions of Zoning	295
	2.		Special Exceptions (Conditional Uses)	296
			Gladden v. District of Columbia Board of Zoning Adjustment	296
			Note on Special Exceptions/Conditional Uses	299
B.			Constraints on Zoning Changes by Legislative Bodies	302
			Note on Dealmaking	303
			Note on the Politics of the Rezoning Process	304
			Background Note on Corruption	308
	1.		Tempered Deference	309
		a.	Spot Zoning	309
			Griswold v. City of Homer	309
			Note on Spot Zoning	315
		b.	Absence of a "Change or Mistake"	317
		c.	"Contract" Zoning	318
			Judith Welch Wegner, Moving Toward the Bargaining Table	318
			Note on Judicial Resistance to Contract Zoning	319
			Chrismon v. Guilford County	322
			Note on the Erosion of the Prohibition on Contract Zoning	326
			Note on Judicial Review of Permitted Contract or Conditional Zoning	327
			Note on Cluster Zoning and Planned-Unit Developments	329
		d.	"Incentive" Zoning	331
			Municipal Art Society v. City of New York	332
			Note on Incentive Zoning	333
		e.	Zoning Without, or in Conflict with, Planning	336
			Haines v. City of Phoenix	337
			Note on Procedures and Standards for Determining Consistency	338
			Note on Barriers to Plan Amendments	340
	2.		Rejection of Deferential Review	341
			Snyder v. Board of County Commissioners	341
			Board of County Commissioners v. Snyder	346
			Note on *Snyder*	347
C.			The Procedural Rights of Developers and Their Neighbors	352
			Developments in the Law — Zoning	352
	1.		Fair Proceedings	353
			Korean Buddhist Dae Won Sa Temple of Hawaii v. Sullivan	353
			Note on What Process Is Due	358
	2.		Qualified Decisionmakers	360
			1000 Friends of Oregon v. Wasco County Court	360
			Note on Bias and the Appearance of Unfairness	364
	3.		Informed Decisionmakers: The Example of Environmental Impact Statements	368
			Note on the Justifications for EIS Requirements	369
		a.	When Is an EIS Required?	370
			Chinese Staff & Workers Association v. City of New York	370
			Note on When an EIS Is Required	374
			Note on Conditioned Negative Declarations	378

        b.   When Is an EIS Adequate?   380
           Laurel Heights Improvement Association v. Regents of the
              University of California   380
           Note on the Adequacy of an EIS   385
        c.   What If an EIS Identifies Adverse Impacts?   387
           Town of Henrietta v. Department of Environmental
              Conservation   387
           Note on the Substantive Impact of EIS Requirements   390
        d.   Assessment   391
  D.   Constraints on Land Use Decisions by Neighbors   393
     1.   Neighbors' Consent Requirements   393
          City of Chicago v. Stratton   393
          Note on "All Power to the Neighborhood"   394
          Cary v. City of Rapid City   396
          Note on Neighbors' Consent Requirements   398
     2.   Initiatives and Referenda   401
          M. Dane Waters, The Initiative and Referendum Almanac   401
          Buckeye Community Hope Foundation v. City of
            Cuyahoga Falls   401
          Note on the Legality of Ballot Box Zoning   403
          Note on the Merits of Plebiscites   405

Chapter Five

Subdivision Regulations, Building Codes, Aesthetic Controls	411

A.   Subdivision Regulations   411
     1.   Coordination of Street Layouts by Means of Official Maps   411
          In re Furman Street   412
          Note on Official Maps   415
     2.   Subdivision Regulation: Rationales and Standards   416
          New Jersey Stat. Ann. §40:55(D)-38   417
          Miles v. Planning Board of Millbury   418
          Note on Subdivision Standards   420
          Note on Street Layouts   421
     3.   The Chronology of a Subdivision   424
          The Saga of a Los Angeles Subdivision   424
     4.   The Vesting of Rights to Subdivide   430
          City of West Hollywood v. Beverly Towers, Inc.   430
          Note on Vesting of Rights to Subdivide   433
     5.   Grounds for Rejection of a Preliminary Map   435
          Richardson v. City of Little Rock Planning Commission   435
          Note on a Local Government's Discretion   437
     6.   Neighbors' Rights   438
          Lyman v. Planning Board of Winchester   438
          Note on Neighbors' Rights   440
     7.   Unregulated Subdivisions   441
B.   Assuring the Quality of Construction: Building Codes   444
          Stephen R. Seidel, Housing Costs and Government
            Regulations   444

	Note on Assurance of Building Quality Through Private Law	445
1.	The Maze of Building Codes	447
	Note on the Basics of Building Codes	447
	Note on Statutory Innovations in Building Regulation	448
2.	Code Administration	452
	a. The Dynamics of Building Regulation	452
	Stephen R. Seidel, *Housing Costs and Government Regulations*	454
	Note on the Dynamics of Building Regulation	454
	b. Remedying Lawless Code Enforcement by Government	456
	Commonwealth v. Collins	456
	Note on Remedies Against Building Departments	457
3.	Evaluation of Building Codes	458
	a. Asserted Inefficiencies	458
	Stephen R. Seidel, *Housing Costs and Government Regulations*	458
	Note on the Costs and Benefits of Codes	459
	b. Builders' Constitutional Challenges to Excessive Code Requirements	461
	Boise Cascade Corp. v. Gwinnett County	461
	Note on the Federal Constitution as a Limitation on Code Requirements	463
	State v. Cook	463
	Note on Licensing of Contractors	465
4.	Applying Standards Retrospectively: Housing Codes	465
	City of St. Louis v. Brune	465
	Note on Housing Codes	468
C.	Aesthetic Regulation	469
	City of Passaic v. Paterson Bill Posting, Advertising & Sign Painting Co.	470
	Stephen F. Williams, *Subjectivity, Expression, and Privacy*	470
	Note on Aesthetics	471
1.	Sign Controls	472
	Metromedia, Inc. v. City of San Diego [Cal. 1980]	472
	Note on Nonspeech Issues Posed by Billboard Regulation	476
	Metromedia, Inc. v. City of San Diego [U.S. 1981]	478
	Note on Commercial Signs and Free Speech	482
	City of Ladue v. Gilleo	484
	Note on Noncommercial Signs and Free Speech	488
2.	Architectural Review	489
	Anderson v. City of Issaquah	489
	Note on Architectural Review by Government	492
3.	Historic Preservation	494
	State by Powderly v. Erickson	494
	Note on Techniques of Historic Preservation	496
	Rector of St. Bartholomew's Church v. City of New York	498
	Note on Constitutional Constraints on Landmarking Buildings	499
	A-S-P Associates v. City of Raleigh	500
	Note on Historic Districts	504

D. Streamlining the Regulatory Process   505
        Report of the President's Commission on Housing   506
        Note on State-Mandated Reforms   507
        Note on State and Federal Permit Requirements:
            The Regulation of Wetlands   508

Chapter Six

Alternatives to Public Regulation: Nuisance Law, Fees and Rewards, Covenants   511

A. The Common Law Rights of Neighbors: Nuisance Law   511
    1. Private Nuisance: The Prima Facie Case   512
            Middlesex Co. v. McCue   512
            Rose v. Chaikin   513
            Robert C. Ellickson, Alternatives to Zoning: Covenants,
                Nuisance Rules, and Fines as Land Use Controls   516
            Note on the Basis of Nuisance Liability   517
            Note on Rights to Light, Air, and View   520
            Note on Solar Access   521
            Falloon v. Schilling   522
            Note on Disfavored People and Low-Cost Housing
                as Nuisances   523
            Note on Governmental Activity as a Nuisance   524
    2. Private Nuisance: Defenses   525
            Kellogg v. Village of Viola   525
            Note on Defenses   527
    3. Private Nuisance: Remedies   528
            Boomer v. Atlantic Cement Co.   528
            Guido Calabresi & A. Douglas Melamed, Property Rules,
                Liability Rules, and Inalienability   532
            Note on Remedial Options   533
    4. Public Nuisance   536
            People v. Mason   536
            Note on Public Nuisance Law   537
    5. Government-Administered Externality Fees   538
B. Beneficence Law (the Converse of Nuisance Law)   539
    1. Common Law Rights to Restitution for Benefits Conferred
            on Neighbors   539
            Campbell v. Mesier   539
            Note on Party Walls   541
            Detroit Base-Ball Club v. Deppert   542
            Note on External Benefits   543
    2. Public Subsidization of Beneficial Uses   544
            Hoffmann v. Clark   544
            Barry Currier, An Analysis of Differential Taxation as a
                Method of Maintaining Agricultural and Open Space
                Land Uses   546
            Note on Government Subsidization of Beneficial Uses   548

C.   Covenants Among Neighbors   550
                    Susan F. French, Tradition and Innovation in the New
                            Restatement of Servitudes: A Report from Midpoint   551
          1.   Validity Between the Contracting Parties   553
               a.   Interpretation   553
               b.   Remedies   553
               c.   Limitations on the Substance of Covenants   554
                    Nahrstedt v. Lakeside Village Condominium Association   554
                    Note on the Validity of Covenants   559
                    Note on Racial Restrictions   559
                    Note on Covenants Restricting Age and Household
                            Composition   561
                    Note on Other Controversial Restrictions   562
          2.   The Running of the Burdens and Benefits of Covenants to
               Succeeding Owners   563
                    Lewis v. Gollner   563
                    Note on the Core Requirements for the Running of
                            Covenant Burdens and Benefits   564
                    Note on Some Archaic(?) Requirements for the Running
                            of Covenants   566
          3.   Tying Up a Subdivision with Covenants   569
               a.   Doing It Right   569
                    Homes Association Handbook   569
                    Note on Restrictions Created by Recorded Declaration   570
               b.   Doing It Sloppily: Judicial Rescue via the "General Plan"
                    Doctrine   571
          4.   Termination   572
                    Cordogan v. Union National Bank of Elgin   573
                    Note on the Doctrine of Changed Conditions   575
                    Blakeley v. Gorin   576
                    Note on Statutory Limits on the Life of Covenants   578
          5.   Conservation and Historic-Preservation Servitudes   580
D.   Residential Community Associations   582
          1.   Functions and Structure   582
                    Note on Private Governments   582
          2.   Developer-Homeowner Relations in a New Community   585
                    Tobin v. Paparone Construction Co.   585
                    Note on Protecting Purchasers' Expectations About
                            Community Quality   586
                    Jan Z. Krasnowiecki, Townhouses with Homes Associations:
                            A New Perspective   587
                    Note on the Transfer of Control of a Residential Community
                            Association from the Developer to Unit Owners   588
                    Note on a Developer's Retention of Discretionary Powers   589
          3.   Judicial Review of Residential Community Associations   590
               a.   Legal Constraints on Association Structure and Procedures   590
               b.   Judicial Review of Association Decisions   591
                    Levandusky v. One Fifth Avenue Apartment Corp.   591
                    Note on Judicial Review of Association Decisionmaking   593
                    Town & Country Estates Association v. Slater   593

Note on Architectural Control by Residential Community
Associations   595
  c. Judicial Review of Board Rulemaking   597
  d. Limitations on Amendments to the Basic Governing Documents   598
    Harrison v. Air Park Estates Zoning Committee   598
    Note on Declaration Amendments   599
 4. Association Finances   601
   Thiess v. Island House Association   601
   Note on Association Fiscal Policies   603
 5. The Merits of Residential Community Associations   605
 6. Retrofitting an Association onto a Previously Subdivided Territory   607
E. Land Use in the Absence of Zoning   607
   Roger W. Lotchin, San Francisco 1846–1856   608
   Note on City Development in the Prezoning Era   610
   Bernard H. Siegan, Non-Zoning in Houston   611
   Note on Houston   612

Chapter Seven

Financing the Urban Infrastructure   615

   Note on the Fiscal Situation of Local Governments   615
   Note on Fiscal-Impact Analysis of a Proposed Development   617
A. Special Assessments   619
   McNally v. Township of Teaneck   619
   Note on Special Assessments   621
   Louisville & Nashville Railroad v. Barber Asphalt Paving Co.   623
   Note on the Different Roles of Federal and State Courts in
    Special Assessment Cases   624
   Richard A. Musgrave & Peggy B. Musgrave, Public Finance
    in Theory and Practice   625
   Note on Special Assessments and Public Goods   627
   Tax Foundation, Inc., Special Assessments and Service
    Charges in Municipal Finance   629
   Note on the Near Death and Eventual Transfiguration of
    Special Assessments   630
   2nd Roc-Jersey Associates v. Town of Morristown   630
   Note on Business Improvement Districts   633
B. Development Exactions   634
   Vicki Been, "Exit" as a Constraint on Land Use Exactions   635
   Note on the Rise of Municipal Exactions   637
 1. State Court Review of Exactions Prior to *Nollan*   637
 2. The Supreme Court Enters the Fray   638
   Nollan v. California Coastal Commission   638
   Note on *Nollan*'s "Essential Nexus"   642
   Dolan v. City of Tigard   643
   Note on *Dolan* and "Rough Proportionality"   650
 3. Who Ultimately Bears the Costs of Exactions?   652
   Henry George, Our Land and Land Policy   652
   Note on the Economics of Land Taxes   654

	4.	A Necessary Aside: Equal Protection Issues Posed by Exactions	658
	5.	Physical Exactions After *Dolan*	659
		Goss v. City of Little Rock	660
		Note on the Exaction of Land and Physical Improvements	661
	6.	Monetary Exactions After *Dolan*	663
		Ehrlich v. City of Culver City	663
		Note on Impact Fees	667
	a.	Impact Fees Placed in Special Accounts to Finance Utility and Transportation Systems	668
	b.	Impact Fees for Schools and Parks	669
		Volusia County v. Aberdeen at Ormond Beach	669
		Note on Monetary Exactions for Schools and Parks	671
	c.	Exactions for Inclusionary Housing	671
	7.	Defenses and Remedies	674
		West Park Avenue, Inc. v. Township of Ocean	674
		Note on Defenses and Remedies	675
	8.	State Statutes Governing Exactions from Developers	676
	9.	General Taxes on Development	678
C.		Municipal Duties to Provide Services	679
	1.	Municipal Obligations to Furnish Equal Services	679
		Hawkins v. Town of Shaw	679
		Note of Inequalities in Municipal Services	681
	2.	Municipal Privileges to Deny Services	683
	a.	The Costs of Extensions to Remote Areas	683
		Moore v. City of Harrodsburg [Moore I]	683
		Moore v. City Council of Harrodsburg [Moore II]	684
		Crowell v. Hackensack Water Co.	684
		Note on Refusal to Serve on Grounds of Unjustifiably High Costs of Service	686
	b.	Lack of Service Capacity	686
		First Peoples Bank of New Jersey v. Township of Medford	686
		Note on Lack of Service Capacity	687
	3.	Rights of Outsiders to Demand the Extension of Municipal Services	688
		Yakima County (West Valley) Fire Protection District No. 12 v. City of Yakima	688
		Note on Annexations and Extraterritorial Utility Service	689
D.		Easing the Fiscal Pressure on Municipalities	689

Chapter Eight

Discriminatory Land Use Controls   691

A.		Discrimination Against Racial and Ethnic Minorities	692
		Nancy A. Denton, Half Empty or Half Full	693
	1.	Constitutional Challenges	697
		Village of Arlington Heights v. Metropolitan Housing Development Corp. [Arlington Heights I]	698
		Note on Racial Motivation	701
		Note on Expulsive Zoning	702

Note on Standing and the Role of Federal Courts in
Discriminatory Zoning Cases   703
2.   The Fair Housing Act   705
*Metropolitan Housing Development Corp. v. Village of
Arlington Heights [Arlington Heights II]*   705
Note on the Fair Housing Act   706
B.   Discrimination Against the Poor   709
C.   Discrimination Against Unconventional Households   710
Village of Belle Terre v. Boraas   710
Moore v. City of East Cleveland   712
Note on Untraditional Families and Households   714
D.   Discrimination Against People with Disabilities   716
1.   Constitutional Challenges   717
City of Cleburne v. Cleburne Living Center   717
Note on *Cleburne*   721
2.   Statutory Protections   722
Smith & Lee Associates v. City of Taylor   722
Note on the Fair Housing Act's Accommodation
Requirement   726
Note on the Fair Housing Act Amendments   727
Note on the Rehabilitation Act of 1973 and the
Americans with Disabilities Act of 1990   730

Chapter Nine

The Regional Obligations of Municipalities   731

A.   Obligations to Consider the Negative Spillover Effects of Uses Located
Near Municipal Borders   733
Borough of Cresskill v. Borough of Dumont   733
Note on Private Challenges to Parochial Decisions   734
City of Del Mar v. City of San Diego   735
Note on Local Governments Litigating Against Other
Local Governments   738
B.   Obligations to Consider Regional Needs for Locally Undesirable
Land Uses   740
1.   Siting LULUs   741
Don Munton, Introduction: The NIMBY Phenomenon and
Approaches to Facility Siting   741
Note on Siting Strategies   745
*Beaver Gasoline Co. v. Zoning Hearing Board of the Borough
of Osborne*   747
Note on Municipal Duties to Allow the Full Spectrum of
Nonresidential Uses   748
2.   The Special Problems Posed by Government Facilities   750
City of Crown Point v. Lake County   750
Note on Governmental Immunities from Municipal
Land Use Regulation   752
3.   Environmental Justice and Other Objections to the Siting of LULUs   754
Note on Environmental Justice   756

Vicki Been, Conceptions of Fairness in Proposals for
        Facility Siting   758
    Note on Fair Siting Proposals   759
C. Obligations to Allow (or Provide) Low- and Moderate-Income Housing   760
        Southern Burlington County NAACP v. Township of
            Mount Laurel [Mount Laurel I]   763
    Note on the Motivations for Exclusionary Zoning   768
    Note on Mount Laurel I   771
        Southern Burlington County NAACP v. Township of
            Mount Laurel [Mount Laurel II]   773
    Note on Mount Laurel II   775
    Note on the Fair Housing Act   776
    David L. Kirp et al., Our Town   779
    Note on the Mount Laurel Trilogy   780
    Note on Legislative Attempts to Curb Exclusionary Zoning   783
    Note on Challenges to Specific Types of Exclusionary
        Measures   788
D. Municipal Obligations to Accommodate Pressures for Regional Growth   788
    1. Justifications for Growth Management   789
            Robert W. Burchell et al., The Costs of Sprawl — 2000   790
        Note on Sprawl   793
        Note on the Danger of Monopolistic Control of City Size   796
            Robert C. Ellickson, Suburban Growth Controls: An
                Economic and Legal Analysis   796
        Note on Monopolistic Homeowners   796
    2. Moratoria   797
            Associated Home Builders, Inc., v. City of Livermore   797
        Note on Moratoria and Interim Zoning   800
        Note on Other Legal Challenges to Moratoria   801
        Note on "Ballot Box" Growth Management   803
    3. Rate of Growth or Quota Programs   804
            Construction Industry Association v. City of Petaluma   804
        Note on Quotas   806
    4. Growth Phasing and Concurrency Programs   808
            Golden v. Planning Board of Town of Ramapo   808
        Note on Phasing Controls   810
        Note on Concurrency, or Adequacy of Public Facilities,
            Requirements   812
    5. Urban Expansion Limits   813
        Note on Urban Growth Boundaries   816
        Note on the Effects of Growth Controls and Growth
            Management Programs   817

Chapter Ten

Government as Landowner, Developer, and Financier — 819

A. Government as Landowner   820
    1. Federal Exurban Lands   820
    2. Federal Urban Lands   822

      3.   State Lands   822

      4.   Local Lands   823

B.   Government as Land Assembler: Eminent Domain   823

      1.   The Public Use Issue   824

           Kelo v. City of New London   824

           Note on the Federal Public Use Requirement   830

           Southwestern Illinois Development Authority v. National

              City Environmental, L.L.C.   832

           Note on the Public Use Issue in the State Courts   836

           Note on Other Legal Limits on the Use of

              Eminent Domain   839

      2.   The Metamorphosis of Urban Renewal: Tax-Increment Financing   840

           Bernard J. Frieden & Marshall Kaplan, The Politics

              of Neglect   840

           Note on the Demise of the Federal Urban Renewal

              Program   841

           Wolper v. City Council of the City of Charleston   842

           Note on Tax-Increment Financed Urban Renewal   844

      3.   Land Assembly by Private Firms   845

           Peter Hellman, How They Assembled the Most Expensive

              Block in New York's History   846

           Note on Land Assembly Without Eminent Domain   853

      4.   Just Compensation   855

           O'Donnell v. State   855

           State v. Caoili   857

           Note on Just Compensation   859

C.   Government as Developer   861

      1.   Federal and State Homebuilding   862

         a.   Early Federal Endeavors   862

         b.   State Homebuilding: The Saga of the New York State Urban

             Development Corporation   862

      2.   Local Homebuilding: The Public Housing Program of 1937   863

           Stephen B. Kinnaird, Note, Public Housing   864

           Note on Public Housing   866

D.   Government as Financier   868

      1.   Government Assistance to Housing Consumers   868

         a.   Federal Assistance to Homebuyers   868

         b.   Federal Assistance to Tenants   870

            John C. Weicher, Privatizing Subsidized Housing   870

            Note on Federal Financial Assistance to Tenants   874

         c.   Federal Low-Income Housing Tax Credits   878

         d.   State and Local Housing Programs   879

      2.   Government Aid to Urban Places   880

         a.   Subsidization of Economic Development   881

            Maready v. City of Winston-Salem   881

            Note on Legal Constraints on Municipal Economic

              Development Activity   883

            William J. Stern, State Capitalism, New York Style   884

            Note on the Merits of Economic Development Programs   887

         b.   Assistance Targeted at Poor Cities and Neighborhoods   888

3. Government Financial Support to Urban Innovators   889
    a. Experimental Urban Designs: The Example of New Towns   889
    b. New Urban Institutions: Community Development Corporations
        and Community Banks   890

Table of Cases   893
Author Index   905
Subject Index   917

Preface

Land is one of America's most precious resources, central not only to our economy, but also to our culture, our social networks, our health and environmental welfare, and our aspirations for "the good life." Not surprisingly, then, differing views about how land should be used lead to highly contentious and hard-fought battles, which have come to be mediated by extensive governmental regulation. This book accordingly views the land-development industry as a regulated industry. It asks students to justify when and why regulation should be preferred to its alternatives — the market, systems of informal norms, private law, such as the law of nuisance, and private ordering through covenants and other formal agreements. It reveals that decisions about whether and how to regulate involve choices among imperfect institutions, and it challenges students to consider how the advantages of each alternative institution might best be harnessed and how the risks of each might be minimized.

Three basic players participate in the land use "game" — landowners/developers, neighbors, and governments (usually local ones). The existing land use regulatory scheme divides power among these three players and creates incentives for each of them. This book describes the many variations of this complex and decentralized regulatory system and repeatedly invites students to evaluate the wisdom of current substantive rules and procedural structures.

A lawyer primarily participates in the incremental design of the land use regulatory system when striving to solve a problem that confronts a client at a particular moment. This book therefore explores the practical problems that vex both attorneys trying to secure development approval for their clients and those trying to block proposed development. It asks students to pay close attention to the facts that underlie typical controversies and the ways in which those facts are developed by attorneys and their clients. It focuses students' attention on the differences between the rights a developer has as plaintiff and those the developer has as defendant (or real party in interest) in a neighbor's lawsuit. It explores the relevance of distinctions between state and federal courts and between administrative and legislative tribunals. It confronts students with the critical difference between winning a lawsuit and building a profitable project, thereby challenging students to strategize not only about rights, but also about remedies and about alternatives to litigation.

This third edition continues to bear the imprint of Dan Tarlock, whose work on the first edition of the book set a standard of excellence we've tried hard to match as we have updated and revised the book. This edition also has benefited from the good fortune we have had to work with some of the nation's best law students. We owe a special debt to the following students for their conscientious and able research, excellent suggestions, and attention to detail: Henry Frampton, Joshua Glasgow, Alana Hoffman, and Christopher Kemmitt from Yale University; and Zabrina Aleguire, Amie Broder, Eileen Connor, Dallas DeLuca, Matthew Hand, Lisa Herman, Qiong Sun, Prashant Tamaskar, Nathan Tasso, and James Temple from New York University.

Students in our classes at Yale and NYU gave us helpful feedback on drafts of the book. Professor Susan French also used a draft in her land use course at the University of California at Los Angeles School of Law, and gave us suggestions about improving the draft. Deans Anthony Kronman and Harold Koh at Yale and Dean Richard Revesz at NYU were gracious and generous in their support, as was the Filomen D'Agostino and Max E. Greenberg Research Fund at New York University School of Law.

Our assistants — Alieta Marie Lynch at Yale and Danielle Scugoza, Mara Steinbugler, Katherine Surrence, and Erica Tate at NYU — made preparation of the manuscript go smoothly. John Devins, Carmen Reid, and Lisa Wehrle at Aspen Publishers all were a pleasure to work with. They showed enormous flexibility and patience when the U.S. Supreme Court inexplicably failed to take our production schedule into account when timing its release in May and June 2005 of the four decisions that we knew we wanted to include.

Like the earlier editions, this book makes use of the usual editorial shorthands: Citations appearing in judicial opinions often (but not always) are deleted without ellipsis marks. Most of the footnotes in excerpted material are deleted without reference. Reprinted footnotes are given the numbers they carry in the original. The editors' footnotes are indicated by "Eds.:". With rare exception, statutory cites carry Westlaw dates rather than those from official or unofficial hard-bound volumes.

Last, but not least, we would like to thank Lynn, Ricky, Joshua, and Sarah for their patience, good humor, gentle ribbing, and moral support, as we obsessed about getting this book just right for another generation of land use students, and for the joy they bring to our lives every day.

Robert C. Ellickson
Vicki L. Been

July 2005

Acknowledgments

The authors acknowledge the permission kindly granted to reproduce excerpts from, and illustrations of, the materials indicated below.

American Law Institute, Model Land Development Code 111-12, 115-16 (1976) (Commentary on Article 3). Reprinted by permission of the American Law Institute.

American Planning Association, Policies and Commentary, *reprinted in* Planning, July 1979, at 24B, 24H. Reprinted by permission from Planning. © July 1979 by the American Planning Association, Suite 1600, 122 South Michigan Avenue, Chicago, IL 60603-6107.

Been, Vicki, Conceptions of Fairness in Proposals for Facility Siting, 5 Md. J. Contemp. Legal Issues 13, 13-17 (1993/94). Reprinted by permission of the Maryland Journal of Contemporary Legal Issues.

Been, Vicki, "Exit" As a Constraint on Land Use Exactions: Rethinking the Unconstitutional Conditions Doctrine, 91 Colum. L. Rev. 473, 474-83 (1991). Reprinted by permission.

Bernhard, Arlyne S. & Mary J. Stott, Milwaukee Revenue Cost Analysis, 36 Urb. Land, Dec. 1977, at 16, 18 (No. 11, Dec. 1977). Reprinted by permission from publisher, ULI – The Urban Land Institute, 1025 Thomas Jefferson Street N.W., Suite 500W, Washington, D.C. 20007-5201.

Blume, Lawrence & Daniel L. Rubinfeld, Compensation for Takings: An Economic Analysis, 72 Cal. L. Rev. 569, 590-92, 610-11, 624 (1984). © 1984 by California Law Review, Inc. Reprinted by permission.

Burchell, Robert W., et al., The Costs of Sprawl – 2000, Transit Cooperative Research Program Rep. 74 Preface, Executive Summary at 9-17 (2002). Reprinted by permission of the Transportation Research Board.

Calabresi, Guido & A. Douglas Melamed, Property Rules, Liability Rules and Inalienability, 85 Harv. L. Rev. 1089, 1092, 1115-19 (1972). Copyright © 1972 by the Harvard Law Review Association. Reprinted by permission of the Harvard Law Review Association.

Calthorpe, Peter, The Next American Metropolis: Ecology, Community and the American Dream 49 (1993). Reprinted by permission of Princeton Architectural Press.

Cashin, Sheryll D., Middle-Class Black Suburbs and the State of Integration: A Post-Integrationist Vision for Metropolitan America, 86 Cornell L. Rev. 729, 735-38 (2001). Reprinted by permission of the Cornell Law Review.

Catanese, Anthony J. & W. Paul Farmer, Personality, Politics, and Planning 180-81, 183-84, 186-90 (1978). Copyright © 1978 by Sage Publications, Inc. Reprinted by permission of Sage Publications, Inc.

Currier, Barry, An Analysis of Differential Taxation as a Method of Maintaining Agriculture and Open Space Land Uses, 30 U. Fla. L. Rev. 821, 824-29, 836-37 (1978). Reprinted by permission of the University of Florida Law Review. Copyright 1978.

Denton, Nancy A., Half Empty or Half Full: Segregation and Segregated Neighborhoods 30 Years After the Fair Housing Act, 4 Cityscape 107, 108-10, 112-14, 116 (1999). Reprinted by permission of the author and publisher.

Denton, Nancy A., The Role of Residential Segregation in Promoting and Maintaining Inequality in Wealth and Property, 34 Ind. L. Rev. 1199, 1205-07 (2001). Reprinted by permission of the Indiana Law Review.

Easley, V. Gail, Staying Inside the Lines: Urban Growth Boundaries (1992). Reprinted by permission from Planning Advisory Service Report No. 440, © Nov. 1992 by the American Planning Association, Suite 1600, 122 South Michigan Avenue, Chicago, IL 60603-6107.

Ellickson, Robert C., Alternatives to Zoning: Covenants, Nuisance Rules, and Fines as Land Use Controls, 40 Univ. Chi. L. Rev. 681, 728-31 (1973). Reprinted by permission of the University of Chicago Law Review.

Ellickson, Robert C., Suburban Growth Controls: An Economic and Legal Analysis, 86 Yale L. J. 385, 400-02, 430-32 (1977). Reprinted by permission of the Yale Law Journal Company and Fred B. Rothman & Company from The Yale Law Journal, Vol. 86, pages 385-511.

Epstein, Richard A., Bargaining with the State 80 (1993). © 1993 by Princeton University Press. Reprinted by permission of Princeton University Press.

Fischel, William A., The Economics of Zoning Laws: A Property Rights Approach to American Land Use Controls 1-5, 234-37 (1985). © John Hopkins University Press. Reprinted by permission of the John Hopkins University Press.

Fischel, William A., The Homevoter Hypothesis 4–6, 12 (2001). Reprinted by permission of the publisher from THE HOMEVOTER HYPOTHESIS: HOW HOME VALUES INFLUENCE LOCAL GOVERNMENT TAXATION, SCHOOL FINANCE, AND LAND-USE POLICIES by William A. Fischel, pp. 4-6, 12, Cambridge, Mass.: Harvard University Press. Copyright © 2001 by the president and Fellows of Harvard College.

Fluck, Timothy Alan, *Euclid v. Ambler* – A Retrospective, 52 J. Am. Plan. Ass'n 326 (Summer 1986). Reprinted by permission of the Journal of the American Planning Association, Vol. 52, Issue 3, 1986.

French, Susan F., Tradition and Innovation in the New Restatement of Servitudes: A Report from Midpoint, 27 Conn. L. Rev. 119, 119-26 (1994). Reprinted by permission of the Connecticut Law Review.

Frieden, Bernard J. & Marshall Kaplan, The Politics of Neglect 24-25 (1975). Reprinted by permission of the authors and Massachusetts Institute of Technology Press.

Fuller, Lon L., Freedom – A Suggested Analysis, 68 Harv. L. Rev. 1305, 1325 (1955). Copyright © 1955 by the Harvard Law Review Association. Reprinted by permission of the Harvard Law Review Association.

Gardiner, John A. & Theodore Lyman, Decisions for Sale: Corruption and Reform in Land-Use and Building Regulation 20-22 (Praeger Publishers 1978). Reprinted by permission of the publisher.

Glaeser, Edward L. & Jesse M. Shapiro, City Growth: Which Places Grew and Why *in* Redefining Urban and Suburban America: Evidence from Census 2000, at 13, 18–25, 28 (Bruce Katz & Robert E. Lang eds., 2003). Reprinted by permission of the Brookings Institution.

Harvard Law Review, Developments in the Law-Zoning, 91 Harv. L. Rev. 1427, 1505-08, 1524 (1978). Copyright © 1978 by the Harvard Law Review Association. Reprinted by permission of the Harvard Law Review Association.

Hayek, Frederick A., The Road to Serfdom 36, 48-50 (1944). © 1944 University of Chicago Press. Reprinted by permission of the University of Chicago Press.

Hellman, Peter, How They Assembled the Most Expensive Block in New York's History, New York Magazine, Feb. 25, 1974, at 31. Reprinted by permission of New York Magazine.

Kaiser, Edward J., & David R. Godschalk, Twentieth Century Land Use Planning: A Stalwart Family Tree, 61 J. Am. Plan. Ass'n 365, 372-73 (1995). Reprinted by permission of the Journal of the American Planning Association, Vol. 61, Issue 3, 1995.

Kinnaird, Stephen B., Note, Public Housing: Abandon HOPE: But Not Privatization, 103 Yale L.J. 961, 966-73, 984-85 (1994). Reprinted by permission of the Yale Law Journal Company and Fred B. Rothman & Company from the Yale Law Journal, Vol. 103, pages 961-995.

Kirp, David L., John P. Dwyer & Larry A. Rosenthal, Our Town: Race, Housing, and the Soul of Suburbia 186-87 (1995). Copyright © 1995 by David L. Kirp, John P. Dwyer and Larry A. Rosenthal. Reprinted by permission of Rutgers University Press.

Komesar, Neil, Housing, Zoning and the Public Interest *in* Burton A. Weisbrod et al., Public Interest Law: An Economic and Institutional Analysis 218, 219-21 (1978). Reprinted by permission of the University of California Press.

Krasnowiecki, Jan Z., Townhouses with Homes Associations: A New Perspective, 123 U. Pa. L. Rev. 711, 742-43 (1975). © 1975 University of Pennsylvania Law Review. Reprinted by permission of the University of Pennsylvania Law Review.

Lassar, Terry Jill, The Limits of Incentive Zoning, Urb. Land, May 1990, at 12, 13. Reprinted with permission from publisher ULI – the Urban Land Institute, 1025 Thomas Jefferson Street, N.W., Suite 500W, Washington, D.C. 20007-5201.

Lindblom, Charles E., The Intelligence of Democracy: Decision Making Through Mutual Adjustment 3-6 (1965). Copyright © 1965 by The Free Press. Reprinted with the permission of The Free Press, a Division of Simon & Schuster, Inc.

Lindblom, Charles E., The Science of "Muddling Through," 19 Pub. Admin. Rev. 79 (Spring 1959). Reprinted with permission from the American Society for Public Administration, 1999.

Lotchin, Roger W., San Francisco 1846-1856: From Hamlet to City pp. vii, 11-13, 17-18, 23-24, 165 (1974). Copyright © 1974 by Oxford University Press, Inc. Used by permission of Oxford University Press, Inc.

Maisel, Sherman J., Real Estate Finance 460-67 (2d ed. 1992). © 1992 by Harcourt, Inc. Reprinted by pemission of the publisher.

McClendon, Dennis, City of Tigard, *in* John Tibbets, Everybody's Taking the Fifth, Planning, Jan. 1995, at 4, 8. Reprinted by permission from Planning © Jan. 1995 by the American Planning Association, Suite 1600, 122 South Michigan Avenue, Chicago, IL 60603-6107.

Michelman, Frank I., Political Markets and Community Self-Determination: Competing Judicial Models of Local Government Legitimacy, 53 Ind. L.J. 145, 147-53 (1977-1978). Reprinted by permission of the Indiana Law Journal and William S. Hein & Co.

Michelman, Frank I., Property, Utility, and Fairness: Comments on the Ethical Foundations of Just Compensation Law, 80 Harv. L. Rev. 1165, 1214-15, 1218-19, 1222-23 (1967). Copyright 1967 by the Harvard Law Review Association. Reprinted by permission of the Harvard Law Review Association.

Mieszkowski, Peter & Edwin S. Mills, The Causes of Metropolitan Suburbanization, 7 J. Econ. Persp. 135-37, 141-42, 144-46 (Summer 1993). Reprinted by permission of the American Economic Association.

Munton, Don, Introduction: The NIMBY Phenomenon and Approaches to Facility Siting *in* Hazardous Waste Siting and Democratic Choice 10-23 (Don Munton ed., 1996). Reprinted by permission of the author and publisher, Georgetown University Press.

Musgrave, Richard & Peggy Musgrave, Public Finance in Theory and Practice 8-9, 43-44, 49 (McGraw-Hill, 5th ed. 1989). © 1989 by The McGraw-Hill Companies. Reprinted by permission of The McGraw-Hill Companies.

Porter, Douglas R., The Lucas Case, Urb. Land, Sept. 1992, at 27, 29. Reprinted by permission from publisher, ULI – The Urban Land Institute, 1025 Thomas Jefferson Street N.W., Suite 500W, Washington, D.C. 20007-5201.

Rahenkamp, John, Land Use Management: An Alternative to Controls *in* Future Land Use 191-92 (Robert W. Burchell & David Listokin eds., 1975). © 1975 Rutgers University, Center for Urban Policy Research, with permission.

Rose, Carol M., Planning and Dealing: Piecemeal Land Controls as a Problem of Local Legitimacy, 71 Calif. L. Rev. 837, 854-56, 868-70 (1983). © 1983 by California Law Review, Inc. Reprinted by permission of the California Law Review.

Scott, James C., Seeing Like a State: How Certain Schemes to Improve the Human Condition Have Failed 142-43 (1998). © 1998 Yale University Press. Reprinted by permission of James C. Scott and the Yale University Press.

Seidel, Stephen R., Housing Costs and Government Regulations 73-75, 77, 88, 90-91 (1978). © 1978 Rutgers University, Center for Urban Policy Research, with permission.

Siegan, Bernard, Non-Zoning in Houston, 13 J.L. & Econ. 71, 142-43 (1970). Copyright 1970 by the University of Chicago. All rights reserved.

Southworth, Michael & Eran Ben-Joseph, Street Standards and the Shaping of Suburbia, 61 J. Am. Plan. Ass'n 65, 79-80, Figures 11, 12 (1995). Reprinted by permission of the Journal of the American Planning Association, Vol. 61, No. 1, Winter 1995.

Steele, Eric H., Participation and Rules – The Functions of Zoning, 1986 Am. B. Found. Res. J. 709, 737-38, 740-41, 749-50. © 1986 American Bar Foundation. Reprinted by permission of the University of Chicago Press.

Stern, William J., State Capitalism, New York Style, City J., Summer 1994, at 70-75. This article is reprinted from the Summer 1994 issue of the Manhattan Institute's City Journal (www.city-journal.org).

Tax Foundation, Inc., Facts and Figures on Government Finance 243 (1979). Source: Tax Foundation.

Tax Foundation, Inc., Facts and Figures on Government Finance 232, 233 (1995). Source: Tax Foundation.

Tax Foundation, Inc., Special Assessments and Service Charges in Municipal Finance 9-10, 19-20 (1970). Source: Tax Foundation.

Treanor, William Michael, The Original Understanding of the Takings Clause and the Political Process, 95 Colum. L. Rev. 782, 785-92, 866-72 (1995). Reprinted by permission.

Urban Land Institute, Homes Association Handbook 197-99 (Urb. Land Inst. Tech. Bull. No. 50, 1966). Reprinted by permission from ULI – The Urban Land Institute, 1025 Thomas Jefferson Street N.W., Suite 500W, Washington, D.C. 20007-5201.

Urban Land Institute, Innovations vs. Traditions in Community Development 24 (Urb. Land Inst. Tech. Bull. No. 47, 1963). Reprinted by permission from ULI – The Urban Land Institute, 1025 Thomas Jefferson Street N.W., Suite 500W, Washington, D.C. 20007-5201.

Waters, M. Dane, The Initiative and Referendum Almanac 11, 6-8, 36 (2003). Reprinted by permission of Carolina Academic Press.

Wegner, Judith Welch, Moving Toward the Bargaining Table: Contract Zoning, Development Agreements, and the Theoretical Foundations of Government Land Use Deals, 65 N.C. L. Rev. 957, 977-78 (1987). Copyright 1987 by the North Carolina Law Review Association. Reprinted by permission.

Weicher, John C., Privatizing Subsidized Housing 3-12, 43-44 (1997). Reprinted by permission of American Enterprise Institute.

Williams, Stephen F., Subjectivity, Expression, and Privacy: Problems of Aesthetic Regulation, 62 Minn. L. Rev. 1, 58 (1977). Reprinted by permission of the Minnesota Law Review.

Land Use Controls

Chapter One

The Land Development Process

Neighbors may become enemies. One landowner's activities can impose losses on others located nearby. Examples are legion: a fast-food restaurant built next to a high-priced house, a copper smelter situated near an orchard, a billboard alongside a scenic highway. This casebook inquires into the legal system that has evolved in the United States to resolve these sorts of conflicts. The issues are challenging because there are many regulatory options, none of them obviously best.

Social and economic trends determine the frequency with which disputes between neighbors arise. In general, rising population and increased economic output mean more land development activity and hence more growing pains. Conflicts also are more likely to occur when land ownership is fragmented as opposed to highly concentrated.

To provide a context for current systems of land use control, this chapter provides an overview of the underlying market forces that affect the allocation of land in the United States. We begin with population trends, a major determinant of the demand for new land uses. Next we turn to the supply side—to land and to the financiers, entrepreneurs, and workers involved in land development. The chapter then examines the products (especially housing) produced by the interaction of these forces of demand and supply. Having introduced the industry being regulated, we end with a look at the chief land use regulators in the United States: units of local government.

A. The Setting

1. Population Trends

a. National Population Growth

Trends in fertility rates. Fertility rates and mortality rates combine with immigration rates to determine national population growth. Demographers define the *total fertility rate* as the predicted number of children born to an average woman in her reproductive lifetime. A fertility rate of 2.1 is the replacement rate, an important benchmark. At that rate, a population can be self-sustaining without net immigration. (The rate is 2.1, not 2.0, both because boy babies slightly outnumber girl babies and because there has to be an allowance for the possibility that a potential mother will die before the end of her reproductive period.) In 1940, the total fertility rate in the United States was 2.3. By 1960, near the height of the baby boom, the rate had risen to 3.7. By 1980, the rate stunningly had been halved to 1.8. By 2000, the total fertility rate had crept back up to around the 2.1 replacement rate.

In March 2005, the United Nations estimated the world fertility rate for 2000–2005 at 2.65. In most developed nations, however, fertility rates have fallen well below the replacement level. Examples: Canada, 1.51; Japan, 1.33; Spain, 1.27. Visit http://esa.un.org/unpp/index.asp?panel=2 for updated figures. What land use policies are appropriate in a country that is depopulating?

Mortality rates. In the United States, the average life expectancy at birth has increased from 49 years in 1900, to 68 years in 1950, to 77 years in 2000. The huge leap in the elderly population has fueled demand for housing for seniors, particularly in Sunbelt locations.

Projections of the future population of the United States. Demographers associated with the Bureau of the Census periodically issue population projections that vary according to assumptions about future rates of fertility, mortality, and immigration. Because fertility has been at around the replacement rate, recent population growth in the United States mainly has stemmed from a combination of increasing life spans and net immigration. Together, these forces boosted the U.S. population from 228 million in 1980 to 289 million in 2002. Will this growth continue? Under a midrange scenario, which assumes a continuing increase in life expectancies, a 2004 Census projection forecasts that the population of the United States will be 420 million in 2050. Non-Hispanic whites are projected to constitute 50 percent of the 2050 population; Hispanics, 24 percent; blacks, 15 percent; Asians, 8 percent; and mixed and other races, 5 percent. Changes in legal rules governing immigration, birth control, euthanasia, stem-cell research, and related practices might profoundly affect national rates of population growth.

b.   Migration Between Regions

Migration within the United States has tended to be toward the south and west. See Figure 1-1, which portrays differences in states' rates of population growth during the 1990s. Land use law plainly takes on more significance where an area is fast-growing. The following selection, in the course of discussing differences in the growth rates of cities, identifies some likely causes of regional variations.

Edward L. Glaeser & Jesse M. Shapiro, City Growth: Which Places Grew and Why
in Redefining Urban and Suburban America: Evidence from Census 2000, at 13, 18–25, 28 (Bruce Katz & Robert E. Lang eds., 2003)

A survey of Census 2000 data reveals the following in regard to U.S. cities with 1990 populations greater than 100,000:

- The median growth rate for cities in the 1990s was 8.7%. . . . An extremely strong correspondence exists between many cities' growth rate in the 1980s and their growth rate in the 1990s.
- Western cities grew the fastest, with an average growth rate of 19%. Cities of the Northeast, on average, declined. Cities in the South grew substantially but at

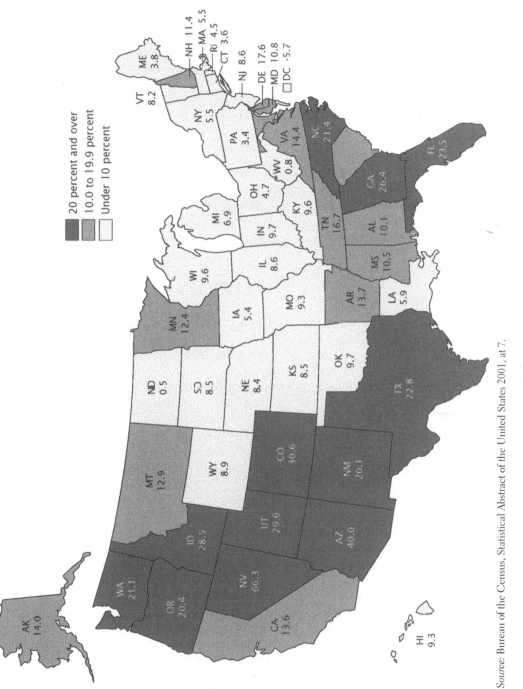

Source: Bureau of the Census, Statistical Abstract of the United States 2001, at 7.

FIGURE 1-1

Percent Change in State Populations, 1990–2000

about half the rate of cities in the West, and cities of the Midwest grew at 3% on average.

- "High-human-capital" cities grew. The levels of residents' education and income are consistent predictors of urban growth.
- Cities with large manufacturing bases grew much more slowly than cities with strong service industries. Cities with high unemployment rates grew more slowly than those with low unemployment rates. Cities built for pedestrians and for mass transit shrank (with a few exceptions), while auto-dependent cities grew. Similarly, older cities declined and younger cities grew.
- Foreign-born residents contributed to strong city growth rates. Cities with more foreign-born residents in 1990 grew more quickly than other cities, up to a point.

. . . [T]here has been a dizzying array of growth rates across cities. Las Vegas (which has generally been the fastest-growing city in the postwar era) grew by 85% [in the 1990s], while St. Louis (one of the reliably declining cities) shrank by almost 13%. It may be tempting to read much into a 9.3% increase in population in New York City or a 4% increase in Chicago, but in fact more than 25% of cities in our sample grew by 18% or more. New York and Chicago are actually among the moderately growing cities—they are not high-fliers.

VARIATION IN GROWTH RATES

Western cities grew the fastest, followed by southern cities and midwestern cities, while northeastern cities lost population. . . .

Why are these regional patterns so strong? One simple explanation is that the growth of the South and West simply reflects the importance of the weather. To examine this hypothesis we first look at the relationship between city growth and average January temperature in a city between 1960 and 1990. Cities with an average daily January temperature of less than 30 degrees Fahrenheit grew by less than 5% on average, while cities with a daily January temperature above 50 degrees grew by more than 15%. We can perform a similar exercise for average annual rainfall. Cities with less than 15 inches of average annual precipitation grew by more than 20% on average, while cities with more than 45 inches of annual precipitation grew by less than 10%.

Why is weather so important a determinant of city growth? There are three schools of thought on this issue. The first view is that the spread to the West and South is the continuation of a nearly 400-year process initiated when European settlers originally came to the cold, wet part of the country and continuing as these settlers' descendants and other immigrants steadily spread out southward and westward. Although this view perhaps holds some truth, the South did not experience relative population growth for the eighty years between 1860 and 1940, which does not corroborate the hypothesis of the steady spreading out of the settlers' descendants. A second view is that technological advances made it easier to live and work in hotter climates. The postwar period has seen the rise of the air conditioner and the elimination of malaria in the South. Both of these advances make warmer climates more appealing. A third view is that location decisions in the past were driven primarily by factors driving the productivity of firms. The Midwest was very desirable to companies because of its proximity to the Great Lakes, for example. But as transport costs have fallen, businesses can now locate much more freely, and the residential tastes of consumers have become more dominant. We suspect that all three hypotheses have some truth.

CITIES AND HUMAN CAPITAL

High-human-capital cities grew in the 1990s, as did cities with wealthier residents. . . . Cities with high percentages of poor people tend to lose population.

What causes this relationship between measures of human capital and later growth? One interpretation of the income and poverty numbers is that these figures are just reflecting bad labor market conditions. This is certainly a possibility, but earlier research has strongly suggested that high poverty levels in cities tend to be permanent features of those cities and reflect the city residents' underlying skill distribution more than they do the local labor markets.

Alternatively, it could be that places with a greater proportion of highly skilled workers have simply gotten more attractive, for various reasons. First, skilled workers may be better at generating new ideas, and these ideas lead to expanding labor market opportunities. Second, people learn from their neighbors, and being around skilled workers may be valuable to prospective residents and may have become even more so as the country enters into a more skill-intensive era. Finally, less-skilled workers may be associated with more social problems, and these social problems may deter prospective residents. Further investigation of this issue is needed. . . .

CARS AND AMERICAN CITIES

Cities built for cars grew [in the 1990s], but cities designed for mass transit and for pedestrians tended to shrink. As incomes have risen and as automobile technology has improved, cars have become an increasingly important element in American life and in American cities. Within metropolitan areas the flight to the suburbs reflects in part a movement toward auto-dependency and away from mass transit, with people moving first and employment following. A parallel shift can be seen in the movement of people between cities. "Driving cities" have grown, and "public transportation cities" have not. Population grew by an average of less than 2% in cities with less than 65% of their commuters driving unaccompanied to their jobs, while other cities grew by an average of more than 12%. This phenomenon is not merely another example of regional growth; it survives controlling for regions, as emphasized by a growth comparison between nondriving cities (such as San Francisco) and driving cities (such as Los Angeles) within the same region. . . .

. . . A huge shift has occurred away from the older walking-oriented and public-transport-oriented cities of the past toward the driving-oriented cities of today. Of course, certain public transport cities such as New York and Chicago were somewhat exceptional during the 1990s in that they actually grew, but they were balanced by shrinking cities like Pittsburgh and Philadelphia.

It may be that the rise of driving cities represents an even broader phenomenon of an urban life cycle. It is possible that in every age, new technologies have come along that have made some of the features of older cities somewhat obsolete. As a result, people have moved to newer cities built around different technologies.

c. *Suburbanization*

Land developers pick their spots. They generally have been more active in metropolitan areas than in rural areas and in suburbs than in central cities. To what extent is the "suburban sprawl" that has resulted a laudable adaptation to new technological conditions and higher levels of wealth? To what extent is it a lamentable outgrowth of suburbanites' racial and class prejudices and of misguided taxation, spending, and regulatory policies?

Peter Mieszkowski & Edwin S. Mills, The Causes of Metropolitan Suburbanization

7 J. Econ. Persp. 135–37, 141–42, 144–46 (Summer 1993)

In the United States, 69% of the population lived in what the government statisticians call metropolitan statistical areas (MSAs) in 1970, 75% in 1980, and 77% in 1990. But while a greater proportion of the population is living in urban areas broadly defined, a smaller proportion is living and working in the central cities. In the 1950s, 57% of MSA residents and 70% of MSA jobs were located in central cities; in 1960, the percentages were 49 and 63; in 1970, they were 43 and 55; in 1980, they were 40 and 50; in 1990, they were about 37 and 45. The United States is approaching the time when only about one-third of the residents within an MSA will live in central cities and only about 40% of MSA jobs will be located there.

Many popular discussions are written as if suburbanization were a postwar U.S. phenomenon, induced by circumstances peculiar to the period. For example, during the 1950s, it was claimed that home mortgage insurance by the federal government was responsible for suburbanization. In the 1960s, the interstate highway system and racial tensions were popular explanations of decentralization. More recently, crime and schooling considerations have been prominent explanations of urban decentralization. While all of these factors have played some role in causing suburbanization, they are all postwar phenomena, and are mostly provincial U.S. problems. In reality, the trend toward suburbanization has been prewar as well as postwar, and has been international in scope.

The growth and suburbanization of MSAs have been international trends. Most high income countries are 60–85% metropolitan, and the growth in U.S. metropolitan population has slowed relative to national population growth as it has approached the upper end of that range. Suburbanization in metropolitan areas has also occurred worldwide during the postwar period, although it has proceeded farther and faster in the United States.

Two classes of theories of suburbanization have been offered. The first, favored by urban theorists and transportation experts, might be called a natural evolution theory. When employment is concentrated at the center of a city, around a port or railhead, residential development takes place from the inside out. To minimize commuting costs for work trips to the Central Business District (CBD), central areas are developed first, and as land in the central city becomes filled in, development moves to open tracts of land in the suburbs. As new housing is built at the periphery, high income groups who can afford larger and more modern housing settle there. The older, smaller, centrally located units, built when average real incomes were lower, filter down to lower income groups. This natural working of the housing market leads to income-stratified neighborhoods, and there is a tendency for low income groups to live in central locations and for affluent households to reside in outlying suburban areas. The majority of the middle class apparently prefers larger single family lots in the suburbs to denser multi-family residences in the central city.

The tendency of the middle class to live in the suburbs has been reinforced by transportation innovations and travel time considerations. During the mid-19th century, when the cost of moving goods and people within cities was high, and urban areas were dense and spatially small, high income groups located at the center, while low income groups walked to work. When streetcars, commuter railroads, and finally the automobile were developed, they were fast but (relative to earnings) expensive modes of transportation; they were initially utilized by the well-to-do, who used these fast modes to commute from suburbs. Increases in real incomes allowed the general public to adopt the faster modes of transportation. Moreover, the falling cost of intra-urban transport following the construction of freeways significantly increased the size of the urban area, decreased residential densities and allowed MSAs to develop in all directions at suburban locations.

The decentralization of residential activity was followed by employment decentralization, made possible in part by the adoption of truck transport for goods. Firms followed the population to the suburbs, both to provide services to suburban residents and to take advantage of lower suburban wages and land costs. This process was self-reinforcing: as large employers became suburbanized, their employees followed them.

This natural evolution theory of urban development emphasizes the distance of residential sites to central work places, the effects of rising real incomes over time, the demand for new housing and land, and the heterogeneity of the housing stock. Other important considerations for this theory are transportation costs, innovations of intra-urban transportation and changes through time in the comparative advantage of different income groups at commuting longer distances to work.

In contrast, a second class of explanations for suburbanization stresses fiscal and social problems of central cities: high taxes, low quality public schools and other government services, racial tensions, crime, congestion, and low environmental quality. These problems lead affluent central city residents to migrate to the suburbs, which leads to a further deterioration of the quality of life and the fiscal situation of central areas, which induces further outmigration.

Those who move to the suburbs often seek to form homogenous communities, for several reasons. There is the preference for residing among individuals of like income, education, race, and ethnicity. By residing in income-stratified communities, the affluent avoid local redistributive taxes. Homogenous community formation is also motivated by varying demands for local public goods, caused by income and taste differences. Homogenous groupings enhance the quality of education, as there is evidence that peer-group effects are important in the production of educational achievement. . . .

. . . [L]and use controls . . . have clearly been an important part of the suburban homogenization process at least since World War II. Once a relatively homogenous group has collected in a suburban jurisdiction, they can exclude people whose housing demands are very different by land use controls on residences. To some extent, they can exclude other types of people by similar controls on commercial development. Land use controls have become increasingly stringent in the 1970s and 1980s, and residential segregation now works increasingly by income, and somewhat less by race and ethnicity.

Also, as affluent groups first had the means to use expensive transportation innovations to commute from suburbs, this natural process was instrumental in the formation of well-financed and high-achieving school districts. Once high quality school districts became established, they became magnets for further suburbanization and attracted other households that placed a high value on education, furthering their quality and reputation. . . .

INTER-COUNTRY COMPARISONS OF SUBURBANIZATION

. . . Casual observation indicates that U.S. MSAs are less dense and more suburbanized than metropolitan areas in other high income countries. These differences have been attributed to the abundance of land in the United States, greater reliance on the automobile, a more extensive system of freeways within urban areas, greater suburban fiscal autonomy, higher crime rates in central cities, and greater ethnic and social diversity in the United States.

In general, the cross-country comparisons . . . confirm the common perception that cities in Japan, Canada, and Germany are relatively less suburbanized. However, it is difficult to decompose these differences into specific factors and explanations.

Evidence developed by Mills and Ohta and reproduced by Glickman demonstrates that central densities and density gradients in Japan are relatively high. Japan is ethnically and socially homogeneous, but it is also relatively land poor and relies to a much greater extent than the United States on public transportation for intra-urban travel.

Glickman used population information for small areas (wards) to estimate density gradients for German and British metropolitan areas for 1960 and 1970. He found that German metropolitan areas are relatively less decentralized and that the rate of suburbanization between 1960 and 1970 was much slower there than in the United States. Somewhat unexpectedly, Glickman demonstrated that, on average, the central density and density gradients in United Kingdom metropolitan areas are similar to those in the United States.

Goldberg and Mercer set out to demonstrate that Canadian metropolitan areas are relatively compact and more centralized than those in the United States. However, the authors conclude from density gradients estimated for the period 1950 to 1975 that Canadian and U.S. metropolitan areas were decentralizing at the same rate. They also conclude that the central densities of Canadian metropolitan areas are roughly twice those of U.S. metropolitan areas, but the average density gradient is the same in both countries. However, larger metropolitan areas, with populations exceeding 500,000, are denser and more decentralized in the United States. . . .

CONCLUSIONS AND POLICY IMPLICATIONS

Our judgment is that both the natural evolution and fiscal-social approaches are important. Much evidence and analysis indicate that MSA size, income levels and distribution, transportation evolution, and housing demand are important in understanding MSA structure and decentralization. On the other hand, no careful study has failed to confirm that central city racial mix and suburban land use controls interact to help explain both the extent and pattern of suburbanization in U.S. MSAs.

However, the relative importance placed on the two theories can lead to different policy conclusions. At issue is the appropriate role of the federal and state governments in shaping urban development. If suburbanization is largely the result of natural evolution and technology- and income-induced changes in the demand for land, then it is appropriate for the public sector to accommodate these demands. State and federal governments should be neutral in allocating development funds between suburbs and the central city. If households prefer to live in low density suburbs, and to use automobiles as their primary means of intra-urban transportation, the public sector should validate these preferences with the appropriate highway and infrastructure investments.

From this view, the requests of central city landowners to prop up their declining fortunes with area-specific transportation investments or subsidies should be resisted. Rail transportation might be justified as part of an overall public investment strategy, but only if it is the best means of satisfying trip demand, whether these work trips are from the suburbs to the central city, from central city to suburbs, or within the central city, and only if rail is cost-effective relative to an alternative means of transportation such as the automobile. . . .

We judge that tax and government service level considerations inhibit central city redevelopment. In many cities, affluent households are willing to pay high prices for housing in secure, high income, centrally located neighborhoods. Yet since 1950, many central cities have lost large amounts of population and appear ripe for redevelopment. This development would be more likely to occur if the vacant or underutilized central city land could be incorporated as an independent jurisdiction. Or equivalently, the centrally located land would be worth more if the landowners could secede from the central-city. The difference between the value of land in a hypothetical independent jurisdiction and its current value is a measure of the welfare loss, for a specific area, of being part of a redistributive central city fiscal system. . . .

A necessary condition for an efficiency-based intervention on behalf of central cities is the demonstration that fiscal and related factors are quantitatively important in affecting the degree of decentralization of MSAs. This evidence would also strengthen the case for equity-based aid to central areas so as to share more equitably the cost of central city government services and to aid low income groups. . . .

Note on Population Movement Within Metropolitan Areas

1. *Filtering in real estate markets.* A spanking-new shopping mall on the outskirts of a small city may destroy the viability of the city's old central business district. Such linkages between real estate markets, usually called "filtering" effects, have been studied most extensively in housing. See generally Jerome Rothenberg et al., The Maze of Urban Housing Markets (1991). For a description of the filtering process at work in the Chicago area, see Brian J.L. Berry, Ghetto Expansion and Single-Family Housing Prices: Chicago, 1968–72, 3 J. Urb. Econ. 397, 416 (1976):

> Between 1960 and 1970, 482,000 new housing units were built in the Chicago SMSA [Standard Metropolitan Statistical Area], while the number of households increased by only 285,000, a ratio of 1.7 new housing units for each new family. This high ratio apparently promoted a massive chain of successive housing moves as upwardly mobile families occupied homes vacated by the new suburban homeowners and renters. The effects of the new construction filtered down the chain of housing values and inward from the suburbs to the core of the city. One consequence was that many families were able to improve their housing condition dramatically during the decade. . . .

Would zoning officials in Chicago's suburbs have taken into account these external benefits when they made land use policy? See pp. 731–33.

2. *The eclipse of the central city?* Many older U.S. cities have suffered steep declines in population. An extreme case is St. Louis, which had nearly 900,000 residents in 1950, but only 348,000 in 2000 (down to 14 percent of the total population of its metropolitan area). In general, middle-class residents and white residents have disproportionately participated in the exodus. As late as 1960, per capita income in central cities in the United States was higher than per capita income in metropolitan-area suburbs. By 1990, however, median incomes in central cities were almost 30 percent *below* those in their suburbs. Margery Austin Turner, Achieving a New Urban Diversity, 8 Hous. Pol'y Debate 295 (1997). Most cities thus have been degentrifying. See generally Kenneth T. Jackson, Crabgrass Frontier: The Suburbanization of the United States (1985); John D. Kasarda et al., Central-City and Suburban Migration Patterns, 8 Hous. Pol'y Debate 307 (1997). Will continuing innovations in the computer and telecommunications industries further strengthen the centrifugal forces at work in metropolitan areas?

Nonetheless, especially after the 1970s, some well-located central-city areas began to attract well-heeled urban professionals. See Rebecca R. Sohmer & Robert E. Lang, Downtown Rebound, *in* Redefining Urban and Suburban America: Evidence from Census 2000, at 63 (Bruce Katz & Robert E. Lang eds., 2003) (marshalling Census data); Edward L. Glaeser et al., Consumer City, 1 J. Econ. Geogr. 27 (2001) (noting the increasing appeal of restaurants and live-performance theaters—local services that central cities have a comparative advantage in providing). Some commentators lament this trend. They fear that landlords in a gentrifying neighborhood will refuse to renew the leases of poor tenants and that an influx of more affluent residents will adversely affect the culture of a poor neighborhood. Should a central city where most neighborhoods are filtering downward ever adopt policies to inhibit the upward filtering of the lesser number of neighborhoods that are gentrifying? For an affirmative answer, see, e.g., Lawrence K. Kolodney, Eviction Free Zones: The Economics of Legal Bricolage in the Fight Against Displacement, 18 Fordham Urb. L.J. 507 (1991). But see Andres Duany, Three Cheers for Gentrification, Am. Enter., Apr./May 2001, at 37:

> Gentrification is usually good news, for there is nothing more unhealthy for a city than a monoculture of poverty. . . . Gentrification rebalances a concentration of poverty by providing the tax base, rub-off work ethic, and political effectiveness of a middle class, and in the process improves the quality of life for all of a community's residents. It is the rising tide that lifts all boats.
>
> Opposition to gentrification often starts from the assumption that it is artificially induced, and controllable. But with few exceptions, neither of those things are true.
>
> . . . [E]xamples of spontaneous gentrification—improvement that takes off without municipal intervention—are legion. New York has undergone a continuous sequence of these, beginning with Greenwich Village and proceeding to SoHo and all the subsequent Hos. Elsewhere around the country, it is hard to believe today that the real estate of Georgetown, Beacon Hill, Charleston, Santa Fe, or Nob Hill was ever down; but it was, before spontaneous gentrification. . . . The government caught up later, sometimes trying to take credit, often interfering with the natural cycle.

For a spirited exchange on the issue, compare J. Peter Byrne, Two Cheers for Gentrification, 46 How. L.J. 405 (2003), with John A. Powell & Marguerite L. Spencer, Giving Them the Old "One-Two": Gentrification and the K.O. of Impoverished Urban Dwellers of Color, id. at 433.

3. *The diversity of suburbs.* During the 1990s, the populations of suburbs in large metropolitan areas grew by 14 percent, a rate almost twice that of their central cities. This aggregate figure, however, obscures significant differences. In fact, 37 percent of suburbs either lost population in the 1990s or remained stable. The decliners tended to be either older inner-ring suburbs or suburbs in declining metropolitan areas, such as Buffalo, Cleveland, Detroit, Philadelphia, and Pittsburgh, in each of which a majority of suburbs lost population. See William H. Lucy & David L. Phillips, Suburbs: Patterns of Growth and Decline, *in* Redefining Urban and Suburban America, supra, at 117.

The prototypical American postwar suburb is Levittown, in Nassau County, Long Island, New York. This community of 17,500 houses was developed by Levitt & Sons, a homebuilding firm that offered only one of two basic house styles—Cape Cod or ranch—per neighborhood. The initial sales price of a Levittown house in 1948 was $7,500. By 2003, an unaltered Levittown house was selling for $255,000. Few remained unaltered, however, because almost all owners had expanded and differentiated their units. See Barbara M. Kelly, Expanding the American Dream: Building and Rebuilding Levittown (1993); John Rather, Built All at Once, No Longer Look-Alikes, N.Y. Times, Mar. 9, 2003, Real Estate Section, at 5.

4. *Is suburbanization a problem?* What regulatory policies, if any, would be appropriate to stem the forces that have led to the depopulation of many central cities and inner-ring suburbs? If the continuing expansion of the urban fringe is a problem, what level of government is best suited to addressing it? Most of the chapters that follow contain some materials that bear on these important questions. See especially Chapter 9, which addresses growth controls and the regional obligations of municipalities.

Sheryll D. Cashin, Middle-Class Black Suburbs and the State of Integration: A Post-Integrationist Vision for Metropolitan America
86 Cornell L. Rev. 729, 735–38 (2001)

Prior to 1950, a modest black population had always existed in communities lying outside central cities. Black suburbanization did not begin in earnest, however, until the 1970s, after the passage of the Civil Rights Act of 1964 and the Fair Housing Act of 1968. In 1970, less than one-sixth of the U.S. black population lived in suburbs, compared to 40% of whites. By 1980, however, over 22% of the black population had moved to suburbia and by 1995 this number had risen to nearly 32%. Thus, between 1970 and 1995, seven million black people moved to the suburbs, a number considerably greater than the 4.4 million blacks who comprised the migration from south to north between 1940 and 1970. Even so, blacks still remain a relatively small percentage of the total suburban population—slightly over 8% in 1995, up from a mere 5.5% in 1950.

Early studies showed that black migrants to the suburbs were "younger, more affluent, and better educated" than their urban counterparts. And, beginning in the 1970s, the majority of black migrants located in predominately white neighborhoods, although many were simply moving across a central city boundary to an older suburban community. According to the latest available census data, this trend of blacks locating in predominately white suburban neighborhoods has continued. In contrast to the "black enclave" phenomenon that is the focus of this Article, most black suburbanites locate in areas with a large number of whites and, according to one analysis of recent census data, they tend to avoid areas with a high concentration of their own group. As this Article discusses below, however, this does not mean that substantial racial integration is being achieved or sustained in American suburbs.

The general trend of black migrants avoiding high concentrations of minority populations may be changing. While blacks have consistently stated a preference for living in an integrated neighborhood, their conception of integration no longer appears to mean "half-black, half-white." Instead, blacks, like whites, now appear to prefer an integrated neighborhood in which their own group is in the majority. For example, in a 1976 survey of the preferences of blacks in the Detroit area regarding neighborhood composition, participants stated the strongest preference (82%) for a neighborhood that was half-black and half-white; by 1992, however, black residents that participated in a similar survey stated their strongest preference (82%) for a neighborhood that was 72% black. While four out of five participants stated a preference for some form of integration, only a distinct minority—29% in 1976 and 22% in 1992—were willing to live in a neighborhood in which they would be outnumbered by whites. At the same time, an even smaller number of survey participants— 17% in 1976 and 20% in 1992—stated a strong preference for living in neighborhoods that were 100% black.

The same surveys also revealed that the tolerance of whites toward black neighbors increased between 1976 and 1992. During this time the level of black presence in a neighborhood that would likely produce an exodus of whites increased from 30% to 40%. However, the majority of whites clearly preferred not to live in a neighborhood in which blacks outnumbered them. . . .

Thus, the prospects for residential integration do not appear strong. The level of residential segregation of African Americans in the United States is still quite high and the pace of their desegregation has been glacial. In 1990, for example, the average black-white segregation index for northern metropolitan regions with the largest black populations was 77.8, where an index of 100 represents complete separation of the races. This figure declined from 80.1 in 1980 and 84.5 in 1970. The average index in 1990 for southern regions with large black populations was 66.5, down from 68.3 in 1980 and 75.3 in 1970.

Thus, the rate of decline in racial segregation in the metropolitan areas where the majority of black Americans live has been unimpressive. . . .

Note on Housing Segregation

1. *Trends in racial segregation.* Edward L. Glaeser & Jacob L. Vigdor, Racial Segregation in the 2000 Census: Promising News, *in* Redefining Urban and Suburban America: Evidence from Census 2000, at 211 (Bruce Katz & Robert E. Lang eds., 2003), reports what the authors regard as dramatic declines in racial segregation since 1970. During the 1990s, 272 out of 291 metropolitan areas the authors analyzed became more integrated, often to a significant degree. However, others, like Cashin, look at similar data and are discouraged by the slowness of the pace of integration. See also, e.g., John R. Logan, Ethnic Diversity Grows, Neighborhood Integration Lags, *in* Redefining Urban and Suburban America, supra, at 235.

One might expect stable interracial neighborhoods to be rare if most people, as Cashin reports, prefer to live in a neighborhood where people of their own race are in the majority. See Thomas C. Schelling, Micromotives and Macrobehavior 140–55 (1978) (analyzing the dynamics of "tipping"). In fact, however, enduringly integrated neighborhoods have become more common. See Ingrid Gould Ellen, Sharing America's Neighborhoods: The Prospects for Stable Racial Integration 21–34 (2000) (reporting that between 1970 and 1990, the percentage of metropolitan-area blacks living in census tracts that were less than half black increased from 33 percent to 46 percent). See also Sean-Shong Hwang & Steve H. Murdock, Racial Attraction or Racial Avoidance in American Suburbs?, 77 Soc. Forces 541 (1998) (finding that Hispanics, Asian Americans, and African Americans are more likely to move to white-majority suburbs than to suburbs dominated by their own or any other racial minority group). These studies suggest that either tastes for racial integration are higher than those reported in the surveys that Cashin cites, or that other attributes of neighborhoods (such as schools, location, or crime rates) have more influence on households' location decisions.

On the legal issues posed by private and public land use controls that foster racial segregation, see respectively pp. 559–61 and 692–709.

2. *Suburbanization of members of minority groups.* Cashin notes the increasing suburbanization of the African American population. In 2000, 39 percent of all metropolitan-area blacks lived in the suburbs. In the Baltimore-Washington, D.C., metropolitan area, 62 percent of blacks were residing outside of Baltimore and Washington proper, many in majority-black suburban areas such as Prince Georges County, Maryland. The suburbanization of members of minority groups is significantly higher in the Sunbelt than in the North, and is higher for both Hispanics and (especially) Asians than it is for blacks. See William H. Frey, Melting Pot Suburbs, *in* Redefining Urban and Suburban America, supra, at 155.

3. *Do blacks pay less or more for housing?* Some analysts predict that African Americans (or members of any group that suffers from discrimination) will end up paying less for housing because others will decline to bid for units in neighborhoods where members of that group predominate. See Richard Muth, Cities and Housing 106–12 (1969). Some empirical studies support this prediction. See, e.g., John F. McDonald, Economic Analysis of an Urban Housing Market 54–61 (1979). But other investigators have concluded that those who suffer from discrimination have to pay more for housing, presumably because many neighborhoods are at least partly closed to them. See, e.g., Caitlin Knowles Myers, Discrimination and Neighborhood Effects: Understanding Racial Differentials in U.S.

Housing Prices, 56 J. Urb. Econ. 279 (2004) (finding blacks have to pay a 10 percent premium). As yet, there is no consensus on this issue.

4. *Segregation by social class.* Households, regardless of race, strongly tend to cluster according to social class. William Julius Wilson's influential work, The Truly Disadvantaged (1987), emphasized the exodus, beginning in the 1960s, of middle-class blacks from the central city. Other observers subsequently documented large increases in the 1980s in the degree to which members of minority groups, particularly African Americans and Hispanics, live in neighborhoods segregated by income. See Paul A. Jargowsky, Take the Money and Run: Economic Segregation in U.S. Metropolitan Areas, 61 Am. Soc. Rev. 984 (1996).

Chapters 8 and 9 explore the link between exclusionary zoning practices and the segregation of different income groups.

2. The Supply of Land

William A. Fischel, The Economics of Zoning Laws
1–5 (1985)

At the beginning of my urban economics course, I pose the following thought experiment to my students: Divide the current U.S. population into households of 4 persons and house them at the "suburban sprawl" density of one acre per household. (An acre is 1/640 of a square mile, or approximately the size of a football field without the end zones.) What percentage of the total land area of the forty-eight contiguous states would be taken up?

Answers to this question typically range from 10% to 70%, with 30% a frequent median guess. Even professionals in urban and land use planning usually offer guesses considerably above the correct answer: 3%. The high guesses may explain why credence is given to lurid warnings about "running out" of farmland or "paving over" America. Most of us live in or near urban areas, and we tend to project our everyday experience on the entire country. But this is a case where everyday experience is misleading, as looking out of the window of an airplane will usually demonstrate.

One may object to my heuristic calculation. Average household size is smaller than 4 [it was 2.58 in 2002—EDS.], and other activities besides housing need to be counted. The facts, however, show that my simple calculation is not far off. Table 1-1 [updated here to 1997—EDS.] shows that land devoted to [urban] uses . . . accounts for only [3.4%] of the land area of the forty-eight states.

Another objection to these figures is that they do not indicate the rate at which rural uses are converted to urban ones. One well-publicized study indicated that this rate had increased alarmingly in the 1970s (National Agricultural Lands Study 1981). The alarm turned out to be false. Subsequent evidence from the 1980 Census and special studies by the Soil Conservation Service proved that there was no acceleration of urban growth in the 1970s.

The issue of urban and suburban development may be put in perspective by looking at Table 1-1, which shows the major classes of land use for the forty-eight contiguous United States. (Including Alaska would increase land area by about one-fifth, most of it in the categories of forests and tundra.) The Table shows that the vast majority [84.1%] of our land is forest, range, pasture, and cropland. Should an "Earth probe" from an alien planet land in a random spot in the United States, it would be unlikely to encounter human habitation.

TABLE 1-1
Major Uses of Land in the Contiguous United States, 1997

	Millions of Acres	Percentage of 48 States' Area
Forests outside of parks	552.0	29.2%
Grassland pasture and range	578.0	30.5
Cropland	455.0	24.0
Wetlands, bare rock, desert, and tundra	102.7	5.4
Rural parks and wildlife reserves	95.2	5.0
Urbanized areas and urban places	64.3	3.4
Rural roads, railroads, and airports	25.4	1.3
Military and nuclear installations	14.6	0.8
Farmsteads and roads on farms	6.8	0.4
Total land area	1,894.0	100.0%

Source: U.S. Dep't of Agric., Major Uses of Land in the U.S., 1997 (Sept. 2001), available at http://www.ers.usda.gov/publications/sb973 [updating the numbers that appeared in Fischel's original table—Eds.].

One hazard in looking at Table 1-1 is the tendency to view each category as if it were fixed for all time or uniquely suited for its present purpose. This is not true, as but one example will show. From the beginning of this century, cropland expanded from 319 million acres to a peak of 478 million in 1949; it then declined to 434 million acres in 1970. This decline did not occur because the land came to be used for urban or other developed purposes. Most of the loss of cropland has been to other rural uses, most commonly pasture or forest land. This process is of course reversible. When world grain prices rose dramatically in the early 1970s, 27 million acres of other rural land were converted to crops to take advantage of the higher prices, so that by 1978 some 461 million acres were classified as cropland. . . .

. . . Kathryn Zeimetz and others selected the fifty-three large counties that grew fastest between 1960 and 1970. They then obtained aerial photographs of them from either end of the decade. The sample was dominated by suburban counties of larger [metropolitan areas]. By careful examination of aerial photographs, they were able to calculate how much of each county was built up in various classifications. Using census data for population, they found that population per acre of all built-up land was about four persons.

The Zeimetz study also gave a useful breakdown of urban and built-up land use. In their entire sample, about half of such land was used for residential purposes, including residential streets. One-quarter was used for other urban transportation, and only about one-sixth of the built-up land area was used for commercial, industrial, or institutional purposes. (The remainder was for recreation or consisted of vacant lots.) Housing is thus the dominant land use in urban areas.

Note on Land and Landowners

1. *The pace of urbanization.* Census data indicate that each year between 1960 and 1990 about 1 million acres (on average) were added to urban areas in the contiguous United States. See Major Uses of Land in the United States, 1997, at 45 (U.S. Dept. Agric. Stat. Bull. No. 973, Aug. 2001). This source, moreover, indicates that the rate of urbanization

increased to 1.7 million acres per year during 1990–1997. At that rate, in each decade an additional 0.9 percent of the land in the 48 states would be urbanized. There are skeptics, however, who assert that some of the lands that the Census Bureau classifies as urban actually don't fit that label.

2. *Land for streets.* About one-quarter of developed urban land is devoted to highway and street rights-of-way. See John H. Niedercorn & Edward F.R. Hearle, Recent Land-Use Trends in Forty-Eight Large American Cities, 40 Land Econ. 105, 106 (1964). A right-of-way typically is considerably wider than the street pavement within it. A city's ownership may extend on each side beyond the pavement to include a planted strip (treebelt) between the sidewalk and curb, a sidewalk, and the first few feet of what appears to be the private front yard of the abutting lot. Because a subdivider must dedicate land for street rights-of-way, the net yield of a subdivision of quarter-acre lots is closer to three lots than to four lots per acre. An acre, by the way, contains 43,560 square feet—as Fischel notes, a little less than the area of a regulation-size football field excluding the end zones.

3. *Variations in cities' lands.* Most undeveloped lands in central cities have gradually been filled in. (In a city such as Detroit, however, where distressed neighborhoods are being abandoned, newly vacant land is plentiful.) Countering the general trend toward less privately owned open space is a definite trend toward more public open space. The median percentage of land in parks in the 11 most populous cities rose from 5.5 percent in 1926 to 8.8 percent in 1960. Seymour M. Gold, Urban Recreation Planning 295 (1973). By 1999, the figure had risen to over 11 percent. Peter Harnik, Inside City Parks 126 (2000).

For figures on the allocation of land in various large cities, see Charles Abrams, The Uses of Land in Cities, Sci. Am., Sept. 1965, at 154.

4. *Who owns developable land?* Most private land in the United States is owned by smallholders such as individuals and co-owning relatives, not by corporations. See Arthur Anderson Real Estate Servs. Group, Who Owns America?, Urb. Land, Oct. 1991, at 30 (reporting that individuals and partnerships together owned 70 percent of the value of U.S. real estate); H. James Brown et al., Land Markets at the Urban Fringe, 47 J. Am. Plan. Ass'n, 131, 133 (Apr. 1981) (asserting that individuals and families owned 82 percent of undeveloped land area located on the peripheries of the Atlanta, Boston, Buffalo, and Sacramento metropolitan areas). See generally Robert G. Healy & James L. Short, The Market for Rural Land (1981).

Much of the land prime for urbanization currently is used for either pasture or cropland. It is likely to be owned either by farmers or by speculating investors who are leasing it to agricultural tenants. See Marion Clawson, Suburban Land Conversion in the United States 62 (1971). If a government were to prohibit speculators from purchasing exurban land, would that prohibition help or hurt farmers?

Individuals who passively own land contribute nothing to the land development process. This truth provides one basis for Henry George's proposal that unearned increments in land value be taxed away. See the excerpt from George at p. 652. However, the owner of land situated at the urban fringe commonly is actively involved in the development process. The owner may assist in land assembly, in financing developer operations, and in the time-consuming process of obtaining development approvals.

Securing development approvals from local officials has become an increasingly risky undertaking. As a result, a developer commonly conditions purchase of land on later success in obtaining specific rezonings, site-plan approvals, and the like from the local government. A conditional land-sale contract makes the land seller and the developer-buyer staunch allies during subsequent dealings with neighbors and local officials. It also helps spread the loss when a local government denies development permission.

B.   *The Land Development Industry*

President's Committee on Urban Housing, A Decent Home
Kaiser Committee Report 113–18 (1969)

The "housing industry"—defined here to include all firms that share in the receipts of expenditures for housing—is one of the most complex in the American economy. The firms that perform the critical function of putting together the finished housing unit make up the heart of the industry. These home assemblers include homebuilders, contractors, home manufacturers (and their dealers) and mobile home producers. These firms procure their materials from an extraordinary range of building products manufacturers, from tiny millwork plants to some of the nation's largest corporations. Distribution of these materials from manufacturer to assembler is carried out primarily by specialized wholesalers and retailers—lumberyards and hardware stores, for example. Acquisition and preparation of land for the ultimate construction of housing commonly involves real estate brokers, lawyers, title-insurance companies, surveyors, and civil engineers, and possibly land planners and landscape architects. Engineers and architects are sometimes involved in design. Much on-site construction work is characteristically performed by specialty subcontractors, for instance, for painting, plumbing, or electrical work. Financing, needed both by the builders to complete construction and development and by buyers to finance purchase of completed units, is available through a battery of lending institutions. Operation of apartments may involve superintendents or management firms. Maintenance of housing adds to the cast of characters—for example, repairmen, janitors, remodeling firms, and domestic workers.

Thus, the housing industry is made up of literally millions of business enterprises. Most are small and specialized, and competition throughout the industry is characteristically fierce. . . .

B. A House Is an Unusual Product

Housing's distinctive characteristics require a production and merchandising system unlike those typical in manufacturing.

Housing Is Tied to Land. The fact that housing developments are inevitably associated with land operations has numerous consequences. Land development has historically been regulated primarily by local governments that typically impose a battery of building and mechanical codes, zoning ordinances, and subdivision regulations on potential builders. The tradition of local regulation of building contributes to the localization of markets. Builders, lenders, and real estate brokers often must learn a new set of rules each time they venture from their home territory. . . .

Housing Is Durable. A house or apartment building, if structurally sound when built, may last for generations. Repair and replacements can remedy whatever deterioration in materials may occur, and may even forestall market obsolescence. The dominance of the existing stock in the market means that housing production can be deferred for long periods (during wars or depressions, for example). The annual rate of production of new housing can—and does—vary widely. In addition, the durability of housing leads to a level of expenditures for repair and maintenance that is usually high in comparison to most other goods.

Housing Is Bulky. The sheer size of housing units and their components places strong pressure on the industry to minimize storage costs and handling expenses and to avoid the transportation of major elements where possible. The shipment of three-dimensional prefabricated houses is costly compared to shipment of the unassembled materials. Manufacturers of sectionalized houses, or mobile homes, who assemble materials at a convenient place and then ship the finished product to final site, have been successful primarily where they have not had to compete with modern line-assembly operations on the sites themselves. Many large homebuilders that have studied the problem believe that, if good production management is used, it is usually more efficient to assemble the structures on their sites. On-site assembly requires a complex system of supply of both materials and labor to diverse and shifting locations. The constant shifting of job sites has brought into being rather unique institutions in the construction labor market. The fact that much of the work is done in the open also means that it is vulnerable to daily weather conditions.

Housing Is a Large Expenditure Item. Housing represents the largest single fraction of most family budgets. As a consequence, both homebuyers and owners of rental units usually make their purchases on credit, characteristically through a loan secured by a mortgage on the property. Housing therefore is tied to the money market and interest rates to a degree far beyond that of any other consumer purchase.

Housing Comes in Many Varieties. . . . The highly individual character of housing demand has forced the housing industry to offer an exceptionally wide range of units. Mass-produced standardized units are often difficult to market because of the variations in consumer demands. In fact, in recent years, over one-third of all new single-family homes have been custom-tailored to the desires of their first occupants. Individuation in the market is increasing. In the early 1950's, large tract builders were able to build and sell thousands of identical units on contiguous parcels. Today, housing consumers are much more discriminating; tract builders now find it necessary to offer a range of models.

C. THE HOUSING INDUSTRY IS UNIQUE AND COMPLEX

The methods of producing housing have evolved in response to these characteristics of its product. Laymen are inclined to wonder why houses are not produced like automobiles through a highly capitalized, factory assembly-line production process. There are several reasons; one is that factory assembly has often proved to be more expensive than on-site assembly, because of high overhead and transportation costs. Much can be done to improve the efficiency of housing production, but even a high-technology housing industry might have little in common with assembly-line manufacturing industries.

With the major exception of the mobile home industry (and to a lesser extent the home manufacturing industry), the present characteristics of the housing industry are these:

Localization. The fact that housing is tied to land and locally regulated has meant that most builders, real estate brokers, and mortgage lenders (at least savings and loan associations) restrict their activities to rather small geographical areas. Only a handful of homebuilders look for nationwide market possibilities.

Fragmentation. The variety of the housing product has led to fragmentation of the industry into an elaborate complex of interlocking producing units. Different structures require different combinations of skills. Thus, the industry tends to work through ad hoc arrangements for each specific job. The practice of subcontracting, which is prevalent in the industry, is not necessarily irrational, and, in fact, is often an efficient response to the need to meet many specialized demands. It is not clear whether greater vertical integration in the industry—that is, permanent alignment of a broader range of skills under the umbrella of a larger organization—would greatly increase efficiency in production. One clearly adverse result of fragmentation, however, has been an inadequate amount of research and development.

Trade associations have evolved to diminish the effect of this fragmentation. For example, in addition to providing technical services to its members, the National Association of Homebuilders has been effectively involved in the councils of government on housing policy, economic issues, and other questions affecting the housing industry.

Lack of Size. With the major exception of some building materials manufacturers and a few distributors and lending institutions, most firms involved in the production and distribution of housing are relatively small. Smallness is characteristic not only of most builders, contractors, and subcontractors, but also of architectural and engineering firms, real estate brokers, and real estate management and maintenance firms. The smallness of these firms results primarily from the industry's localized and fragmented nature. There are, however, additional reasons for the smallness and light capitalization of construction firms. The rate of housing production is rather erratic, both on a national basis, and especially in each local market. The main causes of this instability are seasonal fluctuations in production (which now seem to be based mainly on tradition inasmuch as winter protection has been demonstrated to be completely feasible), the sensitivity of the industry to the supply of credit, and the dominance of the existing stock in the market. The erratic rate of output forces construction firms to try to keep their continuing overhead to a minimum, thus discouraging capital investment and the assembly of large central staffs.

Dependence on Outsiders. The firms that make up the heart of the industry—primarily, homebuilders and contractors—are dependent on larger enterprises not primarily engaged in housing. They are usually too small to bargain on an equal basis with the larger firms on the periphery of the industry. Thus financial institutions probably constitute the single most important locus of power in the industry. . . .

Note on Developers and Homebuilders

1. *The distinction between developers and builders.* The conversion of raw land to finished urban use can be accomplished entirely by one vertically integrated firm, or serially through the complex interweaving of the contributions of many firms providing separate, incremental contributions. Because any particular participant is apt to perform an unconventional cluster of functions, the vocabulary used to describe real estate firms inevitably is imprecise.

The term *land developer* ordinarily connotes a firm that acquires raw land; subdivides the land into lots; installs site improvements such as streets, sewers, and water systems; and then sells the improved lots to buyers who then themselves build on the lots. The lot-buyers may either be intermediaries such as speculative *builders* or final consumers who wish to design their own houses, stores, or factories.

Before World War II, it was unusual for a firm that had developed a large tract of land also to erect buildings on a significant part of that land. Today, however, many of the largest homebuilding firms perform both functions. They subdivide and improve raw land and also design and erect houses, apartments, and related commercial buildings. Some companies still specialize in land development as such. Examples include the firms that develop "new towns," those that subdivide land in recreation areas for sale to small investors or would-be builders of vacation homes, and some developers of shopping centers and industrial parks.

Developers hire civil engineers (and, less often, professional planners) for design services. Builders hire architects (or use stock plans). Developers know about soils, sewers, and subdivision plat maps. Builders know about studs, sheet-rock, and shingles. Merchant homebuilders know about all these things, and also how to market their final product.

Many builders of income property—whether residential, commercial, or industrial—after completing construction soon sell their interests to real estate syndicates or other investors. The few who build, hold, and manage are sometimes called *builder-investors*.

See generally Ned Eichler, The Merchant Builders (1982) (discussing the home-building industry during the period 1945–1980); Leo Grebler, Large Scale Housing and Real Estate Firms (1973).

2. *Stereotype.* Thomas E. Ricks, Small-Scale Developer Earns Big-Time Profits in Orlando, Fla., Boom, Wall St. J., May 29, 1986, at A1, offers a portrait of developer Allan Keen:

> The incomes of Mr. Keen and his peers already resemble those of major-league baseball players. But aside from that, there is little remarkable about the two dozen men who make up Orlando's fraternity of developers.
>
> What is most striking is their sameness. Almost all are white males aged 35 to 45 who attended college in Florida, drive sleek imports—Porsches, Jaguars and Mercedeses—and are casual in manner and business style. Many are slightly overweight. Almost all are "attentive" to politics, as one puts it, but few are ideologically minded. They are outgoing [and] intelligent, but the secret of their success isn't brains.

The secret, according to the article, is building a reputation and having contacts, especially political contacts. Keen estimated that he spends 40 percent of his time on regulatory matters. The article refers to a deal in which Keen bought land for $15,000 per acre, used his contacts to quickly take it through the rezoning and subdivision-approval processes, and then sold it (unaltered) for $27,000 per acre. The jump in price, he said, was "purely the approvals."

3. *Competition among merchant homebuilders.* The land development industry is highly competitive in most localities. Although gradually rising, concentration in the industry remains low. According to Professional Builder, a trade publication, in 2003 the four largest homebuilding firms nationally—Centex, D.R. Horton, Lennar, and Pulte Homes—each sold between 30,000 and 40,000 dwelling units. These four firms together accounted for 8 percent of total national housing starts in 2003.

Market concentrations of course tend to be higher in specific metropolitan areas. A study of the Sacramento County, San Jose, and Fresno markets in the late 1970s found that in each the combined market share of the largest four homebuilders was on the order of 50 percent. John D. Landis, Land Regulation and the Price of New Housing, 52 J. Am. Plan. Ass'n 9 (Winter 1986). Landis cautions local planners to avoid adopting stringent land use controls that confer monopoly power on a small number of homebuilders.

4. *Unionization.* In 1977, about 40 percent of the workers in the construction industry were members of unions. By 2002, the percentage had fallen to 17 percent (a figure nevertheless twice the 2002 figure for the private sector as a whole). Statistical Abstract 2003, at 431. Construction workforces are more unionized in the North (over 50 percent in Buffalo and Chicago) than in the South (0 percent in San Antonio). Organized labor has had more success in heavy construction, including large commercial and industrial projects, than in housebuilding and other light construction. Unionization appears to be associated with significantly higher housing construction costs. See, e.g., Joseph Gyourko & Albert Saiz, The Supply Side of Urban Revival (Wharton Real Est. Ctr., Working Paper No. 453, 2004).

Unions are particularly prominent in public works. When a government finances a construction project, a prevailing wage law is likely to prevent a contractor from reducing costs by hiring workers from the less expensive nonunion sector. The federal statute controlling wages on public works—the Davis-Bacon Act (40 U.S.C. §276(a)–(c) (2004))—has many state and local counterparts. On the effects of these laws, see Daniel P. Kessler & Lawrence F. Katz, Prevailing Wage Laws and Construction Labor Markets, 54 Indus. & Lab. Rel. Rev. 259 (2001) (finding that repeal of a state prevailing-wage law is associated with reduced wages for union members and a narrowing of black/nonblack wage differentials).

Despite their declining ability to organize specific job sites, the building trades unions remain an important force in land development politics. For economic reasons, they tend to be strongly pro-development. They are likely to support all construction projects — even those that are likely to be nonunion — because their members generally benefit from any increase in construction activity. For example, many union members are willing at times to "put their cards in their shoes" — that is, to work at nonunion pay for an unorganized contractor.

Sherman J. Maisel, Real Estate Finance
460–67 (1992)

Developers must solve three problems in obtaining the necessary financing for a project:

1. The first and greatest difficulty is obtaining the actual equity money, called *front money*. This term is used to describe the money developers or promoters must put up prior to the time they can draw on financing through a mortgage. It also includes the amount needed to supplement the funds received through lenders.

2. Developers must obtain take-out commitments. These are promises from lenders that they will fund the project when it is completed. Lenders will make long-term, permanent loans to qualified buyers or to developers if they retain ownership. The commitment makes certain that funds will be available to repay the construction loan.

3. If the developers have take-out commitments in hand, they can borrow for the development and construction process. These short-term loans are paid out as the work progresses and are to be repaid upon completion.

OBTAINING FRONT MONEY

Financing the development of construction projects is difficult because the risks are so high. At this stage many things can go wrong. Indeed, the riskiest period in any project is when the proposals are completely fluid. Anyone putting up front money during this period expects a high reward because of the risks. Developers need capital for their preliminary plans, to make the necessary studies for their presentation, and to control the land they will develop. These expenditures must be made before they can arrange debt financing. As the number of approvals to be obtained and requirements to be met has proliferated, the amount of front money developers need has risen rapidly.

Front money is also needed during the actual process of land development and construction. Even though some loans are available during this period, developers must find enough money to bridge the gaps between the phases or times at which the financing becomes available.

SOURCES OF FUNDS

Developers look to several sources for their front money. One is their own capital, which provides the maximum discretion and fewest restrictions. But only a limited number of developers enjoy the luxury of having substantial financing of their own.

In addition to their own funds, developers can turn to several other sources of front money. One may be a regular credit line from their banks. Another is to obtain as much credit as possible from their suppliers or consultants. It is common to find that the lawyer, the architect, and even the market analyst delay their billing in return for a share of the potential profits.

During the construction phase, suppliers often act in the role of lenders. Even though they may not be compensated for it, they find that their bills are simply paid late. This whole problem of loans during the construction process is one of the factors raising the cost of construction. Suppliers who find themselves with debts continually owed to them reflect this in their prices. Suppliers who must anticipate waiting to be paid for their work will very likely charge higher prices. They add an extra increment both for the time they must wait and—more importantly—for the uncertainty associated with collecting the account at all.

Of greater concern is that the developers' dependence on suppliers for credit may influence the quality of the goods or services the suppliers provide. If payment is not immediately forthcoming, suppliers may be motivated to furnish less than top-quality materials. In the case of consultants providing professional services, their objectivity may be noticeably influenced by what form the payments take. Clearly, consultants whose payments depend on the successful availability of financing will be highly motivated to make sure that such funds become available. Consequently, the soundness of their advice may be impaired.

JOINT VENTURES

Because of the enormous difficulties of coming up with the needed front money, developers often turn to the joint venture in order to find financial partners who can assume the major burden for these expenditures. This is one reason why some of the largest developers have gone into partnerships with insurance companies or pension funds.

If the venture is to be a form of limited partnership, the developer must provide prospective partners with considerable amounts of information before they can be admitted. Therefore, a good deal of the planning must have already taken place. The dimensions of the project must be defined, possible economic benefits must be identified, and there must be a projected set of financial statements. Without considerable detailed information of this type, joint venture partners cannot know whether they ought to become involved.

This means again that substantial resources are required even before a developer is in a position to admit financial partners. Even if the developer seeks to minimize front-money requirements through finding a buyer (preselling) for the project before it becomes necessary to incur capital expenditures, a fair amount of upfront work must have been done, and payments made, to move the venture to the point at which it can be considered by a potential purchaser.

LAND DEVELOPMENT AND SUBDIVIDING OPTIONS

Probably the prime source of front money is through a favorable deal with landowners. Essentially, developers seek to have landowners allow them to defer the time when the money must be put up for the land. One frequent method of ensuring the availability of the land during the planning period is through a series of options. These might include a lease of the land with an option to buy at some later time. The first lease payments could be small, or payments might be deferred until the property is completed and income is being produced. In other cases, developers may buy the land on an extended purchase contract with only small early payments required. Developers usually insist that there be no recourse if they fail to meet the remainder of the contract. The entire security will be the land itself.

In another procedure, the owner retains title while the land is being developed and may even furnish part of the capital for improvements. As individual lots are sold, the owner transfers title to the purchaser. Part of the income from the sale is paid to the owner for his or her land and risk, while part goes as a return to the developer.

In still another method, the builder buys the land but the original owner retains a large purchase-money mortgage against the property. The lien is usually a *blanket mortgage* — that is, one that covers a number of parcels or the entire parcel of land. When an individual lot is sold, the mortgage holder receives payment for somewhat more than the amount of land involved, so that the debt owed becomes an ever-smaller percentage of the value of the still unsold land. Upon receipt of payment, the mortgage holder releases his or her claim and the purchaser receives a clear title. . . .

CREDIT FOR IMPROVEMENTS

If the land is to be built upon or improved before sale, the firm making a construction loan usually requires a subordination agreement. Under such an agreement, the holder of the blanket mortgage agrees to allow his or her claim to be junior, or second, to the construction loan even though it was recorded first in time. The conditions of such subordination clauses and the release clause that specifies the conditions for transferring titles on individual lots are an important part of the bargaining in land sales. Such conditions, as well as the use of options and developing on others' land, are usually paid for through the fact that the price of the land becomes higher than it would be in a cash sale. For example, in the case of land bought for $300,000 including a subordinated mortgage, the cash price might be only $225,000.

Credit for construction of land improvements is expensive, but not quite as difficult to obtain as credit for purchasing raw land. Developers who have used their own capital to buy the land or who have received financing through the owner or another land investor are often able to borrow the money needed for streets, lights, and other improvements from a combination of financial institutions, material suppliers, and subcontractors, in a system similar to that used for the construction of the house. In fact, in much tract development the construction of the house and land improvements proceed and are financed together. . . .

AN EXAMPLE OF A DEVELOPMENT LOAN

A fairly typical case is one in which the developer buys the land but the sellers retain a large purchase-money mortgage. The sellers are willing to subordinate their mortgage to a loan for the construction necessary to develop salable lots. In this example, the developer, John Mason, prepares a proposed development called Fair Oaks. He approaches the DeRosa family to purchase a 22-acre tract from their farm, which lies in the path of the city's development. Roads, sewers, and water are available at the edge of the tract. Mason has already drawn up a budget (see Table 1-2). He can afford to pay $47,000 per acre, or $1,034,000 for the tract, if the DeRosas are willing to accept a $34,000 down payment with a $1 million mortgage.

The mortgage would be due in 2 years and would be subordinated to a first mortgage loan from a savings bank, needed to cover the cost of development. Mason plans to subdivide the tract into 60 lots, believing he could sell each lot at an average price of $29,000.

TABLE 1-2
Budget for Fair Oaks Project

Expenditure	Amount
Land, 22 acres at $47,000 per acre	$1,034,000
Development	
hard costs	355,500
soft costs	60,500
Developer's overhead and profit	290,000
Gross sales of 60 lots at $29,000 each	$1,740,000

First mortgage loan $416,000, including interest, at 3 points and 3% over bank prime

Distribution of Cash Flow from Sales

Total cash flow: 60 lots at $29,000 each	$1,740,000
To landowner: $19,000 per lot × 52.63 lots	$1,000,000
To lender: $7,700 per lot × 54.03 lots	$416,000
To developer: $2,300 per lot × 53 + $29,000 × 7	$324,000

He offers the DeRosas a release price of $19,000 per lot, or 114% of the land mortgage on each one.

The DeRosas would receive $20,000 for a 1-year option to be applied as part of the down payment. Closing would occur, and the remainder of the down payment would be due as soon as Mason received the necessary planning approvals and permits for construction. On the basis of independent estimates that the cash value of their property was about $850,000, the DeRosas agree to the arrangement.

REMAINDER OF THE BUDGET

Mason next approaches Farmer's Savings Bank for a land development loan of $416,000. Of this amount, $39,500 is to cover the lender's interest and points. He submits a complete construction budget, including clearing, excavation, grading and paving, as well as costs for utilities, sewers, and water distribution. Since these costs cover the actual "bricks and mortar," they are sometimes referred to as *hard costs*. The estimated hard costs of $355,500, shown in Table 1-2, include on-site expenses of management and supervision. Also included in the budget are the indirect or *soft costs*, such as loan fees, interest, and legal fees. . . .

Note on Financing Land Development

1. *Tax incentive for landowner financing.* Internal Revenue Code §453 provides an incentive for the seller of undeveloped land to extend purchase-money financing to a developer. Section 453 may permit a seller to spread any income received on a sale over all the years in which purchase-price payments are made. For example, if a seller were to have provided purchase-money financing equal to 80 percent of the total purchase price, the seller's first-year receipts would be 20 percent, and only 20 percent of the gain on the sale would be recognized in that year. Small-time farmers or speculators who own land

that has appreciated greatly in value are likely to welcome the income-spreading effects of §453. "Dealers" generally are unable to select this so-called *installment method*.

2. *The pro-development alliance*. The foregoing excursion into the organization of the land development industry has identified the members of the pro-development alliance. The applicant for a development permit is at the point of attack. Arrayed behind the applicant—perhaps visible, perhaps not—are prior and subsequent landowners, financiers, contractors, construction workers, real estate brokers, and the rest of the land development army. Together, these interest groups constitute a potent and persistent minority faction in almost every political arena. See Harvey Molotch, The City as Growth Machine, 82 Am. J. Soc. 309 (1976) (discussing factions involved in land use politics). But cf. Thomas K. Rudel, Situations and Strategies in American Land-Use Planning (1989), an empirical study of land use politics in western Connecticut towns. Many of Rudel's findings are inconsistent with Molotch's general hypothesis that pro-growth elites dominate the zoning process. For more extended discussions of the role of interest groups in land use politics, see pp. 46–50 and 303–09.

C.   The Product

1.   Housing and Other Structures

a.   The Housing Stock

Structures. The Statistical Abstract of the United States, published annually by the Bureau of the Census, provides an invaluable portrait of the nation. The 2003 edition reports that in 2002 there were 123.3 million housing units. Their median age was 31 years; 18 percent of them were built before 1940. Statistical Abstract 2003, at 619. Throughout the last third of the twentieth century, about three-fourths of American households were living in single-family units, some of them as renters. During that same period, large multifamily buildings became somewhat more prevalent and small multifamily structures less so. See Table 1-3.

Mobile homes (or "manufactured housing units," as the producers' trade association prefers to call them) accounted for 1.4 percent of the housing stock in 1960. By 2001, their share had quintupled to 7 percent of the occupied stock. Mobile homes then were most prevalent in New Mexico and South Carolina, where they constituted over 18 percent of total dwelling units. They were least common in Hawaii (0.2 percent) and Connecticut (0.8 percent). Statistical Abstract 2003, at 620. To what extent might differing regulatory environments be responsible for these variations among states?

TABLE 1-3
Occupied Housing Units, By Type of Structure

Units in Structure	1960	2001
Single-family, detached or attached	76%	77%
2–4 units	13	8
5 units or more	11	15
	100%	100%

Source: Statistical Abstract 2003, at 619.

Homeownership. From 1900 to 1940, slightly less than half of U.S. households were homeowners. By 1960, the massive suburbanization after World War II increased the rate to the range of 62 to 66 percent. See James W. Hughes, Economic Shifts and the Changing Homeownership Trajectory, 7 Hous. Pol'y Debate 293 (1996). The national homeownership rate reached 68.3 percent, an all-time high, in 2003. In that year, West Virginia (78 percent), Delaware, and Minnesota (both 77 percent) had the highest rates of homeownership, and New York (54 percent), Hawaii (58 percent) and California (59 percent) had the lowest. Statistical Abstract 2004-2005, at 612. Again, might variations in state regulatory policies be affecting these numbers?

In 2003, 57 percent of household heads aged 30 to 34 owned their own homes, compared to 83 percent of those aged 65 to 69 (the highest-owning age cohort). Id. at 612. Of households in the richest quintile of income in 2000, 87 percent were homeowners; the figure was 45 percent for households in the poorest quintile. John M. Quigley & Steven Raphael, Is Housing Unaffordable? Why Isn't It More Affordable?, 18 J. Econ. Persp. 191, 193 (2004). In 2003, 75 percent of white household heads were homeowners, compared to 48 percent of blacks, 47 percent of Hispanics, and 57 percent of Asians and others. See Joint Center for Housing Studies, The State of the Nation's Housing 2004, at 35, available at http://www.jchs.harvard.edu.

In the decades after 1980, immigration to the United States surged to over twice the immigration rate during the 1950s. An influx of immigrants tends to dampen increases in homeownership rates because only after several decades in residence do newcomers' homeownership rates come close to the rates of the native-born. See Housing Research News, June 1995, at 5 (reporting that immigrants arriving during the 1980s had a home-ownership rate of about 25 percent in 1990); N. Edward Coulson, Why Are Hispanic and Asian-American Homeownership Rates So Low?, 45 J. Urb. Econ. 209 (1999); Gary Painter et al., Heterogeneity in Asian-American Home-Ownership: The Impact of Household Endowments and Immigrant Status, 40 Urb. Stud. 505 (2003).

Many studies support the notion that homeownership generates significant social benefits. See, e.g., Denise DiPasquale & Edward L. Glaeser, Incentives and Social Capital: Are Homeowners Better Citizens?, 45 J. Urb. Econ. 354 (1999) (finding homeownership tends to promote investment in local amenities and social capital); Richard K. Green & Michelle J. White, Measuring the Benefits of Homeowning: Effects on Children, 41 J. Urb. Econ. 441 (1997) (finding that children of homeowners, particularly of low-income homeowners, stay in school longer). See generally Robert D. Dietz & Donald R. Haurin, The Social and Private Micro-Level Consequences of Homeownership, 54 J. Urb. Econ. 401 (2003) (critically reviewing the literature). Do these findings justify the many Internal Revenue Code provisions that favor homeownership (described at p. 868)?

Housing conditions. The quality of housing in the United States has improved steadily in recent decades for all segments of the population. The proportion of occupied dwellings served by central air conditioning rose from 2 percent in 1960, to 28 percent in 1980, to 60 percent in 2001. Statistical Abstract 2003, at 619. The percentage of housing units lacking complete plumbing facilities fell from 35 percent in 1950, to 7 percent in 1970, to 1 percent in 1990. Statistical Abstract 1995, at 733. Of households in the lowest quarter of the income distribution, 12 percent were living in "crowded" conditions in 1960, compared to 4 percent in 1980. John C. Weicher, Private Production: Has the Rising Tide Lifted All Boats?, *in* Housing America's Poor 45, 50 (Peter Salins ed., 1987).

U.S. housing conditions compare favorably with those in other industrialized nations. A United Nations survey in 1990 found that U.S. households were occupying an average of almost 700 square feet per person, about twice the comparable figure for France and Germany, three times that for the Netherlands, and four times that for Japan. Shlomo Angel,

Housing Policy Matters: A Global Analysis 369 (2000). See also Housing Markets and Housing Institutions: An International Comparison (Bjorn Harsman & John M. Quigley eds., 1991).

These statistics invite several questions:

(a) Is the standard for "decent" or "adequate" housing unvarying, or is it dynamic, changing with prevailing quality levels? If the latter, can we soon expect housing lacking central air conditioning to be regarded as substandard?

(b) Are the availability of plumbing facilities, air conditioning, and so on, trustworthy measures of overall housing quality? What other relevant characteristics should the Bureau of the Census attempt to measure?

(c) The quality of a neighborhood, of course, can decline while the quality of housing units within it is rising. What physical and social indicators might be used to judge neighborhood quality? The three neighborhood conditions that surveyed residents complain about the most are street noise (11 percent), crime (9 percent), and trash in the street (9 percent). Statistical Abstract 2003, at 629.

(d) How might a nation's system of land use regulation affect, for better or worse, its homeownership rate, quality of housing, and quality of neighborhoods?

b. The Pace of New Construction

In recent decades, the annual value of new construction has hovered at around 8% of gross domestic product. Table 1-4 breaks down the $0.9 trillion of construction activity in 2002

TABLE 1-4
Value of New Construction Put in Place, 2002

	$ billions	Percent of Total Construction (rounded)
Private Residential		
Single-Family	$266	31%
Multifamily	33	4
Additions and Alterations to Existing Units	123	14
Private Nonresidential		
Industrial	17	2
Commercial	104	12
Churches, Schools, Hospitals, etc.	39	5
Public Utilities	54	6
Miscellaneous	17	2
Public		
Highways and Streets	60	7
Sewers, Water Supply, Misc.	38	5
Educational	56	6
Other	56	6
TOTAL	$861	100%

Source: Statistical Abstract 2003, at 606.

into its major components. In that year, housing accounted for almost two-thirds of total private construction.

The volume of private construction tends to be cyclical. Because homebuyers and other purchasers prefer to avoid paying high interest rates on mortgage loans, construction falls off when interest rates rise. On the other hand, when money is cheap, as is common during an economic recession, housing starts and related construction indicators begin to perk up. Because private construction tends to recover from recessions (and wilt during booms) prior to activity in other economic sectors, housing starts are regarded as a "leading" economic indicator. The cyclical nature of the housing industry has ramifications in land use litigation. If opponents of a subdivision can succeed in delaying it, the developer may be deprived of an opportunity to exploit a trough in mortgage interest rates.

The Great Depression and World War II caused a great buildup in unsatisfied demand for single-family houses. During the 1950s, almost 90 percent of all new housing units were in one-family structures. Between 1968 and 1973, by contrast, almost 40 percent of new units were in structures designed for five or more households. During that period, the trend toward the undoubling of households containing several unmarried adults, plus the coming of age of the first wave of the postwar baby boom generation, boosted demand for multifamily units. By the early 2000s, however, the production of single-family units (counting manufactured housing) had surged again, and accounted for over 80 percent of housing starts. See Table 1-5.

c.   *Housing Prices*

In 2003, existing single-family houses in the United States sold for a median price of $170,000. In general, houses are less expensive in the South and Midwest and more expensive in the Northeast and West. Table 1-6 shows the wide diversion of median house prices in 2003 in the dozen most populous metropolitan areas. The San Francisco Bay area's median ($558,100) was more than three times the national figure, and the medians for Boston, Los Angeles, and New York more than twice it. At the low end, well below the national median, was the Houston area, where the median house price was $136,400 (just a shade below the figure for Dallas).

In some respects, median sales price is a crude measure of housing costs. It fails to account for differences in the size and quality of units in metropolitan housing stocks. In addition, it ignores the amenities of neighborhoods and regions. House prices might be high in San Francisco primarily because people will pay a premium to live there.

TABLE 1-5
Private Housing Starts: 2002

	(in thousands of dwelling units)
Single-family houses	1,359
In structures with 2–4 units	39
In structures with 5+ units	308
Total Private Housing Starts	1,705
New manufactured (mobile) homes placed	172
Total Housing Production	1,877

Source: Statistical Abstract 2003, at 610, 612.

TABLE 1-6
Median Sales Price of Existing Single-Family
Homes, Most Populous Metropolitan Areas, 2003

Metropolitan Area	Median Home Price
San Francisco Bay	$558,100
Boston	$354,800
Los Angeles	$354,700
New York	$353,000
Washington, D.C.	$286,200
Chicago	$238,900
Miami	$226,800
United States as a whole	$170,000
Philadelphia	$168,000
Atlanta	$152,400
Dallas	$138,400
Houston	$136,400
Detroit	data not available

Source: National Association of Realtors, at http://www.
realtor.org/Research.nsf/Pages/MetroPrice.

Nevertheless, there is increasing evidence that land use regulations—the subject of this book—have significant impact on the cost of housing. In many contexts, regulations that limit the supply of housing or increase production costs raise the price not only of new housing but also of existing housing, which is a close substitute. Houston, where land use controls are unusually lenient (see pp. 611–14), has low house prices. In California and the Northeast, where controls are unusually stringent, housing prices are highest.

Explanations for trends in California's housing prices are examined in William A. Fischel, Regulatory Takings 218–52 (1995). Fischel notes that California housing prices exploded during the 1970s, going from 35 percent above the national median in 1970 to 79 percent above in 1980. After discussing and rejecting other hypotheses, such as that demand for California's amenities might have soared during the 1970s, Fischel attributes much of the house-price increase to legal change. He asserts that California Supreme Court decisions such as Friends of Mammoth v. Board of Supervisors, 502 P.2d 1049 (Cal. 1972), discussed at p. 374, greatly enhanced the power of opponents of development.

A growing number of studies by economists attribute high housing prices in part to excessive regulation. See, e.g., Edward Glaeser & Joseph Gyourko, Zoning's Steep Price, Regulation, Fall 2002, at 24, 29:

> If policy advocates are interested in reducing housing costs, they would do well to start with zoning reform. Building small numbers of subsidized housing units is likely to have a trivial impact on average housing prices . . . , even if well-targeted toward deserving poor households. However, reducing the implied zoning tax on new construction could well have a massive effect on housing prices.

See also Stephen Malpezzi, Housing Prices, Externalities, and Regulation in U.S. Metropolitan Areas, 7 J. Hous. Res. 209 (1996) (finding increased regulation tends to raise both housing prices and housing values, and to lower homeownership rates); John

M. Quigley & Steven Raphael, Is Housing Unaffordable? Why Isn't It More Affordable?, 18 J. Econ. Persp. 191 (2004); Symposium on Regulatory Barriers to Affordable Housing, 8 Cityscape 1 (2005). For trends in residential rent levels and rent burdens faced by low-income renters, see Joint Center for Housing Studies, The State of the Nation's Housing, 2004, available at http://www.jchs.harvard.edu.

D.   *The Regulators: Local Governments*

Public land use regulation in the United States traditionally has been mainly the province of local governments. These conventionally are divided into two types: *general-purpose local governments* (the ones that engage in land use regulation) and *special districts*. The 2002 Census of Governments tallied a total of 3,034 counties; 19,429 municipalities; 16,504 townships (including the "town" governments in the six New England states, Minnesota, New York, and Wisconsin); and 48,558 special districts (including school districts). Statistical Abstract 2003, at 276. Of these, counties and municipalities are highly likely to be general-purpose governments and, depending on state law, townships may be as well. On the varieties of local government, see George W. Liebmann, The New American Local Government, 34 Urb. Law. 93 (2002).

Municipalities. The ease of incorporating a local government varies from state to state. In 2002, Iowa had 948 municipalities while Arizona, with about twice Iowa's area and population, had 87. Counties typically have land use control authority over unincorporated areas (although, as noted below, a state may grant a city some extraterritorial powers).

There is much variation in the relative prominence of a central city and its suburbs. In 2000, 82 percent of the population of metropolitan El Paso lived in the central city; for Boston, the figure was 13 percent. The District of Columbia was considerably less populous than each of three of its suburban counties—Fairfax, Montgomery, and Prince Georges.

Powers. Because local governments are entirely creations of their states, the issue of the reach of local powers often arises in land use litigation. Traditionally, a municipality (or other local governmental unit) had only the powers its state had delegated to it through enabling legislation. Thus the enactment of the Standard State Zoning Enabling Act (SZEA) in many states during the 1920s was a necessary forerunner to the widespread local exercise of zoning power that soon followed. "Dillon's Rule," named for the author of a turn-of-the-century treatise, was a traditional doctrine that required a court to construe narrowly any local powers that a state had conferred through enabling legislation. This rule, along with the SZEA's rather detailed structuring of the zoning process, for many decades made municipal zoning systems surprisingly uniform throughout the United States.

This uniformity has eroded, especially since the 1960s. There are at least three causes. First, more and more states (Oregon and Pennsylvania are conspicuous examples) have enacted tailor-made zoning and planning statutes that depart significantly from the SZEA. Second, courts increasingly have rejected the strictures of Dillon's Rule, and liberally interpret vague statutory language as authorizing innovative types of local land use controls. An instance is Golden v. Planning Board of Town of Ramapo, 285 N.E.2d 291 (N.Y. 1972), excerpted at p. 808 (sustaining the Town of Ramapo's experiment in controlling the timing of development).

The third cause is the pronounced trend toward *home rule* in local governance. In 2000, 40 state constitutions contained provisions that granted general powers to municipalities. An additional 5 states conferred municipal home-rule authority by general statute.

Hawaii, which lacks municipalities, has by constitutional provision granted home-rule powers to its four counties (among them the city-county of Honolulu, which governs the entire island of Oahu). The remaining four states—Alabama, Nevada, New Hampshire, and Vermont—have most staunchly bucked the trend toward home rule. See Dale Krane et al., Home Rule in America: A Fifty-State Handbook 112, 476–77 (2001). In many home-rule states, a municipality or county must adopt a charter to avail itself of its opportunity for home rule. If a local unit does adopt a charter, it can then point to the state constitutional provision or general statute as its source of power, and largely free itself from the strait-jacket of detailed enabling statutes. See, e.g., Ayres v. City Council, 207 P.2d 1 (Cal. 1949) (charter city has power to levy subdivision exactions unless barred by statute or charter provision); White v. City of Dallas, 517 S.W.2d 344 (Tex. Civ. App. 1974) (home-rule city has zoning powers beyond those conferred by enabling act).

The trend toward home rule, however, hardly resolves all controversies over the scope of local power. In California, long a home-rule state, a large majority of municipalities have declined to adopt charters and thus remain general-law cities. Moreover, for several reasons a judge may decide that even a municipality with a charter lacks power to legislate in a particular field. The municipality's own charter may fail to confer the power in controversy. The state grant of home-rule power may be limited in some way (e.g., to "municipal affairs"), and the city may have overstepped those limits. Lastly, state courts generally defer to state legislative efforts to cabin cities' home-rule powers. For example, if a state statute clearly denies local governments a power (e.g., to regulate power plant siting) or explicitly or implicitly preempts the field to the exclusion of local discretion, the courts usually find the subject matter to be one of statewide concern in which the legislature's decision should prevail. See pp. 745–46.

Extraterritorial powers. Many states explicitly grant their municipalities some regula-tory powers over certain adjacent unincorporated areas. A tally taken in the 1970s reported that municipalities had extraterritorial zoning power in 20 states, extraterritorial subdivision-control power in 32 states, and extraterritorial power to impose building codes in 4 states. Daniel R. Mandelker & Dawn Clark Netsch, State and Local Government in a Federal System 447 (1977). One justification for these powers is that an adjacent municipality may eventually annex nearby unincorporated territories and thus is interested in how land is being developed there. In Holt Civic Club v. City of Tuscaloosa, 439 U.S. 60 (1978), the Supreme Court upheld the constitutionality of an Alabama statute that granted a city extraterritorial powers without entitling persons in the affected area to vote in city elections. On this issue, see also Richard Briffault, Who Rules at Home? One Person/One Vote and Local Governments, 60 U. Chi. L. Rev. 339, 385–89 (1993). On extraterritorial powers generally, see Eugene McQuillan, The Law of Municipal Corporations §24.57 (rev. 3d ed. 1997).

For more on the sources and limits of local powers of all types, see Lynn Baker & Clayton P. Gillette, Local Government Law 201–336 (3d ed. 2004).

Chapter Two

Markets and Planners: An Initial Look at Relative Institutional Competence

The central issue of land use policy is how power over physical space should be apportioned between private landowners and government regulators. Few observers approach this issue free of ideological baggage. Stalwarts of public regulation regard government as an essential check on the environmental damage that self-interested landowners might cause if left alone; in addition, many regard the process of civic engagement as a valuable end in itself. Stalwarts of markets, by contrast, regard public regulation as a coercive system that commonly makes urban outcomes worse, not better. There is, however, overwhelming evidence that neither government planners nor market forces are universally trustworthy. This suggests that land use conflicts may be best resolved through an amalgam of institutional arrangements—markets, politics, hierarchies, and various mixtures thereof. In short, land use law is an ideal context for appraising relative institutional competence.

This chapter begins by drawing on economic analysis to explore how private landowners themselves might succeed (or fail) in controlling spillover effects from land use activities. Much neighborly interaction occurs largely beyond the shadow of the legal system. For example, landowners may employ gossip, status rewards, and other informal social devices to enforce norms of neighborliness. Because this is a legal casebook, however, the pertinent issue is how law might be used to facilitate bottom-up systems of interneighbor coordination. While we introduce this important topic here, we defer examination of the legal details of decentralized systems of land use coordination to Chapter 6. There we treat nuisance law (private-law rights that a neighbor may have against a landowner's annoyance) and covenant law (interneighbor contracts). Public officials such as judges and legislators are intimately involved in these private law systems, but largely in the role of enabling private coordination, not in the role of prescribing or proscribing land uses.

To provide contrast to the economic perspective, the middle portion of the chapter introduces a competing vision of local politics: civic republicanism. Those who subscribe to this vision are likely to be more optimistic than market-oriented observers about processes of municipal planning and zoning.

Building on this civic republican bridge, the chapter concludes with a look at the theory and practice of municipal planning. *Planning* is an inherently vague term. In this context, it denotes governmental efforts: (1) to coordinate the future provision of streets, schools, and other public infrastructure; and (2) to impose and enforce (mainly by means of permits) command-and-control regulations on private land users. Even in a relatively lightly regulated city such as Houston, public officials invariably are involved in the former task of shaping the grid of public lands in which private parcels are situated. To what extent should public officials also regulate the use of privately owned lands, as opposed to relegating those decisions to market forces? In the United States, the main traditional forms of municipal land use regulations are zoning ordinances, subdivision regulations, and building codes. In some states, a municipality also may adopt a "comprehensive plan" to integrate and supplement these traditional regulations. The materials at the end of this chapter explore the nature of the planning process, describe the legal framework governing the preparation of a comprehensive plan, and present both defenses and critiques of top-down coordination of land development. This backdrop sets the stage for more detailed treatment, in the ensuing chapters, of zoning and other more focused forms of public land use regulation.

A.   *Economic Analysis of Land Use Conflicts*

Economics provides a theory of the purposive behavior of private landowners, the primary targets of land use regulatory systems. Economists classically assume that a person is self-interested and makes rational choices among available opportunities. See Jack Hirshleifer, The Expanding Domain of Economics, 75 Am. Econ. Rev. 53 (Dec. 1985) (providing a concise description of the classical economic model and its limitations). Beginning in the 1980s, economists began drawing on psychology, sociology, and other disciplines to enhance the realism of the classical paradigm. See, e.g., Christine Jolls, Cass R. Sunstein & Richard Thaler, A Behavioral Approach to Law and Economics, 50 Stan. L. Rev. 1471 (1998) (stressing the limits of individuals' cognitive capacities, self-control, and selfishness); Behavioral Law and Economics (Cass R. Sunstein ed., 2000). Self-interestedness, although softened by kinship altruism, reciprocal altruism, and the like, nevertheless remains a core attribute of *homo economicus*.

1.   *The Potential of Decentralized Decisionmaking*

When can neighbors succeed in coordinating the uses of their land without the aid of a central planner? By analogy, to what extent can a civilization create a language, a culture, or an economy without top-down direction?

Charles E. Lindblom, The Intelligence of Democracy
3–6 (1965)[1]

A simple idea is elaborated in this book: that people can coordinate with each other without anyone's coordinating them, without a dominant common purpose and without rules that fully prescribe their relations to each other. For example, any small number of people can through a series of two-person communications arrange a meeting of them all; no central management is required, nor need they all have originally wanted to organize or attend the meeting. When two masses of pedestrians cross an intersection against each other they will slip through each other, each pedestrian making such threatening, adaptive,

---

[1] Copyright © 1965 by the Free Press, a Division of Macmillan Publishing Co., Inc. Reprinted with permission.

or deferential moves as will permit him to cross, despite the number of bodies apparently in his way. Similarly, the representatives of a dozen unions and the management of an enterprise can coordinate with each other on wages and working conditions through negotiation.

On an immensely larger scale coordination also is often achieved through mutual adjustment of persons not ordered by rule, central management, or dominant common purpose. An American consumer of coffee and a Brazilian supplier are so coordinated. The market mechanism is, both within many countries and among them, a large-scale, highly developed process for coordinating millions of economically interdependent persons without their being deliberately coordinated by a central coordinator, without rules that assign to each person his position relative to all others, and without a dominant common purpose. Market coordination is powered by diverse self-interests. Scholars can hardly fail to note the possibilities of coordination through mutual adjustment of partisans in the market, for a long tradition of theory has produced an increasingly refined explanation of the process.

Development of common law may be another example. The law as laid down by different judges is coordinated, at least in part if not entirely, because the judges have an eye on each other. They are, of course, bound greatly by rules, but on those points at which new law is required, one cannot wholly explain its coordination as no more than a result of rule observance. As to whether judges hold to a dominant purpose or, on the other hand, to diverse purposes hidden under abstract language is a matter of dispute. In any case common-law development, like the other examples, suggests possibilities for coordination through mutual adjustment.

Similarly, to speak a language is to follow rules. But innovations in language — usages that depart from existing rules — are coordinated by mutual adjustment among persons who have no necessary common interest, not even in the improvement of the language. Each person on his own reacts in one way or another to an innovation; the result is that the innovation either fails or is given an agreed meaning or use. It has then been made a coordinate part of a complex system for communication.

The first striking fact about this simple idea is that although significant examples of coordination through mutual adjustment are easy to find and coordination through mutual adjustment is the subject of a body of theory in economics, many informed persons either in effect deny that it is possible or treat it as of little consequence. . . .

The pedestrian of our example and the coffee consumer or supplier play their coordinating roles in mutual adjustment without being aware of it — that is, they do not ordinarily see their problem as one of coordination and, in any case, do not deliberately discharge a coordinating function. What coordination is achieved is not in their minds, nor governed by their minds' concern with coordination. Yet William Yandell Elliott has written, "If a government is ever to be coordinated, it must be coordinated in the minds of the people who authorize it and those who operate it, from the top to the bottom of the structure."[3] The statement comes close to denying the fact of coordination through mutual adjustment — at least in government.

Reinhold Niebuhr has said:

> Human society therefore requires a conscious control and manipulation of the various equilibria which exist in it. There must be an organizing centre within a given field of social vitalities. This centre must arbitrate conflicts from a more impartial perspective than is available to any party of a given conflict. . . . [4]

3. William Yandell Elliott, United States Foreign Policy, a report of a study group for the Woodrow Wilson Foundation (New York, Columbia University Press, 1952), p. 66.
4. Reinhold Niebuhr, The Nature and Destiny of Man (New York, Scribners, 1949) II, p. 266.

It appears that for some reason, despite the obvious usefulness of mutual adjustment elsewhere, it is its coordinating role in politics that is doubted—doubted even in a pluralist society with a pluralist theme in much of its political philosophy and science. . . .

Note on Coordination from Below

Witold Rybczynski, City Life 90 (1995), offers a musical metaphor for the decentralized evolution of a town:

[The layout of Woodstock, Vermont, reveals] a subtle sort of urban design, but it is design, design that proceeds not from a predetermined master plan, but from the process of building itself. A rough framework is established, with individual builders adapting as they come along. If Parisian planning in the grand manner can be likened to carefully scored symphonic music, the New England town is like jazz. Admittedly, it's a very restrained jazz—pianist Bill Evans, say, not Fats Waller. But like jazz, it involves improvisation, and as in jazz, this does not mean that the result is accidental or that there are no rules.

2.   *The Possibility of Coasian Bargaining*

An activity on one site may affect the utility of neighboring sites. A self-interested land user might fail to take these externalities into account. The classic work on how the presence of externalities may prevent competitive markets from achieving efficiency in resource allocation is A.C. Pigou, The Economics of Welfare (4th ed. 1932). Otto A. Davis, Economic Elements in Municipal Zoning Decisions, 39 Land Econ. 375 (1963), is an early application of the theory to land use issues.

Pigou and other classical economists drew a distinction between external costs and external benefits. If uninternalized, either type can lead to inefficiency—on the one hand, too many bad uses, and on the other hand, too few good ones. (The viability of this distinction between negative and positive externalities is explored in conjunction with nuisance law at pp. 516–18.)

The Pigovian view of externalities had to be rethought after the appearance of Ronald Coase's classic article, The Problem of Social Cost, 3 J.L. & Econ. 1 (1960). In brief, Coase argues that, in a world of costless market transactions, there would be no externalities because any outsiders affected by a land use activity would bring home those effects by, for example, offering to pay the land user to alter the activity. Coase's article soon spawned a rich literature, much of it emphasizing the implications of the fact that transaction costs in fact are positive.

Neil K. Komesar, Housing, Zoning, and the Public Interest
in Burton A. Weisbrod et al., Public Interest Law: An Economic and
Institutional Analysis 218, 219–21 (1978)

. . . Consider a tract of land which contains nine five-acre parcels of the form set out in Figure 2-1.

The parcels are lettered to indicate their owners. Assume now that E wishes to erect five high-rise units each containing twenty apartments; that each of his eight neighbors would prefer that E build only single family houses on one acre plots; that each of the neighbors

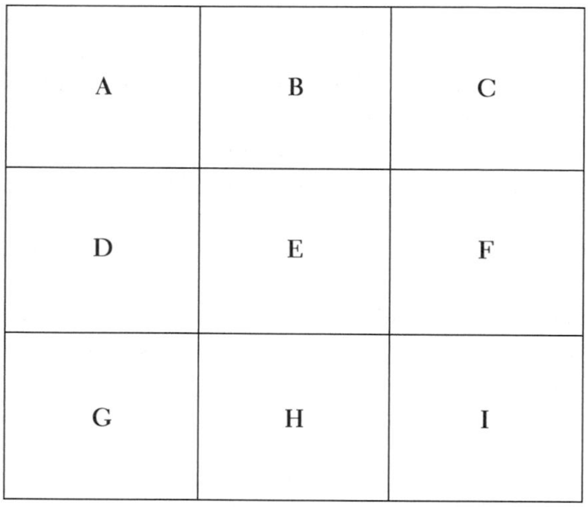

A	B	C
D	E	F
G	H	I

FIGURE 2-1

values the less dense use of E's land by $1,000 (that is, each neighbor would be willing to pay E that sum if E would promise to build only five single-family homes); and that E in turn would gain $6,400 from the high-rise development relative to the less dense use.

The total loss to the neighbors from E's proposed land use, $8,000, exceeds the gain to E, $6,400. But there is still reason to believe that E would build the apartments. There are two means by which "external" costs—external to E's decision—may be internalized by E; that is, included by E in his own cost-benefit analysis. First, E may gain pleasure from benefiting others and may therefore include all or part of his neighbors' losses as his own. In the present instance, if E "felt" more than $6,400 worth of the neighbors' losses, he would not build the apartment houses. Second, the neighbors might bring their losses to E's attention by offering him payment to desist from building the apartments. Thus, if E were offered any amount in excess of $6,400, his own cost-benefit analysis would favor the less dense housing choice—single family homes. In legal terms, he would sell his neighbors an interest in his land—a covenant restricting his land use.

The question becomes how or whether E would be made to consider his neighbors' losses. In the transaction-costless world of Ronald Coase, this removal of the potential externality would occur instantaneously. The neighbors would compensate E an amount ranging from $6,400 to $8,000 in exchange for his promise to restrict his land use to five single family houses. Without the extreme Coase assumptions, however, it remains uncertain whether the neighbors will succeed in purchasing the land use restriction from E. There are eight neighbors, none of whom is threatened with sufficient loss to justify the minimum restriction price of $6,400. Each of the neighbors would prefer that another set of neighbors purchase the restriction, producing a "free rider" situation.[6] There may be

_____

6. If any seven neighbors—for example B, C, D, F, G, H, and I—each expended slightly less than $925 each, they could in combination exceed the minimum price necessary to restrict E without the inclusion of the eighth, A. A would be particularly fortunate if this occurred; he would be saved from E's undesired land use without any expenditure on his part. Here A would be a "free rider." If the process worked just as described, it might produce an unfair distribution of the benefits of the restriction, but it would at least produce the socially preferred land-use pattern. However, each of the neighbors would like to be in A's position and, therefore, each has an incentive to wait to see if the others will purchase the restriction. If each waits, none will act, the restriction will not be purchased, and the socially preferred land-use pattern will not be observed. This ramification of the free rider problem is a form of "prisoners' dilemma" (see note 14).

substantial costs involved in organizing the eight neighbors, determining and levying their share, and bargaining with E, in addition to the incidental costs for lawyers, filings, and so on. If these costs are sufficiently high to block the purchase of the land use restriction, a potential private market failure is present. It is a "failure" because, despite the fact that the "social" or aggregate loss from the proposed apartments exceeds the "social" or aggregate benefits, the private market would still produce the less desirable apartment use. The failure is "potential" since it remains to be seen whether there is an alternative solution from either the public or the voluntary sector that will produce the restriction at costs that are less than the costs of unrestricted land use.[7]

There are several alternative public solutions. First, the neighbors might seek a judicial determination that E's multiple dwellings would constitute a "nuisance"—public or private—and therefore should be enjoined. Nuisance actions are sometimes employed to stop such externalities as smoke or particle pollution, but the nuisance approach generally is not employed in connection with residential use.

Second, the neighbors might attempt to prevail on a legislative or administrative authority to employ an eminent domain power, which could "take" the apartment building use from E and pay E the value of the lost use, an amount determined by the authority. If the nine tracts were a political and taxing jurisdiction (an assumption soon employed more extensively), if each neighbor were in a similar tax position, and if the "correct" value were determined, the eminent domain solution would closely approximate the "Coase" or private solution.[9] The public entity, with its power to impose costs (taxation) and perhaps its economies in factual investigation, would be substituted for private bargaining at presumably lower transaction costs. While the "compensation" scheme might have some marginal function in the housing restriction case, there are several reasons to believe it will be far less frequently used than the third form of public solution: zoning.[10] Since zoning is the most widely used—and the most controversial—public solution, we will discuss it in some detail.

The Zoning Process

The zoning process controls land use without attempting direct compensation for any losses imposed by the controls. We will examine several models of the zoning process and the general form of land use restrictions that each is likely to produce. To aid in the analysis a few facts will be added to the hypothetical. Assume that in addition to preferring one-acre single-family homes to multi-unit dwellings, each of the neighbors would prefer

7. In our hypothetical, the social value of the removal would be $1,600. Presumably, the costs of the public solution would have to be less than $1,600 to justify such a solution.

9. The two solutions would be identical if no tax were imposed on E, *qua* taxpayer, in the process of raising the funds to compensate E, *qua* landowner.

10. One important reason lies in the costs of the compensation scheme—the administrative costs, not the transfer payment. Where a complex land-use regulation is involved, it is difficult to assess the value of the loss and to separate real from illusory claims. In an important sense, the reluctance of courts to declare losses associated with governmental activity as "property" losses and therefore compensable under the Fifth or Fourteenth Amendments of the U.S. Constitution probably lies in a sense of the complexity of assessing the loss. For a similar treatment, see Frank I. Michelman, Property, Utility and Fairness: Comments on the Ethical Foundations of "Just Compensation" Law, 80 Harv. L. Rev. 1165–1258 (1968).

A second reason for the preference of the "zoning" over the "eminent domain" approach stems from the "majoritarian" bias discussed subsequently. Even if the administrative costs associated with compensation were zero, the majority, which may make the decision, may prefer to see a distribution of the benefits and costs of the public program that is favorable to them. Here it is the transfer, not the administrative costs, that controls the decision. Where the courts determine that such a legislative process indeed took place, the courts are likely to override the legislative decision, because it produces a non–cost-justified, unfair distribution of costs and benefits. See, for example, Vernon Park Realty v. City of Mount Vernon, 121 N.E.2d 517 (N.Y. 1954).

vacant land (open space with the natural setting of trees, flowers, and the animals of the forest) to one-acre single-family homes; that each neighbor would receive benefits from such a use of $500; and that E would lose $6,000 if such a restriction were imposed.[11]

The Omniscient Dictator: Allocative Efficiency Criteria. Assume first that land-use decisions are made by a dictator who has the ability to determine costlessly the relative values of many land-use arrangements. He is hired by the 45-acre jurisdiction defined by our nine tracts of land and instructed to seek the most efficient allocation of resources. In particular, he is told to impose land-use restrictions only where the aggregate benefits of the restriction to the citizens of the community exceed the aggregate losses. Given the hypothetical, he would presumably impose the one-acre, single-family restriction, but refuse the more stringent "open space" restriction.[12]

The Majoritarian Model. Assume that the jurisdiction puts each zoning decision to a public vote and the restriction is imposed if a majority (over 50 percent) of the voters favor it. Given the hypothetical, it is quite likely that the more stringent open space restriction would be imposed. There are eight voters who are benefited by the open space restriction and only one who is harmed. The fact that E's harm is greater than the neighbors' benefit is not determinative. The outcome described assumes that E is unable to purchase the votes of at least four of his neighbors, and that the neighbors do not view the vote as a precedent that can produce a future decision of sufficient adversity to them. The presence or absence of laws against vote selling, the size of transaction costs involved in bargaining for and purchasing a sufficient number of votes, and the tastes of the neighbors are all factors that determine the stability of the conclusion. It is sufficient, for the present, to note that it is possible and even substantially probable that the majoritarian system would have the bias suggested.

The Influence Model. Assume that the decision is again made by a dictator, but not an omniscient one. The dictator in fact has none of the information necessary for his land-use decision. He bases each decision solely on the arguments of the interested parties. Assume further that the effectiveness of the argument is a function of the expenditures by the interested parties on investigators, lawyers, and economists, and that there are positive economies of scale in the production of effective argument.

Given the hypothetical, it is now possible that no restriction will be imposed. To the extent that the costs of organization keep the neighbors from pooling their efforts, the information they produce about the single-family house restriction may be less than that produced by E, despite the greater total amount at stake for the neighbors. This would be so because they would duplicate efforts and because each would be faced with the relatively high cost of small scale. In addition, the "free rider" and "prisoner dilemma" problems may lead each neighbor to await the efforts of the others, with the result that the neighbors will produce little or no expenditure to affect the land-use decision.[14]

---

11. It should be emphasized that the restriction to single-family use (over open space) and the restriction to multi-family use (over single-family) are not overlapping, but rather are cumulative. Thus, the loss to E of a restriction to open space is the sum of the loss from the restriction from multi-family to single-family ($6,400) *relative to multi-family use* and the loss from the restriction from single-family to open space ($6,000)—$12,400 in total.

12. As seen previously, the restriction from multi-family to single-family has a net "social" benefit of $1,600 ($8,000 − $6,400). The restriction from single-family to open space would have a net "social" loss of $2,000 ($4,000 − $6,000) and therefore would not be imposed.

14. The term "prisoners' dilemma" arose from a case in game theory where two players must collude for rational benefit, but because of lack of knowledge, each player will perform a less-than-optimal action that will result in less gain than could have been obtained by collusion. The term itself came from an application of the theory to the questioning of suspects in a crime. For a discussion of an application of the "prisoners' dilemma" in the area of land use and urban renewal see Otto A. Davis & Andrew B. Whinston, The Economics of Urban Renewal, 26 L. & Contemp. Prob. 105–112 (1961). Its relationship to free rider problems is pointed out in note 6.

Note on the Coase Theorem and Bargaining Among Neighbors

1. *The relevance of the allocation of property rights.* In *The Problem of Social Cost*, Coase asserts that the shifting of legal entitlements from one party to another does not affect the allocation of resources as long as transaction costs are zero. An extension of Komesar's example helps to illustrate Coase's theorem. Assume first that E has the right to build multifamily structures. If bargaining were costless, Komesar shows that the neighbors would band together to purchase a restrictive covenant forbidding multifamily structures on E's land. The neighbors would be willing to bid up to $8,000 to purchase the covenant, and E would insist on a payment of at least $6,400 (his valuation of multifamily-use rights); the ultimate sales price would lie between those two figures. Now assume that the law is changed so as to entitle each of the neighbors to enjoin E's construction of apartments. Coase asserts that the result would still be that no apartments would be built. Although E would offer up to $6,400 to purchase the neighbors' rights, they would insist on at least $8,000 and therefore no deal would be struck.

In Komesar's example, E's land would be most efficiently used for single-family dwellings. (Efficient, that is, according to Kaldor-Hicks criteria, explained at p. 96.) If use of the land were to be further restricted to open space, that restriction would harm E by $6,000 but help his neighbors by an aggregate of only $4,000. How would Coase argue that (given his assumptions) single-family houses would be built on E's land regardless of whether (a) E had the right to build those houses; or (b) (the less obvious case) the eight neighbors each had the right to enjoin house construction on E's land?

2. *Wealth effects.* Economists now agree that Coase failed to observe that shifts in legal entitlements, by altering the wealth of affected parties, may influence how much the parties value particular entitlements. For example, suppose that E's eight neighbors initially each had the right to enjoin construction of multifamily units on E's land. Assume Komesar is correct when he states that each one would insist on being paid at least $1,000 before selling that right to E. Now suppose that these entitlements were shifted to E by operation of law without compensation being paid to the neighbors. This legal shift would make each neighbor poorer by $1,000. Because they would now be poorer, they would have to husband their remaining wealth more carefully and might now choose to bid less than $1,000 each to stop multifamily construction on E's land. Suppose each would now bid only $500. They would then be able to raise an aggregate bid of only $4,000—less than the $6,400 they would need to buy back the entitlement from E (assuming E's asking price had not increased on account of his added wealth). In this case, the optimal allocation of E's land would have been determined by the original allocation of rights among the parties. Multifamily units would be the Pareto optimal allocation if E had originally been granted the entitlement to build them, but single-family units would be the Pareto optimal allocation if E's neighbors had been given an original entitlement to insist on them. See Harold Demsetz, Wealth Distribution and the Ownership of Rights, 1 J. Legal Stud. 223, 228 (1972); Mark Kelman, Consumption Theory, Production Theory, and Ideology in the Coase Theorem, 52 S. Cal. L. Rev. 669 (1979).

3. *The assumption of zero transaction costs.* In a world of no transaction costs, all land use conflicts would be settled efficiently by bargains between neighbors and, in the eyes of many economists, there would be no role for the city planner other than to coordinate the location and use of public lands. The assumption of zero transaction costs that underlies Coase's theorem is similar to the common assumption in theoretical physics of no friction between bodies. As an empirical matter, both assumptions are false. As Coase himself

stresses, even the simplest of land use conflicts does involve transaction costs—the burdens of organizing, gathering information, negotiating, and so on. Little is known about the magnitude of these costs in actual situations. If the settlement of localized conflicts between neighbors were to entail only trivial transaction costs, planners would have a difficult time showing why their involvement in such conflicts is justified. On the other hand, if transaction costs indeed prove to be high even in localized disputes, the case for some form of governmental regulation is stronger.

4. *Social conditions conducive to cooperation among neighbors.* When a potential land use conflict arises at a particular site, landowners and residents of the immediate neighborhood may know more than city officials do about the merits of various resolutions of the conflict. In addition, they are likely to have sharper incentives than planners do to resolve the dispute cooperatively. See pp. 65–69. On the other hand, as Komesar notes, transaction costs may prevent members of a neighborhood from reaching a cooperative result.

The more closely-knit a group of residents and landowners, the more likely they are to succeed in exercising informal social controls to settle land use disputes at the micro level. For members of an informal group to be closely knit, they must: (1) have good information about both the current situation and who has done what in the past; and (2) be enmeshed in continuing relationships that enable each of them to informally punish uncooperative actions and reward cooperative actions. See generally Robert C. Ellickson, Order Without Law: How Neighbors Settle Disputes 167–83 (1991) (proposing theory derived from study of neighbors in rural Shasta County, California). As the numbers of neighbors affected by a conflict grows, these conditions are less likely to be met, and bottom-up cooperation becomes more difficult.

Valuable studies of actual neighbor interactions include M.P. Baumgartner, The Moral Order of a Suburb (1988) (examining a small city in Westchester County, New York); Gideon Parchomovsky & Peter Siegelman, Selling Mayberry: Communities and Individuals in Law and Economics, 92 Cal. L. Rev. 75 (2004) (on resolution of conflicts created by polluting power plant in Cheshire, Ohio); Mark D. West, The Resolution of Karaoke Disputes: The Calculus of Institutions and Social Capital, 28 J. Japanese Stud. 301 (2002) (investigation into noise disputes in Japan). In general, field investigators find that neighbors turn to lawyers and litigation only as a last resort.

5. *Other limitations of Coasian analysis.* Commentators have challenged Coase's sense of how people bargain, his assumption that people typically look to the legal system to determine their entitlements, and his assumption that a forgone gain of a given amount is the equivalent of the loss of that same amount. For readings on these points, see Robert C. Ellickson, Carol M. Rose & Bruce A. Ackerman, Perspectives on Property Law 200–33 (3d ed. 2002).

6. *An application: rights to sunlight.* Judges have applied common law principles to decide whether erection of a structure that casts a shadow on a neighbor's solar collector is an actionable nuisance. See pp. 521–22. In addition, a number of states have enacted statutes that bear on this issue. See, e.g., Cal. Pub. Res. Code §§25982–86 (West 2004) (enacted 1978). Would you expect the number of solar collectors in use to vary with the substance of these common law doctrines and statutes? Compare Melvin M. Eisenstadt & Albert E. Utton, Solar Rights and Their Effect on Solar Heating and Cooling, 16 Nat. Res. J. 363, 414 (1976) (arguing that use of solar equipment will come to a standstill unless rights to sunlight are established by law), with Stephen F. Williams, Solar Access and Property Rights, 11 Conn. L. Rev. 430 (1979) (anticipating that Coasian bargaining would minimize influence of solar-access laws), and with Ellickson, Order Without Law, supra, at 273 (predicting that most adjoining homeowners would apply informal norms, not legal rules, to resolve disputes over solar access).

Note on Possible Economic Rationales for Zoning

1. *Komesar's update of Pigou.* The Komesar excerpt implies that zoning can enhance the efficiency of land use when the zoning process, flawed as it is, outperforms the interneighbor bargaining process, flawed as it is, in internalizing externalities arising from incompatible land uses. As Komesar observes, the identification of market imperfections does not by itself make a case for government intervention. Under both the "majoritarian" and the "influence" models of politics, a government would choose an inefficient zoning classification for E's land. Komesar also points out that, because it may be costly to administer government programs, some market imperfections may be best left untouched. (Observe that Komesar does not address whether a system of public fees and bonuses (discussed at pp. 538–39 and 544–50) could internalize externalities better than the zoning approach does.)

2. *Hamilton on fiscal free-riding.* When a local government does not charge user fees for public schools and other public services, it may disproportionately attract entrants who expect to consume high levels of local services but pay little in local property taxes. According to Bruce Hamilton, a locality facing this risk must either cut the level of public services (usually an unpalatable choice) or use a strategy such as exclusionary zoning to help ensure that each household pays a significant amount of local property taxes. Bruce W. Hamilton, Zoning and Property Taxation in a System of Local Governments, 12 Urb. Stud. 205 (1975). Hamilton's analysis correctly predicts that municipalities regulate land uses to control fiscal as well as physical spillover effects. Chapter 7 takes up fiscal issues; Chapter 9C addresses exclusionary zoning.

3. *Nonconvexities.* Another—and quite unintuitive—economic rationale for zoning rests on the possible existence of what economists call nonconvexities in production possibilities. See Robert Cooter & Thomas Ulen, Law and Economics 169–74 (3d ed. 2000); Theodore M. Crone, Elements of an Economic Justification for Municipal Zoning, 14 J. Urb. Econ. 168 (1983).

To illustrate, consider the vineyards in the Napa Valley, northeast of San Francisco Bay. In light of the intense demand for housing in the Bay Area, assume that social welfare would be maximized if all Napa vineyards were to be converted en masse to housing development. If so, this all-housing outcome would be what economists call the "global optimum," an outcome better than the current "local optimum" (an all-vineyard allocation). Assume also, however, that a partial-housing outcome in the Napa Valley would be even less efficient than an all-vineyard allocation. Under these assumptions, landowners might not be able to bargain their way away from the status quo. If production possibilities were to be nonconvex, neighboring vintners would be able to offer the first-arriving housing developer enough to stop the developer's incremental introduction of housing into the vineyards. Although a complete shift to the all-housing outcome would be efficient, market forces would tend to stymie any first steps in that direction.

According to this theory, only zoning authorities can be expected to recognize the optimality of the all-housing outcome, a goal they could achieve by banning grape-growing in the region. Expositors of this theory are aware that it may be overly optimistic about the relative capabilities and motivations of zoning officials.

The City of Cerritos in Los Angeles County offers an empirical perspective on the nonconvexity theory. Prior to Cerritos's rapid conversion to housing subdivisions in the late 1960s, the city bore the name Dairy Valley and was a center of the southern California dairy industry. The authors are not aware of the roles that zoning officials and dairy-farm owners played in the sudden transformation of Dairy Valley. The nonconvexity theory supposes that public officials would have been the key actors.

4. *Distributive justice.* The effects of government land use regulations inevitably are uneven. Some persons come out ahead, while others suffer losses. Are land use controls plausible instruments, particularly in comparison to broad taxation and welfare policies, for pursuing goals of distributive justice? Studies of the distributive effects of actual planning and zoning systems include Paul Cheshire & Stephen Sheppard, The Welfare Economics of Land Use Planning, 52 J. Urb. Econ. 242 (2002) (asserting that the planning system in southern England imposes significant net costs and is slightly regressive); Jeremy R. Groves & Eric Helland, Zoning and the Distribution of Land Rents: An Empirical Analysis of Harris County, Texas, 78 Land Econ. 28 (2002) (focusing on differential effects on land values). See also the sources, cited at pp. 27–29 and 613–14, on the effects of zoning systems on housing prices.

3.   *Evidence of Externalities*

William A. Fischel, The Economics of Zoning Laws
234–37 (1985)

The approach of externalities and zoning studies is to take the traditional justification for zoning at face value and see whether its underlying assumptions are valid. The traditional story, at least as it is understood by economists, is that zoning is necessary because in the absence of public controls, activities that adversely affect the value of housing will locate in residential neighborhoods. Other purposes of zoning may be advanced, but preservation of residential amenities appears so often in the literature that it seems reasonable to focus on the apex of the traditional pyramid.

Studies investigating this claim usually find a residential neighborhood that has some nonconforming land use and then compare its housing prices with the prices in a similar neighborhood that lacks the nonconforming use. If the first neighborhood's housing prices are lower than those in the second, it means that buyers of housing viewed the nonconforming use as a nuisance to be avoided and lowered their offers for the site. If this effect is found, many researchers conclude that zoning is justified in order to separate nonconforming uses. If there appear to be no systematic differences between the two neighborhoods, zoning is not justified.

Note that I have changed the question around here. "Does zoning have an effect?" has been subtly replaced by "Is zoning justified?" Many people seem to think that these are the same questions, and they quote different studies indiscriminately. I will argue that the externalities studies do not conclusively answer either question.

It will help nonspecialists to understand my criticism of these studies to learn something about their basic procedure. The technique ordinarily employed is to take a sample of houses or census tracts (at least 40) and employ a statistical technique called multiple regression analysis to determine the "price" of the house. In everyday speech we often refer to the value of a house and its price as the same thing. We speak of a house priced at $80,000, for example. But that is not a satisfactory approach to a good as complex and variable as a house.

A house is a composite of many attributes. These include lot size, number of rooms, square feet of interior space, number of bathrooms, size of the garage, type of flooring, extent of insulation, neighborhood and community characteristics, and proximity to jobs, shopping, and schools. The economists' approach to measuring these attributes is the hedonic price index, in which a house's value is thought to be the sum of the value of each attribute.

The empirical question is how important each attribute is. This is where multiple regression analysis comes in. A simple example would be as follows:

$$\text{House Value} = a \text{ (number of rooms)} + b \text{ (lot size)} +$$

$$c \text{ (miles to employment)} + d \text{ (distance to pulp mill)}$$

The coefficients $a, b, c,$ and d are to be estimated by the regressions, while the attributes (number of rooms, lot size, miles to employment, and distance to pulp mill) constitute the data for the sample. The coefficient estimates impute a dollar value to the attribute. For example, the estimate of coefficient a might turn out to be \$4,129, meaning that at the mean of the sample, an extra room adds \$4,129 to the value of the house, other things held constant. Standard statistical tests are applied to the coefficients to see whether they can be accepted as significantly different from zero.

Now consider what one would expect from performing a statistical experiment like this and how the results can be interpreted. We would ordinarily expect coefficients a and b to be positive: more rooms and a bigger lot are attributes that people are willing to pay to have. Coefficient c would usually be negative: as people move farther from their place of employment, they must suffer the increased expense and irritation of long-distance commuting. Coefficient d, the one relevant to the externalities and zoning studies, is expected to be positive; the closer one gets to a pulp mill (or a commercial district, a busy highway, a dilapidated structure, a high-crime neighborhood) the greater is the disamenity effect and the less potential buyers will value the site.

Researchers who undertake these studies are often surprised to find that coefficient d is not significantly different from zero or, if it is significant, how small it seems to be relative to the noise made at zoning hearings about such prospective uses. From these results, some investigators have concluded or implied that externalities are not very important. (I use the term "externalities" . . . to mean spillovers, regardless of whether property rights in them can be established. This is what most empirical studies take it to mean.) This conclusion is probably not warranted. . . . [E]mpirical studies usually underestimate the importance of negative neighborhood effects. . . .

Suppose in the example . . . that the employment center is the pulp mill. This creates a conflicting incentive on the part of potential buyers of the house (who plan to work in the pulp mill or in some other firm nearby). They will want to live near the mill in order to reduce commuting costs, but not too near, in order to keep away from its disamenities. It might well turn out that the estimates of both coefficients c and d are very low or insignificant, because one offsets the other. This will not always be the case, though, especially in large urban areas, where jobs may be located in many different places. Moreover, careful sample selection can overcome this problem if the researchers are aware of it.

There are other reasons why coefficient d might be low. Suppose that construction of the pulp mill is proposed after the nearby houses are built. The residents of the neighborhood object to the construction of the mill at a zoning board hearing. As a result, the pulp mill owners take some steps to reduce the nuisances or to compensate the neighbors.

There are several methods by which the neighbors might be compensated. The mill might provide a park or some other public facility. It might give money to local charities to finance summer camp programs for children in the area. Alternatively, the community authorities might redirect some of the property taxes paid by the mill for special services for the neighborhood.

Each of the aforementioned compensations is directed at the neighborhood rather than at specific individuals. Compensation thus "runs with the land." When a prospective buyer (or tenant) arrives, he will perceive the nuisance effects of the mill, lowering his offer to buy, but he will also perceive the compensatory benefits, raising it right back up. Unless the compensations are separated from the nuisance effects—something few studies attempt to do—the estimate of the importance of nuisances will be too low.

I do not want to be nihilistic about studies of the effects of nuisances on surrounding property values. With the right sample and careful specification, the hedonic price index approach should reveal reasonable estimates of willingness to pay for neighborhood and community amenities. Moreover, other techniques, such as interview surveys about prospective changes in land use, can reveal some information. Answers to these questions are surely valuable for planning purposes.

I wish to address a different question now: What do studies of the importance of externality have to do with the justification for zoning? Suppose that a study using impeccable statistical techniques showed that some nonconforming use had no appreciable effect on neighboring property values. Would this be an argument against zoning? Not necessarily; the reason that the nonconforming use had no effect might be that the area in question was subject to zoning. Zoning authorities may have seen to it that it stayed innocuous or that it satisfied neighboring residents that the benefits to them clearly outweighed the costs. The use of zoning (or even the prospect of zoning) might be precisely the reason why spillovers are hard to detect. The real question is whether zoning results in a more satisfactory use of land than does some other system.

If this is the question, would not the discovery that spillovers do affect property values be an indictment of zoning? Again, it does not necessarily follow. Just because one land parcel's value is reduced does not mean that total welfare is reduced. Suppose that zoning authorities ignore the objections of neighbors and allow a mill to be constructed on a certain site. Neighbors' property values are reduced by $20,000; however, the utilization of that particular site by the mill allows the value of paper production to rise by $50,000. Is this situation undesirable?

Note on Research on Externalities

1. *Why external effects may be hard to detect.* As Fischel mentions, a number of studies have reached the conclusion that externalities from discordant land uses are not significant in urban land markets. See, e.g., John P. Crecine et al., Urban Property Markets: Some Empirical Results and Their Implications for Municipal Zoning, 10 J.L. & Econ. 79 (1967); S.M. Maser et al., The Effects of Zoning and Externalities on the Price of Land, 20 J.L. & Econ. 111 (1977).

Fischel indicates several possible shortcomings of these studies. Another sort of critique appears in Ronald E. Grieson & James R. White, The Existence and Capitalization of Neighborhood Externalities: A Reassessment, 25 J. Urb. Econ. 68 (1989). Grieson and White note that a house situated next to a commercial district might not sell for less because bidders for the site would take into account its unusually high probability of later being rezoned for commercial use.

Many scholars, especially those analyzing suburban samples, have found that values of single-family houses are sensitive to neighboring land uses. In addition to the more specific studies presented in the next series of notes, see Ronald N. Lafferty & H.E. Frech, Community Environment and the Market Value of Single-Family Homes, 21 J.L. & Econ. 381 (1978) (finding that houses are more valuable when other types of land uses in the same city are spatially concentrated, not dispersed); William J. Stull, Community Environment, Zoning, and the Market Value of Single-Family Homes, 18 J.L. & Econ. 535 (1975) (finding homeowners in Boston suburbs preferred living in homogeneous single-family communities to residing in those containing large amounts of industrial or vacant land). See generally The Economics of Urban Amenities (Douglas B. Diamond, Jr. & George S. Tolley eds., 1982).

2. *Commercial, industrial, and utility facilities.* Few surprises appear in Stanley W. Hamilton & Gregory M. Schwann, Do High Voltage Electric Transmission Lines Affect Property Value?, 71 Land Econ. 436 (1995). The authors report that transmission towers impose negative externalities, primarily visual ones. Properties immediately adjacent lose 6.3 percent of value, but the effect falls off sharply with distance. Negative externalities from a dump appear to decline more slowly with distance. See Arthur C. Nelson et al., Price Effects of Landfills on House Values, 68 Land Econ. 359 (1992). Noise, predictably, depresses nearby property values. Marcel A.J. Theebe, Planes, Trains, and Automobiles: The Impact of Traffic Noise on House Prices, 28 J. Real Est. Fin. & Econ. 209 (2004).

The erection of an 11-story office building in Dallas was found to impose mixed externalities in a pattern that Fischel's pulp-mill example anticipates. See Thomas G. Thibodeau, Estimating the Effect of High-Rise Office Buildings on Residential Property Values, 66 Land Econ. 402, 403 (1990):

> Residential property values for nearby houses are discounted by as much as 15 percent. Alternatively, values for properties 1,000 meters away from the high rise sell for a 5 percent premium. The aggregate effect of the high rise—the positive externality benefits less the negative externality costs summed over all properties within 2,500 meters of Lennox Center—is positive. Lennox Center increased aggregate residential property values about 1 percent.

See also John K. Kain & John M. Quigley, Measuring the Value of House Quality, 65 J. Am. Stat. Ass'n 532 (1970) (finding that presence of commercial or industrial uses on a parcel's face-block had negative effects on values of residential uses).

3. *Institutional uses.* Immediate proximity to a school is usually found to lower the value of residential property. See William S. Hendon, Property Values, Schools, and Park-School Combinations, 49 Land Econ. 216 (1973). Churches have been found to have negative effects up to 850 feet away. See A. Quang Do et al., An Empirical Examination of the Externalities of Neighborhood Churches on Housing Values, 9 J. Real Est. Fin. & Econ. 127 (1994). There is no consensus on the neighborhood effects of group homes for persons with physical or mental disabilities. Compare George Galster et al., Supportive Housing and Neighborhood Property Value Externalities, 80 Land Econ. 33 (2004) (finding positive effects on the value of property located 1,000–2,000 feet away), with Peter F. Colwell et al., The Effect of Group Homes on Neighborhood Property Values, 76 Land Econ. 615 (2000) (finding negative effects on value of nearby property). Do these results support the common municipal practice, treated at pp. 296–302, of requiring a developer of an institutional use to obtain a conditional-use permit?

4. *Parks, open spaces, and wetlands.* Proximity to a park generally enhances the value of nearby residential property. But nearness to a park apparently can be a disadvantage in some situations. Studies indicate that house prices are lower, all else equal, near parks that contain heavily used recreational facilities. In addition, a residential property typically sells for less if it directly abuts either recreational or nonrecreational open space. The loss of privacy and security threatened when a residential lot has a scenic park beside or behind it apparently can outweigh whatever advantages consumers see in being immediately adjacent to a greenway. See generally Mark R. Correll et al., The Effects of Greenbelts on Residential

Property Values, 54 Land Econ. 207 (1978); Thomas R. Hammer et al., The Effect of a Large Park on Real Estate Value, 40 J. Am. Inst. Planners 274 (1974). But cf. A. Quang Do & Gary Grudnitski, Golf Courses and Residential House Prices, 10 J. Real Est. Fin. & Econ. 261 (1995) (finding that a house abutting a golf course sells for a premium in San Diego suburbs); Brent L. Mahan et al., Valuing Urban Wetlands: A Property Price Approach, 76 Land Econ. 100 (2000) (finding proximity to wetlands, regardless of type, increases urban home values).

5. *Multifamily housing.* Most zoning ordinances seek to insulate single-family houses from apartment buildings. There is some evidence—weaker than one might suppose— that proximity to low-density, nonsubsidized multifamily buildings does negatively affect house values. See David M. Grether & Peter Mieszkowski, The Effects of Nonresidential Land Uses on the Prices of Adjacent Housing, 8 J. Urb. Econ. 1 (1980); Keith Ihlanfeldt & Thomas P. Boehm, Government Intervention in the Housing Market: An Empirical Test of the Externalities Rationale, 22 J. Urb. Econ. 276 (1987).

6. *Subsidized housing.* Does proximity to government-assisted housing affect property values for better or worse? The wide variety of both subsidized projects (see pp. 869–80) and neighborhoods complicates the question. For a review of the literature, see Michael H. Schill et al., Revitalizing Inner-City Neighborhoods: New York City's Ten-Year Plan, 13 Hous. Pol'y Debate 529 (2002) (reporting positive effects in the case of New York City's inner-city program).

The findings of various studies are hard to reconcile. For example, on the effects of moderate-income projects that confer shallow subsidies on tenants, compare Joseph S. DeSalvo, Neighborhood Upgrading Effects of Middle Income Housing Projects in New York City, 1 J. Urb. Econ. 269 (1974) (finding that Mitchell-Lama projects enhanced value of city neighborhoods), with Donald C. Guy et al., The Effect of Subsidized Housing on Values of Adjacent Housing, 13 AREUEA J. 378 (1985) (finding that suburban §221(d)(3) and §236 projects had negative impacts). See also Amy Ellen Schwartz et al., The External Effects of Place-Based Subsidized Housing (Furman Center Working Paper, 2005) (generally finding significant and sustained positive effects, perhaps partly as a result of the elimination of prior disamenities).

7. *Owned versus rented houses.* As the fraction of leased (as opposed to owner-occupied) single-family houses rises in a residential neighborhood, property values tend to drop. Ko Wang et al., The Impact of Rental Properties on the Value of Single-Family Residences, 30 J. Urb. Econ. 152 (1991). The authors attribute this result to the likelihood that leased property will be worse maintained than owner-occupied property. Might it also reflect consumer preferences for neighborhoods where residents do not turn over rapidly? See also Chang-Moo Lee et al., The Differential Impacts of Federally Assisted Housing Programs on Nearby Property Values: A Philadelphia Case Study, 10 Hous. Pol'y Debate 75 (1999) (finding that government programs that subsidize homeownership generate positive neighborhood effects).

8. *Relevance.* There is little solid information about how various land uses affect the value of neighboring property. If that is so, how can courts (to anticipate some issues to come): (a) measure damages in nuisance cases? (b) determine when covenants should be terminated because of changed neighborhood conditions? (c) decide whether zoning restrictions meet constitutional or statutory requirements of rationality? and (d) review special assessments or subdivision exactions imposed on landowners to recoup the benefits conferred by public facilities? Are the views of real estate appraisers and brokers—the usual experts consulted when property valuations are in dispute—a sufficiently reliable basis for such decisions?

B.   *Competing Conceptions of Local Politics*

William A. Fischel, The Homevoter Hypothesis
4–6, 12 (2001)

. . . The homevoter hypothesis holds that homeowners, who are the most numerous and politically influential group within most localities, are guided by their concern for the value of their homes to make political decisions that are more efficient than those that would be made at a higher level of government. Homeowners are acutely aware that local amenities, public services, and taxes affect ("are capitalized in") the value of the largest single asset they own. As a result, they pay much closer attention to such policies at the local level than they would at the state or national level. They balance the benefits of local policies against the costs when the policies affect the value of their home, and they will tend to choose those policies that preserve or increase the value of their homes.

The importance of a home for the typical owner can hardly be overstated. Two-thirds of all homes are owner-occupied. For the great majority of these homeowners, the equity in their home is the most important savings they have. . . .

I am arguing both positive and normative positions [here]. I think that, subject to some important qualifications, local governments perform localized services more efficiently than the state or national government would. But readers do not have to accept my normative contentions to find something useful here. The approach that yields the best understanding of local government behavior, and hence the best predictions about what happens when institutional arrangements are changed, is to see that behavior through the eyes of a homeowner. . . .

. . . An increase in local property taxes to add teachers for schools may make the community more attractive to homebuyers. This will, if the program is cost effective, add to the value of all homes in the community, not just of homes currently containing school-age children. The prospect of a capital gain (or the anxiety about a loss if the schools are left to deteriorate) makes the policy more palatable to the majority of voters, even those who do not have children in school. . . .

Attention to home prices will also guide regulatory policies. A town that is asked to rezone property for a low-level nuclear waste dump in exchange for $2 million a year in cash and benefits has to consider not just the value of the cash (which could be used to cut property taxes or to augment local services), but also the effect that harboring the dump will have on the community's reputation and health and hence the value of the voters' homes. This probably accounts for why the actual proffer of such a deal in New Jersey found no takers among that state's 567 municipalities. . . .

. . . Concern about the vulnerability of their largest asset also explains why homeowners are more likely to participate in school board meetings, vote in local elections, and otherwise participate in community affairs. There is hard evidence that they do so. Denise DiPasquale and Edward Glaeser analyzed a national survey of citizen participation in local affairs. Even after controlling for other economic and demographic differences between homeowners and renters, they found that homeowners were more conscientious citizens and more effective in providing community amenities.

The importance and vulnerability of their asset are not the only reasons that homeowners are more likely to be the major local political actors. Living in a home for a long time creates a personal attachment for which changes in the neighborhood and community are upsetting. Surveys indicate that long-term residence by both renters and homeowners is an important factor in community participation. But length of residence does not always mean more protectiveness. Kent Portney found that long-time residents were *less* opposed than newcomers to the establishment of proposed waste-disposal sites in Massachusetts. Less systematically, I have observed that people who have just moved into the neighborhood are often most concerned about proposed land-use changes. Maybe noneconomic attachments to neighborhoods and community are formed that quickly, but I suspect that the size of the down payment and the newly acquired mortgage make new homeowners especially watchful of local activity. The uninsurable-asset aspect of homeownership still seems like the key factor. . . .

Frank I. Michelman, Political Markets and Community Self-Determination: Competing Judicial Models of Local Government Legitimacy
53 Ind. L.J. 145, 147–53 (1977–1978)

. . . [I]t is natural to think that a judge formulating doctrine or deciding cases in [areas of public law] would have somewhere in mind a normative model of government, however indistinct, inarticulate, or intuitive the model might be—a normative model being a general conception of how governmental institutions ideally must be supposed to work in order to satisfy the conditions of a theory of moral justification for such institutions. Governmental institutions tend to occupy morally problematic positions—generate a continuing demand for moral justification—because our world is one in which ultimate ends are generally taken to be those of individuals, and social arrangements, accordingly, tend to be judged by their conduciveness to individual welfare, individual self-realization, and individual freedom.

[This essay hypothesizes] the coexistence in the judicial mentality of two different, and contradictory, models of local-government legitimacy—an economic or "public choice" model and a non-economic "public interest" or "community self-determination" model. . . .

In the economic or public choice model, all substantive values or ends are regarded as strictly private and subjective. The legislature is conceived as a market-like arena in which votes instead of money are the medium of exchange. The rule of majority rule arises strictly in the guise of a technical device for prudently controlling the transaction costs of individualistic exchanges.[15] Legislative intercourse is not public-spirited but self-interested. Legislators do not deliberate towards goals, they dicker towards terms. There is no right answer, there are only struck bargains.[16] There is no public or general or social interest, there are only concatenations of particular interests or private preferences. There is no reason, only strategy;[17] no persuasion, only temptation and threat. There are no good legislators, only shrewd ones; no statesmen, only messengers; no entrusted representatives, only tethered agents.

The opposed, public interest model depends at bottom on a belief in the reality—or at least the possibility—of public or objective values and ends for human action. In this public interest model the legislature is regarded as a forum for identifying or defining and acting towards those ends. The process is one of mutual search through joint deliberation relying on the use of reason supposed to have persuasive force. Majority rule is experienced as the natural way of taking action as and for a group—or as a device for filtering the reasonable from the unreasonable, the persuasive from the unpersuasive, the right from the wrong, and the good from the bad. Moral insight, sociological understanding, and goodwill are all

15. See generally J. Buchanan & G. Tullock, The Calculus of Consent (1962).
16. See, e.g., G. Stigler, The Citizen and the State 114–41 (1975).
17. See, e.g., W. Riker, The Theory of Political Coalitions (1962).

legislative virtues. Representatives are chosen in part for their supposed excellence in such virtues. This model, no doubt, is as sentimental as the public-choice model is unlovely; but though public interest may in that sense be a less "realistic" way of looking at the world than public choice, I doubt that it is less real as a description of our actual way of experiencing and interpreting our political life; nor is it less real—and here is a major thesis of this essay—as a description of the way judges perceive that life.

Coexistence of the two opposed models of legitimacy may be connected with a deep controversy in our philosophical tradition between opposed notions of human freedom and value. On the one hand there is a tradition deeply entrenched in Western thought—chiefly associated with Kant and Rousseau but apparently tracing back at least to Aristotle[27]—that conceives individual freedom in such a way that its attainment depends on the possibility of values that are communal and objective—jointly recognized by members of a group and determinable through reasoned interchange among them. In the conception advanced by Rousseau and Kant, freedom is the state of giving the law to oneself. This conception is, to put it a bit crudely, one of self-regulation as opposed to self-indulgence. It implies that unfettered trade in a perfectly free, competitive market cannot by itself constitute a person's freedom; for by itself free trade can be taken as a reflection of perfect enslavement to wants or appetites that are not chosen but just impinge on one inexplicably and uncontrollably. Freedom in the Kantian view must mean choosing one's ends by an activity of reason. . . . If reason can liberate from appetite, it can do so only insofar as the reasoner can somehow rise above the question of what long-range plan will best satisfy the present wants of the person as he is in the world as it is, to deal rather with a question about how one is to become or remain the person he wants to be, in the world he needs to live in if he is to be that person. Reasoning in such a constitutive mode seems to involve constraint of choice by some principle or set of principles other than the principle of maximizing the satisfaction—even the long-range satisfaction—of one's present wants.

There may be grounds for thinking that, for many if not all individuals, the possibility of such a reasoned choice of ends will depend on the individual's functioning—by participation and commitment—as a member of a group of persons engaged in making choices by which all members are bound. If so, then it is the case not only that freedom for individuals depends upon the possibility of objective ends or values to which one can commit oneself on principle; but also that for individuals in secular society such ends or values will encompass matters of interpersonal relationship, obligation, and respect and, for the freedom-seeking socialized individual, the political process will be both a medium for reasoning towards the ends (and acting towards their attainment) and, at the same time, itself one of the ends. And so the Kantian notion of freedom seems to be a link that connects a public-interest model of politics with an objective stance towards values.

On the other hand there is a strictly individualist and subjectivist conception of human experience, a conception which serves as a foundation for modern economic analysis. . . .

Note on Conceptions of Local Government

1. *The public choice model.* Fischel, p. 46, and Komesar, p. 34, both implicitly embrace what Michelman calls an "economic or public choice model" of local politics. This model

---

27. Compare Aristotle, Politics (J. Warrington tr.) *in* Aristotle's Politics and the Athenian Constitution 156 (Everyman's ed. 1959): "In extreme democracies . . . everyone lives as he pleases, as Euripides says, 'for any end he happens to desire.' But this is an altogether unsatisfactory conception of liberty. It is quite wrong to imagine that life subject to constitutional control is mere slavery; it is in fact salvation." See E. Barker, The Political Thought of Plato and Aristotle 355 (Dover ed. 1959). Durkheim is another notable contributor to this associational conception of freedom. See E. Durkheim, Suicide 169–70, 210–15, 248–49, 289–90, 356 (J. Spaulding & G. Simpson tr., 1951); R. Wolff, The Poverty of Liberalism 143–45 (1968).

includes both descriptive and normative components. Descriptively the model is grounded on what Michelman calls the "unlovely" proposition that voters, politicians, bureaucrats, interest groups, and others all tend to be self-interested. Fischel sees homevoters, for example, as striving to boost the value of their houses. The theory of public finance (presented at pp. 625–27) provides the normative component of the economic model. It basically calls for local governments to pursue cost-effective policies to correct "market failures" such as uninternalized externalities from private land use decisions. More precisely, some economic theorists have proposed that a local government seek to maximize the aggregate value of the land within municipal boundaries. Jon C. Sonstelie & Paul R. Portnoy, Profit Maximizing Communities and the Theory of Local Public Expenditures, 5 J. Urb. Econ. 263 (1978).

The public choice model allows for the possibility, indeed likelihood, of "government failures." In practice, a municipality might act not to maximize the aggregate value of land within it but rather, for example, to maximize the wealth of the median homevoter, perhaps to the detriment of political minorities and owners of undeveloped land. See William A. Fischel, Regulatory Takings 255–59 (1995) (reviewing literature on the median-voter model). See also pp. 303–09 (on the politics of rezoning).

2. *Civic republicanism.* The descriptive and normative components of Michelman's "public interest" or "community self-determination" model, more conventionally called civic republicanism, are quite different. This model conceives of citizens not so much as bringing already formed values to the public sphere, but rather as finding their values there. Civic republicans place less normative weight than economists do on the substantive merits of municipal decisions, and more weight on whether public deliberations promote solidarity, inculcate virtue, and foster citizen self-governance. In the civic republican vision, an advocate's appeal to the "public interest" is not necessarily naive, but perhaps a plausible tactic for evoking the latent altruism harbored by the socialized members of a community. Fischel himself hardly dismisses this possibility out of hand. Elsewhere he states: "What I am arguing as a normative matter is that the world will get more of these good things [public schools and amenable environments] if the motive to do good is lined up with the motive to do well." Homevoter Hypothesis, at 18.

For an analysis stressing the social dimensions of land use decisions, see Michael J. Sandel, Democracy's Discontent 334–36 (1996). Sandel lauds community activists in small towns and cities who oppose the opening of a big-box retailer such as Wal-Mart at a remote highway interchange. The advent of a Wal-Mart, he implies, tends not only to depreciate the physical capital in the older downtown retail district, but also to destroy the social capital that had previously kept the town together. Sandel also praises proponents of the New Urbanism (a movement discussed at pp. 422–24 and 793–95) for favoring pedestrian-friendly designs, front porches, public squares, and other features that might enhance the quality of civic life. Is Sandel's vision overly romantic? Would an adherent of the economic model object to internalizing the effects of a developer's decisions on the stock of social capital?

3. *Implications of competing conceptions.* Should analysts systematically vary their positive and normative conceptions of municipal behavior with the geographic scope, or generality, of the issue that the municipality is confronting? For the argument that quite different models are appropriate for small-scale, piecemeal decisions as opposed to large-scale decisions, see Carol M. Rose, New Models for Local Land Use Decisions, 79 Nw. U. L. Rev. 1155 (1984–1985). Rose asserts that models of legislative lawmaking are inappropriate when a local government addresses a decision that involves only a small site. See also Chapter 4A and 4B (on the law of piecemeal zoning changes).

To what extent should positive and normative models vary with the characteristics of a municipality? For example, how might the political dynamics of a large central city with a diverse population differ from those of a homogeneous suburb, or those of a rural county? See pp. 305–08.

Could the articulation of a normative model of local government itself have real-world effects? For example, might the legitimation of the public choice model engender more selfishness? Many judicial opinions implicitly embrace a public interest model of municipal politics. Might this normative rhetoric serve to raise the aspirations of citizens and officials?

Under either of Michelman's normative models, would a local government that faithfully responded to the concerns of its residents necessarily be promoting the welfare of its metropolitan area and state? On the regional obligations of municipalities, see Chapter 9.

4. *Additional sources.* On the evolving field of public choice, see, e.g., Daniel A. Farber & Philip P. Frickey, Law and Public Choice (1991); Jerry L. Mashaw, Greed, Chaos, and Governance: Using Public Choice to Improve Public Law (1997); and Dennis C. Mueller, Public Choice III (2003). On civic republicanism, see, e.g., Michael J. Sandel, Liberalism and the Limits of Justice (2d ed. 1998); Richard H. Fallon, What Is Republicanism, and Is It Worth Reviving?, 102 Harv. L. Rev. 1695 (1989); Cass Sunstein, Beyond the Republican Revival, 97 Yale L.J. 1539 (1988).

On the dynamics of local government in particular, see Richard Briffault, Our Localism: Part II, 90 Colum. L. Rev. 346, 392–435 (1990) (contrasting local government as "polis" with local government as "firm"). Briffault notes that citizens are less likely to vote in local elections than in state and federal elections. See id. at 397–98. Is this fact consistent with Fischel's homevoter hypothesis? In The City as a Legal Concept, 93 Harv. L. Rev. 1059 (1980), Gerald Frug asserts that the relative powerlessness of local government has led to voter apathy. For counterpoint, see Robert C. Ellickson, Cities and Homeowners Associations, 130 U. Pa. L. Rev. 1519 (1982) (challenging Frug's claim that cities are weak).

For a review of studies of local zoning authorities in action, see Melvyn R. Durchslag, *Village of Euclid v. Ambler Realty Co.*, Seventy-Five Years Later, 51 Case W. Res. L. Rev. 645, 654–60 (2001). Durchslag asserts that local representatives commonly behave in a more public-spirited fashion than a public choice theorist would predict.

C.   Planning, Planners, Plans

Even apart from the allure of civic republicanism, the existence of both externalities and transaction costs should shake the confidence of observers inclined to relegate all land use decisionmaking to private landowners. With market coordination cast into doubt, the agenda now turns to the converse task of fostering uncertainty about the relative competence of a government to plan the use of private land.

Although local land use plans appear in many varieties, a typical one includes a statement of goals and a map that indicates desired land uses (usually less precisely than a zoning map does). The vocabulary of planning is not standardized. Sabo v. Township of Monroe, 232 N.W.2d 584, 594 n.14 (Mich. 1975), quotes Arthur Abba Goldberg, Zoning and Land Use 17 (1972), as follows:

> "Master plan" is but one of many terms that can be used to describe the document which local governments used with varying degrees of success as a guide to the physical development of their communities. Over the years a variety of names have been used to describe this document: official plan, comprehensive plan, and central plan. The term "official plan" was in vogue during the 1930's, while during the 1940's "master plan" was the term used. The 1950's saw the term "comprehensive plan" become popular and in the 1960's it was the "general plan."

Plans have taken on considerable legal importance in many states. This subchapter introduces planning theory and the planning profession, presents illustrative plans and illustrative statutes that require a local government to plan, and concludes with materials that probe the question of when land use planning is worth the candle. (The issue of the legal significance of a local plan is deferred to pp. 336–41.)

1.   The Planning Process

In their influential book on the Chicago public housing program, Meyerson and Banfield explicitly define the steps in the planning process:

> A *course of action* is a sequence of prospective acts which are viewed as a unit of action; the acts which comprise the sequence are mutually related as means to the attainment of ends. A *plan* is a course of action which can be carried into effect, which can be expected to lead to the attainment of the ends sought, and which someone (an effectuating organization) intends to carry into effect. (By contrast, a course of action which could not be carried out, which would not have the consequences intended, or which no one intends to carry out is a "utopian scheme" rather than a plan.)

Martin Meyerson & Edward C. Banfield, Politics, Planning and the Public Interest 312 (1955). The authors essentially define planning as the articulation of goals and the rational consideration of various courses of action for achieving those goals. See id. at 312–15. Thus defined, planning is a pervasive activity practiced to some degree by virtually all individuals and organizations.

City plans vary in a number of basic dimensions: the size of the geographic area covered; the time span of control efforts within that space; and the array of activities controlled. The larger the territory, the longer the time period, and the greater the number of activities regulated, the more "comprehensive" the plan. Early city plans, such as the 1791 L'Enfant Plan for Washington (reproduced at p. 413), mainly were attempts to control the location of streets, parks, and public buildings, not the use of the private parcels situated within this public grid. The City Beautiful movement, triggered by the Columbian Exposition in Chicago in 1893, similarly stressed the design of the public armature. By the mid-twentieth century, however, the scope of public planning had been broadened to encompass the use of private lands.

Writing on the planning of cities dates back at least to Aristotle. See Politics of Aristotle 306–09 (Ernest Barker trans., 1946). On the history of American ideas and efforts, see Alexander Garvin, The American City: What Works, What Doesn't (2d ed. 2002); Jon A. Peterson, The Birth of City Planning in the United States, 1840–1917 (2003); John W. Reps, The Making of Urban America: A History of City Planning in the United States (1965). The most influential critic of planning has been Jane Jacobs, who announces in the first sentence of The Death and Life of Great American Cities 3 (1961) that "This book is an attack on current city planning and building." Jacobs's basic criticism is that planners have tended to segregate differing public and private land uses, while a city thrives only when it allows land uses to be intricately diverse and close-grained. Similarly skeptical is Kenneth L. Kolson, Big Plans: The Allure and Folly of Urban Design (2002).

Land use planning is sometimes associated with the now-repudiated practice of dreaming about how a community might appear on a specific date far in the future. Planners who followed this practice usually chose a round number as their target (the year 2000 was extremely popular during the mid-twentieth century) and prepared futuristic maps and pictures portraying life at that time. "Plans" of this sort have almost never had any significant effect. Meyerson and Banfield describe these as "utopian schemes"; others who have been less charitable have called them "letters to Santa Claus." Influential critiques of these long-range, end-state plans include Melville C. Branch, Continuous City Planning (1981); and Martin Meyerson, Building the Middle-Range Bridge for Comprehensive Planning, 22 J. Am. Inst. Planners 58 (1956).

In the 1950s, the federal government swung its weight behind comprehensive land use planning. In 1954, Congress required that a local government have a "workable program for community improvement" to be eligible for urban renewal funding and other federal grants-in-aid; a "workable program" was defined to include progress toward adoption of a comprehensive plan. The Section 701 program, also begun in 1954, provided federal financial support for plan preparation. The first generation of plans produced in response to this federal impetus did little to add to the prestige of the planning profession. The plans that were adopted usually had little legal effect and tended to be ignored by policymakers. See Alan A. Altshuler, The City Planning Process 84–143 (1965) (devastating critique of how a plan was prepared and adopted in the late 1950s in St. Paul, Minnesota). Moreover, many plans prepared during this period were formally aborted. Even as late as 1970, the planning departments of Los Angeles and New York were producing massive drafts of general plans that ultimately were not adopted by their cities.

By around 1980, virtually all planning professionals had come to recognize both the limits of rationality and the unpredictability of modern civilization. Planners thus have tended to become less ambitious in the dimensions of space and time. "Specific plans" applicable to particular subcity areas have come into vogue. See Note 3, p. 65. Many planners also have come to believe that the planning period should not stretch beyond 25 years (at the very most) and that detailed planning should concentrate on the next 5 years or so. There also is agreement that plans have to be continually revised to take account of new information and events. In sum, flexible, middle-range planning has come to replace long-range, end-state planning. We shall soon see, however, that some critics doubt the wisdom of even these more modest planning efforts, particularly insofar as they apply to use of private lands.

Especially after 1991, the federal government has conditioned portions of federal transportation funding on progress in metropolitan-wide transportation planning. See, e.g., 23 U.S.C. §134 (2004). Would Jacobs object to comprehensive planning of this part of the public grid?

a.   Planning Theory

Daniel Burnham, an influential architect, is famous for the adage, "Make no little plans. They have no magic to stir men's blood. . . . " Burnham, a central figure in the City Beautiful movement, designed the layout of Chicago's Columbian Exposition of 1893 and coauthored the Plan of Chicago (1909), a document privately commissioned by the Commercial Club. Burnham's plan envisioned a new city center, parks, bridges, and boulevards. The plan had some influence on the subsequent development of Chicago's lakefront.

At the time of its formation in the late 1970s as a result of the merger of the American Institute of Planners and the American Society of Planning Officials, the American Planning Association (APA) adopted a set of official policies. Here are some excerpts. To what extent do the APA policies honor Burnham's call for ambition in planning? Echo the stress, in his Chicago plan, on the physical layout of *public* spaces?

American Planning Association, Policies and Commentary
reprinted in Planning, July 1979, at 24B, 24H

THE ROLE OF PLANNING

COMMENTARY:

Definition. Planning is a comprehensive, coordinated and continuing process, the purpose of which is to help public and private decision makers arrive at decisions which promote the common good of society. This process includes: (1) Identification of problems or issues; (2) Research and analysis to provide definitive understanding of such problems or issues; (3) Formulation of goals and objectives to be attained in alleviating problems or resolving issues; (4) Development and evaluation of alternative methods (plans and programs) to attain agreed upon goals and objectives; (5) Recommendation of appropriate courses of action from among the alternatives; (6) Assistance in implementation of approved plans and programs; (7) Evaluation of actions taken to implement approved plans and programs in terms of progress towards agreed upon goals and objectives; and (8) A continuing process of adjusting plans and programs in light of the results of such evaluation or to take into account changed circumstances.

The planning process attempts to identify, accurately reflect and provide means for the significant participation of the diverse interests involved in any planning problem or issue. The interests involved typically include business, labor, concerned citizens, minority groups, governmental units at several levels, various professions and news media.

The planning process provides long range, as well as short range perspectives for decision makers. It attempts to provide public and private decision makers with the best possible information, analyses, and recommendations to promote the public welfare, to help eliminate duplication within government and burdens on the private sector, to help resolve conflicts among public policies and to assist in the rational allocation of human, natural and financial resources.

Scope of Planning. Planning practice now encompasses such functional or topical public policy areas as:

Growth Management
Housing and Community Development
Economic Development
Environmental Quality
Energy and Other Natural Resource Conservation and Development
Aesthetics and Historic Preservation
Transportation
Health, Education and Welfare
Public Safety
Leisure, Recreation and Cultural Opportunities

The planning process may be, and often is, used within each of these areas (functional planning), as well as for coordination among them (comprehensive planning). In addition, this process can be used by competing special interests and individuals as they pursue their own interests and participate in the making of public policy.

Location of the Planning Function. Public planning in the United States as it is known today began as part of a citizen movement for "good government." Most communities first experienced planning in the form of independently appointed advisory planning commissions with some administrative responsibilities. In recent years, the planning function has been moving into the regular departmental structures of government under the chief executives—mayors, county executives, chief administrative officers and governors. Planning commissions sometimes are retained, but without administrative or decision making powers. Within the executive branches, planning responsibilities usually are split between the functional departments and a central planning unit close to the chief executive. Part of the public planning function is also fulfilled by special purpose authorities that are charged with a variety of functions in single or multijurisdictional settings.

The growing interdependence of local communities has caused the need for areawide coordinative planning by multijurisdictional organizations. Also, as the planning function has come increasingly under the influence of chief executives, the need developed for inclusion of state and local legislative bodies into the planning process. Many minority groups, business interests, institutions and citizen organizations also have felt the need for access to planning expertise of their own. To satisfy these needs, planners frequently work for legislative units and help a variety of interest groups to participate in the making of public policy.

Products of the Planning Process. The planning process produces advice to public and private decision makers in many forms. Among these are: (1) Written policy proposals; (2) Plans with maps and other illustrations; (3) Special reports analyzing problems, impacts and issues or evaluating existing programs; (4) Improvement programs projecting ahead several years a series of prioritized capital and operating activities geared to the realization of long term goals; (5) Annual reports, budgets and legislative programs suggesting needed actions for the immediate future; (6) Proposed codes and ordinances needed to regulate development; (7) Recommendations regarding individual cases to be decided under codes, ordinances, budgets and improvement programs; (8) Managerial controls to link current activities with desired goals within a single organization; and (9) Coordinative procedures to link the activities of diverse groups toward the achievement of common goals.

APA POLICIES:

1. Planning (as defined in the above commentary) should be widely practiced by the private sector and by all levels and branches of government, and its fruits should be made readily available both within and outside of government in forms which will be clearly understood by public and private decision makers, the general public and others who may be involved or affected. . . .

BASIC [PLANNING] GOALS

COMMENTARY:

In the broadest terms, planning is concerned with achieving the highest possible quality of life for all in the most cost-effective way. In pursuing this goal, planning operates in the framework of policies aimed at the realization of objectives that deal with only one or another aspect of the quality of our lives. It is useful, therefore, to state the goals which the planning profession accepts as the desired ultimate result of the aggregate of policies with which it deals.

APA POLICIES:

The aggregate of national nondefense oriented policies at all levels of government should aim to achieve the following goals:

a. Increased opportunities for all people to enjoy as many as possible of the benefits which this nation can provide. These include decent shelter and mobility, goods and services, jobs and income, protection under the Constitution, total health care, high quality education and cultural experiences, personal safety, high quality environment and communities, and a chance for personal fulfillment.

b. Increased number of choices that individuals can make in pursuit of their own needs and wants.

c. Increased opportunities for all people to enjoy their heritage within a framework that values all equally.

Note on Planning Theory

1. *Turmoil.* Many planning theorists do not subscribe to the mainstream approach articulated in the APA Policies. For a taste of the ferment of self-criticism that pervades the planning literature, see Edward J. Kaiser & David R. Godschalk, Twentieth Century Land Use Planning, 61 J. Am. Plan. Ass'n 365 (1995); Planning Theory in the 1980s: A Search for Future Directions (Robert W. Burchell & George Sternlieb eds., 1978).

2. *Planning fashions.* Schools of planning theory have tended to rise and ebb within a period of no more than a decade or so. Peter Hall, The Turbulent Eighth Decade, 55 J. Am. Plan. Ass'n 275 (1989), distinguishes ten periods in the history of planning from 1890 to 1989. Notable ones are The City Beautiful (1901–1915), The City Functional (1916–1939), The City Renewable (1937–1964), and The City Enterprising (1980–1989). To what extent does this trendiness caution against attempts at long-range planning?

3. *Planning theory and economic theory.* Would planning theory be strengthened if it were more explicitly based on economics, in particular on the role of the public sector in assisting the internalization of externalities?

4. *Advocacy planning.* Beginning in the late 1960s, one wing of the planning profession began to stress community organizing to empower individuals who are relatively disadvantaged. On this movement, see Norman Krumholz & Pierre Clavel, Reinventing Cities: Equity Planners Tell Their Stories (1994).

b. The Planning Profession

Anthony J. Catanese & W. Paul Farmer, Personality, Politics, and Planning
180–81, 183–84, 186–90 (1978)

[The authors report on their lengthy conversations with the chief planners of seven large central cities.]

. . . We suspected that there might be a gap between theory and practice—we found instead a chasm. There appears to be little congruence between the theoretical works in the field of city planning and the practice that we have been examining. Most of the planners we talked with had little interest in the detail and intricacies of city planning theory, although they were aware of the major writers and overall themes. The specific content and breadth of that body of theory seemed to hold little relevance for these planners.

This is an intriguing finding. Does it signify the often-mentioned academic and impractical bent of theoreticians, usually based in universities or research institutes, or does it allude to the reality of the practice of planning, which may not have the leeway for experimentation? The planners in this set of discussions were clearly of the opinion that the theories were unrealistic or esoteric. Almost all of them had a deep skepticism and, in some cases, cynicism for the theories found in the literature of the field. This skepticism was often focused on the substance of the theory, but in many cases it was focused on the person propounding the theory. It was usually stated that the theories and theoreticians were divorced from the realities of planning practice in large central cities and that the persons writing the theories seemed to be out of touch with local politics and politicians. . . .

This brings us to the clearly discernible characteristic common to all of these planners—politicization. All of the planners in this series made it known that they were working for political leaders and within a political setting and, hence, had to rely upon successful performance in the political arena. It was quite fascinating to hear so many chief planners from such diverse cities explain how they tried to make the nontechnical skills of the politician useful to planners. For example, there was much talk about compromises, forming coalitions, and predicting the political feasibility of plans. While this may seem eminently reasonable, there is very little such discussion in the literature of planning (and what exists is very recent in origin). . . .

One further point should be made concerning this characteristic of politicization—that is, the demise in significance of the "independent planning commission." The history of city planning in the United States really starts with the late nineteenth century and early twentieth century Reform Movements. These led to the peculiar notion of keeping city planning sacrosanct, protecting it from evil politicians by having planners working for a righteous group of public-spirited individuals who composed an independent planning commission (which was usually called the "city planning commission"). The reformers believed that this would allow planners to deal with substantive issues of city growth and development in such a manner that only the objective and nonpolitical aspects of the matter need be examined. In essence, the commissioners shielded the planners from the politicians. To a certain extent, the commissioners thought of themselves as the voice of the people.

All of the planners that we have talked with in this endeavor have abandoned any pretext of belief in that early theory. Some of the planners expressed an arrogance toward the independent planning commission, but most viewed it as a curious relic from the past. One wonders why we bother to have such commissions at all given this low assessment of their efficacy and the shaky foundation of their raison d'etre. All of the planners in this discussion have been oriented toward city planning as an arm of the executive branch of local government. They see the chief executive, not the city planning commission, as the representative of the people. This is certainly the mainstream of contemporary thought in city planning, and it shows that these planners have emerged from the isolation and aloofness sometimes forced by reporting to such an independent planning commission. . . .

. . . We asked the planners to describe the overriding goal for planning in their respective cities. All of them did it without hesitation or protest. We were frankly surprised by this and had expected some protest. . . .

The statements on the overriding goal for planning in each city by the respective planners are arrayed in Table [2-1]. We are not entirely sure of the significance of such statements—or the utility. We are certain that such statements make for fascinating discussion. . . .

We were pleased to see that at least three of the planners identified economic and fiscal matters as overriding goals for their planning. Drew said it most clearly when he described Milwaukee's decision to make "fiscal balance . . . our overall goal." That makes it quite clear that planning will be directed toward development that will produce a favorable cost

TABLE 2-1
Overriding Goal Comparison

Eplan-Atlanta	"to make the city tolerable to live in . . . the basic common denominator there is to design a city where you can raise a child . . . and to help guide the decisions . . . toward a common goal . . . "
Krumholz-Cleveland	"promoting a wider range of choice for those Cleveland residents who have few if any choices."
Carroll-Indianapolis	"input into the goals-setting process . . . [and] budget-making process . . . "
Vitt-Kansas City	"The overriding goal of the department is to help the city as a whole and each subarea . . . work toward performing closer to the potential that exists . . . "
Drew-Milwaukee	"We decided that fiscal balance would be our overall goal and the cornerstone of our comprehensive planning and programming efforts."
Bonner-Portland	"Less is enough is really where it is at."
Spaid-St. Paul	"The overriding goal . . . has two perspectives: neighborhood stability and economic viability."

and benefit ratio. Developments that pay their way through taxes and economic upgrading will receive a high priority in Milwaukee's planning program. . . .

Note on the Planning Profession

1. *Planners' values.* According to one study, most planners tend to be committed to environmental protection and mass transit, but are mildly negative about development. Elizabeth Howe & Jerome Kaufman, The Values of Contemporary American Planners, 47 J. Am. Plan. Ass'n 266 (1981). See also Jerome L. Kaufman, Thinking Alike, 66 J. Am. Plan. Ass'n 34 (2000) (finding that planners of several surveyed nations share these same attitudes). A study of San Diego planners, however, revealed that they had more favorable attitudes toward growth than did members of the general population. Nico Calavita & Roger Caves, Planners' Attitudes Toward Growth, 60 J. Am. Plan. Ass'n 483 (1994). See generally The Profession of City Planning: Changes, Images, and Challenges 1950–2000 (Lloyd Rodwin & Bishwapriya Sanyal eds., 2000).

2. *The evolution of planning education.* The Federal Housing Act of 1954 provided major inducements to municipalities to prepare comprehensive plans. Partly as a result, the yearly number of professional degrees awarded by U.S. planning schools increased from about 100 in 1954 to nearly 1,500 in 1975. Enrollment in planning schools began to decline after 1975, however, as federal and other financial support fell, schools of public policy began to compete with planning schools for students, and young people generally became less idealistic. See William Alonso, The Unplanned Paths of Planning Schools, Pub. Int., No. 82, at 58 (Winter 1986). Planning schools at MIT, the University of Southern California, and elsewhere adapted to the falloff in student demand by offering degrees in real estate development. Many graduates of these programs end up working for developers and lending institutions. See Gayle Berens, Changing with the Times at MIT, Urb. Land, Apr. 1991, at 34.

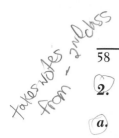

2. *The Comprehensive Plan*

a. *State Statutes That Require a Local Government to Adopt a Plan*

Variations. Some observers assert that about half of the states compel their localities to prepare a comprehensive plan. See, e.g., James Lawlor, State of the Statutes, Planning, Dec. 1992, at 10. See also Patricia E. Salkin, From *Euclid* to Growing Smart, 20 Pace Envtl. L. Rev. 109 (2002) (reviewing legislative activity on this and other fronts). The pertinent state statutes, however, are not easy to classify.

A number of states flatly command each general-purpose local government to adopt and update a comprehensive plan. These include California (Cal. Gov't Code §§65300, 65700 (West 2004), first enacted in 1965); Florida (Fla. Stat. ch. 163.3167 (2004), first enacted in 1975); and Maine (Me. Rev. Stat. Ann. tit. 30A, §§4312–49 (West 2004), first enacted in 1989).

Many states, however, limit their mandates in one fashion or another. For example, Mass. Gen. Laws ch. 41, §§81A, 81D (2004), specifies that a town with a population over 10,000 must establish a planning board, which "shall make a master plan" whenever it "may deem advisable." In Missouri, a municipality has the option of creating a planning commission; if it does, the commission "shall make and adopt a city plan." Mo. Rev. Stat. §§89.310–340 (2004). A city or county in Nebraska must prepare a comprehensive plan to be empowered to adopt zoning regulations. Neb. Rev. Stat. §§19-901, 23-114.03 (2004).

Merits. The wisdom of mandatory planning statutes is debated by law professor Daniel Mandelker and planning professor Lawrence Susskind in an exchange published at Planning 14–22 (July 1978). Ironically, it is Susskind who contends that state governments should not insist on local comprehensive planning. He argues that local compliance will be grudging at best, especially if the state declines to fund planning costs. Mandelker asserts that planning is necessary to ensure that zoning regulations are not invalidated for violating judicial norms of fundamental fairness.

After conducting an empirical study, a team of professors at planning schools concluded that local plans tend to be of higher quality in states that mandate planning. Raymond J. Burby et al., Is State-Mandated Planning Effective?, Land Use L., Oct. 1993, at 3. See also Charles M. Haar, "In Accordance with a Comprehensive Plan," 68 Harv. L. Rev. 1154 (1955) (supporting mandatory planning). But see Model Land Dev. Code §3-101 note 2 (1976) (stating that local planning should be optional); Robert E. Deyle & Richard A. Smith, Local Government Compliance with State Planning Mandates, 64 J. Am. Plan. Ass'n 457 (1998) (suggesting that Florida's planning mandates were "of little consequence without local commitment to the policies contained in the plan"). What statewide interests, if any, are promoted by local comprehensive planning?

A thwarted local revolt. In 1982, voters in Tehama County, situated in the northern portion of the Central Valley of California, narrowly approved an initiative measure entitled the "Landowners Bill of Rights." This sought to sweep away most of the county's land use controls, including its general plan. The ballot argument in favor of the initiative stated in part that its intent was to "Expose the fallacy of governmentally dictated land use control. The current County plan has been declared a failure by the very governmental body that created it." In Patterson v. County of Tehama, 235 Cal. Rptr. 867 (Ct. App. 1987), the central provisions of the initiative were struck down for violating California's mandatory-planning statute.

Consistency requirements. California and about a dozen other states require "consistency" between a municipality's land use decisions and its comprehensive plan. See Stuart

Meck, The Legislative Requirement that Zoning and Land Use Controls Be Consistent with an Independently Adopted Local Comprehensive Plan: A Model Statute, 3 Wash. U. J.L. & Pol'y 295 (2000). In these states, plans have far more legal significance than they do elsewhere. See pp. 336–41.

Remedies for violations of compulsory planning requirements. A local government might ignore a state mandate that it adopt a plan. Or it might adopt one, but violate a statutory requirement that the plan include certain elements, achieve a standard of adequacy, or be internally consistent.

What remedies are available to either developers or neighbors who seek to take advantage of these planning failures? There are three approaches. In Florida, a local government's failure to plan may result in its ceding planning power to a regional planning agency. Fla. Stat. ch. 163.3167(3) (2004). This essentially places the risk of noncompliance on the city itself.

Second, California places much of the risk of city noncompliance on developers. Cal. Gov't Code §§65750–63 (West 2004) generally direct a court that has found that a plan does not "substantially comply" with statutory requirements (1) to order the local government to bring the plan into compliance, and, in the interim, (2) to suspend the locality's power to grant building permits, preliminary subdivision approvals, and zoning changes. See Committee for Responsible Planning v. City of Indian Wells, 257 Cal. Rptr. 635 (Ct. App. 1989) (denying developer relief from suspension of city permit functions). But cf. Cal. Gov't Code §65754.5 (West 2004) (protecting certain housing developments from being stymied by challenges to plan adequacy).

Finally, some courts have concluded that city noncompliance should work in favor of, not against, developers. See, e.g., Sprenger, Grubb & Associates, Inc. v. City of Hailey, 986 P.2d 343 (Idaho 1999), where the court invalidated the city's effort to tighten the zoning restrictions on the plaintiff landowner's tract because the city's comprehensive plan had omitted two state-mandated elements—a land use map and a property rights component. (An earlier decision in the *Sprenger* controversy is excerpted at p. 112.) See also Hoffmeister v. City of San Diego, 64 Cal. Rptr. 2d 684 (Ct. App. 1997), which held that sponsors of facilities for the homeless could use the inadequacy of the housing element in the city's plan as a lever for forcing the granting of conditional use permits.

Fiscal inducements for local planning. To reduce the risk of grudging compliance with a mandatory-planning statute, many states provide technical and financial assistance to local governments. See, e.g., Me. Rev. Stat. Ann. tit. 30A, §4346 (West 2004), whose effects are discussed in Rick Adams, Down Easters Take on Growth Management, Planning, Aug. 1991, at 26. Georgia once threatened to withhold infrastructure funding from recalcitrant jurisdictions. Planning, Apr. 1989, at 36. Are carrots or sticks more appropriate in this context? Will federal inducements for metropolitan transportation planning (mentioned at p. 52) make states more interested in subsidizing local planning? As mentioned, under the Section 701 program, 40 U.S.C. §461 (enacted 1954, repealed 1981), the federal government once made direct grants to localities to help fund planning efforts. Should Congress reauthorize grants of this sort?

b.   State Regulation of the Elements of a Municipality's Plan

In 1975, Florida enacted a statute that required each of its counties and municipalities to prepare a comprehensive plan by July 1, 1979. Another Florida statutory provision, reproduced in heavily edited form below, closely regulates the contents of these plans. Ponder what statewide concerns, if any, support the Florida legislature's directives. Cf.

Buena Vista Gardens Apts. Ass'n v. City of San Diego, 220 Cal. Rptr. 732 (Ct. App. 1985) (holding that state could compel a city to include a housing element in its general plan because housing is a matter of statewide concern). Compare the Florida statute with the simpler South Carolina version, which is reprinted thereafter. In general, these sorts of state statutory mandates are becoming more detailed. Is this trend to be applauded?

Florida Stat. ch. 163.3177
(2003)

Ch. 163.3177 *Required and optional elements of comprehensive plan; studies and surveys*

(1) The comprehensive plan shall consist of materials in such descriptive form, written or graphic, as may be appropriate to the prescription of principles, guidelines, and standards for the orderly and balanced future economic, social, physical, environmental, and fiscal development of the area.

(2) Coordination of the several elements of the local comprehensive plan shall be a major objective of the planning process. The several elements of the comprehensive plan shall be consistent, and the comprehensive plan shall be economically feasible.

(3)(a) The comprehensive plan shall contain a capital improvements element designed to consider the need for and the location of public facilities in order to encourage the efficient utilization of such facilities. . . .

(b) The capital improvements element shall be reviewed on an annual basis and modified as necessary. . . . All public facilities shall be consistent with the capital improvements element.

(4)(a) Coordination of the local comprehensive plan with the comprehensive plans of adjacent municipalities, the county, adjacent counties or the region; . . . with adopted rules pertaining to designated areas of critical state concerns; and with the state comprehensive plan shall be a major objective of the local comprehensive planning process. To that end, in the preparation of a comprehensive plan or element thereof, and in the comprehensive plan or element as adopted, the governing body shall include a specific policy statement indicating the relationship of the proposed development of the area to the comprehensive plans of the adjacent municipalities, the county, adjacent counties, or the region and to the state comprehensive plan, as the case may require and as such adopted plans or plans in preparation may exist. . . .

(5)(a) Each local government comprehensive plan must include at least two planning periods, one covering at least the first 5-year period occurring after the plan's adoption and one covering at least a 10-year period.

(b) The comprehensive plan and its elements shall contain policy recommendations for the implementation of the plan and its elements.

(6) In addition to the requirements of subsections (1)–(5), the comprehensive plan shall include the following elements:

(a) A future land use plan element designating proposed future general distribution, location, and extent of the uses of land for residential uses, commercial uses, industry, agriculture, recreation, conservation, education, public buildings and grounds, other public facilities, and other categories of the public and private uses of land. The future land use plan shall include standards to be followed in the control and distribution of population densities and building and structure intensities. The proposed distribution, location, and extent of the various categories of the land shall be shown on a land use map or map series which shall be supplemented by goals, policies, and measurable objectives. . . .

(b) A traffic circulation element consisting of the types, locations, and extent of existing and proposed major thoroughfares and transportation routes, including bicycle and pedestrian ways.

(c) A general sanitary sewer, solid waste, drainage, potable water, and natural ground water aquifer recharge element. . . . (environment)

(d) A conservation element for the conservation, use, and protection of natural resources in the area, including air, water, water recharge areas, wetlands, waterwells, estuarine marshes, soils, beaches, shores, flood plains, rivers, bays, lakes, harbors, forests, fisheries and wildlife, marine habitat, minerals, and other natural and environmental resources. . . .

(e) A recreation and open space element. . . .

(f) 1. A housing element consisting of standards, plans, and principles to be followed in:

a. The provision of housing for all current and anticipated future residents of the jurisdiction.

b. The elimination of substandard dwelling conditions.

c. The structural and aesthetic improvement of existing housing.

d. The provision of adequate sites for future housing, including housing for low-income, very low-income, and moderate-income families, mobile homes, and group home facilities and foster care facilities, with supporting infrastructure and public facilities. . . .

(g) For those units of local government [in a coastal zone,] a coastal management element. . . .

(h) 1. An intergovernmental coordination element showing relationships and stating principles and guidelines to be used in coordinating the adopted comprehensive plans of adjacent municipalities, the county, adjacent counties, or the region, [and] with the state comprehensive plan. . . .

(7) [This section lists various optional elements that may appear in a comprehensive plan, including a redevelopment element, a historical and scenic preservation element, and any other element that the local government may desire.] . . .

(9) The state land planning agency shall, by February 15, 1986, adopt by rule minimum criteria for the review and determination of compliance of the local government comprehensive plan elements required by this act. . . .

South Carolina Code Ann. §6-29-510
(Law. Co-op. 2004)

[South Carolina does not require a county or municipality to create a local planning commission. If a locality does create one, however, the commission must produce a local comprehensive plan and, according to this 1994 enactment:]   it must include

(D) A local comprehensive plan must include, but not be limited to, the following planning elements:

(1) a population element which considers historic trends and projections, household numbers and sizes, educational levels, and income characteristics;

(2) an economic development element which considers labor force and labor force characteristics, employment by place of work and residence, and analysis of the economic base;

(3) a natural resources element which considers coastal resources, slope characteristics, prime agricultural and forest land, plant and animal habitats, parks and recreation areas, scenic views and sites, wetlands, and soil types . . . ;

(4) a cultural resources element which considers historic buildings and structures, commercial districts, residential districts, unique, natural, or scenic resources, archaeological, and other cultural resources . . . ;

(5) a community facilities element which considers transportation network; water supply, treatment, and distribution; sewage system and wastewater treatment; solid waste collection and disposal, fire protection, emergency medical services, and general government facilities; education facilities; and libraries and other cultural facilities;

(6) a housing element which considers location, types, age and condition of housing, owner and renter occupancy, and affordability of housing; and

(7) a land use element which considers existing and future land use by categories, including residential, commercial, industrial, agricultural, forestry, mining, public and quasi-public, recreation, parks, open space, and vacant or undeveloped.

c. *Sample Plans*

As mentioned, a comprehensive plan typically contains both verbal goals and a schematic map. The map makes general land use designations and shows existing and proposed public facilities such as highways, parks, and schools.

American Law Institute, Model Land Development Code
115–16 (1976) (Commentary on Article 3)

. . . [T]he planning process is said to proceed from the general to the particular. See F. Stuart Chapin, Urban Land Use Planning 349–54 (1965 ed.). In Chapin's view the initial statement of objectives should be at a high order of generality. He quotes with approval the following list taken from a study of regional growth alternatives in the Hartford, Connecticut area:

1. Provide for the orderly growth and development of the region while preserving a measure of diversity among its parts.
2. Allocate land in the region, recognizing that it may become a scarce resource, to be conserved rather than wasted.
3. Satisfy the multiple needs of a society with increasing amounts of leisure time in general, and preserve the amenities associated with the region's "open character" in particular.
4. Maximize the opportunity for a wide range of choice in residential living in general, and serve the varying housing needs of the region's population in particular.
5. Help promote sound economic development and assure employment stability of both the region and the state.
6. Minimize conflicts with residential areas and facilitate the provision of required public services, particularly transportation and utilities.

Thereafter, the planning process should deduce from these general principles lower level objectives and policies.

A difficulty with the approach is that it is nearly impossible to state significant general objectives in the first instance. For example, what does the first of the quoted objectives mean? Specifically what is meant by "orderly" and by "diversity"? Does "orderly" mean development proceeding from present population centers outward rather than "leapfrogging"? Or does it mean starting new population centers in presently undeveloped areas with greenbelts separating the population cores? And what happens if sporadic building is the only practical way to obtain "diversity"? Moreover, even if the objectives were more certainly stated (perhaps number 6 is an example), how can choices rationally be made without knowing their implications?

A major problem with this type of planning is that key decisions are made through a deductive process that reasons from plausible sounding but uncertain statements based on professional standards and predilections whose origins or rationale are only rarely made explicit. See Melvin Webber, The Roles of Intelligence Systems in Urban-Systems Planning, 31 J. Am. Inst. Plan. 289, 291 (1965). Thus, if the plan is effective, there is no assurance that the choices are those which actually would be desired by a majority of the population, or their representatives, if the implications and rationale were known.

Edward J. Kaiser & David R. Godschalk, Twentieth Century Land Use Planning: A Stalwart Family Tree
61 J. Am. Plan. Ass'n 365, 372–73 (1995)

The land use design plan is the most traditional of the [main varieties] of contemporary plans and is the most direct descendent of the Kent-Chapin-701 plans of the 1950s and 1960s. It proposes a long-range future urban form as a pattern of retail, office, industrial, residential, and open spaces, and public land uses and a circulation system. Today's version, however, incorporates environmental processes, and sometimes agriculture and forestry, under the "open space" category of land use. Its land uses often include a "mixed use" category, honoring the neotraditional principle of closer mingling of residential, employment, and shopping areas. In addition, it may include a development strategy map, which is designed to bring about the future urban form and to link strategy to the community's financial capacity to provide infrastructure and services. . . .

. . . While at midcentury, plans unquestioningly accommodated growth, today's plans cast the amount, pace, location, and costs of growth as policy choices to be determined in the planning process.

The 1990 Howard County (Maryland) General Plan, winner of an American Planning Association (APA) award in 1991 for outstanding comprehensive planning, exemplifies contemporary land use design. See Figure 2-2. While clearly a direct descendent of the traditional general plan, the Howard County plan adds new types of goals, policies, and planning techniques. To enhance communication and public understanding, it is organized strategically around six themes/chapters (responsible regionalism, preservation of the rural area, balanced growth, working with nature, community enhancement, and phased growth), instead of the customary plan elements. Along with the traditional land use design, the plan includes a "policy map" (strategy map) for each theme and an overall policies map for the years 2000 and 2010. A planned service area boundary is used to contain urban growth within the eastern urbanized part of the county, home to the well-known Columbia New Town. The plan lays out specific steps to be implemented over the next two years, and defines yardsticks for measuring success. An extensive public participation process for formulating the plan involved a 32-member General Plan Task Force, public opinion polling to discover citizen concerns, circulation of preplan issue papers on development impacts, and consideration of six alternative development scenarios.

Note on the Contents of Comprehensive Plans

1. *Verbal planning goals.* Should a local government weight or rank its articulated planning goals? If it does not, how meaningful will its list of goals be? For a review of scholarship on the effectiveness of actual comprehensive plans, see Emily Talen, Do Plans Get Implemented? A Review of Evaluation in Planning, 10 J. Plan. Liter. 248 (1996).

2. *Maps.* Plan maps typically are more general and suggestive than zoning maps. For example, a suburban city might have five or more different single-family residential

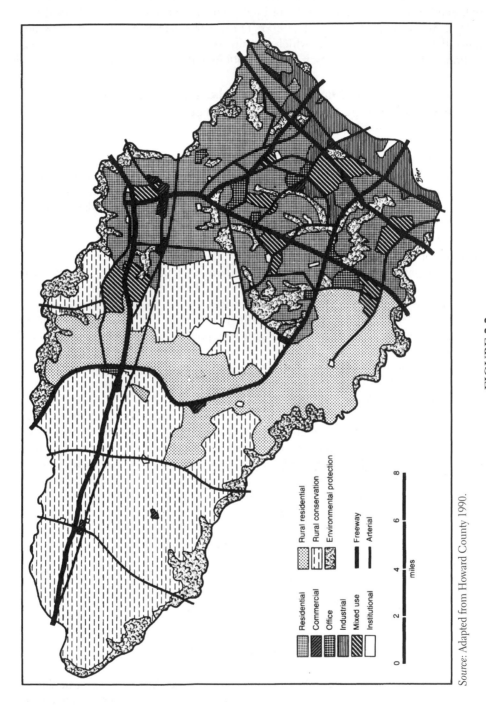

Legend

Residential · **Commercial** · **Office** · **Industrial** · **Mixed use** · **Institutional**

Rural residential · **Rural conservation** · **Environmental protection** · **Freeway** · **Arterial**

miles: 0 2 4 6 8

FIGURE 2-2
Howard County, Maryland, General Plan, Land Use 2010

Source: Adapted from Howard County 1990.

zones with varying minimum lot-area requirements, frontage requirements, and so forth. Nevertheless, the drafters of the city's plan might use a single color to map all single-family areas. Because of these simplifications, use restrictions imposed on plan districts also must be kept general. For example, Palo Alto's 1977–1990 plan allowed zoning densities in its "single-family residential" area to range from 1 to 14 dwelling units per acre. Moreover, the blobs of color on planning maps often are deliberately given rough edges; by contrast, the boundaries of zoning districts are precisely fixed.

3. *Specific plans.* California authorizes its local governments to prepare "specific plans" as well as general plans. See Cal. Gov't Code §§65450–57 (West 2004). A specific plan applies only to a subarea of the enacting jurisdiction and, because it proposes implementing legislation, tends to be much more concrete than a general plan. To achieve a politically acceptable end-product, planners preparing a specific plan may consult closely with nearby residents and also owners of undeveloped land in the affected territory. Case studies include Doug Dahlin, The Evergreen Specific Plan: Proactive Public Planning, Urb. Land, Mar. 1992, at 12 (focusing on area within the City of San Jose); Kenneth C. Topping, Thinking Big in California, Planning, Oct. 1982, at 16 (focusing on Chino Hills area of San Bernardino County). The City of San Jose and San Bernardino County are two localities unusually large in area, a circumstance that may have prompted them to prepare specific plans. If city plans are developed at the neighborhood level after substantial participation by local citizens, how great is the risk that the plans will unduly stress specific neighborhood improvements at the expense of other citywide interests?

4. *Do local politicians favor constraining plans?* A public official may prefer to retain discretion over policy rather than to be locked into implementing prior directives, particularly ones issued by predecessors in office. Having discretion provides leverage to obtain private favors such as campaign contributions and public benefits such as development exactions. See Chapter 4B, which examines deals between local governments and private developers. An official who wishes to retain flexibility in decisionmaking therefore may favor imprecision in a plan's maps and vagueness in its verbal goals. In short, even if a planning agency could establish concrete, prioritized planning goals, the political actors controlling the agency might resist precision in planning.

3. Criticisms of Comprehensive Planning

When a private entity, such as a land development firm, attempts to plan comprehensively, its executives may have difficulty amassing and integrating the pertinent information. As the domain of the firm's plan increases—whether in territory affected, functions included, or time span covered—these difficulties multiply. When a government plans, its agents must surmount these same hurdles and additional ones as well. Even more than private planners, public planners may lack incentives to consider all of the costs and benefits of their efforts and, in a democratic society, may lack the legitimacy to make long-term governmental commitments.

a. Can Planners Gather and Process the Pertinent Information?

Lon L. Fuller, Freedom—A Suggested Analysis
68 Harv. L. Rev. 1305, 1325 (1955)

Imagine a newly settled rural community in which it is apparent that sooner or later a path will be worn through a particular woodland. Suppose the community decides to plan the path in advance. There would be definite advantages in this course. Experts could be brought in. A general view of the whole situation could be obtained that would not be available to any individual wayfarer. What would be lacking would be the contribution of countless small decisions by people actually using the path—the decision, for example, of those whose footprints pulled the path slightly to the east so that they might look at a field of daisies, or of those who detoured around a spot generally dry, but unaccountably wet in August.

I hope the figure of the path will not be taken with more seriousness than it is offered. Lest I be accused of romanticizing the problem, I should like to [relate] an actual incident that seems in point.

Through the foresight of the city fathers the Cambridge Common is provided with an elaborate network of paved sidewalks, carefully planned to serve the convenience of any person wishing to traverse the Common from any angle. It was found, however, that at certain points people perversely insisted on walking across the grass. The usual countermeasures were tried, but failed. Now the city is taking down its barriers and its "keep-off-the-grass" signs and is busily engaged in paving the paths cut by trespassing feet. Those who have had experience with the problem of designing forms for the life of the human animal will see here, I believe, a pattern of events that has repeated itself many, many times.

John Rahenkamp, Land Use Management:
An Alternative to Controls
in Future Land Use 191–92 (Robert W. Burchell & David Listokin eds., 1975)

My experience would suggest that any fixed plan is inevitably wrong. In fact, fixed plans have no logical or legal basis and no sensitivity over time to the fundamental changes which can occur. I think it is extraordinarily clear—as a matter of fact, I am amazed that we have to keep talking about it—that our attempts to project social need or technological change have been historically inaccurate. Our long-term projections are grossly out of line every time. The best we can work with is something approximating three to five years. At best, we can simulate within brackets. But even so, the brackets are so broad that if we are asking society to believe we are operating a system strictly within those brackets, I think we are grossly misleading them.

We should also remember that we are a pluralistic society, and somehow, the reflection of that pluralism ought to be different from the patterns we have seen in the past, different from the patterns in Europe. Let me provide two examples of the way master plans haven't worked. I had dinner the other night with an English new town planner, who had been involved in some of the old "new towns," and pointed out the extraordinary problems of having a fixed master plan. He told me about the 1950 projection of one car for ten units, which now represents about one-quarter of the total, and described having to put blacktop and tarmac on everything to try to get enough parking. Similarly, we are working in Columbia [Maryland] where good planners laid down master plans ten years ago and said the neighborhoods will produce 600 children. Actually, the neighborhoods are producing only two-thirds of that—perhaps because the residents ride bicycles so much.

The best master planners we have in the country inevitably are failures when it comes to prognosticating over a long period of time. The new system of new town planning is simply laying down the infrastructure and letting it happen. That sounds like managed sprawl to me, which is perhaps the logical way to go.

Charles E. Lindblom, The Science of "Muddling Through"
19 Pub. Admin. Rev. 79 (1959)

[In this article, Lindblom compares two methods of policymaking: (1) the rational comprehensive approach and (2) the successive limited comparisons approach. The former approach generally corresponds to comprehensive planning, and the latter to muddling through—that is, the practice of confronting problems piecemeal as they arise. The following table, which appears in the article, succinctly presents the differences between the two methods. Lindblom claims that the muddling-through approach is the one that agencies actually practice. He asserts that the rational comprehensive approach is "impossible" (except for relatively simple problems), because it "assumes intellectual capacities and sources of information that men simply do not possess, and it is even more absurd as an approach to policy when the time and money that can be allocated to a policy problem are limited, as is always the case."]

Rational Comprehensive	*Successive Limited Comparisons*
1a. Clarification of values or objectives distinct from and usually prerequisite to empirical analysis of alternative policies.	1b. Selection of value goals and empirical analysis of the needed action are not distinct from one another but are closely intertwined.
2a. Policy formulation is therefore approached through means-end analysis: First the ends are isolated, then the means to achieve them are sought.	2b. Since means and ends are not distinct, means-end analysis is often inappropriate or limited.
3a. The test of a "good" policy is that it can be shown to be the most appropriate means to desired ends.	3b. The test of a "goods" policy is typically that various analysts find themselves directly agreeing on a policy (without their agreeing that it is the most appropriate means to an agreed objective).
4a. Analysis is comprehensive; every important relevant factor is taken into account.	4b. Analysis is drastically limited: (1) Important possible outcomes are neglected. (2) Important alternative potential policies are neglected. (3) Important affected values are neglected.
5a. Theory is often heavily relied upon.	5b. A succession of comparisons greatly reduces or eliminates reliance on theory.

For a critique of the generality of Lindblom's arguments on behalf of using successive limited comparisons, see Jonathan Bendor, A Model of Muddling Through, 89 Am. Pol. Sci. Rev. 819 (1995).

Friedrich A. Hayek, The Road to Serfdom
36, 48–50 (1944)

Economic liberalism is opposed . . . to competition's being supplanted by inferior methods of co-ordinating individual efforts. And it regards competition as superior not only because it is in most circumstances the most efficient method known but even more because it is the only method by which our activities can be adjusted to each other without coercive or arbitrary intervention of authority. . . .

The assertion that modern technological progress makes planning inevitable can also be interpreted in a different manner. It may mean that the complexity of our modern industrial civilization creates new problems with which we cannot hope to deal effectively except by central planning. In a sense this is true—yet not in the wide sense in which it is claimed. It is, for example, a commonplace that many of the problems created by a modern town, like many other problems caused by close contiguity in space, are not adequately solved by competition.[2] But it is not these problems, like those of the "public utilities," etc., which are uppermost in the minds of those who invoke the complexity of modern civilization as an argument for central planning. What they generally suggest is that the increasing difficulty of obtaining a coherent picture of the complete economic process makes it indispensable that things should be coordinated by some central agency if social life is not to dissolve in chaos.

This argument is based on a complete misapprehension of the working of competition. Far from being appropriate only to comparatively simple conditions, it is the very complexity of the division of labor under modern conditions which makes competition the only method by which such coordination can be adequately brought about. There would be no difficulty about efficient control or planning were conditions so simple that a single person or board could effectively survey all the relevant facts. It is only as the factors which have to be taken into account become so numerous that it is impossible to gain a synoptic view of them that decentralization becomes imperative. . . .

. . . The more complicated the whole, the more dependent we become on that division of knowledge between individuals whose separate efforts are coordinated by the impersonal mechanism for transmitting the relevant information known by us as the price system.

Note on Planners' Weighty Informational Requirements and Limited Cognitive Capacities

1. *Introspection.* Do you engage in much medium- and long-range planning in ordering your personal life? For example, are you a person who adopts and adheres to New Year's resolutions? If not, why not? How detailed are your plans for your career? For the time remaining in the current academic year? To what extent would you chalk up your failures to plan to inadequate information and bounded cognitive capacity, as opposed, say, to inadequate self-control?

2. *Gallows humor.* Notes on Planning Objectives, *in* Richard Hedman & Frederick Haigh Bair, And On the Eighth Day (2d ed. 1967), offers a wry perspective on planners' difficulties in obtaining and weighing information. The authors outline the "basic principles" of four different 20-year master plans that a city might have adopted in 1905, 1935,

---

[2] Eds: Hayek was writing in opposition to central economic planning. Can one construe this sentence to mean that he would favor comprehensive land use planning?

1960, and 1980. The 1905 plan states in part that "Streetcar lines are a major determinant in shaping the frame of the city of tomorrow. . . . Make ample provision for livery stables in the Plan." The 1935 plan notes that "Population approaches its ultimate peak. . . . [T]here will be an oversupply of schools. This is obvious from the drop in the birth rate." The 1960 plan contemplates rapid population growth, and calls for massive expenditures on superhighways and parking structures. The 1980 plan states that "It is functionally pointless to attempt reconstruction of the large-target metropolis," but adds optimistically that "Population of the U.S. will soon be back up to 100 million, barring resumption of hostilities or unforeseen results of radiation exposure."

3. *Theory and practice*. To what extent has mainstream planning theory recognized and adapted to planners' difficulties in acquiring and processing information?

b. Do Planners Have Appropriate Incentives?

Suppose that a tract of land would be most profitably improved with townhouses, but that a homebuilding company were to make a business error and develop detached single-family houses on it instead. The investors and other participants in the firm would bear most if not all of the losses from this mistake. To avoid losses of this sort, the managers of a profit-oriented developer have incentives to gather reliable information about both consumer tastes and the production costs of alternative development schemes.

Now suppose a government planner were to decide whether to allocate the same tract to townhouse or single-family use. Would the planner bear any of the losses resulting from an allocative error? (How might the law of takings, discussed at pp. 134–97, bear on the answer?) Would a planner have adequate nonmonetary incentives to assemble accurate information about market conditions?

One of the arguments for planning is that a government official is more likely than a developer to take into account the external costs that a townhouse (or single-family) development would impose on neighboring landowners. Is this advantage likely to outweigh the disadvantages arising from the relative weakness of a planner's incentives? How great is the risk that planners will not selflessly pursue the "public interest," but instead be captured by one interest group or another, as envisioned in both Komesar's "majoritarian" and "influence" models, presented at p. 37?

c. Can Planning Be Reconciled with Democracy?

American Law Institute, Model Land Development Code
111–12 (1976) (Commentary on Article 3)

William Wheaton, Director of the Institute of Urban and Regional Development at Berkeley, analyzed the metropolitan plans for Denver and Washington and concluded that the patterns of physical development stated were based on five biases of planners, probably not shared by the community at large. The biases were (1) that scattered development is inherently evil; (2) that open space should be preserved; (3) that a city should have a strong, high density core; (4) that the journey to work should be reduced; and (5) that central urban residential locations are preferable to suburbs of single-family homes. Wheaton asks whether objectives like full employment and maximization of opportunities for underprivileged groups are not more important. He admits the present difficulty of designing plans for these objectives, but he argues that physical plans must at least attempt to forecast economic and social consequences which will flow from the stated development pattern. (Wheaton, Operations Research for Metropolitan Planning, 29 J. Am. Inst. Planners 250 (1963).)

James C. Scott, Seeing Like a State: How Certain Schemes to Improve the Human Condition Have Failed
142–43 (1998)

[Scott's chapter on the "high-modernist city" describes the influential ideas of Le Corbusier, a Swiss-born French architect and planner who was active mainly between 1920 and 1960. Le Corbusier favored highly ordered and comprehensive city plans that strictly separated different land uses. The city that most closely accords with Le Corbusier's ideals is Brasilia, the capital of Brazil. Designed in the 1950s by the architects Oscar Niemeyer and Lucio Costa, Brasilia features monumental traffic arteries, huge squares, dramatic public buildings, and large, uniform apartment blocks. In criticizing the sterility of Brasilia and its lack of pedestrian traffic, Scott echoes Jane Jacobs's reservations about comprehensive planning (see p. 51).]

The historic diversity of the city—the source of its value and magnetism—is an unplanned creation of many hands and long historical practice. Most cities are the outcome, the vector sum, of innumerable small acts bearing no discernible overall intention. Despite the best efforts of monarchs, planning bodies, and capitalist speculators, "most city diversity is the creation of incredible numbers of different people and different private organizations, with vastly different ideas and purposes, planning and contriving outside the formal framework of public action."[103] Le Corbusier would have agreed with this description of the existing city, and it was precisely what appalled him. It was just this cacophony of intentions that was responsible for the clutter, ugliness, disorder, and inefficiencies of the unplanned city. Looking at the same social and historical facts, Jacobs sees reason to praise them: "Cities have the capability of providing something for everybody, only because, and only when, they are created by everybody."[104] She is no free-market libertarian, however; she understands clearly that capitalists and speculators are, willy-nilly, transforming the city with their commercial muscle and political influence. But when it comes to urban public policy, she thinks planning ought not to usurp this unplanned city: "The main responsibility of city planning and design should be to develop, insofar as public policy and action can do so, cities that are congenial places for this great range of unofficial plans, ideas, and opportunities to flourish."[105] Whereas Le Corbusier's planner is concerned with the overall form of the cityscape and its efficiency in moving people from point to point, Jacobs's planner consciously makes room for the unexpected, small, informal, and even nonproductive human activities that constitute the vitality of the "lived city."

Note on Planning and Democracy

The articulation of goals seldom is a simple task. Presumably most adults have some ability to set personal goals. Similarly, private organizations often are able to establish

---

103. Jane Jacobs, The Death and Life of Great American Cities (New York, Vintage Books, 1961), p. 241.
104. Ibid., p. 238. The caveat, "and only when," may be a rare recognition by Jacobs that, in the absence of extensive planning in a liberal economy, the asymmetrical market forces which shape the city are hardly democratic.
105. Ibid., p. 241.

goals that attain wide support among members. For example, a corporation may strive to maximize the value of the firm, a religious organization to keep and spread the faith, and a university to climb in academic stature. Public planning efforts, however, usually pose more intractable problems in goal setting. The constituents of political systems often sharply disagree on goals. (This may be ameliorated in part to the extent that like-minded people cluster together in distinct political units.) If voters disagree on goals, governmental policy can be expected to fluctuate from election to election (if not more frequently). One of the purposes of a new election in fact is to permit the electorate to have a new say on governmental goals. In short, there is an inherent tension between democratic government and long-range planning beyond the span of a single term of office. In addition, the American tradition of separation of powers among relatively independent governmental branches inhibits planning efforts by any single branch.

Given that markets and other decentralized systems of coordination are hardly perfect either, how telling are the arguments that public decisionmakers may lack the information, cognitive capacity, incentives, and legitimacy conducive to successful comprehensive planning?

Chapter Three

Zoning and the Rights of Landowners and Developers

A typical land use dispute is a drama featuring three main sets of players:

(1) The *developer* (who usually either owns the land or holds an option to purchase the land) triggers the dispute by desiring to carry out the activity in controversy. The landowner will usually be allied with the developer (if the developer does not yet own the land at issue), as will firms and workers whom the developer would hire to perform the activity. The ultimate consumers of the activity also are potential allies of the developer, but in practice they rarely are sufficiently organized to be of help.

(2) The *neighbors* of the land in dispute (or others situated farther away but still threatened by the negative consequences of the proposed activity) are the developer's first and main line of opposition. Opponents may be individuals, grass-roots community organizations, local civic associations, or local chapters of national environmental organizations. Not infrequently, competitors of the developer who already are carrying out the proposed activity on their own land will be among the opponents.

(3) The *general-purpose local government* in which the land is located is the principal institution for reconciling the competing interests of the developer and the neighbors. Local elected officials, usually advised by planners and other professionals, attempt to resolve the conflict by adopting and administering land use regulations with which the developer must comply. However, the local officials are not simply passive arbitrators. Even if the developer has no opposition from neighbors, the local officials usually will use the approval process to seek funding for local streets, utilities, and other infrastructure from the developer (who may then pass the costs on to the ultimate consumers of the development or to the landowner, if the developer has not yet purchased the land). Developers thus typically regard local officials as part of the opposition they must overcome.

When a local government makes a decision regarding a developer's proposed project, a party aggrieved by the decision may challenge it in court. These materials emphasize instances in which judicial review was in fact sought. It should be remembered, however, that lawsuits are aberrational. Observe also that the party seeking judicial review may be either the developer or, if the local government has sided with the developer, the neighbors. In reading a judicial opinion in a land use case, one's first task is to identify whether it is a developer's or neighbors' lawsuit, a distinction judges themselves rarely emphasize. Attention to this distinction will help dispel some of the confusion in land use law.

Local governments use four main tools to regulate developers and builders:

(1) Comprehensive plans consist principally of (a) statements of goals and (b) maps that establish use and density guidelines for various districts and project future public improvements. The legal developments chronicled in Chapter 2 have elevated plans in some states to the dominant position in the hierarchy of public land use controls.

(2) Zoning ordinances essentially control (a) building bulks, (b) the size and shape of lots, (c) the placement of buildings on lots, and (d) the uses to which the land and buildings may be put. An ordinance typically defines the boundaries of various zones, and the substance of the controls differs from zone to zone.

(3) Subdivision regulations give local officials the power to control the location and design of streets, sewers, parks and other infrastructure, and the leverage to make developers pay for most of these improvements.

(4) Building and related codes regulate the materials and designs permitted in new structures. Some local governments also have aesthetic regulations that control signs, architectural styles, and the alteration of historic buildings.

This chapter is devoted to zoning, the tool local governments have traditionally used most heavily to control land development patterns. After surveying the evolution of zoning, the chapter turns to its main business: exploring the rights developers have to challenge the application of unwanted zoning restrictions to their properties.

A.   The Evolution of Zoning

Zoning flowered suddenly in the United States, precipitated by three important events that occurred within just a decade. First, in 1916 New York City passed the first widely publicized comprehensive zoning ordinance. Second, in 1921 U.S. Secretary of Commerce Herbert Hoover convened the "who's who" of the real estate development and planning worlds as a "committee to consider the question of zones." Richard H. Chused, Euclid's Historical Imagery, 51 Case W. Res. L. Rev. 597, 598 (2001). In 1922, the committee published a widely read zoning primer and promulgated the first version of the Standard State Zoning Enabling Act (SZEA). Finally, in 1926, the Supreme Court sustained the constitutionality of the principle of zoning in Village of Euclid v. Ambler Realty Co., 272 U.S. 365 (1926) excerpted later in this subchapter. The *Euclid* decision remains the foundation of land use law. These three events must be viewed, however, against a rich history of efforts to shape the growth and character of cities.

1.   Zoning Before Euclid

American zoning had two main roots: (1) early single-purpose public land use controls, and (2) the coalescence of the urban reform and architecture movements into the city planning movement.

a.   Early Regulatory Efforts

Prior to the advent of zoning, landowners were hardly free to do whatever they chose. The nuisance law and express contractual agreements (covenants) discussed in Chapter 6 were, and still are, potentially important constraints. Moreover, prior to the New York City zoning ordinance of 1916, some cities had adopted limited-purpose controls on building bulks. For example, in 1898 Massachusetts limited the height of buildings around the statehouse in Boston, and in 1899 Washington, D.C., restricted the height of buildings to preserve the prominence of the national Capitol's dome. In 1906, Boston sought to minimize fire hazards by imposing height limitations that varied between residential and commercial or business areas.

Many cities had adopted controls on specific land uses. Mich. Rev. Stat. 171 (1838) authorized local government officials to "assign certain places for the exercising of any trade or employment offensive to the inhabitants." Courts routinely enforced ordinances that barred specific noxious uses from neighborhoods designated for protection. See, e.g., In re Hang Kie, 10 P. 327 (Cal. 1886) (laundries); Shea v. City of Muncie, 46 N.E. 138 (Ind. 1897) (taverns and liquor stores); Cronin v. People, 82 N.Y. 318 (1880) (slaughtering of cattle).

However, the technique of comprehensively dividing a city into districts and varying building and use regulations from district to district was not pioneered until 1891, in the German city of Frankfurt-on-the-Main. For descriptions of the Frankfurt plan, see Anthony Sutcliffe, Towards the Planned City: Germany, Britain, the United States and France, 1780–1914, at 32 (1981); Thomas H. Logan, The Americanization of German Zoning, 42 J. Am. Inst. Planners 377, 379–80 (1976). In 1909, Los Angeles adopted a comprehensive zoning scheme demarcating one residential and seven industrial districts. See Ex parte Quong Wo, 118 P. 714 (Cal. 1911).

The 1916 New York City ordinance did the most to trigger interest in zoning. The ordinance was designed to cure two specific problems: the invasion of loft factories employing Eastern European garment workers into the prestigious Fifth Avenue commercial district, and the traffic congestion and blockage of light and air caused by proliferating skyscrapers. The ordinance was pushed through by a coalition of three interest groups: Fifth Avenue merchants, real estate owners concerned about keeping skyscrapers from depressing property values, and reformers interested in broader concepts of city planning. In his informative history, Seymour Toll concludes it was "a tiny interest group in the city to which a much larger community acquiesced when the law was eventually passed in 1916." Seymour I. Toll, Zoned American 164 (1969); see also Gregory F. Gilmartin, Shaping the City: New York and the Municipal Arts Society 188–202 (1995); Raphaël Fischler, The Metropolitan Dimension of Early Zoning, 64 J. Am. Plan. Ass'n 170 (1998).

New York City's ordinance helped inspire Herbert Hoover to promulgate the SZEA to assist states in authorizing their cities to zone. The first three sections of the SZEA concisely describe the method and theory of zoning. Section 1 empowers local governments to

> regulate and restrict the height, number of stories, and size of buildings and other structures, the percentage of a lot that may be occupied, the size of yards, courts, and other open spaces, the density of population, and the location and use of buildings, structures, and land for trade, industry, residence, or other purposes.

U.S. Department of Commerce, Standard State Zoning Enabling Act (1926), *reprinted in* 5 Kenneth H. Young, Anderson's American Law of Zoning §32.01 (4th ed. & Supp. 2004).

Section 2 contemplates the particular method by which such powers are to be implemented:

> For any or all of said purposes the local legislative body may divide the municipality into districts of such number, shape, and area as may be deemed best suited to carry out the purposes of this act; and within such districts it may regulate and restrict the erection, construction,

reconstruction, alteration, repair or use of buildings, structures, or land. All such regulations shall be uniform for each class or kind of building throughout each district, but the regulations in one district may differ from those in other districts.

Id. Although Section 1 empowered local government to adopt land use regulations only "for the purpose of promoting health, safety, morals, or the general welfare of the community," Section 3 elaborated further on the permissible goals of regulation:

Such regulations shall be made in accordance with a comprehensive plan and designed to lessen congestion in the streets; to secure safety from fire, panic, and other dangers; to promote health and the general welfare; to provide adequate light and air; to prevent the overcrowding of land; to avoid undue concentration of population; and to facilitate the adequate provision of transportation, water, sewerage, schools, parks, and other public requirements. Such regulations shall be made with reasonable consideration, among other things, to the character of the district and its peculiar suitability for particular uses, and with a view to conserving the value of buildings and encouraging the most appropriate use of land throughout such municipality.

Id. The idea of districting land uses had great political appeal. Reformers thought it would promote the general welfare. Landowners, especially owners of single-family houses, saw zoning as a way of protecting their investments from inferior uses that might locate close by. Even industrialists could see some virtues in zoning; if a manufacturing plant was located in a district designated for industry, it probably would be less likely to be enjoined as a nuisance.

In any event, the practice of zoning spread rapidly. By 1930, 35 states had passed zoning enabling acts patterned after the SZEA. Between 1915 and 1925, the number of cities with zoning rose from a handful to 500. Developments in the Law — Zoning, 91 Harv. L. Rev. 1427, 1434–35 (1978). Today, Houston is the only large city without comprehensive zoning. (For a glimpse of the way things work in Houston, see pp. 607–14.) Most small cities also have zoning schemes.

The state courts split on the constitutionality of the first comprehensive zoning ordinances: Ten or so upheld comprehensive zoning ordinances, but several others held that the technique violated due process by not being sufficiently related to traditional police power concerns. See id. at 1435; Alfred Bettman, Constitutionality of Zoning, 37 Harv. L. Rev. 834 (1924). Then came *Euclid*, the first zoning case to reach the Supreme Court.

2. *The* Euclid *Decision*

Village of Euclid v. Ambler Realty Co.
272 U.S. 365 (1926)

Mr. Justice SUTHERLAND delivered the opinion of the Court.

The Village of Euclid is an Ohio municipal corporation. It adjoins and practically is a suburb of the City of Cleveland. Its estimated population is between 5,000 and 10,000, and its area from twelve to fourteen square miles, the greater part of which is farm lands or unimproved acreage. It lies, roughly, in the form of a parallelogram measuring approximately three and one-half miles each way. East and west it is traversed by three principal highways: Euclid Avenue, through the southerly border, St. Clair Avenue, through the central portion, and Lake Shore Boulevard, through the northerly border in close proximity to the shore of Lake Erie. The Nickel Plate railroad lies from 1,500 to 1,800 feet north of Euclid Avenue, and the Lake Shore railroad 1,600 feet farther to the north. The three highways and the two railroads are substantially parallel.

Appellee is the owner of a tract of land containing 68 acres, situated in the westerly end of the village, abutting on Euclid Avenue to the south and the Nickel Plate railroad to the north. Adjoining this tract, both on the east and on the west, there have been laid out restricted residential plots upon which residences have been erected.

On November 13, 1922, an ordinance was adopted by the Village Council, establishing a comprehensive zoning plan for regulating and restricting the location of trades, industries, apartment houses, two-family houses, single-family houses, etc., the lot area to be built upon, the size and height of buildings, etc.

The entire area of the village is divided by the ordinance into six classes of use districts, denominated U-1 to U-6, inclusive; three classes of height districts, denominated H-1 to H-3, inclusive; and four classes of area districts, denominated A-1 to A-4, inclusive. The use districts are classified in respect of the buildings which may be erected within their respective limits, as follows: U-1 is restricted to single-family dwellings, public parks, water towers and reservoirs, suburban and interurban electric railway passenger stations and rights of way, and farming, non-commercial greenhouse nurseries and truck gardening; U-2 is extended to include two-family dwellings; U-3 is further extended to include apartment houses, hotels, churches, schools, public libraries, museums, private clubs, community center buildings, hospitals, sanitariums, public playgrounds and recreation buildings, and a city hall and courthouse; . . . [U-4 includes retail stores and offices; U-5 includes wholesaling and light manufacturing facilities; U-6 includes plants for sewage disposal, garbage and refuse incineration, junk yards, cemeteries, crematories, correctional institutions, institutions for the insane, storage of oil and gasoline, and manufacturing and industrial operations and public utilities not included in earlier classes.]

Class U-1 is the only district in which buildings are restricted to those enumerated. In the other classes the uses are cumulative; that is to say, uses in class U-2 include those enumerated in the preceding class, U-1; class U-3 includes uses enumerated in the preceding classes, U-2 and U-1; and so on. . . .

Appellee's tract of land comes under U-2, U-3 and U-6. The first strip of 620 feet immediately north of Euclid Avenue falls in class U-2, the next 130 feet to the north, in U-3, and the remainder in U-6. The uses of the first 620 feet, therefore, do not include apartment houses, . . . [and the] uses of the next 130 feet . . . exclude industries, . . . and the various other uses set forth in respect of U-4 to U-6, inclusive. [See Figure 3-1 on p. 82 for the location of the Ambler Realty Co. tract; see Figure 3-2 on p. 83 for the general zoning map of Euclid.]

Annexed to the ordinance, and made a part of it, is a zone map, showing the location and limits of the various use, height and area districts, from which it appears that the three classes overlap one another; that is to say, for example, both U-5 and U-6 use districts are in A-4 area districts, but the former is in H-2 and the latter in H-3 height districts. . . .

The lands lying between the two railroads for the entire length of the village area and extending some distance on either side to the north and south, having an average width of about 1,600 feet, are left open, with slight exceptions, for industrial and all other uses. This includes the larger part of appellee's tract. Approximately one-sixth of the area of the entire village is included in U-5 and U-6 use districts. That part of the village lying south of Euclid Avenue is principally in U-1 districts. The lands lying north of Euclid Avenue and bordering on the long strip just described are included in U-1, U-2, U-3 and U-4 districts, principally in U-2. . . .

The ordinance is assailed on the grounds that it . . . deprives appellee of liberty and property without due process of law and denies it the equal protection of the law, and that it offends against certain provisions of the Constitution of the State of Ohio. The prayer of the bill is for an injunction restraining the enforcement of the ordinance and all attempts to impose or maintain as to appellee's property any of the restrictions, limitations or conditions. The court below held the ordinance to be unconstitutional and void, and enjoined its enforcement. 297 Fed. 307.

Before proceeding to a consideration of the case, it is necessary to determine the scope of the inquiry. The bill alleges that the tract of land in question is vacant and has been held for years for the purpose of selling and developing it for industrial uses, for which it is especially adapted, being immediately in the path of progressive industrial development; that for such uses it has a market value of about $10,000 per acre, but if the use be limited to residential purposes the market value is not in excess of $2,500 per acre; that the first 200 feet of the parcel back from Euclid Avenue, if unrestricted in respect of use, has a value of $150 per front foot, but if limited to residential uses, and ordinary mercantile business be excluded therefrom, its value is not in excess of $50 per front foot.

It is specifically averred that the ordinance attempts to restrict and control the lawful uses of appellee's land so as to confiscate and destroy a great part of its value; that it is being enforced in accordance with its terms; that prospective buyers of land for industrial, commercial and residential uses in the metropolitan district of Cleveland are deterred from buying any part of this land because of the existence of the ordinance and the necessity thereby entailed of conducting burdensome and expensive litigation in order to vindicate the right to use the land for lawful and legitimate purposes; that the ordinance constitutes a cloud upon the land, reduces and destroys its value, and has the effect of diverting the normal industrial, commercial and residential development thereof to other and less favorable locations.

The record goes no farther than to show, as the lower court found, that the normal, and reasonably to be expected, use and development of that part of appellee's land adjoining Euclid Avenue is for general trade and commercial purposes, particularly retail stores and like establishments, and that the normal, and reasonably to be expected, use and development of the residue of the land is for industrial and trade purposes. . . .

A motion was made in the court below to dismiss the bill on the ground that, because [appellee] had made no effort to obtain a building permit or apply to the zoning board of appeals for relief as it might have done under the terms of the ordinance, the suit was premature. The motion was properly overruled. The effect of the allegations of the bill is that the ordinance of its own force operates greatly to reduce the value of appellee's lands and destroy their marketability for industrial, commercial and residential uses; and the attack is directed, not against any specific provision or provisions, but against the ordinance as an entirety. Assuming the premises, the existence and maintenance of the ordinance, in effect, constitutes a present invasion of appellee's property rights and a threat to continue it. Under these circumstances, the equitable jurisdiction is clear.

It is not necessary to set forth the provisions of the Ohio Constitution which are thought to be infringed. The question is the same under both Constitutions, namely, as stated by appellee: Is the ordinance invalid in that it violates the constitutional protection "to the right of property in the appellee by attempted regulations under the guise of the police power, which are unreasonable and confiscatory?"

Building zone laws are of modern origin. They began in this country about twenty-five years ago. Until recent years, urban life was comparatively simple; but with the great increase and concentration of population, problems have developed, and constantly are developing, which require, and will continue to require, additional restrictions in respect of the use and occupation of private lands in urban communities. Regulations, the wisdom, necessity and validity of which, as applied to existing conditions, are so apparent that they are now uniformly sustained, a century ago, or even half a century ago, probably would have been rejected as arbitrary and oppressive. Such regulations are sustained, under the complex conditions of our day, for reasons analogous to those which justify traffic regulations, which, before the advent of automobiles and rapid transit street railways, would have been condemned as fatally arbitrary and unreasonable. And in this there is no inconsistency, for while the meaning of constitutional guaranties never varies, the scope of their application must expand or contract to meet the new and different conditions which are constantly coming within the field of their operation.

The ordinance now under review, and all similar laws and regulations, must find their justification in some aspect of the police power, asserted for the public welfare. The line which in this field separates the legitimate from the illegitimate assumption of power is not capable of precise delimitation. It varies with circumstances and conditions. . . . In solving doubts, the maxim *sic utere tuo ut alienum non laedas*, which lies at the foundation of so much of the common law of nuisances, ordinarily will furnish a fairly helpful clew. And the law of nuisances, likewise, may be consulted, not for the purpose of controlling, but for the helpful aid of its analogies in the process of ascertaining the scope of, the power. Thus the question whether the power exists to forbid the erection of a building of a particular kind or for a particular use, like the question whether a particular thing is a nuisance, is to be determined, not by an abstract consideration of the building or of the thing considered apart, but by considering it in connection with the circumstances and the locality. A nuisance may be merely a right thing in the wrong place, like a pig in the parlor instead of the barnyard. If the validity of the legislative classification for zoning purposes be fairly debatable, the legislative judgment must be allowed to control. Radice v. New York, 264 U.S. 292, 294 (1924).

There is no serious difference of opinion in respect of the validity of laws and regulations fixing the height of buildings within reasonable limits, the character of materials and methods of construction, and the adjoining area which must be left open, in order to minimize the danger of fire or collapse, the evils of over-crowding, and the like, and excluding from residential sections offensive trades, industries and structures likely to create nuisances.

Here, however, the exclusion is in general terms of all industrial establishments, and it may thereby happen that not only offensive or dangerous industries will be excluded, but those which are neither offensive nor dangerous will share the same fate. But this is no more than happens in respect of many practice-forbidding laws which this Court has upheld although drawn in general terms so as to include individual cases that may turn out to be innocuous in themselves. The inclusion of a reasonable margin, to insure effective enforcement, will not put upon a law, otherwise valid, the stamp of invalidity. Such laws may also find their justification in the fact that, in some fields, the bad fades into the good by such insensible degrees that the two are not capable of being readily distinguished and separated in terms of legislation. In the light of these considerations, we are not prepared to say that the end in view was not sufficient to justify the general rule of the ordinance, although some industries of an innocent character might fall within the proscribed class. It cannot be said that the ordinance in this respect "passes the bounds of reason and assumes the character of a merely arbitrary fiat." Purity Extract Co. v. Lynch, 226 U.S. 192 (1912). . . .

It is said that the Village of Euclid is a mere suburb of the City of Cleveland; that the industrial development of that city has now reached and in some degree extended into the village and, in the obvious course of things, will soon absorb the entire area for industrial enterprises; that the effect of the ordinance is to divert this natural development elsewhere with the consequent loss of increased values to the owners of the lands within the village borders. But the village, though physically a suburb of Cleveland, is politically a separate municipality, with powers of its own and authority to govern itself as it sees fit within the limits of the organic law of its creation and the State and Federal Constitutions. Its governing authorities, presumably representing a majority of its inhabitants and voicing their will, have determined, not that industrial development shall cease at its boundaries, but that the course of such development shall proceed within definitely fixed lines. If it be a proper exercise of the police power to relegate industrial establishments to localities separated from residential sections, it is not easy to find a sufficient reason for denying the power because the effect of its exercise is to divert an industrial flow from the course which it would follow, to the injury of the residential public if left alone, to another course where such injury will be obviated. It is not meant by this, however, to exclude the possibility of cases where the general public interest would so far outweigh the interest of the municipality that the municipality would not be allowed to stand in the way.

We find no difficulty in sustaining restrictions of the kind thus far reviewed. The serious question in the case arises over the provisions of the ordinance excluding from residential districts, apartment houses, business houses, retail stores and shops, and other like establishments. This question involves the validity of what is really the crux of the more recent zoning legislation, namely, the creation and maintenance of residential districts, from which business and trade of every sort, including hotels and apartment houses, are excluded. . . .

The matter of zoning has received much attention at the hands of commissions and experts, and the results of their investigations have been set forth in comprehensive reports. [In] these reports, which bear every evidence of painstaking consideration, . . . it is pointed out that the development of detached house sections is greatly retarded by the coming of apartment houses, which has sometimes resulted in destroying the entire section for private house purposes; that in such sections very often the apartment house is a mere parasite, constructed in order to take advantage of the open spaces and attractive surroundings created by the residential character of the district. Moreover, the coming of one apartment house is followed by others, interfering by their height and bulk with the free circulation of air and monopolizing the rays of the sun which otherwise would fall upon the smaller homes, and bringing, as their necessary accompaniments, the disturbing noises incident to increased traffic and business, and the occupation, by means of moving and parked automobiles, of larger portions of the streets, thus detracting from their safety and depriving children of the privilege of quiet and open spaces for play, enjoyed by those in more favored localities, — until, finally, the residential character of the neighborhood and its desirability as a place of detached residences are utterly destroyed. Under these circumstances, apartment houses, which in a different environment would be not only entirely unobjectionable but highly desirable, come very near to being nuisances.

If these reasons, thus summarized, do not demonstrate the wisdom or sound policy in all respects of those restrictions which we have indicated as pertinent to the inquiry, at least the reasons are sufficiently cogent to preclude us from saying, as it must be said before the ordinance can be declared unconstitutional, that such provisions are clearly arbitrary and unreasonable, having no substantial relation to the public health, safety, morals, or general welfare.

It is true that when, if ever, the provisions set forth in the ordinance in tedious and minute detail, come to be concretely applied to particular premises, including those of the appellee, or to particular conditions, or to be considered in connection with specific complaints, some of them, or even many of them, may be found to be clearly arbitrary and unreasonable. But where the equitable remedy of injunction is sought, as it is here, not upon the ground of a present infringement or denial of a specific right, or of a particular injury in process of actual execution, but upon the broad ground that the mere existence and threatened enforcement of the ordinance, by materially and adversely affecting values and curtailing the opportunities of the market, constitute a present and irreparable injury, the court will not scrutinize its provisions, sentence by sentence, to ascertain by a process of piecemeal dissection whether there may be, here and there, provisions of a minor character, or relating to matters of administration, or not shown to contribute to the injury complained of, which, if attacked separately, might not withstand the test of constitutionality. In respect of such provisions, of which specific complaint is not made, it cannot be said that the land owner has suffered or is threatened with an injury which entitles him to challenge their constitutionality. . . .

Decree reversed.

Mr. Justice VAN DEVANTER, Mr. Justice McREYNOLDS and Mr. Justice BUTLER, dissent.

Note on *Euclid*

1. *The landscape*. As Figure 3-1 reveals, Ambler Realty's tract was bounded on one side by the Nickel Plate Railroad. The property along the railroad tracks was undeveloped or mixed use, with 16 industries located along 14 miles of tracks; other areas of the village had been developed for residential use. Indeed, Ambler had sold off properties on the east side of its tract with covenants restricting them for residential use, and Ambler's tract was bounded on the west by a residential development. The zoning of Ambler's tract and neighboring properties reflected both their prior development and a general pattern of zoning the area nearest the railroad tracks for industrial use, the area across from Euclid Avenue for single-family use, and the buffering area in between for apartments and multifamily houses. See Figure 3-2, Euclid's zoning map.

2. *The cast of characters*. Ambler Realty's challenge to Euclid's ordinance involved an unusually star-studded and intertwined cast. Ambler was represented by Newton Baker, who had previously served as mayor of Cleveland and as secretary of war under President Wilson; Euclid was represented by a protegee of Baker's, James Metzenbaum, who chaired Euclid's Board of Zoning Appeals. He was aided by a "Brandeis brief" filed by Alfred Bettman, a municipal reformer and former special assistant to President Wilson's attorney general, who had been one of the authors of the SZEA. The district court judge assigned to hear the case, Dale C. Westenhaver, was a former law partner of Baker's and, in large part, had been nominated to the bench because of Baker's sponsorship. For profiles of the key players in the *Euclid* case, along with discussions of their motivations and strategies in the case, see Arthur V.N. Brooks, The Office File Box — Emanations from the Battlefield, *in* Zoning and the American Dream 3 (Charles M. Haar & Jerold S. Kayden eds., 1989); Laurence C. Gerckens, Bettman of Cincinnati, *in* The American Planner: Biographies and Recollections 120 (Donald A. Krueckeberg ed., 1983); William M. Randle, Professors, Reformers, Bureaucrats, and Cronies: The Players in *Euclid v. Ambler, in* Zoning and the American Dream, supra, at 31; Timothy Alan Fluck, *Euclid v. Ambler*: A Retrospective, 52 J. Am. Plan. Ass'n 326 (1986); Garrett Power, The Advent of Zoning, 4 Plan. Persp. 1 (1989).

3. *Zoning and the poor*. In Ambler Realty Co. v. Village of Euclid, 297 F. 307 (N.D. Ohio 1924), District Judge Westenhaver, after noting that "[t]his case is obviously destined to go higher," concluded his opinion as follows:

> The plain truth is that the true object of the ordinance in question is to place all the property in an undeveloped area of 16 square miles in a strait-jacket. The purpose to be accomplished is really to regulate the mode of living of persons who may hereafter inhabit it. In the last analysis,

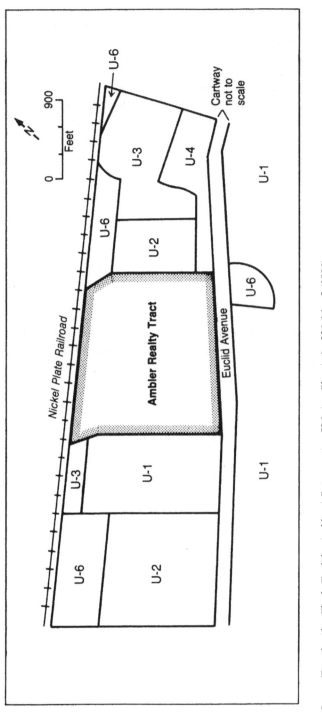

FIGURE 3-1

Zoning of Properties Near the Ambler Realty Tract

Source: Timothy Alan Fluck, *Euclid v. Ambler: A Retrospective,* 52 J. Am. Plan Ass'n. 326, Map 2 (1986).

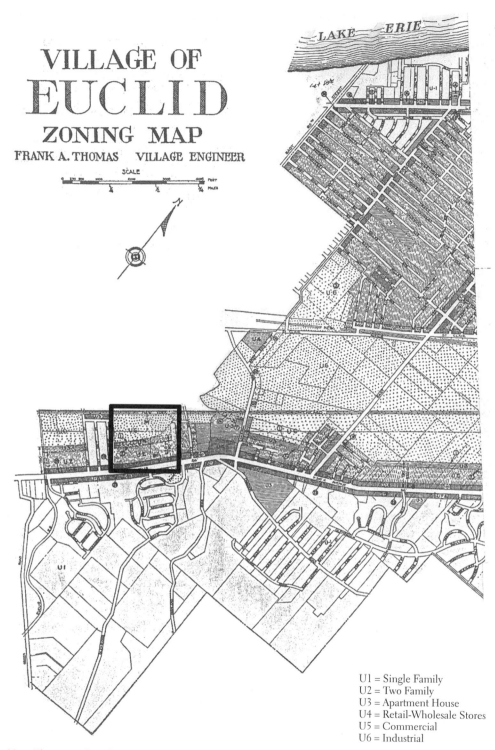

U1 = Single Family
U2 = Two Family
U3 = Apartment House
U4 = Retail-Wholesale Stores
U5 = Commercial
U6 = Industrial

Note: The rectangle indicates the approximate location of the Amber Realty Tract shown in Figure 3-1.
Source: Florence Humphrey, Euclid Historical Society.

FIGURE 3-2
A Portion of Euclid's Zoning Map, 1922

the result to be accomplished is to classify the population and segregate them according to their income or situation in life. The true reason why some persons live in a mansion and others in a shack, why some live in a single-family dwelling and others . . . in an apartment, or why some live in a well-kept apartment and others in a tenement, is primarily economic. It is a matter of income and wealth, plus the labor and difficulty of procuring adequate domestic service. Aside from contributing to these results and furthering such class tendencies, the ordinance has also an esthetic purpose; that is to say, to make this village develop into a city along lines now conceived by the village council to be attractive and beautiful. . . . Whether these purposes and objects would justify the taking of plaintiff's property as and for a public use need not be considered. It is sufficient to say that, in our opinion, and as applied to plaintiff's property, it may not be done without compensation under the guise of exercising the police power.

Id. at 316. Is Justice Sutherland's view that multifamily apartments are "parasite[s]" an adequate answer to concerns about the impact of zoning on the poor? Even assuming that Justice Sutherland was correct in analogizing apartments to nuisances, was it reasonable to extend that analogy to two-family houses? For helpful discussions of the debates about zoning's impact on the poor at the time of *Euclid*, see David Callies, *Village of Euclid v. Ambler Realty Co., in* Property Stories 323, 334–37 (Gerald Korngold & Andrew P. Morriss eds., 2004); Richard H. Chused, *Euclid*'s Historical Imagery, 51 Case W. Res. L. Rev. 597 (2001); Martha A. Lees, Preserving Property Values? Preserving Proper Homes? Preserving Privilege? The Pre-*Euclid* Debate over Zoning for Exclusively Private Residential Areas, 56 U. Pitt. L. Rev. 367 (1994).

4. *Zoning and race.* Euclid's zoning ordinance was drafted against the backdrop of increasing racial tension in Cleveland and its suburbs. Before Euclid adopted its ordinance, several nearby communities, including Lakewood, Cleveland Heights, and East Cleveland, had adopted zoning ordinances drafted by Robert Whitten. Whitten was a strong defender of the use of "race zoning" (indeed, he once proposed a zoning plan for Atlanta that explicitly subdivided residential districts by race). Euclid's ordinance was very similar to the East Cleveland plan Whitten had drafted. William M. Randle, Professors, Reformers, Bureaucrats, and Cronies: The Players in *Euclid v. Ambler, in* Zoning and the American Dream 31, 38–43 (Charles M. Haar & Jerold S. Kayden eds., 1989).

Judge Westenhaver's reasoning in striking down Euclid's ordinance contained a revealing, and ugly, acknowledgment of the role that race played in motivating some zoning efforts. He noted that the U.S. Supreme Court had just a few years before struck down explicit racial zoning in Buchanan v. Warley, 245 U.S. 60 (1917) (discussed at pp. 692–93), and observed:

> It seems to me that no candid mind can deny that more and stronger reasons exist, having a real and substantial relation to the public peace, supporting [the Buchanan] ordinance than can be urged under any aspect of the police power to support the present ordinance as applied to plaintiff's property. And no gift of second sight is required to foresee that if [the explicit racial zoning in *Buchanan*] had been sustained, its provisions would have spread from city to city throughout the length and breadth of the land. And it is equally apparent that the next step in the exercise of this police power would be to apply similar restrictions for the purpose of segregating in like manner various groups of newly arrived immigrants. The blighting of property values and the congesting of the population, whenever the colored or certain foreign races invade a residential section, are so well known as to be within the judicial cognizance.

297 F. at 312–13. In short, then, for Judge Westenhaver, if the Supreme Court would not allow racial zoning, it certainly would not allow a zoning scheme based on even less compelling rationales. See Chused, supra.

For extended discussion of how zoning has been used to exclude and expel people of color from communities, see Chapter 8A.

5. *Sutherland's epiphany?* Justice Sutherland so often joined with Justices Butler, McReynolds, and Van Devanter (the dissenters in *Euclid*) in conservative decisions striking down social legislation that the group became known as the "Four Horsemen." See Barry Cushman, The Secret Lives of the Four Horsemen, 83 Va. L. Rev. 559 (1997). Just a few years before *Euclid*, Justice Sutherland authored, and the *Euclid* dissenters joined, an opinion striking down minimum wage laws for women and children, Adkins v. Children's Hospital, 261 U.S. 525 (1923). That opinion reaffirmed the view (usually associated with Lochner v. New York, 198 U.S. 45 (1905)) that the legislature cannot seek to benefit the poor, workers, or other social groups by interfering with individuals' freedom to contract or individual property rights. Ambler Realty's brief stressed a similar theme. Garrett Power, Advocates at Cross Purposes: The Briefs on Behalf of Zoning in the Supreme Court, 2 J. Sup. Ct. Hist. 79, 84 n.39 (1997).

Why then did Sutherland break with his usual allies to write the decision that "provided the constitutional foundation for an explosive growth in modern zoning, subdivision controls, and other governmental land use regulation that has transformed the organization and development of land and communities"? Gerald Korngold, The Emergence of Private Land Use Controls in Large-Scale Subdivisions: The Companion Story to *Village of Euclid v. Amber Realty Co.*, 51 Case W. Res. L. Rev. 617, 617 (2001). Sutherland's biographer offers the following:

> The opinion makes clear that Sutherland saw in the zoning act not the deprivation of property, but its enhancement. A distinction observed by [Judge] Cooley long before was therefore pertinent. It pointed out "the line between what would be a clear invasion of right on the one hand, and regulations not lessening the value of the right" on the other. On this basis the common law had allowed the abatement of nuisances, and the forbidden industrial plants would approximate nuisances in a residential area such as Euclid. The result of the statute, then, was beneficial to property.

Joel F. Paschal, Mr. Justice Sutherland: A Man Against the State 127 (1951). For other views about what led Justice Sutherland to approve zoning, see Charles M. Haar & Michael Allan Wolf, Commentary, *Euclid* Lives: The Survival of Progressive Jurisprudence, 115 Harv. L. Rev. 2158 (2002); Joseph Gordon Hylton, Prelude to *Euclid*: The United States Supreme Court and the Constitutionality of Land Use Regulation, 1900–1920, 3 Wash. U. J.L. & Pol'y 1 (2000); Robert A. Williams, Jr., Legal Discourse, Social Vision and the Supreme Court's Land Use Planning Law: The Genealogy of the Lochnerian Recurrence in *First English Lutheran Church* and *Nollan*, 59 U. Colo. L. Rev. 427, 439–43 (1988).

6. *Bedrock law.* Although zoning as currently practiced has many critics (see pp. 607–14 for the major criticisms), most commentators agree with the core *Euclid* holding that the federal Constitution should not be construed to prevent cities from segregating industry, creating separate districts for single-family houses, and so forth. But see Richard A. Epstein, Takings 131–34 (1985), and Bernard H. Siegan, Land Use Without Zoning 203–47 (1972), in which leading opponents of zoning express doubts about the constitutionality of the general practice.

7. *Exhaustion of nonjudicial remedies.* In *Euclid*, Justice Sutherland permitted Ambler Realty to mount a constitutional challenge in court, even though the company had neither proposed any particular use for the land nor sought a variance from the zoning board of appeals. Today, facial challenges are extremely hard to win, and developers challenging the application of a zoning ordinance to their land are required to submit a specific proposal for development and seek any available variances (exceptions to the zoning ordinance)

for that specific plan before a court will consider their federal takings claim to be ripe for decision. The current ripeness requirements are discussed at pp. 234–51.

8. *As the world turns.* Euclid's victory failed to protect the site from industrialization because during World War II "the federal government decide[d] it want[ed] a defense plant there." Jeff Piorkowski, Talk in the Town, Euclid Sun J., Apr. 1, 1999, at A5 (quoting then-Mayor Paul Oyaski). Florence Humphrey of the Euclid Historical Society reports that the plant, Cleveland Pneumatic Aerol, went out of business when World War II ended; the site was sold to General Motors in 1947. GM's Fisher Body plant shut down in the early 1990s, and the site was unused for several years. In 1996, the site was sold for $2.5 million, and in 1999, a portion of the plant was converted to an indoor sports facility. The surrounding area is now a hodgepodge of commercial and industrial uses, modest homes, and apartment complexes. Michael Allan Wolf, "Compelled by Conscientious Duty": *Village of Euclid v. Ambler Realty Co.* as Romance, 2 J. Sup. Ct. Hist. 88, 97 (1997).

3.   *The Modern Zoning Ordinance*

Introductory Note on Post-Euclidean Zoning Techniques

1. *The mapping of districts.* A zoning ordinance has two parts: a map and a text. The map classifies the city's land into zoning districts; the text spells out the uses permitted in each zone and details restrictions on lot size, building placement, building height, and similar issues. Figure 3-3 reproduces a portion of the zoning map currently in force in Euclid, Ohio; Figure 3-4 reproduces portions of Euclid's current zoning ordinance.

District boundaries often follow streets and alleys. But as the *Euclid* facts show, classifications along major transportation arteries often are bounded by lines paralleling the artery. When a technique of this sort is used, zoning boundaries will not necessarily correspond to lotlines between property owners.

2. *The evolution of zoning from a static to a dynamic system.* The first generation of zoning ordinances made only modest incursions into the choices of private landowners. Euclidean zoning segregated land uses to minimize conflicts, but it assumed that development would and should occur, and the only issue was where it should go. Early building-bulk and lot-area requirements were rather mild and essentially attempted to establish rights to light and air beyond those recognized by the common law. Modern zoning not only goes much further in its substantive restrictions, but also typically involves a different decisionmaking process.

The original zoning system was built on five crucial assumptions:

> First, a simplistic segregation of uses would result in a quality urban environment. Second, it would be possible, in drawing the zoning map, to formulate an intelligent all-at-once decision to which the market would conform. Third, the governors of the system would rarely change the rules. Fourth, nonconforming uses would go away. Fifth, municipal power would accomplish these goals.

Ira Michael Heyman, Legal Assaults on Municipal Land Use Regulation, 5 Urb. Law. 2 (1973), *reprinted in* The Land Use Awakening: Zoning in the Seventies 51 (Robert H. Freilich & Eric O. Stuhler eds., 1980).

If these assumptions had been correct, local zoning administrators would have had little discretion: They merely would have applied rules set out in advance in zoning ordinances. But it is now widely conceded that these original assumptions were naive.

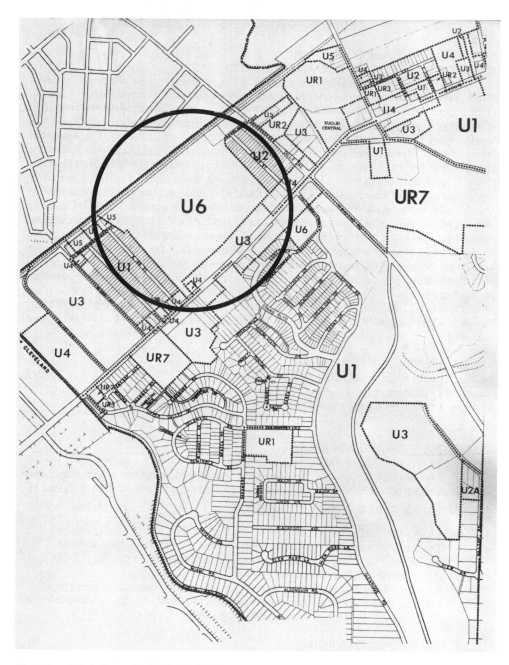

Note: The circle indicates the Ambler Realty Tract.
Source: Euclid, Ohio, City Planning Department.

FIGURE 3-3
Euclid's Current Zoning Map

FIGURE 3-4
Excerpt from Euclid, Ohio, Zoning Ordinance
CODIFIED ORDINANCES OF EUCLID (2004)

TITLE SEVEN - Zoning Districts; Map
1341.01 DISTRICTS AND ZONE MAP ESTABLISHED.
       For the purpose of regulating and restricting the location of trades, industries, apartment houses, two-family houses, single-family houses and other uses of property, the number of square feet of lot area per family housed, the width of lots, the location and size of yards and the size and height of buildings, the City is divided into twelve classes of use districts termed respectively Class UI or Single-Family House Districts, Class U2 or Two-Family House Districts, Class U3 or Apartment House Districts, Class U3E or Elevator Apartment House Districts, Class U3EL or Senior Citizens Use Districts, ASF Attached Single-Family Districts, Class U4 or Local Retail or Wholesale Store Districts, Class U5 or Commercial Districts, Class U6 or Industrial and Manufacturing Districts, Class U7 or Light Industrial Park Districts, Class U8 or Office Building Districts and Class R or Institutional Use Districts; also into three classes of height districts termed respectively Class HI, H2 and H3; and into four classes of area districts termed respectively Class Al, A2, A3 and A4; all districts are as shown on the Zone Map which is declared to be a part hereof. The use, height and area districts designated on the Zone Map are established. The Map designations and the Map designation rules which accompany the Map are declared to be part thereof and hereof. No buildings or premises shall be erected or used except in conformity with the regulations in this Planning and Zoning Code prescribed for the respective use, height and area district in which such building or premises are located. (Ord. 2812. Passed 11-13-22; Ord. 251-1967. Passed 10-2-67; Ord. 29-1969. Passed 2-17-69; Ord. 99-1972. Passed 5-1-72; Ord. 159-1972. Passed 7-10-72; Ord. 9-1983. Passed 1-4-83; Ord. 151-1990. Passed 5-21-90.)

1341.02 CLASSIFICATION OF USES.
       For the purpose of this Zoning Code, the various uses of buildings and premises are divided into groups, classes and subdivisions as set forth in the classification of uses in Title Nine, Zoning Use Districts. (Ord. 28-1957. Passed 1-28-57.)

TITLE NINE - Zoning Use Districts
1351.01 COMPLIANCE REQUIRED.
       In a Class U1 District no building or premises shall be used, and no building shall be erected which is arranged, intended or designed to be used, except for a Class U1 use. (Ord. 2812. Passed 11-13-22.)

1351.02 PERMITTED USES.
       The permitted uses in a Class Ul Single-Family House District shall be as follows:
      (a)   A public park, not including an amusement park operated for profit;
      (b)   A single-family dwelling; and
      (c)   The raising of crops or nurseries, but not including any commercial greenhouses.
      (d)   This section shall not be construed to include a two-family dwelling or a double house.
(Ord. 28-1957. Passed 1-28-57; Ord. 178-1959. Passed 9-14-59.)

1353.01 COMPLIANCE REQUIRED.
       In a Class U2 District no building or premises shall be used, and no building shall be erected which is arranged, intended or designed to be used, except for a Class UI or U2 use.
(Ord. 2812. Passed 11-13-22.)

1353.02 PERMITTED USES.
       The permitted uses in a Class U2 Two-Family House District shall be as follows:
      (a) Uses permitted in Class UI Districts; and
      (b) Two-family dwellings.
(Ord. 28-1957. Passed 1-28-57.)

FIGURE 3-4 (*Continued*)

1355.01 COMPLIANCE REQUIRED.

In a Class U3 District no building or premises shall be used, and no building shall be erected which is arranged, intended or designed to be used, except for a Class U1, U2 or U3 use. (Ord. 2812. Passed 11-13-22.)

1355.02 PERMITTED USES.

The permitted uses in a Class U3 Apartment House District shall be as follows:
(a)   Uses permitted in Class UI and U2 Districts;
(b)   An apartment house; and
(c)   A community center building.
(Ord. 97-1972. Passed 5-1-72.) . . .

1361.01 COMPLIANCE REQUIRED.

In a Class U6 District no building or premises shall be used, and no building shall be erected which is arranged, intended or designed to be used, except for a U6 use. (Ord. 3-1973, Passed 1-2-73.)
. . .

1361.04 PERMITTED USES.

The permitted uses in a Class U6 Industrial and Manufacturing District shall be as follows: Any trade, industry or use, except those prohibited in Chapter 1373, and except those which are or will be injurious, hazardous, noxious or offensive by reason of the emission of odor, dust, smoke, gas, vibration or noise. (Ord. 28-1957. Passed 1-28-57.)

1361.05 SPECIALLY PERMITTED USES.

The location of the uses set forth in this section in a Class U6 Use District shall be conditioned upon the issuance of a special permit by the City Planning and Zoning Commission, which permission shall be confirmed by resolution of Council before becoming effective. As a condition for the issuance of a special permit, the Zoning Commissioner may set a limit on the number of cars, boats or other motorized vehicles to be stored or parked on the premises of a used car lot where such use has been permitted pursuant to subsection (c) hereof. Uses requiring special permits are as follows:

(a) Drive-in restaurant or food establishment;
(b) Dance hall;
(c) Used car or used boat lots;
(d) Roller skating or ice skating rink;
(e) Public recreation center;
(f) Race track, archery range, golf course, golf driving range or miniature golf course;
(g) Animal hospitals, pet shops, animal kennels;
(h) Bowling alley;
(i) Car rental or car leasing companies;
   (Ord. 16-1996. Passed 1-16-96; Eff. 2-16-96.)
(j) Warehousing; and
(k) Office use. (Ord. 161-1996. Passed 9-3-96; Eff. 10-3-96.)

Source: Euclid, Ohio City Planning Department.

Experience quickly revealed that it is not practically possible to predict future market demand, and that zoning provisions that run counter to the market create great political pressure for change and are apt to be amended. Accordingly, as early as the 1930s, planners began to turn away from static end-state plans and to shift the focus of zoning away from fixed advance allocations and toward case-by-case review of landowners' or developers' proposed development plans.

This changed the function of zoning maps. Early zoning maps actually attempted to project desired development patterns. When it became clear that this was impossible (or at least very difficult), zoning maps essentially became "first offers," which described minimum uses that cities would allow; the "final offers" (the real controls) emerged from ad hoc bargaining between landowner and city. To discern a municipality's zoning intentions today, therefore, one must focus not only on the current map, but also on the pattern of amendments the municipality recently has approved.

Modern zoning maps have several general characteristics. First, the map by and large confirms existing use patterns. This practice sidesteps many nonconforming use conflicts, albeit at the price of making zoning maps a maze of oddly shaped, ad hoc districts (and at the price of continuing uses that, absent the gerrymandering, would be nonconforming). Although all use designations are potentially amendable, those in established neighborhoods are the least likely to be open for negotiation. Second, the map assigns most undeveloped tracts to "holding zones" (i.e., zoning classifications more restrictive than the property owners would want and than the city actually may need). The restricted landowners can then be expected to customize their plans and to offer concessions to neighbors and other potential opponents to induce the city to lift some of its restrictions. In the time span between the end of World War II and the late 1960s, zoning thus was largely transformed from a static to a dynamic system that responds in an ad hoc manner to specific development proposals.

Third, the zoning classifications of modern maps are both more narrowly defined and more numerous than those of first generation maps. The 1916 New York City ordinance had only three types of use districts: "residence," "business," and "unrestricted." Lincoln Trust Co. v. Williams Bldg. Corp., 128 N.E. 209, 210 (N.Y. 1920). Today, the New York City ordinance has 176 different use districts. New York, N.Y., Zoning Resolution, art. I, ch. 1, §§11–12 (May 13, 2004). At the time *Euclid* was decided, that city had 6 use districts; today it has 12. The reasons behind this expansion already have been alluded to. The more use districts a city has, the more easily it can allow existing uses to continue while at the same time restricting their expansion. Similarly, creating new zones improves a city's bargaining position because more types of ad hoc deals become possible.

Examining the current map is much easier than discerning patterns in how the municipality has allowed the map to be amended and circumvented. The next Note and Chapter 4 address the ways in which municipalities make their zoning maps more "flexible." Chapter 4 also analyzes the advantages and dangers of dealmaking between local governments and private developers.

3. *Noncumulative zoning.* The zoning scheme at issue in *Euclid* was cumulative. Someone owning land in the U-6 zone, for example, could use it not only for heavy industry, but also for all uses allowed in the U-1 through U-5 zones (e.g., residences). Much of modern zoning, especially for industrial districts, is noncumulative; the owner is permitted to undertake certain specified uses, but not more delicate ones. (In the ordinance now in effect in Euclid, for example, only the U-2 and U-3 zones are cumulative (they allow single-family houses); all others are noncumulative.) See Figure 3-4. The major (though usually unstated) reason for noncumulative zoning is fiscal. Light industrial uses (and even multifamily buildings) are more likely than single-family homes to contribute

taxes sufficient to pay for the municipal services they consume. See pp. 763–71. Local governments also may favor noncumulative zoning because it promotes efficiency where industrial and residential users need different types of infrastructure. Industry may prefer noncumulative zoning because the development of other uses in industrial districts may limit existing industries' abilities to expand, may precipitate conflicts, and may expose the industrial uses to nuisance or toxic tort suits.

4. *Separation of uses.* The ordinance at issue in *Euclid*, like most early zoning ordinances, rested on a definite vision of the city. The "highest" use of land was seen as a neighborhood of single-family houses, unsullied by inconsistent uses. Once this vision was accepted, the notion of a hierarchy of uses and of the need for their rigid segregation followed. The notion that residential areas should be sharply differentiated from nonresidential areas owes much to the landscape architects of the late nineteenth and early twentieth centuries who sought to reconcile the city with the country. See Roy Lubove, The Urban Community: Housing and Planning in the Progressive Era 1–22 (1967), for a brief survey of that tradition.

The rigid separation of uses that marks Euclidean zoning was sharply criticized by Jane Jacobs in her 1961 classic, The Death and Life of Great American Cities. Jacobs argues that a mixture of uses is crucial to a city's vitality, in part because mixed use districts attract different kinds of people whose activities occur over more of the day, thereby making the area safer and more vibrant around the clock, and in part because a mixture of uses promotes "the cross-fertilization of ideas and experiences that is so important to a city's economic and social health." Jay Wickersham, Jane Jacobs's Critique of Zoning: From *Euclid* to Portland and Beyond, 28 B.C. Envtl. Aff. L. Rev. 547, 550–51 (2001); see also pp. 51–52 for a discussion of Jane Jacobs. Today, criticism of Euclidean separation of uses is pressed most strongly by the "New Urbanists," who urge that a mix of uses that allows people to work and shop within walking distance of their homes promotes a greater sense of community and reduces dependence on environmentally unfriendly automobiles. See, e.g., Andres Duany et al., Suburban Nation: The Rise of Sprawl and the Decline of the American Dream 24–25 (2000). Chapters 5A and 9D explore those themes.

5. *Flexibility devices.* Cities now offer a wide variety of procedures by which the zoning rules applicable to a particular piece of land can be changed. Although these change mechanisms are treated in detail in Chapter 4, the balance of this chapter will be less mysterious if some of them are defined at this juncture.

The SZEA provided two basic avenues for change. *Variances* essentially waive the application of specific provisions of the zoning ordinance to a particular plot. The SZEA envisioned that variances would be granted by a quasi-judicial board of zoning appeals to relieve landowners of unnecessary hardship, and would be sufficiently limited to avoid compromising the overall zoning scheme. *Rezonings* (also called *zoning amendments* or *map amendments*) are revisions of the applicable text or map. They are enacted by the local legislative body through the normal legislative process.

Since the 1920s, a variety of other flexibility devices have evolved. The *special exception* (also known as *conditional use*) is one of the most important. The local legislative body identifies relatively unusual uses that are apt to create special siting problems (service stations, houses of worship, schools) and declares in what zones and under what conditions they are to be permitted. Typically, the planning commission first hears applications for these permits. The commission's decision often may be appealed to the local legislative body.

Overlay zoning allows a local government to vary its regulations within the same basic use zone. For example, hillside areas might be identified as warranting special height, grading, or lot-size requirements. These could be imposed through the creation of some entirely new use districts. The overlay technique, however, instead involves the creation of new regulations applicable to the special area; these are overlaid on (added to) the regulations of the zones already in existence there. This also may be done for wetlands, critical habitats for endangered species, or other areas of special environmental importance.

The two modern innovations that most depart from Euclidean thinking are planned-unit development (PUD) ordinances and transferable development rights (TDR) systems. PUD ordinances authorize large-scale developers to ignore the detailed use, bulk, and lot-area regulations on their land and instead to propose specific development plans that meet general density and use criteria. The developer thus can cluster housing units, mix different uses, set aside large areas for open space, and so on. The preset regulations of Euclidean vintage are swept away; what matters is the developer's offer and the municipality's ad hoc response to it.

A municipality using a TDR system authorizes landowners in certain designated areas to buy zoning rights (e.g., permitted building bulk) from landowners in other designated areas. The second (transferor) area is usually a historic district or other area the municipality desires to preserve. Landowners in that area are compensated for restrictions by being given TDRs, and the landowners in the transferee area bear the costs of the preservation program. A TDR ordinance forswears Euclidean thinking because, at least to a degree, it puts zoning classifications on the auction block.

Note on Sanctions Imposed on Violators of Local Land Use Regulations

Local officials seek to ensure that developers comply with zoning ordinances by conditioning the grant of building permits on official approval of building plans, coupled with site inspections of the project as it is being developed. That preventive check helps to keep buildings that would not comply with the ordinance from ever entering the construction phase. Some landowners, however, just ignore the requirement for a building permit. Others ignore the mandates of municipal regulations once they have a building permit in hand or change the use to which land is put without undertaking construction that would trigger the need for a building permit. What risks do those violators run? Section 8 of the SZEA authorized local governments to impose both civil and criminal sanctions, and most states and cities have followed this suggestion. Civil enforcement typically starts with a local official ordering the landowner to remove or modify the offending structure or to cease the unlawful use. If construction is underway, the city may issue a stop-work order or revoke the developer's building permit pending correction of the violation. If the landowner fails to correct the problem, the city may impose a fine or petition a court to issue a mandatory injunction that the landowner comply. See, e.g., Kosciusko County Board of Zoning Appeals v. Wygant, 644 N.E.2d 112 (Ind. 1994) (trial court abused its discretion in denying a mandatory injunction after county had proved a violation of a valid zoning ordinance, at least where the violation threatens "important interests of the community"). A landowner who is a true scofflaw and ignores the court order risks fines and imprisonment for contempt of court. Recalcitrants nevertheless often succeed in delaying compliance. See, e.g., Town of Nottingham v. Bonser, 777 A.2d 851 (N.H. 2001), recounting the 20-year history of the town's efforts to remove mobile homes that violated a zoning ordinance, where the owner was held in civil contempt, fined $1,000 per day, and then found to have fraudulently conveyed the property to avoid the town's efforts to collect more than $1.4 million in fines.

Removing or modifying the noncomplying structure or use may be extremely costly. One such case made headlines when a Florida builder was required to demolish apartments built in violation of a comprehensive plan. Razing of Apartments Makes History in Florida, St. Petersburg Times, Sept. 7, 2002, at 5B; see also Pinecrest Lakes, Inc. v. Shidel, 795 So. 2d 191, 209 (Fla. Dist. Ct. App. 2001). Another notable example arose in New York City, where a developer built a 31-story apartment building in an Upper East Side district zoned for 19 stories. The developer claimed that the violation was caused by an error in the city's maps and fought enforcement efforts in the courts and before the city agency charged with granting variances. After five years of unsuccessful litigation, however, the developer finally agreed to remove the extra 12 stories, at a cost of almost $2 million. David W. Dunlap, Builder Agrees to Decapitate 31-Story Tower, N.Y. Times, Apr. 23, 1991, at B4; Thomas J. Lueck, Court Backs New York's Right to Order Building's Top Razed, N.Y. Times, Feb. 10, 1988, at A1. In other instances in which violations of the zoning code would be extremely costly to correct, cities have allowed developers to escape enforcement by providing amenities for the community. For criticism of that approach, see Paul Goldberger, When Developers Change the Rules During the Game, N.Y. Times, Mar. 19, 1989, §2, at 36.

Enforcement of zoning ordinances is often lax. Many cities do not proactively enforce the regulations but rely instead on citizen complaints to trigger enforcement actions. In addition, enforcement traditionally has been left to building departments rather than planning agencies. Planners complain that building departments lack sufficient knowledge of the zoning ordinance to adequately police compliance, and that they are more concerned about compliance with building codes than adherence to the zoning ordinance. Enforcement is further hindered by the increasing complexity and variability of regulations that are tailored to each property through development agreements, conditional variances or rezonings, and other flexibility devices of recent vintage.

To improve enforcement efforts, some cities have introduced such techniques as neighborhood sweeps to identify violations. Others rely on sophisticated computer systems to keep track of the requirements applicable to each property and to identify offenders. Many cities have reassigned responsibility for enforcement to the planning department or to a centralized agency charged with enforcing all regulations related to property. Others are trying to upgrade the professionalism of the enforcement staff. Some cities encourage planning and enforcement staffs to coordinate their efforts, asking the enforcement officers to review proposed zoning text to ensure that it is clear and enforceable, for example, and asking planners to accompany inspectors on their rounds to identify problems. See Eric Damian Kelly, Enforcing Zoning & Land Use Controls, APA Planning Advisory Service Rep. 409 (1988); Todd W. Bressi, Throwing the Book at Zoning Violators: Communities Are Catching on to More Sophisticated Enforcement Techniques, Planning, Dec. 1988, at 4.

A landowner who escapes the notice of enforcers or who induces local officials to refrain from enforcement is hardly on safe ground. Neighboring landowners also may sue to remedy violations of public land use controls. Illustrative is Frankland v. City of Lake Oswego, 517 P.2d 1042 (Or. 1973), in which neighbors convinced the court that the developer had built apartment buildings in violation of the final plan the city had approved under its planned-unit development ordinance. The case was remanded for a determination of whether the neighbors' remedy should be damages or some form of mandatory injunction. In considering whether to grant an injunction, the Oregon Supreme Court concluded that the trial court should compare the neighbors' injury arising from the violation to the developer's cost of remedying the violation. Would such a balancing of hardship be appropriate if the city had been the party seeking a mandatory injunction?

See City of Aiken v. Cole, 345 S.E.2d 760, 762 (S.C. Ct. App. 1986) (city's request for an injunction ordering removal of satellite dishes erected in violation of zoning law denied; courts must balance the equities between the parties, using a "relative hardship or balance of convenience" standard).

Land use control ordinances also usually provide that violators are subject to criminal sanctions, and prosecutors do occasionally bring criminal charges. Most prosecutions involve owners who keep junkyards on their property, but occasionally, seemingly much less noxious uses are subject to prosecution. See, e.g., People v. Multari, 517 N.Y.S.2d 374 (Albany County Ct. 1987) (upholding imprisonment for student convicted of violating "grouper" ordinance prohibiting more than three unrelated adults from living together in a single-family residence).

B.   Landowners' and Developers' Constitutional Rights As Constraints on Inefficient Zoning Measures

Justice Sutherland's majority opinion in *Euclid* admitted the possibility that zoning controls could restrict the development of specific tracts in such an "arbitrary and unreasonable" way that the constitutional rights of landowners and developers would be abridged. Thus, while *Euclid* forced attorneys for landowners to concede the constitutional validity of the principle of zoning, they remained free to challenge its particular applications. Such a particularized challenge inevitably demands close scrutiny of (1) the value of the parcel in alternative uses, and (2) how each of those different uses would affect neighbors. Although Justice Sutherland had some particularized evidence of this sort about the Ambler Realty tract before him, he chose to discuss the constitutional validity of zoning only "in its general scope," and thus did not focus on this evidence.

Since *Euclid*, landowners and developers aggrieved by zoning controls have filed (probably) tens of thousands of complaints seeking particularized judicial relief for their parcels. Some of these lawsuits have been based on nonconstitutional theories. The city may have violated its own ordinances or the state's zoning enabling act, or may have failed to comply with other specific state statutes limiting the use of zoning. See, e.g., Mass. Gen. Laws Ann. ch. 40A, §3 (West 2004) (no zoning ordinance shall prohibit the use of lands owned by religious sects or denominations for religious or educational purposes). Some landowner suits in recent years have even rested exclusively on provisions of state constitutions or on federal statutes. However, the historic tendency of attorneys for landowners has been to reject (or overlook) these narrower lines of legal attack and to invoke instead the heavy artillery of the federal Constitution.[1]

As will soon be clear, the constitutional law of landowner rights is exasperatingly untidy. Different constitutional doctrines overlap in their purposes and scope. Judges often neglect to reveal which clauses (or even which constitutions) justify their holdings. Further,

---

[1] Most landowner challenges that rest on the federal Constitution invoke language from one of the following three amendments:

Amendment I: Congress shall make no law respecting an establishment of religion, or prohibiting the free exercise thereof; or abridging the freedom of speech, or of the press; . . .

Amendment V: . . . [N]or shall private property by taken for public use, without just compensation.

Amendment XIV: . . . [N]or shall any state deprive any person of life, liberty, or property, without due process of law; nor deny to any person within its jurisdiction the equal protection of the laws.

even when they find that landowners or developers are constitutionally entitled to relief, the courts often have paid too little attention to the issue of remedy.

This subchapter, along with the next two, groups the cases adjudicating landowners' constitutional claims according to the three major types of policy arguments underlying the claims. In brief, these are that the restriction being challenged is (1) inefficient from a social perspective, (2) unfairly burdensome or disruptive of settled expectations, and (3) violative of the landowner's or developer's civil liberties.

Different constitutional clauses are relevant under the three policy headings. Constraints on municipal adoption of inefficient zoning controls traditionally spring from the Due Process Clause of the Fourteenth Amendment, which is construed to require that each zoning restriction be reasonably related to a legitimate government objective. But some courts instead used the Fifth Amendment's Takings Clause to examine the reasonableness of a regulation, until Lingle v. Chevron U.S.A., Inc., 125 S. Ct. 2074 (2005), excerpted at p.193, foreclosed that option. Courts deploy both the Equal Protection Clause of the Fourteenth Amendment and the Takings Clause to protect landowners from having to shoulder unfair burdens. Similarly, both the Due Process Clause and the Takings Clause are used to review a landowner's claim that a regulation interferes too dramatically with settled expectations. The third value at stake, civil liberties, was once protected by the Due Process Clause. Today, the First Amendment's explicit and implicit protection of free expression, free religious exercise, privacy, and association is more commonly used for safeguarding civil liberties.

Division of the case law on landowners' constitutional rights into the functional concerns of "efficiency," "unfair burdens," and "civil liberties" serves to shorten the exposition and to illuminate doctrinal interconnections. However, many judicial opinions inevitably resist this categorization, and the cases exhibit a great deal of confusion about what concern the developer has expressed, and about what constitutional provision the court has relied on in responding to that concern. Several courts have valiantly attempted to put the house in order by providing typologies of claims. See Villas of Lake Jackson, Ltd. v. Leon County, 121 F.3d 610 (11th Cir. 1997); Pearson v. City of Grand Blanc, 961 F.2d 1211 (6th Cir. 1992). Confusion persists, however, in part because of bad (or strategic) lawyering and judging, and in part because the three concerns overlap. The fairness of making a landowner submit to a zoning restriction, for example, may depend in part on the efficiency of the restriction, as Professor Michelman explains in an article excerpted at p. 146.

1. The Substantive Due Process Challenge: Judicial Review of the "Reasonableness" of Legislative Line-Drawing Through Cost/Benefit Analysis

A zoning restriction is inefficient when the burdens on the restricted landowner are greater than the benefits of the restriction to the landowner's neighbors and other interested parties. To illustrate, suppose a landowner would be willing to pay $100,000 to be free of a height limit on new buildings. Suppose all affected neighbors would insist on aggregate compensation of only $20,000 to agree to waive the height limit. If the neighbors in fact had the power of waiver and if transactions could be costlessly arranged, the neighbors would consent to a waiver for a sum between $20,000 and $100,000. Suppose the agreed payment was $40,000. Both parties would be better off because the neighbors would have collected double their perceived damages and the landowner would be ahead by $60,000.

As is discussed at pp. 34–39, in economic language, this waiver of the height limit would be a Pareto superior move — one that made at least some parties better off and left no party worse off.

If a court invalidated this hypothetical height limit on constitutional grounds, it would normally not order the unshackled landowner to compensate the neighbors who valued the height restriction previously in effect. Therefore, judicial invalidation of the measure could not be said to achieve a Pareto superior result. However, invalidation would still be efficient in this instance under the Kaldor-Hicks test, which considers a policy efficient if those who gain from the policy value their gains in an amount greater than the amount the losers from the policy value their losses. Economists prefer to define efficiency as Pareto superiority, but usually recognize that policymakers must inevitably resort to the Kaldor-Hicks definition when compensation of losers is difficult to arrange. *Efficiency* is used in this casebook in the Kaldor-Hicks sense.

In the following cases on the "reasonableness" of zoning classifications, think about whether the courts mean *efficient* when they say *reasonable*, and observe how litigants provide the data courts need to determine reasonableness. Also note how differently trial and appellate courts, state and federal courts, and courts in various states respond when they are asked to second-guess zoning decisions made by local governing bodies.

a.   *The Nature of the Substantive Due Process Inquiry*

Nectow v. City of Cambridge
277 U.S. 183 (1928)

Mr. Justice SUTHERLAND delivered the opinion of the Court.

A zoning ordinance of the City of Cambridge divides the city into three kinds of districts: residential, business and unrestricted. Each of these districts is sub-classified in respect of the kind of buildings which may be erected. . . . The land of plaintiff in error was put in district R-3, in which are permitted only dwellings, hotels, clubs, churches, schools, philanthropic institutions, greenhouses and gardening. . . . [A map of the property appears in Figure 3-5.] The attack upon the ordinance is that, as specifically applied to plaintiff in error, it deprived him of his property without due process of law in contravention of the Fourteenth Amendment.

. . . The case was referred to a master to make and report findings of fact. . . . The case came on to be heard by a justice of the court, who, after confirming the master's report [in favor of the plaintiff in error], reported the case for the determination of the full court. Upon consideration, that court sustained the ordinance as applied to plaintiff in error, and dismissed the bill. 260 Mass. 441.

A condensed statement of facts, taken from the master's report, is all that is necessary. When the zoning ordinance was enacted, plaintiff in error was and still is the owner of a tract of land containing 140,000 square feet, of which the locus here in question is a part. . . . The effect of the zoning is to separate from the west end of plaintiff in error's tract a strip 100 feet in width. The Ford Motor Company has a large auto assembling factory south of the locus; and a soap factory and the tracks of the Boston & Albany Railroad lie near. Opposite the locus, on Brookline street, and included in the same district, there are some residences; and opposite the locus, on Henry street, and in the same district, are other residences. . . . Under the ordinance, business and industry of all sorts are excluded from the locus, while the remainder of the tract is unrestricted. It further appears that provision has been made for widening Brookline street, the effect of which, if carried out, will be

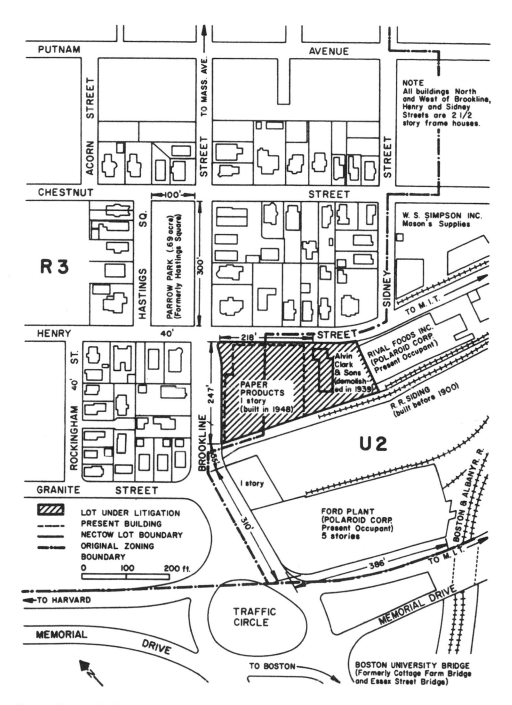

Source: 6 Norman Williams, Jr. & John M. Taylor, Williams American Land Planning Law Plate 15 (2002).

FIGURE 3-5
Property Involved in *Nectow v. City of Cambridge* (As the Area Was About
the Time of the Litigation)

to reduce the depth of the locus to 65 feet. After a statement at length of further facts, the master finds "that no practical use can be made of the land in question for residential purposes, because among other reasons herein related, there would not be adequate return on the amount of any investment for the development of the property." The last finding of the master is:

> I am satisfied that the districting of the plaintiff's land in a residence district would not promote the health, safety, convenience and general welfare of the inhabitants of that part of the defendant City, taking into account the natural development thereof and the character of the district and the resulting benefit to accrue to the whole City and I so find.

It is made pretty clear that because of the industrial and railroad purposes to which the immediately adjoining lands to the south and east have been devoted and for which they are zoned, the locus is of comparatively little value for the limited uses permitted by the ordinance.

We quite agree with the opinion expressed below that a court should not set aside the determination of public officers in such a matter unless it is clear that their action "has no foundation in reason and is a mere arbitrary or irrational exercise of power having no substantial relation to the public health, the public morals, the public safety or the public welfare in its proper sense." Euclid v. Ambler Co., [272 U.S. 365,] 395 [(1926)].

. . . [T]he inclusion of the locus in question is not indispensable to the general plan. The boundary line of the residential district before reaching the locus runs for some distance along the streets, and to exclude the locus from the residential district requires only that such line shall be continued 100 feet further along Henry street and thence south along Brookline street. There does not appear to be any reason why this should not be done. Nevertheless, if that were all, we should not be warranted in substituting our judgment for that of the zoning authorities primarily charged with the duty and responsibility of determining the question. But that is not all. . . . Here, the express finding of the master, already quoted, confirmed by the court below, is that the health, safety, convenience and general welfare of the inhabitants of the part of the city affected will not be promoted by the disposition made by the ordinance of the locus in question. This finding of the master, after a hearing and an inspection of the entire area affected, supported, as we think it is, by other findings of fact, is determinative of the case. That the invasion of the property of plaintiff in error was serious and highly injurious is clearly established, and, since a necessary basis for the support of that invasion is wanting, the action of the zoning authorities comes within the ban of the Fourteenth Amendment and cannot be sustained.

Judgment reversed.

b.   The Role of Federal Courts in Land Use Cases

After *Nectow*, the Supreme Court declined to decide another zoning case for another half-century. Although the Supreme Court has shown renewed interest in land use cases since the late 1970s, especially in recent years, it also has sharply limited landowners' access to federal courts through the ripeness requirements discussed at pp. 234–51. The Supreme Court's many decades of inattention, combined with the ripeness rules, have meant that the lower federal courts and the state courts have borne the brunt of elaborating the federal constitutional rules set out in *Nectow*. As the next case makes clear, the lower federal courts have had limited enthusiasm for cost/benefit balancing like that the *Nectow* special master performed.

Coniston Corp. v. Village of Hoffman Estates
844 F.2d 461 (7th Cir. 1988)

POSNER, Circuit Judge.

The plaintiffs own a tract of several hundred acres of land, originally undeveloped, in the Village of Hoffman Estates, Illinois. Their complaint . . . charges that in turning down the site plan for a 17-acre parcel in the tract, the Village Board of Trustees and its members violated the Constitution and state law. The district court dismissed the complaint for failure to state a claim.

The procedure for land development set forth in the Village's ordinances . . . requires first of all that there be a general plan for development approved by the Village Board of Trustees. This condition was met; . . . . [A]s development proceeds, the developer must submit site plans setting forth his plans for developing particular parcels. The site plan is first submitted to the Village Plan Commission for its recommendation and is then forwarded to the Board of Trustees for its approval or disapproval. No criteria are set forth in the ordinances or anywhere else to guide the Board.

Over the years the plaintiffs have presented a number of site plans for parcels within their tract, and these plans have been approved by both the Plan Commission and the Board of Trustees. For the 17-acre parcel at issue in this case, the plaintiffs submitted a plan that envisaged the construction of five single-story commercial buildings with a total office space of 181,000 square feet. The Plan Commission recommended approval of the plan, finding that it conformed to the general plan for the development of the plaintiffs' tract and to all applicable legal regulations. The Board of Trustees, however, disapproved the plan. It gave no reasons for its action but one of the trustees indicated that the reason (her reason, at any rate) was that the village has a lot of unused office space. (The Plan Commission had also expressed concern with the amount of vacant office space in the village.) . . .

The plaintiffs' only federal claims are that they were denied "substantive" and "procedural" due process. They expressly waived any claim they may have had that the defendants, by preventing them from developing the 17-acre parcel in accordance with the site plan, took their property without paying just compensation, in violation of the Fifth and Fourteenth Amendments. . . .

[One] objection to the due process route in a case such as the present one is that it depends on the idea of "substantive" due process. This is the idea that depriving a person of life, liberty, or property can violate the due process clause of the Fifth and Fourteenth Amendments even if there are no procedural irregularities — even if, for example, the state after due deliberation has passed a statute establishing procedures for taking private homes and giving them to major campaign contributors or people with red hair, and in taking the plaintiff's home has complied scrupulously with the statute's procedural requirements.

Substantive due process is a tenacious but embattled concept. Text and history, at least ancient history, are against it, though perhaps not decisively. . . .

The strongest criticisms of substantive due process are institutional ones. The concept invests judges with an uncanalized discretion to invalidate federal and state legislation. It also and by the same token invites the federal courts to sit in judgment on almost all state action — including, to come back to the present case, all zoning decisions. For it is tempting to view every zoning decision that is adverse to the landowner and in violation of state law as a deprivation of property. Property is not a thing, but a bundle of rights, and if the state confers rights with one hand and takes them away with the other, by a zoning decision that by violating state law deprives the owner of a property right and not just a property interest (the owner's financial interest in being able to employ his land in its most valuable use), why is it not guilty of denying substantive due process?

No one thinks substantive due process should be interpreted so broadly as to protect landowners against erroneous zoning decisions. But it is difficult to come up with limiting concepts that are not completely ad hoc. . . .

The present case is so remote from a plausible violation of substantive due process that we need not decide whether, or to precisely what extent, the concept limits takings by state and local governments; or whether the takings clause does so; or whether both or neither do so and if both whether there is any practical difference except possibly in a case like this where the plaintiff waives any claim based on the takings clause; or, finally, whether the plaintiffs can force us to confront difficult questions of substantive due process by their decision to waive a seemingly more straightforward claim under the takings clause. . . .

. . . Granted, the rejection of the plaintiffs' site plan probably reduced the value of their land. The plan must have represented their best guess about how to maximize the value of the property, and almost certainly a better guess than governmental officials would make even if the officials were trying to maximize that value, which of course they were not. But the plaintiffs do not even argue that the rejection of the site plan reduced the value of their parcel much, let alone that the parcel will be worthless unless it can be used to create 181,000 square feet of office space. . . . The plaintiffs in this case have been deprived of their "right" to create 181,000 square feet of office space on a 17-acre parcel of a much larger tract, and that deprivation is a limited, perhaps minimal, incursion into their property rights. If so it is not a deprivation at all, in the constitutional sense, and the due process clause is not in play.

Considering now the grounds as distinct from the consequences of the defendants' action, it may seem that since the Board of Trustees gave no reason for rejecting the plan we cannot exclude the possibility that the motive for the rejection was private, so that if (but it is a big if, as we have just seen) the rejection amounted to a taking or deprivation of property the plaintiffs' constitutional rights may have been violated. And even if, as seems plausible, the reason given by one trustee was the ground for the Board's rejection of the site plan, this reason seems to amount to nothing more than a desire to protect existing owners of office buildings from new competition, and thus makes the rejection look like an effort to transfer wealth from the plaintiffs to the existing owners. But . . . much governmental action is protectionist or anticompetitive; and nothing is more common in zoning disputes than selfish opposition to zoning changes. The Constitution does not forbid government to yield to such opposition; it does not outlaw the characteristic operations of democratic (perhaps of any) government, operations which are permeated by pressure from special interests. . . .

This case presents a garden-variety zoning dispute dressed up in the trappings of constitutional law. . . . If the plaintiffs can get us to review the merits of the Board of Trustees' decision under state law, we cannot imagine what zoning dispute could not be shoehorned into federal court in this way, there to displace or postpone consideration of some worthier object of federal judicial solicitude. Something more is necessary than dissatisfaction with the rejection of a site plan to turn a zoning case into a federal case; and it should go without saying that the something more cannot be merely a violation of state (or local) law. A violation of state law is not a denial of due process of law.

Thus we agree with the First Circuit's decision in Creative Environments, Inc. v. Estabrook, 680 F.2d 822, 833 (1st Cir. 1982), that the fact "that town officials are motivated by parochial views of local interests which work against plaintiffs' plan and which may contravene state subdivision laws" (or, we add, local ordinances) does not state a claim of denial of substantive due process. . . . Of course if a zoning decision is based on considerations that violate specific constitutional guarantees, it is invalid; but in all other cases the decision can be said to deny substantive due process only if it is irrational. . . .

At worst, the decision here was mistaken and protectionist; it was not irrational, so the claim of a denial of substantive due process fails. But were the plaintiffs denied procedural due process? As often, the line between "procedure" and "substance" is hazy in the setting of the regulation of land uses. The denial of the plaintiffs' site plan without a full statement of reasons is what gives the denial such arbitrary cast as it may have, and thus lends color to the claim of irrationality, which is the substantive due process claim; but the failure to give reasons is also the cornerstone of the procedural due process claim. It is no good saying that if a person is deprived of property for a bad reason it violates substantive due process and if for no reason it violates procedural due process. Unless the bad reason is invidious or irrational, the deprivation is constitutional; and the no-reason case will sometimes be a case of invidious or irrational deprivation, too, depending on the motives and consequences of the challenged action.

The plaintiffs complain not only about the absence of a statement of reasons but also about . . . the absence of any language in the Village's ordinances to indicate that the Board of Trustees is authorized to reject a site plan recommended by the Plan Commission. These complaints might have considerable force if the zoning decision had been adjudicative in nature, but it was not. The very absence of criteria, coupled with the fact that the Village Board of Trustees is the governing body of the Village of Hoffman, suggests that, as is usually true of zoning, the Board's decision to approve or disapprove a site plan is a legislative rather than adjudicative decision. The difference is critical. See Bi-Metallic Investment Co. v. State Board of Equalization, 239 U.S. 441 (1915); City of Eastlake v. Forest City Enterprises, Inc., 426 U.S. 668, 675 n.10 (1976). The Constitution does not require legislatures to use adjudicative-type procedures, to give reasons for their enactments, or to act "reasonably" in the sense in which courts are required to do; as already noted, legislatures can base their actions on considerations — such as the desire of a special-interest group for redistributive legislation in its favor — that would be thought improper in judicial decision-making. . . .

It is not labels that determine whether action is legislative or adjudicative. . . . The decision whether and what kind of land uses to permit does not have the form of a judicial decision. The potential criteria and considerations are too open-ended and ill-defined. Granted, much modern adjudication has this character, but the difference is that even modern courts hesitate to treat the decision-making process as a wide-open search for the result that is just in light of all possible considerations of distributive and corrective justice, while legislatures are free to range widely over ethical and political considerations in deciding what regulations to impose on society. . . .

The Board of Trustees is the Village's legislature, and it has reserved to itself the final decision in zoning matters. Naturally it has not sought to tie its hands with criteria for approval of site plans or with a requirement that it give reasons for its action and always act in a fishbowl. The check on its behavior is purely electoral, but, as the Supreme Court stated in the *City of Eastlake* case, in a democratic polity this method of checking official action cannot be dismissed as inadequate per se.

. . . A statute, unlike a judicial decision, applies directly to a whole class of people, and it is this attribute that makes democratic checking feasible, though it is far from perfect. The smaller the class affected by a nominally legislative act, the weaker the democratic check. . . . The class here is small. This might support an argument that some type of individualized hearing was required. See Londoner v. City of Denver, 210 U.S. 373, 385–86 (1908). *City of Eastlake*, upholding the decision to submit a single landowner's zoning application to a referendum, cuts the other way. In any event, there was a hearing here — maybe not enough of one to satisfy the requirements of due process in an adjudicative setting but enough to give the plaintiffs all the process that due process in zoning could possibly be thought to require after *City of Eastlake*. . . .

Affirmed.

Note on Substantive Due Process Challenges in the Federal Courts

1. *How bad does it have to be to count as "irrational"?* In City of Cuyahoga Falls, Ohio v. Buckeye Community Hope Foundation, 538 U.S. 188 (2003), the Supreme Court rejected a developer's claim that the city violated due process by refusing to grant building permits for a low-income housing project. After the city council approved the project, opponents petitioned to force the council's decision to be submitted to a voter referendum (see pp. 401–09). The city engineer then refused to issue building permits while the petition was pending. The Court held that the refusal to issue the permits:

> in no sense constituted egregious or arbitrary government conduct. See County of Sacramento v. Lewis, 523 U.S. 833, 846 (1998) (noting that in our evaluations of "abusive executive action," we have held that "only the most egregious official conduct can be said to be 'arbitrary in the constitutional sense'").

538 U.S. at 198. The lower courts have split over just how bad conduct has to be to satisfy the "most egregious" standard. Some circuits hold that there is no violation of substantive due process unless the land use regulation at issue "shocks the conscience," a standard taken from the County of Sacramento v. Lewis decision the *Cuyahoga* Court cited. See, e.g., United Artists Theatre Circuit, Inc. v. Township of Warrington, 316 F.3d 392 (3d Cir. 2003); Bowers v. City of Flint, 325 F.3d 758, 763 (6th Cir. 2003); Baker v. Coxe, 230 F.3d 470, 474 (1st Cir. 2000) (noting that the "shocks the conscience" standard leaves "the door slightly ajar for federal relief [only] in truly horrendous situations" and accordingly "observe[s] a marked difference between the inevitable misjudgments, wrongheadedness, and mistakes of local government bureaucracies and the utterly unjustified, malignant, and extreme actions of those who would be parochial potentates").

The Eighth Circuit requires that the government conduct be "truly irrational" such as "attempting to apply a zoning ordinance only to persons whose names begin with a letter in the first half of the alphabet." Chesterfield Development Corp. v. City of Chesterfield, 963 F.2d 1102, 1104 (8th Cir. 1992), or "a zoning board's decision made by flipping a coin," Lemke v. Cass County, 846 F.2d 469, 472 (8th Cir. 1986) (en banc) (per curiam) (Arnold, J. concurring). The D.C. Circuit views only "grave unfairness" as violating substantive due process requirements. George Washington University v. District of Columbia, 318 F.3d 203, 209 (D.C. Cir. 2003) (noting that such unfairness may be shown only by a substantial infringement of state law prompted by personal or group animus or a deliberate flouting of the law that trammels significant personal or property rights).

Not surprisingly, then, substantive due process challenges to the decisions of land use regulators have been voted the "most unlikely to succeed" in federal courts by some commentators. See Joseph D. Richards & Alyssa A. Ruge, "Most Unlikely to Succeed": Substantive Due Process Claims Against Local Governments Applying Land Use Restrictions, 78 Fla. B.J. 34 (2004).

2. *Substantive due process claims substituting for takings claims.* As *Coniston* indicates, litigants may seek to style their complaint as a substantive due process claim that the government's action is "irrational" (or, in some circuits, "arbitrary and capricious") because a takings claim — a claim that the regulation destroyed so much of the value of the property that fairness requires just compensation — is unavailable. In *Coniston*, the takings claim

was foreclosed by waiver, but most commonly the claim is foreclosed by the Supreme Court's stringent ripeness requirements, discussed at pp. 234–51. The federal courts are impatient with such tactics. See, e.g., Forseth v. Village of Sussex, 199 F.3d 363 (7th Cir. 2000). Since 1996, the Ninth Circuit has steadfastly held that "due process claims are precluded where the alleged violation is addressed by the explicit textual provisions of the Fifth Amendment's Takings Clause." Madison v. Graham, 316 F.3d 867, 870–71 (9th Cir. 2002) (citing Armendariz v. Penman, 75 F.2d 1311 (9th Cir. 1996)) (en banc). Several other circuits and state courts have adopted the same rule, see, e.g., South County Sand & Gravel Co., Inc. v. Town of South Kingstown, 160 F.3d 834 (1st Cir. 1998); Bateman v. City of West Bountiful, 89 F.3d 704 (10th Cir. 1996); Mission Springs, Inc. v. City of Spokane, 954 P.2d 250 (Wash. 1998). See Peter J. Rubin, Square Pegs and Round Holes: Substantive Due Process, Procedural Due Process, and the Bill of Rights, 103 Colum. L. Rev. 833 (2003); Robert Ashbrook, Comment, Land Development, the Graham Doctrine, and the Extinction of Economic Substantive Due Process, 150 U. Pa. L. Rev. 1255 (2002).

The difficulty of distinguishing between substantive due process and takings claims, and the importance of doing so, is discussed at pp. 94–95, 179, and 193–97.

3. *Substantive due process claims substituting for First Amendment challenges.* The term "substantive due process" is sometimes used to mean the application of rights guaranteed by the Bill of Rights to the states through the Fourteenth Amendment. Litigants accordingly sometimes argue that a land use regulation is "irrational" and violates due process because it seeks to suppress speech, promote a particular religious belief, or suppress a disfavored religious practice, all of which the First Amendment declares to be illegitimate goals. Some courts have tried to eliminate such confusion by refusing to consider substantive due process challenges if the conduct at issue could be addressed by a First Amendment challenge. See, e.g., Nestor Colon Medina & Sucesores, Inc. v. Custodio, 964 F.2d 32 (1st Cir. 1992) (claim that permit for residential complex was denied in retaliation for developer's outspoken support of rival political party and criticism of government's environmental policies best considered under First Amendment, rather than as a substantive due process claim).

4. *The "property" interest.* Some circuits have refused to consider due process challenges to the denial of discretionary permits such as rezonings or special use permits, reasoning that a developer has no "property" interest in receiving such permits unless "absent the alleged denial of due process, there is either a certainty or a very strong likelihood that the application would have been granted." RRI Realty Corp. v. Incorporated Village of Southampton, 870 F.2d 911, 914–18 (2d Cir. 1989) (quoting Yale Auto Parts, Inc. v. Johnson, 758 F.2d 54, 59 (2d Cir. 1985)). The Seventh Circuit has explicitly rejected the Second Circuit's approach, reasoning: "Otherwise a single local ordinance providing that 'we may put your land in any zone we want, for any reason we feel like' would abolish all property rights in land overnight. The due process and takings clauses are made of sterner stuff." River Park, Inc. v. City of Highland Park, 23 F.3d 164, 166 (7th Cir. 1994). The Third Circuit agrees with the Seventh, holding that an ownership interest in the land itself qualifies for due process protection regardless of the degree of discretion the land use official has to grant or deny the requested permit. DeBlasio v. Zoning Board of Adjustment, 53 F.3d 592, 601 (3d Cir. 1995). The Fourth, Eighth, Tenth, and Eleventh Circuits, however, agree with the Second. See Gardner v. Baltimore, 969 F.2d 63, 68 (4th Cir. 1992); Bituminous Materials v. Rice County, 126 F.3d 1068, 1070 (8th Cir. 1997); Jacobs, Visconsi & Jacobs Co. v. City of Lawrence, 927 F.2d 1111 (10th Cir. 1991); Spence v. Zimmerman, 873 F.2d 256, 258 (11th Cir. 1989). Which position makes more sense? See Kenneth B. Bley & Tina R. Axelrad, The Search for Constitutionally Protected "Property" in Land-Use, 29 Urb. Law. 251 (1997); Daniel R. Mandelker, Entitlement to Substantive Due

Process: Old Versus New Property in Land Use Regulation, 3 Wash. U. J.L. & Pol'y 61 (2000).

5. *Legislative versus administrative or adjudicative decisionmaking.* As *Coniston* indicates, a critical issue in all due process challenges to land use regulations is whether the challenged action should be considered legislative, on the one hand, or administrative or adjudicative (also sometimes called *quasi-judicial*), on the other. If the action is considered legislative, "the 'true' purpose of the [policy], (i.e., the actual purpose that may have motivated its proponents, assuming this can be known) is irrelevant for rational basis analysis. The question is only whether a rational relationship exists between the [policy] and a conceivable legitimate governmental objective." Crider v. Board of County Commissioners of County of Boulder, 246 F.3d 1285, 1289 (10th Cir. 2001) (quoting FM Properties Operating Co. v. City of Austin, 93 F.3d 167, 174–175 (5th Cir. 1996)). If the action is considered administrative, however, the court will review the evidence before the decisionmaker "to determin[e] whether the [decisionmaker] has paid attention to the evidence adduced and acted rationally upon it." Pearson v. City of Grand Blanc, 961 F.2d 1211, 1222 (6th Cir. 1992). The decision may be set aside as arbitrary and capricious only if the record contains no rational basis for the decision. Id. State courts may have stricter standards of review of adjudicative actions. See pp. 341–52. The Supreme Court has hinted that stricter standards may sometimes apply under the Takings Clause when the action challenged is adjudicative rather than legislative. See pp. 643–52.

6. *The protections of democratic processes.* Do the justifications *Coniston* offers for the courts' deference to local zoning decisions make sense? Should the nature of judicial scrutiny depend on how many people are affected by the challenged action? What other features of the local decisionmaking process are likely to be relevant to whether property owners' interests are adequately protected by democratic processes?

c.   The Role of State Courts in Land Use Cases

Because of decisions like *Coniston*, review of reasonableness of land use decisions has fallen primarily on the state courts. Federal law is supreme, so the state courts must at least purport to honor the *Nectow* doctrine. However, the improbability of Supreme Court review (not to mention the conflicting signals sent by the lower federal courts) means that the various state supreme courts have been able to adopt vastly different approaches when reviewing the reasonableness of zoning restrictions.

Twigg v. County of Will
627 N.E.2d 742 (Ill. App. Ct. 1994)

Justice BARRY delivered the opinion of the court.

Defendant County of Will appeals from a judgment of the Circuit Court of Will County declaring defendant's county zoning ordinance void and unconstitutional as applied to the property of plaintiffs John W. and Anna Twigg and granting injunctive relief to restrain defendant from enforcing its A-1 (agricultural) zoning regulation with respect to the subject real estate. The issue in this appeal is whether the trial court's decision is contrary to the manifest weight of the evidence. For reasons that follow, we affirm.

According to the record on appeal, plaintiffs purchased a 35-acre parcel of land in Peotone Township zoned A-1 for $3750 per acre in 1991. John Twigg testified that he knew the zoning classification at the time of the purchase, but he was not aware that the corresponding county ordinance required a minimum of 10 acres per residential unit. He testified that he had intended to divide the real estate into four parcels to provide separate residential lots for himself and his three adult children and to raise and keep horses. However, because of complaints of an adjoining property-owner, plaintiffs sold off the eastern-most 10 acres for $50,000. They then proposed to divide the remaining acreage into two 10-acre lots for one son and their daughter, and to split the last 5 acres into two lots of 2 1/2 acres each for themselves and their other son. Because plaintiffs' plans for the five acres did not conform with the A-1 classification, they petitioned the Will County Board to rezone the five acres from A-1 to E-2, which permits country residential lots of 2 1/2 acres. The Board denied plaintiffs' application, and they brought their complaint for declaratory and injunctive relief in the circuit court.

At trial, plaintiffs presented expert testimony of Thomas Murphy, a land use planner, and Charles Southcomb, a real estate appraiser. Murphy testified that E-2 zoning was a good use of the 5-acre parcel and that it would have a positive effect on the future development of the surrounding area in that it would increase tax values while providing attractive residences in the immediate area. He further opined that the current A-1 zoning had no practical application and its 10-acre limitation was "somewhat arbitrary" as applied to plaintiffs' proposed use. As a former director of the Will County Regional Planning Commission, Murphy testified that in his opinion the county had assigned A-1 classification arbitrarily to all tracts in Will County that were not otherwise used for non-agricultural purposes when the county zoning ordinance was adopted in 1978. He testified that the county had a history of turning down all applications for rezoning to develop parcels of less than 10 acres. Finally, Murphy testified that denial of plaintiffs' proposed use of the 5-acre parcel for two single-family residences adjacent to their daughter's horse-keeping operation would do nothing to preserve the agricultural character of the surrounding area.

Southcomb testified . . . that the market value of the land as currently zoned was $5000 per acre, and that using a comparable sales analysis it would be $12,000 per acre if rezoned E-2.

James Shelby, Director of Planning for Will County, and Bruce Clover, a farmer in the immediate area, testified on defendant's behalf. Shelby testified that there were no parcels zoned E-2 within a 1 1/2-mile radius of the subject property. However, he admitted that there are about five non-conforming parcels with residences on less than 10-acre lots within that 1 1/2-mile radius. These all had been in existence prior to the enactment of the 1978 zoning ordinance. Shelby testified that residential development was generally incompatible with agricultural use because the homeowners complained about farming practices. He also expressed concern about setting a precedent for residential development if the rezoning were allowed in this case.

Clover testified that he had leased the subject real estate from the prior owner and had himself netted about $150 per acre per year on a crop-share basis. He stated that he bore no animosity toward the plaintiffs, but that agricultural use was incompatible with residential development to the extent that mail boxes and garbage cans along the roadways might hinder the movement of farm machinery, or children playing in the area might damage terraces and downspouts. Clover agreed that the soil was "excellent" for growing crops, including alfalfa, and for pasturing horses.

. . . On February 22, 1993, a written decision was entered granting declaratory and injunctive relief for plaintiffs, as aforesaid.

. . . [A] zoning ordinance will be deemed constitutional and its validity upheld if it bears any "substantial relationship to the public health, safety, comfort or welfare." La Grange State Bank v. County of Cook 388 N.E.2d 388, 390–91 (Ill. 1979) (quoting Tomasek v. City of Des Plaines, 354 N.E.2d 899, 903 (Ill. 1976)). A party challenging the validity of a zoning ordinance . . . has the burden of proving by clear and convincing evidence that the application of the ordinance to the property is "unreasonable and arbitrary and bears no substantial relation to public health, safety, morals, or welfare." Cosmopolitan Nat'l Bank v. County of Cook, 469 N.E.2d 183, 187 (Ill. 1984). An appellate court may not reverse the trial court's findings unless such findings are against the manifest weight of the evidence. The trier of fact is in a better position to assess the credibility of the witnesses and their opinions, and the reviewing court may not reverse simply because the reviewing court may have come to a different conclusion.

There are eight factors to consider in determining whether a zoning ordinance is valid. . . . They are: (1) the existing uses and zoning of nearby property; (2) the extent to which property values are diminished by the particular zoning restrictions; (3) the extent to which the destruction of property values of plaintiff promote the health, safety, morals or welfare of the public; (4) the relative gain to the public as compared to the hardship imposed upon the individual property owner; (5) the suitability of the subject property for the zoned purposes; . . . (6) the length of time the property has been vacant as zoned considered in the context of land development in the area in the vicinity of the subject property[;] . . . (7) the care that the community has taken to plan its land use development[;] and (8) the community need for the proposed use. [See La Salle Nat'l Bank v. County of Cook, 145 N.E.2d 65 (Ill. 1957); Sinclair Pipeline Co. v. Village of Richton Park, 167 N.E.2d 406 (Ill. 1960).]

Although no one factor is controlling, the first factor — existing uses and zoning of nearby property — is "of paramount importance." Defendant argues in this appeal that this factor weighs heavily in its favor. We do not agree. As plaintiffs correctly point out, the quarter section in which the subject property is situated is divided into nine other ownerships, three of which contain less than 10 acres. Plaintiffs' 5-acre parcel lies in the northwest corner of the quarter section, and within the 1 1/2-mile radius surrounding it, several residences on parcels of less than 10 acres are established. Although none are zoned E-2 and were existing prior to the 1978 ordinance, the uses of nearby property are not inconsistent with the E-2 use plaintiffs propose for the 5-acre parcel in question. The trial court specifically noted that the existing, non-conforming uses of the surrounding property did not support the county's position in this case. We find that the trial court's conclusion is not contrary to the manifest weight of the evidence.

With regard to the second factor, . . . the evidence presented to the court established that the highest and best use of the property was E-2, and there was no evidence that the value of surrounding property would be diminished by plaintiffs' proposed use. . . .

The third and fourth factors, similarly, support the trial court's conclusion. . . . [T]here was some testimony that farming practices are not compatible with residential use. On the other hand, plaintiffs' expert witnesses testified that the A-1 limitation was not substantially related to issues of public health, safety or general welfare. . . . Defense witnesses' suggestion that rezoning in this case would set an unfavorable precedent for future property owners was purely speculative, self-serving and appropriately discounted by the trial court in weighing the parties' evidence. And, inasmuch as plaintiffs' proposed use of the entire 25-acre parcel was to unite his family and promote animal husbandry, thereby preserving the agricultural character of the area, there is little, if any, public gain to be realized by enforcing the A-1 classification, and great hardship would be imposed on plaintiffs to deny the zoning change.

Factors five and six, as the court noted in its written decision, do not establish the invalidity of the ordinance. There is no dispute that the land is suitable for agricultural use and that it was actively farmed prior to plaintiffs' purchase of it.

With respect to factor seven, the evidence tended to show that the current zoning of the area, including plaintiffs' tract, was assigned in an arbitrary manner without considering the several non-conforming uses existing when the land use plan was adopted and the zoning ordinance was enacted. The former planning director testified that he had expressed his disagreement with the across-the-board A-1 classification, but that he was overruled by the time the plan was presented for approval in 1978. A later Land Resource Management Plan adopted in 1990 pursuant to the State Local Land Resource Management Planning Act similarly failed to take into consideration the various residences on parcels under 10 acres surrounding plaintiffs' property. Thus, despite the county board's consistent denial of petitions for rezoning, the trial court's conclusion that the land use plan was not carefully designed is supported by the evidence of record.

Lastly, although no community need for rezoning was demonstrated (factor eight), a need for rezoning was shown to exist for plaintiffs in order to accommodate their interest in uniting with their adult children in a country environment. Mr. Twigg testified that he had looked at other parcels in other townships, but the size and selling price made this particular 35-acre tract appropriate for his purposes. The promotion of family unity and animal husbandry in this case is consistent with the community interest in preserving A-1 agricultural zoning generally.

Although no one factor definitively established the invalidity of defendant's ordinance in this case, it is clear that the court gave great weight to its finding that plaintiffs' proposed use of the remaining 25 acres of the original 35-acre land purchase was generally in harmony with both the current A-1 agricultural zoning and existing non-conforming uses for smaller residential parcels in the surrounding area. In our opinion, the court acted within its discretion in analyzing the factors and weighting them within the context of the evidence presented here.

In sum, we find that the trial court's conclusion that enforcement of the zoning ordinance prohibiting plaintiffs' proposed development of the 5-acre parcel "is arbitrary and bears no substantial or reasonable relation to public health, safety, morals, comfort and general welfare" is not contrary to the manifest weight of the evidence. Accordingly, we affirm the court's judgment declaring the ordinance void and unconstitutional as applied to plaintiffs' property and enjoining the defendant from prohibiting the building of two residences on the 5-acre parcel as proposed. . . .

Cormier v. County of San Luis Obispo
207 Cal. Rptr. 880 (Ct. App. 1984)

GILBERT, Associate Justice.

. . . On March 10, 1982, Jay Cormier filed a petition for writ of mandate to compel the County of San Luis Obispo (County), its Board of Supervisors (Board) and Planning Commission (Commission) to reclassify and rezone his seven acre parcel of real property. He combined this with a complaint for declaratory relief to determine whether the County's general plan amendment which had down zoned his property was invalid. Cormier alleged, among other things, that the San Luis Obispo Land Use Element/Land Use Ordinance of 1980 was invalid as applied to down zone his property, and that the Board's action was arbitrary, discriminatory, and capricious and constituted an invalid exercise of local police and zoning powers. . . .

We affirm the trial court's decision denying mandamus because the Board acted within its authority in adopting the ordinance . . . and the ordinance is valid and constitutional.

FACTS

In August 1977 Cormier purchased the subject seven acre parcel of unimproved real property near the interchange of U.S. Highway 101 and Thompson Road for $150,000. At that time it was zoned, as shown by the South County General Plan, C-1-D (highway commercial) and Cormier planned to develop the property with a motel-restaurant. Later that year, Cormier discovered that as part of a comprehensive revision to the South County General Plan (hereafter the General Plan) a proposal had been prepared by the staff of the San Luis Obispo County Planning Department (Department) recommending a change of classification and a down zoning of his property to rural-residential. The C-1-D zoning permits development for highway-oriented uses with prior County approval, while rural-residential zoning limits development to a single house or a restaurant with restricted use.

In November 1977 Cormier contacted the Department opposing the proposed zoning change. During 1978 he also contacted a local zoning advisory body called Nipomo Advisory Group (NAG — pardon the acronym) to persuade them to revise their recommendation to down zone his property. He was unsuccessful. . . .

When the Commission began formal hearings in early 1980, Cormier appeared to protest the change. Despite his protest, on July 1, 1980, the Commission adopted a motion recommending reclassification of Cormier's property to rural-residential. It also instructed the Department staff to bring the matter to the attention of the Commission again should NAG change its position with respect to the zoning change.

NAG changed its position on July 3, 1980, and recommended against altering the zoning. William Blount, NAG chairman, hand-delivered a letter announcing this change to Bryce Tingle in the Department's land use section. The staff did not advise the Commission that NAG had changed its position. On July 10, the Commission held a meeting and adopted a formal resolution recommending to the Board the new plan, which down zoned Cormier's property.

On September 3, 1980, Cormier submitted a formal development plan for the motel-restaurant to the County. Thereafter, the Board conducted hearings concerning the new Land Use Element. It received the Commission's recommendation that the rural-residential classification be adopted for Cormier's property. It also considered the testimony of Cormier, who presented a copy of NAG's letter of July 7 which recommended retention of the commercial zoning designation. Bryce Tingle testified that he had never seen the letter before.

 . . . On December 18, 1980, the Board adopted Ordinance No. 2050, the Land Use Ordinance. . . .

[Plaintiff then challenged the plan amendment.] At the hearing in the trial court a real estate appraiser testified that if water and sewer services were available, Cormier's property had a value of $315,000 for commercial use, but a value of only $75,000 for rural-residential use. Cormier testified that he believed the value of the property was $576,000 for commercial use.

The trial court found that the value of the property as down zoned was 25 percent or less of its value as commercial property and that Cormier suffered economic detriment equaling or exceeding $250,000. . . . It nonetheless denied the petition for writ of mandate or declaratory relief. . . .

Cormier . . . contends that the Board's action in down zoning his property was arbitrary, and capricious, constituting an invalid and excessive exercise of the local police and zoning powers. The trial court's finding that the ordinance was constitutionally valid because the Board did not act arbitrarily or unreasonably is supported by the record.

The standard of review which the trial court applied to test the validity of the Board's action in enacting the ordinance was the "fairly debatable" standard set forth in Associated Home Builders, Inc. v. City of Livermore, 557 P.2d 473 (Cal. 1976):

> The constitutional measure by which we judge the validity of a land use ordinance that is assailed as exceeding municipal authority under the police power dates in California from the landmark decision in Miller v. Board of Public Works, 234 P. 381 (Cal. 1925). . . . [There] we declared that an ordinance restricting land use was valid if it had a "real or substantial relation to the public health, safety, moral or general welfare." . . .
>
> In deciding whether a challenged ordinance reasonably relates to the public welfare, the courts recognize that such ordinances are presumed to be constitutional and come before the court with every intendment in their favor. . . . In short, as stated by the Supreme Court in Euclid v. Ambler Co., . . . "If the validity . . . be fairly debatable, the legislative judgment must be allowed to control."

557 P.2d at 486; . . .

Courts are traditionally reluctant to interfere with the activities of the legislative body which has rendered a decision with respect to the zoning and classification of real property. "Denial of rezoning will be held valid unless there is no reasonable relation to the public welfare; and, before the courts will interfere with a zoning ordinance, the plan must be arbitrary." Lockard v. City of Los Angeles, 202 P.2d 38 (Cal. 1949). The sole issue on review of a zoning ordinance is whether or not there is any reasonable basis to support the legislative determination of the governing body, and the appellate court is not bound by the findings of the trial court if the record shows the question is debatable.

Cormier . . . argues that the action of the Board was arbitrary and capricious because the proposed rezoning classification was selected "without consideration of the various zoning alternatives or the best utilization of the property and only because [a rural-residential] zoning classification represented the fullest possible down zoning." Arnel v. City of Costa Mesa, 620 P.2d 565 (Cal. 1980). He asserts that there is nothing in the record to show that the Board or the Department staff considered alternative zoning or that rural-residential zoning was the appropriate choice.

The evidence before the court shows, however, that the change of designation and the down zoning of Cormier's property was part of an ongoing and comprehensive amendment of the County's general plan. The Commission and the Board carefully considered, discussed and reviewed the issues involved in allowing commercial development of real property adjacent to the freeway interchange where Cormier's property is located. The Board had the advice of its Planning Department staff, and it accepted statements from members of the general public. In addition to the original recommendation made by NAG, the Board received and considered the changed recommendation from NAG before it determined that commercial development of the property would not be advisable.

The Commission used the report of the Department staff in adopting a recommendation which it transmitted to the Board and upon which the Board acted. That report listed five negative consequences of commercial zoning for Cormier's property as follows:

1. Commercial uses would introduce urban development into a rural area.
2. There are highway-oriented commercial uses and areas for future development of commercial uses in Nipomo and Arroyo Grande.
3. The area lacks urban service.
4. Nipomo Advisory Group has recommended against establishment of commercial uses at this interchange.
5. The properties in the northwest and northeast quadrants do not have good freeway visibility.

The trial court found that number 4 was untrue and number 5 was of debatable relevance. The first three negative factors it found "were subject to interpretation and debate." . . .

The trial court took cognizance of the restricted scope of its authority on review of cases relating to zoning changes. The court is required to determine " . . . that a land use restriction lies within the public power if it has a 'reasonable relation to the public welfare.'" Associated Home Builders, Inc. v. City of Livermore, 557 P.2d 473 (1976). Therefore, adhering to the appropriate standard of review, the court found that the validity of the Board's enactment was fairly debatable, hence it was constitutional, and both the writ and declaratory relief were properly denied.

The judgment is affirmed.

Note on State Court Review of the Reasonableness of Zoning Restrictions

1. *A tale of two states: California and Illinois.* In *Twigg* and *Cormier*, the California and Illinois appellate courts announced similar rules of decision, but proceeded to interpret and apply them quite differently. These cases are typical of zoning jurisprudence in the two states. The California courts have long been exceedingly deferential to land use controls adopted by local governments. The Illinois courts are at the other pole; they actively conduct their own cost/benefit analyses of challenged land use restrictions and do not hesitate to invalidate restrictions that they regard as inefficient. Most state judiciaries fall somewhere between the extreme deference of California and the extreme activism of Illinois. See 1 Norman Williams, Jr. & John M. Taylor, Williams American Land Planning Law §§6.01–6.43 (1988 rev. & Supp. 2002), and Dennis J. Coyle, Property Rights and the Constitution 10–11 (1993), for discussions of where particular states fall on the continuum. For an exploration of the reasons behind the activist stance of Illinois, see Fred P. Bosselman, The Commodification of "Nature's Metropolis": The Historical Context of Illinois' Unique Zoning Standards, 12 N. Ill. U. L. Rev. 527 (1992).

2. *Presumptions and burdens of proof.* Both federal and state judicial opinions frequently assert that comprehensive zoning ordinances (and usually individual zoning amendments) carry a presumption of constitutionality. In all courts, this presumption is potentially rebuttable, although in a state like California the presumption is close to conclusive. The presumption has two effects. The challenger cannot prevail without submitting evidence to rebut the presumption. The challenger thus carries the "burden of proof" in the sense of the burden of going forward with evidence. The presumption also means that the challenger carries the "burden of proof" in its second meaning, the risk of nonpersuasion. When the evidence is closely balanced, or "fairly debatable," on the point at issue — whether the ordinance bears a rational relationship to the achievement of valid governmental goals — the presumption requires a trial judge to render judgment in favor of the defendant government. See Board of Supervisors v. Stickley, 556 S.E.2d 748 (Va. 2002).

A related issue is the standard by which the challenger's evidence will be judged. Here the approaches vary from "preponderance of the evidence," to "clear and convincing evidence," to the criminal law standard of "proof beyond a reasonable doubt." See John J. Delaney, et al., Land Use Practice and Forms: Handling the Land Use Case §12.2 (2004); 1 Kenneth H. Young, Anderson's American Law of Zoning §3.16 (4th ed. 1996 & Supp. 2004).

3. *Forsaking the presumption*. In some instances, state courts have varied these rules to expedite challenges to exclusionary zoning regulations and to other regulations that bar particular uses from the community. In these special cases, the challenger need only make out the modest prima facie case that the favored use has been excluded; the burden then shifts to the defendant government to produce evidence showing the constitutionality of the exclusion. See, e.g., Southern Burlington County NAACP v. Township of Mount Laurel, 336 A.2d 713 (N.J. 1975), excerpted at p. 763 (excluded modest-cost housing). A few state courts also have varied these rules when the government takes the challenged action without first having a comprehensive plan or when the action is not in accordance with the comprehensive plan. See pp. 336–41. Finally, some state courts have backed away from the presumption by holding that certain local land use decisions are not the sort of legislative acts to which courts normally should defer. Those cases are discussed at pp. 341–52.

Professors Mandelker and Tarlock argue that the use of a presumption of constitutionality to allocate the burden of production and the risk of nonpersuasion is inappropriate in land use cases because "the reasonableness of a zoning decision cannot be proved as the term is used in civil and criminal litigation. Factual questions . . . are relevant to the reasonableness of a decision but ultimately zoning decisions rest on assumptions about the desired city form and the social make-up of the area." Instead, they argue, courts should adopt a "process-based approach . . . that seeks to ensure that decision makers do the two things that are most likely to suffer in community politics: careful consideration of the relationship between individual decisions and the future form and composition of the community and particular attention to voices most likely to be ignored in representative government." Daniel R. Mandelker & A. Dan Tarlock, Shifting the Presumption of Constitutionality in Land Use Law, 24 Urb. Law. 1, 9–10 (1992). Does their argument distinguish land use cases from, for example, decisions about how to structure the tax code? If their argument about the distinctiveness of land use cases is sound, does their alternative process-based approach follow from the argument? See also Robert J. Hopperton, Majoritarian and Counter-Majoritarian Difficulties: Democracy, Distrust, and Disclosure in American Land-Use Jurispruduce — A Response to Professors Mandelker and Tarlock's Reply, 24 B.C. Envtl. Aff. L. Rev. 541 (1997); Daniel R. Mandelker & A. Dan Tarlock, Two Cheers for Shifting the Presumption of Validity: A Reply to Professor Hopperton, 24 B.C. Envtl. Aff. L. Rev. 103 (1997); Robert J. Hopperton, The Presumption of Validity in American Land-Use Law: A Substitute for Analysis, a Source of Significant Confusion, 23 B.C. Envtl. Aff. L. Rev. 301 (1996).

4. *Expert witnesses*. An aggrieved landowner's lawyer normally calls real estate brokers or appraisers to testify as to how the challenged restriction has diminished the value of the client's land. To identify the benefits of the restriction, counsel for the city often counters by calling the city's planning director, traffic engineers, heads of local civic associations, and others familiar with the local situation or the challenged technique. In major cases, both sides may hire expensive planning and zoning consultants as expert witnesses. How reliable will the data generated through this battle of experts be? Which of the opposing sides is helped by the fact that the costs and benefits in question often are extremely difficult to quantify? For a discussion of one area in which the Supreme Court has shifted the burden of proof, see pp. 643–52.

5. *The* Twigg *factors*. Did the *Twigg* court give appropriate weight to the testimony of the former director of the planning commission, whose arguments admittedly failed to convince a majority of the commission? For a discussion of the "wait and see" zoning used in both *Twigg* and *Cormier*, see Chapter 4B.

Was the *Twigg* court right to downplay the zoning of the surrounding areas and focus instead on the existence of nonconforming uses in those areas? For a discussion of the difficulties nonconforming uses pose for land use regulators, see pp. 197–202. Was the court's reasoning about the nonconforming uses consistent with its view that the county's concern about the precedential effect of a rezoning was speculative?

Should courts reviewing land use decisions be concerned about such personal factors as the Twiggs' desire to "unite their adult children in a country environment"? See p. 294 for a discussion of the general rule that such personal factors may not be considered by land use regulators in deciding whether to grant variances from zoning ordinances.

2.   Constraints on the Use of Zoning to Limit Competition

Zoning ordinances reduce competition in the market for consumer goods and services by limiting the entry of business firms into geographic areas. This is a particularly troublesome feature of restrictions on commercial uses. Transportation costs limit the willingness of shoppers to travel to avoid monopoly pricing by retail outlets. Therefore, if the proprietors of an existing supermarket (for example) can persuade city officials to zone out other supermarkets from their area, the proprietors will profit at the expense of consumers.

When a zoning restriction inhibits competition, a developer challenging it can introduce a new factor into the cost/benefit analysis. Besides pointing out its own welfare losses from the restriction, the developer can assert the losses consumers will suffer if its entry is barred. The zoning government must then respond that the benefits of the restriction outweigh (or rationally could be believed to outweigh) both of these costs.

Zoning ordinances also reduce competition in the housing market by restricting the supply of housing and by raising the cost of entry for new developers. In theory, the effect of ordinances that reduce competition in the housing market could be treated in the same way as ordinances that reduce competition in the market for consumer goods and services, but the law tends to treat the former as part of the debates about the appropriateness of exclusionary zoning, addressed in Chapter 9C, and the legitimacy of growth management, addressed in Chapter 9D.

a.   The Substantive Due Process Challenge

Sprenger, Grubb & Associates, Inc. v. City of Hailey
903 P.2d 741 (Idaho 1995)

Silak, Justice

This appeal concerns a decision by the Hailey City Council to change the zoning classification of certain land owned by appellant Sprenger, Grubb & Associates (SGA) from "Business" to "Limited Business." SGA appealed to the district court, and the district court upheld the City Council's action. SGA again appeals. . . .

In 1973, the City of Hailey and . . . the predecessor to SGA, entered into a development agreement which provided for . . . the development of a "master planned residential-recreational neighborhood." . . . The subject of this appeal is 12.6 acres within Woodside [appellant's project], which had been classified as a Business District from 1973 until 1993, when the Hailey City Council adopted Hailey City Ordinance No. 623, rezoning the 12.6 acres to a Limited Business District. The 12.6 acres is completely surrounded by property zoned and developed as General Residential and is one and a half miles south of Hailey's downtown business area. . . .

In 1990, Hailey's Mayor R. Keith Roark supported "downzoning" the 12.6 acres in Woodside based upon the property's distance from the "downtown business core." In July, 1990, the Hailey City Council amended its comprehensive plan, defining the existing business core as a discrete area demarcated by certain city streets within Hailey. The ordinance further prescribed that expansions of the Business and Limited Business Districts were to occur around the "existing core," as defined. The Hailey Planning and Zoning Commission (Zoning Commission) was requested to "downzone" the property in question from Business District to General Residential District in 1990 and again in 1992, and the Zoning Commission denied both requests. Later in 1992, Mayor Roark directed the City Planning and Zoning Administrator to request the Zoning Commission to rezone the 12.6 acres from Business to Limited Business District. Again, the Zoning Commission denied the request. The Zoning Commission decided that the existing Business District classification conformed to the City's comprehensive plan, and that the proposed zone change to Limited Business did not conform to the comprehensive plan.

The City Planning and Zoning Administrator appealed the Zoning Commission's decision to disallow the rezoning request. This appeal was heard by the Hailey City Council in July 1993, in conjunction with a public hearing. The public comment at the hearing was overwhelmingly in favor of rezoning the 12.6 acres in Woodside. . . .

At the conclusion of the hearing, the three attending Hailey City Council members unanimously voted to reverse the Zoning Commission's decision, and thus, to rezone (or downzone) the 12.6 acres in Woodside to Limited Business. . . . In its conclusions of law, the City Council concluded among other things that "the existence of a large retail commercial property outside the Hailey Business Core, as defined in the Hailey Comprehensive Plan, is not in accordance with the current Hailey Comprehensive Plan, adopted in 1983." . . .

SGA claims the rezoning action was an invalid exercise of police powers to protect downtown merchants from retail competition. SGA contends the City Council members had protectionist motives, and sought to regulate competition. One Council member stated at the hearing that allowing business zones in the periphery of our city "pulls the rug out from under those businesses who have invested their hearts and their wallets in our downtown." SGA contends that a desire to prevent competition for the benefit of Hailey's downtown merchants is not a proper application of zoning law and police power principles.

. . . Assuming arguendo, as SGA contends, that protecting downtown merchants from competition is not a goal that may be "properly pursued" by the City through its police power, the record indicates other legitimate purposes supporting the rezoning.

In its findings of fact and conclusions of law . . . the City Council articulated various reasons for its decision to rezone the property. Finding of fact number 6 cites to the Hailey Comprehensive Plan, which states that the Business and Limited Business Districts are to be expanded around the existing business core. Likewise, finding number 12 states that the Hailey Comprehensive Plan requires the City Council to encourage a central business core that will be conducive to economic growth and will contain a concentration of community services, shopping, entertainment and cultural facilities so as to optimize the use of the existing infrastructure and decrease dependency on automobiles. Finding number 14 refers to a statement by the Hailey Police Chief that the Hailey Police Department does not currently have the law enforcement personnel necessary to patrol two business districts within the City of Hailey. Finding of fact number 15 says the overwhelming weight of public comment was that the existence of a large business zone located nearly two miles from the central core of the City was extremely detrimental to the welfare of the public and the integrity of the community. The Council's Conclusions of Law state that "the existence of a large retail commercial property outside the Hailey Business Core . . . is not in accordance with the current Hailey Comprehensive Plan, adopted in 1983," and ". . . will create excessive additional requirements at public cost for public facilities and services." . . .

Determining where particular business uses shall be allowed to expand in a community is normally an appropriate exercise of the police power. Preserving aesthetic values and the economic viability of a community's downtown business core can be a proper zoning purpose. Moreover, SGA's protection from competition argument is defective because nothing in the rezoning ordinance prevents new retail, restaurant, and entertainment businesses from locating in or around the City's downtown core and competing with existing businesses. On this record, we cannot agree with SGA that the only reason for the rezoning was to protect downtown merchants from competition. . . .

The decision by the Hailey City Council to rezone the 12.6 acres to Limited Business . . . is affirmed. . . .

[Although the City of Hailey won this battle, the war was from far from over. In 1996, the landowner succeeded in having the rezoning held invalid because the city had failed to comply with notice requirements under the state's Local Land Use Planning Act (LLUPA). Castle et al. v. City of Hailey, CV-96-2837 (5th Dist., Blaine County 1996). The Hailey City Council then rezoned the property again, this time from Business to General Residential. The landowner again challenged the rezoning, this time on the ground that Hailey's comprehensive plan, upon which the rezoning was based, had omitted two compulsory elements. The Idaho Supreme Court agreed with the landowner. Sprenger, Grubb & Associates, Inc. v. City of Hailey, 986 P.2d 343 (1999).]

Note on Legitimate Purposes for the Exercise of Zoning Power

The *Sprenger* court avoided deciding whether inhibiting competition is ever a permissible goal for zoning officials to pursue. A short detour on the general question of the proper goals of zoning may shed light on this issue.

Section 1 of the SZEA permits zoning "[f]or the purpose of promoting health, safety, morals, or the general welfare of the community." In *Euclid*, the Supreme Court, adhering to accepted constitutional doctrine of that era, held that the Due Process Clause requires that zoning measures be rationally related to one of these same four governmental goals. Hence one finds this orthodox quartet — health, safety, morals, general welfare — repeated over and over in judicial opinions in zoning cases.

For several decades after *Euclid*, courts tried, at the expense of forthrightness, to honor the orthodox quartet. Judges who were concerned that the quartet threatened to limit public enactments developed several ways around the quartet. First, a court might interpret an unlisted goal such as aesthetics as being incorporated within the broadest listed goal, promotion of the general welfare. A more common tack was for the proponents of an ordinance to downplay its true purposes (if those purposes were not members of the orthodox quartet), and to assert, however artificially, that the ordinance was aimed at health, safety, or moral conditions. Thus in St. Louis Gunning Advertisement Co. v. City of St. Louis, 137 S.W. 929 (Mo. 1911), an ordinance regulating construction of ground-level billboards was held justified, not for the aesthetic benefits it would engender, but because rats, criminals, and prostitutes might use such billboards as sanctuaries behind which to hide. See pp. 469–72 for further discussion of the legitimacy of aesthetic controls.

In recent decades, both federal and state courts have succeeded in freeing themselves from the grip of the orthodox quartet. See, e.g., Berman v. Parker, 348 U.S. 26 (1954), discussed at pp. 830-31 (power of eminent domain may be exercised in pursuit of beauty); Village of Belle Terre v. Boraas, 416 U.S. 1 (1974), excerpted at p. 710 (sustaining village's residency restrictions aimed at promoting "family values, youth values, and the blessings of quiet seclusion"). See generally 1 Kenneth H. Young, Anderson's American Law of Zoning §§7.01–7.34 (4th ed. 1996 & Supp. 2002); Developments in the Law — Zoning, 91 Harv. L. Rev. 1427, 1443–62 (1978).

The demise of the orthodox quartet does not mean that courts now interpret the U.S. Constitution to permit local governments to pursue any purposes they choose. For example, discrimination against racial minorities is barred by the Equal Protection Clause. See Chapter 8A. Moreover, a municipality's naked use of zoning power to capture the wealth of isolated landowners is regarded as impermissible. This principle is reflected in judicial decisions that prohibit a city from employing zoning restrictions simply to reduce the size of the condemnation award it will have to pay when it acquires the land. See pp. 133–34.

The detour is now over. It should now be clear why courts traditionally have regarded the suppression of competition as an illegitimate goal for zoning officials to pursue. "Suppressing competition" is not a member of the orthodox quartet. Further, suppressing competition impairs economic efficiency, at least according to the prevailing economic wisdom reflected in antitrust statutes. Moreover, any redistribution of wealth from consumers to monopolists that a zoning ordinance might bring about seems too haphazard to be deemed just. Therefore an ordinance whose sole purpose is to suppress competition should be held to violate the Due Process Clause.

Note on Determining Legislative Motivation

1. *Mixed motives.* As the *Sprenger* court realized, legislation often is motivated by a complex myriad of purposes. To address such "mixed motive" cases, a court can employ either or both of two related yet distinct methods for taking the taint of an anticompetitive purpose into account. First, it could count the consumer losses from monopoly pricing as part of the costs of the measure, and conduct a comprehensive cost/benefit analysis of the measure to determine whether a rational person would conceivably regard its total benefits as exceeding its total costs. This is the standard of review that courts usually employ when the reasonableness (efficiency) of zoning is challenged. Second, a court could inquire about the extent to which the desire to suppress competition influenced the decision, and invalidate decisions in which the influence of the anticompetitive motive reached some threshold level. A court could adopt a rule that any anticompetitive motive would invalidate the rule or, conversely, that any legitimate motive would overcome the taint of the anticompetitive motive and thereby validate the decision. Or the court could adopt the rule applied in cases alleging that decisionmakers were motivated by an intent to discriminate on the basis of race. The inquiry would then be whether the illegitimate purpose was the "but for" cause of the ordinance — would the local government have adopted the challenged measure if it had not harbored the impermissible purpose of suppressing competition? Cf. Mt. Healthy City School District Board of Education v. Doyle, 429 U.S. 274 (1977) (even if teacher's speech played a substantial role in the defendant's refusal to rehire the teacher, defendant can escape liability if it can show that it would have reached the same decision even in the absence of the speech). Which approach did the *Sprenger* court adopt? Which approach is preferable?

2. *Proving anticompetitive motives.* If anticompetitive purposes are impermissible, and if such purposes matter even when intertwined with additional, legitimate, purposes, then courts must decide what evidence proves the existence and strength of legislative motivations. What weight, if any, should the *Sprenger* court have given the city council's findings of fact and conclusions of law? The one council member's statement about "pulling the rug out" from under existing businesses? The obvious anticompetitive consequences of the rezoning?

In Village of Arlington Heights v. Metropolitan Housing Development Corp., 429 U.S. 252 (1977), excerpted at p. 698, the Supreme Court listed factors judges can use to determine whether legislation is tainted by the illegitimate goal of racial discrimination. These include the measure's impact and its historical background. Also relevant are the legislative or administrative history of the measure, especially when there are contemporary statements by members of the decisionmaking body, minutes of its meetings, or reports. Indeed, the Court indicated that in some extraordinary instances the members might be called to the stand at trial to testify concerning the purpose of the official action.

At least in land use matters that do not raise the specter of racial discrimination, however, courts have been quite reluctant to put too much stock in what local legislators say on the record, much less to take testimony about what the legislators might have been thinking when they cast their votes. In rejecting a challenge to a rezoning that prevented the development of a proposed shopping center that would compete with an already approved project, the court in Ensign Bickford Realty Corp. v. City Council, 137 Cal. Rptr. 304 (Ct. App. 1977), articulated some of the reasons behind the reluctance:

> Respondent argues . . . that when a record is made . . . wherein various councilmen in fact state their reasons, the court must consider those reasons in determining whether the decision was arbitrary or unreasonable. . . . To accept respondent's argument would place an oner-ous burden on legislators to carefully articulate for the record all of the reasons and motives behind their decisions. To fail to do so would put their action in peril. . . . Often the discus-sions at a public hearing are guided by the direction taken by members of the public who speak. These discussions may or may not include what is significant to a given member of the agency. . . . There are a host of reasons why the utterances of councilmen at public hearings cannot be said to encompass the totality of their thought processes. It would be manifestly burdensome and unproductive to require that once a councilman started discussing the merits of a decision he was being called upon to make, he must set forth all of his opinions on the subject under discussion. Such an inhibiting factor would lead inevitably to silent council meetings. . . .

Id. at 311.

The problem is compounded when the land use measure is passed or ratified by the electorate directly in an initiative or referendum. See, e.g., International Paper Co. v. Town of Jay, 928 F.2d 480 (1st Cir. 1991) (refusing to consider legislators' motives for passing an ordinance imposing a special exception requirement on polluting industries, even though most of the legislators voting for the ordinance were then on strike against the town's primary polluting industry and substantial evidence suggested that those legislators hoped the ordinance would pressure the company to settle the strike, because ordinance had been approved by the electorate through a referendum). For further discussion of initiatives and referenda on land use matters, see pp. 401–09.

On the unsettled question of how legislative motives are to be proved, see Scott W. Breedlove & Victoria S. Salzmann, The Devil Made Me Do It: The Irrelevance of Legislative Motivation Under the Establishment Clause, 53 Baylor L. Rev. 419 (2001);

Paul Brest, *Palmer v. Thompson*: An Approach to the Problem of Unconstitutional Legislative Motive, 1971 Sup. Ct. Rev. 95, 120–24; Alan E. Brownstein, Illicit Legislative Motive in the Municipal Land Use Regulation Process, 57 U. Cin. L. Rev. 1 (1988); John Hart Ely, Legislative and Administrative Motivation in Constitutional Law, 79 Yale L.J. 1205 (1970); Charles R. Lawrence III, The Id, the Ego, and Equal Protection: Reckoning with Unconscious Racism, 39 Stan. L. Rev. 317, 322–44 (1987); Colloquium, Legislative Motivation, 15 San Diego L. Rev. 925–1183 (1978).

Note on Zoning Techniques That Raise a Red Flag About Anticompetitive Purposes

1. *Protecting downtown stores from suburban shopping centers.* As in *Sprenger*, most courts have allowed cities to protect their downtowns if the challenged decision was part of a comprehensive plan to revitalize or maintain the downtown. See Murray S. Levin, The Antitrust Challenge to Local Government Protection of the Central Business District, 55 U. Colo. L. Rev. 21, 71–78 (1983); Clifford L. Weaver & Christopher J. Duerksen, Central Business Planning and the Control of Outlying Shopping Centers, 14 Urb. L. Ann. 57 (1977). Why should anticompetitive zoning be allowed if it is "comprehensive" but struck down if it is ad hoc? On the role of comprehensive planning in justifying zoning decisions, see pp. 309–17 and 336–41.

2. *Protecting independent stores against the chains.* In recent years, many municipalities have sought to limit "formula businesses" within their jurisdictions. Arcata, California, for example, permits only nine formula restaurants to operate within its borders (there were nine formula restaurants in place when the ordinance passed, so one would have to close before a new restaurant could open). The ordinance defines a formula restaurant as one that is contractually required to have "standardized menus, ingredients, food preparation, decor, uniforms, architecture, signs or similar standardized features and which causes it to be substantially identical to more than eleven other restaurants regardless of ownership or location." Arcata, Cal., Ordinance 1333 (June 5, 2002).

Coronado, California, requires all "formula retail" establishments to obtain a special use permit, which is available only if the city planning commission and city council find that the establishment will be compatible with surrounding existing uses, will not disturb the community's "character and ambiance," is consistent with the local general plan, will contribute to an "appropriate balance of local, regional or national-based businesses in the community," and will contribute to an "appropriate balance of small, medium and large-sized businesses in the community." The California Court of Appeals rejected a claim that the ordinance discriminated against interstate commerce, reasoning that it applies equally to intrastate and interstate chains. See Coronadans Organized for Retail Enhancement v. City of Coronado, 2003 WL 21363665 (Cal. Ct. App. June 13, 2003).

How should challenges based on the anticompetitive nature of such techniques be decided? See William D. McElyea, Playing the Numbers: Local Government Authority to Apply Use Quotas in Neighborhood Commercial Districts, 14 Ecology L.Q. 325 (1987); Richard F. Babcock & R. Marlin Smith, Zoning by the Numbers: A Not-so-Modest Proposal for Legally Limiting Too Much of a Good Thing, Planning, June 1985, at 12.

3. *The Wal-Mart wars*: Many local governments try hard to attract so-called big box stores because of the sales tax revenue they generate, but other communities fight desperately to keep them out. The "Wal-Mart wars" are particularly intense in California, where

grocery worker unions have lobbied for bans on superstores to keep nonunion Wal-Mart Supercenters from competing against unionized regional grocery chains. See, e.g., Turlock Pursues Help on Lawsuits: Council Seeking Legislation Allowing It to Recoup Costs if It Wins Wal-Mart Battle, Modesto Bee, Apr. 13, 2005, at A1 (reporting that Wal-Mart is appealing the California Superior Court's dismissal of its challenge to Turlock, California's ban on stores of more than 100,000 square feet that operate full-service grocery stores, and also is challenging the ban in federal court).

Los Angeles has taken a different tack by requiring builders of stores of more than 100,000 square feet that devote more than 10 percent of their floor space to selling groceries to pay for an economic analysis to determine whether the superstore would "eliminate jobs, depress wages or harm surrounding businesses." Battles over Mega-Stores May Shift to New Studies, L.A. Times, Aug. 12, 2004, at B1. See also In re WalMart Stores, Inc., 702 A.2d 397 (Vt. 1997) (Vermont Environmental Board could consider a proposed Wal-Mart's likely effect on tax revenues from competitors in deciding to deny a permit for the store).

Palm Beach, Florida, appears to have successfully fought big boxes by limiting retailers in its central business district to 2,000 square feet unless they can show that at least 50 percent of their customers are residents or guests at the town's hotels. A Florida appellate court found the purpose of the ordinance was to reduce "the problems of parking and traffic congestion determined to result from establishments of a region-serving scale," and concluded that there was a rational relationship between the ordinance and its valid public purposes. See Handelsman v. Town of Palm Beach, 585 So. 2d 1047 (Fla. Dist. Ct. App. 1991).

For an insightful look at the Wal-Mart wars, see David Porter & Chester L. Mirsky, Megamall on the Hudson: Planning, Wal-Mart and Grassroots Resistance (2003). See also William E. Roper & Elizabeth Humstone, Wal-Mart In Vermont — The Case Against Sprawl, 22 Vt. L. Rev. 755 (1998).

4. *Need-based determinations.* Some cities have attempted to control the proliferation of particular uses by requiring that the developer prove that a need exists for the proposed use in order to qualify for a special use permit. The courts are split. Compare, e.g., Lucky Stores, Inc. v. Board of Appeals, 312 A.2d 758 (Md. 1973) (upholding need-based determinations), with Metro 500, Inc. v. City of Brooklyn Park, 211 N.W.2d 358, 363 (Minn. 1973) ("The number and type of gasoline stations and other permissible uses within a zone should be determined by the interaction of the economic law of supply and demand rather than by the collective opinion of the members of a municipal governing body concerning the needs of the community.").

5. *Minimum spacing requirements.* Some cities prohibit service stations (and occasionally other uses) from being built within a certain distance of one another. In some instances, courts have held that these spacing requirements violate the Due Process Clause by not being rationally related to any legitimate government goal. See, e.g., Exxon Co., U.S.A. v. Township of Livingston, 489 A.2d 1218 (N.J. Super. Ct. App. Div. 1985). More commonly, however, courts have accepted the notion that gasoline stations generate special community problems as justifications for these restraints on competition. See, e.g., Mobil Oil Co. v. Township of Westtown, 345 A.2d 313 (Pa. Commw. Ct. 1975) (gasoline stations present "unique traffic hazards"). Do service stations really pose problems different from those presented by fast-food restaurants, drive-in banks, or any number of other commercial uses? Would distance restrictions on those uses be upheld?

6. *Total exclusions of commercial uses.* What if a town bars all commercial uses? See Missouri ex rel. Chiavola v. Village of Oakwood, 886 S.W.2d 74 (Mo. Ct. App. 1994) (sustaining a town's total exclusion of commercial uses). See also pp. 747–49. What if the ban on commercial uses leaves existing nonconforming uses with a monopoly? Cf. Ex

parte White, 243 P. 396 (Cal. 1925) (invalidating ordinance zoning business enterprises out of all but one acre of the town, an area already occupied by two businesses).

7. *Preventing established enterprises from abusing the land use control process.* As these materials show, proprietors of existing retail outlets often are extremely interested in influencing the number and location of additional commercial uses. When an established firm fails to stop its city from rezoning to allow a competing use, it sometimes challenges the validity of the rezoning in court. In such cases, most courts honor the principle that stifling competition is not a proper function of government by holding that competitive injury does not confer standing for an established firm to bring these challenges. See, e.g., Nautilus of Exeter, Inc. v. Town of Exeter, 656 A.2d 407 (N.H. 1995). The established firm may, however, fund litigation by others whose interest in the matter does confer standing. See Baltimore Scrap Corp. v. David J. Joseph Co., 237 F.3d 394 (4th Cir. 2001), for a particularly sordid tale of a competitor's clandestine funding of a zoning battle.

b. Challenges Under the Federal Antitrust Laws

City of Columbia v. Omni Outdoor Advertising, Inc.
499 U.S. 365 (1991)

Justice SCALIA delivered the opinion of the Court.

This case requires us to clarify the application of the Sherman Act to municipal governments and to the citizens who seek action from them.

I

Petitioner Columbia Outdoor Advertising, Inc. (COA), a South Carolina corporation, entered the billboard business in the city of Columbia, South Carolina (also a petitioner here), in the 1940's. By 1981 it controlled more than 95% of what has been conceded to be the relevant market. COA was a local business owned by a family with deep roots in the community, and enjoyed close relations with the city's political leaders. The mayor and other members of the city council were personal friends of COA's majority owner, and the company and its officers occasionally contributed funds and free billboard space to their campaigns. . . .

In 1981, Omni, a Georgia corporation, began erecting billboards in and around the city. COA responded to this competition in several ways. . . . Finally (and this is what gives rise to the issue we address today), COA executives met with city officials to seek the enactment of zoning ordinances that would restrict billboard construction. COA was not alone in urging this course; concerned about the city's recent explosion of billboards, a number of citizens including writers of articles and editorials in local newspapers advocated restrictions.

. . . In September 1982, after a series of public hearings and numerous meetings involving city officials, Omni, and COA . . . the city council passed a[n] . . . ordinance restricting the size, location, and spacing of billboards. These restrictions, particularly those on spacing, obviously benefited COA, which already had its billboards in place; they severely hindered Omni's ability to compete.

In November 1982, Omni filed suit against COA and the city in Federal District Court, charging that they had violated §§1 and 2 of the Sherman Act, 15 U.S.C. §§1,

2^1 . . . Omni contended, in particular, that the city's billboard ordinances were the result of an anticompetitive conspiracy between city officials and COA that stripped both parties of any immunity they might otherwise enjoy from the federal antitrust laws. In January 1986, after more than two weeks of trial, a jury . . . [found the city and COA had violated the Sherman Act and] awarded damages, before trebling, of $600,000 on the §1 Sherman Act claim, and $400,000 on the §2 claim.[2] . . . Petitioners moved for judgment notwithstanding the verdict, contending among other things that their activities were outside the scope of the federal antitrust laws. In November 1988, the District Court granted the motion.

A divided panel of the United States Court of Appeals for the Fourth Circuit reversed the judgment of the District Court and reinstated the jury verdict on all counts. 891 F.2d 1127 (1989). . . .

II

In the landmark case of Parker v. Brown, 317 U.S. 341 (1943), . . . [r]elying on principles of federalism and state sovereignty, we held that the Sherman Act did not apply to anticompetitive restraints imposed by the States "as an act of government." Id. at 352.

Since *Parker* emphasized the role of sovereign States in a federal system, it was initially unclear whether the governmental actions of political subdivisions enjoyed similar protection. In recent years, we have held that *Parker* immunity does not apply directly to local governments, see Town of Hallie v. City of Eau Claire, 471 U.S. 34, 38 (1985); Community Communications Co. v. City of Boulder, 455 U.S. 40, 50–51 (1982); City of Lafayette, Louisiana v. Louisiana Power & Light Co., 435 U.S. 389, 412–13 (1978) (plurality opinion). We have recognized, however, that a municipality's restriction of competition may sometimes be an authorized implementation of state policy, and have accorded *Parker* immunity where that is the case.

The South Carolina statutes under which the city acted in the present case authorize municipalities to regulate the use of land and the construction of buildings and other structures within their boundaries.[3] It is undisputed that, as a matter of state law, these statutes authorize the city to regulate the size, location, and spacing of billboards. It could be argued, however, that a municipality acts beyond its delegated authority, for *Parker* purposes, whenever the nature of its regulation is substantively or even procedurally defective. On such an analysis it could be contended, for example, that the city's regulation in the present case was not "authorized" by S.C. Code Ann. §5-23-10 (1976), see n.3, supra, if it was not, as that statute requires, adopted "for the purpose of promoting health, safety, morals or the general welfare of the community." As scholarly commentary has noted, such an expansive interpretation of the *Parker*-defense authorization requirement would have unacceptable consequences.

---

1. Section 1 provides in pertinent part: "Every contract, combination in the form of trust or otherwise, or conspiracy, in restraint of trade or commerce among the several States, or with foreign nations, is declared to be illegal." 15 U.S.C. §1. Section 2 provides in pertinent part: "Every person who shall monopolize, or attempt to monopolize, or combine or conspire with any other person or persons, to monopolize any part of the trade or commerce among the several States, or with foreign nations, shall be deemed guilty of a felony." 15 U.S.C. §2.

2. The monetary damages in this case were assessed entirely against COA, the District Court having ruled that the city was immunized by the Local Government Antitrust Act of 1984, 98 Stat. 2750, as amended, 15 U.S.C. §§34–36, which exempts local governments from paying damages for violations of the federal antitrust laws. . . .

3. S.C. Code Ann. §5-23-10 (1976) ("Building and zoning regulations authorized") provides that "[f]or the purpose of promoting health, safety, morals or the general welfare of the community, the legislative body of cities and incorporated towns may by ordinance regulate and restrict the height, number of stories and size of buildings and other structures." . . .

To be sure, state law "authorizes" only agency decisions that are substantively and procedurally correct. Errors of fact, law, or judgment by the agency are not "authorized." Erroneous acts or decisions are subject to reversal by superior tribunals because unauthorized. If the antitrust court demands unqualified "authority" in this sense, it inevitably becomes the standard reviewer not only of federal agency activity but also of state and local activity whenever it is alleged that the governmental body, though possessing the power to engage in the challenged conduct, has actually exercised its power in a manner not authorized by state law. We should not lightly assume that *Lafayette*'s authorization requirement dictates transformation of state administrative review into a federal antitrust job. Yet that would be the consequence of making antitrust liability depend on an undiscriminating and mechanical demand for "authority" in the full administrative law sense.

P. Areeda & H. Hovenkamp, Antitrust Law ¶212.3b, p. 145 (Supp. 1989). We agree with that assessment, and believe that in order to prevent *Parker* from undermining the very interests of federalism it is designed to protect, it is necessary to adopt a concept of authority broader than what is applied to determine the legality of the municipality's action under state law. . . . It suffices for the present to conclude that here no more is needed to establish, for *Parker* purposes, the city's authority to regulate than its unquestioned zoning power over the size, location, and spacing of billboards.

Besides authority to regulate, however, the *Parker* defense also requires authority to suppress competition — more specifically, "clear articulation of a state policy to authorize anticompetitive conduct" by the municipality in connection with its regulation. *Hallie*, 471 U.S. at 40 (internal quotation omitted). We have rejected the contention that this requirement can be met only if the delegating statute explicitly permits the displacement of competition. See id. at 41–42. It is enough, we have held, if suppression of competition is the "foreseeable result" of what the statute authorizes. Id. at 42. That condition is amply met here. The very purpose of zoning regulation is to displace unfettered business freedom in a manner that regularly has the effect of preventing normal acts of competition, particularly on the part of new entrants. A municipal ordinance restricting the size, location, and spacing of billboards (surely a common form of zoning) necessarily protects existing billboards against some competition from newcomers.

The Court of Appeals was therefore correct in its conclusion that the city's restriction of billboard construction was prima facie entitled to *Parker* immunity. The Court of Appeals upheld the jury verdict, however, by invoking a "conspiracy" exception to *Parker* that has been recognized by several Courts of Appeals. . . . *Parker* does not apply, according to the Fourth Circuit, "where politicians or political entities are involved as conspirators" with private actors in the restraint of trade. 891 F.2d at 1134.

There is no such conspiracy exception. . . . The impracticality of such a principle is evident if, for purposes of the exception, "conspiracy" means nothing more than an agreement to impose the regulation in question. Since it is both inevitable and desirable that public officials often agree to do what one or another group of private citizens urges upon them, such an exception would virtually swallow up the *Parker* rule: All anticompetitive regulation would be vulnerable to a "conspiracy" charge.

Omni suggests, however, that "conspiracy" might be limited to instances of governmental "corruption," defined variously as "abandonment of public responsibilities to private interests," Brief for Respondent 42, "corrupt or bad faith decisions," id. at 44, and "selfish or corrupt motives." Id. Ultimately, Omni asks us not to define "corruption" at all, but simply to leave that task to the jury: "[a]t bottom, however, it was within the jury's province to determine what constituted corruption of the governmental process in their community." Id. at 43. Omni's amicus eschews this emphasis on "corruption," instead urging us to define the conspiracy exception as encompassing any governmental act "not in the public interest." Brief for Associated Builders and Contractors, Inc., as Amicus Curiae 5.

A conspiracy exception narrowed along such vague lines is similarly impractical. Few governmental actions are immune from the charge that they are "not in the public interest" or in some sense "corrupt." . . . The fact is that virtually all regulation benefits some segments of the society and harms others; and that it is not universally considered contrary to the public good if the net economic loss to the losers exceeds the net economic gain to the winners. *Parker* was not written in ignorance of the reality that determination of "the public interest" in the manifold areas of government regulation entails not merely economic and mathematical analysis but value judgment, and it was not meant to shift that judgment from elected officials to judges and juries. If the city of Columbia's decision to regulate what one local newspaper called "billboard jungles," Columbia Record, May 21, 1982, p. 14–A, col. 1, is made subject to ex post facto judicial assessment of "the public interest," with personal liability of city officials a possible consequence, we will have gone far to "compromise the States' ability to regulate their domestic commerce," Southern Motor Carriers Rate Conference, Inc. v. United States, 471 U.S. 48, 56 (1985). The situation would not be better, but arguably even worse, if the courts were to apply a subjective test: not whether the action was in the public interest, but whether the officials involved thought it to be so. This would require the sort of deconstruction of the governmental process and probing of the official "intent" that we have consistently sought to avoid.[6] . . .

For these reasons, we reaffirm our rejection of any interpretation of the Sherman Act that would allow plaintiffs to look behind the actions of state sovereigns to base their claims on "perceived conspiracies to restrain trade." Hoover v. Ronwin, 466 U.S. 558, 580 (1984). We reiterate that, with the possible market participant exception, any action that qualifies as state action is "ipso facto . . . exempt from the operation of the antitrust laws." Id. at 568. . . .

III

While *Parker* recognized the States' freedom to engage in anticompetitive regulation, it did not purport to immunize from antitrust liability the private parties who urge them to engage in anticompetitive regulation. However, it is obviously peculiar in a democracy, and perhaps in derogation of the constitutional right "to petition the Government for a redress of grievances," U.S. Const. Amend. I, to establish a category of lawful state action that citizens are not permitted to urge. Thus, beginning with Eastern Railroad Presidents Conference v. Noerr Motor Freight, Inc., 365 U.S. 127 (1961), we have developed a corollary to *Parker*: The federal antitrust laws also do not regulate the conduct of private individuals in seeking anticompetitive action from the government. This doctrine, like *Parker*, rests ultimately upon a recognition that the antitrust laws, "tailored as they are for the business world, are not at all appropriate for application in the political arena." *Noerr*, 365 U.S. at 141. That a private party's political motives are selfish is irrelevant: "*Noerr* shields from the Sherman Act a concerted effort to influence public officials regardless of intent or purpose." UMWA v. Pennington, 381 U.S. 657, 670 (1965).

Noerr recognized, however, what has come to be known as the "sham" exception to its rule: "There may be situations in which a publicity campaign, ostensibly directed toward

---

6. We have proceeded otherwise only in the "very limited and well-defined class of cases where the very nature of the constitutional question requires [this] inquiry." United States v. O'Brien, 391 U.S. 367, 383 n.30 (1968) (bill of attainder). See also Arlington Heights v. Metropolitan Housing Development Corp., 429 U.S. 252, 268 n.18 (1977) (race-based motivation).

influencing governmental action, is a mere sham to cover what is actually nothing more than an attempt to interfere directly with the business relationships of a competitor and the application of the Sherman Act would be justified." 365 U.S. at 144. The Court of Appeals concluded that the jury in this case could have found that COA's activities on behalf of the restrictive billboard ordinances fell within this exception. In our view that was error.

The "sham" exception to *Noerr* encompasses situations in which persons use the governmental process — as opposed to the outcome of that process — as an anticompetitive weapon. A classic example is the filing of frivolous objections to the license application of a competitor, with no expectation of achieving denial of the license but simply in order to impose expense and delay. A "sham" situation involves a defendant whose activities are "not genuinely aimed at procuring favorable government action" at all, Allied Tube & Conduit Corp. v. Indian Head, Inc., 486 U.S. 492, 500 n. 4 (1988), not one "who 'genuinely seeks to achieve his governmental result, but does so through improper means.'" Id. at 508 n.10 (quoting Sessions Tank Liners, Inc. v. Joor Mfg., Inc., 827 F.2d 458, 465 n.5 (9th Cir. 1987)).

. . . Although COA indisputably set out to disrupt Omni's business relationships, it sought to do so not through the very process of lobbying, or of causing the city council to consider zoning measures, but rather through the ultimate product of that lobbying and consideration, viz., the zoning ordinances. . . . "If *Noerr* teaches anything it is that an intent to restrain trade as a result of the government action sought . . . does not foreclose protection." Lawrence A. Sullivan, Developments in the *Noerr* Doctrine, 56 Antitrust L.J. 361, 362 (1987). . . .

IV

Under *Parker* and *Noerr*, therefore, both the city and COA are entitled to immunity from the federal antitrust laws for their activities relating to enactment of the ordinances. . . .

. . . The judgment of the Court of Appeals is reversed. . . .

Justice STEVENS, with whom Justice WHITE and Justice MARSHALL join, dissenting. . . .

Note on the Application of Antitrust Laws to Zoning

1. *The decreased threat of antitrust liability.* In the early 1980s, antitrust actions against zoning officials were viewed as a serious threat to local governments. After finding that a village and county had conspired against a developer, one jury awarded damages that, when trebled under the remedy provisions of the Clayton Act, totaled $28.5 million. Unity Ventures v. County of Lake, 1984-1 Trade Cas. (CCH) ¶65,883 (N.D. Ill. 1983). The verdict was later set aside, 631 F. Supp. 181 (N.D. Ill. 1986), aff'd, 841 F.2d 770 (7th Cir. 1988), but the case created hysteria among local governments. The developments chronicled in *Omni* and described further in the following notes have virtually eliminated the threat. See E. Thomas Sullivan, Antitrust Regulation of Land Use: Federalism's Triumph over Competition, The Last Fifty Years, 3 Wash. U. J.L. & Pol'y 473 (2000).

2. *The authorization prong of the state action exemption.* To qualify for the *Parker v. Brown* state action immunity, the challenged municipal action must satisfy a two-pronged test. First, the state legislature must have authorized the municipal activity. That prong has not been problematic in most land use cases because state zoning enabling acts have been

seen as providing the required authority. Where a local government draws its authority not from the state zoning enabling act but from general home rule provisions, however, the state action exemption does not apply. Community Communications. Co. v. City of Boulder, 455 U.S. 40 (1982).

3. *The intent to authorize displacement of competition prong.* The second prong, which requires that the state legislature must have intended to authorize the municipality to displace competition, has been slightly more troublesome. The courts have not required that the state expressly articulate an intent to allow the local government to engage in anticompetitive conduct, holding instead that the statutory language and legislative history of the enabling act must evidence a "clearly articulated and affirmatively expressed" state policy to displace competition and must show that "the legislature contemplated the kind of action complained of." Town of Hallie v. City of Eau Claire, 471 U.S. 34, 43–44 (1985).

4. *The conspiracy exception.* Prior to *Omni*, several courts had held that municipal zoning actions could trigger the federal antitrust statutes regardless of the state action exception if local officials engaged in a conspiracy with private parties to injure those parties' competitors. See Westborough Mall, Inc. v. City of Cape Girardeau, 693 F.2d 733 (8th Cir. 1982). *Omni* obviously puts that line of attack to rest. What does the *Omni* Court's reasoning portend for the future of substantive due process challenges to anticompetitive zoning practices like that decided in *Sprenger*?

5. *The Local Government Antitrust Act of 1984.* In part because of the panic created by the *Unity Ventures* jury verdict, Congress passed a statute in 1984 that prohibits recovery of damages, costs, or attorney fees under the federal antitrust acts against local governments and their officials (if acting in an official capacity). Pub. L. No. 98-544, 98 Stat. 2750 (1984) (codified at 15 U.S.C. §§34–36 (2005)).

6. *The state action exception as a window on views of local politics.* Arguments for and against the court's exemption from antitrust laws of states and their municipalities (when authorized by the state) rest on competing views of state and local politics that reverberate throughout land use law. The exemption may be justified on the ground that the federal government has no obligation to protect citizens from the consequences of the political processes that they themselves control, at least where those consequences are felt only within the political jurisdiction. Alternatively, the exemption may be defended on the ground that state and local regulation may be preferable to federal regulation because of the peculiarity of local market failures, the need for local knowledge, and the ability of potential victims to protect themselves in the local legislative processes. See Frank Easterbrook, Antitrust and the Economics of Federalism, 26 J.L. & Econ. 23 (1983); Herbert Hovenkamp & John A. MacKerron III, Municipal Regulation and Federal Antitrust Policy, 32 UCLA L. Rev. 719 (1985); John Shepard Wiley, Jr., A Capture Theory of Antitrust Federalism, 99 Harv. L. Rev. 713 (1986).

As you read the cases in the next section, consider which (if either) of those views underlies the courts' attitude toward local governments. Consider also whether the reluctance Justice Scalia shows in *Omni* about efforts to "transform[] state administrative review into a federal antitrust job" is consistent with the rules he advocates in takings cases. Is *Omni* evidence that the Supreme Court's takings jurisprudence is on a "collision course" with the Court's federalism decisions, as some scholars maintain? Robert V. Percival, "Greening" The Constitution — Harmonizing Environmental and Constitutional Values, 32 Envtl. L. 809, 810 (2002). See also, e.g., Richard H. Fallon, Jr., The "Conservative" Paths of the Rehnquist Court's Federalism Decisions, 69 U. Chi. L. Rev. 429 (2002); Frank I. Michelman, Property, Federalism, and Jurisprudence: A Comment On *Lucas* and Judicial Conservatism, 35 Wm. & Mary L. Rev. 301 (1993).

C.   Landowners' and Developers' Constitutional Rights as Constraints on Zoning Measures That Impose Unfair Burdens

In the prior cases, the aggrieved developer or landowner mainly challenged the "reasonableness" (efficiency?) of the zoning restriction at issue. We now turn to instances in which the landowner's arguments are couched mainly in terms of fairness, or, as economists say, distributional considerations. Suppose, as in Caspersen v. Town of Lyme, 661 A.2d 759 (N.H. 1995), that a town has prohibited the owner of land on a mountainside from building more than one residential unit per 50 acres. The owner might conceivably raise four somewhat different forms of fairness arguments in a constitutional challenge to this dramatic restriction on densities.

First, the landowner might complain that the line the restriction drew between the restricted owner and other property owners was unfair. Suppose the town adopted its limitation on residential development on the owner's mountain land in order to keep scenic views unspoiled. But suppose further that most nearby mountainside parcels were not so restricted, and therefore most of the scenery in the area would eventually be spoiled anyway. The owner could then argue that she had not been treated like similarly situated owners, and could claim to be the victim of an irrational classification. Fairness claims of this sort are generally styled as challenges under the Equal Protection Clause, and the issue becomes whether the county had a rational basis for drawing its zoning district boundaries where it did.

Second, the landowner could complain that the restriction was imposed on her because of who she is. She might claim that the property owners restricted by the measure all are members of a particular race or national origin, while those exempted from the regulation are not, and that the restriction was imposed because of racism or prejudice, or has a disparate impact on members of a particular race or national origin. Those types of equal protection challenges, in which the plaintiff claims to be a member of a class of people who are being unfairly burdened because of their race, national origin, gender, social class, age or marital status, or because they are disabled, are discussed in detail in Chapter 8. Similar equal protection challenges that arise when the landowner claims to be the victim of discrimination because of her religious beliefs are discussed at pp. 209-20.

In some cases, however, the landowner does not claim to be a member of any particular racial group or other "class," but instead claims that she is being singled out for mistreatment by local government officials. Suppose that the mountaintop restriction was imposed after the owner vocally criticized the town's land use officials, and the owner is convinced that the restriction was retaliation for those criticisms. Such "class of one" claims again require the court to consider whether the claimant is actually being treated differently from other similarly situated owners, and if so, whether the local government has a rational reason for doing so. Such claims also may implicate the First Amendment's protection of free speech; see pp. 220-31.

Third, the evidence might show that the town could not justify the restriction by reference to the usual concerns of land use law, such as environmental protection, but rather had designed it solely to capture the value of the owner's land. Suppose, for example, that the town intended to acquire this same land later by eminent domain, and restricting its use by regulation would lower the price the town would eventually have to pay for the land (thereby saving money for the county's taxpayers). The density restriction accordingly was designed solely to reduce the acquisition price the town had to pay. In effect, the value of the restricted land would be seized by the town and converted to tax savings, which would be spread among the town's taxpayers. Governments, of course, may redistribute wealth, but judges become nervous when the losers (or winners) from a redistribution are haphazardly chosen. A court thus might invalidate the town's density restriction, perhaps calling it an "arbitrary and capricious" way for the town to have tried to save money.

Because it is unusual for a government to have no "health, safety, morals and general welfare" justification for a zoning restriction, a fourth type of fairness argument is more frequently encountered — that in which the landowner's welfare allegedly is being unfairly sacrificed for the benefit of the community at large. These cases rest on claims that the property has been "taken" — confiscated, destroyed, or rendered valueless — without just compensation, in violation of the Fifth Amendment. If the owner of mountain land brought this sort of constitutional claim against the town, the inquiry would focus on both the losses that the landowner had suffered and the town's reasons for imposing the restriction. Evidence about existing or permitted residential densities in similarly situated areas zoned by the town might be relevant both to assess the cost the restriction imposes on the landowner and to judge the nature of the government's interest in the restriction. Unlike the equal protection cases, however, the uses of (and restrictions on) similar parcels, and the government's reasons for the differences in treatment of similarly situated owners, would not be determinative of the fairness inquiry. An important feature of takings claims is this: A landowner may be entitled to prevail on a claim that a zoning classification is unconstitutionally confiscatory even though the court is convinced that the classification is efficient. For example, a court might deem the town's program to preserve the mountainside to be cost-effective, but nevertheless conclude that the financial burden on the restricted landowner is too unfair for the program to pass constitutional muster. Such a ruling would not preclude the town from preserving the mountainside, but it would force the town to use its eminent domain power to acquire the development rights of the stymied landowners at fair market value, thus achieving the same result in a fairer way.

1. Discriminatory Line Drawing

Layne v. Zoning Board of Adjustment
460 A.2d 1088 (Pa. 1983)

McDermott, Justice.

This case arose from the denial by the Zoning Board of Adjustment of the City of Pittsburgh of appellee's request to occupy the property she leases in Pittsburgh as a boarding house. That decision, as affirmed by the Court of Common Pleas of Allegheny County, was based upon the fact that appellee's property is located in an R-4 residential district where . . . boarding homes are not permitted. The Commonwealth Court, however, reasoned that boarding homes could not be rationally excluded from the R-4 residential districts when rooming houses were allowed in such districts. . . . We now reverse.

Initially, we note that zoning classifications are largely within the judgment of the legislative body and the exercise of that judgment will not be interfered with by the courts except where it is obvious that the classification has no substantial relationship to public health, safety, morals or general welfare. In addition, when the constitutionality of a zoning ordinance is attacked, there is a presumption that the ordinance is valid and that the municipal legislative body acted with the purpose of serving the public welfare. The burden is on the challenger to rebut this presumption and prove that the ordinance in question is clearly unconstitutional.

In the instant case, it is clear that the legislative body of the City of Pittsburgh has classified rooming and boarding houses as different entities for zoning purposes. Section 903.02(b) of the Pittsburgh Code provides, "'Boarding house' means a building or portion thereof, other than a hotel, containing not more than one dwelling unit, if any, *where meals and lodging are provided* for persons not residing in the dwelling unit" (emphasis added). And, Section 903.02(r) notes, "'Rooming house' means a building or portion thereof other than an apartment hotel or a hotel, containing not more than one dwelling unit, if any, *where lodging is provided without meals* for persons not residing in the dwelling unit" (emphasis added).

Despite this meal-service distinction, the Commonwealth Court found no real difference relevant to zoning purposes between the boarding and rooming house. In doing so, they relied primarily upon the testimony of Mr. Brown, a city zoning administrator who noted: "A boarding home, in the general sense, where people merely live there, it's their place of residence and have at least one meal a day provided to them, I don't see much difference between that and a rooming house."

We do not find Mr. Brown's testimony sufficient to rebut the presumption in favor of the constitutionality of the ordinance, nor do we find that the classification distinction between boarding and rooming houses fails to bear a substantial relationship to the health, safety, morals or general welfare of the community. Rather, the record reveals that the legislature's purpose in making a distinction between these entities was to exclude commercial institutions from residential districts.[2]

Within this design, a distinction based upon the availability of meal service — a service which necessarily invokes the city's health code — is sufficiently related to the health, safety and general welfare of the community, so as not to offend the equal protection clause of our constitution. The zoning power is one of the tools of government which, in order to be effective, must not be subjected to judicial interference unless clearly necessary.

For the reasons stated, we do not find it necessary to set aside the determination of the local legislative body in this case.

Therefore, the order of the Commonwealth Court is reversed.

NIX, Justice, files a dissenting opinion in which LARSEN, Justice, joins.

. . . Rooming houses in cities of the class of Pittsburgh are of much, if not more, of a transient trade as boarding homes. Further, I question the accuracy today of equating a boarding home which serves one or even two meals with a commercial restaurant.

Actually, it appears that rooming houses are more commercial in nature because the business of renting rooms in large cities is frequently more transient than boarding homes that are essentially stable residences with a family-type atmosphere.

The majority sees a relationship to the health, safety and general welfare of the community in the distinction based upon the availability of meal service. That distinction has "no real difference relevant to zoning purposes." Especially when an equal protection of the laws challenge is raised we must closely scrutinize to ensure that regulations adopted pursuant to zoning power are not unreasonable, arbitrary or confiscatory. [T]he power to thus regulate does not extend to an arbitrary, unnecessary or unreasonable intermeddling with the private ownership of property, even though such acts be labelled for the preservation of health, safety and general welfare. . . .

2. Mr. Brown, the zoning administrator, testified: "Well, the rationale was set up before my time, some time between 1950 and 1958, and as I gather, through the years, the difference they had in mind at the time was that a boarding house appeared or was more of a commercial use since it's usually more of a transient trade, and *you're feeding people, something of a restaurant type use,* and for that reason they placed a boarding home in a commercial district" (emphasis added).

Therefore I dissent.

FLAHERTY, Justice, dissenting.

I dissent. The city zoning administrator's testimony contained an acknowledgment of the absence of any meaningful distinction between rooming houses and boarding houses, and the city has failed to establish an evidentiary basis for excluding boarding houses from an R-4 district where rooming houses are permitted. Even if a boarding house were regarded as having a "commercial" character, due to its functional similarity to an inn, the nature of a rooming house is no less inn-like, despite its lack of meal-service, and the latter is no less "commercial" than the former. A distinction between boarding houses and rooming houses, based on the availability of meal-service, embodies no significant difference relevant to legitimate zoning goals, and is, therefore, violative of equal protection.

It is to be noted, too, in response to the matter of scope of judicial review of zoning ordinances as addressed by Mr. Justice McDermott, that review must be sufficiently strict to constitute a meaningful inquiry.

Note on Equal Protection

1. *Lines based on who is housed.* Layne provided "meals, lodging, clothes and personal care on a long-term basis" to 17 boarders, ranging in age from 50 to 101 years. Layne v. Zoning Board of Adjustment, 439 A.2d 1311, 1312 (Pa. Commw. Ct. 1982). For discussion of whether her claim would have been more successful if her boarders had a characteristic such as race, religion, or a physical or mental disability in common, and the distinction between her house and other permitted uses was drawn on the basis of that characteristic, see Chapter 8.

What if her boarders were all law students? See Kirsch v. Prince George's County, 626 A.2d 372 (Md. 1993) (zoning ordinance that imposed stricter requirements upon "mini-dormitories" — houses that were occupied by between three and five unrelated students enrolled in institutions of higher learning — held to violate Equal Protection Clause); accord, College Area Renters & Landlord Ass'n v. City of San Diego, 50 Cal. Rptr. 2d 515 (Ct. App. 1996).

2. *Political protections.* If landowners like Layne cannot turn to the courts for relief from arbitrary distinctions, where can they turn? When confronted with the substantive due process challenge in *Coniston,* Judge Posner reasoned that the check on legislatures in zoning matters was "purely electoral." Under what circumstances, if any, would Layne be likely to succeed in using the political process to secure a change in the classifications drawn by the zoning ordinance?

3. *Boundary lines.* As *Nectow* illustrates, the drawing of zoning boundaries invites complaints by landowners who think the grass is greener on the other side of the line. Most courts, however, are hesitant to second-guess line-drawing decisions. As was said in Robinson v. City of Bloomfield Hills, 86 N.W.2d 166 (Mich. 1957):

> Somewhere one zone must end and another start. There will always be peripheral problems. But . . . "[i]t is the province of the municipal body to draw the line of demarcation as to the use and purpose to which property shall be assigned or placed, and it is neither the province nor duty of courts to interfere with the discretion with which such bodies are invested, except where there is a clear showing of an abuse of that discretion, which is not the case where the question is merely debatable. . . . The fixing of zoning lines is a matter of legislative discretion and necessarily results in a different classification of uses on either side of the line. This does

not render limitations on use of property near the boundary line in a more restricted district unreasonable or invalid."

86 N.W.2d at 171–72 (internal citations omitted). For the exceptional case in which a landowner successfully challenged line-drawing, see, e.g., Ross v. City of Yorba Linda, 2 Cal. Rptr. 2d 638 (Ct. App. 1991) (city council's refusal to rezone a lot zoned for one dwelling per acre was irrational when lot was surrounded by smaller parcels and the city's only reason for refusing the rezoning was to prevent "urbanization," though the area was already well developed).

2.   *Discrimination Against a Particular Landowner*

Village of Willowbrook v. Olech
528 U.S. 562 (2000)

PER CURIAM.

Respondent Grace Olech and her late husband Thaddeus asked petitioner Village of Willowbrook (Village) to connect their property to the municipal water supply. The Village at first conditioned the connection on the Olechs granting the Village a 33-foot easement. The Olechs objected, claiming that the Village only required a 15-foot easement from other property owners seeking access to the water supply. After a 3-month delay, the Village relented and agreed to provide water service with only a 15-foot easement. Olech sued the Village, claiming that the Village's demand of an additional 18-foot easement violated the Equal Protection Clause of the Fourteenth Amendment. Olech asserted that the 33-foot easement demand was "irrational and wholly arbitrary"; that the Village's demand was actually motivated by ill will resulting from the Olechs' previous filing of an unrelated, successful lawsuit against the Village; and that the Village acted either with the intent to deprive Olech of her rights or in reckless disregard of her rights.

The District Court dismissed the lawsuit pursuant to Federal Rule of Civil Procedure 12(b)(6) for failure to state a cognizable claim under the Equal Protection Clause. Relying on Circuit precedent, the Court of Appeals for the Seventh Circuit reversed, holding that a plaintiff can allege an equal protection violation by asserting that state action was motivated solely by a "'spiteful effort to "get" him for reasons wholly unrelated to any legitimate state objective.'" 160 F.3d 386, 387 (1998) (quoting Esmail v. Macrane, 53 F.3d 176, 180 (7th Cir. 1995)). It determined that Olech's complaint sufficiently alleged such a claim. 160 F.3d at 388. We granted certiorari to determine whether the Equal Protection Clause gives rise to a cause of action on behalf of a "class of one" where the plaintiff did not allege membership in a class or group.[1]

Our cases have recognized successful equal protection claims brought by a "class of one," where the plaintiff alleges that she has been intentionally treated differently from others similarly situated and that there is no rational basis for the difference in treatment. See Sioux City Bridge Co. v. Dakota County, 260 U.S. 441 (1923); . . . . In so doing, we have

---

1. We note that the complaint in this case could be read to allege a class of five. In addition to Grace and Thaddeus Olech, their neighbors Rodney and Phyllis Zimmer and Howard Brinkman requested to be connected to the municipal water supply, and the Village initially demanded the 33-foot easement from all of them. The Zimmers and Mr. Brinkman were also involved in the previous, successful lawsuit against the Village, which allegedly created the ill will motivating the excessive easement demand. Whether the complaint alleges a class of one or of five is of no consequence because we conclude that the number of individuals in a class is immaterial for equal protection analysis.

explained that " '[t]he purpose of the equal protection clause of the Fourteenth Amendment is to secure every person within the State's jurisdiction against intentional and arbitrary discrimination, whether occasioned by express terms of a statute or by its improper execution through duly constituted agents.' " Sioux City Bridge Co., supra, at 445 (quoting Sunday Lake Iron Co. v. Township of Wakefield, 247 U.S. 350, 352 (1918)).

That reasoning is applicable to this case. Olech's complaint can fairly be construed as alleging that the Village intentionally demanded a 33-foot easement as a condition of connecting her property to the municipal water supply where the Village required only a 15-foot easement from other similarly situated property owners. . . . The complaint also alleged that the Village's demand was "irrational and wholly arbitrary" and that the Village ultimately connected her property after receiving a clearly adequate 15-foot easement. These allegations, quite apart from the Village's subjective motivation, are sufficient to state a claim for relief under traditional equal protection analysis. We therefore affirm the judgment of the Court of Appeals, but do not reach the alternative theory of "subjective ill will" relied on by that court.

It is so ordered.

Mr. Justice BREYER, concurring in the result.

The Solicitor General and the village of Willowbrook have expressed concern lest we interpret the Equal Protection Clause in this case in a way that would transform many ordinary violations of city or state law into violations of the Constitution. It might be thought that a rule that looks only to an intentional difference in treatment and a lack of a rational basis for that different treatment would work such a transformation. Zoning decisions, for example, will often, perhaps almost always, treat one landowner differently from another, and one might claim that, when a city's zoning authority takes an action that fails to conform to a city zoning regulation, it lacks a "rational basis" for its action (at least if the regulation in question is reasonably clear).

This case, however, does not directly raise the question whether the simple and common instance of a faulty zoning decision would violate the Equal Protection Clause. That is because the Court of Appeals found that in this case respondent had alleged an extra factor as well — a factor that the Court of Appeals called "vindictive action," "illegitimate animus," or "ill will." 160 F.3d 386, 388 (7th Cir. 1998). And, in that respect, the court said this case resembled Esmail v. Macrane, 53 F.3d 176 (7th Cir. 1995), because the Esmail plaintiff had alleged that the municipality's differential treatment "was the result not of prosecutorial discretion honestly (even if ineptly — even if arbitrarily) exercised but of an illegitimate desire to 'get' him." 160 F.3d at 388.

In my view, the presence of that added factor in this case is sufficient to minimize any concern about transforming run-of-the-mill zoning cases into cases of constitutional right. For this reason, along with the others mentioned by the Court, I concur in the result.

Note on *Olech* and "Class of One" Challenges

1. *Opening the floodgates?* Judge Posner's opinion for the Seventh Circuit noted:

Of course we are troubled, as was the district judge, by the prospect of turning every squabble over municipal services, of which there must be tens or even hundreds of thousands every year, into a federal constitutional case. But bear in mind that the "vindictive action" class of equal protection cases requires proof that the cause of the differential treatment of which the plaintiff complains was a totally illegitimate animus toward the plaintiff by the defendant. If the defendant would have taken the complained-of action anyway, even if it didn't have the animus, the animus would not condemn the action; a tincture of ill will does not invalidate governmental action.

Olech v. Village of Willowbrook, 160 F.3d 386, 388 (7th Cir. 1998), rev'd, 528 U.S. 562 (2000).

The Supreme Court's *per curiam* opinion did not adopt Judge Posner's "ill will" requirement, of course, and it is difficult to tell what Justice Breyer's concurrence bodes for whether the Court will adopt that limitation in the future. After *Olech*, then, how will the federal courts avoid the "garden variety zoning dispute[s] dressed up in the trappings of constitutional law" that so bothered Judge Posner in *Coniston*?

2. *Proof of the flood?* One scholar has studied the post-*Olech* litigation and found the following:

> During a recent twenty-five year period, the Supreme Court decided one hundred ten rational basis cases and the plaintiff prevailed in only ten of these, for a success rate of only nine percent. One would imagine then, that "class of one" equal protection claims, which rarely involve suspect classes or fundamental rights, would rarely be successful. After *Olech*, that is no longer true. In the first eighty-six federal district court opinions after *Olech* that cite *Olech* and the term "class of one," plaintiffs prevailed in thirty, for a success rate of thirty-five percent. This is an unexpectedly high percentage which suggests both that *Olech* is having a significant impact on the federal courts, and that Justice Breyer's and Judge Posner's concerns about the explosion of federal cases were well-justified.

Robert C. Farrell, Classes, Persons, Equal Protection, and *Village of Willowbrook v. Olech*, 78 Wash. L. Rev. 367, 416–17 (2003). Putting aside issues about the workload of the federal courts, does Farrell's analysis suggest cause for alarm, or signal that regulatory abuses that were going unchecked now are being appropriately vindicated?

3. *The persistence of the "ill will" requirement.* Perhaps because of concern about the flood of litigation, some lower courts have been unwilling to give up on the "ill will" requirement. The persistence of that requirement has created a great deal of confusion about what must be alleged and proved to establish a "class of one" claim. For a description of the confusion and a plug for his original formulation of the "class of one" cause of action in *Olech*, see Judge Posner's concurrence in Bell v. Duperrault, 367 F.3d 703, 711 (7th Cir. 2004) (Posner, J., concurring).

Did the Supreme Court shy away from the ill will limitation because it did not want to open the door to inquiries about the decisionmaker's intent that decisions like *Coniston* and *Omni* have kept firmly closed? See Erwin Chemerinsky, Suing the Government for Arbitrary Actions, Trial, May 2004, at 89, 90 (suggesting that the *Olech* Court was concerned that "issues of motivation focus on the government's actual purpose, while rational basis review looks solely to whether there is a conceivable permissible purpose for the government's action"). What else might explain the Court's reluctance to cabin equal protection claims by imposing an ill will requirement? If an ill will requirement is not the right way to cabin the claims, what other limiting principle should the courts use?

4. *Squaring* Olech *with the due process cases.* Should "class of one" challenges be subject to the limitations imposed on federal due process challenges that were discussed at pp. 98–104? See, e.g., Timothy Zick, Angry White Males: The Equal Protection Clause and "Classes of One," 89 Ky. L.J. 69, 134 (2000–2001) ("Under the Court's substantive due process jurisprudence, only those executive acts that 'shock the conscience' are constitutionally significant and thus call for a federal remedy. All other cases are the province of state law. Unless *Olech* is so limited, federal courts will be expounding not a constitution,

but a 'font' of administrative law."). Note that in those jurisdictions that limit substantive due process claims by holding that discretionary permits are not a property interest, as discussed in the previous subchapter, *Olech* claims have the decided advantage not only of a standard that is easier than the "shocks the conscience" requirement, but also of not being tied to a property interest.

5. *The intentionality requirement.* Some lower courts have interpreted the Court's statement that "plaintiff must allege that she has been intentionally treated differently" to require proof that the government intended to discriminate against the landowner. In Giordano v. City of New York, 274 F.3d 740, 751 (2d Cir. 2001), for example, the Second Circuit affirmed a grant of summary judgment to the government on an employee's "class of one" equal protection claim because the plaintiff had "pointed to no evidence in the record that would support a jury finding that those responsible for terminating him . . . knew that they were treating him differently from anyone else."

6. *How similarly situated?* Other courts are seeking to rein in the "class of one" complaints by imposing strict requirements for the plaintiff's allegations that she was treated differently from similarly situated landowners. In Lakeside Builders, Inc. v. Planning Board of Town of Franklin, 2002 WL 31655250 (D. Mass. Mar. 21, 2002), for example, the court dismissed a complaint alleging that a local government's refusal to grant waivers from its subdivision regulations violated equal protection, noting:

> The complaint does not propose any standard by which to judge whether one applicant for a waiver was "similarly situated" to another. Rather, it simply asserts in conclusory fashion that the plaintiffs were treated differently from other similarly situated applicants. Such a conclusory allegation conveys no factual meaning unless it is explained by at least some specifics. . . .

Id. at 2-3. But see Marchese v. Umstead, 110 F. Supp. 2d 361 (E.D. Pa. 2000) (plaintiff's allegation that "others" were treated differently by land use officials was sufficient to withstand a motion to dismiss). Cf. Futernick v. Sumpter Township, 78 F.3d 1051, 1058–59 (6th Cir. 1996) (noting in a "selective prosecution" equal protection challenge that "we are uncertain if a focus on similarly situated persons works as a screening device. Determining 'all relevant aspects' of similar situations usually depends on too many facts (and too much discovery) to allow dismissal on a Rule 12(b)(6) motion. If we require defendants to wait until summary judgment, we burden local and state officials with the regular prospect of 'fishing expeditions' and meritless suits. In the meantime we federalize and constitutionalize what are essentially issues of local law and policy.").

7. *Getting past the pleading stage.* Under traditional equal protection analysis, the burden is upon the challenging party to negative " 'any reasonably conceivable state of facts that could provide a rational basis for the classification.' " Board of Trustees of University of Alabama v. Garrett, 531 U.S. 356, 367 (2001) (citations omitted). That makes it difficult for plaintiffs to survive a motion to dismiss or a summary judgment motion because if defendants can offer, or a judge can imagine, a rational basis, there is no need for discovery and trial. Professor Farrell reports that: "Probably the most significant effect of the U.S. Supreme Court's *Olech* opinion is that it is now far more difficult for government defendants to have a case dismissed on the pleadings. Although it has never been possible for local government officials to prevent equal protection law suits from being filed against them, the damage from those suits to local government can be minimized if the suits can be dismissed at a very early stage, before discovery has taken place, before trial preparations have been made, and before the trial itself." 78 Wash. L. Rev. at 418. The ability of "class of one" claimants to get past the pleading stage stems both from courts confused about how to reconcile the traditional rules of deference with liberal rules of pleading when confronted with *Olech* claims, and to the introduction of the element of ill will, which creates a disputed

fact about the state of mind of the decisionmaker. See Shaun M. Gehan, Comment, With Malice Toward One: Malice and the Substantive Law in "Class of One" Equal Protection Claims in the Wake of *Village of Willowbrook v. Olech*, 54 Me. L. Rev. 329, 363, 385 (2002).

3.   Arbitrary Wealth Redistributions: Zoning for Purely Fiscal Purposes

When a local government imposes a land use restriction for the sole purpose of decreasing the value of land it plans to acquire through eminent domain, the courts have uniformly struck down the restriction. Riggs v. Township of Long Beach, 538 A.2d 808 (N.J. 1988), is a good example. In 1977, Riggs applied for a permit to subdivide his beachfront parcel into four lots, consistent with its zoning, which allowed lots of 5,000 square feet. The Township advised the owner that it planned to acquire the property for open space and therefore would not approve the application. After substantial delay, the Township offered $234,500 — the parcel's appraised value in 1978 — to purchase the property. Negotiations dragged on for several years, and in 1980, a new appraisal valued the property at $400,000. Both appraisals reflected the value of the parcel as zoned for four lots. The Township's mayor then asked Riggs if he would donate the $160,000 increase in the property's value to the Township, so that the Township's cost of acquisition would remain at the 1978 level. Riggs refused, and negotiations ended. The Township then amended its zoning ordinance to increase the minimum lot size for land in the area to 10,000 square feet, thereby reducing to two the number of lots the Riggs parcel could contain. Because the Township had acquired all the other land in the area, the amendment effectively applied only to Riggs's property. Although the Township asserted that the downzoning "promotes open space, controls population density, and prevents urban sprawl and the degradation of the environment," the Supreme Court of New Jersey found that "objective facts establish that the sole purpose of the ordinance was to permit the Township to purchase the property more cheaply." Id. at 814. The ordinance accordingly "does not fulfill a valid zoning purpose." Id. at 812.

Similarly, courts have struck down land use restrictions intended solely to force the owner to use the land in a way that would maximize the local government's tax revenues. See, e.g., Mindel v. Township Council, 400 A.2d 1244 (N.J. Super. Ct. Law Div. 1979) (township's refusal to allow owner to farm the land, which he wished to do to qualify for lower property tax assessments under the state's Farmland Assessment Act, had sole purpose of protecting the Township's tax revenue, and therefore was arbitrary and unreasonable).

But as discussed at pp. 112–17, it is fairly rare for a court to find that an illegitimate purpose is the sole reason for a land use regulation. In Crider v. Board of County Commissioners of County of Boulder, 246 F.3d 1285, 1290 (10th Cir. 2001), for example, the court dismissed a substantive due process challenge to the designation of land as rural preservation, noting that although plaintiffs alleged "a conspiracy on the part of the defendants to obtain [the property] at decreased cost," the complaint failed to allege that the county had no conceivable rational basis for the classification.

Note on Zoning for Fiscal Purposes

1. *Precondemnation versus no-condemnation.* What if the Township of Long Beach had not announced that it planned to acquire the land for "public open space," but instead

had rezoned it so restrictively that effectively it would be left as "private open space"? The community would not enjoy exactly the same benefits — it could not traverse the land, for example — but it would enjoy protected views, and some of the other advantages of open space. The owner's rights in that case are not so clear. See the discussion of takings challenges at pp. 134–97. Why should rezoning to reduce the cost of acquiring open space be unreasonable, but rezoning to achieve some of advantages of open space, with none of the acquisition costs, be upheld?

2. *Preventing tax burdens.* In his famous majority opinion in Southern Burlington County NAACP v. Township of Mount Laurel, 336 A.2d 713, 731 (N.J. 1975), excerpted at p. 763, Justice Hall declared: "We have no hesitancy in now saying, and do so emphatically, that, considering the basic importance of the opportunity for appropriate housing for all classes of our citizenry, no municipality may exclude or limit categories of housing for [a fiscal] reason or purpose." However, outside the context of exclusionary zoning (and, other than in New Jersey and a few other states, even in that context), many land use restrictions are motivated and justified, at least in part, by the desire to avoid tax burdens. See, e.g., the discussion of exactions at pp. 652–59. If avoiding tax burdens is a legitimate land use purpose, why isn't increasing tax revenues?

4. Confiscatory Zoning Classifications (The Takings Issue)

a. The Original Focus on Physical Takings

William Michael Treanor, The Original Understanding of the Takings Clause and the Political Process
95 Colum. L. Rev. 782, 785–92 (1995)

. . . In colonial America, government routinely acted in ways that affected private property, and the political process determined when compensation was due. No judicially enforceable compensation requirement existed during this period. Even after the establishment of a compensation requirement, it applied only to interference with physical ownership, and government routinely acted in ways that diminished the value of private property without providing compensation.

A. Takings Law Before the Fifth Amendment

Precedents for the Fifth Amendment's Takings Clause were relatively few in number and narrow in application. Even with respect to physical seizures of property by the government, the compensation requirement was not generally recognized at the time of the framing of the Fifth Amendment. Moreover, no colonial charter or state constitution recognized that regulations could give rise to a requirement of compensation. . . .

Only two fundamental documents of the colonial era provided even limited recognition of a right to compensation. A provision of the Massachusetts Body of Liberties, adopted in 1641, imposed a compensation requirement, but it was limited to the seizure of personal property. . . .

The 1669 Fundamental Constitutions of Carolina, drafted by John Locke and never fully implemented, provided compensation for the seizure of real property. They authorized the High Steward's Court to erect buildings and lay highways, adding: "The damage the owner of such lands (on or through which any such public things shall be made) shall receive thereby shall be valued, and satisfaction made by such ways as the grand council shall appoint."

None of the other colonial charters recognized a compensation requirement, either for personal or real property. Where they protected personal or real property, the colonial charters did so by imposing a requirement of procedural regularity, rather than by recognizing a substantive right. . . .

. . . In practice, compensation was the norm when the state took private property. For example, in the case of road-building, the most common occasion in colonial America for the exercise of the eminent domain power, the authorizing statutes typically provided for juries to award compensation for the land taken. At the same time, however, colonial governments often took private property without providing compensation. In particular, all colonies except Massachusetts provided that undeveloped land could be taken for roads without compensation. . . . Moreover, uncompensated takings occurred outside the context of physical takings of land. For example, . . . Virginia statutes aimed at protecting the state's reputation as a producer of quality tobacco empowered the state to seize without compensation processed tobacco of less than premium quality. . . .

Although colonies clearly limited the ways in which individuals could use property, no colonial charter mandated compensation when regulations affected the value of property. Furthermore, courts did not direct compensation for such regulations. Land use was subject to extensive regulations. In colonial Virginia, for example, various statutes barred overplanting of tobacco and required the growing of crops other than tobacco. Boston had zoning regulations governing the location of bakeries, slaughterhouses, stills, and tallowchandlers, and violators were subject to prosecution. New York City and Charlestown enacted ordinances barring further operation of slaughterhouses within city limits. . . .

. . . The first state constitutions of the revolutionary era followed colonial precedent. None of the state constitutions adopted in 1776 had just compensation requirements. The three that contained eminent domain clauses simply echoed Article 39 of Magna Carta, providing that the consent of the owner or of the legislature was needed for the state to exercise its eminent domain power.

The Revolution increased governmental actions that challenged or destroyed property rights. The revolutionary army seized private goods without compensation. States passed statutes limiting wages and prices and barring forestalling and engrossing. A variety of statutes undercut the property interests of British citizens and American loyalists. . . . [D]ivestment acts and bills of attainder effected the confiscation of loyalist property worth, by one historian's estimates, twenty million dollars at a time when the value of all improved real estate in the country was two hundred million dollars. Equally significant, revolutionary era governmental actions also had the effect of redistributing wealth among Americans. . . . State legislators aided debtors, and thus deprived creditors of property rights, by passing statutes that stayed execution of debts, that made valueless land legal tender, and that permitted payment of debts in depreciated paper money.

The first state constitution to contain a compensation requirement was the Vermont Constitution of 1777, which declared that "whenever any particular man's property is taken for the use of the public, the owner ought to receive an equivalent in money." The Massachusetts Constitution of 1780 provided that "whenever the public exigencies require that the property of any individual should be appropriated to public uses, he shall receive a reasonable compensation therefor." The final revolutionary era document to contain a compensation requirement was the Northwest Ordinance of 1787, which the Continental Congress passed as the governance instrument for the Northwest Territories. It stated: "[S]hould the public exigencies make it necessary, for the common preservation, to take any person's property, or to demand his particular services, full compensation shall be made for the same." In each case, a plain language reading of the text indicates that it protected property only against physical confiscation, and the early judicial decisions construed them in this way.

B. THE FIFTH AMENDMENT'S TAKINGS CLAUSE

Despite this precedent for a constitutional compensation requirement, states did not demand a similar limitation on the federal government in the Bill of Rights. State ratifying conventions sought as amendments to the Constitution every provision in the Bill of Rights except the Takings Clause. There are apparently no records of discussion about the meaning of the clause in either Congress or, after its proposal, in the states. [Because James Madison initially proposed the Fifth Amendment,] Madison's statements . . . provide unusually significant evidence about what the clause was originally understood to mean (and about why Madison thought this particular protection of property necessary). As will be discussed, those statements uniformly indicate that the clause only mandated compensation when the government physically took property. . . .

C. EARLY INTERPRETATIONS OF THE TAKINGS CLAUSE AND ITS STATE COUNTERPARTS

Most of the early case law came from state courts. These courts held that compensation was required if government physically took property, but not if it merely regulated the owner's use of property. When the Supreme Court eventually began to resolve takings issues under the federal Constitution, its holdings accorded with these earlier state decisions. . . .

Mugler v. Kansas
123 U.S. 623 (1887)

Mr. Justice HARLAN delivered the opinion of the court. . . .

[In 1880, Kansas amended its constitution to prohibit the manufacture and sale of liquor. One section of the legislation passed to effectuate the amendment declared all places where liquor was manufactured or sold to be common nuisances and allowed such places to be closed down upon a judicial finding of nuisance. Pursuant to the legislation, state authorities filed an action to have the defendants' brewery declared a nuisance and to enjoin its use for the sale of liquor. The suit was dismissed; the state appealed.] . . .

. . . [I]t is contended that, as . . . their respective breweries were erected when it was lawful to engage in the manufacture of beer for every purpose; as such establishments will become of no value as property, or, at least, will be materially diminished in value, if not employed in the manufacture of beer for every purpose; the prohibition upon their being so employed is, in effect, a taking of property for public use without compensation, and depriving the citizen of his property without due process of law. In other words, although the State, in the exercise of her police powers, may lawfully prohibit the manufacture and sale, within her limits, of intoxicating liquors to be used as a beverage, legislation having that object in view cannot be enforced against those who, at the time, happen to own property, the chief value of which consists in its fitness for such manufacturing purposes, unless compensation is first made for the diminution in the value of their property, resulting from such prohibitory enactments. . . .

. . . A prohibition simply upon the use of property for purposes that are declared, by valid legislation, to be injurious to the health, morals, or safety of the community, cannot, in any just sense, be deemed a taking or an appropriation of property for the public benefit. Such legislation does not disturb the owner in the control or use of his property for lawful purposes, nor restrict his right to dispose of it, but is only a declaration by the State that its use by any one, for certain forbidden purposes, is prejudicial to the public interests. . . . The power which the States have of prohibiting such use by individuals of their property as will be prejudicial to the health, the morals, or the safety of the public, is not — and, consistently with the existence and safety of organized society, cannot be — burdened with the condition that the State must compensate such individual owners for pecuniary losses they may sustain, by reason of their not being permitted, by a noxious use of their property, to inflict injury upon the community. The exercise of the police power by the destruction of property which is itself a public nuisance, or the prohibition of its use in a particular way, whereby its value becomes depreciated, is very different from taking property for public use, or from depriving a person of his property without due process of law. In the one case, a nuisance only is abated; in the other, unoffending property is taken away from an innocent owner. It is true, that, when the defendants in these cases purchased or erected their breweries, the laws of the State did not forbid the manufacture of intoxicating liquors. But the State did not thereby give any assurance, or come under an obligation, that its legislation upon that subject would remain unchanged. . . .

Note on the Original Focus of the Takings Clause

1. *The physical/regulatory distinction.* According to one reading of *Mugler,* the Court draws a distinction between physical appropriation or possession and regulation. That distinction is consistent with Professor Treanor's account of the original understanding of the Takings Clause. For additional support for Treanor's account, see, e.g., Morton J. Horwitz, The Transformation of American Law: 1780–1860, at 63–66 (1977); William J. Novak, The People's Welfare: Law and Regulation in Nineteenth-Century America (1996); James W. Ely, Jr., "That Due Satisfaction May Be Made": The Fifth Amendment and the Origins of the Compensation Principle, 36 Am. J. Legal Hist. 1 (1992); John F. Hart, Land Use Law in the Early Republic and the Original Meaning of the Takings Clause, 94 Nw. U. L. Rev. 1099, 1107–31 (2000); John F. Hart, Colonial Land Use Law and Its Significance for Modern Takings Doctrine, 109 Harv. L. Rev. 1252 (1996); William B. Stoebuck, A General Theory of Eminent Domain, 47 Wash. L. Rev. 553 (1972).

Professor Treanor's history increasingly is contested, however. See Eric R. Claeys, Takings, Regulations, and Natural Property Rights, 88 Cornell L. Rev. 1549, 1553 (2003) (nineteenth-century state regulatory takings law is "profoundly misunderst[oo]d"); Andrew Gold, Regulatory Takings and Original Intent: The Direct, Physical Takings Thesis "Goes Too Far," 49 Am. U. L. Rev. 181, 241 (1999) (the historical record is ambiguous; there is "enough material for a party on either side of the regulatory takings debate to muster an argument for his or her position"); Kris W. Kobach, The Origins of Regulatory Takings: Setting the Record Straight, 1996 Utah L. Rev. 1211, 1213 (in the early 1800s, "state courts interpreting the takings clauses of their constitutions and refining state common law . . . embraced what we might now describe as regulatory takings"); David A. Thomas, Finding More Pieces for the Takings Puzzle: How Correcting History Can Clarify Doctrine, 75 U. Colo. L. Rev. 497, 520 (2004) ("the idea that compensation would be owed for deprivation of property rights short of complete appropriation was widely accepted, even if not often tested" in the early cases).

Whether compensation ought to be paid when regulation affects the value of property but leaves it physically in the possession of the owner depends, at least in part, on what purposes compensation is meant to serve. That issue is addressed in the sections that follow. First, however, let us explore alternative readings of *Mugler*.

2. A *"nuisance exception"?* In Penn Central Transportation Co. v. City of New York, 438 U.S. 104 (1978), excerpted at p. 158, Justice Rehnquist described *Mugler* as establishing a "nuisance exception to the taking guarantee," but argued that the exception applies only to "noxious uses" of property. Id. at 144–46 & n.8 (Rehnquist J., dissenting). Could those injured by drunkenness or alcoholism, or neighbors of a property used for brewing alcohol, have sued the brewery under common law principles of nuisance? See pp. 511–24; see also Richard A. Epstein, Takings 130–31 (1985) (questioning whether the producers of alcohol would have been found to have "caused" any nuisance posed by alcoholism or public drunkenness). Assuming that the brewery was a nuisance and assuming further that the *Mugler* Court's decision turned on that fact, is Justice Rehnquist necessarily correct that the exception he reads *Mugler* as creating was limited to common law nuisances? As we will see, Justice Rehnquist's emphasis on common law nuisances enjoyed something of a revival in Lucas v. South Carolina Coastal Council, 505 U.S. 1003 (1992), excerpted at p. 169.

If *Mugler* is appropriately read as allowing a nuisance exception to the compensation requirement, should governments regulating nuisances be limited to those remedies that neighbors who complain of nuisance would receive? In Spur Industries, Inc. v. Del E. Webb Development Co., 494 P.2d 700 (Ariz. 1972), discussed at pp. 534–35, for example, a feed lot was ordered to stop its operations because they were annoying to the residents of a new subdivision that had been constructed next door. But the injunction became effective only if the subdivider paid the feed lot owner the costs of moving or shutting down the operation.

In a case closely tracking *Spur Industries*, however, the Supreme Court refused to find a taking when Los Angeles prohibited the manufacture of brick within a particular district, in order to close down a brickyard that had become an annoyance to the homeowners who moved into the area. Hadacheck v. Sebastian, 239 U.S. 394 (1915). Should the homeowners who moved in next to the brickyard also bear some responsibility for the conflict and be forced (through taxation) to pay for the brickyard owner's losses? See Lawrence Berger, Public Use, Substantive Due Process and Takings — An Integration, 74 Neb. L. Rev. 843, 877 (1995); Claeys, supra, at 1613–15.

3. *The harm/benefit distinction. Mugler* sometimes is said to rest on an argument Professor Ernst Freund advanced in an influential treatise in the beginning of the twentieth century: Government need not compensate for injuries arising from regulations aimed at preventing harms, but should provide compensation if its regulations were designed to extract benefits. Ernst Freund, The Police Power: Public Policy and Constitutional Rights 546–47 (1904). Professor Freund's argument has had considerable influence over takings law, although the Supreme Court recently repudiated the harm/benefit distinction, at least in some of its guises. See Lucas v. South Carolina Coastal Council, supra, excerpted at p. 169.

How can one identify which regulations prevent "harms" rather than secure "benefits"? Miller v. Schoene, 276 U.S. 272 (1928), illustrates the difficulty. In *Miller*, the Virginia legislature authorized the destruction of any red cedar trees growing within a specified distance from an apple orchard because red cedar trees harbor a fungus that, while harmless to the cedar trees, can do serious damage to apple trees. When the owners of the cedar trees challenged the legislation as a violation of due process, the Supreme Court rejected their argument, reasoning that the Constitution permitted the state to destroy "one class of property in order to save another which, in the judgment of the legislature, is of greater value to the public." Id. at 279.

Does the fact that the cedar trees produce less of a benefit to society as a whole than apple trees mean that the cedar trees cause harm by harboring the fungus? Professor Fischel has argued that "prices make rights," and the "public's demand for the favored species' product" provided a "widely shared, non-legal norm" that the Court correctly used in *Miller* to uphold the preference the legislature showed for apple growers. William A. Fischel, The Law and Economics of Cedar-Apple Rust: State Action and Just Compensation in *Miller v. Schoene* 2, 20, 56–57 (Dartmouth College Economics Dep't Working Paper, Apr. 23, 2004). See also James M. Buchanan, Politics, Property, and the Law: An Alternative Interpretation of *Miller et al. v. Schoene*, 15 J.L. & Econ. 439 (1972).

Or are the apple tree owners seeking the benefit of a less stressful environment for their apples, at the expense of the cedar tree owners? See Ronald Coase, The Problem of Social Cost, 3 J.L. & Econ. 1 (1960) (arguing that if two property uses are incompatible, it is senseless to think of one as "at fault" because both impose reciprocal costs on the other). But see Thomas W. Merrill & Henry E. Smith, Essay, What Happened to Property in Law and Economics?, 111 Yale L.J. 357, 391–95 (2001) (taking issue with Coase's "causal agnosticism").

Can ordinary language provide the baseline from which decisionmakers can determine whether a land use causes "harm"? After all, an activity most people engage in generally is not one that can be easily characterized as "harmful"; that derogatory adjective is usually employed in ordinary language only to describe conduct that falls below what is common. See Robert C. Ellickson, Alternatives to Zoning: Covenants, Nuisance Rules, and Fines as Land Use Controls, 40 U. Chi. L. Rev. 681 (1973), excerpted at p. 516. See also William A. Fischel, Regulatory Takings: Law, Economics, and Politics 352–61 (1995).

Another option, suggested by the previous note, would be to use the common law of nuisance (discussed at pp. 511–38) as the baseline. See Richard A. Epstein, Takings 107–25 (1985). We'll return to the role that nuisance law should play in determining whether compensation should be required for regulatory intrusions when we discuss Lucas v. South Carolina Coastal Council, supra, excerpted at p. 169.

For further discussion of the baselines that might be used, and the conceptual difficulties each raises, see Jeremy Paul, The Hidden Structure of Takings Law, 64 S. Cal. L. Rev. 1393, 1433–64 (1991).

4. *Variations on the harm/benefit theme.* The harm/benefit test has enjoyed several refinements since Professor Freund first articulated the theory. Professor Joseph Sax, for example, argues that when government acts to control negative externalities, or spillover effects, it should not be required to compensate. Joseph L. Sax, Takings, Private Property and Public Rights, 81 Yale L.J. 149 (1971). See also, e.g., Robert C. Ellickson, Suburban Growth Controls: An Economic and Legal Analysis, 86 Yale L.J. 385, 418–24 (1977) (no taking occurs if government prohibits "subnormal" land uses, unless the prohibition is "grossly inefficient"); Andrea L. Peterson, The Takings Clause: In Search of Underlying Principles Part II — Takings as Intentional Deprivations of Property Without Moral Justification, 78 Cal. L. Rev. 53 (1990) (no taking occurs if government is preventing or punishing wrongdoing).

For sharp criticisms of the various formulations of the harm/benefit principle, see, e.g., Glynn S. Lunney, Jr., Responsibility, Causation and the Harm-Benefit Line in Takings Jurisprudence, 6 Fordham Envtl. L.J. 433 (1995). For defenses of the principle, see, e.g., Douglas W. Kmiec, The Original Understanding of the Taking Clauses Is Neither Weak Nor Obtuse, 88 Colum. L. Rev. 1630, 1635–38 (1988); Lynda J. Oswald, The Role of the "Harm/Benefit" and "Average Reciprocity of Advantage" Rules in a Comprehensive Takings Analysis, 50 Vand. L. Rev. 1449 (1997).

5. *The problem of legal transitions.* Takings law is so difficult (and untidy, as we are about to see) in part because takings controversies tend to arise during transitions — times when society is undergoing some radical shift in the way that it thinks about an issue. Prohibition

was one such shift, because it banned "a remarkably profitable activity . . . that previously enjoyed the sanction of law." William J. Novak, The People's Welfare 177 (1996). Thomas Cooley posed the transitional fairness issues most starkly:

> The trade in alcoholic drinks being lawful, and the capital employed in it fully protected by the law, the legislature then steps in, and by enactment based on general reasons of public utility, annihilates the traffic, destroys altogether the employment, and reduces to a nominal value the property on hand. . . . The merchant of yesterday becomes the criminal of today, and the very building in which he lives becomes perhaps a nuisance.

Thomas M. Cooley, A Treatise on the Constitutional Limitations Which Rest upon the Legislative Power of the States of the American Union 583–84 (7th ed. 1903).

The problem of how to be fair to landowners who acquired property under one set of rules, only to see the uses of the property drastically limited as morals, technology, or scientific understanding change, is a recurring theme in the materials that follow. For an overview of the problem, see Holly Doremus, Takings and Transitions, 19 J. Land Use & Envtl. L. 1 (2003).

b.   Going Too Far

Pennsylvania Coal Co. v. Mahon
260 U.S. 393 (1922)

Mr. Justice HOLMES delivered the opinion of the Court.

This is a bill in equity brought by the defendants in error to prevent the Pennsylvania Coal Company from mining under their property in such way as to remove the supports and cause a subsidence of the surface and of their house. The . . . deed executed by the Coal Company in 1878, under which the plaintiffs claim . . . conveys the surface, but in express terms reserves the right to remove all the coal under the same, and the grantee takes the premises with the risk, and waives all claim for damages that may arise from mining out the coal. But the plaintiffs say that whatever may have been the Coal Company's rights, they were taken away by an Act of Pennsylvania, approved May 27, 1921, P.L. 1198, commonly known there as the Kohler Act. . . .

The statute forbids the mining of anthracite coal in such way as to cause the subsidence of, among other things, any structure used as a human habitation, with certain exceptions. . . . As applied to this case the statute is admitted to destroy previously existing rights of property and contract. The question is whether the police power can be stretched so far.

Government hardly could go on if to some extent values incident to property could not be diminished without paying for every such change in the general law. As long recognized, some values are enjoyed under an implied limitation and must yield to the police power. But obviously the implied limitation must have its limits, or the contract and due process clauses are gone. One fact for consideration in determining such limits is the extent of the diminution. When it reaches a certain magnitude, in most if not in all cases there must be an exercise of eminent domain and compensation to sustain the act. So the question depends upon the particular facts. . . .

This is the case of a single private house. No doubt there is a public interest even in this, . . . [b]ut usually in ordinary private affairs the public interest does not warrant much of this kind of interference. . . . A source of damage to such a house is not a public nuisance. . . . The damage is not common or public. The extent of the public interest is shown by the statute to be limited, since the statute ordinarily does not apply to land when the surface is owned by the owner of the coal. Furthermore, it is not justified as a protection of personal safety. That could be provided for by notice. . . . On the other hand the extent of the taking is great. It purports to abolish what is recognized in Pennsylvania as an estate in land — a very valuable estate — and what is declared by the Court below to be a contract hitherto binding the plaintiffs. If we were called upon to deal with the plaintiffs' position alone, we should think it clear that the statute does not disclose a public interest sufficient to warrant so extensive a destruction of the defendant's constitutionally protected rights.

But the case has been treated as one in which the general validity of the act should be discussed. . . .

It is our opinion that the act cannot be sustained as an exercise of the police power. . . . What makes the right to mine coal valuable is that it can be exercised with profit. To make it commercially impracticable to mine certain coal has very nearly the same effect for constitutional purposes as appropriating or destroying it. This we think that we are warranted in assuming that the statute does.

It is true that in Plymouth Coal Co. v. Pennsylvania, 232 U.S. 531 (1914), it was held competent for the legislature to require a pillar of coal to be left along the line of adjoining property, that, with the pillar on the other side of the line, would be a barrier sufficient for the safety of the employees of either mine in case the other should be abandoned and allowed to fill with water. But that was a requirement for the safety of employees invited into the mine, and secured an average reciprocity of advantage that has been recognized as a justification of various laws. . . .

The general rule at least is, that while property may be regulated to a certain extent, if regulation goes too far it will be recognized as a taking. It may be doubted how far exceptional cases, like the blowing up of a house to stop a conflagration, go — and if they go beyond the general rule, whether they do not stand as much upon tradition as upon principle. In general it is not plain that a man's misfortunes or necessities will justify his shifting the damages to his neighbor's shoulders. We are in danger of forgetting that a strong public desire to improve the public condition is not enough to warrant achieving the desire by a shorter cut than the constitutional way of paying for the change. As we already have said, this is a question of degree — and therefore cannot be disposed of by general propositions. . . .

. . . [T]he question at bottom is upon whom the loss of the changes desired should fall. So far as private persons or communities have seen fit to take the risk of acquiring only surface rights, we cannot see that the fact that their risk has become a danger warrants the giving to them greater rights than they bought.

Decree reversed.

Mr. Justice BRANDEIS, dissenting.

. . . Coal in place is land; and the right of the owner to use his land is not absolute. He may not so use it as to create a public nuisance; and uses, once harmless, may, owing to changed conditions, seriously threaten the public welfare. Whenever they do, the legislature has power to prohibit such uses without paying compensation; and the power to prohibit extends alike to the manner, the character and the purpose of the use. . . .

. . . [A] restriction imposed to protect the public health, safety or morals from dangers threatened is not a taking. The restriction here in question is merely the prohibition of a noxious use. The property so restricted remains in the possession of its owner. The State does not appropriate it or make any use of it. The State merely prevents the owner from making a use which interferes with paramount rights of the public. Whenever the use prohibited ceases to be noxious, — as it may because of further change in local or social conditions, — the restriction will have to be removed and the owner will again be free to enjoy his property as heretofore.

. . . If by mining anthracite coal the owner would necessarily unloose poisonous gasses, I suppose no one would doubt the power of the State to prevent the mining, without buying his coal fields. And why may not the State, likewise, without paying compensation, prohibit one from digging so deep or excavating so near the surface, as to expose the community to like dangers? In the latter case, as in the former, carrying on the business would be a public nuisance.

It is said that one fact for consideration in determining whether the limits of the police power have been exceeded is the extent of the resulting diminution in value; and that here the restriction destroys existing rights of property and contract. But values are relative. If we are to consider the value of the coal kept in place by the restriction, we should compare it with the value of all other parts of the land. That is, with the value not of the coal alone, but with the value of the whole property. The rights of an owner as against the public are not increased by dividing the interests in his property into surface and subsoil. The sum of the rights in the parts cannot be greater than the rights in the whole. . . .

Note on *Pennsylvania Coal*

1. *What happened to* Mugler? Why did Pennsylvania go too far in prohibiting the mining of coal, if Kansas hadn't gone too far in prohibiting the manufacture of alcohol? Were the effects of manufacturing alcohol more clearly a "harm" than the effects of causing subsidence? Was the diminution in value of the coal greater than the diminution in value of the brewery? Were the efficiency gains of the Kohler Act less than the efficiency gains of prohibition? Is *Pennsylvania Coal* different from *Mugler* because of the existence of the deed explicitly waiving the rights the Mahons later wanted to have? Do the two holdings simply reflect the difference between a takings challenge and a due process challenge? In short, can *Pennsylvania Coal* reasonably be distinguished from *Mugler*, or should it be read to overrule *Mugler* (which Justice Holmes did not even cite)?

While we're on the subject of missing citations, what should one make of the fact that *Euclid* (in which Justice Holmes voted with the majority) made no attempt to distinguish *Pennsylvania Coal*, even though *Euclid* was decided just four years later and the trial court's opinion striking down Euclid's zoning ordinance relied extensively on Justice Holmes's opinion in *Pennsylvania Coal*?

2. *What, and how big, is the property?* The debate between Justice Holmes and Justice Brandeis exposes two critical issues underlying the takings puzzle that are even yet unresolved, as the materials that follow will make clear. First, there's the question that Justice Brandeis raises in the last few sentences of the excerpt: What is the "whole" property against which a diminution in value should be measured? We'll return to this "denominator problem" at the end of this note and at pp. 185–93. Second, there is the issue of what kinds of interests should count as property, a problem we already saw arise in the context of substantive due process challenges. All interpretations of the Takings Clause are inextricably intertwined with views about what property is and what role property serves in society. Some of the best discussions of those issues are found in Jennifer Nedelsky, Private Property and the Limits of American Constitutionalism (1990); Jeremy Waldron, The Right to Private Property (1988); Craig Anthony Arnold, The Reconstitution of Property: Property as a Web of Interests, 26 Harv. Envtl. L. Rev. 281 (2002); Michael A. Heller, The Boundaries of Private Property, 108 Yale L.J. 1163 (1999); Carol M. Rose, Property as

the Keystone Right?, 71 Notre Dame L. Rev. 329 (1996); Laura S. Underkuffler-Freund, Property: A Special Right, 71 Notre Dame L. Rev. 1033 (1996).

3. *Line-drawing or balancing?* Is the test Justice Holmes sets forth a line-drawing rule — regulations that cross a line in diminishing too much of the value of property require compensation, while those that fall on the other side of the line do not — or is it a balancing test, in which the extent of the diminution in value is weighed against the importance of the government's interest? Many students of the opinion have viewed it as drawing a line and have been puzzled by the opinion's seeming departure from Justice Holmes's general view that judges should defer to legislatures engaged in economic regulation, see, e.g., Lochner v. New York, 198 U.S. 45, 76 (1905) (Holmes, J., dissenting), just as court-watchers were confused by Justice Sutherland's vote in *Euclid.*

Professor William Treanor argues, however, that when viewed against the background of Justice Holmes's previous takings opinions, *Pennsylvania Coal* must be read as rejecting the categorical rules that had previously dominated takings jurisprudence (such as the physical/regulatory or harm/benefit distinctions attributed to *Mugler*) and as adopting a balancing test. Because a balancing test applied by a judge deferential to the legislature's view of the public interest would leave much, if not most, economic regulation intact, *Pennsylvania Coal* should be seen as consistent with Holmes's rejection of *Lochner.* William Michael Treanor, Jam for Justice Holmes: Reassessing the Significance of *Mahon*, 86 Geo. L.J. 813 (1998). See also the critiques of Treanor's arguments by D. Benjamin Barros, The Police Power and the Takings Clause, 58 U. Miami L. Rev. 471, 498–509 (2004); Richard A. Epstein, *Pennsylvania Coal v. Mahon*: The Erratic Takings Jurisprudence of Justice Holmes, 86 Geo. L.J. 875 (1998), and Robert Brauneis, Treanor's *Mahon*, 86 Geo. L.J. 907 (1998). Professor Treanor responds to the critics in Understanding *Mahon* in Historical Context, 86 Geo. L.J. 933 (1998).

4. *The options available to the Pennsylvania Coal Company.* The Kohler Act was passed as part of a package that included legislation known as the Fowler Act. The Fowler Act provided that every owner of an anthracite coal mine had to elect either to come under the terms of the Kohler Act or to pay a yearly fee of 2 percent of the market price of all anthracite coal the company mined that year in Pennsylvania. The fee would be used to compensate victims of subsidence damage for personal injuries and property losses. William A. Fischel, Regulatory Takings 32–33 (1995); Lawrence M. Friedman, A Search for Seizure: *Pennsylvania Coal Co. v. Mahon* in Context, 4 Law & Hist. Rev. 1, 21 (1986).

Should the fact that the Pennsylvania Coal Company could have mined all the coal it wanted, regardless of subsidence, if it paid the 2 percent yearly fee, change the outcome of the case?

5. *Regulation versus taxation.* What if Pennsylvania had chosen to impose a tax on all anthracite coal mined in the state, rather than prohibiting mining that caused subsidence but waiving the prohibition for those who "volunteered" to pay the yearly fee? The state may not have chosen that option because of concern about its power to levy such a tax. But assuming that Pennsylvania had authority to impose such a tax, should courts be more comfortable with the political processes states use to impose taxes than with state land use processes? That is a subject to which we return in Chapter 7A and 7B. If governments (and their taxpayers) are not able or willing to tax and spend to reach a particular result, should they ever be able to accomplish the same goal through uncompensated regulation?

6. *The original assignment of rights.* Does the appropriateness of Justice Holmes's holding depend on an analysis of the bargain the owners of the surface estates struck? What if the coal companies selling the surface estates had a virtual monopoly on the land close enough to the mines to be suitable for housing mineworkers? What if the import of the bargain had changed because mining technology and the skyrocketing value of coal

made it feasible and desirable to mine support pillars that never would have been touched in the late 1800s, when the Mahons' predecessor in interest waived support rights? See Carol M. Rose, *Mahon* Reconstructed: Why the Takings Issue Is Still a Muddle, 57 S. Cal. L. Rev. 561, 577 (1984). Should the issue of whether compensation is due depend in part on the "correctness" (which could mean efficiency, or could mean fairness or morality) of the original assignment of rights? Should it depend on whether any initial "incorrectness" could have been fixed through Coasian bargaining? See pp. 34–39.

7. *Redistributing rights.* Professor Rose argues that *Pennsylvania Coal* "turned not on the question of 'too much' taking, but on the fact that the statute transferred rights from one finite class of property owners to another." Rose, supra, at 581. She contends that "[n]one of the possible public purposes withstands analysis; transfers of rights brought about by the statute resulted in no net social gain, perhaps not even in the case of transfers to municipalities. The various beneficiaries of the Act represented no more than a collection of private interests." Id. at 580.

Are the beneficiaries of regulation always just "a collection of private interests"? If not, does Rose's observation distinguish *Pennsylvania Coal* from *Mugler*? Should redistributive regulation always trigger a compensation requirement? See Rose, supra, at 583–87. See also Richard A. Epstein, Takings (1985).

8. *The protections of the political process.* Professor Fischel concludes his detailed analysis of the history and aftermath of the decision with the following:

> The Kohler Act was passed by a representative body responsive to those in a good position to reap the benefits and bear the costs of the regulation. Coal was important to the general prosperity of the state and to the Scranton area in particular. The idea that the state, at the urging of the city, would pass a regulation that would foul its own economic nest seems paternalistic. . . . There is little evidence for the idea that coal mine owners lacked sympathizers in the legislature. The U.S. Supreme Court's decision to review *Pennsylvania Coal* was questionable because it imposed a judicial discipline in a place where political calculation might be expected to work to protect each party's interests.

Fischel, supra, at 46. Are you persuaded?

9. *Private ordering.* Why didn't the individual surface owners simply negotiate with the owners of the mineral estates to buy back the support estates? Indeed, in 1911 and 1917, coal companies responded to calls for regulation by a group of local citizens called the "Surface Protective Association" by voluntarily agreeing "[w]henever the danger of surface subsidence is imminent . . . to sell for a fair consideration to owners of the structures exceeding $5,000 [in value], such pillar coal as they may reasonably desire to purchase for the support of said structures. The price of this coal was later fixed at 35¢ a ton." Fischel, supra, at 30 (quoting George E. Stevenson, Reflections of an Anthracite Engineer (1931)). Anthracite coal was then selling for approximately $1 per ton in place, so the bargain was a good one for the surface owners. Fischel, supra, at 30. The companies also agreed to repair subsidence damage to homes valued at $5,000 or less, and to preserve public highways and streets.

What justification might there be for legislative intervention, given the proven ability of the parties to work the problem out through private ordering? How should the fact that private bargains could and did take place affect the determination whether compensation should be paid?

10. *The aftermath of the decision.* Even the principal author of the Kohler Act, whose briefs supporting the act were filled with predictions of doom should the Kohler Act fail, admitted later that the Supreme Court's decision had limited real-world impact. The companies continued to abide by their voluntary agreements to repair subsidence damage.

Fischel, supra, at 40 (citing Philip V. Mattes, Tales of Scranton (1974)). Why might the coal companies have decided not to press their victory? What does that suggest about the need for regulation? About the appropriateness of the Court's holding?

11. *Anthracite versus bituminous coal.* In Keystone Bituminous Coal Ass'n v. DeBenedictis, 480 U.S. 470 (1987), the Supreme Court revisited Pennsylvania's attempts to control subsidence from coal mining. *Keystone* involved a challenge to the Bituminous Mine Subsidence and Land Conservation Act, legislation very similar to the Kohler Act, except for the type of coal regulated. In a five-to-four decision, the Court rejected the challenger's assertion that the case was controlled by *Mahon*, and refused to find that the Subsidence Act effected a taking. Justice Stevens, writing for the majority, distinguished *Mahon* because (among other reasons) Justice Holmes had found that the Kohler Act made the mining of "certain coal" commercially impracticable, but the *Keystone* challengers had not shown that they were denied economically viable use of their property "[w]hen the coal that must remain beneath the ground is viewed in the context of any reasonable unit of petitioners' coal mining operations and financial-backed expectations." Id. at 499. The Court rejected in *Keystone* the argument that the focus should be on the support estate as a separate interest in land, noting that the support estate's value "is merely a part of the entire bundle of rights possessed by the owner of either the coal or the surface." Id. at 1250. But even if the support estate were viewed as a distinct segment of property, the takings claim would still fail, the Court said, because petitioners owned many support estates and had not shown what percentage of those was affected by the regulation.

Justice Rehnquist, joined by Justices Powell, O'Connor, and Scalia, filed a spirited dissent, finding *Keystone* "strikingly similar" to *Mahon.* For illustrative examples of the scholarly reaction to the majority's characterization of *Mahon*, see Richard Epstein, Takings: Descent and Resurrection, 1987 Sup. Ct. Rev. 1, 14-15, 19 (Justice Stevens's reading of *Mahon* was "incredible"); Douglas W. Kmiec, The Original Understanding of the Takings Clause Is Neither Weak Nor Obtuse, 88 Colum. L. Rev. 1630, 1631-33 (1988) ("revisionist" and "disingenuous"); Frank Michelman, Takings, 1987, 88 Colum. L. Rev. 1600, 1600 n.2 (1988) (an "amazing reconstruction").

We'll return to the controversy over how to define the relevant unit of property at pp. 185-93.

12. *Heaps of mischief.* Felix Frankfurter's notes of his conversations with Justice Brandeis include the following reference: Frankfurter "spoke of Holmes' occasional indulgence of a large phrase, 'general principles which do not decide concrete cases' which begets heaps of mischief, as in [the] *Mahon* case. . . . " Melvin I. Urofsky, The Brandeis-Frankfurter Conversations, 1985 Sup. Ct. Rev. 299, 334. As you read the remainder of the takings cases, consider whether Frankfurter was right.

c. *Justifications for the Compensation Requirement*

Before turning to how the courts have struggled with Justice Holmes's "large phrase," it is useful to step back for a moment to think about why the government should compensate those from whom it takes property. The justifications are usually divided into two categories: concerns about efficiency — the need to maximize the aggregate welfare — and concerns about fairness — the need to prevent "government from forcing some people alone to bear public burdens which, in all fairness and justice, should be borne by the public as a whole." Armstrong v. United States, 364 U.S. 40, 49 (1960).

Efficiency rationales for the compensation requirement most commonly argue that compensation is necessary because governments will not pay sufficient attention to the costs their regulations impose unless they are forced to compensate those whose property values are diminished by the regulation. If a government must pay those costs, this cost-internalization theory continues, regulators will be much more likely to adopt only those measures that produce greater benefits than costs. Other efficiency theorists suggest that unless compensation is mandatory, investors' decisions will be so distorted by their fear that government regulation might destroy the fruits of their labor that they will not put resources to their most efficient use. This insurance rationale argues that the way to counter investors' aversion to the risk of regulatory losses is to insure property owners against such losses by requiring compensation.

Fairness rationales argue that compensation is required to correct for failures in the democratic process or to force government to treat similar property owners equally. Influential statements of each of these leading theories follow.

Frank I. Michelman, Property, Utility, and Fairness: Comments on the Ethical Foundations of "Just Compensation" Law
80 Harv. L. Rev. 1165, 1214–15, 1218–19, 1222–23 (1967)

A. Compensation and Utility

A strictly utilitarian argument leading to the specific identification of "compensable" occasions would have a quasi-mathematical structure. Let us define three quantities to be known as "efficiency gains," "demoralization costs," and "settlement costs." "Efficiency gains" we define as the excess of benefits produced by a measure over losses inflicted by it, where benefits are measured by the total number of dollars which prospective gainers would be willing to pay to secure adoption, and losses are measured by the total number of dollars which prospective losers would insist on as the price of agreeing to adoption. "Demoralization costs" are defined as the total of (1) the dollar value necessary to offset disutilities which accrue to losers and their sympathizers specifically from the realization that no compensation is offered, and (2) the present capitalized dollar value of lost future production (reflecting either impaired incentives or social unrest) caused by demoralization of uncompensated losers, their sympathizers, and other observers disturbed by the thought that they themselves may be subjected to similar treatment on some other occasion. "Settlement costs" are measured by the dollar value of the time, effort, and resources which would be required in order to reach compensation settlements adequate to avoid demoralization costs. Included are the costs of settling not only the particular compensation claims presented, but also those of all persons so affected by the measure in question or similar measures as to have claims not obviously distinguishable by the available settlement apparatus.

A measure attended by positive efficiency gains is, under utilitarian ethics, prima facie desirable. But felicific calculation under the definition given for efficiency gains is imperfect because it takes no account of demoralization costs caused by a capricious redistribution, or alternatively, of the settlement costs necessary to avoid such demoralization costs. When pursuit of efficiency gains entails capricious redistribution, either demoralization costs or settlement costs must be incurred. It follows that if, for any measure, both demoralization costs and settlement costs (whichever were chosen) would exceed efficiency gains, the measure is to be rejected; but that otherwise, since either demoralization costs or settlement costs must be paid, it is the lower of these two costs which should be paid. The compensation rule which then clearly emerges is that compensation is to be paid whenever settlement costs are lower than both demoralization costs and efficiency gains. But if settlement costs, while lower than demoralization costs, exceed efficiency gains, then the measure is improper regardless of whether compensation is paid. The correct utilitarian statement, then, insofar as *the issue of compensability* is concerned, is that compensation is due whenever demoralization costs exceed settlement costs, and not otherwise. . . .

B. COMPENSATION AND FAIRNESS

. . . We must consider whether, in the name of justice, a person might not claim compensation (or society might not refuse compensation) regardless of the consequences for the net social product. . . .

Previous discussion helps us identify the relevant risks. The risk associated with the more stringent compensation practice is that its settlement costs will force abandonment of efficient projects. . . . The risk associated with the less stringent compensation practice is that of sustaining concentrated losses from efficiency-motivated social projects which otherwise would not have been sustained — losses which may partially or totally exclude their bearer from sharing in the general gains from social activity.

The question, then, is whether the more or the less stringent compensation practice minimizes the sum of these risks. . . . A decision not to compensate is not unfair as long as the disappointed claimant ought to be able to appreciate how such decisions might fit into a consistent practice which holds forth a lesser long-run risk to people like him than would any consistent practice which is naturally suggested by the opposite decision.

If we set about to make practical use of this approach, we shall find ourselves asking much the same questions to determine whether a compensability decision is fair as were suggested by the utilitarian approach. The relevant risks plainly are minimized by insistence on compensation when settlement costs are low, when efficiency gains are dubious, and when the harm concentrated on one individual is unusually great. They are also minimized if insistence on compensation is relaxed when there are visible reciprocities of burden and benefit, or when burdens similar to that for which compensation is denied are concomitantly imposed on many other people (indicating that settlement costs are high and that those sustaining the burden are probably incurring relatively small net losses — else, being many, they probably could have been mobilized to deflect the measure which burdens them). . . .

Note on Utilitarian Theories of Compensation

1. *Michelman's efficiency formula.* Michelman's utilitarian argument is summarized as:

- If B (benefits) < C (costs other than demoralization costs), do not regulate.
- If B > C, but (B − C) (efficiency gains) < the lower of S (settlement costs) or D (demoralization costs), do not regulate.
- If B > C, and (B − C) > the lower of S or D, regulate.
  - If S < D, compensate.
  - If D < S, do not compensate.

The costs against which the benefits of the measure are to be compared in the first step of the formula include diminutions in property value occasioned by the regulation. The settlement or demoralization costs considered in the second step should not count these property value impacts again, but should focus instead on the administrative costs of settlement. See William W. Fisher III, The Significance of Public Perceptions of the Takings Doctrine, 88 Colum. L. Rev. 1774, 1776–81 (1988).

Who should determine the first three steps of Michelman's formula, which address whether to regulate? The last two steps, which address whether to compensate? See Glynn S. Lunney, Jr., A Critical Reexamination of the Takings Jurisprudence, 90 Mich. L. Rev. 1892, 1943 (1992) (Michelman's theory fails to explain why the legislature cannot be trusted with both sets of questions). If the legislative or administrative body addresses both, should the reviewing court give the two types of decisions the same level of deference?

2. *The tale of two pies.* Professor Richard Epstein offers a different utilitarian argument for the compensation requirement, which he articulates through the "Tale of Two Pies" shown in Figure 3-6. The smaller pie is the distribution of holdings under a system of private property. The outer ring represents gains that can be achieved by a reassignment of property rights through collective action by the government when transaction costs preclude voluntary trades. The government should make only those changes in property rules that will result in a net social gain (i.e., make the pie larger). Further, those social gains must be distributed pro rata, according to preexisting property rights, such that no one is worse off for the change in rules, and each person's piece of the pie remains the same relative to others' pieces. Richard A. Epstein, Takings (1985). Epstein argues that the "no net losers" requirement of his compensation rule is necessary because "[b]y forcing the winners to fully compensate the losers for the deprivation of their rights, the losses that the winning coalition could otherwise externalize on losers are brought back to bear on them." Richard A. Epstein, Bargaining with the State 85 (1993). The pro rata distribution requirement is necessary to prevent the social gains from the change in property rights from being dissipated by interest groups "striv[ing] to obtain the largest share of the surplus for themselves." Id. at 93.

Professor Epstein would allow changes in property rights to escape a requirement of cash compensation if they were accompanied by implicit, or in-kind, compensation or if they would do no more than apply prohibitions against fraud or theft that the law currently allows an individual to invoke against another's misuse of property. Nevertheless, critics assert that Epstein's takings theory would eliminate most zoning rules, progressive taxation schemes, and welfare and social security programs.

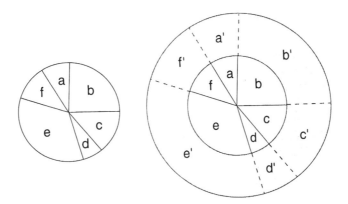

Source: Richard A. Epstein, Bargaining with the State 80 (1993).

FIGURE 3-6
The Tale of Two Pies

Epstein's theory has generated volumes of debate. For a representative sample, see Symposium on Richard Epstein's Takings, 41 U. Miami L. Rev. 49 (1986); Thomas W. Merrill, Rent Seeking and the Compensation Principle, 80 Nw. U. L. Rev. 1561 (1987) (book review); Jeremy Paul, Searching for the Status Quo, 7 Cardozo L. Rev. 743 (1986) (book review).

3. *Working at cross purposes?* One function of land use regulation is to force those who use property in a particular way to bear the full cost of that use. Requiring compensation in those circumstances would undermine the whole purpose of the regulation. Can either Michelman or Epstein address that problem without falling back on the harm/benefit distinction discussed at pp. 138–39?

Note on Compensation as Cost Internalization

1. *Fiscal illusion.* A primary function of the just compensation requirement, under both Michelman's and Epstein's theories, is to force government to internalize the costs of its regulation. The cost-internalization argument often is referred to as one of "fiscal illusion" because it asserts that government policymakers will undervalue costs they do not bear and thus act under an illusion about the efficiency and value of their policies.

The cost-internalization rationale for compensation enjoys widespread support. See, e.g., Pennell v. City of San Jose, 485 U.S. 1, 22 (1988) (Scalia, J., concurring in part and dissenting in part); Richard A. Posner, Economic Analysis of Law 54–57 (6th ed. 2003); William A. Fischel & Perry Shapiro, Takings, Insurance, and Michelman: Comments on Economic Interpretations of "Just Compensation" Law, 17 J. Legal Stud. 269 (1988); Michael A. Heller & James E. Krier, Deterrence and Distribution in the Law of Takings, 112 Harv. L. Rev. 997, 1017–18 (1999); Thomas W. Merrill, *Dolan v. City of Tigard*: Constitutional Rights as Public Goods, 72 Denver U. L. Rev. 859, 882–83 (1995); Thomas J. Miceli & Kathleen Segerson, Regulatory Takings: When Should Compensation Be Paid?, 23 J. Legal Stud. 749, 758–59 (1994).

2. *Does cost internalization work when applied to governments?* Professor Daryl Levinson has argued that the cost-internalization theory for compensation, which is derived from private law models that assume that firms in a market environment will rationally seek to maximize wealth by weighing the economic costs and benefits of their activity, is based on a mistaken analogy:

> [G]overnment does not internalize costs in the same way as a private firm. Government actors respond to political incentives, not financial ones — to votes, not dollars. We cannot assume that government will internalize social costs just because it is forced to make a budgetary outlay. While imposing financial outflows on government will ultimately create political costs (and benefits), the mechanism is complicated and depends on the model of government behavior used to translate between market costs and benefits and political costs and benefits.

Daryl J. Levinson, Making Government Pay: Markets, Politics, and the Allocation of Constitutional Costs, 67 U. Chi. L. Rev. 345, 345 (2000). After exploring the most common models of government behavior — "public interest" models, simple majority rule models, and models that reflect interest group analysis and theories of bureaucracy — Levinson concludes that the "difficulty of making any confident predictions of how government will behave in response to constitutional cost remedies" should "cast considerable doubt on the assumptions about the deterrent effects of constitutional cost remedies currently taken for granted by courts and commentators." Id. at 361–62. Indeed, he argues that "the incentive effects of constitutional cost remedies are, as a general matter, simply indeterminate — perhaps as likely to be perverse as beneficial." Id. at 387.

Is Levinson correct? If he is, does that necessarily mean that compensation should not be required when regulations diminish the value of property? Imperfect as it is, should we nevertheless prefer the flaws of cost internalization to the alternative of allowing regulators to escape any financial consequences for the costs regulations impose?

3. *Bearing the cost or passing it on?* When a government is required to pay compensation because the value of someone's property is diminished by a regulation, the government regulators will not bear the cost of compensation directly but will pass costs along to taxpayers, to the government's insurer (and other members of the insurance pool), or to the beneficiaries of other programs that must be reduced to fund compensation payments. Whether a compensation requirement will result in more efficient regulation, then, should depend on how direct, immediate, and transparent the tax increase (or benefit reduction) is to those who elect the regulators (or the elected officials who appoint or control the regulators). It should depend as well on whether the compensation award, when spread over taxpayers or beneficiaries of programs reduced to pay the compensation award, is significant enough to motivate a taxpayer to express her displeasure. Finally, it should depend on how clearly and effectively those who pay the costs of the compensation award can communicate their displeasure back to government officials. See Vicki Been & Joel C. Beauvais, The Global Fifth Amendment? Nafta's Investment Protections and the Misguided Quest for an International "Regulatory Takings" Doctrine, 78 N.Y.U. L. Rev. 30, 90–96 (2003); Susan Rose-Ackerman, Against Ad Hocery, 88 Colum. L. Rev. 1697, 1706 (1988). As you read the developing law of regulatory takings, consider whether the doctrines reflect concern about any of those issues.

4. *Internalizing benefits?* If compensation to property owners hurt by regulations should be required to force governments to internalize the *costs* of regulations, should restitution — compensation from property owners benefited by regulations — be required to ensure that the government fully internalizes the *benefits* of regulations? See Windfalls for Wipeouts: Land Value and Compensation (Donald Hagman & Dean Misczynski eds., 1978); Daniel D. Barnhizer, Givings Recapture: Funding Public Acquisition of Private Property Interests on the Coasts, 27 Harv. Envtl. L. Rev. 295 (2003); Abraham Bell & Gideon Parchomovsky, Givings, 111 Yale L.J. 547 (2001); Eric Kades, Windfalls, 108 Yale L.J. 1489 (1999). Professor Levinson argues that takings theories:

> mysteriously assume[] that government policymakers discount social costs that are not translated into budgetary expenditures, but do not similarly discount the social benefits derived from government programs. For purposes of internalizing costs, in other words, government behaves like a private actor in a market environment. For purposes of internalizing benefits, however, government exhibits a more altruistic, public-regarding welfare function, weighing externalized benefits as if they were enjoyed by government itself. One searches the takings literature in vain for some explanation of this puzzling asymmetry.

Levinson, supra, at 350. Professor Been and Joel Beauvais have analyzed possible explanations for the asymmetry:

> One reason a government might seek to generate benefits, even if it cannot capture the monetary value of those benefits, is that those benefited will respond to the "giving" by voting for the government official responsible and by contributing funds to ensure the reelection of that official. But the same could be said of those who lose from a regulation. . . . A second reason the government might generate benefits even if it could not fully capture those benefits is that it might be able to capture some of the benefits through taxation. If, for example, a local government passes a land use restriction that benefits neighboring land by either protecting or

> increasing its value, the government will capture at least some of that avoided loss (or gain) through property taxes. . . . But again, the same can be said about costs — the government will bear a portion of the costs of such measures in the form of reduced property taxes on the restricted land. . . .

Been & Beauvais, supra, at 97. They conclude that neither explanation suffices to explain the one-sidedness of the internalization argument. Are there more satisfying explanations for the asymmetry?

5. *Cost/benefit analysis.* Would a requirement that regulators prepare, and consider, a cost/benefit analysis for every proposed regulation (and its alternatives) force internalization as (or more) effectively as a compensation requirement? For discussions of analogous requirements, see pp. 275–76, 368–93.

6. *Selling exemptions rather than compensating for regulations.* If forcing the government to bear the costs of its regulations is a primary goal of a compensation requirement, could that goal be achieved as well by allowing the government to sell exemptions from its regulations? After all, if the government chooses not to sell, it bears the cost of its regulations by forgoing income. See William A. Fischel, The Economics of Zoning Laws, 179–84 (1985); Note, Taking Back Takings: A Coasean Approach to Regulation, 106 Harv. L. Rev. 914, 923–24 (1993). For discussion of instances in which, some would argue, governments are allowed to sell exemptions from regulations, see pp. 331–36 and 634–79.

7. *Uncoupling takings and compensation.* Might there be instances in which the need to force government to internalize the costs of its regulations suggests that the government should compensate for a taking, but it would be inefficient to pay the compensation to the actual victims of the taking? Or conversely, might there be instances in which efficiency or fairness suggests that the victims of a taking should receive compensation, but those same concerns suggest that the government actor at issue should not be forced to pay the compensation? Professors Heller and Krier argue that the law should recognize that a taking does not necessarily require compensation to specific victims, but could instead give rise to "general" compensation — to a special fund, for example. Similarly, they argue that a taking does not necessarily require compensation from the government entity effecting the taking, but could instead give rise to compensation from a general fund. Those remedial options would allow courts to address instances in which the deterrence, or cost-internalization, concern of compensation conflicts with the fairness concern. Michael A. Heller & James E. Krier, Deterrence and Distribution in the Law of Takings, 112 Harv. L. Rev. 997 (1999).

Lawrence Blume & Daniel L. Rubinfeld, Compensation for Takings: An Economic Analysis
72 Cal. L. Rev. 569, 590–92, 610–11, 624 (1984)

Consider the following simple example. . . .

An individual homeowner is contemplating the purchase of a parcel of land and a house, valued at $100,000. At the time of purchase the individual is aware that there is a 0.5 probability that the government will choose to rezone neighboring land to permit dumping of toxic chemicals. This would create noxious odors and lower the value of the house to $50,000.

Assuming that the individual homeowner correctly perceives the risks involved in the regulatory process, we can calculate the expected return on the property with or without compensation after the rezoning. With compensation, the property would be worth $100,000 to the investor, whether or not the regulation is enacted. On the other hand, without compensation, the expected return on the land would be $75,000 ($100,000 × 0.5 + $50,000 × 0.5). . . .

. . . [W]hen a homeowner purchases a parcel of land, the investment in the land and structure often represents a substantial portion of that individual's net worth. When purchasing an asset that makes up such a large portion of one's wealth, one is likely to be very wary of undertaking risk. Individuals would presumably be willing to pay something to insure against the prospect of a factory moving nearby and imposing substantial externalities. Thus, even though the probability of government action reducing the value of land may be relatively low, the potential consequences in terms of the expected losses and the effect on landowners can be very large.

As a consequence of their risk aversion, such investors would consider the possibility of buying insurance sufficient to cover themselves against future losses. . . . The availability of . . . insurance allows the individual to turn a risky investment into a certain one. Thus, rather than paying $75,000 for the parcel with the risk of earning either $100,000 or $50,000 depending upon governmental action, the individual pays $75,000 for the parcel as before, but purchases an insurance contract for $25,000. With the insurance contract, the individual has paid $100,000 independent of any government action. If no taking occurs, the market value of the land is $100,000; if the zoning regulation is changed, the value falls to $50,000, and the insurance payment of $50,000 compensates for the loss. Thus, with full information and competitive markets, including the market for insurance, the allocation of resources will be an efficient one in which risk-averse individuals purchase full insurance against all uncertainties. . . .

While contracts that provide some kind of insurance occur frequently in private land markets, arrangements that provide insurance against the actions of the government are rare. When purchasing land, why do individuals not write contracts which require compensation if the land is physically taken or severely regulated? Or, why do private insurance companies not sell takings insurance? The answer lies in the fact that markets for insurance against such governmental actions are not perfect. . . .

[The authors go on to explain why the private market fails to provide insurance against government regulation, and how a policy of requiring compensation for some diminutions in value caused by regulation can serve the same purpose as private market insurance.]

. . . [T]wo conditions must be satisfied in order for compensation to be efficient. First, the loss must be substantial. The loss is considered substantial if it significantly reduces the owner's net worth. Second, the party that is harmed must be substantially averse to risk. In general, we will assume that the more wealthy the plaintiff, the less likely that she will be risk averse (in relative terms). . . .

Apart from any considerations of equity, compensation can improve the efficiency of the land market by eliminating some or all of the risk of governmental regulation that risk-averse landowners face. This reduction of risk will also reduce any distortions in land use decisions that are created by differing attitudes toward risk. The risk-insurance approach to the taking question can provide a theoretical foundation upon which support for the diminution in value compensation theory can be built. With individuals who have decreasing relative risk aversion, large risks, associated with large percentage losses, are those most likely to be insured. Therefore, large risks are those that ought to be compensated. . . .

Note on Using Compensation to Reduce Risk

1. *Moral hazard.* Insurance markets are plagued by a phenomenon called *moral hazard*, which occurs when the insured can affect the likelihood or extent of the event that triggers payment. Fire insurance, for example, poses a moral hazard because the availability of the insurance may encourage the insured to invest more in fire-prone buildings or to

take fewer precautions against fire. If compensation is awarded for changes in legal rules, will landowners be prone to invest more than the socially optimal amount in land or development activities that are at risk of physical or regulatory takings? See Blume & Rubinfeld, *supra*, at 593–95. See also Steve P. Calandrillo, Eminent Domain Economics: Should "Just Compensation" Be Abolished, and Would "Takings Insurance" Work Instead?, 64 Ohio St. L.J. 451, 513–16, 525–27 (2003); Richard Craswell, Instrumental Theories of Compensation: A Survey, 40 San Diego L. Rev. 1135, 1147–49, 1154–55 (2003); Hanoch Dagan, Takings and Distributive Justice, 85 Va. L. Rev. 741, 749 (1999); William A. Fischel & Perry Shapiro, Takings, Insurance, and Michelman: Comments on Economic Interpretations of "Just Compensation" Law, 17 J. Legal Stud. 269, 270–74 (1988); Eric Kades, Avoiding Takings "Accidents," 28 U. Rich. L. Rev. 1235 (1994); Louis Kaplow, An Economic Analysis of Legal Transitions, 99 Harv. L. Rev. 509 (1986).

Will the availability of compensation make landowners less vigilant in monitoring, or less vocal in opposing, proposed legal changes? See Susan Rose-Ackerman & Jim Rossi, Disentangling Deregulatory Takings, 86 Va. L. Rev. 1435, 1483 (2000) ("Takings jurisprudence should not make investors indifferent to the government's capital-destroying actions. A no-compensation rule for broad policy initiatives would encourage investors to lobby the state to refrain from its wasteful policies.").

Another form of moral hazard occurs when the availability of compensation causes property owners to act strategically to secure more compensation. Professor Fischel found an interesting example of that phenomenon while investigating the apple tree versus cedar tree controversy that resulted in Miller v. Schoene, 276 U.S. 272 (1928):

> The law . . . actually did contemplate compensation for those few owners who had cedars that added value to their property. [The compensation was financed through a tax on apple tree growers.] The problem that developed was exactly that which economists have labeled the "moral hazard" problem in takings: Cedar owners who prior to the law had no apparent interest in their value sometimes feigned a strong affection for them after its passage for the apparent reason of additional compensation. . . . Only after this abuse began to threaten the viability of the program did apple growers actively resist payment of compensation.

William A. Fischel, The Law and Economics of Cedar-Apple Rust: State Action and Just Compensation in *Miller v. Schoene* 57 (Dartmouth College Economics Dep't Working Paper, Apr. 23, 2004).

How should the inefficiencies of these various types of moral hazard be balanced against the danger that the government will impose inefficient restrictions unless forced to bear the costs of those restrictions?

2. *Private insurance.* Professors Blume and Rubinfeld argue that the market will not provide insurance against governmental regulation because of the problems of moral hazard and adverse selection (only those people who know they are most at risk for regulation will buy the insurance). Another problem is the potential for corruption: Government officials could warn landowners that they might want to consider purchasing insurance (and in return, the grateful landowners might give the officials some share of the insurance proceeds or some other gratuity).

Nevertheless, insurance against the risk that regulatory changes will destroy the value of property is beginning to appear in the international investment context. The major capital-exporting countries provide national investment insurance programs that cover some of the risks of expropriation for their investors. The Multilateral Investment Guarantee Agency provides similar coverage, as do many private insurers. See Vicki Been & Joel C. Beauvais, The Global Fifth Amendment? Nafta's Investment Protections and the Misguided Quest for an International "Regulatory Takings" Doctrine, 78 N.Y.U. L. Rev.

30, 111–14 (2003). If similar developments occur within the United States, and the private insurance market began to make insurance against regulatory changes available, would private insurance necessarily be preferable to compensation? Would an insurance payment adequately assuage the demoralization costs, such as feelings about being treated unfairly, that worried Professor Michelman? See Fischel & Shapiro, supra (arguing that it would not).

3. *Limits of economic analysis?* How valid is the following criticism of both Michelman's utilitarian theory and the insurance theory of compensation?

> The common feature of [constitutional] rights is that they stand against any ordinary cost/benefit calculus of social welfare. . . .
>
> To economize the Compensation Clause — to hold that the right to just compensation should be suspended whenever society would produce more efficiently by dishonoring it — would misapprehend the central idea of our foundational law. It would turn the Constitution on its head. The constitutional right to compensation, to be a constitutional right, must stand precisely when the felicific or economic calculus would count against it.

Jed Rubenfeld, Usings, 102 Yale L.J. 1077, 1133–34 (1993). Jed Rubenfeld (the lawyer, as opposed to Dan Rubinfeld, the economist) argues that the justification for the compensation requirement lies not in efficiency but in the need to protect liberty:

> When the state puts a person's things to use, the individual does not merely suffer economic injury. A servitude is forced upon him. He is made in a small or large way an instrumentality of the state.

Id. at 1143. Jed Rubenfeld would require compensation whenever the government "conscripts someone's property for state use." Id. at 1080. A zoning regulation that requires property to be used only for a parking lot would therefore require compensation because "it is as if the state had condemned the property for this specific use." Id. at 1155. But a regulation that allowed a mix of commercial uses would not require compensation.

Jed Rubenfeld's concern about the threat government regulation of property poses to liberty is shared by many. Professor Epstein, for example, justifies his proposals for a sweeping compensation requirement (see pp. 148–49) in part by arguing that "[a] nation in which private property is protected contains independent, decentralized sources of power that can be used against the state, reducing thereby the possibility that any group will be able to seize control over the sources of information or the levers of political power." Richard A. Epstein, Takings 138 (1985). See also Bernard H. Siegan, Economic Liberties and the Constitution (1980).

4. *What is special about regulation?* Many government activities other than land use regulations, such as decisions about where to site highways, transit stations, or other public facilities, may have dramatic impacts on property values. Is there any reason to treat those risks differently from the risk of regulatory changes? See Richard A. Epstein, *Lucas v. South Carolina Coastal Council*: A Tangled Web of Expectations, 45 Stan. L. Rev. 1369, 1376 (1993) (arguing that siting of a highway is a form of competition against which landowners should not be protected).

William Michael Treanor, The Original Understanding of the Takings Clause and the Political Process
95 Colum. L. Rev. 782, 866–72 (1995)

[See pp. 134–36 for Professor Treanor's description of the origins of the Takings Clause.]

In recent years, Professors Farber,[2] Fischel,[3] and Levmore[4] have offered public choice theories of the Takings Clause. Like the original understanding of the Takings Clause, these theories treat the central concern of the Takings Clause as protecting those who suffer property losses because of process failure. . . .

Fischel's model offers the broadest protection to property owners. He argues that courts construing the Takings Clause should direct compensation when property owners are "victims of democratic excess." Fischel provides the following test for the identification of such "victims": "[T]hey are a minority in a jurisdiction in which the usual minoritarian political processes are attenuated — that is, they are subject to local governments or to politically insulated special commissions, and they possess assets whose regulation cannot be escaped by moving them to other jurisdictions or other employments." The governmental entity making the decision is of critical significance in Fischel's theory: "[C]ourts can save some of their scarce political capital by ignoring all but the most extreme regulations enacted by larger units of governments, such as the United States Congress, most states, and some large cities and counties." In our system, larger units of government are characterized by pluralist politics — with logrolling and the opportunity for deal-making — and this gives property owners "a realistic opportunity to politically protect themselves." In contrast, empirical studies indicate that local government decisionmaking is characterized by majoritarian politics, rather than by deal-making. Because local governments typically have one legislative chamber, rather than two, and because their legislative agenda has a relatively limited number of items, there are fewer opportunities for logrolling. As a result, special interests are likely to lose consistently. Such interests will not be able to bargain in order to protect themselves, and therefore need judicial protection. When a larger unit of government is involved, such protection is generally unnecessary. . . .

[Fischel's theory] fails to accord enough respect to the Takings Clause's limiting principle — the principle of deference to the political process, except where it is most prone to failure. Fischel's theory imposes a high level of judicial scrutiny on decisions made by most localities. . . .

The weakness of this argument, however, is that our system affords those who lose local struggles an opportunity for political redress; they can challenge adverse decisions at the state level. . . .

. . . Farber argues that the principal purpose of the Takings Clause is "horizontal equity." Public choice theory shows that even in the absence of a constitutional requirement, democratic legislatures would normally compensate when they physically took property. Only the politically unprotected will not be compensated: "[I]n a world where government compensation is often available, it is unacceptable that some groups are denied compensation because of their unusual political vulnerability." This principle requires compensation whenever the government physically takes property. In order to ensure that government will not strategically evade the Takings Clause, the principle must be extended to situations in which the government seeks to transfer property from one private citizen to another. For the same reason, it must also extend to "regulations that are functionally equivalent to government acquisitions." . . .

. . . [Farber's] conception of process failure is too broad, for reasons suggested by Fischel's explanation of how special interests are able to use pluralist politics to protect their property claims. . . . [T]he regulations for which he would require compensation

[2] EDS.: Daniel A. Farber, Public Choice and Just Compensation, 9 Const. Comment. 279 (1992).

[3] EDS.: William A. Fischel, Exploring the Kozinski Paradox: Why Is More Efficient Regulation a Taking of Property?, 67 Chi.-Kent L. Rev. 865, 897–98 (1991); William A. Fischel, Introduction: Utilitarian Balancing and Formalism in Takings, 88 Colum. L. Rev. 1581, 1582–84 (1988).

[4] EDS.: Saul Levmore, Takings, Torts, and Special Interests, 77 Va. L. Rev. 1333 (1991).

will often not be the product of process failure. . . . Farber would provide compensation for regulatory takings that are similar to physical takings, even though this class of regulatory takings as a whole is not one in which process failure is particularly likely.

Professor Levmore has advanced a third public choice approach to the Takings Clause, one that focuses on singling out. He argues that process failure is likely when an individual or small group of people has been singled out and that compensation is particularly appropriate in such situations. When a proposed statute or regulation affects a great many people, they can protect themselves through the political process, engaging in logrolling to ensure that they do not receive an unfair share of the public's burden. But the situation is very different when a proposed governmental action affects only a few people or, worse, a single person. Professor Levmore writes: "It is unlikely that such individuals can compete effectively in the political arena and it would be undesirable for them to try; the transaction cost of individual involvement in politics is, after all, quite great." For example, if the government were to take my home, in the absence of a just-compensation clause I would be poorly positioned to go to the legislature or Congress and obtain redress. Thus, Levmore argues that takings law properly protects individual actors and small groups of actors who are affected by governmental actions but cannot effectively engage in interest group politics because they are not repeat players and because they are a tiny part of the polity.

. . . Levmore's theory . . . [is flawed] because it provides for compensation of a small group whose property interests are affected, even when a larger group would not be compensated. For example, a court will order compensation in the case of an individual whose property suffers a particularly sharp decrease in value because of airplane overflights, but not when overflights affect a larger group. . . .

[Professor Treanor then argues that a synthesis of Farber's and Levmore's theories provides the best "translation" of the original understanding of the Takings Clause:] Compensation is due when a governmental action affects only the property interests of an individual or a small group of people and when, in the absence of compensation, there would be a lack of horizontal equity (i.e., when compensation is the norm in similar circumstances). Such a theory does what the Takings Clause was initially interpreted to do; it defers to majoritarian decisionmaking in most instances but defends those most likely to be the victims of process failure. . . .

Note on Political Process Failure Theories

1. *Equal protection.* By emphasizing "horizontal equity," the political process theories appear to ask the Takings Clause to do the work of the Equal Protection Clause. Professor Fee has been more explicit: He argues that regulatory takings doctrine mistakenly has treated takings claims as similar to due process cases, and has understood the Fifth Amendment as a "defense for individuals against government actions that are extreme and unreasonable as applied to the individual." It should be interpreted, he maintains, "as a guarantee of equal treatment among members of a community." He claims:

> . . . [T]he Fifth Amendment Takings Clause, like the Equal Protection Clause, is designed to protect the legal rights of individual citizens relative to others, not to protect individual expectations of wealth or to provide an insurance policy against unreasonable governmental burdens. The right of just compensation accorded to every property owner by the Takings Clause is fundamentally an antidiscrimination principle. This explains, for example, why general taxes have never been understood to violate the Takings Clause, although taxes do diminish

a person's private wealth for public use. It also explains why general criminal laws, liability rules, or business regulations should not be considered takings, no matter how financially burdensome they may be to some owners. The default "bundle of rights" inherent in private property includes an affirmative "right to use" one's private assets, which may not be denied without compensation. This right to use, however, is inherently bounded by the government's power to restrict an owner's conduct through general laws. The proper role of the Takings Clause is to require compensation in those circumstances where the government legitimately targets merely one or a few owners to bear a unique legal burden for the benefit of the general community.

John E. Fee, The Takings Clause as a Comparative Right, 76 S. Cal. L. Rev. 1003, 1004, 1007 (2003).

Is the risk of discrimination against property owners greater than the risk of discrimination against other classes? Is the nature or effect of the discrimination more troublesome? If not, why read the Takings Clause as addressing a problem the Equal Protection Clause is more clearly targeted to solve?

2. *Internalization, again.* Professor Fischel's theory derives from the same internalization-forcing impetus that drove the utilitarian formulas discussed previously. Professor Fischel would have a court reviewing a regulation ask "what standards voters would impose if the economic effects fell on themselves." If the regulation approximates that standard, its costs have been sufficiently internalized by the decisionmaker, and compensation should not be due. If the regulation deviates from the standard, the likelihood of a political process failure is sufficiently high that the court should require compensation. William A. Fischel, Regulatory Takings: Law, Economics, and Politics 6 (1995). Do departures from Fischel's version of the Golden Rule necessarily signal a political process failure?

3. *The level of government.* Professor Fischel's theory depends heavily on the level and size of the government imposing the regulation. He believes that large republics are less prone to majoritarian tyranny than smaller governments, and has faith in the ability of property owners to protect their interests before large governments by lobbying, exerting interest group pressure, and using other forms of "voice." Are you persuaded by Professor Treanor's retort that those who suffer at the hands of majoritarian local governments can protect themselves by appealing to the state or other larger governments? Is Fischel's view of the influence landowners have on larger governments unduly rosy? This issue also is addressed at pp. 731–40.

4. *Physical invasions.* Are those whose land is physically appropriated more or less likely to suffer political process failures than those whose property values are diminished by regulation? Compare Saul Levmore, Takings, Torts, and Special Interests, 77 Va. L. Rev. 1333 (1991) (victims of physical takings are unlikely to be well represented in political process because they are an unorganized "ad hoc" group, face significant organizational hurdles, and are not repeat players in the political realm who can ally with other groups), with Daniel A. Farber, Public Choice and Just Compensation, 9 Const. Comment. 279, 289 (1992) (victims of physical takings are better able to organize than taxpayers at large because they are usually few in number, have high stakes, and share a geographical connection that will aid organization). See also Jeffry A. Frieden, Towards a Political Economy of Takings, 3 Wash. U. J.L. & Pol'y 137, 138, 146 (2000); Henry A. Span, Public Choice Theory and the Political Utility of the Takings Clause, 40 Idaho L. Rev. 11, 30 (2003).

5. *Dodge ball?* Noting the debate among the process theorists about physical invasions, Professor Krier asserts: "Rather than advancing the ball, Fischel, and the process theorists generally, tend instead just to move it laterally: disputes and disagreements that might

before have been framed in one set of terms (for example, does a particular regulation 'go too far'?) will now, at most, be framed in another set (was the political process 'working' here?) about which there is likely to be little (if any) more consensus than before." James E. Krier, Takings from Freund to Fischel, 84 Geo. L.J. 1895, 1911 (1996) (book review). What defense might the process theorists offer to that charge?

6. *Process theories generally.* For critiques of process theories in general, see, e.g., Daniel R. Ortiz, Pursuing a Perfect Politics: The Allure and Failure of Process Theory, 77 Va. L. Rev. 721 (1991); Laurence H. Tribe, The Puzzling Persistence of Process-Based Constitutional Theories, 89 Yale L.J. 1063, 1065–72 (1980).

d.   *The Ad Hoc Balancing Test*

Penn Central Transportation Co. v. City of New York
438 U.S. 104 (1978)

Mr. Justice BRENNAN delivered the opinion of the Court.

The question presented is whether a city may, as part of a comprehensive program to preserve historic landmarks and historic districts, place restrictions on the development of individual historic landmarks — in addition to those imposed by applicable zoning ordinances — without effecting a "taking" requiring the payment of "just compensation." . . .

I

A

Over the past 50 years, all 50 States and over 500 municipalities have enacted laws to encourage or require the preservation of buildings and areas with historic or aesthetic importance. . . .

New York City, responding to similar concerns and acting pursuant to a New York State enabling act, adopted its Landmarks Preservation Law in 1965. See New York City Charter and Administrative Code, ch. 8-A, §205–1.0 et seq. (1976). . . .

The New York City law is typical of many urban landmark laws in that its primary method of achieving its goals is not by acquisitions of historic properties,[6] but rather by involving public entities in land use decisions affecting these properties and providing services, standards, controls, and incentives that will encourage preservation by private owners and users. . . .

. . . The primary responsibility for administering the Act is vested in the Landmarks Preservation Commission (Commission). . . . The Commission first . . . [identifies] properties and areas that have "a special character or special historical or aesthetic interest or value as part of the development, heritage, or cultural characteristics of the city, state or nation." §207–1.0(n); see §207–1.0(h). If the Commission determines, after giving all interested parties an opportunity to be heard, that a building or area satisfies the ordinance's

---

6. The consensus is that widespread public ownership of historic properties in urban settings is neither feasible nor wise. Public ownership reduces the tax base, burdens the public budget with costs of acquisitions and maintenance and results in the preservation of public buildings as museums and similar facilities, rather than as economically productive features of the urban scene. See Wilson & Winkler, The Response of State Legislation to Historic Preservation, 36 Law & Contemp. Prob. 329, 330–331, 339–340 (1971).

criteria, it will designate a building to be a "landmark," . . . or will designate an area to be a "historic district." . . .

Final designation as a landmark results in restrictions upon the property owner's options concerning use of the landmark site. . . . [T]he Commission must approve in advance any proposal to alter the exterior architectural features of the landmark or to construct any exterior improvement on the landmark site, thus ensuring that decisions concerning construction on the landmark site are made with due consideration of both the public interest in the maintenance of the structure and the landowner's interest in use of the property.

. . . [T]hree separate procedures are available through which administrative approval may be obtained. First, the owner may apply to the Commission for a "certificate of no effect on protected architectural features"; that is, for an order approving the improvement or alteration on the ground that it will not change or affect any architectural feature of the landmark and will be in harmony therewith. . . .

Second, the owner may apply to the Commission for a certificate of "appropriateness." Such certificates will be granted if the Commission concludes — focusing upon aesthetic, historical, and architectural values — that the proposed construction on the landmark site would not unduly hinder the protection, enhancement, perpetuation, and use of the landmark. . . . The final procedure — seeking a certificate of appropriateness on the ground of "insufficient return," — provides special mechanisms, which vary depending on whether or not the landmark enjoys a tax exemption, to ensure that designation does not cause economic hardship.

Although the designation of a landmark and landmark site restricts the owner's control over the parcel, designation also enhances the economic position of the landmark owner in one significant respect. Under New York City's zoning laws, owners of real property who have not developed their property to the full extent permitted by the applicable zoning laws are allowed to transfer development rights to [certain other nearby parcels].

B

This case involves the application of New York City's Landmark Preservation Law to Grand Central Terminal (Terminal). The Terminal, which is owned by the Penn Central Transportation Company and its affiliates (Penn Central), is one of New York City's most famous buildings. Opened in 1913, it is regarded not only as providing an ingenious engineering solution to the problems presented by urban railroad stations, but also as a magnificent example of the French Beaux Arts style.

The Terminal is located in midtown Manhattan. . . . Although a 20-story office tower, to have been located above the Terminal, was part of the original design, the planned tower was never constructed. The Terminal itself is an eight-story structure which Penn Central uses as a railroad station and in which it rents space not needed for railroad purposes to a variety of commercial interests. . . .

On August 2, 1967, following a public hearing, the Commission designated the Terminal a "landmark." . . . Although appellant Penn Central had opposed the designation before the Commission, it did not seek judicial review of the final designation decision.

On January 22, 1968, appellant Penn Central, to increase its income, entered into a renewable 50-year lease and sublease agreement with appellant UGP Properties, Inc. (UGP). . . . Under the terms of the agreement, UGP was to construct a multistory office building above the Terminal. . . .

Appellants UGP and Penn Central then applied to the Commission for permission to construct an office building atop the Terminal. Two separate plans, both designed by architect Marcel Breuer and both apparently satisfying the terms of the applicable zoning ordinance, were submitted to the Commission for approval. The first, Breuer I, provided for the construction of a 55-story office building, to be cantilevered above the existing facade and to rest on the roof of the Terminal. The second, Breuer II Revised, called for tearing down a portion of the Terminal that included the 42nd Street facade, stripping off some of the remaining features of the Terminal's facade, and constructing a 53-story office building. The Commission denied a certificate of no exterior effect on September 20, 1968. Appellants then applied for a certificate of "appropriateness" as to both proposals. After four days of hearings at which over 80 witnesses testified, the Commission denied this application as to both proposals.

The Commission's reasons for rejecting certificates respecting Breuer II Revised are summarized in the following statement: "To protect a landmark, one does not tear it down. To perpetuate its architectural features, one does not strip them off." Record 2255. Breuer I, which would have preserved the existing vertical facades of the present structure, received more sympathetic consideration. The Commission first focused on the effect that the proposed tower would have on one desirable feature created by the present structure and its surroundings: the dramatic view of the Terminal from Park Avenue South. Although appellants had contended that the Pan Am Building had already destroyed the silhouette of the south facade and that one additional tower could do no further damage and might even provide a better background for the facade, the Commission disagreed, stating that it found the majestic approach from the south to be still unique in the city and that a 55-story tower atop the Terminal would be far more detrimental to its south facade than the Pan Am Building 375 feet away. Moreover, the Commission found that from closer vantage points, the Pan Am Building and the other towers were largely cut off from view, which would not be the case of the mass on top of the Terminal planned under Breuer I. . . .

Appellants did not seek judicial review of the denial of either certificate. . . . Instead, appellants filed suit in New York Supreme Court, Trial Term, claiming, inter alia, that the application of the Landmarks Preservation Law had "taken" their property without just compensation in violation of the Fifth and Fourteenth Amendment and arbitrarily deprived them of their property without Due Process of Law in violation of the Fourteenth Amendment. Appellants sought a declaratory judgment, injunctive relief barring the city from using the Landmarks Law to impede the construction of any structure that may otherwise lawfully be constructed on the Terminal site, and damages for the "temporary taking" that occurred between August 2, 1967, the designation date, and the date when the restrictions arising from the Landmarks Law are lifted. The trial court granted the injunctive and declaratory relief, but severed the question of damages for a "temporary taking." . . .

[The New York Appellate Division reversed the trial court's grant of injunctive and declaratory relief. The New York Court of Appeals affirmed that reversal. Penn Central then appealed to the Supreme Court.]

. . . We affirm.

II

The issues presented by appellants are (1) whether the restrictions imposed by New York City's law upon appellants' exploitation of the Terminal site effect a "taking" of appellants' property for a public use within the meaning of the Fifth Amendment, which of course is made applicable to the States through the Fourteenth Amendment, see Chicago B. & Q.R.R. Co. v. Chicago, 166 U.S. 226, 239 (1897) and, (2) if so, whether the transferable development rights afforded appellants constitute "just compensation" within the meaning of the Fifth Amendment. We need only address the question whether a "taking" has occurred.[25]

Only need to address the first 2

A

. . . The question of what constitutes a "taking" for purposes of the Fifth Amendment has proved to be a problem of considerable difficulty. While this Court has recognized that the "Fifth Amendment's guarantee [is] designed to bar Government from forcing some people alone to bear public burdens which, in all fairness and justice, should be borne by the public as a whole," Armstrong v. United States, 364 U.S. 40, 49 (1960), this Court, quite simply, has been unable to develop any "set formula" for determining when "justice and fairness" require that economic injuries caused by public action be compensated by the Government, rather than remain disproportionately concentrated on a few persons. See Goldblatt v. Town of Hempstead, 369 U.S. 590 (1962). Indeed, we have frequently observed that whether a particular restriction will be rendered invalid by the Government's failure to pay for any losses proximately caused by it depends largely "upon the particular circumstances [in that] case." United States v. Central Eureka Mining Co., 357 U.S. 155, 168 (1958).

have been unable to develop a set formula

largely depends on particular circumstances of the case

In engaging in these essentially ad hoc, factual inquiries, the Court's decisions have identified several factors that have particular significance. The economic impact of the regulation on the claimant and, particularly, the extent to which the regulation has interfered with distinct investment backed expectations are of course relevant considerations. See Goldblatt, supra, 369 U.S. at 594. So too is the character of the governmental action. A "taking" may more readily be found when the interference with property can be characterized as a physical invasion by Government . . . than when interference arises from some public program adjusting the benefits and burdens of economic life to promote the common good. . . .

easier to find a taking where it's physical vs public program

. . . [A]ppellants do not challenge any of the specific factual premises of the decision below. They accept for present purposes both that the parcel of land occupied by Grand Central Terminal must, in its present state, be regarded as capable of earning a reasonable return, and that the transferable development rights afforded appellants by virtue of the Terminal's designation as a landmark are valuable, even if not as valuable as the rights to construct above the Terminal. In appellants' view none of these factors derogate from their claim that New York City's law has effected a "taking."

Ps → air use is valuable + the law prevents us from using it

They first observe that the air space above the Terminal is a valuable property interest. . . . They urge that the Landmarks Law has deprived them of any gainful use of their "air rights" above the Terminal and that, irrespective of the value of the remainder of their parcel, the city has "taken" their right to this superadjacent air space, thus entitling them to "just compensation" measured by the fair market value of these air rights.

. . . [T]he submission that appellants may establish a "taking" simply by showing that they have been denied the ability to exploit a property interest that they heretofore had believed was available for development is quite simply untenable. . . . "Taking" jurisprudence does not divide a single parcel into discrete segments and attempt to determine whether rights in a particular segment have been entirely abrogated. In deciding whether a particular governmental action has effected a taking, this Court focuses rather both on the character of the action and on the nature and extent of the interference with rights in the parcel as a whole, here, the city tax block designated as the "landmark site."

CT says not good enough to say taking occurs where you've been denied the right to exploit a prop. interest

25. As is implicit in our opinion, we do not embrace the proposition that a "taking" can never occur unless Government has transferred physical control over a portion of a parcel.

Secondly, appellants, focusing on the character and impact of the New York City law, argue that it effects a "taking" because its operation has significantly diminished the value of the Terminal site. Appellants concede that the decisions sustaining other land-use regulations, which, like the New York law, are reasonably related to the promotion of the general welfare, uniformly reject the proposition that diminution in property value, standing alone, can establish a taking, see Village of Euclid v. Ambler Realty Co., [272 U.S. 365 (1926)] (75% diminution in value caused by zoning law). . . .

. . . It is of course true that the Landmarks Law has a more severe impact on some landowners than on others, but that in itself does not mean that the law effects a "taking." Legislation designed to promote the general welfare commonly burdens some more than others. . . . [30] . . .

In any event, appellants' repeated suggestions that they are solely burdened and unbenefited is factually inaccurate. This contention overlooks the fact that the New York City law applies to vast numbers of structures in the city in addition to the Terminal — all the structures contained in the 31 historic districts and over 400 individual landmarks, many of which are close to the Terminal. Unless we are to reject the judgment of the New York City Council that the preservation of landmarks benefit all New York citizens and all structures, both economically and by improving the quality of life in the city as a whole — which we are unwilling to do — we cannot conclude that the owners of the Terminal have in no sense been benefited by the Landmarks Law. Doubtless appellants believe they are more burdened than benefited by the law, but that must have been true too of the property owners in . . . *Hadacheck* [v. Sebastian, 239 U.S. 394 (1915)], *Euclid*, and [other cases in which a taking was not found]. . . .

C

. . . We now must consider whether the interference with appellants' property is of such a magnitude that "there must be an exercise of eminent domain and compensation to sustain [it]." Pennsylvania Coal Co. [v. Mahon, 260 U.S. 393, 413 (1922)]. That inquiry may be narrowed to the question of the severity of the impact of the law on appellants' parcel, and its resolution in turn requires a careful assessment of the impact of the regulation on the Terminal site.

. . . [T]he New York City law does not interfere in any way with the present uses of the Terminal. Its designation as a landmark not only permits but contemplates that appellants may continue to use the property precisely as it has for the past 65 years: as a railroad terminal containing office space and concessions. So the law does not interfere with what must be regarded as Penn Central's primary expectation concerning the use of the parcel. More importantly, on this record, we must regard the New York City law as

30. Appellants attempt to distinguish these cases on the ground that, in each, Government was prohibiting a "noxious" use of land and that in the present case, in contrast, appellants' proposed construction above the Terminal would be beneficial. We observe that the uses in issue in *Hadacheck* . . . were perfectly lawful in themselves. They involved no "blameworthiness, . . . moral wrongdoing, or conscious act of dangerous risk-taking which induce[d society] to shift the cost to a particular individual." Sax, Takings and the Police Power, 74 Yale L.J. 36, 50 (1964). These cases are better understood as resting not on any supposed "noxious" quality of the prohibited uses but rather on the ground that the restrictions were reasonably related to the implementation of a policy — not unlike historic preservation — expected to produce a widespread public benefit and applicable to all similarly situated property.

Nor, correlatively, can it be asserted that the destruction or fundamental alteration of a historic landmark is not harmful. The suggestion that the beneficial quality of appellants' proposed construction is established by the fact the construction would have been consistent with applicable zoning laws ignores the development in sensibilities and ideals reflected in landmark legislation like New York City's.

— P profits + obtains a reasonable return on its investment

permitting Penn Central not only to profit from the Terminal but to obtain a "reasonable return" on its investment.

Appellants, moreover, exaggerate the effect of the Act on its ability to make use of the air rights above the Terminal in two respects. First, . . . [s]ince appellants have not sought approval for the construction of a smaller structure, we do not know that appellants will be denied any use of any portion of the airspace above the Terminal.

Second, to the extent appellants have been denied the right to build above the Terminal, it is not literally accurate to say that they have been denied all use of even those pre-existing air rights. Their ability to use these rights has not been abrogated; they are made transferable to at least eight parcels in the vicinity of the Terminal, one or two of which have been found suitable for the construction of new office buildings. Although appellants and others have argued that New York City's transferable development rights program is far from ideal, the New York courts here supportably found that, at least in the case of the Terminal, the rights afforded are valuable. While these rights may well not have constituted "just compensation" if a "taking" had occurred, the rights nevertheless undoubtedly mitigate whatever financial burdens the law has imposed on appellants and, for that reason, are to be taken into account in considering the impact of regulation. . . .

On this record we conclude that the application of New York City's Landmarks Preservation Law has not effected a "taking" of appellants' property. The restrictions imposed are substantially related to the promotion of the general welfare and not only permit reasonable beneficial use of the landmark site but afford appellants opportunities further to enhance not only the Terminal site proper but also other properties.[36]

Law has not effected a taking of the property

Affirmed.

Mr. Justice REHNQUIST, with whom THE CHIEF JUSTICE and Mr. Justice STEVENS join, dissenting. . . .

Note on *Penn Central*

1. *The economic impact of the regulation.* Why is the extent of the diminution in value, to use the language of *Mahon*, or the economic impact of the regulation, to use Justice Brennan's formulation, relevant to whether there has been a taking, as opposed to the calculation of compensation due? Does the Fifth Amendment allow the government to take a little, but not a lot?

The Supreme Court decided in 1992 that a 100 percent diminution of value falls outside the *Penn Central* balancing test and always will require compensation unless the regulation simply codifies already inherent limitations on the owner's title. See Lucas v. South Carolina Coastal Council, 505 U.S. 1003 (1992), excerpted at p. 169. Anything short of a 100 percent diminution, however, must be decided within *Penn Central's* framework. The extent of diminution in value depends, of course, on the size of the denominator in the fraction. As *Penn Central* recognizes, how the court defines the property that should serve as the denominator is therefore critical. We'll return to that subject at pp. 185-93.

---

36. We emphasize that our holding today is on the present record which in turn is based on Penn Central's present ability to use the Terminal for its intended purposes and in a gainful fashion. The city conceded at oral argument that if appellants can demonstrate at some point in the future that circumstances have changed such that the Terminal ceases to be, in the city's counsel's words, "economically viable," appellants may obtain relief. See Tr. of Oral Arg. 42-43.

In considering the economic impact of the regulation, should the courts focus on the percentage of value lost or on the absolute dollar amount lost? Is loss of 50 percent of the $10,000 value of a plot of land more harmful to its owner than the loss of $5,000 on a property worth $1 million? Does the percentage diminution in value factor disfavor owners with deeper pockets?

In measuring the economic impact, should the courts compare the property's current market value as restricted by the regulation to its current market value if the regulation was not imposed on the property? Or is the correct comparison between the price the owner originally paid for the property and the property's current market value as restricted? See, e.g., Walcek v. United States, 303 F.3d 1349 (Fed. Cl. 2002) (approving the second comparison). These issues are discussed more fully at pp. 267–74 because they arise most clearly when courts are determining how much compensation is due once a taking has been established.

2. *The character of the governmental action.* At the time *Penn Central* was decided, the cases in which the plaintiff had successfully invoked the Takings Clause, other than *Pennsylvania Coal*, had involved physical invasions (or "constructive" physical invasions) of the plaintiff's property. Justice Brennan's inclusion of the "character of the governmental action" in the balancing test therefore can be understood as weighting the scales to account for the historically special character of physical occupations or intrusions onto land. Several years after *Penn Central*, however, the Court took many physical invasions out of the ad hoc analysis by announcing that permanent physical occupations of land are such an affront to the rights of the landowner that they always count as a taking. Loretto v. Teleprompter Manhattan CATV Corp., 458 U.S. 419 (1982), discussed at pp. 167–69.

In light of *Loretto*, then, the "character of the governmental action" prong of *Penn Central* has lost its mooring. It sometimes is invoked to examine more carefully regulations that the court considers most closely analogous to physical occupations. See, e.g., Cienega Gardens v. United States, 331 F.3d 1319, 1338 (Fed. Cir. 2003) (federal statute preventing owners of low-income apartments from prepaying their federally subsidized mortgages to free themselves from regulatory restrictions governing the mortgages effected a taking, because the statute is "akin" to a physical invasion whereby the government "effectively rented apartment buildings from the owners beyond the term of the agreed leasehold and then sublet apartments to low-income tenants"). The prong sometimes is used to scrutinize the nature of the government's purpose in imposing the challenged regulation. See, e.g., Keystone Bituminous Coal Ass'n v. DeBenedictis, 480 U.S. 470, 485 (1987), discussed at p. 145 ("[T]he character of the governmental action involved here leans heavily against finding a taking; the Commonwealth of Pennsylvania has acted to arrest what it perceives to be a significant threat to the common welfare."). The Supreme Court also has invoked the prong to examine the causal relationship between a property owner's conduct and the burden imposed by the challenged regulation. See Eastern Enterprises v. Apfel, 524 U.S. 498 (1998) (plurality opinion). Some have suggested that the character prong should focus on whether the regulation targets one or a few landowners or instead applies broadly across the community. John D. Echeverria, Georgetown Environmental Law & Policy Institute "Top Ten" Takings Issues, SJ086 ALI-ABA 297, 303 (2004). Increasingly, for reasons that will become clear following the discussion of Lucas v. South Carolina Coastal Council (U.S. 1992), excerpted at p. 169, the prong is used in the lower federal courts to examine the relationship between the challenged regulation and nuisance law. See Steven J. Eagle, "Character of the Governmental Action" in Takings Law: Past, Present, and Future, SJ052 ALI-ABA 459 (2004).

3. *Interference with "distinct investment-backed expectations."* What are investment-backed expectations? Do gifts or inheritances count? See Hodel v. Irving, 481 U.S. 704, 715

(1987) (striking law prohibiting devise or intestate succession of certain fractionated Indian lands, but noting in dicta that because almost all of the owners had acquired their interests by gift, descent, or devise, it was "dubious" that any had "investment-backed expectations in passing on [the] property").

For helpful discussions of the notion of reasonable investment-backed expectations, or "RIBE," see, e.g., Daniel R. Mandelker, Investment-Backed Expectations in Taking Law, 27 Urb. Law. 215 (1995); Lynda J. Oswald, Cornering the Quark: Investment-Backed Expectations and Economically Viable Uses in Takings Analysis, 70 Wash. L. Rev. 91 (1995); Robert M. Washburn, "Reasonable Investment Backed Expectations" as a Factor in Defining Property Interest, 49 Wash. U. J. Urb. & Contemp. L. 63 (1996). For excellent reviews of all the *Penn Central* factors, and takings jurisprudence in general, see Robert Meltz et al., The Takings Issue (1999). For a treatise on takings, see Jan G. Laitos, Law of Property Rights Protection (1998 & Supp. 2004).

4. *Coming to the taking.* Can a property owner who invests in property knowing that the government has adopted or is likely to adopt a regulation that would diminish the value of the property claim a RIBE? Compare the doctrine of self-created hardship in the law of variances (see p. 293); compare also the "coming to the nuisance" doctrine (see pp. 525–28). We'll return to this issue at pp. 180–85.

Note on Transferable Development Rights

1. *What are they?* Think of the maximum development potential of a building lot as a three-dimensional mold, with height, width, and depth. If a building fits within this mold or "envelope" with room to spare, by being only 5 stories high when the envelope allows 20 stories, for example, the building has unused development potential. The concept of transferable development rights (TDRs) permits the transfer of that unused potential to other buildings that are bursting at the seams of their envelope. Similarly, if a tract of land is currently undeveloped, although zoned for two units per acre, a TDR program would allow the unused potential to be transferred to some tract for which a developer wanted to build beyond the allowed density.

2. Penn Central's *tortured efforts to use those TDRs.* In 1979, Penn Central transferred 74,665 square feet of air rights to Philip Morris Inc. for a 26-story building across from Grand Central. Penn Central then sought to sell 800,000 square feet of air rights to the First Boston Corp., which planned to erect a 72-story building on Madison Avenue between 46th and 47th Streets. The City objected, disputing the number of air rights that Penn Central owned and its right to transfer the rights to the 46th Street parcel. Under New York's zoning ordinance, TDRs could be transferred to lots that were contiguous to, catercornered from, or directly facing the transferor parcel. In addition, TDRs could be transferred to "any chain of adjacent lots in the same ownership as the landmark site." Penn Central argued that the 46th Street parcel was in a chain of adjacent lots because Penn Central owned subsurface lots (which housed train tracks and other such facilities) that ran from Grand Central to the 46th Street parcel (and indeed, all the way to Yonkers, north of the City). The City insisted that subsurface lots were not what the zoning resolution had in mind as a "chain of adjacent lots." The City also asserted that even if the subsurface rights could satisfy the transferral requirements, the proposal nevertheless would have to be denied because the planned tower was just too big.

Penn Central sued, and four days later, the City came forward with a proposal to more than double the area to which the TDRs could be transferred, but to cap the number of rights that could be transferred to any one site. In 1992, the City formally adopted the plan, creating a midtown "subdistrict" that would allow Penn Central's TDRs to be transferred to 21 different lots. Finally, in January 1999, the City Planning Commission approved the transfer of 285,865 square feet of development rights to the 46th Street lot, 383 Madison Avenue. The transfer allowed a 44 percent increase in the square footage of the 45-story Bear Stearns building built on the lot. Another 67,679 square feet were transferred to the CIBC World Markets building at 300 Madison Avenue; and 19,582 square feet were transferred to 360 Madison Avenue. In 2003, the current owner of the remaining 1,264,364 square feet of TDRs, American Financial of Cincinnati, valued those rights at between $50 and $60 million.

For the saga of the air rights, see Harry Berkowitz, City Backs Air Rights Transfer, Newsday, Nov. 4, 1989, at 6; Michael H. Cottman, Manhattan Neighborhoods, Newsday, July 7, 1992, at 25; David W. Dunlap, 25 Years Ago, Landmarks Law Stopped a Skyscraper, N.Y. Times, June 26, 2003, at B3; David Dunlap, Builders Lose Bid to Transfer Air Rights, N.Y. Times, Aug. 24, 1989, at B1; Martin Gottlieb, Zoning Fight Again Imperils Grand Central, N.Y. Times, Oct. 14, 1986, at B1; Steven D. Kowaloff, Grand Central Zoning Game: Project Symbolized Contest Between City and Developer, N.Y.L.J., Sept. 20, 1989, at 33.

3. *No taking, or just compensation?* The Supreme Court confronted TDRs again in *Suitum v. Tahoe Regional Planning Agency*, 520 U.S. 725 (1997). Mrs. Suitum alleged that regulations foreclosing development of her property near Lake Tahoe effected a taking, regardless of the availability of TDRs, which she had never attempted to use. The Ninth Circuit held the claim was not ripe (for discussion of the ripeness requirements for takings challenges, see pp. 234-51). In the Supreme Court, the majority's opinion focused on the ripeness issue, holding that the property owner did not need to try to sell or transfer the TDRs to bring her claim. The concurring opinion of Justice Scalia, joined by Justices O'Connor and Thomas, however, tackled the issue lurking in *Penn Central*:

> Just as a cash payment from the government would not relate to whether the regulation "goes too far" (i.e., restricts use of the land so severely as to constitute a taking), but rather to whether there has been adequate compensation for the taking; . . . so also the marketable TDR, a peculiar type of chit which enables a third party not to get cash from the government but to use his land in ways the government would otherwise not permit, relates not to taking but to compensation. . . .
>
> Putting TDRs on the taking rather than the just compensation side of the equation (as the Ninth Circuit did below) is a clever, albeit transparent, device that seeks to take advantage of a peculiarity of our takings clause jurisprudence: Whereas once there is a taking, the Constitution requires just (i.e., full) compensation, a regulatory taking generally does not occur so long as the land retains substantial (albeit not its full) value. If money that the government regulator gives to the landowner can be counted on the question of whether there is a taking (causing the courts to say that the land retains substantial value, and has thus not been taken), rather than on the question of whether the compensation for the taking is adequate, the government can get away with paying much less. That is all that is going on here. . . .

Id. at 747-48 (Scalia, J., concurring). Justice Scalia distinguished *Penn Central* on the ground that the challenger there owned at least some of the lots to which the TDRs could be transferred. The relevant property therefore could be said to be an aggregation of the owners' parcels subject to the regulation (or at least the contiguous parcels), and the use of that land, as a whole, had not been diminished. Justice Scalia added: "If Penn Central's one-paragraph expedition into the realm of TDRs were not distinguishable in this fashion, it would deserve to be overruled." Id. at 749. For helpful analyses of *Suitum*, see, e.g., James

E. Holloway & Donald C. Guy, The Utility and Validity of TDRs Under the Takings Clause and the Role of TDRs in the Takings Equation Under Legal Theory, 11 Penn St. Envtl. L. Rev. 45 (2002); Andrew J. Miller, Transferable Development Rights in the Constitutional Landscape: Has *Penn Central* Failed to Weather the Storm?, 39 Nat. Resources J. 459 (1999).

4. *Obtaining compensation funds from TDR purchasers.* However the debate that surfaced in *Suitum* eventually comes out, a TDR program can produce another set of Constitution-quoting plaintiffs — the owners of land in the receiving area. These owners may assert that a TDR program is essentially a way for a city to raise funds by selling zoning in the receiving district. The city must make TDRs valuable to beat back constitutional challenges by transferors. To make TDRs valuable, the city may restrict permitted densities in the receiving area below what the city otherwise would have been willing to permit. Receiving-district landowners therefore might argue that the extra restrictions they face were adopted for purely fiscal purposes (cf. pp. 133–34), and that they have been unfairly singled out to finance a program of no particular benefit to them (cf. the discussion of exactions at pp. 634–78).

Barancik v. County of Marin, 872 F.2d 834 (9th Cir. 1988), offers scant hope to landowners in receiving areas, however. The county's zoning had restricted residential development in a ranching region to one unit per 60 acres, but did designate the region a receiving area for TDRs. A rancher who sought to develop one unit per 20 acres was unable to purchase the needed TDRs from neighbors. The rancher also fruitlessly applied for a rezoning to permit development at one unit per 20 acres. Exasperated, the rancher challenged the county's denial of rezoning on substantive due process grounds, but the court held the county's TDR program to be rationally related to its conservation goals. See also Fisher v. Giuliani, 720 N.Y.S.2d 50 (App. Div. 2001) (rejecting challenge by receiving area that TDR scheme was not within scope of legitimate zoning power). For analysis of how such receiving area claims should be evaluated, see Matthew C. Garvey, Student Article, When Political Muscle Is Enough: The Case for Limited Judicial Review of Long Distance Transfers of Development Rights, 11 N.Y.U. Envtl. L.J. 798 (2003).

5. *Realpolitik.* TDR systems typically funnel part of a city's potential proceeds from its land use control system into outlays for the preservation of open space or historic buildings. These "expenditures" are not easily detected or controlled by legislators or voters. To what extent are advocates of TDRs drawn to the technique because they fear that it is politically impossible to persuade politicians to appropriate much general revenue for these purposes? Land use policymakers probably place more value on physical amenities than ordinary citizens do. If so, it would not be surprising if these policymakers favored devices that channel municipal benefits from land use controls into spending on physical amenities, as opposed to, say, spending on social services.

6. *Bibliography.* For further reading, see Dorothy J. Glancy, Preserving Rockefeller Center, 24 Urb. Law. 423 (1992); Conrad Julian Juergensmeyer et al., Transferable Development Rights and Alternatives After *Suitum*, 30 Urb. Law. 441, 456–57 (1998); James T.B. Tripp & Daniel J. Dudek, Institutional Guidelines for Designing Successful Transferable Rights Programs, 6 Yale J. Reg. 369 (1989).

e. *Per Se Takings — Exceptions to* Penn Central

Just a few years after announcing the balancing test of *Penn Central*, the Supreme Court seemed to change course in Loretto v. Teleprompter Manhattan CATV Corp., 458 U.S.

419 (1982). *Loretto* involved a challenge to a New York law requiring landlords to permit cable television companies to install cable equipment on their buildings. Although the equipment amounted only to approximately 36 feet of half-inch cable on the side of Ms. Loretto's townhouse, and two 4-inch by 4-inch metal boxes on the roof, the Court held that a permanent physical occupation of property by a third party authorized by government regulation always is a taking, "without regard to whether the action achieves an important public benefit or has only minimal economic impact on the owner." Id. at 434–35. The majority opinion, authored by Justice Marshall, based the holding upon the long line of cases that it interpreted to "consider a physical intrusion by government to be a property restriction of an unusually serious character." Id. at 427. The Court also reasoned that a permanent physical occupation "effectively destroys" each of the rights to possess, use, and dispose of the affected property. Id. at 435. Such occupations are, the Court asserted, "qualitatively more severe than a regulation of the use of property." Id. at 436. Further, permanent physical occupations "present relatively few problems of proof," thereby rendering the application of the multi-factored *Penn Central* test unnecessary. Id. at 437.

Justice Blackmun wrote a caustic dissent, joined by Justice Brennan and Justice White, arguing that the cable requirement is indistinguishable from "other garden-variety landlord-tenant legislation" such as requirements that landlords install locks or fire protection systems in their rental property, and that the opinion therefore threatens a vast array of regulations. Id. at 442, 452 (Blackmun, J., dissenting).

Note on the Per Se Rule Against Permanent Physical Occupations

1. *Hollow victory?* On remand from the Supreme Court's decision in *Loretto*, the New York Court of Appeals upheld the portion of the challenged statute that authorized the Commission on Cable Television to determine what compensation was due landlords. The Commission made only nominal awards of $1, reasoning that the presence of cable television usually increased, rather than decreased, a building's value. The Commission rejected Loretto's argument that "just compensation" should be the amount customarily paid to landlords before the adoption of the statute, which was 5 percent of Teleprompter's gross revenues. Loretto v. Teleprompter Manhattan CATV Corp., 446 N.E.2d 428 (N.Y. 1983). Was the $1 in compensation inadequate, or was Loretto trying to use her locational advantage to "hold up" Teleprompter? See also Loretto v. Group W. Cable, 522 N.Y.S.2d 543 (App. Div. 1987) (denying Loretto's claim for attorney fees as the prevailing party).

Should courts separate the question of whether compensation is required from the question of how much compensation is due, as the *Loretto* Court did? Compare Brown v. Legal Foundation of Washington, 538 U.S. 216 (2003) (law requiring lawyers to place client funds that could not otherwise generate earnings into a special account, then requiring that the interest on that account be used to fund programs providing legal services for the poor did not violate the Takings Clause because compensation should be measured by what is lost to the property owner, not what is gained by the legal services program, and the property owner lost nothing).

2. *Shoehorning claims into the physical takings category.* The dissenting opinion in *Loretto* warned that the majority's opinion would "encourage litigants to manipulate their factual allegations . . . to shoehorn insubstantial takings claims into [the per se rule's] 'set formula.'" 458 U.S at 451. Consistent with that prediction, litigants began to claim that various landlord-tenant regulations, such as mobile home rent control, constituted

"permanent physical invasions" by the protected tenant. See, e.g., Hall v. City of Santa Barbara, 833 F.2d 1270 (9th Cir. 1986) (plaintiffs stated a claim for a physical taking by alleging that the rent control ordinance transferred a possessory interest in the land to tenants). The Supreme Court then clarified *Loretto* in Federal Communications Commission v. Florida Power Corp., 480 U.S. 245 (1987). Rejecting a claim by the owners of utility poles that the Federal Communications Commission's regulation of the rent the utilities could charge to carry cable television cables on their poles effected a physical taking, the Court distinguished *Loretto* because nothing in the FCC regulations "gives cable companies any right to occupy space on utility poles, or prohibits utility companies from refusing to enter into attachment agreements with cable operators." Id. at 251. The Court held: "The line which separates these cases from *Loretto* is the unambiguous distinction between a commercial lessee and an interloper with a government license." Id. at 252–53.

Nevertheless, litigants continued to try to bring their challenges within *Loretto*, and a few courts accepted the ploy. See, e.g., Seawall Associates v. City of New York, 542 N.E.2d 1059 (N.Y. 1989) (ordinance prohibiting demolition or warehousing of single-room occupancy housing and requiring owners to restore and lease the housing at controlled rents constituted a physical invasion and therefore required compensation).

The Supreme Court put a more decisive end to the foray, however, in Yee v. City of Escondido, 503 U.S. 519 (1992), in which mobile home park owners claimed that a rent control ordinance effected a physical taking:

> The government effects a physical taking only where it requires the landowner to submit to the physical occupation of his land. . . .
>
>   But the Escondido rent control ordinance . . . authorizes no such thing. Petitioners voluntarily rented their land to mobile home owners. . . . Put bluntly, no government has required any physical invasion of petitioners' property. Petitioners' tenants were invited by petitioners, not forced upon them by the government. . . .
>
>   . . . A different case would be presented were the statute, on its face or as applied, to compel a landowner over objection to rent his property or to refrain in perpetuity from terminating a tenancy. . . .

Id. at 527–28.

Aggressive and creative lawyers continue to try to push the boundaries of the physical occupation per se rule, however, and sometimes succeed. The Supreme Court accepted one such stratagem in Brown v. Legal Foundation of Washington, supra, finding that a requirement that interest earned on accounts containing client funds that could not generate income for their owners be used to fund programs to provide legal services to the poor was "akin to the occupation of a small amount of rooftop space in *Loretto*" and therefore subject to *Loretto*'s per se rule. 538 U.S. at 234.

Lucas v. South Carolina Coastal Council
505 U.S. 1003 (1992)

Justice SCALIA delivered the opinion of the Court.

In 1986, petitioner David H. Lucas paid $975,000 for two residential lots on the Isle of Palms in Charleston County, South Carolina, on which he intended to build single-family homes. In 1988, however, the South Carolina Legislature enacted the Beachfront Management Act, S.C. Code §48-39-250 et seq. (Supp. 1990) (Act), which had the direct effect of barring petitioner from erecting any permanent habitable structures on his two parcels. A state trial court found that this prohibition rendered Lucas's parcels "valueless." This case requires us to decide whether the Act's dramatic effect on the economic value of Lucas's lots accomplished a taking of private property under the Fifth and Fourteenth Amendments requiring the payment of "just compensation."

I

A

. . . In the late 1970's, Lucas and others began extensive residential development of the Isle of Palms, a barrier island situated eastward of the City of Charleston. Toward the close of the development cycle for one residential subdivision known as "Beachwood East," Lucas in 1986 purchased the two lots at issue in this litigation for his own account. . . . His intention with respect to the lots was to do what the owners of the immediately adjacent parcels had already done: erect single-family residences. . . .

The Beachfront Management Act brought Lucas's plans to an abrupt end. Under that 1988 legislation, the Council was directed to establish a "baseline" connecting the landward-most "point[s] of erosion . . . during the past forty years" in the region of the Isle of Palms that includes Lucas's lots. S.C. Code §48-39-280(A)(2). In action not challenged here, the Council fixed this baseline landward of Lucas's parcels. [See Figure 3-7 for a map showing the baseline.] That was significant, for under the Act construction of occupiable improvements was flatly prohibited seaward of a line drawn 20 feet landward of, and parallel to, the baseline. The Act provided no exceptions.

B

Lucas promptly filed suit in the South Carolina Court of Common Pleas, contending that the Beachfront Management Act's construction bar effected a taking of his property without just compensation. . . . Following a bench trial, the court agreed. Among its factual determinations was the finding that . . . the Beachfront Management Act decreed a permanent ban on construction insofar as Lucas's lots were concerned, and that this prohibition "deprive[d] Lucas of any reasonable economic use of the lots, . . . eliminated the unrestricted right of use, and render[ed] them valueless." The court thus concluded that Lucas's properties had been "taken" by operation of the Act, and it ordered respondent to pay "just compensation" in the amount of $1,232,387.50.

The Supreme Court of South Carolina reversed. . . . The Court ruled that when a regulation respecting the use of property is designed "to prevent serious public harm," Id. at 383 (citing, inter alia, Mugler v. Kansas, 123 U.S. 623 (1887)), no compensation is owing under the Takings Clause regardless of the regulation's effect on the property's value. . . .

III

A . . .

. . . In 70-odd years of succeeding "regulatory takings" jurisprudence [since Justice Holmes's decision in *Mahon*,] we have generally eschewed any "set formula" for determining how far is too far, preferring to "engag[e] in . . . essentially ad hoc, factual inquiries," Penn Cent. Transp. Co. v. City of New York, 438 U.S. 104, 124 (1978). . . . We have, however, described at least two discrete categories of regulatory action as compensable without

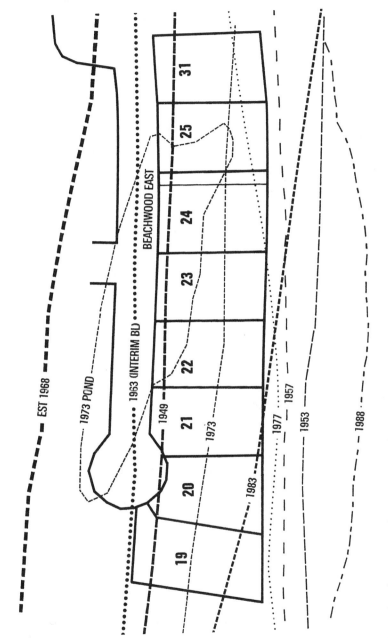

Source: Douglas R. Porter, The *Lucas* Case, Urb. Land, Sept. 1992, at 27, 29.

FIGURE 3-7

Map of the Land Involved in *Lucas*

Lucas's beachfront lots (numbers 22 and 24) are founded literally on shifting sands. Surveys along the coastline over several decades have established that the waterline has moved hundreds of feet back and forth as the beach has alternately eroded and built up. At one point, Lucas's lots lay under the surf; at another, most of his lots and the surrounding area were covered by a pool of water. In recent years, erosion has nibbled large chunks of beach away from some homesites. Moreover, the South Carolina coastline, like much of the Atlantic Coast, is extremely vulnerable to the high winds and water of frequent hurricanes.

case-specific inquiry into the public interest advanced in support of the restraint. The first encompasses regulations that compel the property owner to suffer a physical "invasion" of his property. In general (at least with regard to permanent invasions), no matter how minute the intrusion, and no matter how weighty the public purpose behind it, we have required compensation. . . .

The second situation in which we have found categorical treatment appropriate is where regulation denies all economically beneficial or productive use of land. See Agins v. City of Tiburon, 447 U.S. 255, 260 [(1980)]; . . . . As we have said on numerous occasions, the Fifth Amendment is violated when land-use regulation "does not substantially advance legitimate state interests *or denies an owner economically viable use of his land.*" Agins, supra, 447 U.S. at 260, (citations omitted) (emphasis added).[7]

We have never set forth the justification for this rule. Perhaps it is simply, as Justice Brennan suggested, that total deprivation of beneficial use is, from the landowner's point of view, the equivalent of a physical appropriation. See San Diego Gas & Elec. Co. v. City of San Diego, 450 U.S. 621, 652 (1981) (Brennan, J., dissenting). . . . Surely, at least, in the extraordinary circumstance when *no* productive or economically beneficial use of land is permitted, it is less realistic to indulge our usual assumption that the legislature is simply "adjusting the benefits and burdens of economic life," *Penn Cent. Transp. Co.*, 438 U.S. at 124, in a manner that secures an "average reciprocity of advantage" to everyone concerned. [Pennsylvania Coal Co. v. Mahon, 260 U.S. 393, 415 (1922).] And the *functional* basis for permitting the government, by regulation, to affect property values without compensation — that "Government hardly could go on if to some extent values incident to property could not be diminished without paying for every such change in the general law," id. at 413 — does not apply to the relatively rare situations where the government has deprived a landowner of all economically beneficial uses.

On the other side of the balance, affirmatively supporting a compensation requirement, is the fact that regulations that leave the owner of land without economically beneficial or productive options for its use — typically, as here, by requiring land to be left substantially in its natural state — carry with them a heightened risk that private property is being pressed into some form of public service under the guise of mitigating serious public harm. . . . The many statutes on the books, both state and federal, that provide for the use of eminent domain to impose servitudes on private scenic lands preventing developmental uses, or to acquire such lands altogether, suggest the practical equivalence in this setting of negative regulation and appropriation.

We think, in short, that there are good reasons for our frequently expressed belief that when the owner of real property has been called upon to sacrifice all economically beneficial uses in the name of the common good, that is, to leave his property economically idle, he has suffered a taking.

---

7. Regrettably, the rhetorical force of our "deprivation of all economically feasible use" rule is greater than its precision, since the rule does not make clear the "property interest" against which the loss of value is to be measured. When, for example, a regulation requires a developer to leave 90% of a rural tract in its natural state, it is unclear whether we would analyze the situation as one in which the owner has been deprived of all economically beneficial use of the burdened portion of the tract, or as one in which the owner has suffered a mere diminution in value of the tract as a whole. . . . The answer to this difficult question may lie in how the owner's reasonable expectations have been shaped by the State's law of property — i.e., whether and to what degree the State's law has accorded legal recognition and protection to the particular interest in land with respect to which the takings claimant alleges a diminution in (or elimination of) value. In any event, we avoid this difficulty in the present case, since the "interest in land" that Lucas has pleaded (a fee simple interest) is an estate with a rich tradition of protection at common law, and since the South Carolina Court of Common Pleas found that the Beachfront Management Act left each of Lucas's beachfront lots without economic value.

B

        . . . In the [South Carolina Supreme Court's] view, . . . [Lucas's concession that "discouraging new construction in close proximity to the beach/dune area is necessary to prevent a great public harm"] brought petitioner's challenge within a long line of this Court's cases sustaining against Due Process and Takings Clause challenges the State's use of its "police powers" to enjoin a property owner from activities akin to public nuisances. See Mugler v. Kansas, 123 U.S. 623 (1887). . . .

        It is correct that many of our prior opinions have suggested that "harmful or noxious uses" of property may be proscribed by government regulation without the requirement of compensation. For a number of reasons, however, we think the South Carolina Supreme Court was too quick to conclude that that principle decides the present case. . . .

        . . . [T]he distinction between "harm-preventing" and "benefit-conferring" regulation is often in the eye of the beholder. It is quite possible, for example, to describe in either fashion the ecological, economic, and aesthetic concerns that inspired the South Carolina legislature in the present case. One could say that imposing a servitude on Lucas's land is necessary in order to prevent his use of it from "harming" South Carolina's ecological resources; or, instead, in order to achieve the "benefits" of an ecological preserve. Whether one or the other of the competing characterizations will come to one's lips in a particular case depends primarily upon one's evaluation of the worth of competing uses of real estate. A given restraint will be seen as mitigating "harm" to the adjacent parcels or securing a "benefit" for them, depending upon the observer's evaluation of the relative importance of the use that the restraint favors. . . . [12]

        When it is understood that . . . the distinction between regulation that "prevents harmful use" and that which "confers benefits" is difficult, if not impossible, to discern on an objective, value-free basis[,] it becomes self-evident that noxious-use logic cannot serve as a touchstone to distinguish regulatory "takings" — which require compensation — from regulatory deprivations that do not require compensation. . . . The South Carolina Supreme Court's approach would essentially nullify *Mahon*'s affirmation of limits to the noncompensable exercise of the police power. Our cases provide no support for this: None of them that employed the logic of "harmful use" prevention to sustain a regulation involved an allegation that the regulation wholly eliminated the value of the claimant's land.

        Where the State seeks to sustain regulation that deprives land of all economically beneficial use, we think it may resist compensation only if the logically antecedent inquiry into the nature of the owner's estate shows that the proscribed use interests were not part of his title to begin with.[14] This accords, we think, with our "takings" jurisprudence, which has traditionally been guided by the understandings of our citizens regarding the content of, and the State's power over, the "bundle of rights" that they acquire when they obtain

        12. In Justice BLACKMUN's view, even with respect to regulations that deprive an owner of all developmental or economically beneficial land uses, the test for required compensation is whether the legislature has recited a harm-preventing justification for its action. Since such a justification can be formulated in practically every case, this amounts to a test of whether the legislature has a stupid staff. We think the Takings Clause requires courts to do more than insist upon artful harm-preventing characterizations.

        14. Drawing on our First Amendment jurisprudence, Justice STEVENS would "loo[k] to the generality of a regulation of property" to determine whether compensation is owing. The Beachfront Management Act is general, in his view, because it "regulates the use of the coastline of the entire state." There may be some validity to the principle Justice STEVENS proposes, but it does not properly apply to the present case. . . . [Perhaps] a law that destroys the value of land without being aimed at land . . . — the generally applicable criminal prohibition on the manufacturing of alcoholic beverages challenged in *Mugler* comes to mind — cannot constitute a compensable taking. But a regulation specifically directed to land-use no more acquires immunity by plundering landowners generally than does a law specifically directed at religious practice acquire immunity by prohibiting all religions. Justice STEVENS' approach renders the Takings Clause little more than a particularized restatement of the Equal Protection Clause.

title to property. It seems to us that the property owner necessarily expects the uses of his property to be restricted, from time to time, by various measures newly enacted by the State in legitimate exercise of its police powers; "[a]s long recognized, some values are enjoyed under an implied limitation and must yield to the police power." *Pennsylvania Coal Co.*, 260 U.S. at 413. And in the case of personal property, by reason of the State's traditionally high degree of control over commercial dealings, he ought to be aware of the possibility that new regulation might even render his property economically worthless (at least if the property's only economically productive use is sale or manufacture for sale), see Andrus v. Allard, 444 U.S. 51, 66–67 (1979) (prohibition on sale of eagle feathers). In the case of land, however, we think the notion pressed by the Council that title is somehow held subject to the "implied limitation" that the State may subsequently eliminate all economically valuable use is inconsistent with the historical compact recorded in the Takings Clause that has become part of our constitutional culture.

Where "permanent physical occupation" of land is concerned, we have refused to allow the government to decree it anew (without compensation), no matter how weighty the asserted "public interests" involved, Loretto v. Teleprompter Manhattan CATV Corp., 458 U.S. at 426 — though we assuredly would permit the government to assert a permanent easement that was a pre-existing limitation upon the landowner's title. We believe similar treatment must be accorded confiscatory regulations, i.e., regulations that prohibit all economically beneficial use of land. Any limitation so severe cannot be newly legislated or decreed (without compensation), but must inhere in the title itself, in the restrictions that background principles of the State's law of property and nuisance already place upon land ownership. A law or decree with such an effect must, in other words, do no more than duplicate the result that could have been achieved in the courts — by adjacent landowners (or other uniquely affected persons) under the State's law of private nuisance, or by the State under its complementary power to abate nuisances that affect the public generally, or otherwise.[16]

On this analysis, the owner of a lake bed, for example, would not be entitled to compensation when he is denied the requisite permit to engage in a landfilling operation that would have the effect of flooding others' land. Nor the corporate owner of a nuclear generating plant, when it is directed to remove all improvements from its land upon discovery that the plant sits astride an earthquake fault. Such regulatory action may well have the effect of eliminating the land's only economically productive use, but it does not proscribe a productive use that was previously permissible under relevant property and nuisance principles. The use of these properties for what are now expressly prohibited purposes was always unlawful, and (subject to other constitutional limitations) it was open to the State at any point to make the implication of those background principles of nuisance and property law explicit. In light of our traditional resort to "existing rules or understandings that stem from an independent source such as state law" to define the range of interests that qualify for protection as "property" under the Fifth (and Fourteenth) amendments, Board of Regents of State Colleges v. Roth, 408 U.S. 564, 577 (1972); . . . this recognition that the Takings Clause does not require compensation when an owner is barred from putting land to a use that is proscribed by those "existing rules or understandings" is surely unexceptional. When, however, a regulation that declares "off-limits" all economically

---

16. The principal "otherwise" that we have in mind is litigation absolving the State (or private parties) of liability for the destruction of "real and personal property, in cases of actual necessity, to prevent the spreading of a fire" or to forestall other grave threats to the lives and property of others.

productive or beneficial uses of land goes beyond what the relevant background principles would dictate, compensation must be paid to sustain it.

The "total taking" inquiry we require today will ordinarily entail (as the application of state nuisance law ordinarily entails) analysis of, among other things, the degree of harm to public lands and resources, or adjacent private property, posed by the claimant's proposed activities, see, e.g., Restatement (Second) of Torts §§826, 827, the social value of the claimant's activities and their suitability to the locality in question, and the relative ease with which the alleged harm can be avoided through measures taken by the claimant and the government (or adjacent private landowners) alike. The fact that a particular use has long been engaged in by similarly situated owners ordinarily imports a lack of any common-law prohibition (though changed circumstances or new knowledge may make what was previously permissible no longer so). So also does the fact that other landowners, similarly situated, are permitted to continue the use denied to the claimant.

It seems unlikely that common-law principles would have prevented the erection of any habitable or productive improvements on petitioner's land; they rarely support prohibition of the "essential use" of land. Curtin v. Benson, 222 U.S. 78, 86 (1911). The question, however, is one of state law to be dealt with on remand. We emphasize that to win its case South Carolina must do more than proffer the legislature's declaration that the uses Lucas desires are inconsistent with the public interest, or the conclusory assertion that they violate a common-law maxim such as *sic utere tuo ut alienum non laedas*. As we have said, a "State, by *ipse dixit*, may not transform private property into public property without compensation. . . . " Webb's Fabulous Pharmacies, Inc. v. Beckwith, 449 U.S. 155, 164 (1980). Instead, as it would be required to do if it sought to restrain Lucas in a common-law action for public nuisance, South Carolina must identify background principles of nuisance and property law that prohibit the uses he now intends in the circumstances in which the property is presently found. Only on this showing can the State fairly claim that, in proscribing all such beneficial uses, the Beachfront Management Act is taking nothing.[18]

The judgment is reversed and the cause remanded for proceedings not inconsistent with this opinion.

Justice KENNEDY, concurring in the judgment.

. . . The common law of nuisance is too narrow a confine for the exercise of regulatory power in a complex and interdependent society. The State should not be prevented from enacting new regulatory initiatives in response to changing conditions, and courts must consider all reasonable expectations whatever their source. The Takings Clause does not require a static body of state property law; it protects private expectations to ensure private investment. I agree with the Court that nuisance prevention accords with the most common expectations of property owners who face regulation, but I do not believe this can be the sole source of state authority to impose severe restrictions. Coastal property may present such unique concerns for a fragile land system that the State can go further in regulating its development and use than the common law of nuisance might otherwise permit. . . .

18. Justice BLACKMUN decries our reliance on background nuisance principles at least in part because he believes those principles to be as manipulable as we find the "harm prevention"/"benefit conferral" dichotomy. There is no doubt some leeway in a court's interpretation of what existing state law permits — but not remotely as much, we think, as in a legislative crafting of the reasons for its confiscatory regulation. We stress that an affirmative decree eliminating all economically beneficial uses may be defended only if an objectively reasonable application of relevant precedents would exclude those beneficial uses in the circumstances in which the land is presently found.

Justice BLACKMUN, dissenting.

. . . [The Court] creates simultaneously a new categorical rule and an exception (neither of which is rooted in our prior case law, common law, or common sense). . . .

IV . . .

A . . .

Ultimately even the Court cannot embrace the full implications of its per se rule: it eventually agrees that there cannot be a categorical rule for a taking based on economic value that wholly disregards the public need asserted. Instead, the Court decides that it will permit a State to regulate all economic value only if the State prohibits uses that would not be permitted under "background principles of nuisance and property law."[15] . . .

. . . [T]he Court's reliance on common-law principles of nuisance in its quest for a value-free taking jurisprudence [is perplexing]. In determining what is a nuisance at common law, state courts make exactly the decision that the Court finds so troubling when made by the South Carolina General Assembly today: they determine whether the use is harmful. Common-law public and private nuisance law is simply a determination whether a particular use causes harm. There is nothing magical in the reasoning of judges long dead. They determined a harm in the same way as state judges and legislatures do today. If judges in the 18th and 19th centuries can distinguish a harm from a benefit, why not judges in the 20th century, and if judges can, why not legislators? . . .

Justice STEVENS, dissenting. . . .

THE NUISANCE EXCEPTION . . .

The Court's holding today effectively freezes the State's common law, denying the legislature much of its traditional power to revise the law governing the rights and uses of property. . . .

Arresting the development of the common law is not only a departure from our prior decisions; it is also profoundly unwise. The human condition is one of constant learning and evolution — both moral and practical. Legislatures implement that new learning; in doing so they must often revise the definition of property and the rights of property owners. Thus, when the Nation came to understand that slavery was morally wrong and mandated the emancipation of all slaves, it, in effect, redefined "property." . . . New appreciation of the significance of endangered species; the importance of wetlands; and the vulnerability of coastal lands, shapes our evolving understandings of property rights.

Of course, some legislative redefinitions of property will effect a taking and must be compensated — but it certainly cannot be the case that every movement away from common law does so. There is no reason, and less sense, in such an absolute rule. . . .

15. Although it refers to state nuisance and property law, the Court apparently does not mean just any state nuisance and property law. Public nuisance was first a common-law creation, see Newark, The Boundaries of Nuisance, 65 L.Q. Rev. 480, 482 (1949) (attributing development of nuisance to 1535), but by the 1800s in both the United States and England, legislatures had the power to define what is a public nuisance, and particular uses often have been selectively targeted. See Prosser, Private Action for Public Nuisance, 52 Va. L. Rev. 997, 999–1000 (1966); J.F. Stephen, A General View of the Criminal Law of England 105–07 (2d ed. 1890). The Court's references to "common-law" background principles, however, indicate that legislative determinations do not constitute "state nuisance and property law" for the Court.

III . . .

In considering Lucas' claim, the generality of the Beachfront Management Act is significant. The Act does not target particular landowners, but rather regulates the use of the coastline of the entire State. Indeed, . . . every coastal State has implemented coastline regulations. Moreover, the Act did not single out owners of undeveloped land. The Act also prohibited owners of developed land from rebuilding if their structures were destroyed, and what is equally significant, from repairing erosion control devices, such as seawalls. . . . In short, the South Carolina Act imposed substantial burdens on owners of developed and undeveloped land alike. This generality indicates that the Act is not an effort to expropriate owners of undeveloped land. . . .

In view of all of these factors, even assuming that petitioner's property was rendered valueless, the risk inherent in investments of the sort made by petitioner, the generality of the Act, and the compelling purpose motivating the South Carolina Legislature persuade me that the Act did not effect a taking of petitioner's property. . . . *NO taking*

Statement of Justice SOUTER. . . . [Justice Souter would dismiss the writ of certiorari because it was "abundantly clear" that the unreviewable finding of the state trial court that the regulation had destroyed the entire value of the property was so questionable that it was imprudent to use the case as a vehicle for addressing the issue of what constitutes a total deprivation, and whether and when a total deprivation might require compensation.]

Note on *Lucas*

1. *Aftermath.* On remand, the South Carolina Supreme Court determined that no "common law basis" justified the restraint on the Lucas lots, and remanded the case to the trial court for a determination of what would constitute just compensation. Lucas v. South Carolina Coastal Council, 424 S.E.2d 484 (S.C. 1992). The parties then settled the case, with South Carolina agreeing to pay $850,000 for the property ($60,000 less than Lucas had paid), $514,000 in attorney fees, and $136,000 in interest and other related costs. The state decided that the gated nature of the community precluded it from using the lots for a public park and sold the property for $730,000. H. Jane Lehman, Accord Ends Fight over Use of Land, Wash. Post, July 17, 1993, at E1. The lots now sport four- and five-bedroom homes. Vicki Been, Lucas v. The Green Machine: Using the Takings Clause to Promote More Efficient Regulation?, *in* Property Stories 221, 239 (Gerald Korngold & Andrew P. Morriss eds., 2004).

Shortly after houses were built on the lots, the beach on which the lots sit suffered a "temporary erosion episode," and lost 200 feet of shoreline. High tides swept within 10 to 15 feet of the new houses, prompting the purchaser of one of the lots to join with neighboring property owners to petition for a permit to protect their homes with either a rock wall or a 6-foot high wall of sand bags or tubes. When the successor agency to the Coastal Council denied the permit, some of the property owners sued, claiming that the denial of permission for erosion control barriers constituted a taking. The same trial judge who had decided in favor of Lucas held that the Coastal Zone Management Act, which authorized denial of the erosion permits, was an inherent limitation on title that defeated the takings claim. Jerozal v. South Carolina Department of Health & Environmental Control, No. 95-CP-10-4365 (County of Charleston Ct. C. P. 1996). The controversy came to an end, however, when the erosion shifted north, abating the threat to the properties (at least for the moment), reports Mary Shahid, former counsel for the South Carolina Department of Health and Environmental Control, Office of Coastal and Resource Management. See Been, supra, at 239–40.

2. *Evidence for the cost-internalization justification for takings?* Professor William Fischel has argued that the *Lucas* aftermath "exquisitely illustrates" the validity of the cost-internalization rationale for requiring compensation when regulations diminish the value of property. He writes:

> . . . Prior to the *Lucas* decision, South Carolina perceived the price of Lucas's lot (and others like it) as being low, since it did not expect to have to pay for them. At that price — zero dollars and zero cents — even the least environmentally sensitive legislator would have to concede that environmental values should prevail. . . .
>
> Once the state came into possession of the land, however, it had reason to pay attention to its market price relative to its environmental value. . . . The state's agents then surely noticed that developers were willing to pay nearly half a million dollars for each of the lots, and the state's agents did what rational and faithful public servants should do: they sold the lots to developers. . . .
>
> . . . Having to pay money out of scarce budgetary resources makes officials calculate whether it is worthwhile to undertake a particular project. . . .

William A. Fischel, Takings and Public Choice: The Persuasion of Price, *in* The Encyclopedia of Public Choice 549, 552 (Charles Kershaw Rowley ed., 2003). See also Joseph W. Trefzger, Efficient Compensation for Regulatory Takings: Some Thoughts Following the *Lucas* Ruling, 23 Real Est. L.J. 191 (1995). Is Fischel's argument persuasive? See Been, supra, for one response.

3. *Regulations that diminish less than all value of the land.* How persuasive is Justice Scalia's distinction between total and less-than-total diminutions in value? If a "total" destruction in value is equivalent to a physical appropriation, why is a partial destruction not equivalent to a partial physical appropriation such as the 1 1/2 cubic feet at issue in *Loretto*? See Richard A. Epstein, *Lucas v. South Carolina Coastal Council*: A Tangled Web of Expectations, 45 Stan. L. Rev. 1369, 1374 (1993).

The Court reaffirmed its bright-line totality rule in Palazzolo v. Rhode Island, 533 U.S. 606 (2001), excerpted at p. 180.

4. *Common versus positive law.* Should statutes and regulations trigger the "inherent limitation in title" exception, or did the Court mean to limit the exception to constraints common law nuisance imposed on title, as Justice Blackmun supposes? For an argument that there is no justification for such a limit, see Lynn E. Blais, Takings, Statutes, and the Common Law: Considering Inherent Limitations on Title, 70 S. Cal. L. Rev. 1 (1996). See also American Pelagic Fishing Co. v. United States, 379 F.3d 1363 (Fed. Cir. 2004) (holding that because federal Magnusson Act, which assumed sovereignty for the United States over the management and conservation of fishery resources, was in effect when investor bought ship and had it retrofitted for mackerel fishing, it was an inherent limitation on title, such that ship's owner had no property right to use the ship to fish for mackerel in U.S. waters).

5. *Judicial takings?* Are common law judges, whose rulings may radically change a property owner's rights, exempt from the requirements of the Takings Clause? Should they be? See, e.g., David J. Bederman, The Curious Resurrection of Custom: Beach Access and Judicial Takings, 96 Colum. L. Rev. 1375 (1996); Paul B. Stephan, Redistributive Litigation — Judicial Innovation, Private Expectations, and the Shadow of International Law, 88 Va. L. Rev. 789 (2002); Barton H. Thompson, Jr., Judicial Takings, 76 Va. L. Rev. 1449 (1990); W. David Sarratt, Note, Judicial Takings and the Course Pursued, 90 Va. L. Rev. 1487 (2004). See also Stevens v. Cannon Beach, 510 U.S. 1207 (1994) (Scalia & O'Connor, JJ., dissenting from denial of certiorari).

6. *The early bird gets to build.* Was the *Lucas* majority right to have qualms about denying Lucas the right to build when so many neighbors already had built? Are the arguments that Justice Stevens raises about the burdens imposed on the existing homes persuasive? Which is the more important value: equity for those who simply want to do what others have done before them, or flexibility for governments faced with the realization that earlier policies were mistaken? For provocative discussions of how the law should address "the reality that any type of human land use, however benign the use and however appropriate the location, can prove harmful when too many acres are devoted to it," see Eric T. Freyfogle, The Owning and Taking of Sensitive Lands, 43 UCLA L. Rev. 77, 79 (1995). See also Mark Sagoff, Muddle or Muddle Through? Takings Jurisprudence Meets the Endangered Species Act, 38 Wm. & Mary L. Rev. 825 (1997).

Was Lucas an appropriate plaintiff to merit such concerns about equity? Lucas was not a latecomer to the Isle of Palms — indeed, the partnership Lucas created, known as Wild Dune Associates, had developed the subdivision in which the lots were located. Should the fact that the remainder of the Wild Dunes development was completed before the coastal development rules changed mean that the Takings Clause should be interpreted to protect investors like Lucas from the risk of evolving regulatory regimes? See Been, supra, at 225–26.

7. *Rights in land versus personal property.* Is the distinction Justice Scalia draws between the expectations of those who hold their wealth in personal property and those who hold land sound? See William W. Fisher III, The Trouble with *Lucas*, 45 Stan. L. Rev. 1393, 1400–01 (1993). See also Daniel W. Bromley, Regulatory Takings: Coherent Concept or Logical Contradiction?, 17 Vt. L. Rev. 647, 676–78 (1993).

8. *Takings and Due Process. Lucas* relies on language from Agins v. City of Tiburon, 447 U.S. 255, 260 (1980) that seems to imply that a taking may arise not only when a regulation destroys all economically viable use of land, but also whenever the regulation "does not substantially advance legitimate state interests." The challenge in *Agins* rested on the plaintiff's allegation that the city's zoning ordinance on its face had completely destroyed the value of the property, and there was little question about the legitimacy of the city's purposes, so the *Agins* Court did not confront the issue whether a failure to substantially advance legitimate state interests, standing alone, would constitute a violation of the Takings Clause. Justice Scalia's invocation of the language from *Agins* in *Lucas*, however, reinvigorated long-running debates about the relationship between the Takings and Due Process Clauses. See, e.g., Kenneth Salzberg, "Takings" as Due Process, or Due Process as "Takings"?, 36 Val. U. L. Rev. 413 (2002); Mark Tunick, Constitutional Protections of Private Property: Decoupling the Takings and Due Process Clauses, 3 U. Pa. J. Const. L. 885 (2001). In 2005, the Supreme Court resolved the debate, see p. 193.

9. *Per se rules versus "ad hocery."* What are the costs and benefits of moving from the informal, open-ended, and multifactored balancing test of *Penn Central* to more formal per se rules? Professor Michelman argues that "balancing — or better, the judicial practice of situated judgment or practical reason" is necessary in takings jurisprudence because of the inherent difficulty of reconciling private property and democracy. Frank Michelman, Takings, 1987, 88 Colum. L. Rev. 1600 (1988). In response, Professor Rose-Ackerman claims that the uncertainty created by ad hoc balancing will lead to inefficient levels of investment and "act as a force for conservatism among public officials." Susan Rose-Ackerman, Against Ad Hocery: A Comment on Michelman, 88 Colum. L. Rev. 1697 (1988). Michelman's reply is at 88 Colum. L. Rev. 1712 (1988). See also Marc Poirier, The Virtue of Vagueness in Takings Doctrine, 24 Cardozo L. Rev. 93 (2002); Stewart Sterk, The Federalist Dimension of Regulatory Takings Jurisprudence, 114 Yale L.J. 203 (2004); Barton H. Thompson, Jr., The Allure of Consequential Fit, 51 Ala. L. Rev. 1261, 1270 (2000).

f. | *Tensions Between* **Penn Central** *and the Per Se Rules of*
    | **Loretto** *and* **Lucas**

Palazzolo v. Rhode Island

533 U.S. 606 (2001)

Justice K~~ENNEDY~~ delivered the opinion of the Court. . . .

I

The town of Westerly is on an edge of the Rhode Island coastline. . . . Westerly today has about 20,000 year-round residents, and thousands of summer visitors come to enjoy its beaches and coastal advantages.

One of the more popular attractions is Misquamicut State Beach, a lengthy expanse of coastline facing Block Island Sound and beyond to the Atlantic Ocean. The primary point of access to the beach is Atlantic Avenue. . . .

In 1959 petitioner, a lifelong Westerly resident, decided to invest in three undeveloped, adjoining parcels along . . . Atlantic Avenue. To the north, the property faces, and borders upon, Winnapaug Pond; the south of the property faces Atlantic Avenue and the beachfront homes abutting it on the other side, and beyond that the dunes and the beach. To purchase and hold the property, petitioner and associates formed Shore Gardens, Inc. (SGI). After SGI purchased the property petitioner bought out his associates and became the sole shareholder. In the first decade of SGI's ownership of the property the corporation submitted a plat to the town subdividing the property into 80 lots; and it engaged in various transactions that left it with 74 lots, which together encompassed about 20 acres. During the same period SGI also made initial attempts to develop the property and submitted intermittent applications to state agencies to fill substantial portions of the parcel. Most of the property was then, as it is now, salt marsh subject to tidal flooding. The wet ground and permeable soil would require considerable fill — as much as six feet in some places — before significant structures could be built. SGI's proposal, submitted in 1962 to the Rhode Island Division of Harbors and Rivers (DHR), sought to dredge from Winnapaug Pond and fill the entire property. The application was denied for lack of essential information. A second, similar proposal followed a year later. A third application, submitted in 1966 while the second application was pending, proposed more limited filling of the land for use as a private beach club. These latter two applications were referred to the Rhode Island Department of Natural Resources, which indicated initial assent. The agency later withdrew approval, however, citing adverse environmental impacts. SGI did not contest the ruling.

No further attempts to develop the property were made for over a decade. Two intervening events, however, become important to the issues presented. First, in 1971, Rhode Island enacted legislation creating the Council, an agency charged with the duty of protecting the State's coastal properties. 1971 R.I. Pub. Laws, ch. 279, §1 et seq. Regulations promulgated by the Council designated salt marshes like those on SGI's property as protected "coastal wetlands," Rhode Island Coastal Resources Management Program (CRMP) §210.3, on which development is limited to a great extent. Second, in 1978, SGI's corporate charter was revoked for failure to pay corporate income taxes; and title to the property passed, by operation of state law, to petitioner as the corporation's sole shareholder.

In 1983, petitioner, now the owner, renewed the efforts to develop the property. An application to the Council, resembling the 1962 submission, requested permission to construct a wooden bulkhead along the shore of Winnapaug Pond and to fill the entire marshland area. The Council rejected the application. . . .

Petitioner went back to the drawing board, this time hiring counsel and preparing a more specific and limited proposal for use of the property. The new application, submitted to the Council in 1985, echoed the 1966 request to build a private beach club. The details do not tend to inspire the reader with an idyllic coastal image, for the proposal was to fill 11 acres of the property with gravel to accommodate "50 cars with boat trailers, a dumpster, port-a-johns, picnic tables, barbecue pits of concrete, and other trash receptacles."

The application fared no better with the Council than previous ones. Under the agency's regulations, a landowner wishing to fill salt marsh on Winnapaug Pond needed a "special exception" from the Council. CRMP §130. In a short opinion the Council said the beach club proposal conflicted with the regulatory standard for a special exception. . . . This time petitioner appealed the decision to the Rhode Island courts, challenging the Council's conclusion as contrary to principles of state administrative law. The Council's decision was affirmed.

Petitioner filed an inverse condemnation action in Rhode Island Superior Court, asserting that the State's wetlands regulations, as applied by the Council to his parcel, had taken the property without compensation in violation of the Fifth and Fourteenth Amendments. The suit alleged the Council's action deprived him of "economically, beneficial use" of his property, resulting in a total taking requiring compensation under Lucas v. South Carolina Coastal Council, 505 U.S. 1003 (1992). He sought damages in the amount of $3,150,000, a figure derived from an appraiser's estimate as to the value of a 74-lot residential subdivision. . . . After a bench trial, a justice of the Superior Court ruled against petitioner. . . .

The Rhode Island Supreme Court affirmed. . . . The court held . . . that petitioner had no right to challenge regulations predating 1978, when he succeeded to legal ownership of the property from SGI. . . . In addition . . . the court concluded he could not recover under the more general test of Penn Central Transp. Co. v. City New York, 438 U.S. 104 (1978). On this claim, too, the date of acquisition of the parcel was found determinative, and the court held he could have had "no reasonable investment-backed expectations that were affected by this regulation" because it predated his ownership.

We disagree with the Supreme Court of Rhode Island [on the pre-acquisition notice issue]; . . . we hold [that] . . . the owner is not deprived of all economic use of his property because the value of upland portions is substantial. We remand for further consideration of the claim under the principles set forth in Penn Central.

II . . .

B

. . . When the Council promulgated its wetlands regulations, the disputed parcel was owned not by petitioner but by the corporation of which he was sole shareholder. When title was transferred to petitioner by operation of law, the wetlands regulations were in force. The state court held the postregulation acquisition of title was fatal to the claim for deprivation of all economic use, and to the Penn Central claim. . . . [T]he two holdings together amount to a single, sweeping, rule: A purchaser or a successive title holder like petitioner is deemed to have notice of an earlier-enacted restriction and is barred from claiming that it effects a taking.

The theory underlying the argument that postenactment purchasers cannot challenge a regulation under the Takings Clause seems to run on these lines: Property rights are created by the State. So, the argument goes, by prospective legislation the State can shape and define property rights and reasonable investment-backed expectations, and subsequent owners cannot claim any injury from lost value. After all, they purchased or took title with notice of the limitation.

The State may not put so potent a Hobbesian stick into the Lockean bundle. The right to improve property, of course, is subject to the reasonable exercise of state authority, including the enforcement of valid zoning and land-use restrictions. . . . The Takings Clause, however, in certain circumstances allows a landowner to assert that a particular exercise of the State's regulatory power is so unreasonable or onerous as to compel compensation. Just as a prospective enactment, such as a new zoning ordinance, can limit the value of land without effecting a taking because it can be understood as reasonable by all concerned, other enactments are unreasonable and do not become less so through passage of time or title. Were we to accept the State's rule, the postenactment transfer of title would absolve the State of its obligation to defend any action restricting land use, no matter how extreme or unreasonable. A State would be allowed, in effect, to put an expiration date on the Takings Clause. This ought not to be the rule. Future generations, too, have a right to challenge unreasonable limitations on the use and value of land.

Nor does the justification of notice take into account the effect on owners at the time of enactment, who are prejudiced as well. Should an owner attempt to challenge a new regulation, but not survive the process of ripening his or her claim (which, as this case demonstrates, will often take years), under the proposed rule the right to compensation may not be asserted by an heir or successor, and so may not be asserted at all. The State's rule would work a critical alteration to the nature of property, as the newly regulated landowner is stripped of the ability to transfer the interest which was possessed prior to the regulation. The State may not by this means secure a windfall for itself. The proposed rule is, furthermore, capricious in effect. The young owner contrasted with the older owner, the owner with the resources to hold contrasted with the owner with the need to sell, would be in different positions. The Takings Clause is not so quixotic. A blanket rule that purchasers with notice have no compensation right when a claim becomes ripe is too blunt an instrument to accord with the duty to compensate for what is taken. . . .

. . . It is asserted here that *Lucas* stands for the proposition that any new regulation, once enacted, becomes a background principle of property law which cannot be challenged by those who acquire title after the enactment.

We have no occasion to consider the precise circumstances when a legislative enactment can be deemed a background principle of state law or whether those circumstances are present here. It suffices to say that a regulation that otherwise would be unconstitutional absent compensation is not transformed into a background principle of the State's law by mere virtue of the passage of title. This relative standard would be incompatible with our description of the concept in *Lucas*, which is explained in terms of those common, shared understandings of permissible limitations derived from a State's legal tradition. . . .

III

As . . . the date of transfer of title does not bar petitioner's takings claim, we have before us the alternative ground relied upon by the Rhode Island Supreme Court in ruling upon the merits of the takings claims. It held that all economically beneficial use was not deprived because the uplands portion of the property can still be improved. On this point, we agree with the court's decision. Petitioner accepts the Council's contention and the state trial court's finding that his parcel retains $200,000 in development value under the State's wetlands regulations. He asserts, nonetheless, that he has suffered a total taking and contends the Council cannot sidestep the holding in *Lucas* "by the simple expedient of leaving a landowner a few crumbs of value." Brief for Petitioner 37.

Assuming a taking is otherwise established, a State may not evade the duty to compensate on the premise that the landowner is left with a token interest. This is not the situation of the landowner in this case, however. A regulation permitting a landowner to build a substantial residence on an 18-acre parcel does not leave the property "economically idle." *Lucas*, supra, at 1019. . . .

For the reasons we have discussed, the State Supreme Court erred . . . in ruling that acquisition of title after the effective date of the regulations barred the takings claims. The court did not err in finding that petitioner failed to establish a deprivation of all economic value, for it is undisputed that the parcel retains significant worth for construction of a residence. The claims under the *Penn Central* analysis were not examined, and for this purpose the case should be remanded.

The judgment of the Rhode Island Supreme Court is affirmed in part and reversed in part, and the case is remanded for further proceedings not inconsistent with this opinion.

Justice O'CONNOR, concurring. . . .

. . . Today's holding does not mean that the timing of the regulation's enactment relative to the acquisition of title is immaterial to the *Penn Central* analysis. Indeed, it would be just as much error to expunge this consideration from the takings inquiry as it would be to accord it exclusive significance. Our polestar instead remains the principles set forth in *Penn Central* itself and our other cases that govern partial regulatory takings. Under these cases, interference with investment-backed expectations is one of a number of factors that a court must examine. Further, the regulatory regime in place at the time the claimant acquires the property at issue helps to shape the reasonableness of those expectations. . . .

. . . If investment-backed expectations are given exclusive significance in the *Penn Central* analysis and existing regulations dictate the reasonableness of those expectations in every instance, then the State wields far too much power to redefine property rights upon passage of title. On the other hand, if existing regulations do nothing to inform the analysis, then some property owners may reap windfalls and an important indicium of fairness is lost. As I understand it, our decision today does not remove the regulatory backdrop against which an owner takes title to property from the purview of the *Penn Central* inquiry. It simply restores balance to that inquiry. Courts properly consider the effect of existing regulations under the rubric of investment-backed expectations in determining whether a compensable taking has occurred. As before, the salience of these facts cannot be reduced to any "set formula." *Penn Central*, 438 U.S. at 124. The temptation to adopt what amount to per se rules in either direction must be resisted. The Takings Clause requires careful examination and weighing of all the relevant circumstances in this context. The court below therefore must consider on remand the array of relevant factors under *Penn Central* before deciding whether any compensation is due.

Justice SCALIA, concurring.

I write separately to make clear that my understanding of how the issues discussed in Part II-B of the Court's opinion must be considered on remand is not Justice O'Connor's.

. . . In my view, the fact that a restriction existed at the time the purchaser took title (other than a restriction forming part of the "background principles of the State's law of property and nuisance," *Lucas*) should have no bearing upon the determination of whether the restriction is so substantial as to constitute a taking. The "investment-backed expectations" that the law will take into account do not include the assumed validity of a restriction that in fact deprives property of so much of its value as to be unconstitutional.

Which is to say that a *Penn Central* taking, no less than a total taking, is not absolved by the transfer of title.

Justice STEVENS, concurring in part and dissenting in part.

. . . [W]hile I join Part II-A of the opinion, I dissent from the judgment and, in particular, from Part II-B. . . .

To the extent that the adoption of the regulations constitute the challenged taking, petitioner is simply the wrong party to be bringing this action. If the regulations imposed a compensable injury on anyone, it was on the owner of the property at the moment the regulations were adopted. Given the trial court's finding that petitioner did not own the property at that time, in my judgment it is pellucidly clear that he has no standing to claim that the promulgation of the regulations constituted a taking of any part of the property that he subsequently acquired. . . .

Justice GINSBURG, with whom Justice SOUTER and Justice BREYER join, dissenting [on ripeness grounds]. . . .

Justice BREYER, dissenting.

. . . [G]iven this Court's precedents, I would agree with Justice O'CONNOR that the simple fact that a piece of property has changed hands (for example, by inheritance) does not always and *automatically* bar a takings claim. Here, for example, without in any way suggesting that Palazzolo has any valid takings claim, I believe his postregulatory acquisition of the property (through automatic operation of law) by itself should not prove dispositive.

As Justice O'CONNOR explains, under *Penn Central*, much depends upon whether, or how, the timing and circumstances of a change of ownership affect whatever reasonable investment-backed expectations might otherwise exist. Ordinarily, such expectations will diminish in force and significance — rapidly and dramatically — as property continues to change hands over time. I believe that such factors can adequately be taken into account within the *Penn Central* framework. . . .

Note on the Notice Question

1. *Aftermath.* On remand, the Rhode Island Superior Court rejected the takings claim. Applying the *Penn Central* factors, the court found that the proposed development would constitute a public nuisance, and that the cost of the proposed subdivision would be so high that Palazzolo would be better off selling the tract for one homesite. Palazzolo v. Rhode Island, C.A. No. WM 88-0297 (R.I. Super. Ct. July 5, 2005).

2. *The role of notice.* Who has the better of the argument between Justices O'Connor and Scalia about what role notice should play in a *Penn Central* analysis? See Daniel R. Mandelker, The Notice Rule in Investment-Backed Expectations, *in* Taking Sides on Takings Issues: Public and Private Perspectives 21 (Thomas E. Roberts ed., 2002); Steven J. Eagle, The 1997 Regulatory Takings Quartet: Retreating from the "Rule of Law," 42 N.Y.L. Sch. L. Rev. 345 (1998); Donald C. Guy & James E. Holloway, Finding the Development Value of Wetlands and Other Environmentally Sensitive Lands Under the Extent of Interference with Reasonable Investment-Backed Expectations, 19 J. Land Use & Envtl. L. 297 (2004); Max Gibbons, Comment, Of Windfalls and Property Rights: *Palazzolo* and the Regulatory Takings Notice Debate, 50 UCLA L. Rev. 1259 (2003).

3. *Takings and transitions.* Consider the argument advanced by Professor Doremus that not only should notice be dispositive of a takings claim, but that a change in the applicable rules should be *required* to support a takings claim:

Regulatory transitions are inevitable over the long run, and often represent socially adaptive responses to changed circumstances or increased information. They are difficult to achieve, however, because substantial psychological and political barriers stand in the way. Compensation requirements should be narrowly drawn to avoid over deterrence of regulatory change. Courts should require takings claimants to prove that they have been the victims of a change in the principles governing use or ownership of their property, to avoid playing into the human tendencies to resist change and to read vague legal principles as inapplicable to one's own activities. . . . [W]hen a change in the legal rules does occur, the decision as to whether or not compensation is required should take into account the justifications for the change; the extent to which it could have been foreseen; the ability of the landowner to take action, before or after the change, to reduce its impacts or respond to it; the pace of the change; and the extent to which its costs have been spread to all similarly situated landowners.

Holly Doremus, Takings and Transitions, 19 J. Land Use & Envtl. L. 1, 45 (2003). See also Louis Kaplow, An Economic Analysis of Legal Transitions, 99 Harv. L. Rev. 509 (1986); Saul Levmore, Changes, Anticipations, and Reparations, 99 Colum. L. Rev. 1657, 1673 (1999); Michael P. Van Alstine, The Costs of Legal Change, 49 UCLA L. Rev. 789 (2002).

4. *Coming to the taking?* Should it matter if the purchaser paid less for the property because of uncertainty about whether it could be developed for a particular use? If the purchaser on notice paid less because of the uncertainty, should the seller have a takings claim for the reduction in the price received? If so, why shouldn't the seller then be able to transfer that claim to the buyer? See, e.g., William A. Fischel & Perry Shapiro, Takings, Insurance, and Michelman, 17 J. Legal Stud. 269, 287–89 (1988) (arguing that a land seller should be entitled to transfer a valid takings claim to a buyer); Gregory M. Stein, Who Gets the Takings Claim? Changes in Land Use Law, Pre-Enactment Owners, and Post-Enactment Buyers, 61 Ohio St. L.J. 89, 135 (2000).

What if a purchaser pays a premium for the property under the (mistaken) belief that development can occur — should the premium serve as the basis for a takings claim? Compare the doctrine of self-created hardship in the law of variances (see p. 293); compare also the "coming to the nuisance" doctrine (see pp. 525–28). See Samuel Taylor Hirzel II, *Palazzolo v. Rhode Island*: Preserving a Constitutional Safety Valve in the Murky Waters of the Self-Imposed Hardship Rule, 107 Dick. L. Rev. 919 (2003).

5. *Involuntary transfers.* Should it matter whether the acquirer with notice purchased the property or took by inheritance, gift, intestate succession, or another type of "involuntary" transfer? See Carol Necole Brown, Taking the Takings Claim: A Policy and Economic Analysis of the Survival of Takings Claims After Property Transfers, 36 Conn. L. Rev. 7 (2003).

6. *Other relevant factors.* What other factors should the trial court consider in determining the importance of notice under Justice O'Connor's approach?

7. *Ripeness.* The notice issue is substantially complicated by the Supreme Court's rules regarding when takings claims are considered ripe, a subject we take up at pp. 234–51. For an explanation of how the ripeness rules affect the notice issue after *Palazzolo*, see Gregory M. Stein, The Effect of *Palazzolo v. Rhode Island* on the Role of Reasonable Investment-Backed Expectations, *in* Taking Sides on Takings Issues: Public and Private Perspectives 41 (Thomas E. Roberts ed., 2002).

Tahoe-Sierra Preservation Council, Inc. v. Tahoe Regional Planning Agency

535 U.S. 302 (2002)

Justice STEVENS delivered the opinion of the Court.

The question presented is whether a moratorium on development imposed during the process of devising a comprehensive land-use plan constitutes a per se taking of property requiring compensation under the Takings Clause of the United States Constitution. This case actually involves two moratoria ordered by respondent Tahoe Regional Planning Agency (TRPA) to maintain the status quo while studying the impact of development on Lake Tahoe and designing a strategy for environmentally sound growth. . . . As a result of these two directives, virtually all development on a substantial portion of the property subject to TRPA's jurisdiction was prohibited for a period of 32 months. Although the question we decide relates only to that 32-month period, a brief description of the events leading up to the moratoria and a comment on the two permanent plans that TRPA adopted thereafter will clarify the narrow scope of our holding.

I . . .

Lake Tahoe's exceptional clarity is attributed to the absence of algae that obscures the waters of most other lakes. Historically, the lack of nitrogen and phosphorous, which nourish the growth of algae, has ensured the transparency of its waters. Unfortunately, the lake's pristine state has deteriorated rapidly over the past 40 years; increased land development in the Lake Tahoe Basin (Basin) has threatened the " 'noble sheet of blue water' " beloved by Twain and countless others. [Tahoe-Sierra Preservation Council, Inc. v. Tahoe Regional Planning Agency, 34 F. Supp. 2d 1226, 1230 (D. Nev. 1999)]. . . .

The upsurge of development in the area has caused "increased nutrient loading of the lake largely because of the increase in impervious coverage of land in the Basin resulting from that development." Ibid. . . . Given this trend, the District Court predicted that "unless the process is stopped, the lake will lose its clarity and its trademark blue color, becoming green and opaque for eternity." . . .

Those areas in the Basin that have steeper slopes produce more runoff; therefore, they are usually considered "high hazard" lands. Moreover, certain areas near streams or wetlands known as "Stream Environment Zones" (SEZs) are especially vulnerable to the impact of development because, in their natural state, they act as filters for much of the debris that runoff carries. Because "[t]he most obvious response to this problem . . . is to restrict development around the lake — especially in SEZ lands, as well as in areas already naturally prone to runoff," id. at 1232, conservation efforts have focused on controlling growth in these high hazard areas.

In the 1960's, when the problems associated with the burgeoning development began to receive significant attention, jurisdiction over the Basin, which occupies 501 square miles, was shared by the States of California and Nevada, five counties, several municipalities, and the Forest Service of the Federal Government. In 1968, the legislatures of the two States adopted the Tahoe Regional Planning Compact. . . .

[The Compact, as amended in 1980, set deadlines for TRPA's adoption of a permanent plan imposing regional standards for development.] . . .

. . . Despite the fact that TRPA performed these obligations in "good faith and to the best of its ability," 34 F. Supp. 2d, at 1233, after a few months it concluded that it could not meet the deadlines in the Compact. On June 25, 1981, it therefore enacted Ordinance 81-5 imposing the first of the two moratoria on development that petitioners challenge in this proceeding. . . .

. . . It is undisputed . . . that Ordinance 81-5 prohibited the construction of any new residences on SEZ lands in either State and on class 1, 2, and 3 lands in California.

. . . Under a liberal reading of the Compact, TRPA then had until August 26, 1983, to adopt a new regional plan. 94 Stat. 3240. "Unfortunately, but again not surprisingly, no regional plan was in place as of that date." 34 F. Supp. 2d, at 1235. TRPA therefore adopted Resolution 83-21, "which completely suspended all project reviews and approvals, including the acceptance of new proposals," and which remained in effect until a new regional plan was adopted on April 26, 1984. Thus, Resolution 83-21 imposed an 8-month moratorium prohibiting all construction on high hazard lands in either State. In combination, Ordinance 81-5 and Resolution 83-21 effectively prohibited all construction on sensitive lands in California and on all SEZ lands in the entire Basin for 32 months. . . .

I

. . . The petitioners include the Tahoe-Sierra Preservation Council, Inc., a nonprofit membership corporation representing about 2,000 owners of both improved and unimproved parcels of real estate in the Lake Tahoe Basin, and a class of some 400 individual owners of vacant lots located either on SEZ lands or in other parts of districts 1, 2, or 3. Those individuals purchased their properties prior to the effective date of the 1980 Compact, App. 34, primarily for the purpose of constructing "at a time of their choosing" a single-family home "to serve as a permanent, retirement or vacation residence," id. at 36. When they made those purchases, they did so with the understanding that such construction was authorized provided that "they complied with all reasonable requirements for building." Ibid.

Petitioners' complaints gave rise to protracted litigation that has produced four opinions by the Court of Appeals for the Ninth Circuit and several published District Court opinions. . . . [W]e limit our discussion to the lower courts' disposition of the claims based on the 2-year moratorium (Ordinance 81-5) and the ensuing 8-month moratorium (Resolution 83-21). . . .

Emphasizing the temporary nature of the regulations, the testimony that the "average holding time of a lot in the Tahoe area between lot purchase and home construction is twenty-five years," and the failure of petitioners to offer specific evidence of harm, the District Court concluded that "consideration of the *Penn Central* factors clearly leads to the conclusion that there was no taking." 34 F. Supp. 2d, at 1240. . . .

The District Court had more difficulty with the "total taking" issue. Although it was satisfied that petitioners' property did retain some value during the moratoria, it found that they had been temporarily deprived of "all economically viable use of their land." Id. at 1245. The court concluded that those actions therefore constituted "categorical" takings under our decision in Lucas v. South Carolina Coastal Council, 505 U.S. 1003 (1992). . . .

Contrary to the District Court, the Court of Appeals held that because the regulations had only a temporary impact on petitioners' fee interest in the properties, no categorical taking had occurred. . . . Because of the importance of the case, we granted certiorari limited to the question stated at the beginning of this opinion. 533 U.S. 948 (2001). We now affirm.

III

Petitioners make only a facial attack on Ordinance 81-5 and Resolution 83-21. They contend that the mere enactment of a temporary regulation that, while in effect, denies a property owner all viable economic use of her property gives rise to an unqualified constitutional obligation to compensate her for the value of its use during that period. Hence, they "face an uphill battle," Keystone Bituminous Coal Assn. v. DeBenedictis, 480 U.S. 470, 495 (1987), that is made especially steep by their desire for a categorical rule requiring compensation whenever the government imposes such a moratorium on development. Under their proposed rule, there is no need to evaluate the landowners' investment-backed expectations, the actual impact of the regulation on any individual, the importance of the public interest served by the regulation, or the reasons for imposing the temporary restriction. For petitioners, it is enough that a regulation imposes a temporary deprivation — no matter how brief — of all economically viable use to trigger a per se rule that a taking has occurred. . . . We shall first explain why our cases do not support their proposed categorical rule — indeed, fairly read, they implicitly reject it. . . . In our view the answer to the abstract question whether a temporary moratorium effects a taking is neither "yes, always" nor "no, never"; the answer depends upon the particular circumstances of the case.[16] Resisting "[t]he temptation to adopt what amount to per se rules in either direction," *Palazzolo v. Rhode Island*, 533 U.S. 606, 636 (2001) (O'CONNOR, J., concurring), we conclude that the circumstances in this case are best analyzed within the *Penn Central* framework.

IV . . .

When the government physically takes possession of an interest in property for some public purpose, it has a categorical duty to compensate the former owner, *United States v. Pewee Coal Co.*, 341 U.S. 114, 115 (1951), regardless of whether the interest that is taken constitutes an entire parcel or merely a part thereof. Thus, compensation is mandated when a leasehold is taken and the government occupies the property for its own purposes, even though that use is temporary. *United States v. General Motors Corp.*, 323 U.S. 373 1945. . . . But a government regulation that . . . bans certain private uses of a portion of an owner's property, *Village of Euclid v. Ambler Realty Co.*, 272 U.S. 365 (1926); *Keystone Bituminous Coal Assn. v. DeBenedictis*, 480 U.S. 470 (1987); or that forbids the private use of certain airspace, *Penn Central Transp. Co. v. New York City*, 438 U.S. 104 (1978), does not constitute a categorical taking. "The first category of cases requires courts to apply a clear rule; the second necessarily entails complex factual assessments of the purposes and economic effects of government actions." *Yee v. Escondido*, 503 U.S. 519, 523 (1992). . . .

. . . Land-use regulations are ubiquitous and most of them impact property values in some tangential way — often in completely unanticipated ways. Treating them all as per se takings would transform government regulation into a luxury few governments could afford. By contrast, physical appropriations are relatively rare, easily identified, and usually represent a greater affront to individual property rights. . . .

In the decades following [Justice Holmes's opinion in *Pennsylvania Coal Co. v. Mahon*, 260 U.S. 393 (1922)], we have "generally eschewed" any set formula for determining how far is too far, choosing instead to engage in " 'essentially ad hoc, factual inquiries.' " *Lucas*, 505 U.S. at 1015 (quoting *Penn Central*, 438 U.S. at 124). Indeed, we still resist the temptation to adopt per se rules in our cases involving partial regulatory takings, preferring to examine "a number of factors" rather than a simple "mathematically precise" formula. Justice Brennan's opinion for the Court in *Penn Central* did, however, make it clear that even though multiple factors are relevant in the analysis of regulatory takings claims, in such cases we must focus on "the parcel as a whole":

16. Despite our clear refusal to hold that a moratorium never effects a taking, the CHIEF JUSTICE accuses us of "allow[ing] the government to ' . . . take private property without paying for it.' " It may be true that under a *Penn Central* analysis petitioners' land was taken and compensation would be due. But petitioners failed to challenge the District Court's conclusion that there was no taking under *Penn Central*.

> "Taking" jurisprudence does not divide a single parcel into discrete segments and attempt to determine whether rights in a particular segment have been entirely abrogated. In deciding whether a particular governmental action has effected a taking, this Court focuses rather both on the character of the action and on the nature and extent of the interference with rights in the parcel as a whole — here, the city tax block designated as the "landmark site."

438 U.S. at 130–131. . . .

This requirement that "the aggregate must be viewed in its entirety" explains why, for example, a regulation that prohibited commercial transactions in eagle feathers, but did not bar other uses or impose any physical invasion or restraint upon them, was not a taking. Andrus v. Allard, 444 U.S. 51, 66 (1979). It also clarifies why restrictions on the use of only limited portions of the parcel, such as setback ordinances, Gorieb v. Fox, 274 U.S. 603 (1927), or a requirement that coal pillars be left in place to prevent mine subsidence, Keystone Bituminous Coal Assn. v. DeBenedictis, 480 U.S. at 498, were not considered regulatory takings. In each of these cases, we affirmed that "where an owner possesses a full 'bundle' of property rights, the destruction of one 'strand' of the bundle is not a taking." Andrus, 444 U.S. at 65–66. . . .

. . . Petitioners seek to bring this case under the rule announced in Lucas by arguing that we can effectively sever a 32-month segment from the remainder of each landowner's fee simple estate, and then ask whether that segment has been taken in its entirety by the moratoria. Of course, defining the property interest taken in terms of the very regulation being challenged is circular. With property so divided, every delay would become a total ban; the moratorium and the normal permit process alike would constitute categorical takings. Petitioners' "conceptual severance" argument is unavailing because it ignores Penn Central's admonition that in regulatory takings cases we must focus on "the parcel as a whole." 438 U.S. at 130–131. We have consistently rejected such an approach to the "denominator" question. See Keystone, 480 U.S. at 497. . . . Thus, the District Court erred when it disaggregated petitioners' property into temporal segments corresponding to the regulations at issue and then analyzed whether petitioners were deprived of all economically viable use during each period. 34 F. Supp. 2d, at 1242–1245. The starting point for the court's analysis should have been to ask whether there was a total taking of the entire parcel; if not, then Penn Central was the proper framework.

An interest in real property is defined by the metes and bounds that describe its geographic dimensions and the term of years that describes the temporal aspect of the owner's interest. Both dimensions must be considered if the interest is to be viewed in its entirety. Hence, a permanent deprivation of the owner's use of the entire area is a taking of "the parcel as a whole," whereas a temporary restriction that merely causes a diminution in value is not. Logically, a fee simple estate cannot be rendered valueless by a temporary prohibition on economic use, because the property will recover value as soon as the prohibition is lifted. . . .

. . . [Our] cases make clear that the categorical rule in Lucas was carved out for the "extraordinary case" in which a regulation permanently deprives property of all value; the default rule remains that, in the regulatory taking context, we require a more fact specific inquiry. . . .

V

Considerations of "fairness and justice" arguably could support the conclusion that TRPA's moratoria were takings of petitioners' property based on any of seven different theories. First, even though we have not previously done so, we might now announce a categorical rule that, in the interest of fairness and justice, compensation is required whenever government temporarily deprives an owner of all economically viable use of her property. Second, we could craft a narrower rule that would cover all temporary land-use restrictions except those "normal delays in obtaining building permits, changes in zoning ordinances, variances, and the like" which were put to one side in our opinion in [First English Evangelical Lutheran Church of Glendale v. County of Los Angeles, 482 U.S. 304, 321 (1987)]. Third, we could adopt a rule like the one suggested by an amicus supporting petitioners that would "allow a short fixed period for deliberations to take place without compensation — say maximum one year — after which the just compensation requirements" would "kick in." Fourth, with the benefit of hindsight, we might characterize the successive actions of TRPA as a "series of rolling moratoria" that were the functional equivalent of a permanent taking. Fifth, were it not for the findings of the District Court that TRPA acted diligently and in good faith, we might have concluded that the agency was stalling in order to avoid promulgating the environmental threshold carrying capacities and regional plan mandated by the 1980 Compact. Cf. Monterey v. Del Monte Dunes at Monterey, Ltd., 526 U.S. 687, 698 (1999). Sixth, apart from the District Court's finding that TRPA's actions represented a proportional response to a serious risk of harm to the lake, petitioners might have argued that the moratoria did not substantially advance a legitimate state interest, see [Agins v. City of Tiburon, 447 U.S. 255, 260 (1980)] and *Monterey*. Finally, if petitioners had challenged the application of the moratoria to their individual parcels, instead of making a facial challenge, some of them might have prevailed under a *Penn Central* analysis.

As the case comes to us, however, none of the last four theories is available. The "rolling moratoria" theory was presented in the petition for certiorari, but our order granting review did not encompass that issue, 533 U.S. 948 (2001); the case was tried in the District Court and reviewed in the Court of Appeals on the theory that each of the two moratoria was a separate taking, one for a 2-year period and the other for an 8-month period. [Tahoe-Sierra Preservation Council, Inc. v. Tahoe Regional Planning Agency, 216 F.3d 764, 769 (9th Cir. 2000).] And, as we have already noted, recovery on either a bad faith theory or a theory that the state interests were insubstantial is foreclosed by the District Court's unchallenged findings of fact. Recovery under a *Penn Central* analysis is also foreclosed both because petitioners expressly disavowed that theory, and because they did not appeal from the District Court's conclusion that the evidence would not support it. Nonetheless, each of the three per se theories is fairly encompassed within the question that we decided to answer.

With respect to these theories, the ultimate constitutional question is whether the concepts of "fairness and justice" that underlie the Takings Clause will be better served by one of these categorical rules or by a *Penn Central* inquiry into all of the relevant circumstances in particular cases. From that perspective, the extreme categorical rule that any deprivation of all economic use, no matter how brief, constitutes a compensable taking surely cannot be sustained. Petitioners' broad submission would apply to numerous "normal delays in obtaining building permits, changes in zoning ordinances, variances, and the like," [*First English*,] 482 U.S. at 321, as well as to orders temporarily prohibiting access to crime scenes, businesses that violate health codes, fire-damaged buildings, or other areas that we cannot now foresee. Such a rule would undoubtedly require changes in numerous practices that have long been considered permissible exercises of the police power. As Justice Holmes warned in *Mahon*, "[g]overnment hardly could go on if to some extent values incident to property could not be diminished without paying for every such change in the general law." 260 U.S. at 413. A rule that required compensation for every delay in the use of property would render routine government processes prohibitively expensive

[handwritten margin note: that's for leg Not cT]

or encourage hasty decisionmaking. Such an important change in the law should be the product of legislative rulemaking rather than adjudication.

More importantly, for reasons set out at some length by Justice O'CONNOR in her *[handwritten: 's concurrence in Palazzolo]* concurring opinion in Palazzolo v. Rhode Island, 533 U.S. at 636, we are persuaded that the better approach to claims that a regulation has effected a temporary taking "requires careful examination and weighing of all the relevant circumstances." . . . In rejecting petitioners' per se rule, we do not hold that the temporary nature of a land-use restriction precludes finding that it effects a taking; we simply recognize that it should not be given exclusive significance one way or the other.

A narrower rule that excluded the normal delays associated with processing permits, or that covered only delays of more than a year, would certainly have a less severe impact on prevailing practices, but it would still impose serious financial constraints on the planning process. Unlike the "extraordinary circumstance" in which the government deprives a property owner of all economic use, *Lucas*, 505 U.S. at 1017, moratoria like Ordinance 81-5 and Resolution 83-21 are used widely among land-use planners to preserve the status quo while formulating a more permanent development strategy. In fact, the consensus in the planning community appears to be that moratoria, or "interim development controls" as they are often called, are an essential tool of successful development. Yet even the weak version of petitioners' categorical rule would treat these interim measures as takings regardless of the good faith of the planners, the reasonable expectations of the landowners, or the actual impact of the moratorium on property values.

The interest in facilitating informed decisionmaking by regulatory agencies counsels against adopting a per se rule that would impose such severe costs on their deliberations. Otherwise, the financial constraints of compensating property owners during a moratorium may force officials to rush through the planning process or to abandon the practice altogether. To the extent that communities are forced to abandon using moratoria, landowners will have incentives to develop their property quickly before a comprehensive plan can be enacted, thereby fostering inefficient and ill-conceived growth. A finding in the 1980 Compact itself, which presumably was endorsed by all three legislative bodies that participated in its enactment, attests to the importance of that concern. 94 Stat. 3243 ("The legislatures of the States of California and Nevada find that in order to make effective the regional plan as revised by the agency, it is necessary to halt temporarily works of development in the region which might otherwise absorb the entire capability of the region for further development or direct it out of harmony with the ultimate plan"). . . .

It may well be true that any moratorium that lasts for more than one year should be viewed with special skepticism. But given the fact that the District Court found that the 32 months required by TRPA to formulate the 1984 Regional Plan was not unreasonable, we could not possibly conclude that every delay of over one year is constitutionally unacceptable. Formulating a general rule of this kind is a suitable task for state legislatures. In our view, the duration of the restriction is one of the important factors that a court must consider in the appraisal of a regulatory takings claim, but with respect to that factor as with respect to other factors, the "temptation to adopt what amount to per se rules in either direction must be resisted." *Palazzolo*, 533 U.S. at 636 (O'CONNOR, J., concurring). There may be moratoria that last longer than one year which interfere with reasonable investment-backed expectations, but as the District Court's opinion illustrates, petitioners' proposed rule is simply "too blunt an instrument" for identifying those cases. Id. at 628. We conclude, therefore, that the interest in "fairness and justice" will be best served by relying on the familiar *Penn Central* approach when deciding cases like this, rather than by attempting to craft a new categorical rule.

Accordingly, the judgment of the Court of Appeals is affirmed.

[handwritten margin note: As for time of moratorium ⟶ DC found 32 mos. wasn't unreasonable]

Chief Justice REHNQUIST, with whom Justice SCALIA and Justice THOMAS join, dissenting. . . .

II

. . . *Lucas* reaffirmed our "frequently expressed" view that "when the owner of real property has been called upon to sacrifice all economically beneficial uses in the name of the common good, that is, to leave his property economically idle, he has suffered a taking." 505 U.S. at 1019. . . . But the Court refuses to apply *Lucas* on the ground that the deprivation was "temporary."

Neither the Takings Clause nor our case law supports such a distinction. For one thing, a distinction between "temporary" and "permanent" prohibitions is tenuous. The "temporary" prohibition in this case that the Court finds is not a taking lasted almost six years. The "permanent" prohibition that the Court held to be a taking in *Lucas* lasted less than two years. See 505 U.S. at 1011–1012. . . . Under the Court's decision today, the takings question turns entirely on the initial label given a regulation, a label that is often without much meaning. There is every incentive for government to simply label any prohibition on development "temporary," or to fix a set number of years. As in this case, this initial designation does not preclude the government from repeatedly extending the "temporary" prohibition into a long-term ban on all development. . . .

III . . . When a regulation merely delays a final land-use decision, we have recognized that there are other background principles of state property law that prevent the delay from being deemed a taking. We thus noted in *First English* that our discussion of temporary takings did not apply "in the case of normal delays in obtaining building permits, changes in zoning ordinances, variances, and the like." 482 U.S. at 321. . . . Thus, the short-term delays attendant to zoning and permit regimes are a longstanding feature of state property law and part of a landowner's reasonable investment-backed expectations. . . .

[T]his case does not require us to decide as a categorical matter whether moratoria prohibiting all economic use are an implied limitation of state property law, because the duration of this "moratorium" far exceeds that of ordinary moratoria. . . .

Lake Tahoe is a national treasure, and I do not doubt that respondent's efforts at preventing further degradation of the lake were made in good faith in furtherance of the public interest. But, as is the case with most governmental action that furthers the public interest, the Constitution requires that the costs and burdens be borne by the public at large, not by a few targeted citizens. . . .

Justice THOMAS, with whom Justice SCALIA joins, dissenting. . . .

I would hold that regulations prohibiting all productive uses of property are subject to *Lucas'* per se rule, regardless of whether the property so burdened retains theoretical useful life and value if, and when, the "temporary" moratorium is lifted. To my mind, such potential future value bears on the amount of compensation due and has nothing to do with the question whether there was a taking in the first place. . . .

Note on the Denominator Problem

1. *Conceptual severance.* Professor Radin coined the term *conceptual severance* to describe the strategy of "delineating a property interest consisting of just what the

government action has removed from the owner . . . [t]hus . . . 'sever[ing]' from the whole bundle of rights just those strands that are interfered with by the regulation, and then hypothetically or conceptually constru[ing] those strands in the aggregate as a separate whole thing." Margaret Jane Radin, The Liberal Conception of Property: Cross Currents in the Jurisprudence of Takings, 88 Colum. L. Rev. 1667, 1676 (1988). Does *Tahoe-Sierra's* rejection of conceptual severance in the moratorium context finally put to rest the "parcel as a whole" question that footnote 7 of *Lucas* maintained was still open?

2. *Advantages and disadvantages of a narrow definition of property.* What do each of the theories of compensation outlined at pp. 145–58 suggest about how broadly property ought to be defined? See, e.g., Susan Rose-Ackerman, Against Ad Hocery, 88 Colum. L. Rev. 1697, 1705 (1988) (under insurance theory of compensation, broad view of property is warranted because an individual's aversion to risk depends on the threat the risk poses to one's total wealth).

3. *The multifactored, ad hoc denominator test.* The lower federal courts and state courts generally have converged on a multifactored, ad hoc test to define the denominator. The factors they examine include the degree of contiguity between the various plots; the dates of acquisition; how the landowner's investment-backed expectations regarded the parcel; whether any land that could be part of the denominator was sold or developed prior to the regulation's enactment or enforcement; the extent to which the parcel has been treated as a single unit for the purposes of, for example, financing, insurance, or taxation; and the extent to which the protected land enhances the value of the remaining land. Ciampitti v. United States, 22 Cl. Ct. 310 (1991).

For good reviews of the cases, see Joel R. Burcat & Julia M. Glencer, Is the Relevant Parcel Still Relevant?, SJ052 ALI-ABA 99 (2004); Dwight H. Merriam, Rules for the Relevant Parcel, 25 U. Haw. L. Rev. 353 (2003). For overviews of the theoretical problems posed by the denominator issue, see, e.g., Benjamin Allee, Drawing the Line in Regulatory Takings Law: How a Benefits Fraction Supports the Fee Simple Approach to the Denominator Problem, 70 Fordham L. Rev. 1957, 1970 (2002); John E. Fee, Unearthing the Denominator in Regulatory Taking Claims, 61 U. Chi. L. Rev. 1535, 1552 (1994); Danaya C. Wright, A New Time for Denominators: Toward a Dynamic Theory of Property in the Regulatory Takings Relevant Parcel Analysis, 34 Envtl. L. 175 (2004).

4. *Jurisdictional limits?* When determining the relevant parcel, should the court take into account the jurisdictional boundaries of the regulating authority? See, e.g., Vulcan Materials Co. v. City of Tehuacana, 369 F.3d 882, 890 (5th Cir. 2004) (relevant parcel was 48 acres of land located within city borders and subject to city's ban on quarrying, even though owner was able to quarry the 250 adjacent acres that were outside the city's jurisdiction, because denominator should not include property beyond the regulator's reach).

5. *Ad hocery, again.* Perhaps the most significant aspect of *Palazzolo* and *Tahoe-Sierra* is the Court's backtracking from the per se tests that the Court seemed to be embracing in *Lucas*. See also p. 179.

Lingle v. Chevron U.S.A., Inc.
125 S. Ct. 2074 (2005)

Justice O'CONNOR delivered the opinion of the Court.

. . . A quarter century ago, in Agins v. City of Tiburon, 447 U.S. 255, the Court declared that government regulation of private property "effects a taking if [such regulation] does not substantially advance legitimate state interests. . . ." Id. at 260. Through reiteration in a half dozen or so decisions since *Agins*, this language has been ensconced in our Fifth Amendment takings jurisprudence. See Monterey v. Del Monte Dunes at Monterey, Ltd., 526 U.S. 687, 704 (1999) (citing cases).

In the case before us, the lower courts applied *Agins*' "substantially advances" formula to strike down a Hawaii statute that limits the rent that oil companies may charge to dealers who lease service stations owned by the companies. . . . This case requires us to decide whether the "substantially advances" formula announced in *Agins* is an appropriate test for determining whether a regulation effects a Fifth Amendment taking. We conclude that it is not. . . .

II

A . . .

[The Court explains the two per se rules of Loretto v. Teleprompter Manhattan CATV Corp., 458 U.S. 419 (1982), discussed at pp. 167–69, and Lucas v. South Carolina Coastal Council, 505 U.S. 1003 (1992), excerpted at p. 169, and notes that "outside these two categories" and the special context of land-use exactions, discussed at pp. 634–52, regulatory takings challenges are governed by Penn Central Transportation Co. v. New York City, 438 U.S. 104 (1976), excerpted at p. 158).]

Although our regulatory takings jurisprudence cannot be characterized as unified, these three inquiries (reflected in *Loretto, Lucas,* and *Penn Central*) share a common touchstone. Each aims to identify regulatory actions that are functionally equivalent to the classic taking in which government directly appropriates private property or ousts the owner from his domain. Accordingly, each of these tests focuses directly upon the severity of the burden that government imposes upon private property rights. . . .

B

. . . The "substantially advances" formula suggests a means-ends test: It asks, in essence, whether a regulation of private property is *effective* in achieving some legitimate public purpose. An inquiry of this nature has some logic in the context of a due process challenge, for a regulation that fails to serve any legitimate governmental objective may be so arbitrary or irrational that it runs afoul of the Due Process Clause. But such a test is not a valid method of discerning whether private property has been "taken" for purposes of the Fifth Amendment.

In stark contrast to the three regulatory takings tests discussed above, the "substantially advances" inquiry reveals nothing about the *magnitude or character of the burden* a particular regulation imposes upon private property rights. Nor does it provide any information about how any regulatory burden is *distributed* among property owners. In consequence, this test does not help to identify those regulations whose effects are functionally comparable to government appropriation or invasion of private property; it is tethered neither to the text of the Takings Clause nor to the basic justification for allowing regulatory actions to be challenged under the Clause.

. . . A test that tells us nothing about the actual burden imposed on property rights, or how that burden is allocated cannot tell us when justice might require that the burden be spread among taxpayers through the payment of compensation. The owner of a property subject to a regulation that *effectively* serves a legitimate state interest may be just as singled out and just as burdened as the owner of a property subject to an *ineffective* regulation. It would make little sense to say that the second owner has suffered a taking while the first has not. Likewise, an ineffective regulation may not significantly burden property rights at all, and it may distribute any burden broadly and evenly among property owners. The notion that such a regulation nevertheless "takes" private property for public use merely by virtue of its ineffectiveness or foolishness is untenable.

Instead of addressing a challenged regulation's effect on private property, the "substantially advances" inquiry probes the regulation's underlying validity. But such an inquiry is logically prior to and distinct from the question whether a regulation effects a taking, for the Takings Clause presupposes that the government has acted in pursuit of a valid public purpose. The Clause expressly requires compensation where government takes private property "*for public use.*" It does not bar government from interfering with property rights, but rather requires compensation "in the event of *otherwise proper interference* amounting to a taking." First English Evangelical Lutheran Church [of Glendale v. County of Los Angeles], 482 U.S. [304], 315 [(1987)] (emphasis added). Conversely, if a government action is found to be impermissible—for instance because it fails to meet the "public use" requirement or is so arbitrary as to violate due process—that is the end of the inquiry. No amount of compensation can authorize such action.

Chevron's challenge to the Hawaii statute in this case illustrates the flaws in the "substantially advances" theory. To begin with, it is unclear how significantly Hawaii's rent cap actually burdens Chevron's property rights. The parties stipulated below that the cap would reduce Chevron's aggregate rental income on 11 of its 64 lessee-dealer stations by about $207,000 per year, but that Chevron nevertheless expects to receive a return on its investment in these stations that satisfies any constitutional standard. Moreover, Chevron asserted below, and the District Court found, that Chevron would recoup any reductions in its rental income by raising wholesale gasoline prices. In short, Chevron has not clearly argued—let alone established—that it has been singled out to bear any particularly severe regulatory burden. Rather, the gravamen of Chevron's claim is simply that Hawaii's rent cap will not actually serve the State's legitimate interest in protecting consumers against high gasoline prices. Whatever the merits of that claim, it does not sound under the Takings Clause. Chevron plainly does not seek compensation for a taking of its property for a legitimate public use, but rather an injunction against the enforcement of a regulation that it alleges to be fundamentally arbitrary and irrational.

Finally, the "substantially advances" formula is not only *doctrinally* untenable as a takings test—its application as such would also present serious practical difficulties. The *Agins* formula can be read to demand heightened means-ends review of virtually any regulation of private property. If so interpreted, it would require courts to scrutinize the efficacy of a vast array of state and federal regulations—a task for which courts are not well suited. Moreover, it would empower—and might often require—courts to substitute their predictive judgments for those of elected legislatures and expert agencies.

Although the instant case is only the tip of the proverbial iceberg, it foreshadows the hazards of placing courts in this role. To resolve Chevron's takings claim, the District Court was required to choose between the views of two opposing economists as to whether Hawaii's rent control statute would help to prevent concentration and supracompetitive prices in the State's retail gasoline market. Finding one expert to be "more persuasive" than the other, the court concluded that the Hawaii Legislature's chosen regulatory strategy would not actually achieve its objectives. . . . We find the proceedings below remarkable, to say the least, given that we have long eschewed such heightened scrutiny when addressing substantive due process challenges to government regulation. See, e.g., Exxon Corp. v. Governor of Maryland, 437 U.S. 117, 124–125 (1978). The reasons for deference to legislative judgments about the need for, and likely effectiveness of, regulatory actions are by now well established, and we think they are no less applicable here. . . .

III

. . . Today we correct course. We hold that the "substantially advances" formula is not a valid takings test, and indeed conclude that it has no proper place in our takings jurisprudence. . . . Because Chevron argued only a "substantially advances" theory in support of its takings claim, it was not entitled to summary judgment on that claim. Accordingly, we reverse the judgment of the Ninth Circuit and remand the case for further proceedings consistent with this opinion.

Justice KENNEDY, concurring. . . .

No SS for Chevron

Note on the Relationship Between the Takings Clause and the Due Process Clause

1. *The longstanding debate*. The controversy *Lingle* puts to rest had been simmering for decades. For representative recent discussions of the merits and demerits of including a due process inquiry in the takings analysis, see, e.g., Steven J. Eagle, Substantive Due Process and Regulatory Takings: A Reappraisal, 51 Ala. L. Rev. 977 (2000); John D. Echeverria & Sharon Dennis, The Takings Issue and the Due Process Clause: A Way Out of a Doctrinal Confusion, 17 Vt. L. Rev. 695 (1993); Ronald J. Krotoszynski, Jr., Expropriatory Intent: Defining the Proper Boundaries of Substantive Due Process and the Takings Clause, 80 N.C. L. Rev. 713 (2002); R.S. Radford, The "Substantial Advancement" Test and the Supreme Court's Regulatory Takings Doctrine, SJ052 ALI-ABA 341 (2004); Kenneth Salzberg, "Takings" as Due Process, or Due Process as "Takings"?, 36 Val. U. L. Rev. 413 (2002); Edward J. Sullivan, Emperors and Clothes: The Genealogy and Operation of the *Agins'* Tests, 33 Urb. Law. 343 (2001); Mark Tunick, Constitutional Protections of Private Property: Decoupling the Takings and Due Process Clauses, 3 U. Pa. J. Const. L. 885 (2001).

2. *Claims about money rather than real property*. Although *Lingle* resolved the debate over whether courts should incorporate the Due Process Clause into takings analysis, questions still remain about the kinds of challenges best addressed under each clause, a problem we first saw at p. 95. In Eastern Enterprises v. Apfel, 524 U.S. 498 (1998), for example, a former coal company challenged provisions of the Coal Industry Retiree Health Benefit Act of 1992 under both the Takings and Due Process Clauses. The act required Eastern to fund health care benefits for retired miners who had worked for the company prior to 1966. Justice O'Connor, joined by Justices Rehnquist, Scalia, and Thomas, believed the act constituted a taking under the *Penn Central* factors because it "single[d] out certain employers to bear a burden that is substantial in amount, based on the employers' conduct far in the past, and unrelated to any commitment that the employers made or to any injury they caused." Id. at 537. Justice Kennedy concurred in the judgment holding the act unconstitutional, but argued that the act was appropriately analyzed under the Due Process Clause, not the Takings Clause. The Takings Clause, he reasoned, applies to regulations that affect a specific and identified property or right, not to those that impose monetary liability on the plaintiff. Because of the retroactive nature of the act, however, Justice Kennedy believed it violated the Due Process Clause. Justice Stevens, joined by Justices Souter, Ginsburg, and Breyer, agreed with Justice Kennedy that the Takings Clause did not apply, but disagreed that the act violated the Due Process Clause.

3. *Levels of scrutiny*. In Nollan v. California Coastal Commission, 483 U.S. 825 (1987), which we won't reach in full until Chapter 7 (see p. 638), the Supreme Court decided

a takings challenge to an exaction demanded by the California Coastal Commission in exchange for the Commission's permission to develop beachfront property. The majority asserted that "[o]ur cases have not elaborated on the standards for determining what constitutes a 'legitimate state interest' or what type of connection between the regulation and the state interest satisfies the requirement that the former 'substantially advance' the latter." Id. at 834. Invoking *Agins*, the *Nollan* Court then hinted that the level of scrutiny (or conversely, degree of deference shown) in takings cases might be higher than that traditionally used in due process or equal protection cases. See id. at 834 n.3.

Lingle seems to dispose of any notion that the Takings Clause should be used, outside the exactions context we'll discuss in Chapter 7, to give property owners the benefit of greater judicial scrutiny of legislative decisions than is usually imposed. For discussion of the deference due the legislature in takings challenges, see Robert J. Hopperton, Standards of Judicial Review in Supreme Court Land Use Opinions: A Taxonomy, an Analytical Framework, and a Synthesis, 51 Wash. U. J. Urb. & Contemp. L. 1 (1997); Nathaniel S. Lawrence, Means, Motives, and Takings: The Nexus Test of *Nollan v. California Coastal Commission*, 12 Harv. Envtl. L. Rev. 231 (1988); Frank Michelman, Takings, 1987, 88 Colum. L. Rev. 1600, 1605–14 (1988).

g. The Special Problem of Nonconforming Uses and Vested Rights

In *Penn Central*, the Court hinted that it might have reached a different outcome if the challenged regulation had prevented Grand Central from being used as it always had been. The state courts have long regarded government actions that interfere with a long-standing use of property, or change the rules once a development project is underway, as posing special threats of unfairness. Accordingly, the state courts (and increasingly, state legislatures) have developed two related doctrines — the law of nonconforming uses and the law of vested rights (as well as the closely connected law of estoppel) — to address those threats.

Village of Valatie v. Smith
632 N.E.2d 1264 (N.Y. 1994)

SIMONS, Judge.

This appeal challenges the facial validity of . . . a local law that terminates the nonconforming use of a mobile home upon the transfer of ownership of either the mobile home or the land upon which it sits. Defendant argues that it is unconstitutional for the Village to use a change in ownership as the termination date for a nonconforming use. We conclude, however, that defendant has failed to carry her burden of showing that the local law is unreasonable on its face. . . .

In 1968, the Village enacted chapter 85 to prohibit the placement of mobile homes outside mobile home parks. Under the law, any existing mobile home located outside a park which met certain health standards was allowed to remain as a nonconforming use until either ownership of the land or ownership of the mobile home changed. According to the Village, six mobile homes, including one owned by defendant's father, fell within this exception at the time the law was passed.

In 1989, defendant inherited the mobile home from her father and the Village instituted this action to enforce the law and have the unit removed. . . . [On cross-motions for summary judgment], the court characterized defendant's mobile home as a lawful non-conforming use — i.e., a use that was legally in place at the time the municipality enacted legislation prohibiting the use. Reasoning that the right to continue a nonconforming use runs with the land, the court held that the portion of the ordinance setting termination at the transfer of ownership was unconstitutional. The Appellate Division affirmed. . . . 596 N.Y.S.2d 581.

Preliminarily, it is important to note that the question presented is the facial validity of the local law. The Court is not called upon to decide whether the local law as applied so deprived defendant of the value of her property as to constitute a governmental taking under the Fifth Amendment. . . .

Thus, the narrow issue is whether the Village acted unreasonably by establishing an amortization period that uses the transfer of ownership as an end point.

The policy of allowing nonconforming uses to continue originated in concerns that the application of land use regulations to uses existing prior to the regulations' enactment might be construed as confiscatory and unconstitutional. While it was initially assumed that nonconforming uses would disappear with time, just the opposite proved to be true in many instances, with the nonconforming use thriving in the absence of any new lawful competition. In light of the problems presented by continuing nonconforming uses, this Court has characterized the law's allowance of such uses as a "grudging tolerance," and we have recognized the right of municipalities to take reasonable measures to eliminate them. See Matter of Pelham Esplanade v. Board of Trustees, 565 N.E.2d 508 (N.Y. 1990).

Most often, elimination has been effected by establishing amortization periods, at the conclusion of which the nonconforming use must end. . . . "Amortization period" simply designates a period of time granted to owners of nonconforming uses during which they may phase out their operations as they see fit and make other arrangements. It is, in effect, a grace period, putting owners on fair notice of the law and giving them a fair opportunity to recoup their investment. . . .

The validity of an amortization period depends on its reasonableness. Matter of Harbison v. City of Buffalo, 152 N.E.2d 42 (N.Y. 1958). We have avoided any fixed formula for determining what constitutes a reasonable period. Instead, we have held that an amortization period is presumed valid, and the owner must carry the heavy burden of overcoming that presumption by demonstrating that the loss suffered is so substantial that it outweighs the public benefit to be gained by the exercise of the police power. Matter of Town of Islip v. Caviglia, 540 N.E.2d 215 (N.Y. 1989). . . .

Defendant here does not challenge the local law's constitutionality under our established balancing test for amortization periods — i.e., whether the individual loss outweighs the public benefit. Instead, the challenge is a more basic due process claim: that the means of eliminating nonconforming uses is not reasonably related to the Village's legitimate interest in land use planning. More particularly, defendant makes two arguments: first, that the length of an amortization period must be related either to land use objectives or to the financial recoupment needs of the owner and, second, that the local law violates the principle that zoning is to regulate land use rather than ownership. Neither argument withstands analysis.

We have never required that the length of the amortization period be based on a municipality's land use objectives. To the contrary, the periods are routinely calculated to protect the rights of individual owners at the temporary expense of public land use objectives. Typically, the period of time allowed has been measured for reasonableness by considering whether the owners had adequate time to recoup their investment in the use. Patently, such protection of an individual's interest is unrelated to land use objectives. Indeed, were land use objectives the only permissible criteria for scheduling amortization, the law would require immediate elimination of nonconforming uses in all instances. Instead, the setting of the amortization period involves balancing the interests of the individual and those of the public. Thus, the real issue here is whether it was irrational for the Village, in striking that balance, to consider a nonfinancial interest of the individual owners — specifically, the individual's interest in not being displaced involuntarily.

It is significant that the six properties involved here are residential. In our previous cases dealing with amortization, we have focused almost exclusively on commercial properties, where the owner's interest is easily reduced to financial considerations. The same may not be true for the owners of residential properties, especially in instances where the property is the primary residence of the owner. Simply being able to recoup one's financial investment may be a secondary concern to staying in a neighborhood or remaining on a particular piece of land. Indeed, when mobile homes are involved, there may actually be little or no financial loss, given that the owner often will be able to relocate the structure and sell the land for legal development. Here, rather than focusing solely on financial recoupment, the Village apparently took a broader view of "an individual's interest in maintaining the present use" of the property. See Modjeska Sign Studios v. Berle, 373 N.E.2d 255 (N.Y. 1977). It enacted a law that allowed owners to keep their mobile homes in place until they decided to sell, even though they may have recouped their investment long ago. By doing so, it saved the owners from a forced relocation at the end of a predetermined amortization period set by the Village. Defendant has not demonstrated why such an approach is irrational or explained why a municipality should be barred constitutionally from considering the nonfinancial interests of the owners in setting an amortization schedule. . . .

Defendant's second argument is premised on the "fundamental rule that zoning deals basically with land use and not with the person who owns or occupies it." Matter of Dexter v. Town Board, 324 N.E.2d 870 (N.Y. 1975). In essence, the rule is a prohibition against ad hominem zoning decisions. In *Dexter*, for instance, a zoning change needed to allow a supermarket was to be effective only if a certain corporation developed the site. We voided the action on the ground that the identity of the site's owner was irrelevant to its suitability for a certain type of development. Likewise, variances to accommodate the personal physical needs of the occupants have been denied on the basis that such needs are unrelated to land use. See Matter of Fuhst v. Foley, 382 N.E.2d 756 (N.Y. 1978). . . .

. . . The hallmark of cases like *Dexter* and *Fuhst* is that an identifiable individual is singled out for special treatment in land use regulation. No such individualized treatment is involved in the present case. All similarly situated owners are treated identically. The same is true for all prospective buyers. The only preferential treatment identified by defendant is that the owner in 1968 has rights that no future owner will enjoy. But the law has long recognized the special status of those who have a preexisting use at the time land controls are adopted. Indeed, the allowance of a nonconforming use in the first instance is based on that recognition. . . .

Thus, we conclude that defendant has failed to prevail on her facial challenge to the Village law. . . .

Note on Nonconforming Uses

1. *Opposing views.* A substantial minority of courts refuse to countenance any amortization or rollback of nonconforming uses, either on state constitutional grounds, see, e.g., PA Northwestern Distributors, Inc. v. Zoning Hearing Board, 584 A.2d 1372 (Pa. 1991), or on the ground that amortization is not authorized by the state's zoning enabling act. See, e.g., State v. Bates, 305 N.W.2d 426 (Iowa 1981). For a catalog of the various

states' positions, see Jay M. Zitter, Annotation, Validity of Provisions for Amortization of Nonconforming Uses, 8 A.L.R.5th 391 (1992 & 2004 Supp.). Dissenters from the majority view augment their constitutional and authority arguments with dire predictions that amortization of nonconforming uses will deter investment by putting any landowner's reasonable expectations at risk and will result in deterioration as owners refuse to maintain their properties. See *PA Northwestern*, supra. See also Harbison v. City of Buffalo, 152 N.E.2d 42, 47 (N.Y. 1958) (Van Voorhis, J., dissenting). For analysis of those arguments, see, e.g., Craig A. Peterson & Claire McCarthy, Amortization of Legal Land Use Nonconformities as Regulatory Takings: An Uncertain Future, 35 Wash. U. J. Urb. & Contemp. L. 37 (1989).

2. *Statutory prohibitions on amortization.* Many state zoning enabling acts protect nonconforming uses against interference. See, e.g., Ariz. Rev. Stat. Ann. §9-462.02 (West 2005) ("Nothing in an ordinance or regulation authorized by this article shall affect existing property or the right to its continued use for the purpose used at the time the ordinance or regulation takes effect, nor to any reasonable repairs or alterations in buildings or property used for such existing purpose"); N.J. Stat. Ann. §40:55D-68 (West 2005) ("Any nonconforming use or structure existing at the time of the passage of an ordinance may be continued upon the lot or in the structure so occupied and any such structure may be restored or repaired in the event of partial destruction thereof").

3. *Determining the reasonableness of an amortization period.* As *Valatie's* dicta reveal, many courts hold that the reasonableness of an amortization period depends on whether the public benefits from termination of a use outweigh the landowner's cost of losing that use. If a city can immediately terminate a brewery without paying compensation (see *Mugler*, pp. 136–37), why should it have to compensate in order to immediately terminate a nonconforming mobile home? Is the only difference between *Mugler* and *Valatie* whether the use at issue is a nuisance? If a nonconforming use is a nuisance, does the cost/benefit analysis mean that a city must tolerate continuation of the use so long as the nuisance is cost-justified? See pp. 511–20.

If the nonconforming use is not a nuisance, why should it be treated any differently from any other land use? Surely a city could not (without compensating the owner) force the demolition of a single-family house a few years after it was built just because razing the house would generate great public benefits — for example, by opening up a previously blocked view. But see Lone v. Montgomery County, 584 A.2d 142 (Md. Ct. Spec. App. 1991) (upholding ten-year amortization period to convert nonconforming multifamily housing to single-family use). Why then, should that be the rule for nonconforming uses? The Missouri Supreme Court invalidated an amortization period in Hoffmann v. Kinealy, 389 S.W.2d 745, 753 (Mo. 1965), reasoning that "it would be a strange and novel doctrine indeed which would approve a municipality taking private property . . . without compensation if the property was not too valuable and the taking was not too soon. . . . " How would you answer that argument?

What factors are relevant in determining the reasonableness of an amortization period? Should the owners of expensive nonconforming improvements have a longer amortization period than owners of cheaper ones? See, e.g., Red Roof Inns, Inc. v. City of Ridgeland, 797 So.2d 898 (Miss. 2001) (upholding amortization of signs based upon original cost of construction); Town of Islip v. Caviglia, 540 N.E.2d 215, 224 (N.Y. 1989) (noting that "the period of amortization will normally increase as the amount invested increases"). See also Jay Campbell, Amortization in the Twenty-Second Century, Zoning & Plan. L. Rep., Jan. 2004, at 1; Margaret Collins, Methods of Determining Amortization Periods for Non-Conforming Uses, 3 Wash. U. J.L. & Pol'y 215 (2000); Zitter, supra.

4. *Personality interest?* Is *Valatie* correct in holding that amortization periods can take into account such "nonfinancial" concerns as the owner's "personality interest" in the property? See Margaret Jane Radin, Property and Personhood, 34 Stan. L. Rev. 957 (1982). If nonconforming use status is meant to protect personality interests, would it be reasonable to require amortization after a number of years rather than after death or transfer of the property as in *Valatie?* May amortization schedules be tied to how long the person has lived on the property? Should they be? Could an amortization scheme take into account other "nonfinancial" concerns, such as the owner's illness or special care needs? As *Valatie* indicates, that is not the law when landowners seek a variance: there, the personal needs of an individual owner may not be considered. See p. 294. Are the two situations distinguishable?

5. *Buying time.* Property owners challenging amortization periods sometimes use litigation to delay enforcement of valid amortization programs for years. What remedies (such as appeals bonds or liability for the city's interim damages) would deter a landowner from pursuing meritless lawsuits to buy time?

6. *Alteration and expansion of nonconforming uses.* When zoning first gained momentum in the 1920s, its application to existing cities inevitably created many nonconforming uses, despite the tendency of officials to draw zoning boundaries to legitimize existing uses. During the early years of zoning, officials hoped that these nonconforming uses would slowly wither away. To expedite this withering, most ordinances placed limitations on the expansion and alteration of such uses. Because natural withering was expected and was less controversial politically than imposition of a cutoff date, many cities also declined to pursue mandatory phaseout programs. In combination, these policies produced unexpected results. A nonconforming grocery store in a residential neighborhood, for example, may not wither away, but instead may prosper because zoning prevents competitors from opening up nearby. However, because of limitations on expansion, the grocery's owners may be forced to continue operating in obsolete and shabby quarters, often to the increasing dismay of immediate neighbors.

When the owner of a nonconforming use seeks permission to modernize the use, a local government thus faces a dilemma. Granting the request often results in immediate environmental benefits, but perpetuates a use that is inconsistent with the official plan for the city.

A local government that allows a nonconforming use to modernize may run afoul of the state's zoning enabling act. In Avalon Home & Land Owner's Ass'n v. Avalon, 543 A.2d 950 (N.J. 1988), for example, the New Jersey Supreme Court invalidated a local ordinance that allowed owners of nonconforming structures to replace or renovate such a structure as long as the replacement did not exceed the size of the existing structure. The court considered the local ordinance inconsistent with the state's zoning enabling act, which allowed restoration of a nonconforming use when the use was partially destroyed. The court expressed sympathy for the local government's desire to encourage renovation of nonconforming uses, but opined that the proper way to accomplish that goal was for the local government to rezone to make the uses conforming or to grant use variances to the nonconforming uses.

A zoning ordinance that authorizes the continuation of nonconforming uses may sometimes be construed to allow such uses to expand. Moreover, some courts hold that a property owner has a constitutional right to expand a lawful nonconforming use to meet natural business expansion so long as the health, safety, and welfare of the community are not jeopardized. Township of Chartiers v. William H. Martin, Inc., 542 A.2d 985 (Pa. 1988) ("natural expansion" doctrine gives landfill operators absolute right to increase intake). Cf. Smith v. Zoning Hearing Board, 619 A.2d 399 (Pa. Commw. Ct. 1992) (natural expansion doctrine does not give hospital right to expand nonconforming parking lot to properties bought after the date the zoning ordinance went into effect). Most other courts, however, limit nonconforming uses fairly strictly. See, e.g., Rotter v. Coconino County, 818 P.2d 704 (Ariz. 1991) (refusing to allow expansion); In re Stowe Club Highlands, 668 A.2d 1271 (Vt. 1995) (upholding refusal to allow landowner to tear down nonconforming barn and replace it with a better building). Cf. Peabody v. Town of Windham, 703 A.2d 886 (N.H. 1997) (allowing local government to impose reasonable conditions on expansion of nonconforming use).

May the owner of a nonconforming grocery store convert the premises to another nonconforming use — for example, a drugstore? Some zoning ordinances prohibit any change in use except to a conforming use. However, many ordinances allow changes so long as one moves up the Euclidean scale or at least stays at the same level. See, e.g., Adolphson v. Zoning Board of Appeals, 535 A.2d 799 (Conn. 1988) (owners of nonconforming foundry were entitled to a variance to allow them to change the foundry to a "less offensive" use). See 4A Norman Williams, Jr. & John M. Taylor, Williams American Land Planning Law §112 (1998 & Supp. 2002), for a discussion of the cases (§112.14 has a particularly useful chart portraying the change in use cases by state, category of existing and proposed use, and result).

7. *Abandonment and destruction.* Ordinances frequently provide that if a nonconforming use is abandoned, subsequent uses must conform to the zoning regulations. Most courts apply the common law definition of abandonment and hold that a municipality must prove both a period of nonuse and that the landowner intended to abandon the old use. Washington Arcade Associates v. Zoning Board of Review, 528 A.2d 736 (R.I. 1987). However, as at common law, intent to abandon may sometimes be inferred from a long period of nonuse, absent extenuating circumstances. Occasionally an ordinance will provide that a landowner forfeits the right to maintain a nonconforming use if that use is discontinued for a set period of time, usually one year; no intent to abandon need be found. Hartley v. City of Colorado Springs, 764 P.2d 1216 (Colo. 1988) (en banc). Which approach is easier to apply? Which best protects the landowner's probable expectations?

If a nonconforming structure burns down or is otherwise destroyed, may its owner rebuild it? See, e.g., Ruby v. Carlisle Zoning Hearing Board, 488 A.2d 655 (Pa. Commw. Ct. 1985) (ordinance terminating nonconforming use on damage to 50 percent of the value or bulk of the use was unreasonable restriction on owner's right to continue a lawful nonconforming use).

Valley View Industrial Park v. City of Redmond
733 P.2d 182 (Wash. 1987) (en banc)

CALLOW, Justice.

This appeal involves the vested rights doctrine as it pertains to property zoning changes. . . . The property involved is located as shown on the map in the appendix. [See Figure 3-8 on p. 203.] . . .

Valley View intends to develop an industrial park on a 26.71-acre parcel of property in the Sammamish River Valley. The valley historically was an agricultural area; the soil is some of the richest in King County. In recent years the agricultural character of the Sammamish River Valley has changed drastically. The population has increased significantly. Commercial and residential development has replaced many of the farms and the accompanying agricultural support services, including feed and fertilizer dealers, farm equipment sellers, and grain elevators. The area around the Valley View parcel reflects this

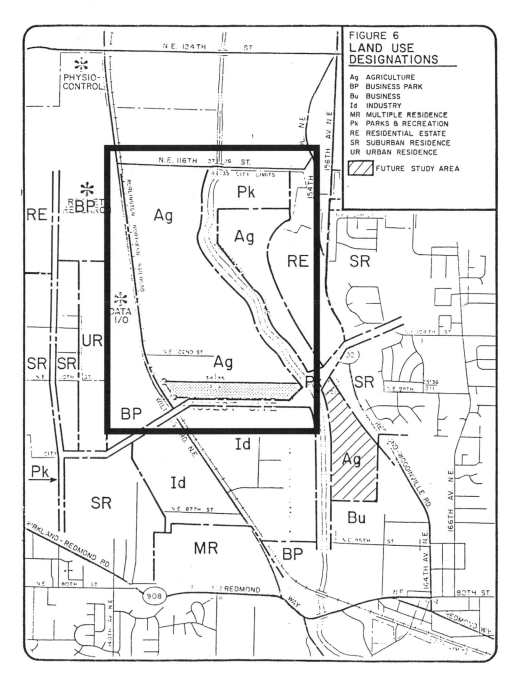

Note. The square indicates the parcel at issue in Valley View.
Source: 733 P.2d at 203.

FIGURE 3-8
Rezoning Map at Issue in *Valley View*

transition. The property immediately to the north remains zoned for agricultural uses. To the northwest, across the road from Valley View, are three large industrial developments. Puget Sound Power and Light holds a 250-foot right of way on Valley View's south border. South of that right of way is another industrial park and property zoned for expected commercial and residential development. The Sammamish River marks the east edge of the Valley View property. Across the river, to the southeast, is the site of a proposed regional shopping center.

The City of Redmond annexed the Valley View parcel from King County in 1964, and changed the zoning of the parcel from agricultural to "light industrial." In 1970, the City adopted a comprehensive land use plan setting forth the City's official policies and goals for future regulation and use of property.

The City began revising and updating its land use regulations to achieve conformity with the 1970 comprehensive plan. Concurrently, the farmlands preservation movement became a force in King County and applied pressure for agricultural zoning of the parcel. In 1977, a citizen's advisory committee was formed for the purpose of formulating recommendations on the land use plan and regulatory revisions. The committee conducted numerous public hearings and meetings, culminating in an official committee proposal which was forwarded to the city council. Following receipt of the proposal, the city council conducted extensive deliberations, including additional public hearings upon the proposal. On June 5, 1979, the council passed ordinance 875, which adopted the City's revised land use goals, policies, plans, regulations and procedures in a volume entitled Community Development Guide.

The Community Development Guide included an amended zoning map which adjusted the boundary between the agricultural and industrial zones in the Sammamish Valley. The citizen advisory committee recommended that the council shift the boundary between the agricultural and light industrial uses to the south, in alignment with a 250-foot-wide power transmission line right of way, thereby providing a visible and spatial separation of the agricultural and industrial uses. The city council adopted this recommendation as a part of its comprehensive zoning revisions. With adoption of the revised zoning map, the boundary line was extended to the southern boundary of the Valley View property to adjoin the 250-foot power line right of way. The zoning of the Valley View property thus was revised from light industrial to agricultural use.

Valley View formulated and proceeded with plans to develop an industrial park on the tract. Valley View intended the industrial park to consist of 12 buildings, developed in phases. In the first phase, it intended to build the infrastructure (i.e., the road, utilities, etc.) and the shell of the first building. It then intended to market the project and construct additional buildings as it found tenants for those buildings. . . .

Valley View first initiated contact with the city planning department on September 3, 1978, by submitting a preliminary site plan for the proposed development. A city planner informed Valley View representatives that the proposed industrial park would be subject to site plan review under Redmond ordinance 733, which provided that no building permit could be issued for a commercial or industrial development without prior site plan approval. . . .

During the conversation on September 3, Valley View was requested to file, and as a result on September 7, 1978 Valley View did file, a more detailed site plan, a SEPA environmental checklist, a shoreline substantial development permit application and plans for the first of 12 buildings to be constructed in the industrial park. . . .

In a September 18 letter, city officials wrote Valley View for additional information. In response, [on October 18] Valley View provided some information on sewers and storm drainage, as well as a revised SEPA checklist, a revised site plan and a proposed protective covenant. . . .

The City requested no additional information for 3 months. In the interim, it approved a plan to connect the Valley View property to the storm sewer system in place at the industrial park to the south [and] . . . collected $2,500 from Valley View to pay for the extension. On January 22, 1979, the City informed Valley View that an environmental impact statement [EIS] was necessary.

On February 2, Valley View submitted the names of three consultants to prepare the EIS. The City responded on March 6, by selecting a consultant not on the Valley View list. Attempting to avoid further delay, Valley View sought an appeal of the EIS decision on March 7. The City stated that no appeal was possible, but suggested a modification of the project proposal to obviate the need for an EIS. Valley View submitted a new proposal according to the City's suggested modifications.

In early 1979, Redmond officials informed Valley View that it would have to file additional building permit applications in order to vest its rights to construct the entire project if the City downzoned the property. At that time, the City's site plan review process for the project had not been completed. Valley View then filed four additional building permit applications. The five buildings, for which building permit applications were filed, totaled approximately 108,000 square feet of space out of the 466,914 square feet contemplated by the site plan as a whole. Five was the maximum number of buildings which Valley View concluded it was feasible to build prior to obtaining tenants for them.

On May 22, 1979, Valley View submitted an enlarged site plan and revised protective covenants and offered to negotiate with the City concerning dedication to the City of a buffer zone to the north of the Valley View property. On June 5, 1979, the Redmond City Council enacted the revised zoning code which downzoned the Valley View property from light industrial to agricultural use. . . .

When the City refused to allow Valley View to proceed with the . . . development, this suit was commenced on July 10, 1981. . . .

Due process requires governments to treat citizens in a fundamentally fair manner. West Main Assocs. v. Bellevue, 720 P.2d 782 (Wash. 1986). Consequently, citizens must be protected from the fluctuations of legislative policy, [id.] at 785 (citing The Federalist No. 44, at 301 (J. Madison) (J. Cooke ed. 1961)), so that they can plan their conduct with reasonable certainty as to the legal consequences.

These due process considerations require that developers be able to take recognized action under fixed rules governing the development of their land. [Id.] at 785. We have rejected the rule of many jurisdictions which requires a change of position and a substantial reliance on the building permit before equitable estoppel arises to rescue the by then financially extended landowner. 1 R. Anderson, Zoning §6.24, 408–09 (2d ed. 1976). See Hull v. Hunt, 331 P.2d 856 (Wash. 1958).

Washington's "date certain vesting rights doctrine" aims at insuring that new land-use ordinances do not unduly oppress development rights, thereby denying a property owner's right to due process under the law. . . .

In the ordinary course of events, a developer's right to develop in accordance with a particular zoning designation vests only if the developer files a building permit application that (1) is sufficiently complete, (2) complies with existing zoning ordinances and building codes, and (3) is filed during the effective period of the zoning ordinances under which the developer seeks to develop. West Main Assocs., 720 P.2d at 785. Due process considerations of fundamental fairness require this court to look beyond these . . . requirements to the conduct of the parties only in the rare case where city officials clearly frustrate a developer's diligent, good faith efforts to complete the permit application process. See . . . Parkridge v. Seattle, 573 P.2d 359 (Wash. 1978). . . .

. . . The trial court's findings clearly demonstrate the presence of each of the *Parkridge* elements: (1) Valley View diligently and in good faith attempted to obtain building permits; (2) Redmond officials explicitly frustrated Valley View's attempts; and (3) as a result, Valley View's building permit applications were incomplete. Thus, Valley View has a vested right to complete the five buildings for which it filed building permit applications under the light industrial zoning classifications.

Whether Valley View's vested right also encompasses the remaining seven buildings is a question of first impression for the court. . . . Because we have held that Valley View has a vested right to build the five permit application buildings, we consider those buildings as having been constructed, and review the validity of Redmond's downzoning of Valley View's property. . . .

. . . [W]hen Valley View constructs the five buildings covered by permit applications, the buildings would be so located on the 26.71 acres that its preservation and use as farmland is no longer feasible. In addition, with five buildings already built on the property, the power line no longer provides a break between industrial and agricultural land. . . .

Five buildings plus necessary access roads, parking and utility ingress and egress will so cut up the property that any agricultural use on the remaining portions of the property could well be uneconomic. Furthermore nothing in the record indicates that the right to build just five buildings makes financial sense. The practical result of changing the zoning to agricultural could place Valley View in a situation where economic realities dictate that no buildings will be built. This would deny Valley View its rights which vested upon the filing of the five building permit applications.

. . . Moreover, the rezoning does not bear a substantial relationship to the public welfare in light of the evidence that changes in the Redmond area made Valley View's property extremely undesirable for agricultural use, land to the south and west has been, or rapidly is being, developed for industrial and commercial purposes, and the Valley View parcel does not qualify for the King County Agricultural Lands Preservation Program.

Had the City not explicitly frustrated the building permit process, Valley View would have constructed five buildings ranging over the complete area of its single tract of land. Consequently, the City's subsequent action to downzone would not have withstood scrutiny. Therefore, the City may no longer preclude development of the Valley View property consistent with the code requirements and restrictions pertaining to the light industrial classification in effect at the time the building permit applications were filed. . . .

We hold that (1) Valley View has the vested right to have its five building permit applications processed under the light industrial use classification in existence at the time such building permit applications were filed; (2) the entire property must remain zoned as light industrial with the possibility of additional light industrial buildings being constructed on the property subject to compliance with existing City ordinances. . . .

DORE, Justice (dissenting). . . .

Note on Vested Rights

1. *Early versus late vesting.* As the *Valley View* court recognizes, Washington's very early vesting rule runs counter to the rule in most states. Most courts will recognize vested rights only if the owner has made substantial expenditures in good faith reliance on the issuance of a building permit or other approval. For those courts, the critical variables in

vested rights cases are (1) how far the developer had progressed in obtaining necessary governmental approvals, (2) the amount of unrecoverable expenses incurred in good faith, and (3) whether the expenditures were for preliminary activities or for construction. For useful surveys of the cases, see Daniel R. Mandelker, Land Use Law §§6.12-6.22 (5th ed. 2003); John J. Delaney & Emily J. Vaias, Recognizing Vested Development Rights as Protected Property in Fifth Amendment Due Process and Takings Claims, SK002 ALI-ABA 1113 (2004); Daniel R. Mandelker, Vested Rights and Nonconforming Uses, SK002 ALI-ABA 1103 (2004).

2. *Source of the protection.* The *Valley View* court grounded its doctrine in the Due Process Clause, focusing on the need to protect landowners from fluctuations in governmental policy. Other courts describe the vested rights doctrine as required by the Takings Clause. They point to *Penn Central's* emphasis on "investment-backed expectations" to argue that the Takings Clause mandates compensation if vested rights are infringed. Still other courts derive their rules regarding when a right to develop vests by asking when work on a development is sufficiently far along for the development to qualify as a nonconforming use. See, e.g., H.R.D.E., Inc. v. Zoning Officer, 430 S.E.2d 341 (W. Va. 1993) (requiring proof of substantial expenditures that would be wasted). How might the way in which the court grounds the doctrine influence whether it chooses a late or early vesting rule?

3. *The need for certainty versus the need for change.* At what point is the local government's need to respond to new learning and changed circumstances appropriately balanced against the property owner's need for certainty? In adopting the early vesting rule, the Washington court focused on the administrative costs of a late vesting rule:

> Notwithstanding the weight of authority, we prefer to have a date certain upon which the right vests to construct in accordance with the building permit. We prefer not to adopt a rule which forces the court to search through (to quote from Ogden v. Bellevue, [275 P.2d 899 (Wash. 1954)]) "the moves and countermoves of . . . parties . . . by way of passing ordinances and bringing actions for injunctions" — to which may be added the stalling or acceleration of administrative action in the issuance of permits — to find that date upon which the substantial change of position is made which finally vests the right. The more practical rule to administer, we feel, is that the right vests when the party, property owner or not, applies for his building permit, if that permit is thereafter issued.

Hull v. Hunt, 331 P.2d 856, 859 (Wash. 1958). The disadvantage of per se rules, of course, is their inability to address the factors that might make an individual case more or less compelling. In *Valley View*, for example, had the court applied a more ad hoc late vesting rule, it would have taken into account the fact that the landowner had been on notice for many years that a rezoning was under consideration and enjoyed support from the agricultural preservation movement. Similarly, a court applying a late vesting rule probably would have been troubled by the fact that the developer had expended relatively little on the project. Is it better to have a bright-line rule or to be able to factor those considerations into the decision? See, e.g., John J. Delaney, Vesting Verities and the Development Chronology: A Gaping Disconnect?, 3 Wash. U. J.L. & Pol'y 603 (2000); Gregory Overstreet & Diana M. Kirchheim, The Quest for the Best Test to Vest: Washington's Vested Rights Doctrine Beats the Rest, 23 Seattle U. L. Rev. 1043 (2000); Roger D. Wynne, Washington's Vested Rights Doctrine: How We Have Muddled a Simple Concept and How We Can Reclaim It, 24 Seattle U. L. Rev. 851 (2001); Karen L. Crocker, Student Note, Vested Rights and Zoning: Avoiding All-or-Nothing Results, 43 B.C. L. Rev. 935 (2002).

How bright is Washington's bright-line rule after *Valley View*? Does the court's willingness to bend the "complete application" rule to address the government's foot-dragging, as well as the court's decision to essentially rezone the land to protect the seven buildings for which the landowner had not yet sought permits, reintroduce considerable attention to "the moves and countermoves of . . . parties"?

4. *Vesting and estoppel*. A rule closely related to vested rights, which may have been lurking beneath the surface of *Valley View*, is the doctrine of estoppel. The doctrine of equitable estoppel bars a local government from enforcing its zoning rules when a property owner:

> (1) relying in good faith
> (2) upon some act or omission of the government
> (3) has made such a substantial change in position or incurred such extensive obligations and expenses that it would be highly inequitable and unjust to destroy the rights he has acquired.

Town of Largo v. Imperial Homes Corp., 309 So. 2d 571, 572–73 (Fla. Dist. Ct. App. 1975) (town is estopped from enforcing rezoning to single-family use, where contract of sale for property was contingent on zoning that would expressly allow multifamily development, town rezoned the property for multifamily housing knowing that fact, and landowner then bought the property and spent $69,000 in architectural fees and other development costs). Generally, estoppel cases focus on assurances or actions of the local government that reasonably invoked reliance by a landowner. The differences between vested rights and estoppel are blurry, and the terms often are used interchangeably.

5. *The scope of* Valley View's *vested rights*. The dissent in *Valley View* argued that the majority had essentially rezoned the property by granting vested rights to the seven buildings for which the landowner had not yet sought building permits. In this view, the land development business is just too speculative to assume, as the majority did, that the project would proceed as the developer envisioned. Because even the first five buildings might never be built, the dissent would have left for another day the question whether rezoning the land to agricultural use was rational in light of the industrial nature of the five buildings for which vested rights were recognized. Who has the better of that argument?

In fact, none of the buildings was built, reports Dianna Broadie, Long-Range Planner for the City of Redmond. The land sat vacant until the mid-1990s, when a church purchased it and built a 5,138-seat house of worship (which the zoning ordinance allowed as a special use in the industrial zone). For further developments in the City's efforts to preserve agricultural land, see City of Redmond v. Central Puget Sound Growth Management Hearings Board, 959 P.2d 1091 (Wash. 1998) (en banc).

6. *Statutory protections*. Many states have adopted statutes more protective of property owners than the common law. Texas, for example, requires regulatory agencies to consider applications for permits only on the basis of regulations in effect at the time the original application was filed. Furthermore:

> If a series of permits is required for a project, the . . . [laws, regulations, etc.] in effect at the time the original application for the first permit in that series is filed shall be the sole basis for consideration of all subsequent permits required for the completion of the project.

Tex. Loc. Gov't Code Ann. §245.002 (2004). See also Terry D. Morgan, Vested Rights Legislation, 34 Urb. Law. 131 (2002).

When the legislature has not spoken, can a local government adopt its own rules as to when rights vest under its procedures? See, e.g., West Main Associates v. City of Bellevue,

720 P.2d 782 (Wash. 1986) (en banc) (not when the rule is less protective than the state's common law vested rights doctrine).

7. *Development agreements.* In some states, developers can protect themselves against changes in land use regulations that might interfere with completion of the project by entering into development agreements with the local government. Development agreements are discussed at pp. 434–35.

D. Constraints on Zoning Measures That Threaten Civil Liberties

1. Freedom of Religion

The First Amendment declares: "Congress shall make no law respecting an establishment of religion, or prohibiting the free exercise thereof." Until fairly recently, most state courts interpreting the religion clauses were quite skeptical of land use regulations that zoned religious uses out of substantial portions of the city or imposed requirements that made it costly for a religion to establish its use on a chosen site. Traditionally, most state courts struck down ordinances that excluded houses of worship from all residential districts, for example. Those courts sometimes based their decision on the notion that religious uses of land are "inherently beneficial," and so obviously further the public health, safety, and welfare that attempts to bar them from residential districts are irrational. See, e.g., Diocese of Rochester v. Planning Board, 136 N.E.2d 827 (N.Y. 1956). Indeed, some courts granted religious uses a virtual exemption from zoning. See, e.g., Jewish Reconstructionist Synagogue v. Incorporated Village of Roslyn Harbor, 342 N.E.2d 534 (N.Y. 1975). But cf. Cornell University v. Bagnardi, 503 N.E.2d 509 (N.Y. 1986) (backing away from that position). See generally 3 Kenneth H. Young, Anderson's American Law of Zoning § 12.22 (4th ed. 1996 & Supp. 2004); R.P. Davis, Annotation, Zoning Regulations as Affecting Churches, 74 A.L.R.2d 377 (1960 & Supp. 2002).

In the early 1980s, several important lower federal court decisions broke sharply from the traditional state court view. In Lakewood, Ohio Congregation of Jehovah's Witnesses, Inc. v. City of Lakewood, 699 F.2d 303 (6th Cir. 1983), for example, the Sixth Circuit upheld a zoning ordinance that limited the construction of church buildings to office, retail, and high-density multifamily zones, which amounted to only 10 percent of the city's land. In rejecting the plaintiff's free exercise claim, the court found that the ordinance did not infringe on religious freedom because the "construction of a church building in a residential district . . . has no religious or ritualistic significance," at least for Jehovah's Witnesses. Id. at 306–07. In response to the argument that the ordinance "effectively eliminates religious worship from the city," the court responded that the "ordinance merely frustrates the Congregation's desire to locate itself in a more pleasant, more convenient and less expensive location. Such desires, however are not protected by the Constitution." Id. at 307, 309. See also Grosz v. City of Miami Beach, 721 F.2d 729 (11th Cir. 1983) (rejecting the claim of Orthodox Jews that an ordinance prohibiting religious uses in single-family districts violated the First Amendment, because the incidental burden on religion did not outweigh the government's interest in maintaining the residential quality of the neighborhood).

The Supreme Court put further pressure on the traditional view in 1990, when it decided Employment Division, Department of Human Resources v. Smith, 494 U.S. 872

(1990). *Smith* involved two employees of a drug rehabilitation center who were fired after they admitted they had used peyote in a sacramental ceremony at the Native American Church. The employees then were denied unemployment benefits on the ground that their dismissal was based on work-related "misconduct." The Supreme Court held that "the right of free exercise does not relieve an individual of the obligation to comply with a valid and neutral law of general applicability on the ground that the law proscribes (or prescribes) conduct that his religion prescribes (or proscribes)." Id. at 879 (internal quotations omitted). Accordingly, a generally applicable criminal law that has the incidental effect of burdening a particular religious practice need not be justified by a compelling governmental interest, but need only meet the usual rational basis standard.

Smith was denounced by many religious and civil liberties organizations, who argued that the decision would allow communities to zone all religious uses, or disfavored religions, out of their jurisdictions. Congress responded to *Smith* by passing the Religious Freedom Restoration Act of 1993, Pub. L. No. 103–141, 107 Stat. 1488 (1993) (codified at 42 U.S.C. §2000bb (2005)). RFRA provided that "government shall not substantially burden a person's exercise of religion even if the burden results from a rule of general applicability," unless the government demonstrates that "1) it is in furtherance of a compelling governmental interest; and 2) is the least restrictive means of furthering that compelling governmental interest." 42 U.S.C. §2000bb-1. RFRA therefore effectively overruled *Smith* and reinstated the compelling state interest test of Sherbert v. Verner, 374 U.S. 398 (1963).

RFRA was declared an unconstitutional restriction of the states in City of Boerne v. Flores, 521 U.S. 507 (1997), a challenge to the designation of a church as a historic landmark, on the ground that Congress had exceeded its enforcement powers under §5 of the Fourteenth Amendment in enacting RFRA. Three years later, Congress responded by passing the Religious Land Use and Institutionalized Persons Act of 2000 (RLUIPA), Pub. L. No. 106–274, 114 Stat. 803–807 (codified at 42 U.S.C. §§2000cc et seq. (2005)).

Congregation Kol Ami v. Abington Township

2004 WL 1837037 (E.D. Pa. Aug. 17, 2004), as amended on denial of reconsideration by 2004 WL 2137819 (E.D. Pa. Sept. 21, 2004)

NEWCOMER, Justice.

This is a religious rights case. The action is premised on violations of the Federal and Pennsylvania constitutions, the Pennsylvania Religious Freedom Restoration Act ("Pa-RFRA"), and 42 U.S.C. §§2000cc, et seq., which is commonly referred to as the Religious Land Use and Institutionalized Persons Act ("RLUIPA"). . . .

I. FACTS

Plaintiff Congregation Kol Ami (the "Plaintiff") is a Reform Jewish Synagogue. . . . It conducts religious services, Hebrew classes, and other related activities at various locations in eastern Montgomery County. . . .

Defendant Abington Township (the "Township") . . . has the power to regulate and restrict the use of land and structures within its borders. . . . Defendant Board of Commissioners (the "Board") is the duly elected executive body of the Township.

The Zoning Hearing Board of Abington Township (the "ZHB") is a separate entity from the Township whose members are elected by the Board. The ZHB's primary function is to hear and render final adjudication on: 1) appeals concerning the zoning ordinance at issue — the May 9, 1996 Revised Abington Township Zoning Ordinance (the "Ordinance"); 2) special exceptions to the Ordinance; and 3) variances from the terms of the Ordinance. . . .

A. HISTORY OF THE RELEVANT ZONING ORDINANCE

In 1978 the Township enacted Ordinance No. 1469 (the "1978 Ordinance"), which established a V-Residence Zoning District . . . [that] permitted several land uses by right: single-family detached dwellings, tilling of soil, township administrative buildings, public libraries, parks, and play or recreational areas. Those seeking to use this area for religious institutions such as churches, rectories, parish houses, convents, monasteries, etc., could petition the ZHB for a special exception.

On March 8, 1990, the Township . . . amended . . . the 1978 Ordinance to eliminate all uses except single-family detached dwellings . . . . All uses previously permitted by special exemption, including "religious uses," were eliminated.

On May 9, 1996 the Township again modified its Comprehensive plan . . . [changing] the zoning designation of the Township's low density residential district . . . [to R-1, which] permit[s] the following uses by right: agriculture, livestock, single-family detached dwellings, conservation, and recreation preserves. The Ordinance also permitted the following uses by special exception: kennels, riding academies, municipal complexes, outdoor recreation, emergency services, and utility facilities. . . .

Churches and other religious institutions looking to relocate to a R-1 Residential District must apply for a variance with the ZHB. . . . The variance standard is much different from the special exception standard, with the most notable difference being that the variance standard requires the applicant to demonstrate unnecessary hardship . . . [while] an applicant seeking a special exception . . . need only establish that the zoning ordinance allows the use, and that the particular use applied for is consistent with the public interest. . . .

Religious institutions are permitted, by right, to locate in areas designated by the Ordinance as either CS-Community Service Districts or M-Mixed Use Districts, and by special exception in A-O Apartment/Office Districts. . . . Twenty-nine of the thirty-six churches and synagogues currently operating in the Township existed prior to the Ordinance, and are legal, nonconforming uses outside of the CS, M, and A-O Districts. Twenty-five of those places of worship are located in residential districts.

B. HISTORY OF THE PROPERTY AT ISSUE

The property in question, located at 1908 Robert Road, is zoned R-1 Residential and consists of several buildings situated on a 10.9 acre parcel of land. In 1951, the property was purchased by the Sisters of Nazareth, an Order of Roman Catholic Nuns. The property was used as a convent. . . . In 1995, the Sisters leased the property to a community of Greek Orthodox Monks for religious services, family retreats, religious study, and prayer. To conform to the 1990 amendments, the Monks . . . [sought and received] a variance from the Ordinance to use the property as a monastery. . . . [T]he surrounding area is completely residential.

C. HISTORY OF THE CURRENT LITIGATION

In August 1999, the Plaintiffs entered into an agreement with the Sisters to purchase the property for use as a place of worship. By January 2000, the Plaintiffs filed an application with the ZHB seeking either a variance, a special exception, or permission to use the property as an existing non-conforming use. At that time, the Plaintiffs also petitioned for the right to use the property for Shabbat services on alternate Fridays and Saturdays, Hebrew classes on Wednesdays, and religious classes for two hours on Sunday mornings. Other proposed uses would include four High Holy Day services in the fall, religious meetings, Bar and Bat Mitzvah services, outdoor wedding ceremonies, and other similar celebrations and receptions. The Plaintiffs also planned to expand the existing parking from twenty spaces to at least one hundred and thirty seven spaces.

On March 20, 2001, the ZHB issued an Opinion and Order denying Plaintiffs' requests, finding that the proposed use of the property differed from the Sisters' use and would cause more traffic, noise, and other neighborhood disruptions. The ZHB further concluded that the Plaintiffs had failed to show that they were entitled to a variance because there were no unique physical features of the property that would preclude it from being used as zoned, and that the Plaintiffs failed to demonstrate unnecessary hardship.

II. OUTLINE OF THE PLAINTIFFS' CLAIMS

. . . Under the U.S. Constitution, the Plaintiffs allege claims for: (1) violation of the right to free exercise of religion under the First and Fourteenth Amendments, . . . (4) violation of the Equal Protection Clause of the Fourteenth Amendment. . . . [Plaintiffs also allege claims under the Pennsylvania Constitution.]

The Plaintiffs further allege: (1) violations of the RLUIPA, 42 U.S.C. §§2000cc(b)(1) and (2), claiming that the Defendants discriminated on the basis of religion and treated Plaintiffs on less than equal terms with non-religious institutions; (2) violation of the RLUIPA, 42 U.S.C. §2000cc(a), claiming that the Defendants imposed a substantial burden on the Plaintiffs' free exercise of religion; (3) violation of the RLUIPA, 42 U.S.C. §2000cc(b)(3)(B), claiming that the Defendants unreasonably limited religious assemblies in the Township. . . .

III. FREE EXERCISE OF RELIGION

A. PLAINTIFFS' FIRST AMENDMENT RIGHTS WERE NOT VIOLATED UNDER PRE-RFRA AND PRE-RLUIPA JURISPRUDENCE

The Plaintiffs argue that strict scrutiny should be applied to the Ordinance and to the denial of the variance by the ZHB because the Ordinance, on its face and as applied, infringes on their right to freely exercise their religion. The Court concludes that the burden placed on religion, however, is not sufficient to raise a free exercise violation under our First Amendment jurisprudence before the adoption of the RLUIPA.[1]

The First Amendment provides that "Congress shall make no law respecting an establishment of religion, or *prohibiting the free exercise thereof.*" U.S. Const. Amend. I (emphasis added). Because the Amendment only forbids the making of laws which "prohibit" free exercise, it is a basic precept of free exercise jurisprudence that not every governmental act

---

1. As will be explained infra, there is a marked break in the case law between pre- and post-RLUIPA cases. Read without recognizing the deviation brought about by the RLUIPA, as both parties would have us do, the cases appear to be hopelessly contradictory. Viewed in the light that the RLUIPA effectively changed the type of burdens that require judicial intervention, it appears that there are two types of "burdens" on the exercise of religion: Those defined by free exercise case law both prior to and during the effectiveness of the RFRA, and those that have been recognized since the passage of the RLUIPA.

that affects religion violates the First Amendment. The First Amendment is only offended if there is a substantial burden on religious exercise. *To decide burden:*

In deciding what burdens amount to a prohibition of free exercise, the nature and centrality of the religious activity is a major consideration.[2] Free exercise is substantially burdened, in a First Amendment context, when the government coerces a person not to engage in activity that is warranted by a fundamental tenet of his religious beliefs, Wisconsin v. Yoder, 406 U.S. 205 (1972); or, when following the basic tenets of your religious beliefs forces you to forfeit your right to needed government benefits. Sherbert v. Verner, 374 U.S. 398, 404 (1963). *Before cases*

Cases decided before the passage of the RFRA found no violation of the Free Exercise Clause when the burden imposed on religion was merely incidental, economic, or aesthetic. In Braunfield v. Brown, 366 U.S. 599 (1961), the Supreme Court found that a government regulation that made practicing one's religion more expensive does not affect religious freedom. The case involved a challenge to Pennsylvania's Sunday Closing law, which when combined with the plaintiff's religious obligation to refrain from Saturday work imposed a financial hardship. Id. There was no free exercise issue, however, because although the law made practicing one's religion more difficult by increasing the financial hardship, it did not interfere with or impede a religious observation. Id. at 605. In [Lakewood, Ohio Cong. of Jehovah's Witnesses, Inc. v. City of Lakewood, 699 F.2d 303, 306 (1983)], the Sixth Circuit rejected a free exercise challenge against a zoning ordinance that prohibited churches from locating in residential areas. That ordinance required the church to either build in the ten percent of the City not zoned residential, or to purchase an existing church. Id. at 307. The court found that the City's imposition on the church's financial and aesthetic interests, including its desire to build in a residential area, did not amount to an infringement on the church's freedom of religion rights. . . .

Under the substantial burden analysis of the RFRA, courts continued to hold that indirect, financial, and aesthetic burdens did not warrant judicial intervention.[3] . . .

Considering this pre-RLUIPA case law defining free exercise burdens, it is clear that the prohibition against developing the property at 1908 Robert Road or in locating a new synagogue in other residential areas of the Township does not meet the applicable substantial burdens test. It is undisputed that the government regulation does not restrict the Plaintiffs' beliefs, but only their conduct. The regulation prevents them from developing and using the property at 1908 Robert Road as a synagogue and from developing any other property not currently being used as a house of worship located in residential zones. The Plaintiffs, however, do not claim that locating their house of worship in a residential area is a basic tenet of their faith. . . . *P says land in other zoning areas isn't suitable for our purposes*

The Plaintiffs' assertion that locations in the other three zoning areas where houses of worship are permitted "are unsuitable for Plaintiff's religious purposes" does not change this analysis. The First Amendment does not guarantee a perfect fit between available land and proposed religious purposes. See Love Church v. City of Evanston, 896 F.2d 1082, 1086 (7th Cir. 1990) ("the harsh reality of the marketplace sometimes dictates that certain facilities are not available to those who desire them."). The Plaintiffs have not shown that any law, ordinance, or regulation would prevent it from engaging in its proposed institutional uses in these available zones. The Court must conclude that the burden

---

2. In determining whether a specific religious exercise is central to a plaintiff's belief system, the court must be careful not to question what is asserted by the plaintiff. See DeHart v. Horn, 227 F.3d 47, 50 (3d Cir. 2000) (restating that it is not for a court to determine if a religious belief is doctrinally correct).

3. Although the RFRA was eventually found unconstitutional for impermissibly expanding free exercise rights, the law did not attempt to change the definition of what constituted a substantial burden on free exercise. . . .

imposed on the Plaintiffs does not prevent conduct mandated by a central tenet of its religion, and that it is only an indirect financial and aesthetic burden. Thus, the Plaintiffs' claim under the First Amendment's Free Exercise Clause cannot survive. . . .

V. The RLUIPA

A. THE RLUIPA APPLIES TO THIS CASE

The Court must next decide whether the §(a)(1) of RLUIPA applies to the instant case.[5] Despite the fact that there is no substantial burden as defined by pre-RLUIPA case law, the Court holds that the RLUIPA imposes a broad test for determining what is a substantial burden on religious exercise. Both the textual changes made by Congress to the definition of free exercise of religion (with the adoption of the RLUIPA), and the case law, support this Court's finding that the Plaintiffs are facing a "substantial burden" in this case.

In passing the RLUIPA, Congress changed the definition of religious exercise from what it had been under the RFRA . . . RFRA left the Courts to apply the definition of free exercise as it existed under precedent. Therefore, the courts continued to apply the same threshold requirements to RFRA challenges as they had to free exercise challenges. This scenario led to many cases being dismissed without the application of strict scrutiny because courts found that the burden on free exercise was merely incidental and not sufficient to fall within the ambit of "free exercise." When the RLUIPA was adopted, Congress amended the definition section to provide:

> (7) Religious exercise. —
>   (A) In general. — The term "religious exercise" includes any exercise of religion, whether or not compelled by, or central to, a system of religious belief.
>   (B) Rule. — The use, building, or conversion of real property for the purpose of religious exercise shall be considered to be religious exercise of the person or entity that uses or intends to use the property for that purpose. Pub. L. 106-274, §8, Sept. 22, 2000.

Section 7(A) lessened the emphasis courts should place on the nature and centrality of the exercise that is being burdened. Subsection (B) undermines the relevance of holdings in cases like *Lakewood*. . . . Those cases held that all-out prohibitions against the development of a particular piece of real property into a place of worship do not violate the First Amendment or the RFRA. It is doubtful that those cases would have been decided the same under the above cited definition of religious exercise. Under the RLUIPA, the development of these properties would have been deemed "religious exercise." This exercise was substantially burdened, and in fact prohibited by, the challenged government action. . . .

Evaluating the instant case with the understanding that the RLUIPA changed the standard for the type of burdens on free exercise that are actionable, . . . it is clear that the Ordinance and the denial of a variance to the Plaintiffs are substantial burdens on their free exercise rights. This case is precisely the type of case contemplated by the drafters in their

5. Section (a)(1), which states the General Rule of the RLUIPA, provides:

(a) Substantial burdens. (1) General rule. No government shall impose or implement a land use regulation in a manner that imposes a substantial burden on the religious exercise of a person, including a religious assembly or institution, unless the government demonstrates that imposition of the burden on that person, assembly, or institution —
    (A) is in furtherance of a compelling governmental interest; and
    (B) is the least restrictive means of furthering that compelling governmental interest.

drafters had this kind of case in mind.

definition of free exercise under the RLUIPA. Under the statute, developing and operating a place of worship at 1908 Robert Road is free exercise. There can be no reasonable dispute that the Ordinance and the denial of the variance, which have effectively prevented the Plaintiffs from engaging in this "free exercise," create a substantial burden within the meaning of the Act.

B. THE RLUIPA IS CONSTITUTIONAL

Now that it has been concluded that the RLUIPA applies to the instant case, the next question this Court must decide is whether the RLUIPA is constitutional. The Plaintiffs argue that the RLUIPA is constitutional under 42 U.S.C. §2000cc(a)(2)(B) or (C). These sections provide that:

Yes it is

> Scope of application. This subsection applies in any case in which —
>
>   (A) . . .
>   (B) the substantial burden affects, or removal of that substantial burden would affect, commerce with foreign nations, among the several States, or with Indian tribes, even if the burden results from a rule of general applicability; or
>   (C) the substantial burden is imposed in the implementation of a land use regulation or system of land use regulations, under which a government makes, or has in place formal or informal procedures or practices that permit the government to make, individualized assessments of the proposed uses for the property involved.

— w/in Congress's Commerce Clause power or through the enforcement Clause of the 14th A.

Section (a)(2)(B) justifies the RLUIPA's application because it is within Congress's authority under the Commerce Clause. Section (a)(2)(C) purports to allow the application of the RLUIPA through the Enforcement Clause of the Fourteenth Amendment. The Court finds that RLUIPA is constitutionally permissible under both.

1. The RLUIPA Is a Valid Exercise of Congressional Authority Under Section V of the Fourteenth Amendment

. . . [T]he RLUIPA expands upon the case law because, as discussed at length supra, it applies to cases where the burdens on free exercise are less than those that were previously actionable. . . . Nonetheless, it is proper remedial legislation within Congress's power under the Fourteenth Amendment.

. . . The RLUIPA may constitutionally apply if Congress has merely set out to remedy violations of constitutional rights, rather than to define substantive rights under the Amendment. . . . To qualify as remedial legislation, "[t]here must be a congruence and proportionality between the injury to be prevented or remedied and the means adopted to that end." [City of Boerne v. Flores, 521 U.S. 507, 520 (1997).] In *Boerne*, the Supreme Court rejected the RLUIPA's predecessor — the RFRA — as not being sufficiently proportional and congruent to fall within the enforcement power; accordingly, the Court shall start its proportionality and congruence analysis by comparing the two acts.

Unlike the RFRA, the RLUIPA does not have "[s]weeping coverage ensur[ing] its intrusion at every level of government, displacing laws and prohibiting official actions of almost every description and regardless of subject matter." *Boerne*, 521 U.S. at 532. The RLUIPA applies only to a very limited subject matter. The RFRA, on the other hand, sought to make laws in nearly every conceivable arena — from family law to criminal law to wildlife protection — justify burdens on religion by satisfying strict scrutiny. In stark contrast, the RLUIPA applies only to land use and regulations affecting institutionalized persons.

The RFRA, because its stated goal was to effectively overrule *Smith*, precipitated a change in the level of scrutiny in the majority of cases to which it would apply. The

RLUIPA only applies, under Section 2(a)(C), when a land use decision turns on issues of individualized exemptions, which opens the door for local land use bodies to cloak religious hostility under a veil of discretion. Rather than change the constitutional standard, the RLUIPA, in almost all of its applications, will only reinforce the level of scrutiny applicable to systems of individualized exemptions. See Hale O Kaula Church v. Maui Planning Com'n, 229 F. Supp. 2d 1056, 1073 (D. Hawai'i 2002) (finding that RLUIPA codifies existing Supreme Court precedent on individualized exemptions and that "[r]egardless of RLUIPA, . . . the substantive test before the court is strict scrutiny"); . . .

The RLUIPA also differs from the RFRA in the legislative findings supporting its passage. The RFRA's legislative findings lacked any showing of modern laws of general applicability which passed for reasons of religious bigotry. *Boerne*, 521 U.S. at 530. In contrast, the RLUIPA's record is replete with zoning actions, in the form of individualized decisions, which adversely affect religious institutions. Restrictive zoning is a relatively modern invention, and based upon the record presented to Congress, its use to burden religious minorities is likely to increase. See Religious Liberty Protection Act of 1998: Hearing on H.R. 4019 Before Subcommittee on the Constitution of the House Committee on the Judiciary, 105th Cong., 2d Sess., at 405, 415–16 (discussing Gallup Poll showing hostile attitudes to religious minorities).

The RLUIPA is sufficiently congruent and proportional to fall under Section V of the Fourteenth Amendment. First, the RLUIPA will only apply to a small number of additional zoning actions that are constitutional under the First Amendment because the burden placed on religion was not substantial under pre-existing jurisprudence. This wider berth of substantial burdens will help both legislatures and Courts by simplifying limitations on the authority of zoning commissions and by eliminating any need to determine whether a particular activity is mandated by religion. This slight expansion of rights is warranted based on a review of the congressional record, which documents a history of the use of individualized assessments in zoning to violate the rights of religious practitioners, especially those of religious minorities.[7] Unlike the RFRA, which drove a substantive change in the constitutional standard, the RLUIPA clarifies the definition of an already-accepted individualized assessment doctrine and reinforces its application. This is the type of remedial legislation allowed by the Fourteenth Amendment. . . .

3. The RLUIPA Does Not Violate the Establishment Clause[9]

The Defendants argue that the RLUIPA is unconstitutional on its face because it violates the First Amendment's prohibition against laws "respecting an establishment of religion." . . .

7. The congressional record (146 Cong. Rec. S7774) supports the notion that zoning laws are often enacted and enforced out of hostility to religion. This discriminatory application of zoning laws is common because of the discretionary nature of the laws. Congress's findings were backed by statistical and anecdotal evidence, which was paired with testimony by expert witnesses who affirmed that the anecdotes were representative of the frequent discriminatory application of zoning laws. Douglas Laycock, State RFRAs and Land Use Regulation, 32 U.C. Davis L. Rev. 755, 770 (1999). There exists a vast array of cases in which courts have echoed these congressional findings. See, e.g., Family Christian Fellowship v. County of Winnebago, 503 N.E.2d 367 (Ill. App. 1986) (city's refusal to permit church use of existing buildings was arbitrary and capricious); Islamic Center of Mississippi, Inc. v. City of Starkville, 840 F.2d 293 (5th Cir. 1988) (city denied a Muslim organization a special use permit three times while granting such permits to every Christian church that had applied); Marks v. City of Chesapeake, 883 F.2d 308, 309–10 (4th Cir. 1989) (city, acting "arbitrarily and capriciously," refused to grant a use permit because neighbors disapproved of the religious practices of the applicant).

9. If we followed the reasoning of some courts, we could reject Defendants' establishment clause argument based on the earlier conclusion that the RLUIPA enforces the free exercise protections of the First Amendment.

test to pass scrutiny:

. . . To pass scrutiny under the *Lemon* test, "the statute must have a secular legislative purpose, . . . its principal or primary effect must be one that neither advances nor inhibits religion, . . . [and] the statute must not foster 'an excessive government entanglement with religion.'" [Lemon v. Kurtzman, 403 U.S. 602,] 612–613 [(1971)] (quoting Walz v. Tax Comm'n, 397 U.S. 664, 674 (1970)). . . .

ct: it has a secular purpose?

a. The RLUIPA Has a Secular Purpose

The RLUIPA has a legitimate secular purpose. The fact that an accommodation statute, such as the RLUIPA, mentions or even singles out religion does not prevent it from having a secular purpose. The government need not be "oblivious to impositions that legitimate exercises of state power may place on religious belief and practice." [Board of Education of Kiryas Joel Village School v. Grumet, 512 U.S. 687, 705 (1994).] It is an acceptable stated purpose to act "to alleviate significant governmental interference with the ability of religious organizations to define and carry out their religious missions." [Corporation of Presiding Bishop v. Amos, 483 U.S. 327, 335 (1987)]. The RLUIPA has exactly that purpose.

b. The RLUIPA Does Not Have an Impermissible Effect on Religion

The RLUIPA does not have the primary effect of advancing religion merely because it benefits religion. Scores of statutes alleviate burdens on religious organizations, making it easier for those organizations to disseminate their message. In *Amos*, the Supreme Court stated that statutes that accommodate religion do not have an impermissible effect merely because they allow churches to advance religion. Id. at 337. . . .

To run afoul of the second prong of the *Lemon* test, "it must be fair to say that the government itself has advanced religion through its own activities and influence." *Amos*, 483 U.S. at 337. "[F]or the men who wrote the Religion Clauses of the First Amendment the 'establishment' of religion connoted a sponsorship, financial support, and active involvement of the sovereign in religious activity." *Walz*, 397 U.S. at 668. The RLUIPA, by its own terms, has done nothing to actively advance religion. All it has done is advance the ability of people to engage in the free exercise of their religious beliefs without unnecessary government burdens. This fact does not make it unconstitutional.

c. The RLUIPA Does Not Create Excessive Entanglement with Religion

The RLUIPA does not create excessive entanglement as argued by the Defendants. . . . RLUIPA requires no more expertise in religious practices than does current First Amendment jurisprudence. Local officials, before RLUIPA, have had to determine whether their limitations would violate the Free Exercise Clause. If anything, Congress's elimination of any inquiry into whether a particular activity is a central tenet of a religion will reduce entanglement between local land use boards and religious organizations. Contrary to the Defendants' claim that the RLUIPA compels municipal governments to consider "every potential religious objection to every land use law from the perspective

---

The mere fact that the RLUIPA, as applied through section (a)(2)(C), is an enforcement of free exercise rights logically prevents it from violating the establishment clause. To hold to the contrary would be stating that while in large part it would be unconstitutional to enact or implement certain zoning laws that burden religion, it would be equally unconstitutional to prohibit them. . . .

of each religious believer," the RLUIPA only requires the ZHB to consider whether the reasons behind their decisions are the least restrictive means of achieving a compelling government interest. This determination is not entanglement because that decision turns purely on the government's secular motivation and means. It neither requires oversight of religious beliefs nor creates situations where the government could be accused of endorsing particular religious beliefs or religion in general. . . .

C. IT IS UNNECESSARY TO DETERMINE IF STRICT SCRUTINY HAS BEEN MET

Having found that the RLUIPA is constitutional and properly applies to this case, we need only briefly touch on the actual substance of the statute. Under the RLUIPA, a land use action can only place a substantial burden on the free exercise of religion if it "(A) is in furtherance of a compelling governmental interest; and (B) is the least restrictive means of furthering that compelling governmental interest." 42 U.S.C. §2000cc(a)(1). Because the Defendants do not argue that the denial of the Plaintiffs' permit furthers a compelling government interest, the Court does not need to analyze whether strict scrutiny is satisfied at this time. The Court thus concludes that the Defendants' Motion for Summary Judgment as to Count XI must be denied. . . .

Note on the Free Exercise of Religion

1. *Protection or privilege?* Is the protection afforded religious uses under RLUIPA (and that previously provided under the traditional state court rulings) consistent with the First Amendment's Establishment Clause? As *Kol Ami* notes, most of the courts that have reached the issue have rejected the Establishment Clause challenge. In Cutter v. Wilkinson, 125 S. Ct. 2113 (2005), a challenge to RLUIPA's application to prisons, the Court held that RLUIPA's provisions relating to institutionalized persons do not violate the Establishment Clause.

For a strong argument that most challenges to zoning ordinances by religious institutions are "at bottom . . . about money and convenience," not about religious belief, and that "the bald favoritism to religion" shown by the traditional decisions (and presumably by RLUIPA) "undermine[s] rather than fulfill[s] the constitutional ideal of religious liberty," see Christopher L. Eisgruber & Lawrence G. Sager, Congressional Power and Religious Liberty After *City of Boerne v. Flores*, 1997 Sup. Ct. Rev. 79, 106–08. For others skeptical of the whether RLUIPA merely protects, or actually favors religion, see Mark Tushnet, Questioning the Value of Accommodating Religion, *in* Law and Religion: A Critical Anthology 245, 251–52 (Stephen M. Feldman ed., 2000); Richard C. Schragger, The Role of the Local in the Doctrine and Discourse of Religious Liberty, 117 Harv. L. Rev. 1810 (2004). For defenses of the act, see, e.g., Gregory P. Magarian, How to Apply the Religious Freedom Restoration Act to Federal Law Without Violating the Constitution, 99 Mich. L. Rev. 1903 (2001); Kevin M. Powers, The Sword and the Shield: RLUIPA and the New Battle Ground of Religious Freedom, 22 Buff. Pub. Int. L.J. 145 (2004); Roman P. Storzer & Anthony R. Picarello, Jr., The Religious Land Use and Institutionalized Persons Act of 2000: A Constitutional Response to Unconstitutional Zoning Practices, 9 Geo. Mason L. Rev. 929, 977 (2001).

2. *How widespread is the problem of discrimination against religious uses?* The evidence presented to Congress during hearings on RFRA and RLUIPA (and on a precursor to RLUIPA — the Religious Liberties Protection Act, or RLPA) included a report of a survey conducted for Brigham & Young University, which found that:

> Minority religions representing less than 9% of the population were involved in over 49% of the cases regarding the right to locate religious buildings at a particular site, and in over 33% of the cases seeking approval of accessory uses. . . . While a study of this type can at best give a rough picture of what is happening, the conclusion seems inescapable that illicit motivation is [sic] affecting disputes in the land use area.

Religious Liberty Protection Act of 1998: Hearings on H.R. 4019 Before the Subcomm. on the Constitution of the House Comm. on the Judiciary, 105th Cong. 131, 136 (1998) (testimony of Prof. Cole W. Durham, Jr., Brigham Young University Law School).

Another study, by Professor Mark Chaves and William Tsitsos, Are Congregations Constrained by Government? Empirical Results from the National Congregations Study, 42 J. Church & State 335, 337 (2000), reached very different conclusions. Based on data from the 1998 National Congregations Study, the authors found that only 1 percent of the religious institutions seeking a permit or license had their requests denied. Of those six congregations that encountered problems in the zoning process, five were from mainstream religious groups. The study was brought to the attention of Congress, but the authors were not asked to testify, and the study was not made part of the record.

None of the hearings on RFRA, RLPA, or RLUIPA included testimony from state and local land use officials, or from experts on land use matters. Requests to participate from local government representatives such as the National League of Cities and the National Association of Counties were denied. For the history of RLUIPA, see Marci A. Hamilton, Federalism and the Public Good: The True Story Behind the Religious Land Use and Institutionalized Persons Act, 78 Ind. L.J. 311, 335–41 (2003).

3. *State RFRAs.* The federalism concerns that motivated the Court to find RFRA unconstitutional do not apply to state laws. Unless RLUIPA is struck down on Establishment Clause grounds, then, states remain free to adopt protections for religious uses in state versions of RFRA or RLUIPA. About a dozen states have done so. For a survey of the state acts, see James A. Hanson, Missouri's Religious Freedom Restoration Act: A New Approach to the Cause of Conscience, 69 Mo. L. Rev. 853 (2004); Gregory W. McCracken & Robert I. McMurry, Update on First Amendment Issues: Religious Activities and Signs and Adult Uses, SK002 ALI-ABA 913 (2004). Some of the state statutes or constitutional amendments provide greater protections than RFRA, and some go even further than RLUIPA. See, e.g., Connecticut Act Concerning Religious Freedom, Conn. Gen. Stat. §52-571b (2005) (requiring that any burden (not just a substantial burden) on the exercise of religion further a substantial state interest by the least restrictive means available); Illinois Religious Freedom Restoration Act, 775 Ill. Comp. Stat. 35/15 (2005) (government may not substantially burden a person's exercise of religion (even if the burden results from a rule of generally applicability) unless it demonstrates that the burden is the least restrictive means of furthering a compelling government interest).

4. *Laws of "general applicability."* If, as *Congregation Kol Ami* presumes, RLUIPA only applies "when a land use decision turns on issues of individualized exemptions," should it apply to special exceptions? Ordinances that allow religious landowners to obtain variances on a showing of particularized hardship? Schemes in which religious uses sometimes are granted rezonings? Historic preservation laws, which typically require designation of individual properties? For further discussion of special exceptions, variances and rezonings, see Chapter 4; for discussion of historic preservation, see pp. 494–505. Compare Douglas Laycock, Conceptual Gulfs in *City of Boerne v. Flores*, 39 Wm. & Mary L. Rev. 743, 781 (1998) ("[t]he process[] of administering zoning laws . . . [is] highly individualized," "[s]tandards tend to be vague and manipulable," "zoning for a parcel is easily changed if those in power desire to change it," and land use laws "are almost never generally applicable

in any meaningful sense"), with Alan C. Weinstein, Zoning and Landmark Regulation of Religious Institutions After *City of Boerne v. Flores*, Plan. & L. Div. Newsl. (Am. Plan. Ass'n), Summer 1998, at 1, 5 (landmarking designation is "individualized" only in the same sense that a criminal prosecution involves the "individualized" application of neutral standards to particular defendants).

5. *Zoning ordinances that discriminate against a religion.* In Church of the Lukumi Babalu Aye, Inc. v. City of Hialeah, 508 U.S. 520 (1993), the Court made clear that a zoning ordinance that "targets" a particular religion for exclusion from the community will not withstand scrutiny. In *Lukumi*, the city adopted a zoning ordinance, along with three other ordinances, addressing religious animal sacrifice, which was practiced within the community by adherents of the Santeria religion. After examining the history of the city council's concerns about animal sacrifice, as well as the terms of the ordinances, the Court found that the object of the ordinances had been to suppress the Santeria religion, and that the city had failed to demonstrate a compelling governmental justification for the ordinances. See also Islamic Center v. City of Starkville, 840 F.2d 293 (5th Cir. 1988) (city's denial of special exception to a Muslim mosque, after it had granted exceptions to nine Christian churches, violated First Amendment).

6. *Condemnation of religious uses.* Religious institutions also have invoked RLUIPA to fight attempts by local governments to condemn property that is owned by religious institutions. Those issues are covered at p. 839.

2.   *Freedom of Speech*

City of Renton v. Playtime Theatres, Inc.
475 U.S. 41 (1986)

Justice REHNQUIST delivered the opinion of the Court.

This case involves a constitutional challenge to a zoning ordinance, enacted by appellant city of Renton, Washington, that prohibits adult motion picture theaters from locating within 1,000 feet of any residential zone, single- or multiple-family dwelling, church, park, or school. Appellees, . . . [sought] a declaratory judgment that the Renton ordinance violated the First and Fourteenth Amendments and a permanent injunction against its enforcement. The District Court ruled in favor of Renton and denied the permanent injunction, but the Court of Appeals for the Ninth Circuit reversed and remanded for reconsideration. . . .

In April 1981, . . . the City Council enacted Ordinance No. 3526. The ordinance prohibited any "adult motion picture theater" from locating within 1,000 feet of any residential zone, single- or multiple-family dwelling, church, or park, and within one mile of any school. The term "adult motion picture theater" was defined as "[an] enclosed building used for presenting motion picture films, video cassettes, cable television, or any other such visual media, distinguished or [characterized] by an emphasis on matter depicting, describing or relating to 'specified sexual activities' or 'specified anatomical areas' . . . for observation by patrons therein."

In early 1982, respondents acquired two existing theaters in downtown Renton, with the intention of using them to exhibit feature-length adult films. The theaters were located within the area proscribed by Ordinance No. 3526. . . .

In our view, the resolution of this case is largely dictated by our decision in Young v. American Mini Theatres, Inc., [427 U.S. 50 (1976)]. . . . The Renton ordinance, like the one in *American Mini Theatres*, does not ban adult theaters altogether, but merely provides

certain distance

that such theaters may not be located within 1,000 feet of any residential zone, single- or multiple-family dwelling, church, park, or school. The ordinance is therefore properly analyzed as a form of time, place, and manner regulation. Id. at 63 & n.18; id. at 78–79 (Powell, J., concurring).

Describing the ordinance as a time, place, and manner regulation is, of course, only the first step in our inquiry. This Court has long held that regulations enacted for the purpose of restraining speech on the basis of its content presumptively violate the First Amendment. See Carey v. Brown, 447 U.S. 455, 462–63, & n.7 (1980). On the other hand, so-called "content-neutral" time, place, and manner regulations are acceptable so long as they are designed to serve a substantial governmental interest and do not unreasonably limit alternative avenues of communication. See Clark v. Community for Creative Non-Violence, 468 U.S. 288, 293 (1984).

here hard to say if its

At first glance, the Renton ordinance, like the ordinance in *American Mini Theatres*, does not appear to fit neatly into either the "content-based" or the "content-neutral" category. To be sure, the ordinance treats theaters that specialize in adult films differently from *c+* other kinds of theaters. Nevertheless, as the District Court concluded, the Renton ordinance is aimed not at the content of the films shown at "adult motion picture theatres," but rather at the secondary effects of such theaters on the surrounding community. The District Court found that the City Council's "predominate concerns" were with the secondary effects of adult theaters, and not with the content of adult films themselves. . . . The District Court's finding as to "predominate" intent, left undisturbed by the Court of Appeals, is more than adequate to establish that the city's pursuit of its zoning interests here was unrelated to the suppression of free expression. The ordinance by its terms is designed to *c+e* prevent crime, protect the city's retail trade, maintain property values, and generally "[protect] and [preserve] the quality of [the city's] neighborhoods, commercial districts, and the quality of urban life," not to suppress the expression of unpopular views. As Justice Powell observed in *American Mini Theatres*, "[i]f [the city] had been concerned with restricting the message purveyed by adult theaters, it would have tried to close them or restrict their number rather than circumscribe their choice as to location." 427 U.S. at 82, n.4. . . .

So review under content neutral

It was with this understanding in mind that, in *American Mini Theatres*, a majority of this Court decided that, at least with respect to businesses that purvey sexually explicit materials,[2] zoning ordinances designed to combat the undesirable secondary effects of such businesses are to be reviewed under the standards applicable to "content-neutral" time, place, and manner regulations. . . .   *So:*

The appropriate inquiry in this case, then, is whether the Renton ordinance is designed to serve a substantial governmental interest and allows for reasonable alternative avenues of communication. It is clear that the ordinance meets such a standard. As a majority of this   *Yes.* Court recognized in *American Mini Theatres*, a city's "interest in attempting to preserve the quality of urban life is one that must be accorded high respect." 427 U.S. at 71 (plurality opinion). . . .

The Court of Appeals ruled, however, that because the Renton ordinance was enacted without the benefit of studies specifically relating to "the particular problems or needs of Renton," the city's justifications for the ordinance were "conclusory and speculative." We think the Court of Appeals imposed on the city an unnecessarily rigid burden of proof. The record in this case reveals that Renton relied heavily on the experience of, and studies produced by, the city of Seattle. . . .

---

2. See *American Mini Theatres*, 427 U.S. at 70 (plurality opinion) ("[It] is manifest that society's interest in protecting this type of expression is of a wholly different, and lesser, magnitude than the interest in untrammeled political debate . . . ").

We hold that Renton was entitled to rely on the experiences of Seattle and other cities . . . in enacting its adult theater zoning ordinance. The First Amendment does not require a city, before enacting such an ordinance, to conduct new studies or produce evidence independent of that already generated by other cities, so long as whatever evidence the city relies upon is reasonably believed to be relevant to the problem that the city addresses. That was the case here. . . .

Finally, turning to the question whether the Renton ordinance allows for reasonable alternative avenues of communication, we note that the ordinance leaves some 520 acres, or more than five percent of the entire land area of Renton, open to use as adult theater sites. The District Court found, and the Court of Appeals did not dispute the finding, that the 520 acres of land consists of "[ample], accessible real estate," including "acreage in all stages of development from raw land to developed, industrial, warehouse, office, and shopping space that is criss-crossed by freeways, highways, and roads."

Respondents argue, however, that some of the land in question is already occupied by existing businesses, that "practically none" of the undeveloped land is currently for sale or lease, and that in general there are no "commercially viable" adult theater sites within the 520 acres left open by the Renton ordinance. . . . That respondents must fend for themselves in the real estate market, on an equal footing with other prospective purchasers and lessees, does not give rise to a First Amendment violation. And although we have cautioned against the enactment of zoning regulations that have "the effect of suppressing, or greatly restricting access to, lawful speech," *American Mini Theatres*, 427 U.S. at 71, n.35 (plurality opinion), we have never suggested that the First Amendment compels the Government to ensure that adult theaters, or any other kinds of speech-related businesses for that matter, will be able to obtain sites at bargain prices. See id. at 78 (Powell, J., concurring) ("The inquiry for First Amendment purposes is not concerned with economic impact"). . . .

In sum, we find that the Renton ordinance represents a valid governmental response to the "admittedly serious problems" created by adult theaters. See id. at 71 (plurality opinion). Renton has not used "the power to zone as a pretext for suppressing expression," id. at 84 (Powell, J., concurring), but rather has sought to make some areas available for adult theaters and their patrons, while at the same time preserving the quality of life in the community at large by preventing those theaters from locating in other areas. This, after all, is the essence of zoning. Here, as in *American Mini Theatres*, the city has enacted a zoning ordinance that meets these goals while also satisfying the dictates of the First Amendment. The judgment of the Court of Appeals is therefore reversed.

Justice BLACKMUN concurs in the result. . . .

Justice BRENNAN, with whom Justice MARSHALL joins, dissenting.
Renton's zoning ordinance selectively imposes limitations on the location of a movie theater based exclusively on the content of the films shown there. The constitutionality of the ordinance is therefore not correctly analyzed under standards applied to content-neutral time, place, and manner restrictions. . . .

City of Los Angeles v. Alameda Books, Inc.
535 U.S. 425 (2002)

[In 1977, Los Angeles studied adult entertainment businesses and concluded that concentrations of such businesses were associated with higher rates of prostitution, robbery, assaults and theft in surrounding neighborhoods. The City then passed an ordinance similar to that challenged in *Renton*, but which also forbade adult entertainment businesses from locating within 1000 feet of another such business. Concerned that adult businesses would seek to evade the law by concentrating several adult businesses within a single structure, the City later amended its ordinance to forbid more than one adult entertainment business in the same building. The amendment defined an adult entertainment business as each operation that could be considered an adult arcade, bookstore, cabaret, and so on, even if each operation was within the same establishment.

Alameda Books, Inc. rents sexually oriented videocassettes and provides booths where patrons can view them. Its operations therefore counted as both an adult bookstore and a cabaret, and accordingly violated the anti-concentration ordinance. Alameda sued under 42 U.S.C. §1983 for declaratory and injunctive relief to prevent enforcement of the ordinance.

The District Court granted summary judgment to Alameda. It held that *Renton* was inapplicable because the City's study did not support a reasonable belief that multiple-use adult businesses produced secondary effects. It therefore applied strict scrutiny, and found that the city could not show that the content-based prohibition was necessary to serve a compelling governmental interest. The Court of Appeals for the Ninth Circuit affirmed on different grounds. It did not decide whether the ordinance was content based, because it found that even if content-neutral, the City had failed to prove that its regulation of multiple-use establishments was designed to serve the city's interest in reducing crime, as required by *Renton*.]

Justice O'CONNOR announced the judgment of the Court and delivered an opinion, in which THE CHIEF JUSTICE, Justice SCALIA, and Justice THOMAS join. . . .

II . . .

The Court of Appeals found that the 1977 study did not reasonably support the inference that a concentration of adult operations within a single adult establishment produced greater levels of criminal activity because the study focused on the effect that a concentration of establishments — not a concentration of operations within a single establishment — had on crime rates. The Court of Appeals pointed out that the study treated combination adult bookstore/arcades as single establishments and did not study the effect of any separate-standing adult bookstore or arcade. [Alameda Books, Inc. v. City of Los Angeles, 222 F.3d 719, 724 (9th Cir. 2000)]. . . .

The error that the Court of Appeals made is that it required the city to prove that its theory about a concentration of adult operations attracting crowds of customers, much like a minimall or department store does, is a necessary consequence of the 1977 study. . . .

In *Renton*, we specifically refused to set such a high bar for municipalities that want to address merely the secondary effects of protected speech. We held that a municipality may rely on any evidence that is "reasonably believed to be relevant" for demonstrating a connection between speech and a substantial, independent government interest. 475 U.S. at 51–52. This is not to say that a municipality can get away with shoddy data or reasoning. The municipality's evidence must fairly support the municipality's rationale for its ordinance. If plaintiffs fail to cast direct doubt on this rationale, either by demonstrating that the municipality's evidence does not support its rationale or by furnishing evidence that disputes the municipality's factual findings, the municipality meets the standard set forth in *Renton*. If plaintiffs succeed in casting doubt on a municipality's rationale in either manner, the burden shifts back to the municipality to supplement the record with evidence renewing support for a theory that justifies its ordinance. See, e.g., Erie v. Pap's A.M., 529 U.S. 277, 298 (2000) (plurality opinion). This case is at a very early stage in this process.

It arrives on a summary judgment motion by respondents defended only by complaints that the 1977 study fails to prove that the city's justification for its ordinance is necessarily correct. Therefore, we conclude that the city, at this stage of the litigation, has complied with the evidentiary requirement in *Renton*.

In effect, Justice SOUTER asks the city to demonstrate, not merely by appeal to common sense, but also with empirical data, that its ordinance will successfully lower crime. Our cases have never required that municipalities make such a showing, certainly not without actual and convincing evidence from plaintiffs to the contrary. Such a requirement would go too far in undermining our settled position that municipalities must be given a "'reasonable opportunity to experiment with solutions'" to address the secondary effects of protected speech. *Renton*, supra, at 52 (quoting Young v. American Mini Theatres, Inc., 427 U.S. 50, 71 (1976) (plurality opinion)). A municipality considering an innovative solution may not have data that could demonstrate the efficacy of its proposal because the solution would, by definition, not have been implemented previously. The city's ordinance banning multiple-use adult establishments is such a solution. . . .

Our deference to the evidence presented by the city of Los Angeles is the product of a careful balance between competing interests. On the one hand, we have an "obligation to exercise independent judgment when First Amendment rights are implicated." Turner Broadcasting System, Inc. v. FCC, 512 U.S. 622, 666 (1994) (plurality opinion). On the other hand, we must acknowledge that the Los Angeles City Council is in a better position than the Judiciary to gather and evaluate data on local problems. See *Turner*, supra, at 665–666. We are also guided by the fact that *Renton* requires that municipal ordinances receive only intermediate scrutiny if they are content neutral. 475 U.S. at 48–50. There is less reason to be concerned that municipalities will use these ordinances to discriminate against unpopular speech. See *Erie*, supra, at 298–299.

Justice SOUTER would have us rethink this balance, and indeed the entire *Renton* framework. In *Renton*, the Court distinguished the inquiry into whether a municipal ordinance is content neutral from the inquiry into whether it is "designed to serve a substantial government[al] interest and [does] not unreasonably limit alternative avenues of communication." 475 U.S. at 47–54. The former requires courts to verify that the "predominate concerns" motivating the ordinance "were with the secondary effects of adult [speech], and not with the content of adult [speech]." Id. at 47 (emphasis deleted). The latter inquiry goes one step further and asks whether the municipality can demonstrate a connection between the speech regulated by the ordinance and the secondary effects that motivated the adoption of the ordinance. Only at this stage did *Renton* contemplate that courts would examine evidence concerning regulated speech and secondary effects. Id. at 50–52. Justice SOUTER would either merge these two inquiries or move the evidentiary analysis into the inquiry on content neutrality, and raise the evidentiary bar that a municipality must pass. His logic is that verifying that the ordinance actually reduces the secondary effects asserted would ensure that zoning regulations are not merely content-based regulations in disguise. See *post*.

We think this proposal unwise. First, none of the parties request the Court to depart from the *Renton* framework. . . . Second, there is no evidence suggesting that courts have difficulty determining whether municipal ordinances are motivated primarily by the content of adult speech or by its secondary effects without looking to evidence connecting such speech to the asserted secondary effects. . . . Finally, Justice SOUTER does not clarify the sort of evidence upon which municipalities may rely to meet the evidentiary burden he would require. It is easy to say that courts must demand evidence when "common experience" or "common assumptions" are incorrect, see *post*, but it is difficult for courts to know ahead of time whether that condition is met. Municipalities will, in general, have greater experience with and understanding of the secondary effects that follow certain protected speech than will the courts. See *Erie*, 529 U.S. at 297–298 (plurality opinion). For this reason our cases require only that municipalities rely upon evidence that is "'reasonably believed to be relevant'" to the secondary effects that they seek to address. Id. at 296.

III . . .

Accordingly, we reverse the Court of Appeals' judgment granting summary judgment to respondents and remand the case for further proceedings.

Justice SCALIA, concurring.
. . . As I have said elsewhere . . . [t]he Constitution does not prevent those communities that wish to do so from regulating, or indeed entirely suppressing, the business of pandering sex.

Justice KENNEDY, concurring in the judgment. . . .

I

. . . If a city can decrease the crime and blight associated with certain speech by the traditional exercise of its zoning power, and at the same time leave the quantity and accessibility of the speech substantially undiminished, there is no First Amendment objection. This is so even if the measure identifies the problem outside by reference to the speech inside — that is, even if the measure is in that sense content based.

On the other hand, a city may not regulate the secondary effects of speech by suppressing the speech itself. A city may not, for example, impose a content-based fee or tax. See Arkansas Writers' Project, Inc. v. Ragland, 481 U.S. 221, 230 (1987) ("[O]fficial scrutiny of the content of publications as the basis for imposing a tax is entirely incompatible with the First Amendment's guarantee of freedom of the press"). This is true even if the government purports to justify the fee by reference to secondary effects. Though the inference may be inexorable that a city could reduce secondary effects by reducing speech, this is not a permissible strategy. The purpose and effect of a zoning ordinance must be to reduce secondary effects and not to reduce speech.

A zoning measure can be consistent with the First Amendment if it is likely to cause a significant decrease in secondary effects and a trivial decrease in the quantity of speech. . . .

II

In *Renton*, . . . [t]he ordinance "by its terms [was] designed to prevent crime, protect the city's retail trade, maintain property values, and generally protec[t] and preserv[e] the quality of [the city's] neighborhoods, commercial districts, and the quality of urban life, not to suppress the expression of unpopular views." 475 U.S. at 48 (internal quotation marks omitted). On this premise, the Court designated the restriction "content neutral." Ibid.

The Court appeared to recognize, however, that the designation was something of a fiction, which, perhaps, is why it kept the phrase in quotes. After all, whether a statute is content neutral or content based is something that can be determined on the face of it; if the statute describes speech by content then it is content based. And the ordinance in *Renton* "treat[ed] theaters that specialize in adult films differently from other kinds of theaters." Id. at 47. The fiction that this sort of ordinance is content neutral — or "content neutral" — is perhaps more confusing than helpful, as Justice SOUTER demonstrates, see *post* (dissenting opinion). . . . These ordinances are content based, and we should call them so.

Nevertheless . . . the central holding of *Renton* is sound: A zoning restriction that is designed to decrease secondary effects and not speech should be subject to intermediate rather than strict scrutiny. . . .

III . . .

At the outset, we must identify the claim a city must make in order to justify a content-based zoning ordinance. As discussed above, a city must advance some basis to show that its regulation has the purpose and effect of suppressing secondary effects, while leaving the quantity and accessibility of speech substantially intact. The ordinance may identify the speech based on content, but only as a shorthand for identifying the secondary effects outside. A city may not assert that it will reduce secondary effects by reducing speech in the same proportion. On this point, I agree with Justice SOUTER. The rationale of the ordinance must be that it will suppress secondary effects — and not by suppressing speech. . . .

The analysis requires a few more steps. If two adult businesses are under the same roof, an ordinance requiring them to separate will have one of two results: One business will either move elsewhere or close. The city's premise cannot be the latter. . . .

The premise, therefore, must be that businesses — even those that have always been under one roof — will for the most part disperse rather than shut down. . . .

Only after identifying the proposition to be proved can we ask the second part of the question presented: is there sufficient evidence to support the proposition? As to this, we have consistently held that a city must have latitude to experiment, at least at the outset, and that very little evidence is required. . . . The Los Angeles City Council knows the streets of Los Angeles better than we do. It is entitled to rely on that knowledge; and if its inferences appear reasonable, we should not say there is no basis for its conclusion. . . .

. . . The city could reach the reasonable conclusion that knocking down the wall between two adult businesses does not ameliorate any undesirable secondary effects of their proximity to one another. If the city's first ordinance was justified, therefore, then the second is too. Dispersing two adult businesses under one roof is reasonably likely to cause a substantial reduction in secondary effects while reducing speech very little.

IV

These propositions are well established in common experience and in zoning policies that we have already examined, and for these reasons this ordinance is not invalid on its face. If these assumptions can be proved unsound at trial, then the ordinance might not withstand intermediate scrutiny. The ordinance does, however, survive the summary judgment motion that the Court of Appeals ordered granted in this case.

Justice SOUTER, with whom Justice STEVENS and Justice GINSBURG join, and with whom Justice BREYER joins as to Part II, dissenting. . . .

I . . .

Although this type of land-use restriction has even been called a variety of time, place, or manner regulation, [*Renton*, 475 U.S. at 46], equating a secondary-effects zoning regulation with a mere regulation of time, place, or manner jumps over an important difference between them. A restriction on loudspeakers has no obvious relationship to the substance of what is broadcast, while a zoning regulation of businesses in adult expression just as obviously does. And while it may be true that an adult business is burdened only because of its secondary effects, it is clearly burdened only if its expressive products have adult content. Thus, the Court has recognized that this kind of regulation, though called content neutral, occupies a kind of limbo between full-blown, content-based restrictions and regulations that apply without any reference to the substance of what is said. Id. at 47.

It would in fact make sense to give this kind of zoning regulation a First Amendment label of its own, and if we called it content correlated, we would not only describe it for what it is, but keep alert to a risk of content-based regulation that it poses. The risk lies in the fact that when a law applies selectively only to speech of particular content, the more precisely the content is identified, the greater is the opportunity for government censorship. Adult speech refers not merely to sexually explicit content, but to speech reflecting a favorable view of being explicit about sex and a favorable view of the practices it depicts; a restriction on adult content is thus also a restriction turning on a particular viewpoint, of which the government may disapprove.

This risk of viewpoint discrimination is subject to a relatively simple safeguard, however. If combating secondary effects of property devaluation and crime is truly the reason for the regulation, it is possible to show by empirical evidence that the effects exist, that they are caused by the expressive activity subject to the zoning, and that the zoning can be expected either to ameliorate them or to enhance the capacity of the government to combat them (say, by concentrating them in one area), without suppressing the expressive activity itself. This capacity of zoning regulation to address the practical problems without eliminating the speech is, after all, the only possible excuse for speaking of secondary-effects zoning as akin to time, place, or manner regulations. . . .

. . . In this case, however, the government has not shown that bookstores containing viewing booths, isolated from other adult establishments, increase crime or produce other negative secondary effects in surrounding neighborhoods, and we are thus left without substantial justification for viewing the city's First Amendment restriction as content correlated but not simply content based. . . .

. . . If we take the city's breakup policy at its face, enforcing it will mean that in every case two establishments will operate instead of the traditional one. Since the city presumably does not wish merely to multiply adult establishments, it makes sense to ask what offsetting gain the city may obtain from its new breakup policy. The answer may lie in the fact that two establishments in place of one will entail two business overheads in place of one: two monthly rents, two electricity bills, two payrolls. Every month business will be more expensive than it used to be, perhaps even twice as much. That sounds like a good strategy for driving out expressive adult businesses. It sounds, in other words, like a policy of content-based regulation.

I respectfully dissent.

Note on Adult Entertainment

1. *Content or secondary effects?* Under *Renton* or under Justice O'Connor's plurality opinion in *Alameda,* the determination whether an ordinance is "content neutral" requires an analysis whether the local government truly was "predominantly" concerned with secondary effects rather than content. The difficulties of relying on tests related to the

regulator's intent were discussed at pp. 115–17. How could the law of "adult entertainment" zoning be recrafted to get behind boilerplate statements of purpose, yet still allow cities room to address true secondary effects? What are the risks of Justice Souter's proposal to test the motivation for the regulation by measuring whether the law actually achieves the purpose of reducing the secondary effects?

Does *Alameda* signal that the categorical rules for content-neutral and content-based regulation, like per se rules in takings doctrine, are giving way (or moving back) to more of an ad hoc multifactored test like the *Penn Central* analysis for takings? See Wilson R. Huhn, Assessing the Constitutionality of Laws That Are Both Content-Based and Content-Neutral: The Emerging Constitutional Calculus, 79 Ind. L.J. 801 (2004).

2. *The secondary effects studies.* In Dolan v. City of Tigard, 512 U.S. 374 (1994), excerpted at p. 643, the Supreme Court held that when a developer challenges an exaction that a local government has imposed as a condition for permission to develop, the local government bears the burden of proving that it has made "some sort of individualized determination that the required dedication is related both in nature and extent to the impact of the proposed development." Id. at 391. *Dolan* also required the local government to bear the burden of justifying the required dedication. How does the standard and burden of proof required by *Alameda* compare with the requirements of *Dolan*? Should adult use restrictions be treated the same as the exactions at issue in *Dolan*?

Studies refuting the allegation that adult uses produce secondary effects have begun to be proffered by adult use plaintiffs. See, e.g., Daniel Linz et al., An Examination of the Assumption That Adult Businesses Are Associated with Crime in Surrounding Areas: A Secondary Effects Study in Charlotte, North Carolina, 38 Law & Soc'y Rev. 69 (2004); Bryant Paul et al., Government Regulation of "Adult" Businesses Through Zoning and Anti-Nudity Ordinances: Debunking the Legal Myth of Negative Secondary Effects, 6 Comm. L. & Pol'y 355 (2001). At least one court has overturned a grant of summary judgment to the local government because of the strength of the adult use's evidence disputing the allegation of secondary effects. Peek-A-Boo Lounge of Bradenton, Inc. v. Manatee County, Fla., 337 F.3d 1251 (11th Cir. 2003). But see Clay Calvert & Robert D. Richards, Stripping Away First Amendment Rights: The Legislative Assault On Sexually Oriented Businesses, 7 N.Y.U. J. Legis. & Pub. Pol'y 287, 325–27 (2003–2004).

What if "analysis of the hard data regarding the relationship between adult uses and urban ills [fails to] yield conclusive results," but survey evidence shows "that the negative perception of adult enterprises held by the business community and the public itself results in disinvestment, with the concomitant deterioration in the social and economic well-being of the surrounding area"? See Stringfellow's of New York, Ltd. v. City of New York, 694 N.E.2d 407, 416 (N.Y. 1998) (upholding the adult use zoning). Is such a perception "content-based" discrimination? If the concerns of neighbors are shown to be based on "unsubstantiated fears," can the local government's claim to be regulating on the basis of secondary effects rather than content withstand analysis? Cf. City of Cleburne v. Cleburne Living Center, 473 U.S. 432 (1985), excerpted at p. 717.

3. *The limits of the secondary effects rationale?* Can the secondary effects rationale justify restrictions on businesses that sell adult-oriented material for "take home" or off-premises use only? Compare Encore Videos, Inc. v. City of San Antonio, 330 F.3d 288 (5th Cir. 2003) (finding that the dispersion ordinance was not narrowly tailored to serve a substantial governmental interest because it was based on secondary effects studies of in-store adult uses, or studies that failed to separate out the effects of in-store and take-home adult entertainment), with Z.J. Gifts, D-2 L.L.C. v. City of Aurora, 136 F.3d 683, 687 (10th Cir. 1998) (differences in the mode of delivery of sexually oriented materials are constitutionally insignificant for purposes of determining an ordinance's content-neutrality).

Should tax evasion or fraud count as a secondary effect sufficient to trigger the content-neutral test? See, e.g., SOB, Inc. v. County of Benton, 317 F.3d 856, 863 (8th Cir. 2003) ("A ban on live nude dancing . . . may address other adverse secondary effects, such as the likelihood that an establishment whose dancers and customers routinely violate long-established standards of public decency will foster illegal activity such as drug use, prostitution, tax evasion, and fraud.").

Should the secondary effects doctrine apply to zoning ordinances aimed at homes in which pornography is filmed? See Francesca Ortiz, Zoning the Voyeur Dorm: Regulating Home-Based Voyeur Web Sites Through Land Use Laws, 34 U.C. Davis L. Rev. 929 (2001).

4. *"Reasonably" available?* The following excerpt from Topanga Press, Inc. v. City of Los Angeles, 989 F.2d 1524 (9th Cir. 1993), illustrates the difficulties the state and lower federal courts have had in applying the "reasonable alternative avenues of communication" prong of *Renton*'s holding:

> The Supreme Court . . . has not stated what sort of factors may be considered when deciding whether the relocation sites provided by a city are reasonable. Some courts have attempted to draw a distinction between economically unsuitable land and physically or practically unsuitable land. See Woodall v. City of El Paso, 959 F.2d 1305, 1306 (5th Cir.) (per curiam) modifying 950 F.2d 255 (5th Cir. 1992); Alexander v. City of Minneapolis, 928 F.2d 278, 283 (8th Cir. 1991). . . .
>
> The problem, however, is that the distinction between economically unsuitable and physically or practically unsuitable land is difficult to maintain. Nearly all forms of physical and legal unsuitability may be couched in terms of economic unsuitability. Conversely, problems of economic suitability may be couched in terms of physical unsuitability. For example, in the instant case, some of the definitionally "available" land is currently used as runways for the Los Angeles airport. One could argue that this land is physically unsuitable for a business. On the other hand, one could argue that it is merely economically unsuitable, since there is nothing to prevent an adult business from physically relocating to this site; rather it is prevented by a consideration of the cost of tearing down part of an airstrip and then building a storefront. . . .
>
> . . . [A] particular relocation site may be considered part of the relevant real estate market when the following conditions are met. First, although *Renton* stressed that the First Amendment only requires a relocation site to be potentially available rather than actually available, . . . property is not "potentially" available when it is unreasonable to believe that it would ever become available to any commercial enterprise.
>
> Second . . . within manufacturing or industrial zones, relocation sites that are reasonably accessible to the general public may also be part of the market. Third, areas in manufacturing zones which have a proper infrastructure such as sidewalks, roads and lighting may be included in the market. Fourth, when a relocation site suits some generic commercial enterprise, although not every particular enterprise, it too may be said to be part of the real estate market. While it is constitutionally irrelevant whether relocation sites located in industrial or manufacturing zones suit the particular needs of an adult business, potential sites must be reasonable relocation sites for some commercial enterprise before they can be considered part of the relevant market. . . .
>
> Fifth, and most obvious, those relocation sites which are commercially zoned are part of the market.
>
> We emphasize that assuming a relocation site is part of the relevant market, it is not relevant whether a relocation site will result in lost profits, higher overhead costs, or even prove to be commercially infeasible for an adult business. The issue is whether any site is part of an actual market for commercial enterprises generally. . . .

Id. at 1529–32. Is the *Topanga* approach sound? Is it consistent with *Renton*? Should a local government have to identify the specific sites "available" for adult uses to carry its burden of proving that reasonable alternative avenues of communication remain available? See Ashley C. Phillips, Comment, Matter of Arithmetic: Using Supply and Demand to Determine the Constitutionality of Adult Entertainment Zoning Ordinances, 51 Emory L.J. 319 (2002).

5. *Broader prohibitions.* May a small town attack pornography by barring all movie houses within its boundaries? In Schad v. Borough of Mount Ephraim, 452 U.S. 61 (1981), the Court struck down a zoning ordinance that prohibited "live entertainment" of all kinds (including the commercial production of all plays, concerts and musicals) within the Borough of Mount Ephraim, New Jersey. The Court reasoned that the restriction at issue in *American Mini Theatres* did not affect the number of adult movie theaters that could operate in the city; but merely dispersed them, and accordingly did not govern a complete restriction. The Court rejected the Borough's argument that it sought to limit its commercial zone to firms that cater only to the "immediate needs" of their residents, such as milk, eggs, and bread that residents forget to buy elsewhere, noting that "virtually the only item or service that may not be sold . . . is . . . live entertainment." It also rejected the Borough's claim that the ban was necessary to address parking, trash, and police protection problems caused by live entertainment, reasoning that the Borough had presented no evidence that those problems were different from the problems posed by permitted commercial establishments. Id. at 72–73. Finally, the Court found that the ordinance did not leave open adequate alternative channels of communication, noting that the Borough had not proved its contention that live entertainment was available in other nearby communities. Id. at 76.

In concurring and dissenting opinions, five justices appeared to endorse the notion that a community could ban all commercial public entertainment under some circumstances. See id. at 79 (Powell, J., concurring, joined by Stewart, J.); id. at 85, n.11 (Stevens, J., concurring); id. at 87 (Burger, C.J., dissenting, joined by Rehnquist, J.). The state and lower federal courts have had little occasion to reckon with the issue, however, in part because most communities are savvy enough to zone at least some land within the jurisdiction for the use of pornographic businesses.

6. *Retroactive application of "adult entertainment" zoning ordinances.* The ordinances at issue in *American Mini Theatres, Schad, Renton* and *Alameda* all applied only prospectively to new businesses. A few courts have distinguished ordinances that apply retroactively to require existing businesses to close. See, e.g., Walnut Properties, Inc. v. City of Whittier, 861 F.2d 1102, 1110 (9th Cir. 1988) (finding that an ordinance that "would force the only existing adult theater . . . to close at its present location with no definite prospect of a place to relocate" was unconstitutional, distinguishing *Renton* and *American Mini Theatres* because the ordinances at issue there were prospective only); People Tags, Inc. v. Jackson County Legislature, 636 F. Supp. 1345 (W.D. Mo. 1986) (finding an ordinance "intended to prevent the continued operation" of an existing "adult bookstore . . . and theatre" was content based). The majority of courts, however, uphold provisions requiring existing businesses to phase out or come into compliance with the ordinance as long as the amortization period is reasonable. See, e.g., World Wide Video of Wash., Inc. v. City of Spokane, 368 F.3d 1186 (9th Cir. 2004); Jake's, Ltd., Inc. v. City of Coates, 284 F.3d 884 (8th Cir. 2002). See pp. 197–202 for further discussion of the problems of retroactivity.

7. *Piecemeal purification.* Although the owners of adult uses most often bring facial challenges to zoning ordinances restricting the location of adult uses, owners sometimes challenge the denial of a variance, rezoning, special exception, or other discretionary permit for a proposed adult use, arguing that the denial is content based. Compare U.S. Partners Financial Corp. v. Kansas City, 707 F. Supp. 1090 (W.D. Mo. 1989) (denial of rezoning

for adult use was content-neutral decision based on legitimate concerns about secondary effects), with Bayou Landing, Ltd. v. Watts, 563 F.2d 1172 (5th Cir. 1977) (invalidating city's refusal to renew an occupancy permit for adult bookstore, finding that refusal was based at least in part on neighbor's objections to the nature of the business), and Gascoe, Ltd. v. Newtown Township, 699 F. Supp. 1092 (E. D. Pa. 1988) (denial of special use permit on the ground that rental of adult films "will not further the public welfare" violates First Amendment).

8. *Permitting schemes.* Where a city tries to regulate sexually oriented businesses through licensing or discretionary permitting schemes (such as special exceptions), the rules regarding prior restraints on speech apply. See FW/PBS, Inc. v. City of Dallas, 493 U.S. 215 (1990). Such ordinances must not place "unbridled discretion in the hands of a government official or agency." Id. at 225 (O'Connor, J., joined by Stevens & Kennedy, JJ.). Further, "the licensor must make the decision whether to issue the license within a specified and reasonable time period during which the status quo is maintained, and there must be the possibility of prompt judicial review in the event that the license is erroneously denied." Id. at 228; see also id. at 239 (Brennan, J., joined by Marshall & Blackmun, JJ.). See generally Jules B. Gerard, Local Regulation of Adult Businesses (2003).

9. *Neighborhood consent.* What if a city prohibited adult uses within a specified distance of residential neighborhoods, but allowed a majority of a neighborhood's residents to waive the prohibition? See County of Cook v. World Wide News Agency, 424 N.E.2d 1173 (Ill. App. Ct. 1981) (holding the ordinance unconstitutional). See also pp. 393–400 for discussion of neighborhood consent provisions generally.

10. *Pornography and the rights of women.* Andrea Dworkin and Catharine A. MacKinnon (among others) argue that pornography is discrimination on the basis of sex and therefore violates women's civil rights. See, e.g., Andrea Dworkin & Catharine A. MacKinnon, Pornography and Civil Rights: A New Day for Women's Equality (1988). For dissent, see, e.g., Nadine Strossen, Defending Pornography: Free Speech, Sex, and the Fight for Women's Rights (1995). What if the "purposes" section of an ordinance cited the protection of women's equality and the prevention of violence against women, rather than the usual "secondary effects," as justification for the ordinance? Cf. Boos v. Barry, 485 U.S. 312, 321 (1988) (O'Connor, J., joined by Stevens and Scalia, JJ.) (arguing that if the ordinance in *Renton* had been justified by the city's "desire to prevent the psychological damage it felt was associated with viewing adult movies" the ordinance would have been content based).

11. *Billboards and other means of disseminating information.* First Amendment protections also come into play when local governments try to regulate communications media and technology ranging from billboards to cellular phone transmitting stations. Because those issues have been integrally connected with the legitimacy of aesthetic concerns as governmental interests, they are addressed at pp. 469–89.

3.   *Other Fundamental Rights*

Land use regulations sometimes infringe on other fundamental rights, such as the right of privacy recognized in Roe v. Wade, 410 U.S. 113 (1973). In Cleveland, Ohio, for example, the city council adopted an "emergency" zoning measure to prohibit the provision of abortions in local retail business districts, in response to public opposition to an organization's plans to establish a first trimester abortion clinic in such a district. West Side Women's

Servs., Inc. v. City of Cleveland, 573 F. Supp. 504 (N.D. Ohio 1983). When the organization challenged the measure, the court surveyed the U.S. Supreme Court's confusing pronouncements on abortion, and then concluded:

> [R]egulations having a substantial burden on the abortion decision . . . must be justified by a compelling state interest, and will be deemed invalid if the proffered justifications are not substantial enough to justify the burden imposed. On the other hand, if the challenged regulation imposes only a de minimis burden on the abortion decision, the rational relationship test will be used. . . .
>
> Applying the aforementioned principles to the facts of the instant case, the Court finds that the ordinance in question imposes a sufficiently substantial burden on access to abortions to warrant the application of the strict scrutiny test. The basis for this finding lies primarily in the nature of the ordinance. First, this ordinance cannot be said to fall within the category of abortion regulations that place "no obstacle — absolute or otherwise — in the pregnant woman's path to an abortion." Maher [v. Roe, 432 U.S. 464,] 474 [(1977)]. Nor is this an example of mere "state encouragement of an alternative activity consonant with legislative policy." Id. at 475. Rather, in this instance, a municipality has created an obstacle to a woman's exercise of her protected right, an obstacle which did not previously exist and which, therefore, constitutes "direct state interference with a protected activity." . . . Defendants argue, however, that this case does not involve any fundamental right. Rather, the only issue at stake is whether plaintiffs have a right to operate their business wherever they choose. . . . Defendants also argue that the impact of the ordinance in question upon the physician-patient relationship, and, consequently, upon the woman's decision to have an abortion, is minimal since the ordinance only applies to a very small portion of Cleveland and since abortion services are available elsewhere in the City.
>
> Defendants' arguments are unavailing. First, they address only the degree of the burden and fail to take into account the nature of the interference with the abortion decision. Second, and more importantly, an ordinance which interferes with a woman's exercise of her fundamental right is not safe from constitutional challenge merely because it is limited in its geographical scope. The Supreme Court in Maher noted that "a state-created obstacle [to obtaining an abortion] need not be absolute to be impermissible." Maher, 432 U.S. at 473. Indeed, the same holds true for laws impinging on other fundamental rights. In the Schad case, the Court, quoting Schneider v. New Jersey, 308 U.S. 147, 163 (1939), stated: "One is not to have the exercise of his liberty of expression in appropriate places abridged on the plea that it may be exercised in some other place." Schad v. Borough of Mt. Ephraim, 452 U.S. 61, 76–77 (1981). . . .

573 F. Supp. at 517–18. The court went on to find that none of the possible justifications the city could offer for its zoning measure survived strict scrutiny. Id.

Are you persuaded by the court's response to the argument that lesser scrutiny should apply because abortion services were available in other parts of Cleveland? If the constitutionality of infringements of religious liberty or freedom of speech may turn, in part, on whether the local government left alternative sites available, should the constitutionality of burdens on the right to choose to have an abortion also depend on the availability of alternative locations for abortion clinics? Should Renton's "secondary effects" analysis apply where zoning officials justify their exclusion of abortion clinics on the ground that the public health and welfare is likely to be threatened by the noise, aggravation, and danger posed by protest likely to accompany the operation of the clinic? See Elizabeth B. Meyer, Exclusionary Zoning of Abortion Facilities, 32 Wash. U. J. Urb. & Contemp. L. 361 (1987); Jan Ryan Novak, Zoning Control of Abortion Clinics, 28 Clev. St. L. Rev. 507 (1979).

E.   Procedural and Remedial Aspects of Landowners' and Developers' Constitutional Rights

1.   Jurisdiction

A landowner or developer who wishes to bring a takings challenge to any federal regulation limiting the use of land generally must proceed under the Tucker Act, 28 U.S.C. §1491, in the U.S. Court of Federal Claims. See Robert Meltz, Takings Claims Against the Federal Government, SC 43 ALI-ABA 57 (1998). If the challenge to the federal regulation involves a due process, equal protection, or civil liberties claim, the jurisdictional basis for the challenge is 28 U.S.C. §1331(a) ("The district courts shall have original jurisdiction of all civil actions arising under the Constitution, laws, or treaties of the United States."). A property owner who seeks both to invalidate a regulation on due process or other grounds, and to claim that the regulation effected a taking while (improperly) in effect, thus must litigate in two different courts: the Court of Federal Claims will have jurisdiction only over the takings claim, seeking compensation; a federal district court will have jurisdiction only on the claim seeking invalidation of the (wrongful) regulation. For a discussion of the problems arising from this "Tucker Act Shuffle," see Robert Meltz, The Impact of *Eastern Enterprises* and Possible Legislation on the Jurisdiction and Remedies of the U.S. Court of Federal Claims, 51 Ala. L. Rev. 1161 (2000).

    If the developer or landowner believes that state or local land use regulations violate the federal constitution or federal laws, the developer may sue in federal court under the federal civil rights statute, 42 U.S.C. §1983, which provides:

> Every person who, under color of any statute, ordinance, regulation, custom, or usage, of any State or Territory or the District of Columbia, subjects, or causes to be subjected, any citizen of the United States or any other person within the jurisdiction thereof to the deprivation of any rights, privileges, or immunities secured by the Constitution and laws, shall be liable to the party injured in an action at law, suit in equity, or other proper proceeding for redress. . . .

Jurisdiction for §1983 claims is derived from either 28 U.S.C. §1331(a)[5] or 28 U.S.C. §1343.[6] It is possible that jurisdiction over federal constitutional claims against state and local land use officials also may be derived from 28 U.S.C. §1331(a) on the theory that the federal constitutional provisions in question provide an implied right of action. See Davis v. Passman, 442 U.S. 228 (1979) (recognizing an implied right of action under the Fifth Amendment for claims against federal officers); Lake Country Estates, Inc. v. Tahoe Regional Planning Agency, 440 U.S. 391, 400 (1979) (noting that whether there is an implied right of action under the Fifth or Fourteenth Amendments is an unresolved question). But see Azul-Pacifico, Inc. v. City of Los Angeles, 973 F.2d 704 (9th Cir. 1992) (no cause of action for a taking lies directly under the U.S. Constitution).

---

[5] "The district courts shall have original jurisdiction of all civil actions arising under the Constitution, laws, or treaties of the United States."

[6] "The district courts shall have original jurisdiction of any civil action authorized by law to be commenced by any person: . . .

> (3) To redress the deprivation, under color of any State law, statute, ordinance, regulation, custom or usage, of any right, privilege or immunity secured by the Constitution of the United States or by any Act of Congress providing for equal rights of citizens or of all persons within the jurisdiction of the United States. . . . "

A developer may sue in state court under 42 U.S.C. §1983 because federal district courts have original but not exclusive jurisdiction over §1983 claims. For an extremely helpful overview of §1983 actions in land use matters, see Kenneth B. Bley, Use of the Civil Rights Acts to Recover Damages in Land Use Cases, in American Law Institute–American Bar Association, Inverse Condemnation and Related Government Liability 179 (Apr. 22–24, 2004).

2.   *Ripeness*

Williamson County Regional Planning Commission v. Hamilton Bank
473 U.S. 172 (1985)

Justice BLACKMUN delivered the opinion of the Court.

Respondent, the owner of a tract of land it was developing as a residential subdivision, sued petitioners, the Williamson County (Tennessee) Regional Planning Commission and its members and staff, in United States District Court, alleging that petitioners' application of various zoning laws and regulations to respondent's property amounted to a "taking" of that property. . . . Petitioners and their amici urge this Court to overturn the jury's award on the ground that a temporary regulatory interference with an investor's profit expectation does not constitute a "taking" within the meaning of the Just Compensation Clause of the Fifth Amendment, or, alternatively, on the ground that even if such interference does constitute a taking, the Just Compensation Clause does not require money damages as recompense. Before we reach those contentions, we examine the procedural posture of respondent's claim.

I

A

. . . As required by . . . [state law], respondent's predecessor-in-interest (developer) in 1973 submitted a preliminary plat for the cluster development of its tract, the Temple Hills Country Club Estates (Temple Hills), to the Williamson County Regional Planning Commission for approval. At that time, the county's zoning ordinance and the Commission's subdivision regulations required . . . [t]he developer first . . . to submit for approval a preliminary plat, or "initial sketch plan," indicating, among other things, the boundaries and acreage of the site, the number of dwelling units and their basic design, the location of existing and proposed roads, structures, lots, utility layouts, and open space, and the contour of the land. Once approved, the preliminary plat served as a basis for the preparation of a final plat. Under the Commission's regulations, however, approval of a preliminary plat "will not constitute acceptance of the final plat." . . .

On May 3, 1973, the Commission approved the developer's preliminary plat for Temple Hills. The plat indicated that the development was to include 676 acres, of which 260 acres would be open space, primarily in the form of a golf course. A notation on the plat indicated that the number of "allowable dwelling units for total development" was 736, but lot lines were drawn in for only 469 units. The areas in which the remaining 276 units were to be placed were left blank and bore the notation "this parcel not to be developed until approved by the planning commission." . . . The density of 736 allowable dwelling units was calculated by multiplying the number of acres (676) by the number of units allowed per acre (1.089). . . .

P's predecessor:

Upon approval of the preliminary plat, the developer . . . spent approximately $3 million building the golf course, and another $500,000 installing sewer and water facilities. Before housing construction was to begin on a particular section, a final plat of that section was submitted for approval. Several sections, containing a total of 212 units, were given final approval by 1979. . . .

In 1977, the county changed its zoning ordinance to require that calculations of allowable density exclude 10% of the total acreage to account for roads and utilities. In addition, the number of allowable units was changed to one per acre from the 1.089 per acre allowed in 1973. . . .

In January 1980, the Commission asked the developer to submit a revised preliminary plat before it sought final approval for the remaining sections of the subdivision. The Commission reasoned that this was necessary because the original preliminary plat contained a number of surveying errors, the land available in the subdivision had been decreased inasmuch as the State had condemned part of the land for a parkway, and the areas marked "reserved for future development" had never been platted. A special committee (Temple Hills Committee) was appointed to work with the developer on the revision of the preliminary plat.

The developer submitted a revised preliminary plat for approval in October 1980. Upon review, the Commission's staff and the Temple Hills Committee noted . . . [eight] problems with the revised plat. . . . [The problems involved allowable density, the length of certain cul-de-sac roads, the grade of some of the roads, the grade of certain housing lots, requirements related to the construction and maintenance of the main road, the adequacy of fire protection services and children's recreational space, and road frontage.]

The Temple Hills Committee recommended that the Commission grant a waiver of the regulations regarding the length of the cul-de-sacs, the maximum grade of the roads, and the minimum frontage requirement. Without addressing the suggestion that those three requirements be waived, the Commission disapproved the plat on two other grounds: first, the plat did not comply with the density requirements of the zoning ordinance or subdivision regulations . . . and second, lots were placed on slopes with a grade greater than 25%. . . .

On November 26, respondent, Hamilton Bank of Johnson City, acquired through foreclosure the property in the Temple Hills subdivision that had not yet been developed, a total of 257.65 acres. . . . In June 1981, respondent submitted two preliminary plats to the Commission — the plat that had been approved in 1973 and subsequently reapproved several times, and a plat indicating respondent's plans for the undeveloped areas, which was similar to the plat submitted by the developer in 1980. The new plat proposed the development of 688 units; the reduction from 736 units represented respondent's concession that 18.5 acres should be removed from the acreage because that land had been taken for the parkway.

On June 18, the Commission disapproved the plat for eight reasons, including the density and grade problems cited in the October 1980 denial, as well as the [remaining] objections the Temple Hills Committee had raised in 1980. . . .

B

Respondent then filed this suit in the United States District Court for the Middle District of Tennessee, pursuant to 42 U.S.C. §1983, alleging that the Commission had taken its property without just compensation and asserting that the Commission should be estopped under state law from denying approval of the project. Respondent's expert witnesses testified that the design that would meet each of the Commission's eight objections would allow respondent to build only 67 units, 409 fewer than respondent claims it is entitled to build,[5] and that the development of only 67 sites would result in a net loss of over $1 million. . . .

After a three-week trial, the jury found that respondent had been denied the "economically viable" use of its property in violation of the Just Compensation Clause, and that the Commission was estopped under state law from requiring respondent to comply with the current zoning ordinance and subdivision regulations rather than those in effect in 1973. The jury awarded damages of $350,000 for the temporary taking of respondent's property. . . .

The court then granted judgment notwithstanding the verdict in favor of the Commission on the taking claim, reasoning in part that respondent was unable to derive economic benefit from its property on a temporary basis only, and that such a temporary deprivation, as a matter of law, cannot constitute a taking. . . . [The court entered a permanent injunction] to require the Commission . . . to apply the zoning ordinance and subdivision regulations in effect in 1973 to the project, rather than requiring approval of the plat, in order to allow the parties to resolve "legitimate technical questions of whether plaintiff meets the requirements of the 1973 regulations" through the applicable state and local appeals procedures.[7]

A divided panel of the United States Court of Appeals for the Sixth Circuit reversed. . . .

The court rejected the District Court's holding that the taking verdict could not stand as a matter of law. A temporary denial of property could be a taking, and was to be analyzed in the same manner as a permanent taking. Finally, relying upon the dissent in *San Diego Gas & Electric Co. v. City of San Diego*, 450 U.S. 621 (1981), the court determined that damages are required to compensate for a temporary taking.

II

We granted certiorari to address the question whether Federal, State, and Local governments must pay money damages to a landowner whose property allegedly has been "taken" temporarily by the application of government regulations. 469 U.S. 815 (1984). . . . The Court twice has left this issue undecided. *San Diego Gas & Electric Co.*, 450 U.S. 621; *Agins v. City of Tiburon*, 447 U.S. 255, 263 (1980). Once again, we find that the question is not properly presented, and must be left for another day. For whether we examine the Planning Commission's application of its regulations under Fifth Amendment "taking" jurisprudence, or under the precept of due process, we conclude that respondent's claim is premature.

III

. . . [T]he jury verdict in this case cannot be upheld. Because respondent has not yet obtained a final decision regarding the application of the zoning ordinance and subdivision

---

5. Respondent claimed it was entitled to build 476 units: the 736 units allegedly approved in 1973 minus the 212 units already built or given final approval and minus 48 units that were no longer available because land had been taken from the subdivision for the parkway.

7. While respondent's appeal was pending before the Court of Appeals, the parties reached an agreement whereby the Commission granted a variance from its cul-de-sac and road-grade regulations and approved the development of 476 units, and respondent agreed, among other things, to rebuild existing roads, and build all new roads, according to current regulations.

regulations to its property, nor utilized the procedures Tennessee provides for obtaining just compensation, respondent's claim is not ripe.

A

As the Court has made clear in several recent decisions, a claim that the application of government regulations effects a taking of a property interest is not ripe until the government entity charged with implementing the regulations has reached a final decision regarding the application of the regulations to the property at issue. In Hodel v. Virginia Surface Mining & Reclamation Ass'n, 452 U.S. 264 (1981), for example, the Court rejected a claim that the Surface Mining Control and Reclamation Act of 1977 effected a taking because: "There is no indication in the record that appellees have availed themselves of the opportunities provided by the Act to obtain administrative relief by requesting either a variance from the approximate-original-contour requirement . . . or a waiver from the surface mining restrictions. . . . If [the property owners] were to seek administrative relief under these procedures, a mutually acceptable solution might well be reached with regard to individual properties, thereby obviating any need to address the constitutional questions. The potential for such administrative solutions confirms the conclusion that the taking issue decided by the District Court simply is not ripe for judicial resolution." 452 U.S. at 297 (footnote omitted).

Similarly, in Agins v. City of Tiburon, the Court held that a challenge to the application of a zoning ordinance was not ripe because the property owners had not yet submitted a plan for development of their property. 447 U.S. at 260. In Penn Central Transportation Co. v. City of New York, the Court declined to find that the application of New York City's Landmarks Preservation Law to Grand Central Terminal effected a taking because, although the Landmarks Preservation Commission had disapproved a plan for a 50-story office building above the terminal, the property owners had not sought approval for any other plan, and it therefore was not clear whether the Commission would deny approval for all uses that would enable the plaintiffs to derive economic benefit from the property. 438 U.S. 104, 136–37 (1978).

Respondent's claim is in a posture similar to the claims the Court held premature in *Hodel*. Respondent has submitted a plan for developing its property, and thus has passed beyond the *Agins* threshold. But, like the *Hodel* plaintiffs, respondent did not then seek variances that would have allowed it to develop the property according to its proposed plat, notwithstanding the Commission's finding that the plat did not comply with the zoning ordinance and subdivision regulations. It appears that variances could have been granted to resolve at least five of the Commission's eight objections to the plat. The Board of Zoning Appeals had the power to grant certain variances from the zoning ordinance, including the ordinance's density requirements and its restriction on placing units on land with slopes having a grade in excess of 25%. The Commission had the power to grant variances from the subdivision regulations, including the cul-de-sac, road-grade, and frontage requirements. Indeed, the Temple Hills Committee had recommended that the Commission grant variances from those regulations. Nevertheless, respondent did not seek variances from either the Board or the Commission. . . .

As in *Hodel*, *Agins*, and *Penn Central*, then, respondent has not yet obtained a final decision regarding how it will be allowed to develop its property. Our reluctance to examine taking claims until such a final decision has been made is compelled by the very nature of the inquiry required by the Just Compensation Clause. Although "[t]he question of what constitutes a 'taking' for purposes of the Fifth Amendment has proved to be a problem of considerable difficulty," *Penn Central Transportation Co.*, 438 U.S. at 123,

One factor under Penn:

this Court consistently has indicated that among the factors of particular significance in the inquiry are the economic impact of the challenged action and the extent to which it interferes with reasonable investment-backed expectations. Id. at 124. Those factors simply cannot be evaluated until the administrative agency has arrived at a final, definitive position regarding how it will apply the regulations at issue to the particular land in question.

Here, for example, the jury's verdict indicates only that it found that respondent would be denied the economically feasible use of its property if it were forced to develop the subdivision in a manner that would meet each of the Commission's eight objections. It is not clear whether the jury would have found that the respondent had been denied all reasonable beneficial use of the property had any of the eight objections been met through the grant of a variance. Indeed, the expert witness who testified regarding the economic impact of the Commission's actions did not itemize the effect of each of the eight objections, so the jury would have been unable to discern how a grant of a variance from any one of the regulations at issue would have affected the profitability of the development. Accordingly, until the Commission determines that no variances will be granted, it is impossible for the jury to find, on this record, whether respondent "will be unable to derive economic benefit" from the land.

P argues under 1983 –

Respondent asserts that it should not be required to seek variances from the regulations because its suit is predicated upon 42 U.S.C. §1983, and there is no requirement that a plaintiff exhaust administrative remedies before bringing a §1983 action. Patsy v. Board of Regents, 457 U.S. 496 (1982). The question whether administrative remedies must be exhausted is conceptually distinct, however, from the question whether an administrative action must be final before it is judicially reviewable. While the policies underlying the two concepts often overlap, the finality requirement is concerned with whether the initial decisionmaker has arrived at a definitive position on the issue that inflicts an actual, concrete injury; the exhaustion requirement generally refers to administrative and judicial procedures by which an injured party may seek review of an adverse decision and obtain a remedy if the decision is found to be unlawful or otherwise inappropriate. Patsy concerned the latter, not the former.

ct seems to think Π is confusing exhaustion w/ final action being judicially reviewable (ripeness)

The difference is best illustrated by comparing the procedure for seeking a variance with the procedures that, under Patsy, respondent would not be required to exhaust. While it appears that the State provides procedures by which an aggrieved property owner may seek a declaratory judgment regarding the validity of zoning and planning actions taken by county authorities, respondent would not be required to resort to those procedures before bringing its §1983 action, because those procedures clearly are remedial. Similarly, respondent would not be required to appeal the Commission's rejection of the preliminary plat to the Board of Zoning Appeals, because the Board was empowered, at most, to review that rejection, not to participate in the Commission's decisionmaking.

Resort to those procedures would result in a judgment whether the Commission's actions violated any of respondent's rights. In contrast, resort to the procedure for obtaining variances would result in a conclusive determination by the Commission whether it would allow respondent to develop the subdivision in the manner respondent proposed. The Commission's refusal to approve the preliminary plat does not determine that issue; it prevents respondent from developing its subdivision without obtaining the necessary variances, but leaves open the possibility that respondent may develop the subdivision according to its plat after obtaining the variances. In short, the Commission's denial of approval does not conclusively determine whether respondent will be denied all reasonable beneficial use of its property, and therefore is not a final, reviewable decision.

B

A second reason the taking claim is not yet ripe is that respondent did not seek compensation through the procedures the State has provided for doing so. The Fifth Amendment does not proscribe the taking of property; it proscribes taking without just compensation. Nor does the Fifth Amendment require that just compensation be paid in advance of, or contemporaneously with, the taking; all that is required is that a "'reasonable, certain and adequate provision for obtaining compensation'" exist at the time of the taking. Regional Rail Reorganization Act Cases, 419 U.S. 102, 124–25 (1974) (quoting Cherokee Nation v. Southern Kan. Ry. Co., 135 U.S. 641 (1890)). If the government has provided an adequate process for obtaining compensation, and if resort to that process "yield[s] just compensation," then the property owner "has no claim against the Government" for a taking. Ruckelshaus v. Monsanto Co., 467 U.S. 986, 1013, 1018 n.21 (1984). Thus, we have held that taking claims against the Federal Government are premature until the property owner has availed itself of the process provided by the Tucker Act, 28 U.S.C. §1491. *Monsanto*, 467 U.S. at 1016–20. Similarly, if a State provides an adequate procedure for seeking just compensation, the property owner cannot claim a violation of the Just Compensation Clause until it has used the procedure and been denied just compensation. . . .

. . . The Tennessee state courts have interpreted . . . [state law] to allow recovery through inverse condemnation where the "taking" is effected by restrictive zoning laws or development regulations. Respondent has not shown that the inverse condemnation procedure is unavailable or inadequate, and until it has utilized that procedure, its taking claim is premature. . . .

Justice WHITE dissents from the holding that the issues in this case are not ripe for decision at this time.

Justice POWELL took no part in the decision of this case.

Justice BRENNAN, with whom Justice MARSHALL joins, concurring. . . .

Justice STEVENS, concurring in the judgment. . . .

Note on When the Ripeness Requirements Apply

1. *Facial versus as-applied claims.* A facial takings challenge must assert that the "mere enactment" of the challenged regulation deprives the landowner of all economically viable use of the property. Agins v. City of Tiburon, 447 U.S. 255, 260 (1980). Such claims are not subject to the "final determination" prong of *Williamson County*'s ripeness requirements. See Keystone Bituminous Coal Ass'n v. DeBenedictis, 480 U.S. 470 (1987); Yee v. City of Escondido, 503 U.S. 519 (1992) (addressing the merits of facial claims without requiring the plaintiffs to satisfy *Williamson County*'s final determination requirement). See also Suitum v. Tahoe Regional Planning Agency, 520 U.S. 725, 736 n.10 (1997) (stating that facial claims are generally ripe the moment the challenged regulation is passed).

Nor does the "state remedies" prong of *Williamson County* apply to such facial takings claims. See San Remo Hotel, L.P. v. City & County of San Francisco, 125 S. Ct. 2491, 2503 n.23 (2005), excerpted at p. 245.

2. *Substantive due process, procedural due process, equal protection, and civil liberties claims.* Although the second prong of *Williamson County*'s ripeness requirements is by its very nature limited to takings claims, the courts have struggled with whether to apply the first, final determination, prong to as-applied arbitrary and capricious substantive due process claims. Compare Sameric Corp. of Delaware v. City of Philadelphia, 142 F.3d 582 (3d Cir. 1998) (final determination requirement applies), with Restigouche, Inc. v. Town of

Jupiter, 59 F.3d 1208, 1212 (11th Cir. 1995) ("Because substantive due process and takings challenges to the zoning process scrutinize that process in slightly different ways, . . . [the] claims mature at different points in the process."). See also David S. Mendel, Determining Ripeness of Substantive Due Process Claims Brought by Landowners Against Local Governments, 95 Mich. L. Rev. 492 (1996).

Similarly, the courts are split over whether the final determination requirement applies to equal protection claims. Compare Christopher Lake Development Co. v. St. Louis County, 35 F.3d 1269 (8th Cir. 1994) (yes), with Forseth v. Village of Sussex, 199 F.3d 363, 371 (7th Cir. 2000) (no). As to procedural due process claims, compare, e.g., Dougherty v. Town of North Hempstead Board of Zoning, 282 F.3d 83, 87 (2d Cir. 2002) (yes), with Nasierowski Bros. Investment Co. v. City of Sterling Heights, 949 F.2d 890 (6th Cir. 1991) (no). For a review of the cases, see Stephen E. Abraham, *Williamson County* Fifteen Years Later: When Is a Takings Claim (Ever) Ripe?, 36 Real Prop. Prob. & Tr. J. 101 (2001).

3. *Jurisdictional or prudential ripeness?* Must the landowner meet the requirements of *Williamson County* for the court to have subject matter jurisdiction over the case, or are the requirements merely "prudential"? In *Lucas*, Justice Blackmun argued in dissent that the property owner's failure to seek a special permit from the coastal zone regulations imposed "jurisdictional barriers" to the Court's review. 505 U.S. at 1041–43 (Blackmun J., dissenting). The majority responded: "That there is a discretionary special permit procedure by which he may regain — for the future, at least — beneficial use of his land goes only to the prudential 'ripeness' of Lucas's challenge, and for the reasons discussed we do not think it prudent to apply that prudential requirement here." Id. at 1012. In *Suitum*, described at pp. 166–67, the majority again seemed to think of the final determination prong of *Williamson County* only as prudential. 520 U.S. 725, 733 n.7. Some lower courts nevertheless treat the final determination requirement as jurisdictional. See, e.g., Gavlak v. Town of Somers, 267 F. Supp. 2d 214, 218 (D. Conn. 2003) (addressing ripeness issues sua sponte because final determination prong implicates subject matter jurisdiction).

Note on the "Final Determination" Requirement

1. *What kind of application?* To meet the final determination requirement, the landowner must show that it submitted at least one "meaningful" application for development, and that the local government denied that application. See, e.g., Southern Pacific Transportation Co. v. City of Los Angeles, 922 F.2d 498, 503–04 (9th Cir. 1990). The application must be "essentially complete, must realistically describe the desired use, and must be reasonably current (or, at least, if it has been pending for some time, the agency's rejection of it must be reasonably fresh)." Gilbert v. City of Cambridge, 932 F.2d 51, 63 n.15 (1st Cir. 1991).

2. *How many applications?* In MacDonald, Sommer & Frates v. County of Yolo, 477 U.S. 340 (1986), the owner's subdivision plans, which called for 159 single- and multiple-family lots, were rejected on the grounds that the subdivision would have inadequate access to public streets, would have no public water or sewer service, and would strain the local government's police services. The Court held that the landowner had not satisfied *Williamson County*'s final determination requirement: "Rejection of exceedingly grandiose development plans does not logically imply that less ambitious plans will receive similarly unfavorable reviews." Id. at 353 n.9. The Court noted that "[a] property owner is of course

not required to resort to piecemeal litigation or otherwise unfair procedures in order to obtain this determination." Id. at 350 n.7.

Palazzolo v. Rhode Island, 533 U.S. 606 (2001), excerpted at p. 180, sheds some light on where the line falls between grandiose applications and unfair procedures requiring futile reapplications. In *Palazzolo*, the Court overturned a finding that the property owner's claim was not ripe because his several applications had proposed to fill all, or nearly all, of the wetlands but had not explored less grandiose development options. The Supreme Court found that "the Council's decisions make plain that the agency interpreted its regulations to bar petitioner from engaging in *any* filling or development activity on the wetlands." 533 U.S. at 621 (emphasis added). The Court noted that the *Williamson County* rule was necessary because of the "high degree of discretion characteristically possessed by land-use boards," but reasoned that "once it becomes clear that the agency lacks the discretion to permit any development, or the permissible uses of the property are known to a reasonable degree of certainty, a takings claim is likely to have ripened." Id. at 620–21. The Court distinguished *MacDonald*, *Williamson County*, and *Agins*, which it characterized as involving denials of "substantial" projects that left doubt whether a "more modest submission" might be accepted. In contrast, the Court emphasized the "unequivocal nature of the wetland regulations at issue" and Rhode Island's candid admission that it would not allow fill of the wetlands for any "likely or foreseeable use." Id.

Many developers submit proposals that leave them room to negotiate with the local government. Are such "opening bids" necessarily "exceedingly grandiose"? If a developer submits successively more modest proposals, but still fails to win approval and decides to litigate, are the more modest proposals a "concession" that the developer had no right to its original proposal? See Gregory Overstreet, Update on the Continuing and Dramatic Effect of the Ripeness Doctrine on Federal Land Use Litigation, Zoning & Plan. L. Rep., Mar. 1997, at 21, 22.

3. *The futility exception*: Once a meaningful application has been filed, adequately pursued, and rejected, *Williamson County* then requires the developer to seek a variance, special permit, or other discretionary relief from whatever regulation was invoked to deny the application. *Palazzolo* makes clear, however, that a plaintiff need not apply for such discretionary relief if the application would be "futile." 533 U.S. at 626. See also *MacDonald*, 477 U.S. at 352 n.8. The lower courts have struggled to define the parameters of the futility exception. If there are no variances available under the zoning ordinance, the developer obviously should not need to apply for one. Greenbriar, Ltd. v. City of Alabaster, 881 F.2d 1570 (11th Cir. 1989). But what if local government officials just hint that an application will not be successful? See, e.g., Gilbert v. City of Cambridge, 932 F.2d 51, 61 (1st Cir. 1991) ("To come within the exception, a sort of inevitability is required: the prospect of refusal must be certain (or nearly so)."); Kinzli v. City of Santa Cruz, 818 F.2d 1449, 1452 (9th Cir.) (claim not ripe where developer abandoned application after staff engineer for Department of Public Works said city could not provide water to property, because process of securing approval involves many different agencies and entails negotiation), amended by 830 F.2d 968 (9th Cir. 1987). What purpose (if any) is served by having developers pursue applications in the face of such informal dissuasion?

4. *The burden of proof*: James Burling, an attorney with the Pacific Legal Foundation, reads *Palazzolo* to put the burden of proving futility on the government defendant:

> What may become the most significant aspect of the ripeness holding in *Palazzolo* is the suggestion that once a landowner has a meaningful permit application denied, the burden shifts to the government to indicate what, if any, other uses of the property may be available. Several times in the opinion the Court implies that the government must "explain" or give an

"indication" of its potential acceptance of another or a reduced use. First, the Court implied that a landowner must first submit an application to provide the agency with an opportunity to "explain" the reach of its restrictions: "a landowner may not establish a taking before a land-use authority has the opportunity, using its own reasonable procedures, to decide and explain the reach of a challenged regulation." Next, after noting that the 11.4 acre beach club had been rejected under a "compelling public purpose" standard the Court notes, "[t]here is no indication the Council would have accepted the application had petitioner's proposed beach club occupied a smaller surface area." Finally, the Court put it more directly later in the opinion when it found "the limitations the wetland regulations imposed were clear from the Council's denial of his applications, and there is no indication that any use involving any substantial structures or improvements would have been allowed." The lesson here is that once an applicant submits and has rejected a meaningful application to put real property to an economically viable use, an agency must at the very least come forward and suggest other uses that might be available for the property. Such uses must, of course, be economically meaningful.

James S. Burling, When Is a Claim Against the Government Ripe? Takings, Equal Protection, Due Process, and First Amendment Challenges, SJ052 ALI-ABA 35, 46 (2004) (citations omitted). Is Burling's analysis persuasive? Who should bear the burden of proving that any further applications to the local government would be futile? See also pp. 276–81, discussing Florida's efforts to clarify when a local government has rendered a final determination.

5. *The risk of abuse.* Under *Williamson County*, *MacDonald*, and *Palazzolo*, can a local government "string out" the developer by indicating a willingness to accept different, or more modest, proposals? See, e.g., Del Monte Dunes at Monterey, Ltd. v. City of Monterey, 920 F.2d 1496 (9th Cir. 1990), aff'd, 526 U.S. 687 (1999) (reversing the district court's finding that the takings claim was not ripe, when the developer had submitted a proposal for 344 units; then after being told that 264 units would be favorably received, submitted a second proposal for 264 units; then after being told that 224 units would be favorably received, submitted a third proposal for 224 units; then after the city council overturned denial of that proposal with instructions to approve a 190-unit proposal, submitted a fourth proposal for 190 units, which was conditionally approved; then submitted a fifth proposal for 190 units that met all the conditions imposed, but nevertheless was denied permission to build).

Given that delay may be just as harmful to a developer as denial of the application, how can a developer fight a local government that misuses *Williamson County*? Will the threat of a compensation award in the (unlikely) event that the local government is found to have effected a taking be a sufficient deterrent for abuse? Compare e.g., Vicki Been, The Finality Requirement in Takings Litigation after *Palazzolo*, in Taking Sides on Takings Issues: Public and Private Perspectives 485, 497-500 (Thomas E. Roberts ed., 2002) (questioning the evidence that such abuse is widespread, and exploring possible constraints on abuse); Michael M. Berger, The "Ripeness" Mess in Federal Land Use Cases or How the Supreme Court Converted Federal Judges into Fruit Peddlers, 1991 Inst. on Plan. Zoning & Eminent Domain, ch. 7 (complaining of abuse).

Even if the local government does not seek to abuse the ripeness requirements, do the requirements nevertheless serve as an unduly formidable financial barrier for disappointed landowners considering whether to sue? See Gregory M. Stein, Regulatory Takings and Ripeness in Federal Courts, 48 Vand. L. Rev. 1, 43 (1995) ("Practically speaking, the universe of plaintiffs with the financial ability to survive the lengthy ripening process is small.").

6. *Variances versus rezonings.* Where a variance is unavailable, must the developer seek a rezoning or an amendment to the comprehensive plan? See Tahoe-Sierra Preservation

Council, Inc. v. Tahoe Regional Planning Agency, 911 F.2d 1331 (9th Cir. 1990) [*Tahoe I*] (plaintiffs should have sought amendment to defendant's regional plan); but see Tahoe-Sierra Preservation Council, Inc. v. Tahoe Regional Planning Agency, 938 F.2d 153 (9th Cir. 1991) (refusing to follow *Tahoe I* in a parallel case). Is requiring a developer to seek legislative as opposed to administrative relief from a regulation consistent with the reasoning of *Williamson County*? See Gregory Overstreet, The Ripeness Doctrine of the Taking Clause: A Survey of Decisions Showing Just How Far Federal Courts Will Go to Avoid Adjudicating Land-Use Cases, 10 J. Land Use & Envtl. L. 91, 111–12 (1994). What if the state at issue classifies rezonings as adjudicative rather than legislative? See pp. 341–52.

7. *TDRs*. In *Suitum*, described at pp. 166–67, the Supreme Court held that a landowner has no obligation to attempt to actually sell the TDRs the government has provided to soften the impact of its regulations in order to establish a ripe takings challenge to the regulations, because "valuation of Suitum's TDR's is . . . simply an issue of fact about possible market prices." 520 U.S. at 741. Is that rule consistent with the reasons for *Williamson County*'s final determination requirement if TDRs are considered to be compensation, as discussed at pp. 166–67? If they are thought instead to be one of the factors that should be taken into account in the determination whether there has been a taking? See 520 U.S. at 746 (Scalia, J., concurring in part and concurring in the judgment) ("The focus of the 'final decision' inquiry is on ascertaining the extent of the governmental restriction on land use, not what the government has given the landowner in exchange for that restriction.").

8. *Criticisms of* Williamson County. Many academics and practitioners are extremely critical of *Williamson County*. See, e.g., Berger, supra; Peter A. Buchsbaum, Should Land Use Be Different? Reflections on *Williamson County Regional Planning Board v. Hamilton Bank*, *in* Taking Sides on Takings Issues: Public and Private Perspectives 471 (Thomas E. Roberts ed., 2002); Gideon Kanner, Hunting the Snark, Not the Quark: Has the U.S. Supreme Court Been Competent in Its Effort to Formulate Coherent Regulatory Takings Law?, 30 Urb. Law. 307 (1998); Timothy V. Kassouni, The Ripeness Doctrine and the Judicial Relegation of Constitutionally Protected Property Rights, 29 Cal. W. L. Rev. 1 (1992); Overstreet, supra; Henry Paul Monaghan, Comment, State Law Wrongs, State Law Remedies, and the Fourteenth Amendment, 86 Colum. L. Rev. 979, 988–90 (1986). For defenses of the finality and state remedies requirements, see Been, supra; R. Jeffrey Lyman, Finality Ripeness in Federal Land-Use Cases from *Hamilton Bank* to *Lucas*, 9 J. Land Use & Envtl. L. 101, 127 (1993) (concluding that despite "despair" of scholars and practitioners, the lower courts have been "remarkably tolerant of developers' efforts to reach the federal courts"); Thomas E. Roberts, Procedural Implications of *Williamson County/First English* in Regulatory Takings Litigation: Herein of Reservations, Removal, Diversity, Supplemental Jurisdiction, *Rooker-Feldman*, and Res Judicata, 31 Envtl. L. Rep. 10353 (2001).

Critics of the state remedies prong of *Williamson County* have convinced at least four justices that the requirement should be revisited. See *San Remo*, excerpted at p. 245. The final determination prong, however, appears firmly ensconced. See id. Legislative attacks on both prongs are discussed at pp. 274–82.

9. *State ripeness requirements*. Many states have adopted ripeness requirements for takings claims brought under state constitutions. See, e.g., Martin County v. Section 28 Partnership, Ltd., 668 So. 2d 672 (Fla. Dist. Ct. App. 1996). Does that reflect the wisdom of *Williamson County* or an uncritical adoption of federal precedents?

In *Palazzolo*, the State and its amici argued that the property owner's applications, which sought permission to fill wetlands in order to construct a beach club, should not be allowed to ripen his eventual takings claim, which alleged that the State took his right to construct a 74-unit residential subdivision. They pointed out that the defendant agency, the Coastal Resources Management Council, would not have entertained an application for residential use until Palazzolo had obtained the appropriate zoning permits from the town and sewage disposal permits from the State's Department of Environmental Resources. By short-circuiting those processes and preventing the State from using them to develop a record about the potential harms of such intensive use, they argued, Palazzolo used "a hide the ball strategy of submitting applications for more modest uses to the Council, only to assert later a takings action predicated on the purported inability to build a much larger project." 533 U.S. at 624. The Court granted the validity of the State's concern that "landowners could demand damages for a taking based on a project that could not have been constructed under other, valid zoning restrictions quite apart from the regulation being challenged" and disclaimed any intent to "cast doubt upon" the authority of a state "to insist . . . that landowners follow normal planning procedures or to enact rules to control damage awards based on hypothetical uses that should have been reviewed in the normal course." Id. at 625. Professor Been has suggested that "[r]egulatory agencies should respond to the Court's discussion by strictly enforcing their rules about the sequencing of reviews where more than one agency has an interest in a proposed development, and by insisting on meticulous adherence to all requirements for a permit application." Been, supra, at 497.

Note on the "State Remedies" Requirement

1. *Effect of* First English. In 1987, the Supreme Court finally reached the question it left unanswered in *Williamson County*, deciding that the Fifth Amendment requires compensation for temporary regulatory takings. First English Evangelical Lutheran Church of Glendale v. County of Los Angeles, 482 U.S. 304 (1987), excerpted at p. 258. Under *First English*, every state court finding a regulatory taking under the federal Constitution should require the state to compensate for the taking. Does the juxtaposition of *Williamson County* and *First English* therefore mean that *no* federal takings challenge to a state or local land use decision will be ripe unless the federal claim is first pursued in state court?

2. *Adequacy of the state procedures.* What might make the state court remedies that *First English* mandates "unavailable or inadequate"? If the success rate for landowners in a particular state's courts is significantly lower than the rate in federal courts (or other states' courts), would *Williamson County* excuse resort to the state's courts? See J. David Breemer, Overcoming *Williamson County*'s Troubling State Procedures Rule: How the *England* Reservation, Issue Preclusion Exceptions, and the Inadequacy Exception Open the Federal Courthouse Door to Ripe Takings Claims, 18 J. Land Use & Envtl. L. 209, 260 (2003) (arguing that the statistics show that in California, the state court remedy is "non-existent as a practical and theoretical matter"). What if the state court has announced an interpretation of the state constitution that arguably is out of step with the federal courts' interpretation of the Fifth Amendment? See Thomas E. Roberts, Procedural Implications of *Williamson County/First English* in Regulatory Takings Litigation: Herein of Reservations, Removal, Diversity, Supplemental Jurisdiction, *Rooker-Feldman*, and Res Judicata, 31 Envtl. L. Rep. 10353 (2001).

The landowner bears the burden of proving that state court remedies are inadequate, and evidence that the remedies are just uncertain is not sufficient. See, e.g., Carson Harbor Village, Ltd. v. City of Carson, 353 F.3d 824, 830 (9th Cir. 2004) (the considerable uncertainty over the procedures California imposes on landlords claiming that rent control regulations effectuate a taking is not enough to render those remedies inadequate); John Corp. v. City of Houston, 214 F.3d 573, 581 (5th Cir. 2000) (plaintiff had not met burden of proving that it "almost certainly" would not be compensated under Texas law).

3. *A lopsided rule?* If a landowner files a takings claim in state court, as *Williamson County* requires, but includes federal claims in the complaint, can the governmental defendant remove the case to federal court? In City of Chicago v. International College of Surgeons, 522 U.S. 156 (1997), a landowner sought permits to demolish all but the facades of two mansions designated as historic landmarks. When the application for the permits and a subsequent application for a hardship exception to the landmark rules were denied, the landowner sued in state court, raising federal due process, equal protection, and takings claims, as well as takings and other claims under state law. The City (perhaps after reading Coniston Corp. v. Village of Hoffman Estates, 844 F.2d 461 (7th Cir. 1988), excerpted at p. 99) removed the cases to federal court, asserting that the federal courts had original jurisdiction over the federal claims and should exercise supplemental jurisdiction, under 28 U.S.C. §1367, over the state claims. The district court exercised jurisdiction, decided that the denial of the permit had not effected a taking, and dismissed the action. The Seventh Circuit reversed, holding that the district court had no jurisdiction over the cases. The Supreme Court reversed, agreeing with the district court.

Neither the majority nor the dissenting Supreme Court opinions even mentioned *Williamson County*. Could *International College of Surgeons* mean that government defendants can remove takings claims to federal courts without regard to the requirements of *Williamson County*, even though those requirements bar property owners from bringing such claims in federal court? The lower courts have declined to read *International College of Surgeons* as modifying *Williamson County*'s ripeness rules for landowners. See, e.g, Kottschade v. City of Rochester, 319 F.3d 1038, 1040–41 (8th Cir. 2003). In some cases, however, that means a case is dismissed, after years of litigation in federal courts occasioned by the *local government's* removal, because of the plaintiff's failure to pursue state court remedies. See, e.g, Sandy Creek Investors, Ltd. v. City of Jonestown, Tex., 325 F.3d 623 (5th Cir. 2003). For discussion of the "Catch-22" between *Williamson County* and *International College of Surgeons*, see Michael M. Berger & Gideon Kanner, Shell Game! You Can't Get There from Here: Supreme Court Ripeness Jurisprudence in Takings Cases at Long Last Reaches the Self-Parody Stage, 36 Urb. Law. 671, 677 (2004).

4. *Diversity jurisdiction and* Williamson County? Should a plaintiff who is a citizen of a different state than the defendant government be able to bring its state takings claim in federal court under the diversity jurisdiction provisions, rather than bringing the claim in state court? See, e.g., Vulcan Materials Co. v. City of Tehuacana, 238 F.3d 382, 385 (5th Cir. 2001) (although plaintiff could not bring a *federal* takings claim in federal court until it had pursued its state takings claim, it could bring the *state* claim in federal court if it qualified for diversity jurisdiction).

5. *Ripening to preclusion?* If the juxtaposition of *Williamson County* and *First English* means that all litigants bringing as-applied takings claims must pursue state compensation remedies, can a landowner *then* have its federal takings claim heard in federal court? Once the landowner has ripened the claim, will it then be barred by principles of issue or claim preclusion?

San Remo Hotel, L.P. v. City & County of San Francisco
125 S. Ct. 2491 (2005)

Justice STEVENS delivered the opinion of the Court. . . .

This case presents the question whether federal courts may craft an exception to the full faith and credit statute, 28 U.S.C. §1738, for claims brought under the Takings Clause of the Fifth Amendment.

Petitioners, who own and operate a hotel in San Francisco, California (hereinafter City), initiated this litigation in response to the application of a city ordinance that required them to pay a $567,000 "conversion fee" in 1996. After the California courts rejected petitioners' various state-law takings claims, they advanced in the Federal District Court a series of federal takings claims that depended on issues identical to those that had previously been resolved in the state-court action. In order to avoid the bar of issue preclusion, petitioners asked the District Court to exempt from §1738's reach claims brought under the Takings Clause of the Fifth Amendment.

Petitioners' argument is predicated on Williamson County Regional Planning Comm'n v. Hamilton Bank of Johnson City, 473 U.S. 172 (1985), which held that takings claims are not ripe until a State fails "to provide adequate compensation for the taking." Id. at 195. Unless courts disregard §1738 in takings cases, petitioners argue, plaintiffs will be forced to litigate their claims in state court without any realistic possibility of ever obtaining review in a federal forum. The Ninth Circuit's rejection of this argument conflicted with the Second Circuit's decision in Santini v. Connecticut Hazardous Waste Management Service, 342 F.3d 118 (2003). We granted certiorari to resolve the conflict, and now affirm the judgment of the Ninth Circuit.

I

The San Remo Hotel is a three-story, 62-unit hotel in the Fisherman's Wharf neighborhood in San Francisco. . . .

[In 1981, San Francisco responded to "a severe shortage" of affordable rental housing by enacting a Hotel Conversion Ordinance (HCO) that required a hotel owner to obtain a permit to convert residential units into tourist units. An owner could obtain the permit only by constructing new, or rehabilitating old, residential units or by paying a conversion fee into the City's Residential Hotel Preservation Fund. After the lessee of the San Remo erroneously reported to the City that all the rooms in the hotel were "residential units," the City zoned the San Remo Hotel as a "residential" hotel. That classification meant that although the San Remo Hotel had operated in practice as a tourist hotel for many years, petitioners were required to apply for a permit to do business officially as a "tourist" hotel. In 1993, the City Planning Commission granted the permit, but only after imposing several conditions, including a requirement that petitioners pay $567,000 in conversion fees.]

In March 1993, Petitioners filed for a writ of administrative mandamus in California Superior Court. . . . [T]he parties ultimately agreed to stay that action. . . .

Petitioners filed in federal court for the first time on May 4, 1993 . . . [alleging] due process (substantive and procedural) and takings (facial and as-applied) violations under the Fifth and Fourteenth Amendments to the United States Constitution, . . . and one pendent state-law claim. The District Court granted respondents summary judgment. . . . [finding] that petitioners' facial takings claim was untimely under the applicable statute of limitations, and that the as-applied takings claim was unripe under Williamson County.

On appeal to the Court of Appeals for the Ninth Circuit, petitioners took the unusual position that the court should not decide their federal claims, but instead should abstain under Railroad Comm'n of Tex. v. Pullman Co., 312 U.S. 496 (1941), because a return to state court could conceivably moot the remaining federal questions. The Court of Appeals obliged petitioners' request with respect to the facial challenge, . . . reason[ing that it] was "ripe the instant the 1990 HCO was enacted," and appropriate for Pullman abstention principally because petitioners' "entire case" hinged on the propriety of the planning commission's zoning designation—the precise subject of the pending state mandamus action. The court, however, affirmed the District Court's determination that petitioners' as-applied takings claim . . . was unripe . . . [b]ecause petitioners had failed to pursue an inverse condemnation action in state court . . .

. . . [T]he court appended a footnote stating that . . . [if petitioners] wanted to "retain [their] right to return to federal court for adjudication of [their] federal claim, [they] must make an appropriate reservation in state court." [145 F.3d 1095] at 1106, n.7 [(9th Cir. 1998)].[6] That is precisely what petitioners attempted to do when they reactivated the dormant California case. . . . The state trial court dismissed petitioners' amended complaint, but the intermediate appellate court reversed. The court held that . . . the "in lieu" fee effected a taking. . . .

The California Supreme Court reversed. . . . The court initially noted that petitioners had reserved their federal causes of action and had sought no relief for any violation of the Federal Constitution. 41 P.3d [87], 91, n. 1 [(Cal. 2002)]. In the portion of its opinion discussing the Takings Clause of the California Constitution, however, the court noted that "we appear to have construed the clauses congruently." Id. at 100–101 (citing cases). Accordingly, despite the fact that petitioners sought relief only under California law, the state court decided to "analyze their takings claim under the relevant decisions of both this court and the United States Supreme Court." Ibid. at 101. . . .

. . . [T]he court upheld the HCO on its face and as-applied to petitioners. . . .

Petitioners . . . returned to Federal District Court . . . The District Court held that petitioners' facial attack on the HCO was . . . barred by . . . the general rule of issue preclusion. . . . Because California courts had interpreted the relevant substantive state takings law coextensively with federal law, petitioners' federal claims constituted the same claims that had already been resolved in state court.

The Court of Appeals affirmed. . . . We granted certiorari and now affirm.

II

Article IV, §1, of the United States Constitution demands that "Full Faith and Credit shall be given in each State to the public Acts, Records, and judicial Proceedings of every other State. And the Congress may by general Laws prescribe the Manner in which such Acts, Records and Proceedings shall be proved, and the Effect thereof." . . . The modern version of the [implementing] statute, 28 U.S.C. §1738, provides that "judicial proceedings . . . shall have the same full faith and credit in every court within the United States and its Territories and Possessions as they have by law or usage in the courts of such State. . . . " This statute has long been understood to encompass the doctrines of res judicata, or "claim preclusion," and collateral estoppel, or "issue preclusion." See Allen v. McCurry, 449 U.S. 90, 94–96 (1980).[16] . . .

The essence of petitioners' argument is as follows: because no claim that a state agency has violated the federal Takings Clause can be heard in federal court until the property owner has "been denied just compensation" through an available state compensation procedure, [*Williamson County*] at 195, "federal courts [should be] required to disregard the decision of the state court" in order to ensure that federal takings claims can be "considered on the merits in . . . federal court." See Brief for Petitioners 8, 14. Therefore, the argument goes, whenever plaintiffs reserve their claims under England v. Louisiana Bd. of Medical

---

6. The reservation discussed in the Ninth Circuit's opinion was the common reservation of federal claims made in state litigation under England v. Louisiana Bd. of Medical Examiners, 375 U.S. 411, 420–421 (1964).

16. "Under res judicata, a final judgment on the merits of an action precludes the parties or their privies from relitigating issues that were or could have been raised in that action. Under collateral estoppel, once a court has decided an issue of fact or law necessary to its judgment, that decision may preclude relitigation of the issue in a suit on a different cause of action involving a party to the first case." Allen v. McCurry, [449 U.S. 90, 94 (1980).]

Examiners, 375 U.S. 411 (1964), federal courts should review the reserved federal claims de novo, regardless of what issues the state court may have decided or how it may have decided them.

We reject petitioners' contention. Although petitioners were certainly entitled to reserve some of their federal claims, as we shall explain, *England* does not support their erroneous expectation that their reservation would fully negate the preclusive effect of the state-court judgment with respect to any and all federal issues that might arise in the future federal litigation. Federal courts, moreover, are not free to disregard 28 U.S.C. §1738 simply to guarantee that all takings plaintiffs can have their day in federal court. We turn first to *England*.

III

[In] *England . . .* we held that when a federal court abstains from deciding a federal constitutional issue to enable the state courts to address an antecedent state-law issue, the plaintiff may reserve his right to return to federal court for the disposition of his federal claims. [375 U.S.] at 419. . . . "Typical" *England* cases generally involve federal constitutional challenges to a state statute that can be avoided if a state court construes the statute in a particular manner. In such cases, the purpose of abstention is not to afford state courts an opportunity to adjudicate an issue that is functionally identical to the federal question. To the contrary, the purpose of *Pullman* abstention in such cases is to avoid resolving the federal question by encouraging a state-law determination that may moot the federal controversy. See 375 U.S. at 416–417, and n.7. . . .

Our holding in *England* does not support petitioners' attempt to relitigate issues resolved by the California courts. With respect to petitioners' facial takings claims, the Court of Appeals invoked *Pullman* abstention after determining that a ripe federal question existed—namely, "the facial takings challenge to the 1990 HCO." 145 F.3d at 1105.[23] . . . Thus, petitioners were entitled to insulate from preclusive effect one federal issue—their facial constitutional challenge to the HCO—while they returned to state court to resolve their petition for writ of mandate.

Petitioners, however, chose to advance broader issues than the limited issues contained within their state petition for writ of administrative mandamus on which the Ninth Circuit relied when it invoked *Pullman* abstention. In their state action, petitioners advanced not only their request for a writ of administrative mandate, but also their various claims that the HCO was unconstitutional on its face and as applied for (1) its failure to substantially advance a legitimate interest, (2) its lack of a nexus between the required fees and the ultimate objectives sought to be achieved via the ordinance, and (3) its imposition of an undue economic burden on individual property owners. 41 P.3d at 106–109. By broadening their state action beyond the mandamus petition to include their "substantially advances" claims, petitioners effectively asked the state court to resolve the same federal issues they asked it to reserve. *England* does not support the exercise of any such right.

Petitioners' as-applied takings claims fare no better. . . . [T]he Court of Appeals . . . found that they were unripe under *Williamson County*. The court therefore affirmed the district court's dismissal of those claims. 145 F.3d at 1106. Unlike their "substantially advances" claims, petitioners' as-applied claims were never properly before the District Court, and there was no reason to expect that they could be relitigated in full if

---

23. Petitioners' facial challenges to the HCO were ripe, of course, under Yee v. Escondido, 503 U.S. 519, 534 (1992), in which we held that facial challenges based on the "substantially advances" test need not be ripened in state court—the claims do "not depend on the extent to which petitioners are deprived of the economic use of their particular pieces of property or the extent to which these particular petitioners are compensated." *Ibid.*

advanced in the state proceedings. See Allen, 449 U.S. at 101, n. 17. In short, our opinion in *England* does not support petitioners' attempt to circumvent §1738.

IV

In *Santini,* the Second Circuit held that parties "who litigate state-law takings claims in state court involuntarily" pursuant to *Williamson County* cannot be precluded from having those very claims resolved "by a federal court." 342 F.3d at 130. The court . . . reasoned that "[i]t would be both ironic and unfair if the very procedure that the Supreme Court required [plaintiffs] to follow before bringing a Fifth Amendment takings claim . . . also precluded [them] from ever bringing a Fifth Amendment takings claim." Ibid. We find this reasoning unpersuasive for several reasons.

First, both petitioners and *Santini* ultimately depend on an assumption that plaintiffs have a right to vindicate their federal claims in a federal forum. We have repeatedly held, to the contrary, that issues actually decided in valid state-court judgments may well deprive plaintiffs of the "right" to have their federal claims relitigated in federal court. See, e.g., Migra v. Warren City School Dist. Bd. of Ed., 465 U.S. 75, 84 (1984); *Allen,* 449 U.S. at 103–104. This is so even when the plaintiff would have preferred not to litigate in state court, but was required to do so by statute or prudential rules. See id. at 104. . . .

. . . Unfortunately for petitioners, it is entirely unclear why their preference for a federal forum should matter for constitutional or statutory purposes. . . .

The second reason we find petitioners' argument unpersuasive is that it assumes that courts may simply create exceptions to 28 U.S.C. §1738 wherever courts deem them appropriate. Even conceding, arguendo, the laudable policy goal of making federal forums available to deserving litigants, we have expressly rejected petitioners' view. "Such a fundamental departure from traditional rules of preclusion, enacted into federal law, can be justified only if plainly stated by Congress." Kremer v. Chemical Constr. Corp., 456 U.S. 461, 485 (1982). . . .

. . . Congress has not expressed any intent to exempt from the full faith and credit statute federal takings claims. . . .

Third, petitioners have overstated the reach of *Williamson County* throughout this litigation. Petitioners were never required to ripen the heart of their complaint—the claim that the HCO was facially invalid because it failed to substantially advance a legitimate state interest—in state court. See Yee v. Escondido, 503 U.S. 519, 534 (1992). Petitioners therefore could have raised most of their facial takings challenges, which by their nature requested relief distinct from the provision of "just compensation," directly in federal court.[25] Alternatively, petitioners had the option of reserving their facial claims while pursuing their as-applied claims along with their petition for writ of administrative mandamus. Petitioners did not have the right, however, to seek state review of the same substantive issues they sought to reserve. The purpose of the *England* reservation is not to grant plaintiffs a second bite at the apple in their forum of choice.

With respect to those federal claims that did require ripening, we reject petitioners' contention that *Williamson County* forbids plaintiffs from advancing their federal claims in state courts. The requirement that aggrieved property owners must seek "compensation through the procedures the State has provided for doing so," 473 U.S. at 194, does not preclude state courts from hearing simultaneously a plaintiff's request for compensation under state law and the claim that, in the alternative, the denial of compensation would violate the

---

25. In all events, petitioners may no longer advance such claims given our recent holding that the "'substantially advances' formula is not a valid takings test, and indeed . . . has no proper place in our takings jurisprudence." *Lingle,* 125 S. Ct. 2074 (2005).

Fifth Amendment of the Federal Constitution. Reading *Williamson County* to preclude plaintiffs from raising such claims in the alternative would erroneously interpret our cases as requiring property owners to "resort to piecemeal litigation or otherwise unfair procedures." MacDonald, Sommer & Frates v. Yolo County, 477 U.S. 340, 350, n. 7 (1986). . . .

Moreover, this is not the only area of law in which we have recognized limits to plaintiffs' ability to press their federal claims in federal courts. See, e.g., Fair Assessment in Real Estate Assn., Inc. v. McNary, 454 U.S. 100, 116 (1981) (holding that taxpayers are "barred by the principle of comity from asserting §1983 actions against the validity of state tax systems in federal courts"). State courts are fully competent to adjudicate constitutional challenges to local land-use decisions. Indeed, state courts undoubtedly have more experience than federal courts do in resolving the complex factual, technical, and legal questions related to zoning and land-use regulations.

At base, petitioners' claim amounts to little more than the concern that it is unfair to give preclusive effect to state-court proceedings that are not chosen, but are instead required in order to ripen federal takings claims. Whatever the merits of that concern may be, we are not free to disregard the full faith and credit statute solely to preserve the availability of a federal forum. The Court of Appeals was correct to decline petitioners' invitation to ignore the requirements of 28 U.S.C. §1738. The judgment of the Court of Appeals is therefore affirmed.

Chief Justice REHNQUIST, with whom Justice O'CONNOR, Justice KENNEDY, and Justice THOMAS join, concurring in the judgment.

I agree that the judgment of the Court of Appeals should be affirmed. . . . I write separately . . . [because although] I joined the opinion of the Court in *Williamson County* . . . further reflection and experience lead me to think that the justifications for its state-litigation requirement are suspect, while its impact on takings plaintiffs is dramatic. . . . In an appropriate case, I believe the Court should reconsider whether plaintiffs asserting a Fifth Amendment takings claim based on the final decision of a state or local government entity must first seek compensation in state courts. . . .

Note on *Williamson County* and Issue or Claim Preclusion

1. *Bait and switch?* Although the Supreme Court decided *San Remo* just as this book was going to press, so that it was not possible to report the reactions of critics, the early returns tracked the bitter complaints that critics had registered about the lower courts' navigation of the interstices of *Williamson County* and issue or claim preclusion. Michael Berger had lamented, for example:

> [The courts] cannot, with any degree of intellectual honesty, apply by rote the general precepts of claim and issue preclusion without noting the destructive impact on those general rules of the core holding of *Williamson County*. . . . Whether by design or blunder, the Supreme Court justices created a system in which they instructed property owners with constitutional claims to litigate the same factual case twice: once, under state law in state court, and then, if they so chose, again in federal court under federal law. It is simply impermissible to say that when the Supreme Court did so, it meant to create a system in which property owners are deliberately duped into giving up their right to federal litigation of federal constitutional issues because they do their best to comply with *Williamson County*'s clear holding. . . .

Michael M. Berger, Supreme Bait and Switch: The Ripeness Ruse in Regulatory Takings, 3 Wash. U. J.L. & Pol'y 99, 131–32 (2000).

2. *The attraction of (need for?) a federal forum.* Why are property owners so eager to be in federal court? Consider the arguments advanced by Brian W. Blaesser, Closing the

Federal Courthouse Door on Property Owners: The Ripeness and Abstention Doctrines in Section 1983 Land Use Cases, 2 Hofstra Prop. L.J. 73 (1988):

> The reasons why section 1983 suits should have a federal forum are at least threefold. First, where there are allegations that a wrong was committed under color of state law, there is "an inherent potential for bias" in the state court. Second, judicial review of allegations involving activities that are unpopular locally is best conducted by life-tenure federal judges whose jobs are not subject to parochial pressures. Finally, because the essence of a section 1983 action is the assertion of a national right, federal judges may have a greater understanding of and sympathy with constitutional goals. Review of their decisions through the federal appellate system will help ensure the uniform application of civil rights principles.

Id. at 74. See also Jeremy Paul, The Hidden Structure of Takings Law, 64 S. Cal. L. Rev. 1393, 1412 (1991) (federal court review of state action is necessary to prevent state overreaching).

How valid are those concerns? See Stewart Sterk, The Federalist Dimension of Regulatory Takings Jurisprudence, 114 Yale L.J. 203, 233–36 (2004) (reviewing the arguments that federal court review is necessary and finding them unpersuasive). Can the arguments be reconciled with the hostility some federal courts show toward land use claims, as evidenced by *Coniston*, excerpted at p. 99? Are landowners attracted to federal courts by the structural protections Blaesser discusses or (more cynically) by the number of federal judges appointed in recent years whose sympathies tend to be pro-landowner? To what extent do matters such as the relative "quality" of the federal and state benches or the relative speediness of the courts inform litigators' choice of forum? Should the evaluation of cases like *San Remo* turn on whether litigators prefer federal courts because of the structural protections they may provide or because of matters better described as "forum shopping"?

Does the public have an interest, independent of the parties' concerns, in the allocation of responsibility between the federal and state courts? See, e.g., Barry Friedman, Under the Law of Federal Jurisdiction: Allocating Cases Between Federal and State Courts, 104 Colum. L. Rev. 1211, 1235–46 (2004).

3. Abstention

In those instances in which ripeness or preclusion rules do not prevent (or at least delay) landowners' efforts to have a federal court decide their federal takings claims, abstention rules may.

Sinclair Oil Corp. v. County of Santa Barbara
96 F.3d 401 (9th Cir. 1996)

FLOYD R. GIBSON, Circuit Judge: . . .
. . . In 1993, the County . . . enacted [a] Community Plan, which was applicable to a particular geographic region known as Goleta, [and] . . . contemporaneously . . . designat[ed] certain areas as environmentally sensitive habitats. Once land has been specified as an environmentally sensitive habitat, its use is significantly restricted and subject to severe limitations.

Sinclair owns 265 acres of undeveloped coastal land in Santa Barbara County; this property, known as "More Mesa," is subject to the Goleta Community Plan ("the Plan"). The Plan substantially affects Sinclair's property, as it reduced from 300 to 70 the number of homes potentially allowable on More Mesa. Furthermore, the Plan designated a large portion of the land as an environmentally sensitive habitat. The Plan did create an administrative procedure through which Sinclair could petition to develop more than 70 residences on the site. To date, though, Sinclair has not submitted to the County a proposal for development of More Mesa, and it has also failed to seek compensation from the County.

On November 17, 1993, Sinclair filed this lawsuit in the United States District Court for the Central District of California.[1] The complaint asserted that the Plan, on its face, effected a taking of Sinclair's property requiring just compensation under the California and United States Constitutions. . . . In addition, Sinclair claimed that the County's adoption of the Plan violated Sinclair's substantive due process rights. . . .

The district court granted the [County's] motion [to dismiss], labeling as unripe . . . Sinclair's . . . causes of action. . . .

Before this Court, Sinclair maintains the district court improperly concluded that its facial challenges to the land use regulations are not ripe for federal adjudication. The County remonstrates that the court correctly determined the claims are not yet justiciable. In the alternative, the County contends the federal courts should abstain from hearing this case. . . .

[The Court read Sinclair's takings claims as "facial" challenges that (1) the Plan does not substantially advance legitimate state interests, and (2) the Plan denied Sinclair the economically viable use of its land. As to the first, the court found that neither prong of ripeness requirements applied, and the claim was therefore ripe. As to the second, the court held that the final determination prong of *Williamson County* did not apply because the challenge was facial rather than as-applied, but that the second, state remedies, prong of *Williamson County* did apply, so the claim was not ripe.

The court found that Sinclair's substantive due process claims failed to state a cause of action, under its holding in Armendariz v. Penman, 75 F.3d 1311 (9th Cir. 1996) (en banc), see p. 103, that "[s]ubstantive due process analysis has no place in contexts already addressed by explicit textual provisions of constitutional protection."

Finally, the court held that Sinclair's state takings claims, while within the district court's jurisdiction because of diversity of citizenship, nevertheless were not ripe under California's equivalent of *Williamson County*.]

To recapitulate, we have decided that the district court correctly dismissed all of Sinclair's grounds for relief except the company's federal facial taking claim to the extent it asserts the Plan does not substantially advance a legitimate state interest. We now determine that the district court should refrain from presently addressing this claim under the reasoning of Railroad Comm'n v. Pullman Co., 312 U.S. 496 (1941).

This Court has in multiple land use cases approved a district court's decision to employ *Pullman* abstention. See, e.g., Sederquist v. City of Tiburon, 590 F.2d 278 (9th Cir. 1978). *Pullman* abstention is appropriate where:

(1)   The complaint touches a sensitive area of social policy upon which the federal courts ought not to enter unless no alternative to its adjudication is open.

(2)   Such constitutional adjudication plainly can be avoided if a definitive ruling on the state issue would terminate the controversy.

(3)   The possibly determinative issue of state law is doubtful.

---

1. Sinclair also filed, in September of 1993, a suit in state court seeking to nullify the Plan as inconsistent with California's Environmental Quality Act and the California Coastal Act. In its state court prayer for relief, Sinclair does not request damages or "just compensation." Instead, the company merely desires a peremptory writ invalidating the Plan. Furthermore, the parties informed this Court by letter that the state litigation has been voluntarily stayed until October 24, 1996.

Pearl Inv. Co. v. City & County of San Francisco, 774 F.2d 1460, 1463 (9th Cir. 1985) (quotations omitted). This case meets each of these requirements.

First, this Court has consistently held that "land use planning is a sensitive area of social policy that meets the first requirement for *Pullman* abstention." Kollsman v. City of Los Angeles, 737 F.2d 830, 833 (9th Cir. 1984). Furthermore, the second prerequisite is met because, "Given [an] opportunity, a state court might avoid the federal constitutional issues by deciding that an illegal taking under the California Constitution has occurred." *Sederquist*, 590 F.2d at 282. Certainly, if the California courts provide Sinclair just compensation for a taking under state law, it might be unnecessary to address the oil company's federal taking claim. Of course, adjudication of the state claims is not absolutely certain to obviate the need for considering the federal constitutional issues. Sinclair might, for example, object to the amount of compensation received. For *Pullman* purposes, though, it is sufficient if the state law issues might "narrow" the federal constitutional questions. *Pearl*, 774 F.2d at 1464. Resolution of the California law issues would most certainly narrow a federal court's constitutional inquiry in this case.

Finally, we find that the determinative issues of state law are uncertain. To be sure, the conventional inverse condemnation claim advanced by Sinclair does not appear to be particularly extraordinary or unique, and Sinclair does not raise a novel claim of statutory interpretation. Still, the Plan itself has not yet been challenged in the state courts. In a somewhat similar case, this Court observed that a local government's enactment of land use regulations "is by nature a question turning on the peculiar facts of each case in light of the many [applicable] local and state-wide land use laws. . . . " Santa Fe Land Improvement Co. v. City of Chula Vista, 596 F.2d 838, 841 (9th Cir. 1979) (quotation omitted). The court continued, "We do not claim the ability to predict whether a state court would decide that the [local government] here abused its discretion." Id. (quotation omitted). But see *Pearl*, 774 F.2d at 1465 (criticizing this Court's liberal approach toward *Pullman*'s third requirement in land use cases, but nonetheless following that reasoning as controlling precedent).

We recognize that we cannot appropriately direct the district court to refrain from exercising its jurisdiction over this litigation solely because the suit involves an inverse condemnation action. Nevertheless, it is apparent to us that this case meets the criteria for *Pullman* abstention. See *Kollsman*, 737 F.2d at 836 n.18 ("[A]bstention often will be appropriate when state land use regulations are challenged on state and federal grounds."). We therefore instruct the district court to abstain from considering Sinclair's only cause of action that is currently ripe for adjudication.[6] . . .

Note on Abstention

1. *The* Pullman *factors.* What makes land use a "sensitive area of social policy upon which the federal courts ought not to enter"? Is it the local nature of land use regulation? Would the Ninth Circuit take a similar stance on cases raising freedom of speech challenges to a local school's policies, given that education is another quintessentially "local" matter? Cf. Pearl Inv. Co. v. City & County of San Francisco, 774 F.2d 1460 (9th Cir. 1985) (recognizing that the Ninth Circuit had "at times declined to abstain in cases dealing with arguably more sensitive social issues" than land use, but nevertheless finding that land use

---

6. Because this federal taking claim is an action "at law" for just compensation, the district court should retain jurisdiction and enter a stay deferring consideration of this ground for relief until Sinclair's state law claims are definitively resolved in the California courts. See Quackenbush v. Allstate Ins. Co., 517 U.S. 706, 731 (1996) (concluding that federal courts can dismiss based on abstention only where the relief sought is equitable or otherwise discretionary).

met the first *Pullman* requirement). Or is the Ninth Circuit really drawing a distinction between "important" constitutional protections and "mere" property rights?

What exactly is uncertain about how the state court will interpret the state's takings clause? Would the resolution of any takings claim (or any constitutional challenge, for that matter) be uncertain under the court's reasoning? Is the Ninth Circuit adopting a per se rule of abstention for federal takings claims? Land use cases in general?

2. *Claim and issue preclusion after abstention.* Footnote 6 of *Sinclair* states that the federal court should not dismiss the action, but should instead "stay" the action until the state court resolves the state court issues. Under *San Remo*, what is likely to happen when the case returns to federal court? In *San Remo*, the issue on which the federal court abstained was the propriety of the City's designation of the hotel as "residential," and the Supreme Court made clear that had the plaintiff limited its claims in state court to that state law issue, claim preclusion would not have barred the federal facial takings claim when the case returned to federal court. In *Sinclair*, on the other hand, the state law issue upon which the federal court based its decision to abstain on the federal takings claim was a state *takings* claim. Under *San Remo*, is there anything the plaintiff can do to avoid claim preclusion in that circumstance? Even if the plaintiff could avoid *claim* preclusion, might the claimant nevertheless still suffer the effects of *issue* preclusion? See Instructional Systems, Inc. v. Computer Curriculum Corp., 35 F.3d 813 (3d Cir. 1994).

Note that the federal takings claim in *Sinclair* would now be precluded by the Court's decision in *Lingle*, supra.

3. Burford *abstention.* A second kind of abstention sometimes invoked in land use cases stems from Burford v. Sun Oil Co., 319 U.S. 315 (1943). *Burford* involved a challenge to an order by the Texas Railroad Commission granting a permit to drill for oil in a certain oil field. Because of the need for uniform regulation of competing claims to common pools of oil and gas, Texas had given the Commission exclusive regulatory authority, and had vested authority to review the Commission's orders in a single set of state courts. The Supreme Court held that the federal courts sitting in equity could decline to exercise jurisdiction out of "proper regard for the rightful independence of state governments in carrying out their domestic policy." Id. at 317–18. The Court stressed that the "thorny" nature of oil and gas regulation, the demonstrated need for uniform regulation, and the detrimental impact of conflicts that already had developed as a result of federal review of Commission orders all justified abstention. For elaborations on *Burford*, see Quackenbush v. Allstate Insurance Co., 517 U.S. 706 (1996); New Orleans Public Serv., Inc. v. Council of New Orleans, 491 U.S. 350 (1989); Colorado River Water Conservation District v. United States, 424 U.S. 800 (1976).

Is land use similar to the oil and gas regulatory scheme in *Burford*? In Pomponio v. Fauquier County Board of Supervisors, 21 F.3d 1319 (4th Cir. 1994), the landowner alleged that zoning officials had misconstrued the applicable ordinances in denying his application for subdivision approval and thereby had violated his rights to procedural due process, substantive due process, and equal protection. The Fourth Circuit held: "In cases in which plaintiffs' federal claims stem solely from construction of state or local land use or zoning law, not involving the constitutional validity of the same and absent exceptional circumstances not present here, the district courts should abstain under the *Burford* doctrine to avoid interference with the State's or locality's land use policy." Id. at 1327. The court reasoned that

> cases involving questions of state and local land use and zoning law are a classic example of situations in which "the 'exercise of federal review of the question in a case and in similar cases would be disruptive of state efforts to establish a coherent policy with respect to a matter of

substantial public concern.'" *New Orleans Public Service*, 491 U.S. at 361. We can conceive of few matters of public concern more substantial than zoning and land use laws. . . . It is also clear that in most of these cases requiring *Burford* abstention, the federal claim cannot be untangled from the state or local zoning or land use law. Therefore, we believe that in the usual case federal courts should not leave their indelible print on local and state land use and zoning law by entertaining these cases and, in effect, sitting as a zoning board of appeals. . . .

Id.

Other circuits are more skeptical of *Burford* abstention in land use cases. See, e.g., Dittmer v. County of Suffolk, 146 F.3d 113 (2d Cir. 1998) (reversing district court's decision to abstain in case involving due process and equal protection challenges to the Long Island Pine Barrens Protection Act); International College of Surgeons v. City of Chicago, 153 F.3d 356 (7th Cir. 1998) (*Burford* abstention inappropriate in case challenging Landmarks Commission's refusal to grant permits to allow owner to demolish certain buildings because there was no specialized court to review Commission's orders like that in *Burford*).

4. Younger *abstention*. In Younger v. Harris, 401 U.S. 37 (1971), the Supreme Court held that a federal court should not enjoin an ongoing state criminal proceeding absent extraordinary circumstances. The *Younger* doctrine has been extended to require the federal courts to abstain from hearing a federal claim against a state (or its agents) if the state has an action pending in the state courts that seeks to exercise coercive power over the federal plaintiff. See, e.g., Huffman v. Pursue, 420 U.S. 592 (1974) (federal court should have abstained from deciding constitutional challenge to state statute allowing theater to be declared a nuisance if it showed pornographic films, where state nuisance action had been decided against the federal plaintiff but the federal plaintiff had not exhausted the state appellate remedies). The lower federal courts occasionally invoke *Younger* in land use cases. See, e.g., Lui v. Commission on Adult Entertainment Establishments, 369 F.3d 319 (3d Cir. 2004) (where owner of Fantasia Restaurant & Lounge was defending a criminal prosecution in state court for allegedly failing to obtain an adult entertainment establishment zoning certification, federal court would abstain under *Younger* from hearing his federal constitutional challenges to the zoning ordinance and the prosecution).

5. *The* Rooker-Feldman *doctrine*. In addition to the abstention doctrines, some lower federal courts have applied the *Rooker-Feldman* doctrine when the state court rejects a state takings claim. The *Rooker-Feldman* doctrine, articulated in Rooker v. Fidelity Trust Co., 263 U.S. 413 (1923), and District of Columbia Ct. of App. v. Feldman, 460 U.S. 462 (1983), holds that a party cannot appeal an adverse state court decision to a federal district court, but must instead petition for a writ of certiorari from the U.S. Supreme Court. Some lower federal courts interpreted that to mean that the federal courts could not address federal takings claims where the state courts have rejected a state takings claim based on the same facts. See, e.g., Johnson v. City of Shorewood, Minn., 360 F.3d 810 (8th Cir. 2004). In 2005 the Supreme Court sharply limited the *Rooker-Feldman* doctrine, confining it to "cases brought by state-court losers complaining of injuries caused by state-court judgments rendered before the district court proceedings commenced and inviting district court review and rejection of those judgments." Exxon Mobil Corp. v. Saudi Basic Industries Corp. 125 S. Ct. 1517, 1521-22 (2005). The concurrence in *San Remo*, supra, indicated that the *Rooker-Feldman* doctrine might very well continue to apply in takings cases, however. See 125 S. Ct. at 2509 (Rehnquist, C.J., concurring).

6. *The prevalence of abstention*. The Supreme Court repeatedly has warned that *Pullman* and *Burford* are "extraordinary and narrow exception[s] to the duty of the District Court to adjudicate a controversy properly before it." *Colorado River*, 424 U.S. at 813 (internal quotations omitted). Nevertheless, a review of federal cases involving land use

regulation decided between 1972 and 1988 found that the federal courts abstained in about half the cases, with the Fourth, Sixth, Eighth, and Ninth Circuits being the most likely to abstain. Brian W. Blaesser, Closing the Federal Courthouse Door on Property Owners: The Ripeness and Abstention Doctrines in Section 1983 Land Use Cases, 2 Hofstra Prop. L.J. 73 (1988). Without knowing how the courts treated comparable cases (such as §1983 cases not involving land use regulation), one cannot draw a firm conclusion that abstention is exercised too frequently, but the numbers certainly raise that suspicion.

7. *Malpractice?* In light of the hostility shown to land use cases in decisions like *Coniston* (see pp. 99–104), the ripeness requirements of *Williamson County* (see pp. 234–45), the issue preclusive effects of those ripeness requirements as illustrated by *San Remo* (see pp. 245–51), the abstention doctrines reviewed here, and the *Rooker-Feldman* doctrine, when is it appropriate for a lawyer to file a land use challenge in federal court?

4.   Remedies

Introductory Note on the "Compensation" Question

Until 1987, if a court concluded that a zoning restriction deprived a landowner of federal constitutional rights, the court would remedy that violation by proclaiming the restriction to be "void" or "invalid." See, e.g., Board of Supervisors v. Rowe, 216 S.E.2d 199 (Va. 1975). Invalidation was the normal remedy regardless of the constitutional clause at issue, or whether the judicial intervention was motivated to prevent inefficiency, guard against unfairness, or protect civil liberties. Even if the court held that the application of a government regulation constituted a "taking" of private property, it would provide as a remedy not the "just compensation" that the constitutional text implies should be made available, but rather some form of injunctive relief against enforcement of the regulation. See, e.g., AMG Associates v. Township of Springfield, 319 A.2d 705 (N.J. 1974).

That practice came under intense pressure from landowners and their attorneys, who argued that the remedy for takings effected by regulation should be just compensation rather than invalidation. See, e.g., Michael M. Berger & Gideon Kanner, Thoughts on *The White River Junction Manifesto*: A Reply to the "Gang of Five's" Views on Just Compensation for Regulatory Taking of Property, 19 Loy. L.A. L. Rev. 685 (1986). Several state courts firmly rejected the argument. See Agins v. City of Tiburon, 598 P.2d 25 (Cal. 1979), aff'd on other grounds, 447 U.S. 255 (1980); Charles v. Diamond, 360 N.E.2d 1295 (N.Y. 1977); Superior Uptown, Inc. v. City of Cleveland, 313 N.E.2d 820 (Ohio 1974).

The U.S. Supreme Court, however, signaled some sympathy for the landowners' argument. In San Diego Gas & Electric Co. v. City of San Diego, 450 U.S. 621 (1981), the majority refused to reach the issue, but Justice Brennan (joined by Justices Stewart, Marshall, and Powell) argued in dissent that just compensation would have to be paid on a finding that a regulation effected a taking:

> In my view, once a court establishes that there was a regulatory "taking," the Constitution demands that the government entity pay just compensation for the period commencing on the date the regulation first effected the "taking," and ending on the date the government entity chooses to rescind or . . . amend the regulation. This interpretation, I believe, is supported by the express words and purpose of the Just Compensation Clause, as well as by cases of this Court construing it.
>
> The language of the Fifth Amendment prohibits the "tak[ing]" of private property for "public use" without payment of "just compensation." As soon as private property has been

taken, whether through formal condemnation proceedings, occupancy, physical invasion, or regulation, the landowner has already suffered a constitutional violation, and "'the self-executing character of the constitutional provision with respect to compensation,'" United States v. Clarke, 445 U.S. 253, 257 (1980), quoting 6 J. Sackman, Nichols' Law of Eminent Domain §25.41 (rev. 3d ed. 1980), is triggered. This Court has consistently recognized that the just compensation requirement in the Fifth Amendment is not precatory: once there is a "taking," compensation must be awarded. . . . Invalidation unaccompanied by payment of damages would hardly compensate the landowner for any economic loss suffered during the time his property was taken.[22]

Moreover, mere invalidation would fall far short of fulfilling the fundamental purpose of the Just Compensation Clause. That guarantee was designed to bar the government from forcing some individuals to bear burdens which, in all fairness, should be borne by the public as a whole. Armstrong v. United States, 364 U.S. 40, 49 (1960). . . . Because police power regulations must be substantially related to the advancement of the public health, safety, morals, or general welfare, see Village of Euclid v. Ambler Realty Co., 272 U.S. 365, 395 (1926), it is axiomatic that the public receives a benefit while the offending regulation is in effect. If the regulation denies the private property owner the use and enjoyment of his land and is found to effect a "taking," it is only fair that the public bear the cost of benefits received during the interim period between application of the regulation and the government entity's rescission of it. The payment of just compensation serves to place the landowner in the same position monetarily as he would have occupied if his property had not been taken.

The fact that a regulatory "taking" may be temporary, by virtue of the government's power to rescind or amend the regulation, does not make it any less of a constitutional "taking." Nothing in the Just Compensation Clause suggests that "takings" must be permanent and irrevocable. Nor does the temporary reversible quality of a regulatory "taking" render compensation for the time of the "taking" any less obligatory. This Court more than once has recognized that temporary reversible "takings" should be analyzed according to the same constitutional framework applied to permanent irreversible "takings." . . . In Agins v. City of Tiburon, 598 P.2d [25,] 29 [(Cal. 1979), aff'd on other grounds, 447 U.S. 255 (1980)], the California Supreme Court was "persuaded by various policy considerations to the view that inverse condemnation is an inappropriate and undesirable remedy in cases in which unconstitutional regulation is alleged." In particular, the court cited "the need for preserving a degree of freedom in land-use planning function, and the inhibiting financial force which inheres in the inverse condemnation remedy," in reaching its conclusion. Id. at 31. But the applicability of express constitutional guarantees is not a matter to be determined on the basis of policy judgments made by the

---

22. The instant litigation is a good case in point. The trial court, on April 9, 1976, found that the city's actions effected a "taking" of appellant's property on June 19, 1973. If true, then appellant has been deprived of all beneficial use of its property in violation of the Just Compensation Clause for the past seven years.

Invalidation hardly prevents enactment of subsequent unconstitutional regulations by the government entity. At the 1974 annual conference of the National Institute of Municipal Law Officers in California, a California City Attorney gave fellow City Attorneys the following advice:

IF ALL ELSE FAILS, MERELY AMEND THE REGULATION AND START OVER AGAIN.
If legal preventive maintenance does not work, and you still receive a claim attacking the land use regulation, or if you try the case and lose, don't worry about it. All is not lost. One of the extra "goodies" contained in the recent [California] Supreme Court case of Selby Realty Co. v. City of San Buenaventura, 514 P.2d 111 (Cal. 1973), appears to allow the City to change the regulation in question, even after trial and judgment, make it more reasonable, more restrictive, or whatever, and everybody starts over again. . . .
See how easy it is to be a City Attorney. Sometimes you can lose the battle and still win the war. Good luck.

Longtin, Avoiding and Defending Constitutional Attacks on Land-Use Regulations (Including Inverse Condemnation), in 38B NIMLO Municipal Law Review 192–93 (1975) (emphasis in original). . . .

legislative, executive, or judicial branches.[26] Nor can the vindication of those rights depend on the expense in doing so. . . .

450 U.S. at 653–61. After four false starts caused by ripeness problems, the Court finally reached the issue.

First English Evangelical Lutheran Church of Glendale v. County of Los Angeles
482 U.S. 304 (1987)

Chief Justice REHNQUIST delivered the opinion of the Court.

In this case the California Court of Appeal held that a landowner who claims that his property has been "taken" by a land-use regulation may not recover damages for the time before it is finally determined that the regulation constitutes a "taking" of his property. We disagree, and conclude that in these circumstances the Fifth and Fourteenth Amendments to the United States Constitution would require compensation for that period.

In 1957, appellant First English Evangelical Lutheran Church purchased a 21-acre parcel of land in a canyon along the banks of the Middle Fork of Mill Creek in the Angeles National Forest. . . . Twelve of the acres owned by the church are flat land, and contained a dining hall, two bunkhouses, a caretaker's lodge, an outdoor chapel, and a footbridge across the creek. The church operated on the site a campground, known as "Lutherglen," as a retreat center and a recreational area for handicapped children.

In July 1977, a forest fire denuded the hills upstream from Lutherglen, destroying approximately 3,860 acres of the watershed area and creating a serious flood hazard. Such flooding occurred on February 9 and 10, 1978, when a storm dropped 11 inches of rain in the watershed. The runoff from the storm overflowed the banks of the Mill Creek, flooding Lutherglen and destroying its buildings.

In response to the flooding of the canyon, appellee County of Los Angeles adopted Interim Ordinance No. 11,855 in January 1979. The ordinance provided that "[a] person shall not construct, reconstruct, place or enlarge any building or structure, any portion of which is, or will be, located within the outer boundary lines of the interim flood protection area located in Mill Creek Canyon. . . . " The ordinance was effective immediately because the county determined that it was "required for the immediate preservation of the public health and safety. . . . " The interim flood protection area described by the ordinance included the flat areas on either side of Mill Creek on which Lutherglen had stood.

The church filed a complaint in the Superior Court of California a little more than a month after the ordinance was adopted. . . . The first [claim] alleged . . . that "Ordinance No. 11,855 denies [appellant] all use of Lutherglen." . . . Appellant sought damages . . . for loss of use of Lutherglen. The defendants moved to strike the portions

---

26. Even if I were to concede a role for policy considerations, I am not so sure that they would militate against requiring payment of just compensation. Indeed, land-use planning commentators have suggested that the threat of financial liability for unconstitutional police power regulations would help to produce a more rational basis of decisionmaking that weighs the costs of restrictions against their benefits. Dunham, From Rural Enclosure to Re-Enclosure of Urban Land, 35 N.Y.U. L. Rev. 1238, 1253–54 (1960). Such liability might also encourage municipalities to err on the constitutional side of police power regulations, and to develop internal rules and operating procedures to minimize overzealous regulatory attempts. Cf. Owen v. City of Independence, 445 U.S. 622, 651–52 (1980). After all, if a policeman must know the Constitution, then why not a planner? In any event, one may wonder as an empirical matter whether the threat of just compensation will greatly impede the efforts of planners. Cf. id. at 656.

of the complaint alleging that the county's ordinance denied all use of Lutherglen, on the view that the California Supreme Court's decision in Agins v. Tiburon, 24 Cal. 3d 266 (1979), aff'd on other grounds, 447 U.S. 255 (1980), rendered the allegation "entirely immaterial and irrelevant[, with] no bearing upon any conceivable cause of action herein."

In Agins v. Tiburon, supra, the California Supreme Court decided that a landowner may not maintain an inverse condemnation suit in the courts of that State based upon a "regulatory" taking. . . . Under this decision, then, compensation is not required until the challenged regulation or ordinance has been held excessive in an action for declaratory relief or a writ of mandamus and the government has nevertheless decided to continue the regulation in effect. Based on this decision, the trial court in the present case granted the motion to strike the allegation that the church had been denied all use of Lutherglen. It explained that "a careful re-reading of the *Agins* case persuades the Court that when an ordinance, even a non-zoning ordinance, deprives a person of the total use of his lands, his challenge to the ordinance is by way of declaratory relief or possibly mandamus." Because the appellant alleged a regulatory taking and sought only damages, the allegation that the ordinance denied all use of Lutherglen was deemed irrelevant.[2]

On appeal, the California Court of Appeal read the complaint as one seeking "damages for the uncompensated taking of all use of Lutherglen by County Ordinance No. 11,855. . . ." It too relied on the California Supreme Court's decision in *Agins* in rejecting the cause of action. . . . It accordingly affirmed the trial court's decision to strike the allegations concerning appellee's ordinance. The California Supreme Court denied review.

This appeal followed. . . . Appellant asks us to hold that the California Supreme Court erred in Agins v. Tiburon in determining that the Fifth Amendment, as made applicable to the States through the Fourteenth Amendment, does not require compensation as a remedy for "temporary" regulatory takings — those regulatory takings which are ultimately invalidated by the courts. Four times this decade, we have considered similar claims and have found ourselves for one reason or another unable to consider the merits of the *Agins* rule. See MacDonald, Sommer & Frates v. Yolo County, 477 U.S. 340 (1986); Williamson County Regional Planning Comm'n v. Hamilton Bank, 473 U.S. 172 (1985); San Diego Gas & Elec. Co. [v. San Diego, 450 U.S. 621 (1981)]; Agins v. Tiburon, supra. For the reasons explained below, however, we find the constitutional claim properly presented in this case, and hold that on these facts the California courts have decided the compensation question inconsistently with the requirements of the Fifth Amendment.

I . . .

. . . The California Court of Appeal has thus held that, regardless of the correctness of appellant's claim that the challenged ordinance denies it "all use of Lutherglen," appellant may not recover damages until the ordinance is finally declared unconstitutional, and then only for any period after that declaration for which the county seeks to enforce it. The constitutional question pretermitted in our earlier cases is therefore squarely presented here.

We reject appellee's suggestion that, regardless of the state court's treatment of the question, we must independently evaluate the adequacy of the complaint and resolve the takings claim on the merits before we can reach the remedial question. However "cryptic" — to use appellee's description — the allegations with respect to the taking were,

---

2. . . . At the close of plaintiff's evidence, the trial court granted a nonsuit on behalf of defendants, dismissing the entire complaint.

the California courts deemed them sufficient to present the issue. We accordingly have no occasion to decide whether the ordinance at issue actually denied appellant all use of its property or whether the county might avoid the conclusion that a compensable taking had occurred by establishing that the denial of all use was insulated as a part of the State's authority to enact safety regulations. See, e.g., . . . Mugler v. Kansas, 123 U.S. 623 (1887). These questions, of course, remain open for decision on the remand we direct today. . . .

II

Consideration of the compensation question must begin with direct reference to the language of the Fifth Amendment, which provides in relevant part that "private property [shall not] be taken for public use, without just compensation." . . .

It has also been established doctrine at least since Justice Holmes's opinion for the Court in Pennsylvania Coal Co. v. Mahon, 260 U.S. 393 (1922), that "[t]he general rule at least is, that while property may be regulated to a certain extent, if regulation goes too far it will be recognized as a taking." Id. at 415. While the typical taking occurs when the government acts to condemn property in the exercise of its power of eminent domain, the entire doctrine of inverse condemnation is predicated on the proposition that a taking may occur without such formal proceedings. In Pumpelly v. Green Bay Co., 13 Wall. 166, 177–78 (1872), construing a provision in the Wisconsin Constitution identical to the Just Compensation Clause, this Court said:

> It would be a very curious and unsatisfactory result, if . . . it shall be held that if the government refrains from the absolute conversion of real property to the uses of the public it can destroy its value entirely, can inflict irreparable and permanent injury to any extent, can, in effect, subject it to total destruction without making any compensation, because, in the narrowest sense of that word, it is not taken for the public use.

Later cases have unhesitatingly applied this principle. See, e.g., Kaiser Aetna v. United States, 444 U.S. 164 (1979).

While the California Supreme Court may not have actually disavowed this general rule in *Agins*, we believe that it has truncated the rule by disallowing damages that occurred prior to the ultimate invalidation of the challenged regulation. The California Supreme Court justified its conclusion at length in the *Agins* opinion, concluding that:

> In combination, the need for preserving a degree of freedom in the land-use planning function, and the inhibiting financial force which inheres in the inverse condemnation remedy, persuade us that on balance mandamus or declaratory relief rather than inverse condemnation is the appropriate relief under the circumstances.

24 Cal. 3d, at 276–77.

We, of course, are not unmindful of these considerations, but they must be evaluated in the light of the command of the Just Compensation Clause of the Fifth Amendment. The Court has recognized in more than one case that the government may elect to abandon its intrusion or discontinue regulations. See, e.g., Kirby Forest Industries, Inc. v. United States, [467 U.S. 1 (1946)]. Similarly, a governmental body may acquiesce in a judicial declaration that one of its ordinances has effected an unconstitutional taking of property; the landowner has no right under the Just Compensation Clause to insist that a "temporary" taking be deemed a permanent taking. But we have not resolved whether abandonment by the government requires payment of compensation for the period of time during which regulations deny a landowner all use of his land.

In considering this question, we find substantial guidance in cases where the government has only temporarily exercised its right to use private property. In United States v. Dow, [357 U.S. 17, 26 (1958)], though rejecting a claim that the Government may not abandon condemnation proceedings, the Court observed that abandonment "results in an alteration in the property interest taken — from [one of] full ownership to one of temporary use and occupation. . . . In such cases compensation would be measured by the principles normally governing the taking of a right to use property temporarily. See Kimball Laundry Co. v. United States, 338 U.S. 1 [(1949)]; United States v. Petty Motor Co., 327 U.S. 372 [(1946)]; United States v. General Motors Corp., 323 U.S. 373 [(1945)]." Each of the cases cited by the *Dow* Court involved appropriation of private property by the United States for use during World War II. Though the takings were in fact "temporary," see Petty Motor Co., supra, 327 U.S. at 375, there was no question that compensation would be required for the Government's interference with the use of the property. . . .

These cases reflect the fact that "temporary" takings which, as here, deny a landowner all use of his property, are not different in kind from permanent takings, for which the Constitution clearly requires compensation. Cf. *San Diego Gas & Electric Co.*, 450 U.S. at 657 (BRENNAN, J., dissenting) ("Nothing in the Just Compensation Clause suggests that 'takings' must be permanent and irrevocable"). . . . In the present case the interim ordinance was adopted by the County of Los Angeles in January 1979, and became effective immediately. Appellant filed suit within a month after the effective date of the ordinance and yet when the California Supreme Court denied a hearing in the case on October 17, 1985, the merits of appellant's claim had yet to be determined. The United States has been required to pay compensation for leasehold interests of shorter duration than this. The value of a leasehold interest in property for a period of years may be substantial, and the burden on the property owner in extinguishing such an interest for a period of years may be great indeed. See, e.g., United States v. General Motors, supra. Where this burden results from governmental action that amounted to a taking, the Just Compensation Clause of the Fifth Amendment requires that the government pay the landowner for the value of the use of the land during this period. . . . Invalidation of the ordinance or its successor ordinance after this period of time, though converting the taking into a "temporary" one, is not a sufficient remedy to meet the demands of the Just Compensation Clause. . . .

Nothing we say today is intended to abrogate the principle that the decision to exercise the power of eminent domain is a legislative function " 'for Congress and Congress alone to determine.' " Hawaii Housing Authority v. Midkiff, 467 U.S. 229, 240 (1984), quoting Berman v. Parker, 348 U.S. 26 (1954). Once a court determines that a taking has occurred, the government retains the whole range of options already available — amendment of the regulation, withdrawal of the invalidated regulation, or exercise of eminent domain. Thus we do not, as the Solicitor General suggests, "permit a court, at the behest of a private person, to require the . . . Government to exercise the power of eminent domain. . . . " Brief for United States as Amicus Curiae 22. We merely hold that where the government's activities have already worked a taking of all use of property, no subsequent action by the government can relieve it of the duty to provide compensation for the period during which the taking was effective.

We also point out that the allegation of the complaint which we treat as true for purposes of our decision was that the ordinance in question denied appellant all use of its property. We limit our holding to the facts presented, and of course do not deal with the quite different questions that would arise in the case of normal delays in obtaining building permits, changes in zoning ordinances, variances, and the like which are not before us. We realize that even our present holding will undoubtedly lessen to some extent the freedom and flexibility of land-use planners and governing bodies of municipal corporations when enacting land-use regulations. But such consequences necessarily flow from any decision upholding a claim of constitutional right; many of the provisions of the Constitution are designed to limit the flexibility and freedom of governmental authorities, and the Just Compensation Clause of the Fifth Amendment is one of them. As Justice Holmes aptly noted more than 50 years ago, "a strong public desire to improve the public condition is not enough to warrant achieving the desire by a shorter cut than the constitutional way of paying for the change." Pennsylvania Coal Co. v. Mahon, 260 U.S. at 416.

Here we must assume that the Los Angeles County ordinance has denied appellant all use of its property for a considerable period of years, and we hold that invalidation of the ordinance without payment of fair value for the use of the property during this period of time would be a constitutionally insufficient remedy. The judgment of the California Court of Appeal is therefore reversed, and the case is remanded for further proceedings not inconsistent with this opinion.

Justice STEVENS, with whom Justice BLACKMUN and Justice O'CONNOR join as to Parts I and III, dissenting. . . .

II . . .

A temporary interference with an owner's use of his property may constitute a taking for which the Constitution requires that compensation be paid. At least with respect to physical takings, the Court has so held. Thus, if the government appropriates a leasehold interest and uses it for a public purpose, the return of the premises at the expiration of the lease would obviously not erase the fact of the government's temporary occupation. . . . These examples are consistent with the rule that even minimal physical occupations constitute takings which give rise to a duty to compensate. See Loretto v. Teleprompter Manhattan CATV Corp., 458 U.S. 419 (1982).

But our cases also make it clear that regulatory takings and physical takings are very different in this, as well as other, respects. While virtually all physical invasions are deemed takings, see, e.g., *Loretto*, supra, . . . a regulatory program that adversely affects property values does not constitute a taking unless it destroys a major portion of the property's value. See [Keystone Bituminous Coal Ass'n v. DeBenedictis, 480 U.S. 470, 493–502 (1987)]; . . . Agins v. Tiburon, 447 U.S. 255, 260 (1980). This diminution of value inquiry is unique to regulatory takings. Unlike physical invasions, which are relatively rare and easily identifiable without making any economic analysis, regulatory programs constantly affect property values in countless ways, and only the most extreme regulations can constitute takings. Some dividing line must be established between everyday regulatory inconveniences and those so severe that they constitute takings. The diminution of value inquiry has long been used in identifying that line. . . . It is this basic distinction between regulatory and physical takings that the Court ignores today.

Regulations are three dimensional; they have depth, width, and length. As for depth, regulations define the extent to which the owner may not use the property in question. With respect to width, regulations define the amount of property encompassed by the restrictions. Finally, and for purposes of this case, essentially, regulations set forth the duration of the restrictions. It is obvious that no one of these elements can be analyzed alone to evaluate the impact of a regulation, and hence to determine whether a taking has occurred. For example, in *Keystone Bituminous* we declined to focus in on any discrete segment of the coal in the petitioners' mines, but rather looked to the effect that the restriction had on their entire mining project. See 480 U.S. at 493–502. . . . Similarly, in *Penn Central*, the Court concluded that it was error to focus on the nature of the uses which were prohibited without also examining the many profitable uses to which the property could still be put. Both of these factors are essential to a meaningful analysis of the economic effect that regulations have on the value of property and on an owner's reasonable investment-based expectations with respect to the property.

Just as it would be senseless to ignore these first two factors in assessing the economic effect of a regulation, one cannot conduct the inquiry without considering the duration of the restriction. For example, . . . I am confident that even the dissenters in *Keystone Bituminous* would not have concluded that the restriction on bituminous coal mining would have constituted a taking had it simply required the mining companies to delay their operations until an appropriate safety inspection could be made.

On the other hand, I am willing to assume that some cases may arise in which a property owner can show that prospective invalidation of the regulation cannot cure the taking — that the temporary operation of a regulation has caused such a significant diminution in the property's value that compensation must be afforded for the taking that has already occurred. For this ever to happen, the restriction on the use of the property would not only have to be a substantial one, but it would also have to remain in effect for a significant percentage of the property's useful life. In such a case an application of our test for regulatory takings would obviously require an inquiry into the duration of the restriction, as well as its scope and severity.

The cases that the Court relies upon for the proposition that there is no distinction between temporary and permanent takings, are inapposite, for they all deal with physical takings — where the diminution of value test is inapplicable. None of those cases is controversial; the state certainly may not occupy an individual's home for a month and then escape compensation by leaving and declaring the occupation "temporary." But what does that have to do with the proper inquiry for regulatory takings? Why should there be a constitutional distinction between a permanent restriction that only reduces the economic value of the property by a fraction — perhaps one-third — and a restriction that merely postpones the development of a property for a fraction of its useful life — presumably far less than a third? In the former instance, no taking has occurred; in the latter case, the Court now proclaims that compensation for a taking must be provided. The Court makes no effort to explain these irreconcilable results. Instead, without any attempt to fit its proclamation into our regulatory takings cases, the Court boldly announces that once a property owner makes out a claim that a regulation would constitute a taking if allowed to stand, then he or she is entitled to damages for the period of time between its enactment and its invalidation. . . .

The Court's reasoning also suffers from severe internal inconsistency. Although it purports to put to one side "normal delays in obtaining building permits, changes in zoning ordinances, variances and the like," the Court does not explain why there is a constitutional distinction between a total denial of all use of property during such "normal delays" and an equally total denial for the same length of time in order to determine whether a regulation has "gone too far" to be sustained unless the government is prepared to condemn the property. Precisely the same interference with a real estate developer's plans may be occasioned by protracted proceedings which terminate with a zoning board's decision that the public interest would be served by modification of its regulation and equally protracted litigation which ends with a judicial determination that the existing zoning restraint has "gone too far," and that the board must therefore grant the developer a variance. The Court's analysis takes no cognizance of these realities. Instead, it appears to erect an artificial distinction between "normal delays" and the delays involved in obtaining a court declaration that the regulation constitutes a taking. . . .

IV . . .

The policy implications of today's decision are obvious and, I fear, far reaching. Cautious local officials and land-use planners may avoid taking any action that might later be challenged and thus give rise to a damages action. Much important regulation will never be enacted,[17] even perhaps in the health and safety area. Were this result mandated by the Constitution, these serious implications would have to be ignored. But the loose cannon the Court fires today is not only unattached to the Constitution, but it also takes aim at a long line of precedents in the regulatory takings area. It would be the better part of valor simply to decide the case at hand instead of igniting the kind of litigation explosion that this decision will undoubtedly touch off.

I respectfully dissent.

Note on *First English*

1. *The taking that never was.* On remand, the California court found that the church had not suffered a taking. First, relying heavily on *Mugler*, see p. 136, the court held that the ordinance was justified by a "public safety" exception to the compensation requirement. Second, the regulation did not destroy all the value of the land. It allowed the church to occupy any buildings that had not been destroyed by the flood, and to use the property for any purpose other than the reconstruction of demolished buildings or the erection of new ones. First English Evangelical Lutheran Church of Glendale v. County of Los Angeles, 258 Cal. Rptr. 893 (Ct. App. 1989), cert. denied, 493 U.S. 1056 (1990).

2. *Reconciling* Tahoe-Sierra *and* First English. The lower courts and commentators have identified several types of temporary takings:

> First, a temporary taking occurs when what would otherwise be a permanent taking is temporally cut short. Temporary takings of this category may result when a court invalidates a regulation that had previously effected a taking; when the government elects to discontinue regulations after a taking has occurred; or when the government denies a permit and at some later point reconsiders the earlier denial and grants a permit (or revokes the permitting requirement). The essential element of this type of temporary taking is a finite start and end to the taking.
>
> Alternatively, a temporary taking may occur by reason of extraordinary delay in the governmental decision making process. In such a case, a property owner may be entitled to compensation for property loss incurred while the government was in the process of deciding whether to allow the contested activity. This type of temporary takings claim may be asserted notwithstanding the failure of the government to deny a permit or affirmatively prohibit a certain use of the property.

Seiber v. United States, 364 F.3d 1356, 1364 (Fed. Cir. 2003) (internal quotations and citations omitted). The first type of temporary taking has been referred to as a "retrospectively

---

17. It is no answer to say that "[a]fter all, if a policeman must know the Constitution, then why not a planner?" San Diego Gas & Electric Co. v. San Diego, 450 U.S. 621, 661, n.26 (1981) (BRENNAN, J., dissenting). To begin with, the Court has repeatedly recognized that it itself cannot establish any objective rules to assess when a regulation becomes a taking. See Hodel v. Irving, 481 U.S. 704, 713–14 (1987); Andrus v. Allard, 444 U.S. 51, 65 [(1979)]; *Penn Central*, 438 U.S. at 123–24. How then can it demand that land planners do any better? However confusing some of our criminal procedure cases may be, I do not believe they have been as open-ended and standardless as our regulatory takings cases are. As one commentator concluded: "The chaotic state of taking law makes it especially likely that availability of the damages remedy will induce land-use planning officials to stay well back of the invisible line that they dare not cross." Johnson, Compensation for Invalid Land-Use Regulations, 15 Ga. L. Rev. 559, 594 (1981). . . .

temporary" taking. See, e.g., Keshbro, Inc. v. City of Miami, 801 So. 2d 864, 873 (Fla. 2001). The second type has been referred to as a "permitting delay" taking. Both those takings have been distinguished from "prospectively temporary takings" such as moratoria.

Tahoe-Sierra, excerpted at p. 185, concerned a moratorium. Because Justice Steven's majority opinion in *Tahoe-Sierra* reads suspiciously like his dissent in *First English*, some have questioned whether *Tahoe-Sierra*'s holding that the *Penn Central* analysis rather than a *Lucas* per se test determines whether a "prospectively temporary" regulation constitutes a taking may be extended as well to a retrospectively temporary regulation or to a claim that a permitting delay has effected a temporary taking. *Tahoe-Sierra*'s admonition that courts must look at the "parcel as a whole" — the value of the property over the entire life span of the interest — would make it difficult for courts to find a taking in most cases of a permitting delay or a retrospectively temporary regulation. See, e.g., Appolo Fuels, Inc. v. United States, 381 F.3d 1338, 1352 (Fed. Cir. 2004) (applying *Penn Central* to a claim that a permitting delay constituted a temporary taking and finding no taking).

Is there a qualitative difference between a prospectively temporary regulation and a regulation whose effect is rendered temporary by judicial action? See Frank Michelman, Takings, 1987, 88 Colum. L. Rev. 1600, 1616–21 (arguing that *First English* would not reach a regulation that was expressly designed to be temporary because it would not have the same "lawless" character as a regulation that destroys the value of property and was meant to be permanent or of indefinite duration).

For attempts to square the holding in *Tahoe-Sierra* with that of *First English*, see, e.g., Michael M. Berger, *Tahoe Sierra*: Much Ado About — What?, 25 U. Haw. L. Rev. 295 (2003); Steven J. Eagle, Planning Moratoria and Regulatory Takings: The Supreme Court's Fairness Mandate Benefits Landowners, 31 Fla. St. U. L. Rev. 429, 444 45 (2004); Thomas E. Roberts, An Analysis of *Tahoe-Sierra* and Its Help and Hindrance in Understanding the Concept of a Temporary Regulatory Taking, 25 U. Haw. L. Rev. 417 (2003).

3. *"Partial" temporary takings?* Even if *Tahoe-Sierra*'s "parcel as a whole" rule is limited to prospectively temporary takings, might the government nevertheless escape a finding that a retrospectively temporary regulation or a permitting delay effected a taking if the property retains some value or use during the period of the alleged taking? The majority opinion in *First English* was careful to point out that the property owner was alleged to have been denied *all* use of the property for the period in which the dispute was working its way through the courts. Some courts have therefore applied *Penn Central* to determine whether a retrospectively temporary regulation effected a taking if some use was left in the property during the dispute. See, e.g., Cooley v. United States, 324 F.3d 1297 (Fed. Cir. 2003) (where the denial of a permit reduced the value of the property by 98.8 percent rather than 100 percent, appropriate test to determine whether there was a temporary taking during the period between the original denial of the permit and the subsequent grant of the permit is the *Penn Central* test).

4. *"Takings" effected by unauthorized regulations.* Should a property owner be entitled to compensation under *First English* if the regulation alleged to have effected the temporary taking was ultra vires — beyond the enacting government's authority? See, e.g., Board Machine, Inc. v. United States, 49 Fed. Cl. 325, 334 (2001) (dismissing takings challenge to Food and Drug Administration tobacco regulations held to have been prohibited by Congress and holding that a government regulation that was ultra vires cannot be a taking, at least as long as the "lack of authority . . . [is] predicated on a showing of clear preclusion of the jurisdiction or failure to follow procedures necessary to secure authority"). But see Osprey Pacific Corp. v. United States, 41 Fed. Cl. 150, 157 (1998) (it is no defense to a takings claim for the government to claim that it lacked authority to take the property); Steinbergh v. City of Cambridge, 604 N.E.2d 1269 (Mass. 1992) (considering a regulatory

takings challenge to a city rent control ordinance despite a prior ruling that the ordinance was ultra vires). See also Matthew D. Zinn, Note, Ultra Vires Takings, 97 Mich. L. Rev. 245 (1998) (unauthorized governmental actions should trigger due process or tort remedies, but should not trigger the requirement of just compensation).

5. *"Takings" effected by invalid regulations.* What if the regulation is within the government's authority, but invalid because, for example, it doesn't rationally further a legitimate governmental purpose and therefore violates substantive due process? Consider Professor John E. Fee's argument:

> The Takings Clause presupposes that government may take private property only for "public use," or in other words, to serve a legitimate governmental interest. If a government action fails to serve a legitimate public purpose, the proper remedy is invalidation, not compensation. Unlike many other constitutional doctrines that must balance the public interest, the compensation requirement of the Fifth Amendment is not designed to prohibit invalid governmental action; it is more accurately concerned with who should bear the cost of legitimate governmental action.

John E. Fee, The Takings Clause as a Comparative Right, 75 S. Cal. L. Rev. 1003, 1035–36 (2003). See also John D. Echeverria, Takings and Errors, 51 Ala. L. Rev. 1047 (2000); Alan I. Saltman, The Government's Liability for Actions of its Agents That Are Not Specifically Authorized: The Continuing Influence of *Merrill* and *Richmond*, 32 Pub. Contract L.J. 775, 775 (2003); Jed Michael Silversmith, Takings, Torts and Turmoil: Reviewing the Authority Requirement of the Just Compensation Clause, 19 UCLA J. Envtl. L. & Pol'y 359 (2001–2002).

6. *Normal delays.* What exactly are the "normal delays" the Court refers to? Does the Court mean only that the "normal" time spent successfully securing permits, standing alone, could never constitute a taking? If an ordinance effects a taking on its face (because, for example, its mere enactment destroys 100 percent of the value of the property), is the time a landowner spends litigating the facial validity of the ordinance a "normal delay"? What if the ordinance is not unconstitutional on its face, but as applied — is the time the landowner spends seeking a variance (or otherwise establishing a "final determination" under *Williamson County*), then seeking compensation a "normal delay"? See *Tahoe-Sierra*, excerpted at p. 185 (noting that it "would create a perverse system of incentives were we to hold that landowners must wait for a takings claim to ripen so that planners can make well-reasoned decisions while, at the same time, holding that those planners must compensate landowners for the delay"). See also Gregory M. Stein, Regulatory Takings and Ripeness in the Federal Courts, 48 Vand. L. Rev. 1, 60–61 (1995) (arguing that a taking becomes effective only on denial of the landowner's last required variance application, because time spent pursuing variances is a "normal" delay); William David Taylor III, Comment, He Who Calls the Tune Must Pay the Piper: Compensation for Regulatory Takings of Property After *First English Evangelical Lutheran Church v. County of Los Angeles*, 53 Mo. L. Rev. 69 (1988).

Is a delay resulting from government error "normal"? In Landgate, Inc. v. California Coastal Commission, 953 P.2d 1188 (Cal. 1998), the Commission refused to grant a permit to allow Landgate to build a large house in a coastal zone, asserting that a lotline adjustment made earlier by county authorities had been illegal because the Commission, rather than the county, had jurisdiction over such adjustments. The landowner challenged the Commission's assertion of jurisdiction, and prevailed in the state courts. The landowner then argued that the Commission's erroneous assertion of jurisdiction had denied all use of the land for the two-year period of the dispute, and sought compensation. The California

Supreme Court, over spirited dissents, held that no taking had occurred: "an error by a governmental agency in the development approval process does not necessarily amount to a taking even if the error in some way diminishes the value of the subject property." Instead, such errors, "are part of a reasonable regulatory process" and therefore come within the "normal delays" *First English* said did not trigger the compensation requirement. The court noted, however, that "[i]t would be . . . a different question if . . . the Commission's position . . . was so unreasonable from a legal standpoint as to lead to the conclusion that it was taken for no purpose other than to delay the development project before it." Id. at 1199.

When might a permitting delay rise to the level of a taking? See, e.g., Bass Enterprises Production Co. v. United States, 381 F.3d 1360 (Fed. Cir. 2004) (45-month delay not unreasonable); Wyatt v. United States, 271 F.3d 1090 (Fed. Cir. 2001) (7-year delay not unreasonable).

7. *The risk of a chilling effect.* If one of the goals of the Takings Clause is to promote better decisionmaking by forcing decisionmakers to consider the costs of regulations, see pp. 145–51, one would want *First English* to have some deterrent effect on government officials. But at some point, the deterrent effect might inhibit desirable regulations for which compensation would not be due because fear of liability might make decisionmakers err too much on the side of caution. What factors might determine whether a compensation requirement has sufficient deterrent effect? Too much deterrent effect? What if the average tenure of a government official is less than the average time between the imposition of the regulation and the compensation award? What if the regulating agency's budget is not held directly liable for compensation awards? What if the regulating agency is insured? For discussions of the likelihood of chilling, see, e.g., Vicki Been & Joel C. Beauvais, The Global Fifth Amendment? Nafta's Investment Protections and the Misguided Quest for an International "Regulatory Takings" Doctrine, 78 N.Y.U. L. Rev. 30, 90–96, 132–35 (2003); Theodore M. Cooperstein, Sensing Leave for One's Takings: Interim Damages and Land Use Regulation, 7 Stan. Envtl. L.J. 49 (1987–1988). For empirical evidence that at least some of the Supreme Court's takings decisions have caused local governments to reform land use practices, but also suggesting that land use regulators view those decisions positively, see Ann E. Carlson & Daniel Pollak, Takings on the Ground: How the Supreme Court's Takings Jurisprudence Affects Local Land Use Decisions, 35 U.C. Davis L. Rev. 103, 141–43 (2001).

Wheeler v. City of Pleasant Grove (*Wheeler III*)
833 F.2d 267 (11th Cir. 1987)

TJOFLAT, Circuit Judge:

This appeal marks the third time this case has been before us. The present appeal is limited to the issue of whether the district court applied the correct measure of damages.

In 1978, Cliff Development Corp. (Cliff Development) contracted with Joseph and Clarice Wheeler (the Wheelers) to buy a parcel of land in Pleasant Grove, Alabama, for the sum of $160,000. Cliff Development planned to build a 120-unit apartment complex on the site. Pursuant to the contract, Cliff Development made a downpayment of $1,000 to the Wheelers. After finding that the proposed land use complied with applicable zoning ordinances, the Pleasant Grove Planning Commission issued a building permit. Cliff Development paid the city $6,165 for the permit and commenced work in preparation for construction.

Strong community opposition to the proposed development soon arose. Two mass public meetings were held, followed by a referendum in which a majority of the citizens of Pleasant Grove expressed opposition to construction of the apartments. In the wake of the referendum, the City Council in July 1978 passed Ordinance No. 216, which outlawed construction of apartment complexes in Pleasant Grove. . . .

[Cliff Development and the Wheelers sued the City of Pleasant Grove and city officials, alleging violations of the Fifth and Fourteenth Amendments. The district court found that the ordinance was arbitrary and capricious and was "confiscatory in nature." The court permanently enjoined the city from enforcing the ordinance, but refused to grant plaintiffs monetary relief, finding that defendants were shielded by a qualified immunity. On appeal, the Fifth Circuit affirmed the finding that the application of the ordinance to the plaintiffs was unconstitutional, but held that a good faith defense was not available to municipalities in §1983 actions, and remanded for a determination of damages. Wheeler v. City of Pleasant Grove, 664 F.2d 99 (5th Cir. 1981) (*Wheeler I*).

On remand, the district court again refused to award damages, finding that the ordinance had not proximately caused any compensable injury to plaintiffs. The Eleventh Circuit reversed, holding that the district court's original finding of liability had "at least by necessary implication[] decided that the unconstitutional conduct upon which that finding was predicated had damaged plaintiffs." Wheeler v. City of Pleasant Grove, 746 F.2d 1437, 1441 (11th Cir. 1984) (*Wheeler II*). The Eleventh Circuit again remanded for a determination of damages.

On the second remand, the district court found that the value of the Wheelers' land had gone up since the original enactment of the ordinance, and awarded them nominal damages of $1. Cliff Development was awarded damages equal to the increased costs of construction and temporary financing. Pleasant Grove appealed, and plaintiffs cross-appealed.]

At the time *Wheeler I* and *Wheeler II* were decided, the Supreme Court had not yet ruled on the issue of whether a landowner could recover damages for a temporary regulatory taking — that is, a taking that is ultimately invalidated by a court. . . . The Supreme Court, however, has since affirmed our position in *Wheeler I* and *Wheeler II* by holding that the Constitution requires compensation for a temporary regulatory taking. See First English Evangelical Lutheran Church of Glendale v. County of Los Angeles, 482 U.S. 304 (1987). In this appeal, we confront the difficult issue of how to calculate the compensation due when such a taking has occurred. . . .

It is well settled that in determining the compensation due for a taking, "the question is, What has the owner lost?" Boston Chamber of Commerce v. City of Boston, 217 U.S. 189, 195 (1910). The owner's loss is measured by the extent to which governmental action has deprived him of an interest in property. See United States v. General Motors Corp., 323 U.S. 373, 378 (1945). The value of that interest, in turn, is determined by isolating it as a component of the overall fair market value of the affected property. See Kimball Laundry Co. v. United States, 338 U.S. 1, 7 (1949).

In the case of a temporary regulatory taking, the landowner's loss takes the form of an injury to the property's potential for producing income or an expected profit. See generally 7 P. Rohan, Zoning and Land Use Controls §52A.03(2) (1986 & Supp. 1987). The landowner's compensable interest, therefore, is the return on the portion of fair market value that is lost as a result of the regulatory restriction. Accordingly, the landowner should be awarded the market rate return computed over the period of the temporary taking on the difference between the property's fair market value without the regulatory restriction and its fair market value with the restriction. See Nemmers v. City of Dubuque, 764 F.2d 502, 505 (8th Cir. 1985). Under this approach, the landowner recovers what he lost. To award any affected party additional compensation for lost profits or increased costs of development would be to award double recovery: the relevant fair market values by definition reflect a market estimation of future profits and development costs with respect to the particular property at issue. . . .

Assuming that the Wheelers had a total interest in the property, the district court plainly applied an incorrect measure of damages. The court concluded that the Wheelers had suffered no compensable loss because the property's value after the lifting of the regulatory restriction was greater than its value before the restriction came into effect. The district court's analysis fails to account for their loss as measured by the formula we set forth above, that is, the loss in income-producing potential suffered over the sixteen months that Ordinance No. 216 was in effect.[5] On remand, the district court must determine the amount of that loss. . . .

Note on Determining Compensation for Temporary Regulatory Takings

1. *Wheeler IV*. On remand, the trial court once again found that the Wheelers were entitled to no compensation, reasoning that because the value of the property had increased despite the ordinance, there had been no diminution in the fair market value of the land. The Court of Appeals again reversed. Wheeler v. City of Pleasant Grove (*Wheeler IV*), 896 F.2d 1347 (11th Cir. 1990). Leaving nothing to the district court's discretion, the *Wheeler IV* court calculated the compensation due according to the following formula:

Owner's Equity in Market Value Without Restriction (25% of $2.3 million)
− Owner's Equity in Market Value with Restriction (25% of $200,000)
_____

= Owner's Lost Value from Restriction (25% of $2.1 million = $525,000)
× Market Rate of Return (9.77% per year, or 0.814166% per month)
× Length of Restriction (14 months)
_____

= Lost Return ($59,841.23)

2. *Apples to apples?* Was the *Wheeler IV* court comparing apples and oranges in subtracting the value of the undeveloped lot from the value of the hypothetical apartment complex? Would a buyer pay $2.3 million for the lot as is, even if assured that the challenged ordinance would not be applied? See Corn v. City of Lauderdale Lakes, 771 F. Supp. 1557, 1570–71 (S.D. Fla. 1991) (criticizing *Wheeler IV* because " 'The property's fair market value without the regulatory restriction' was defined . . . as the value of 'the complex which appellants had the right to build,' as if it were completed, and without regard to the cost of construction."), aff'd in part, rev'd in part, 997 F.2d 1369 (11th Cir. 1993). See also Cooley v. United States, 46 Fed. Cl. 538, 551 (Fed. Cl. 2000) (reducing as-developed value of property by estimated cost of sales, promotion and advertising, direct development

_____

5. In the analogous context of temporary physical takings, the Supreme Court has rejected the measure of compensation used by the district court — that is, the difference between the market value of the owner's interest in the property before its taking and the market value on the date of its return. See Kimball Laundry Co. v. United States, 338 U.S. 1, 7 (1949). Because the market value of the property often would not have decreased, the Court observed, this approach would frequently result in no compensation for the owner, despite the identifiable loss he suffered over the period of the temporary taking. The same concern moves us to reject that approach in the context of a temporary regulatory taking.

costs, indirect costs such as real estate taxes and liability insurance and holding costs such as interest and financing), aff'd in part, vacated in part, 324 F.3d 1297 (Fed. Cir. 2003).

Given that the $2.3 million reflects the value once built, should that figure have been discounted to its present value? See Robert Meltz et al., The Takings Issue 483–510 (1999); Richard J. Roddewig & Christopher J. Duerksen, Measuring Damages in Takings Cases: The Next Frontier, *in* 1993 Zoning & Planning Law Handbook 273, 285 (Kenneth H. Young ed.).

The market values of the property without and with the restriction sometimes are referred to as the "before" and "after" values. But if the lost value is based on market valuations of the land at two different times, should the compensation award be adjusted to reflect increases (decreases) in the market value of the property due to appreciation (depreciation) in land prices generally? Otherwise, if the land has appreciated sufficiently for the "after" value to equal the "before" (unregulated) value, the owner would be entitled to no compensation. But why should the government, rather than the property owner, enjoy the benefit of such increases?

In Nemmers v. City of Dubuque, 764 F.2d 502 (8th Cir. 1985), which *Wheeler III* cited, the court used a market rate of return method similar to *Wheeler IV*'s, but allowed the landowner to recover on the full difference between the value of the property with and without the regulation, not just on the owner's equity interest in that value. Which approach is preferable?

3. *Market value as affected by permissible but unenacted regulations?* The *Wheeler IV* court's valuation of the complex assumes that the complex will be built if Ordinance No. 216 is not applied. But the complex might never be built for any number of reasons other than the offending ordinance, including the possibility that some regulation short of a total ban on apartments might be enacted and survive constitutional scrutiny. Should the court have based compensation on the value of the land regulated to the maximum extent that would not constitute a taking? On the value of the land so regulated, discounted by the probability that such a regulation would be enacted? See Christopher Serkin, The Meaning of Value: Assessing Just Compensation for Regulatory Takings, 99 Nw. U. L. Rev. 677 (2005). How easy is it for courts (or government regulators) to ascertain exactly what regulation would stop just short of a taking? See Joseph LaRusso, "Paying for the Change": *First English Evangelical Lutheran Church of Glendale v. County of Los Angeles* and the Calculation of Interim Damages for Regulatory Takings, 17 B.C. Envtl. Aff. L. Rev. 551 (1990) (basing compensation on the value of the land regulated to the permissible extent is too speculative). If the court had based its calculations on the market value of the unrestricted undeveloped lot (rather than the hypothetical complex), would the market value account for the possibility of other regulations?

4. *The "probability" method.* In Herrington v. County of Sonoma, 790 F. Supp. 909 (N.D. Cal. 1992), the County argued that because plaintiff's application for a subdivision had been denied at an early stage, compensation was not due because such a preliminary decision "would have no effect on the price a willing buyer would pay for the property." Id. at 914. The court responded by awarding compensation based on probability: The court found that plaintiff had one chance in three of winning approval for the subdivision, valued at $1.3 million, considering the indeterminate outcome of a pending environmental impact report, as well as still unresolved issues regarding the availability of adequate water and sewage facilities. The land without the approval was valued at $490,000. Multiplying the chance of approval by the value of the land with the approval (0.33 × $1,300,000) and the chance of nonapproval by the value of the land without the approval (0.67 × $490,000), it added the products and arrived at a probability-derived "value" of the property without the taking, which it then used to calculate plaintiff's damages. Id. at 915–22.

Herrington's formula is:

$$[(aX + bY) - Y] Rt + ac = Damages$$

where: a is the probability that the property will be developed as proposed
       b is the probability that the proposed plans will not be approved
       X is the value of the land developed as proposed
       Y is the value of the land if the proposal is not approved
       R is the rate of interest
       t is the duration of the temporary taking
       c is the increased cost of development due to the delay

Herrington has been praised for understanding the risks inherent in real estate development and lauded as the model for future calculations of compensation. Roddewig & Duerksen, supra, at 283–85 (acknowledging, however, that "there is an infinite set of development probabilities, not just two"). How should a court determine the probability that the land will ever be developed as proposed? Note the various kinds of risk involved: regulation by other agencies or governments; changes in tax laws or other laws or regulations affecting the feasibility of the project; changes in the real estate market or the broader economy; increases in financing or other costs; discovery of hazardous materials or unforeseen site conditions on the property; and changes in financial feasibility due to design errors or delays, supplier or subcontractor defaults or problems in performance, construction defects or delays, and cost estimating errors. Jesse B. Grove, III, Risk Allocation from the Contractor's Perspective: Philosophies of Risk Allocation, 167 PLI/Rcal 41, 125 (2001).

Are the risks of development, and the probability that those risks will occur, built into the market's valuation of the undeveloped land? What advantage is there to using the court's assessment of that probability, rather than the market's? Are there other theoretical or practical problems with *Herrington*?

5. *Rental value.* When property is physically taken on a temporary basis, the courts have required the government to pay the owner the fair market rental value of the property. Kimball Laundry Co. v. United States, 338 U.S. 1 (1949). Some courts have applied the same rule to temporary regulatory takings. See, e.g., Yuba Natural Resources, Inc. v. United States, 904 F.2d 1577 (Fed. Cir. 1990) (fair market rental value of mineral rights is appropriate measure of compensation where United States prohibited dredging necessary to mine gold). See also Garrett Power, Comment, Multiple Permits, Temporary Takings, and Just Compensation, 23 Urb. Law. 449, 456 (1991) ("the 'rental that probably could have been obtained' . . . seems appropriate in inverse condemnation cases", citing *Kimball Laundry*).

Landowners who suffer a temporary taking nevertheless often have some rights to the land during the period of the taking (for agricultural use or for lower density use than the landowner wished). Should the "rent" due for the temporary taking be based only on those rights actually taken? If, for example, a developer seeks to build a 32-unit subdivision (and it turns out, should have been allowed to build all those units), but is limited to a 20-unit subdivision, should the government be charged the rent due on the difference between 32 and 20 units or on the rent for all 32 units? Given that neither 32 units nor 20 units actually have been built, is the imaginary rental of the right to build 32 rather than 20 units simply too speculative to be appropriate? What if we drop the assumption that the landowner would have the right to build 32 units but for the unconstitutional regulation, and introduce uncertainty about what limitations could have been applied without triggering the right to compensation?

Why would a court ever prefer the rental value method to *Wheeler IV*'s methodology? Would market rents ever be easier to determine than market rates of return on similar investments? For further discussion of the rental value approach, see Donald G. Hagman, Temporary or Interim Damages Awards in Land Use Control Cases, *in* 1982 Zoning & Planning Law Handbook 201, 219 (Fredric A. Strom ed.); Jay Harris Rabin, Note, It's Not Just Compensation, It's a Theory of Valuation as Well: Valuing "Just Compensation" for Temporary Regulatory Takings, 14 Colum. J. Envtl. L. 247, 259–60 (1989); J. Margaret Tretbar, Comment, Calculating Compensation for Temporary Regulatory Takings, 42 U. Kan. L. Rev. 201, 219 (1993).

6. *Option value.* The New Jersey courts have treated temporary takings as equivalent to holding an option on the land, and award compensation for the value of an option to buy the land for the period of the taking. Sheerr v. Township of Evesham, 445 A.2d 46 (N.J. Super. Ct. Law Div. 1982). As long as the option market is sufficiently robust that the valuation of the option will be reasonably accurate, the option value method may be a good approximation of what the government received by delaying development, but is it a good measure of what the owner lost?

7. *Cost of delay.* A few courts have based compensation on the difference between the return on the cash flows the developer would have enjoyed with and without the regulation, reasoning that in the case of temporary takings that delay development, the real issue is "what would [the developer] have charged to delay development" for the period of the taking? In SDDS, Inc. v. South Dakota, 650 N.W.2d 1 (S.D. 2002), for example, the property owner's plans to develop a 1,200-acre parcel into a municipal solid waste storage facility were stymied for several years when voters passed an initiative requiring legislative approval of the facility and when the legislature didn't take the hint, later passed a referendum overturning the legislature's approval. After the referendum was invalidated, a jury awarded $10.1 million in compensation for the temporary taking, after being instructed to calculate damages on the basis of the fair market rental value of the property for the period of the taking, the option value, or lost return on investment on the portion of fair market value lost over the period of the taking (essentially the *Wheeler* method). The South Dakota Supreme Court reversed, finding that the best measure of compensation was instead the difference between the interest the developer would have received on the cash flow that the developer "was reasonably certain to have received without the delay" and the interest the developer would have received on the cash flow of the project given the delay caused by the temporary taking. Id. at 19. See also Bass Enterprises Production Co. v. United States, 48 Fed. Cl. 621 (2001), rev'd on other grounds upon reconsideration, 54 Fed. Cl. 400 (2002).

Is *SDDS* correct that the lost return on cash flow is a more accurate measure of damages than the lost return on diminution in market value used by *Wheeler*? What if the delay caused by the temporary taking causes the developer to lose a competitive advantage or causes the development to come to market under less favorable conditions? See *SDDS*, supra, at 17 n.13 (those are the normal risks of development and therefore not compensable).

8. *The ad hoc approach.* In Corrigan v. City of Scottsdale, 720 P.2d 513 (Ariz. 1986), the Supreme Court of Arizona anticipated *First English* by holding that the Arizona Constitution required compensation for temporary regulatory takings. The court then surveyed the various measures of damages, and concluded:

> Each of these damage measures works well in some "taking" cases and inequitably, if at all, in others. This is because no one rule adequately fits each of the many factual situations that may be present in a particular case. Such problems as: whether the losses are speculative; when the taking actually occurred; whether it caused any damage; and whether it was an acquisitory

or nonacquisitory setting combine to make each measure of damages, in some cases, a "guessing game" between too little compensation on the one hand and providing a windfall on the other.

Recognizing this problem, we feel the best approach is not to require the application of any particular damage rule to all temporary taking cases. Instead we hold that the proper measure of damages in a particular case is an issue to be decided on the facts of each individual case. It is our intent to compensate a person for the losses he has actually suffered by virtue of the taking. . . .

Id. at 515. The *Corrigan* court's flexible approach to measuring damages has been adopted by other courts. See, e.g., Lucas v. South Carolina Coastal Council, 424 S.E.2d 484, 486 (S.C. 1992). See also Joseph P. Mikitish, Note, Measuring Damages for Temporary Regulatory Takings: Against Undue Formalism, 32 Ariz. L. Rev. 985, 993 (1990). The costs and benefits of an ad hoc approach should now be familiar. See p. 179.

9. *Actual losses.* *Corrigan* holds that only actual losses, such as increased construction costs, should be compensated in a temporary regulatory taking case. See 720 P.2d at 518–19. Several other courts have taken the same tack. See, e.g., Carter v. City of Porterville, 22 Cal. Rptr. 2d 76, 87 (Ct. App. 1993); Poirier v. Grand Blanc Township, 481 N.W.2d 762, 766 (Mich. Ct. App. 1992). The actual losses rule has been criticized by many commentators, however, who argue that actual losses are very difficult to prove or measure. See, e.g., Corwin W. Johnson, Compensation for Invalid Land-Use Regulations, 15 Ga. L. Rev. 559, 595 (1981); Douglas W. Kmiec, Regulatory Takings: The Supreme Court Runs Out of Gas in San Diego, 57 Ind. L.J. 45, 65 (1982). Others argue that compensating only for actual loss violates the Fifth Amendment, which requires that government pay for the property interest taken, not the loss to the owner. See Rabin, supra, at 254–55. For support of actual losses as a measure of compensation, see, e.g., Cynthia J. Barnes, Comment, Just Compensation or Just Damages: The Measure of Damages for Temporary Regulatory Takings in *Wheeler v. City of Pleasant Grove*, 74 Iowa L. Rev. 1243, 1256 (1989).

10. *Value added by the regulation.* *Wheeler* compared the value of the property with and without the challenged regulation. What if the value of the property without the regulation derives in part from the fact that other land suitable for the use is regulated and therefore not available for the use? Or what if the value of the property without the restriction derives in part from the fact that the challenged restriction increases property values in the neighborhood generally by preventing disamenities or providing amenities? Should the compensation award be adjusted to reflect such "windfalls" or "givings" to the property owner? See also pp. 150–51 for a discussion of how the analysis of whether a regulation effects a taking should account for "givings."

11. *Measuring the time of the taking.* An indispensable variable in the calculation of compensation is the length of the taking. Most courts have held compensation to be due from the date of the challenged regulatory action. See, e.g., France Stone Co., Inc. v. Charter Township of Monroe, 802 F. Supp. 90, 107 (E.D. Mich. 1992) (taking began on date of denial of rezoning). Should the clock start to run instead on the date that satisfies *Williamson County*'s finality requirement? Cf. Hernandez v. City of Lafayette, 643 F.2d 1188, 1200 (5th Cir. 1981) (taking "does not occur until the municipality's governing body is given a realistic opportunity and reasonable time within which to review its zoning legislation vis-à-vis the particular property and to correct the inequity"). See David A. Arrensen, Compensation for Regulatory Takings: Finality of Local Decisionmaking and the Measure of Compensation, 63 Ind. L.J. 649, 661 (1988).

Land use regulations often are proposed and debated months or even years before they are enacted. The probability that a proposed regulation will be enacted accordingly may affect property values even before the effective date of the regulation. Should the date of the regulatory taking account for such preregulation effects, just as some courts award compensation for "precondemnation blight" in condemnation cases? See Serkin, supra, at 697–98; for a description of how courts address the precondemnation blight issue, see Paul R. Scott, The Double-Edged Sword of Project Influence, SJ051 ALI-ABA 157 (2004).

12. *Mitigation of damages.* Does the landowner have any obligation to mitigate damages and thereby reduce the compensation due for a temporary taking? Should the compensation due in *Wheeler*, for example, have been reduced if Cliff Development could have built a "rent-payer" (a temporary structure used to pay the rent until the final development can be built), or used the lot for other temporary purposes? Cf. Miller & Son Paving, Inc., v. Plumstead Township, 717 A.2d 483 (Pa. 1998) (no compensation for invalid prohibition on quarrying because owner could have used the land for residential purposes while challenging the prohibition). What if the landowner could have reduced the time spent securing the compensation (during which the compensation bill was increasing) by paying more careful attention to ripeness, abstention, and finality rules?

13. *Who decides: judge or jury?* In cases against state and local governments, the courts generally agree that questions about the amount of compensation due for a taking may be submitted to a jury (determining the appropriate standard by which damages are to be measured is, of course, the judge's responsibility). Whether questions of liability are matters for the jury is less clear. In City of Monterey v. Del Monte Dunes at Monterey, Ltd., 526 U.S. 687 (1999), the Supreme Court held, by a five-to-four vote, that a landowner seeking compensation through a §1983 action in federal court was entitled to a jury trial both on issues of liability and on the amount of compensation. The procedural posture of *Del Monte Dunes* was unusual, however, in that the landowner was able to bring the case in federal court without first seeking compensation in state court, despite *Williamson County*, because the case arose prior to *First English* and California state courts did not then provide a remedy for temporary takings. The Court limited its holding to that factual situation, which is unlikely to arise again because states now provide inverse condemnation remedies pursuant to *First English*. The majority emphasized that it did not "address the jury's role in an ordinary inverse condemnation suit." Id. at 721. The Court also declined to "attempt a precise demarcation of the respective provinces of judge and jury." Id.

In takings suits against the federal government, the Seventh Amendment does not apply, so landowners are not entitled to a jury trial on either liability or the amount of damages.

14. *The methods of valuing compensation and the underlying theories of takings.* Christopher Serkin has argued that the courts' decisions about how to calculate the compensation due for regulatory takings reflect implicit substantive disagreements both about property rights and about the justifications for a compensation requirement for regulatory takings (canvassed at pp. 145–58). Careful attention to the relationship between valuation methods and underlying theories of takings is necessary, he maintains, to ensure that valuation methods advance the substantive goals of the Takings Clause. Serkin, supra, at 680–81.

F. Legislative Initiatives to Increase Landowners' and Developers' Rights

Dissatisfied with the confusing and, to some people's minds, hostile takings rules established by the courts, property rights advocates have turned to the legislative and executive branches for help. For various perspectives on the property rights movement, see, e.g., Land Rights: The 1990s Property Rights Rebellion (Bruce Yandle ed., 1995); Let the People Judge: A Reader on the Wise Use Movement (John Echeverria & Raymond B. Eby eds., 1995); David Helvarg, Legal Assault on the Environment: The Property Rights Movement, The Nation, Jan. 30, 1995, at 126.

President Reagan responded in 1988 with Executive Order 12,630, 53 Fed. Reg. 8859 (1988), reprinted as amended in 5 U.S.C. §601 (2005), which instructed all executive agencies to conduct a "takings impact assessment" (TIA) for any action that might effect a taking. The TIA required the agency to evaluate the cost the proposed regulation would impose on affected property owners, and to determine whether there were any alternative actions that could accomplish the same goal without imposing those costs. Although the Executive Order remains in force, it has been largely ignored. General Accounting Office, Regulatory Takings: Implementation of Executive Order of Government Actions Affecting Private Property Use (2003) ("agency officials said that they fully consider the potential takings implications of their regulatory actions, but provided us with limited documentary evidence to support this claim"); Kirk Emerson & Charles R. Wise, Statutory Approaches to Regulatory Takings: State Property Rights Legislation Issues and Implications for Public Administration, 57 Pub. Admin. Rev. 411 (1997). The courts have refused to recognize a private right of action to enforce the order. McKinley v. United States, 828 F. Supp. 888 (D.N.M. 1993) (order was intended only to "improve the internal management of the executive branch and is not intended to create any right or benefit, substantive or procedural, enforceable at law"). For discussions of the Order, see, e.g., Jerry Jackson & Lyle D. Albaugh, A Critique of the Takings Executive Order in the Context of Environmental Regulation, 18 Envtl. L. Rep. 10463 (1988).

Congress jumped into the fray in 1990, considering a floor amendment to a farm bill that would have codified the Executive Order. Since then, various bills have been introduced. See, e.g., the Private Property Owners' Bill of Rights, S. 953, 105th Cong. (1997); the Landowners Equal Treatment Act, H.R. 1142, 106th Cong. (1999); and the Life, Liberty, and Property Protection Act, H.R. 5709, 107th Cong. (2002). A proposal to modify the ripeness requirements discussed at pp. 234–51, The Private Property Rights Implementation Act of 1997, H.R. 1534, 105th Cong. (1997), passed the House of Representatives in the fall of 1997, but a motion in the Senate to "proceed to the consideration" of the bill failed to muster the required three-fifths vote. For reviews of the federal bills, see Robert Meltz, Property Rights Legislation: Analysis and Update, CA 24 ALI-ABA 17 (1996); Frank I. Michelman, A Skeptical View of "Property Rights" Legislation, 6 Fordham Envtl. L.J. 409 (1995); Carol M. Rose, A Dozen Propositions on Private Property, Public Rights and the New Takings Legislation, 53 Wash. & Lee L. Rev. 265 (1996); Lois J. Schiffer, Taking Stock of the Takings Debate, 38 Santa Clara L. Rev. 153 (1997).

In the state legislatures and in the initiative process, property rights advocates have been much more successful. Hundreds of takings bills have been considered by the state legislatures in the last decade, and about half the states have adopted some form of takings legislation. Steven J. Eagle, Protecting Property from Unjust Deprivations Beyond Takings: Substantive Due Process, Equal Protection, and State Legislation, in Taking Sides on Takings Issues: Public and Private Perspectives 507, 535 (Thomas E. Roberts ed., 2002); Emerson & Wise, supra.

The state takings statutes impose either "assessment" requirements or "compensation" requirements, or both. Assessment requirements primarily are modeled on the takings impact statement introduced by President Reagan's Executive Order. They require state agencies — and, in a few instances, local governments — to assess whether a proposed action or regulation would effect a taking. Most define "taking" by reference to existing case law. For a summary of the definitions, see David A. Thomas, The Illusory Restraints and

Empty Promises of New Property Protection Laws, 28 Urb. Law. 223, 244–46 (1996). Some assessment requirements incorporate the review into existing processes. See, e.g., Mont. Code Ann. §75-1-201 (2005) (requiring that environmental impact statements regarding proposed rules analyze regulatory impacts on private property and examine alternatives). Others assign the review to the state attorney general. See, e.g., Del. Code Ann. tit. 29, §605 (2004). Most, however, require each agency to conduct a review of its own proposed rules or action, sometimes according to guidelines established by the state attorney general. See, e.g., Kan. Stat. Ann. §77-704 (2005).

Impact assessment bills differ primarily in the breadth of their requirements: Some include only a few agencies, see, e.g., W. Va. Code §§22-1A-1 to 22-1A-6 (2005) (applicable only to state division of environmental protection), while others reach a broader group of state agencies, see, e.g., Wyo. Stat. Ann. §§9-5-301 to 9-5-305 (2005), and a few reach both state agencies and local governments. See, e.g., Idaho Code §67-8003 (2005). Some assessment requirements apply only to proposed rules and regulations. See, e.g., N.D. Cent. Code §28-32-09 (2005). Others extend the requirement to proposed legislation. See, e.g., Kan. Stat. Ann. §77-703 (2005). A few extend the requirement to permitting decisions. See, e.g., Mich. Comp. Laws Ann. §24.422 (2005). For reviews of the assessment requirements, see Mark W. Cordes, Leapfrogging the Constitution: The Rise of State Takings Legislation, 24 Ecology L.Q. 187 (1997); David Coursen, Property Rights Legislation: A Survey of Federal and State Compensation Measures, 26 Envtl. L. Rep. 10239 (1996); Marilyn F. Drees, Do State Legislatures Have a Role in Resolving the "Just Compensation" Dilemma? Some Lessons from Public Choice and Positive Political Theory, 66 Fordham L. Rev. 787 (1997); Carl P. Marcellino, Note, The Evolution of State Takings Legislation and the Proposals Considered During the 1997–1998 Legislative Session, 2 N.Y.U. J. Legis. & Pub. Pol'y 143, 152–54 (1998–1999).

As noted, some state takings statutes impose compensation requirements.

Bert J. Harris, Jr., Private Property Rights Protection Act
Florida Stat. Ann. §70.001 (West 2005) (effective Oct. 1, 1995)

(1) . . . The Legislature recognizes that some laws, regulations, and ordinances of the state and political entities in the state, as applied, may inordinately burden, restrict, or limit private property rights without amounting to a taking under the State Constitution or the United States Constitution. The Legislature determines that there is an important state interest in protecting the interests of private property owners from such inordinate burdens. Therefore, it is the intent of the Legislature that, as a separate and distinct cause of action from the law of takings, the Legislature herein provides for relief, or payment of compensation, when a new law, rule, regulation, or ordinance of the state or a political entity in the state, as applied, unfairly affects real property. . . .

(3) For purposes of this section: . . .

(c) The term "governmental entity" includes an agency of the state, a regional or a local government created by the State Constitution or by general or special act, any county or municipality, or any other entity that independently exercises governmental authority. . . .

(d) The term "action of a governmental entity" means a specific action of a governmental entity which affects real property, including action on an application or permit.

(e) The terms "inordinate burden" or "inordinately burdened" mean that an action of one or more governmental entities has directly restricted or limited the use of real property such that the property owner is permanently unable to attain the reasonable, investment-backed expectation for the existing use of the real property or a vested right to a specific use of the real property with respect to the real property as a whole, or that the property owner is left with existing or vested uses that are unreasonable such that the property owner bears permanently a disproportionate share of a burden imposed for the good of the public, which in fairness should be borne by the public at large. The terms "inordinate burden" or "inordinately burdened" do not include temporary impacts to real property; impacts to real property occasioned by governmental abatement, prohibition, prevention, or remediation of a public nuisance at common law or a noxious use of private property; or impacts to real property caused by an action of a governmental entity taken to grant relief to a property owner under this section. . . .

(4) (a) Not less than 180 days prior to filing an action under this section against a governmental entity, a property owner who seeks compensation under this section must present the claim in writing to the head of the governmental entity. . . .

(c) During the 180-day-notice period, unless extended by agreement of the parties, the governmental entity shall make a written settlement offer to effectuate:

1. An adjustment of land development or permit standards or other provisions controlling the development or use of land.

2. Increases or modifications in the density, intensity, or use of areas of development.

3. The transfer of developmental rights.

4. Land swaps or exchanges.

5. Mitigation, including payments in lieu of onsite mitigation.

6. Location on the least sensitive portion of the property.

7. Conditioning the amount of development or use permitted.

8. A requirement that issues be addressed on a more comprehensive basis than a single proposed use or development.

9. Issuance of the development order, a variance, special exception, or other extraordinary relief.

10. Purchase of the real property, or an interest therein, by an appropriate governmental entity.

11. No changes to the action of the governmental entity.

If the property owner accepts the settlement offer, the governmental entity may implement the settlement offer by appropriate development agreement; by issuing a variance, special exception, or other extraordinary relief; or by other appropriate method, subject to paragraph (d). . . .

(d) . . .

2. Whenever a governmental entity enters into a settlement agreement under this section which would have the effect of contravening the application of a statute as it would otherwise apply to the subject real property, the governmental entity and the property owner shall jointly file an action in the circuit court where the real property is located for approval of the settlement agreement by the court to ensure that the relief granted protects the public interest served by the statute at issue and is the appropriate relief necessary to prevent the governmental regulatory effort from inordinately burdening the real property.

(5) (a) During the 180-day-notice period, unless a settlement offer is accepted by the property owner, each of the governmental entities . . . shall issue a written ripeness decision identifying the allowable uses to which the subject property may be put. . . . The ripeness decision, as a matter of law, constitutes the last prerequisite to judicial review, and

the matter shall be deemed ripe or final for the purposes of the judicial proceeding created by this section, notwithstanding the availability of other administrative remedies. . . .

(9) This section provides a cause of action for governmental actions that may not rise to the level of a taking under the State Constitution or the United States Constitution. . . .

As pp. 401–09 explains, many states allow voters to enact legislation through an "initiative" process, whereby a measure may be placed on the ballot by securing a specified number of signatures. The following measure was adopted by 61 percent of the Oregon voters casting ballots in the 2004 general election.

Oregon Initiative Measure No. 37: Governments Must Pay Owners, or Forgo Enforcement, When Certain Land Use Restrictions Reduce Property Value

The following provisions are added to and made a part of Or. Rev. Stat. chapter 197. [Chapter 197 concerns "Comprehensive Land Use Planning Coordination."]

(1) If a public entity enacts or enforces a new land use regulation or enforces a land use regulation enacted prior to the effective date of this amendment that restricts the use of private real property or any interest therein and has the effect of reducing the fair market value of the property, or any interest therein, then the owner of the property shall be paid just compensation.

(2) Just compensation shall be equal to the reduction in the fair market value of the affected property interest resulting from enactment or enforcement of the land use regulation as of the date the owner makes written demand for compensation under this act.

(3) Subsection (1) of this act shall not apply to land use regulations:

(A) Restricting or prohibiting activities commonly and historically recognized as public nuisances under common law. This subsection shall be construed narrowly in favor of a finding of compensation under this act;

(B) Restricting or prohibiting activities for the protection of public health and safety, such as fire and building codes, health and sanitation regulations, solid or hazardous waste regulations, and pollution control regulations;

(C) To the extent the land use regulation is required to comply with federal law;

(D) Restricting or prohibiting the use of a property for the purpose of selling pornography or performing nude dancing. Nothing in this subsection, however, is intended to affect or alter rights provided by the Oregon or United States [Constitution]; or

(E) Enacted prior to the date of acquisition of the property by the owner or a family member of the owner who owned the subject property prior to acquisition or inheritance by the owner, whichever occurred first.

(4) Just compensation under subsection (1) of this act shall be due the owner of the property if the land use regulation continues to be enforced against the property 180 days after the owner of the property makes written demand for compensation under this section to the public entity enacting or enforcing the land use regulation.

(5) For claims arising from land use regulations enacted prior to the effective date of this act, written demand for compensation under subsection (4) shall be made within two years of the effective date of this act, or the date the public entity applies the land use regulation as an approval criteria to an application submitted by the owner of the property,

whichever is later. For claims arising from land use regulations enacted after the effective date of this act, written demand for compensation under subsection (4) shall be made within two years of the enactment of the land use regulation, or the date the owner of the property submits a land use application in which the land use regulation is an approval criteria, whichever is later.

(6) If a land use regulation continues to apply to the subject property more than 180 days after the present owner of the property has made written demand for compensation under this act, the present owner of the property, or any interest therein, shall have a cause of action for compensation under this act in the circuit court in which the real property is located, and the present owner of the real property shall be entitled to reasonable attorney fees, expenses, costs, and other disbursements reasonably incurred to collect the compensation. . . .

(8) Notwithstanding any other state statute or the availability of funds under subsection (10) of this act, in lieu of payment of just compensation under this act, the governing body responsible for enacting the land use regulation may modify, remove, or not to apply the land use regulation or land use regulations to allow the owner to use the property for a use permitted at the time the owner acquired the property. . . .

(10) Claims made under this section shall be paid from funds, if any, specifically allocated by the legislature, city, county, or metropolitan service district for payment of claims under this act. Notwithstanding the availability of funds under this subsection, a metropolitan service district, city, county, or state agency shall have discretion to use available funds to pay claims or to modify, remove, or not apply a land use regulation or land use regulations pursuant to subsection (6) of this act. If a claim has not been paid within two years from the date on which it accrues, the owner shall be allowed to use the property as permitted at the time the owner acquired the property. . . .

(11) Definitions — for purposes of this section:

(A) "Family member" shall include the wife, husband, son, daughter, mother, father, brother, brother-in-law, sister, sister-in-law, son-in-law, daughter-in-law, mother-in-law, father-in-law, aunt, uncle, niece, nephew, stepparent, stepchild, grandparent, or grandchild of the owner of the property, an estate of any of the foregoing family members, or a legal entity owned by any one or combination of these family members or the owner of the property.

(B) "Land use regulation" shall include:

(i) Any statute regulating the use of land or any interest therein;

(ii) Administrative rules and goals of the Land Conservation and Development Commission;

(iii) Local government comprehensive plans, zoning ordinances, land division ordinances, and transportation ordinances;

(iv) Metropolitan service district regional framework plans, functional plans, planning goals and objectives; and

(v) Statutes and administrative rules regulating farming and forest practices. . . .

Note on Takings Statutes

1. *State versus local focus.* Why do relatively few of the statutes extend to local governments? Are takings more likely to occur at the state level? Are the prophylactics used by the statutes less likely to work at the local level? Are there certain local governments more likely to take property or more likely to be disciplined by the provisions of the statutes?

As you study the next chapter, which reviews judicial attempts to rein in local parochialism, consider how the view of local governments reflected in those decisions differs from the view inherent in the takings statutes.

2. *Enforcement.* How should the assessment requirements be enforced? Should disaffected property owners who believe the assessment was not made, or if made, was not adequate, have a cause of action? A few statutes explicitly preclude judicial review of assessments, see, e.g., Kan. Stat. Ann. §77-710 (2005); but most are silent on the question. Texas allows affected property owners to bring an action to invalidate any governmental action for which a required assessment was not prepared. Tex. Gov't Code Ann. §2007.044(a) (West 2005). For a discussion of the problems raised by judicial review, see Mark W. Cordes, Leapfrogging the Constitution: The Rise of State Takings Legislation, 24 Ecology L.Q. 187, 210–12, 222 (1997); Robert C. Ellickson, Takings Legislation: A Comment, 20 Harv. J.L. & Pub. Pol'y 75 (1996).

3. *Facial challenges.* Under the assessment statutes, most TIAs will be prepared for what courts would consider facial challenges — evaluations of how the statute or regulation on its face will affect property values. What does the courts' skepticism about facial challenges, see pp. 185–88, suggest about how helpful such TIAs are likely to be?

4. *Why are assessment statutes necessary?* Property owners are given notice and an opportunity to comment in almost any situation in which legislation, regulation, or administrative action might affect their interests. Why are those forums not sufficient to force decisionmakers to think about the takings implications of their actions? Why isn't the threat of liability for a compensation award enough to force decisionmakers to consider the takings implications of their actions (and what does that tell us about the cost-internalization rationale for requiring compensation for regulatory takings discussed at pp. 145–51)? If those attention-getting mechanisms are not working, how likely is it that TIA statements will make administrators pay more serious attention to the costs of agency decisions? See pp. 391–93 for a discussion of the effectiveness of analogous environmental impact statements. See also Barton H. Thompson, Jr., The Endangered Species Act: A Case Study in Takings and Incentives, 49 Stan. L. Rev. 305, 336–38 (1997) (reporting that TIAs filed by the Fish and Wildlife Service are "cookie cutter" documents).

Should agencies considering proposals to weaken regulation or applications for variances or rezonings have to file a TIA to assess the likely impact on neighboring property values? See George E. Grimes, Jr., Comment, Texas Private Real Property Rights Preservation Act: A Political Solution to the Regulatory Takings Problem, 27 St. Mary's L.J. 557 (1996) (reporting on environmentalists' calls for an "even-handed" TIA requirement).

5. *Responding to a "positive" TIA.* What should an agency do if its TIA concludes that the regulation at issue will effect a taking? If it believes that its mandate nevertheless requires the action, may it go ahead with the proposed action? Or must it seek authorization for the taking from the executive or the legislature? If the agency decides to regulate, may the TIA be used against the agency in any litigation over whether a taking occurred?

6. *Line-drawing in compensation statutes.* Which is preferable: the seemingly absolutist rule of the Oregon initiative or the "inordinate burden" standard Florida uses? How well does the line-drawing in each of the measures satisfy the concerns about fairness, efficiency, or political process failures that motivate the compensation requirement? Michael A. Culpepper, Comment, The Strategic Alternative: How State Takings Statutes May Resolve the Unanswered Questions of *Palazzolo*, 36 U. Rich. L. Rev. 509 (2002).

7. *Defining the property.* How do measures define the property against which any reduction in value (Oregon), or the "inordinate burden" (Florida) are to be measured? How should the courts interpret Oregon's "real property or any interest therein" provision? See William Michael Treanor, The Armstrong Principle, The Narratives of Takings, and

Compensation Statutes, 38 Wm. & Mary L. Rev. 1151 (1997) (arguing that the "horror stories" that have proved very powerful weapons for proponents of the takings legislation reveal a "cultural convention" that fairness requires compensation in "cases in which unanticipated regulations destroy a significant portion of the total assets of a property owner" but that state takings legislation has gone much further than that cultural convention).

8. *Oregon's waiver option.* What rights, if any, will neighbors have if a local government chooses to waive the regulation as to a particular property rather than pay compensation? Should neighbors receive notice of the fact that a claim has been filed and might result in a waiver? An opportunity to be heard on the wisdom of granting a waiver rather than paying any compensation due? Will a waiver run with the land, or be valid only for the owner of the land who received the waiver in settlement of a compensation claim? Which governmental body should decide whether to waive the regulation or pay compensation — the legislature or the administrative body charged with granting variances, for example? See Edward J. Sullivan, Oregon's Measure 37: Crisis and Opportunity for Planning, Plan. & Envtl. L., March 2005, at 3, 6-7.

Some of the compensation statutes forbid the government from asking a landowner to forgo rights under the statute in exchange for permission to build. See Miss. Code Ann. §49-33-11 (2005). What effect are such provisions likely to have on the development process? Oregon's Measure 37 is silent on whether a government can exact a covenant not to sue from a landowner, but the issue undoubtedly will arise soon.

9. *Givings, again.* Oregon has given farmers, ranchers, and the owners of forest lands approximately $5.4 billion in tax waivers to keep the lands in agricultural or conservation use. Sullivan, supra, at 8. If one of the recipients of favorable tax treatment claims a right to compensation under Measure 37 for a land use restriction, should the compensation be offset by the value of those tax breaks? What if the tax breaks were given instead by the federal government?

10. *Ripeness.* Does the Florida statute solve the problems that critics of *Williamson County* have asserted plagues the federal ripeness rules? Are there any disadvantages to the Florida approach? Compare Sylvia R. Lazos Vargas, Florida's Property Rights Act: A Political Quick Fix Results in a Mixed Bag of Tricks, 23 Fla. St. U. L. Rev. 315, 370–72, 386-96 (1995) (critiquing the act's ripeness provisions), with Patrick W. Maraist, The Ripeness Doctrine in Florida Land Use Law, Fla. B.J., Feb. 1997, at 58 (defending the act). Is Oregon's rule that a cause of action accrues 180 days after a landowner files a demand for compensation preferable?

The Florida statute recognizes that protecting private property rights may come at the expense of protecting public health and safety. Does the requirement that a judge approve settlements under the act adequately ensure that the balance is struck correctly? See Lazos Vargas, supra. See also Thomas G. Douglass, Jr., Note, Have They Gone Too Far? An Evaluation and Comparison of 1995 State Takings Legislation, 30 Ga. L. Rev. 1061 (1996).

11. *Political reception for compensation requirements.* Although at least 25 states have considered compensation requirements, only Florida, Oregon, and Texas (see Tex. Gov't Code Ann. §2007 (West 2005)) have broad compensation requirements in effect. Two other states have compensation requirements in very limited circumstances. See La. Stat. Ann. §§3:3601–3612 (West 2005) (agricultural land); Miss. Code Ann. §§49-33-1–49-33-17 (2005) (regulation of agricultural or forest land).

Washington's compensation statute, which required compensation for any diminution in value, was recalled by a referendum just one year after it was enacted, by a 60 to 40 percent vote. Frank A. Vickory & Barry A. Diskin, Advances in Private Property Protection Rights: The States in the Vanguard, 34 Am. Bus. L.J. 561 (1997). In Colorado, the governor vetoed measures passed by the legislature. See Colorado Governor Vetos Takings Bill, 27 Env't Rep. (BNA) 419 (1996). The Oregon initiative measure enacts legislation that may be amended by the legislature. What is your prediction about how the legislature will respond to that opportunity?

What does the success of the compensation measures in two of the states known for their leadership in land use planning (see Chapter 4B) and growth management (see Chapter 9D) say about the political process failure arguments discussed at pp. 154–58?

12. *Success or failure?* Evaluations of the effect of the Florida compensation require- ment reveal that it has not resulted in the flood of litigation that critics feared. Although there is some anecdotal evidence that the statute has had a chilling effect on local gov- ernments, causing them to back away from open space and historic preservation programs and to grant landowners' requests for rezonings more readily than they otherwise would, the statute seems to have led more to negotiated settlements in individual disputes than to wide-ranging changes in legislative or regulatory policy. See Stacey S. White, State Prop- erty Rights Laws: Recent Impacts and Future Implications, Land Use L. & Zoning Dig., July 2000, at 3–9. See also Susan L. Trevarthen, Advising the Client Regarding Protection of Property Rights: Harris Act and Inverse Condemnation Claims, *in* 2004 Update: Emi- nent Domain's Role in Redevelopment, SK002 ALI-ABA 185 (Theodore C. Taub 2004); Ronald L. Weaver & Nicole S. Sayfie, 1999 Update on the Bert J. Harris Private Property Rights Protection, Fla. B.J., Mar. 1999, at 49.

In the first three months after Oregon's Measure 37 went into effect, at least 200 claims were filed under its provisions. Sullivan, supra, at 6. For an update on the evolving legal environment in Oregon, visit http://www.oregon.gov/LCD/measure37.shtml.

Chapter Four

Zoning Changes and the Rights of Neighbors

Landowners who wish to develop their property in ways that contravene the zoning ordinances may work around the existing zoning in several ways. The enabling acts modeled on the Standard State Zoning Enabling Act (SZEA) specifically contemplated that there would be a need for exceptions to and modifications of any zoning ordinance. They therefore generally provide for three "traditional" means of securing zoning changes: variances, special exceptions (also known as special use permits or conditional uses), and rezonings or map amendments.

Modern zoning practices increasingly use what has come to be known as "wait and see" zoning, in which undeveloped land is placed in a "holding category" such as agricultural use until someone expresses an interest in the land. When the land becomes attractive to a developer, the developer makes a proposal to the local zoning authorities and, after considerable give and take, the city rezones the land from the holding category to the category appropriate for the proposed development. Local governments have devised a variety of modern flexibility devices that make "wait and see" zoning possible, including contract and conditional zoning, cluster zoning, floating zones, planned-unit development (PUD) approval procedures, and site plan reviews.

Chapter 3 chronicled battles between developers and local governments. This chapter features the third category of antagonists in land use controversies — persons who own land near the site where development is proposed, referred to here as "neighbors." When a local government considers removing a zoning restriction from a particular site, either through the traditional avenues of zoning change or through the newer flexibility devices, it must essentially choose between denying the change (and thus offending the landowner) or granting the change (and possibly offending the neighbors). This chapter explores the process of zoning-change decisions and the rights the offended parties have to challenge the decision reached. The materials emphasize neighbors' rights and thus mainly involve situations where local officials have sided with the developer-landowner. Developers may be able to take advantage of the doctrines developed in neighbors' cases, however, either to insist on an entitlement, to obtain administrative relief from literal enforcement of ordinance standards, or to challenge zoning changes that are adverse to them. This chapter examines these rights of landowners, which of course supplement the rights canvassed in the preceding chapter.

The materials emphasize the inherent tension between local officials' quest for flexibility and judicial concern about the dangers of discretionary decisionmaking. To put it more bluntly, we are about to discover the gulf between the Euclidean dream of comprehensive planning and the reality of chronic dealmaking between local governments and developers.

The chapter begins with an exploration of the major techniques the courts and state legislatures have used to control local governments' use of both the traditional avenues for zoning change and the flexibility devices that have come into use with the advent of "wait and see" zoning. The chapter examines four of the primary control strategies: (1) elaborating and enforcing substantive criteria for the grant of zoning changes by administrative agencies; (2) using various danger signals to trigger more searching cost/benefit review of zoning changes granted by legislative bodies; (3) reducing the deference given to certain kinds of legislative decisions; and (4) imposing procedural, ethical, and informational protections.

The chapter concludes by discussing the role neighbors play in seeking to influence land use policy through consent requirements and initiative and referenda measures.

Background Note on Government Structures

The organization of local governments varies considerably from state to state. Nevertheless, the SZEA so influenced the evolution of zoning that, at least until recent years, there has been surprisingly little variation among states in the governmental structures used to process zoning changes. The SZEA envisioned that the local legislative body would be able to delegate some requests for changes to an administrative agency, which would have the following organizational structure and allocation of powers:

SEC. 7. BOARD OF ADJUSTMENT

Such local legislative body may provide for the appointment of a board of adjustment, and in the regulations and restrictions adopted pursuant to the authority of this act, may provide that the said board of adjustment may, in appropriate cases and subject to appropriate conditions and safeguards, make special exceptions to the terms of the ordinance in harmony with its general purpose and intent and in accordance with general or specific rules therein contained. . . .

The board of adjustment shall have the following powers:

1. To hear and decide appeals where it is alleged that there is error in any order, requirement, decision, or determination made by an administrative official in the enforcement of this act or of any ordinance adopted pursuant thereto.
2. To hear and decide special exceptions to the terms of the ordinance upon which such board is required to pass under such ordinance.
3. To authorize, upon appeal in specific cases, such variance from the terms of the ordinance as will not be contrary to the public interest, where, owing to special conditions, a literal enforcement of the provisions of the ordinance will result in unnecessary hardship, and so that the spirit of the ordinance shall be observed and substantial justice done. . . .

As the SZEA envisioned, in almost all states today, the general-purpose *local legislative body* (known variously as the city council, board of aldermen, board of county supervisors or county commissioners, or township board) is the only entity that can amend the text or map of a zoning ordinance.

In most jurisdictions today, two bodies of laypersons appointed by the local legislative body or local executive each shoulder part of the load of administering zoning changes. In many states, their roles are still largely defined as they were in the SZEA and its sibling, the Standard City Planning Enabling Act.

One body, the *planning commission*, holds public hearings on proposed zoning amendments and reports its recommendations to the legislative body. Most jurisdictions authorize affected landowners (as well as the commission and legislative body) to propose zoning amendments, thereby triggering the hearing process. The planning commission typically also has a major (and sometimes final) role in processing special exceptions, in considering proposed subdivision maps and site plans, and in preparing comprehensive plans. Usually, however, major decisions of the planning commission are reviewed by the legislative body. Because the planning commission is a part-time lay body (often populated by attorneys, real estate brokers, civic activists, university professors, and others without formal training in planning), it requires staff support. This comes either from the local government's *planning department*, or, especially if the government is too small to have such staff, from consultants.

The other lay body, which the SZEA called the *board of adjustment*, now often has a more descriptive title, such as the *board of zoning appeals* (BZA). The BZA makes final decisions on what often are relatively minor matters — applications for variances in cases of hardship and appeals from building-permit denials by yet another agency, the local government's *building department*.

The foregoing description is becoming less reliable as time passes. A growing number of states are straying from the original SZEA. Moreover, there is a definite trend toward professionalization of zoning administration. In some large cities, for example, a *zoning administrator* may be empowered to make decisions in the simpler cases within the jurisdiction of the BZA. In addition, to relieve the members of the lay bodies from the tedium of endless hearings, local governments increasingly are employing hearing examiners to take evidence and make recommendations.

Note on Problems Posed by Overlapping Government Structures

1. *Weight given to recommendations of subordinate staff or agencies.* When a local legislative body decides an issue contrary to the recommendations of its staff and/or its planning commission, should a court count that as evidence that the legislative decision is arbitrary? There are many holdings and dicta to the effect that the choices of the legislative body should not be restricted in this way. See, e.g., American National Bank & Trust Co. v. Village of Skokie, 536 N.E.2d 926 (Ill. App. Ct. 1989) (legislative body may grant site plan approval under the special exception provisions of zoning ordinance even though the village's plan commission recommended that approval be denied). Some zoning ordinances, however, make approval by the administrative agency a condition precedent to the legislative body's approval of a zoning change or proposed development. See, e.g., Webster Associates v. Town of Webster, 451 N.E.2d 189 (N.Y. 1983) (relying on such a condition-precedent clause in invalidating town board's approval of development plan that planning board had disapproved). In others, a negative recommendation by the planning commission may be overcome only by a supermajority vote of the legislative body. See, e.g., Del. Code Ann. tit. 9, §2614 (2004) (if a proposed change is not recommended by the Department of Land Use, the legislative body can approve the proposal only if two-thirds of the legislators concur). Regardless of the professed rules, any legal realist who examined the decisional law would quickly discern that judges are less likely to sustain a legislative body's zoning decisions when they run contrary to the recommendations of administrative advisors.

2. *Reviewing appeals from administrative decisions*. When the local legislative body has delegated decisionmaking authority, such as the power to grant or deny variances to an administrative agency, but allows parties to "appeal" the decision to the legislative body, does the legislative body "review" the decision in the same way a court would, or may it make an independent decision based on either the record before the administrative agency or its own hearings or receipt of evidence? See, e.g., King v. Caddo Parish Commission, 719 So. 2d 410 (La. 1998) (legislative body was not limited to reviewing whether the zoning board of appeal's decision to deny a special exception was arbitrary and capricious, but could decide the issue independently).

3. *Excessive delegation*. A local legislative body may violate the zoning enabling statute by delegating too much authority to its lay bodies, or by delegating authority to a different agency than the zoning enabling act envisions. See, e.g., PRB Enterprises, Inc. v. South Brunswick Planning Board, 518 A.2d 1099 (N.J. 1987) (legislative body cannot delegate to planning board the power to determine uses to be allowed within a zone); Diller & Fisher Co. v. Architectural Review Board, 587 A.2d 674 (N.J. Super. Ct. Law Div. 1990) (municipality improperly delegated to an architectural review board decisionmaking powers that should have resided in planning or zoning boards).

4. *Independence of related land use decisionmakers from each other*. Agencies (or their members) sometimes try to lobby other agencies. Such efforts may be prohibited outright — see, e.g., Sander v. Planning Board, 356 A.2d 411 (N.J. Super. Ct. App. Div. 1976) (planning board's unsolicited letter to a board of adjustment opposing an application for a variance was beyond the board's statutory authority) — or may give rise to conflict of interest and bias charges. Compare, e.g., Prin v. Council of Monroeville, 645 A.2d 450 (Pa. Commw. Ct. 1994) (town council member's appearance before planning commission to oppose application should have precluded him from later voting on the commission's recommendation that the application be denied), with Breakzone Billiards v. City of Torrance, 81 Cal. App. 4th 1205 (2000) (fact that a member of the planning commission, who was also a member of the city council, appealed the commission's ruling granting the conditional use permit to the city council for a de novo hearing, then participated in the hearing, did not make the proceeding unfair or violate due process).

Agencies sometimes try to limit or usurp the authority of their counterparts. See, e.g., Zoning Board of Appeals v. Planning & Zoning Commission, 605 A.2d 885 (Conn. App. Ct. 1992) (commission acted beyond its authority when it tried to restrict the board's power to grant use variances). Agencies or legislative bodies also sometimes resort to the courts to block actions by competing agencies. See, e.g., Board of Supervisors v. Board of Zoning Appeals, 604 S.E.2d 7 (Va. 2004) (county's legislative body has standing to challenge grant of variance by its BZA).

A.   *Constraints on Zoning Changes by Administrative Bodies*

1.   *Variances*

Matthew v. Smith
707 S.W.2d 411 (Mo. 1986)

WELLIVER, Justice.
. . . The Brandts own a tract of land comprising one and one-half plotted lots. When they purchased the property in March of 1980, there already were two houses on the land,

one toward the front of Erie Street and one in the rear. Each of the buildings is occupied by one residential family as tenants of the Brandts. The two houses apparently have been used as separate residences for the past 30 years, with only intermittent vacancies. The property is zoned for Single Family Residences. At the suggestion of a city official, the Brandts applied for a variance which would allow them to rent both houses with a single family in each house. After some delay, including two hearings by the Board of Zoning Adjustment of Kansas City, the Board granted the application. Appellant, Jon Matthew, a neighboring landowner challenged the grant of the variance. . . . The circuit court affirmed the Board's order; on appeal, the court of appeals held that the Board was without authority to grant the requested variance. A dissenting judge certified the case to this Court. . . .

Under most zoning acts, [Boards of Zoning Adjustments] . . . have the authority to grant variances from the strict letter of the zoning ordinance. The variance procedure "fulfils a sort of 'escape hatch' or 'safety valve' function for individual landowners who would suffer special hardship from the literal application of the . . . zoning ordinance." City & Borough of Juneau v. Thibodeau, 595 P.2d 626, 633 (Alaska 1979). It is often said that "the variance provides an administrative alternative for individual relief that can avoid the damage that can occur to a zoning ordinance as a result of as applied taking litigation." D. Mandelker, Land Use Law 169 (1982). The general rule is that the authority to grant a variance should be exercised sparingly and only under exceptional circumstances. See, e.g., A. Rathkopf, [3 The Law of Zoning and Planning] §37.06, at 69 [(1979)].

Both the majority of courts and the commentators recognize two types of variances: an area (nonuse) variance and a use variance. . . .

> As the name indicates, a use variance is one which permits a use other than one of those prescribed by the zoning ordinance in the particular district; it permits a use which the ordinance prohibits. A nonuse variance authorizes deviations from restrictions which relate to a permitted use, rather than limitations on the use itself, that is, restrictions on the bulk of buildings, or relating to their height, size, and extent of lot coverage, or minimum habitable area therein, or on the placement of buildings and structures on the lot with respect to required yards. Variances made necessary by the physical characteristics of the lot itself are nonuse variances of a kind commonly termed "area variances."

Rathkopf, supra, at §38.01. Many zoning acts or ordinances expressly distinguish between the two types of variances. N. Williams, Jr. [5 American Land Planning Law] §129.07, at 17 [1985]. When the distinction is not statutory, "the courts have always distinguished use from area variances." Mandelker, supra, at 167. Some jurisdictions, whether by express statutory directive or by court interpretation, do not permit the grant of a use variance.

Past decisions in this State have placed Missouri within those jurisdictions not permitting a use variance. This line of cases would suggest that the Brandts are not entitled to the variance. They seek a variance to use the property in a manner not permitted under the permissible uses established by the ordinance. . . .

. . . These past cases, beginning with State ex rel. Nigro v. Kansas City, 27 S.W.2d 1030 (Mo. 1930), are based upon the premise that the granting of a use variance would be an unconstitutional delegation of power to the Board to amend the ordinance. See generally Mandelker, Delegation of Power and Function In Zoning Administration, 1963 Wash. U. L.Q. 60, 68-71. This view has long since been repudiated by most jurisdictions, and it is contrary to the express language of Mo. Rev. Stat. §89.090 (1978), which grants the Board the "power to vary or modify the application of any of the regulations or provisions of such ordinance relating to the *use*, construction or alteration of buildings or structures, or the *use of land*" (emphasis added). We, therefore, hold that under the proper circumstances an applicant may obtain a use variance.

Mo. Rev. Stat. §89.090 (1978) delegates to the Board of Adjustment the power to grant a variance when the applicant establishes "practical difficulties or unnecessary hardship in the way of carrying out the strict letter of such ordinance . . . so that the spirit of the ordinance shall be observed, public safety and welfare secured and substantial justice done." Missouri lifted this language out of the 1920 amendment to the General City Law of New York. . . . The New York statute served as the first general model for other jurisdictions; soon thereafter, however, many states adopted the Standard Zoning [Enabling] Act that had been prepared in the early 1920's under the aegis of the United States Department of Commerce. . . .

Before further examining the contours of unnecessary hardship, jurisdictions such as Missouri that follow the New York model rather than the Standard Act need to address the significance of the statutory dual standard of "unnecessary hardship" or "practical difficulties." Generally, this dual standard has been treated in one of two ways. On the one hand, many courts view the two terms as interchangeable. On the other hand, a number of jurisdictions follow the approach of New York, the jurisdiction where the language originated, and hold that "practical difficulties" is a slightly lesser standard than "unnecessary hardship" and only applies to the granting of an area variance and not a use variance. The rationale for this approach is that an area variance is a relaxation of one or more incidental limitations to a permitted use and does not alter the character of the district as much as a use not permitted by the ordinance.

In light of our decision to permit the granting of a use variance, we are persuaded that the New York rule reflects the sound approach for treating the distinction between area and use variances. To obtain a use variance, an applicant must demonstrate, inter alia, unnecessary hardship; and, to obtain an area variance, an applicant must establish, inter alia, the existence of conditions slightly less rigorous than unnecessary hardship.

While today we enter a field not yet developed by case law in our own jurisdiction, other jurisdictions provide some guidance for determining what is required to establish unnecessary hardship when granting a use variance. It is generally said that Otto v. Steinhilber, 24 N.E.2d 851, 853 (N.Y. 1939) contains the classic definition of unnecessary hardship:

> the Board may exercise its discretion and grant a variance upon the ground of unnecessary hardship, the record must show that (1) the land in question cannot yield a reasonable return if used only for a purpose allowed in that zone; (2) that the plight of the owner is due to unique circumstances and not to the general conditions in the neighborhood which may reflect the unreasonableness of the zoning ordinance itself; and (3) that the use to be authorized by the variance will not alter the essential character of the locality.

Quite often the existence of unnecessary hardship depends upon whether the landowner can establish that without the variance the property cannot yield a reasonable return. "Reasonable return is not maximum return." Curtis v. Main, 482 A.2d 1253, 1257 (Me. 1984). Rather, the landowner must demonstrate that he or she will be deprived of all beneficial use of the property under any of the permitted uses. . . . Most courts agree that mere conclusory and lay opinion concerning the lack of any reasonable return is not sufficient; there must be actual proof, often in the form of dollars and cents evidence. In a well-reasoned opinion, Judge Meyer of the New York Court of Appeals stated:

> Whether the existing zoning permits of a reasonable return requires proof from which can be determined the rate of return earned by like property in the community and proof in dollars and cents form of the owner's investment in the property as well as the return that the property will produce from the various uses permissible under the existing classification.

Northern Westchester Prof'l Park Assocs. v. Town of Bedford, 458 N.E.2d 809, 814 (N.Y. 1983). Such pronouncements and requirements of the vast majority of jurisdictions illustrate that, if the law of variances is to have any viability, only in the exceptional case will a use variance be justified.

The record before this Court is . . . without sufficient evidence to establish unnecessary hardship.[8] The only evidence in the record is the conclusory opinion of Brandt that they would be deprived of a reasonable return if not allowed to rent both houses. No evidence of land values was offered; and, no dollars and cents proof was presented to demonstrate that they would be deprived of all beneficial use of their property. Appellant, in fact, was not permitted to introduce such evidence. The Board, therefore, was without authority to grant a use variance upon this record. . . .

The judgment of the circuit court is reversed and the cause is remanded back to the circuit court with directions that the cause be remanded back to the Board of Adjustment with directions that the applicants be permitted to present evidence warranting the grant of a variance. . . .

EDWARD D. ROBERTSON, JR., J., concurring in result. . . .

Note on Variances

1. *Area versus use variances.* The concurring opinion in *Matthew* argued that the variance requested by the Brandts was not a use variance because the use of the land was single-family residential, as the zoning mandated. Rather, he argued, the Brandts needed an area variance because the two single-family homes were located on a lot too small to accommodate both houses under the applicable zoning. As that argument indicates, it is not always easy to differentiate between use and area variances, especially when the variance sought involves an increase in density. See, e.g., Commercial Realty & Resources Corp. v. First Atlantic Properties Co., 585 A.2d 928 (N.J. 1991) (density and floor-area-ratio variances must be treated like use variances, but height variances are area variances). As *Matthew* and the following notes reveal, the classification of a variance application determines both the availability of variances in general and the specific test applied to the application.

2. *Special limitations on use variances.* Use variances tend to be more controversial than area variances because the widespread granting of use variances can quickly undermine Euclidean efforts to segregate different activities. Several legal developments have limited the incidence of use variances. First, as illustrated by *Matthew*'s discussion of the need to overrule *State ex rel. Nigro*, some state courts initially interpreted statutes modeled after the SZEA to bar the award of use variances on the theory that a use variance is a rezoning and that the power to amend the ordinance has not been delegated to the BZA.

---

8. The Constitution requires that the decision of the Board be reviewed to determine if it is authorized by law and supported by competent and substantial evidence. Mo. Const. art. V, §18. When the Brandts initially applied for a variance and a hearing was held, there were no minutes of the proceeding and the circuit court had to send the case back to the Board before it could review the Board's order. Nothing in the record indicates why this occurred, but the statute [Mo. Rev. Stat. §89.080 (1978)] expressly requires that such minutes be transcribed. . . . Compliance with this requirement is necessary if there is to be any meaningful review exercised by the circuit court upon the issuance of a writ of certiorari. . . .

Although the circuit court does not exercise de novo review, the statute nonetheless contemplates a meaningful review that may extend beyond the record before the Board. While not deciding the point, it might be noted that both the ordinance and a growing number of jurisdictions suggest that the Board should issue findings of fact.

Second, as in *Matthew*, many state courts have creatively construed the relevant statutes and ordinances to impose tougher criteria for the award of use variances ("undue hardship") than for area variances ("practical difficulties"). Many courts also apply the self-created hardship rule, discussed later in this note, more readily when a use variance is being sought.

Third, some cities have adopted zoning ordinances that prohibit the grant of use variances. Where the city is governed by a zoning enabling act, and that act has been interpreted to confer the authority to grant use variances, the local government's attempt to prohibit such variances may be rejected as inconsistent with the enabling act. See, e.g., North Fork Properties v. Bath Township, 2004 WL 57564 (Ohio Ct. App. Jan. 14, 2004) (unpublished opinion). In states that offer their cities home-rule powers, however, or in states whose enabling act gives local governments a choice whether to exercise the power to grant use variances, the local government will be able to define the powers of a board of adjustment to exclude use variances.

Fourth, state legislatures have amended their enabling acts to either eliminate or toughen standards for use variances. See, e.g., Cal. Gov't Code §65906 (West 2004) (prohibiting use variances); N.J. Stat. Ann. §40:55D-70 (West 2004) (allowing use variances only on a supermajority vote).

3. *Variances as a safety valve.* New Hampshire recently loosened its unnecessary hardship standard for a use variance, finding that its previous standard — "that the deprivation resulting from the enforcement of the ordinance had to be so great as to effectively prevent the landowner from making any reasonable use of the property" — was too restrictive "in light of the constitutional protections by which it must be tempered." Simplex Technologies v. Town of Newington, 766 A.2d 713, 716–17 (N.H. 2001). The new less restrictive standard for unnecessary hardship requires the landowner to prove:

1. a zoning restriction as applied to their property interferes with their reasonable use of the property, considering the unique setting of the property in its environment;
2. no fair and substantial relationship exists between the general purposes of the zoning ordinance and the specific restriction on the property; and
3. the variance would not injure the public or private rights of others.

Id. at 717. Apparently, then, the *Simplex* court views the availability of variances as a safety valve not only to avoid takings claims, but to avoid substantive due process claims as well. Should a BZA be allowed to grant a variance anytime it believes the landowner would prevail in litigation against the local government regarding the restriction?

Other courts also recently have indicated that the unnecessary hardship standard for variances is not as strict as the standard for a taking. See, e.g., Lewis v. Department of Natural Resources, 833 A.2d 563, 581 (Md. Ct. App. 2003). What dangers, if any, lie in setting the variance standard loose from its mooring in the Takings Clause? See David W. Owens, The Zoning Variance: Reappraisal and Recommendations for Reform of a Much-Maligned Tool, 29 Colum. J. Envtl. L. 279, 317 (2004) (arguing that variances should be used not only as a constitutional safeguard, but also as a simple, cost-effective means of providing modest adjustments to the regulatory scheme, and the standard should reflect that second purpose).

4. *Variances and nonconforming uses.* Why did the Brandts seek a variance for houses that appeared to constitute nonconforming uses? See pp. 197–202. Why would the neighbor object to the grant of a variance for houses that were being used in the same way they had been for the past 30 years? Why was the case so important that the parties would endure the expense of litigating all the way to the state supreme court?

5. *The practical difficulties standard for area variances.* While many states apply the same unnecessary hardship test to both area and use variances, others apply either a modified (and less stringent) version of the unnecessary hardship test to area variances, see, e.g., State v. Waushara County Board of Adjustment, 679 N.W.2d 514 (Wis. 2004), or apply what *Matthew* refers to as the "New York rule" that a developer seeking an area variance must prove only "practical difficulties" rather than unnecessary hardship. See, e.g., Marriott Corp. v. Concord Hotel Management, 578 A.2d 1097 (Del. 1990). The Supreme Court of Ohio describes its version of the practical difficulties standard as follows:

> The practical difficulties standard differs from the unnecessary hardship standard normally applied in use variance cases, because no single factor controls in a determination of practical difficulties . . .
>
> The factors to be considered and weighed in determining whether a property owner seeking an area variance has encountered practical difficulties in the use of his property include, but are not limited to: (1) whether the property in question will yield a reasonable return or whether there can be any beneficial use of the property without the variance; (2) whether the variance is substantial; (3) whether the essential character of the neighborhood would be substantially altered or whether adjoining properties would suffer a substantial detriment as a result of the variance; (4) whether the variance would adversely affect the delivery of governmental services (e.g. water, sewer, garbage); (5) whether the property owner purchased the property with knowledge of the zoning restriction; (6) whether the property owner's predicament feasibly can be obviated through some method other than a variance; (7) whether the spirit and intent behind the zoning requirement would be observed and substantial justice done by granting the variance.

Duncan v. Village of Middlefield, 491 N.E.2d 692, 695 (Ohio 1986).

Does it make sense to impose a lower standard for area variances than for use variances? Does that depend on whether variances to increase density are classified as use or area variances?

New York has abandoned the practical difficulties test in favor of an explicit balancing of the benefit of the variance to the property owner against the harm the variance would cause to the health, safety and welfare of the neighborhood. N.Y. Town Law §267-b(3)(b) (McKinney 2004). In doing that balancing, though, the courts examine many of the same factors that *Duncan* identifies as essential to the practical difficulties test. See, e.g., Sasso v. Osgood, 657 N.E.2d 254 (N.Y. 1995). Is an explicit cost/benefit balancing preferable to the ad hoc practical difficulties standard?

6. *Findings requirements.* As footnote 8 in *Matthew* indicates, it is difficult for courts to enforce substantive standards for the grant of variances if the record on appeal is cursory. The California courts first addressed this problem in Topanga Association for a Scenic Community v. County of Los Angeles, 522 P.2d 12, 18 (Cal. 1974), holding that the variance board "must render findings sufficient both to enable the parties to determine whether and on what basis they should seek review and, in the event of review, to apprise a reviewing court of the basis for the board's action." The court reasoned that findings were necessary to "persuade the parties that administrative decision-making is careful, reasoned, and equitable" and to promote "vigorous and meaningful" judicial review of variance decisions. It added:

> [C]ourts must meaningfully review grants of variances in order to protect the interests of those who hold rights in property nearby the parcel for which a variance is sought. A zoning scheme, after all, is similar in some respects to a contract; each party [forgoes] rights to use its land as it wishes in return for the assurance that the use of neighboring property will be

similarly restricted, the rationale being that such mutual restriction can enhance total community welfare. . . . If the interest of these parties in preventing unjustified variance awards for neighboring land is not sufficiently protected, the consequence will be subversion of the critical reciprocity upon which zoning regulation rests.

. . . Significantly, many zoning boards employ adjudicatory procedures that may be characterized as casual. The availability of careful judicial review may help conduce these boards to insure that all parties have an opportunity fully to present their evidence and arguments. Further, although we emphasize that we have no reason to believe that such a circumstance exists in the case at bar, the membership of some zoning boards may be inadequately insulated from the interests whose advocates most frequently seek variances. Vigorous judicial review thus can serve to mitigate the effects of insufficiently independent decision-making. . . .

Id. at 19. Decisions in other jurisdictions have imposed *Topanga*-like fact-finding requirements on boards of adjustment. See, e.g., New York SMSA v. Board of Adjustment, 851 A.2d 110 (N.J. Super. Ct. 2004). Some states have amended their zoning enabling acts to require written findings of fact. See, e.g., Ind. Code §36-7-4-915 (2004). What costs do fact-finding requirements and "vigorous" judicial review impose? Are there any circumstances under which those costs might outweigh the benefits *Topanga* identifies?

7. *The role of community opposition.* Which interest groups probably are most interested in who is appointed to low-visibility boards of adjustment? How might a board member be expected to act on a technically unjustified application for a variance if all nearby neighbors were notified of the application and none opposed it? Should the test for the availability of a variance be reformulated so that it is explicit that the outcome is based primarily on the degree of neighborhood opposition, with applicants encouraged to marshal the support of their neighbors? See pp. 393–400 for a discussion of neighbor consent requirements.

8. *The unrepresented consumer interest.* Most litigation over variances involves bitter fights between a landowner or developer and the developer's neighbors, with local officials caught in between. In this instance, and in most other land use controversies, however, the outcome affects yet another group — consumers of the land use activity that the developer is proposing. Who speaks for the Brandts' tenants in *Matthew*? Certainly no one directly represented them in this litigation, and they were probably unrepresented at the board's hearing as well. Consumers seldom overcome the free-rider problem that prevents them from organizing to defend themselves. Consumers are many in number, and they usually have small individual stakes in any given outcome. Their interests are usually aligned with the developer's. For example, homebuilders largely represent the interests of housing consumers, if only by proxy. However, a consumer may value a land use activity more than the developer charges for it. For instance, the Brandts' tenants may have developed an attachment to the neighborhood that gave the tenancy a value beyond the amount of rent paid. Unless consumers organize to offer to help finance the litigation, a developer has no financial incentive to take consumer surplus of this sort into account; the developer might therefore abandon an appeal that consumers would prefer be continued. See also p. 740 for discussion of how the problem of the unrepresented consumer interest contributes to the problem of siting locally undesirable land uses.

9. *Preferred uses?* Should a board or reviewing court take into account the social utility of the project for which the variance is requested? In New York, for example, public utilities are entitled to a more favorable version of the unnecessary hardship test than are other uses. Consolidated Edison Co. v. Hoffman, 374 N.E.2d 105 (N.Y. 1978) (board had been arbitrary and capricious in denying area and use variances for a 565-foot cooling tower at an operating nuclear power plant). In New Jersey, "inherently beneficial" commercial uses (such as for-profit senior citizen care facilities or day care centers) enjoy a more favorable variance test than other commercial uses. Sica v. Board of Adjustment, 603 A.2d 30

(N.J. 1992). But see Cell South of New Jersey, Inc. v. Zoning Board of Adjustment, 796 A.2d 247 (N.J. 2002) (refusing to find that cell phone towers are an inherently beneficial use). In other states, however, the socially valuable nature of the proposed use does not entitle the applicant to any special consideration. See, e.g., Zaruta v. Zoning Hearing Board, 543 A.2d 1282 (Pa. Commw. Ct. 1988) (where unique and unnecessary hardship was not proven, variance could not be granted even though the community badly needed the proposed homeless shelter).

10. *Self-created hardship.* In a number of states, a variance is not available if the hardship is self-created; in other states, the self-created nature of the claimed hardship weighs against, but does not necessarily foreclose, the grant of a variance. Self-created hardship can arise in three ways: (1) the applicant subdivides a tract to create a lot that will be difficult or impossible to develop in conformity with the applicable zoning restrictions; (2) the applicant develops the property in violation of applicable zoning restrictions; or (3) the applicant purchases the property knowing that it is not economically feasible to develop it unless a variance is obtained. Denial of a variance is understandable in the first two classes of cases. See, e.g., Sciacca v. Caruso, 769 A.2d 578 (R.I. 2001) (applicant who subdivided a single-conforming lot into two substandard-sized parcels was not entitled to variance because hardship was self-created).

The courts are divided, however, on whether landowners should also be denied variances in the third class of cases — those in which the applicant has merely bought into a hardship situation. Compare, e.g., Pecoraro v. Board of Appeals, 814 N.E.2d 404 (N.Y. 2004) (denial of variance appropriate where applicant knew the parcel did not meet zoning requirements), with Richard Roeser Professional Builder, Inc. v. Anne Arundel County, 793 A.2d 545 (Md. 2002) (purchase with notice does not count as a self-created hardship). Such cases should be divided into two categories: those in which the prior owners themselves could not have obtained variances, and those in which the prior owner would have been entitled to a variance but did not seek one. If the prior owner could not obtain a variance, there is no reason that a purchaser should be entitled to a variance, even if the purchaser paid an inflated price for the land on the expectation of receiving a variance.

But where a prior owner would be entitled to a variance, should the same relief be denied to someone who purchases the land with knowledge of the restriction? Would such a rule needlessly impair the transferability of land? Would it result in inefficient development of the land by the original owner? Such a rule would be inconsistent with the general rule that variances run with the land rather than being personal to the owner. Judicial opinions increasingly perceive the inapplicability of the self-created hardship defense in those situations. See, e.g., Twigg v. Town of Kennebunk, 662 A.2d 914 (Me. 1995) (self-created hardship not found where applicant had purchased from a seller who had obtained a variance but had let the variance expire). See generally Osborne M. Reynolds, Jr., Self-Induced Hardship in Zoning Variances: Does a Purchaser Have No One But Himself to Blame?, 20 Urb. Law. 1 (1988).

Does *Palazzolo*, excerpted at p. 180, require states that prohibit variances if the applicant bought the property with notice of the problem to soften their rule? Compare also the rules that apply when a plaintiff is accused of having come to a nuisance, see pp. 525–28.

It bears repeating that despite rules such as those prohibiting the grant of variances for self-created hardships, zoning boards of adjustment frequently grant variances in contravention of the rules, especially when the application is unopposed. Indeed, one study of BZA practices showed that people who built first and sought variances later were more successful in obtaining variances than those who proceeded lawfully. David L. Kent, The Presumption in Favor of Granting Zoning Variances, N.H.B.J., June 1993, at 29, 32.

11. *Neighbors' offers to purchase.* Should a neighbor's offer to pay fair market value for an undeveloped lot for which a variance is sought preclude the grant of a variance? New Jersey recognizes a "conditional variance," by which a variance is denied subject to the condition that the neighbors purchase the property at a "fair" price. "A conditional variance recognizes that adjacent owners have a heightened interest in the sale and development of adjoining property. . . . Conditioning the . . . [denial] of a variance on an adjacent owner's offer to purchase prevents the strict application of an ordinance from zoning property into inutility, while avoiding the possible intrusion of substandard lots or structures into a neighborhood." Davis Enterprises v. Karpf, 523 A.2d 137, 140 (N.J. 1987). The New Jersey courts have held, however, that because a conditional variance is "strong medicine" and "subordinates an owner's ability to use his or her property to another's desire to purchase it," a neighbor's offer to purchase does not necessarily foreclose the grant of a variance. Id. at 141. In a jurisdiction that does not recognize conditional variances, should the failure or refusal of objecting neighbors to offer to purchase the property in question nevertheless enter into the board's assessment of the validity of the neighbors' objections?

12. *Personal hardship.* As *Matthew* makes clear, the focus of the variance inquiry is on the characteristics of the land, not the needs of particular owners. That inattention to personal needs, while necessary because variances run with the land and not with the owner, can work real hardships. See, e.g., David Gonzalez, Love Is Blind: Unfortunately, So Is the Law, N.Y. Times, May 28, 1997, at B1 (blind newlyweds not entitled to variance needed to expand bride's house to accommodate her husband, even though denial meant woman would have to leave her home of 20 years and learn her way around a new neighborhood). To address such problems, should a jurisdiction fashion a new kind of personal hardship variance that does not run with the land?

Note on the "Steady Leak"

One critique of variance practices has charged that "the board of appeals variance procedure, conceived as the 'safety valve' of the zoning ordinance, has ruptured into a steady leak." Clifford L. Weaver & Richard F. Babcock, City Zoning: The Once and Future Frontier 272 (1979). Indeed, numerous empirical studies have documented that BZAs tend to grant between 50 percent and almost 90 percent of landowners' requests for variances. See, e.g., Municipal Art Society, Zoning Variances and the New York City Board of Standards and Appeals 21 (2004), *available at* http://www.mas. org/ContentLibrary/MAS%20BSA%20Report.pdf (93 percent of variance applications decided in 2001 and 2002 were granted); David L. Kent, The Presumption in Favor of Granting Zoning Variances, N.H.B.J., June 1993, at 29 (the probability of gaining a variance before five diverse communities in New Hampshire between 1987 and 1992 was 70 percent); David W. Owens, The Zoning Variance: Reappraisal and Recommendations for Reform of a Much-Maligned Tool, 29 Colum. J. Envtl. L. 279 (2004) (survey of North Carolina cities and counties in 2002 revealed that 72 percent of variances requested in the prior 12 months were granted).

The high number of variance requests granted may signal that the zoning ordinance is inappropriately restrictive, that BZAs are granting requests even when the legal requirements of unique and unnecessary hardship have not or cannot be shown (as in *Matthew*), or both. For an insightful discussion of the first proposition, see David P. Bryden, The Impact of Variances: A Study of Statewide Zoning, 61 Minn. L. Rev. 769 (1977). The evidence regarding the latter proposition is mixed. Different studies have found different rates of reversal. Compare e.g., Municipal Art Society, supra, at 42 (review of judicial decisions regarding variances between 1962 and 2003 found that only 15 percent were overturned), and Owens, supra, at 316 (only 7 percent of the North Carolina cities and counties reported judicial challenges to variance decisions, and the courts affirmed the board's decision in almost 60 percent of the challenges), with Kent, supra, at 30 (between 1987 and 1992, the New Hampshire Supreme Court reversed all ten grants of variances it reviewed). Scholarly reviews of the records in variance cases contend that a low percentage of the requests meet the unique and unnecessary hardship requirement, but those reviews are quite dated. See, e.g., Joseph H. Bornong & Bradley R. Peyton, Contemporary Studies Project, Rural Land Use Regulation in Iowa: An Empirical Analysis of County Board of Adjustment Practices, 68 Iowa L. Rev. 1083, 1161 (1983) (boards failed to apply the unnecessary hardship standard properly, and their reasons for granting variances "rarely satisfy the legal requirements").

Critics of local governments' variance policies argue that the liberal grant of variances undermines the predictability of land use regulation, and thereby increases the risk of ownership and diminishes property values. The introduction of new uses or building types into a neighborhood through the variance process is said to contribute to neighborhood decline, and to undermine the comprehensive plan by creating pressure for amendments to make the plan conform to the pattern of variances granted. Kent, supra, at 29. Finally, the frequency with which boards grant variances may take away communities' incentive to zone carefully, leading to sloppy zoning. Roderick M. Bryden, Zoning: Rigid, Flexible, or Fluid?, 44 J. Urb. L. 287, 299 (1967).

But (as usual) there is another way to think about evidence that boards grant variances relatively freely. In addition to the following excerpt, see Carol M. Rose, Planning and Dealing: Piecemeal Land Controls as a Problem of Local Legitimacy, 71 Cal. L. Rev. 837 (1983).

Eric H. Steele, Participation and Rules — The Functions of Zoning
1986 Am. B. Found. Res. J. 709, 737-38, 740-41, 749-50

Zoning is usually conceived of as the enforcement of a set of positive rules governing land use. This is a top-down, rule-oriented view of regulation that characterizes zoning as the mandating of a master plan defining what may be built and what land and buildings may be used for. . . .

[This] objective model of zoning is most effective in undeveloped, growing areas where large-scale, new development predominates, where there is little or very weak pre-existing community sentiment, and where the interests being regulated are fungible and investment oriented. . . .

But where strong, mature, well-organized, and cohesive residential communities exist and communities are already heavily built up, zoning tends more toward the participatory model and relates to a broader range of interests to be regulated. In such situations, people, residences, businesses, and institutions are in close proximity and are highly interdependent. . . . Such built-up, dense urban communities are often also characterized by well-developed and institutionalized sociopolitical organization that is commonly formalized in ongoing community organizations. Such organizations embody and express . . . a claim of rights to represent the collective interests of the community and to negotiate on behalf of shared interests when significant community change is proposed. In such communities zoning serves to institutionalize and embody this collective claim to a "voice" in decisions on significant community change.

The complex rules of zoning operate as guidelines indicating the types of proposals that may cause significant change affecting the community's legitimate collective interests. This responsive view of zoning rules as signals that community input is appropriate, as tripwires for community notice and hearing, is quite different from the rule-oriented autonomous view of zoning rules as prescriptive and legislative, akin to architectural specifications to be followed regardless of the context. In the responsive view, zoning rules flag issues for discussion almost more than they control land use and building design or prejudge the outcome of disputes over permitted construction and use. . . .

One would expect, under this view, that many matters identified as potentially problematic would actually generate little participation or comment and would be routinely granted by default. A large proportion of the proposed zoning changes identified by the zoning rules as potentially important community issues are not disputed — they are "false positives" in the identification process. If there are too many false positives of a particular type, then there is pressure to amend the zoning rules to eliminate or loosen the criterion. . . .

The granting of a significant proportion of piecemeal zoning change applications by default is not to be interpreted as evidence of the failure of zoning. It is completely consistent with the effective functioning of zoning boards. The criteria of identifying potentially problematic proposals and presenting them to the community for comment are intended to include a broader range of cases than those that actually are serious threats to the community. A large proportion of false positives reflects a conservative set of zoning rules and solicits community participation on a broad range of potentially significant proposed changes, many of which are not problematic and therefore elicit no comment from the community. This analysis would suggest, in fact, that if the process turned up very few false positives, it might be missing some true positives, and that the zoning criteria should be tightened to identify a broader range of potential problem cases. . . .

While the physical standards embodied in the zoning ordinances are only crude and indirect indicators of acceptable change, they function, together with community participation, to maintain the shifting balance between community cohesion and stability and necessary change. Where there is a high degree of cohesion to be conserved, the zoning rules tend to be enforced more rigidly to deter substantial change. This tendency is reinforced by community participation. These participatory zoning processes are most viable in strong, stable, single-family neighborhoods where many families and children live and turnover is low. Where there is a lower degree of cohesion and stability, less community participation is generated to resist change (i.e., for strict rule enforcement) and the process tends to adjust itself to grant a larger proportion of change applications by default and thus to enforce less restraint on proposed change.

2. *Special Exceptions (Conditional Uses)*

Gladden v. District of Columbia Board of Zoning Adjustment
659 A.2d 249 (D.C. 1995)

KERN, Senior Judge:
A District of Columbia property owner submitted an application to the District of Columbia Board of Zoning Adjustment ("BZA") for a special exception from the zoning laws in order to establish in his house a youth rehabilitation home. Petitioners, . . . who live in close proximity to the proposed youth rehabilitation home, opposed the application on the grounds that the home would have an adverse [e]ffect on the neighborhood. The BZA, after a hearing, approved the exception with several special conditions. . . .

The record reflects the following. The co-owner of a house and real property located at No. 2 T Street, N.E. filed an application before the BZA for a special exception under 11

DCMR §335.1 to establish a youth rehabilitation home for ten youths, ages 13–19.[1] The BZA held a hearing on June 9, 1993. There was evidence that the three-story building for which the exception is sought contains nine bedrooms and four bathrooms. This property was to be leased to . . . Gateway Youth Home Educational Designs, Inc. ("Gateway"). The purpose of the home is to provide counseling and discipline in a non-institutional setting in order to rehabilitate the residents for reintegration into society.

The proposed home would have eight full-time and four part-time employees, would include counselors and mental health specialists, and would not be open to drug users. The residents would go to school during the day and would be allowed to return to their families on the weekends. The rehabilitation home was to be Gateway's third operating project. Witnesses testified that Gateway has one of the best rehabilitation programs in the city.

The District of Columbia Office of Planning recommended approval of the project with several conditions. The Office informed the Board that no other community-based residential facilities were within a 500-foot radius of the project, but noted that two were located in the vicinity. The Office of Planning concluded that the project would not adversely affect the community and would have no significant impact in terms of traffic and noise. . . .

. . . The Neighborhood Advisory Commission ("ANC") and several neighbors testified against granting the exception. The ANC noted that the area is already "saturated" with group homes, including five in the surrounding five-block area and 21 altogether in Ward 5C. . . . Many residents of the area testified that another facility was just too many for the area and that the proposed home would be located in a high crime area. . . .

On November 18, 1993, the BZA issued a written decision granting a special exception for this property to be used as a youth rehabilitation home for two years. The Board concluded that there would be no adverse affect on the neighborhood. . . . The BZA further concluded that "while there may be a number of other facilities located in Ward 5, the Board is bound by the Zoning regulations which allow facilities to be approved if they are not within 500 feet of each other or within the same square." . . .

Petitioners . . . [argue that] the record does not support the BZA's conclusion that the facility will not adversely affect the neighborhood. . . .

First, we address the sufficiency of the BZA's findings based upon the evidence of record. We note that a BZA decision will be upheld "if there is a rational basis for it" and if the facts found by the Board have "substantial support in the evidence." Citizens Coalition v. District of Columbia Bd. of Zoning Adjustment, 619 A.2d 940, 947 (D.C. 1993). . . . Our review is summarized as follows:

> A decision by the BZA will not be set aside if: (1) the decision was accompanied by findings of fact sufficient to enable a reviewing court to reach a decision; (2) the decision reached by the agency follows as a matter of law from the facts; and (3) the facts so stated have substantial support in the evidence.
>
> Accordingly, our scope of review is "limited to whether the Board's interpretation is legally consistent with the regulations and whether the decision is clearly arbitrary and capricious in both a factual and a legal context." Salsbery v. District of Columbia Bd. of Zoning Adjustment, 318 A.2d 894, 896 (D.C. 1974) (citations omitted).

[*Citizens Coalition*, 619 A.2d at 947.]

___

1. "Youth rehabilitation homes . . . for one (1) to fifteen (15) persons, not including resident supervisors or staff and their families, shall be permitted in an R-4 district if approved by the Board of Zoning Adjustment in accordance with the conditions specified in §3108 of chapter 31 of this title, subject to the provisions of this section." 11 DCMR §335.1.

. . . Petitioners challenge . . . aspects of the BZA's conclusions as either not supported by the evidence or not adequately addressed or explained in the BZA's findings and conclusions. These . . . issues are . . . (2) the rate of abscondence from the Gateway facilities; (3) the impact of the proposed home on the neighborhood. . . .

Petitioners challenge the BZA's findings of fact Nos. 8 and 9 which state that the Gateway program will "prevent the youths from adversely impacting the surrounding neighborhood" and will "operate to prevent the impact that crime and other adverse neighborhood conditions will have on the residents of the facility." Specifically, petitioners question these findings in light of Gateway's 38% abscondence rate at its other facilities. However, Board member Bennett pointed out that "the testimony reflected the fact that when youth run, they try to get as far away from the facility as possible. . . . So while their abscondence probably is detrimental to the District of Columbia as a whole, it is not necessarily detrimental to that neighborhood. At least, the record does not reflect that." There was testimony that those youths who abscond "just take off" and, if caught, go back to court. No contrary evidence was presented and Gateway submitted numerous letters of support from people who live or work near their other facilities. In our review of the record, particularly Board Member Bennett's observation, we are persuaded that findings of fact Nos. 8 and 9 are sufficiently supported by the evidence.

Petitioners also assert error in the BZA's finding of fact No. 12 which stated that the "proposed use, combined with similar facilities in the area will not adversely affect the neighborhood." The BZA concluded that "while there may be a number of other facilities located in Ward 5, the Board is bound by the Zoning Regulations which allow facilities to be approved if they are not within 500 feet of each other or within the same square." Petitioners assert that by reaching this conclusion the BZA . . . ignored the evidence in the record. . . .

As Chairman Clarens correctly observed there is "no evidence [in the record] that this particular facility would have an actual adverse impact on the community." Clearly, the record reflects that the ANC and members of the community were very concerned that Ward 5C presently contains a disproportionate number of community-based residential facilities. There was evidence presented to the BZA that this subsection of the city already had 21 community-based residential facilities, seven other residential facilities primarily for homeless people and six facilities providing social services to homeless persons and drug abusers. Petitioners assert that the BZA simply ignored their concerns that the city was "dumping" all these facilities in one Ward subsection. Petitioners in support of this argument point to Hubbard v. District of Columbia Bd. of Zoning Adjustment, 366 A.2d 427 (D.C. 1976). There, this court, in dicta, commented that no one section of a community should have to bear a disproportionate share of the burden which community-based residential facilities and social service centers impose on local neighborhoods. . . .

Nevertheless, we are constrained to note that since our 1976 decision in *Hubbard*, new zoning regulations have been promulgated. These new regulations regarding rehabilitation and substance abusers' homes state that "[t]here shall be no other property containing a community-based residential facility for seven (7) or more persons within a radius of five hundred feet (500 ft.) from any portion of the subject property," 11 DCMR §335.3, and the "facility shall not have an adverse impact on the neighborhood because of traffic, noise, operations, or the number of similar facilities in the area." 11 DCMR §335.6.

We have stated that "'[s]pecial exceptions, unlike variances, are expressly provided for in the Zoning Regulations. The Board's discretion to grant special exceptions is limited to a determination whether the exception sought meets the requirements of the regulation.'" First Baptist Church v. District of Columbia Bd. of Zoning Adjustment, 432 A.2d 695, 701 (D.C. 1981) (quoting Stewart v. District of Columbia Bd. of Zoning Adjustment, 305 A.2d

516, 518 (D.C. 1973)). . . . Thus, we must agree with the BZA's conclusion that as long as the proposed facility did not have another facility within 500 feet and there was no adverse impact on the neighborhood the Board was bound to approve the exception requested by the applicant. In our view the regulations require the Board only to determine whether the "number of similar facilities in the area," in and of itself, has "an adverse impact on the neighborhood" rather than determine whether a section of the city bears "a disproportionate share" of such facilities. Petitioner's concerns regarding the "dumping" of community-based residential facilities in their ward is a concern for the Zoning Commission with its power to amend BZA regulations and the comprehensive plan rather than the BZA with its limited powers. . . .

. . . We affirm the BZA's decision [as to the grant of the special exception]. . . .

Note on Special Exceptions/Conditional Uses

1. *Function.* The role of these devices is explained in Zylka v. City of Crystal, 167 N.W.2d 45 (Minn. 1969):

> Provisions such as the one contained in defendant city's ordinance providing for special-use permits, sometimes called "special exception permits" or "conditional use permits," were introduced into zoning ordinances as flexibility devices. They are designed to meet the problem which arises where certain uses, although generally compatible with the basic use classification of a particular zone, should not be permitted to be located as a matter of right in every area included within the zone because of hazards inherent in the use itself or special problems which its proposed location may present. By this device, certain uses (e.g., gasoline service stations, electric substations, hospitals, schools, churches, country clubs, and the like) which may be considered essentially desirable to the community, but which should not be authorized generally in a particular zone because of considerations such as current and anticipated traffic congestion, population density, noise, effect on adjoining land values, or other considerations involving public health, safety, or general welfare, may be permitted upon a proposed site depending upon the facts and circumstances of the particular case. Unlike a variance provision which permits particular property to be used in a manner forbidden by the ordinance by varying the terms of the ordinance, a special-use provision permits property, within the discretion of the governing body, to be used in a manner expressly authorized by the ordinance. In theory, if not in practice, provisions authorizing the issuance of special-use permits are intended to provide more flexibility in land use control than provisions authorizing a variance. While the administering body, be it the council itself or a planning commission to which power to act is delegated, has broad discretionary power to deny an application for a special-use permit, it cannot do so arbitrarily.

Id. at 48–49.

2. *Differences between variances and special exceptions.* Neighbors' challenges to the grant of variances succeed more often than their challenges to the grant of special exceptions. Courts presume that variances should be granted rarely (see, e.g., Matthew v. Smith), but presume that special exceptions are too frequently denied. The opposing presumptions stem in part from the differences between the two devices that *Zylka* highlights. See Elliot Gardner, Student Note, To Defer or Not to Defer: Judicial Review of Zoning Board Decisions in New York, 2 Cardozo Pub. L. Pol'y & Ethics J. 421 (2004). They also arise because the courts understand that many of the land uses typically subject to special exceptions are "NIMBY" (not-in-my-back-yard) uses, which tend to arouse passionate resistance from neighbors. See Chapter 9B and 9C.

3. *Standards.* The courts' greater solicitude for applicants for special exceptions threatens to deprive local governments of discretion, and thus to take away their leverage to exact tribute from landowners. Many local governments make it difficult for an applicant to prove compliance with ordinance requirements, however, by adopting deliberately vague standards for the availability of special exceptions — often some variant of a "promote the general welfare" test. Ordinances of this type may be challenged as providing inadequate guidance to decisionmakers. Courts uniformly insist that if a legislative body delegates the power to grant or deny special exceptions to an administrative body, the legislature must provide standards to guide the administrative body's discretion. See, e.g., Dinsmore Development Co. v. Cherokee County, 398 S.E.2d 539 (Ga. 1990); Meszaros v. Planning Board, 852 A.2d 236 (N.J. Super. Ct. 2004). But most courts do not insist that the standards be very specific. Edward Kraemer & Sons v. Sauk County Board of Adjustment, 515 N.W.2d 256 (Wis. 1994), for example, upheld a requirement that the board consider whether the proposed special exception will "avoid harm to the public health, safety and welfare," reasoning:

> The purpose of the special exception-conditional use technique is to confer a degree of flexibility in the land use regulations. This would be lost if overly detailed standards covering each specific situation in which the use is to be granted . . . were required to be placed in the ordinance.

Id. at 261 (internal quotations omitted).

A few courts, however, demand more precision. Maine's highest court, for example, struck down a requirement that the proposed use be "compatible with existing uses in the neighborhood, with respect to physical size, visual impact, intensity of use, proximity to other structures and density of development." The court reasoned:

> . . . Absent specific standards giving content to the term "intensity of use," whether that term means "two persons per acre" or "twenty persons per acre," or something else entirely, is a matter of conjecture. Similarly, absent specific standards giving content to the term "density of development," whether that term signifies a ratio of built-upon acreage to unbuilt-upon acreage, or the number of structures on a particular lot, or something else entirely, is also a matter of conjecture. From the ordinance an applicant cannot even tell whether compatibility with his project's surroundings requires the same intensity of use and density of development, or less, or more. Such uncertainty is impermissible. . . .
>
> The lack of specific standards in the Yarmouth ordinance permits the Board to go beyond its proper quasi-judicial function. Rather than restricting itself to its narrow task of finding whether a proposed "special exception" use satisfies defined factual requirements, the Board can roam at large in policy-making. . . . The ordinance opens the door wide to favoritism and discrimination by permitting the Board to grant or deny special exceptions for reasons that are unconnected to the ordinance but that masquerade as quasi-judicial findings of fact.

Wakelin v. Town of Yarmouth, 523 A.2d 575 (Me. 1987). See also Kosalka v. Town of Georgetown, 752 A.2d 183, 187 (Me. 2000) (provision of special use permit ordinance that required developments to "conserve natural beauty" is "totally lacking in cognizable, quantitative standards"); Orlando E. Delogu & Susan E. Spokes, The Long-Standing Requirement That Delegations of Land Use Control Power Contain "Meaningful" Standards to Restrain and Guide Decision-Makers Should Not Be Weakened, 48 Me. L. Rev. 49 (1996). Who has the better of the argument?

Some state enabling acts allow the legislative body of a local government to retain the power to grant special permits. See, e.g., N.C. Gen. Stat. §160A-381(a) (2004). In those states, should courts require that standards guide the authority to issue special permits even when that authority is exercised by a legislative body? See, e.g., Cummings v. Town Board, 466 N.E.2d 147 (N.Y. 1984) (standard need not be specified).

4. *Supermajority requirements.* Some local governments have sought to impose super-majority requirements on the grant of a special exception. The courts have been unwilling to accept that tactic, holding that supermajority requirements must be specifically authorized by the zoning enabling act. See, e.g., Mossburg v. Montgomery County, 620 A.2d 886 (Md. 1993). Why might a local government want a supermajority requirement?

5. *Burdens of proof.* To account for the vagueness of many of the criteria for special exceptions, the courts of some states have held that the applicant for a special exception bears the burden of proof on the specific or "objective" requirements, but that once the applicant has met that burden, the burden then shifts to objectors to prove that the proposed use would "pose a substantial threat to the community" or violate other similarly general criteria. See, e.g., Visionquest National, Ltd. v. Board of Supervisors, 569 A.2d 915 (Pa. 1990).

Does that allocation of the burden of proof make sense? A dissenting judge in a Pennsylvania case overturning the denial of a special exception for a prerelease facility for state prisoners argued strenuously that shifting the burden of proof to objectors, and requiring that they present "studies, police records, property valuations" or other objective evidence to substantiate their fears about the impact of the facility, "guarantees that facilities like the prerelease center herein will never be placed in wealthy communities. This is so because the majority places a burden upon objectors . . . that none but the well-to-do could possibly afford." Commonwealth v. City of Pittsburgh, 532 A.2d 12, 16 (Pa. 1987) (Larsen, J., dissenting). See pp. 754–60 for further discussion of concerns that undesirable land uses are disproportionately placed in poorer neighborhoods.

6. *Baselines.* The Maryland courts have held that a decisionmaker determining whether a proposed special use would have an adverse impact on neighboring properties must evaluate whether the asserted adverse effects are "above and beyond those inherently associated with such a special exception use." Schultz v. Pritts, 432 A.2d 1319, 1327 (Md. 1981). *Schultz* reasoned that although a funeral home has an "inherent depressing and disturbing psychological effect" that may affect neighboring property values, the fact that the legislative body designated funeral homes as special exceptions indicates that the legislature determined that funeral homes should be allowed in the zone notwithstanding those effects. To deny a special exception on the basis of its inherent adverse effects, therefore, would be improper; instead, an exception should be denied only on proof that the proposed use would result in an adverse effect on neighboring properties "unique and different" from the inherently adverse effect that would result from the development of any funeral home in the zone. Did *Schultz* set the baseline correctly?

7. *Can every use be a conditional use?* Local officials are understandably attracted by the discretionary character of conditional use permits and can be expected to stretch their authority to be able to employ the device. The mechanism gives them considerable leverage over an applicant because approval can be made contingent on the applicant's meeting neighbors' objections and also contributing fees and improvements to local coffers.

Hardin County, Kentucky, provides an example of how far the conditional use permit technique can be stretched. In 1984, the county designated its entire unincorporated area as one zone. In that zone, agricultural and single-family residential uses were "uses-by-right," various uses such as flashing signs were designated "prohibited uses," and everything else was designated as a "conditional use." Under the scheme, applicants for conditional use permits first submitted their proposal to the planning commission for a "growth guidance assessment" in which points were awarded for criteria such as the project's proximity to previously developed areas and amenities. If the proposal scored 150 points, it then was submitted for a "compatibility assessment," in which the applicant, neighbors, and the planning commission staff met informally to discuss the proposal. If no consensus about the desirability of the project was reached in that informal meeting, the commission convened a public hearing. The Kentucky Court of Appeals invalidated the scheme, reasoning that it failed to give notice to property owners about what uses they could make of their property, it vested "absolute and arbitrary power" in the administrative agency, and it improperly allowed zoning decisions to be based solely on the complaints of neighbors. Hardin County v. Jost, 897 S.W.2d 592 (Ky. Ct. App. 1995).

Some courts, however, have allowed expansive use of conditional use permitting schemes. See, e.g., Gage v. Town of Egremont, 566 N.E.2d 597 (Mass. 1991) (upholding ordinance establishing one zoning district, in which single-family and two-family uses were allowed as of right, and all multifamily dwellings, retail businesses, and consumer-service establishments required special exceptions, but striking provision that authorized special exceptions for "any other use determined by the Planning Board and not offensive or detrimental to the neighborhood").

8. *Findings requirements.* Like the *Topanga* court in the variance context, see pp. 291–92, many courts confronting special exceptions have imposed a requirement that the agency deciding the application state on the record its reasons for granting the exception. See, e.g., Henry v. Jefferson County Planning Commission, 496 S.E.2d 239 (W. Va. 1997) (one-sentence order was not sufficient). In some cases, the courts have imposed the findings requirement even when the body granting the special exception was the local government's legislative body. See Earthburners, Inc. v. County of Carlton, 513 N.W.2d 460 (Minn. 1994).

9. *Equality principles.* Judicial review of both variances and special exceptions focuses primarily on whether the local government adhered to the standards set forth in the zoning ordinance or enabling act. Occasionally, however, an unsuccessful applicant (or the neighbors of successful applicants) raise equal protection claims, arguing that the denial of the zoning change was inconsistent with previous grants of similar applications (or that the grant was inconsistent with previous denials). As the cases discussed on pp. 125–33 revealed, those are hard claims to win. See, e.g., Board of Supervisors v. McDonald's Corp., 544 S.E.2d 334 (Va. 2001). But cf. Knight v. Amelkin, 503 N.E.2d 106 (N.Y. 1986) (requiring BZA to explain why its decision on the application varied from earlier determinations in factually similar cases).

10. *Conditional special exceptions?* Should a BZA be able to impose conditions on its grant of a special exception? That is a topic to which we'll turn shortly. In the meantime, see the remarkable example of The President & Directors of Georgetown College v. District of Columbia Board of Zoning Adjustment, 837 A.2d 58, 70 n.11, 77 (D.C. Ct. App. 2003) (BZA can impose conditions, but "a university — even a law school — is not to be presumed, for purposes of the Zoning Regulations, to be the land use equivalent of the bubonic plague," and conditions that "involve the Board in the details and mechanics of the University's enforcement of student discipline" are "far removed from the BZA's expertise and area of responsibility").

B.   Constraints on Zoning Changes by Legislative Bodies

As discussed at pp. 98–112, landowners and developers who challenge restrictive land use regulations under the Due Process Clause often are disappointed to find that courts review the reasonableness of legislation through a very deferential cost/benefit analysis.

Neighbors challenging rezonings and map amendments initially were confronted with similarly deferential judicial review. In Ferris v. City of Alhambra, 189 Cal. App. 2d 517 (Dist. Ct. App. 1961), for example, neighbors challenged the rezoning of a 30-acre parcel from single-family residential to commercial shopping center. Although a majority of neighboring property owners protested the rezoning, the city's planning commission did not recommend the rezoning, and the city's engineer raised questions about the suitability of the land for the shopping center, the appellate court overturned the trial court's decision favoring the neighbors, reasoning that "[i]f the matter is debatable, if reasonable minds may differ upon the question of whether the zoning is required by or consistent with the public welfare, the courts may not interfere." Id. at 524-25.

In response to concerns that rezonings are granted too frequently and for the wrong reasons, the courts and state legislatures gradually have developed doctrines to strengthen judicial review of rezonings. Those doctrines fall into two categories. In the first, courts continue to espouse traditional deference to legislative decisionmaking but temper that deference in cases presenting certain danger signals. Some courts scrutinize the costs and benefits of the rezoning more closely, for example, if the rezoning has the characteristics of "spot zoning." Others are skeptical of rezonings unless they are justified by a change in circumstances or discovery of a mistake in the original zoning. Some courts are reluctant to uphold rezonings that obviously result from a "contract" between the applicant and the local government, or that seem to be a quid pro quo for benefits the developer provided the local government. Finally, some courts are suspicious of rezonings that are inconsistent with the comprehensive plan. In many cases, these categories blur; inconsistency with the comprehensive plan is one element of the definition of spot zoning, for example, so those categories are sometimes hard to distinguish. The materials in the next subsection focus on these "tempered" deference doctrines.

The discussion then turns to the second category of cases, in which courts have rejected the view that all rezonings are legislative and therefore must be reviewed under a deferential standard. Both of the strategies for increasing judicial scrutiny of rezonings are based on a suspicion that, at least where certain "red flags" are raised, local government decisionmaking processes are insufficiently protective of neighbors' (and sometimes landowners') interests. The following introductory notes explore features of the rezoning process that may give rise to that suspicion.

Note on Dealmaking

The relaxation of an enforceable zoning restriction creates development rights that may be quite valuable. If a local government were to grant such a relaxation free of charge, the landowner would receive a "windfall" (would that always be a correct characterization?), and the local government would squander an opportunity to capture part of the value for its own benefit or, more precisely, for the benefit of whatever interest groups the local government's policies favor.

When a local government pursues an aboveboard "planning" approach to land use controls, it loses most of its leverage over persons who own lands in areas it has slated for unusually intensive development. If a comprehensive plan and accompanying zoning ordinance authorize such landowners to proceed with intensive development, those landowners, if later resisted by the local government, may be able to persuade a court to order the issuance of whatever minor permits the landowner needs. Local officials accordingly are naturally drawn to another approach, one that maintains their leverage over developers. The hallmark of the "dealmaking" strategy (as opposed to a "planning" strategy) is that most undeveloped lands are placed in holding zones that prohibit those lands from being developed into their most profitable (and efficient?) uses. When any such parcel of undeveloped land becomes ripe for development, its owner can be expected to come to city hall to try to strike a deal. To obtain a rezoning, the owner will agree to comply with conditions that will transfer some of the owner's financial gain from the rezoning to whomever local officials select to receive a share of those benefits.

There are four natural objects of a local government's affections. The winds of politics determine how these four fare in any given municipality. The first group might loosely be called the *community-at-large* (although in fact, this group is defined more accurately as the owners of already-developed land in the municipality). This group gains when local officials compel a would-be developer to pay cash exactions to the general treasury or to install an improvement of communitywide benefit, such as an off-site road.

Neighbors, the second group, are a subclass of the community-at-large. Their special interests are served when the deal struck between the local government and developer provides localized external benefits. Examples include conditions requiring the developer to install landscaped buffer strips or to provide a local playground readily accessible to neighbors.

Third, *local officials* may use their leverage to enrich themselves. When the developer kicks in part of the anticipated gain from a rezoning as an overt campaign contribution, this payment is still widely regarded as an allowable part of the rough-and-tumble of politics. If the payment (perhaps cash, perhaps a free remodeling) is made under the table, the parties on both sides will have engaged in some form of criminal bribery. See pp. 308–09 for further discussion of corruption in the land use process.

The fourth group of possible beneficiaries of dealmaking consists of both the *landowners* who succeed in obtaining rezonings and their agents (*zoning consultants*) who help them along the way. The rezoning process can be an avenue to a fast fortune. A winner's key steps are to: (1) pay $X for land situated in what appears to be a permanently restricted zone; (2) massage the rezoning process with key contributions and concessions, thereby obtaining an unexpected relaxation in the zoning; and (3) sell the rezoned land to a developer for $2X, $3X, or more. This scenario works only when the increment in land value produced by the rezoning is sufficient to cover the landowner's holding costs, administrative costs, and costs of meeting any requirements the local government imposes as a condition for the rezoning. A landowner who lacks the necessary political connections may have to share some of the gains with zoning consultants who will provide, for a fee, the requisite massaging.

Note on the Politics of the Rezoning Process

When do municipalities typically adhere to a planning strategy and when to a deal-making strategy? If a municipality uses a planning strategy, how do local officials weigh competing interests in formulating the plan? Are some groups more influential in that process than others, and if so, when and why? If a municipality uses the bargaining approach, under what circumstances will local officials tend to allocate the proceeds of their deals to the community-at-large, to neighbors, to landowners, or to themselves? To answer such questions, scholars must both provide theoretical models of how local officials behave and test those models through systematic empirical studies of rezoning practices. Unfortunately, less work has been done on both forms of research than is needed.

Several theoretical models may help to explain the politics of the rezoning process. As discussed at pp. 46–50, models of local government behavior often are divided into "public interest" and "public choice" models. Under the public interest model, local government officials deciding rezoning requests seek to promote either the most efficient allocation of resources or some other vision of the greater good. Under the public choice model, in contrast, legislators confronted with rezoning requests seek to maximize their chances of reelection, even if acceding to a campaign contributor's pleas for a rezoning will be inefficient or otherwise contrary to the public interest. See generally Daniel A. Farber & Philip P. Frickey, Law and Public Choice (1991).

The public choice model suggests that the politics of rezonings should differ depending on the size and homogeneity of the jurisdiction's populace and the number of issues the jurisdiction regularly decides. Under the model, a politician will vote for a proposed rezoning if the politician thinks that a majority of the voters would favor it. In a jurisdiction where the electorate is small and the issues are few, a politician can read the sentiment of the electorate, and the electorate can monitor and respond to a politician's stance on the issues. Politics therefore are likely to be "majoritarian": An interest group's influence over a rezoning decision is determined by that group's voting strength in general elections. See pp. 46–50; see also Robert C. Ellickson, Suburban Growth Controls: An Economic and Legal Analysis, 86 Yale L.J. 385, 404–05 (1977).

In most smaller suburban municipalities, people who own homes in the community constitute a substantial majority of the voters. Their interests in land use matters often coincide. Land use regulation is the primary function of local governments, so land use issues dominate local elections. The majoritarian model therefore predicts that:

> [D]evelopment in suburban areas takes place because existing residents — who are largely homeowners — either seek to have it (for fiscal reasons) or find it sufficiently harmless to their interest that they do not bother to object. . . . In most zoning cases, . . . the evidence is fairly strong that a relatively small group of neighboring homeowners can succeed in blocking rezonings.

William A. Fischel, The Economics of Zoning Laws 209 (1985). See also Richard F. Babcock, The Zoning Game: Municipal Practices and Policies 141 (1966); Richard F. Babcock & Charles L. Siemon, The Zoning Game Revisited 12 (1985).

Homeowners are interested in maximizing their own wealth and accordingly are likely to oppose rezoning requests that would increase their tax burdens, decrease the amenities (including community character) they have grown used to, or bring new housing to the community (because that housing will compete with their own homes in the sale and rental markets). See Ellickson, supra, at 394–401. Indeed, in The Homevoter Hypothesis (2001), excerpted at p. 46, William A. Fischel argues that local governments are likely to exercise more efficient control over land use than higher levels of government precisely because of "homevoters'" concern about the value of their homes. For an insightful critique of that argument, see Lee Anne Fennell, Homes Rule, 112 Yale L.J. 617 (2002) (book review).

In larger, more diverse jurisdictions where the issues are more numerous, however, the politician's calculus is more complicated. Because the politician is less likely to have a good sense of what the majority of the electorate thinks about a particular issue, the politician must rely more on organized interest groups to provide information about various constituencies. The relative abilities of interest groups to organize an effective lobbying effort therefore become quite important. At the same time, the politician must invest considerable effort, such as campaign advertising, to communicate to voters his or her position on the issues. An interest group's ability to contribute resources to the politician's efforts therefore also is important. Further, as the complexity of the government increases, the majority's view on any single issue is less likely to prevail because minority interest groups can "logroll" or trade votes on several different issues to form a majority coalition on the packaged issues. Thus, under an "influence" model of politics:

> [T]he strength of an interest group is purely a function of its ability to contribute money, manpower, or other political assets to election campaigns. The most powerful groups are those that can best organize to raise campaign contributions and those whose members have the greatest wealth.

Ellickson, supra, at 407. For accessible overviews of the literature on interest-group theory, see Farber & Frickey, supra; Einer R. Elhauge, Does Interest Group Theory Justify More Intrusive Judicial Review?, 101 Yale L.J. 31 (1991). A good collection of the most important works in the field is found in Dennis C. Mueller, Public Choice III (2003).

Real estate interests are major campaign contributors. See, e.g., Urban Fortunes: The Political Economy of Place 230–32 (John R. Logan & Harvey L. Molotch eds., 1987) (describing the role of real estate interests in elections in New York City, San Francisco, and Los Angeles). They are likely to be better organized, and therefore better able to communicate their interests (and the strength of their vote) to politicians than are existing homeowners, who are a larger, more diffuse group of people whose individual stake in each controversy may not be sufficiently large to overcome the costs of organizing. See generally Russell Hardin, Collective Action (1982); Mancur Olson, The Logic of Collective Action (2d ed. 1971). In addition to organizing advantages, pro-development forces are aided by the fact that politics in larger cities involve a wide range of issues, so that "[a] city councilman from a district whose residents oppose the proposed development may favor it (or not vigorously oppose it) because he expects other council members or the mayor to vote for an issue that is even more important to his constituents." Fischel, Economics, supra, at 214. The influence model of politics predicts, therefore, that at least in larger cities, development interests often will prevail over homeowner opposition to rezoning proposals (although the development interests may have to offer some concessions or compromise). See Ellickson, supra, at 407–08; Fischel, Economics, supra, at 214.

Another strand of the public choice model of local governments focuses on the ability of developers to "capture" the administrative and political rezoning processes through means other than campaign contributions. Many members of appointed planning commissions are involved in some aspect of real estate and therefore, by background and training, may be more sympathetic toward development interests than to neighbors' interests. Even those members who are not currently (or were not formerly) employed in the real estate industry may hope to become so employed on leaving the administrative body and therefore may be concerned about staying on the good side of developers. In addition, real estate interests tend to be repeat players before the commissions and legislative bodies; accordingly, they may develop personal relationships with members that may compromise the appointed or elected officials' ability to assess the worth of a particular proposal. See generally Richard A. Posner, Theories of Economic Regulation, 5 Bell J. Econ. & Mgmt. Sci. 335 (1974). For a sophisticated analysis, see Ian Ayres & John Braithwaite, Responsive Regulation 54–100 (1992).

Finally, the "growth machine" model of local government behavior predicts that governments will support developers' requests for rezoning if the proposed development will increase the city's net tax revenues (or decrease the city's outlays for infrastructure and public services). The growth machine model is based on the same assumptions about the self-interested nature of constituent and legislator behavior as the public choice model, but focuses particularly on the role that the quest for economic growth plays in local politics. See, e.g., Logan & Molotch, supra, at 50–98, 154–62; Paul E. Peterson, City Limits (1981).

Existing empirical evidence regarding rezonings is limited and does not directly test the various public choice and public interest models of local government. A study of rezoning requests filed in 51 different local governments in the Atlanta metropolitan area during 1984 concluded that because citizens testified or wrote in opposition to just 39.1 percent of all applications, "the image of rezoning as a highly charged political process controlled by public protest is misleading." Arnold Fleischmann, Politics, Administration, and Local Land-Use Regulation: Analyzing Zoning as a Policy Process, 49 Pub. Admin. Rev. 337, 342 (1989). The study found that citizen protest had a significant, but hardly dispositive effect: When there was no citizen objection to a proposal, only 6.9 percent were denied; when citizens did oppose the rezoning, 40.3 percent of the requests were denied outright, but 50.1 percent were approved either as submitted or, more often, with some type of compromise included in the approval. Id. at 340. See also Arnold Fleischmann & Carol A. Pierannunzi, Citizens, Development Interests, and Local Land Use Regulation, 52 J. Politics 838 (1990) (finding no relationship between presence of citizen opposition or applicant's status as a developer and the outcome of rezoning decisions). Cf. Judy B. Rosener, Making Bureaucrats Responsive: A Study of the Impact of Citizen Participation and Staff Recommendations on Regulatory Decision Making, 42 Pub. Admin. Rev. 339, 341–45 (1982) (analysis of 1,816 development permit applications for which hearings were held before 6 regional coastal commissions in California showed that citizens opposed the application in only 34 percent of the cases, that the denial rate in those cases was three times higher than in cases in which there was no opposition, but that 82 percent of all applications were granted, including 15 percent of the applications in which the staff had recommended denial).

Eric Steele's study of a sample of rezoning requests filed between 1948 and 1983 in Evanston, Illinois (a medium-sized, fully built-up, residentially oriented community) found much higher rates of citizen participation (in 66 percent of all cases). He also found citizen opposition to be a more important determinant of the advisory committee's disposition of the application: When there was no citizen support for or opposition to an application, 14 percent were recommended for denial; 38 percent were recommended for approval with modifications, and 48 percent were recommended for approval outright. When there was citizen opposition to the proposal and no citizen support, 69 percent of the applications were recommended for denial, 18 percent for approval with modifications, and only 14 percent for approval outright. Eric H. Steele, Participation and Rules — The Functions of Zoning, 1986 Am. B. Found. Res. J. 709.

These studies do not provide enough information about the characteristics of the jurisdictions studied to reveal whether differences in the extent and effectiveness of public participation correlate with the size and nature of the local governments studied. Further, although both the Fleischmann and the Steele studies show that compromises are common, without more information about those compromises it is hard to classify the outcomes as pro-homeowner or pro-development. If the compromise adequately addresses the neighbors' concerns, compromise would suggest that citizens are able to protect themselves against development interests. But if the benefits the government secures in the compromise fall short of compensating for the harms the development imposes, the prevalence of compromises might evidence pro-development politics.

How could one evaluate the compromises? Some studies have shown that cities get a tiny fraction of the value of the zoning change when negotiating compromises with developers. See, e.g., Bernard J. Frieden, Center City Transformed: Planners as Developers, 56 J. Am. Plan. Ass'n 423, 426 (1990) (reporting a study showing that New York City received public amenities worth approximately $5 million in exchange for zoning waivers worth $108 million to the developers). Does the low ratio of value extracted to value added indicate that neighbors' interests are insufficiently protected?

Background Note on Corruption

Underlying much of the judicial suspicion of local governments is concern about the seamier side of public land use processes. In many communities, the reality of zoning administration contrasts sharply with the idealistic expectations harbored by the early proponents of zoning and still harbored by many recent graduates of law and planning schools.

The land use control system has long been tainted with discoveries and allegations of corruption. One author, who has surveyed corrupt practices in several contexts, asserts that land use control is the government activity "most closely associated with corruption in the public's mind." George Amick, The American Way of Graft 77 (1976). See also John A. Gardiner & Theodore R. Lyman, Decisions for Sale: Corruption and Reform in Land-Use and Building Regulation (1978) (reporting instances of corruption in six states and proposing reforms). Although some of those images stem from the days of Tammany Hall, they retain current vitality. See, e.g., Brenda Moore, FBI's Operation Rezone Nabs Seven Californians, Planning, Oct. 1995, at 20 (FBI sting operation results in charges that at least 7 and possibly as many as 20 political and development figures in Fresno County traded money for favorable land use votes); J. Jioni Palmer & Ann Givens, Brookhaven Plea, Newsday, Apr. 16, 2004, at A2 (zoning board member admits to demanding and receiving $2,000 per lot for voting to approve a builder's subdivision plans).

The seeds of zoning corruption are obvious. On one side of the deal is a landowner who realizes that a rezoning can increase the value of land twentyfold. The temptation to approach a decisionmaker with a bribe therefore may prove irresistible. On the other side are local zoning officials who are asked repeatedly to make decisions that transfer large amounts of wealth. Their jobs lack glamour and usually are quite poorly compensated. As Sanford Halberstadter, an Elizabeth, New Jersey, lawyer observes, "You get a man sitting night after night on long planning board hearings without salary, and even if he is a good person he's got to feel that he is doing more than his share and should get something for it." Amick, supra, at 169. It takes little imagination for a public official to perceive that it would be possible to persuade the beneficiaries of governmental actions to kick back part of their gains as a "tip" for services the official rendered. In multilevel review procedures, there are many such officials, increasing the opportunities for corruption. Because time is money, developers have incentives to use "tips" not only to influence the outcome of the decision, but also to move the proposal to the top of a decisionmaker's priority list.

Compounding the problem is the fact that corruption is relatively easy to hide. In many jurisdictions, rezonings take place in processes marked by informality: hearings are not transcribed and decisions are issued without findings of fact or statements of reasons. The standards by which rezoning applications are to be evaluated are ambiguous. Officials on administrative boards and elected legislators range from citizen volunteers with no training or expertise in administration or land use, to persons chosen more for their political connections than for their expertise or wisdom, to professionals. Whether a decisionmaker is voting according to conscience, in over his or her head, or corrupt therefore is far from obvious. Those features of the zoning process also make it difficult for the media and "good government" groups to detect corruption. Further, judicial review is unlikely to uncover evidence of corruption because in many jurisdictions the state of the record, the open-ended nature of the decisionmaking criteria, and the "fairly debatable" standard of review all hamper a court's ability to discern the arbitrariness that might signal corruption. See generally, U.S. Department of Justice, Law Enforcement Assistance Administration, National Institute of Law Enforcement and Criminal Justice, Program for the Study of Corruption in Local Government, An Analysis of Zoning Reforms: Minimizing the Incentive for Corruption (1979).

As you study the next few sections, which chronicle the efforts of judges and state legislatures striving to strike the right balance between oversight and deference to local government land use decisions, consider how that struggle is affected by the perception that corruption plagues land use systems. Consider also whether corruption has any virtues. If a rezoning will result in a great increase in land value, that may be evidence that the newly permitted use has been excessively suppressed in the past. If so, consumers of that use would stand to gain from the rezoning. Would the successful suppression of zoning graft have the unfortunate side effect of obscuring economic signals that regulations are too restrictive or cumbersome? See Andrei Shleifer & Robert W. Vishny, Corruption, 108 Q.J. Econ. 599, 600 (1993). See generally Peter De Leon, Thinking About Political Corruption 25–46 (1993) (exploring whether corruption may serve a useful social function by allowing people to get around imperfections in organizational rules and structures).

1. Tempered Deference

a. Spot Zoning

Griswold v. City of Homer
925 P.2d 1015 (Alaska 1996)

EASTAUGH, Justice. . . .
In 1992 the Homer City Council adopted Ordinance 92-18 amending Homer's zoning and planning code to allow motor vehicle sales and services on thirteen lots in Homer's Central Business District. Frank Griswold claims Ordinance 92-18 is invalid because it constitutes spot zoning. . . .

The City adopted a comprehensive land use plan in 1983 and revised it in 1989. The City Council enacted zoning ordinances to implement the plans. Motor vehicle sales and services were not a permissible use within the Central Business District (CBD). Several businesses provided automobile services in the CBD before the City adopted the zoning ordinances. Those businesses were "grandfathered" into the zoning district and allowed to continue to provide those services as nonconforming uses. . . . [Figure 4-1 on p. 310 reproduces the zoning map for Homer, Alaska.]

Guy Rosi Sr. owns a parcel (Lot 13) in the CBD . . . [on which he] has continuously operated an automobile repair service. . . . His repair business remains a valid nonconforming use in the CBD. Rosi Sr. also operated an automobile dealership on Lot 13 until sometime prior to 1990, but lost the right to continue that nonconforming use on that lot by discontinuing the vehicle sales business for more than one year.

Guy Rosi Jr. owns Lot 12, which is adjacent to his father's lot. . . . [In 1986, Lot 12 was rezoned to General Commercial 1 (GC1), allowing its use for vehicle sales.]

. . . In September 1990 Rosi Sr. requested that the CBD be rezoned to allow vehicle sales and related services. In August 1991 Rosi Sr., stating that he had not received any response to his earlier request, asked that Lot 13 be rezoned to allow vehicle sales and related services. . . .

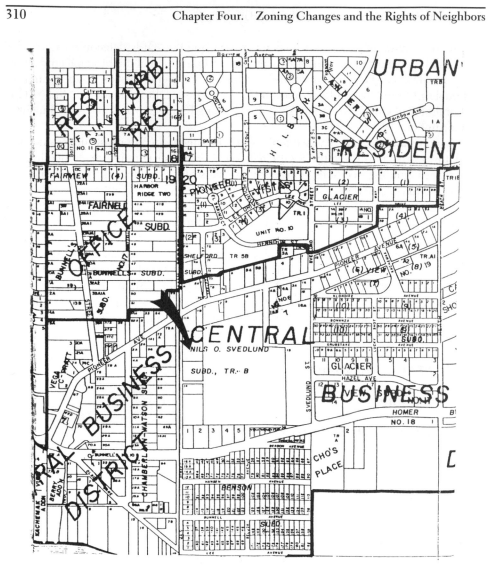

Note: The arrow indicates Lot 13, the parcel owned by Guy Rosi Sr.
Source: Homer, Alaska, Planning and Zoning Department.

FIGURE 4-1
Zoning Map for Homer, Alaska

In January 1992 a commission memorandum informed the City Manager that the commission had been wrestling with several possible amendments to the zoning code since 1990, and that "[c]entral to the issue is the Commission's desire to rezone the Guy Rosi property to allow for vehicle sales." The commission noted that a proposed ordinance would allow automobile-related services in the CBD only on Main Street from Pioneer Avenue to the Homer Bypass, excluding corner lots with frontage on Pioneer Avenue and the Homer Bypass Road. However, the commission staff recommended that the council pass an ordinance which would allow automobile-related services "everywhere in the Central Business District or nowhere." The memo stated that the City Attorney felt the proposed ordinance would be difficult to enforce and defend.

In April the City Council adopted Ordinance 92-18, which amended HCC 21.48.020 by adding the following section:

> *hh.* Automobile and vehicle repair, vehicle maintenance, public garage, and motor vehicle sales, showrooms and sales lots, but only on Main Street from Pioneer Avenue to the Homer Bypass Road, excluding corner lots with frontage on Pioneer Avenue or the Homer Bypass Road, be allowed as a permitted use. . . .

Frank Griswold, the plaintiff in this case, owns an automobile repair shop in the CBD. Its operation was grandfathered in under the zoning code. He also lives in the CBD. . . . Griswold brought suit against the City, alleging under several theories that Ordinance 92-18 is an invalid exercise of the City's zoning power. . . . Following a bench trial, the superior court found against Griswold on all issues. It later ordered him to pay a portion of the City's court costs and attorney's fees. Griswold appeals.

III. DISCUSSION

We have repeatedly held that it is the role of elected representatives rather than the courts to decide whether a particular statute or ordinance is a wise one. . . . In Concerned Citizens of S. Kenai Peninsula v. Kenai Peninsula Borough, 527 P.2d 447, 452 (Alaska 1974), we stated:

> A court's inquiry into arbitrariness begins with the presumption that the action of the legislature is proper. The party claiming a denial of substantive due process has the burden of demonstrating that no rational basis for the challenged legislation exists. This burden is a heavy one, for if any conceivable legitimate public policy for the enactment is apparent on its face or is offered by those defending the enactment, the opponents of the measure must disprove the factual basis for such a justification.

(Footnote omitted.) . . .

However, we will invalidate zoning decisions which are the result of prejudice, arbitrary decision-making, or improper motives. . . . Similarly, a legislative body's zoning decision violates substantive due process if it has no reasonable relationship to a legitimate government purpose. . . . [4] In this case, Griswold argues that the City's Ordinance does not have a legitimate basis but rather is arbitrary spot zoning. . . .

A. CLAIM OF SPOT ZONING

The "classic" definition of spot zoning is "the process of singling out a small parcel of land for a use classification totally different from that of the surrounding area, for the benefit of the owner of such property and to the detriment of other owners. . . . " [1 Robert M.] Anderson, [American Law of Zoning] §5.12, at 359 [(1986)]. Spot zoning "is the very antithesis of planned zoning." Id. . . . Professor Ziegler states:

> Faced with an allegation of spot zoning, courts determine first whether the rezoning is compatible with the comprehensive plan or, where no plan exists, with surrounding uses. Courts then examine the degree of public benefit gained and the characteristics of land, including parcel

---

4. We have held that, although a planning commission is not required to make specific findings supporting its decisions, it must articulate reasons for its decisions sufficient to assist the parties preparing for review and to restrain agencies within the bounds of their jurisdiction. South Anchorage Concerned Coalition v. Coffey, 862 P.2d 168, 175 (Alaska 1993).

size and other factors indicating that any reclassification should have embraced a larger area containing the subject parcel rather than that parcel alone. No one particular characteristic associated with spot zoning, except a failure to comply with at least the spirit of a comprehensive plan, is necessarily fatal to the amendment. Spot zoning analysis depends primarily on the facts and circumstances of the particular case. Therefore the criteria are flexible and provide guidelines for judicial balancing of interests.

Depends on all the circumstances

3 Edward H. Ziegler Jr., Rathkopf's The Law of Zoning and Planning §28.01, at 28-3 (4th ed. 1995). . . .

1. Consistency with the comprehensive plan . . .

Homer's comprehensive plan . . . states, "The City shall encourage a mix of business/commercial and public/governmental activities in areas zoned or planned as central business district." The plan states that the CBD is "intended primarily for retail sales and services occurring within enclosed structures." The plan's objectives for the CBD are (1) to guide growth and development to provide a centrally located business and commercial area and focal point for the community; (2) to encourage infilling of the area already designated CBD before expanding the area; (3) to promote a safe, attractive, and easily accessible business and commercial core for pedestrian and vehicular visitors and residents; (4) to attract and accommodate a variety of uses to fill the business and commercial needs of downtown Homer; and (5) to tie into state and federal programs that beautify the business and commercial core.

Griswold . . . notes however, that . . . the planning commission previously denied a conditional use permit for auto-related services on Main Street, specifically finding, inter alia, that automobile sales were not consistent with the purpose of the CBD and were not in harmony with the comprehensive plan. He also notes that the comprehensive plan provides that the CBD was meant primarily for retail sales and services occurring within enclosed structures. Further, the fact that the City began phasing out auto-related services in the CBD when it adopted the comprehensive plan, while simultaneously specifically permitting these services in the General Commercial I District, indicates to Griswold that auto-related sales and services were, at least at one time, considered incompatible with the CBD.

trial ct: The superior court concluded that the Ordinance was consistent with the comprehensive plan. In so concluding, it considered the policy statement implementing the Ordinance, and found that the Ordinance "encourages private investment and infilling" and "enhances convenient access to other parts of the CBD which are designated for other uses." . . .

Griswold points to trial evidence that the expansion of auto-related services in the CBD does not further all the goals of the comprehensive plan, but he fails to demonstrate that the superior court's finding — that the Ordinance is consistent with the plan — is clearly erroneous. . . . [The] evidence does not compel a finding that auto-related uses are in fact incompatible with the CBD or comprehensive plan, or that the City Council's 1992 change of opinion is unsupportable and arbitrary. . . .

2. Effect of small-parcel zoning on owner and community

Perhaps the most important factor in determining whether a small-parcel zoning amendment will be upheld is whether the amendment provides a benefit to the public, rather than primarily a benefit to a private owner. Courts generally do not assume that a zoning amendment is primarily for the benefit of a landowner merely because the amendment was adopted at the request of the landowner. If the owner's benefit is merely incidental to the general community's benefit, the amendment will be upheld. The City argues that Ordinance 92-18 serves the interests of the general community rather than primarily the interests of the Rosis. We agree.

a. *Benefits and detriments to the community*

Griswold . . . presented evidence that a newspaper article quoted Planning Commissioner Cushing as saying that public opinion was overwhelmingly against allowing auto-related services in the CBD and that many Homer citizens expressed the opinion that their homes and businesses would be harmed by introducing auto-related services into the area. A real estate agent testified that property in the CBD has a higher value than property in the GC1 District. . . .

However, despite this negative aspect of Ordinance 92-18, it appears that the Ordinance will result in genuine benefits for the City of Homer. The City notes that before adopting Ordinance 92-18, for a year and a half it deliberated proposals which would allow auto-related uses in the CBD and delineated the many benefits which it believed the Ordinance will confer upon the community. These benefits include encouraging filling in vacant places in the CBD; increasing the tax base and employment in the CBD;[9] increasing convenience and accessibility for local and regional customers for vehicle repairs or purchases; and promoting orderly growth and development in the CBD. Homer's city planner testified that the Ordinance provides a convenience to the public and guides growth and development to a centrally located area, while restricting such uses to areas away from tourists or to areas for visitors and pedestrians.

The superior court stated that Ordinance 92-18 advances legitimate legislative goals articulated in HCC 21.28.020 including but not limited to regulating and limiting the density of populations; conserving and stabilizing the value of properties; providing adequate open spaces for light and air; preventing undue concentration of population; lessening congestion on streets and highways; and promoting health, safety and general welfare. The court found "as a matter of fact and law that Ordinance No. 92-18 bears a substantial relationship between legitimate legislative goals and the means chosen to achieve those goals."

Griswold has demonstrated that there are some negative aspects of allowing auto-related uses in the CBD. Nonetheless, giving proper deference to the City Council as legislative policymaker and to the superior court as finder of fact, we cannot conclude

---

9. Not all of the goals articulated by the City can be considered legitimate per se. For example, any zoning change which eases restrictions on property use could be said to further the goal of "filling in vacant places." Similarly, increasing the tax base and the employment of a community is not automatically a legitimate zoning goal. See Concerned Citizens for McHenry, Inc. v. City of McHenry, 395 N.E.2d 944, 950 (Ill. 1979) (an increase in the tax base of the community as the primary justification for a rezone is "totally violative of all the basic principles of zoning"). . . . Thus, the goal of increasing the tax base and employment opportunities is usually legitimate only if the ordinance is otherwise reasonable and in accordance with the comprehensive plan.

Some courts have allowed inconsistent small or single parcel rezoning in order to raise tax revenues or stimulate needed industry if the public receives higher tax revenue or employment industries. Generally, the facility being built must be indisputably needed, and the city must have secured assurance as to the existence and amount of increased employment and tax revenue. For example, in Information Please Inc. v. County Comm'rs of Morgan County, 600 P.2d 86 (Colo. Ct. App. 1979), the county rezoned agricultural area to industrial to accommodate an electric utility after determining the plant would add $46,000,000 to the tax base of the county, and provide approximately 250 jobs after it was completed. Id. at 88. . . .

that these detriments so outweigh the benefits of Ordinance 92-18 that we must hold the Ordinance was arbitrarily and capriciously adopted.

b. *Benefit to the landowner*

It appears that initially the City was primarily concerned with Rosi Sr.'s interests. Rosi Sr. initiated the inquiry into rezoning the CBD. Before the City amended the zoning code, the planning commission chair stated that "[c]entral to the issue is the Commission's desire to rezone the Guy Rosi property to allow for vehicle sales." In 1991 commissioners "voiced their dislike for spot zoning but felt it important to right a wrong [done to Mr. Rosi]." The City planning staff stated that "'spot zoning' is not good planning; however there are extenuating circumstances that support the proposed change in zone." The commission supported these conclusions with the following findings of fact: (1) the property owner had owned and operated a business on the property since the early 1950's; (2) public testimony and response to staff were positive; (3) the City Attorney's response was positive; and (4) the business was an expensive business to establish and maintain. This desire to accommodate the needs of a businessman who had been in the community for decades is understandable. Nevertheless, small-parcel zoning designed merely to benefit one owner constitutes unwarranted discrimination and arbitrary decision-making, unless the ordinance amendment is designed to achieve the statutory objectives of the City's own zoning scheme, even where the purpose of the change is to bring a nonconforming use into conformance or allow it to expand. Otherwise, the City would be forced either to discriminate arbitrarily among landowners seeking relaxed restrictions or to abandon the concept of planned zoning altogether. Thus, if assisting Guy Rosi Sr. was the primary purpose of the Ordinance, we would invalidate it even if it was not the product of discriminatory animus.

However, it appears that the City Council was ultimately motivated to pass the Ordinance because of the community benefits the council perceived rather than because of the benefit the Ordinance would confer upon Rosi Sr. The Ordinance restricted auto-related uses to one street not because its real intent was to benefit Rosi Sr.'s property, but, as Homer's city planner testified, because the City desired to minimize the negative impact of auto-related uses, especially the impact of such uses on more pedestrian and tourist-oriented areas such as Pioneer Avenue. . . . Similarly, it appears that vacant lots located farther from Pioneer Avenue were excluded not because Rosi did not own these lots, but in an attempt to prevent urban sprawl by filling in vacant places in developed areas before expanding development. These reasons are legitimate, nondiscriminatory justifications for enacting the Ordinance.

3. Size of "rezoned" area

Ordinance 92-18 directly affects 7.29 acres. The size of the area reclassified has been called "more significant [than all other factors] in determining the presence of spot zoning." Anderson, supra, §5.15, at 378. The rationale for that statement is that "[i]t is inherently difficult to relate a reclassification of a single lot to the comprehensive plan; it is less troublesome to demonstrate that a change which affects a larger area is in accordance with a plan to control development for the benefit of all." Id. at 379.

We believe that . . . the size of the area rezoned should not be considered more significant than other factors in determining whether spot zoning has occurred. A parcel cannot be too large per se to preclude a finding of spot zoning, nor can it be so small that it mandates a finding of spot zoning occurred. Although Anderson notes that reclassifications of parcels under three acres are nearly always found invalid, while reclassifications of parcels over thirteen acres are nearly always found valid, id., as Ziegler notes, the relative size of the parcel is invariably considered by courts. Ziegler, supra, §28.04, at 28-14. One court found spot zoning where the reclassified parcel was 635 acres in an affected area of 7,680 acres. Chrobuck v. Snohomish County, 480 P.2d 489, 497 (Wash. 1971).

Nor does the reclassification of more than one parcel negate the possibility of finding spot zoning. In this case, there was some evidence that the reclassified area may have been expanded to avoid a charge of spot zoning. Other courts have invalidated zoning amendments after finding that a multiple-parcel reclassification was a subterfuge to obscure the actual purpose of special treatment for a particular landowner. See Atherton v. Selectmen of Bourne, 149 N.E.2d 232, 235 (Mass. 1958) (holding that the amendment is "no less 'spot zoning' by the inclusion of the additional six lots than it would be without them" where proponents of a zoning change apparently anticipated a charge of spot zoning and enlarged the area to include the three lots on either side of the lot in question).

Homer's CBD is over 400 acres; the reclassified area is 7.29 acres. The CBD appears to contain approximately 500 lots; the reclassified area contains 13 lots. A comparison of the size of the area rezoned and the size of the entire CBD is not in itself sufficient to persuade us that the City's decision was the product of prejudice, arbitrary decision-making, or improper motives. . . .

We hold that Ordinance 92-18 does not constitute spot zoning, and consequently affirm that aspect of the judgment below. . . .

RABINOWITZ, Justice, dissenting in part. . . .

Note on Spot Zoning

1. *Conclusion or trigger?* In *Griswold*, the court engaged in a relatively searching cost/benefit analysis to determine whether the challenged rezoning was spot zoning, believing that if the cost/benefit analysis, along with consideration of the size of the parcel and the rezoning's relationship to the comprehensive plan, resulted in a conclusion that the rezoning was spot zoning, it therefore would be illegal. Some courts separate the inquiry into two steps. They look first at whether such factors as the size of the parcel or the rezoning's inconsistency with the comprehensive plan signal that spot zoning has occurred. If it has, the courts then engage in a cost/benefit analysis to determine whether the spot zoning is justified. In those courts, spot zoning is not necessarily illegal, but simply serves to trigger a more searching review of the asserted justifications for the rezoning. Most recent decisions adopt the latter view. See, e.g., Save Sunset Beach Coalition v. City & County of Honolulu, 78 P.3d 1, 9 (Haw. 2003).

2. *Other factors that may betray the presence of spot zoning.* In addition to the factors the *Griswold* court took into account, courts typically look at the following in reviewing allegations of spot zoning.

a. *"Spots" versus "slops."* Note that in *Griswold*, the rezone allowed Rosi Sr. to establish the same use that was allowed on his son's adjacent parcel. (Rosi Jr.'s property had been rezoned for car sales through a "contract zone," which is addressed at pp. 318–29.) Courts often find spot zoning in situations where the newly implanted zone is entirely surrounded by other zones, but are less likely to find spot zoning when the rezoning has "slopped over" by extending the perimeter of an existing zone to include the rezoned area. See, e.g., Sharp v. Zoning Hearing Board, 628 A.2d 1223 (Pa. Commw. Ct. 1993) (expansion of planned institutional zone to accommodate Villanova University's need for additional dormitories was not spot zoning).

b. *Neighborhood character.* A related consideration is whether the lands surrounding the rezoned area are devoted to uses compatible with the new uses the rezoning would permit. Courts are more likely to invoke spot-zoning doctrines to protect stable residential areas than to protect areas characterized by mixed uses, or areas in transition. Might that result in underprotection of those neighborhoods that most need stability? Should it matter if the uses compatible with the rezoning are allowed in the area only as nonconforming uses? Recall the court's determination in Twigg v. County of Will, 627 N.E.2d 742 (Ill. App. Ct. 1994), excerpted at p. 104, that the existence of compatible, albeit nonconforming, uses in the surrounding area suggested that a refusal to rezone was unconstitutional.

c. *Motive.* As *Griswold's* discussion of the city's solicitude for "the needs of a business-man who had been in the community for decades" illustrates, courts look hard at whether the rezoning was solely, or even primarily, motivated by a desire to benefit a particular individual rather than the public at large. How does that compare with the motive inquiry used in the suppression of competition cases studied at pp. 112–17? If the rezoning brings net benefits to the community, why should it matter if the primary motive was to benefit the landowner? Should the court also consider the motives of those opposing the rezoning (in *Griswold*, a competitor able to satisfy standing requirements because he also resided in the area)?

d. *Procedural irregularities.* Courts are suspicious of rezonings that result from expe-dited or otherwise irregular procedures. See, e.g., Baker v. Chartiers Township Zoning Hearing Board, 677 A.2d 1274, 1278 (Pa. Commw. Ct. 1996) (finding spot zoning where failure to follow normal procedures for comparing the proposed rezoning to the compre-hensive plan indicated that "the deliberation process was expedited to the detriment of the public interest"). Although the *Griswold* court apparently did not focus on the fact that the rezoning went against the advice of the commission staff and the city attorney, many courts look on such situations with suspicion.

3. *Constitutional or statutory basis?* Like *Griswold*, many courts view the rule against spot zoning as simply the familiar substantive due process requirement that rezonings be rationally related to a legitimate state interest. Others seem to view the rule as a check on discrimination, grounded in equal protection principles. See, e.g., Rando v. Town of North Attleborough, 692 N.E.2d 544 (Mass. App. Ct. 1998). Some state courts rest the rule on the grounds that the rezoning does not serve any of the permissible statutory purposes for the exercise of zoning power. See, e.g., Clark v. City of Boulder, 362 P.2d 160 (Colo. 1961).

4. *An unhelpful term?* Consider the conclusion of Osborne M. Reynolds, Jr., "Spot Zoning" — A Spot That Could Be Removed from the Law, 48 Wash. U. J. Urb. & Contemp. L. 117, 135–37 (1995):

> The term "spot zoning," . . . [a]t best, . . . [is] but a description of a process of singling-out a particular piece of property for treatment that differs from that accorded neighboring properties. If and when courts declare such zoning invalid, they must base this declaration on one or more of . . . [three] grounds: lack of connection to a police power purpose, lack of conformity to a comprehensive plan, or unreasonable inequality in treatment of similarly situated lands. . . .
>
> The public and the immediately involved landowners are entitled to know the specific grounds for the invalidation. Use of the term "spot zoning" only clouds the question, for the term covers a number of grounds and lacks precision. . . . In order to serve the public welfare, the zoning law must reasonably relate to a police power purpose, must be enacted in furtherance of a comprehensive plan, and must be applied without unreasonable discrimination. . . . If the zoning does not meet one of these requirements, the courts should set forth the requirement and note the ways in which the law fails to meet it. Only then can the local legislature possibly correct the deficiency, or at least avoid the pitfall in the future. Only then can the affected landowners know the scope of their protection against government restriction. "Spot zoning"

as a legal term adds nothing to the analysis and courts should remove the black spot from the law.

Does the term have any redeeming value?

5. *Down- versus upzoning.* Although the spot-zoning doctrine originally was formulated to address rezonings to less restrictive districts that allowed the landowner to develop the land more intensively (upzonings), it now often is applied to rezonings that move the property into more restrictive districts (downzonings), against the owner's wishes, or to so-called reverse spot zoning in which the property surrounding a tract is rezoned for more intense use, but the local government refuses to extend that rezoning to the tract in controversy. See, e.g., In re Realen Valley Forge Greenes Associates, 838 A.2d 718 (Pa. 2003) (refusals to rezone the tract next to one of the nation's largest shopping malls from restrictive agricultural zoning to secure the property as "green space" was unlawful "reverse spot zoning").

b.   *Absence of a "Change or Mistake"*

Courts in Maryland have adopted a rule that a local governing body may adopt a piecemeal zoning-map amendment only when there has been substantial change in the character of the neighborhood where the rezoned property is located, or when there was a mistake in the prior zoning classification. Wakefield v. Kraft, 96 A.2d 27 (Md. 1953). In 1970, the Maryland legislature incorporated the rule into the zoning enabling act. See Md. Ann. Code art. 66B, §4.05 (2004). The burden is on the supporters of the rezoning to introduce evidence of neighborhood change or original mistake, and a Maryland court will bow to the decision to rezone if the evidence is fairly debatable.

The rule does not apply to "comprehensive" rezonings, which are judged by the usual (more lenient) substantive due process test. See, e.g., People's Counsel for Baltimore County v. Beachwood 1 Ltd. Partnership, 670 A.2d 484 (Md. Ct. Spec. App. 1995) (rezoning of 148-acre parcel pursuant to a comprehensive rezoning not subject to change or mistake rule). Accordingly, although both neighbors and landowners can invoke the change or mistake rule, landowners challenging rezonings that place land in more restrictive categories often are denied the benefit of the doctrine on the ground that the rezoning is comprehensive.

The change or mistake rule substantially extends the rule prohibiting spot zoning and severely limits the possibility of small zoning changes. Consider the following criticism of the rule:

> The Maryland "change-or-mistake" rule is a clear example of a legal doctrine based upon a misunderstanding of the nature of the planning process. . . . In the nature of planning, several situations arise where a "piecemeal" change of zoning is appropriate. . . . The first involves simply a change of policy: a municipality may decide that greater emphasis should be given to housing for its aged, or that a discount store (or one more supermarket) would be handy, and may thus rezone a tract or two for this purpose. If these are new problems, the rezoning can perhaps be justified under "change"; but if they are longstanding problems, . . . it is a little absurd that this should militate against the use of zoning to take care of them. . . . Second, a similar change of policy . . . may be justified not by any change of conditions, but by a more complete understanding of long-established conditions and trends — for example, by a realization that there are new zoning techniques which may encourage better design, or provide a better transition between residential and commercial areas. Or the forecasts upon which a

plan was based may not have come true. Third, . . . [a comprehensive plan] will normally provide for changes in land use in the future — for example, a priority order for the sequence of development on vacant land in the outer areas, and redevelopment of an industrial slum for residential use in the future. In this instance the future master plan designation and the interim zoning will be different, and the zoning will be changed to conform when the time comes for development. Finally, in the normal situation the first zoning ordinance is a rather weak and inadequate thing, with substantial overzoning for commercial; once people get used to the idea, a more effective ordinance can often be passed easily. The really effective (and realistic) zoning thus often comes by rezoning. In this latter instance a comprehensive rezoning would clearly be better, but may be politically impractical in some instances; it would be a harsh rule to prevent any other upgrading. . . .

1 Norman Williams, Jr. & John M. Taylor, Williams American Land Planning Law §32.01 (1988). See also Chapman v. Montgomery County Council, 271 A.2d 156, 161 (Md. 1970) (Barnes, J., dissenting).

The change or mistake rule has been explicitly rejected in some states. See, e.g., Lum Yip Kee, Ltd. v. City of Honolulu, 767 P.2d 815 (Haw. 1989); Neuzil v. City of Iowa City, 451 N.W.2d 159 (Iowa 1990); Palermo Land Co. v. Planning Commission, 561 So. 2d 482 (La. 1990). Nevertheless, several other states have adopted the rule, either for all rezonings or for those rezonings that are not in accord with a comprehensive plan. See, e.g., King's Mill Homeowners Association v. City of Westminster, 557 P.2d 1186 (Colo. 1976) (en banc); Board of Aldermen v. Conerly, 509 So. 2d 877 (Miss. 1987); Davis v. City of Albuquerque, 648 P.2d 777 (N.M. 1982); Seabrooke Partners v. City of Chesapeake, 393 S.E.2d 191 (Va. 1990); Parkridge v. City of Seattle, 573 P.2d 359 (Wash. 1978). See also Ky. Rev. Stat. Ann. §100.213 (2004). See generally Barlow Burke, Jr., The Change-Mistake Rule and Zoning in Maryland, 25 Am. U. L. Rev. 631 (1976) (defending rule and discussing its influence in other states).

c.   *"Contract" Zoning*

Judith Welch Wegner, Moving Toward the Bargaining Table: Contract Zoning, Development Agreements, and the Theoretical Foundations of Government Land Use Deals
65 N.C. L. Rev. 957, 977–78 (1987)

A variety of techniques have been developed in recent years in response to local governments' perceived need to tailor land use requirements more closely to the circumstances and characteristics of particular parcels and affected areas. The need for such individualization is particularly great in the context of rezoning petitions that request zoning-map amendments. Rezoning decisions are a chronic source of litigation, because deeply held expectations of neighborhood stability are often at war with deep-seated desires for handsome profits, against a backdrop of uncertain jurisprudence and unpredictable judicial dispositions. Carefully constructed compromises that focus on the legitimate concerns of residents, developers, and local governments offer an appealing alternative.

Such compromises may take several forms and may be implemented in several different ways. Often it may be desirable to limit the types of use that may be made of particular property, notwithstanding the wider range of uses otherwise permissible in a given district: for example, residential neighbors may find a rezoning to commercial use more palatable if only certain types of uses are allowed. Other requirements might mitigate adverse environmental effects, by, for example, restricting building placement or specifying that a property owner utilize buffering and landscaping. Alternatively, adverse effects on community structure might be addressed by specifying that a property owner dedicate land, undertake construction, or contribute funds for road improvements or for other purposes. These and other compromises might be incorporated in express or implied agreements between a developer and a local government, in covenants between a developer and a neighborhood association, or in rezoning ordinances passed by local legislative bodies.

Note on Judicial Resistance to Contract Zoning

1. *The courts' initial reactions.* Courts confronted with the express or implied agreements Professor Wegner describes at first were quite hostile to the idea of "contract" zoning. Typical of the reactions was Allred v. City of Raleigh, 178 S.E.2d 432 (N.C. 1971), which rejected a rezoning from an R-4 to a R-10 to allow the developer to build a luxury high rise, reasoning:

> Consideration of the minutes of the Planning Commission and of the City Council show beyond doubt that the City Council did not determine that the . . . tract and the existing circumstances justified the rezoning of the . . . tract so as to permit all uses permissible in an R-10 district. On the contrary, it appears clearly that the ground on which the City Council based its action was its approval of the specific plans of the applicant to construct . . . "luxury apartments . . . in twin high-rise towers." We assume the City Council was fully justified in accepting the assurances of the applicant that the . . . tract would be developed in accordance with the particular and impressive plans submitted to the Planning Commission and to the City Council. However, "[i]n enacting a zoning ordinance, a municipality is engaged in legislating and not in contracting."

Id. at 440 (citations omitted).

2. *The evils of contract zoning.* What exactly is wrong with contract zoning? Some early decisions rejecting contract zoning were based on authority grounds, reasoning that the enabling act did not provide for the imposition of conditions or the use of contracts in rezoning. Other courts invoked various substantive objections:

a. *Procedural due process.* Some courts struck down the practice as violating at least the spirit of procedural requirements:

> A contract in which a municipality promises to zone property in a specified manner is illegal because, in making such a promise, a municipality preempts the power of the zoning authority to zone the property according to prescribed legislative procedures. Our statutes require notice and a public hearing prior to passage, amendment, supplement, or repeal of any zoning regulation. The statutes also grant to citizens and parties in interest the opportunity to be heard at the hearing. By making a promise to zone before a zoning hearing occurs, a municipality denigrates the statutory process because it purports to commit itself to certain action before listening to the public comments on that action. . . .

Dacy v. Village of Ruidoso, 845 P.2d 793, 797 (N.M. 1992). Compare Warner Co. v. Sutton, 644 A.2d 656 (N.J. Super. Ct. App. Div. 1994) (rejecting settlement agreement that provided for rezoning because "contract zoning" frustrates the public's right to be heard), with Gandolfi v. Town of Hammonton, 843 A.2d 1175 (N.J. Super. Ct. App. Div. 2004) (where plan discussed in settlement negotiations was subject to independent and exhaustive public scrutiny, public's right to be heard and to participate was "vindicated"). See generally Richard S. Cohen et al., Settling Land Use Litigation While Protecting the Public Interest: Whose Lawsuit Is This Anyway?, 23 Seton Hall L. Rev. 844 (1993).

Could procedural objections be met by conditioning the contract on the city's determination, after the required public hearings, that the contract served the public interest? Cf. Chung v. Sarasota County, 686 So. 2d 1358, 1360 (Fla. Dist. Ct. App. 1996) (agreement to settle litigation that obligated county to rezone was improper contract zoning because even though the rezoning would follow public hearings, those hearings would be a "pro forma exercise," and the county's obligation to follow various procedures "is an obligation that must be exercised prior to the decision-making, not afterwards"). What if the contract rezoning were submitted to the affected neighborhood, or the city as a whole, for approval, through a referendum-like process? See pp. 401–09 for discussion of referenda.

b. *Uniformity requirements.* Section 2 of the SZEA requires that "regulations shall be uniform for each class or kind of buildings throughout each district." Some courts reject contract zoning as inconsistent with uniformity requirements. See, e.g., Board of County Commissioners v. H. Manny Holtz, Inc., 501 A.2d 489, 493 (Md. Ct. Spec. App. 1985) (rejected a rezoning that imposed various conditions limiting uses of the property to four of the eight uses authorized in the zone on the ground that such limitations would create "a unique mini-district," and the "piecemeal proliferations of these mini-districts would totally emasculate the uniformity requirement of the zoning ordinance"); Campion v. Board of Aldermen, 859 A.2d 586, 601 (Conn. App. Ct. 2004) (ordinance providing for a "planned development district" that could be subject to conditions was unauthorized because the ordinance failed to contain uniform standards).

To get around the uniformity requirement, could the government reach the same result as contract zoning — albeit less speedily — by inventing and applying a brand-new zone tailored to allow only the landowner's proposed use? Why would that route be preferable to contract zoning? Could the purposes of the uniformity requirement be satisfied by an equal protection analysis of a landowner's complaint that the local government refused to offer a contract rezoning on the same terms as other landowners had received, or a neighbor's complaint that the local government imposed fewer or less protective restrictions on a contract rezoning than were imposed in other neighborhoods? See, e.g., Giger v. City of Omaha, 442 N.W.2d 182 (Neb. 1989) (uniformity requirement does not prevent distinctions between properties within a zone resulting from "conditional rezoning" as long as those distinctions are reasonable and serve public policy).

c. *Corruption or the appearance of favoritism.* Still other courts base their rejection of contract zoning on the notion that it allows the "zoning power . . . [to be] prostituted for the special benefit" of the developer, Midtown Properties, Inc. v. Madison Township, 172 A.2d 40, 44 (N.J. Super. Ct. Law Div. 1961), aff'd, 189 A.2d 226 (N.J. Super. Ct. App. Div. 1963), or that it destroys "that confidence in the integrity and discretion of public action which is essential to the preservation of civilized society." City of Knoxville v. Ambrister, 263 S.W.2d 528, 530 (Tenn. 1953).

Is an explicit contract securing protections for neighbors more likely to have been the product of corruption or undue influence than a rezoning with no (apparent) strings attached? Is a regime that allows contract zoning likely to grant more or fewer rezonings? If it grants more, is that necessarily a sign that the public officials have been "captured" by developers and are not serving the public interest? What would Steele's argument, excerpted at p. 295, suggest about contract rezonings?

For good overviews of the courts' early reactions to contract zoning, see Judith Welch Wegner, Moving Toward the Bargaining Table: Contract Zoning, Development Agreements, and the Theoretical Foundations of Government Land Use Deals, 65 N.C. L. Rev. 957, 983–86 (1987); Bruce R. Bailey, Comment, The Use and Abuse of Contract Zoning, 12 UCLA L. Rev. 897 (1965).

3. *Is contract zoning efficient?* Might government imposition of express conditions to protect neighbors be a sign that officials have faithfully served members of the public, not betrayed them? Consider the argument advanced in Jennifer G. Brown, Concomitant Agreement Zoning: An Economic Analysis, 1 U. Ill. L. Rev. 89, 110 (1985):

> Euclidean zoning fails to recognize that a restrictive zoning classification sometimes imposes costs on a landowner that exceed potential damage to the community from a rezoning of the landowner's property. Mandatory compliance with a restrictive zoning classification can result in inefficient land use, because the landowner loses the chance to compensate the community for costs that would result if the landowner's property were rezoned to a classification less restrictive and more beneficial to the landowner. . . .
>
> Concomitant agreement zoning [another name for contract zoning] overcomes this sort of inefficiency by giving the landowner the chance to develop the land more intensively and bear the costs that may result from the more intensive development. . . . When the costs of restrictively zoning a parcel of land are greater than the costs of developing the land more intensively, CAZ allows the landowner to develop the land but bear the costs of development. CAZ permits the kind of land use decision making that maximizes the aggregate welfare, because it improves the landowner's situation without damaging that of others.

See also Robert C. Ellickson, Alternatives to Zoning: Covenants, Nuisance Rules, and Fines as Land Use Controls, 40 U. Chi. L. Rev. 681, 708 (1973); Lee Anne Fennell, Hard Bargains and Real Steals: Land Use Exactions Revisited, 86 Iowa L. Rev. 1, 14–25 (2000); William A. Fischel, Equity and Efficiency Aspects of Zoning Reform, 27 Pub. Pol'y 301 (1979).

If contract zoning is to increase efficiency, the developer must be forced to internalize all the costs of the rezoning. If the government fails to anticipate all the costs of the rezoning or fails to charge them all to the developer, the neighbors can rightfully charge that the government has "sold out" to the developer. Further, even if the government charges the developer with all the costs, it is possible that the government might not distribute the revenues or benefits to those actually harmed by the development. See, e.g., Prock v. Town of Danville, 655 N.E.2d 553 (Ind. Ct. App. 1995) (neighbors' unsuccessful challenge to rezoning of land for use as a landfill, where developer had promised, among other things, three annual payments of $50,000 to the local Chamber of Commerce). In that situation, the neighbors have a claim that the contract rezoning, although Kaldor-Hicks efficient, sacrificed their interests.

4. *Escaping from illegal contracts.* *Allred* illustrates that where contract zoning is illegal, neighbors and other third parties can have the deal voided and the rezoning rolled back. Can the parties to the deal invoke its illegality to renege on their promises? In City of Knoxville v. Ambrister, 263 S.W.2d 528 (Tenn. 1953), a developer promised in a letter to dedicate part of his land to the city if a certain rezoning were to occur. When the rezoning did occur, the developer proceeded with his planned construction and later refused to honor the promise to dedicate. The city's suit to require the dedication failed because the Supreme Court of Tennessee would not tolerate contract zoning. Could the city then sue to have its own rezoning nullified? See Cederberg v. City of Rockford, 291 N.E.2d 249 (Ill. App. Ct. 1972) (remanding for a determination whether city should be estopped from rescinding the rezoning). If the rezoning were nullified, would the city be entitled to have the buildings razed on the theory that they were completed pursuant to invalid permits? See pp. 92–94. For discussions of the enforcement problems arising when contract rezoning is considered illegal, see Nolan M. Kennedy, Jr., Note, Contract and Conditional Zoning: A Tool for Zoning Flexibility, 23 Hastings L.J. 825, 836–37 (1972).

Chrismon v. Guilford County
370 S.E.2d 579 (N.C. 1988)

MEYER, Justice.

This was an action by plaintiffs for a declaratory judgment . . . that the amendment to the ordinance adopted 20 December 1982 rezoning defendant Bruce Clapp's 8.57 acres of land was unlawful and therefore void. . . .

. . . Defendant Bruce Clapp . . . had been operating a business on a 3.18-acre tract of property adjacent to his residence in Rock Creek Township, Guilford County, since 1948. Mr. Clapp's business consisted, first, of buying, drying, storing, and selling grain and, second, of selling and distributing lime, fertilizer, pesticides, and other agricultural chemicals. . . .

In 1964, Guilford County adopted a comprehensive zoning ordinance. The ordinance zoned Mr. Clapp's 3.18-acre tract, as well as an extensive area surrounding his tract, as "A-1 Agricultural" (hereinafter "A-1"). Under this particular zoning classification, one element of the business — namely, the grain drying and storing operation — constituted a permitted use. Significantly, however, the sale and distribution of the lime, fertilizer, pesticides, and other agricultural chemicals were not uses permitted by the A-1 classification. However, because this latter activity pre-existed the ordinance, Mr. Clapp was allowed to continue to sell agricultural chemicals on the 3.18-acre tract adjacent to his own home. . . .

In 1969, plaintiffs William and Evelyn Chrismon bought a tract of land from Mr. Clapp and built a home there. Plaintiffs' lot is located at the south side of the intersection of North Carolina Highway 61 and Gun Shop Road. . . . Mr. Clapp's residence is located on the north side of the intersection, directly across Gun Shop Road from plaintiffs' residence. Adjacent to plaintiffs' lot is an additional 5.06-acre tract, also owned by Mr. Clapp. . . .

Beginning in 1980, . . . Mr. Clapp moved some portion of his business operation from the 3.18-acre tract [adjacent to his home] . . . to the 5.06-acre tract . . . directly adjacent to plaintiffs' lot. . . . Concerned by the increased noise, dust, and traffic caused by Mr. Clapp's expansion, plaintiffs filed a complaint with the Guilford County Inspections Department. The Inspections Department subsequently notified Mr. Clapp, by letter dated 22 July 1982 . . . that, though his activity was impermissible under the ordinance, should he so desire, he could request a rezoning of the property.

Shortly thereafter, Mr. Clapp applied to have . . . the 3.18-acre tract north of Gun Shop Road and the 5.06-acre tract south of Gun Shop Road, rezoned from A-1 to "Conditional Use Industrial District" (hereinafter CU-M-2). He also applied for a conditional use permit, specifying in the application that he would use the property as it was then being used and listing those improvements he would like to make in the next five years. Under the CU-M-2 classification, Clapp's agricultural chemical operation would become a permitted use upon the issuance of the conditional use permit. The Guilford County Planning Board . . . voted to approve the recommendation of the Planning Division that the property be rezoned consistent with Mr. Clapp's request.

. . . [After a public hearing], the Guilford County Board of Commissioners . . . voted to rezone the tracts in question from A-1 to CU-M-2, and as a part of the same resolution, they also voted to approve the conditional use permit application.

. . . [P]laintiffs brought this action seeking to have both the zoning amendment and the conditional use permit declared invalid. After a trial without a jury, the trial court found, among other things, that the sale and distribution of the agricultural chemicals were uses compatible with the agricultural needs of the surrounding area. The trial court concluded further that the rezoning was neither "spot zoning" nor "contract zoning" and also that the County had not acted arbitrarily in making its decision . . .

. . . [T]he Court of Appeals reversed the decision of the trial court. It held, first, that . . . the rezoning of Mr. Clapp's 8.57 acres from A-1 to CU-M-2 constituted an illegal form of "spot zoning" and was therefore void. . . .

The Court of Appeals held, second, that the rezoning in question also constituted illegal "contract zoning" and was therefore also void for that alternative reason. Here, stated the Court of Appeals, the rezoning was accomplished upon the assurance that Mr. Clapp would submit an application for a conditional use permit specifying that he would use the property only in a certain manner. The Court of Appeals concluded that, in essence, the rezoning here was accomplished through a bargain between the applicant and the Board rather than through a proper and valid exercise of Guilford County's legislative discretion. According to the Court of Appeals, this activity constituted illegal "contract zoning" and was therefore void.

. . . The questions plainly before us are these: first, did the rezoning of defendant Clapp's tract from A-1 to CU-M-2 by the Guilford County Board of Commissioners constitute illegal spot zoning; and second, did the same rezoning constitute illegal contract zoning. . . . We conclude that the correct answer to both questions is "no."

I . . .

. . . Comprehensive zoning systems, though effective in preserving the character of ongoing uses, are often criticized for not allowing for the degree of flexibility needed to allow local officials to respond appropriately to "constantly shifting conditions and public needs." Brough, Flexibility Without Arbitrariness In The Zoning System: Observations On North Carolina Special Exception and Zoning Amendment Cases, 53 N.C. L. Rev. 925, 925 (1975).

The practice of conditional use zoning — like that used by Guilford County in this case — is one of several vehicles by which greater zoning flexibility can be and has been acquired by zoning authorities. Conditional use zoning anticipates that when the rezoning of certain property . . . would constitute an unacceptably drastic change, such a rezoning could still be accomplished through the addition of certain conditions or use limitations. Specifically, conditional use zoning occurs when a governmental body, without committing its own authority, secures a given property owner's agreement to limit the use of his property to a particular use or to subject his tract to certain restrictions as a precondition to any rezoning. D. Hagman & J. Juergensmeyer, Urban Planning and Land Development Control Law §5.5 (2d ed. 1986); Shapiro, The Case for Conditional Rezoning, 41 Temp. L.Q. 267 (1968). . . .

Steven E. Davenport and Philip P. Green, Jr., of our own Institute of Government, . . . [have explained] the benefits of conditional use zoning:

> The City of Greensboro's conditional-use approach to rezoning arose from the theory that of the hundreds of pieces of property in the city, many — because of particular physical or locational attributes — did not fit well into any of the classes of general zoning districts available at that time. For example, perhaps a lot zoned "residential" adjoining a "commercial area" should not reasonably be "residential," but rezoning it commercial (with all legal uses permitted) would only aggravate the land use problem. But if the rezoning was accompanied by certain conditions or use limitations, or both, a rezoning could perhaps not only offer a reasonable use for the property but also solve a land-use relationship problem.

Davenport & Green, Special Use and Conditional Use Districts: A Way to Impose More Specific Zoning Controls at 13 (Institute of Government, The University of North Carolina at Chapel Hill, 1980).

. . . [T]he action here is consistent with the observations of . . . Davenport and Green. . . . While the rezoning of the two tracts to M-2 Industrial would clearly allow the desired agricultural chemical operation, it would also clearly allow for activities substantially inconsistent with the surrounding A-1 areas.[2] Herein lies the usefulness of conditional use zoning. By rezoning these tracts CU-M-2, the desired activity becomes a conforming use, but by virtue of the attendant conditions, uses undesirable under these circumstances can be limited or avoided altogether.

Notwithstanding the manifest benefits of conditional use zoning, there has, over the course of time, been some divergence of opinion amongst courts and commentators alike as to the legal status of the practice. In fact, the initial judicial response to conditional use zoning was to condemn the practice as invalid per se. See, e.g., Hartnett v. Austin, 93 So. 2d 86 (Fla. 1956); V.F. Zahodiakin Engineering Corp. v. Zoning Board of Adjustment, 86 A.2d 127 (N.J. 1952). . . .

The benefits of the additional zoning and planning flexibility inherent in conditional use zoning have apparently not escaped the attention of jurisdictions which have addressed the issue more recently. Many jurisdictions now approve of the practice of conditional use zoning, so long as the action of the local zoning authority in accomplishing the zoning is reasonable, neither arbitrary nor unduly discriminatory, and in the public interest. These jurisdictions, which comprise a growing trend, have concluded, among other things, that zoning legislation provides ample authority for the practice; that the use under the practice of carefully tailored restraints advanced, rather than injured, the interests of adjacent landowners; and that the practice is an appropriate means of harmonizing private interests in land and thus of benefitting the public interest. Wegner, Moving Toward the Bargaining Table: Contract Zoning, Development Agreements, and the Theoretical Foundations of Government Land Use Deals, 65 N.C. L. Rev. 957, 983–84 (1987).

Today, we join this growing trend of jurisdictions in recognizing the validity of properly employed conditional use zoning. . . .

. . . In our view, the "all or nothing" approach of traditional zoning techniques is insufficient in today's world of rapid industrial expansion and pressing urban and rural social and economic problems.

Having so stated, we hasten to add that, just as this type of zoning can provide much-needed and valuable flexibility to the planning efforts of local zoning authorities, it could also be as easily abused. We recognize that critics of the practice are to a limited extent justified in their concern that the unrestricted use of conditional use zoning could lead to private or public abuse of governmental power. We have said, however, that, in order to be legal and proper, conditional use zoning, like any type of zoning, must be reasonable, neither arbitrary nor unduly discriminatory, and in the public interest. It goes without saying that it also cannot constitute illegal spot zoning or illegal contract zoning as those two concepts are developed in the pages which follow. The benefits of the flexibility of conditional use zoning can be fairly achieved only when these limiting standards are consistently and carefully applied. . . .

. . . [In rejecting conditional zoning] the Court of Appeals improperly relied upon our decision in *Allred* [v. City of Raleigh, 178 S.E.2d 432 (N.C. 1971), discussed at p. 319], a general and not a conditional use zoning case. In *Allred* . . . [t]he complained-of rezoning was that from one general district or zone, R-4, to another general district or zone, R-10. This Court held that the property in question could be rezoned "only if and

---

2. For example, permitted uses in a district zoned under the M-2 Industrial classification would include, among other things, manufacturing facilities of virtually any kind, fuel oil dealerships, waste recycling facilities, and public utility storage depots.

when its location and the surrounding circumstances are such that the property should be made available for all uses permitted in an R-10 district." Id. at 440–41. While this is an accurate statement of North Carolina law with regard to rezoning from one general district to another general district, it is not authority in cases such as this involving rezoning from a general district to a conditional use district. . . .

III

. . . In the view of this Court, the Court of Appeals, in its approach to the question of whether the rezoning at issue in this case constituted illegal contract zoning, improperly considered as equals two very different concepts — namely, valid conditional use zoning and illegal contract zoning. . . . In fact, for the reasons we will develop below, the two concepts are not to be considered synonymous. . . .

Illegal contract zoning properly connotes a transaction wherein both the landowner who is seeking a certain zoning action and the zoning authority itself undertake reciprocal obligations in the context of a bilateral contract. One commentator provides as illustration the following example:

> A Council enters into an agreement with the landowner and then enacts a zoning amendment. *The agreement, however, includes not merely the promise of the owner to subject his property to deed restrictions; the Council also binds itself to enact the amendment and not to alter the zoning change for a specified period of time.* Most courts will conclude that by agreeing to curtail its legislative power, the Council acted ultra vires. Such contract zoning is illegal and the rezoning is therefore a nullity.

Shapiro, supra, at 269 (emphasis added).

As the excerpted illustration suggests, contract zoning of this type is objectionable primarily because it represents an abandonment on the part of the zoning authority of its duty to exercise independent judgment in making zoning decisions.

As we indicated in Part I above, valid conditional use zoning, on the other hand, is an entirely different matter . . . :

> An orthodox conditional zoning situation occurs when a zoning authority, *without committing its own power,* secures a property owner's agreement to subject his tract to certain restrictions as a prerequisite to rezoning. These restrictions may require that the rezoned property be limited to just one of the uses permitted in the new classification; or particular physical improvements and maintenance requirements may be imposed.

Shapiro, supra, at 270–71 (emphasis added).

In our view, therefore, the principal differences between valid conditional use zoning and illegal contract zoning are related and are essentially two in number. First, valid conditional use zoning features merely a unilateral promise from the landowner to the local zoning authority as to the landowner's intended use of the land in question, while illegal contract zoning anticipates a bilateral contract in which the landowner and the zoning authority make reciprocal promises. Second, in the context of conditional use zoning, the local zoning authority maintains its independent decision-making authority, while in the contract zoning scenario, it abandons that authority by binding itself contractually with the landowner seeking a zoning amendment.

. . . [W]e find what occurred in the case before us to constitute valid conditional use zoning and not illegal contract zoning.

First, having carefully reviewed the record in the case, we find no evidence that the local zoning authority — here, the Guilford County Board of Commissioners — entered into anything approaching a bilateral contract with the landowner — here, Mr. Clapp. The facts of the case reveal that, pursuant to a filed complaint from the Chrismons, the Guilford County Inspections Department, by a letter dated 22 July 1982, . . . informed Mr. Clapp of his various options in the following manner:

> Mr. Clapp, there are several courses of action available to you in an effort to resolve your Zoning Ordinance violations: . . .
>
> 2. You may request rezoning of that portion of your land involved in the violations. This is not a guaranteed option.

. . . [W]e are quite satisfied that the only promises made in this case were unilateral — specifically, those from Mr. Clapp to the Board in the form of the substance of his conditional use permit application. As the letter excerpted above makes clear, no promises whatever were made by the Board in exchange, and this rezoning does not therefore fall into the category of illegal contract zoning.

Second, and perhaps more important, the Board did not, by virtue of its actions in this case, abandon its position as an independent decision-maker. . . . On the contrary, we find that the Board made its decision in this matter only after a lengthy deliberation completely consistent with both the procedure called for by the relevant zoning ordinance and the rules prohibiting illegal contract zoning. . . .

Accordingly, the decision of Court of Appeals is hereby reversed. . . .

[Dissenting opinions omitted].

Note on the Erosion of the Prohibition on Contract Zoning

1. *Direct assaults on the prohibition.* Most recent decisions abandon the prohibition on contract zoning, at least for those contracts now euphemistically styled as "conditional" zoning. See, e.g., Super Wash, Inc. v. City of White Settlement, 131 S.W.3d 249 (Tex. App. 2004). Further, some states have adopted statutes that appear to legitimize contract or conditional zoning. Maine's is more explicit than most:

§4301. DEFINITIONS . . .

4. Conditional zoning. "Conditional zoning" means the process by which the municipal legislative body may rezone property to permit the use of that property subject to conditions not generally applicable to other properties similarly zoned.

5. Contract zoning. "Contract zoning" means the process by which the property owner, in consideration of the rezoning of that person's property, agrees to the imposition of certain conditions or restrictions not imposed on other similarly zoned properties.

§4352. ZONING ORDINANCES . . .

8. Conditional and contract rezoning. A zoning ordinance may include provisions for conditional or contract zoning. All rezoning under this subsection must:

A. Be consistent with the local growth management program adopted under this chapter;

B. Establish rezoned areas that are consistent with the existing and permitted uses within the original zones; and

C. Only include conditions and restrictions that relate to the physical development or operation of the property. . . .

Me. Rev. Stat. Ann. tit. 30A §§4301, 4352 (West 2004). For a much more restrictive statute, see, e.g., Md. Code Ann. art. 66B, §4.01(c) (2004).

2. *End runs around prohibitions.* What if special conditions are contained in a declaration of covenants to neighbors, executed prior to the rezoning, rather than in a promise to the local government? See, e.g., State ex rel. Zupancic v. Schimenz, 174 N.W.2d 533 (Wis. 1970) (such an arrangement is not "contract" or "conditional" zoning). If a developer who needs a rezoning works out a settlement with neighbors, and the local government rezones on the basis of that settlement, does the neighbors' involvement adequately address concerns the courts initially had about contract zoning? For a discussion of problems raised by neighbors' consent requirements, see pp. 393–400.

The Maryland courts have adopted the view that illegal contract zoning occurs only when the ultimate zoning authority — the legislative body itself — is a party to the contract, not when advisory bodies such as a planning commission are parties. See, e.g., People's Counsel for Baltimore County v. Beachwood I Ltd. Partnership, 670 A.2d 484 (Md. Ct. Spec. App. 1995) (if contract existed, it was between the developer and the planning board, which was not the ultimate zoning authority, and therefore any such contract did not violate prohibition on contract zoning). What makes a deal between a landowner and advisory boards less troublesome than a deal between a landowner and elected officials?

3. *A distinction without a difference?* Do the purported differences between "contract" and "conditional" (also known as "concomitant agreement," "unilateral contract" and "contingent") rezoning justify the distinctive legal treatment the practices receive?

4. *Conditional use zoning.* The rezoning technique approved in *Chrismon* arguably is different from what most courts and commentators label conditional zoning because it rezones the applicant's land to a conditional *use* district, which would seem to imply that no uses are permitted as of right, but that the landowner can seek a conditional use permit for the specific use proposed. Indeed, one lower court overturned a "conditional use district permit" issued by a city council as part of the rezoning, finding that the procedure envisioned by *Chrismon* involved a two-step process: a legislative rezoning to a conditional use district, followed by an administrative determination whether to grant the landowner's application for a conditional use permit. Both the legislature and the intermediate court of appeals rejected that reading, however. Massey v. City of Charlotte, 550 S.E.2d 838 (N.C. Ct. App. 2001); 2000 N.C. Sess. Laws ch. 84, §1(e). Accordingly, in North Carolina, *conditional use* zoning is equivalent to other states' *conditional* zoning. Would it be preferable to have the two-step procedure that *Chrismon*'s language implied and the trial court envisioned?

Note on Judicial Review of Permitted Contract or Conditional Zoning

1. *The rezoning stands alone.* When judges review contract or conditional rezoning, they typically evaluate the underlying decision to rezone by the same tests that apply to regular rezonings — the spot-zoning, change or mistake, and consistency doctrines. Some courts assert that the underlying rezoning must be valid standing alone, "without the imposition of restrictive conditions," Collard v. Incorporated Village of Flower Hill, 421 N.E. 2d 818, 851 (N.Y. 1981), while others evaluate the rezoning as conditioned. Which approach is better? Compare Jennifer G. Brown, Concomitant Agreement Zoning: An Economic Analysis, 1 U. Ill. L. Rev. 89, 104–05, 111 (1985) (*Collard* approach appropriately recognizes that the rezoning, not just the conditions that accompany the rezoning, should benefit the public), with Bruce Kramer, Contract Zoning — Old Myths and New Realities, Land Use L. & Zoning Dig., Aug. 1982, at 4, 10 (*Collard* approach will preclude use of conditional zoning that would be beneficial to community as a whole).

2. *Constraints on the conditions.* What limits should the courts or state legislatures place on the nature of the benefits the property owner offers during the rezoning process? The Massachusetts Supreme Judicial Court recently rejected neighbors' claims that a rezoning was invalid because the property owner had offered to give the town $8 million, which the town could spend on projects wholly unrelated to the proposed development, if the rezoning was approved. The court reasoned that the rezoning was valid standing alone, and that the developer's voluntary offer was not an adequate ground "to set aside an otherwise valid legislative act." Durand v. IDC Bellingham, LLC, 793 N.E.2d 359 (Mass. 2003). See also Paul D. Wilson, Contract Zoning and Development Exactions: *IDC Bellingham* and Its Implications, Boston B.J., May/June 2004, at 10.

What limits should be placed on conditions that the developer does not initially offer but that he agrees to after the local government puts them on the bargaining table? If the agreed-on condition were instead a required dedication (or even perhaps a required impact fee), the nexus and proportionality tests the Supreme Court has articulated for dedications, see pp. 637–52, would apply. Should those tests apply as well to conditions the developer accepts as part of a conditional rezoning? See, e.g., Hayes v. City of Seattle, 934 P.2d 1179 (Wash. 1997) (en banc) (city council's grant of a "master use permit" conditioned on developer reducing the length of the proposed building by 15 feet was arbitrary and capricious because council failed to describe the adverse impact of the proposed building or to explain how reducing the size would mitigate those impacts); Board of Supervisors v. Reed's Landing Corp., 463 S.E.2d 668, 669–70 (Va. 1995) (agreeing with property owner that county acted unlawfully in refusing to rezone after developer had balked at the county's "recommended" proffer of $2,439 per lot "to help defray costs of capital facilities related to new development" because county is "not empowered to require a specified proffer as a condition precedent to a rezoning" but may accept proffers of conditions "made voluntarily").

Note that the Maine statute excerpted at p. 326 limits conditions to those "that relate to the physical development or operation of the property." Does that limit make sense? What other limits might be desirable? How might the legislature or the courts prevent a local government from overusing the conditional rezoning process to impose conditions that should be generally applicable?

If a condition is found to be unreasonable, should the condition be stricken but the rezoning left in place, or should both be voided? See, e.g., *Collard*, 421 N.E. 2d at 823 (suggesting that if the condition was unreasonable, the rezoning would have to be voided).

3. *Enforcement.* If a local government reneges in a state that permits contract zoning, can the developer force specific performance? Recover damages? See City of Orange Beach v. Perdido Pass Developers, 631 So. 2d 850 (Ala. 1993) (affirming jury award of $4.5 million to developer for city's breach of a contract to rezone).

What if the developer reneges? Can the local government then revoke the rezoning without violating the property owner's property rights? See, e.g., Agripost, Inc. v. Metropolitan Miami-Dade County, 845 So. 2d 918 (Fla. Ct. App. 2003) (county's revocation of conditional "unusual use zoning approval" on property owner's failure to abide by conditions did not constitute a taking). What about the property owner's procedural due process rights? See, e.g., City of Homer v. Campbell, 719 P.2d 683 (Alaska 1986) (property owner has a due process right to notice and an opportunity to be heard before city revokes contract rezoning as a remedy for the landowner's alleged breaches of the contract). Can the conditional rezoning itself include an automatic reverter clause that restores the original zoning in the event of a breach of conditions? Compare Super Wash, Inc. v. City of White Settlement, 131 S.W.3d 249 (Tex. App. 2004) (automatic reverter

clause is an invalid delegation of the city's legislative power because a zoning regulation, even a conditional rezoning, should be amended only if the public interest requires
the amendment), with Konkel v. Common Council, 229 N.W.2d 606 (Wis. 1975) (automatic reverter clause can be valid if subject to notice and hearing before the original
rezoning).

Can the local government refuse any approvals the reneging developer still needs,
such as the building permits or certificates of occupancy that are discussed at pp. 428–30?

Note on Cluster Zoning and Planned-Unit Developments

Traditional zoning assumed that single-family houses would be built one at a time
on individual lots in a grid pattern, rigidly separated from nonresidential uses. With the
exception of a few "new towns" (such as Radburn, New Jersey, and Palos Verdes Estates,
California), most jurisdictions hewed to that model through rigid Euclidean zoning. The
result was a remarkably consistent, and boring, "cookie-cutter" development pattern. The
traditional model began to come under considerable pressure in the 1960s, when developers moved from building on single lots to developing large subdivisions; local governments
struggled to provide schools, parks, fire protection and other services to such large-scale
developments; and both developers and local governments faced increasing pressure to
minimize the environmental impacts of development and to preserve environmentally
sensitive areas. Those pressures led to the wide-scale adoption of cluster zoning and
planned-unit developments (PUDs). Under cluster zoning, the local government allows
deviations from the minimum lot-area, setback, and frontage requirements to encourage
the developer to cluster housing together and dedicate the "saved" land for recreational
areas or open space. Cluster zoning allows the overall density of a project to remain the
same, but increases the density of the land actually developed. The increased density
reduces the cost of roads and other infrastructure, allows natural features and environmentally sensitive areas to be preserved, makes open space and common recreational areas
possible, and provides a greater range of housing choice for consumers.

Cluster zoning did not challenge the Euclidean principle that single-family homes
had to be separated from other housing types and residential uses had to be separated from
other uses. PUDs broke that barrier by allowing a mix of housing types, from single-family
detached homes to multifamily townhouses or apartments, within a single development.
Indeed PUDs can incorporate retail shopping, office buildings, and other uses into primarily residential developments, or can be used to allow a range of uses within primarily
industrial or retail developments. The difference between Euclidean zoning and cluster
and PUD zoning is illustrated by Figure 4-2.

Because they mix housing types and (sometimes) uses, PUDs were difficult to accommodate through special exceptions or subdivision regulation reviews. Instead, they required
a new approach:

> While planned unit development ordinances vary, the most common type provides for the
> creation of a planned unit development district through a two step legislative process. The
> initial ordinance describes a planned unit development district, and outlines the enactment
> procedure, but it does not locate the district on the zoning map of the municipality. Actual
> creation of such a district must be accomplished by a second legislative act — an amendment
> to the zoning ordinance. The final legislative step is preceded by a full dress review of the plans
> by a planning board, and a recommendation by that agency.

2 Kenneth H. Young, Anderson's American Law of Zoning §11.15 (4th ed. 1996). Because a

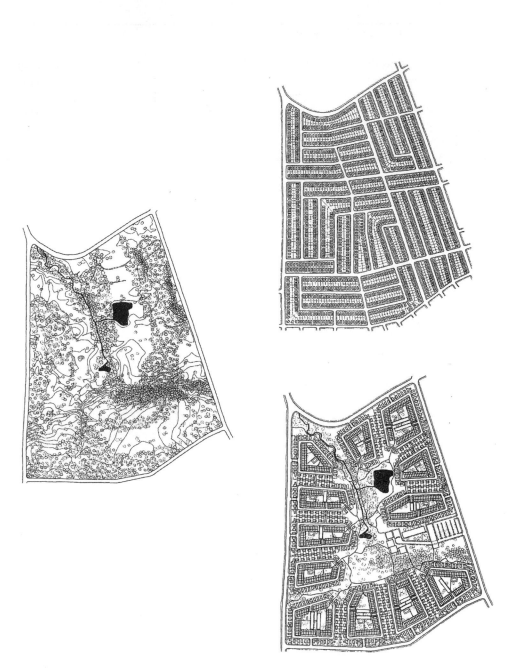

Left: contour map showing existing features (trees, ponds, creek, and bounding road) of a 205-acre undeveloped site. Top right: site plan showing conventional street grid (with 1,427 single-family house lots) that destroys the natural character of the site. Bottom right: plan generated by using the cluster zoning approach would preserve the natural features of the site, provide for an elementary school and shopping facilities, and accommodate 1,445 housing units in a range of house types (detached and semidetached houses, townhouses, and attached row houses).

Source: New York City Department of City Planning, *reprinted in* Alexander Garvin, The American City: What Works, What Doesn't 279 (1996).

FIGURE 4-2
Cluster Zoning and Planned Unit Development

PUD ordinance does not use command-and-control restrictions to detail precisely what uses are allowed or how they must be situated, but instead sets out broad performance-oriented principles, developers are given considerable freedom to design developments in accord with their judgments about market demand. That flexibility necessitates considerable give-and-take, or dealmaking, between the developer and planners.

Not surprisingly, cluster zoning, PUDs, and related techniques such as "floating zones" (zones specified in the zoning text, but not "anchored" in the zoning map until a specific project is proposed, at which time the zoning map is amended to incorporate the zone) faced some initial skepticism in the courts. See, e.g., Eves v. Zoning Board of Adjustment, 164 A.2d 7 (Pa. 1960). The techniques soon became accepted, however. See, e.g., Chrinko v. South Brunswick Township Planning Board, 187 A.2d 221 (N.J. Super. Ct. Law Div. 1963) (upholding cluster zoning); Rodgers v. Village of Tarrytown, 96 N.E.2d 731 (N.Y. 1951) (upholding floating zone); Cheney v. Village 2 at New Hope, Inc., 241 A.2d 81 (Pa. 1968) (upholding PUD ordinance).

Many states have adopted statutes that explicitly authorize their local governments to enact PUD statutes. See, e.g., Colo. Rev. Stat. §§24-67-101–24-67-108 (2004). For a model statute and a good collection of articles about PUDs, see Symposium, Planned Unit Development, 114 U. Pa. L. Rev. 1 (1965). For other helpful discussions, see, e.g., Michael Fedun, A Proposal for Improving Vermont's Statutory Requirements for Planned Unit Development, 14 Vt. L. Rev. 591 (1990); Clyde W. Forrest, Planned Unit Development and Takings Post *Dolan*, 15 N. Ill. U. L. Rev. 571 (1995).

Local governments continue to experiment with new forms of flexibility devices, and as in the past, the initial reaction of the courts tends to be skeptical. See, e.g., Louisville & Jefferson County Planning Commission v. Schmidt, 83 S.W.3d 449 (Ky. 2001) (county's "Innovative Residential Development Regulations" were an unconstitutional delegation of legislative power).

d.   "Incentive" Zoning

Under the law surveyed at pp. 134–97, government engages in regulation but compensates landowners who suffer losses on account of it, at least in limited circumstances. These systems are applications of what Calabresi and Melamed, excerpted at p. 532, call the "rule-two" approach: a liability rule protecting a landowner. As Calabresi and Melamed observe, a liability rule also can operate in the opposite direction. In the land regulation context, the "rule-four" approach entitles a landowner to free itself from regulation by compensating the government.

Incentive zoning (or bonus zoning) employs the rule-four approach. A government stipulates in advance some basic terms of deregulatory deals that it will accept, entitling landowners to "buy" their way out of regulation at preset "prices." For example, the government may announce that developers can receive an increase in allowable floor area, or an exemption from height and setback requirements, or a reduction in the required number of parking spaces the project must provide if the developer agrees to provide specified public amenities. In the dealmaking between a developer and local government described in *Allred* and *Chrismon* by contrast, the local government did not indicate in advance what it would demand in return for a regulatory approval.

Does incentive zoning have any advantages over ad hoc contract or conditional zoning? Does it pose any greater risks?

Municipal Art Society v. City of New York
522 N.Y.S.2d 800 (Sup. Ct. 1987)

EDWARD H. LEHNER, Judge.

The threshold issue . . . is whether the contract for the sale of the Coliseum site was illegal by reason of the inclusion of a provision for a $57 million reduction in the purchase price in the event the developer is denied a bonus permitting an increase in the allowable floor area for the project. The court finds such provision illegal, and declares the resolutions approving the transaction to be null and void. . . .

These proceedings involve the site of the New York Coliseum and an adjoining office building located on the west side of Columbus Circle in Manhattan extending from 58th to 60th Street.

In 1953 the City of New York (the "City") acquired the property by eminent domain, and sold it to the Triborough Bridge and Tunnel Authority ("TBTA"), an affiliate of the Metropolitan Transportation Authority ("MTA"), both of which are public authorities created by the State. On that site, the TBTA constructed and operated the office building and Coliseum. . . .

The Coliseum is located in a zone which permits construction as of right of floor space up to a maximum of 15 times the square footage of the lot. This floor area ratio ("FAR") is subject to being increased by up to 20% in exchange for the developer agreeing to "provide major improvements for adjacent subway stations," provided that "the zoning lot for the development . . . on which a floor area bonus is requested shall be adjacent to the mezzanine or concourse of the subway station for which the improvement is proposed or an existing connecting passageway to the station." Zoning Resolution of The City of New York, §81-53.

In December 1984 the City and the TBTA agreed to sell the site for private development. In February 1985, TBTA . . . offered the property for sale pursuant to a Request for Proposals ("RFP").

The RFP provided that: i) the amount of the purchase price offered "will be the primary consideration," and the criteria for acceptance would also include "the economic viability of the proposal, the developer's experience and financial capacity" as well as "the overall benefit to the City"; ii) the designated developer "must apply for and use its best efforts to obtain the maximum twenty percent Subway Bonus" (448,500 additional square feet); iii) if any FAR bonus is granted, the developer must agree to construct the subway station improvements "as set forth in concept" in the RFP, with such obligation to exist even if the maximum bonus is not granted, so long as any FAR bonus is approved; iv) the amount of the bid "must assume the maximum twenty percent FAR Subway Bonus will be granted"; v) the purchase price will be reduced by a specified formula if the full 20% FAR bonus is not granted, with such amount to be $57 million if no bonus is granted. . . .

By May 1, 1985, 15 proposals were received in response to the RFP, and although one bid was received for $477 million, a committee of City and MTA officials selected the bid of $455,100,000 from Boston Properties. A contract of sale dated September 30, 1985 was thereafter entered into which provides for a mixed use project. . . . The building would have two towers, one 925 feet (68 stories) and the other 802 feet (58 stories), with a total of 9,300 people expected to be employed at the site.

The contract provides that if no FAR bonus is granted, the purchase price will be reduced by $57 million. The estimated cost of improvements to be made by the purchaser to the adjoining Columbus Circle (59th Street) subway station is between $35 and $40 million, although the estimated cost at the time of the execution of the contract is claimed to have been between $20 and $25 million. . . .

[The New York City Planning Commission [CPC] and the Board of Estimate (the local governing body) approved the proposed project and also granted the maximum 20 percent FAR bonus.]

In the Article 78 proceeding instituted by the Municipal Art Society of New York ("MAS") and others, the following arguments are raised:

1) The City illegally sold a zoning bonus because the price is reduced by $57 million in the event a subway bonus is not granted. . . .

. . . [T]he claim of illegality relates solely to the $57 million. This sum, which the City and the TBTA will receive as a result of the grant of the bonus, is not earmarked for the improvement of any local facility. . . .

Although the transaction may well have been structured to paint a different picture, the clear fact of the matter is that in return for the grant by the CPC of the twenty percent floor area ratio bonus, the City is obtaining not only $35 to $40 million of local subway improvements, but an additional $57 million in cash to be employed for other purposes. This is not contemplated by the Zoning Resolution. . . .

. . . Increasing the bulk of a project imposes a certain burden on the local community. The Zoning Resolution provides a means by which, in return for the imposition of that burden, a benefit is granted to the community.

Here, the major portion of the benefit which the purchaser is willing to pay for the right to construct a building of greater density than is permitted "as of right" is to be paid to the City to be employed for purposes other than local improvements. A proper quid pro quo for the grant of the right to increase the bulk of a building may not be the payment of additional cash into the City's coffers for citywide use.

Although the members of the CPC may well in good faith have approved the full 20% FAR bonus as a fair incentive for the developer agreeing to make $35 to $40 million of subway station improvements, the developer and the City officials who approved the contract obviously recognized that this bonus was worth a great deal more. However, government may not place itself in the position of reaping a cash premium because one of its agencies bestows a zoning benefit upon a developer. Zoning benefits are not cash items. . . .

In conclusion, the court finds that the contract with the developer provides for an illegal payment. Consequently, the approvals thereof by the City and TBTA are null and void. . . .

Note on Incentive Zoning

1. *Cold cash.* Why was trading a zoning benefit for cash illegal in this instance? Does a cash deal inherently delegitimize zoning in a way that an in-kind trade between a city and a developer does not? Or was the court mostly bothered by the fact that the municipal agencies entering into the sale did not have to spend the $57 million within the vicinity of Columbus Circle, the neighborhood that the increased floor area ratio would most affect? If the latter, might that concern better be addressed by a "nexus" requirement similar to that used for exactions? See pp. 637–52. For analysis of *Municipal Art Society*, see Jerold S. Kayden, Zoning for Dollars: New Rules for an Old Game?, 39 Wash. U. J. Urb. & Contemp. L. 3 (1991).

2. *Piggybacking incentives.* Figure 4-3 indicates how one developer took advantage of Seattle's incentive zoning.

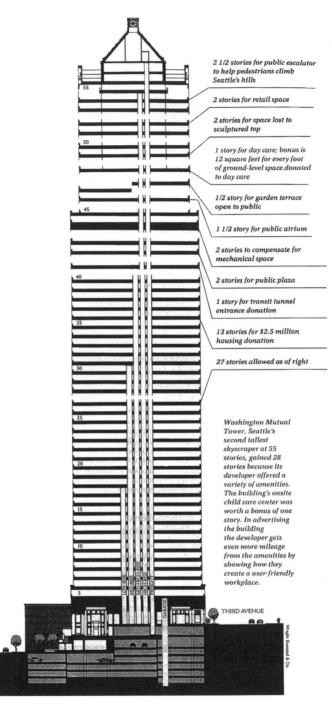

2 1/2 stories for public escalator to help pedestrians climb Seattle's hills

2 stories for retail space

2 stories for space lost to sculptured top

1 story for day care; bonus is 12 square feet for every foot of ground-level space donated to day care

1/2 story for garden terrace open to public

1 1/2 story for public atrium

2 stories to compensate for mechanical space

2 stories for public plaza

1 story for transit tunnel entrance donation

13 stories for $2.5 million housing donation

27 stories allowed as of right

Washington Mutual Tower, Seattle's second tallest skyscraper at 55 stories, gained 28 stories because its developer offered a variety of amenities. The building's onsite child care center was worth a bonus of one story. In advertising the building the developer gets even more mileage from the amenities by showing how they create a user-friendly workplace.

THIRD AVENUE

Source: Terry Jill Lassar, The Limits of Incentive Zoning, Urb. Land, May 1990, at 12, 13.

FIGURE 4-3
Piggybacking Incentives

3. *The pricing of incentives*. How hard a bargain are local governments likely to drive in structuring incentive zoning? Consider the following:

> Unfortunately, the experience in many United States cities shows a consistent pattern of underpricing incentives by granting more of them than is necessary to encourage the desired private behavior. The reasons for this practice include a paucity of on-staff real estate financial expertise, the utilization of inadequate or incorrect analytical frameworks for evaluating deals, and the absence of any market-driven imperative for government to negotiate the best deal.

Jerold S. Kayden, Market-Based Regulatory Approaches: A Comparative Discussion of Environmental and Land Use Techniques in the United States, 19 B.C. Envtl. Aff. L. Rev. 565 (1992). What role, if any, should the courts play in ensuring that local governments do not give bonuses away too freely?

4. *Effect on the restrictiveness of zoning regulations.* Will desire for the subway improvements or other amenities that trigger bonus zoning drive officials to set the underlying regulations (the floor area ratios in *Municipal Art Society*, for example) too restrictively, so that developers are more likely to resort to the bonus zoning scheme? Should a court's view of the legality of bonus zoning schemes depend on whether the bonus scheme was added onto existing zoning regulations (presumably promulgated without bonuses in mind) or was established as part of a comprehensive program (where officials' thinking about the baseline might have been influenced by the need to make the bonuses attractive)?

5. *Other forms of bonus zoning.* The cluster zoning discussed at pp. 329-31 was an early form of incentive zoning: Developers were given waivers from area and setback requirements to encourage them to preserve open space and provide common recreational areas. Inclusionary zoning programs commonly include explicit density bonuses to induce builders to provide affordable housing, as discussed at pp. 671-74. Neither cluster zoning nor inclusionary zoning bonuses have met with the hostility the court showed in *Municipal Art Society*. Is the difference between cluster or inclusionary zoning and the "cashout" of the FAR bonus a matter of degree or kind? Are the courts likely to soften their views about cashout bonuses as they did in the transition between *Allred* and *Chrismon*? Cf. Durand v. IDC Bellingham, LLC, 793 N.E.2d 359 (Mass. 2003) (upholding a conditional rezoning in which the developer offered $8 million that the local government could use for projects unrelated to the impact of the development).

6. *Enforcement.* Like contract and conditional zoning, bonus zoning raises difficult issues of enforcement. Once the building is built, what is a city to do about amenities never provided or provided at low quality? What happens when an "amenity" such as a public plaza turns out to be a haven for crime or other disturbing behavior? Professor Jerold Kayden examined over 500 plazas and other public places for which New York City provided bonus zoning, and offered a scathing indictment of their value to the public. Jerold S. Kayden et al., Privately Owned Public Space: The New York City Experience (2000). He also found that over half of the buildings with public spaces were out of compliance with the regulations intended to ensure their value to the public. In part because of dissatisfaction with the "amenities" received through incentive zoning, the chairman of New York City's City Planning Commission recommended in April 1999 that incentive zoning be abandoned. Thomas J. Lueck, Giuliani to Propose Some Height Limits on City Skyscrapers, N.Y. Times, Apr. 20, 1999, at A1. More recently, however, New York City has agressively used inclusionary zoning bonuses to induce developers in areas being rezoned to provide affordable housing. See Diane Cardwell, City Backs Makeover for Decaying Brooklyn Waterfront, N.Y. Times, May 3, 2005 at A1.

7. *Irony or vindication?* The *Municipal Art Society* decision delayed the redevelopment of the coliseum site for many years, but eventually the site was developed as the

Time Warner Center, a 2.8 million square foot mixed use complex. On December 8, 2004, the Municipal Art Society awarded the Center two of its 2003 MASterworks Awards for Excellence in Urban Design: for "Best New Building" and for "Best New Privately Owned Public Space." Real Estate Wkly., Dec. 22, 2004, at 1.

e. Zoning Without, or in Conflict with, Planning

Section 3 of the SZEA begins: "[Zoning] regulations shall be made in accordance with a comprehensive plan. . . . " About three-quarters of the states adopted that or similar language in their zoning enabling acts. Initially, most state courts refused to construe such provisions to mean that a government must adopt a formal plan before beginning to zone. Instead, as one leading case reasoned:

> Without venturing an exact definition, it may be said for present purposes that "plan" connotes an integrated product of a rational process and "comprehensive" requires something beyond a piecemeal approach, both to be revealed by the ordinance considered in relation to the physical facts and the purposes authorized by [the enabling act]. Such being the requirements of a comprehensive plan, no reason is perceived why we should infer the Legislature intended by necessary implication that the comprehensive plan be portrayed in some physical form outside the ordinance itself. A plan may readily be revealed in an end product — here the zoning ordinance — and no more is required by the statute.

Kozesnik v. Township of Montgomery, 131 A.2d 1 (N.J. 1957).

Courts continue to invoke the rationale of *Kozesnik* to avoid the "in accordance with" language of the SZEA when local governments have not adopted a plan. See, e.g., Iowa Coal Mining Co. v. Monroe County, 494 N.W.2d 664 (Iowa 1993). But see Heine Farms v. Yankton County, 649 N.W.2d 597, 601–02 (S.D. 2002) (striking down zoning ordinance adopted through initiative procedure because the enabling act defined a zoning ordinance as "any ordinance adopted . . . to implement the comprehensive plan by regulating the location and use of buildings and uses of land," and the county had no comprehensive plan). See also Edward J. Sullivan & Thomas G. Pelham, The Evolving Role of the Comprehensive Plan, 29 Urb. Law. 363 (1997). Nevertheless, the importance of *Kozesnik* has decreased because, as discussed at pp. 58–59, as many as half the states have passed legislation specifically requiring local governments to engage in comprehensive planning, at least in some circumstances.

When a jurisdiction has adopted a comprehensive plan, how ought the content of that plan affect how courts review zoning changes? The Oregon Supreme Court provided a pioneering analysis of the relationship between planning and zoning in Baker v. City of Milwaukie, 533 P.2d 772 (Or. 1975). The court upheld a challenge to the grant of a building permit in an area zoned for more intensive use than the city's comprehensive plan envisioned:

> In order to answer the question of whether a city, once it has adopted a comprehensive plan, has a duty to zone in accord with that plan, it is first necessary to discuss the relationship between planning and zoning.
>
> This court has recently recognized the controlling effect of the comprehensive plan on land use planning in a community: "The basic instrument for county or municipal land use planning is the 'comprehensive plan.' . . . The plan has been described as a general plan to control and direct the use and development of property in a municipality. . . . " Fasano v. Board of County Comm'rs, 507 P.2d 23, 27 (Or. 1973).
>
> Zoning, on the other hand, is the means by which the comprehensive plan is effectuated. . . .

Some writers have likened the comprehensive plan to a constitution. Thus it has been said that a comprehensive plan is a "constitution for all future development within the city." O'Loane v. O'Rourke, 42 Cal. Rptr. 283, 288 (Cal. Dist. Ct. App. 1965). . . .

While this analogy between a comprehensive plan and a constitution may be helpful in determining the relationship between planning and zoning, it must be remembered that the comprehensive plan is flexible and subject to change when the needs of the community demand. "[U]nlike [a constitution] it is subject to amendatory procedures not significantly different from the course followed in enacting ordinary legislation." [Charles M.] Haar, [The Master Plan: An Impermanent Constitution, 20 Law & Contemp. Probs. 353, 375 (1955)]. . . .

. . . If that plan is to have any efficacy as the basic planning tool for the City of Milwaukie, it must be given preference over conflicting prior zoning ordinances. To hold otherwise would allow a city to go through the motions and expense of formulating a comprehensive plan and then relegating that document to oblivion through continued reliance on the older zoning ordinances. . . .

533 P.2d at 775-76.

Baker stood alone for many years, and outside of Oregon, no state supreme court has required, without a clear statutory directive, that zoning ordinances be consistent with, and subservient to, comprehensive plans. See, e.g., State by Rochester Association of Neighborhoods v. City of Rochester, 268 N.W.2d 885 (Minn. 1978) (rejecting *Baker* by name). As discussed at pp. 58-59, more than a dozen states require that zoning be consistent with comprehensive plans the local government has adopted. The provisions of the statutes vary, as do state court interpretations of the meaning of consistency requirements. For a state-by-state review, see Edward J. Sullivan & Matthew J. Michel, *Ramapo* Plus Thirty: The Changing Role of the Plan in Land Use Regulation, 35 Urb. Law. 75 (2003).

Haines v. City of Phoenix
727 P.2d 339 (Ariz. Ct. App. 1986)

[As required by state statute, in 1979 Phoenix adopted a general plan. The plan limited the height of buildings along a portion of Central Avenue to no more than 250 feet. In 1984, the city council approved a rezoning that authorized the construction of a 500-foot-high office building in the same area. In his attack on the zoning change, Haines invoked an Arizona consistency statute, Ariz. Rev. Stat. §9-462.01(E), which requires that "[a]ll zoning ordinances or regulations adopted under this article shall be consistent with the adopted general or specific plans of the municipality." The trial court granted summary judgment in favor of the city.]

HATHAWAY, Chief Judge. . . .

If we were to apply the rational basis review to the current situation, we would presume the rezoning to be valid and would uphold its validity if we could hypothesize any reason why the city council may have believed the rezoning was consistent with the general plan. Some courts have taken this approach to deciding whether a zoning amendment is consistent with a general plan. Barret v. County of Shelby, 619 S.W.2d 390 (Tenn. App. 1981); see also Environmental Council of Sacramento v. Board of Supervisors, 185 Cal. Rptr. 363 ([Ct. App.] 1982). Appellant argues, however, that the passage of §9-462.01(E) vitiates the . . . normal level of review. He argues that if rational basis review is utilized, the legislative mandate requiring consistency between zoning and the general plan is without any force. Appellant argues instead that, due to the statute, there be no presumption of legislative validity and the city council be required to make written findings and articulate reasons for any deviation from the general plan. There is support for this approach. See Love v. Board of County Comm'rs, 671 P.2d 471 (Idaho 1983).

We, however, reject both of the above approaches. By the enactment of §9-462.01(E), the legislature has provided a standard by which to review zoning decisions in addition to the usual constitutional standard. That standard is consistency with the general plan. In our review, however, we will not substitute our judgment for that of the duly elected legislative body, the city council. Therefore our review will consist of viewing the record that was before the city council and determining if, from that evidence, the council could have decided that despite the deviation from the letter of the plan there was consistency. The burden of proof will still be on the plaintiff to show inconsistency.

Consistency has been defined as "basic harmony." J. Di Mento, The Consistency Doctrine and the Limits of Planning (1980). Therefore in the current situation if from the evidence before it the city council could have determined that the rezoning was in basic harmony with the general plan, the rezoning is valid. Of course in cases where the rezoning does not deviate from the general plan, rational basis review will still be utilized.

This rezoning did deviate from the general plan in that it surpassed by a large margin the 250-foot height restriction. The plan, however, has other goals for that area. The plan does provide that gradient areas where this proposed building lies will have some concentrations of land use in sub cores. Also there is a provision for commercial development of the Central Avenue corridor. The building height restrictions are only stated in precatory language. Additionally, the plan provided for open space in the gradient, encouragement of landscaping, areas for people to enjoy and commercial development. The city council had before it evidence that this building would be commercially beneficial, would provide open spaces and recreational areas, landscaping, etc. The council also heard testimony that the developer could build two 20-story buildings which would leave less open space and less potential recreational areas. In viewing the above evidence, we cannot say the city council was wrong in finding the rezoning in basic harmony with the general plan. We do not need specific findings by the council to come to this conclusion since we have viewed the same evidence the council viewed. Certainly written findings would be preferable, but they are not mandatory. . . .

Affirmed.

Note on Procedures and Standards for Determining Consistency

1. *Which decisions must be consistent?* The Arizona statute involved in *Haines* required "zoning ordinances or regulations" to be consistent with a city's plan. Do "adjudicative" actions such as the grant of special exceptions, variances, or building permits fall within this category? Compare, e.g., Enterprise Citizens Action Commission v. Clark County Board of Commissioners, 918 P.2d 305 (Nev. 1996) (variances must be consistent), with Hawkins v. County of Marin, 126 Cal. Rptr. 754 (Ct. App. 1976) (conditional use permits need not be consistent with the plan), and Elysian Heights Residents Association v. Los Angeles, 227 Cal. Rptr. 226 (Ct. App. 1986) (building permits need not be consistent). Note that in many jurisdictions, the criteria for granting a variance or special exception include consistency with the comprehensive plan, so application of the consistency statute itself may not be necessary.

2. *Spot zoning?* Would the rezoning at issue in *Haines* constitute spot zoning under the decisions discussed at pp. 309–17? Should consistency with the comprehensive plan be sufficient to defeat a charge of spot zoning regardless of other factors, such as the size of the parcel or incompatibility with surrounding land uses?

3. *Consistency through vagueness.* Does *Haines* encourage local governments to adopt vague or internally inconsistent plans in order to withstand consistency challenges? Should a court try to prevent such end runs around the consistency requirements? If so, how? Should the *Haines* court have considered the very specific height limit more important than the more general goals of increasing open space, encouraging landscaping, and so on?

4. *Rational basis review?* How exactly does the standard of review the *Haines* court adopted differ from the normal rational basis test discussed at pp. 95–112?

5. *Written findings?* In some states, a local agency may be required to prepare written findings to support the plan consistency of certain of its decisions. As a result, opponents of a zoning change may be able to buy time by arguing that express findings either were not made or were not adequately supported by the evidence. See, e.g., Love v. Board of County Commissioners of Bingham County, 671 P.2d 471, 473 (Idaho 1983). The American Planning Association's Growing Smart project has proposed a model zoning enabling act that would require the local planning agency to conduct a written analysis of consistency with the comprehensive plan for all proposed rezonings or discretionary land use actions. For an analysis of the model act, see Stuart Meck, The Legislative Requirement That Zoning and Land Use Controls Be Consistent with an Independently Adopted Local Comprehensive Plan: A Model Statute, 3 Wash. U. J.L. & Pol'y 295 (2000).

6. *Plans are ceilings, but not floors.* In Marracci v. City of Scappoose, 552 P.2d 552 (Or. Ct. App. 1976), the city denied plaintiff's application for a special exception to construct multifamily housing even though the city's comprehensive plan designated plaintiff's land for "higher density residential" use. Citing *Baker*, the Oregon Court of Appeals sustained the denial, saying in part:

> The applicable comprehensive plan contains no timetable or other guidance on the question of when more restrictive zoning ordinances will evolve toward conformity with more permissive provisions of the plan. In such a situation, we hold the determination of when to conform more restrictive zoning ordinances with the plan is a legislative judgment to be made by a local governing body, and only subject to limited judicial review for patent arbitrariness. In adopting a comprehensive plan, a governing body necessarily makes a great number of legislative and policy judgments about what the future use of land might and should be. It is just as much a legislative judgment when the local governing body is called upon to decide whether "the future has arrived" and it is therefore appropriate to conform zoning with planning.
>
> There is no suggestion in the present record that the defendant city's determination that it was premature to move toward the more intensive multiple-family residential use allowed by the plan was in any sense arbitrary.

Id. at 553. See also Board of County Commissioners v. Snyder, 627 So. 2d 469 (Fla. 1993), excerpted at p. 341. The *Marracci* rule, requiring a developer to comply with the stricter of the plan and zoning provisions, has been adopted in some of the states that have consistency statutes. In Manalapan Realty, L.P. v. Township Committee, 658 A.2d 1230 (N.J. 1995), for example, the township's master plan had designated a district for "mixed commercial uses." To thwart a proposed Home Depot outlet, opponents persuaded the township to amend the zoning ordinance to prohibit retail stores in the district from selling lumber and building materials. The New Jersey Supreme Court held that this amendment did not violate a statute requiring zoning to be "substantially consistent" with a master plan. *Manalapan* implies that, in practice, consistency statutes do little to elevate the legal importance of the comprehensive plan, at least in developer challenges. But there also is authority on the other side. See, e.g., Lesher Communications, Inc. v. City of Walnut Creek, 802 P.2d 317 (Cal. 1990) (initiative measure limiting municipal growth found to conflict with comprehensive plan, which was growth oriented).

7. *The wisdom of consistency requirements.* In light of the obstacles to rational planning discussed at pp. 65–71, what are the costs and benefits of a consistency requirement? See, e.g., Robert C. Apgar, Essay, Comprehensive Plans in the Twenty-First Century: Suggestions to Improve a Valuable Process, 30 Stetson L. Rev. 965 (2001) (reviewing serious problems resulting from the consistency requirement in Florida); Gus Bauman, APA Growing Smart Legislation: Consistency of Land Use Regulations with the Local Comprehensive Plan, SG021 ALI-ABA 613 (2001) (consistency requirements introduce uncertainty into land use development process and may produce unfairness when a property owner has relied on a rezoning or approval later found to be inconsistent with the plan); George Lefcoe, California's Land Planning Requirements: The Case for Deregulation, 54 S. Cal. L. Rev. 447 (1981) (consistency requirements interfere with local autonomy, fail to reduce corruption in the zoning process, and embrace a view of comprehensive social engineering that is unrealistic); A. Dan Tarlock, Consistency with Adopted Land Use Plans as a Standard of Judicial Review: The Case Against, 9 Urb. L. Ann. 69 (1975) (planning theory has never won widespread support and plans are likely to allocate land in an inefficient and arbitrary way).

Professor Mandelker, one of the leading proponents of planning, espouses the opposite view, mainly because he believes formal plans help to ensure that zoning decisions are not arbitrary. Daniel R. Mandelker, Planning and the Law, 20 Vt. L. Rev. 657 (1996); Daniel R. Mandelker, The Role of the Local Comprehensive Plan in Land Use Regulation, 74 Mich. L. Rev. 899 (1976). See also Joseph F. Di Mento, The Consistency Doctrine and the Limits of Planning (1980).

Note on Barriers to Plan Amendments

As this chapter has chronicled, the zoning system has evolved from rigid, end-state zoning to more flexible dealmaking. For dealmaking to be possible, a municipality must have the power both to place a tract with development potential into a restrictive (holding) classification and also to free the tract from the classification once the developer has agreed to make various contributions and design concessions.

A strict interpretation of consistency requirements is likely to alter the land use regulation process in two fundamental ways. First, it encourages a local government to favor plans that severely restrict development. If a liberal plan provision would trump a stricter zoning provision, only draconian planning preserves a municipality's bargaining power with developers. If a locality uses a plan to create "holding zones" that it may later bargain away, will the plan serve the purposes of planning discussed at pp. 50–55?

Second, strict construction of consistency requirements is likely to encourage increasing numbers of ad hoc amendments to comprehensive plans. Consistency requirements would mean little if a local governing body could amend its comprehensive plan as easily as its zoning map. A restricted landowner would then apply simultaneously for both plan and zoning-map amendments. The local agencies would hold simultaneous hearings on both applications (a procedure approved in Tierney v. Duris, 536 P.2d 435 (Or. Ct. App. 1975)), and if willing, would approve both amendments. Instant consistency! But see Price v. Payette County Board of County Commissioners, 958 P.2d 583 (Idaho 1998) (plan amendment held unlawful where record suggested that board considered rezoning first, then amended the plan to conform to the rezoning).

The judges, legislators, and others who envision the planning process as a method for controlling piecemeal decisions may attempt to counter the impetus toward dealmaking by making it harder for a municipality to amend a plan than a zoning map. See, e.g., South of Sunnyside Neighborhood League v. Board of Commissioners, 569 P.2d 1063 (Or. 1977) (when a comprehensive plan map is amended to change the permissible use of a single tract of land, without any change in the plan's underlying policies, the proponent of the change has the burden of proving that the change in the plan map is consistent with the goals and policies expressed in the plan as a whole). But see Karlson v. City of Camarillo, 161 Cal. Rptr. 260 (Ct. App. 1980) (rejecting a neighbor's allegations that two plan-map amendments that would have permitted denser development were inconsistent with other provisions of the plan, applying an undemanding "arbitrary and capricious" standard of review).

Some states have attempted to limit plan amendments by restricting the number of amendments that may be made in any year. See, e.g., Cal. Gov't Code §65358(b) (West 2004) (plan may not be amended more than four times per year).

Suppose a county were to switch a small tract of land lying within a large territory planned for agricultural use to a "heavy industrial" plan designation. Could distraught neighbors challenge this "spot planning" on constitutional grounds? Cf. the discussion of spot zoning on pp. 309–17. Or would that suit be premature until the city had, for example, also amended its zoning ordinance to permit heavy industry? Cf. 1000 Friends of Oregon v. Land Conservation & Development Commission, 591 P.2d 387 (Or. Ct. App. 1979) (neighbors' attack on abstract planning decision rejected on ripeness grounds).

2. Rejection of Deferential Review

Snyder v. Board of County Commissioners

595 So. 2d 65 (Fla. Dist. Ct. App. 1991), quashed, 627 So. 2d 469 (Fla. 1993)

PER CURIAM, ...

Petitioners, owners of a one-half acre parcel of land zoned GU (General Use) under the Brevard County Comprehensive Zoning Plan ordinance, desire to erect a multi-unit dwelling of their property and petitioned the governmental zoning authority, the Board of County Commissioners of Brevard County, to rezone their land to a RU-2-15 medium density multiple-family dwelling zoning classification.

... Upon receiving the rezoning application from the landowners, the staff of the Brevard County Comprehensive Planning and Zoning Department (P & ZD) reviewed it and ... [found that it was consistent with the comprehensive plan, met all requirements relating to essential facilities, and was compatible with the zoning of surrounding lands]. However, the staff noted ... that this parcel of land appeared to be located within a 100 year flood plain and because, for environmental reasons, the maximum residential density in a 100 year flood plain was two units per acre, that for this reason alone, the rezoning request should not be approved. ...

[After a public hearing, at which it was revealed that the proposed development was *not* in the 100-year flood plain, the Planning and Zoning Board recommended approval of the zoning change.]

At a subsequent public hearing before the Brevard County Board of Commissioners ... a number of residents living in single-family homes north of the property sought to be rezoned appeared and spoke against the rezoning request. The objecting citizens expressed the usual concerns about traffic and parking problems, that they considered the neighborhood to be mainly single-family, that there was already multifamily zoning in the area that was not selling and that the residents did not want multifamily use in the area. ...

The Board of County Commissioners overruled the Planning and Zoning Board's recommendation and denied the rezoning request without giving any reason.

The landowners filed in the circuit court a Petition for Writ of Certiorari alleging that the . . . denial [of the rezoning] was arbitrary and unreasonable and had no substantial relation to the public health, safety, morals or general welfare and was not according to the essential requirements of law. . . .

[After the circuit court denied the petition,] [t]he landowners filed this petition for certiorari in this court. . . .

. . . The essential issue in this case is whether the decision by the County Commissioners to deny the landowners' rezoning request in this instance was a legislative act to which, under the constitutional separation of powers doctrine, the judiciary must give a deferential standard of review and uphold if "fairly debatable." . . .

[The Court begins its answer to that question with an impassioned exegesis about the Anglo-American conception of private property, concluding that "the right of a citizen to own property is one of the most fundamental and cherished rights and is the cornerstone that anchors the capitalistic form of government guaranteed by the federal and state constitutions."]

IV. Rezoning — Is It Executive, Legislative or Judicial Action?

IV. (A) SOME BASIC ZONING AND REZONING CONCEPTS

Historically, zoning developed as a governmental effort to create a fixed blue-print of development. The original zoning ordinances were to have broad uniform application to all. It was believed that the local governmental body would allow or disallow under fixed terms, applicable to all, a particular type of development in a particular area. Development was seen as a matter of right if the fixed criteria of the zoning ordinances was satisfied. . . .

However, in reality most development has not occurred "as-of-right" under actual zoning practices. Most communities in actual practice have zoned their undeveloped land under a highly restrictive classification such as "general use" and agriculture. Typically, in such "zones" the most development allowed was one single-family residence on very large parcels. The original intent was not to permanently preclude more intensive development but to adopt a "wait and see" attitude toward the direction of future development. Most government officials have little motivation to incur the "wrath of neighbors by zoning vacant land for industrial, commercial, or intensive residential development in advance of an actual proposal for development."

In reality, therefore, at the inception of zoning most land was zoned according to its then use, exceptions were grandfathered in and most vacant land was underzoned or "short-zoned." In order for development to proceed, rezoning becomes not the exception, but the rule. The burden is thus then placed on the landowner, who wishes to exercise his constitutional right to use his vacant property or make a more intense use of his underzoned land, to first obtain permission from the government. Whereas prior to zoning the burden was on government to allege and prove that protection of the public required a restriction on the use of private property, after zoning is adopted the roles are reversed and use of land is not only frozen but the burden is shifted to the landowner to obtain governmental permission to use privately owned property. Furthermore, rezoning is granted not solely on the basis of the land's suitability to the new zoning classification and compatibility with the use of surrounding acreage, but, also, and perhaps foremost, on local political considerations including who the owner is, who the objectors are, the particular and exact land improvement and use that is intended to be made and whose ox is being fattened or gored by the granting or denial of the rezoning request.

In this context, local governments frequently use governmental authority to make a rezoning decision as leverage in order to negotiate, impose, coerce and compel concessions and conditions on the developer. . . .

When land is restricted and regulated by zoning ordinances several things occur. Immediately and over time land that can be used more freely under zoning increases in market value as compared to similar land the use of which is more restricted by zoning. The value of land zoned and used for residential purposes is further enhanced because of the spaciousness occasioned by the non-use of nearby land, the use of which is restricted by zoning.

For these and other reasons persons owning or using land naturally prefer that nearby lands not be used at all and that their use be continued to be restricted by zoning regulations. The legislative and executive are the political branches of government and the governmental zoning bodies exercising those functions have politicized the "re-zoning" process by forming the issues and considering and determining them at public meetings to which nearby landowners are encouraged to appear and oppose requests for rezoning and the issue-forming, fact-finding and decision-making is conducted in a politicized forum and atmosphere rather than in a neutral forum by an independent deliberative body determining facts in a detached manner and applying general legislative rules of law impartially to individual cases or specific instances.

Because the procedure in considering the rezoning of individual parcels has been made political and the decision to grant them has been traditionally made in the form of enacting amendments to the general ordinances, general zoning bodies have often successfully urged that such decisions are legislative in character and that a proper respect for the separation of powers doctrine requires the courts to avoid involvement and that to the extent the court is involved it must defer to the "legislative" action by upholding it if it can be justified as being even "fairly debatable."

IV. (B) TRADITIONAL JUDICIAL REVIEW . .

It has frequently been broadly stated that a rezoning action is a legislative action, not a quasi-judicial action. In Schauer v. City of Miami Beach, 112 So. 2d 838, 839 (Fla. 1959), the supreme court stated:

> It is obvious to us that the enactment of the original zoning ordinance was a legislative function and *we cannot reason that the amendment of it was of different character.* (Emphasis added).

The answer is that there are two distinctly different types of amendments to zoning ordinances, one of which is legislative and the other of which is not, Schauer involved the enactment of a change in general policy of widespread applicability affecting a large area of the community rather than a "rezoning" that relates only to the application of an existing general legislated policy (i.e., a general rule of law) to a particular parcel of land and to owners whose property interests were easily identifiable. . . .

Broad judicial statements suggesting that all rezonings are legislative in nature are out of step with the realities of zoning practice and also with the evolvement of zoning law. Since . . . Schauer, the mechanics of zoning has come to be better known and understood and there have been significant changes in zoning law. . . .

In 1985, the Florida Legislature enacted the Local Government Comprehensive Planning and Land Development Regulation Act. Rezonings under the new act are required to be consistent with the local comprehensive plan. . . . As a result, Florida courts have adopted a standard of strict scrutiny in reviewing the consistency between local development orders (which include rezoning decisions) and the local comprehensive plan (which represents general legislative policy).

Moreover, Florida courts, in order to curb the favoritism, abuses and inconsistencies resulting from piecemeal rezoning decisions being treated as legislative in character, have developed a number of judicial doctrines not normally applied to legislative decisions. For example, "spot zoning" is likely to occur when local rezoning decisions are given the deference of legislative actions. The "change or mistake" rule has been developed to curb some of the abuses of "spot zoning." . . .

IV. (C) FASANO V. BOARD OF COUNTY COMMISSIONERS

. . . Other courts have moved away from the fairly debatable standard toward stricter scrutiny by reasoning that local rezonings are quasi-judicial in character and are not due the judicial deference inherent in the fairly debatable standard. The leading case expounding this latter view is the landmark decision of the Oregon Supreme Court in Fasano v. Board of County Comm'rs, 507 P.2d 23 (1973) (en banc).

In *Fasano*, the Board of County Commissioners had rezoned thirty-two acres of land zoned single-family residential to planned residential which allowed the construction of a mobile home park. The adjacent homeowners unsuccessfully opposed the rezoning. On appeal to the Oregon Supreme Court, the commissioners argued that the commissioners' decision was presumptively valid and that the homeowners had to show the decision was arbitrary and capricious to obtain relief.

The Oregon Supreme Court rejected this argument, stating:

> At this juncture we feel we would be ignoring reality to rigidly view all zoning decisions by local governing bodies as legislative acts to be accorded a full presumption of validity and shielded from less than constitutional scrutiny by the theory of separation of powers.

The *Fasano* court . . . [held that] the action was judicial in nature because it did not entail the development of a general policy applicable to a large portion of the public but the application of a general policy to specific identifiable parties and interests. The court used the following test to distinguish judicial from legislative actions:

> Basically, this test involves the determination of whether action produces a general rule or policy which is applicable to an open class of individuals, interests, or situations, or whether it entails the application of a general rule or policy to specific individuals, interests or situations. If the former determination is satisfied, there is legislative action; if the latter determination is satisfied, the action is quasi-judicial. . . .

The *Fasano* court reasoned that even though applying a greater scrutiny to rezoning actions might mean county commissioners could not adjust as freely to changed conditions, the "dangers of making desirable change more difficult" was to be less feared than "the dangers of the almost irresistible pressures that can be asserted by private economic interests on local government." The court concluded an adequate record with findings of fact must support a rezoning decision.

An increasing number of jurisdictions have either adopted the *Fasano* standard or accepted it in limited form. Besides Oregon, the supreme courts in the following states have adopted the *Fasano* approach: Washington, Idaho, [and] Kansas. The District of Columbia uses the quasi-judicial approach to rezonings as the result of legislation. States that have accepted the doctrine in limited form or expressed an inclination toward quasi-judicial review of rezonings are Virginia, Nevada, Illinois, Hawaii, Colorado and Montana. . . .

IV. (D) TOWARD A FUNCTIONAL ANALYSIS

We agree with the *Fasano* approach and conclude that rezonings are not legislative in nature. One writer has cogently contrasted legislative and judicial or quasi-judicial action in the following way:

> First, judicial action is narrow in scope, focusing on special individuals or on specific situations, while legislative action is open-ended, affecting a broad class of individuals or situations. . . .
>
> Secondly, legislative action results in the formulation of a general rule of policy, while judicial action results in the application of a general rule of policy. . . .
>
> Thirdly, it is generally stated that judicial action is retrospective, determining "[t]he rights and duties of parties under existing law and with relation to existing facts. . . . " By contrast, legislative action is said to be prospective, determining "[w]hat the law shall be in future cases". . . .

Peckingpaugh, Burden of Proof In Land Use Regulation: A Unified Approach and Application to Florida, 8 Fla. St. U. L. Rev. 499, 504 (1980). Initial zoning enactments and comprehensive rezonings or rezonings affecting a large portion of the public are legislative in character. However, rezoning actions which have an impact on a limited number of persons or property owners, on identifiable parties and interests, where the decision is contingent on a fact or facts arrived at from distinct alternatives presented at a hearing, and where the decision can be functionally viewed as policy application, rather than policy setting, are in the nature of executive or judicial or quasi-judicial action but are definitely not legislative in character. . . .

. . . [T]he manner in which the decision was made in this case was not legislative in nature. A hearing was held after notice to the parties and the decision was contingent on the evidence adduced as at an executive, (administrative), or judicial proceeding. This zoning action was not an action producing a policy of general applicability to a wide portion of the public, but an application of policy to a specific individual and a single parcel of land after a proceeding in which a decision was made between two distinct alternatives. . . .

V. CONCLUSION

We hold that: . . .

Since a property owner's right to own and use his property is constitutionally protected, review of any governmental action denying or abridging that right is subject to close judicial scrutiny. Effective judicial review, constitutional due process and other essential requirements of law, all necessitate that the governmental agency (by whatever name it may be characterized) applying legislated land use restrictions to particular parcels of privately owned lands, must state reasons for action that denies the owner the use of his land[68] and must make findings of fact and a record of its proceedings, sufficient for judicial review

---

68. Ordinances and statutes give certain classes of persons the right to oppose rezoning requests by landowners. However, neither such objectors nor the governmental zoning authority has a constitutional right to prevent a private landowner from enjoying his constitutionally protected right to own and use private property. Therefore, all presumptions should be in favor of the correctness of a decision granting a landowner's request for rezoning and that decision should be upheld by the courts if "fairly debatable."

of: the legal sufficiency of the evidence to support the findings of fact made, the legal sufficiency of the findings of fact supporting the reasons given and the legal adequacy, under applicable law (i.e., under general comprehensive zoning ordinances, applicable state and case law and state and federal constitutional provisions) of the reasons given for the result of the action taken.

The initial burden is upon the landowner to demonstrate that his petition or application for use of privately owned lands (rezoning, special exception, conditional use permit, variance, site plan approval, etc.) complies with the reasonable procedural requirements of the ordinance and that the use sought is consistent with the applicable comprehensive zoning plan. Upon such a showing the landowner is presumptively entitled to use his property in the manner he seeks unless the opposing governmental agency asserts and proves by clear and convincing evidence that a specifically stated public necessity requires a specified, more restrictive, use. After such a showing the burden shifts to the landowner to assert and prove that such specified more restrictive land use constitutes a taking of his property for public use for which he is entitled to compensation under the taking provisions of the state or federal constitutions.

Applying these principles to the facts of this case, we find (1) that the landowners' petition to the zoning authority for a zoning classification of RU-2-15 for their parcel of land demonstrated conclusively that such use was consistent with the county comprehensive plan of the county general zoning ordinance, (2) that there was no assertion or evidence that a more restrictive zoning classification was necessary to protect the health, safety, morals or welfare of the general public and (3) that the petitioning landowners were entitled to the zoning classification sought and its denial without given reasons supported by facts was, as a matter of law, arbitrary and unreasonable and judicially reviewable and reversible.

. . . Accordingly, the petition for certiorari in this case is granted, . . . and this cause is remanded for proceedings consistent with this opinion. . . .

Board of County Commissioners v. Snyder
627 So. 2d 469 (Fla. 1993)

GRIMES, Justice. . . .

We review Snyder v. Board of County Comm'rs, 595 So. 2d 65 (Fla. Dist. Ct. App. 1991), because of its conflict with Schauer v. City of Miami Beach, 112 So. 2d 838 (Fla. 1959). . . .

. . . [C]omprehensive rezonings affecting a large portion of the public are legislative in nature. However, we agree with the court below . . . [that] the board's action on Snyder's application was in the nature of a quasi-judicial proceeding. . . .

[The Court also agreed that the board's denial of the rezoning application therefore was subject to heightened scrutiny.]

At this point, we depart from the rationale of the court below. In the first place, the opinion overlooks the premise that the comprehensive plan is intended to provide for the future use of land, which contemplates a gradual and ordered growth. See City of Jacksonville Beach v. Grubbs, 461 So. 2d 160, 163 (Fla. Dist. Ct. App. 1984), in which the following statement from Marracci v. City of Scappoose, 552 P.2d 552, 553 (Or. Ct. App. 1976), was approved:

> [A] comprehensive plan only establishes a long-range maximum limit on the possible intensity of land use; a plan does not simultaneously establish an immediate minimum limit on the possible intensity of land use. The present use of land may, by zoning ordinance, continue to be more limited than the future use contemplated by the comprehensive plan.

Even where a denial of a zoning application would be inconsistent with the plan, the local government should have the discretion to decide that the maximum development density should not be allowed provided the governmental body approves some development that is consistent with the plan and the government's decision is supported by substantial, competent evidence.

Further, we cannot accept the proposition that once the landowner demonstrates that the proposed use is consistent with the comprehensive plan, he is presumptively entitled to this use unless the opposing governmental agency proves by clear and convincing evidence that specifically stated public necessity requires a more restricted use. We do not believe that a property owner is necessarily entitled to relief by proving consistency when the board action is also consistent with the plan. . . .

Upon consideration, we hold that a landowner seeking to rezone property has the burden of proving that the proposal is consistent with the comprehensive plan and complies with all procedural requirements of the zoning ordinance. At this point, the burden shifts to the governmental board to demonstrate that maintaining the existing zoning classification with respect to the property accomplishes a legitimate public purpose. In effect, the landowners' traditional remedies will be subsumed within this rule, and the board will now have the burden of showing that the refusal to rezone the property is not arbitrary, discriminatory, or unreasonable. If the board carries its burden, the application should be denied.

While they may be useful, the board will not be required to make findings of fact. However, in order to sustain the board's action, upon review by certiorari in the circuit court it must be shown that there was competent substantial evidence presented to the board to support its ruling. . . .

Based on the foregoing, we quash the decision below . . . . [W]e believe that justice would be best served by permitting [the Snyders] to file a new application for rezoning of the property. The application will . . . allow the process to begin anew according to the procedure outlined in our opinion.   — follow procedure outlined

BARKETT, C.J., and OVERTON, MCDONALD, KOGAN and HARDING, JJ., concur.

SHAW, J., dissents.

Note on *Snyder*   D.C. of Appeal — Wanted wait + re zoning

1. *What's behind "wait and see" zoning?* The *Snyder* District Court of Appeal's view of how land use control systems currently work enjoys wide anecdotal support. For classic descriptions, see, e.g., Richard F. Babcock, The Zoning Game 90–92 (1966); Richard F. Babcock & Charles L. Siemon, The Zoning Game Revisited (1985); Ira M. Heyman, Innovative Land Regulation and Comprehensive Planning, 13 Santa Clara Law. 183, 187–200 (1972); Jan Z. Krasnowiecki, Zoning Litigation — How to Win Without Really Losing, 1976 Inst. on Planning, Zoning & Eminent Domain 1, 3–4.

Why do local governments rely on "wait and see" zoning? In addition to the answers offered by the *Snyder* court, consider the explanation given by the Douglas Commission, an interdisciplinary panel of experts appointed by President Lyndon B. Johnson to examine housing and urban problems:

> *First,* these provisions enable communities to relate their regulatory process more closely to the process of development. Especially in undeveloped areas, detailed decisionmaking can be postponed until the pertinent facts become available. Depending on how carefully general

policies and requirements are determined in advance, this approach may carry out a plan or mark the absence of one.

Second, municipal discretion provides great opportunities to overcome some imperfections in the usual process used to achieve development that is compatible with its immediate surroundings. Most regulations rely essentially on probabilities to achieve such compatibility: regulations thus permit uses, buildings, densities and public facilities that will probably fit together properly. From the standpoint of development quality, such reliance on probabilities is a weakness of current regulations. Because the focus is on what will probably happen, regulation must often prohibit the good as well as the bad — or permit some bad as well as the good. (For example, such arbitrary standards as a limit of eight row houses in a row or a requirement for twenty-foot side yards may be salutary when dealing with usual low-quality design; but they also prohibit innovation — and would even prohibit some of the great urban designs of the past.) "Wait and see" provisions permit local reviewing agencies to exercise more refined, particularized control. Instead of having to be content with probabilities, they may consider all the special circumstances of the individual case — lot shape, traffic consequences, landscaping, sometimes even style of architecture, and many more.

Third, "wait and see" permits localities to obtain concessions that may be — or are feared to be — beyond local legal powers to demand directly. The concessions may have exclusionary objectives. . . . They may be aimed at achieving particularized design control. Or they may involve land dedications — especially for parks and school sites, but also for street widening or other public uses: the developer "voluntarily" provides these in return for development permission.

National Commission on Urban Problems, Building the American City: Douglas Commission Report, H.R. Doc. No. 91–34, at 206–08 (1968).

2. Snyder's *"troublesome suspicion" of local governments.* What justifies the great deference courts usually pay to legislative decisions? Why do both *Snyder* courts believe that justification is unwarranted in land use matters? If rezonings truly are granted on the basis of "political considerations" such as "whose ox is being fattened or gored," does that distinguish the process from, for example, the way in which tax codes are amended? Consider Professor Rose's explanation for what she refers to as a "troublesome suspicion" of local legislative bodies reflected in *Fasano* (and presumably its progeny):

Madison[] . . . [suggested] the qualities that make a legislature's decisions fair and reliable.

Madison's essay begins with the argument that the chief obstacle to fairness in a legislative body is "faction": the tendency of one interest group to impose its will at the expense of others. The antidote to faction, Madison says, lies in a constituency of sufficient size and variety. . . . Where the constituency is large, action is possible only through persuasion and coalitions of interest groups. Through a pattern of shifting alliances and vote trading, every interest can obtain at least partial satisfaction in the legislature. . . .

That all of the participating parties can expect some satisfaction of at least some of their desires is one assurance of fairness in legislation. Fairness is also advanced by the conditions that attend coalition-building itself: no interest group can safely go for the jugular of another, because all know that they may need to call on each other in different coalitions. . . .

. . . [A] second characteristic of . . . [the] legislature . . . [that] assures due consideration of the public interest [is that] the clash of multiple interests prevents hasty and ill-considered decisions and forces the legislators to take the time to reflect on the true public welfare. Because of these factors, then, the courts can safely trust the larger legislature to make fair and careful decisions under most circumstances, and can give broad leeway to those decisions. . . .

But this justification of large legislatures' decisions contains an implicit criticism of small-scale government: A legislative body drawn from too small or too homogeneous a constituency may be dominated by a single interest or faction. Factional domination may take varying forms.

One is sheer corruption, made possible in smaller representative bodies because a limited number of persons have influence which must be bought. . . . Finally, and perhaps most feared by Madison, is the factional domination created by a popular "passion" — sometimes a sudden whim, sometimes a longstanding prejudice — that carries a majority before it. Under any of these various forms of factional domination, all of which are far more likely to occur in a smaller legislature than in a larger one, a dominant group may subject others to sudden destruction or to permanent political disability.

In a small-scale government, then, there may be no clash of multiple interests leading to at least temporary stasis and ultimately to an adequate and careful consideration of the public well-being. Moreover, . . . there may not be enough items of political interest to permit the development of coalitions and the benefit-trading and mutual forbearance they entail. Thus, a local representative council cannot (or cannot always) be trusted to act with the "legislative due process" envisioned by The Federalist No. 10 in a larger legislature.

Carol M. Rose, Planning and Dealing: Piecemeal Land Controls as a Problem of Local Legitimacy, 71 Cal. L. Rev. 837, 854–56 (1983). Professor Rose goes on to reject the Madisonian critique, finding alternative sources of local government fairness in participation and the opportunity for choice. Nevertheless, the Madisonian critique raises issues: If *Snyder* is based on the premise that local governments are "too small and homogeneous" and do not deal with enough issues to promote coalitions and vote-trading, should *Snyder* apply to Miami? Should that depend on whether the rezoning decision challenged affects only a few single-issue interest groups?

3. *The analogy to adjudicative actions by administrative agencies.* If *Snyder* is correct that all local legislative bodies do not provide the protections against faction that justify judicial deference to legislative decisions, does it follow that rezonings should be considered "quasi-judicial"? Professor Rose argues that the courts have gone wrong in invoking the quasi-judicial model:

> According to plan jurisprudence, the courts view local governing bodies as if they, like administrative agencies, could move back and forth between the traditional legislative and judicial functions, wearing a judicial hat when, for a particular task, the "legislative" rubric cannot ensure fairness and due consideration. This raises a question: Are local bodies equipped to make these switches so that, when they supposedly act judicially, fairness and due consideration are ensured?
>
> The judicial or quasi-judicial function has its own criteria for fairness and due consideration, notably the presence of preexisting standards and procedural rules that channel discussion and decision of each individual case toward those standards. But The Federalist's examination of judicial due consideration and fairness had another element as well: secure tenure of office, in order to promote judicial steadiness, impartiality, and insulation from irrelevant pressures. Administrative agencies, and, even more, elective local governing officials, lack this additional legitimizing aspect of the federal judicial branch.
>
> In the traditional doctrine of administrative law, the chief substitute for the guarantee of institutional competence provided by life tenure is technical expertise; mastery of the subject matter ensures that the agency will come to the correct conclusion. Even in many administrative agencies, technical expertise has become more debatable of late as an assurance of sound decisions, though no very good alternative has been identified. But in local governments' land changes, technical expertise is no assurance at all, because local governments simply do not have it.
>
> Administrative agencies traditionally exercise their discretionary powers within a defined subject matter — consumer product safety, for example, or environmental protection, or a given form of transportation. Local governing bodies, on the other hand, exercise general powers of government, limited by geographic area rather than by subject matter. Land use

issues might to some degree be regarded as specialized matters, but on closer examination their specialized quality evaporates. It is true that local governments are advised by planning commissions, but the commissioners are normally ordinary citizens with no special expertise. Planning commission advisory staffs are professionals, but even professional planners have come to see their tasks as more political than technical. The local governing bodies who pass zoning ordinances and amendments have more and more come to use land use controls as a general means of governing. If they have any "expertise" in land as such, it derives less from professional or technical education or information than from sheer familiarity with a locality taken as a whole, in all its complexity. This expertise is of a quite different order from that which substitutes for life tenure, and the difference has bedeviled the quasi-judicialization of local land use decisions.

Indeed, any notion of adjudicative impartiality is threatened by the kind of expertise local decisionmakers do have: namely, political expertise. Can local decisionmakers really be expected to be impartial in their quasi-judicial capacity when they are not in their other capacities?

Rose, supra, at 868–70. Professor Rose proposes that the courts instead view a local government that decides piecemeal land use changes as acting in a "mediative" role. Judicial scrutiny of a local government's decisions would then focus on whether interested parties had an opportunity to participate in the mediation process, whether the local government fully explored the issues those interests raised, whether the local government disclosed and explained the norms it used and the tradeoffs it made in reaching a decision, and whether the decision reached was reasonably foreseeable by individuals who had some opportunity to exit the community. Id. at 894–900, 908–10.

4. *Protection for landowners or neighbors?* Footnote 68 of the *Snyder* lower court's opinion limits the higher scrutiny of rezonings to situations in which the landowner challenges the rezoning, on the ground that neighbors have no right to interfere with landowners' constitutional property rights and therefore should be entitled only to traditional deferential scrutiny for their challenges. *Fasano*, on the other hand, was a neighbor's case, and was based in substantial part on the court's concern about the "irresistible pressures that can be asserted by private economic interests on local governments." 507 P.2d at 29. Indeed, many of the doctrines courts have developed for limiting local government discretion have assumed that the problem is disproportionate influence by development interests. Those doctrines have rarely been limited to neighbors' cases, however. Given the evidence discussed earlier on pp. 304–08 that local rezoning politics differ depending on the size, diversity, and complexity of the jurisdiction, is there any justification for relegating neighbors to traditional deferential review, while granting property owners higher scrutiny (or vice versa)? If property owners' rights are infringed by overreaching neighbors, why aren't the remedies available under the Takings Clause, discussed at pp. 134–97, sufficient to address the problem?

5. *The illusive distinction between legislative and quasi-judicial rezonings.* How easy will it be for litigants and courts to distinguish between what the Florida Supreme Court refers to as comprehensive rezonings, subject to traditional deference, and limited impact rezonings, subject to greater scrutiny? That problem bedeviled Oregon courts in the few years following *Fasano*, until the Oregon Supreme Court decided that the rezoning of a 601-acre parcel of land was a quasi-judicial decision. The court reasoned that the rezoning affected a relatively small number of identifiable persons, required the application of established criteria to a specific factual setting, and involved a process that was "bound to result in a decision" among a relatively constrained set of options. The court dismissed the claim that the decision involved policy considerations regarding the provision of governmental services and intergovernmental cooperation, reasoning that such policy considerations

were inherent in all decisions about large-scale projects. Neuberger v. City of Portland, 603 P.2d 771 (Or. 1979). After *Neuberger*, can one imagine a map amendment that the Supreme Court of Oregon would *not* regard as quasi-judicial? See also Todd W. Prall, Comment, Dysfunctional Distinctions in Land Use: The Failure of Legislative/Adjudicative Distinctions in Utah and the Case for a Uniform Standard of Review, 2004 B.Y.U. L. Rev. 1049.

Snyder's distinction between comprehensive and limited impact rezonings has been criticized as logically inconsistent: If the consistency requirement justifies greater scrutiny of smaller-scale rezonings, and comprehensive rezonings also are subject to the consistency requirement, why should the latter enjoy traditional deference? Thomas G. Pelham, Quasi-Judicial Rezonings: A Commentary on the *Snyder* Decision and the Consistency Requirement, 9 J. Land Use & Envtl. L. 243, 284–85 (1994). See also Jeffrey M. Taylor, Note, Untangling the Law of Site-Specific Rezoning in Florida: A Critical Evaluation of the Functional Approach, 45 Fla. L. Rev. 873, 908–10 (1993).

If impact on a limited number of persons or property and applying rather than making policy are the hallmarks of quasi-judicial decisions in Florida, should at least some amendments to the comprehensive plan be classified as quasi-judicial? See Minnaugh v. County Commission of Broward County, 783 So. 2d 1054 (Fla. 2001) (rejecting extension of *Snyder* to very small scale plan amendments); Martin County v. Yusem, 690 So. 2d 1288 (Fla. 1997) (rejecting extension of *Snyder* to amendments to local comprehensive plans, even though the amendment at issue was for one 54-acre parcel, was sought in connection with a proposed rezoning, and was the subject of a hearing at which the property owner presented detailed evidence of the facts relating to his particular property).

6. *Relationship to other doctrines.* In states that adopt the *Fasano/Snyder* rule, is there any further need for the "tempered deference" rules described earlier at pp. 309–41? If not, should the Florida Supreme Court declare those rules to be superseded?

7. *The costs of* Snyder. There is no such thing as free due process. Consider the arguments advanced in Pelham, supra, at 278–80:

> [L]ocal governments and their officials have an interest in maintaining a manageable local zoning process which is not so cumbersome and time-consuming that it overtaxes the resources and capabilities of local decision-making bodies. This interest is of special concern to small local governments with limited staffs and financial resources. . . . [P]roperty owners and other affected citizens have a strong interest in a rational local decision-making process that affords fair treatment and due process and produces decisions based on previously established policies and standards rather than the undue political influence of a particular applicant, industry or constituency. On the other hand, these same groups have an interest in ensuring that the zoning process does not become so judicialized that effective participation requires the employment of lawyers and other professionals for even the most routine rezoning application.
>
> Application of the quasi-judicial model to rezoning adversely affects several of these interests. Requiring local governments to conduct a formal, judicial-type proceeding on every quasi-judicial rezoning application, no matter how small or insignificant and regardless of whether anyone desires to challenge the decision, greatly complicates the local decision-making process and places a heavy strain on the time and resources of local governments. Although property owners and affected citizens are ensured of a more rational local decision-making process, one may legitimately question whether this requires more process than necessary. Indeed, some property owners and other affected citizens may be unduly burdened by the necessity of employing attorneys and other experts to present their cases to the local zoning authority. . . .

See also Craig Coller, Should The Narrowing Scope of Second-Tier Certiorari Mandate Findings of Fact in Local Government Quasi-Judicial Decisions?, Fla. B.J., July/Aug. 2002, at 67. An additional problem arises because decisionmakers in quasi-judicial proceedings are typically precluded from ex parte contacts, such as might occur if a local council member is questioned or lobbied by a constituent about a particular rezoning.

8. *The distinction between legislative and quasi-judicial decisions.* Numerous issues in land use law turn on whether a governmental decision can be characterized as legislative. This characterization may affect, in addition to the appropriate standard of judicial review, such matters as (1) when the decision is ripe for review, (2) the immunity of a local official from §1983 damage suits, (3) the procedures to be followed when the decision is made, (4) the procedures litigants must follow to secure judicial review, and (5) whether the decision may be submitted to popular vote. Ironically, in Florida, the designation of limited impact rezonings as quasi-judicial limits the nature of the trial court's review, and the nature of the appellate court's review of the trial court's decision, in ways that have created considerable confusion and some consternation that *Snyder*'s bold move will have less impact on local land use than its supporters hoped. Graham C. Penn, Student Note, Trying to Fit an Elephant in a Volkswagen: Six Years of the *Snyder* Decision in Florida Land Use Law, 52 Fla. L. Rev. 217, 239–40 (2000).

C.   The Procedural Rights of Developers and Their Neighbors

Developments in the Law — Zoning
91 Harv. L. Rev. 1427, 1505–08, 1524 (1978)

A functional analysis of due process suggests that at least three distinct interests are served by extending process rights. First, due process assures that governmental decisions affecting individuals are made correctly and efficiently (the efficiency interest). Second, it permits the person affected by a decision to argue before the relevant body about the substantive rules that are to be applied and how they should be interpreted in the particular instance (the representational interest). Third, and last, it protects individual dignity by requiring that the government explain its actions to those directly affected (the dignity interest). . . .

. . . Within the context of zoning decisions, efficiency interests are clearly implicated, for example, in the specific requirements that zoning boards consistently and accurately implement the statutory grant of zoning authority, that decisions be supported by substantial evidence, and that a record be made to facilitate review of whether decisionmaking criteria have been correctly applied.

The efficiency interest takes as given the rules being used to reach a decision, and demands only that these rules be accurately applied. The representational function, on the other hand, relates due process directly to the substantive rules of decision by promoting debate over the merits and correct interpretation of the rules themselves. Courts frequently characterize hearings as an "informal give and take," thus recognizing that a function of due process is to allow the individual to question the substantive scope of the relevant legal rules and the acceptability of the outcome for the specific situation. The representational function becomes particularly important where, as is true in many zoning cases, the criteria of decisionmaking are inherently imprecise. Zoning variances illustrate this aspect of the representational function. Most variance ordinances require that "undue hardship" be demonstrated before the variance is granted. Hearings on variance applications serve the representational interest by allowing interested parties to argue how "undue hardship" should be characterized and how such a characterization should be applied to the specific facts. The hearing, of course, also serves the efficiency and dignity interests by bringing all relevant information to the decisionmaker's attention, and by allowing persons to feel that they are not being subjected to some "secret, one-sided determination of facts decisive of rights."

Unlike the efficiency or representational aspects of due process, the dignity function is not concerned with the individual's right to argue for a different outcome in his particular case. Instead, participation is required because human dignity mandates consultation with an individual prior to taking any action vitally affecting his interests. The Supreme Court has recognized that participation is the surest means of fostering the belief that government may not act against the governed in a clandestine or arbitrary manner. As Justice Frankfurter noted in his famous concurrence in Joint Anti-Fascist Refugee Committee v. McGrath:[28] "Nor has a better way been found [than procedural due process] for generating the feeling, so important to a popular government, that justice has been done." . . .

As a general constitutional matter, the Supreme Court has stressed that "due process is flexible and calls for such procedural protections as the particular situation demands."[100] The Court has articulated a balancing test to determine the requirements of due process in any given situation: the private interest affected by the government interest, and the value of additional procedures in guarding against erroneous deprivations of that interest, are weighed against the fiscal and administrative burdens that the additional procedures would impose upon the government.[101]

1. Fair Proceedings

Korean Buddhist Dae Won Sa Temple of Hawaii v. Sullivan
953 P.2d 1315 (Haw. 1998)

LEVINSON, Justice. . . .

On September 25, 1986, the Honolulu Building Department issued a building permit to the Temple to expand the construction on its compound (then consisting of several buildings, a courtyard, and statuary) in an "R-5" residential district. . . . The permit authorized the construction of the Hall, which the Temple expected to use for "offices, [a] library, [a] museum and [an] exhibition room intended to further the understanding of the Korean Buddhist religion." The permit approved the Temple's building plans accompanying its permit request, which indicated that the height of the Hall would be approximately 66 feet above grade. No revision of the building plans was ever submitted to the Building Department. . . . However, after the Hall was actually built, a DLU [Department of Land Utilization] inspector determined that an extra floor had been built and that the structure's height was 74 to 75 feet — 9 feet higher than authorized by the building permit and 6.88 feet higher than the maximum height allowed by [the zoning ordinance]. . . . Accordingly, the inspector issued a notice of violation on February 23, 1988, ordering the Temple to stop work on the Hall.

---

28. 341 U.S. 123 (1951).

100. Morrissey v. Brewer, 408 U.S. 471, 481 (1972).

101. See Mathews v. Eldridge, 424 U.S. 319, 335 (1976); Mashaw, The Supreme Court's Due Process Calculus for Administrative Adjudication in *Mathews v. Eldridge*: Three Factors in Search of a Theory of Value, 44 U. Chi. L. Rev. 28 (1976); Note, Specifying the Procedures Required by Due Process: Toward Limits on the Use of Interest Balancing, 88 Harv. L. Rev. 1510.

The Temple filed its first application for a variance on June 15, 1988. The Director denied the application on September 16, 1988, after a public hearing . . . [ruling] that the Temple had not met the standards for hardship that were required for a variance by the Revised Charter of the City and County of Honolulu (1973) (RCCCH or the City Charter). . . .

The Temple filed a second variance application for a height overage on February 1, 1993. The Director considered the application "because the rules and regulations pertaining to variance applications permit an applicant to reapply for the same or substantially the same variance one year from the effective date of the denial." Public hearings were held on the 1993 variance application on September 2, 1993 and October 14, 1993. . . .

Despite the Temple's insistence that it was entitled to a trial-like "contested case" hearing, the hearings officer (HO) treated the hearings as "public," allowing all witnesses to testify briefly without being subject to direct or cross-examination. The HO denied the Temple's repeated requests to cross-examine witnesses, but allowed the Temple to proffer rebuttal witnesses and arguments. In addition to the legal argument by counsel, fifty-three witnesses testified in support of the Temple's application, and twelve spoke in opposition, including representatives of the neighborhood organizations, "Concerned Citizens of Palolo" and "Life of the Land." Numerous letters, written statements, photographs, charts, and other exhibits, including evidence that other Buddhist temples in Korea and Hawaii are not as large as the Hall and copies of a petition in support of the variance request allegedly signed by over 15,000 people. . . .

Abbot Dae Won Ki, the spiritual leader of the Temple, introduced written testimony, in which he explained . . .

> [o]ur Buddhist order emphasizes meditation and all of the buildings and other parts of the Temple compound are very sensitively designed to be in balance and harmony with each other and the mountains which surround the Temple. The individual [b]uildings[,] and the individual parts of the buildings, serve more than a secular purpose[;] they add up to a whole, more like a religious work of art. Removing the peak of the roof of the Main Temple Hall would be comparable to removing the hand of God from Michelangelo's painting on the ceiling of the Sistine chapel, or the head of Mary on the Pieta. This balance and harmony is an integral part of the religious teaching and experience which leads to Enlightenment. The Main Temple Hall is an integral part of this balance and harmony[;] it is not too tall and it is not too short[;] it is as it should be.

Finally, Abbot Ki stated that traditional Korean "temple builders" had been brought in from Korea to design and construct the project after the initial plans had been submitted to the Building Department. In order to "create the necessary balance and harmony" the builders had altered the plans and, thus, had extended the Hall to its present height. Describing the act of reducing the height of the Hall as a "desecration of the worst kind," the abbot asserted that it would also cause extreme financial hardship to the Temple. . . .

. . . Those testifying in opposition to the variance voiced a number of complaints, ranging from damage, noise, pollution, and other interference with their property — all of which had resulted from the sustained construction on the Temple site — to parking congestion and the effects of the imposing size of the Hall, including loss of views, declining property values, and a sense of being overshadowed in their homes and yards. . . .

The Director . . . examined the facts in light of the three findings required for the issuance of a variance outlined in RCCCH §6-910:(1) that without the variance the applicant would be denied reasonable use; (2) that the hardship is based on unique circumstances; and (3) that the variance does not alter the essential character of the neighborhood or act contrary to the intent and purpose of the zoning ordinance.

With respect to the first factor, the Director found that the Temple would have reasonable use of its land without a variance. . . . The Director . . . rejected the Temple's religious, architectural, and historical arguments that the roof must be higher than originally permitted, noting that the Temple itself had initially submitted plans calling for a height no greater that 66 feet. . . .

Regarding the second factor, the Director ruled that no unique circumstances had been demonstrated. He found that the topographical conditions were not unusual for the neighborhood. He also rejected the Temple's arguments that it would be especially costly to lower the roof, reasoning that the hardship was self-created.

Finally, with respect to the third factor, and relying on the opposition testimony of neighbors and the considerable height of the building, the Director ruled that the height overage altered the essential residential character of the neighborhood. . . .

Accordingly, the Director denied the Temple's variance application and ordered removal of that portion of the Hall exceeding 66 feet in height. . . .

The Temple appealed the Director's decision and order regarding its request for a variance. . . .

The ZBA held consolidated hearings on the Temple's . . . appeals over six dates between February 17, 1994 and July 14, 1994. At a pre-hearing scheduling session, the Temple asked . . . whether the Temple would be allowed to introduce new evidence. The Chair of the ZBA . . . ruled that the ZBA would not "accept any new evidence because we're looking to see if the Director was arbitrary and capricious based on the facts known to him at the time he made his decision."

In the course of the ZBA hearings, the parties were permitted to call and cross-examine witnesses. Nevertheless, the Temple declined to call any witnesses, opting instead to present its case through the documentary record and through cross-examination of the City's witnesses (all of whom were employees of the DLU). On cross-examination, the Director testified that his staff had proffered evidence to him that had not been formally introduced at the public hearing conducted by the HO and that this was common practice:

> Q (By [the Temple's counsel:]) The bottom line, though[,] is that evidence was considered that didn't — that wasn't introduced at the hearings officer's hearing.
> A There's lots of evidence that was considered that wasn't introduced at the hearings officer's —
> Q What other kind of evidence?
> A Anything that's submitted. We're not in a court of law when we're doing this. We accept documents from the neighborhood. We accept documents from anybody who wants to submit them to us. The public hearing is a requirement by law, and those who wish to participate in that may; but that's not the only information we use. That would be terrible. We're not in a court of law. . . .
> Q . . . Is there any provision that you have in the way you operate that allows an applicant to address things that you're considering that the applicant doesn't know you're considering?
> A The applicant can review the files at any time.
> Q How does the applicant know what you're considering?
> A If the applicant [is] concerned, they'll go and review the files and find out what's in there.

Among the items submitted to the Director by his staff in connection with the Temple's variance application were "drawings in a book that related to Buddhist religion in Korea," the title and author of which the Director could not remember. These drawings purportedly suggested that the teachings of Buddhism did not require the Hall to be of the height to which it was built. Additionally, the staff had undertaken to proffer testimony regarding the nature of Buddhism, to be given by a "qualified individual." The Director testified that his staff had brought this testimony to his attention in response to the Temple's evidence on the subject, but that he had not actually considered it in making his decision and, for that reason, had decided not to make it part of the record:

> These are things that they . . . mentioned to me and showed me, but they are not part of the file . . . because the religious aspects of this building are not at issue in the variance.
> You brought it up as it were, but in my opinion in looking at the charter and looking at the criteria for judgment, the religious significance of the structure, the height or the things that you mentioned is not a factor in my . . . giving a variance or denying a variance. . . . The religious aspects of this, regardless of what they are, had no bearing on the variance.

The ZBA Chair sustained the City's objection to the Temple's continued examination as to the identity of the "qualified individual," on the basis that the Director had not considered the matter in rendering his decision.

The ZBA rejected the positions advanced [by the Temple] . . . entering findings of fact and conclusions of law similar to those of the Director. . . . [The Temple appealed to the circuit court, which rejected the Temple's claims.] . . .

III. Discussion

The Temple asserts . . . that it was denied its right to procedural due process under the fourteenth amendment to the United States Constitution and article I, section 5[28] of the Hawaii Constitution (1978). . . .

As noted above, the only significant limitation to which the Temple was subjected in the ZBA proceedings was that it was afforded no opportunity to cross-examine those witnesses who had testified at the public hearing but not before the ZBA. The question before this court, therefore, is whether that restriction of access to cross-examination violated the Temple's right to procedural due process.

We have repeatedly recognized that . . .

> The full rights of due process present in a court of law, including presentation of witnesses and cross-examination, do not automatically attach to a quasi-judicial hearing. See Goss v. Lopez, 419 U.S. 565 (1975); Arnett v. Kennedy, 416 U.S. 134 (1974). . . .
> Determination of the specific procedures required to satisfy due process requires a balancing of several factors: (1) the private interest which will be affected; (2) the risk of an erroneous deprivation of such interest through the procedures actually used, and the probable value, if any, of additional or alternative procedural safeguards; and (3) the governmental interest, including the burden that additional procedural safeguards would entail. Mathews v. Eldridge, 424 U.S. at 335. . . .

Sandy Beach Defense Fund [v. City Council], 773 P.2d [250], 261 [(Haw. 1989)].

This court has never, however, directly considered the issue of cross-examination within the context of zoning proceedings. . . .

Other jurisdictions are split as to whether zoning variance hearings and similar proceedings may validly be conducted without according the parties the right to cross-examine all adverse witnesses. Compare, e.g., Chongris v. Board of Appeals, 811 F.2d 36, 42 (1st Cir. 1987) ("[O]mitting cross-examination at a zoning hearing or kindred event does not

---

28. Article I, section 5 of the Hawaii Constitution provides in relevant part that "[n]o person shall be deprived of life, liberty or property without due process of law[.]"

amount to a denial of due process in violation of the fourteenth amendment."), . . . with Kelly Supply Co., Inc. v. City of Anchorage, 516 P.2d 1206, 1209 (Alaska 1973) ("[T]he right of cross-examination undoubtedly exists in hearings on zoning matters[.]"), and Humble Oil & Refining Co. v. Board of Aldermen, 202 S.E.2d 129, 137 (N.C. 1974) ("[A] zoning board of adjustment, or a board of aldermen conducting a quasi-judicial hearing, can dispense with no essential element of a fair trial . . . [including the right to] cross-examine witnesses[.]"). See generally 3 Edward H. Ziegler, Jr., Rathkopf's Law of Zoning and Planning §37.06(5) (Supp. 1997) (listing cases on both sides of the issue).

An independent examination of the Sandy Beach Defense Fund/Mathews factors suggests that the DLU's variance application procedures are cause for concern, at least in the abstract. With regard to the first factor, it is clear that the Temple has an important property interest at stake in its variance application. With regard to the second, the absence of the opportunity for cross-examination in the ZBA's proceedings creates the potential "risk of an erroneous deprivation" in the form of the loss of potentially vital evidence. As noted above, even if the Temple had subpoenaed witnesses to testify at . . . the ZBA's hearings, the limitations imposed on the ZBA's scope of review could conceivably hamper the Temple's ability to examine them fully. At least one of the RCCCH §6-610 factors — the inquiry into whether the applicant's land possesses "unique characteristics" — would seem to invite testimony that is technical in nature. Fully testing the strength of the opinions of architects or similar adversarial witnesses through cross-examination (or though leading questions of a hostile witness on direct examination) would likewise seem to be worthwhile. Finally, with regard to the third factor, although the City argues that it would be unthinkably burdensome on the DLU to offer full trial-like hearings before the Director were to render his decision as to each variance request, all variance applications were presumably afforded such protections in the ZBA prior to 1987, when the mayor shifted power over the determination of variance requests from the ZBA to the Director. Thus, the City was evidently capable of coping with these procedures in the past without undue administrative burden.

Nevertheless, despite the potential for unfairness that is subsumed within the DLU's processes, it appears that the Temple suffered no demonstrable prejudice in this case. As noted above, the Temple adduced extensive oral and documentary evidence and was permitted to rebut the testimony of opposing witnesses. No expert witnesses testified in opposition to the Temple at the public hearing before the HO, with the exception of a DLU employee, who also testified in the course of the ZBA hearings, where the Temple subjected her to intensive cross-examination. Only neighbors and community leaders, whose testimony generally related to their subjective feelings and legal arguments about the Hall's size, were exempted from cross-examination in this case.

A constitutional error is harmless so long as "the court . . . [is] able to declare a belief that it was harmless beyond a reasonable doubt." Chapman v. California, 386 U.S. 18, 24 (1966). . . . Although some constitutional rights are considered so fundamental that their denial may never be considered harmless, . . . the harmless error standard nevertheless applies to infringements on the right to cross-examine witnesses. See Delaware v. Van Arsdall, 475 U.S. 673 (1986) (addressing a criminal defendant's right to confrontation).

On the record before us, we hold that the Temple's inability to cross-examine its neighbors regarding whether they actually "felt" oppressed by the Hall's size was harmless beyond a reasonable doubt. Wholly separate and apart from their testimony, there was substantial support in the record for the Director's and ZBA's decisions. It is virtually inconceivable that cross-examination of the witnesses in question would have altered the decisions in any way. . . .

Similarly, we hold that the Director's exposure to material outside the record — relating to the nature of Buddhism — was constitutionally harmless beyond a reasonable doubt because the question of "religious hardship" was immaterial to the issue before the Director, and, moreover, the Director expressly declined to consider the material in rendering his decision. . . .

Accordingly, although the DLU's review procedures governing variance applications are flawed and have the potential for violating the rights of litigants to procedural due process, we hold beyond a reasonable doubt that any procedural errors committed in this case did not prejudice the Temple and were, therefore, harmless. . . .

Note on What Process Is Due

1. *Aftermath.* Following this decision, Honolulu's planning and permitting director ruled that the temple had to be lowered by 6.2 feet. To be "unarguably in compliance," the temple was lowered 6.8 feet and renamed "Mu-Ryang-Sa," which translates to "broken ridge temple," to account for the alteration. Two organizations — "Concerned Citizens of Palolo" and "Life of the Land" — were irate that the city had not demanded removal of the full 9 feet and went back to court, but lost in further proceedings. Honolulu Star-Bulletin, Aug. 7, 2001, *available* (with photos!) *at* http://starbulletin.com/2001/08/07/news/story2.html.

2. *Sources of procedural rights.* The due process clauses of the federal and state constitutions provide bedrock procedural rights. These rights are usually confirmed, and often supplemented, by other legal authorities, such as the state zoning enabling act and the local zoning ordinance. See, e.g., State ex rel. Battershell v. City of Albuquerque, 777 P.2d 386 (N.M. Ct. App. 1989) (right to cross-examine witnesses opposing application for conditional use permit found implicit in provision of city's zoning code that required parties to "be afforded an opportunity to present evidence and argument and to question witnesses on all relevant issues"); Relosky v. Sacco, 523 A.2d 1112 (Pa. 1987) (construing zoning enabling act to require opportunity for cross-examination).

3. *Remedy.* If the Supreme Court of Hawaii had found constitutional error and had found that the error was not harmless, would the correct remedy be to order a new hearing before the director or to award damages?

4. *Legislative versus adjudicative decisionmaking, again.* Should the right of cross-examination extend to hearings regarding rezoning requests that are held by advisory agencies such as planning commissions? To hearings before the local governing body on the commission's recommendation? Compare Hyson v. Montgomery County Council, 217 A.2d 578 (Md. 1966) (right to cross-examine at hearing where local governing body is considering piecemeal change), with Montgomery County v. Woodward & Lothrop, Inc., 376 A.2d 483 (Md. 1977) (right to cross-examine does not apply where local governing body is considering comprehensive rezoning). To hearings regarding comprehensive plan amendments? See, e.g., Holbrook, Inc. v. Clark County, 49 P.3d 142, 149 (Wash. Ct. App. 2002) (no right to individual notice of hearings on comprehensive plan amendments that did not specifically target the land at issue because they were "quasi-legislative"). What if the various bodies decide to hold a joint hearing on a proposal that will involve both a legislative decision such as a rezoning and an adjudicative decision such as a special use permit? See, e.g., Klaeren v. Village of Lisle, 781 N.E.2d 223 (Ill. 2002) (if the joint hearing involves an adjudicative decision, interested parties must be given the right to cross-examine witnesses).

5. *Notice and opportunity to be heard.* State enabling acts often specify to whom notice must be given and the minimum form of the notice. See, e.g., N.J. Stat. Ann. §40:55D-12(b)

(West 2004). Many enabling acts require that neighbors within a specified number of feet of the subject property receive notice by personal service or certified mail. More distant neighbors, and the general public, may be notified by newspaper publication or public posting.

Other enabling acts leave notice requirements to the discretion of the agency. See, e.g., Ind. Code §36-7-4-920 (2004) (BZA "shall, by rule, determine who are interested parties, how notice is to be given to them, and who is required to give that notice"). The agency's requirements then are vulnerable to challenge. In California, for example, where the enabling act allows notice to be given by publication or posting and "in any other manner [the local agency] deems necessary or desirable," Cal. Gov't Code §65090 (West 2004), the California Supreme Court requires the adequacy of notice to be tested against federal due process standards on a case-by-case basis:

> We deliberately refrain from describing a specific formula which details the nature, content, and timing of the requisite notice. Rather, we leave to the affected local governments these determinations. We do observe, however, that depending on (1) the magnitude of the project, and (2) the degree to which a particular landowner's interests may be affected, acceptable techniques might include notice by mail to the owners of record of property situate within a designated radius of the subject property, or by the posting of notice at or near the project site, or both. Notice must, of course, occur sufficiently prior to a final decision to permit a "meaningful" predeprivation hearing to affected landowners.

Horn v. County of Ventura, 596 P.2d 1134 (Cal. 1979). Consequently, the notice provided in particular cases is the subject of considerable litigation. See, e.g., Hayssen v. Sonoma County Board of Zoning Adjustments, 217 Cal. Rptr. 464 (Ct. App. 1985) (notice by posting of conditional use permit hearing for a sawmill constitutionally sufficient).

Technical mistakes in the notice or insufficiently specific notices may violate due process guarantees. See, e.g., Paquette v. Zoning Board of Review, 372 A.2d 973 (R.I. 1977) (nullifying a special exception granted after a public hearing at which about 100 protestors appeared because the notice for the hearing had said lots 736 and 754 on Eagle Street would be affected, when it should have said lots 736 and 574); Peters v. Environmental Protection Board, 593 A.2d 975 (Conn. App. Ct. 1991) (notice of hearing "to consider information relevant to Application #8843, Transcon Builder, Inc., for activities on Stillwater Road" inadequate to apprise neighbors of plan to build 120-bed nursing home).

The American Planning Association has drafted a model enabling act that seeks to refine notice requirements to encourage earlier participation in zoning and planning decisions. See Daniel R. Mandelker, Model Legislation for Land Use Decisions, 35 Urb. Law. 635 (2003); Douglas A. Jorden & Michele A. Hentrich, Public Participation Is on the Rise: A Review of the Changes in the Notice and Hearing Requirements for the Adoption and Amendment of General Plans and Rezonings Nationwide and in Recent Arizona Land Use Legislation, 43 Nat. Resources J. 865 (2003).

6. *Transcripts.* For a court to review an agency's adjudicative decision, it must be able to examine a record to determine whether there is sufficient evidence supporting the local agency's findings. Partly in response to this need to facilitate judicial review, statutes, ordinances, and judicial decisions increasingly require the preparation of verbatim transcripts of nonlegislative zoning proceedings. See, e.g., Cooper v. Board of County Commissioners, 614 P.2d 947 (Idaho 1980). Transcripts are of utmost importance when a reviewing court is confined to the evidence received by the administrative body. See, e.g., Cal. Civ. Proc. Code §1094.5(e) (West 2004) (when the substantial evidence test applies, and the court finds there is relevant evidence the agency did not receive, the court must remand the controversy to the administrative body for reconsideration). But see Ohio

Rev. Code Ann. §2506.03 (West 2004) (court must take any additional evidence offered by either party); Pa. Stat. Ann. tit. 53, §11005-A (West 2004) (court may take additional evidence or remand).

7. *Sunshine laws.* A number of states have enacted statutes that require specified public agencies to carry out all phases of their deliberations on certain types of decisions in meetings that are open to the public. These "sunshine laws" may provide yet another means for a person aggrieved by a zoning change to attack that change. See, e.g., Wesley Chapel Bluemount Association v. Baltimore County, 699 A.2d 434 (Md. 1997) (county board of appeal's discussion of subdivision development plan had to comply with open-meeting law). But cf. Griswold v. City of Homer, 55 P.3d 64 (Alaska 2002) (zoning board of adjustment hearing exempt from open meeting law because it is quasi-judicial).

8. *Who bears the risks of procedural error?* As counsel for a developer seeking a zoning change, what steps should one take if one concludes that a local agency willing to approve the requested change has made significant errors in processing it? Does counsel for neighbors opposing the change have to point out the procedural errors, or can he or she remain silent and use them as the basis for a subsequent appeal?

2.   *Qualified Decisionmakers*

In 1981, followers of Bhagwan Shree Rajneesh, an Indian mystic, bought a 64,000 acre ranch known as the Big Muddy in Central Oregon, renamed it Rancho Rajneesh, and founded a spiritual community. The community, known as Rajneeshpuram, eventually housed approximately 3000 residents, with as many as 10,000–15,000 followers attending annual celebrations there. The commune was very controversial, in part because of Bhagwan's extravagances (he is said to have owned 93 Rolls Royces at one time) and the drug use and sexual practices attributed to followers. The community disintegrated in the early 1990s, after Bhagwan was deported for immigration fraud and several followers were prosecuted for crimes that included burning the county planning offices and poisoning a county commissioner. See Glen O. Robinson, Communities, 83 Va. L. Rev. 269, 295 n.6 (1997). For more background about the controversies the commune caused, see the summaries and collection of citations in United States v. Croft, 124 F.3d 1109 (9th Cir. 1997) and Connecticut General Life Ins. Co. v. Department of Revenue, June 21, 1993 WL 247787 (Or. Tax).

In 1981, their first year at the ranch, the members of the commune took steps to incorporate as a municipality. The next case arose out of the intense opposition to that effort.

1000 Friends of Oregon v. Wasco County Court
742 P.2d 39 (Or. 1987) (en banc)

LINDE, Justice.
The issue before us is whether a 2–1 decision by a board of county commissioners to call an election on a proposal to incorporate a city was invalid because one of the favorable votes was cast by a member who had undisclosed business dealings with proponents of the incorporation. The Land Use Board of Appeals (LUBA), after taking evidence on the transactions, rejected this challenge to the county board's action. On review, the Court of Appeals reversed LUBA's order and invalidated the county board's decision because one

of the participants was not impartial. We reverse the Court of Appeals and affirm LUBA's order. . . .

LUBA's findings of fact may be summarized as follows. On two occasions [in 1981] when Cantrell [a member of the board] visited the ranch, representatives of its residents, the petitioners for incorporation, told him that they were interested in buying cattle. Cantrell by letter offered to sell cattle to the ranch, asking prices somewhat higher than the prevailing market prices. He told his fellow commissioners of the intended sale but did not make it public. The representatives of the ranch accepted Cantrell's offer at his asking price. They decided to do so because they "needed him," and they consciously kept the transaction "low key" in order not to embarrass Cantrell. They also overlooked certain irregularities in the quality, weighing and transportation of the cattle, which LUBA found to have no significance for its decision. LUBA concluded:

> In sum, the evidence is that the sale was irregular in some respects. Overall, the sale reflects an eager buyer, i.e., one who was less concerned with obtaining the best bargain possible than with meeting the requirements of the seller. The buyers and their associates may have believed this transaction would improve their chances of favorable treatment concerning the incorporation and related proceedings. There is no proof, however, that the transaction was expressly contingent on Cantrell's vote of November 4, 1981. Indeed, the evidence does not show any discussion at all between Cantrell and the cattle purchasers about the incorporation petition then pending before the county. Nor do we find that the transaction was so one-sided as to constitute a sham or an implicit "pay-off" for his vote. Thus, we conclude petitioners have not carried the burden of proving disqualifying bias.

LUBA also considered whether the county board's decision was tainted by Cantrell's failure publicly to disclose his private dealings with the proponents of the incorporation. The majority opinion observed that the facts did not meet Oregon's statutory definition of a "potential conflict of interest," ORS 244.020(4), because the effect of the incorporation decision would not be to Cantrell's private benefit or detriment, and in any event, the government ethics law expressly provides that an official's failure to disclose a potential conflict of interest shall not lead to invalidating the official's action by a "court." ORS 244.130(2). . . .

In reversing LUBA's affirmance of the county board's action, the Court of Appeals held that LUBA's findings of fact were supported by substantial evidence. . . . The court held the action was "quasi-judicial" . . . and therefore required decision by impartial board members under Fasano v. Board of County Comm'rs, 507 P.2d 23 (Or. 1973). . . .

. . . Without pursuing the question here, we shall accept the assumption that a county board's decision on a petition for an election to incorporate a city is "quasi-judicial," because we agree with the LUBA majority that even so, the decision need not be set aside on the facts found by LUBA.

OREGON LAW . . .

. . . The prefix "quasi," we recently said in another context, "means that a thing is treated as if it were something it resembles but is not." State ex rel. Eckles v. Woolley, 726 P.2d 918 (Or. 1986). The quasi-judicial decisions of local general-purpose governing bodies resemble, or should resemble, adjudications in important respects that bear on the procedural fairness and substantive correctness of the decision, but in other respects these bodies remain more "quasi" than judicial. Their members are politically elected to positions that do not separate legislative from executive and judicial power on the state or federal model; characteristically they combine lawmaking with administration that is sometimes executive and sometimes adjudicative. The combination leaves little room to demand that an elected board member who actively pursues a particular view of the community's interest in his policymaking role must maintain an appearance of having no such view when the decision is to be made by an adjudicatory procedure. Also, the members of most governing bodies in this state serve part-time and without pay, making their livings from the ordinary pursuits and private transactions of their communities. Restrictions on permissible business activities and sources of outside income imposed on judges for the sake of appearance do not apply by analogy to such board members.

. . . [In] Swift v. Island County, 552 P.2d 175 (Wash. 1976), . . . an officer of a lending institution participated as a county commissioner in approving a development that could indirectly benefit his company. The Washington court, however, went beyond the commissioner's actual interest and set aside the vote of approval for "lacking an 'appearance of fairness.' " 552 P.2d at 183. The court continued:

> This doctrine has been developed to preserve the highest public confidence in those governmental processes which bring about zoning changes or which formulate property use and land planning measures. . . . It is the possible range of mental impressions made upon the public's mind, rather than the intent of the acting governmental employee, that matters. The question to be asked is this: Would a disinterested person, having been apprised of the totality of a board member's personal interest in a matter being acted upon, be reasonably justified in thinking that partiality may exist? If answered in the affirmative, such deliberations, and any course of conduct reached thereon, should be voided.

Id. (citations omitted). . . .

We do not minimize the value of evident as well as actual objectivity and disinterestedness in governmental decisions. Its importance is recognized in the government ethics law, ORS chapter 244, and elsewhere. Lawmakers have chosen to promote confidence in official probity by means of periodic disclosure of specified economic interests by state officials. ORS 244.050 to 244.110. The requirement extends to local officials if local voters so choose. ORS 244.160 to 244.201. The law also requires public officials to announce potential conflicts of interest before acting in the matter involving the potential conflict. ORS 244.120 to 244.130. Beyond these disclosure requirements, ORS 244.040 proscribes the actual use of an official's position or office to obtain financial gain for the public official or for closely associated persons. The Oregon Government Ethics Commission is responsible for enforcing the statute against officials . . . , but the statute does not prescribe the effect of a violation on the official's action. ORS 244.350 to 244.390.

If actual bias or self-interest will invalidate . . . quasi-judicial action, a prophylactic rule invalidating action for "lacking an 'appearance of fairness,' " Swift v. Island County, supra, may seem merely a desirable further step toward the same goal. That is not necessarily so. Of course, a reviewing body may find it less painful to order reconsideration of an official's action for insufficient respect for appearances than to determine whether the official in fact acted under the influence of bias or self-interest. But the two standards serve different interests. Actual impartiality protects the substantive quality of the official action as well as the parties' interest in its fairness. Invalidation for appearance alone, as the Swift court said, aims to preserve public confidence, and it does so regardless whether the decision in fact was both correct and fair. The price of such invalidation is delay of what, but for appearances, is a proper application of public policy, at potentially heavy cost to an innocently successful proponent as well as to the agency.

Public confidence in judicial institutions is given such priority over efficiency even in a fairly and correctly decided case. Even for decisions of elected boards that, as we have said, are more "quasi" than judicial, this priority for public confidence may be the desirable choice. But it is not a choice for this court to impose in the name of public policy. The contrary choice of policy toward appearances alone is implied by the provision in Oregon's governmental ethics law against invalidating actions for failure to disclose a potential conflict of interest, ORS 244.130(2).

DUE PROCESS

The Court of Appeals believed that Cantrell's participation tainted the county board's vote on the incorporation petition for failure to meet federal standards of due process under the 14th amendment. . . .

The Court of Appeals wrote that a "decision on the merits by an adjudicator with a personal interest in the outcome is a violation of due process," noting that this "rule applies to administrative as well as judicial adjudications." 723 P.2d 1034. In support of these propositions, the court cited Ward v. Village of Monroeville, 409 U.S. 57 (1972); Tumey v. Ohio, 273 U.S. 510 (1927); Gibson v. Berryhill, 411 U.S. 564, 578–579 (1973); . . . and Commonwealth Corp. v. Casualty Co., [393 U.S. 145 (1968)]. The general proposition is unexceptionable, though it rather grandly passes over the key question what kind of interests are distinctively "personal" and how directly they must be at stake in the outcome.

In *Tumey*, which originated this line of cases, the personal interest was financial and immediate: The compensation of the adjudicating officer (a mayor) included the costs assessed against those defendants whom he found guilty. An equally direct financial gain from the fines of convicted offenders was involved in *Ward*, with the significant difference that the income went to village operations for which the mayor was responsible rather than to himself. Also these cases involved classic adjudications, decisions that an individual had violated a law, there was nothing "quasi-judicial" about them.

Gibson v. Berryhill, supra, found a denial of due process when optometrists working for a corporate employer were penalized for "unprofessional conduct" by a state board of optometry composed of independent practitioners, who, according to the trial court's findings, would gain financially along with other private practitioners from driving the corporation out of business. 411 U.S. at 571. The tribunal in *Gibson* was an administrative board applying a professional licensing law, but as in *Tumey*, the holding rested on the board members' personal financial gains from the substance of the decision at issue. Id. at 579. . . .

Finally, the Court of Appeals considered the "case closest to this one on its facts" to be Commonwealth Corp. v. Casualty Co., supra, from which it quoted the proposition that "any tribunal permitted by law to try cases and controversies not only must be unbiased but also must avoid even the appearance of bias." 393 U.S. at 150, quoted in 723 P.2d 1034. In *Commonwealth Corp.*, the Supreme Court invalidated an arbitration of a contract dispute under the United States Arbitration Act because the prevailing party earlier had employed the firm of the neutral member of the arbitration panel, who in fact had performed services on the projects involved in the dispute, and neither the prevailing party nor the arbitrator had disclosed this to the other party. We are not persuaded that the quoted generalization will stretch from that context to invalidate under the 14th amendment a county commissioner's vote under circumstances like the present.

. . . In short, the role of the arbitrators in *Commonwealth Corp.*, or at least of the supposedly neutral member, was more "judicial" and less "quasi," more that of a "tribunal permitted by law to try cases and controversies" (a phrase drawn from the definition of federal judicial power under article III of the United States Constitution), than the role performed by the Wasco County commissioners in deciding whether to approve an election on the petition to incorporate the City of Rajneeshpuram.

The cases do not easily yield a single, simple rule, but it seems that 14th amendment standards for disqualification tighten with three separate variables: first, the more the officer or agency purports to act as a court (*Tumey* . . .); second, the closer the issues and interests at stake resemble those in traditional adjudications (*Commonwealth Corp.*); and third, as the disqualifying element moves from appearances through possible temptation and generic self-interest (*Gibson*) to actual personal interest in the outcome of the decision (*Tumey*). In the present case each element is at the low end of the scale.

In sum, the disagreement between the LUBA majority and the dissenting member was whether due process required Cantrell's disqualification because his sale of cattle to proponents of Rajneeshpuram on favorable terms was likely to have predisposed him to support their petition. Neither found that Cantrell gained anything from voting to submit the incorporation petition to an election. Without reaching any issue of disqualification for actual bias, the Court of Appeals held that Cantrell's failure to disclose his dealings with the proponents sufficed under the 14th amendment to disqualify him from voting. That holding pushes general propositions from cases involving courts, administrative adjudications and arbitrations further than we think the United States Supreme Court would go in a decision of this kind. As the factfinding agency, LUBA here found that Cantrell was not disqualified by financial interest or actual bias in favor of the proponents. We agree with LUBA that there is no legal basis for invalidating the decision of the Wasco County commissioners.

The decision of the Court of Appeals is reversed. . . .

Note on Bias and the Appearance of Unfairness

1. *The "quasi" in quasi-judicial.* Is the *1000 Friends* court's justification for holding quasi-judicial officials to a somewhat more lenient standard than "real" judges persuasive? See also Petrowski v. Norwich Free Academy, 506 A.2d 139, 142 (Conn. 1986) ("Such a rarefied atmosphere of impartiality cannot practically be achieved where the persons acting as administrative adjudicators, whose decisions are normally subject to judicial review, often have other employment or associations in the community they serve. It would be difficult to find competent people willing to serve, commonly without recompense, upon the numerous boards and commissions in this state if any connection with such agencies, however remotely related to the matters they are called upon to decide were deemed to disqualify them.").

2. *Quasi-judicial decisions by legislative bodies.* Where there are no conflict-of-interest statutes or ordinances, courts traditionally have declined to invalidate decisions of legislative bodies because some participating legislators were tainted by bias or self-interest. An extreme example of this hands-off approach is Schauer v. City of Miami Beach, 112 So. 2d 838 (Fla. 1959), discussed in *Snyder* at p. 343, where a rezoning was upheld even though a councilman who cast a vote crucial to the passage of the ordinance stood to gain $600,000 in increased property value if it passed. The rationale for the hands-off approach presumably is that courts can and should leave the policing of legislators to the electoral process.

As *1000 Friends* makes clear, the *Fasano/Snyder* rule that small rezonings are essentially quasi-judicial decisions has helped erode the traditional hands-off rule. Even in states that have not adopted *Fasano/Snyder*, courts increasingly apply conflict-of-interest restrictions to members of the local governing body voting on piecemeal zoning changes. See, e.g., Barrett v. Union Township Committee, 553 A.2d 62 (N.J. Super. Ct. App. Div. 1989) (council member whose mother resided in nursing home owned by persons who would be favored by passage of rezoning disqualified from voting on rezoning).

But

In some states, conflict-of-interest statutes specifically apply to zoning decisions by legislators as well as administrative officials. See, e.g., Ind. Code §36-7-4-223 (2004). In interpreting statutes applicable to legislative officials, however, courts continue to distinguish between legislative and quasi-judicial officials. See, e.g., Perry-Worth Concerned Citizens v. Board of Commissioners, 723 N.E.2d 457 (Ind. Ct. App. 2000) (refusing to read an appearance of fairness requirement into a statute governing conflicts of interests by legislative officials, in light of the differences between legislative and quasi-judicial roles).

3. *Actual bias.* Some states and cities have statutes and ordinances that are designed to disqualify a zoning official from voting or otherwise participating in a matter in which the official has a personal or financial interest. See, e.g., Ga. Code Ann. §36-67A-1 to -6 (2004) (legislators and members of planning commission); Ind. Code §§36-7-4-223, 36-7-4-909 (2004) (planning commission and boards of adjustment). In some other states, general conflict-of-interest statutes govern the activities of zoning officials.

Critics contend the statutes are much too vague to protect against bias:

> While there are some clear cases of direct financial interest, such as a developer whose project is before the board, the statutes do not specify whether a more remote interest — such as a real estate agent who hopes to sell lots in the new development — would also be disqualifying. Disqualification for "personal interest" is even harder to interpret. Perhaps being the brother-in-law of the developer would be a clear case, but what if you are a member of the country club that is making the application for rezoning?

Jerry L. Anderson & Erin Sass, Is the Wheel Unbalanced? A Study of Bias on Zoning Boards, 36 Urb. Law. 447, 451–52 (2004). How might the statutes be drafted to be more helpful?

4. *Apparent bias.* The Washington appearance-of-fairness doctrine *1000 Friends* rejects is much stricter than the conflict-of-interest rules in effect in most other states. The doctrine was first announced in Smith v. Skagit County, 453 P.2d 832 (Wash. 1969), which involved an ex parte meeting with the proponents of a rezoning. The court extended the doctrine to legislators acting on rezoning matters in Fleming v. City of Tacoma, 502 P.2d 327 (Wash. 1972), which invalidated a rezoning because one of the members of the six-to-three majority began working for the developers who sought the rezoning less than 48 hours after the vote.

The Washington legislature modified the appearance-of-fairness doctrine in 1982, however, to limit its application to quasi-judicial actions, which the statute defines to exclude legislative actions adopting "area-wide zoning ordinances" or zoning amendments of "area-wide significance." Wash. Rev. Code §42.36.010 (2004). See also Raynes v. City of Leavenworth, 821 P.2d 1204 (Wash. 1992) (en banc) (overruling *Fleming* and holding the appearance-of-fairness doctrine inapplicable to a zoning amendment). For analysis of the Washington appearance-of-fairness doctrine, see, e.g., Mark W. Cordes, Policing Bias and Conflicts of Interest in Zoning Decisionmaking, 65 N.D. L. Rev. 161, 200–02 (1989); Carolyn M. Van Noy, Comment, The Appearance of Fairness Doctrine: A Conflict in Values, 61 Wash. L. Rev. 533 (1986); W.T. Watterson, Comment, What Ever Happened to the Appearance of Fairness Doctrine? Local Land Use Decisions in an Age of Statutory Process, 21 Seattle U. L. Rev. 653 (1998).

5. *Institutional bias.* Jerry Anderson and Erin Sass have argued that state and local governments should enact legislation regarding the occupational composition of zoning boards. They surveyed local governments in Iowa and found that about one-half of the members of the BZAs or planning commissions were in occupations likely to be biased in favor of development (such as real estate lawyers, architects, brokers, or lenders). Anderson & Sass, supra, at 472–73. They acknowledge that people from such occupations are

likely to bring expertise to the job, but believe that occupations related to real estate and development are overrepresented. What would be the optimal occupational composition of a BZA or planning commission? Should the composition of such boards be the same regardless of the town's size or the nature of its industry?

6. *Campaign contributions.* In Woodland Hills Residents Association v. City Council, 153 Cal. Rptr. 651 (Ct. App. 1979), neighbors challenged the Los Angeles city council's approval of a preliminary subdivision map for 123 lots in the Santa Monica Mountains on the ground that, in the three years prior to the approval, the subdivider and its engineering and law firms had made publicly reported campaign contributions to 13 of the 15 members of the city council. (The highest total received from these sources by any council member appears to have been $1,625.)

The California Court of Appeals invalidated the map approval, holding that the council had violated a California statute that guarantees a "fair trial." Citing the Washington appearance-of-fairness cases, among others, the majority concluded that the issue was not whether the decisionmakers actually had been biased, but rather whether there had been an appearance of unfairness. On appeal, the California Supreme Court reversed. Woodland Hills Residents Association v. City Council, 609 P.2d 1029 (Cal. 1980). Justice Clark, writing for the court, reasoned:

> Political contribution involves an exercise of fundamental freedom protected by the First Amendment to the United States Constitution and article I, section 2 of the California Constitution. . . . To disqualify a city council member from acting on a development proposal because the developer had made a campaign contribution to that member would threaten constitutionally protected political speech and associational freedoms.
>
> Governmental restraint on political activity must be strictly scrutinized and justified only by compelling state interest. Buckley v. Valeo, 424 U.S. 1, 25 (1975). While disqualifying contribution recipients from voting would not prohibit contributions, it would curtail contributors' constitutional rights. Representative government would be thwarted by depriving certain classes of voters (i.e., developers, builders, engineers, and attorneys who are related in some fashion to developers) of the constitutional right to participate in the electoral process.
>
> Public policy strongly encourages the giving and receiving of campaign contributions. Such contributions do not automatically create an appearance of unfairness. Adequate protection against corruption and bias is afforded through the Political Reform Act and criminal sanctions.

Id. at 1033. See also Snohomish County Improvement Alliance v. Snohomish County, 808 P.2d 781 (Wash. Ct. App. 1991) (receipt of campaign contributions does not violate either appearance-of-fairness doctrine or prohibition against ex parte communications).

7. *Campaign promises.* If an elected official speaks out about a proposed development during his or her election campaign, is it a conflict of interest for the official to participate in proceedings regarding the development? See, e.g., Madison River R.V. Ltd. v. Town of Ennis, 994 P.2d 1098 (Mont. 2000) (claim that elected town council member should not have expressed views on the proposal "is the antithesis of our political process, in which candidates run for election based on espoused political platforms and on promises of what they will do — if elected — concerning various issues of public interest"; as long as council member did not have an "irrevocably closed" mind on the subject, town was not required to disqualify him from participating).

8. *Inattentiveness.* Does a property owner or neighbor have a right to have a decisionmaker who is awake and attentive during the proceedings? Compare Lacy Street Hospitality Service, Inc. v. City of Los Angeles, 2004 WL 3016280 (Cal. Ct. App. Dec. 30, 2004) (where videotape showed that few council members were even in their seats during the hearing,

and most of those who were spent their time talking on cell phones, talking with each other or with aides, or doing paperwork, "the council cannot be said to have made a reasoned decision based upon hearing all the evidence and argument, which is the essence of sound decision making and . . . due process"), with Rural Area Concerned Citizens, Inc. v. Fayette County Zoning Hearing Board, 646 A.2d 717, 725 (Pa. Commw. Ct. 1994) ("the mere appearance of dozing may not be taken as a clear indication that an individual is asleep, and is missing relevant testimony").

9. *Discovery?* Should opponents be allowed discovery to try to uncover evidence of bias? Should they be allowed to introduce such evidence if it is not in the record of the hearing, even though judicial scrutiny of land use decisions usually is limited to the record? See, e.g., Sills v. Walworth County Land Management Committee, 648 N.W.2d 878, 891 (Wis. Ct. App. 2002) (public policy of promoting confidence in impartial tribunals may justify expansion of the record where evidence outside the record demonstrates procedural unfairness; but before a court allows discovery or expansion of the record, the party alleging bias must make a prima facie showing of an impermissibly high risk of bias).

10. *Remedies when a conflict of interest is found.* When a biased decisionmaker casts the dispositive vote, courts generally invalidate the decision. A harder question arises when the biased final decisionmaker's vote was unnecessary for the majority decision, or when the biased decisionmaker served only on an advisory board that made a recommendation to the final decisionmaker. In Griswold v. City of Homer, 925 P.2d 1015 (Alaska 1996), excepted at p. 309, the court held that one member of the city council had a conflict of interest because he owned property in the rezoned area. In deciding what effect the disqualification should have, the court reasoned:

> Thus, without counting Sweiven's vote, Ordinance 92-18 would have passed. The superior court held that even if Sweiven had a disqualifying conflict of interest, his participation and voting would not invalidate the result. In support it cited Waikiki Resort Hotel v. City of Honolulu, 624 P.2d 1353, 1370–71 (Haw. 1981).
>
> *Waikiki* followed the rule, also articulated in several other jurisdictions, that where the required majority exists without the vote of the disqualified member, the member's participation in deliberation and voting will not invalidate the result. 624 P.2d at 1371. . . .
>
> . . . [O]ther jurisdictions hold[] that a vote cast by a disqualified member vitiates the decision in which the member participated, even if the vote does not change the outcome of the decision. . . . Buell v. City of Bremerton, 495 P.2d 1358 (Wash. 1972). . . .
>
> We decline to follow the vote-counting approach adopted in *Waikiki*, notwithstanding its appealing ease of application. A council member's role in the adoption or rejection of an ordinance cannot necessarily be measured solely by that member's vote. A conflicted member's participation in discussion and debate culminating in the final vote may influence the votes of the member's colleagues. Moreover, the integrity required of public officeholders demands that the appearance of impropriety be avoided; the approach adopted in *Waikiki* will not always do so. . . .
>
> We also decline, however, to adopt the rule of automatic invalidation endorsed in cases such as *Buell*, 495 P.2d at 1362–63. The vote and participation of a conflicted member will not invariably alter the votes of other members or affect the merits of the council's decision. This is especially true if the conflict is disclosed or well-known, allowing other members to assess the merits of the conflicted member's comments in light of his or her interest. Automatic invalidation could needlessly overturn well-considered measures which would have been adopted even if the disqualified member had refrained from participating. Automatic invalidation has the potential for thwarting legislative enactments which are not in fact the result of improper influence. . . .
>
> Guided by these basic policy concerns, we conclude that the following analysis should be applied in determining the effect of a conflicted vote. Initially the court must determine

whether a member with a disqualifying interest cast the decisive vote. If so, the ordinance must be invalidated. If the ordinance would have passed without the vote of the conflicted member, the court should examine the following three factors: (1) whether the member disclosed the interest or the other council members were fully aware of it; (2) the extent of the member's participation in the decision; and (3) the magnitude of the member's interest. The first two factors squarely bear on the accuracy of the council's decision. All three factors directly relate to any appearance of impropriety.

If the interest is undisclosed, the ordinance will generally be invalid; it can stand only if the magnitude of the member's interest, and the extent of his or her participation, are minimal. If the interest is disclosed, the ordinance will be valid unless the member's interest and participation are so great as to create an intolerable appearance of impropriety. The party challenging the ordinance bears the burden of proving its invalidity. We recognize that this analysis is more difficult to apply than the vote-counting and automatic invalidation rules. Simple to apply, those rules are unacceptably rigid. . . .

925 P.2d at 1027–29. Is *Homer's* approach an improvement on the vote-counting or automatic invalidation rules? For additional analysis of those rules, see Mark W. Cordes, Policing Bias and Conflicts of Interest in Zoning Decisionmaking, 65 N.D. L. Rev. 161, 200–02 (1989).

11. *Ex ante disqualifications.* Suppose two voting members of a zoning body conclude that they have a conflict of interest in a certain decision and disqualify themselves before the vote. Should applicable statutes and ordinances: (1) reduce the majority vote subsequently required for approval? (2) count the abstaining members in determining whether a quorum is present? Compare, e.g., N.J. Stat. Ann. §40:55D-69.1 (West 2004) (allowing additional members to be appointed to boards of adjustment and planning boards to constitute a quorum lacking because of disqualification), with Croaff v. Evans, 636 P.2d 131 (Ariz. Ct. App. 1981) (required number of votes is based on membership remaining after disqualification), and with Tippitt v. City of Hernando, 780 So. 2d 649 (Miss. Ct. App. 2000) (a person who fails to vote for any reason, including conflict of interest, counts against the total membership).

3. *Informed Decisionmakers: The Example of Environmental Impact Statements*

The National Environmental Policy Act of 1969 (NEPA), 42 U.S.C. §§4321–4370d (2004), which became effective on January 1, 1970, requires that all federal agencies:

> include in every recommendation or report on proposals for legislation and other major Federal actions significantly affecting the quality of the human environment, a detailed statement by the responsible official on —
>   (i) the environmental impact of the proposed action,
>   (ii) any adverse environmental effects which cannot be avoided should the proposal be implemented,
>   (iii) alternatives to the proposed action. . . .

42 U.S.C. §4332(C).

This innovation has trickled down, in one form or another, to about half of the states. Most of the state requirements originally were modeled after NEPA (and therefore are commonly referred to as "SEPAs" or "little NEPAs"), and the state courts often have looked to federal NEPA precedents in interpreting the state acts. As time has passed, however, the states have customized their requirements, so some state requirements now differ significantly from NEPA.

Because NEPA extends only to "major Federal actions" and therefore rarely applies to run-of-the-mill land use controversies, the following materials emphasize state requirements. They draw most heavily on the California Environmental Quality Act (CEQA), Cal. Pub. Res. Code §§21000–21177 (West 2004), and the New York Environmental Quality Review Act (SEQRA), N.Y. Envtl. Conserv. Law §§8-0101–8-0117 (McKinney 2004). Those two states generate the lion's share of litigation over the environmental impact statement (EIS) requirement, and along with Massachusetts, Minnesota, and Washington, have the best-developed bodies of EIS law. For citations and summaries of the state requirements, see 5 Zoning and Land Use Controls §§28.01, 28.02[1] (Patrick J. Rohan ed., 2004); 4 Frank Grad, Treatise on Environmental Law §9.08 (2004).

Although the state requirements differ, the major legal issues they raise are fairly uniform: (1) when is an EIS (referred to in California as an environmental impact report, or EIR) required; (2) when is an EIS "adequate"; and (3) what consequences, if any, follow if an EIS contains information that a proposed project will have adverse environmental effects? This section explores those issues and then turns to the broader question of whether the environmental impact reporting process is a sensible one.

Note on the Justifications for EIS Requirements

Normally, of course, we rely on interest group politics to inform decisionmakers about the costs and benefits of particular proposals or policies, including those related to land use. Why should a legislature insist on the availability of environmental impact information, but not other information that an efficiency-minded decisionmaker would need to carry out a complete cost/benefit analysis of a proposed project, such as estimates of the project's likely effect on employment or housing costs?

The rationales of the legislatures enacting NEPA and its progeny are far from clear. See, e.g., Daniel A. Dreyfus & Helen M. Ingram, The National Environmental Policy Act: A View of Intent and Practice, 16 Nat. Resources J. 243 (1976); Joseph L. Sax, The (Unhappy) Truth About NEPA, 26 Okla. L. Rev. 239, 240 (1973). Professor Stewart Sterk explores four justifications that might have motivated the acts: (1) government officials generally fail to give adequate weight to the future effects of decisions; (2) political pressures often cause officials to overvalue concentrated, concrete economic benefits and to undervalue diffuse environmental benefits; (3) officials can be insensitive to environmental concerns; and (4) ordinary political processes do not always generate sufficient information to enable officials to make good decisions. Professor Sterk argues that the first three concerns do not explain EIS requirements, but finds some merit in the sufficiency of information concern:

Developers are hardly likely to volunteer information about the adverse environmental effects their projects will produce. Indeed, developers have little incentive to investigate those environmental effects in the first place. Civic organizations and individual members of the public have more of an interest in providing decisionmakers with information about adverse environmental impact, but they face freerider problems in organizing to advance their mutual interest. As a result, civic organizations and individuals may underinvest in apprising officials about environmental impact.

Of course, the public choice literature suggests that political processes generally underrepresent interests held by the public at large. With environmental issues, however, the problem is compounded because the public at large may have no easy mechanism for identifying its own interests. Because environmental impact is often not apparent, and because technical studies are frequently necessary to determine potential environmental consequences, individuals and civic groups concerned with the environment cannot know whether they should lobby with public officials until they first expend resources to ascertain whether particular projects raise environmental issues. If freerider problems are difficult to overcome when interested citizens know their own interests, those problems might become insurmountable when an individual or group seeks to raise money to investigate potential environmental consequences that are not readily apparent.

Moreover, the accumulated experience of government decisionmakers is not likely to overcome any deficits in information provided by interested parties. In most cases involving land use decisions (as with many other important government decisions), decisionmakers are lawyers or businesspeople . . . unlikely to have the technical expertise necessary to evaluate environmental consequences. . . . The basic point is that some form of information gathering process is essential if environmental decisions are to be rational; the environmental impact statement requirement produces such a process, and enables governments to pass the cost of information gathering to those parties with the greatest economic stake in the project. . . .

Stewart E. Sterk, Environmental Review in the Land Use Process: New York's Experience with SEQRA, 13 Cardozo L. Rev. 2041, 2052-53 (1992).

Professor Karkkainen, however, argues that the information-forcing rationale for EISs is wrong-headed because it naively assumes that "the agency is capable of acquiring comprehensive information and generating accurate predictions about the full range of environmental impacts of the proposed action and its alternatives without undue expenditure of time, effort, or money." Bradley C. Karkkainen, Toward a Smarter NEPA: Monitoring and Managing Government's Environmental Performance, 102 Colum. L. Rev. 903, 926 (2002). In fact, Karkkainen argues, the statements end up being "exhaustive compilations of recycled information, sometimes of dubious quality" that is revealed too late in the decision process to be helpful. Id. at 923-25. The real value of the EIS, Karkkainen asserts, is the prophylactic effect the requirement has on planners, who structure their projects to avoid embarrassing disclosures and the cost, burden, and risk of the EIS process. Id. at 920-21.

If EIS requirements cause decisionmakers to receive a disproportionate amount of information about one facet of a decision, will they tend to overemphasize (or underemphasize) that factor? Instead of just making a project's proponent identify its external costs, why not make them liable for those costs under, for example, the nuisance law discussed in Chapter 6A?

a.   When Is an EIS Required?

Figure 4-4 presents the decision tree an agency should follow in implementing CEQA. For good overviews of CEQA and SEQRA, see Michael H. Remy et al., Guide to the California Environmental Quality Act (11th ed. 2005) and Michael B. Gerrard et al., Environmental Impact Review in New York (2004).

The following case addresses the third box in the flow chart — whether the project will have a significant effect on the environment and therefore require preparation of an EIS.

Chinese Staff & Workers Association v. City of New York
502 N.E.2d 176 (N.Y. 1986)

ALEXANDER, Judge. . . .

This controversy arises out of the proposed construction of Henry Street Tower, a high-rise luxury condominium, on a vacant lot in the Chinatown section of New York

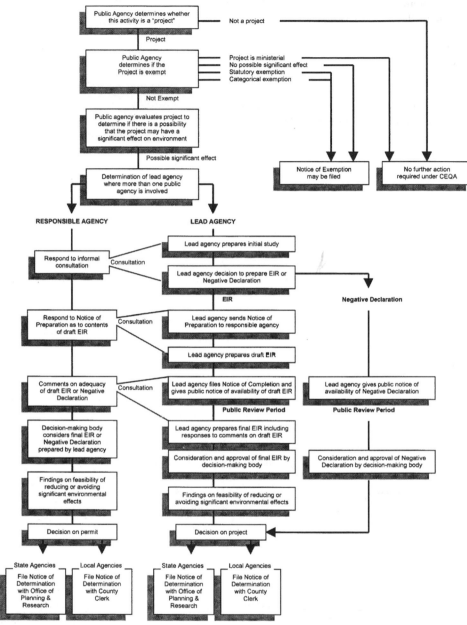

CEQA Process Flow Chart

Source: Cal. Admin. Code tit. 14, ch. 3, app. A (2004).

FIGURE 4-4
Environmental Impact Assessment Process Flow Chart

City. . . . An application for a special permit for Henry Street Tower was submitted by the developer, Henry Street Partners, to the Department of City Planning and the Department of Environmental Protection, the colead agencies responsible for implementing SEQRA in the City of New York.

Following a thorough environmental review of the effects of the project on the physical environment, the agencies issued a conditional negative declaration asserting that the project will not have any significant effect on the environment if certain modifications were adopted by the developer. The modifications were accepted by the developer and the application for a special permit was thereafter approved by the City Planning Commission and the Board of Estimate. [The Board of Estimate was the city's legislative body at the time; it has been replaced by the city council.]

A[n] . . . action . . . was commenced by various members of the Chinatown community challenging the Board of Estimate approval of the special permit. [They alleged] . . . violations of SEQRA and CEQR,[1] . . . and sought, among other things, a declaration that the special permit was null and void. . . . [R]espondents' motion for . . . summary judgment was granted. . . . The Appellate Division affirmed and petitioners were granted leave to appeal by this court.

. . . [P]etitioners argue that the city's environmental review was arbitrary and capricious because of the failure of the lead agencies to consider whether the introduction of luxury housing into the Chinatown community would accelerate the displacement of local low-income residents and businesses or alter the character of the community. Respondents contend that absent a determination that the proposed action will have a significant adverse impact on an area's physical environment, SEQRA and CEQR do not require consideration of any social or economic impacts such as those asserted by petitioners.

II

In reviewing administrative proceedings in general and SEQRA determinations in particular, we are limited to considering "whether a determination was made in violation of lawful procedure, was affected by an error of law or was arbitrary and capricious or an abuse of discretion." N.Y. C.P.L.R. §7803(3). As we stated in Matter of Jackson v. New York State Urban Dev. Corp., 494 N.E.2d 429 (N.Y. 1986), "it is not the role of the courts to weigh the desirability of any action or choose among alternatives, but to assure that the agency itself has satisfied SEQRA, procedurally and substantively." Thus . . . [t]he limited issue presented for our review is whether the respondents identified the relevant areas of environmental concern, took a "hard look" at them, and made a "reasoned elaboration" of the basis for their determination. Id. . . .

The initial determination to be made under SEQRA and CEQR is whether an EIS is required, which in turn depends on whether an action may or will not have a significant effect on the environment. N.Y. Envtl. Conserv. Law §8-0109(2); CEQR 7(a). . . . The threshold at which the requirement that an EIS be prepared is triggered is relatively low: it need only be demonstrated that the action may have a significant effect on the environment.[6]

---

[1] Eds.: SEQRA requires agencies (including local governments) to adopt regulations to implement SEQRA's provisions and authorizes agencies to go beyond SEQRA by promulgating regulations more protective of the environment. CEQR ("City Environmental Quality Review") refers to New York City's implementing regulations. New York City Exec. Order No. 91, Aug. 24, 1977.

6. In this regard, it is interesting to compare the parallel provision of the National Environmental Policy Act of 1969, which requires the preparation of an impact statement if the proposal will "significantly [affect] the

here: how broad is the term environ?

The dispute here concerns the reach of the term "environment," which is defined as "the *physical conditions* which will be affected by a proposed action, including land, *ooo* air, water, minerals, flora, fauna, noise, objects of historic or aesthetic significance, *existing patterns of population concentration, distribution, or growth, and existing community or neighborhood character.*" N.Y. Envtl. Conserv. Law §8-0105(6); CEQR 1(f) (emphasis supplied). Petitioners argue that the displacement of neighborhood residents and businesses caused by a proposed project is an environmental impact within the purview of SEQRA and CEQR, and the failure of respondents to consider these potential effects renders their environmental analysis invalid. Respondents contend that any impacts that are not either directly related to a primary physical impact or will not impinge upon the physical environment in a significant manner are outside the scope of the definition of "environment," and that the lead agencies were therefore not required to investigate the potential effects alleged by petitioners.

Ct says environ is broadly defined

Respondents' limited view of the parameters of the term "environment" is contrary to the plain meaning of SEQRA and the city's regulations and must be rejected. . . . It is clear from the express terms of the statute and the regulations that environment is broadly defined . . . and expressly includes as physical conditions such considerations as "existing patterns of population concentration, distribution, or growth, and existing community or neighborhood character."[7] Thus, the impact that a project may have on population patterns or existing community character, with or without a separate impact on the physical environment, is a relevant concern in an environmental analysis since the statute includes these concerns as elements of the environment. That these factors might generally be regarded as social or economic is irrelevant in view of this explicit definition. By their express terms, therefore, both SEQRA and CEQR require a lead agency to consider more than impacts upon the physical environment in determining whether to require the preparation of an EIS. . . .

here

Turning to the specific allegations in this case, we conclude that under CEQR the potential displacement of local residents and businesses is an effect on population patterns and neighborhood character which must be considered in determining whether the requirement for an EIS is triggered. . . .

. . . The fact that the actual construction on the proposed site will not cause the displacement of any residents or businesses is not dispositive for displacement can occur in the community surrounding a project as well as on the site of a project. . . . As we have indicated in a related context, land development impacts not only on the actual property involved but on the community in general. Berenson v. Town of New Castle, 341 N.E.2d 236 (N.Y. 1975). CEQR does not merely require that the displacement caused by the actual physical construction on this one site be considered. In fact, it specifically requires that "[f]or the purpose of determining whether an action [may have a significant effect on the environment], the action shall be deemed to include other contemporaneous or subsequent actions which are included in any long-range comprehensive integrated plan of which the action under consideration is a part." CEQR 6(b). . . . Thus, in considering the . . . effects of this project on population patterns and neighborhood character, respondents must look to more than the potential effects of this one parcel and must consider the potential impacts on the surrounding community.

---

quality of the human environment," 42 U.S.C. §4332(2)(C), a demonstrably higher threshold requirement. See, Orloff, SEQRA: New York's Reformation of NEPA, 46 Alb. L. Rev. 1128 [(1982)]. . . .

7. Again, comparison with the National Environmental Policy Act (NEPA) is instructive. An EIS is required under NEPA when a proposed Federal action will affect the quality of the "human environment," 42 U.S.C. §4332, which has been interpreted to be limited to effects on the natural or physical environment. See Image of Greater San Antonio v. Brown, 570 F.2d 517 (5th Cir. 1978).

[handwritten margin note: cf not judging the merits of the case, rather]

We do not decide whether these impacts will in fact flow from the construction of Henry Street Tower nor do we express any opinion on the merits of the proposed project. Our holding is limited to a determination that existing patterns of population concentration, distribution or growth and existing community or neighborhood character are physical conditions such that the regulations adopted by the City of New York pursuant to SEQRA require an agency to consider the potential long-term secondary displacement of residents and businesses in determining whether a proposed project may have a significant effect on the environment. Since respondents did not consider these potential effects on the environment in their environmental analysis, their determination does not comply with the statutory mandate and therefore is arbitrary and capricious. . . .

WACHTLER, Chief Judge, and HANCOCK, Judge (concurring and dissenting in part). . . .

Note on When an EIS Is Required

1. *Private development projects.* When NEPA and California's CEQA were first enacted in 1970, it was widely believed that they applied only to the government's own projects, such as highways or dams. In 1972, however, in Friends of Mammoth v. Board of Supervisors, 502 P.2d 1049 (Cal. 1972) (en banc), the California Supreme Court invalidated Mono County's decision to issue a conditional use permit for a condominium project in a ski resort community without preparing an EIR. The developer argued that CEQA's requirement that local governments prepare EIRs "on any project they intend to carry out" could refer only to public works and other public projects, not to private developments. However, Justice Mosk, speaking for the majority, concluded that the term *project* should include any private project that required a public permit.

The California legislature quickly responded to *Friends of Mammoth* by amending CEQA to exempt private projects *already in process* from EIR requirements, but to subject *future* private projects to the requirements. Cal. Pub. Res. Code §21080 (West 2004) (originally enacted as ch. 1154, §2.3, Stats. 1972). See generally Donald G. Hagman, NEPA's Progeny Inhabit the States: Were the Genes Defective?, 7 Urb. L. Ann. 3 (1974); Carl J. Seneker, The Legislative Response to *Friends of Mammoth*, 48 Cal. St. B.J. 127 (1973).

The New York legislature followed suit, requiring state and local agencies to prepare an EIS on "any action they propose or approve which may have a significant effect on the environment" and defining "action" to include "issuance . . . of a lease, permit, license, certificate, or other entitlement for use or permission to act." N.Y. Envtl. Conserv. Law §8-0105 (McKinney 2004). A handful of other states also require EISs for private development projects. See, e.g., D.C. Code Ann. §8-109.01 (2004); Mass. Gen. Laws. ch. 30, §62 (2004); Minn. Stat. §116D.04 (2004); S.D. Codified Laws §34A-9-2(3) (Michie 2004). See also N.C. Gen. Stat. §113A-8 (2004) (authorizing local governments to require developers of major projects to submit EISs).

2. *State versus local actions.* New York and California, along with a few other states, apply their EIS requirements to county and/or local governments. See, e.g., Cal. Pub. Res. Code §21063 (West 2004); Haw. Rev. Stat. §343-2 (2004); Minn. Stat. §116D.04 (2004); N.Y. Envtl. Conserv. Law §8-0105(2) (McKinney 2004); Wash. Rev. Code §43.21C.030 (2004). What is a state's interest in whether its local governments consider environmental impacts in their decisionmaking? Where an environmental impact will be contained within the local government's borders, is a state-mandated EIS procedure undue interference with local autonomy?

3. *The ministerial/discretionary distinction*. Many states have tried to cabin their little NEPAs by excepting "ministerial" acts from the requirement. See, e.g., Conn. Gen. Stat. §22a-1c (2004); N.Y. Comp. Codes R. & Regs. tit. 6, §617.5(c)(19) (2004). Although the distinction between "ministerial" and "discretionary" acts has generated substantial litigation, most courts have given the exception for "ministerial" acts a narrow interpretation. See, e.g., Miller v. City of Hermosa Beach, 17 Cal. Rptr. 2d 408 (Ct. App. 1993) (issuance of a building permit was not ministerial where city used the permitting process to require some modifications in the plans and had helped to "shape[] the project" to avoid potential environmental consequences). Cf. Incorporated Village of Atlantic Beach v. Gavalas, 615 N.E.2d 608 (N.Y. 1993) (while the agency had some discretion in reviewing applications for building permits, that discretion was unrelated to environmental or land use concerns, so the decision to grant the permit did not count as "discretionary" for the purposes of SEQRA).

4. *Legislation*. When reviewing either a negative declaration (known in the business as a "neg dec") or an EIS issued by the legislature for statutes it enacts, should the court impose any more or less scrutiny than it gives an administrative agency's neg decs or EISs regarding proposed regulations or permitting decisions? In New York City Coalition to End Lead Poisoning, Inc. v. Vallone, 794 N.E.2d 672 (N.Y. 2003), for example, the New York City Council adopted legislation regarding the removal of lead paint hazards from apartments in which children reside, along with a resolution finding that the legislation would not have a significant impact on the environment. When opponents challenged the neg dec, the city council responded that the legislative process — the hearings, written submissions, and record of the city council's deliberations — established "exhaustive consideration of the claimed advantages and disadvantages of all of the debated provisions of [the legislation]." Id. at 678. The court disagreed:

> While the record of this legislative process reveals concerned lawmakers struggling with the undoubtedly weighty social, economic and environmental consequences of their decisions, the negative declaration offers little qualitative analysis of the myriad factors inherent in the ultimate passage of Local Law 38 and no assurances that the environmental and public health concerns presented took "their proper place alongside economic interests." The City Council may have had sufficient information to render a proper determination that the new law would not pose any significant adverse environmental impacts, thereby not requiring an EIS. The negative declaration, however, fails to provide an adequate basis upon which a reviewing court can ascertain this because the document does not contain a reasoned elaboration explaining why the City Council reached this conclusion.

Id. at 679 (internal citations omitted).

Should an EIS be required before citizens vote on an initiative or referenda that might have environmental impacts? See, e.g., Friends of Sierra Madre v. City of Sierra Madre, 19 P.3d 567 (Cal. 2001) (no as to voter-sponsored initiatives, but yes as to initiatives generated by a city council).

5. *The list approach*. California and several other states list relatively few exemptions from the EIS requirement, and therefore leave to the courts the task of determining what kinds of proposed projects trigger the requirement. New York's implementing regulations, on the other hand, contain detailed lists of three categories of projects: Type I (presumed likely to have a significant effect and therefore may require an EIS); Type II (presumed to have no significant effect on the environment and therefore not subject to the EIS requirement); and "unlisted" (no presumption either for or against a significant effect, so that a preliminary assessment is necessary). N.Y. Comp. Codes R. & Regs. tit. 6, §617 (2004).

Which approach is likely to promote greater consistency, predictability, and efficiency? See Sean Stuart Varner, Comment, The California Environmental Quality Act (CEQA) After Two Decades: Relevant Problems and Ideas for Necessary Reform, 19 Pepp. L. Rev. 1447 (1992) (preferring the list approach).

6. *The threshold.* Like New York, many states adopted a lower threshold to trigger the EIS requirement than NEPA. See, e.g., Communities for a Better Environment v. California Resources Agency, 126 Cal. Rptr. 2d 441, 446 (Ct. App. 2002) (EIS should be prepared "whenever it can be fairly argued on the basis of substantial evidence that the project may have a significant environmental effect"); Norway Hill Preservation & Protection Association v. King County Council, 552 P.2d 674, 680 (Wash. 1976) (en banc) (EIS should be prepared "whenever more than a moderate effect on the quality of the environment is a reasonable probability").

7. *The possibility or probability of future development.* When a proposed action will not itself change existing land use patterns in any way but may open the door for, or be related to, other actions that might have an adverse impact, is an EIS required? Compare King County v. Washington State Boundary Review Board, 860 P.2d 1024, 1033 (Wash. 1993) (en banc) (requiring EIS for proposed annexation of land to protect city's watershed, despite the absence of any proposals to develop the property, because the likelihood that the land would eventually be developed was "unquestionable" and decisionmakers "need to be apprised of the environmental consequences *before* the project picks up momentum, not after"), with Silveira v. Las Gallinas Valley Sanitary District, 63 Cal. Rptr. 2d 244 (Ct. App. 1997) (district did not have to prepare an EIS before acquiring plaintiff's property for an "odor buffer zone" to separate the sanitation facility from residential development, because acquisition currently would change nothing except the distance between the plant and residential uses; if the acquisition was really just the first step toward a facility expansion, that could be dealt with when a specific proposal for expansion was made). At what point between *King County* and *Silveira* should the probability of future development be considered too low to trigger the EIS requirement?

In Heninger v. Board of Supervisors, 231 Cal. Rptr. 11 (Ct. App. 1986), a landowner applied for a permit to install an "alternative" septic system so that she could build a home on land that was unsuitable for conventional septic systems. The county's ordinances did not provide authority for granting such a permit, so the Board of Supervisors amended the code to allow such systems for single-family homes after issuing a neg dec. The court disagreed with the board's determination of no significant impact, after parsing the statute, regulations, and precedents, but did so with great reluctance:

> In this case, . . . the only plan of which we are aware is that of one landowner who is apparently willing to shoulder the burdens of installing and maintaining an alternative sewage disposal system. No EIR would be required for implementation of that plan by itself, which proposes a system to handle wastewater produced by a two-bedroom house. Guidelines, §15303. An EIR is required in this case, only because of a potential for other alternative sewage disposal proposals for other sites in the future.
>
> This case illustrates how, with some well-directed legal effort, an opponent of development can delay or, sometimes, abort a project. The expense of delay, and the expense of an EIR itself, can force cancellation of plans having little or no environmental impact. This case also illustrates how easily courts can, or must, cause that result even when the substance of the required EIR must be speculative and conjectural, its geographic scope huge, its cost staggering, and its ultimate utility highly questionable, at best.
>
> Due to the unspecified nature of future proposals for alternative sewage disposal systems, the preparer of an EIR in this case would be obliged, among other things, to review "all available literature" on the various types of alternative sewage disposal systems available and their

performance in varying climactic and soil conditions, to do a county-wide study to determine the areas not served by sewers and the soil conditions therein, a study of past problems with sewage pollution, a study of possible future population densities, and a study of potential for future pollution problems and attendant public health hazards. . . . We deal here with a potential for many different plans, involving different systems, in different places, in a county covering 1,300 square miles of varied topography and soil conditions. If we assume that someone is willing to undertake the cost of such a report (and the county seems the only candidate for paying the bill), there is no assurance that the report will be useful to anyone. After an EIR is prepared, if the Board chooses to order one, and by the time another ordinance amendment is enacted, the one known applicant may well have lost interest and others may not materialize. The invitation will be out to other property owners, after great public expense and after considerable delay, but will anyone come to the party?

Expenditure of limited governmental resources on speculative studies is contrary to sound policy and contrary to the legislative intent in enacting CEQA, as we perceive them. The route which the Board followed in this case, adoption of a negative declaration, avoided such foolishness and was suitable to the facts which the Board faced. Nevertheless, we are bound by the pronouncements of the California Supreme Court as to what constitutes sound policy and as to what prompted the Legislature to enact CEQA. . . .[13]

231 Cal. Rptr. at 16–17. The majority's lament was sharply contested by Judge Newsom, concurring:

I find nothing "absurd" in the view that pouring septic effluents into a leach field near a public reservoir should constitute a "project" under applicable law, if only because, as the majority opinion puts it, "the history of conventional septic tank use in Santa Clara . . . is one of environmental degradation." And, indeed, as the majority further notes, the Santa Clara Board itself recognized the "growth inducing potential" of the system proposed in the present case.

. . . [E]ven before specific projects are commenced the City may be able to state — at least in general terms — that the ordinance will have an impact upon the environment, or to dismiss that possibility. Without a threshold evaluation, however, the City leaves its constituents in ignorance of the avoidable dangers CEQA intended to avert. . . .

I wish also to state my entire disagreement with the majority's view that this case serves to illustrate "how an opponent of development can delay, or, sometimes, abort a project." To my mind, it serves rather to illustrate the wisdom of a law which permits citizens vigilant in the public interest to force local government to think before it acts.

Id. at 17–18. Who has the better of the argument? How would you draft implementing regulations to provide guidance to local governments about how and when they should take into account the future environmental impacts that might flow from a particular action?

One approach to the problem is a "generic" EIS, which addresses a multiphase project or a "conceptual" proposal such as a comprehensive plan or transferable development rights program in the abstract — by identifying the important elements of the resources and ecological system potentially affected, discussing "in general terms the constraints and consequences of any narrowing of future options," and "analyz[ing] in general terms a few hypothetical scenarios that could and are likely to occur." N.Y. Comp. Codes R. & Regs. tit. 6, §617.10 (2004). Once the project or proposal has become more concrete, a supplemental

---

13. It is implicit in these pronouncements and the holding of this opinion, that a narrowly drawn ordinance, significantly limiting the number, type, and location of alternative sewage disposal systems which may be installed in Santa Clara County, should not face the problems of the ordinance amendment. An EIR prepared in connection with the enactment of such an ordinance would be manageable in scope and minimally speculative. It should offer real assistance in protecting the environment and serve a real function in informing the Board and the public.

EIS can then be prepared to address the specifics of the project. For a discussion of the use of generic environmental impact review to promote early public participation in debates over the rebuilding of the World Trade Towers site, see James B. Tripp & Nathan G. Alley, Streamlining NEPA's Environmental Review Process: Suggestions for Agency Reform, 12 N.Y.U. Envtl. L.J. 74, 107–09 (2003).

8. *Segmentation.* A problem closely related to the issue of cumulative impact of the proposed project is the problem of segmentation — "the division of the environmental review of an action such that various activities or stages are addressed . . . as though they were independent, unrelated activities. . . . " Forman v. Trustees of State University of New York, 757 N.Y.S.2d 180, 181 (App. Div. 2003) (finding no improper segmentation when projects were not contiguous or interdependent, and were planned and funded separately). See also Long Island Pine Barrens Society v. Planning Board, 606 N.E.2d 1373, 1378 (N.Y. 1992) (no need for review of cumulative impact of 224 separate proposals to build in ecologically sensitive area: the "only element they share — their common placement in the Central Pine Barrens — is an insufficient predicate . . . for mandatory cumulative impact analyses as preconditions to a myriad of local land use determinations"). See also Keith H. Hirokawa, The Gap Between Informational Goals and the Duty to Gather Information: Challenging Piecemealed Review Under the Washington State Environmental Policy, 25 Seattle U. L. Rev. 343 (2001).

9. *Disapprovals?* Most controversies over whether an EIS must be completed involve assertions by project opponents that the project should not be permitted until an EIS is completed. In Main San Gabriel Basin Watermaster v. State Water Resources Control Board, 16 Cal. Rptr. 2d 288 (Ct. App. 1993), however, defendant was challenged for failing to prepare an EIS before disapproving an application to expand a landfill. The court had no sympathy for the challenge. Might there be cases in which an EIS should be required before the project could be denied? In general, should EISs be required for agency inaction? See Note, Does NEPA Require an Impact Statement on Inaction?, 81 Mich. L. Rev. 1337 (1983). Might EIS review of disapprovals of proposed higher density projects be a tool for controlling the sprawl discussed at pp. 788-818?

10. *Socioeconomic, psychological, aesthetic, and other impacts.* Is New York's expansive definition of the effects that will trigger the EIS requirement consistent with the justifications for environmental impact review given by Professor Sterk? For praise of SEQRA's role in filling the gap to protect aesthetic values, see John W. Caffry, The Substantive Reach of SEQRA: Aesthetics, Findings, and Non-Enforcement of SEQRA's Substantive Mandate, 65 Alb. L. Rev. 393 (2001); for criticism, see Jerry J. Salama et al., Reducing the Cost of New Housing Construction in New York City: 2005 Update 53-54 (2005).

Note on Conditioned Negative Declarations

1. *Contract or conditional rezoning, redux?* The plaintiffs in *Chinese Staff Workers* were challenging a "conditional negative declaration," which is issued when the action as originally proposed may result in significant adverse effects, but the lead agency believes that mitigation measures will modify the proposed action so that no significant environmental impacts will result. See, e.g., Merson v. McNally, 688 N.E.2d 479 (N.Y. 1997). The problems posed by conditioned neg decs (or to use the language of NEPA and some of the states — findings of no significant impact, or FONSIs) are similar to the problems posed by the dealmaking discussed at pp. 318–29: Will the process of mitigation lead to overreaching by an agency willing to issue a neg dec in exchange for valuable concessions by

the developer, and (or) will it cause agencies to pay too little attention to the environmental concerns a project might pose?

2. *Constraints on mitigated neg decs.* Is the ability of affected groups to challenge the neg dec a sufficient deterrent to such abuses? Should the court apply heightened scrutiny to neg decs that involve such mitigation measures, as *Snyder* required for piecemeal rezonings? Should the court insist that the mitigation measures actually resolve the problems to which they are addressed? See pp. 637–52 for a discussion of related concerns in the context of exactions.

3. *Enforcement.* What happens if the developer fails to follow through on mitigation measures, or they turn out to be ineffective? Should the lead agency be required to monitor the environmental impacts of the development and adjust the mitigation requirements accordingly?

4. *The predominance of neg decs or FONSIs.* Professor Karkkainen provides this assessment of the relative importance of the process leading to neg decs or FONSIs:

> A recent study for the Federal Highway Administration — one of the leading generators of EISs — found that on average an EIS required 3.6 years to complete, with some taking as long as twelve years. . . .
>
> . . . Because a litigation proof EIS will be burdensome and time consuming to produce, the agency's most important objective becomes to avoid the statutory EIS tripwire in the first place. An agency can often do this by producing just enough information to justify a finding that the proposed action will have "no significant impact" on the environment (a "Finding of No Significant Impact," or "FONSI"). That route requires a less thorough environmental assessment (EA) under a truncated procedure that typically leaves less room for citizen input. . . .
>
> . . . Indeed, the number of EISs produced annually has declined steadily over the years despite growth in both the scale and scope of federal activity, while the number of EAs and FONSIs has soared. Only about 500 EISs are performed annually, and EAs now outnumber EISs by a factor of at least 100 to 1. These figures actually overstate the frequency with which federal agency actions are subject to the EIS process, because the recorded number of EISs includes draft, final, and supplemental documents. . . . In all probability, the number of distinct agency actions subject to the EIS process averages something less than 250 per year — a very small number indeed, given the scope and scale of the federal enterprise.
>
> The perverse consequence of NEPA's seemingly insatiable demand for information, then, is to create powerful incentives for agencies to structure and characterize their activities so as to avoid the full NEPA-mandated EIS inquiry. Despite NEPA's lofty goal of "fully informed" agency decisionmaking, most of the government's NEPA machinery is now devoted not to producing Environmental Impact Statements, but to producing just enough information to justify the conclusion that the "fully informed" EIS inquiry is unnecessary.

Bradley C. Karkkainen, Toward a Smarter NEPA: Monitoring and Managing Government's Environmental Performance, 102 Colum. L. Rev. 903, 918–21 (2002).

5. *Sign of success or failure?* Professor Karkkainen claims that "mitigated FONSIs might be considered evidence that NEPA is having a tangible, proactive, environmentally beneficial effect on agency decisionmaking, not dissimilar to the one NEPA's authors intended, albeit through an unexpected route":

> NEPA's authors thought it would be the information revealed in the EIS itself, together with political pressure produced by public disclosure of that information, that would inform the selection of alternatives and drive improvements in environmental performance. Instead, they managed to construct a formal EIS process so ungainly that agencies have strong incentives to avoid it, if necessary, by investing in environmentally beneficial project modifications. Ironically, then, EIS production becomes not the direct vehicle for environmental improvement

through informed decisionmaking, but a kind of penalty default that kicks in only if agencies are unable to identify alternatives or mitigation measures that would bring the expected environmental impacts of their proposed actions below the threshold level of "significant." The EIS, in short, becomes not the predecision means by which the agency learns to avoid or mitigate adverse environmental impacts, but rather the postdecision price the agency pays for failing to avoid or mitigate adverse environmental impacts.

Id. at 935–36.

b.   *When Is an EIS Adequate?*

Laurel Heights Improvement Association v. Regents of the University of California
764 P.2d 278 (Cal. 1988) (en banc)

EAGLESON, Justice.

In this action, we determine the sufficiency of an environmental impact report (EIR) on the proposed relocation within the City of San Francisco of biomedical research facilities of the School of Pharmacy at the University of California, San Francisco (UCSF). . . .

We find the EIR was inadequate because: (1) it fails to discuss the anticipated future uses of the new facility and the environmental effects of those uses, and (2) the discussion of alternatives is inadequate under CEQA. . . .

Because the EIR is invalid in part, a new EIR must be prepared, submitted for public review and comment, and certified in accord with CEQA procedures. . . .

FACTS . . .

The UCSF Parnassus campus in San Francisco is the site of the University's Schools of Medicine, Nursing, Pharmacy, and Dentistry. . . .

To alleviate . . . space constraints [at the Parnassus campus], in February 1985 the Regents of the University of California purchased the Presidio Corporate Center, . . . located in the Laurel Heights neighborhood of San Francisco. . . . The Laurel Heights neighborhood is a mixture of residential and commercial development. The facility purchased by the Regents is a 10-acre site containing a 354,000 square-foot building (exclusive of parking area) and a 13,000 square-foot annex. . . .

UCSF prepared a draft EIR, which stated that "The UCSF proposal is to move the School of Pharmacy basic science research units from the UCSF Parnassus campus to Laurel Heights." . . . The draft EIR disclosed that the basic science research units to be relocated included a number of facilities that handled possibly toxic chemicals, possible carcinogens, and radioactive substances; that various substances would be vented from the building into the outside air; that hazardous wastes would be generated; and that harmful exposure to hazardous substances could occur through worker negligence, accidents, or unidentified risks. . . . [The draft EIR therefore identified potential environmental effects related to air quality, human health, noise, traffic congestion, and parking.]

. . . After a 45-day period for public review of the EIR and comment, . . . UCSF proposed measures to mitigate the identified environmental effects and prepared a final EIR, concluding that the environmental effects had been "reduced to a level of insignificance." The Regents certified the final EIR.

The Laurel Heights Neighborhood Improvement Association, Inc. (Association) then petitioned for a writ of mandate setting aside the EIR approval. The superior court denied the petition. . . .

The Court of Appeal reversed on three primary grounds. First, it found the EIR . . . did not discuss the future cumulative effects of the relocation of additional UCSF operations to the Laurel Heights site. Second, the Court of Appeal found inadequate the EIR's discussion of project alternatives. Third, the court found no substantial evidence to support the Regents' conclusion that all significant environmental effects will be mitigated. . . .

DISCUSSION . . .

Under CEQA, . . . [t]he lead agency must certify that the final EIR has been completed in compliance with CEQA and that the information in the final EIR was considered by the agency before approving the project. Guidelines, §15090. Before approving the project, the agency must also find either that the project's significant environmental effects identified in the EIR have been avoided or mitigated, or that unmitigated effects are outweighed by the project's benefits. Cal. Pub. Res. Code §§21002, 21002.1, 21081; Guidelines, §§15091–15093.

. . . An EIR is an "environmental 'alarm bell' whose purpose it is to alert the public and its responsible officials to environmental changes before they have reached ecological points of no return." County of Inyo v. Yorty, 108 Cal. Rptr. 377 (Ct. App. 1973). The EIR is also intended "to demonstrate to an apprehensive citizenry that the agency has, in fact, analyzed and considered the ecological implications of its action." No Oil, Inc. v. City of Los Angeles, 529 P.2d 66 (Cal. 1974). . . . Because the EIR must be certified or rejected by public officials, it is a document of accountability. If CEQA is scrupulously followed, the public will know the basis on which its responsible officials either approve or reject environmentally significant action, and the public, being duly informed, can respond accordingly to action with which it disagrees. The EIR process protects not only the environment but also informed self-government.

Section 21168.5 provides that a court's inquiry in an action to set aside an agency's decision under CEQA "shall extend only to whether there was a prejudicial abuse of discretion. Abuse of discretion is established if the agency has not proceeded in a manner required by law or if the determination or decision is not supported by substantial evidence." As a result of this standard, "The court does not pass upon the correctness of the EIR's environmental conclusions, but only upon its sufficiency as an informative document." County of Inyo v. City of Los Angeles, 139 Cal. Rptr. 396 (Ct. App. 1977).

. . . In applying the substantial evidence standard, "the reviewing court must resolve reasonable doubts in favor of the administrative finding and decision." Topanga Ass'n for a Scenic Community v. County of Los Angeles, 522 P.2d 12 (Cal. 1974). The Guidelines define "substantial evidence" as "enough relevant information and reasonable inferences from this information that a fair argument can be made to support a conclusion, even though other conclusions might also be reached." Guidelines, §15384, subd. (a).

A court may not set aside an agency's approval of an EIR on the ground that an opposite conclusion would have been equally or more reasonable. A court's task is not to weigh conflicting evidence and determine who has the better argument when the dispute is whether adverse effects have been mitigated or could be better mitigated. We have neither the resources nor scientific expertise to engage in such analysis, even if the statutorily prescribed standard of review permitted us to do so. . . .

I

The EIR's analysis of future activity and effects is inadequate under CEQA.

The EIR before us defined the project as "mov[ing] the School of Pharmacy basic science research units from the UCSF Parnassus campus to Laurel Heights." The building to which those research units are to be moved is approximately 354,000 square feet in size, but only 100,000 square feet are now available to UCSF because one-half of the building is occupied by the California Department of Transportation (CALTRANS) pursuant to a lease with the University that expires in 1990 with an option to extend tenancy until 1995. . . . The EIR does not discuss the additional environmental effects, if any, that will result from UCSF's use of the remaining 254,000 square feet when it becomes available, perhaps as soon as 1990. . . .

The . . . question is what circumstances require consideration in an EIR of future action related to the proposed project. A basic tenet of CEQA is that an environmental analysis "should be prepared as early as feasible in the planning process to enable environmental considerations to influence project program and design and yet late enough to provide meaningful information for environmental assessment." Guidelines, §15004, subd. (b); *No Oil*, supra, 529 P.2d 66. The Regents correctly note that "where future development is unspecified and uncertain, no purpose can be served by requiring an EIR to engage in sheer speculation as to future environmental consequences." Lake County Energy Council v. County of Lake, 139 Cal. Rptr. 176 (Ct. App. 1977). We agree that environmental resources and the public fisc may be ill served if the environmental review is too early. On the other hand, the later the environmental review process begins, the more bureaucratic and financial momentum there is behind a proposed project, thus providing a strong incentive to ignore environmental concerns that could be dealt with more easily at an early stage of the project. This problem may be exacerbated where, as here, the public agency prepares *and* approves the EIR for its own project. For that reason, "EIRs should be prepared as early in the planning process as possible to enable environmental considerations to influence project, program or design." Bozung [v. Local Agency Formation Comm'n], 529 P.2d 1017 [(Cal. 1975)]. . . .

We hold that an EIR must include a analysis of the environmental effects of future expansion or other action if: (1) it is a reasonably foreseeable consequence of the initial project; and (2) the future expansion or action will be significant in that it will likely change the scope or nature of the initial project or its environmental effects. Absent these two circumstances, the future expansion need not be considered in the EIR for the proposed project. Of course, if the future action is not considered at that time, it will have to be discussed in a subsequent EIR before the future action can be approved under CEQA.

This standard is consistent with the principle that "environmental considerations do not become submerged by chopping a large project into many little ones — each with a minimal potential impact on the environment — which cumulatively may have disastrous consequences." *Bozung*, supra, 529 P.2d 1017. The standard also gives due deference to the fact that premature environmental analysis may be meaningless and financially wasteful. Under this standard, the facts of each case will determine whether and to what extent an EIR must analyze future expansion or other action.

The draft EIR acknowledged that UCSF will occupy the entire Laurel Heights facility when the remainder of the space becomes available. In response to public inquiry as to plans for the facility, UCSF explained that it intends to use the facility for the School of Pharmacy's basic science group and UCSF's Office of the Dean. . . . Under the standard we have announced, it is therefore indisputable that the future expansion and general type of future use is reasonably foreseeable. This is not the type of situation where it is unclear as to whether a parcel of land will be developed or as to whether activity will commence. . . .

We also find the future action will be significant in that it will likely change the scope or nature of the proposed initial project and its environmental effects. . . . The anticipated eventual use of the entire Laurel Heights facility would include an increase in the amount of space used from approximately 100,000 square feet to 354,000 square feet and an increase in occupants from approximately 460 to 860. This is obviously a change in the scope of the project and perhaps its nature as well.

We believe the Regents can provide meaningful, reliable data in the EIR as to future activity at Laurel Heights and thus must do so. . . . UCSF should have discussed in the EIR at least the general effects of the reasonably foreseeable future uses of the Laurel Heights facility, the environmental effects of those uses, and the currently anticipated measures for mitigating those effects. . . .

We do not require prophecy. . . . A detailed environmental analysis of every precise use that may conceivably occur is not necessary at this stage. The fact that precision may not be possible, however, does not mean that no analysis is required. "Drafting an EIR . . . involves some degree of forecasting. While foreseeing the unforeseeable is not possible, an agency must use its best efforts to find out and disclose all that it reasonably can." Guidelines, §15144. . . .

II

The EIR is inadequate under CEQA because the EIR does not contain an adequate description of project alternatives. . . .

UCSF's treatment of alternatives was cursory at best. The draft EIR identified three types of alternatives: no project anywhere, alternative sites on the UCSF Parnassus campus, and alternative sites off-campus. The three categories received a scant one and one-half pages of text in an EIR of more than 250 pages. The EIR stated the obvious conclusion that the "no project" alternative, i.e., no relocation to Laurel Heights, would not have the environmental effects identified in the EIR. It then stated in a mere two-sentence paragraph that " . . . no alternative sites on [the Parnassus] campus were evaluated as possible candidates for the location of the basic science units of the School of Pharmacy." . . . The treatment of off-campus sites is equally deficient. It reads in its entirety: "Currently, the University has facilities at numerous other locations in the City of San Francisco, as shown in Exhibit V-1 [a map]. None of these sites had space available of sufficient size to accommodate the School of Pharmacy units that are to be moved." It defies common sense for the Regents to characterize this as a *discussion* of any kind; it is barely an *identification* of alternatives, if even that. . . .

Even if the Regents are correct in their conclusion that there are no feasible alternatives to the Laurel Heights site, the EIR is nonetheless defective under CEQA. As we stated in a context similar to CEQA, there must be a disclosure of the "analytic route the . . . agency traveled from evidence to action." Topanga Ass'n for a Scenic Community v. County of Los Angeles, 522 P.2d 12 (Cal. 1974). . . .

The Regents argue that alternatives had already been considered and found to be infeasible during the University's various internal planning processes and that an EIR need not discuss a clearly infeasible project alternative. The Regents apparently believe that, because they and UCSF were already fully informed as to the alleged infeasibility of alternatives, there was no need to discuss them in the EIR.

The Regents miss the critical point that the public must be equally informed. Without meaningful analysis of alternatives in the EIR, neither the courts nor the public can fulfill their proper roles in the CEQA process. We do not impugn the integrity of the Regents, but neither can we countenance a result that would require blind trust by the public, especially in light of CEQA's fundamental goal that the public be fully informed as to the environmental consequences of action by their public officials. . . . An EIR must include detail sufficient to enable those who did not participate in its preparation to understand and to consider meaningfully the issues raised by the proposed project. . . .

The Regents also contend the Association failed to point to any evidence in the record that demonstrates reasonable alternatives to moving the School of Pharmacy research units to Laurel Heights. . . . It is the project proponent's responsibility to provide an adequate discussion of alternatives. Guidelines, § 15126, subd. (d). That responsibility is not dependent in the first instance on a showing by the public that there are feasible alternatives. . . .

We hold the discussion in the EIR of project alternatives is legally inadequate under CEQA. UCSF must explain in meaningful detail in a new EIR a range of alternatives to the proposed project and, if UCSF finds them to be infeasible, the reasons and facts that UCSF claims support its conclusion.

Because a new EIR is required, we believe it necessary to provide brief guidance to the parties as to the level of analysis of alternatives that must be included. As we have already explained, the analysis must be specific enough to permit informed decision making and public participation. . . . The need for thorough discussion and analysis is not to be construed unreasonably, however, to serve as an easy way of defeating projects. . . . As with the range of alternatives that must be discussed, the level of analysis is subject to a rule of reason.

III

There is substantial evidence to support the Regents' finding that the potential environmental effects of the project, as it is now defined in the EIR, will be mitigated. . . .

As we have explained, a court's proper role in reviewing a challenged EIR is not to determine whether the EIR's ultimate conclusions are correct but only whether they are supported by substantial evidence and whether the EIR is sufficient as an informational document. The Association, however, invites us to disregard this limitation on our review by weighing competing technical data and arguments. The Association relies on evidence in the record that the Association claims supports conclusions contrary to those reached by the Regents. The question, however, is not whether there is substantial evidence to support the *Association's* position; the question is only whether there is substantial evidence to support the *Regents'* conclusion.

In answering that question, the reviewing court must consider the evidence as a whole. That an EIR's discussion of mitigation measures might be imperfect in various particulars does not necessarily mean it is inadequate. We do not suggest that a reviewing court should refrain from carefully scrutinizing the record. . . . The often technical nature of challenges to EIR's . . . requires particular attention to detail by a reviewing court. The proper judicial goal, however, is not to review each item of evidence in the record with such exactitude that the court loses sight of the rule that the evidence must be considered as a whole. . . .

. . . The Parnassus campus research facility has been in operation for many years. The final EIR described two environmental sampling studies conducted at the Parnassus campus in 1984 and 1986, which established that research activities had not resulted in statistically significant increases in the deposition of organic chemicals or radioactive materials in the vicinity of the campus. We believe the trial court was correct in viewing these studies as evidence in support of the Regents' finding of mitigation.

The Court of Appeal found the studies wanting in various particulars. For example, the Court of Appeal noted that these studies were of soil and vegetation and faulted them for not explaining why examination at ground level alone is sufficient to demonstrate an absence of harmful emissions. The Regents contend such studies are more reliable and informative than air samples. The Court of Appeal also faulted the 1986 study for failing to explain that most measurements of gross gamma radiation were on the average greater than the control level. The Regents contend the court misunderstood the concept of statistical significance. . . .

The Court of Appeal in effect performed its own scientific critique of the studies and found the Regents should not have relied on them. This approach is inconsistent with the principle that "The court does not have the duty of passing on the validity of the conclusions expressed in the EIR, but only on the sufficiency of the report as an informative document." Environmental Defense Fund v. Coastside County Water Dist., 104 Cal. Rptr. 197 (Ct. App. 1972). It is also well established that "[d]isagreement among experts does not make an EIR inadequate." Karlson v. City of Camarillo, 161 Cal. Rptr. 260 (Ct. App. 1980).

We commend the Court of Appeal's thoroughness in reviewing the two studies and the other evidence offered by the Regents in support of their finding of mitigation. As we have explained, such scrutiny is necessary under CEQA. The relevant point, however, is not that the two studies might be lacking in certain particulars or that the studies may not conclusively demonstrate a lack of environmental effect at the Parnassus campus or, inferentially, at Laurel Heights. Stated differently, the issue is not whether the studies are irrefutable or whether they could have been better. The relevant issue is only whether the studies are sufficiently credible to be considered *as part of* the total evidence that supports the Regents' finding of mitigation. We find the studies are sufficient for that purpose. They do tend to show a lack of harmful effects at the Parnassus campus and therefore support at least an inference that the Laurel Heights operations will also have no harmful effects.[12] . . .

. . . [W]e conclude that, when considered individually, some of the evidence proffered by the Regents is subject to reasonable criticism. The EIR might be a more useful document if it included some of the information the Association seeks. That some items or types of evidence, however, are less than conclusive does not mean the evidence as a whole is not substantial. As we have explained in a related context, "the reviewing court must resolve reasonable doubts in favor of the administrative findings and decision." Topanga Ass'n for a Scenic Community v. County of Los Angeles, supra, 522 P.2d 12. To paraphrase the Guidelines, a fair argument can be made to support the Regents' conclusion, even though other conclusions might also be reached. Guidelines, §15384, subd. (a). We hold that, taken as a whole, there was substantial evidence to support the Regents' conclusion that the environmental effects of the project, as now defined, will be mitigated. . . .

For the reasons discussed above, we affirm the Court of Appeal's decision that the EIR should have addressed anticipated future uses and their environmental effects and that the discussion of project alternatives is inadequate under CEQA. . . . We reverse the Court of Appeal's decision that the Regents' finding as to mitigation is inadequate. . . .

Note on the Adequacy of an EIS

1. *Cumulative environmental impacts, again.* Recall the debate in *Heninger*, excerpted at pp. 376–77. Should a court reviewing the *adequacy* of an EIS be more or less willing to require cumulative impact analysis than a court reviewing an agency's decision about

---

12. We do not suggest that a court must uncritically rely on every study or analysis presented by a project proponent in support of its position. A clearly inadequate or unsupported study is entitled to no judicial deference. The Association, however, has failed to demonstrate that the two studies are clearly inadequate or unsupported.

the *need* for an EIS? Does the *Laurel Heights* court's insistence that future projects be a "reasonably foreseeable consequence" of the initial project strike the right balance between the dangers of premature analysis and the dangers of "segmentation"? See, e.g., Berkeley Keep Jets Over the Bay Committee v. Board of Port Commissioners, 111 Cal. Rptr. 2d 598, 610 (Ct. App. 2001) ("mere fact" that a lead agency acknowledges that it contemplates a future project as part of its master plan is not, by itself, sufficient to conclude that the future project is a "reasonably foreseeable consequence of the initial project"). In cases decided under NEPA, the courts have articulated a variety of factors to be considered in determining whether future or related development should be considered within the EIS, such as whether the segment or phase of the project at issue has utility independent of the future development and whether it makes the construction of the second project likely. See Daniel R. Mandelker, NEPA Law and Litigation §§10:42, 12:20 (2d ed. 2003).

2. *How many and which alternatives must be considered?* CEQA states the legislature's intent that "public agencies should not approve projects as proposed if there are feasible alternatives or feasible mitigation measures available which would substantially lessen the significant environmental effects of such projects." Cal. Pub. Res. Code §21002 (West 2004). *Feasible* is defined as "capable of being accomplished in a successful manner within a reasonable period of time, taking into account economic, environmental, social, and technological factors." Id. §21061.1. Given that language, how would you advise a developer about how many or what types of alternatives should be analyzed in an EIS? Must the EIS consider "any alternative that has a champion," as some commentators have suggested? See Robin Gregory et al., Adapting the Environmental Impact Statement Process to Inform Decisionmakers, 11 J. Pol'y Analysis & Mgmt. 58, 60 (1992); Jason J. Czarnezki, Comment, Defining the Project Purpose Under NEPA: Promoting Consideration of Viable EIS Alternatives, 70 U. Chi. L. Rev. 599 (2003).

The California Supreme Court confronted the alternatives requirement in Citizens of Goleta Valley v. Board of Supervisors, 801 P.2d 1161 (Cal. 1990). There, project opponents challenged the approval of an EIR for a proposed resort hotel on 73 acres of oceanfront land in Santa Barbara County on the ground that the EIR had failed to consider a number of alternatives. The court held that the EIR's consideration of six "reduced scale" alternatives, a "no-project" alternative, and one off-site alternative was adequate consideration of alternatives. The court upheld the board's determination that several sites suggested by project opponents were infeasible because they were zoned for uses inconsistent with a major resort, reasoning that city and county comprehensive plans, as well as a "local coastal program," had already addressed whether particular sites were suitable for resort development, and "an EIR is not ordinarily an occasion for the reconsideration or overhaul of fundamental land use policy." Id. at 1173.

The board's determination that various sites were infeasible because they were not owned by the developer also was proper because "surely whether a property is owned or can reasonably be acquired by the project proponent has a strong bearing on the likelihood of a project's ultimate cost and the chances for an expeditious and 'successful accomplishment.'" Id. at 1174. The court noted that in cases in which a private developer owns or controls alternative sites or was in a position to purchase or lease such sites, or otherwise have access to feasible alternatives, consideration of alternative sites would be required. See also Horn v. International Business Machine Corp., 493 N.Y.S.2d 184 (App. Div. 1985) (private developer need not consider as wide a variety of alternative sites as public agency with eminent domain power).

In *Goleta*, the "local coastal program" had specifically considered and rejected resort zoning for the various alternative sites that opponents suggested. If there was no evidence in the record that resort zoning had been specifically rejected for alternative sites, how telling would the lack of alternative sites zoned for resort use be? What if the proposed alternative sites were in a "wait and see" holding zone?

3. *The "no-build" alternative.* If land is zoned to allow some development as of right, must the alternatives considered in the EIS include a "no-build" alternative, or is the as-of-right zoning the baseline from which the environmental impact should be measured? Compare, e.g., Committee to Preserve Brighton Beach v. Council of City of New York, 625 N.Y.S.2d 134 (App. Div. 1995) (as-of-right development is appropriate baseline), with Defreestville Area Neighborhoods Association v. Town Board of North Greenbush, 750 N.Y.S.2d 164 (App. Div. 2002) (environmental impact review should have considered the actual change in *use* from an undeveloped meadow to a retail shopping center, rather than focusing on the change in *zoning*).

4. *Uncertainty.* The implementing regulations for NEPA once required that if information relevant to an agency's evaluation of the proposed action was either unavailable or too costly to obtain, the agency had to include in the EIS a "worst case analysis and an indication of the probability or improbability of its occurrence." The regulations later abandoned that requirement, and the Supreme Court held that it was not mandated by NEPA. Robertson v. Methow Valley Citizens Council, 490 U.S. 332 (1989). New York also rejected worst-case analysis requirements, except in cases of "reasonably foreseeable catastrophic impacts." N.Y. Comp. Codes R. & Regs. tit. 6, §617.9(b)(6) (2004). How should an EIS address gaps in information or knowledge needed to assess likely environmental impacts? See Carla Mattix & Kathleen Becker, Scientific Uncertainty Under the National Environmental Policy Act, 54 Admin. L. Rev. 1125 (2002); Cass Sunstein, Probability Neglect: Emotions, Worst Cases, and the Law, 112 Yale L.J. 61, 96–97 (2002).

c. What If an EIS Identifies Adverse Impacts?

Town of Henrietta v. Department of Environmental Conservation
430 N.Y.S.2d 440 (App. Div. 1980)

CALLAHAN, Justice.

. . . [P]etitioners Miracle Mile Associates and the Town of Henrietta, seek to vacate certain conditions imposed upon permits granted by respondent, Department of Environmental Conservation.

Petitioner Miracle Mile Associates, developer of a regional shopping center to be known as "The Marketplace," received final site approval from the Town of Henrietta in 1974 on a 125 acre tract simultaneously rezoned commercial for this project. . . .

In June 1978, the Commissioner of Environmental Conservation noted that it was still practicable to modify the proposed project in such a way as to mitigate adverse environmental impacts within the purview of the State Environmental Quality Review Act (hereinafter SEQRA). He invoked his authority pursuant to that Act to require the preparation of an environmental impact statement (hereinafter EIS) for this project. The Department of Environmental Conservation (hereinafter DEC) was designated as lead agency for the purpose of carrying out the environmental impact review of the project, which designation placed upon DEC the responsibility of preparing an adequate final EIS.

On May 10, 1979, Miracle Mile Associates submitted to DEC an amended Draft Environmental Impact Statement (hereinafter DEIS) which contained a discussion and analysis of the project's total environmental setting, cumulative environmental and socioeconomic impacts expected to result from the project, and various mitigating measures proposed by petitioner to minimize adverse environmental effects. The proposed mitigation measures included ecosystem and wetland considerations, drainage and flooding abatement measures, and air pollution and noise pollution abatement measures, as well as abatement measures to mitigate aesthetic impacts, traffic impacts, and interference with community activities. . . .

. . . DEC adopted the findings, conclusions and recommendations of the Administrative Law Judge and granted the permits subject to 18 conditions therein set forth. It is these conclusions which frame the basis for the permit conditions challenged by the petitioners.

According to DEC the . . . conditions were intended to fulfill DEC's obligation under SEQRA . . . to insure that all of the project's adverse environmental effects revealed in the EIS are minimized or avoided.

Petitioners seek in this proceeding to annul the conditions imposed upon the approvals granted by the DEC, contending that SEQRA does not authorize DEC to attach conditions to a permit or approval where such conditions have no relevance to the permit or approval sought. Although the attack in their petition was addressed to all 18 conditions, petitioners in their brief expressly limit their challenges to conditions 4(c), 8, 10, 11, 12, 17 and 18.[2] . . .

. . . Federal courts have recognized the significant role of an EIS under National Environmental Policy Act of 1969 (42 U.S.C. §4321 et seq., hereinafter NEPA), the federal environmental statute upon which the New York act was modeled. Moreover, federal courts have clearly enunciated that NEPA is more than just a mere disclosure statute (as petitioners would characterize SEQR). Rather, NEPA requires full consideration by federal decision makers of the environmental consequences and project alternatives indicated in the EIS. This clearly means that NEPA requires federal agencies to take into account all environmental consequences of their projects before they decide to undertake them, regardless of whether or not the specific environmental concern was previously within their mandate, as well as all possible and feasible mitigation measures. The states of Washington and California with analogous statutes have similarly construed their environmental statutes. . . .

A reasonable interpretation of the New York statute indicates that the Legislature intended an EIS under SEQRA to have a similar broad scope. . . . The statute cannot be construed as merely procedural or informational since it states that all approving agencies

---

2. [The challenged conditions are:]
   4. Detailed construction plans shall be submitted to the Department for review and approval prior to beginning construction on each of the following aspects of work: . . .
       (c) all landscaping, particularly with respect to the outer boundaries of the Site;
   8. To insure maximum wildlife utilization of detention/retention basins, dense vegetative screens of low-lying conifers and shrub species, such as autumn olive and dogwood, shall be planted along the basin perimeters.
   10. The area identified on Appendix "A" as "Future Development Area A" Between Ponds "A" and "B," at the southeasterly boundary of the Site, shall be maintained in an undeveloped condition for the life of the mall project.
   11. The water line that would extend from the looped system of distribution mains that is proposed as part of the overall water supply system for The Marketplace to the "Future Development Area" in the southeast portion of the Site for the purpose of serving that area in the future shall be eliminated from the water supply plans, and shall not be installed as part of the development of the 125-acre Site.
   12. Parking areas for the completed project shall not exceed a total of 5,515 spaces.
   17. An energy conservation plan pursuant to Energy Law shall be submitted to the Town and the Department concurrently upon the completion of preliminary design plans for the project or the submission of applications for building permits, whichever is earlier.
   18. Prior to operation of the mall, the Applicant shall submit to the Department for approval a plan to monitor carbon monoxide at the Site and a proposal for remedial action in the event of violation of applicable air standards.

involved in an action must actually consider the EIS and formulate its decision on the basis of all the adverse environmental impacts disclosed therein. [N.Y. Envtl. Conserv. Law §8-0109(2).] Since SEQRA requires an approving agency to act affirmatively upon the adverse environmental impacts revealed in an EIS, §8-0109, subds. (1) and (8), an EIS filed pursuant to SEQRA must also be recognized as not a mere disclosure statement but rather as an aid in an agency's decision-making process to evaluate and balance the competing factors. . . .

. . . SEQRA therefore requires a decision maker to balance the benefits of a proposed project against its unavoidable environmental risks in determining whether to approve the project. While an EIS does not require a public agency to act in any particular manner, it constitutes evidence which must be considered by the public agency along with other evidence which may be presented to such agency. . . .

We must be ever cognizant that environmental amenities will often be in conflict with economic and technical considerations. To consider the former along with the latter must involve a balancing process. In some instances, environmental costs may well outweigh economic and technical benefits while in other instances they may not; but SEQRA mandates a rather finely tuned and systematic balancing analysis in every instance. . . . Failure to employ this balancing analysis may be grounds for nullifying an administrative decision. . . .

. . . [T]he regulations in accord with the statutory provisions of SEQRA, make clear that an agency in approving an action must make a written finding that it has imposed whatever conditions are necessary to minimize or avoid all adverse environmental impacts revealed in the EIS.

We caution, however, that SEQRA must be construed in the light of reason. Any limitations or conditions imposed accordingly must be governed by a "reasonableness test" if they are to survive judicial review. . . .

Having found that DEC did have authority to attach the challenged conditions to the permits it issued petitioners, our duty then is to scrutinize the record and determine whether substantial evidence supports the administrative agency's findings and whether these findings support the agency's decision. In making these determinations, we must resolve reasonable doubts in favor of the administrative findings and decisions. . . .

As we view it, condition 10, leaving area A undeveloped, is pivotal in its scope and directly affects conditions 4(c), 8 and 11. It is intended to mitigate the development's impact on wildlife habitat. The EIS specifically concluded that the mall would result in a total elimination of wildlife species on the portion of the site proposed for development. Petitioners' draft EIS proposed to mitigate this adverse impact by leaving three undisturbed areas totaling 12 acres. However, two of the three areas were designated by Miracle Mile for "future development." The hearing report/EIS firmly concluded that such temporary measures did not adequately mitigate the mall's impact on wildlife habitat. Consequently, condition 10 requiring only one of three undisturbed areas designated by Miracle Mile for future development to remain undeveloped clearly has a rational basis in the record. Likewise does condition 11 prohibiting extension of a water line to service this portion of the site, as well as condition 4(c), requiring approval of perimeter landscaping, which was intended to insure maximum wildlife utilization of the mall site's undeveloped areas. . . .

Condition 18 requires the developers to submit to DEC for approval a plan to monitor carbon monoxide at the site. Air quality is recognized as a valid concern of SEQRA and any adverse impact on air quality caused by the mall site should be identified and mitigated if possible. The difficulty, as we see it, with condition 18 arises in DEC's requiring and relying upon any sort of air quality analysis regarding highway traffic around the mall and then imposing the condition of air monitoring on the applicant for any alleged inadequacy in such a study. The record discloses that there are too many unquantifiable variables present, making it unreasonable to determine how much traffic near the mall is generated solely on account of the mall. Any air monitoring system imposed by the DEC would suffer from the same inadequacies. Condition 18, therefore, should be stricken as arbitrary and unreasonable. . . .

Accordingly, we hold that SEQRA requires an approving agency to consider fully the environmental consequences revealed in an EIS and to take these consequences into account when reaching a decision whether or not to approve an action. Moreover, the statute authorizes the approving agency to implement measures designed to mitigate the adverse environmental impacts identified, so long as these measures are reasonable in scope and are reasonably related to the adverse impacts identified in the EIS. . . .

CARDAMONE, J.P., and SIMONS, DOERR and MOULE, JJ., concur.

Note on the Substantive Impact of EIS Requirements

1. *The balance struck.* Should the court have any role in reviewing the agency's balancing of the costs and benefits of the proposed action other than to make sure the agency did take environmental impacts into consideration? What if there were substantial evidence in the record that the shopping center at issue in *Henrietta* would merely divert jobs, shopping opportunities, and tax revenues from existing downtown businesses, such that the public benefits of the shopping center were minimal, but the local government nevertheless determined that such minor benefits outweighed significant adverse environmental impacts?

2. *The federal perspective.* Strycker's Bay Neighborhood Council, Inc. v. Karlen, 444 U.S. 223 (1980), was a neighbors' suit invoking NEPA to delay construction of low-income housing on the Upper West Side of Manhattan. The Supreme Court reversed a decision of the Second Circuit ordering the U.S. Department of Housing and Urban Development (HUD) to give "determinative weight" to environmental considerations when evaluating alternative plans. The Court's per curiam opinion asserted that NEPA is designed to ensure only that decisionmakers are well informed and does not require them to "elevate environmental considerations over other appropriate considerations." NEPA was designed, the Court said, " 'to insure a fully informed and well-considered decision' but not necessarily 'a decision the judges of the Court of Appeals or this Court would have reached had they been members of the decisionmaking unit of the agency.' " 444 U.S. at 227 (quoting Vermont Yankee Nuclear Power Corp. v. Natural Resources Defense Council, Inc., 435 U.S. 519, 558 (1978)). The Court reiterated its view that NEPA imposes no substantive requirements in Robertson v. Methow Valley Citizens Council, 490 U.S. 332, 351 (1989), stating that "NEPA merely prohibits uninformed — rather than unwise — agency action." NEPA's proceduralist focus is discussed further on pp. 391-92.

3. *Factors in the balance.* Minnesota's EIS requirement prohibits the grant of a permit "likely to cause pollution, impairment, or destruction of . . . natural resources located within the state, so long as there is a feasible and prudent alternative. . . . Economic considerations alone shall not justify such conduct." Minn. Stat. §116D.04(6) (2004). How should a court interpret that mandate? In Reserve Mining Co. v. Herbst, 256 N.W.2d 808 (Minn. 1977), there was evidence that shutdown of the mine (which was threatened if permits for the project under review were not granted) would cause loss of a total yearly payroll of $55 million, yearly local purchases of $45 million, and state and local taxes of nearly $16 million. The court interpreted the limitations of §116D.04(6) as follows:

[S]tate agencies and courts are required by statute to consider both the economic impact and the environmental impact in rendering decisions dealing with environmental matters. Minn. Stat. . . . §116D.04, subd. 6. Where, as here, the evidence of potential detriment to public health is unsubstantial and inconclusive, and there is evidence that effective measures to mitigate air pollution will be taken, we must take into consideration human factors which inevitably bear on a decision having serious personal consequences in the lives and well-being of those closest to the problem. As we construe the statutes . . . if there were substantial evidence that Reserve's proposed tailings site at Mile Post 7 would have significantly adverse medical effects on the residents of Silver Bay, no further consideration would be given to the economic consequences of a total shutdown and the site would be rejected. We are not free to barter the health of residents at Silver Bay for their economic security, even if that were their intention, which it is not. It is only where the likelihood of danger to the public is remote and speculative that economic impacts which are devastating and certain may be weighed in the balance to arrive at an environmentally sound decision.

Id. at 841. Is the court's interpretation sound?

4. *Review of mitigation requirements, again.* By what standard should courts review mitigation requirements imposed as a result of an EIS? Should the standard be different for mitigation measures imposed after a full EIS than for mitigation measures imposed as part of a mitigated negative declaration? Different than the standards applied to conditional zoning? See pp. 318–36. The standards applied to exactions? See pp. 637–52.

5. *Monitoring.* Who should bear the responsibility of monitoring mitigation efforts to ensure that they indeed do minimize or offset adverse environmental impacts? If the mitigation efforts prove less effective than planned, can the mitigation requirements be increased? Can the permits based on the EIS be revoked?

d. Assessment

The EIS process has been roundly criticized by a wide variety of academics, judges, practitioners, and government officials. It has many staunch defenders, however, and has been widely copied, both in other areas of law and around the globe. Kevin R. Gray, International Environmental Impact Assessment, 11 Colo. J. Int'l Envtl. L. & Pol'y 83 (2000); Tim Iglesias, Housing Impact Assessments: Opening New Doors For State Housing Regulation While Localism Persists, 82 Or. L. Rev. 433 (2003); William H. Rodgers, Jr., NEPA at Twenty: Mimicry and Recruitment in Environmental Law, 20 Envtl. L. 485, 488 (1990). Indeed, one commentator has quipped that NEPA has "the unusual honor of being the most successful environmental law in the world and the most disappointing." Oliver A. Houck, Is That All? A Review of the National Environmental Policy Act: An Agenda for the Future by Lynton Keith Caldwell, 111 Duke Envtl. L. & Pol'y F. 171, 171 (2000).

In brief, the criticisms fall into three major categories:

1. *Procedural, rather than substantive, focus.* Many argue that NEPA and some little NEPAs are toothless because they are divorced from any substantive requirement that decisionmakers avoid taking actions that the EIS reveals are environmentally harmful. Professor Richard Stewart has argued, for example:

> [O]ne is left with the impression that NEPA has not deterred agencies from following their bent in most cases after going through the motions of devising an impact statement.
>
> It is perhaps surprising that any different outcome should have been expected. As long as agency discretion to set substantive policy is unconstrained by legislative directives or any other exogenous limits, formal procedures may serve to delineate conflicting claims, but procedures alone cannot resolve them.

Richard B. Stewart, The Reformation of American Administrative Law, 88 Harv. L. Rev. 1669, 1780–81 (1975) (footnotes omitted). More colorfully, Professor Joseph Sax opined: "I know of no solid evidence to support the belief that requiring articulation, detailed findings or reasoned opinions enhances the integrity or propriety of the administrative decisions. I think the emphasis on the redemptive quality of procedural reform is about nine parts myth and one part coconut oil." Joseph L. Sax, The (Unhappy) Truth About NEPA, 26 Okla. L. Rev. 239, 239 (1973). Not only does NEPA's procedural focus fail to improve agency decisions, some critics lament, it also provides an "illusion that our decisions are environmentally sensitive." David R. Hodas, NEPA, Ecosystem Management and Environmental Accounting, 14 Nat. Resources & Env't 185 (2000). See also Lynton Keith Caldwell, National Environmental Policy Act: An Agenda for the Future (1999); Philip Michael Ferester, Revitalizing the National Environmental Policy Act: Substantive Law Adaptations from NEPA's Progeny, 16 Harv. Envtl. L. Rev. 297 (1992); Thomas France, NEPA — The Next Twenty Years, 25 Land & Water L. Rev. 133 (1990); Nicholas C. Yost, NEPA's Promise — Partially Fulfilled, 20 Envtl. L. 533 (1990). For provocative case studies of battles over impact statements that reach similar conclusions, see Daniel Ackman, Highway to Nowhere: NEPA, Environmental Review and the Westway Case, 21 Colum. J.L. & Soc. Probs. 325 (1988); Chester Mirsky & David Porter, Ambushing the Public: The Socio-Political and Legal Consequences of SEQRA Decision-Making, 6 Alb. L. Envtl. Outlook J. 1 (2002).

Professor Sax, however, has since admitted that he "underestimated the influence of NEPA's 'soft law' elements" and that "legitimating public participation, and demanding openness in planning and decisionmaking, has been indispensible to a permanent and powerful increase in environmental protection." Joseph L. Sax, More Than Just a Passing Fad, 29 U. Mich. J.L. Reform 797, 804 & n.28 (1986). Others have affirmatively defended NEPA's proceduralist focus. See, e.g., Michael Herz, Parallel Universes: NEPA Lessons for the New Property, 93 Colum. L. Rev. 1668 (1993); Eric W. Orts, Reflexive Environmental Law, 89 Nw. U. L. Rev. 1227 (1995).

Several critics have recently suggested that the failings of environmental impact review resulting from its proceduralist focus could be alleviated by increasing the monitoring of both the environmental impacts resulting from development and the success of mitigation measures at preventing environmental harm, and by subjecting those who prepare and approve EISs to greater accountability when their estimates of impact turn out to be widely off the mark. See, e.g., Hodas, supra, at 188–89; Bradley Karkkainen, Toward a Smarter NEPA: Monitoring and Managing Government's Environmental Performance, 102 Colum. L. Rev. 903, 927–31 (2002).

As the Council on Environmental Quality (CEQ), the executive agency charged with overseeing NEPA's implementation, has noted, it is hard to quantify the effectiveness of a statute designed to make people think about environmental impacts. Nevertheless, several studies have attempted to measure changes in substantive outcomes attributable to EIS requirements. One such study found that NEPA had a significant effect on the decisions of the U.S. Corps of Engineers and the Forest Service. Serge Taylor, Making Bureaucracies Think (1984). See also Council on Environmental Quality, Environmental Quality, Environmental Impact Statements: An Analysis of Six Years' Experience by Seventy Federal Agencies (1976); Council on Environmental Quality, Fourth Annual Report 247 (1973). Many anecdotal reports assert that the EIS process has led to significant changes in project design. In an extensive study of NEPA occasioned by the twenty-fifth year of its passage, the CEQ found that NEPA "can make it easier to discourage poor proposals . . . and support innovation." Council on Environmental Quality, The National Environmental Policy Act: A Study of Its Effectiveness After Twenty-Five Years ix (1997).

Other studies have found that the environmental review process has had significant benefits quite apart from changing substantive outcomes. The requirement is credited with increasing public participation in agency actions and thereby "democratizing" land use and environmental decisionmaking. See Leonard Ortolano, Environmental Planning and Decision-Making 146–47 (1984). It also is credited with exposing differences of opinion among or within agencies, thereby giving opponents of a project potential allies within the government itself and decreasing the court's willingness to defer to one agency's views. See Wendy Espeland, The Struggle for Water 135–81 (1998); Michael Blumm & Steve Brown, Pluralism and the Environment: The Role of Comment Agencies in NEPA Litigation, 14 Harv. Envtl. L. Rev. 277 (1990).

2. *EISs fail to provide sufficient or objective information.* EISs often are criticized as being too long and too technical on the one hand, and too shallow or conclusory on the other. Both supporters and opponents of the project also often charge that EISs are biased. Are such criticisms inevitable, given that the "audience" for any EIS is composed of multiple interest groups with conflicting concerns and that "objectivity" is likely to be in the eye of the beholder? See M. O'Hare et al., Facility Siting and Public Opposition 99–117 (1983) (arguing that the nature of information makes it impossible for "supply side strategies for information provision" — like EIS requirements — to satisfy users' demands, and suggesting that EIS statutes should require only that "public good" information that all interested groups would want to know, but that government perhaps should subsidize the efforts of individual interest groups to obtain more specific information about the group's particular concerns). See also Karkkainen, supra, at 906–07, arguing that NEPA "ambitiously, and naively demands the impossible: comprehensive, synoptic rationality, in the form of an exhaustive, one-shot set of ex ante predictions of expected impacts."

3. *Opportunity for abuse.* Professor Stewart Sterk argues that "[c]ase law does not sufficiently capture the instances in which decisionmakers use the environmental review process to delay, recast, or kill development projects for ends unrelated to environmental goals." Stewart E. Sterk, Environmental Review in the Land Use Process: New York's Experience with SEQRA, 13 Cardozo L. Rev. 2041, 2055 (1992). See also Philip Weinberg, SEQRA's Too Valuable to Trash: A Reply to Stewart Sterk, 14 Cardozo L. Rev. 1959 (1993). How could such "opportunistic" use of EIS requirements be discouraged? Should successful defendants in EIS challenges be able to recover attorney fees? See, e.g., Mark Vandervelden, Is the State Environmental Act an Endangered Species?, Cal. Law., Apr. 1984, at 45 (discussing such proposals).

D.   Constraints on Land Use Decisions by Neighbors

1.   Neighbors' Consent Requirements

City of Chicago v. Stratton
44 N.E. 853 (Ill. 1896)

This was a suit . . . to recover the penalty for a violation of . . . [section 49 of the building ordinance]:

> Sec. 49. It shall not be lawful for any person to locate, build, construct or keep in any block in which two-thirds of the buildings are devoted to exclusive residence purposes, a livery boarding or sales stable, gas house, gas reservoir, paint, oil or varnish works, within 200 feet of such

residence, on either side of the street, unless the owners of a majority of the lots in such block fronting or abutting on the street consent in writing . . .

It is conceded by the appellees that they are engaged in keeping a livery, boarding, and sale stable at Nos. 211 and 213 Evanston Avenue, in the city of Chicago; . . . and that they did not procure the consent of the owners of a majority of the lots in such block fronting or abutting on the street before the erection of said building. . . .

Upon the trial before the court, a jury having been waived, . . . the court held the section of the ordinance to be invalid, and entered a finding for the defendants. . . . The . . . appellate court . . . affirmed. . . .

MAGRUDER, J. (after stating the facts).

. . . The power to make laws which the constitution confers upon the legislature cannot be delegated by the legislature to any other body or authority. . . . The question, then, in the present case is whether the power to direct the location of livery stables and regulate their use and construction which has been conferred upon the common council of the city of Chicago by the city and village act is delegated by section 49 of the building ordinance to the owners of a majority of the lots in the blocks therein specified. . . .

The prohibition against the location of a stable in a residence block is for the benefit of those who reside there. If those for whose benefit the prohibition is created make no objection to the location of such a stable in their midst, an enforcement of the prohibition as to that block would seem to be unnecessary. By section 49 the lot owners are not clothed with the power to locate livery stables, but are merely given the privilege of consenting that an existing ordinance against the location of a livery stable in such a block as theirs may not be enforced as against their block. They are simply allowed to waive the right to insist upon the enforcement of a legal prohibition which was adopted for their benefit and comfort. . . .

. . . Delegation of power to make the law is forbidden, as necessarily involving a discretion as to what the law shall be; but there can be no valid objection to a law which confers an authority or discretion as to its execution, to be exercised under and in pursuance of the law itself. Here the provision in reference to the consent of the lot owners affects the execution of the ordinance, rather than its enactment. The ordinance in question does not delegate to a majority of the lot owners the right to pass, or even approve of, it. On the contrary, their consent is in the nature of a condition subsequent which may defeat the operation of the prohibition against the location of a livery stable in a block where two-thirds of the buildings are devoted to exclusive residence purposes, but which was never intended to confer upon the ordinance validity as an expression of the legislative will. . . . In determining the question of the location of a livery stable the common council may properly consult the wishes and ascertain the needs of the residents of the block where the stable is to be kept, and to that end make their written consent the basis of the action of the commissioner of buildings in issuing the permit. In matters of purely local concern the parties immediately interested may fairly be supposed to be more competent to judge of their needs than any central authority. . . .

For the reasons stated, we are of the opinion that the ordinance here in question is not void as being a delegation of legislative power. . . .

Reversed and remanded.

Note on "All Power to the Neighborhood"

1. *An alternative to administrative agencies?* The Chicago ordinance essentially gave neighboring landowners complete authority to grant permits for potentially controversial

land uses proposed by developers. The pioneering New York City zoning ordinance, adopted 20 years after *Stratton*, delegated these same decisions to government agencies. Would Chicago's approach have been more likely than New York's to result in efficient and equitable decisions? See Robert H. Nelson, Zoning and Property Rights (1977); A. Dan Tarlock, An Economic Analysis of Direct Voter Participation in Zoning Change, 1 J. Envtl. L. 31 (1980).

2. *A failure of nuisance law?* How did the rights the Chicago ordinance conferred on neighbors differ from the rights those neighbors already had under the private nuisance law discussed in Chapter 6A? Consider this rendition of the history of the Chicago ordinances:

> In the late nineteenth century, most of the transportation on the streets of Chicago was by horse-drawn vehicle. The horses needed a place to reside when they were not working and this function was performed by the livery stable. Livery stables produced certain externalities that their neighbors often found undesirable. In addition to the accumulation of horse manure, the stables typically brought noise and lights late in the evening and early in the morning and created the nineteenth century equivalent of what we would call traffic and parking problems.
>
> The courts had struggled with the issue of how such stables should be treated under nuisance law. Typically, Illinois courts said that a stable was not a nuisance per se so they would not enjoin its construction but would wait until the stable was built and in operation before determining whether it turned out to be a nuisance and whether the neighbors would be entitled to damages or an injunction. Consequently, the threat to build a livery stable in a residential neighborhood foreshadowed a substantial period of insecurity for the residents followed by no assurance of a satisfactory remedy.
>
> . . . Any threat to construct a livery stable had to be taken seriously by residential neighbors. Some people developed a regular practice of buying vacant lots in residential subdivisions, threatening to build a stable, and then extorting a steep price from the neighbors to be bought out. This became such a widespread practice that it became known as the livery stable scam. . . .
>
> The Chicago Real Estate Board was offended by what it saw as this abuse of the free market system, but was reluctant to suggest that the government be given substantial discretion in the location of stables. Instead they proposed an ordinance prohibiting any new livery stables abutting or within 75 feet of any "residence street" unless the owners of all property within 600 feet gave their consent in writing. This ordinance was adopted in 1887 and eventually upheld by the Illinois Supreme Court in the case of City of Chicago v. Stratton.

Fred P. Bosselman, The Commodification of "Nature's Metropolis": The Historical Context of Illinois' Unique Zoning Standards, 12 N. Ill. U. L. Rev. 527, 569–71 (1992). For a more complete treatment, see Andrew J. King, Law and Land Use in Chicago: A Prehistory of Modern Zoning 229–414 (1986).

3. *How many neighbors have to approve?* Was Chicago wise to require no more than majority approval? Certainly unanimous approval would be too much to insist on because some neighbors might then withhold their consents for strategic reasons. Cf. the discussion at pp. 845–54 on land assembly by private firms.

4. *The Supreme Court muddle.* The U.S. Supreme Court first confronted consent provisions in Eubank v. City of Richmond, 226 U.S. 137 (1912). Richmond passed a statute providing that whenever the owners of two-thirds of the property abutting on a street petitioned the city's committee on streets to establish a building line, the committee would do so, and no permit would be issued for the construction of any building on the street that failed to comply with the line. Mr. Eubank received a permit to build a house in December, but in January, the committee on streets responded to the neighbors' petition by establishing a building line that fell behind the bay window Eubank had planned for the house. Eubank sued, and the Supreme Court invalidated the ordinance, reasoning:

The statute and ordinance, while conferring the power on some property holders to virtually control and dispose of the property rights of others, creates no standard by which the power thus given is to be exercised; in other words, the property holders who desire and have the authority to establish the line may do so solely for their own interest, or even capriciously. Taste (for even so arbitrary a thin[g] as taste may control) or judgment may vary in localities, indeed, in the same locality. . . . There may be one taste or judgment of comfort or convenience on one side of a street and a different one on the other. There may be diversity in other blocks; and, viewing them in succession, their building lines may be continuous or staggering (to adopt a word of the mechanical arts) as the interests of certain of the property owners may prompt against the interests of others. . . . It is hard to understand how public comfort or convenience, much less public health, can be promoted by a line which may be so variously disposed. . . .

Id. at 143–46.

A few years later, the Court confronted an ordinance that prohibited billboards on any block in which one-half of the buildings were used solely for residential purposes, unless the owners of a majority of the property on the block consented to the billboard. Thomas Cusack Co. v. City of Chicago, 242 U.S. 526 (1917). The Court upheld the ordinance, finding that the property owner "cannot be injured, but obviously may be benefited, by this provision, for without it the prohibition of the erection of such billboards . . . is absolute." *Eubank* was "plain[ly]" distinguishable: "The one ordinance permits two-thirds of the lot owners to impose restrictions upon the other property in the block, while the other permits one-half of the lot owners to remove a restriction from the other property owners." Id. at 531.

Finally, in Washington ex rel. Seattle Title Trust Co. v. Roberge, 278 U.S. 116 (1928), the Court invalidated a statute that allowed "a philanthropic home for children or for old people" to be located within a residential district when two-thirds of the owners of property within 400 feet of the proposed building consented. The Court again found troubling the fact that neighbors were "uncontrolled by any standard or rule" and were free to "withhold consent for selfish reasons or arbitrarily." *Cusack* was distinguishable because it involved billboards, which "by reason of their nature are liable to be offensive," while the record contained no suggestion that the proposed home for the aged would be a nuisance. Id. at 122.

The next case illustrates how the lower federal courts and state courts currently are trying to make sense of these confusing precedents.

Cary v. City of Rapid City
559 N.W.2d 891 (S.D. 1997)

MILLER, Chief Justice. . . .

Cary's property, which is located in southwestern Rapid City, was annexed into the City on September 8, 1992. . . . Following annexation, City placed a street assessment of approximately $90,000 on the western portion of the property. Additionally, the property's real estate taxes were increased from $122.36 in 1990 to $3,678.48 in 1995. The property, however, continued to be used as a horse pasture and generated rental income of $150 per year.

On December 6, 1993, City adopted an ordinance rezoning Cary's property as "general agriculture" property. . . .

As a result of the street assessment and increased property taxes, Cary decided to sell the property. In 1995, she received an offer to purchase which was contingent on the property being rezoned as "medium density residential" to allow construction of apartment buildings. According to the buyers, a medium density residential designation was the lowest zoning classification which would be cost effective and economically viable for the property.

In an attempt to comply with the buyers' condition, Cary filed a petition with City seeking to rezone the property. She complied with all requirements for rezoning. The Rapid City Fire Department, Engineering Department, Building Inspector and City Planning Department recommended approval of the petition. On September 5, 1995, City approved Ordinance 3224 rezoning Cary's property as medium density residential property. . . . On September 21, 1995, more than 40 percent of the neighboring property owners filed a written protest pursuant to [S.D. Codified Laws §]11-4-5. The protesters owned less than 18 percent of the property neighboring Cary's property. Based on the protest, City took the appropriate legal position that the ordinance could not be effectuated because of the provisions of [§]11-4-5.

Cary then . . . asked the trial court to declare Ordinance 3224 effective and require City to rezone the property in compliance with her petition. Additionally, she requested that [§]11-4-5 be declared inapplicable to the property or, in the alternative, be declared unconstitutional. The trial court denied her requests. Cary appeals. . . .

[Section] 11-4-5 provides:

> If such [a proposed zoning] ordinance be adopted, the same shall be published and take effect as other ordinances unless the referendum be invoked, or unless a written protest be filed with the auditor or clerk, signed by at least 40 percent of the owners of equity in the lots included in any proposed district and the lands within 150 feet from any part of such proposed district measured by excluding streets and alleys. . . . In the event such a protest be filed, the ordinance shall not become effective as to the proposed district against which the protest has been filed. . . .

. . . [T] trial court determined [§]11-4-5 to be constitutional. On appeal, Cary argues the protest provision of the statute is unconstitutional because it does not provide standards and guidelines for the delegation of legislative authority, nor does it contain a legislative bypass provision to remove the ultimate legislative authority and lawmaking power from the protesters. She claims the absence of such provisions is an unlawful delegation of legislative power that results in a small number of property owners being able to prevent a landowner's use of property. . . .

For the reasons set forth below, we . . . conclude [§]11-4-5 is unconstitutional. . . .

Legislative power is vested in the legislature and this essential power may not be abdicated or delegated. . . . When a legislative body retains a police power, articulated standards and guidelines to limit the exercise of the police power are unnecessary. Police powers which are delegated, however, must include minimum standards and guidelines for their application. The failure to provide standards and guidelines for the application of the police power constitutes a delegation of legislative power repugnant to the due process clause of the Fourteenth Amendment. *Seattle Title Trust Co. v. Roberge*, 278 U.S. 116, 122 (1928). . . .

In the instant case, [§]11-4-5 does not provide guidelines or standards for protesting an adopted ordinance. So long as a certain number of neighboring property owners file a written petition, those property owners may impose or create restrictions on neighboring property without reason or justification.

A person's right to use his or her land for any legitimate purpose is constitutionally protected. *Seattle Trust*, 278 U.S. at 121. Section 11-4-5, however, allows the use of a person's property to be held hostage by the will and whims of neighboring landowners without adherence or application of any standards or guidelines. Under [§]11-4-5, "the property holders who desire to have the authority to establish [a restriction] may do so solely for their own interests or even capriciously. Taste (for even so arbitrary a thing as taste may control) or judgment may vary[.]" Eubank [v. City of Richmond], 226 U.S. [137], 144 [(1912)]. Such a standardless protest statute allows for unequal treatment under the law and is in clear contradiction of the protections of the due process clause of the Fourteenth Amendment. See id.

Furthermore, [§]11-4-5 provides no legislative bypass to allow for review of a protest. The filing of a written protest requires that the adopted ordinance "shall not become effective." [§]11-4-5. By allowing 40 percent of the neighboring property owners to block the effectuation of an adopted ordinance approved by City, as being consistent with the best interests of the public, [§]11-4-5 allows a potentially small number of neighboring property owners to make the ultimate determination of the public's best interest.[2] The absence of a review provision or some method by which a protest is reviewed by a legislative body makes the protest filed under [§]11-4-5 determinative and final. The ultimate determination of the public's best interest is for the legislative body, not a minority of neighboring property owners. See Eubank, 226 U.S. at 143. Delegations of legislative authority which allow this ultimate decision to be made by a minority of property owners without an opportunity for review are unlawful. Id.

The protest provision of [§]11-4-5 is unconstitutional. . . .

Note on Neighbors' Consent Requirements

1. *The establish/waive distinction.* The *Eubank*, *Cusack*, and *Roberge* trilogy identifies two variables as having constitutional relevance. The first is whether neighbors are being empowered to establish a restriction or instead to waive one that otherwise would be in effect. Was *Cary* correct in considering the protest statute more like establishing a restriction than waiving a restriction?

If a government can prohibit activity X but then empower a neighborhood group to allow X, why shouldn't the government be able to allow X but then enable a neighborhood group to prohibit it? Might developers actually prefer the system challenged in *Cary* to that in *Cusack*? Will local governments be more prone to pass prohibitions if they know the "safety valve" of neighborhood waiver is present? Note also that the *Cusack* waiver requirement imposed the burden of circulating a petition on the developer, while a requirement like that in *Cary* imposes the burden of taking the lead on the neighbors.

To take advantage of the establish/waive distinction, could a city simply prohibit all development, or all development of a particular kind, but then allow neighbors to waive that prohibition when they wished? In effect, the jurisdiction would be deeming all uses as special exceptions with neighbors' consent one of the criteria for the grant of the special exception. Cf. Minton v. City of Fort Worth Planning Commission, 786 S.W.2d 563 (Tex. Ct. App. 1990) (requirement that two-thirds of nearby owners consent to the replatting of land is not a valid "waiver" provision because city could not constitutionally prohibit all replatting).

2. *Noxiousness.* The second variable, identified in *Roberge*, is the noxiousness of the proposed use. The state courts have repeatedly invalidated consent requirements for uses that are not noxious, but upheld those for uses that are. Compare, e.g., Bourque v. Dettore,

---

2. As presently written, [§]11-4-5 would allow the owner of one small parcel of land within 150 feet of a large parcel of land to effectively block any proposed use of the large parcel of land so long as the small parcel owner constituted 40 percent of neighboring property owners and a written protest was filed.

589 A.2d 815 (R.I. 1991) (grant of license for recycling facility could be conditioned on consent of neighbors because, as in *Cusack*, the use involved was nuisance-like), with Town of Gardiner v. Stanley Orchards, Inc., 432 N.Y.S.2d 335 (Sup. Ct. 1980) (invalidating requirement that all landowners within 500 feet of property consent to the placement of any mobile home, in part because mobile homes are not "nuisances") (for a discussion of exclusionary zoning of mobile homes, see p. 788). Local governments are constitutionally permitted to control the location of inoffensive activities. Why should courts be reluctant to permit neighbors to share that power?

Where the alleged noxiousness of the proposed use is based on the content of speech or the nature of religious belief or practice, consent requirements are particularly problematic for the reasons discussed at pp. 209-32. See, e.g., Young v. City of Simi Valley, 216 F.3d 807, 817 (9th Cir. 2000) (ordinance allowing permit for adult use to be denied if a neighbor showed that the adult use would affect the neighbor's "sensitive use" — such as a youth center — violates the First Amendment).

3. *Religious uses as neighbors.* When the neighbor whose consent is required is a church, synagogue, or other religious use, the Establishment Clause of the First Amendment poses another barrier to consent provisions. In Larkin v. Grendel's Den, Inc., 459 U.S. 116 (1982), the Supreme Court struck down a Massachusetts statute that gave the governing bodies of churches and schools the power to veto applications for liquor licenses within a 500-foot radius of their buildings. The Court reasoned that the statute violated all three prongs of the then prevailing test of Lemon v. Kurtzman, 403 U.S. 602, 614 (1971). Although the ordinance was motivated by valid secular purposes, those purposes could be met by other, less troublesome means; the veto power could be used by a church for explicitly religious goals, such as favoring liquor licenses for members of that congregation or adherents of that faith; and the ordinance entangled churches in governmental matters by substituting "the unilateral and absolute power of a church for the reasoned decisionmaking of a public legislative body acting on evidence and guided by standards, on issues with significant economic and political implications." 459 U.S. at 127. For further discussion of the Establishment Clause, see pp. 209-20.

4. *Buying the approval of neighbors.* Criminal statutes bar the buying and selling of votes in public elections. Should there be any legal barrier to the trading of rights of the sort created by the Massachusetts statute involved in *Grendel's Den*? The District of Columbia Court of Appeals confronted that issue in upholding a statute that required owners of apartment buildings to secure the consent of 50 percent of the tenants before converting to condominiums:

> [The legislative body] . . . undoubtedly recognized that the residents of a particular rental complex might well act in their own financial interest and consent to conversion only if the owners would sweeten the pie by buying them out at an attractive price. . . .
>
> . . . The Act permits tenants to dispense with the protection provided by the general ban on conversions if they can negotiate a better bargain for themselves. It may not be pretty, but we do not think it is unconstitutional.

Hornstein v. Barry, 560 A.2d 530, 534–35 (D.C. 1989). A plaintiff who wins the right to enjoin a use as a nuisance usually is entitled to forgo the injunction in exchange for a cash settlement, as discussed at pp. 532–36. Why shouldn't the neighbors for whose benefit a zoning law was passed similarly be entitled to waive the law in exchange for cash?

If sales for cash are too "ugly" to be unconstitutional, what about a sale in return for a promise to close the Grendel's Den tavern on Sunday?

5. *Consent requirements and models of local politics.* Professor Michelman has attempted to construct public choice and civic republican explanations of the results of

the neighbor consent cases. In his view, public choice analysis suggests that neighborhood voting should be impermissible (1) when only small numbers of landowners have a stake in the outcome (because then there is no justification for collective control of permissible uses) or (2) when the neighborhood voting process is invoked too seldom to permit logrolling (agreements to trade votes). Michelman asserts that a civic republican analysis, by contrast, would be interested in facilitating the communal definition of shared goals and would be hostile to neighborhood voting if the voting format were one that would tend to make participants think and act in a self-interested, as opposed to a public-spirited, way. Frank I. Michelman, Political Markets and Community Self-Determination: Competing Judicial Models of Local Government Legitimacy, 53 Ind. L.J. 145 (1977–1978), excerpted at p. 47. Which explanation best explains the different results in *Cusack* and *Roberge*?

6. *The mechanics of neighborhood voting.* There are countless ways to construct neighborhood consent mechanisms. The basic design decisions are

(a)   how to draw the perimeter that defines the eligible electorate;

(b)   how to identify the "owners" who are eligible to vote (e.g., what about long-term lessees, remaindermen, or concurrent owners?);

(c)   how to weigh owners' votes against each other (e.g., by lot area, by property value, one vote per lot, one vote per owner), especially in view of the conceivable applicability of constitutional requirements that each adult resident be allocated one vote;

(d)   whether to use a simple majority or some other decision rule;

(e)   whether owners of lands closest to the proposed development should be given additional electoral power;

(f)   whether the buying of votes should be expressly authorized; and

(g)   whether a positive vote by the neighborhood should decide whatever is at issue or, instead, just affect the subsequent procedures to be followed by official zoning agencies.

Examine how each of these issues is dealt with in Section 5 of the SZEA:

[Zoning] regulations, restrictions, and boundaries may from time to time be amended, supplemented, changed, modified, or repealed. In case, however, of a protest against such change, signed by the owners of 20 percent or more either of the area of the lots included in such proposed change, or of those immediately adjacent in the rear thereof extending ____ feet therefrom, or of those directly opposite thereto extending ____ feet from the street frontage of such opposite lots, such amendment shall not become effective except by the favorable vote of three-fourths of all the members of the legislative body of such municipality. . . .

The design of consent provisions can lead to tactical maneuvering by applicants for map amendments. For example, in Schwarz v. City of Glendale, 950 P.2d 167 (Ariz. Ct. App. 1997), a hospital bought a 15.1 acre tract adjacent to a residential area and sought to rezone 11.76 acres to allow construction of a medical building, while leaving the remaining 3.34 acres as a buffer zone that would defeat the protest rights of the residential neighbors. The Arizona court upheld the hospital's employment of the buffer zone to "disenfranchise" potential protesters. But see Herrington v. County of Peoria, 295 N.E.2d 729 (Ill. App. Ct. 1973) (three strips of land created as a buffer zone were so "mutually dependent" on the property being rezoned that the purpose of the protest statute would not be served by allowing the buffer to destroy the right of neighbors to protest).

2. Initiatives and Referenda

M. Dane Waters, The Initiative and Referendum Almanac
6-8, 11, 36 (2003)

Initiatives are when the citizens, collecting signatures on a petition, place advisory questions, memorials, statutes or constitutional amendments on the ballot for the citizens to adopt or reject. Twenty-four states have the initiative process. . . .

In many of the same states the citizens have the ability to reject laws or amendments proposed by the state legislature. This process is commonly referred to as the referendum process. . . . Popular referendum, which is available in 24 states . . . is when the people have the power to refer, by collecting signatures on a petition, specific legislation that was enacted by the legislature for the people to either accept or reject. Legislative referendum, which is possible in all states, is when the state legislatures, an elected official, state appointed constitutional revision commission or other government agency or department submits propositions (constitutional amendments, statutes, bond issues, etc.) to the people for their approval or rejection. . . .

. . . On Election Day 2002, voters cast their ballots on 202 statewide ballot measures in 40 states. . . . Fifty-three were placed on the ballot by the people, and 149 were placed on the ballot by the state legislatures. Of the measures placed on the ballot by the people, 45% were approved. . . .

. . . [F]ar more Americans have access to I & R in their local government than have access in their state government. . . .

- Most large cities provide for the initiative, including 15 of the 20 largest.
- One-third to one-half of American cities provide for initiatives.
- Approximately 61 to 71 percent of citizens have the initiative available in their cities. . . .

Buckeye Community Hope Foundation v. City of Cuyahoga Falls
697 N.E.2d 181 (Ohio 1998)

Appellant Buckeye Community Hope Foundation ("Buckeye Hope"), a nonprofit Ohio corporation, develops housing for individuals through the use of state grants and tax credits. . . .

In 1995, Buckeye . . . purchased a tract of land in Cuyahoga Falls for the purpose of building a seventy-two unit apartment complex. The land was zoned for multifamily use. Subsequently, the Cuyahoga Falls Planning Commission unanimously approved a site plan concerning the proposed complex. . . .

On April 1, 1996, the city council ratified the decision of the planning commission by passing Ordinance No. 48-1996. . . .

Following passage of the ordinance, a group of residents of Cuyahoga Falls filed referendum petitions with the clerk of city council. The petitions sought a referendum to approve or reject Ordinance No. 48-1996, pursuant to Section 2, Article IX of the municipal charter, which provides, in relevant part, that the citizens of Cuyahoga Falls "have the power to approve or reject at the polls *any ordinance or resolution passed by the Council.* . . ." (Emphasis added.) The Summit County Board of Elections then certified that the petitions contained a sufficient number of valid signatures to be placed on the November 1996 ballot.

On May 1, 1996, the appellants filed a complaint against the appellees in the Court of Common Pleas of Summit County, requesting injunctive relief and a declaration that the ordinance could not be challenged by referendum because its passage by the city council was an administrative, rather than legislative, action. Appellants claimed that Section 1f, Article II of the Ohio Constitution did not grant powers of referendum to citizens of municipalities on administrative actions taken by municipal legislative bodies.

The trial court . . . determined that the Charter of Cuyahoga Falls permitted the residents of the city to exercise powers of referendum on any action taken by the city council, regardless of whether the action taken was legislative or administrative in nature. . . . The court of appeals affirmed the judgment of the trial court. . . .

Pursuant to the allowance of a discretionary appeal, this court affirmed the judgment of the court of appeals. Buckeye Community Hope Found. v. Cuyahoga Falls, 692 N.E.2d 997 (Ohio 1998).

The cause is now before this court upon a motion for reconsideration filed by the appellants.

MOYER, Chief Justice.
. . . For the reasons that follow, we grant the appellants' motion for reconsideration and reverse the judgment of the court of appeals.

I . . .

The City Charter of Cuyahoga Falls provides that voters may exercise powers of referendum on any ordinance or resolution passed by the city council. The appellants contend that this provision conflicts with Section 1f, Article II of the Constitution. . . .

Section 1f, Article II provides initiative and referendum powers only on those questions that municipalities "may now or hereafter be authorized by law to control by legislative action." We have interpreted this phrase to exclude, from referendum proceedings, administrative actions taken by a city council. In Myers v. Schiering, 271 N.E.2d 864 (Ohio 1971), we held that "[u]nder Section 1f of Article II of the Ohio Constitution, municipal referendum powers are limited to questions which municipalities are 'authorized by law to control by legislative action.'" There, we determined that the passage of a resolution "granting a permit for the operation of a sanitary landfill, pursuant to an existing zoning regulation, constitutes administrative action and is not subject to referendum proceedings." Id. . . .

The section of the Charter of Cuyahoga Falls providing that voters may exercise powers of referendum on any ordinance or resolution passed by the city council is constitutionally invalid. Voters of Cuyahoga Falls may exercise powers of referendum on any ordinance or resolution that constitutes legislative action. Section 1f, Article II does not authorize the residents of Cuyahoga Falls to initiate referendum proceedings on an action taken by the city council that is not legislative in nature. . . .

II

The remaining question for our determination is whether the approval of the site plan by the city council constituted administrative or legislative action. . . .
. . . Donnelly v. Fairview Park, 233 N.E.2d 500 (Ohio 1968) . . . requires that the nature of the action taken determines whether it is legislative or administrative, i.e., whether the action creates or establishes law, or whether the action merely applies existing law to a given situation. [Id.] at 502. . . .

The action taken by the city council here was clearly administrative in nature. Ordinance No. 48-1996 . . . merely approves the planning commission's application of existing zoning regulations to the plan submitted by the appellants. The ordinance has no general, prospective application such that the action taken would fit within the usual and customary meaning of the phrase "legislative action" contained in Section 1f, Article II. See Black's Law Dictionary (6 Ed. 1990) 899 (defining "legislative act" as "[l]aw . . . passed by legislature in contrast to court-made law. One which prescribes what the law shall be in future cases arising under its provisions."). Rather, the city council determined the rights of the appellants by applying existing law to the site plan submitted by the appellants. Accordingly, adoption of Ordinance No. 48-1996 was an administrative act, and therefore was not a legislative action that could be subjected to referendum proceedings pursuant to Section 1f, Article II. . . .

Note on the Legality of Ballot Box Zoning

1. *The federal perspective.* In an earlier cases involving another referendum in Ohio, City of Eastlake v. Forest City Enterprises, Inc., 426 U.S. 668 (1976), the Supreme Court rejected a claim that a city charter provision requiring proposed land use changes to be ratified by 55 percent of the votes cast violates the due process rights of a landowner who applies for a zoning change. The Court reversed the Ohio Supreme Court's decision, which had relied on *Roberge*, *Cusack*, and *Eubank* in holding that because the popular referendum requirement lacked standards to guide the decision of the voters, it permitted the police power to be exercised in a standardless, and therefore arbitrary and capricious, manner, and thus constituted an unlawful delegation of legislative power.

The U.S. Supreme Court reasoned, however, that the referendum could not be characterized as a delegation of power because all power derives from the people, and in establishing legislative bodies, the people can reserve to themselves power to deal directly with matters that might otherwise be assigned to the legislature. The Court held that rules involving the delegation of power from a legislature to an administrative agency were inapplicable because the referendum provision did not involve a delegation of power from the legislature but a reservation of power by the people. The Court distinguished *Eubank* and *Roberge* because "the standardless delegation of power to a limited group of property owners" condemned in those cases "is not to be equated with decisionmaking by the people through the referendum process." Id. at 678.

The U.S. Supreme Court weighed in again as part of the aftermath of the *Buckeye* decision. Before the Ohio Supreme Court reached its decision, the referendum took place, and the voters rejected the site plan. Buckeye filed an action in federal court, alleging that the referendum procedure violated the Equal Protection and Due Process Clauses of the federal Constitution. The U.S. Supreme Court rejected the equal protection claim, finding that the plaintiffs had not proved that the city intended to discriminate against Buckeye because of race. See pp. 698–702. It also rejected the due process claim:

> As a matter of federal constitutional law, we have rejected the distinction that respondents ask us to draw, and that the Ohio Supreme Court drew as a matter of state law, between legislative and administrative referendums. In Eastlake v. Forest City Enterprises, Inc., 426 U.S. at 672, 675, we made clear that because all power stems from the people, "[a] referendum cannot . . . be characterized as a delegation of power," unlawful unless accompanied by "discernible standards." The people retain the power to govern through referendum " 'with respect to any matter, legislative or administrative, within the realm of local affairs.' " Id. at 674, n.9.

Though the "substantive result" of a referendum may be invalid if it is "arbitrary and capricious," Eastlake v. Forest City Enterprises, supra, at 676, respondents do not challenge the referendum itself. The subjection of the site-plan ordinance to the City's referendum process, regardless of whether that ordinance reflected an administrative or legislative decision, did not constitute per se arbitrary government conduct in violation of due process.

City of Cuyahoga Falls, Ohio v. Buckeye Community Hope Foundation, 538 U.S. 188, 199 (2003).

Despite the federal perspective, a significant number of state courts, like the Ohio Supreme Court, have been hostile to popular elections for all or some land use matters. In addition to the legislative/adjudicative (or, in Ohio, administrative) distinction, the courts have used familiar tools to tackle the issue of "ballot box zoning": procedural due process requirements, authority limits, and the requirement that zoning changes be consistent with the comprehensive plan. For general discussions of the state courts' treatment of challenges to the use of direct democracy in land use matters, see Peter G. Glenn, State Law Limitations on the Use of Initiatives and Referenda in Connection with Zoning Amendments, 51 S. Cal. L. Rev. 265 (1978); Jon E. Goetz, Direct Democracy in Land Use Planning: The State Response to *Eastlake*, 19 Pac. L.J. 793 (1987); Daniel P. Selmi, Reconsidering the Use of Direct Democracy in Making Land Use Decisions, 19 UCLA J. Envtl. L. & Pol'y 293 (2001–2002); Nicolas M. Kublicki, Comment, Land Use by, for, and of the People: Problems with the Application of Initiatives and Referenda to the Zoning Process, 19 Pepp. L. Rev. 99 (1991).

2. *The legislative/adjudicative distinction.* The state courts differ markedly in the tests they apply to determine which land use decisions are legislative and accordingly may be subject to initiative or referendum. Compare, e.g., City of Idaho Springs v. Blackwell, 731 P.2d 1250 (Colo. 1987) (actions that relate to subjects of a permanent or general character are legislative, while those that are temporary are not; acts constituting a declaration of public policy are legislative, while acts that are necessary to carry out existing legislative policies are not), with Garvin v. Ninth Judicial District Court, 59 P.3d 1180 (Nev. 2002) (to be legislative, the action must propose policy; changes to established zoning policies are not legislative).

Apparently a decision can be legislative for some purposes but not for others: In a few states that have adopted the *Fasano/Snyder* rule that rezonings are adjudicative for the purpose of determining what level of deference is due the rezoning, the courts nevertheless have held that rezonings can be the subject of initiative and referenda. See, e.g., Margolis v. District Court, 638 P.2d 297, 305 (Colo. 1981).

3. *Ballot box zoning and the comprehensive plan.* The Hawaii Supreme Court has held that "zoning by initiative is inconsistent with the goal of long range comprehensive planning" and that the legislative history of the zoning enabling act and the state constitution made it "abundantly clear that the legislature in its wisdom established a public policy of not effectuating land use zoning through the initiative process." Kaiser Hawaii Kai Development Co. v. City of Honolulu, 777 P.2d 244 (Haw. 1989) (overturning an initiative that rezoned land near a popular public beach from single-family residential to a "preservation" category). See also Township of Sparta v. Spillane, 312 A.2d 154, 157–58 (N.J. Super. Ct. App. Div. 1973) (referenda on rezonings would jeopardize comprehensive planning); I'On, L.L.C. v. Town of Mt. Pleasant, 526 S.E.2d 716, 721 (S.C. 2000) (allowing land use matters to be decided by initiative and referendum could "nullify a carefully established zoning system or master plan developed after debate among many interested persons and entities, resulting in arbitrary decisions and patchwork zoning with little rhyme or reason"); Leonard v. City of Bothell, 557 P.2d 1306 (Wash. 1976) (referenda

on rezonings inconsistent with careful planning needed for land use decisions). But see R.G. Moore Building Corp. v. Committee for Repeal, 391 S.E.2d 587 (Va. 1990) (rejecting argument that zoning by referendum was inconsistent with comprehensive planning).

4. *Initiatives and procedural due process.* A few courts have held that initiative measures are inappropriate means to decide land use matters because they violate the notice and public hearing requirements of the zoning enabling act. See, e.g., Transamerica Title Insurance Co. v. City of Tucson, 757 P.2d 1055 (Ariz. 1988) (initiative to establish buffer zones around existing open space reserves violates notice and public hearing requirements of zoning enabling act). But see Associated Home Builders v. City of Livermore, 557 P.2d 473, 479 (Cal. 1976) (procedural requirements applicable to legislative bodies simply do not apply to direct democracy); Margolis v. District Court, 638 P.2d 297, 305 (Colo. 1981) (procedural requirements are met by election campaign processes). Should the *Transamerica* reasoning apply to referenda? See LaBranche v. A.J. Lane & Co., 537 N.E.2d 119 (Mass. 1989) (referenda process is not inconsistent with the notice and hearing requirements of the zoning enabling act).

Some courts reason that if the state zoning enabling act specifies that a municipality's legislative body has the power to amend the zoning ordinance, the people themselves do not also have that authority. See, e.g., State ex rel. Foster v. City of Morgantown, 432 S.E.2d 195 (W. Va. 1993) (referendum).

5. *Seeking advice.* In a state that prohibits initiatives or binding referenda on land use matters, should the local legislative body be able to submit land use proposals to the electorate for an "advisory" referendum? Given the role that community opposition plays in influencing the outcome of land use decisions, as discussed on pp. 304–08, how "advisory" is any strong expression of community sentiment? See Great Atlantic & Pacific Tea Co. v. Borough of Point Pleasant, 644 A.2d 598 (N.J. 1994) (allowing nonbinding referendum).

Note on the Merits of Plebiscites

1. *Uses of plebiscites.* Zoning by initiative and referenda generally takes four different forms. First, an initiative may attempt broad or systemic reform of a jurisdiction's land use processes. Initiatives that enact systematic growth-control programs are an example. Second, an initiative may seek to zone property more restrictively than the legislature has chosen, and therefore benefit neighbors of the affected property at the expense of the landowner. Third, a referenda may seek to undo a zoning change that the legislative body has granted to a landowner, essentially blocking the legislative body from loosening restrictions and thereby transferring wealth from neighbors to the landowner. Fourth, on a few occasions, landowners have used the initiative process to secure relief from restrictions where a majority of voters perceived benefits from the development that the legislative body apparently found unpersuasive. See generally Peter G. Glenn, State Law Limitations on the Use of Initiatives and Referenda in Connection with Zoning Amendments, 51 S. Cal. L. Rev. 265, 274–75 (1978); Daniel P. Selmi, Reconsidering the Use of Direct Democracy in Making Land Use Decisions, 19 UCLA J. Envtl. L. & Pol'y 293 (2001–2002).

The use of ballot box zoning can significantly affect the nature of land use development. In Parma, Ohio, for example, where rezonings are subject to mandatory referenda, only one plot was rezoned between 1975 (when the referenda law was imposed) and 1988. Iver Peterson, Land Use Decisions Via the Ballot Box, N.Y. Times, May 22, 1988, at 1 (Real Estate Section).

2. *Advantages of direct democracy.* Thomas E. Cronin, Direct Democracy: The Politics of Initiative, Referendum, and Recall (1989), summarizes the virtues that advocates claim direct democracy offers:

> Citizens' initiatives will promote government responsiveness and accountability. If officials ignore the voice of the people, the people will have an available means to make needed law.
>
> Initiatives are freer from special interest domination than the legislative branches of most states, and so provide a desirable safeguard that can be called into use when legislators are corrupt, irresponsible, or dominated by privileged special interests.
>
> The initiative and referendum will produce open, educational debate on critical issues that otherwise might be inadequately discussed. . . .
>
> Direct democracy increases voter interest and election-day turnout. Perhaps, too, giving the citizen more of a role in governmental processes might lessen alienation and apathy.
>
> Finally (although this hardly exhausts the claims), citizen initiatives are needed because legislators often evade the tough issues. . . .

Id. at 10–11.

3. *The inefficiencies of failing to account for intensity of preferences.* Some social scientists are critical of referenda and initiatives because, among other shortcomings, these processes take little account of the intensity of voter preferences. See, e.g., Steven H. Hanke & A. Carbonell, Democratic Methods of Defining Property Rights: A Study of California's Coastal Zone, 2 Water Supply & Mgmt. 483 (1978). The authors note that from 1970 to 1972, the California legislature repeatedly defeated bills calling for state regulation of land use in the coastal zone. Nevertheless, in 1972, California voters approved an initiative measure imposing such a program. Hanke and Carbonell assume that developers and landowners were strongly opposed to the program, but that most Californians were mildly for it. They continue:

> Given these constituencies, the repeated failure of the state legislature to act favorably on coastal-zone bills can be interpreted through economic analysis. Even though the majority of California's voters favored, in varying degrees, more restrictive regulations on the use of coastal-zone lands, these regulations were defeated in the legislature because those who preferred the retention of existing land use regulations had much stronger preferences than those who opposed their retention. With logrolling the representatives of the intense minority were able to vote-trade and defeat attempts by the less-intense majority to introduce more restrictive regulations.
>
> If this analysis is correct, the outcome of the legislative process can be interpreted as being rational. The external costs that would have been imposed on the intense minority, if the legislation had passed, were of a higher magnitude than the benefits that would have been received by the less-intense majority.
>
> Given the failure of the legislature to pass more stringent controls, the [initiative] can be interpreted as a case in which the minority interests were not protected. Although about 55 percent of the voters preferred more stringent land use controls, the value of these controls to this majority was less than the external costs they imposed on the minority. . . .
>
> The use of simple-majority referenda with no side-payments is becoming a more generally accepted way of collectively determining the "proper" limitations on property rights in land. Our analysis questions the desirability of using this process, and suggests that, if referenda are used to determine property rights, something in excess of a simple-majority voting rule is desirable.

Id. at 486. Would these authors favor limiting campaign contributions by developers?

4. *Ignorant decisionmakers?* Many critics of the use of direct democracy measures in land use matters argue that the electors are not sufficiently informed about the competing policy concerns to make the decision. See, e.g., Jonathan S. Paris, Note, The Proper Use of Referenda in Rezoning, 29 Stan. L. Rev. 819 (1977) (results of a survey of voters involved in the Eastlake referenda showed that few knew basic information about the rezoning at issue). See also Michael Durkee et al., Land Use Initiatives and Referenda in California 143 (1990); Cynthia L. Fountaine, Note, Lousy Lawmaking: Questioning the Desirability and Constitutionality of Legislating by Initiative, 61 S. Cal. L. Rev. 733, 738–46 (1988). In some states, legislative decisions on land use matters are subject to the environmental impact review processes described at pp. 368–93, but citizen-placed initiatives are not. See, e.g., Friends of Sierra Madre v. City of Sierra Madre, 19 P.3d 567 (Cal. 2001). Citizens thus have less information and less expertise with which to evaluate the information available than do the members of administrative planning boards or legislative bodies who frequently confront land use matters. See generally Cronin, supra, at 60–89; David B. Magleby, Direct Legislation: Voting on Ballot Propositions in the United States 127–44 (1984); Julian N. Eule, Judicial Review of Direct Democracy, 99 Yale L.J. 1503, 1516–19 (1990).

5. *Unreflective decisionmakers.* Professor Larry Sager has argued that *Eastlake* "simply missed the central point" about the use of initiative and referenda in rezonings: "the unreflective, nondeliberative aggregate will of the electorate as the basis for lot-by-lot determinations of zoning status." Lawrence Gene Sager, Insular Majorities Unabated, 91 Harv. L. Rev. 1373, 1411 (1978). He argues that a right to a "due process of lawmaking" should mandate that "some legislative actions be undertaken only by a government entity which is so structured and so charged as to make possible a reflective determination that the action contemplated is fair, reasonable, and not at odds with a specific prohibitions in the constitution." Id. at 1414. See also Hans A. Linde, Due Process of Lawmaking, 55 Neb. L. Rev. 197 (1976); Glen Staszewski, Rejecting the Myth of Popular Sovereignty and Applying an Agency Model to Direct Democracy, 56 Vand. L. Rev. 395 (2003). Does Professor Sager's argument rest on an accurate view of the deliberativeness that marks local land use officials' decisionmaking? See Richard Briffault, Distrust of Democracy, 63 Tex. L. Rev. 1347, 1362–63 (1985) (book review). Is decisionmaking reflective if the decisionmakers discuss, debate, and think hard about the issue, or does reflectiveness also require compromise or even accommodation in the form of vote-trading?

6. *The influence of special interests.* Small numbers of people can determine the outcome of initiatives and referenda. See Mark August Nitikman, Note, Instant Planning — Land Use Regulation by Initiative in California, 61 S. Cal. L. Rev. 497, 520 & n.129 (1988) (describing land use initiative approved by only 12 percent of voters). The amount of money proponents or opponents of the measure have to spend also helps determine the outcome. See Cronin, supra, at 99–116. Some critics of direct democracy therefore argue that initiative and referenda processes are prone to "capture" by special interest groups. See, e.g., David S. Broder, Democracy Derailed: Initiative Campaigns and the Power of Money (2000); Elisabeth R. Gerber, The Populist Paradox: Interest Group Influence and the Promise of Direct Legislation (1999); Magleby, supra, at 145–51, 182, 198–99. But see Clayton P. Gillette, Plebiscites, Participation, and Collective Action in Local Government Law, 86 Mich. L. Rev. 930, 974–84 (1988) (arguing that legislative processes are just as subject to capture).

Are the "special interest" groups likely to capture land use initiative and referenda processes different from those likely to capture legislative processes? What explains the difference? How do the politics of ballot box zoning square with the politics of rezoning discussed at pp. 304–08? For an interesting description of the efforts the building and real estate interests have made to restrict ballot box zoning in California, see William Fulton,

Ballot Box Zoning, Cal. Law., May 1988, at 43–44. But for an example of the use of the initiative process to restrict land use regulation and otherwise augment landowners' rights, see Patterson v. County of Tehama, 235 Cal. Rptr. 867 (Ct. App. 1987).

7. *Direct democracy and discrimination.* Other critics of direct democracy in land use matters claim that plebiscites are even more parochial than legislative decisionmaking processes and therefore result in more exclusionary zoning or other measures that disadvantage racial or other minorities, who tend to be significantly underrepresented in the electorate of initiatives and referenda. For representative debate on the exclusionary aspects of the use of initiative and referenda in land use matters, compare, e.g., Derrick A. Bell, Jr., The Referendum: Democracy's Barrier to Racial Equality, 54 Wash. L. Rev. 1 (1978); David L. Callies et al., Ballot Box Zoning: Initiative, Referendum and the Law, 39 Wash. U. J. Urb. & Contemp. L. 53, 94–97 (1991); and Julian N. Eule, Representative Government: The People's Choice, 67 Chi.-Kent L. Rev. 777 (1991), with Lynn A. Baker, Direct Democracy and Discrimination: A Public Choice Perspective, 67 Chi.-Kent L. Rev. 707 (1991) (contesting the claim that direct democracy is more likely to disadvantage racial minorities than representative democracy); and Briffault, supra, at 1364–67 (same).

Is there a tension between the argument that plebescites are more likely than representative processes to be captured by special interests and the claim that plebescites are less likely to protect minority interests?

If the legislature enacts a zoning ordinance with the intent to discriminate against racial minorities, the Equal Protection Clause requires invalidation of the law. Proof of intent to discriminate is difficult to muster under any circumstance, as discussed at pp. 698–702. Is the requirement insurmountable for initiatives or referenda? Compare Hunter v. Erickson, 393 U.S. 385 (1969) (amendment to city charter that prevented city council from implementing any ordinance dealing with racial, religious, or ancestral discrimination in housing without the approval of the majority of the voters violates equal protection because it places special burden on racial minorities), with James v. Valtierra, 402 U.S. 137 (1971) (upholding a constitutional amendment mandating a referendum on all local public housing projects because the amendment was facially neutral and there was no evidence that it was "aimed at" a racial minority). See Sager, supra, at 1420–21; Jane S. Schacter, The Pursuit of "Popular Intent": Interpretive Dilemmas in Direct Democracy, 105 Yale L.J. 107 (1995).

8. *Judicial review.* Should a court reviewing a land use matter passed through an initiative or referendum give the electorate the same level of deference courts accord legislative decisions? See Robin Charlow, Judicial Review, Equal Protection and the Problem with Plebiscites, 79 Cornell L. Rev. 527 (1994); Julian N. Eule, Judicial Review of Direct Democracy, 99 Yale L.J. 1503, 1558–72 (1990); Mihui Pak, The Counter-Majoritarian Difficulty in Focus: Judicial Review of Initiatives, 32 Colum. J.L. & Soc. Probs. 237, 262–73 (1999).

Land use initiatives and referenda may be attacked on any of the grounds landowners could use to challenge a legislative decision that were discussed in Chapter 3. See, e.g., Fry v. City of Hayward, 701 F. Supp. 179 (N.D. Cal. 1988) (initiative mandating that one particular property owner could not obtain a rezoning without voter approval violated Equal Protection Clause). Where the initiative or referendum is alleged to effect a taking, the local government may have an incentive to defend it vigorously to avoid paying compensation, but suppose a landowner challenges, on grounds other than the Takings Clause, a referendum that overturned a local government's zoning decision, or an initiative that enacted a law the local government's legislative body had refused to pass. Must the local government defend the referendum or initiative?

9. *Reforms.* How should ballot box zoning be reformed to address the criticisms just canvassed? Consider the following package of reform measures:

> Initiative petitions should be reviewed for their constitutionality and conformance to planning, before being circulated for signatures. . . .
>
> The review, itself, should be conducted by the planning board that has jurisdiction over the [a]ffected property, and in jurisdictions recognizing a regional general welfare concept, the planning boards of other [a]ffected jurisdictions. Local and regional planning boards should advise of the proposal's impact on planning policy and conformance to the city's comprehensive plan. Attention should also be placed on the measure's compliance with state and federal environmental protection acts. Finally, the city attorney should review the proposal to screen drafting errors and violations of constitutional and statutory law. . . .
>
> Presently, long and complicated proposals combined with a lack of voter education skew direct legislation in favor of the educated upper classes. . . . To make the process more representative, ballots should be kept short, by limiting the number of issues presented and by applying a plain language statutory requirement.
>
> Issue comprehension by voters is facilitated by the promulgation of information from unbiased sources. Election boards and other civic-minded groups can provide a symposium of views both pro and con, by mailing pamphlets to each registered voter. . . .
>
> Signature requirements can be used to ensure that an issue is of city wide magnitude and capable of generating voter interest. While a low signature requirement invites frivolous matters, a high signature requirement can bar legitimate issues; therefore, a moderate position that requires a geographic representation of the entire entity can best accommodate both concerns. Requiring a minimum percentage of qualified voters to cast a decision also indicates that the determination is made by the entire city, and not by one segment. In conjunction, ballots should measure voter intensity by offering multiple responses, such as a "none of the above" box, which, when chosen would not be applied to satisfy the minimum vote requirement.
>
> Most importantly, direct legislation in land use issues should be limited to propositions that create land use policy. . . .

Robert H. Freilich & Derek B. Guemmer, Removing Artificial Barriers to Public Participation in Land Use Policy: Effective Zoning and Planning by Initiative and Referenda, 21 Urb. Law. 511, 554–55 (1989). See also Richard B. Collins & Dale Oesterle, Structuring the Ballot Initiative: Procedures That Do and Don't Work, 66 U. Colo. L. Rev. 47 (1995).

Chapter Five

Subdivision Regulations, Building Codes, Aesthetic Controls

The prior three chapters focused on zoning and planning. This chapter introduces other important land use regulations. These pose a variety of legal issues, some fresh, some familiar.

The land-development control system in the United States typically demands that a developer obtain multiple approvals. For example, even if successful in obtaining a rezoning from the local governing body, a developer commonly must apply for subdivision-map or site-plan approval from the planning commission (and, perhaps, from the local governing body as well). Whether the proposal will win approval depends not only on its consistency with the zoning ordinance (and, in some states, with the comprehensive plan), but also on separate statutes and ordinances that govern land subdivisions and site plans. In addition, building construction must await a building permit from the local building department, the agency charged with enforcing building codes, the most textually complex of all land use controls. Separate housing codes, health codes, architectural-design review ordinances, and so on, may produce yet more public protection — or red tape — as the case may be.

Some observers have been highly critical of this system of multiple reviews. They assert that the regulatory maze is needlessly complex and duplicative, produces unnecessary delays, and raises development costs. The final part of the chapter explores these allegations and examines proposals for simplification of public land use regulation.

A. Subdivision Regulations

1. Coordination of Street Layouts by Means of Official Maps

Perhaps the most fundamental planning responsibility of city officials is the coordination of street locations in areas soon to be engulfed by urban expansion. In the nineteenth century, private developers and builders forged great American cities without the benefit of zoning and comprehensive planning systems. See John Reps, The Making of Urban America (1965). However, small-scale developers pursuing their self-interest are unlikely

411

to produce an efficient circulation system for a city. Suppose, for example, that a collector street currently were to dead-end at a developer's tract. Absent regulation, the developer might choose not to extend the street, even though landowners beyond would want the artery to pass through the developer's tract to their lands.

Because landowners would not be likely to devise an efficient street system through voluntary coordination, city officials early assumed responsibility for mapping streets for undeveloped areas. The persons hired for this task commonly were engineers, who typically adopted a functional, if unimaginative, checkerboard layout. A notable exception was the L'Enfant plan for Washington, D.C., first published in 1791, which featured diagonal avenues, and squares and circles at avenue intersections. Visitors to Washington still find this layout refreshing, if somewhat confusing. See Figure 5-1. Downtown Boston illustrates the chaos (quaintness) that the absence of a street plan can produce. Boston contrasts interestingly with downtown Philadelphia, which was shaped by William Penn's gridiron street plan of 1683.

Manhattan perhaps best demonstrates the profound influence of an official map. The oldest part of Manhattan — the portion south of Houston Street — remains a crazy quilt. By contrast, an official map of 1811 laid out virtually all of the area north of Houston Street in a famously regular grid of rectangular blocks. On the advent of street mapping in Manhattan, see Hendrik Hartog, Public Property and Private Power: The Corporation of the City of New York in American Law, 1730–1870, at 159–75 (1983).

In re Furman Street
17 Wend. 649 (N.Y. Sup. Ct. 1836)

BRONSON, Justice . . .
The village of Brooklyn was incorporated on the 12th April, 1816 (Laws of N.Y. vol. 4, p.90, a). By the 18th section of the act, . . . it was made the duty of the trustees "to cause a survey of said village to be made, by some capable person or persons, together with a fair map thereof, exhibiting the streets, roads and alleys to be permanently laid out, and accompanied by such remarks as the nature of the subject may require and admit, which map, with the accompanying remarks, shall be signed by the president of the board of trustees, for the time being, and kept by the clerk of the corporation, subject, however, to the inspection of any inhabitant of the village, who may have an interest therein, in order that no resident may plead ignorance of the permanent plan to be adopted for opening, laying out, leveling, and regulating the streets of the said village of Brooklyn." In pursuance of this authority, a survey and map of the village were made under the direction of the trustees in the year 1818, by Jeremiah Lott and William M. Stewart, surveyors. The map after having been approved by the trustees, was signed by the president, and filed with the clerk of the corporation, on the 8th April, 1819. On this map Furman Street was laid down, where it is now proposed to open the same. . . .

It is objected on behalf of the persons interested in the four last appeals, that the commissioners erred in refusing to allow damages for buildings erected on the site of Furman Street since the filing of the map or permanent plan of the village in 1819. I think the commissioners have given a most reasonable and just interpretation to the act of 1816, under which the survey and map were made; and that this is the only construction which will not render the statute utterly nugatory. . . . [T]he legislature evidently looked forward to the period when Brooklyn was to be a great and flourishing town: and they provided for the opening of new avenues, as the public interests might require, without imposing any

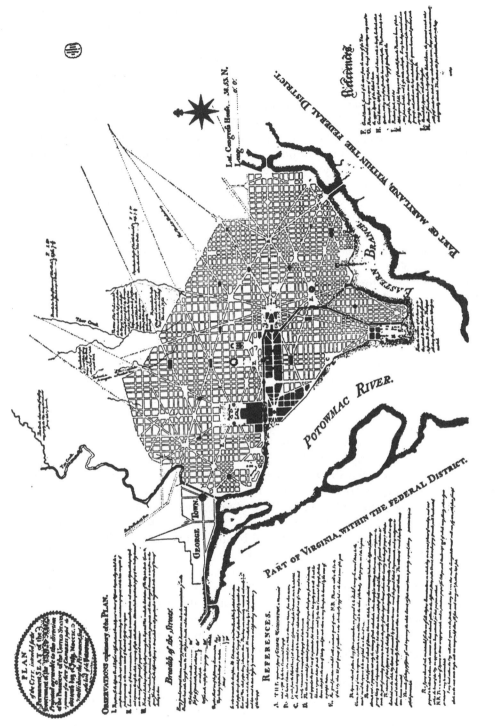

FIGURE 5-1
The L'Enfant Plan

413

unnecessary burden either upon individuals or the town. The owner of land then used for agricultural purposes, was advised on the one hand where to place his buildings, and how to lay out and sell his village lots, so as to derive all the advantages of a new street in prospect; and on the other, he was admonished that if he occupied the designate site of the street with his buildings he was doing a wrong to others for which he should not be compensated in damages when the time arrived for opening the new thoroughfare. . . . Until the time arrived for opening the street, it remained his farm or his garden, with the undoubted right to use it in any way that his interest or his pleasure might suggest, with the single admonition that if he made erections on the site of the street he should not charge the expense to his neighbor. The time for opening the street did not depend upon the will or the caprice of individuals, but was to be decided by the corporation, with a just regard to the public interest; and when the owner was deprived of the use of his property he was to be paid the enhanced value which it had derived from the permanent plan and settlement of the town. In this case, the commissioners have allowed about one dollar on the average for every square foot of land taken for the street, and the owners complain that they have not been allowed more than half enough. Whether commissioners have erred in estimating the value of the land or not, I entertain no doubt that their appraisal exceeds by more than ten times the value of the same property in 1819; and that is much more than the property would have brought at this time if the survey and map had not been made.

If upon the true construction of the act of 1816, the land owners are not to be paid for the buildings which they have erected on the site of the streets, since the map was filed, it was then objected, that the act was unconstitutional. It is perhaps a sufficient answer to this objection, that the provision on which it is based, that private property shall not be taken for public use, without just compensation, was not contained in our constitution at the time the act was passed and the map filed. If the land was in truth appropriated to public purposes in 1819, there was nothing in the constitution to forbid such a course, however injurious it may have been to the owners. But waiving this consideration, the right to take private property for public use, is not conferred by the constitution. It is a right inseparably connected with the sovereign power of the state, in whatever hands that power may reside; and the constitution has only regulated its exercise, by requiring that just compensation be made to the owner. At what time, and in what particular manner, the owner shall receive his recompense, rests in the discretion of the legislature, with no other limitation or restriction than that it shall be just compensation. There is nothing in the constitution, nothing in the natural equity or justice of the case, which forbids that this recompense should be made in property instead of money, or in any other form which secures the owner a fair equivalent for the land of which he has been deprived. It is upon this principle that benefits were set off against damages under the canal laws, and if the land of a farmer of the value of one hundred or one thousand dollars was taken to construct the work, and the canal when completed would enhance the value of his remaining property to an equal or greater amount, no other compensation was made to him. . . .

. . . The loss of the privilege of building on the streets, if it can properly be called an injury, has been greatly overbalanced by the benefits resulting from the permanent and uniform plan which was adopted for the enlargement of the town. . . .

[The court held that the city commissioners may have been mistaken about the elevation proposed for the surface of Furman Street and referred some of the appeals back to them for reconsideration of the compensation that the landowners were entitled to receive.]

Note on Official Maps

1. *As a city grows.* . . . Over a century later, the doubled-decked Brooklyn-Queens Expressway was erected along and over a portion of Furman Street. See In re Brooklyn-Queens Connecting Highway (Furman Street), 89 N.Y.S.2d 428 (Sup. Ct. 1947).

2. *Compensation for a structure built on a site after it had been mapped for public use.* *Furman Street* holds that a landowner who erects a building within the path of a previously mapped street may have no constitutional right to receive compensation for the structure once the street opens. If compensation were to be routinely paid in these situations, a landowner would have no incentive to mitigate damages and would tend to overinvest capital on sites designated for future public acquisition. On the other hand, if a municipality could freely prevent improvements in a proposed public space, a budget-conscious agency might map far more land than it would if it had to consider landowners' costs. On these conflicting considerations, see William A. Fischel & Perry Shapiro, Takings, Insurance, and Michelman, 17 J. Legal Stud. 269 (1988). See also the discussion of moral hazard on pp. 152–53.

3. *Compensation for loss of land in a mapped right-of-way.* The Supreme Court of Florida has vacillated on the issue of when the official mapping of a site for public use constitutes an unconstitutional taking of the land itself. In Joint Ventures, Inc. v. Department of Transportation, 563 So. 2d 622 (Fla. 1990), the state had mapped almost 80 percent of the plaintiff landowner's vacant 8.3 acres for a highway-widening project. By a four-to-three margin, the Supreme Court of Florida sustained the plaintiff's takings claims. Four years later, in Tampa-Hillsborough County Expressway Authority v. A.G.W.S. Corp., 640 So. 2d 54 (Fla. 1994), the court unanimously reversed field. It held that the *Joint Ventures* decision should not be construed to hold that any governmental mapping of a contemplated right-of-way is a per se taking. In the future, it ruled, a Florida landowner who had suffered a mapping could pursue an inverse condemnation action for compensation, but to prevail, that landowner would have to show that the mapping "denie[d] substantially all economically beneficial or productive use of land." Should a mapping be regarded as a regulatory action or as a physical occupation of land (to which Loretto v. Teleprompter Manhattan CATV Corp., 458 U.S. 419 (1982), cited at p. 167, applies)?

When a government insists that a developer *dedicate* mapped lands as a condition of receiving a permit, it has to prove a "rough proportionality" between the amount of land it is demanding and the burdens on the public that development of the land would create. See Dolan v. City of Tigard, 512 U.S. 374 (1994), excerpted at p. 643. Should courts apply a takings test of a similar sort when a landowner is protesting a mapping?

4. *Ripeness.* Courts regard an official map, like a comprehensive plan, to be tentative and subject to amendment prior to actual development. They therefore may hold that a developer's challenge to a map is premature. See, e.g., Selby Realty Co. v. City of San Buenaventura, 514 P.2d 111 (Cal. 1973); Arnold v. Prince George's County, 311 A.2d 223 (Md. 1973). Ripeness is not a barrier, however, to a developer who has been aggrieved by a local decision based on an official map. For example, in City of Houston v. Kolb, 982 S.W.2d 949 (Tex. App. 1999), a property owner was denied subdivision approval for land in the pathway of a planned expressway. The court regarded the claim to be ripe because further appeals would have been futile, and upheld an inverse condemnation award against the city.

5. *A developer's rights to vary the placement of streets from mapped locations.* In Nigro v. Planning Board, 584 A.2d 1350 (N.J. 1991), the board had disapproved Nigro's application for preliminary approval of a major subdivision because Nigro was proposing to build an

access road at a location where the borough's official map did not show a road. A New Jersey statute provided that an "official map shall be deemed conclusive with respect to the location . . . of streets." The Supreme Court of New Jersey nevertheless held that the planning board should not have been so rigid:

> . . . With respect to the designation of major streets, drainage facilities, flood control basins, and public areas, a municipality may properly insist on substantial adherence to the planning choices reflected on its official map, allowing deviations in subdivision or site plan proposals only when reasonably justified by the particular conditions and circumstances. But with respect to its designation of minor roadways, such as the proposed street . . . , a municipality should not insist on rigid compliance with its official map. To adopt Saddle River's position would be to elevate the official map to the status of uncompromising forecaster of future development within a municipality. Such a strict view does not comport with the underlying goal of municipal planning: to promote the general welfare. Planning must ultimately be a flexible process, and the fact that the location of a proposed street on an official map differs from that of a street proposed by a developer does not by itself allow or require a planning board to withhold approval of a development proposal. The Board's position unnecessarily restricts the planning process.

2.   *Subdivision Regulation: Rationales and Standards*

Just as the Standard State Zoning Enabling Act (SZEA) spurred the practice of zoning, the enactment of state enabling legislation spawned municipal subdivision regulation. The earliest subdivision map acts, which aimed only to improve boundary descriptions in land documents, typically required a developer to record a map only as a precondition to selling lots in a tract. California's first statute of this kind was enacted in 1893. See Gardner v. County of Sonoma, 62 P.3d 103 (Cal. 2003); Marc A. Weiss, The Rise of the Community Builders 107–40 (1987) (on evolution of subdivision regulation in California). Nevertheless, some cities were regulating the layouts of internal streets in new subdivisions as early as 1870. See Andrew J. Cappel, Note, A Walk Along Willow, 101 Yale L.J. 617, 627 (1991) (describing practices in New Haven). Municipal review of subdivision layouts blossomed after 1928, the year the federal government published the Standard City Plan Enabling Act. See David Listokin & Carole Walker, The Subdivision and Site Plan Handbook 142–50 (1989).

The review of proposed subdivision maps is one of a municipality's most important powers. This process helps enable the municipality (1) to enforce lot-dimension requirements appearing in its zoning ordinance, (2) to obtain lands designated for public uses on its official map or comprehensive plan, (3) to apply standards for subdivision improvements, and (4) to exact contributions and design modifications from the subdivider. See generally Robert H. Freilich & Michael M. Shultz, Model Subdivision Regulations (2d ed. 1995).

According to Marygold S. Melli, Subdivision Control in Wisconsin, 1953 Wis. L. Rev. 389, 391–97, the regulation of subdivisions confers benefits on a number of different groups. First, *prospective lot owners* in a subdivision benefit from the recording of a final subdivision map that accurately describes each lot within it. This helps forestall subsequent boundary disputes. It also enables an owner to describe land in a legal document simply by referring to a lot number on a recorded subdivision map, rather than using metes and bounds or some other cumbersome description system. Lot buyers are also said to benefit from the imposition and enforcement of subdivision design standards. The buyers are assured, for example, that roads will be wide enough to accommodate firefighting equipment, that sewer capacities will be adequate, that improvements will actually be installed as planned, and so on. Are lot purchasers too ill-informed or lacking in bargaining power to look out for themselves? For a critical look at conditions in unregulated Texas border subdivisions known as *colonias*, see Jane E. Larson, Free Markets Deep in the Heart of Texas, 84 Geo. L.J. 179 (1995) (noting that, while housing in *colonias* is cheap, sanitary conditions are poor). If developers were to be made liable for design and construction defects in subdivisions, would the consumer-protection rationale for subdivision regulation lose force? See p. 444.

Second, subdivision regulation may benefit the *immediate neighbors* of a new subdivision. Local officials can help ensure, for example, that local streets connect together at subdivision boundaries, that street names are not confusing, and that surface water escaping from a new development will be properly channeled.

Third, the *community-at-large* benefits from the coordination of major transportation arteries and other public infrastructure. Municipal taxpayers also have an interest in minimizing the costs of servicing new subdivisions. For example, a police car can patrol a loop street more efficiently than it can a cul-de-sac because less doubling back is required. If streets are well paved, street repair costs are lower. Most significantly, taxpayers can gain when their municipality conditions approval of a subdivision on the subdivider's making cash contributions to the municipal treasury or paying to install improvements (e.g., street trees, playgrounds) that, in existing neighborhoods, are financed out of general municipal revenues.

Professor Melli identifies a fourth class of beneficiaries:

> Subdivision control by the community also benefits the subdividers themselves. Excessive subdivision and the platting of areas which are too far from community services or which are not good for development frequently spell financial ruin for the subdivider. In discouraging this type of subdivision, the community is therefore protecting his interests as well as those of the public and of potential buyers.

1953 Wis. L. Rev. at 397. Is this persuasive?

New Jersey Stat. Ann. §40:55(D)-38
(West Supp. 2004)

40:55D-38. CONTENTS OF ORDINANCE

An ordinance requiring approval by the planning board of either subdivisions or site plans, or both, shall include the following:

a. Provisions, not inconsistent with other provisions of this act, for submission and processing of applications for development, including standards for preliminary and final approval and provisions for processing of final approval by stages or sections of development;

b. Provisions ensuring:

(1)   Consistency of the layout or arrangement of the subdivision or land development with the requirements of the zoning ordinance;

(2)   Streets in the subdivision or land development of sufficient width and suitable grade and suitably located to accommodate prospective traffic and to provide access for firefighting and emergency equipment to buildings and coordinated so as to compose a convenient system consistent with the official map, if any, and the circulation element of the master plan, if any, and so oriented as to permit, consistent with the reasonable utilization of land, the buildings constructed thereon to maximize solar gain; provided

that no street of a width greater than 50 feet within the right-of-way lines shall be required unless said street constitutes an extension of an existing street of the greater width or already has been shown on the master plan at the greater width, or already has been shown in greater width on the official map;

(3)   Adequate water supply, drainage, shade trees, sewerage facilities and other utilities necessary for essential services to residents and occupants;

(4)   Suitable size, shape and location for any area reserved for public use . . . ; . . .

(13) Protection of potable water supply reservoirs from pollution or other degradation of water quality resulting from the development or other uses of surrounding land areas, which provisions shall be in accordance with any siting, performance or other standards or guidelines adopted therefor by the Department of Environmental Protection. . . .

c. Provisions governing the standards for grading, improvement and construction of streets or drives and for any required walkways, curbs, gutters, streetlights, shade trees, fire hydrants and water, and drainage and sewerage facilities and other improvements as shall be found necessary and provisions ensuring that such facilities shall be completed either prior to or subsequent to final approval of the subdivision or site plan by allowing the posting of performance bonds by the developer;

d. Provisions ensuring that when a municipal zoning ordinance is in effect, a subdivision or site plan shall conform to the applicable provisions of the zoning ordinance, and where there is no zoning ordinance, appropriate standards shall be specified in an ordinance pursuant to this article; and

e. Provisions ensuring performance in substantial accordance with the final development plan; provided that the planning board may permit a deviation from the final plan if caused by change of conditions beyond the control of the developer since the date of final approval, and the deviation would not substantially alter the character of the development or substantially impair the intent and purpose of the master plan and zoning ordinance.

Review the following design requirements, quoted and paraphrased from ordinances and regulations of the City of Los Angeles. See, e.g., L.A. Mun. Code §17.05 (2004). Whom are these requirements intended to benefit? Who might object to them?

(1)   *Block lengths.* "Blocks shall not exceed 1,700 feet in length, except in hilly areas."
(2)   *Street slopes.* Unless a city agency has provided a variance, each local street shall have a minimum grade of four-tenths of one percent and a maximum grade of 15 percent.
(3)   *Street intersections.* Street intersections shall be as near to right-angle as is possible. Jogs of streets at intersections shall be minimized.
(4)   *Utilities.* Utility lines, including electricity, street lighting, and cable television lines necessary for the lots in the subdivisions shall be included.
(5)   *Storm drains.* "In areas without sumps, storm drains shall be designed to remove all runoff from a storm of ten-year frequency."

Miles v. Planning Board of Millbury

536 N.E.2d 328 (Mass. 1989)

ABRAMS, Justice.

The planning board of Millbury (board) approved the plaintiffs' plan of subdivision subject to three conditions. First, a concrete sidewalk had to be constructed on one side of the street. Second, a sloped granite curbing had to be installed on both sides of the street. Third, all utility lines had to be buried underground. The plaintiffs appealed to the Superior Court, alleging that the board exceeded its statutory authority under a proviso added to G.L. c. 41, §81Q, by St. 1981, c. 459, in imposing the three conditions. After hearing, the judge concluded that the board did not exceed its authority. . . . We affirm the judgment of the Superior Court.

The plaintiffs are real estate developers engaged in the construction of homes in Millbury. The plaintiffs submitted a plan to subdivide and develop six acres of land into seven residential lots ending in a cul-de-sac. The three conditions accord with the board's rules and regulations adopted pursuant to G.L. c. 41, §81Q.[4] . . .

The burden of proof is on the plaintiffs to prove that the planning board exceeded its authority in imposing the three conditions. Strand v. Planning Bd. of Sudbury, 390 N.E. 2d 1411 (Mass. 1979). To meet their burden, the plaintiffs point to the following four examples of "construction and/or maintenance" which occurred after 1982 to prove that the board exceeded its own building standards in imposing the three conditions. (1) The town reconstructed Holman Road, a dirt road; now, a paved street runs to a carpentry school at the street's end. There are no curbs or sidewalks on Holman Road, and the electric wires are not buried underground. (2) The town reconstructed Farnsworth Court, a street located in a commercially zoned district. Farnsworth Court does not have granite curbing or sidewalks. (3) The Commonwealth reconstructed Gagliardi Way, now a town road, as part of the reconstruction of Route 146. Gagliardi Way also does not have granite curbing or sidewalks. (4) The Commonwealth contracted to reconstruct Grafton Street with joint State, county, and local funding, pursuant to G.L. c. 90. Grafton Street was rebuilt to Commonwealth specifications. This street does not have granite curbs or concrete sidewalks, and the electric utility lines are not buried underground. . . .

General Laws c. 41, §81Q, as amended through St. 1981, c. 459, provides that the planning boards of cities and towns should adopt "reasonable rules and regulations relative to subdivision control." "In establishing such requirements regarding ways, due regard shall be paid to the prospective character of different subdivisions, whether open residence, dense residence, business or industrial, and the prospective amount of travel upon the various ways therein, and to adjustment of the requirements accordingly; *provided, however,* that in no case shall a city or town establish rules or regulations regarding the laying out, construction, alteration, or maintenance of ways within a particular subdivision which exceed the standards and criteria commonly applied by that city or town to the laying out, construction, alteration, or maintenance of its publicly financed ways located in similarly zoned districts within such city or town" (emphasis supplied). [The legislature had enacted the proviso in 1981 in response to the report of a state commission whose "findings emphasized what it viewed as the unfortunate role played by local government in increasing the cost of new housing by setting standards beyond those necessary for the health and safety of residents."]

The plaintiffs argue that the four examples of post-1982 reconstruction of town roads, as well as the building standards of the town in the early 1970's, did not fulfill the three contested conditions. Thus, the conditions imposed exceeded those commonly applied by Millbury. . . . We agree with the board.

---

4. The conditions represent a partial waiver by the board of its strict rules and regulations concerning a new residential subdivision. The Board's rules actually require the installation of sidewalks on both sides of the street and the installation of upright curbing, as opposed to the less expensive sloped curbing. A board may waive strict compliance with its rules and regulations, although it is not required to do so. See, e.g., Mac-Rich Realty Constr., Inc. v. Planning Bd. of Southborough, 4 Mass. App. Ct. 79, 85 (1976).

As an initial matter, the proviso requires adherence to standards "commonly applied" by the town. . . . The standards "commonly applied" by the town today may not be the standards which were applicable in the early 1970's. Thus, there was no error in the judge's determination that examples of early 1970's construction were not relevant. The judge correctly determined that G.L. c. 41, §81Q, does not require "a town to be forever fixed regarding its standards, only that once such standards are adopted, they be fairly applied. . . . [Otherwise], a municipality could never upgrade its subdivisions." The judge also concluded that the plaintiffs failed to prove "that the board has not commonly applied these conditions to similar projects funded by the town . . . since . . . 1982."

The statute is clear that the town need look only to its standards in "similarly zoned districts." Thus, there was no error in not considering the standards of Farnsworth Court, which was commercially zoned. Further, the statute applies only to town standards in connection with "its publicly financed ways." This clause ensures that the town will be bound only by projects which are financed by the town in such a manner that the projects are built to town specifications. Examples of construction done with Commonwealth funding and built to Commonwealth specifications, therefore, were not relevant. Thus, two of the plaintiffs' four examples (Gagliardi Way and Grafton Street) were not applicable. . . .

. . . [Finally] boards may be guided by different policy considerations in imposing different standards on the laying out of new streets as opposed to the reconstruction of already existing streets.[7] . . . Thus, the plaintiffs cannot rely on the example of Holman Road, because that road was reconstructed rather than newly constructed. . . .

Judgment of the Superior Court affirmed.

Note on Subdivision Standards

1. *Street widths.* Traffic engineers recognize, in descending order, a hierarchy of streets: arterial, collector, subcollector (local), and access (cul-de-sac or loop). One authoritative source suggests that local streets require a pavement width of only 26 feet (or 28 feet if there is to be curbside parking on both sides). American Society of Civil Engineering et al., Residential Streets 38 (2d ed. 1990). Nevertheless, municipalities in developing areas commonly insist that developers install local streets with pavements 31 feet to 39 feet wide. Robert Burchell & David Listokin, Design Standards in Developing Areas, *in* America's Housing: Prospects and Problems 359, 364 (George Sternlieb & James Hughes eds., 1980). The City of Los Angeles used to require, except in hilly areas, that local cul-de-sac and loop streets have a right-of-way at least 54 feet in width and a pavement at least 36 feet in width. Was the city wise to repeal that requirement? Why might the fire department have objected? For additional criticism of municipal insistence on wide road pavements in residential areas, see The Report of the President's Commission on Housing 206 (1982); pp. 422–24 (on the New Urbanism).

A street right-of-way accommodates not only the street pavement but also sidewalks and parkways. (See Figure 5-3 on p. 423.) Burchell and Listokin found the conventional minimum width for a local right-of-way in a developing area is 50 feet. In Bevan v. Brandon

---

7. The range of improvements which could be provided to a street during reconstruction might be limited by space constraints due to preexisting structures and by other such considerations which are not present when a new road is laid. A town that wishes to upgrade its new streets is not required to meet those standards just to reconstruct other streets. For example, according to the plaintiffs' argument, if a town wished to require all public or private building of new streets to have electric utility wires buried underground, the town would have to bury electric wires of old streets underground each time it reconstructs a preexisting street. The proviso in G.L. c. 41, §81Q, does not require such a result.

Township, 475 N.W.2d 37 (Mich. 1991), two lot owners who had access by way of a 20-foot wide easement challenged the township's requirement that they widen the easement to 66 feet before constructing dwellings on both lots. The lower courts enjoined the township's enforcement of this condition on the ground that it constituted a taking of property, only to be reversed by the Supreme Court of Michigan.

2. *Criticism of other subdivision standards.* Engineers and planners have asserted that other design standards also tend to be unduly costly. See Jack Newville (an engineer), New Engineering Concepts in Community Development, Urb. Land Inst. Tech. Bull. No. 59 (1967); John Rahenkamp (a planner), The Environmental Scene, House & Home, May 1973. Newville observes that during the 1930s, storm drains were designed only to handle the most severe storm expected to occur in a two- to five-year period; he questions whether the trend toward requiring a drain to handle a storm of ten-year frequency can be justified by cost/benefit analysis. Rahenkamp argues that street curbs often can be eliminated, with the water runoff from streets accommodated by swaling. (Swales are shallow, unpaved channels.) The critics assert that their proposals would not only reduce development and maintenance costs, but also cause new subdivisions to do less violence to the natural environment.

3. *Controlling municipal abuses.* If state limits on local subdivision standards are appropriate, should they be statutory, constitutional, or both? Did the *Miles* opinion give adequate weight to the Massachusetts legislature's intent in adding the proviso? Compare New Jersey State League of Municipalities v. Department of Community Affairs, 708 A.2d 708 (N.J. Super. Ct. App. Div. 1998) (rebuffing municipalities' attack on state's efforts to curtail municipal imposition of excessive subdivision standards); Town of Coventry Zoning Board of Review v. Omni Development Corp., 814 A.2d 889 (R.I. 2003) (on state's efforts to prevent stringent subdivision standards from interfering with construction of housing projects for low- and moderate-income households).

4. *The politics of subdivision standards.* Recall Melli's mention of the stakes that prospective lot-owners, immediate neighbors, and members of the community-at-large have in the design of subdivisions. See pp. 416–17. Is it plausible that a primary beneficiary of subdivision regulation actually is the public-works lobby — the contractors, suppliers, and workers who engage in heavy construction?

Note on Street Layouts

1. *Professional jealousy.* Subdivision mapping is largely the domain of civil engineers. Planners, of course, may prepare initial sketches that influence subdivision layouts. But collaboration between the two professions is less common than one might suppose. Engineers often stereotype planners as starry-eyed dreamers who lack both technical skills and an adequate awareness of development costs. Planners often stereotype engineers as persons lacking both creativity and ecological sensitivity. Engineers claim to have the last laugh because they, not planners, have had (and in most places still have) the greatest influence over the shape of American cities and towns.

2. A *design exercise.* The key decisions in subdivision design involve the location of streets and lotlines. Even when a small parcel is being subdivided, the design alternatives are numerous. Consider, for example, Figure 5-2, which depicts four designs for a 10-acre tract surrounded on three sides by existing streets. (D.U. denotes dwelling units; L.F. St. means linear feet of internal and external streets.) Which of these designs promises to maximize the aggregate market value of the lots produced? Which design would maximize the developer's profits? (Why is this question different from the previous one?) Which

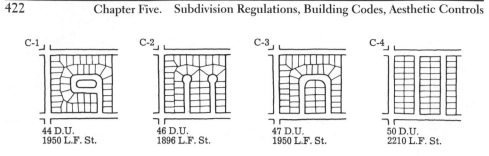

C-1   C-2   C-3   C-4

44 D.U.   46 D.U.   47 D.U.   50 D.U.
1950 L.F. St.   1896 L.F. St.   1950 L.F. St.   2210 L.F. St.

Source: Innovations vs. Traditions in Community Development, Urb. Land Inst. Tech. Bull. No. 47, at 24 (1963).

FIGURE 5-2
Alternative Designs of a 10-Acre Subdivision

design is "best for the community"? Are cul-de-sacs desirable? A statistical study in Halifax, Nova Scotia, indicated that a house on a cul-de-sac sold for a 29 percent premium over a house on a street set in a rectilinear grid. Paul K. Asabere, The Value of a Neighborhood Street with Reference to the Cul-de-Sac, 3 J. Real Est. Fin. & Econ. 185 (1990). See also D. Gordon Bagby, The Effects of Traffic Flow on Residential Property Values, 46 J. Am. Plan. Ass'n 88 (1980). But consider this complication: Although a small cul-de-sac may contribute to social bonding among those neighbors who live on it, it also may impair social bridging between those residents and residents of other streets. If these street-layout issues are challenging when only a 10-acre tract is involved, imagine the difficulty of designing a much larger subdivision!

3. *The rectilinear grid.* A gridiron pattern simplifies surveying and lot descriptions, results in lots suited for rectilinear structures, and is highly legible to pedestrians and drivers. On the evolution and subtle merits of the grid, see Kenneth T. Jackson, Crabgrass Frontier 74–75 (1985); William H. Whyte, City 316–19 (1988). But compare Lewis Mumford (as quoted in Jackson at 74): "The rectangular parceling of ground promoted speculation in land-units and the ready exchange of real property; it had no relation whatever to the essential purposes for which a city exists." Mumford's view was ascendant during most of the latter half of the twentieth century, when subdivision regulators usually favored curvilinear streets, loops, and cul-de-sacs.

4. *New Urbanist subdivisions.* In the early 1980s, the husband-wife team of Andres Duany and Elizabeth Plater-Zyberk spearheaded the "New Urbanism," a movement that has restored the traditional street grid to respectability. On New Urbanism, see generally Peter Calthorpe, The Next American Metropolis (1993); Andres Duany et al., Suburban Nation: The Rise of Sprawl and the Decline of the American Dream (2000); and pp. 608 and 793–95. Instead of curved streets, loops, and cul-de-sacs, neotraditionalists generally favor a return to rectilinear street patterns. They also advocate narrow street pavements, alleys, and curbside parking spaces interrupted at intervals by street trees in concrete wells that protrude into the street. (See Figure 5-3.) (Other New Urbanist ideals, such as mixed use neighborhoods and shallow building setbacks, challenge conventional zoning practices.)

The pioneering New Urbanist subdivisions — Seaside, Florida; Kentlands, Maryland; and Laguna West, California — were successful enough to inspire many imitations, notably the heavily scrutinized Celebration at Disney World. See Douglas Frantz & Catherine Collins, Celebration, U.S.A.: Living in Disney's Brave New Town (1999), and Andrew Ross, The Celebration Chronicles: Life, Liberty, and the Pursuit of Property Value in Disney's

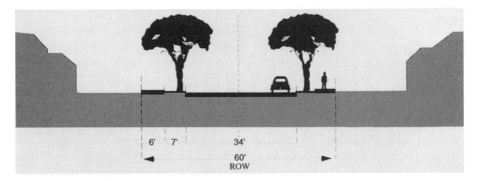

A. Cross-Section of a typical Institute of Transportation Engineers Street

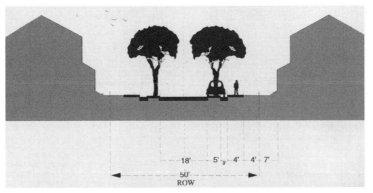

B. Cross-Section of street at Laguna West, California, 1991

Source: Michael Southworth & Eran Ben-Joseph, Street Standards and the Shaping of Suburbia, 61 J. Am. Plan. Ass'n 65, 79–80 (1995).

FIGURE 5-3
Cross-Sections of Conventional and New-Urbanist Streets

New Town (1999) (two largely critical books authored by former residents); Andres Duany, In Celebration, Urb. Land, Jan. 2002, at 57 (offering a mixed assessment).

New Urbanists contend that traditional neighborhood designs not only cater to market preferences, but also increase residents' sense of community. Scholarly assessments of the effectiveness of New Urbanist layouts, however, have been mixed. Yan Song & Gerrit-Jan Knaap, New Urbanism and Housing Values, 54 J. Urb. Econ. 218 (2003), is a study of house values in a suburban county west of Portland, Oregon. The authors found, in brief:

> . . . [R]esidents are willing to pay premiums for houses in neighborhoods with more connec-
> tive street networks; more streets; shorter dead-end streets; more and smaller blocks; better
> pedestrian accessibility to commercial uses; more evenly distributed mixed land uses in the
> neighborhood; and proximity to operating light rail stations. We also find residents are willing
> to pay less for houses in neighborhoods that are dense, contain more commercial, mul-
> tifamily, and public uses (relative to single-family uses), and contain major transportation
> arterials.

Id. at 236. See also Barbara B. Brown & Vivian L. Cropper, New Urban and Standard Suburban Subdivisions, 67 J. Am. Plan. Ass'n 402 (2001), a comparative study of subdivisions in Salt Lake City. Brown and Cropper report that residents of both neotraditional and standard suburban developments report similar levels of "sense of community." Even less encouraging results are reported in Hazel A. Morrow-Jones et al., Consumer Preference for Neotraditional Neighborhood Characteristics, 15 Hous. Pol'y Debate 171 (2004), a survey of Columbus, Ohio, area homeowners. Most survey respondents preferred lower-density cul-de-sac neighborhoods to higher-density rectilinear New Urbanist designs.

A municipality typically must amend its subdivision standards to enable development of a New Urbanist subdivision. See, e.g., Wis. Stat. §66.1027 (Supp. 2004) (enabling municipalities to adopt ordinances friendly to neotraditional layouts); Austin, Tex., City Code §25-3-51 (2003) (providing special subdivision rules for "Traditional Neighborhood Developments" (TNDs)). See Jeremy R. Meredith, Note, Sprawl and the New Urbanist Solution, 89 Va. L. Rev. 447 (2003) (discussing TND ordinances). Do the scattered successes of the New Urbanist movement indicate that conventional subdivision standards are unsound? That a municipality is apt to be flexible when an innovator asks? That municipalities should leave street designs "to the market"?

5. *Bibliography*. Michael Southworth & Eran Ben-Joseph, Streets and the Shaping of Towns and Cities (2d ed. 2003) (a superb historical review); Institute of Transp. Engineers, Recommended Guidelines for Subdivision Streets (1984); Michael C. Poulton, The Best Pattern of Residential Streets, 48 J. Am. Plan. Ass'n 466 (1982).

3.   *The Chronology of a Subdivision*

The process of subdivision review typically involves three phases. First, the developer submits a *sketch plan* of the proposed subdivision, usually prepared by a civil engineer, to municipal officials. The officials may suggest changes at this stage, enabling the subdivider to make revisions without expending large sums of money. Next, the developer presents a more detailed *preliminary* (or *tentative*) *subdivision map*. This shows the exact dimensions of roads and lots, and reveals the planned drainage system. The municipal planning board and governing body both are likely to hold a public hearing when considering a preliminary map, partly because the right to subdivide typically vests on its approval. See pp. 430–35. Finally, after the preliminary map has been approved, the developer's engineer drafts a highly detailed *final subdivision map* consistent with the preliminary design.

The Saga of a Los Angeles Subdivision

To illustrate the dynamics of the subdivision approval process, this note presents a series of maps drafted for a subdivision proposed for an unincorporated area several miles north of the city of Los Angeles.[1] Land use controls in this area are exercised by the County of Los Angeles.

The original sketch plan. The first tentative map for Tract No. 35363 (Figure 5-4) is a reworking of the sketch plat that the consulting engineers first submitted to county staff

---

[1]   The maps in Figures 5-4, 5-5, and 5-6 were made available through the courtesy of Jack Newville and A.E. Béran of the Engineering Service Corporation, Marina Del Rey, California. The discussion in the text mostly refers to the law in force in 1978, when the tentative maps were prepared.

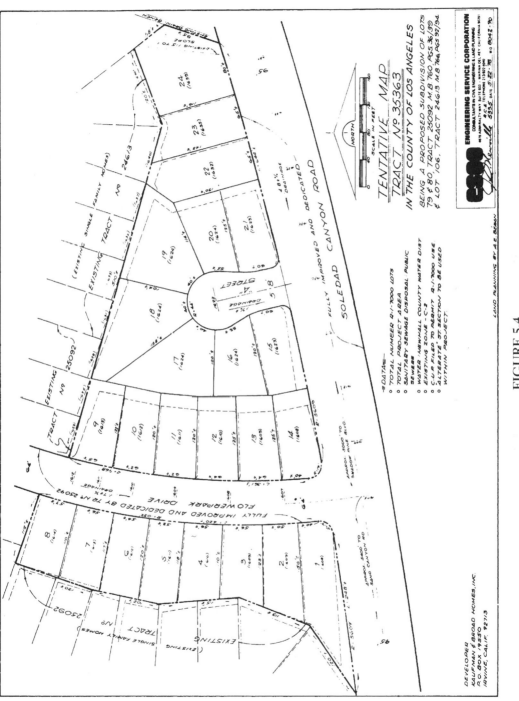

FIGURE 5-4

The Tentative Map That Was Rejected

for comment. Although sketch plats tend to be less polished than Figure 5-4, they typically incorporate much of the same information, especially about neighboring uses.

Observe that each lot in the proposed subdivision is numbered sequentially from 1 through 24. The approximate frontages and lengths of each lot are indicated by the ± dimensions along the lotlines. The number in parentheses immediately below the lot number is the elevation of the graded lot-pad. The dashed lines inside the solid lotlines in Figures 5-4 and 5-5 indicate a grade change. By comparing the elevations of adjacent lots, one may determine which way the grade runs. The presence of a grade change does not necessarily mean that a higher lot will discharge surface water onto a lower lot. Los Angeles County requires each lot to drain into the street on which it fronts. Thus, lot 17 in Figure 5-4 would drain into "A" Street, not into lots 9–12.

In this instance, Flowerpark Drive and Soledad Canyon Road were existing streets that had been improved and dedicated by previous subdividers. The tract was zoned C-2, which allowed development of a commercial use such as a small shopping center. However, because the county had amended its general plan to reduce the permitted residential density in the surrounding area, a shopping center was not economically feasible. The conditional use permit imposed a minimum lot-area requirement of 7,000 square feet; under a county ordinance provision applicable to this subdivision, a lot's area is computed as if it extended 6 feet into the street on which it fronts.

The revised tentative map. When the Figure 5-4 plan was submitted, the county planning staff suggested several changes. The Antelope Valley Freeway parallels Soledad Canyon Road immediately south of the subdivision. The county staff believed that the proposed layout was unnecessarily vulnerable to noise and air pollution from the freeway, and was not as aesthetically pleasing as it might have been. Furthermore, the plan in Figure 5-4 required that Soledad Canyon Road, a major highway, intersect not only the cul-de-sac, but also the driveways on lots 22–24.

The county staff therefore suggested the repositioning of the mouth of the cul-de-sac to Flowerpark Drive, and the elimination of all direct access between the subdivision and Soledad Canyon Road. The consulting engineers then drafted the revised tentative map (Figure 5-5), which altered the orientation and configuration of all but the eight lots located on the west side of Flowerpark Drive. By increasing the grade and length of the cul-de-sac, the Figure 5-5 plan raised the velocity of surface water runoff, required more paving, and reduced the size of abutting lots.

The county planning commission referred the tentative map in Figure 5-5 to 12 county departments and divisions for comment. After receiving their replies and suggestions for conditions to impose, the commission approved the Figure 5-5 map in November 1978, three months after it had been submitted. As required by Cal. Gov't Code §66473.5 (West Supp. 2004), the commission expressly found the proposed subdivision to be consistent with the county's general plan. In California, an environmental impact report must accompany a tentative map for any subdivision that will have a significant effect on the environment. Cal. Pub. Res. Code §21080(a) (West Supp. 2004). The commission found that the subdivision would not have any significant environmental effects, and therefore adopted a Negative Declaration stating that no EIR was needed for this subdivision. The commission also imposed numerous conditions for approval of the tentative map. These conditions required the developer, among other things, to (1) install all internal streets, curbs, sidewalks, street lights, street trees, water lines, sewer lines, and drainage facilities; (2) erect a masonry wall to separate the subdivision from Soledad Canyon Road; (3) pave the driveways providing access to lots 16–18; and (4) either pay a $4,108 park site fee or dedicate 0.28 acres of land suitable for a park site.

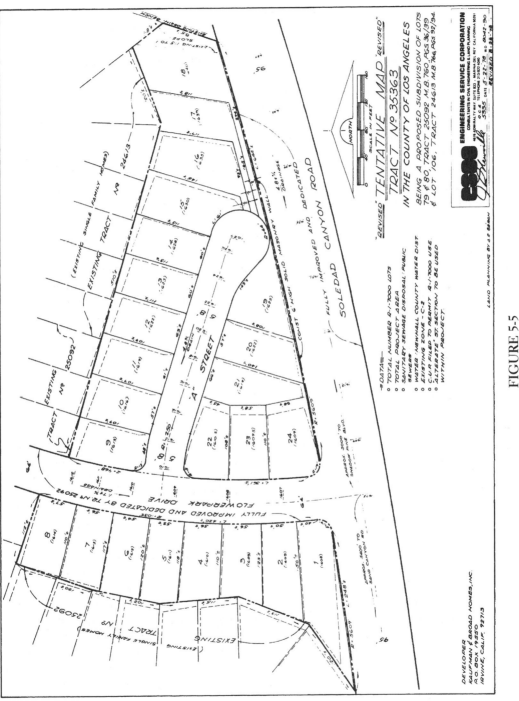

FIGURE 5-5
Tentative Map

427

The commission's rather prompt action in reviewing the proposed map was necessitated by statutory provisions of a type found in more than half of the states. These provisions deem a map to be approved as a matter of law if the local agency does not approve or disapprove it within a specified time period of rather short duration. See Cal. Gov't Code §66452.2–.4 (West Supp. 2004), and sources cited at p. 507. Subdivision statutes and ordinances typically entitle subdividers and their neighbors to appeal tentative-map decisions, including the conditions imposed, to the local governing body. Thereafter, a grievant may pursue judicial review.

Once the Los Angeles County Planning Commission had approved the tentative map pictured in Figure 5-5, the consulting engineer took an accurate survey and drafted detailed working drawings for the subdivision (showing grading plans, fire hydrant locations, and so on). Construction of subdivision improvements could have begun at this point.

The final map. The next processing steps were preparation and approval of the final map. Figure 5-6 shows a portion of the final map for the Los Angeles tract. The form and contents of final maps are specified by statute. Note that the consulting engineer used the survey to locate precisely lot and easement boundaries. As a general rule, a local government must approve a final map if (1) it conforms to the layout in the approved tentative map and (2) the developer has complied or will comply with the conditions for approval.

Cal. Gov't Code §66463.5(a) (West Supp. 2004) requires that a final map be submitted within 24 months of the approval of a tentative map (except when the local government has granted an extension). However, the final layer of asphalt on a street is best laid after a street has had some travel; this particular improvement, as well as many others, is not likely to be complete when the final map is submitted. If so, the local government will typically arrange for bonds or other assurances that improvements will be completed. See Richard Kelley & Michael M. Shultz, " . . . Or Other Adequate Security": Using, Structuring, and Managing the Standby Letter of Credit to Ensure the Completion of Subdivision Improvements, 19 Urb. Law. 39 (1987).

In the final map in Figure 5-6, "A" Street was renamed Poppyseed Lane. Los Angeles County has established a Street Naming Committee, with jurisdiction over the county's unincorporated areas, consisting of representatives from the planning commission, county road and fire departments, county and city engineer's offices, and the U.S. Postal Service. The committee prefers to let a subdivider name the streets, but does review proposed names to avoid duplications, homonyms in nearby neighborhoods, and vulgarities. In this case, Poppyseed Lane was the name of another cul-de-sac just west of Flowerpark Drive, and L.A. County Ord. No. 4478, §148, discourages the changing of street names when streets are in line with one another.

After being certified by the engineer or surveyor who drafted it, a final map is then reviewed by the local government's engineer, and ultimately goes to the local governing body for final approval. This elected body is involved in part because the final map contains an offer by the subdivider to dedicate roadways and perhaps other lands to the local government. The local governing body should formally accept or reject these offers when it approves the final map. See Cal. Gov't Code §66477.1 (West Supp. 2004). If the parties are careless, title to such lands will ultimately have to be determined according to rules of implied dedication and implied acceptance. See, e.g., LaSalle National Bank v. City of Chicago, 312 N.E.2d 322 (Ill. 1974) (holding that city had implicitly accepted mapped but unimproved streets dedicated by plat recorded 50 years earlier); Ponderosa Home Site Lot Owners v. Garfield Bay Resort, Inc., 85 P.3d 675 (Idaho 2004) (holding that subdivider had not intended to dedicate to the public a parcel of lakefront property designated on recorded map as "lake access," but remanding for determination of whether owners of subdivision

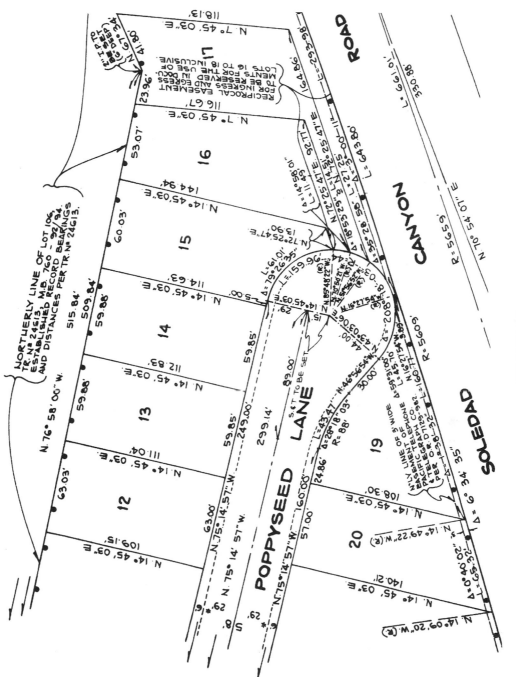

FIGURE 5-6
A Portion of the Final Map

429

lots had private rights in this parcel). After the final plat is approved by the local governing body, it is recorded. Only then can the subdivider begin both to sell lots and to apply for building permits for structures to be placed on the lots.

A California subdivider has another regulatory hurdle to jump. The California Subdivided Lands Act (Cal. Bus. & Prof. Code §§11000–11200 (West Supp. 2004)) requires the state real estate commissioner to prepare a "public report" on each significant subdivision. A subdivider must submit the pertinent information to the commissioner, cannot begin sales until the report is ready, and must provide a copy of the report to all purchasers.

4.   The Vesting of Rights to Subdivide

City of West Hollywood v. Beverly Towers, Inc.
805 P.2d 329 (Cal. 1991)

MOSK, Justice.

Defendants, the owners of apartment buildings in the City of West Hollywood (City), seek review of a Court of Appeal judgment ordering them to comply with a City ordinance requiring a conditional use permit for the conversion of apartments into condominiums. Defendants contend they are exempt from the ordinance because at the time it was enacted they had secured final subdivision map approval and permission from the California Department of Real Estate to sell individual units in their buildings as condominiums.

For the reasons stated below, we agree with defendants and reverse the judgment of the Court of Appeal to the effect that the owners cannot convert their buildings into condominiums until they have complied with local conversion regulations, including those adopted after they received all the necessary approvals granted under the state regulatory scheme.

The citizens of West Hollywood voted to incorporate as a separate municipality on November 29, 1984, thereby assuming land use power that had been vested in the County of Los Angeles (County). On that date, the newly created city council enacted a moratorium on conversions of rental housing until a regulatory system could be instituted; nine months later, the council adopted ordinance No. 114U (Ordinance 114U), which amended the West Hollywood zoning ordinance by adding comprehensive regulations governing the conversion of multiple family rental units into condominiums.

In addition to establishing certain design standards — e.g., storage space, off-street parking — ordinance 114U requires that the City make certain findings of fact before a conditional use permit for conversion can be approved, for example: (1) that the conversion will not adversely affect the supply of rental housing in the City, especially low- and moderate-income housing; and (2) that the vacancy factor of rental housing units in the City has exceeded 5 percent of the total housing inventory for a period of 90 days prior to conversion approval, unless (a) a new rental unit has been or will be added for each rental unit removed by conversion, (b) the developer will provide "inclusionary units or in-lieu fees," or (c) 80 percent of the existing tenants agree to purchase the units and no "substantial dislocation" of tenants will occur.

Prior to the City's incorporation, however, a number of apartment building owners within the City's future borders obtained tentative and final subdivision tract maps from the County to convert their existing rental units into condominiums, and, pursuant to a public report issued by the Department of Real Estate, secured approval for the sale of such condominiums. In 1986 the City filed a complaint for declaratory and injunctive relief, seeking to impose its condominium conversion regulations on the owners in this group who had not yet sold any units. The complaint alleged that 30 specific buildings with over 600 apartment units were subject to the ordinance. . . .

We granted review to decide whether defendants have a right under state law to convert their apartment units into condominiums because they complied with the state subdivision scheme.

To accomplish a condominium conversion, an apartment building owner must comply with numerous government regulations. The owner must conform the conversion to the requirements of the Subdivision Map Act (Cal. Govt. Code, §66410 et seq.) (Map Act), which regulates the design, improvement and sale of subdivisions and authorizes conditions for approval of subdivision maps, and the Davis-Stirling Common Interest Development Act (Cal. Civ. Code, §1350 et seq.), which establishes a uniform set of laws applicable to common interest developments. In addition, the sale of five or more condominiums requires a public report from the Department of Real Estate pursuant to the Subdivided Lands Act (Cal. Bus. & Prof. Code, §§11000–11200). . . .

. . . [S]ome of the Map Act's provisions are designed to safeguard the investments and expectations of developers involved in conversion projects. (See, e.g., §§66474.1, 66474.2, 65961.) We believe that setting a definite date for an owner to proceed with a condominium conversion free of subsequently enacted regulation comports with this intent.

Similar principles of fairness formed the basis of our unanimous holding in Youngblood v. Board of Supervisors, 586 P.2d 556 (Cal. 1978). In that case we held that a county lacked discretion under the Map Act to deny a final subdivision map if the application showed the development substantially conformed to the tentative map and its attendant conditions. We reasoned, "the date when the tentative map comes before the governing body for approval is the crucial date when that body should decide whether to permit the proposed subdivision. Once the tentative map is approved, the developer often must expend substantial sums to comply with the conditions attached to that approval. These expenditures will result in the construction of improvements consistent with the proposed subdivision, but often inconsistent with alternative uses of land. Consequently it is only fair to the developer and to the public interest to require the governing body to render its discretionary decision whether and upon what conditions to approve the proposed subdivision when it acts on the tentative map." (Id. at 562.) . . .

Nor is this case controlled by Avco Community Developers, Inc. v. South Coast Regional Comm., 553 P.2d 546 (Cal. 1976). In Avco, while the developer had obtained final map approval, it had not secured a necessary building permit prior to the effective date of a statute requiring a permit from the California Coastal Zone Commission. Consequently, we held the developer did not have a vested right to proceed without complying with the laws in effect at the time the building permit was issued, including the laws that were enacted after the application for the permit. (Id. at 552–53, and cases cited.) Here, final map approval and issuance of the public report were the last approvals defendants needed to sell a unit as a condominium; they did not require any further discretionary permits.

Nor are we confronted by the same policy consideration that inspired the Avco decision. In that case we were concerned that to grant a developer a vested right to proceed on issuance of a subdivision map, or any other preliminary approval, would impair the government's right to control land use policy by impressing lots previously subdivided — but on which no building had been constructed — with an "exemption of indeterminate duration from the requirements of any future zoning laws." . . . No such concern arises here.

We thus reject the City's contention that subsequently enacted legislation must be enforceable against a subdivider, absent a vested right to proceed, in order for cities to exercise meaningful planning and land use control. In this case we are concerned only with landowners in defendants' position, i.e., those who secured every necessary permit for a conversion project that required no further construction, and thus no additional government approvals. That defendants have yet to sell a unit is a trivial factor that has no effect on the City's zoning and planning power. Indeed, consequences to the zoning power are scarcely different from what inevitably results whenever a permit is deemed to be final. . . .

We also reject the City's claim that even though defendants have all the discretionary approvals necessary for condominium conversion, they still need, in the absence of vested rights, either a vesting tentative map or a development agreement in order to proceed free of subsequent local regulation.[6]

The purpose of the vesting tentative map and the development agreement is to allow a developer who needs additional discretionary approvals to complete a long-term development project as approved, regardless of any intervening changes in local regulations. (See Januta & Boyd, Development Agreements and Uncertainties in the Development Approval Process, 5 Real Prop. L. Rptr. 49 (1982); Cal. Govt. Code §66498.9 [vesting tentative map].) In this instance defendants did not need a vesting tentative map or a development agreement with the City because no further discretionary permits were required in order for them to proceed. . . .

The judgment of the Court of Appeal is reversed with directions to affirm the order of dismissal.

BROUSSARD, Justice, dissenting. . . .

The majority opinion is inconsistent with legislative intent, as well as with case law and commentary. The Legislature does not consider final subdivision map approval under Cal. Govt. Code §§66473–66474.10 as the point at which developers can claim a vested right to proceed free of the requirements of new enactments. In response to the hardship and uncertainty that it perceived that the vested rights doctrine sometimes imposes on developers, the Legislature has adopted a special "Vested Subdivision Map" application process which does assure the developer that the local laws applicable at the time of the tentative map approval will continue to apply throughout the map approval and permit process. See Cal. Gov. Code §§66498.1–66498.7, added by Stats. 1984 . . . ; see also Nadel, This Land Is Your Land . . . Or Is It? Making Sense of Vested Rights in California, 22 Loy. L.A. L. Rev. 791, 819 (1989). . . .

Whether or not subdivision map approval is the last application process through which the state regulatory scheme requires the condominium developer who plans no building to go, approval of the map should not bar the application of later changes in land use law unless the developer can demonstrate detrimental reliance on the map approval. The developer in this case has not even attempted to demonstrate such detrimental reliance. I fail to see how a developer who merely plans to change the nature of ownership of a building, without undertaking any construction or other expenses, has detrimentally relied on the subdivision map approval to the extent that he or she is equitably entitled

6. Landowners may apply for a vesting tentative map whenever the Map Act requires a tentative map. The vesting tentative map gives a developer a vested right to proceed with development, including the right to obtain all necessary building permits and discretionary approvals, in accordance with the local ordinances, policies and standards in effect when the application for the vesting tentative map was complete. Cal. Govt. Code §66498.1.

Similarly, development agreements (§§65864–65869.5) between a developer and a local government limit the power of that government to apply newly enacted ordinances to ongoing developments. Unless otherwise provided in the agreement, the rules, regulations, and official policies governing permitted uses, density, design, improvement, and construction are those in effect when the agreement is executed. §65866.

to estop the government from applying its general land use regulations to his property. The majority silently erode the vested rights doctrine when they confer what can only be termed a vested right to develop without requiring any showing of detrimental reliance.

KENNARD, Justice, concurs.

Note on Vesting of Rights to Subdivide

1. *Question about* West Hollywood. Compare *West Hollywood* with City of Key West v. R.L.J.S. Corp., 537 So. 2d 641 (Fla. Ct. App. 1989). In that instance, the developer of a condominium apartment building had obtained all required permits and sold a substantial number of units. The city then enacted an ordinance that imposed impact fees (treated at pp. 663–74) on new dwelling units built within the city and sought to levy those fees on both the developer's sold and unsold units. The Florida court held that the vested rights doctrine did not shield the developer because the doctrine protects a landowner only from changes in building regulations, not from new taxes. Is this distinction sound?

2. *Comparison with vested rights to build.* Some states do not protect a builder from a zoning change until the builder has both obtained a building permit and spent substantial funds on actual construction. See pp. 202–09. Subdividers generally fare better. Today most local governments have subdivision regulations, so a landowner rarely can subdivide without going through the formal subdivision approval process. If the subdivider submits a tentative (preliminary) map and the local government approves it, statutory provisions in force in most states will protect the right to complete the subdivision, provided that this is accomplished with reasonable dispatch. Why should there be automatic statutory protection of approved engineering drawings for a subdivision, but not for approved architectural drawings for a building?

Even more protective of the subdivider is Wash. Rev. Code §58.17.033 (2004), which proclaims that a proposed preliminary map is to be judged by the local policies in effect on the date the map is first *submitted* for approval. See Noble Manor Co. v. Pierce County, 943 P.2d 1378 (Wash. 1997). For a criticism of the uncertainty of vesting law in other states, see John J. Delaney, Vesting Verities and the Development Chronology: A Gaping Disconnect?, 3 Wash. U. J.L. & Pol'y 603 (2000).

The general statutory rule that a subdivision vests on tentative-map approval means that a developer who has complied with all conditions can obtain a court order that the local government approve a timely submitted final map that substantially conforms to the approved tentative map. See, e.g., Cal. Gov't Code §66458 (West Supp. 2004); Hakim v. Board of Commissioners, 366 A.2d 1306 (Pa. 1976).

There is an important political lesson here for a developer. If antidevelopment forces are apt to oust pro-development politicians in the next local election, a developer should consider seeking immediate approval of preliminary subdivision maps to protect against planning or zoning changes.

3. *When a developer dawdles in completing a subdivision.* In AWL Power, Inc. v. City of Rochester, 813 A.2d 517 (N.H. 2002), after initial subdivision approval the developer spent over $250,000 on infrastructure and built houses on 6 of the 18 lots. The housing market then turned sour and the developer ceased construction for a ten-year period, during which the city toughened its zoning requirements. The court held that the developer's earlier outlays had created a vested right to complete the subdivision as originally planned.

4. *Does the vesting of subdivision rights imply the vesting of building rights?* As *AWL Power* illustrates, the vesting of a right to subdivide is empty unless it also encompasses the

right to build on the subdivision's lots. Not all judges recognize this. In Slagle Construction Co. v. County of Contra Costa, 136 Cal. Rptr. 748 (Ct. App. 1977), the county had approved Slagle's tentative and final subdivision maps without requiring Slagle to bury existing overhead utility wires along a certain road. When Slagle applied for building permits for houses within the subdivision, however, the county would not issue them unless Slagle buried the existing telephone cable along this road. When Slagle sued for damages for a wrongful refusal to award building permits, the court held that their issuance was discretionary and declined to award damages against the county. But see Cal. Gov't Code §65961 (West 2004) (added 1982) (protecting a developer in a situation like Slagle's); Hartsell v. Town of Talty, 130 S.W.3d 325 (Tex. App. 2004) (holding that Texas's vesting statute protected a developer, who had previously obtained preliminary subdivision approval, from a municipality's subsequent effort to extend its building code extraterritorily).

5. *Vesting when a municipality engages in site plan review.* A municipality may subject a development proposal that is exempt from subdivision review to a similar application process, site plan review. See Edward H. Ziegler, Shaping Megalopolis: The Transformation of Euclidean Zoning by Special Zoning Districts and Site-Specific Development Review Techniques, 15 Zoning & Plan. L. Rep. 57 (1992). In Board of Supervisors v. Medical Structures, Inc., 192 S.E.2d 799 (Va. 1972), the county had granted a special use permit authorizing the construction of a nursing home. The permittee's successor prepared a site plan that complied with the terms of the permit. At the stage of site plan review, however, the county rejected the project because it had changed the underlying zoning in the interim. The court noted that the applicant had expended substantial sums on planning and held that its rights to proceed had vested. After the Supreme Court of Virginia diluted this holding in subsequent decisions, the legislature reinstituted it by statute. See Va. Code Ann. §15.2-2307 (2004).

6. *Development agreements.* At least ten states have enacted legislation that authorizes a local government to enter into a "development agreement." A development agreement — essentially a contract between a developer and a government — typically grants the developer a "freeze period" during which subsequently enacted laws or regulations will not be applied to the project, except in specified (usually emergency) situations. Both sides can benefit from a development agreement. The developer obtains greater certainty, which is especially important when a project has multiple phases and requires large early investments. In return for granting this certainty, a local government may be able to secure the developer's agreement to provide more public facilities and mitigation measures. An initial agreement also is likely to reduce the risks of later litigation between the contracting parties. Under what circumstances should an attorney advise a California developer to use either the "vesting tentative map" or "development agreement" options identified in footnote 6 of *West Hollywood*?

The use of development agreements may raise a number of legal issues: whether the state has conferred power on local governments to enter into such an agreement (is special legislation indeed necessary?); whether such agreements violate the proscriptions on "contract" zoning discussed at pp. 318–29; whether development agreements must meet the consistency-with-comprehensive-plan requirements discussed at pp. 336–41; and what rights neighbors and other third parties have to participate in negotiations leading up to an agreement, to challenge the agreement, or to enforce the agreement.

Sources on this topic include Development Agreements: Practice Policy, and Prospects (Douglas R. Porter & Lindell L. Marsh eds., 1989); David L. Callies & Julie A. Tappendorf, Unconstitutional Land Development Conditions and the Development Agreement Solution, 51 Case W. Res. L. Rev. 663 (2001); Judith Welch Wegner, Moving Toward the Bargaining Table: Contract Zoning, Development Agreements, and the

Theoretical Foundations of Government Land Use Deals, 65 N.C. L. Rev. 957 (1987). See also pp. 318–29.

5. *Grounds for Rejection of a Preliminary Map*

Richardson v. City of Little Rock Planning Commission
747 S.W.2d 116 (Ark. 1988)

JOHN NORMAN HARKEY, Special Justice.

The Little Rock Planning Commission disapproved a subdivision application submitted by Robert Richardson. An appeal of this decision to circuit court was unsuccessful. The circuit judge concluded that certain technical violations (which presumably would have been corrected in the final plat) were not the basis for the denial, and then ruled that the Commission had discretionary authority to disapprove.

This is a case of first impression in Arkansas, insofar as it relates to the discretionary authority of planning commissions, and that it is a difficult case is evidenced by the division among members of this court.

The issue is whether a planning commission has discretionary power to disapprove a subdivision plat which meets minimum requirements set forth in the subdivision ordinance. . . .

When a subdivision ordinance specifies minimum standards to which a preliminary plat must conform, it is arbitrary as a matter of law to deny approval of a plat that meets those standards. Odell v. City of Eagan, 348 N.W.2d 792 (Minn. Ct. App. 1984). Accordingly, if the plat is within the use permitted by the zoning classification and meets the development regulations set forth in the subdivision ordinance, then the plat by definition is in "harmony" with the existing subdivisions. Interladco, Inc. v. Billings, 538 P.2d 496 (Colo. Ct. App. 1975).

A primary purpose of these provisions is to ensure that a landowner's plat will be objectively measured against the concrete standards of the subdivision ordinance in effect. Thus, these provisions balance the interests of planned community growth with the private rights of landowners.

The record clearly demonstrates that appellee denied approval of the plat based upon considerations not authorized by the ordinance. Pursuant to the subdivision ordinance Section 37.14(e)(3), appellant received a letter setting forth two reasons for denial: (1) Proximity of a proposed cul-de-sac to the adjacent lots and (2) Marginal development potential of the land, resulting in unusual lot shapes and means for access. The final plat submission from which appellant appeals does not contain a cul-de-sac, and the subdivision ordinance does not contain the term "marginal development potential." In fact, there is testimony to the effect that the term "marginal development potential" was formulated ad hoc as a reason for denying appellant's plat.

In short, a planning commission may not disregard the regulations set forth in the subdivision ordinance and substitute its own discretion in lieu of fixed standards applying to all cases similarly situated. RK Dev. Corp. [v. City of Norwalk], 242 A.2d 781 [(Conn. 1968)]. A planning commission is authorized and required to determine whether a plat presented is in compliance with the particular subdivision regulations. Once compliance is had, no discretionary power to disapprove exists. To rule otherwise would sublimate objective requirements, and instead substitute subjective thinking by individual members of a particular planning commission. This was never contemplated by the law.

We reverse.

HICKMAN, Justice, dissenting.

This is a case of a private developer who bought land on a steep hillside in west Little Rock not suitable to easy development and then refused to change his plan because it would cost him money. The commission decided that until he met their requirements it would not be an acceptable subdivision. It is our duty to review the evidence in the light most favorable to the appellee and affirm the judgment if there is any substantial evidence to support it. Rhea v. Harris, 737 S.W.2d 626 (Ark. 1987). Furthermore, it is our duty to affirm an administrative agency's decision unless it is arbitrary. See Green v. Carder, 667 S.W.2d 660 (Ark. 1984). There is no suggestion the decision was arbitrary. Using this formula, this case should be affirmed.

The majority states the issue is whether a planning commission has discretionary power to disapprove a subdivision plat which meets minimum requirements of a subdivision ordinance; but the majority ignores the fact that the appellant's plan does not comply with the minimum requirements. The street does not meet the minimum requirement for adequate site [sic] distance on a curve. The side lot lines were not at right angles with the street as required by the subdivision ordinance. There was also testimony offered that one of the lots was more than three times as deep as it was wide, which is prohibited by the ordinance. Richardson, the developer, admitted that there were inconsistencies between the plat and the subdivision ordinance requirements; yet he blindly contends that he was in strict and total compliance with the ordinance. There was testimony offered that the nonconformities in the plat could be corrected at the final platting time. However, Richardson's own witness said that he did not know whether the changes could still be made and allow for the 15 lots Richardson insists on having in the subdivision. Richardson stated that he did not want to reduce the number of lots from 15 to 12 because "they stood to lose $100,000 to $150,000." There was also testimony offered that the development would cause erosion in adjacent Robinwood Subdivision and depreciation of the value of some of the homes in Robinwood. . . .

. . . The planning commission clearly has some discretion under the ordinance. If it had no discretion or could use no judgment, then there would be no need for a planning commission. The planning commission would consist of a single bureaucrat who could stamp a yes or no on a developer's plan. . . .

Surely the commission has the discretion to consider the lot shapes in deciding whether to approve a preliminary plat. The ordinance specifically provides:

> The size, shape and orientation of lots shall be appropriate for the location of the subdivision and for the type of development and use contemplated.

Little Rock, Ark., Code of Ordinances §37-24. . . .

The commission gave two reasons for the denial of the appellant's plat: "(1) proximity of [the] proposed cul-de-sac to the adjacent, existing lots and (2) marginal development potential of the land, resulting in unusual lot shapes and means for access." The appellant submitted two plats; one plat had a cul-de-sac and one did not. Both the appellant and the majority opinion focus on the term "marginal development potential" and ignore the language "resulting in unusual lot shapes and means for access." The subdivision ordinance clearly provides that the commission can consider the lot shapes and means of access in deciding whether to approve a preliminary plat. . . .

It comes down to whether the duly constituted authority to govern city planning and development or a private developer will decide what is best for the city. I would affirm the trial court's decision which upheld the city planning commission.

DUDLEY and NEWBERN, JJ., join in the dissent.

Note on a Local Government's Discretion

1. *Dealmaking revisited.* Local officials savor having the discretion to approve or disapprove specific development proposals. See Chapter 4B. Among other things, this discretion provides them with the leverage to exact maximum concessions and payments from developers. By contrast, developers bristle at local discretion. If a development company's engineers have drafted a preliminary subdivision map that complies with the applicable general plan, zoning ordinance, and subdivision regulations, it is apt to conclude that it has done enough, and that it should have a right to force the local government to approve the map. A developer is particularly likely to be incensed when local officials invent an ad hoc rationale for denying map approval. Local officials themselves may be fearful that courts will not look kindly on opportunistic reasons for rejection of a plan; they therefore may attempt to protect themselves by including in the subdivision ordinance a vague provision such as the Little Rock requirement that the "size, shape and orientation of lots . . . be appropriate."

The case law reviewing municipal processing of proposed subdivisions is erratic. Like the majority in *Richardson,* some opinions stress the importance of articulated, nondiscretionary "rules." See, e.g., Board of Supervisors v. Countryside Investment Co., 522 S.E.2d 610 (Va. 1999) (invalidating, as inconsistent with state enabling statute, county ordinance authorizing denial of subdivision application when county authorities deem the land "unsuitable for subdivision"). Other judges are more accepting of a municipality's application of general "standards." For a thorough review, see Laurie Reynolds, Local Subdivision Regulation: Formulaic Constraints in an Age of Discretion, 24 Ga. L. Rev. 525 (1990).

2. *The administrative law of subdivision processing.* A number of leading state courts have held that a local government's decision on a proposed preliminary subdivision map is adjudicative and therefore subject to the protections of procedural due process. (Cf. Chapter 4B, on judicial review of zoning map amendments.) In particular this means that both the subdivider and neighbors are entitled to (1) a hearing, (2) reasonable notice that the hearing is to be held, (3) articulated standards for decision, and (4) express findings supported by substantial evidence. See Horn v. County of Ventura, 596 P.2d 1134 (Cal. 1979); Chapel Road Associates, L.L.C. v. Town of Wells, 787 A.2d 137 (Me. 2001) (asserting that express findings of fact are essential to enable meaningful appellate review). Should the *Richardson* majority have been especially bothered by: (1) the vagueness of Little Rock's standards, (2) the insubstantiality of the evidence supporting the planning commission's findings, or (3) the failure of the planning commission to link its reasons for denial to rationales that the Little Rock ordinance authorized?

3. *Waivers of subdivision standards.* A subdivider may succeed in challenging a board's refusal to relax a waivable standard. See Green Meadows at Montville, L.L.C. v. Planning Board, 746 A.2d 1009 (N.J. Super. Ct. App. Div. 2000) (holding planning board's refusal to waive maximum limit on length of dead-end street to be "arbitrary and unreasonable"); Mill Realty Associates v. Zoning Board of Review, 721 A.2d 887 (R.I. 1998) (holding town should have granted exception to permit subdivider to install gravel road).

4. *Rejection on account of the developer's track record.* Many precedents assert that local governments are empowered only to control land uses, not the identity of the land users. See, e.g., Dexter v. Town Board, 324 N.E.2d 870, 871 (N.Y. 1975). Jan Krasnowiecki sharply criticizes this principle in Abolish Zoning, 31 Syracuse L. Rev. 719, 730–31 (1980):

> . . . I believe that the idea that land use controls cannot deal with individual characteristics is utterly naive. There is no local government that is not interested in a developer's financial

capacity, reputation for quality, and record of good management. Denying that this is so has done zoning no good.

My objection to the traditional view is not confined to its obvious lack of realism. I think that local governments have a legitimate interest in a developer's capacity to complete and manage the project and they should have the right to reject a developer who does not demonstrate such a capacity. In addition, local governments should have the right to control any subventuring or assignments by the developer, at least through the critical construction phase. . . .

Krasnowiecki would authorize a local government to deny subdivision approval to an applicant on the ground that the applicant had a "track record of half-finished projects, cheating on specifications for public improvements, and the like. . . . " Id. at 731 n.50. He anticipates that suburbs would be less hostile to development if they had this authority.

5. *Rejection for fiscal reasons.* Traditionally courts did not condone a municipality's ad hoc refusal to approve a map simply because the proposed project might prove to be a drain on the local budget. See Beach v. Planning & Zoning Commission, 103 A.2d 814 (Conn. 1954) (holding planning commission that had denied map approval for fiscal reasons had acted without statutory authority and was guilty of the worst kind of standard-less decisionmaking). Cf. Southern Burlington County NAACP v. Township of Mount Laurel (*Mount Laurel I*), 336 A.2d 713 (N.J. 1975), excerpted at p. 763 (denying legitimacy of a municipality's basing zoning decisions on fiscal considerations). But times are changing. See pp. 812–13, which describes how many municipalities now condition development approval on the concurrent availability of adequate public facilities. See also pp. 634–78, on the substantial (although hardly unlimited) power of a local government to make its approval of a subdivision map contingent on the subdivider's willingness to contribute land, land improvements, and impact fees.

6. *Municipal discretion to reject a proposed site plan.* Most of the issues just canvassed also arise in the context of site plan review. In Prudential Insurance Co. of America v. Board of Appeals, 502 N.E.2d 137 (Mass. App. Ct. 1986), the court held that if the town was concerned about the traffic impacts of a proposed office-building project, it could not reject the site plan outright but instead only attach reasonable permit conditions to ameliorate traffic problems. But compare City of Colorado Springs v. Securcare Self Storage, Inc., 10 P.3d 1244 (Colo. 2000) (upholding, over a vigorous dissent, city's decision to deny site plan approval of proposed commercial project that met zoning requirements on ground that project would be "incompatible" with surrounding residential neighborhood).

7. *Developers' remedies.* Normally, as in *Richardson*, when a court determines that a municipality has wrongly withheld subdivision or site plan approval, it orders that that approval be granted. Should a municipality or local officials ever be held liable in damages to a wronged applicant? See First English Evangelical Lutheran Church of Glendale v. County of Los Angeles, 482 U.S. 304 (1987), excerpted at p. 258, on the possibility of a takings claim for a wrongful delay.

6.   Neighbors' Rights

Lyman v. Planning Board of Winchester
224 N.E.2d 493 (Mass. 1967)

CUTTER, Justice.

Lyman filed an appeal in the Superior Court with respect to the Winchester planning board's approval of a definitive subdivision plan filed by Frank Catalano, Inc. (Catalano) on January 4, 1965. See G.L. c. 41, §81BB (as amended through St. 1957, c. 199, §2). Catalano was allowed to intervene. Lyman has now appealed to this court from a final decree dismissing the bill. The case is before us upon the evidence and a report of material facts.

Catalano owned about seven and one-half acres of vacant land in Winchester in an area largely developed to the north and east. On the south and west Catalano's land is almost entirely bounded by over thirty-two acres of undeveloped land owned by Lyman. The Catalano land slopes down northerly from a high point at its boundary with the Lyman land. The Lyman land slopes down for about 120 feet south from the Catalano boundary, then dips into a valley.

The Lyman land is in part woodland with outcroppings of ledge, is potentially a fine residential area, and is largely surrounded by other privately owned land and town land. It abuts on a public way (High Street) only at its extreme southwest corner on a frontage of 111 feet. The access from High Street to the Lyman land narrows, not far from the highway, to a width of twenty feet at one point. . . . To have appropriate access to a development on his land, Lyman . . . would be obliged to buy additional land near High Street (to widen his access from that direction) or to obtain other access.

The controversy in the present case arises from the planning board's rules and regulations. . . . Certain of these regulations provide that a definitive plan shall take into account conditions and facilities on property adjoining the land being subdivided.[3]

In 1961 Catalano filed a preliminary subdivision plan which showed one way extending as a dead-end street south to the boundary between the Catalano land and the Lyman land. It also showed an extension to that boundary of sewer, storm drainage, and water lines. These extensions were eliminated in the definitive plan, upon the recommendation of the planning board. At a public hearing on February 1, 1965, Lyman objected to approval of the definitive plan because it did not give him access to the proposed roads on the Catalano land (at a time when it seemed that he might lose his access to High Street) and because it did not comply with the regulations. The board approved the plan on February 18, 1965.

One member of the board, in testimony on which the trial judge obviously relied, gave as the reason for the board's failure to require the extension of roads and sewer lines to the Catalano–Lyman boundary the topographical irregularities of both parcels. He pointed out (a) that the extension of one of the roads proposed for construction on Catalano's land would necessitate a grade not acceptable under the town's regulations and (b) that any method of solving the grade problem would either "injure Catalano seriously and . . . be of no gain to . . . [a possible] Lyman development" or would "seriously injure the Lyman land and . . . be of no gain to Catalano interests." He testified that the contour of the land was such that drainage from the Lyman land to the Catalano land could not be accomplished in "a gravity system." The evidence, including expert testimony and contour maps, shows that these views were justified. . . .

The evidence justifies the trial judge's findings concerning the Catalano and Lyman parcels and his conclusion that the planning board's decision "was based upon valid engineering and . . . factors governing sound planning and development." He correctly ruled that the board's regulations did not preclude it from approving Catalano's plan without requiring it to project its roads, water lines, and sewers to the boundary. . . .

[Affirmed.]

3. Section 111-1 (Street System) reads, in part, "(e) If adjoining property is not subdivided but is, in the opinion of the [b]oard, suitable for ultimate development, provision shall be made for proper projection of streets into such property by continuing appropriate streets within the subdivision to the exterior boundary thereof." [EDS.: Other sections of the regulations similarly called for extension of appropriate drainage, water, and sewer lines to the exterior boundary of a subdivision in order to serve adjacent property.]

Note on Neighbors' Rights

1. *The sizing of shared utility mains.* In Caruso v. Planning Board, 238 N.E.2d 872 (Mass. 1968), the developer of Green Acres had concluded that an off-site sewer main of at least 14 inches was needed to serve its proposed subdivision. The developer of Colonial Acres owned the land situated between Green Acres and an existing 14-inch main. The Colonial Acres developer had won planning board approval of a subdivision map that called for the installation of a mere 8-inch main across this intermediate stretch. When Colonial Acres insisted on being paid $3,000 by Green Acres to upgrade the connecting main to 14 inches, Green Acres unsuccessfully challenged the planning board's approval of the smaller main.

2. *Opposition from existing residents.* Homeowners living on adjoining subdivided acreage may oppose a new subdivision on the ground that it would increase traffic and otherwise disturb the status quo. In one case in Ridgewood, New Jersey, several Wall Street fat cats with houses on a secluded lane mounted a vigorous campaign against a proposed subdivision containing eight lots suitable for million-dollar houses. The campaign forced the planning board to hold at least ten public hearings on the proposal. The opponents threatened that, if the board were to approve the preliminary map, they would seek judicial review, a process that they estimated would take a minimum of three years. Michael Winerip, Urban Blight: New Homes at $1 Million, N.Y. Times, Apr. 23, 1987, at 12. On what terms might these antagonists have settled their dispute?

When a municipality approves a subdivision map that violates its zoning regulations, a neighbor can succeed in persuading a court to invalidate the approval. See, e.g., Save Centennial Valley Association v. Schultz, 284 N.W.2d 452 (S.D. 1979) (also holding that map violated comprehensive plan). But cf. Urrutia v. Blaine County, 2 P.3d 738 (Idaho 2000) (holding that noncompliance with comprehensive plan is insufficient justification for denial of subdivision application).

When a municipality has granted a developer waivers from certain subdivision standards, a neighbor may object that the waived standards were mandatory, not discretionary. Compare Anthony v. Snyder, 10 Cal. Rptr. 3d 505 (Ct. App. 2004) (holding waiver of width requirement for road to be permissible), with Sawyer v. Town of Cape Elizabeth, 852 A.2d 58 (Me. 2004) (remanding, because of absence of articulated findings, planning board's decision to waive requirement for a vegetative buffer at boundary of subdivision).

3. *Neighbors' remedies.* Instead of invalidating an improperly approved map, would it ever be appropriate for a court itself to alter the street arrangement or impose additional conditions? See Strand v. Planning Board, 358 N.E.2d 842 (Mass. 1977), which held that the trial court had wrongly amplified conditions designed to protect neighbors from flooding.

What about the possibility of subdivider liability to neighbors? Four basic rules could be applied to resolve a neighbor's suit to recover damages stemming from a developer's installation of subdivision improvements: (1) no liability, (2) strict liability, (3) strict liability only for the spillover effects of uncommonly injurious activities, and (4) negligence liability. (Cf. the possible formulations of the prima facie case for nuisance, at pp. 517–18.) Each of these four rules has been used at various times to resolve surface-water disputes. See discussion in, e.g., Butler v. Bruno, 341 A.2d 735 (R.I. 1975) (reviewing "common enemy," "civil law," and "reasonable-use" rules).

In Beck v. Bel Air Properties, Inc., 286 P.2d 503 (Cal. 1955), defendant, in grading a number of lots at the top of a canyon, had loosened the compaction of the hillside. Six years later, heavy rains caused rocks and soil to flow downward onto plaintiff's residence at the bottom of the canyon. Plaintiff sought to recover for his personal injuries and property damages on a strict liability theory. The court held that, because subdividing and grading hills is not an ultrahazardous activity, the trial court had erred in instructing the jury to apply a strict liability rule; rather, it said, defendant's conduct should be judged by a negligence standard.

7.   Unregulated Subdivisions

Most states and local governments decline to impose the full-blown review process on all subdivisions of land. The purposes of subdivision control — protection of neighbors, the community-at-large, and prospective subdivision residents — would rarely be served, for example, by governmental review of the proposed division of a large farm into two smaller farms. Should the creation of condominium units be subjected to subdivision regulations? What about the sale by a homeowner of the back 3 feet of a lot to the neighbor in the rear?

Legal definitions of regulated subdivisions. For several reasons, landowners are vitally interested in how applicable enabling acts and ordinances define the "subdivisions" that must be submitted for review. First, the review process often causes delay because the regulations customarily prohibit the sale of lots and the building of structures until after a final map has been approved. See, e.g., Wis. Stat. §236.31.3 (2004) (sale of lot in an illegal subdivision is voidable at the option of the purchaser). Second, design standards for improvements in controlled subdivisions often are higher than the standards the subdivider would adopt in the absence of regulation. Third, a subdivider who does not need subdivision approval may be able to elude municipal exactions.

A New Jersey statute defined a minor subdivision as "the division of a lot, tract or parcel of land into two or more lots, sites or other divisions of land for the purpose, whether immediate or future, of sale or building development. . . . " Plaintiff owned land burdened by an express road easement that defendant was using for access to its appurtenant tract. In a vain attempt to have this easement expunged, plaintiff argued that the creation of the easement constituted a minor subdivision, which was illegal because the city planning commission had not approved it. The court summarily rejected plaintiff's claim in Hutchinson v. Damin Corp., 381 A.2d 405 (N.J. 1977).

Maine used to identify a subdivision as "the division of a tract or parcel of land into three or more lots within any five-year period . . . whether accomplished by sale, lease, development, building or otherwise. . . . " Me. Rev. Stat. Ann. tit. 30, §4956(1) (West 1978). In Town of Arundel v. Swaim, 374 A.2d 317 (Me. 1977), the town asserted that this definition encompassed a campground with 101 campsites. However, the court held otherwise because there was no evidence that the campsites were so clearly delineated as to constitute lots, a lot being defined in Webster's Dictionary as "a measured parcel of land having fixed boundaries." Although land in the campground would be divided so as to give each customer a space to occupy for a certain time (as in a parking lot or drive-in theater), the court concluded that a camper's temporary occupancy of a campsite was not the sort of "division" of land that the legislature intended to regulate. The court cited as inapplicable to the instant case a fundamental purpose of subdivision regulation — protecting the purchaser or lessee from an unscrupulous developer. But cf. Planning Board v. Michaud, 444 A.2d 40 (Me. 1982) (sale of perpetual rights of exclusive use of particular camp sites resulted in subdivision); Cowboy Country Estates v. Ellis County, 692 S.W.2d 882 (Tex. App. 1985) (leasing of discrete spaces in mobile home park constituted a subdivision).

A state's statutory definition of a subdivision generally preempts municipal efforts to loosen or tighten the regulatory net. In Kenai Peninsula Borough v. Kenai Peninsula Board of Realtors, 652 P.2d 471 (Alaska 1982), a borough ordinance that exempted lots of 10 or more acres from subdivision regulation was invalidated because the Alaska subdivision statute required local review of all subdivisions. In Pennobscot, Inc. v. Board of Commissioners, 642 P.2d 915 (Colo. 1982), Pitkin County, the site of staunchly antigrowth Aspen, was deemed unable to override a state statutory exemption of lots of 35 acres or more. What statewide concerns, if any, justify state preemption of local discretion over what subdivisions to review?

Attempts to evade subdivision regulations. Gifford v. Planning Board of Nantucket, 383 N.E.2d 1123 (Mass. 1978), illustrates the extraordinary steps a developer may take to avoid subdivision regulation. The map in Figure 5-7 shows about half of a developer's proposed lot layout for a tract on the island of Nantucket. The design sought to exploit Mass. Gen. Laws ch. 41, §81L (2004), which exempts a tract from local subdivision regulation "if every lot within the tract so divided has frontage on a public way." The developer's maze design fulfilled this requirement, as well as the Town of Nantucket's zoning requirement of a minimum of 75 feet of street frontage for each lot. When the Nantucket Planning Board agreed with the developer that board approval of the plan was not required, neighbors succeeded in obtaining a judicial reversal of the decision. Kaplan, J., noted that a major purpose of lot-frontage requirements is to ensure that police and fire personnel have easy access to structures. The frontages in the proposed development did not serve that purpose because some of the "rat tails" not only were at places narrower than the narrowest fire vehicle in use on Nantucket, but also made directional changes too sharp for most vehicles and approached the main streets at bad angles. The town safety officers in effect testified that if they were to see a building burning, they would undoubtedly start driving down the wrong accessway. This testimony assumed that the developer would provide individual accessways to each lot. Instead of that, could the developer have been planning to use easements to create, for example, a single dead-end street to serve the southern cluster of lots? See also Pratt v. Adams, 40 Cal. Rptr. 505 (Ct. App. 1964) (rebuffing evasion attempt that had utilized procedures for judicial partition of concurrently owned property).

Some developers attempt to create large unregulated subdivisions by sequentially taking advantage of exemptions from subdivision regulation. In California prior to 1975, a subdivision of four or fewer lots was exempt from both local subdivision regulation and the Subdivided Lands Act (a consumer-protection statute mentioned on p. 430). These exemptions gave rise to the process of "four-by-fouring." The owner of a large tract of mountain forest might split the tract into four pieces; each grantee would repeat the process; and so on. See People v. Byers, 153 Cal. Rptr. 249 (Ct. App. 1979) (affirming convictions of subdividers who "four-by-foured" after the pertinent California statutes had been amended). Cf. Gerard v. San Juan County, 715 P.2d 149 (Wash. Ct. App. 1986) (holding legislature did not intend to allow developer to create 18 parcels by sequentially taking advantage of various exemptions in subdivision statute).

The use of lot-splits to avoid subdivision regulation continues and is particularly controversial in the West. See generally Michael M. Shultz & Jeffrey B. Groy, The Failure of Subdivision Control in the Western United States, 1988 Utah L. Rev. 569 (an exceptionally thorough review). Lot-split developments commonly lack basic municipal services such as paved roads and sewers. Critics point to poor access for emergency vehicles, lower property values, and environmental degradation. Proponents note that residents can buy lots more cheaply and are burdened with lower property taxes than are their regulated counterparts. See Mark Robichaux, Arizona's Rural Sprawl: Fast Growth Spawns "Wildcat" Subdivisions, Wall St. J., Jan. 30, 2001, at A1. See also the discussion of the Texas *colonias* at p. 417.

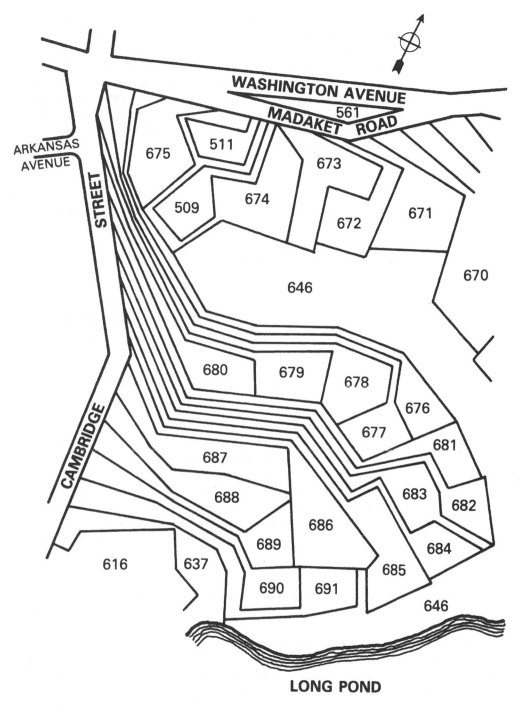

Source: 383 N.E.2d 1123, 1128 (Mass. 1978).

FIGURE 5-7
Gifford v. Planning Board of Nantucket

Subdivision activity raises issues analogous to those arising in products liability law. See, e.g., Stepanov v. Gavrilovich, 594 P.2d 30 (Alaska 1979) (applying negligence standard to resolve issue of a subdivider's liability to lot purchasers damaged by melting of previously undiscovered permafrost). Should a subdivider be entitled to win exemption from the consumer-protection aspects of subdivision regulation by agreeing both (1) to be strictly liable to lot purchasers for subdivision defects, and (2) to post a bond to assure payment of any such liabilities? More generally, to what extent, if any, is private litigation a viable alternative to public regulation of the subdivision process? Could the threat of lawsuits by lot purchasers and neighbors adequately deter abuses by subdividers?

B.   Assuring the Quality of Construction: Building Codes

Shoddy building practices have a long history. The Code of Hammurabi, who ruled Babylonia during the period 1792–1750 B.C., provided in part:

> 229. If a builder constructs a house for a man but does not make his work sound, and the house that he constructs collapses and causes the death of the householder, that builder shall be killed.
> 230. If it should cause the death of a son of the householder, they shall kill a son of that builder. . . .
> 233. If a builder constructs a house for a man but does not make it conform to specifications so that a wall then buckles, that builder shall make that wall sound using his own silver.

Martha T. Roth, Law Collections from Mesopotamia and Asia Minor 125 (1995).

Especially prior to the twentieth century, cities were stalked by fire and pestilence. The Great Fire of 1666 destroyed five-sixths of the buildings in London, but at the same time cleansed the city of the Plague, which had just claimed 70,000 lives. Rome burned most famously in A.D. 64; Chicago, in 1871. Nor were smaller cities free of these dangers. More than 1,000 wooden buildings were engulfed in flames in Charleston (1838), Pittsburgh (1845), Quebec (1845), and San Francisco (1851). Events like these created acute public concern about building designs, building materials, and the provision of sanitary facilities.

Stephen R. Seidel, Housing Costs and Government Regulations
73–74 (1978)

The threshold issue which must be addressed in evaluating building codes is why government has deemed it essential to regulate the private construction market. In other words, if left to follow its own course, would the private market be capable of achieving the same objectives as those attained through building codes?

Two specific areas of experience suggest that some form of government intervention in building construction may be necessary.

The complexity of today's construction methods renders it unlikely that the prospective home buyer will have sufficient technical knowledge to make an informed decision about the structural integrity of the unit. Building codes serve as a substitute for complete knowledge on the part of the consumer by ensuring that at least a minimum level of quality is built into the unit. Without codes there would be little incentive for builders to incorporate more than a minimal degree of structural integrity in their product because most consumers are not capable of distinguishing between varying degrees of structural soundness.

The second market imperfection which suggests the need for government intervention relates to externalities. For instance, home buyers would tend to underinvest in safety features, thinking only of the potential damage to their own properties, without considering the effect of fire or a collapsing building on surrounding properties. Building codes have the effect of readjusting this parochial investment decision by requiring that the potential external costs be considered in deciding how much safety will be built into the unit.

If experience dictates that some form of intervention in the building industry is necessary, it does not demand that those codes be legislated by the government. In France, there is no government promulgated building code. Instead, codes are written by the liability insurance companies, this being the result of a provision in the Napoleonic Code which places liability for major construction defects during a ten year period on architects and contractors. To protect themselves against possible liability, those in the construction field obtain insurance which is made contingent on their compliance with minimum construction standards as established by the insurance companies.

Note on Assurance of Building Quality Through Private Law

1. *Builder liability to the original purchaser.* As Seidel notes, the merits of building codes depend in part on the merits of private-law alternatives. In sharp contrast to the Napoleonic Code, a rule of the caveat emptor applied to the sale of new housing in most of the United States until the 1960s. The rule's reign then came to an abrupt close. See, e.g., Schipper v. Levitt & Sons, 207 A.2d 314 (N.J. 1965) (imposing strict liability on mass homebuilder for house defects); Humber v. Morton, 426 S.W.2d 554 (Tex. 1968) (following *Schipper*). A number of state legislatures also have become involved in protecting purchasers of new houses. See Debra Pogrund Stark & Andrew Cook, Pay It Forward: A Proactive Model to Resolving Construction Defects and Market Failure, 38 Val. U. L. Rev. 1 (2003) (analyzing statutes in Maryland and New Jersey). The upsurge in lawsuits arising out of construction defects has dramatically increased homebuilders' costs of insuring against this litigation risk. See Robert Gavin, Home Builders Face Insurance Woes, Wall St. J., Feb. 27, 2002, at B7.

Should a builder-seller of a single house (and not just a mass developer) be strictly liable for construction defects? Compare McDonald v. Mianecki, 398 A.2d 1283 (N.J. 1979) (yes), with Oliver v. Superior Court, 259 Cal. Rptr. 160 (Ct. App. 1989) (no). Does a builder-seller immutably warrant the quality of an apartment building or commercial structure? See Frickel v. Sunnyside Enterprises, Inc., 725 P.2d 422 (Wash. 1986) (honoring apartment-house buyer's waiver of warranty of fitness); Frona M. Powell & Jane P. Mallor, The Case for an Implied Warranty of Quality in Sales of Commercial Real Estate, 68 Wash. U. L.Q. 305 (1990).

2. *The liabilities of parties other than the builder.* Because many parties have some control over a building's quality, the victim of a defect may be able to choose among a multitude of potential defendants. Architects and engineers, for example, are liable to foreseeable plaintiffs for negligence in design or supervision (see, e.g., Aldrich v. ADD Inc., 770 N.E.2d 447 (Mass. 2002)), but as providers of "services" (as opposed to "products") are not strictly liable for construction defects. Stuart v. Crestview Mutual Water Co., 110 Cal. Rptr. 543 (Ct. App. 1973). Construction lenders, unless specially involved in the development process, are unlikely to be held liable to purchasers to defective buildings.

See Cal. Civ. Code §3434 (West 2004); Melissa Cassedy, The Doctrine of Lender Liability, 40 U. Fla. L. Rev. 165 (1988).

3. *Statutes of repose.* A traditional statute of limitations requires a plaintiff to bring suit within a specified period after the cause of action arises. In a case involving a latent defect in a building, the cause of action does not arise until the defect has been discovered. In some instances, builders and contractors have found themselves to be targets of suits involving construction performed decades earlier. See, e.g., Bradler v. Craig, 79 Cal. Rptr. 401 (Ct. App. 1969) (rejecting action to recover damages from general contractor and construction lender for soil failure that occurred in 1966 under house built in 1948).

To relieve homebuilders and designers of possibly unending exposure to liability, by 2001 all states other than New York and Vermont had enacted a statute of repose for construction-defect litigation. See Allen Holt Gwyn & Paul E. Davis, Statutes of Repose, Constr. Law., Summer 2001, at 33. The time limit in such a statute begins to run on completion of the project (or, in some states, on completion of a defendant subcontractor's work on the project) regardless of when the defect is discovered or causes injury. Time limits vary by jurisdiction and typically range from 4 to 20 years. See, e.g., Ga. Code Ann. §9-3-51 (2004) (eight years); Mich. Comp. Laws §600.5839(1) (2004) (ten years).

4. *A builder's liability to subsequent purchasers.* The decline of the privity limitation in product-defect cases has enhanced the importance of statutes of repose. See, e.g., Gupta v. Ritter Homes, 646 S.W.2d 168 (Tex. 1983) (builder's implied warranty of fitness extends to second purchaser despite lack of privity). See generally Dean J. Zipzer, Note, Builders' Liability for Latent Defects in Used Homes, 32 Stan. L. Rev. 607 (1980). To what extent does the availability of this remedy undercut the consumer-protection rationale for building codes?

5. *A builder's liability for damage to neighbors.* What if a negligent builder were to have erected a firetrap that later ignited and caused damage to both the occupants and owners of an adjacent lot? Contemporary tort doctrine is likely to enable these foreseeable bystanders to recover damages from the builder. These claimants also might have a cause of action against the owner of the building whose defects led to the conflagration. See Alderman v. Shanks, 536 N.W.2d 4 (Minn. 1995). To what extent does the availability of these remedies vitiate the neighbor-protection rationale for building codes?

6. *Learning from the Napoleonic Code?* Like the Code of Hammurabi, most ancient building regulations imposed liability instead of prescribing methods of construction. The Roman Civil Law adopted this approach. From there, it was incorporated into the Napoleonic Code. As Seidel notes, it remains the primary mode of building regulation in France. See also La. Civ. Code Ann. art. 2762 (West 2004) (imposing liability on architects and contractors for defective construction).

When reading the upcoming materials on building codes, consider the viability of a privatized alternative to public regulation of building quality. In 1968, the Kaiser Committee suggested that "warranties on housing units extended by housing producers (backed by bonds or insurance if necessary) might have some potential as a voluntary alternative to building codes." President's Committee on Urban Housing, A Decent Home 202 (1968).

In 1974, the National Association of Home Builders (NAHB) inaugurated its Home Owners Warranty (HOW) program. Member builders who choose to participate in the program provide buyers of their new homes with a ten-year express warranty. The HOW warranty is backed by an insurance policy guaranteeing that the buyer's damages will be paid should the builder become insolvent. (On the scope and structure of HOW coverage, see Cobert v. Home Owners Warranty Corp., 391 S.E.2d 263 (Va. 1990).) Should homebuilders participating in a HOW-type program be exempt from all building code requirements? For affirmative answers to this question, see Peter F. Colwell & James B.

Kau, The Economics of Building Codes and Standards, 11 J. AREUEA 11 (1983); Thomas Schalow, Note, The Home Buyers' Protection Act: An Alternative to Building Codes for Single Family Homes, 54 S. Cal. L. Rev. 529 (1981).

1. The Maze of Building Codes

Note on the Basics of Building Codes

1. *History.* In contrast to the French approach, Anglo-American governments generally have relied on public regulations that prohibit the erection of buildings that fail to utilize prescribed materials and techniques. This system first evolved in medieval London. For example, to reduce fire dangers a London ordinance adopted in 1607 required certain outer walls to be built of brick or stone. In 1667, Parliament passed a relatively comprehensive set of regulations detailing permissible materials and techniques for the reconstruction of London after the Great Fire. See generally C.C. Knowles & P.H. Pitt, The History of Building Regulations in London: 1189–1972 (1972).

The English approach was transported to North America. In 1630, a fire in a Boston house spread to the thatch roof of a neighboring house. The governor of the colony responded by prohibiting thatch roofs and wooden chimneys. On pre-1860 exercises of police power to reduce risks of fire, see William J. Novak, The People's Welfare 51–82 (1996). In 1850, New York City became the first American city to adopt a building code. After the fire of 1871, the City of Chicago, under threat of boycott from the National Board of Fire Underwriters (an insurance trade organization), embraced a comprehensive code. See generally Jon C. Teaford, The Unheralded Triumph: City Government in America, 1870–1900, at 198–203 (1984) (on influence of fire underwriters on code adoption).

2. *A glimpse inside a codebook.* A building code is a technical document, whose level of difficulty at places may rival that of the Internal Revenue Code. Two relatively simple sections of a leading model code appear below. The first section deals with requirements for the structural members of a wood-frame wall; "studs" are the vertical members of the wall frame; "plates," the horizontal members.

INTERNATIONAL CODE COUNCIL, 2003 INTERNATIONAL BUILDING CODE

§2308.9.3 *Nonbearing walls and partitions.* In nonbearing walls and partitions, studs shall be spaced not more than 28 inches (711 mm) o.c. [on center] and are permitted to be set with the long dimension parallel to the wall. Interior nonbearing partitions shall be capped with no less than a single top plate installed to provide overlapping at corners and intersections with other walls and partitions. The plate shall be continuously tied at joints by solid blocking at least 16 inches (406 mm) in length and equal to the plate or by $1/2$ inch by $1 1/2$ inch (12.7 mm by 38 mm) metal ties with spliced sections fastened with two 16d nails on each side of the joint.

§3109.4.1 [Residential swimming pool] *Barrier height and clearances.* The top of the barrier shall be at least 48 inches (1219 mm) above grade measured on the side of the barrier that faces away from the swimming pool. The maximum vertical clearance between grade and the bottom of the barrier shall be 2 inches (51 mm) measured on the side of the barrier that faces away from the swimming pool. Where the top of the pool structure is above grade, the barrier is authorized to be at ground level or mounted on top of the pool structure, the maximum vertical clearance between the top of the pool structure and the bottom of the barrier shall be 4 inches (102 mm).

3. *Specification versus performance standards.* The first of these code sections identifies two permissible technologies for joining a plate with another wall or partition. In lieu of these alternative *specification standards,* the code could have identified a *performance standard,* for example, that a plate joint be strong enough to withstand a specified lateral force. Performance standards are promulgated by major national standard-setting organizations such as the American Society for Testing and Materials (ASTM), the American Plywood Association, the U.S. Department of Commerce, and Underwriters' Laboratories. Unlike specification standards, performance standards encourage the development and dissemination of innovative technologies. Builders and building officials, however, usually find specification standards much easier to understand. Code drafters may be able to exploit the advantages of both approaches by articulating a performance standard and then listing, as safe harbors, several specification standards that satisfy it.

4. *The distinction between building and housing codes.* Building codes are mostly prospective. They govern the design, materials, and construction techniques to be used in the erection of new structures or the alteration of existing structures. Other types of ordinances may apply retrospectively. For example, a municipality might require that barriers be installed around *existing* residential swimming pools, that certain existing commercial buildings be retrofitted with firefighting sprinkler systems, or that existing houses be served by both hot and cold running water. Ordinances that apply retrospectively usually are referred to as safety codes, health codes, or (most commonly) housing codes. On these laws, see pp. 465–69.

5. *When does a project require a building permit?* Building codes identify the types, sizes, and costs of structures that require permits. Should code drafters require a property owner to obtain a building permit before erecting a 6-foot-high prefabricated bird-feeder purchased at Home Depot? See Levy v. Alfano, 47 F. Supp. 2d 488 (S.D.N.Y. 1999) (discussing state court decision holding that bird feeder was not a "structure" under the local building code). Compare Josephine County v. Garnier, 987 P.2d 1263 (Or. Ct. App. 1999) (enjoining defendant from renting four tree houses, constructed without building permits, to overnight guests).

Farm construction commonly is exempt from building codes. See, e.g., Braden Trust v. County of Yuma, 69 P.3d 510 (Ariz. Ct. App. 2003) (holding structures built to house farm workers were exempt by statute from building codes because structures were "incidental to agriculture"). How persuasive in a rural context are the consumer- and neighbor-protection rationales for code enforcement?

After Florida exempted Disney World from most local building code regulation, the Disney Company imposed its own building standards. See Richard E. Foglesong, Married to the Mouse: Walt Disney World and Orlando 81–97 (2001). Did this exemption unduly increase risks of harms to consumers and neighbors?

Note on Statutory Innovations in Building Regulation

1. *Model codes.* Prior to the 1990s, the building code field was dominated by four model code associations, whose influence varied by region of the United States. Building officials and participants in the construction industry made up the memberships of these associations. Although some states and localities drafted their own codes, most adopted one or another of the model codes, often adding or subtracting specific provisions. See James A. Gardiner & Theodore R. Lyman, Decisions for Sale: Corruption and Reform in Land Use and Building Regulation 20–22 (1978).

In 1994, the three most important regional associations merged to form the International Code Council (ICC). In 2000, the ICC released the first edition of the International Building Code, along with several specialty codes, such as the International Plumbing Code. In 2003, the ICC reported that 39 states had adopted at least one International Code at the statewide level. See David Listokin & David Hattis, Building Codes and Housing, 8 Cityscape 21 (2005). In addition, municipalities in several of the remaining states had adopted various of the International Codes. California, by contrast, chose to embrace the National Fire Protection Association code, the reported preference of fire officials and labor unions.

2. *State building codes.* In the mid-1970s, 22 states had statewide building codes. By 2003, that figure had risen to 46. The extent of state control should not be exaggerated, however. Nine state codes apply only to public buildings. Only 28 state codes govern single-family dwellings. Moreover, while a few states such as Connecticut and New Jersey prevent localities from stiffening state code standards (see, e.g., N.J. Stat. Ann. §§52:27D-119 to -141 (West 2004)), most do not preempt local action. See, e.g., Cal. Health & Safety Code §17958.5 (West Supp. 2004); Mass. Gen. Laws ch. 143, §98 (2004); Ohio Rev. Code Ann. §3781.01 (Anderson 2004). See generally Listokin & Hattis, supra.

3. *Rehabilitation codes.* As noted, building codes apply prospectively to new construction, while housing codes apply retrospectively to existing structures. What code should apply to an existing building about to undergo significant rehabilitation? Traditionally, code officials applied a 25/50 rule. If renovations exceeded 50 percent of the building's total value, they would enforce the building code against the entire building. If the total was between 25 percent and 50 percent, they would apply the building code only to the renovated portions. For projects below 25 percent, officials had wide latitude to determine how stringently to apply the codes.

The 25/50 rule discouraged rehabilitation in two ways. First, local inspectors' discretion over smaller projects made it difficult for contractors to make accurate estimates of rehabilitation costs. Second, given the high costs of selective demolition and rehabilitation, a project that exceeded the 50 percent threshold commonly ended up being far more expensive than constructing a new building from scratch.

Recognizing these problems, in 1997 New Jersey adopted a statewide rehabilitation code (or "smart code"), now codified at N.J. Admin. Code tit. 5, §§23-6.1 to 6.33 (2004). The code immunized existing buildings from the requirements applicable to new construction and established separate requirements for five different levels of rehabilitation. In the year following its enactment, the New Jersey code triggered a 60 percent increase in rehabilitation-related construction in the state's five largest cities. Lori Montgomery, "Smart Code" Targets Crumbling Buildings, Wash. Post, Apr. 24, 2000, at B1.

In 2000, Maryland and Rhode Island passed similar legislation. In 2003, the ICC released the first edition of the International Existing Building Code, which was promptly adopted in Michigan (Mich. Admin. Code r. 408.30551 (Supp. 2004)), and Pennsylvania (34 Pa. Code §403.27(b) (2003)). Several large cities, including St. Louis and Wilmington, also have joined the parade.

4. *A federal code for manufactured housing.* In 1974 Congress enacted the National Manufactured Housing Construction and Safety Standards Act. The statute preempts state and local standards applicable to the construction of mobile homes. See 42 U.S.C. §4503(d) (2004). What policy and political factors make mobile home regulation a prime candidate for federal regulation? What clause of Article One of the Constitution provided Congress the power to enact this statute? See Douglas Kmiec, Manufactured Home Siting: Regulatory Challenges and a Proposal for Federal Deregulation, Part II, 6 Zoning & Plan. L. Rep. 113 (1983).

What sorts of municipal regulations does this federal statute preempt? Compare Scurlock v. City of Lynn Haven, 858 F.2d 1521 (11th Cir. 1998) (holding statute preempted application of municipal building code), with King v. City of Bainbridge, 577 S.E.2d 772 (Ga. 2003) (holding that statute did not preempt city's use of zoning powers to restrict mobile homes to mobile home parks). On the legality of local policies that exclude manufactured housing, see also p. 788.

5. *Frontiers of code regulation.* The scope of building regulation seems to be ever expanding. For example:

a. *Energy efficiency.* The energy crisis of the 1970s spawned code innovations designed to promote conservation and use of alternative energy sources. Governments at all levels took initiatives that have stimulated greater use of insulation, insulated windows, fluorescent lighting, and other energy-saving features. State public utility commissions also have pressed utility companies to offer customers incentives to reduce consumption. In the Energy Policy and Conservation Act of 1992, Congress mandated that a home toilet use not more than 1.6 gallons per flush. 42 U.S.C. §6295(k)(1)(A) (2004). Why shouldn't housing consumers be free to choose to install uninsulated windows or traditional toilets that consume 3.5 gallons per flush? What imperfections in energy pricing conceivably might justify these ostensibly paternalistic controls? What if a local government were to impose onerous energy standards, such as solar hot-water heating, on new construction for the purpose of controlling growth and driving up the price of existing housing? See Chapter 9D.

b. *Access for the disabled.* Code requirements designed to improve access for wheelchair users, blind persons, and other disabled individuals have markedly affected the layouts of both new and existing buildings. Two pioneering measures were New York City's Local Law 58, approved in 1987, and the New Jersey Handicapped Access Law, N.J. Stat. Ann. §§52:32-4 to -16 (West 2004), which dates from the 1970s. On the latter, see D.I.A.L. v. Department of Consumer Affairs, 603 A.2d 967 (N.J. Super. Ct. App. Div. 1992) (holding Handicapped Access Law did not exempt designated historic landmarks from retrofit requirements). The federal Fair Housing Amendments Act of 1988 required providers of new multifamily dwellings to include some units with doors, hallways, kitchens, and bathrooms that accommodate wheelchair users. 42 U.S.C. §3604(f)(3)(C) (2004).

The provisions of the Americans with Disabilities Act (ADA) of 1990, 42 U.S.C. §12183 (2004), which govern the design of new and altered public accommodations, reach much further. In Pinnock v. International House of Pancakes Franchisee, 844 F. Supp. 574 (S.D. Cal. 1993), provisions of the ADA that require the owner of a place of public accommodation to retrofit for wheelchair access were held not to be unconstitutionally vague and also not to effect a taking of property. Detailed ADA regulations appear in 28 C.F.R. §§36.101–608 & Pt. 36, App. A ("ADA Accessibility Guidelines") (2003). Examine and appraise the provisions in Figure 5-8, a page from the Guidelines.

The ADA authorizes private actions against owners, lessees, lessors, and operators of noncompliant public accommodations. See 42 U.S.C. §12182 (2004). Is an architect who has designed an inaccessible public accommodation also vulnerable to suit under the ADA? Compare United States v. Ellerbe Becket, Inc., 976 F. Supp. 1262 (D. Minn. 1997) (yes), with Lonberg v. Sanborn Theaters, Inc., 259 F.3d 1029 (9th Cir. 2001) (no, but not reaching question of architect's possible contractual and tort liabilities). See also Adam A. Milani, "Oh, Say, Can I See — and Who Do I Sue If I Can't?": Wheelchair Users, Sightlines over Standing Spectators, and Architect Liability Under the Americans with Disabilities Act, 3 Fla. L. Rev. 523 (2000) (arguing that architects are in the best position to ensure compliance).

stall and any obstruction may be reduced to a minimum of 42 in (1065 mm) (Fig. 30).

4.17.6 Grab Bars. Grab bars complying with the length and positioning shown in Fig. 30(a), (b), (c), and (d) shall be provided. Grab bars may be mounted with any desired method as long as they have a gripping surface at the locations shown and do not obstruct the required clear floor area. Grab bars shall comply with 4.26.

4.18 Urinals.

4.18.1 General. Accessible urinals shall comply with 4.18.

4.18.2 Height. Urinals shall be stall-type or wall-hung with an elongated rim at a maximum of 17 in (430 mm) above the finish floor.

4.18.3 Clear Floor Space. A clear floor space 30 in by 48 in (760 mm by 1220 mm) shall be provided in front of urinals to allow forward approach. This clear space shall adjoin or overlap an accessible route and shall comply with 4.2.4. *Urinal shields that do not extend beyond the front edge of the urinal rim may be provided with 29 in (735 mm) clearance between them.*

4.18.4 Flush Controls. Flush controls shall be hand operated or automatic, and shall comply with 4.27.4, and shall be mounted no more than 44 in (1120 mm) above the finish floor.

4.19 Lavatories and Mirrors.

4.19.1 General. The requirements of 4.19 shall apply to lavatory fixtures, vanities, and built-in lavatories.

4.19.2 Height and Clearances. Lavatories shall be mounted with *the rim or counter surface no higher than 34 in (865 mm) above the finish floor.* Provide a clearance of at least 29 in (735 mm) above the finish floor to the bottom of the apron. Knee and toe clearance shall comply with Fig. 31.

4.19.3 Clear Floor Space. A clear floor space 30 in by 48 in (760 mm by 1220 mm) complying with 4.2.4 shall be provided in front of a lavatory to allow forward approach. Such

clear floor space shall adjoin or overlap an accessible route and shall extend a maximum of 19 in (485 mm) underneath the lavatory (see Fig. 32).

4.19.4 Exposed Pipes and Surfaces. Hot water and drain pipes under lavatories shall be insulated or otherwise *configured to protect against contact.* There shall be no sharp or abrasive surfaces under lavatories.

4.19.5 Faucets. Faucets shall comply with 4.27.4. Lever-operated, push-type, and electronically controlled mechanisms are examples of acceptable designs. *If self-closing valves are*

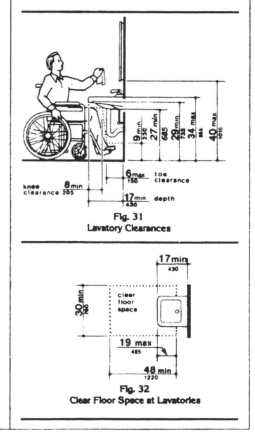

Fig. 31
Lavatory Clearances

Fig. 32
Clear Floor Space at Lavatories

44

Source: 28 C.F.R., Pt. 36, App. A, p. 44 (Lavatories and Mirrors) (2003).

FIGURE 5-8
Excerpt from Americans with Disabilities Act Accessibility Guidelines

A successful ADA complainant can win injunctive relief and attorney fees, but not an award of damages. The statute nevertheless has given rise to a spate of test litigation. Some observers contend that courts have been too reluctant to recognize standing to bring an ADA action. See Adam A. Milani, Wheelchair Users Who Lack "Standing": Another Procedural Threshold Blocking Enforcement of Titles II and III of the ADA, 39 Wake Forest L. Rev. 69 (2004).

The ADA also has drawn criticism. Some observers assert that it gives rise to frivolous litigation, for example, to a Miami attorney who filed 700 complaints in a three-year period, typically settling for $3,000 to $5,000 and a promise from the defendant to correct the violations. See Walter Olson, The ADA Shakedown Racket, City J., Winter 2004, at 80, 82. Other critics contend that various provisions in accessibility laws are not cost-justified. See, e.g., Jack Richman, A New York Law that Disables Builders, N.Y. Times, Nov. 23, 1988, at A23; James Taranto, Mindless Law in Topless Bar, City J., Summer 1991, at 12. And some commentators are concerned about the ADA's potential negative effects on historic preservation efforts. See Grant P. Fondo, Access Reigns Supreme: Title III of the Americans with Disabilities Act and Historic Preservation, 9 B.Y.U. J. Pub. L. 99 (1994).

On challenges to zoning restrictions based on the ADA and other legal authorities that protect the disabled, see pp. 716–30.

c. *Earthquake safety*. States, local governments, and drafters of uniform codes have been stiffening earthquake safety standards for both new and existing construction. See, e.g., California's Unreinforced Masonry Building Law, Cal. Gov't Code §§8875–8875.95 (West 2004) (first enacted in 1986); William D. Schulze, Benefits and Costs of Earthquake Resistant Buildings, 53 S. Econ. J. 934 (1987); Michael D. Turner, Paradigms, Pigeonholes, and Precedent: Reflections on Regulatory Control of Residential Construction, 23 Whittier L. Rev. 3, 62–64 (2001).

d. *Protection against terrorism*. Following the terrorist attacks of September 11, 2001, New York City appointed a task force to assess the adequacy of the city building code. The panel recommended several measures, for example, to protect against bioterrorism, a requirement that air intake ducts be located at least 20 feet above street level. See New York City Dep't of Buildings, World Trade Center Building Code Task Force, Findings and Recommendations, Feb. 2003. An office in the U.S. Commerce Department also began considering development of national building and fire code standards for skyscrapers. See Bill Miller, Attacks May Bring Changes in Building Codes, Wash. Post, Mar. 7, 2002, at A2. Cf. Neal Kumar Katyal, Architecture as Crime Control, 111 Yale L.J. 1039 (2002).

2.   Code Administration

a.   The Dynamics of Building Regulation

The Babel Development Company (Babel) sought to construct a high-rise apartment building in the city of Shinar. The project, named Babel Towers, called for erection of a 15-story masonry-clad building on land owned by Babel and located in Shinar's fire zone number three. The land was zoned for multifamily residential structures. Shinar has a local building code based on the ICC's International Residential Code (2000) with substantial modifications. The city's Department of Building and Engineering Safety administers Shinar's building code. The department also administers the plumbing, electrical, and heating codes of the state of Canaan in which Shinar is situated.

On June 13, Babel submitted to the department two sets of plans (scale drawings) and specifications (lists of materials to be used) for Babel Towers, along with completed

"Application for Building Permit" and "Request for Plan Review" forms. Based on the estimated valuation ($28 million), Babel paid a plan-checking fee of $14,200.

One set of plans was then reviewed by one of the building department's plan examiners to assure conformance with applicable code and zoning requirements. The other circulated to the urban planning, fire, and health departments for approval.

Six weeks after submitting the plan and application, Babel received a "Plan Correction Sheet" from the Department of Building and Engineering Safety. The department declined to approve the plans because they failed to indicate required soil bearing data and because required wet standpipes had been omitted.

Babel Development corrected the plans and the department approved them. Babel then paid the building-permit fee of $14,200 (based on the $28 million valuation) and obtained the building permit. One copy of the building permit and approved plans and specifications was sent to the construction site, and construction commenced.

After the excavation for the concrete foundation had been completed and the forms and reinforcing rods positioned, work ceased. A phone call was placed to the Building Department so the department could send an inspector. The inspector examined the soil, forms, reinforcing rods, and concrete mixture. He then recorded his approval on the building permit and authorized the work to continue.

At this point, the subcontractors who had been hired to install the plumbing, electrical, and heating systems mailed their plans and permit applications to the Department of Building and Engineering Safety. The department found the mechanical plans and mechanical contractors' licenses to be in order. Therefore, the mechanical permits were issued on payment of the appropriate fees.

After the foundation had been poured and back-filled, a crisis arose. Moab's Mud, Inc., canceled a contract to supply mortar for the brick exterior walls of Babel Towers. Forty days of heavy rains had filled Moab's sand pits. Although Babel tried to locate a substitute mortar supply, the rains and resultant flooding had created a great demand for sand for use in building levees and rebuilding damaged buildings. Because of the severe sand shortage, Babel could obtain no mortar. Work on the Babel Towers project ceased.

When 120 days had passed without any work, the building permit expired by its own terms. Shortly thereafter, Babel learned that an oil company named Arko was marketing bitumen, a petroleum derivative, as a mortar substitute. Supplies were virtually unlimited since a number of Arko tankers had ridden out the flooding. Arko agreed to supply enough bitumen to meet Babel's needs.

Because the original permit had expired, Babel had to apply for a new building permit. Babel's new specifications did not indicate that bitumen was to be used to bond the brick walls. Because the building department had received complaints about Babel's abandonment of the project, the department required Babel to post a $500,000 completion bond to cover the cost of demolition should Babel abandon the project permanently. After Babel paid a reissuance fee of $14,400, the department issued a new permit.

After the exterior walls were complete and the roof, plumbing, and heating systems in place, a second inspection was made. On noticing the use of bitumen, the inspector issued a stop-work order because the bitumen was not permitted by the Shinar building code. He ordered Nathan Nimrod, president of Babel Development, to appear at a building department hearing to show cause why a demolition order for the brick walls should not be issued.

At the hearing before the chief building official, the inspector described Babel's use of bitumen instead of mortar. An engineer from Arko testified on Babel's behalf, introducing laboratory reports that indicated that relevant ASTM tests had shown bitumen to have compressive strength and bonding characteristics equal to ordinary mortar. The chief building official explained that, although bitumen seemed a reasonable substitute for the mortar called for by the code, his ministerial position did not give him authority to approve substitutions. Babel would have to obtain a variance from the appeals board.

The appeals board for the Department of Building and Engineering Safety consisted of five citizens appointed by the mayor. There were two engineers, one architect, a contractor, and a university professor. The chief building official sat ex officio and acted as recording secretary. Babel's case was considered at the board's regular monthly meeting. The board members agreed that bitumen seemed to have bonding characteristics equivalent to mortar.

However, the board was concerned about what would happen to the bitumen in the event of a fire. It was agreed that the board would approve Babel's use of bitumen in this instance contingent on the results of independent testing of its fire resistance. If the bitumen joints proved less fire resistant than standard mortar joints, Babel would be required to compensate by installing automatic sprinklers throughout Babel Towers.

Tests were conducted by a laboratory approved by the building department and were paid for by Babel. They indicated that although bitumen, unlike mortar, was flammable, the bitumen/brick system resisted fire just as well as the standard mortar/brick system. The chief building official authorized the completion of Babel Towers without automatic sprinklers.

Work on the Babel Towers was then completed without incident. The building passed the required electrical, plumbing, boiler, elevator, interior wallboard, and final inspections. A certificate of occupancy was issued. Babel Development began leasing the apartments and within six months the building achieved 95 percent occupancy. The use of bitumen in lieu of mortar never caused any problems. But for some inexplicable reason, the building's intercom system never seemed to work properly. Cf. GEN. 11: 1–9.

Stephen R. Seidel, Housing Costs and Government Regulations
88 (1978)

Code Implementation in New York City. Two recent reports, one by the New York Times and the other by New York's Department of Investigations, have uncovered widespread corruption in the city's Building Department. The Department of Investigation's undercover unit reported that: " . . . we found virtually 100 percent of the City employees with whom we had contact were directly involved in corrupt acts or had knowledge of their existence." The report estimated that the "average corrupt inspector or supervisor" could at least double his salary through illicit cash payments. The New York Times report estimated that about 1 percent of total construction costs or $25 million annually was paid out as graft. Both these investigations noted that a considerable number of these bribes were not used to get building officials to approve construction which falls below code standards. Rather developers simply wish to avoid harassment by building officials and to avoid costly delays in obtaining the many approvals required during the construction process.

Note on the Dynamics of Building Regulation

1. *Dispute resolution without lawyers.* Time is of the essence during construction. As a result, participants in a building project are unlikely to turn to lawyers and drawn-out legal processes to resolve disputes with building officials. Architects and building owners instead

commonly employ nonlawyer consultants and expediters to help navigate the process. See Sarah Bartlett, A New York Trade Thrives on Red Tape, N.Y. Times, Sept. 13, 1991, at A1 (reporting existence of 300 to 400 expediters in New York City (prior to the reforms mentioned below)). A builder's need for speedy approvals gives building officials great leverage and leads, in some jurisdictions, to graft.

2. *New York, New York.* Although most municipalities adopt a model code, New York City long has had its own. Critics of the nearly 2,000-page document call it "stringent, voluminous, detailed, complex, cumbersome and arcane," and an impediment to the construction of affordable housing. Jerry J. Salama et al., Reducing the Cost of New Housing Construction in New York City 94–95, 102 (1999). The 2005 edition of the Salama et al. study, however, describes momentum in New York City toward adoption of the International Building Code and other model codes, albeit with amendments. On the history of corruption among city building inspectors, see New York State Organized Crime Task Force, Corruption and Racketeering in the New York City Construction Industry 109–16 (1990). The task force recommended that the city privatize inspections, either by hiring firms to perform them or by authorizing supervising architects and engineers to certify that the work performed satisfied code requirements. Id. at 234–35. The city later adopted the latter recommendation, easing the burden of the overworked Department of Buildings. For mixed reviews of this innovation, see Dennis Hevesi, When Builders Are Inspectors, N.Y. Times, Dec. 3, 2000, §11, at 1.

Although New York traditionally has surpassed most other cities in corruption, it is hardly alone. See, e.g., Cruz v. Town of Cicero, 275 F.3d 579 (7th Cir. 2001) (affirming award of $402,000 and attorney fees against Illinois town for corruptly delaying issuance of certificates of compliance).

3. *Walk right in.* A building inspector typically does not need a warrant to enter a building site because only minimal expectations of privacy are at stake. See Frey v. Panza, 621 F.2d 596 (3d Cir. 1980).

4. *The temptation to evade regulation.* A typical homeowner, while unlikely to erect a new building, may well desire to transform a basement into a family room, an attic into a bedroom, or a yard into an enclosed patio. Although the local building code may require a permit for any of these alterations, in practice, many renovators fail to procure one. A homeowner on a quiet residential street stands a good chance of being able to complete a substantial alteration without the building department's knowledge. Evasion is even simpler in rural areas. See Project, Rural Land Use Regulation in Iowa, 68 Iowa L. Rev. 1083, 1134, 1270 (1983) (noting that many rural owners commence construction without required permits). Young people experimenting with back-to-nature lifestyles are notorious for building without notifying the local government. See Ann Japenga, Housing Rights in Sonoma County: Rural Dwellers Seek Own Style, L.A. Times, Aug. 23, 1981, §4, at 1.

By evading code enforcement, a builder saves permit and plan-inspection fees, the additional costs of any code-required overengineering, and perhaps a good deal of time and red tape. In addition, the tax assessor may not get wind of the improvements. While serving as mayor of Philadelphia, Frank Rizzo is alleged to have installed $340,000 in home renovations without a permit, apparently to avoid a higher property-tax assessment. L.A. Times, Sept. 10, 1975, §1, at 13.

When a builder is caught in an attempt to "bootleg" a construction project (i.e., build without a permit), the building department may insist that the project be brought up to code before it will issue a certificate of occupancy. Compare pp. 92–94, a discussion of sanctions imposed on violators of zoning ordinances. In addition, when an owner desires to sell, subcode work performed without a permit may create apprehensions on the part of potential buyers (and their lenders).

b.   *Remedying Lawless Code Enforcement by Government*

Commonwealth v. Collins
654 S.W.2d 608 (Ky. Ct. App. 1983)

HOWARD, Judge.

This is an appeal from a negligence case in which the trial court upheld an award of the Board of Claims in favor of the appellee in the sum of approximately $35,000.

The appellee ("Collins"), in 1978, owned three parcels of land in Campbell County, Kentucky. All 127 acres were located outside any city limits and were not served by a public water supply. In the Spring of 1978, Collins proceeded with plans to build a retirement home on the smallest of his three parcels, that being about 3.48 acres. He had sold his home in Cincinnati the previous year and moved with his family into an apartment until their new home could be built. From the sale of the Cincinnati home, Collins realized a capital gain of $21,150.00, which he hoped to defer by occupying his newly constructed home within two (2) years, pursuant to the Internal Revenue Code.

In May, 1978, Collins applied for and received a building permit. Appellant Frank Weibel approved this permit in his capacity as a State Plumbing Inspector. On November 15, 1978, Collins was granted a plumbing construction permit, also signed by Weibel. In conjunction with this permit, Collins signed an affidavit stating that he would install plumbing in compliance with K.R.S. Chapter 318, the State Plumbing Law.

On November 17, 1978, Weibel visited the building site and observed plastic pipe in the ground, which was at that time prohibited by state law. Weibel placed a stop plumbing work order on the job site and the construction on the house ceased. Collins immediately protested the stop work order, realizing that work on his house could not proceed until it was resolved. He refused to remove the plastic pipe.

On October 3, 1979, appellant, Department of Housing, Building and Construction ("Department") filed a criminal complaint against Collins and on November 30, 1979, he was convicted in district court of violating the State Plumbing Code. Collins filed for dismissal in district court and on February 15, 1980, the case was dismissed.

After this criminal violation was dismissed, about fifteen months after the stop work order was issued, Collins became ill and was unable to continue work on his house until the Fall of 1980. By this time, prices and interest rates had gone up considerably and he was unable to procure financing for building. On January 21, 1981, Collins filed a claim with the Kentucky Board of Claims ("Board") alleging negligence on the part of the Department based on the actions of its employees in halting construction on Collins' house. The Board determined that the Department and its employees were negligent in their acts toward Collins and awarded him $35,359. The Department appealed to Campbell Circuit Court and the trial court agreed with the Board and upheld the award. We affirm. . . .

As Collins points out, he did not claim that the inspections and subsequent stop work order were performed negligently but that the Department was negligent in performing them at all and that he sustained substantial loss as a result of these acts. Collins is correct in his assertion that since the code provision under which his work was ordered stopped does not apply to him, the Department was negligent in continuing to pursue its enforcement. K.R.S. Chapter 318, the State Plumbing Law under which Collins was prosecuted, specifically exempts "farmsteads" from its provisions. K.R.S. 318.015(3). The Department was, or should have been, aware of the fact that Collins' property was not serviced by any city water system, was not located within a municipality and appeared to be a farm. By issuing the stop work order, the appellants violated their duty of care, creating an "actionable negligence" resulting in injury to Collins. M&T Chem., Inc. v. Westrick, 525 S.W.2d 740 (Ky. 1974).

The appellants also argue that the Department was engaging in the ultimate function of government by "protecting the public through enforcement of the State Plumbing Code." They appear to be saying that they are therefore immune from liability. If they had been indeed enforcing the code, this argument may have had merit since K.R.S. 318 obviously exists to regulate plumbing practices in an effort to protect the public health. However, the code expressly excludes applicability to farmsteads and no public purpose or government function was being advanced by its injurious application here. . . .

Note on Remedies Against Building Departments

1. *Remedial options.* Why did Collins seek damages instead of a mandatory injunction to free himself from the regulatory snare?

2. *Damages for wrongful denial of a building permit.* A California statute immunizes governments and officials from liability for wrongfully withholding a building permit. See Burns v. City Council, 107 Cal. Rptr. 787 (Ct. App. 1973). How constitutionally vulnerable is this statute? In Ali v. City of Los Angeles, 91 Cal. Rptr. 2d 458 (Ct. App. 1999), the court found a temporary taking when the city had refused to approve a demolition permit, thereby preventing the owner from clearing a fire-damaged hotel from his property. The next-to-last paragraph of Justice Rehnquist's opinion in *First English*, at p. 261, implies that interim damages may be available under the federal Takings Clause for losses that exceed those incurred as a result of "normal delays in obtaining building permits." A developer who suffers an abnormal delay therefore may pursue a §1983 action for a taking or, as in the following two cases, a denial of due process. As is common in land use litigation, a claim of this sort is likely to fare better in state court than in federal court. In Mission Springs, Inc. v. City of Spokane, 954 P.2d 250 (Wash. 1998), the court remanded for trial a damages action against city and local elected officials who had improperly denied a grading permit for a 790-unit apartment complex. But see Natale v. Town of Ridgefield, 170 F.3d 258 (2d Cir. 1999) (reversing jury award of $1 million against town). How significant would a vested right to build (see pp. 202–09) be if a locality were never held liable for delay damages?

3. *Damages for wrongful delays after construction has started.* Courts tend to be particularly sympathetic to a claim for interim damages stemming (as in *Collins*) from an abnormal delay that a government unlawfully caused *after* construction had commenced. See, e.g., Samaritan Inns, Inc. v. District of Columbia, 114 F.3d 1227 (D.C. Cir. 1997) (generally affirming awards of damages against both District and its officials on account of unlawful order interrupting nonprofit corporation's construction of facility for former drug and alcohol abusers); Town of Orangetown v. Magee, 665 N.E.2d 1061 (N.Y. 1996) (affirming award of $5.1 million to developer of industrial building whose building permit had been wrongly revoked in midst of construction to placate neighbors opposed to project). But cf. Raben-Pastel v. City of Coconut Creek, 573 So. 2d 298 (Fla. 1990) (trial court properly set aside verdict of $2.5 million against city because building officer's actions did not represent official city policy).

4. *Damages for lax enforcement?* In Dinsky v. Town of Framingham, 438 N.E.2d 51 (Mass. 1982), the buyers of a new house who had suffered from flooding of their lot sought to recover damages from the town for negligent code enforcement during construction. The court rejected the claim, adopting the majority rule that building officials do not owe a duty of care to private citizens. The court worried that municipalities, if potentially liable, might refrain from "enacting regulations designed for the protection and welfare of the public." Id. at 56. What about the risk that, if liable, municipalities would be too stickling in code enforcement? In Wisconsin, where a municipality may be liable for negligent enforcement, a statute sets a ceiling of $25,000 on recoveries. See Wood v. Milin, 397

N.W.2d 479 (Wis. 1986). See generally Scott J. Barth, Comment, Municipal Tort Liability for Wrongful Issuance of Building Permits: A National Survey, 58 Wash. L. Rev. 537 (1983).

5. *Neighbor's rights to halt a project.* Neighbors must seek judicial review promptly if they deem that a building permit has been granted improperly. Otherwise the builder may successfully assert a defense based on estoppel or the expiration of the (usually short) statute of limitations. See Shors v. Johnson, 581 N.W.2d 648 (Iowa 1998) (holding that prior failure to exhaust administrative remedies barred neighbor from seeking judicial review of building permit); Trenkamp v. Township of Burlington, 406 A.2d 218 (N.J. 1979) (comprehensively reviewing New Jersey law on neighbor suits to stop building projects). Should a neighbor who ultimately loses a suit of this sort be liable to the builder for interim damages caused?

6. *Procedural due process.* When a builder or neighbor appeals a building official's decision to a local board of appeals, must the board provide a noticed hearing? Have express standards to guide its decisions? Issue written findings and an opinion? What standard of judicial review of board decisions is appropriate? Is it relevant that the issuance of a building permit is routinely regarded as a "ministerial" act? Compare the materials on judicial review of zoning decisions in Chapter 4 and on subdivision-map decisions in Chapter 5A.

3.   *Evaluation of Building Codes*

a.   *Asserted Inefficiencies*

Stephen R. Seidel, Housing Costs and Government Regulations
73–75, 77, 90–91 (1978)

The most extensive evaluation of building codes dates back to the 1968 report prepared by the Douglas Commission. Unnecessary costs are inherent in building codes that:

1. Delay construction,
2. Prevent the use of modern materials,
3. Inhibit creative design,
4. Include antiquated and outdated provisions,
5. Lack effective procedures for updating,
6. Are controlled by a small group of special interests,
7. Are enforced by inadequately trained and qualified officials,
8. Lack a proper appeal procedure,
9. Are often arbitrarily enforced by local officials,
10. Inhibit the marketing of mobile homes and prefab units,
11. Prevent large-scale building,
12. Should be administered at the state level.

Summing up these inefficiencies, two commentators writing for the Kaiser Committee estimated that building code reform could achieve savings ranging from 1.5 to 7 percent of the total cost of a unit. . . .

MARKET DISTORTIONS CAUSED BY BUILDING CODES

While ensuring that certain public goals are met, building codes do create inefficiencies in the free market. Codes establish minimum levels of housing quality and require that all consumers, regardless of their individual consumption preferences, purchase at least a minimum package of quality and safety features. Such requirements prevent the market from reaching its own equilibrium point. Yet granting that government must establish the minimum level of standards, there is no feasible method for determining the optimum level of safety and stability to be required by building codes. For example, several additional safety features, such as smoke detectors and ground fault interruptors, have recently been added to the list of requirements in many jurisdictions, often without adequate consideration of either their cost-effectiveness or consumer preference.

The second market distortion caused by the minimum standards of building codes is that they require home buyers to invest present dollars to ensure future soundness. This is required despite the fact that most home buyers' incomes will increase rapidly over the years and they would therefore be better capable of affording these structural improvements at some later date. Nonetheless, building codes impose those costs on them at the time of the initial purchase of the unit, a time when they least can afford it. This problem is further compounded by traditional mortgage availability criteria which is based entirely on present earnings. . . .

The Code Approval Process: The Story of Plastic Pipes

A new building product has little chance of gaining a foothold in the market unless it first is incorporated into building codes. Nor is this a simple achievement; it can take many years and cost millions of dollars. While probably not typical of the approval process, the fate of plastic pipes serves as a warning of what may happen to those who seek to market a new building product.

Acrylonitrile-butadiene-styrene (ABS) pipe was invented by the U.S. Rubber Company in 1948. Its first widespread use was in the mobile home industry, where it became an established feature as early as 1958. Two years later, the Federal Housing Authority (FHA) approved of its use for residential construction in drain, waste and vent (DWV) plumbing. It was not until 1966 that the first model code group, the Southern Building Code Congress, approved of its use for DWV plumbing. However, once model code approval is received, the war is still not won. It then becomes necessary for local governments, who are not obligated to adopt model code changes, to decide for themselves whether or not to accept this material. As shown by our code currency survey questions, roughly 30 percent of the municipalities sampled still prohibit the use of this material.

For many years, the Plastic Pipe Institute, in an attempt to gain regulatory acceptance of its product, has lobbied before such groups as model code meetings, state legislatures, Congress, and, most frequently, local building departments. It estimates that approximately $500,000 has been spent annually to support these lobbying efforts. Much of the resistance has been generated by the Cast Iron Soil Pipe Institute, the trade association for competitive pipes currently accepted by model codes. Other dissenting voices were those of labor unions fearing that the ease of installing plastic pipe would eliminate their jobs. This illustration suggests that the administration of building codes has a significant dampening effect on innovation in the building materials industry. . . .

Note on the Costs and Benefits of Codes

1. *Another code war*. In Allied Tube & Conduit Corp. v. Indian Head, Inc., 486 U.S. 492 (1988), the Supreme Court held that the *Noerr* doctrine does not exempt from antitrust liability persons who urge a private code-writing organization to engage in anticompetitive action. The case arose out of efforts by a manufacturer of a plastic conduit for electrical

wires to have its product approved by the association that publishes the highly influential National Electrical Code. Justice Brennan's majority opinion describes the key events:

> . . . Following approval by one of the Association's professional panels, this proposal was scheduled for consideration at the 1980 annual meeting, where it could be adopted or rejected by a simple majority of the members present. Alarmed that, if approved, respondent's product might pose a competitive threat to steel conduit, petitioner, the Nation's largest producer of steel conduit, met to plan strategy with, among others, members of the steel industry, other steel conduit manufacturers, and its independent sales agents. They collectively agreed to exclude respondent's product from the 1981 Code by packing the upcoming annual meeting with new Association members whose only function would be to vote against the polyvinyl chloride proposal.
>
> Combined, the steel interests recruited 230 persons to join the Association and to attend the annual meeting to vote against the proposal. Petitioner alone recruited 155 persons — including employees, executives, sales agents, the agents' employees, employees from two divisions that did not sell electrical products, and the wife of a national sales director. Petitioner and the other steel interests also paid over $100,000 for the membership, registration, and attendance expenses of these voters. At the annual meeting, the steel group voters were instructed where to sit and how and when to vote by group leaders who used walkie-talkies and hand signals to facilitate communication. Few of the steel group voters had any of the technical documentation necessary to follow the meeting. None of them spoke at the meeting to give their reasons for opposing the proposal to approve polyvinyl chloride conduit. Nonetheless, with their solid vote in opposition, the proposal was rejected and returned to committee by a vote of 394 to 390. Respondent appealed the membership's vote to the Association's Board of Directors, but the Board denied the appeal on the ground that, although the Association's rules had been circumvented, they had not been violated.[1]

Id. at 496–97. Would the steel interests have behaved in the same manner after the *Allied Tube* decision? For more on federal antitrust law, see pp. 119–24.

2. *Measuring costs.* Every ten years or so, the president appoints a national commission that ends up bemoaning the cost-inflating features of building codes (as well as other land use regulations). See, e.g., Advisory Commission on Regulatory Barriers to Affordable Housing, "Not in My Back Yard": Removing Barriers to Affordable Housing (1991) (Keane Commission); Report of the President's Commission on Housing 216–22 (1982); National Commission on Urban Problems, Building the American City 254–72 (1968) (Douglas Commission).

One of the most sophisticated efforts to quantify the costs of building codes appears in Richard F. Muth & Elliot Wetzler, The Effect of Constraints on House Costs, 3 J. Urb. Econ. 57 (1976). Using FHA-supplied data, the authors performed a regression analysis to determine variables correlated with higher construction costs. They found (perhaps surprisingly) that the presence of a locally drafted building code did not correlate with higher construction costs. However, if a local government had adopted a model code and then modified it, the authors' data indicated that construction costs would be 2 percent higher in that jurisdiction than in one that had adopted a model code and not tampered with it. The biggest "constraint" the authors found was unionization of the building trades, which produced a 4 percent increase in construction costs.

See also Charles G. Field & Steven R. Rivkin, The Building Code Burden (1975); Jerry J. Salama et al., Reducing the Cost of New Housing Construction in New York City: 2005 Update (2005); Raymond J. Burby et al., Building Code Enforcement Burdens and

---

1. . . . The Association subsequently approved use of polyvinyl chloride conduit for buildings of less than three stories in the 1984 Code, and for all buildings in the 1987 Code.

Central City Decline, 66 J. Am. Plan. Ass'n 143 (2000); Eric Damian Kelly, Fair Housing, Good Housing or Expensive Housing? Are Building Codes Part of the Problem or Part of the Solution?, 29 J. Marshall L. Rev. 349 (1996); Eli Noam, The Interaction of Building Codes and Housing Prices, 10 AREUEA J. 394 (1983).

3. *Measuring benefits.* According to National Safety Council data, in the United States the annual death rate from fire fell from 100 per million in 1918, to 40 per million in 1960, to 12 per million in 2000. Would it be possible to determine how much of this reduction in fire risks was attributable to building codes?

4. *Toward more flexible administration?* In The Death of Common Sense (1994), Philip Howard criticizes two trends that he identifies: a proliferation of legal rules and a decline in administrative judgment. Howard begins with a tale of New York City's insistence that Mother Teresa's order of nuns include an elevator in a four-story structure they intended to renovate into a facility for the homeless. The nuns' vows would have barred them from using the elevator, which would have cost upward of $100,000. When the city refused to relax the requirement, the nuns scuttled the project. Howard also recounts New York City's abandonment of a proposed experiment with coin-operated sidewalk toilet kiosks when protesters noted that the individual kiosks would not be wheelchair accessible. Id. at 113–16. The overarching reform that Howard proposes is an increase in the discretion of field staff: "Decision making must be transferred, from words on a page back to people on the spot. This requires legal frameworks that are open, not open-and-shut." Id. at 186. In an "open" framework, what would be the nature of judicial review of building officials' decisions? Should Howard instead have recommended a general scaling back of regulation?

b.   Builders' Constitutional Challenges to Excessive Code Requirements

Boise Cascade Corp. v. Gwinnett County
272 F. Supp. 847 (N.D. Ga. 1967)

SIDNEY O. SMITH, JR., District Judge.

This is the final trial of a petition by the plaintiff prefabricated-home builder against defendant seeking to enjoin enforcement of a county building code. The case was extensively argued and tried on the preliminary injunction. See 248 F. Supp. 765 (1966). Since the decision in that case, the defendant county has completely revamped its building code and, in effect, has adopted the "Southern Standard Building Code" with three minor amendments. As was indicated earlier there is no dispute over the Southern Standard Building Code itself. Both parties and the court consider it a reasonable exercise of the police power. However, a dispute remains as to two amendments which provide:

(1)   "Where any ceiling joist shall be spaced more than 16 inches on center and a plywood decking is used, said decking must be at least 1/2 inch in thickness."

(2)   "All residential dwellings must be braced at the corner with a minimum of a 1/2 inch plywood corner brace, or a 1/2 corner brace, or a 2/4 corner brace."

The case came on for trial before the court on the issue as to whether such exercise of the police power met the standard of "reasonableness" required and specifically (a) whether the public generally, as distinguished from those of a particular class, require such provisions and (b) whether the provisions are reasonably necessary for the accomplishment of the purpose and not unduly oppressive upon individuals. Lawton v. Steele, 152 U.S. 133,

137 (1894); Mestre v. City of Atlanta, 255 F.2d 401 (5th Cir. 1958). On such trial the court makes the following findings:

(1) Roof Decking

Contrary to the building code, plaintiff uses in its prefabricated home plywood roof-decking of 3/8″ thickness, grade-marked 24/0. Such construction is permitted by the Southern Standard Code as well as VA, FHA, and other recognized national standards. The inquiry into the propriety of plaintiff's construction was complicated but at the same time answered by an industrywide change in the plywood standards which occurred on December 1, 1966. While it is not revealed by the evidence, the court is convinced that such changes were unknown to the county at the time of adoption of its present requirement.

In the constant and continuing progress in research and development in wood materials, manufacturing techniques and standards have changed radically in the last ten years. Originally such changes are initiated by processors, then adopted by the industry trade association (American Plywood Association), and eventually accepted by various standard building codes. The Plywood Association, besides being a promotional and research group, maintains strict quality controls over its members. Compliance is a prime prerequisite to use of trade and grade-marks widely accepted by the public.

Originally, classification of plywood for building purposes related to thickness and species, i.e., Douglas Fir, Southern Pine, spruce, hemlock, etc. As technological advances produced the use of more and more species as well as more and more lamination improvements, the number of standards in existence became cumbersome, as they related to three different use or strength standards and some thirty different species, allocated to various groups. The result was that the public had to perform complicated research to ascertain the building utility of a particular piece of plywood grade marked only as to listed species.

To solve this dilemma, one consolidated standard was adopted to supplant the many pre-existing classifications. In essence, the new standard substitutes a strength test for a species and size test. Thus all plywoods, regardless of species, size, or thickness, are graded by new symbols, indicating strength and rigidity for building purposes. Plywood sheathing panels are now marked 12/0 up to 48/24 indicating comparative strengths, regardless of thickness.

It is abundantly shown both by the standards and codes and by direct evidence of specific deflexion tests conducted by reputable engineering testing companies that the 3/8″ 24/0 plywood used by the plaintiff is the equivalent of the 1/2 plywood required by the code under the old system. Thus, except for certain structural groupings not at issue here, the two requirements are identical and have the same rigidity and strength. Accordingly, there is no hesitancy in concluding that the specific requirement of 1/2 plywood decking is unreasonable and therefore unenforceable, and that the 24/0 requirements of the Southern Standard Building Code is acceptable in all respects for the area in question.

[Discussion of corner-bracing omitted.]

While the county is justified in adopting a building code and specifically in adopting a code specifically covering roof-decking and corner-bracing, the court finds under the evidence that the two provisions adopted in this respect are unreasonable to accomplish this protection of the general public and, therefore, "not reasonably necessary" for such purpose.

Evidence offered by the defendant to the effect that some of plaintiff's homes are being poorly constructed is rejected as irrelevant. Such matters address themselves to compliance with a code rather than the legality of its provisions.

Accordingly, relief will be granted to prevent enforcement of the two amendments attacked, as the plaintiff is otherwise entitled to injunctive relief on the facts proved at the first hearing. See 248 F. Supp. 768. It would appear to the court that this action leaves the Southern Standard Building Code, 1965, as successively amended, in effect in Gwinnett County, but certainly it does not prohibit the adoption of the specific provisions of that Code or any other reasonable building requirement in accordance with this decision. . . .

Note on the Federal Constitution as a Limitation on Code Requirements

1. *Substantive due process.* See also E.J. Bach v. County of St. Clair, 576 N.E.2d 1236 (Ill. Ct. App. 1991), which held that a 14-foot minimum-width requirement for mobile homes lacked a rational basis. See generally Charles G. Field, Judicial Solutions to the Tension Between Construction Codes and Innovation, 4 Urb. L. & Pol'y 107 (1981). But see Levitt & Sons, Inc. v. Young, 74 N.Y.S.2d 120 (Sup. Ct. 1947) (finding a town building code that called for use of 3/4-inch diagonal boards, rather than 5/16-inch plywood, for exterior sheathing was not arbitrary and unreasonable).

2. *Free exercise.* Should building codes apply to someone who objects to modern building methods for religious reasons? Compare State v. Gingerich, 1996 WL 72597 (Ohio Ct. App. Jan. 2, 1996) (upholding fine and three-day jail sentence imposed on Amish man who had refused to comply with plumbing regulations), with Carey v. Town of Westmoreland, 415 A.2d 333 (N.H. 1980) (holding town had been arbitrary and unreasonable in refusing to grant variance from requirement of a septic tank system to Quaker couple whose religious principles led them to prefer using dry compost toilet on rural lot). See also Lisa W. Foderaro, No Wiggle Room in a Window War, N.Y. Times, Nov. 15, 2003, at B1 (documenting the State of New York's attempts to enforce the state building code requirement that bedroom windows be at least 5.7 square feet against an Amish sect whose teachings mandate windows of exactly 5 square feet). In what situations, if any, would RLUIPA, discussed at pp. 210-20, help religious objectors to code enforcement?

3. *Equal protection.* What if code officials especially target the building projects of members of a racial minority? See Boyd v. Board of Councilmen, 77 S.W. 669 (Ky. 1903) (enjoining City of Frankfort from interfering with construction of black church). See also Chapter 8A.

State v. Cook
433 P.2d 677 (Wash. 1967)

FINLEY, Chief Justice.

Appellant, petitioner below, purchased a single-family dwelling and moved it to his lot in Everett. He intended to rent the house, and in preparing it for rental found it necessary to do some plumbing work therein. He applied for a permit to do the plumbing, intending to purchase the materials and do the work himself. Appellant is not a certified plumbing contractor, and made no application for such certification. The permit was denied because the plumbing he intended to do was not in a house occupied or designed to be occupied by him.

Snohomish County has adopted the Uniform Plumbing Code, 1961 Edition, promulgated by the Western Plumbing Officials Association. The preamble to this code states that it is:

An ordinance providing for the protection of the public health and safety, and the qualification and registration of persons engaged in the business of plumbing, or laboring at the trade of plumbing; requiring a permit and inspection for the installation or alteration of plumbing and drainage systems. . . .

Section 1.8 of said code provides that no plumbing work shall be commenced in any building without a permit. The challenged portion of the code, section 1.10, provides that no permit shall be issued for any plumbing or drainage work regulated by the code except to a person holding a valid, unexpired and unrevoked plumbing contractors certificate of qualification.

However, subsection (c) to said section 1.10 contains an exception to the certification requirement under six conditions:

(1)   When the person desires to do plumbing or drainage work in a single family dwelling;
(2)   When such dwelling is to be used exclusively for living purposes;
(3)   When the person who will do the work is the bona fide owner of the dwelling;
(4)   When the dwelling is occupied or designed to be occupied by said owner;
(5)   Provided that said owner shall personally purchase all material;
(6)   Provided that such owner shall personally perform all labor in connection therewith. . . .

Appellant petitioned the trial court for a writ of mandamus, requiring respondent to issue a plumbing permit to appellant. [The trial court denied the writ.]

Appellant contends that since he intends to comply with the code standards, the requirement that nonresident homeowners be licensed to do plumbing on their own premises is not reasonably related to the public health, and therefore unduly restricts his lawful activities upon private property, in violation of the due process provisions of the Washington State Constitution, art. 1, §3, and in violation of the fourteenth amendment to the United States Constitution. . . .

We conclude that the requirement in section 1.10 for certification of nonresident homeowners is part of the total enforcement scheme of the code, and as such is reasonably related to the public health and safety. Such requirement is a valid exercise of the police power, and is not a violation of federal or state due process standards.

This conclusion is based upon the reasoning that a property owner who does plumbing for others, i.e. for prospective tenants or purchasers of this property, has a similar impact upon the public to a commercial plumber. He is to some extent carrying on a commercial activity, since plumbing is an integral part of the property he intends to rent or sell.

Appellant concedes that licensing of commercial plumbers is reasonably related to the public health and safety. Likewise, it must be conceded that one who does any amount of plumbing for others than himself and his immediate family, although it be more limited than that done by commercial plumbers, is in a position similar to commercial plumbers, and can be required to be certified as to requisite skills.

Although one who does plumbing in a residence which he intends to rent or sell is subject to the laws of landlord-tenant, or of contract, such laws are not designed to protect the public health and safety. Nor are such laws adequate for this purpose.

Testimony at trial indicated that some plumbing defects are extremely difficult to detect, even under the detailed inspection required by the plumbing code, and that the plumbing inspectors rely to some extent upon the skill and care of commercial plumbers. Licensed plumbers generally do better work than do nonlicensed plumbers. It is, therefore, reasonable to limit noncertified work, and even though all work must be inspected, there is a legitimate reason for the certification requirement set out in section 1.10.

We cannot say that there is no reasonable relation to public health and safety in the requirement that nonresident homeowners be licensed to do plumbing for others; nor can we say that appellant has been arbitrarily deprived of a lawful right. . . .

The judgment of the trial court is affirmed.

WEAVER, Judge (dissenting). . . .

It should be observed that the ordinance contains no requirement that a resident owner continue to live in his house for any particular length of time. An owner may obtain a permit, do his plumbing work in compliance with the code, live in the house for a time, be it ever so short, and then sell or lease it to others. In no material respect would such an owner differ from one who, from the beginning, plans to rent his house to others and who personally performs identical work with full code compliance. In each case there is the possibility of evasion of the law insofar as bona fide ownership is concerned. In each case the public health and safety is protected by exacting full compliance with code requirements. . . .

Note on Licensing of Contractors

Michael Naturile desired to build a house in Elizabeth, New Jersey, for his family. The city refused to grant him a plumbing permit because he was not a licensed plumber. The city then sought a declaratory judgment sustaining the validity of its application of its licensing requirement in this instance. The court held that the prohibition on an unlicensed person's installing plumbing in his own house violated constitutionally protected property rights (whose exact source the court failed to identify). However, the opinion went on to note that the city might have to spend more time inspecting the work of amateur plumbers than the work of licensed plumbers. If so, the court observed, the city could charge amateurs higher inspection fees. City Council v. Naturile, 345 A.2d 363 (N.J. Super. Ct. Law Div. 1975). Most courts, however, are more deferential to government licensing efforts. See N.J. Marini, Annotation, Validity of Regulations as to Plumbers and Plumbing, 22 A.L.R.2d 816 (1952).

Does a state that preempts a municipality's licensing rules violate the municipality's rights to home rule? See Century Electric Service & Repair, Inc. v. Stone, 564 P.2d 953 (Colo. 1977) (holding Colorado's statewide interests were sufficient for it to preempt Denver's licensing of electricians).

See generally Morris M. Kleiner, Occupational Licensing, 14 J. Econ. Persp. 189 (2000) (analyzing whether these barriers to entry can be justified on grounds of consumer protection).

4.   Applying Standards Retrospectively: Housing Codes

City of St. Louis v. Brune
515 S.W.2d 471 (Mo. 1974)

HENRY I. EAGER, Special Commissioner.

The defendant, appellant, was convicted in the St. Louis Court of Criminal Correction of two violations of a St. Louis Ordinance prescribing minimum housing standards. . . . Section 391.040 required that every dwelling unit "shall have a tub or shower bath in good working condition, properly connected to approved hot and cold water and sewer systems in the toilet room or in a separate room adjacent to such dwelling unit."

Defendant concedes that his units did not and do not contain tubs or showers so connected. . . . The cases were tried together without a jury, the Court found defendant guilty in each case and assessed a fine of $100 and costs against him in each case. No special findings were requested or made. Defendant filed motions to set aside the judgments and for a new trial, specifically raising the point that the Court had erred in sustaining the validity of Section 391.040, supra, because it was unreasonable, arbitrary and confiscatory, that it bore no reasonable relationship to health, welfare or safety, and that it denied to defendant due process under the 14th Amendment to the United States Constitution and took his property for public use without just compensation. . . .

A physician, Dr. Herman Blumenthal, specializing in pathology, testified for defendant: that the purpose of bathing is to remove dirt; that bathing can be done in various ways, and that "there is no special effect in method"; that there is no medical requirement of pipes and a tub; that hot and cold water can be used in any tub or container, and that the absence of a tub or shower from an apartment unit would not, in his opinion, be detrimental to the occupants. . . .

In rebuttal, the city produced Dr. William Blanton who testified: that any dwelling unit without hot water is detrimental to health because of the relative difficulty in removing bacteria without it; that bathing is necessary from a public health standpoint, and that one cannot effectively perform the function of bathing without a tub or shower connected to hot water. . . .

Certain principles seem to have been more or less generally accepted; these are, in substance, the following. Owners of property hold it subject to the reasonable exercise of the police power. The ordinance or other law must, as stated above, bear a reasonable and substantial relation to the public health, welfare or safety; if it does, the power may be exercised without compensation. The cost of the improvement to the owner is not alone decisive of the question, but it may be a material element in a consideration of the reasonableness of the law. In the first instance the legislature has a rather wide discretion and, while the courts may invalidate such a law if arbitrary and unreasonable, they will not in so doing substitute their judgments for those of the legislative bodies; and there is a presumption of constitutionality. On the other hand, there comes a point where the reasonable exercise of the police power ceases, the enforcement of the law becomes confiscatory, and only the right of eminent domain remains; and differences in "degree" constitute material distinctions. . . .

In general, the following requirements have been held valid in other states as to existing buildings, usually apartments or "tenement" houses; rent regulation (Block v. Hirsh, 256 U.S. 135 (1921)); safety and sanitary improvements costing $5,000 on a forty-room tenement assessed at $13,500, details not explained (Adamec v. Post, 7 N.E.2d 120 (N.Y. 1937)); water on each floor in suitable "appliances" (Health Dept. of the City of New York v. Rector, Church Wardens & Vestrymen of Trinity Church, 39 N.E. 833 (N.Y. 1895)); a tub or shower, sink, and toilet with running water (Richards v. City of Columbia, 88 S.E.2d 683 (S.C. 1955), a 3–2 decision); separate lavatories, adequate tubs, sinks (Apple v. City & County of Denver, 390 P.2d 91 (Colo. 1964)); demolition of building which had become a nuisance (Perepletchikoff v. City of Los Angeles, 345 P.2d 261 (Cal. Ct. App. 1959)); adequate fire escapes (City of Seattle v. Hinckley, 82 P. 747 (Wash. 1905)); prohibition of glass panel doors (Kaukas v. City of Chicago, 188 N.E.2d 700 (Ill. 1963)). . . .

In Safer v. City of Jacksonville, 237 So. 2d 8 (Fla. Ct. App. 1970), the city had charged many violations of a municipal housing code, but the ones principally discussed were the absence of lavatories in some units and the lack of hot water to lavatories, tubs or showers in others. The building was valued at about $40,000, and all of the required improvements would have cost approximately $20,000; some of the tenants had been there for 30 years. A jury found that most of the supposed defects were insubstantial. The Court on appeal held that the failure to furnish hot water to the tubs or showers did not adversely affect the health of the tenants, that in this respect, and in view of the cost, the ordinance bore no reasonable relation to the public health and welfare, and that its enforcement would be confiscatory.

In Dente v. City of Mt. Vernon, 272 N.Y.S.2d 65 (N.Y. Sup. Ct. 1966), the Court held unconstitutional, as applied to plaintiff's property, an amended ordinance which required a tub or shower, hot water and a wash basin in all apartment units. Plaintiff owned a building with eleven three-room units, all of which had toilets. The additional cost would have been about $11,000. . . .

As held in some of the cases, supra, we do not in this opinion decide the validity of the ordinance generally; its effect and its reasonableness vary as to each property affected, and a decision must be made on each separate state of facts as they arise. As to the two properties involved here, we have decided that the application of that part of Section 391.040, quoted above, would be arbitrary and unreasonable and hence a deprivation of due process to the defendant.

We recognize that in all probability a majority of the cases involving the general question (but certainly not on identical facts) have held such ordinances to be valid. We have determined that the facts as stated here impel us to a contrary conclusion. These buildings have no sale value, and no loan value. The buildings are 70 years old. No one will purchase them and people simply do not want to live in that neighborhood. This evidence, though coming from the defendant himself, is uncontroverted and we accept it. The locality has been largely vandalized and many of the buildings are vacant. When a building becomes vacant it is almost immediately vandalized and, as defendant said, it "disappears." Most of defendant's tenants are living on welfare or social security. This record does not show that any tenants have complained of existing conditions; they apparently do have flush toilets and lavatories with hot and cold water. The cost to defendant of the improvements demanded would total approximately $7,800 for each building, according to defendant's testimony. This figure was objected to as hearsay, but estimates had been received and defendant was an experienced real estate operator and owner. The evidence was admissible. Also, according to two witnesses who actually made estimates, the total cost of the improvements so estimated would total $7,260 per building. In the alteration the kitchens would be reduced to "closet" size. There was testimony from the defendant that in order to recoup such expense, he would have to charge monthly rentals of $60 over a five-year period and that this was simply not obtainable. The net result would seem to be vacancies, vandalism, and probably a total loss of the buildings.

The problem here is not actually one of public health; it is wholly different from those cases involving outside privies, sewage, etc. While the situation is by no means ideal, it really involves a matter of inconvenience to those tenants who choose to pay a minimum rent in return for incomplete facilities. The tenants may still bathe if they want to, and we are not convinced of any great danger that diseases will be spread. . . .

The judgments appealed from are reversed and the cases are remanded with directions to discharge the defendant.

PER CURIAM:

The foregoing opinion by Henry I. Eager, Special Commissioner, is adopted as the opinion of the Court en Banc. . . .

FINCH, Judge (dissenting). . . .

. . . [I]f it be decided that a particular building requirement is not arbitrary and unreasonable and is a proper exercise of the police power to protect the public health and safety, its enforcement should not depend upon the economic situation of or the economic results to the owner of the property. To hold to the contrary means that the worst housing is exempted from public health and safety requirements and that the hands of the City are tied when it attempts to require that tenements be brought to minimum standards.

Note on Housing Codes

1. *Federal constitutional challenges.* In Hutchinson v. City of Valdosta, 227 U.S. 303 (1913), the city had passed an ordinance requiring persons residing on streets served by sanitary sewer mains to cease using outhouses and to install flush toilets in their houses. Plaintiff alleged that she had lived on a one-acre lot for 20 years and that, despite her outhouse, her lot was clean, healthy, and "free of miasmic conditions." She sought to restrain enforcement of the ordinance. A unanimous Supreme Court was unsympathetic and held that the ordinance was not an arbitrary exercise of the police power and thus did not violate the Due Process Clause.

The owner of a lodging house on the Bowery in New York City fared no better in Queenside Hills Realty Co. v. Saxl, 328 U.S. 80 (1946). The owner alleged that its building had a market value of about $25,000; that the automatic wet-pipe sprinkler system the city had ordered it to install would cost $7,500; and that the benefits of the sprinkler system would be negligible because the building did not pose a fire hazard. Speaking for a unanimous court, Justice Douglas dismissed the owner's due process argument: "[T]he legislature may choose not to take the chance that human life will be lost in lodging house fires and adopt the most conservative course which science and engineering offer." Id. at 83. What if the owner had installed the sprinklers and then sought compensation for an unconstitutional taking of property? See Stern v. Halligan, 158 F.3d 729 (3d Cir. 1998) (holding that township violated neither the Due Process nor the Takings Clause when it compelled former user of private well to connect to public water system). See also pp. 197–202 (on nonconforming uses). Can a tenant ousted as a result of a housing code enforcement program recover damages from the city for the taking of the tenant's leasehold? See Devines v. Maier, 728 F.2d 876 (7th Cir. 1984) (no).

Are there constitutional limits on the amount of fines for housing code violations? In City & County of San Francisco v. Sainez, 92 Cal. Rptr. 2d 418 (Ct. App. 2000), the landlord of a building valued at $300,000 had been fined $663,000 ($1,000 dollars per day for a continuing violation). Emphasizing the defendant's net worth of $2.3 million, the court rejected the landlord's battery of challenges, including one based on the Eighth Amendment's prohibition on excessive fines.

2. *Back to nature?* Defendant allowed his 315-acre ranch located north of San Francisco to be used as a back-to-nature commune. The residents lived in 77 structures — tents, plastic-covered shelters, and the like — and relied on four chemical toilets. In People v. Wheeler, 106 Cal. Rptr. 260 (Ct. App. 1972), the court affirmed the validity of a county order that the occupants either tear down their structures or bring them up to code. If tent living is permissible in a campground, why shouldn't it be on a private ranch?

3. *Enforcement on change of occupancy.* A few cities have enacted ordinances that require that a residential property be inspected for code consistency each time a new occupant is about to move in. The owner receives a residential occupancy permit only if the housing is found to be up-to-code. See Otto J. Hetzel, The Search for Effective and Cost-Efficient Housing Strategies: Enforcing Housing Condition Standards Through Code Inspections at Time of Sale or Transfer, 36 J. Urb. & Contemp. L. 25 (1989).

4. *Enforcement by tenants.* In some states, the provisions of housing codes set the standard of quality for the warranty of habitability implied in residential leases. In these

jurisdictions, could municipal officials leave code-enforcement initiatives entirely to tenants? Or focus exclusively on code violations that pose risks to residents of neighboring properties?

5. *The merits of housing codes.* Critics assert that housing codes can impair the welfare of poor households by forcing them to purchase housing of a higher quality than they would choose voluntarily. See, e.g., Richard A. Posner, Economic Analysis of Law 482–85 (6th ed. 2003); Michael L. Walden, Effects of Housing Codes on Local Housing Markets, 15 AREUEA J. 13 (1987). In *Brune,* for example, St. Louis in effect was forbidding tenants from occupying single-room occupancy (SRO) units serviced by a shower and bath facility located in a hall bathroom. While many housing reformers of the 1950s would have applauded enforcement of this standard, their counterparts a generation later had come to recognize that low-income persons have much to gain from preservation of the SRO housing stock. See SROs: A Poor Stepchild Comes of Age, Zoning News, Aug. 1990, at 1. Cf. San Joaquin Motel & Hotel Property Owners Association v. City of Stockton, 2003 WL 22255839 (Cal. Ct. App. Oct. 2, 2003) (affirming injunction issued to prevent city from employing code requirements in manner that might drive owners of older, downtown hotels out of business); Seawall Associates v. City of New York, 542 N.E.2d 1059 (N.Y. 1989) (holding that New York City's regulations limiting conversion and demolition of SRO units constituted an unconstitutional taking of property).

In Briseno v. City of Santa Ana, 8 Cal. Rptr. 2d 486 (Ct. App. 1992), attorneys for a family of five living in a one-bedroom apartment successfully challenged, on statutory grounds, a city ordinance that would have prohibited habitation at that density. On which side of this dispute would an idealistic lawyer want to be?

Many commentators defend housing code enforcement under certain conditions, particularly when enforcement efforts would be unlikely to raise rents or when enforcement would help persons other than occupying adults, such as neighbors or children. See Bruce A. Ackerman, Regulating Slum Housing Markets on Behalf of the Poor: Of Housing Codes, Housing Subsidies and Income Redistribution Policy, 80 Yale L.J. 1093 (1971); Richard Markovits, The Distributive Impact, Allocative Efficiency, and Overall Desirability of Ideal Housing Codes, 89 Harv. L. Rev. 1815 (1976). See also Nicole Stelle Garnett, Ordering (and Order in) the City, 57 Stan. L. Rev. 1, 11–20 (2004).

Valuable empirical studies include Sarah H. Ramsey & Fredrick Zolna, A Piece in the Puzzle of Providing Adequate Housing: Court Effectiveness in Code Enforcement, 19 Fordham Urb. L.J. 605 (1991) (on practice in Syracuse); H. Laurence Ross, Housing Code Enforcement as Law in Action, 17 Law & Pol'y 133 (1995). Ross finds that housing code enforcement is more simplified and flexible than formal code provisions would imply, but that it commonly gives rise to arbitrary outcomes. He concludes that code enforcement is a largely ineffective response to the problem of urban decline because blight fundamentally is caused by poverty, racism, crime, drugs, and inadequate social institutions such as police departments and school systems.

C.   Aesthetic Regulation

Conventional land use regulations affect the visual appeal of the built environment. For example, front-yard setback requirements in zoning ordinances and street standards in subdivision regulations both influence the attractiveness of streetscapes. This subchapter focuses, however, on three varieties of municipal regulation whose thrust is predominantly aesthetic: sign regulations, architectural review procedures, and historic preservation programs. These sorts of regulations are less ubiquitous than conventional public land use controls, and they have been especially vulnerable to constitutional attack.

City of Passaic v. Paterson Bill Posting, Advertising & Sign Painting Co.
62 A. 267 (N.J. 1905)

SWAYZE, J.

The plaintiff in error was convicted of the violation of an ordinance of the city of Passaic regulating signs or billboards and the conviction was affirmed by the Supreme Court. 71 N.J.L. 75, 58 Atl. 343. The ordinance provides that no sign or billboard shall be at any point more than eight feet above the surface of the ground, and requires that it shall be constructed not less than ten feet from the street line. The statutory authority for this ordinance is the act of April 8, 1903 (P.L. 1903, p.513, c.240), which authorizes the governing body of any city to regulate the size, height, location, position, and material of all fences, signs, billboards, and advertisements. The statute does not limit the power of the municipal authorities to cases where the structures may be in a condition dangerous to the public safety, and the first section of the ordinance absolutely prohibits signs and billboards within ten feet of the street line. In the present case, the billboard was erected in 1902, prior to the passage of the act, and the police justice has certified that no evidence was offered of it being dangerous to life or limb because of insecure fastening. . . .

. . . The very fact that this ordinance is directed against signs and billboards only, and not against fences, indicates that some consideration other than the public safety led to its passage. It is obvious from the face of the ordinance that the object of the first section was not to secure the public safety; that section contains no reference to a dangerous condition of billboards, while the second section expressly undertakes to deal with those that become dangerous.

We think the control attempted to be exercised is in excess of that essential to effect the security of the public. It is probable that the enactment of section 1 of the ordinance was due rather to aesthetic considerations than to considerations of the public safety. No case has been cited, nor are we aware of any case which holds that a man may be deprived of his property because his tastes are not those of his neighbors. Aesthetic considerations are a matter of luxury and indulgence rather than of necessity, and it is necessity alone which justifies the exercise of the police power to take private property without compensation. . . . Since the effect of the ordinance is to take private property without compensation, and cannot be justified as an exercise of the police power, it is invalid.

The judgment of the Supreme Court should be reversed, and a judgment entered reversing the conviction.

Stephen F. Williams, Subjectivity, Expression, and Privacy: Problems of Aesthetic Regulation
62 Minn. L. Rev. 1, 58 (1977)

. . . There was merit in the intuitive judicial anxiety about purely aesthetic purposes which led to the requirement of some nonaesthetic state interest to support the regulation. All that was lacking was an explicit recognition that the factors underlying that uneasiness were the dangers of vagueness and of governmental suppression of aesthetic expression solely on the basis of majoritarian tastes. The absence of a clear understanding of the nature of the problem led some of the earlier courts to accept too readily the protection of property values and the tourist trade as legitimate government interests unrelated to suppression of expression despite the fact that these interests are ultimately rooted in the same interests that make a purely aesthetic purpose suspect. Nonetheless, the anxiety about state intervention in aesthetics is sound. All that is needed is a closer focus on the reasons for that anxiety, for once those reasons are identified, the problem of aesthetic regulation has much in common with many other forms of legislation and can be dealt with in much the same way.

Note on Aesthetics

1. *Academic perspectives*. What is beauty? To architect Robert Venturi and his associates, it is the messy vitality of the Las Vegas Strip. See Robert Venturi et al., Learning from Las Vegas (1972).

A significant article on aesthetic regulation is John J. Costonis, Law and Aesthetics: A Critique and a Reformulation of the Dilemmas, 80 Mich. L. Rev. 355 (1982). (John J. Costonis, Icons and Aliens (1989), is the illustrated version.) Costonis compares two rationales for aesthetic controls. The conventional one is a "visual beauty rationale." Costonis asserts, however, that a "cultural stability rationale" better identifies the impetus for aesthetic regulation:

> . . . [T]he visual beauty interest, insofar as it has any discernible legal content, is subsumed under the stability interest. It is true, of course, that viewers respond affirmatively to particular visual configurations in the environment. Their responses, in fact, are often sufficiently patterned to refute the objection that aesthetics is too subjective to warrant legal protection. But these configurations are compelling because they signify values that stabilize cultural, group, or individual identity, not because their visual qualities conform to the canons of one or another school of aesthetic formalism.

Id. at 357-58. Costonis goes on to consider the constitutional problems — for example, First Amendment issues — that government programs to stabilize cultural values are apt to pose.

2. *Empirical yardsticks for beauty*. One study asked observers to evaluate pictures of highway corridors before and after the removal of different structures. The removal of utility poles was found to have a greater impact on the viewer than the removal of billboards. Aside from utility poles, the study concluded that "it would probably be safe to say that the removal of on-premise signs was the single most important factor in producing a re-evaluation." Cyril Herrman, Human Response to Visual Environments in Urban Areas, *in* Outdoor Advertising 57, 75 (John Houck ed., 1969). Empirical research on aesthetic evaluations of natural areas is summarized in Note, Beyond the Eye of the Beholder: Aesthetics and Objectivity, 71 Mich. L. Rev. 1438, 1442-48 (1973).

To sidestep the ancient philosophical debate over the basis for aesthetic judgments, Professor Michelman has suggested that the legal system look to the impacts that various land uses have on neighboring property values. If an activity causes the value of nearby land to decline, Michelman asserts that this is objective evidence that the activity is "by a social consensus deemed intrinsically ugly, negatively suggestive, or destructive of prior existing beauty." Frank Michelman, Toward a Practical Standard for Aesthetic Regulation, 15 Prac. Law. 36, 37 (Feb. 1969). Cf. Note 6 on pp. 519-20 (exploring how the law of nuisance grapples with the problem of aesthetic harm).

3. *Varieties of aesthetic regulation.* In addition to the principal programs featured below, a municipality may have a number of low-level regulations whose basic thrust is to prevent visual blight. See, e.g., People v. Tolman, 168 Cal. Rptr. 328 (App. Dep't Super. Ct. 1980) (affirming conviction for parking of truck tractor in driveway in residential zone); People v. Jack Resnick & Sons, Inc., 487 N.Y.S.2d 988 (City Ct. of Yonkers 1985) (refusing to dismiss prosecution for failure to cut weeds naturally growing on property); Berberian v. Housing Authority, 315 A.2d 747 (R.I. 1974) (holding city's police powers entitled it to compel homeowner to paint his house); Patricia Leigh Brown, With Neighborliness Fading, Fences Turn Inward, N.Y. Times, Mar. 14, 1999, §1, at 1 (describing ordinances that require a builder of a wooden stockade fence to place the smooth side on the surface facing the neighbor). Are these sorts of localized issues better left to resolution through informal social controls? Some localities also graft innovative aesthetic regulations onto more land use conventional controls. See, e.g., Greater Atlanta Homebuilders Association v. DeKalb County, 588 S.E.2d 694 (Ga. 2003) (holding that ordinance requiring applicants for building and land development permits to submit a tree protection plan did not constitute a taking).

1.   Sign Controls

Metromedia, Inc. v. City of San Diego
610 P.2d 407 (Cal. 1980), *reversed*, 453 U.S. 490 (1981)

TOBRINER, Justice. . . .

The present case concerns the constitutionality of San Diego Ordinance No. 10795 (New Series), enacted March 14, 1972. With limited exceptions specified in the footnote,[1] the ordinance as subsequently amended prohibits all off-site "outdoor advertising display signs." Off-site signs are defined as those which do not identify a use, facility or service located on the premises or a product which is produced, sold or manufactured on the premises. All existing signs which do not conform to the requirements of the ordinance must be removed following expiration of an amortization period, ranging from 90 days to 4 years depending upon the location and depreciated value of the sign.

Plaintiffs, Metromedia, Inc., and Pacific Outdoor Advertising Co., Inc., are engaged in the outdoor advertising business and own a substantial number of off-site billboards subject to removal under Ordinance No. 10795. Plaintiffs filed separate actions against the city, attacking the validity of the ordinance. . . .

To facilitate the determination of the motion for summary judgment the parties entered into a stipulation of facts. The following portions of that stipulation are particularly pertinent to the present appeal:

> 2.   If enforced as written Ordinance No. 10795 will eliminate the outdoor advertising business in the City of San Diego. . . .

---

1. The original ordinance permitted the following off-site signs: Signs maintained in the discharge of a governmental function; bench advertising signs; commemorative plaques, religious symbols, holiday decorations and similar such signs; signs located within shopping malls not visible from any point on the boundary of the premises; signs designating premises for sale, rent or lease; public service signs depicting time, temperature or news; signs on vehicles conforming to city regulations; and temporary off-premises subdivision directional signs.

As originally enacted, the ordinance contained no exception for political signs. On October 19, 1977, the city council amended the ordinance to permit "Temporary political campaign signs, including their supporting structures, which are erected or maintained for no longer than 90 days and, which are removed within 10 days after the election to which they pertain." . . .

13.   Each of the plaintiffs are the owners of a substantial number of outdoor advertising displays (approximately 500 to 800) in the City of San Diego. . . .

17.   The displays have varying values depending upon their size, nature and location.

18.   Each of the displays has a fair market value as a part of an income-producing system of between $2,500 and $25,000.

19.   Each display has a remaining useful income-producing life in excess of 25 years.

20.   All of the signs owned by plaintiffs in the City of San Diego are located in areas zoned for commercial and industrial purposes. . . .

28.   Outdoor advertising increases the sales of products and produces numerous direct and indirect benefits to the public. Valuable commercial, political and social information is communicated to the public through the use of outdoor advertising. Many businesses and politicians and other persons rely upon outdoor advertising because other forms of advertising are insufficient, inappropriate and prohibitively expensive. . . .

31.   Many of plaintiffs' signs are within 660 feet and others are within 500 feet of interstate or federal primary high-ways. . . .

34.   The amortization provisions of Ordinance No. 10795 have no reasonable relationship to the fair market value, useful life or income generated by the signs and were not designed to have such a relationship.

The trial court filed a memorandum opinion stating that the ordinance was invalid as an unreasonable exercise of police power and an abridgment of First Amendment guaranties of freedom of speech and press. The court then entered judgment enjoining enforcement of the ordinance. The city appeals from that judgment.

2. THE SUMMARY JUDGMENT CANNOT BE SUSTAINED ON THE GROUND THAT THE SAN DIEGO ORDINANCE EXCEEDS THE CITY'S AUTHORITY UNDER THE POLICE POWER.

The San Diego ordinance, as we shall explain, represents a proper application of municipal authority over zoning and land use for the purpose of promoting the public safety and welfare. The ordinance recites the purposes for which it was enacted, including the elimination of traffic hazards brought about by distracting advertising displays and the improvement of the appearance of the city. Since these goals are proper objectives for the exercise of the city's police power, the city council, asserting its legislative judgment, could reasonably believe the instant ordinance would further those objectives. . . .

Billboards are intended to, and undoubtedly do, divert a driver's attention from the roadway. . . . Many other decisions have upheld billboard ordinances on the ground that such ordinances reasonably relate to traffic safety; we cannot find it manifestly unreasonable for the San Diego City Council to reach the same conclusion. . . .

We further hold that even if, as plaintiffs maintain, the principal purpose of the ordinance is not to promote traffic safety but to improve the appearance of the community, such a purpose falls within the city's authority under the police power. In contending that aesthetic considerations cannot justify the exercise of the police power to prohibit billboards, plaintiffs rely on Varney & Green v. Williams, 100 P. 867 (Cal. 1909), which held unconstitutional an ordinance of the City of East San Jose prohibiting all advertising billboards. Asserting that the ordinance rested solely on the "promotion of aesthetic or artistic considerations," we stated that "it has never been held that these considerations alone will justify, as an exercise of the police power, a radical restriction of the right of an owner of property. . . . " (Id. at 868, quoting City of Passaic v. Patterson Bill Posting Co., 62 A. 267 (N.J.L. 1905).) . . .

. . . [W]e could distinguish the present case from Varney & Green v. Williams, on the ground that the present ordinance was not enacted exclusively for aesthetic purposes. We believe, however, that the holding of Varney & Green v. Williams, that aesthetic purposes alone cannot justify assertion of the police power to ban billboards, is unworkable, discordant with modern thought as to the scope of the police power, and therefore compels forthright repudiation.

Because this state relies on its scenery to attract tourists and commerce, aesthetic considerations assume economic value. Consequently any distinction between aesthetic and economic grounds as a justification for billboard regulation must fail. . . .

The holding of Varney & Green v. Williams also conflicts with present concepts of the police power. Most jurisdictions now concur with the broad declaration of Justice Douglas in Berman v. Parker, 348 U.S. 26 (1954): "The concept of the public welfare is broad and inclusive. . . . The values it represents are spiritual as well as physical, aesthetic as well as monetary. It is within the power of the legislature to determine that the community should be beautiful as well as healthy, spacious as well as clean, well-balanced as well as carefully patrolled." (Id. at 33.) Although Justice Douglas tendered this description in a case upholding the exercise of the power of eminent domain for community redevelopment, it has since been recognized as a correct description of the authority of a state or city to enact legislation under the police power. (Village of Belle Terre v. Boraas, 416 U.S. 1, 5–6 (1974).)

Present day city planning would be virtually impossible under a doctrine which denied a city authority to legislate for aesthetic purposes under the police power. Virtually every city in this state has enacted zoning ordinances for the purpose of improving the appearance of the urban environment and the quality of metropolitan life. . . .

. . . We conclude that the summary judgment cannot be sustained on the ground that the ordinance exceeds the city's authority under the police power.[12]

3. THE SUMMARY JUDGMENT CANNOT BE SUSTAINED ON THE GROUND THAT THE SAN DIEGO ORDINANCE ON ITS FACE ABRIDGES FREEDOM OF SPEECH. . . .

. . . [T]he ordinance leaves open adequate alternative means of communication. In upholding a Maine statute which imposed a statewide ban on off-site commercial billboards, the federal district court observed that the act "leaves open ample alternative channels for communication of the information now carried by off-premises outdoor advertising. . . . Many, if not all, of the commercial messages displayed on off-premises signs can be conveyed to the traveling public through on-premises advertising, official business directional signs, and tourist information centers and publications, all of which are sanctioned by the Act. . . . Other forms of print media, which, like outdoor advertising, enjoy the advantage of being relatively low in cost, such as pamphleting and leafleting, lie beyond the scope of the Act altogether. . . . " (John Donnelly & Sons v. Mallar, 453 F. Supp. 1272, 1279–1280 (D. Me. 1978).)[14] . . .

12. Varney & Green v. Williams, supra, 100 P. 867, is hereby overruled. . . .

14. Plaintiffs call attention to stipulation No. 28, which states in part that "Many businesses, politicians, and other persons rely upon outdoor advertising because other forms of advertising are insufficient, inappropriate and prohibitively expensive." The possibility that the ordinance may impede an occasional advertiser from communicating his message to the public, however, is not sufficient to invalidate the ordinance on its face. In the present litigation, which pits only the owners of the billboards against the city, individual advertisers are not parties; such an advertiser retains the ability to assert that, owing to the absence of reasonable alternative means of communication, the ordinance cannot constitutionally be applied to prevent him from using a billboard to proclaim his message. [Footnote relocated. — EDS.]

4. The San Diego ordinance is preempted by the Outdoor Advertising Act to the extent that the ordinance requires removal without compensation of billboards within 660 feet of federal interstate and primary highways.

[The federal Highway Beautification Act of 1965 (23 U.S.C. §131), as amended in 1978, denies 10 percent of federal-aid highway funds to any state that fails to control outdoor advertising signs located near the primary system of federal highways. The Act also requires, however, that just compensation be paid to the owner of a sign that is removed. Federal funds, if appropriated, are to reimburse lower-level governments for 75 percent of the compensation they pay. California enacted the Outdoor Advertising Act, Cal. Bus. & Prof. Code §§5200 et seq., in order to avoid losing 10 percent of its federal highway funds. The California Act forbade San Diego from ordering the removal of a federally protected billboard without compensation.]

We believe that the Highway Beautification Act as amended requires the payment of compensation for removal of all billboards existing or subject to litigation on November 6, 1978, located within 660 feet of federal interstate or primary highways within San Diego and visible from the main traveled way of such highways. We reach that conclusion reluctantly, since its effect in this case and in future cases will probably frustrate the original intent of the Highway Beautification Act: to accelerate the removal of billboards. . . .

6. The summary judgment cannot be sustained on the ground that the amortization period prescribed by the ordinance as applied to all or any of plaintiffs' signs is unreasonably short.

The San Diego ordinance requires abatement of all off-site billboards following expiration of an amortization period. That period is computed in the following manner: First, the owner determines the original cost of the sign, including the cost of installation. Second, he deducts 10 percent of that cost for each year the sign has been standing prior to the effective date of the ordinance, arriving at a figure which the ordinance refers to as "the adjusted market value." The ordinance then provides an abatement schedule ranging from one year for signs with an "adjusted market value" of less than $500 to four years for signs with an "adjusted market value" in excess of $20,000.

Finally, the ordinance states that notwithstanding the abatement schedule in the ordinance, any signs located within 500 feet of freeways or scenic highways must be removed within 90 days. This provision is based on the fact that such signs were rendered nonconforming uses by prior city zoning ordinances. Since those prior ordinances had been in force for about 3 years before the effective date of Ordinance No. 10795, the signs in question received an actual amortization period of at least 3 years and 90 days.

. . . As the parties stipulated, the abatement schedule is not computed on the basis of current fair market value, useful life, or income generated by the signs. Relying on that stipulation, plaintiffs contend that the amortization period is unreasonable on its face and hence that the ordinance, to the extent that it requires removal of billboards without compensation or a reasonable amortization period, denies due process of law. . . .

. . . The determination of the length of a reasonable period of amortization is not merely a matter of accounting. "It is not required that the nonconforming property concerned have no value at the termination date." (Art Neon Co. v. City & County of Denver, 488 F.2d 118, 121 (10th Cir. 1973).) The determination instead involves a process of weighing the public gain to be derived from a speedy removal of the nonconforming use against the private loss which removal of the use would entail. (Hadacheck v. Sebastian, 239 U.S. 394 (1915).)

In reviewing the constitutionality of an ordinance providing for amortization of non-conforming billboards we held in National Advertising Co. v. County of Monterey, 464 P.2d 33 (1970), that a one-year amortization period was unreasonable except as to signs which had been fully depreciated for federal income tax purposes. Other decisions have also stated that a one-year amortization period is generally unreasonable . . . but have upheld amortization periods ranging from two years and eight months . . . to five years. . . . In light of those decisions we conclude that the amortization period provided in the instant ordinance which ranges from one to four years, depending upon the depreciated value of the sign, is not unreasonable on its face.

Our conclusion that the amortization schedule established in the San Diego ordinance is not facially unreasonable does not demonstrate its validity as applied to each of plaintiffs' signs. The reasonableness of an amortization period as applied to each billboard depends in part upon facts peculiar to that structure. Such facts include the cost of the billboard, its depreciated value, remaining useful life, the length and remaining term of the lease under which it is maintained, and the harm to the public if the structure remains standing beyond the prescribed amortization period.

8. CONCLUSION

In summary, we conclude that neither the federal nor the state Constitution bars a municipality from enacting a zoning ordinance which prohibits off-site billboards and requires removal of existing billboards after expiration of a reasonable amortization period. The Outdoor Advertising Act, however, preempts local law to bar the uncompensated removal of existing billboards located within 660 feet of federal interstate or primary high-ways. Plaintiffs accordingly may avoid uncompensated removal for any billboards falling within the preemptive scope of the Outdoor Advertising Act; plaintiffs also retain the right to show that the amortization period prescribed by the San Diego ordinance is unreasonably short as applied to some or all of their structures. Because plaintiffs have failed to demonstrate the invalidity of the ordinance on its face, however, the trial court erred in granting their motion for summary judgment.

To hold that a city cannot prohibit off-site commercial billboards for the purpose of protecting and preserving the beauty of the environment is to succumb to a bleak materialism. We conclude with the pungent words of Ogden Nash:

> I think that I shall never see
> A billboard lovely as a tree.
> Indeed, unless the billboards fall,
> I'll never see a tree at all.

The judgment is reversed.

[Justice CLARK dissented, arguing that the San Diego ordinance violated the First Amendment.]

Note on Nonspeech Issues Posed by Billboard Regulation

1. *Ogden Nash reconsidered.* Government prohibition of off-site billboards may be constitutional, but is it desirable? In the late twentieth century, the Wall Drug Store in Wall, South Dakota, became internationally renowned on account of its creative billboard

advertising. For example, during the war years, Wall Drug had 127 billboards in Vietnam. At its peak, Wall Drug pulled in over half of the tourists driving through South Dakota on Interstate 90 during the summer months. See David Russell, Another Roadside Attraction, Am. Demographics, Dec. 1, 1990, at 50. Would the prohibition of off-site billboard advertising by Wall Drug (or an analogue such as South of the Border in South Carolina) enhance the pleasure of transcontinental motorists?

If there are good signs, such as those displaying the humorous Burma-Shave jingles of the mid-twentieth century, would it be possible to define these and exempt them from regulation? How might the Venturis defend the billboards along Sunset Strip in Hollywood that promote the latest records and movies? Billboards in the New Jersey Meadowlands announcing the current run of Broadway shows? The neon glitter of Times Square, where a 1987 New York City ordinance mandates that new buildings sport big signs and bright lights? See New York, N.Y., Zoning Resolution §81-732 (1999). (Billboards actually were far more common in Manhattan a century ago. See Christopher Gray, The Battles over Outdoor Ads Go Back a Century, N.Y. Times, June 17, 2001, Real Estate Section, at 9.) See generally Catherine Gudis, Buyways: Billboards, Automobiles, and the American Landscape (2004); Sally Henderson & Robert Landau, Billboard Art (1980).

2. *Judicial acceptance of aesthetic objectives.* In an important early opinion holding that aesthetic objectives alone allow a community to ban all off-premises billboards, Judge Breitel of the New York Court of Appeals wrote:

> . . . The exercise of the police power should not extend to every artistic conformity or nonconformity. Rather, what is involved are those esthetic considerations which bear substantially on the economic, social, and cultural patterns of a community or district. Advertising signs and billboards, if misplaced, often are egregious examples of ugliness, distraction, and deterioration. They are just as much subject to reasonable controls, including prohibition, as enterprises which emit offensive noises, odors, or debris. The eye is entitled to as much recognition as the other senses, but, of course, the offense to the eye must be substantial and be deemed to have material effect on the community or district pattern.

Cromwell v. Ferrier, 225 N.E.2d 749 (N.Y. 1967). See also Oregon City v. Hartke, 400 P.2d 255 (Or. 1965) (junkyard).

An increasing number of state courts have held that aesthetic considerations alone can justify exercise of the police power. Besides *Metromedia*, see, e.g., Temple Baptist Church, Inc. v. City of Albuquerque, 646 P.2d 565 (N.M. 1982); Samuel Bufford, Beyond the Eye of the Beholder: A New Majority of Jurisdictions Authorize Aesthetic Regulation, 48 UMKC L. Rev. 125 (1980). See also Village of Hudson v. Albrecht, Inc., 458 N.E.2d 852 (Ohio 1984) (tiptoeing up to, but ultimately stepping back from, proposition that a government can legislate solely for aesthetic purposes). The issue remains contested, however, and there are conspicuous holdouts. See, e.g., Mayor & City Council of Baltimore v. Mano Swartz, Inc., 299 A.2d 828 (Md. 1973) (holding that police power does not authorize an ordinance solely or primarily enacted for aesthetic purposes); Board of Supervisors v. Rowe, 216 S.E.2d 199 (Va. 1975) (similar).

3. *Amortization periods for billboards.* The *Metromedia* decision asserts that a landowner's constitutional right to maintain an existing billboard turns on the balance between public gains and private losses that would result were the billboard to be razed. This balancing approach is just one of many approaches that courts have used to decide takings cases in general, see pp. 134-97, and amortization cases in particular, see pp. 197-201.

Another conventional test for takings rests on the distinction between the prevention of harms and the extraction of benefits. If a billboard properly can be characterized as harmful, this second test would permit it to be phased out immediately without compensation. See

People v. Adco Advertisers, 110 Cal. Rptr. 849 (Ct. App. 1973) (billboards that are public nuisances can be banned without amortization period).

See generally Deepa Varadarajan, Note, Billboards and Big Utilities: Borrowing Land-Use Concepts to Regulate "Nonconforming" Sources Under the Clean Air Act, 112 Yale L.J. 2553 (2003).

4. *Federal involvement.* The Highway Beautification Act of 1965, 23 U.S.C. §131 (2004), was a favored cause of Lady Bird Johnson, wife of the then president. As it has evolved, the act has been a boon for the billboard industry and has retarded the elimination of billboards in many areas. Prior to 1974, the act's provisions on new signs mainly sought to induce states to stem billboard erection within 660 feet of federally aided highways in rural areas. This policy led to the construction of enormous billboards situated just beyond that line, a pattern that slowed after 1974 when the act was amended to target all new billboards within a motorist's field of vision. In 1978, Congress modified the act to entitle the owner of an existing billboard located alongside a federally aided highway to compensation in the event that a government sought to abate the use. To some critics, this amendment was a classic instance of the capture of a regulatory program by a regulated industry. During the 1980s, Congress ceased appropriating funds for the 75 percent federal share of the compensatory payments, and billboard-removal efforts along federally aided highways were largely suspended. See General Accounting Office, The Outdoor Advertising Control Program Needs to be Reassessed (1985) (reporting that, because of loopholes, during 1983 the number of new billboards installed along federally aided highways was three times the number removed); Craig J. Albert, Your Ad Goes Here: How the Highway Beautification Act of 1965 Thwarts Highway Beautification, 48 U. Kan. L. Rev. 463 (2000); Charles F. Floyd, Requiem for the Highway Beautification Act, 48 J. Am. Plan. Ass'n 441 (1982) (describing how billboard interests obtain "phony" commercial and industrial zoning along rural highways to evade statutory prohibitions).

For decades after passage of the 1965 act, South Dakota tussled with the federal government and succeeded in preserving many of the Wall Drug billboards in the state. Is there adequate justification for a federal override of a state's approach to billboard issues?

Metromedia, Inc. v. City of San Diego
453 U.S. 490 (1981)

[The case evoked five opinions from the Justices of the Supreme Court. Although no opinion commanded a majority, the Court held that certain features of the ordinance violated the First Amendment.]

Justice WHITE announced the judgment of the Court and delivered an opinion, in which Justices STEWART, MARSHALL, and POWELL joined. . . .

Billboards are a well-established medium of communication, used to convey a broad range of different kinds of messages. As Justice Clark noted in his dissent below: "The outdoor sign or symbol is a venerable medium for expressing political, social and commercial ideas. From the poster or 'broadside' to the billboard, outdoor signs have played a prominent role throughout American history, rallying support for political and social causes." 610 P.2d at 430–31. The record in this case indicates that besides the typical commercial uses, San Diego billboards have been used "to publicize the 'City in motion' campaign of the City of San Diego, to communicate messages from candidates for municipal, state and national offices, including candidates for judicial office, to propose marriage, to seek employment, to encourage the use of seat belts, to denounce the United Nations, to seek support for Prisoners of War and Missing in Action, to promote the United Crusade and a variety of other charitable and socially-related endeavors and to provide directions to the traveling public."

But whatever its communicative function, the billboard remains a "large, immobile, and permanent structure which like other structures is subject to . . . regulation." 610 P.2d at 419. Moreover, because it is designed to stand out and apart from its surroundings, the billboard creates a unique set of problems for land-use planning and development.

Billboards, then, like other media of communication, combine communicative and noncommunicative aspects. As with other media, the government has legitimate interests in controlling the noncommunicative aspects of the medium, but the First and Fourteenth Amendments foreclose a similar interest in controlling the communicative aspects. Because regulation of the noncommunicative aspects of a medium often impinges to some degree on the communicative aspects, it has been necessary for the courts to reconcile the government's regulatory interests with the individual's right to expression. . . .

As construed by the California Supreme Court, the ordinance restricts the use of certain kinds of outdoor signs. . . .

. . . [U]nder the ordinance (1) a sign advertising goods or services available on the property where the sign is located is allowed; (2) a sign on a building or other property advertising goods or services produced or offered elsewhere is barred; (3) noncommercial advertising, unless within one of the specific exceptions, is everywhere prohibited. The occupant of property may advertise his own goods or services; he may not advertise the goods or services of others, nor may he display most noncommercial messages.

IV

Appellants' principal submission is that enforcement of the ordinance will eliminate the outdoor advertising business in San Diego and that the First and Fourteenth Amendments prohibit the elimination of this medium of communication. . . . [W]e consider separately the effect of the ordinance on commercial and noncommercial speech. . . .

. . . [I]n Central Hudson Gas & Electric Corp. v. Public Service Comm'n, 447 U.S. 557 (1980), we held: "The Constitution . . . accords a lesser protection to commercial speech than to other constitutionally guaranteed expression. The protection available for a particular commercial expression turns on the nature both of the expression and of the governmental interests served by its regulation." Id. at 562–563 (citation omitted). We then adopted a four-part test for determining the validity of government restrictions on commercial speech as distinguished from more fully protected speech. (1) The First Amendment protects commercial speech only if that speech concerns lawful activity and is not misleading. A restriction on otherwise protected commercial speech is valid only if it (2) seeks to implement a substantial governmental interest, (3) directly advances that interest, and (4) reaches no further than necessary to accomplish the given objective. Id. at 563–566.

Appellants agree that the proper approach to be taken in determining the validity of the restrictions on commercial speech is that which was articulated in *Central Hudson*, but assert that the San Diego ordinance fails that test. We do not agree.

There can be little controversy over the application of the first, second, and fourth criteria. There is no suggestion that the commercial advertising at issue here involves unlawful activity or is misleading. Nor can there be substantial doubt that the twin goals that the ordinance seeks to further — traffic safety and the appearance of the city — are substantial governmental goals. It is far too late to contend otherwise with respect to either traffic safety, Railway Express Agency, Inc. v. New York, 336 U.S. 106 (1949), or esthetics, see Penn Central Transportation Co. v. New York City, 438 U.S. 104 (1978); Village of Belle Terre v. Boraas, 416 U.S. 1 (1974); Berman v. Parker, 348 U.S. 26, 33 (1954). Similarly, we reject appellants' claim that the ordinance is broader than necessary and, therefore, fails the fourth part of the *Central Hudson* test. If the city has a sufficient basis for believing that billboards are traffic hazards and are unattractive, then obviously the most direct and perhaps the only effective approach to solving the problems they create is to prohibit them. The city has gone no further than necessary in seeking to meet its ends. Indeed, it has stopped short of fully accomplishing its ends: It has not prohibited all billboards, but allows onsite advertising and some other specifically exempted signs.

The more serious question, then, concerns the third of the *Central Hudson* criteria: Does the ordinance "directly advance" governmental interests in traffic safety and in the appearance of the city? . . .

It is . . . argued that the city denigrates its interest in traffic safety and beauty and defeats its own case by permitting onsite advertising and other specified signs. Appellants question whether the distinction between onsite and offsite advertising on the same property is justifiable in terms of either esthetics or traffic safety. The ordinance permits the occupant of property to use billboards located on that property to advertise goods and services offered at that location; identical billboards, equally distracting and unattractive, that advertise goods or services available elsewhere are prohibited even if permitting the latter would not multiply the number of billboards. . . .

. . . San Diego has obviously chosen to value one kind of commercial speech — onsite advertising — more than another kind of commercial speech — offsite advertising. The ordinance reflects a decision by the city that the former interest, but not the latter, is stronger than the city's interests in traffic safety and esthetics. The city has decided that in a limited instance — onsite commercial advertising — its interests should yield. We do not reject that judgment. As we see it, the city could reasonably conclude that a commercial enterprise — as well as the interested public — has a stronger interest in identifying its place of business and advertising the products or services available there than it has in using or leasing its available space for the purpose of advertising commercial enterprises located elsewhere. It does not follow from the fact that the city has concluded that some commercial interests outweigh its municipal interests in this context that it must give similar weight to all other commercial advertising. Thus, offsite commercial billboards may be prohibited while onsite commercial billboards are permitted. . . .

. . . In sum, insofar as it regulates commercial speech the San Diego ordinance meets the constitutional requirements of *Central Hudson*, supra.

V

It does not follow, however, that San Diego's general ban on signs carrying noncommercial advertising is also valid under the First and Fourteenth Amendments. The fact that the city may value commercial messages relating to onsite goods and services more than it values commercial communications relating to offsite goods and services does not justify prohibiting an occupant from displaying its own ideas or those of others.

As indicated above, our recent commercial speech cases have consistently accorded noncommercial speech a greater degree of protection than commercial speech. San Diego effectively inverts this judgment, by affording a greater degree of protection to commercial than to noncommercial speech. There is a broad exception for onsite commercial advertisements, but there is no similar exception for noncommercial speech. The use of onsite billboards to carry commercial messages related to the commercial use of the premises is freely permitted, but the use of otherwise identical billboards to carry noncommercial messages is generally prohibited. The city does not explain how or why noncommercial billboards located in places where commercial billboards are permitted would be more threatening to safe driving or would detract more from the beauty of the city. Insofar as the city tolerates billboards at all, it cannot choose to limit their content to commercial messages; the city may not conclude that the communication of commercial information concerning goods and services connected with a particular site is of greater value than the communication of noncommercial messages.

Furthermore, the ordinance contains exceptions that permit various kinds of noncommercial signs, whether on property where goods and services are offered or not, that would otherwise be within the general ban. A fixed sign may be used to identify any piece of property and its owner. Any piece of property may carry or display religious symbols, commemorative plaques of recognized historical societies and organizations, signs carrying news items or telling the time or temperature, signs erected in discharge of any governmental function, or temporary political campaign signs. No other noncommercial or ideological signs meeting the structural definition are permitted, regardless of their effect on traffic safety or esthetics.

Although the city may distinguish between the relative value of different categories of commercial speech, the city does not have the same range of choice in the area of noncommercial speech to evaluate the strength of, or distinguish between, various communicative interests. See Carey v. Brown, 447 U.S. at 462. With respect to noncommercial speech, the city may not choose the appropriate subjects for public discourse: "To allow a government the choice of permissible subjects for public debate would be to allow that government control over the search for political truth." Consolidated Edison Co. [v. Public Service Commission, 447 U.S. 530, 538 (1980)]. Because some noncommercial messages may be conveyed on billboards throughout the commercial and industrial zones, San Diego must similarly allow billboards conveying other noncommercial messages throughout those zones. . . .

VII

Because the San Diego ordinance reaches too far into the realm of protected speech, we conclude that it is unconstitutional on its face. The judgment of the California Supreme Court is reversed, and the case is remanded to that court. . . .

Justice BRENNAN, with whom Justice BLACKMUN joins, concurring in the judgment. . . .

. . . [M]y view is that the practical effect of the San Diego ordinance is to eliminate the billboard as an effective medium of communication. . . .

. . . I would apply the tests this Court has developed to analyze content-neutral prohibitions of particular media of communication. . . .

. . . In the case of billboards, I would hold that a city may totally ban them if it can show that a sufficiently substantial governmental interest is directly furthered by the total ban, and that any more narrowly drawn restriction, i.e., anything less than a total ban, would promote less well the achievement of that goal.

Applying that test to the instant case, I would invalidate the San Diego ordinance. . . .

Chief Justice BURGER, dissenting.

Today the Court takes an extraordinary — even a bizarre — step by severely limiting the power of a city to act on risks it perceives to traffic safety and the environment posed by large, permanent billboards. Those joining the plurality opinion invalidate a city's effort to minimize these traffic hazards and eyesores simply because, in exercising rational legislative judgment, it has chosen to permit a narrow class of signs that serve special needs.

Relying on simplistic platitudes about content, subject matter, and the dearth of other means to communicate, the billboard industry attempts to escape the real and growing problems every municipality faces in protecting safety and preserving the environment in an urban area. The Court's disposition of the serious issues involved exhibits insensitivity to the impact of these billboards on those who must live with them and the delicacy of the legislative judgments involved in regulating them. American cities desiring to mitigate the dangers mentioned must, as a matter of *federal constitutional law*, elect between two unsatisfactory options: (a) allowing all "noncommercial" signs, no matter how many, how dangerous, or how damaging to the environment; or (b) forbidding signs altogether. Indeed, lurking in the recesses of today's opinions is a not-so-veiled threat that the second option, too, may soon be withdrawn. This is the long arm and voracious appetite of federal power — this time judicial power — with a vengeance, reaching and absorbing traditional concepts of local authority. . . .

[The opinions of Justice REHNQUIST, dissenting, and of Justice STEVENS, dissenting in part, have been omitted.]

Note on Commercial Signs and Free Speech

1. Metromedia, *continued*. On remand, the Supreme Court of California held that the San Diego ordinance could not be saved. Justice Broussard, writing for the majority, reasoned:

> [W]e can salvage the constitutionality of the ordinance only by limiting its scope to prohibit only commercial signs. Such a construction would be inconsistent with the language of the ordinance and the original intent of the city council at the time of enacting the ordinance. The resulting legislation would compel the city to distinguish between commercial and noncommercial speech, a task rife with constitutional enigmas, and might not effectively achieve the city's objective of promoting traffic safety and improving community appearance. We therefore conclude that the ordinance cannot fairly and reasonably be construed in a manner that would preserve its constitutionality.

Metromedia, Inc. v. City of San Diego, 649 P.2d 902, 903 (Cal. 1982).

In 1984, the City of San Diego worked out a compromise with its billboard industry. It enacted a new ordinance that placed a ceiling of slightly less than 1,000 on the number of billboards and mandated that they gradually be relocated to commercial and industrial zones.

2. *Regulation of sign designs*. To what extent does the First Amendment constrain governmental control of the "manner" of outdoor advertising, that is, aspects such as size, height, color, and materials? See, e.g., Wallace v. Brown County Area Plan Commission, 689 N.E.2d 491 (Ind. Ct. App. 1998) (rejecting challenge to prohibition on neon signs); State v. Dahl, 676 N.W.2d 305 (Minn. Ct. App. 2004) (rejecting challenge to ban on signs that move or create an illusion of movement). A total ban on portable signs was sustained over First Amendment objections in Harnish v. Manatee County, 783 F.2d 1535 (11th Cir. 1986). What aesthetic or safety problems do portable signs pose?

The federal Lanham Act prohibits a state or local government from requiring alteration of a federally registered trademark. Would this prevent a city from forcing a

McDonald's or Burger King franchisee to change the font and color of the sign identifying a restaurant? From controlling the dimensions of the sign? See Lisa's Party City, Inc. v. Town of Henrietta, 185 F.3d 12 (2d Cir. 1999) (upholding town's rejection of proposed sign designed to replicate enterprise's trademarked color-combination); Roberta Rosenthal Kwall, Regulating Trademarks on Exterior Signs, 71 S. Cal. L. Rev. 1105 (1998).

3. *On-site commercial signs*. The San Diego ordinance gave on-site commercial advertisers special legislative protection. See also Mass. Gen. Laws ch. 40A, §6 (2004), which prohibits localities from regulating existing on-site signs. Do on-site commercial speakers also warrant special *constitutional* protection? See R. Douglass Bond, Note, Making Sense of Billboard Law: Justifying Prohibitions and Exemptions, 88 Mich. L. Rev. 2482 (1990) (arguing that a sign that "identifies" the premises on which it is placed warrants heightened First Amendment protection because the owner has no other equally good channel for broadcasting this relationship).

Many decisions address the rights of brokers and property owners to post a "For Sale" sign at a listed property. See, e.g., Schoen v. Township of Hillside, 382 A.2d 704 (N.J. Super. Ct. Law Div. 1977), which struck down, for violating the First Amendment, size limits and color restrictions on these signs. However, *Schoen* went on to sustain ordinance provisions that limited signs advertising a garage sale (1) to a size of 10 inches by 14 inches; (2) to the message "Garage Sale," set in black letters on a white background; and (3) to locations set back 15 feet from the "street line." Did the court assure the availability of adequate channels for advertising a garage sale? See also Linmark Associates v. Willingboro Township, 431 U.S. 85 (1977) (invalidating content-based ordinance that had limited the posting of "For Sale" signs to stem white flight). But compare Long Island Board of Realtors, Inc. v. Incorporated Village of Massapequa Park, 277 F.3d 622 (2d Cir. 2002), sustaining validity of ordinance that limited size of signs, including For Sale signs, to 15 inches by 15 inches.

Invoking the notion that adults uses have negative secondary effects, could a municipality impose special burdens on on-site signs advertising these uses, or would that constitute impermissible discrimination based on the content of speech? See pp. 220–31 (on the regulation of adult uses).

4. *Off-site commercial signs*. *Metromedia* holds that the First Amendment provides only limited protection to commercial firms that employ signs to advertise goods or services not available at the location of the sign. See Ackerley Communications of Northwest, Inc. v. Krochalis, 108 F.3d 1095 (9th Cir. 1997) (rebuffing First Amendment challenge to Seattle's off-site billboard regulations). But see Lorillard Tobacco Co. v. Reilly, 533 U.S. 525 (2001), a challenge to Massachusetts regulations that restricted the advertising of tobacco products within 1,000 feet of a school or playground. Justice O'Connor's opinion for the five-to-four majority first held that a federal statute preempted state regulation of both on-site and off-site advertising of cigarettes. In a ruling with much broader implications, she then held that Massachusetts's selective territorial prohibition on off-site advertising of cigars and chewing tobacco violated the fourth prong of *Central Hudson*, which requires a reasonable fit between the ends and means of a regulatory scheme. "In some geographical areas, these regulations would constitute nearly a complete ban on communication of truthful information about smokeless tobacco and cigars to adult consumers," and the state had not "demonstrate[d] a careful calculation of the speech interests involved." Id. at 562. After *Lorillard*, could a city adopt a content-based regulation completely barring off-site billboard advertising specifically of cigars? A content-neutral regulatory scheme that barred commercial off-site advertising of all goods and services, including cigars?

5. *Taxation of expression*. A California state senator once proposed that the state levy an annual tax of 50 cents per square foot on all off-site billboards. Cal. Sen. Bill 708 (1972). Would this program violate the First Amendment? Cf. Clear Channel Outdoor,

Inc. v. City of Los Angeles, 340 F.3d 810 (9th Cir. 2003) (vacating preliminary injunction against city's collection of inspection fee imposed on owners of off-site billboards). But cf. Forsyth County v. Nationalist Movement, 505 U.S. 123 (1992) (invalidating parade fees that administrators were to adjust according to the estimated costs of maintaining public order). Could any taxes or fees imposed on owners of *on-site* signs pass constitutional muster?

6. *State regulatory programs.* In 1967, Vermont adopted one of the earliest and most restrictive state regulatory systems for outdoor advertising. See Vt. Stat. Ann., tit. 10, §§481–505 (2004). Section 493 regulates the size, height, and content of on-premises signs (forbidding, for example, a broker's placement of a "sold" sign). The Vermont statute also limits a merchant to four off-premises directional signs, and authorizes a state agency to "regulate the size, shape, color, lighting, manner of display, and lettering" of directional signs. Id. at §490(a). Is it wise for a government to regulate signs in such detail? What statewide interest might justify state, as opposed to local, control of these matters? Are First Amendment questions raised more sharply when a state does the regulating? For other statewide programs regulating outdoor advertising, see, e.g., Me. Rev. Stat. Ann. tit. 23, §§1901–1925 (West 2004) (enacted 1977); Or. Rev. Stat. §§377.700–377.992 (2004) (enacted 1971).

By contrast, a California statute preempts a local government's power to force a reduction in the height or size of an on-site sign if the reduction would materially impair communication with the traveling public. See Cal. Bus. & Prof. Code §5499 (West 2004); Denny's, Inc. v. City of Agoura Hills, 66 Cal. Rptr. 2d 382 (Ct. App. 1997) (invoking statute to sustain rights of plaintiff owners of fast-food restaurants and service stations to maintain freestanding pole signs along freeway). Why do sign owners fare better in California's legislature than in Vermont's?

7. *Economic consequences of sign regulation.* By crimping a major channel of communication with touring motorists, do billboard controls contribute to the growth of nationally franchised motel and restaurant chains at the expense of mom-and-pop enterprises? Cf. Keith B. Leffler, The Prohibition of Billboard Advertising: An Economic Analysis of the *Metromedia* Decision, 1 Sup. Ct. Econ. Rev. 113 (1983).

8. *The politics of outdoor advertising.* Politicians commonly hire the services of billboard owners during their campaigns for office. How might this affect elected officials' stances on issues of sign regulation? On the rough-and-tumble of billboard politics, see City of Columbia v. Omni Outdoor Advertising, Inc., 499 U.S. 365 (1991), excerpted at p. 119.

City of Ladue v. Gilleo
512 U.S. 43 (1994)

Justice STEVENS delivered the opinion of the Court.

An ordinance of the City of Ladue prohibits homeowners from displaying any signs on their property except "residence identification" signs, "for sale" signs, and signs warning of safety hazards. The ordinance permits commercial establishments, churches, and non-profit organizations to erect certain signs that are not allowed at residences. The question presented is whether the ordinance violates a Ladue resident's right to free speech.

I

Respondent Margaret P. Gilleo owns one of the 57 single-family homes in the Willow Hill subdivision of Ladue. On December 8, 1990, she placed on her front lawn a 24- by

36-inch sign printed with the words "Say No to War in the Persian Gulf, Call Congress Now." After that sign disappeared, Gilleo put up another but it was knocked to the ground. When Gilleo reported these incidents to the police, they advised her that such signs were prohibited in Ladue. The City Council denied her petition for a variance. Gilleo then filed this action under 42 U.S.C. §1983 against the City, the Mayor, and members of the City Council, alleging that Ladue's sign ordinance violated her First Amendment right of free speech.

The District Court issued a preliminary injunction against enforcement of the ordinance. 774 F. Supp. 1559 (E.D. Mo. 1991). Gilleo then placed an 8.5- by 11-inch sign in the second story window of her home stating, "For Peace in the Gulf." The Ladue City Council responded to the injunction by repealing its ordinance and enacting a replacement. Like its predecessor, the new ordinance contains a general prohibition of "signs" and defines that term broadly. The ordinance prohibits all signs except those that fall within one of ten exemptions. Thus, "residential identification signs" no larger than one square foot are allowed, as are signs advertising "that the property is for sale, lease or exchange" and identifying the owner or agent. §35-10, App. to Pet. for Cert. 45a. Also exempted are signs "for churches, religious institutions, and schools," "commercial signs in commercially or industrial zoned districts," and on-site signs advertising "gasoline filling stations." Unlike its predecessor, the new ordinance contains a lengthy "Declaration of Findings, Policies, Interests, and Purposes," part of which recites that the

> "proliferation of an unlimited number of signs in private, residential, commercial, industrial, and public areas of the City of Ladue would create ugliness, visual blight and clutter, tarnish the natural beauty of the landscape as well as the residential and commercial architecture, impair property values, substantially impinge upon the privacy and special ambience of the community, and may cause safety and traffic hazards to motorists, pedestrians, and children[.]" Id., at 36a.

Gilleo amended her complaint to challenge the new ordinance, which explicitly prohibits window signs like hers. The District Court held the ordinance unconstitutional, and the Court of Appeals affirmed. . . .

We . . . now affirm.

II

While signs are a form of expression protected by the Free Speech Clause, they pose distinctive problems that are subject to municipalities' police powers. Unlike oral speech, signs take up space and may obstruct views, distract motorists, displace alternative uses for land, and pose other problems that legitimately call for regulation. It is common ground that governments may regulate the physical characteristics of signs — just as they can, within reasonable bounds and absent censorial purpose, regulate audible expression in its capacity as noise. See, e.g., Ward v. Rock Against Racism, 491 U.S. 781 (1989); Kovacs v. Cooper, 336 U.S. 77 (1949). However, because regulation of a medium inevitably affects communication itself, it is not surprising that we have had occasion to review the constitutionality of municipal ordinances prohibiting the display of certain outdoor signs.

In Linmark Associates, Inc. v. Willingboro, 431 U.S. 85 (1977), we addressed an ordinance that sought to maintain stable, integrated neighborhoods by prohibiting homeowners from placing "For Sale" or "Sold" signs on their property. Although we recognized the importance of Willingboro's objective, we held that the First Amendment prevented the township from "achieving its goal by restricting the free flow of truthful information." Id., at 95. In some respects *Linmark* is the mirror image of this case. For instead of prohibiting "For Sale" signs without banning any other signs, Ladue has exempted such signs from an otherwise virtually complete ban. Moreover, whereas in *Linmark* we noted that the ordinance was not concerned with the promotion of aesthetic values unrelated to the content of the prohibited speech, id., at 93–94, here Ladue relies squarely on that content-neutral justification for its ordinance.

In *Metromedia*, we reviewed an ordinance imposing substantial prohibitions on outdoor advertising displays within the City of San Diego in the interest of traffic safety and aesthetics. . . .

These decisions identify two analytically distinct grounds for challenging the constitutionality of a municipal ordinance regulating the display of signs. One is that the measure in effect restricts too little speech because its exemptions discriminate on the basis of the signs' messages. See *Metromedia*, 453 U.S., at 512–517 (opinion of White, J.). Alternatively, such provisions are subject to attack on the ground that they simply prohibit too much protected speech. See id. at 525–534 (Brennan, J., concurring in judgment). . . .

III

While surprising at first glance, the notion that a regulation of speech may be impermissibly underinclusive is firmly grounded in basic First Amendment principles. Thus, an exemption from an otherwise permissible regulation of speech may represent a governmental "attempt to give one side of a debatable public question an advantage in expressing its views to the people." First Nat. Bank of Boston v. Bellotti, 435 U.S. 765 (1978). . . .

Exemptions from an otherwise legitimate regulation of a medium of speech may be noteworthy for a reason quite apart from the risks of viewpoint and content discrimination: they may diminish the credibility of the government's rationale for restricting speech in the first place. See, e.g., Cincinnati v. Discovery Network, Inc., 507 U.S. 410, 424–426 (1993). In this case, at the very least, the exemptions from Ladue's ordinance demonstrate that Ladue has concluded that the interest in allowing certain messages to be conveyed by means of residential signs outweighs the City's aesthetic interest in eliminating outdoor signs. Ladue has not imposed a flat ban on signs because it has determined that at least some of them are too vital to be banned.

Under the Court of Appeals' content discrimination rationale, the City might theoretically remove the defects in its ordinance by simply repealing all of the exemptions. If, however, the ordinance is also vulnerable because it prohibits too much speech, that solution would not save it. . . .

IV

In *Linmark* we held that the City's interest in maintaining a stable, racially integrated neighborhood was not sufficient to support a prohibition of residential "For Sale" signs. We recognized that even such a narrow sign prohibition would have a deleterious effect on residents' ability to convey important information because alternatives were "far from satisfactory." 431 U.S., at 93. Ladue's sign ordinance is supported principally by the City's interest in minimizing the visual clutter associated with signs, an interest that is concededly valid but certainly no more compelling than the interests at stake in *Linmark*. Moreover, whereas the ordinance in *Linmark* applied only to a form of commercial speech, Ladue's ordinance covers even such absolutely pivotal speech as a sign protesting an imminent governmental decision to go to war.

The impact on free communication of Ladue's broad sign prohibition, moreover, is manifestly greater than in *Linmark*. Gilleo and other residents of Ladue are forbidden to display virtually any "sign" on their property. . . .

. . . Ladue has almost completely foreclosed a venerable means of communication that is both unique and important. It has totally foreclosed that medium to political, religious, or personal messages. Signs that react to a local happening or express a view on a controversial issue both reflect and animate change in the life of a community. Often placed on lawns or in windows, residential signs play an important part in political campaigns, during which they are displayed to signal the resident's support for particular candidates, parties, or causes. They may not afford the same opportunities for conveying complex ideas as do other media, but residential signs have long been an important and distinct medium of expression.

Our prior decisions have voiced particular concern with laws that foreclose an entire medium of expression. Thus, we have held invalid ordinances that completely banned the distribution of pamphlets within the municipality, Lovell v. Griffin, 303 U.S. 444, 451–452 (1938); handbills on the public streets, Jamison v. Texas, 318 U.S. 413, 416 (1943); the door-to-door distribution of literature, Martin v. Struthers, 319 U.S. 141, 145–149 (1943); Schneider v. State, 308 U.S. 147, 164–165 (1939), and live entertainment, Schad v. Mount Ephraim, 452 U.S. 61, 75–76 (1981). . . .

Ladue contends, however, that its ordinance is a mere regulation of the "time, place, or manner" of speech because residents remain free to convey their desired messages by other means, such as *hand-held* signs, "letters, handbills, flyers, telephone calls, newspaper advertisements, bumper stickers, speeches, and neighborhood or community meetings." Brief for Petitioners 41. However, even regulations that do not foreclose an entire medium of expression, but merely shift the time, place, or manner of its use, must "leave open ample alternative channels for communication." Clark v. Community for Creative Non-Violence, 468 U.S. 288, 293 (1984). In this case, we are not persuaded that adequate substitutes exist for the important medium of speech that Ladue has closed off.

Displaying a sign from one's own residence often carries a message quite distinct from placing the same sign someplace else, or conveying the same text or picture by other means. Precisely because of their location, such signs provide information about the identity of the "speaker." As an early and eminent student of rhetoric observed, the identity of the speaker is an important component of many attempts to persuade.[14] A sign advocating "Peace in the Gulf" in the front lawn of a retired general or decorated war veteran may provoke a different reaction than the same sign in a 10-year-old child's bedroom window or the same message on a bumper sticker of a passing automobile. An espousal of socialism may carry different implications when displayed on the grounds of a stately mansion than when posted on a factory wall or an ambulatory sandwich board.

Residential signs are an unusually cheap and convenient form of communication. Especially for persons of modest means or limited mobility, a yard or window sign may have no practical substitute. Even for the affluent, the added costs in money or time of taking out a newspaper advertisement, handing out leaflets on the street, or standing in front of one's house with a hand-held sign may make the difference between participating and not participating in some public debate. Furthermore, a person who puts up a sign at her residence often intends to reach neighbors, an audience that could not be reached nearly as well by other means. . . .

---

14. See Aristotle 2, Rhetoric, Book 1, ch. 2, in 8 Great Books of the Western World, Encyclopedia Britannica 595 (M. Adler ed., 2d ed. 1990) ("We believe good men more fully and more readily than others: this is true generally whatever the question is, and absolutely true where exact certainty is impossible and opinions are divided").

Our decision that Ladue's ban on almost all residential signs violates the First Amendment by no means leaves the City powerless to address the ills that may be associated with residential signs.[17] It bears mentioning that individual residents themselves have strong incentives to keep their own property values up and to prevent "visual clutter" in their own yards and neighborhoods — incentives markedly different from those of persons who erect signs on others' land, in others' neighborhoods, or on public property. Residents' self-interest diminishes the danger of the "unlimited" proliferation of residential signs that concerns the City of Ladue. We are confident that more temperate measures could in large part satisfy Ladue's stated regulatory needs without harm to the First Amendment rights of its citizens. As currently framed, however, the ordinance abridges those rights.

Accordingly, the judgment of the Court of Appeals is affirmed.

[Justice O'CONNOR wrote a concurring opinion.]

Note on Noncommercial Signs and Free Speech

1. *The scope of* Ladue. What if Gilleo's home antiwar sign had been 32 square feet in area, not 6? See Lombardo v. Warner, 353 F.3d 774 (9th Cir. 2003) (rejecting sign-poster's challenge to enforcement of Oregon billboard controls, including assertion that the state improperly was giving preference to on-site commercial speech over on-site political speech).

In Texas Department of Transportation v. Barber, 111 S.W.3d 86 (Tex. 2003), Barber had erected, on nonresidential land he owned adjacent to an interstate highway, an 8-foot by 16-foot billboard. On the billboard, he had placed the message, "Just say NO to Searches," which reflected his concern about police entries into vehicles. Citing the First Amendment and the Liberty of Speech Section of the Texas Constitution, he unsuccessfully sought to annul a state administrative decision that his billboard violated the Texas Highway Beautification Act and had to be razed. The three dissenting justices of the Texas Supreme Court asserted (correctly?) that the case was indistinguishable from *Ladue*.

See generally Mark Cordes, Sign Regulation After *Ladue*, 74 Neb. L. Rev. 36 (1995).

2. *Election signs.* Courts repeatedly have held that the First Amendment forbids stringent local restrictions on the posting of political-campaign signs at the poster's home or place of business. For example, in City of Painesville Building Department v. Dworken & Bernstein Co., 733 N.E.2d 1152 (Ohio 2000), a city ordinance limited display of political signs to 17 days before, and 2 days after, an election. The court ruled in favor of a lawyer prosecuted for posting a sign at his law office building prior to the permitted period. Compare Ross v. Goshi, 351 F. Supp. 949 (D. Haw. 1972) (holding that First Amendment prevented the County of Maui from barring political candidates from using outdoor advertising signs).

3. *Artistic expression.* In City of Indio v. Arroyo, 191 Cal. Rptr. 565 (Ct. App. 1983), the city had invoked its sign-control ordinance to force the removal of a mural painted on a wall of the Arroyos' convenience store. The mural, 110 square feet in area, consisted of scenes depicting aspects of the Arroyos' Mexican heritage. The regulation at issue was held to be both overbroad and unconstitutionally vague.

17. Nor do we hold that every kind of sign must be permitted in residential areas. Different considerations might well apply, for example, in the case of signs (whether political or otherwise) displayed by residents for a fee, or in the case of off-site commercial advertisements on residential property. We also are not confronted here with mere regulations short of a ban.

Elizabeth Maker, Get That Sculpture Off Your Lawn!, N.Y. Times, Mar. 9, 2003, §14CN, at 1, is a report on two Connecticut towns where historic preservationists are opposing the placement of modernist outdoor sculpture in historic districts. Does the First Amendment ever protect a homeowner's or shopkeeper's right to install a work of outdoor sculpture?

2. Architectural Review

Prior to 1970, the City of Ladue, the well-to-do St. Louis suburb involved in the preceding case, established an Architectural Review Board. The board had three members, all required to be architects, who were charged with reviewing plans for buildings in the city. In a leading case, State ex rel. Stoyanoff v. Berkeley, 458 S.W.2d 305 (Mo. 1970), a lot owner had sought approval to construct an ultramodern residence with a pyramidal shape, flat top, and triangular windows at the corners. Most houses in the vicinity were of conventional Colonial, French Provincial, or English design. The board denied the permit, and the Supreme Court of Missouri sustained its decision. The court held first that the Missouri Zoning Enabling Act, copied from the SZEA, authorized architectural review. Second, it deemed the aesthetic objectives of the program permissible when coupled with the city's interests in promoting the general welfare and maintaining property values. Third, the court ruled that the board's standard for decision — to prevent the erection of an "unsightly, grotesque or unsuitable structure in appearance, detrimental to the welfare of the surrounding property or residents" — was not so inadequate as to entail an unconstitutional delegation of power.

Anderson v. City of Issaquah
851 P.2d 744 (Wash. Ct. App. 1993)

Kennedy, Judge.

[Anderson challenges the denial of his] application for a land use certification, arguing, inter alia, that the building design requirements contained in Issaquah Municipal Code (IMC) 16.16.060 are unconstitutionally vague. The Superior Court rejected this constitutional challenge. We reverse and direct that Anderson's land use certification be issued. . . .

Anderson owns property located at 145 N.W. Gilman Boulevard in the city of Issaquah (City). In 1988, Anderson applied to the City for a land use certification to develop the property. The property is zoned for general commercial use. Anderson desired to build a 6800 square foot commercial building for several retail tenants.

After obtaining architectural plans, Anderson submitted the project to various City departments for the necessary approvals. The process went smoothly until the approval of the Issaquah Development Commission (Development Commission) was sought. This commission was created to administer and enforce the City's land use regulations. It has the authority to approve or deny applications for land use certification.

Chapter 16.16.060 of the IMC enumerates various building design objectives which the Development Commission is required to administer and enforce. . . .

As initially designed, Anderson's proposed structure was to be faced with off-white stucco and was to have a blue metal roof. It was designed in a "modern" style with an unbroken "warehouse" appearance in the rear, and large retail-style windows in the front.

The City moved a Victorian era residence, the "Alexander House," onto the neighboring property to serve as a visitors' center. Across the street from the Anderson site is a gasoline station that looks like a gasoline station. Located nearby and within view from the proposed building site are two more gasoline stations, the First Mutual Bank Building built in the "Issaquah territorial style," an Elks hall which is described in the record by the Mayor of Issaquah as a "box building," an auto repair shop, and a veterinary clinic with a cyclone-fenced dog run. The area is described in the record as "a natural transition area between old downtown Issaquah and the new village style construction of Gilman [Boulevard]."

The Development Commission reviewed Anderson's application for the first time at a public hearing on December 21, 1988. Commissioner Nash commented that "the facade did not fit with the concept of the surrounding area." Commissioner McGinnis agreed. Commissioner Nash expressed concern about the building color and stated that he did not think the building was compatible with the image of Issaquah. Commissioner Larson said that he would like to see more depth to the building facade. Commissioner Nash said there should be some interest created along the blank back wall. Commissioner Garrison suggested that the rear facade needed to be redesigned.

At the conclusion of the meeting, the Development Commission voted to continue the hearing to give Anderson an opportunity to modify the building design.

On January 18, 1989, Anderson came back before the Development Commission with modified plans which included changing the roofing from metal to tile, changing the color of the structure from off-white to "Cape Cod" gray with "Tahoe" blue trim, and adding brick to the front facade. During the ensuing discussion among the commissioners, Commissioner Larson stated that the revisions to the front facade had not satisfied his concerns from the last meeting. In response to Anderson's request for more specific design guidelines, Commissioner McGinnis stated that the Development Commission had "been giving direction; it is the applicant's responsibility to take the direction/suggestions and incorporate them into a revised plan that reflects the changes." Commissioner Larson then suggested that "the facade can be broken up with sculptures, benches, fountains, etc." Commissioner Nash suggested that Anderson "drive up and down Gilman and look at both good and bad examples of what has been done with flat facades." . . .

Commissioner Nash continued, stating that he "personally liked the introduction of brick and the use of tiles rather than metal on the roof." Commissioner Larson stated that he would like to see a review of the blue to be used: "Tahoe blue may be too dark." Commissioner Steinwachs agreed. Commissioner Larson noted that "the front of the building could be modulated [to] have other design techniques employed to make the front facade more interesting."

With this, the Development Commission voted to continue the discussion to a future hearing.

On February 15, 1989, Anderson came back before the Development Commission. In the meantime, Anderson's architects had added a 5-foot overhang and a 7-foot accent overhang to the plans for the front of the building. More brick had been added to the front of the building. Wood trim and accent colors had been added to the back of the building and trees were added to the landscaping to further break up the rear facade.

Anderson explained the plans still called for large, floor to ceiling windows as this was to be a retail premises: "[A] glass front is necessary to rent the space. . . . " Commissioner Steinwachs stated that he had driven Gilman Boulevard and taken notes. The following verbatim statement by Steinwachs was placed into the minutes:

> *"My General Observation From Driving Up and Down Gilman Boulevard."* I see certain design elements and techniques used in various combinations in various locations to achieve a visual

effect that is sensitive to the unique character of our Signature Street. I see heavy use of brick, wood, and tile. I see minimal use of stucco. I see colors that are mostly earthtones, avoiding extreme contrasts. I see various methods used to provide modulation in both horizontal and vertical lines, such as gables, bay windows, recesses in front faces, porches, rails, many vertical columns, and breaks in roof lines. I see long, sloping, conspicuous roofs with large overhangs. I see windows with panels above and below windows. I see no windows that extend down to floor level. This is the impression I have of Gilman Boulevard as it relates to building design.

Commissioner Nash agreed stating, "There is a certain feeling you get when you drive along Gilman Boulevard, and this building does not give this same feeling." Commissioner Steinwachs wondered if the applicant had any option but to start "from scratch." Anderson responded that he would be willing to change from stucco to wood facing but that, after working on the project for 9 months and experiencing total frustration, he was not willing to make additional design changes.

At that point, the Development Commission denied Anderson's application. . . .

Anderson, who by this time had an estimated $250,000 into the project, timely appealed the adverse ruling to the Issaquah City Council (City Council). After a lengthy hearing and much debate, the City Council decided to affirm the Development Commission's decision by a vote of 4 to 3. . . .

2. Constitutionality of IMC 16.16.060 (Building Design Provisions)

[A] statute which either forbids or requires the doing of an act in terms so vague that men [and women] of common intelligence must necessarily guess at its meaning and differ as to its application, violates the first essential of due process of law.

Connally v. General Constr. Co., 269 U.S. 385 (1926). . . . The vagueness test does not require a statute to meet impossible standards of specificity. Chicago, M., St. P. & P.R.R. v. State Human Rights Comm'n, 557 P.2d 307, 310 (Wash. 1976).

In the area of land use, a court looks not only at the face of the ordinance but also at its application to the person who has sought to comply with the ordinance and/or who is alleged to have failed to comply. The purpose of the void for vagueness doctrine is to limit arbitrary and discretionary enforcements of the law. . . .

Looking first at the face of the building design sections of IMC 16.16.060, we note that an ordinary citizen reading these sections would learn only that a given building project should bear a good relationship with the Issaquah Valley and surrounding mountains; its windows, doors, eaves and parapets should be of "appropriate proportions," its colors should be "harmonious" and seldom "bright" or "brilliant"; its mechanical equipment should be screened from public view; its exterior lighting should be "harmonious" with the building design and "monotony should be avoided." The project should also be "interesting." IMC 16.16.060(D)(1)-(6). If the building is not "compatible" with adjacent buildings, it should be "made compatible" by the use of screens and site breaks "or other suitable methods and materials." "Harmony in texture, lines, and masses [is] encouraged." The landscaping should provide an "attractive . . . transition" to adjoining properties. IMC 16.16.060(B)(1)–(3).

As is stated in the brief of amicus curiae,[9] we conclude that these code sections "do not give effective or meaningful guidance" to applicants, to design professionals, or to the

---

9. The amicus curiae is the Seattle Chapter of the American Institute of Architects, the Washington Council of the American Institute of Architects, and the Washington Chapter of the American Society of Landscape Architects.

public officials of Issaquah who are responsible for enforcing the code. Brief of Amicus Curiae, at 1. Although it is clear from the code sections here at issue that mechanical equipment must be screened from public view and that, probably, earthtones or pastels located within the cool and muted ranges of the color wheel are going to be preferred, there is nothing in the code from which an applicant can determine whether his or her project is going to be seen by the Development Commission as "interesting" versus "monotonous" and as "harmonious" with the valley and the mountains. Neither is it clear from the code just what else, besides the valley and the mountains, a particular project is supposed to be harmonious with, although "harmony in texture, lines, and masses" is certainly encouraged. IMC 16.16.060(B)(2).

In attempting to interpret and apply this code, the commissioners charged with that task were left with only their own individual, subjective "feelings" about the "image of Issaquah" and as to whether this project was "compatible" or "interesting." . . .

The point we make here is that neither Anderson nor the commissioners may constitutionally be required or allowed to guess at the meaning of the code's building design requirements by driving up and down Gilman Boulevard looking at "good and bad" examples of what has been done with other buildings, recently or in the past. We hold that the code sections here at issue are unconstitutionally vague on their face. The words employed are not technical words which are commonly understood within the professional building design industry. Neither do these words have a settled common law meaning.

As they were applied to Anderson, it is also clear the code sections at issue fail to pass constitutional muster. . . . The commissioners enforced not a building design code but their own arbitrary concept of the provisions of an unwritten "statement" to be made on Gilman Boulevard. The commissioners' individual concepts were as vague and undefined as those written in the code. This is the very epitome of discretionary, arbitrary enforcement of the law. . . .

As well illustrated by the appendices to the brief of amicus curiae, aesthetic considerations are not impossible to define in a code or ordinance.[14] Moreover, the procedural safeguards contained in the Issaquah Municipal Code (providing for appeal to the City Council and to the courts) do not cure the constitutional defects here apparent. . . . [T]he appellate process is to no avail where the statute at issue contains no ascertainable standards. . . .

. . . We order that Anderson's land use certificate be issued, provided however, that those changes which Anderson agreed to through the hearing before the City Council may validly be imposed.

Note on Architectural Review by Government

1. *Administrative structure and the role of architects.* The City of Issaquah had assigned responsibility for architectural review to its general-purpose land use agency, not to a special-purpose review board, such as the one in the City of Ladue. Which administrative structure is preferable? Was the City of Ladue wise to appoint a review board consisting entirely of architects? In *City of Issaquah*, why did chapters of architects' associations appear as amici on behalf of Anderson? If the purpose of architectural review is enhancement of

---

14. Appendix A to the brief of amicus curiae is a portion of the design objectives plan for entryway corridors for Bozeman, Montana. Appendix B is a portion of the development code for San Bernardino, California. Both codes contain extensive written criteria illustrated by schematic drawings and photographs. The illustrations clarify a number of concepts which otherwise might be difficult to describe with the requisite degree of clarity.

property values, are appraisers and real estate brokers better qualified than architects to judge proposed designs?

2. *Vague standards.* Compare Rolling Pines Limited Partnership v. City of Little Rock, 40 S.W.3d 828 (Ark. Ct. App. 2001). As house sales in a new subdivision of brick homes slowed, the developer sought to switch to manufactured housing units clad in vinyl siding. When the owners of the existing brick houses objected, the planning commission and local governing body in turn disapproved the proposed houses on the basis of an ordinance provision that required new land uses to be "compatible with" the neighborhood. Distinguishing *City of Issaquah*, the court held that this standard was not impermissibly vague.

3. *Making a statement.* Could the design-review process abridge guarantees of free expression? See John Nivala, Constitutional Architecture: The First Amendment and the Single Family House, 33 San Diego L. Rev. 291 (1996), which argues that many architectural controls threaten First Amendment values. Would the constitutional problem be avoided if a review board were not authorized to veto a design, but only to compel the builder of a controversial house to compensate neighbors?

4. *Standard of review.* How actively should a reviewing court second-guess the merits of an architectural review decision? See Friends of Davis v. City of Davis, 100 Cal. Rptr. 2d 413 (Ct. App. 2000) (deferring to city's refusal to use design-review process to prevent the Borders chain from opening bookstore); Breneric Associates v. City of Del Mar, 81 Cal. Rptr. 2d 324 (Ct. App. 1998) (applying the deferential substantial evidence test and denying damage award sought by disappointed applicant).

5. *Coordination with private design-review procedures.* As pp. 593–96 explain, in many modern subdivisions, covenants authorize either the developer or the residential community association to exercise design review. Should a local ordinance exempt these subdivisions from the public review process? If there is no rational basis for piggybacking public controls on top of private ones, is this exemption constitutionally required?

6. *Compulsory upgrading.* Architectural review typically is exclusively prospective: Only a landowner who wishes to build or renovate must submit plans for municipal scrutiny. Should a city ever authorize its architectural review agency to survey existing structures and compel owners to make architectural improvements that would enhance the beauty of the cityscape? Would a retrospective effort of this sort be politically untenable? Exceed municipal powers under state enabling acts? Violate the takings clause or other constitutional constraints? Compare Parking Association of Georgia, Inc. v. City of Atlanta, 450 S.E.2d 200 (Ga. 1994) (holding that ordinance that required owners of existing downtown parking lots to install curbs, trees, and landscaping did not violate Takings, Due Process, or Equal Protection Clause). See also Charlie LeDuff, Good Fences, Uneasy Neighbors, a Frosty Dispute, N.Y. Times, Jan. 13, 2003, at A11, a report that Glendale, California, had just begun to enforce against 1,500 violators an 80-year-old ordinance prohibiting fences in front yards.

7. *Merits of architectural review.* Apart from its constitutionality, is governmental architectural review sound policy? An owner who wished to build a single-family house on a one-acre coastal lot in Pacific Grove, California, reports having to endure 20 public hearings over the course of two years, and an out-of-pocket cost of $600,000, to obtain all necessary permits. Stephen J.L. Pace, "In My Former Life as a Seagull," Wall. St. J., Dec. 27, 1994, at A16. In Santa Fe, architectural controls that generally dictate brown adobe buildings with flat roofs have led to bitter interneighbor disputes. Calvin Trillin, U.S. Journal: Santa Fe, N.M.: Thy Neighbor's Roof, New Yorker, Mar. 29, 1982, at 124. See generally Kathryn Shattuck, Beware the Cry of "Niyby": Not in *Your* Backyard, N.Y.

Times, May 11, 2000, at F2. What legal innovations might deter neighbors and members of an architectural review board from being too meddlesome?

Portland, Oregon, has sought to stem the spread of "snout houses" — those with a garage protruding toward the street. In 1999, the city adopted an ordinance that limits garage width to no more than 50 percent of the house frontage and bans placement of a front door more than 8 feet behind the front-most wall. As one city commissioner explained, "[W]e want a house to pass the 'trick or treat' test. So when kids come around to trick or treat, they actually get a sense that somebody lives in the house, and they can find the door." Local homebuilders assert that the ordinance is cost-inflating and inconsistent with consumer preferences. See Timothy Egan, In Portland, Houses Are Friendly. Or Else., N.Y. Times, Apr. 20, 2000, at F1. Why might a city be wise to regulate the design of a house proposed for an existing neighborhood more stringently that the designs of houses in a new subdivision? Does the desirability of architectural review increase or decrease with population density? Cf. Georgette C. Poindexter, Light, Air, or Manhattanization? Communal Aesthetics in Zoning Central City Real Estate Development, 78 B.U. L. Rev. 445 (1998).

Douglas E. Hough & Charles G. Kratz, Can "Good" Architecture Meet the Market Test?, 14 J. Urb. Econ. 40, 51–52 (1983):

> . . . We found that [Chicago] tenants are willing to pay a premium to be in new architecturally significant office buildings, but apparently see no benefits associated with old office buildings that express recognized aesthetic excellence.
>
> The policy implications of these findings are clear. At least in Chicago, those concerned about a city's ambience need not worry much about the architectural quality of new buildings; the market for office space will respond favorably to "good" new architecture. However, that same market does not register any discernible demand by tenants for "good" old space. If these buildings are to survive, those who value them must devise feasible non-market mechanisms so that their preferences for these buildings are revealed and their dollars are contributed.

But cf. Paul K. Asabere et al., Architecture, Historic Zoning, and the Value of Homes, 2 J. Real Est. Fin. & Econ. 181 (1989) (reporting that purchasers of houses in Newburyport, Massachusetts, paid premium prices for houses in older architectural quality styles such as colonial, federal, garrison, and Victorian). In what contexts, if any, do market forces and informal norms adequately reward architectural quality?

3. *Historic Preservation*

State by Powderly v. Erickson
285 N.W.2d 84 (Minn. 1979)

[Erickson owned a small shopping center fronting on a state highway in Red Wing, Minnesota. With an eye toward expansion, he purchased an adjoining set of code-violating row houses. Shortly after Erickson had obtained a permit to demolish the houses, the area was placed in the Heritage Mall Preservation District. Three citizens then invoked the Minnesota Environmental Rights Act (MERA), Minn. Stat. ch. 116B, in an effort to enjoin the proposed demolition. The Minnesota Supreme Court granted the injunction, holding, inter alia, that the buildings were historical.]

WAHL, Justice.
. . . Under MERA, plaintiffs have the burden of proving (1) the existence of a protectable natural resource, and (2) the pollution, impairment, or destruction of that resource.

County of Freeborn v. Bryson, 210 N.W.2d 290 (Minn. 1973); Minn. Stat. 116B.04. In the instant case there is no dispute that demolition would destroy the row houses; the only issue is whether they are protectable natural resources within the meaning of MERA.

For purposes of MERA, natural resources are defined as "all mineral, animal, botanical, air, water, land, timber, soil, quietude, recreational and historical resources." Minn. Stat. 116B.02, subd. 4. No cases define the term "historical resources," although there are extensive local, state, and federal programs for historical preservation. See, 16 U.S.C. §§461–470t; Minn. Stat. 138.51–.65, 138.71–.75; Red Wing City Code, §§2.53–.66. Buildings, sites, and structures of local, state, or national significance are eligible for inclusion on the national register of historic sites under the following criteria:

> . . . The quality of significance in American history, architecture, archeology, and culture is present in districts, sites, buildings, structures and objects of State and local importance that possess integrity of location, design, setting, materials, workmanship, feeling and association and:
>
> (1) That are associated with events that have made a significant contribution to the broad patterns of our history; or
>
> (2) That are associated with the lives of persons significant in our past; or
>
> (3) That embody the distinctive characteristics of a type, period, or method of construction, or that represent the work of a master, or that possess high artistic values, or that represent a significant and distinguishable entity whose components may lack individual distinction; or
>
> (4) That have yielded, or may be likely to yield, information important in prehistory or history. (36 C.F.R. §800.10(a).)

Although these criteria do not control our decision, they do indicate what factors should be considered in determining whether the row houses are historical resources.

In the instant case Russell Fridley, Director of the Minnesota Historical Society and the State Preservation Officer, defined an historical resource as a building, structure, or site possessing historical, archeological, or architectural value. He stated that although age was one factor to consider, not all old buildings were historically significant. Other factors Mr. Fridley considered important were: (1) who built the structure; (2) who lived in it; (3) its location; (4) its architecture; (5) unique materials; (6) quality of workmanship; (7) the structure's association with builders or important people or events in the area; and (8) its interaction with other buildings. In his opinion, the row houses are historical resources because of their age, their construction, and their association with local historical events. The north row house was built in 1870 by James Lawther, an Irish immigrant, who was highly successful in real estate. Lawther had a tremendous impact on building in Red Wing and was one of the town's greatest philanthropists. The south house was built in 1882 by Silas Foot, a mayor and famous civic leader of Red Wing, who was involved in the Foot Tanning Company. The style of the houses, although common in other parts of the country during the 19th century, was unusual in Minnesota. The row houses also occupy a key position on the mall and act as a buffer between the highway and the Heritage Mall Preservation District. Mr. Fridley also testified that both the row houses and the Heritage Mall Preservation District would be eligible for nomination to the national register.

Defendants did not rebut this evidence. Their only rebuttal witness was a registered architect who testified that he had seen buildings of similar style in the Twin Cities. He admitted that he had no prior professional experience in historical renovation or preservation, nor was he familiar with a number of local renovation projects. We find there is sufficient evidence to sustain the trial court's finding that the row houses are historical resources within the meaning of MERA.

[Remanded for issuance of permanent injunction.]

Note on Techniques of Historic Preservation

1. *What to save?* A structure may be historically significant for a variety of reasons. First, a building might be noteworthy for events that occurred on the premises — for example, the Old North Church, Ford's Theatre, the Alamo. Second, a building might be singled out for its architectural excellence. An example would be an antebellum plantation manor in the Deep South or an office building designed by a noteworthy architect such as Louis Sullivan. Third, some buildings that typify construction practices during a prior era may be worth preserving to memorialize customary living patterns. Current sightseers take interest in log cabins and sod houses. Might not preservationists therefore be wise to single out representative New York "dumbbell" tenements, Baltimore row houses, and California bungalows for posterity? See Evelyn Nieves, Wanted in Levittown: Just One Little Box with Ticky Tacky Intact, N.Y. Times, Nov. 11, 1995, at B1.

In 1958, architects designed a new bank building for the central business district of Burlington, Vermont, in the then-fashionable "International Style." The building's dominant feature was a front facade consisting of a curtain wall composed of green and clear glass panels. Thirty years later, bank officials sought to install a brick facade to replace the glass panels, which they regarded as "cold, outdated, and uninviting." Should preservationists support or oppose the bank's renovation plans? See In re Vermont National Bank, 597 A.2d 317 (Vt. 1991) (rebuffing city's eleventh-hour efforts to preserve the International Style facade).

Professor Rose asserts that the underlying rationale of historic preservation is the strengthening of the social ties that bind a community together. See Carol M. Rose, Preservation and Community: New Directions in the Law of Historic Preservation, 33 Stan. L. Rev. 473 (1981). Her analysis is in harmony with Costonis's suggestion that all types of aesthetic regulation are aimed to enhance cultural stability. John J. Costonis, Law and Aesthetics, 80 Mich. L. Rev. 355 (1982). These ideas prefigured the kindred notion of social capital developed in James S. Coleman, Foundations of Social Theory (1990), and Robert D. Putnam, Bowling Alone: The Collapse and Revival of American Community (2000).

To appraise the social-capital perspective, consider the following two controversies over the landmarking of perceived symbols of popular American culture. The California Historical Resources Commission once nominated to the National Register of Historic Places the last surviving McDonald's restaurant built in the original "golden arches" design. The then 30-year-old restaurant was located in a shopping center in Downey, a suburb of Los Angeles. The commission staff's report asked rhetorically, "Are we then required to register the oldest Burger King, Shakey's Pizza Parlor or Bob's Big Boy Restaurant? The answer is, probably not. The factor that sets this property apart from the rest, is that the McDonald brothers' concept revolutionized eating habits in America, creating the first successful franchising of an idea which has now become an American way of life." Bill Soiffer, Beef over a Burger Stand, S.F. Chron., Nov. 28, 1983, at 5.

In Boston, preservationists lobbied to have the city's most conspicuous neon sign designated an historic landmark. In 1965, the Cities Service Company erected a 3,600-square-foot sign to publicize the name CITGO, its new moniker. Located high over Kenmore Square and just behind the famous left field wall of Fenway Park, the sign executes computer-synchronized light displays of the CITGO logo. Reacting in part to rising energy costs, company officials turned off the sign in 1979 and, in 1982, began to talk of removing it. In response to an outpouring of public support for preserving the sign, in 1983 CITGO agreed to turn the sign back on, and since then has continued to operate it. See http://www.redsoxconnection.com/citgo.html.

2. *The National Register.* The National Historic Preservation Act of 1966, 16 U.S.C. §§470–470x (2004), established a National Register of Historic Places. By 2004, the Register included 77,000 listings — mainly buildings, but also geographic districts and sites. Federal agencies must "take into account the effects" of their decisions on registered places. See id. at §470f (§106 of the act). Opponents of federally approved projects have invoked this section, but rarely with success, perhaps because most federal agencies have learned how to satisfy its requirements for advance consultations with historic preservation agencies. See, e.g., Dangerfield Island Protective Society v. Babbitt, 40 F.3d 442 (D.C. Cir. 1994) (rebuffing challenge to federal involvement in highway interchange project). But compare Old Town Neighborhood Association v. Kauffman, 333 F.3d 732 (7th Cir. 2003) (enjoining city, which sought to avoid bite of §106, from seeking federal funding of street-widening project after widening had been completed).

Members of an elite subset of 2,300 places have been singled out in the Register for a more exalted designation: National Historic Landmark. A federal agency considering an action that would adversely affect a landmark it owns or controls must "to the maximum extent possible . . . minimize harm to [the] landmark." 16 U.S.C. §470h-2(f) (2005).

The existence of the National Register obscures the reality that historic preservation efforts are largely decentralized to state and local governments, which may not only nominate properties for inclusion in the Register, but also adopt independent procedures for designating landmarks and restricting their alteration. See, for example, Penn Central Transportation Co. v. City of New York, 438 U.S. 104 (1978), excerpted at p. 158 (describing New York City's procedures). Does a local historical society have standing to sue to enforce these regulations? See Dover Historical Society v. City of Dover Planning Commission, 838 A.2d 1103 (Del. 2003) (yes).

3. *Federal and state tax credits.* Since 1976, the Internal Revenue Code has included incentives for the rehabilitation of historic buildings that are either themselves registered or else situated in a registered district. In real dollars, Congress offered the most generous tax carrots between 1981 and 1986, a period when preservation activity boomed. The Interior Department's National Park Service, which determines a rehabilitator's eligibility, approved tax credits of $2.4 billion in 1985, the peak early year of the program.

The Tax Reform Act of 1986 significantly narrowed the scope of rehabilitation tax shelters. See I.R.C. §47 (2004); Carolyn Ells Cheverine & Charlotte Mariah Hays, Note, Rehabilitation Tax Credit: Does It Still Provide Incentives?, 10 Va. Tax Rev. 167 (1990). The 1986 act reduced the maximum tax credit (available only to rehabilitators of certified historic structures) from 25 percent to 20 percent, and required that the amount of any credit be deducted from the building's new basis, thus lowering the cost-recovery deductions that taxpayers previously had been able to take. Perhaps most importantly, the 1986 act enabled a high-income taxpayer to offset the credit only against tax due on "passive" income. As a result, syndicators increasingly began to market interests in rehabilitation projects to "plump cats" as opposed to "fat cats." After 2000, although the tax provisions had remained unchanged, the use of historic preservation tax credits began to creep back toward pre-1986 levels.

During the 1976–2003 period, the federal credit helped enable the rehabilitation of 31,000 historic properties. In addition, over a dozen states — notably Maryland, Missouri, and North Carolina — confer significant state income tax credits on renovators of historic properties. See Nancy D. Holt, In St. Louis, Developers Bank on Tax Credits, Wall St. J., Dec. 8, 1999, at B10. See generally Roberta F. Mann, Tax Incentives for Historic Preservation: An Antidote to Sprawl?, 8 Widener L. Symp. J. 207 (2002).

4. *Preservation through acquisition.* A government or preservation trust can acquire by consensual purchase (or, when authorized, by eminent domain) an easement over the

historically important facades of a building. Interpretation of an easement of this sort was at issue in Foundation for the Preservation of Georgetown v. Arnold, 651 A.2d 794 (D.C. Ct. App. 1994) (construing ambiguous easement language in favor of free use of land). The potential of preservation easements is featured in Dorothy J. Glancy, Preserving Rockefeller Center, 24 Urb. Law. 423 (1992), a marvelous case study. See also pp. 580–82.

5. *Preservation of building interiors.* Teachers Insurance & Annuity Association v. City of New York, 623 N.E.2d 526 (N.Y. 1993), held that the New York City Landmarks Law authorized a city commission to order the preservation of the interior of the Four Seasons Restaurant, located on the first two floors of Mies van der Rohe's renowned Seagram Building on Park Avenue. The lessees of the Four Seasons had sought this landmark designation to enhance their bargaining position with the landlord when their lease later came up for renewal. See David W. Dunlap, New Lease on Luxury Dining for the Four Seasons Restaurant, N.Y. Times, Nov. 11, 1998, at B7. The landlord had fought the landmarking. What benefits of preserving an interior, if any, would a landlord not have an incentive to take into account in the absence of landmarking? Compare United Artists' Theater Circuit, Inc. v. City of Philadelphia, 635 A.2d 612 (Pa. 1993) (holding that city lacked statutory authority to designate the interior of a building, in this instance an art deco movie theater).

Rector of St. Bartholomew's Church v. City of New York
914 F.2d 348 (2d Cir. 1990)

WINTER, Circuit Judge:
[In 1967, the city designated as historic landmarks both St. Bartholomew's main church and its community house, an adjacent auxiliary building. The two are located on Park Avenue near 50th Street in Manhattan. In 1984, the church desired to raze the community house and replace it with a 47-story office tower, a plausible business venture at this extraordinary site. When the city's Landmarks Preservation Commission denied it permission to demolish, the church asserted that its rights under both the Free Exercise Clause and the Takings Clause had been violated. The district court rejected both arguments and, on appeal, a panel of the Second Circuit affirmed both holdings.]

The Church argues that the Landmarks Law substantially burdens religion in violation of the First Amendment [because it impairs] the Church's ability to carry on and expand the ministerial and charitable activities that are central to its religious mission. It argues that the Community House is no longer a sufficient facility for its activities, and that the Church's financial base has eroded. The construction of an office tower similar to those that now surround St. Bartholomew's in midtown Manhattan, the Church asserts, is a means to provide better space for some of the Church's programs and income to support and expand its various ministerial and community activities. The Church thus argues that even if the proposed office tower will not house all of the Church's programs, the revenue generated by renting commercial office space will enable the Church to move some of its programs — such as sheltering the homeless — off-site.

[Judge Winter held that Employment Division v. Smith, 494 U.S. 872 (1990), required the court to reject the free exercise claim. The landmarks law was facially neutral, not a regulation targeted at religious beliefs as such.]

It is true that the Landmarks Law affects many religious buildings. The Church thus asserts that of the six hundred landmarked sites, over fifteen percent are religious properties and over five percent are Episcopal churches. Nevertheless, we do not understand those facts to demonstrate a lack of neutrality or general applicability. Because of the importance of religion, and of particular churches, in our social and cultural history, and because many churches are designed to be architecturally attractive, many religious structures are likely to fall within the neutral criteria — having "special character or special historical or aesthetic interest or value" — set forth by the Landmarks Law. N.Y.C. Admin. Code §25-302(n) (1986). This, however, is not evidence of an intent to discriminate against, or impinge on, religious belief in the designation of landmark sites.

The Church's brief cites commentators, including a former chair of the Commission, who are highly critical of the Landmarks Law on grounds that it accords great discretion to the Commission and that persons who have interests other than the preservation of historic sites or aesthetic structures may influence Commission decisions.[3] Nevertheless, absent proof of the discriminatory exercise of discretion, there is no constitutional relevance to these observations. . . .

The Church also claims that the Landmarks Law so severely restricts its ability to use its property that it constitutes confiscation of property without just compensation in violation of the Fifth and Fourteenth Amendments. However, the Supreme Court's decision in Penn Central [Transportation Co. v. City of New York, 438 U.S. 104 (1978)] compels us to hold otherwise. . . .

Applying the *Penn Central* standard to property used for charitable purposes, the constitutional question is whether the land-use regulation impairs the continued operation of the property in its originally expected use. We conclude that the Landmarks Law does not effect an unconstitutional taking because the Church can continue its existing charitable and religious activities in its current facilities. Although the regulation may "freeze" the Church's property in its existing use and prevent the Church from expanding or altering its activities, *Penn Central* explicitly permits this. . . .

[Affirmed.]

Note on Constitutional Constraints on Landmarking Buildings

1. *Cause célèbre.* The St. Bart's controversy pitted the rector, Reverend Thomas Dix Bowers, who sought to raise funds mainly for programs for the needy, against some members of the Manhattan upper crust. Philip Johnson, the renowned architect, Brendan Gill, the New Yorker theater critic, Jacqueline Onassis, and Brooke Astor headed the committee that fought against St. Bart's building plans. See Marie Brenner, Holy War on Park Avenue, New York, Dec. 14, 1981, at 34.

2. *Free exercise claims.* On free exercise issues, see also pp. 209–20. As noted there, in 1993 Congress enacted the Religious Freedom Restoration Act (RFRA) to "overrule" Employment Division v. Smith. In City of Boerne v. Flores, 521 U.S. 507 (1997), however, the Supreme Court held that in enacting RFRA, Congress had exceeded its powers to enforce the Fourteenth Amendment. *City of Boerne* itself arose out of a dispute over historic preservation. A Roman Catholic archbishop, acting on behalf of a parish in the Texas Hill Country, had invoked RFRA to challenge the city's prohibition on the razing of a portion of the parish's church. After the Supreme Court held RFRA unconstitutional, the parties agreed to a settlement that allowed the church to pursue a major expansion provided that it also preserve 80 percent of its existing building. N.Y. Times, Aug. 14, 1997, at A21.

---

3. The Landmarks Law made a cameo appearance in a recent best-selling novel as a vehicle for political retaliation against a clerical official seeking to develop Church property. See T. Wolfe, Bonfire of the Vanities 569 (1987) ("Mort? You know that church, St. Timothy's? . . . Right . . . LANDMARK THE SON OF A BITCH!").

The Religious Land Use and Institutionalized Persons Act of 2000 (RLUIPA), discussed at pp. 210–20, requires a government, when it makes a burdensome "individualized assessment" of a proposed religious land use, to have a "compelling government interest" that it is pursuing by the "least restrictive means." What result in a case like *St. Bart's* if the church were to invoke RLUIPA (assuming RLUIPA survives Supreme Court scrutiny)? Compare Episcopal Student Foundation v. City of Ann Arbor, 341 F. Supp. 2d 691 (E.D. Mich. 2004) (holding that city's refusal to permit razing of religious organization's historic building did not "substantially burden" free exercise rights protected by RLUIPA).

3. *Establishment issues when religious buildings are exempt from designation.* Since 1993, the California legislature has immunized the buildings of religious organizations from the exercise of statutorily conferred powers that counties and cities have to designate historic landmarks. In East Bay Asian Local Development Corp. v. State, 13 P.3d 1122 (Cal. 2000), cert. denied, 532 U.S. 1008 (2001), the Supreme Court of California, in a four-to-three decision, held that this exemption violated neither the federal nor the California constitutional prohibition on establishment of religion.

4. *Takings claims.* Some studies indicate that historic designation of a property creates significant positive externalities for owners of neighboring lands. See N. Edward Coulson & Robin M. Leichenko, The Internal and External Impact of Historical Designation on Property Values, 23 J. Real Est. Fin. & Econ. 113 (2001). However, because landmarking singles out a landowner for special burdens, a local government commonly confers a palliative such as a property tax reduction or transferable development rights. If New York City hadn't provided these cushions in both *St. Bart's* and *Penn Central*, excerpted at p. 158, would it still have prevailed against these takings challenges?

5. *Perverse incentives?* An owner who finds landmarking burdensome may respond in a socially destructive manner. See Robert Guenther, Arsonists Increasingly Hitting Buildings in Historic Districts, Wall St. J., Apr. 7, 1982, at 29; Shawn G. Kennedy, Landmarking's Double-Edged Sword: Sometimes It Works Against Preservation, N.Y. Times, Jan. 13, 1991, §10, at 1 (reporting that some owners decide to let their buildings deteriorate rather than incur the costs of obtaining commission approval for facade improvements). For the assertion that historic-preservation laws discourage present-day developers from hiring standout architects, see District Intown Properties Ltd. Partnership v. District of Columbia, 198 F.3d 874, 889–90 (D.C. Cir. 1999) (Williams, J., concurring).

A-S-P Associates v. City of Raleigh
258 S.E.2d 444 (N.C. 1979)

Plaintiff brought this action seeking a declaratory judgment that two ordinances adopted on 3 June 1975 by the City of Raleigh are invalid both on constitutional and statutory grounds. The two ordinances (hereinafter referred to collectively as the Oakwood Ordinance) amended the City's zoning ordinance to create a 98 acre, overlay historic district in the City's Oakwood neighborhood (hereinafter referred to as the Historic District), established the Raleigh Historic District Commission (hereinafter referred to as the Historic District Commission), adopted architectural guidelines and design standards to be applied by the Historic District Commission in its administration of the Oakwood Ordinance, and provided civil and criminal penalties for failure to comply with the Oakwood Ordinance.

The Ordinance was adopted pursuant to G.S. §§160A-395 through 399, which authorize municipalities to designate historic districts and to require that after the designation of a historic district any property owner within it who desires to erect, alter, restore, or move the exterior portion of any building or other structure first obtain a certificate of appropriateness from a historic district commission. A historic district commission's action is limited . . . to "preventing [outcomes] incongruous with the historic aspects of the district."

In May of 1974, the Division of Archives and History of the North Carolina Department of Cultural Resources nominated Raleigh's Oakwood neighborhood for inclusion on the United States Department of Interior's National Register of Historic Places. In the required statement of significance, the Division's Survey and Planning Unit observed:

> Oakwood, a twenty-block area representing the only intact nineteenth century neighborhood remaining in Raleigh, is composed predominantly of Victorian houses built between the Civil War and 1914. Its depressed economic state during most of the twentieth century preserved the neighborhood until 1971, when individuals began its revitalization. The great variety of Victorian architectural styles represented by the houses reflects the primarily middle-class tastes of the business and political leaders of Raleigh for whom they were built, as well as the skill of local architects and builders. Oakwood is a valuable physical document of Southern suburban life during the last quarter of the nineteenth century.

On 25 June 1974, the Oakwood neighborhood was placed on the National Register.

At the request of The Society for the Preservation of Historic Oakwood, the Planning Department of the City of Raleigh conducted a study of the Oakwood neighborhood in 1974. Those conducting the study found that a high rate of absentee ownership existed in the neighborhood, that banks were reticent to lend money in the Oakwood area as a result of its unstable property values, that significant private efforts to preserve the historic aspects of the neighborhood had been undertaken, and that the neighborhood was at a transition point with an uncertain future. The recommendation of the study was that the City take affirmative action in one of two ways: (1) Plan and zone the neighborhood for high density residential and commercial development, which would result in the loss of most aspects of the historic significance of the neighborhood, or (2) maintain the neighborhood as medium density residential with an emphasis on preserving its historic aspects.

In January of 1975, the Planning Department submitted to the City Council "A Proposal for the Designation of Oakwood as an Historic District." . . . On 3 June 1975 the City Council adopted the Oakwood Ordinance.

The Historic District thus created is an overlay zoning district. All zoning regulations in the area in effect prior to passage of the Oakwood Ordinance remain in effect. Compliance with the Oakwood Ordinance is required in addition to compliance with the pre-existing, underlying zoning regulations. Most of the area covered by the Historic District is zoned residential. A relatively small portion of the area covered by it is zoned as office and institutional. Associates own a vacant lot, located within the Historic District at 210 North Person Street. The lot is within the office and institutional zoning district.

On 22 July 1975 Associates brought this action challenging the validity of the Ordinance on constitutional and statutory grounds. . . . On 30 June 1977, the superior court entered an order denying Associates' motion for summary judgment and granting summary judgment in favor of defendant City on all claims raised by the complaint. The Court of Appeals reversed the case on several grounds. . . .

BROCK, Justice. . . .

Associates' first contentions are that the Oakwood Ordinance deprives them of their property without due process of law in contravention of the Fourteenth Amendment to the United States Constitution, and that it deprives them of their property otherwise than by the law of the land in contravention of Article I, Section 19, of the North Carolina Constitution.

The terms "law of the land" and "due process of law" are synonymous. Horton v. Gulledge, 177 S.E.2d 885 (N.C. 1970).

Associates' claim is premised on a line of cases in which this Court has indicated that a statute or ordinance based purely on aesthetic considerations, without any real or substantial relation to the public health, safety or morals, or the general welfare, deprives individuals of due process of law. State v. Vestal, 189 S.E. 2d 152 (N.C. 1972). . . . Associates contend that the Oakwood Ordinance falls within the scope of such impermissible exercise of the police power because it focuses entirely on the exterior appearance of structures within the Historic District. Associates further contend that even if the Ordinance is a valid exercise of the police power insofar as it is applied to historic structures, it is invalid when applied to new construction on property such as Associates' vacant lot. . . .

Legislative exercise of the police power to regulate private property in the interest of historic preservation has met with increasing acceptance by the courts of other jurisdictions. E.g., Maher v. City of New Orleans, 516 F. 2d 1051 (5th Cir. 1975); Rehman v. City of Springfield, 250 N.E.2d 282 (Ill. App. Ct. 1969); Opinion of the Justices, 128 N.E.2d 557 (Mass. 1955) [Nantucket]; Opinion of the Justices, 128 N.E.2d 563 (Mass. 1955) [Beacon Hill]; and City of Santa Fe v. Gamble-Skogmo, Inc., 389 P.2d 13 (N.M. 1964). Historic district legislation similar to the provisions of G.S. §§160A-395 through 399 has now been enacted by at least thirty-nine states. Beckwith, Developments in the Law of Historic Preservation and a Reflection on Liberty, 12 Wake Forest L. Rev. 93, 95 n.18 (1976). More than 500 cities and towns have passed local landmark or historic district ordinances. National Trust for Historic Preservation, Historic Preservation and the Law, Part IV, ch. 5, p. 3 (1978).

In Maher v. City of New Orleans, supra, plaintiff challenged an ordinance that regulates the preservation and maintenance of buildings in the historic Vieux Carre section of that City. In rejecting the plaintiff's contention that the architectural controls imposed by the ordinance were not within the parameters of police power regulation, the Court observed: "[p]roper state purposes may encompass not only the goal of abating undesirable conditions, but of fostering ends the community deems worthy. . . . Nor need the values advanced be solely economic or directed at health and safety in their narrowest senses. The police power inhering in the lawmaker is more generous, comprehending more subtle and ephemeral societal interests." Id. at 1060.

In State v. Vestal, 189 S. E.2d 152 (N.C. 1972), we took note of the growing body of authority in other jurisdictions recognizing that the police power may be broad enough to include reasonable regulation of property for aesthetic reasons alone. Although we are not now prepared to endorse such a broad concept of the scope of the police power, we find no difficulty in holding that the police power encompasses the right to control the exterior appearance of private property when the object of such control is the preservation of the State's legacy of historically significant structures. "While most aesthetic ordinances are concerned with good taste and beauty . . . a historic district zoning ordinance . . . is not primarily concerned with whether the subject of regulation is beautiful or tasteful, but rather with preserving it as it is, representative of what it was, for such educational, cultural, or economic values as it may have. Cases dealing with purely aesthetic regulations are distinguishable from those dealing with preservation of a historical area or a historical style of architecture." A. Rathkopf, The Law of Zoning and Planning, §15.01 p.15-4 (4th ed. 1975).

The preservation of historically significant residential and commercial districts protects and promotes the general welfare in distinct yet intricately related ways. It provides a visual, educational medium by which an understanding of our country's historic and cultural heritage may be imparted to present and future generations. . . . It can stimulate revitalization of deteriorating residential and commercial districts in urban areas, thus contributing to their economic and social stability. . . . It also has the potential, documented in numerous instances, e.g., in the Vieux Carre section of New Orleans, of generating substantial tourism revenues. . . .

. . . Associates' contention that the provisions in the Oakwood Ordinance requiring issuance of a certificate of appropriateness for new construction is unreasonable, particularly when applied to Associates' plans to construct an office building on its now vacant lot, is without merit. It is widely recognized that preservation of the historic aspects of a district requires more than simply the preservation of those buildings of historical and architectural significance within the district. In rejecting a similar challenge, the District Court in Maher v. City of New Orleans, 371 F. Supp. 653, 663 (E.D. La. 1974) observed: "just as important is the preservation and protection of the setting or scene in which [structures of architectural and historical significance] are situated." This "tout ensemble" doctrine, as it is now often termed, is an integral and reasonable part of effective historic preservation. . . .

Associates next contend that the superior court erred as a matter of law in ruling that the Oakwood Ordinance does not delegate legislative power to the Historic District Commission. . . .

Although the neighborhood encompassed by the Historic District is to a considerable extent an architectural mélange, that heterogeneity of architectural style is not such as to render the standard of "incongruity" meaningless. The predominant architectural style found in the area is Victorian, the characteristics of which are readily identifiable. . . .

Associates' third contention is that the superior court erred in concluding that defendant City did not deny Associates' equal protection of the laws by including Associates' property in the Historic District while excluding property owned by the North Carolina Medical Association, which is located in the same block. . . .

. . . Associates' vacant lot is located at 210 North Person Street. Adjacent to it at 216 North Person Street is the former Mansion Square Inn, built in the nineteenth century. The State Medical Society's large, four story office building is located at 222 North Person Street. These three pieces of property and a fourth at 204 North Person have been included since 1961 in an office and institutional zoning district. At the request of the State Medical Society, the property on which its building is located and two other adjacent lots owned by the Society in the same block were excluded from the overlay, Historic District. Associates' request that their vacant lot be similarly excluded was denied and theirs and all other property in the same block was included in the Historic District. Associates' equal protection claim is based on its allegations that defendant City acted arbitrarily and capriciously in setting the boundaries of the Oakwood Historic District because the included and excluded pieces of property are similarly located. . . .

. . . The State Medical Society's building is a large (four story), modern structure; virtually all elements of its architectural style are, by contrast with the structures on property included in the Historic District, extremely incongruous with its historic aspects; the Medical Society made substantial investments in the foundations of the building in order that two additional stories can be added at some point in the future; the adjacent lots owned by the Society, which were also excluded from the District, were acquired to provide additional offstreet parking necessary to future expansion of the building; Associates' property, when purchased in 1972 had on it a dilapidated structure, which was subsequently demolished, and the property has remained vacant since; other pieces of property in the same block are either vacant or have structures on them which are reasonably compatible in terms of scale, orientations, setback and architectural style with the historic aspects of the District.

Bearing in mind the touchstone of judicial review of a particular legislative classification, the object of the legislative exercise of the police power, we cannot say that the superior court erred in its conclusion of law that a reasonable basis existed for the exclusion of the Medical Society's property while other property in the same block was included in the Historic District. Associates' property, other property in the same block, and that owned by the Medical Society are indeed *similarly located*. They are not, however, similarly situated, insofar as the purpose of the Historic District Ordinance is concerned. Substantial and material differences exist, as clearly shown by the uncontroverted evidence presented, which support the superior court's conclusion of law.

Exclusion from the Historic District of only that property owned by the Medical Society on which its building is located might have been a wiser choice. But it is well settled that legislative bodies may make rational distinctions with substantially less than mathematical exactitude. New Orleans v. Dukes, 427 U.S. 297 (1976). . . .

The decision of the Court of Appeals is reversed, and the entry of summary judgment by the superior court in favor of defendant City on all claims raised by Associates' complaint is affirmed.

Note on Historic Districts

1. *Attentiveness or pettiness?* Why did A-S-P Associates oppose inclusion of their lot in the district? One reason may have been the restrictiveness of historic preservation rules. See, e.g., Anderson v. Old King's Highway Regional Historic District Commission, 493 N.E.2d 188 (Mass. 1986) (affirming denial of certificate of appropriateness for use of vinyl clapboards to replace painted shingles on back of addition to house); Richard Bernstein, Critics Says Details Entrap Landmarks Panel, N.Y. Times, Apr. 28, 1993, at B1 (reporting protests against commission's prohibition against planting of trees in SoHo district); Michael T. Kaufman, Preservation Panel Slams Two Deviant Windows Shut, N.Y. Times, Mar. 27, 1993, at 23 (reporting that New York City Landmarks Preservation Commission had ordered owner of Park Avenue cooperative apartment to replace two windows because they lacked divided panes). Is this level of strictness worth the strife?

2. *Landowners' constitutional claims.* A landowner's takings argument is less plausible when a city is trying to preserve not just an isolated landmark, such as St. Bart's, but all older structures in a larger historic district, such as Beacon Hill in Boston or the French Quarter in New Orleans. Because a larger number of landowners are subjected to district-wide controls, an individual owner has a weaker claim of having been singled out and forced to confer a benefit. Moreover, a landowner may receive a "reciprocity of advantage" from district-wide controls. As several studies indicate, a landowner's benefits from being included in the preserved area may outweigh the costs of inclusion. See Robin M. Leichenko et al., Historic Preservation and Residential Property Values: An Analysis of Texas Cities, 11 Urb. Stud. 1973 (2001) (citing studies finding that a district designation raises property values). But cf. Paul K. Asabere et al., The Adverse Impacts of Local Historic Designation: The Case of Small Apartment Buildings in Philadelphia, 8 J. Real Est. Fin. & Econ. 225, 232 (1994) ("The results imply that historic designation (as practiced in Philadelphia) is confiscatory. . . . "). Does the soundness of historic districting turn entirely on its having a positive effect on district property values?

In Nevel v. Village of Schaumburg, 297 F.3d 673 (7th Cir. 2002), the owners of a village-landmarked house built in 1930 sought to install vinyl siding, a material that would cost $93,000 less than wood siding. When the village denied permission, the owners asserted — without success — a denial of equal protection because the village previously had allowed vinyl siding on other historic properties. But cf. Norton v. City of Danville, 602 S.E.2d 126 (Va. 2004) (holding city had been "unreasonable" to order owner of historic house to maintain original front-door style when that design had given rise to three burglaries).

3. *Is an historic district a boon or bane for gentrifiers?* Some commentators have been concerned that the designation of an area as an historic district might lead to the displacement of poor households. See David B. Fein, Note, Historic Districts: Preserving City Neighborhoods for the Privileged, 60 N.Y.U. L. Rev. 64 (1985). Cf. pp. 9–10, on gentrification. Could an historic district designation both reduce property values (see supra Note 2) *and* displace the poor?

4. *Will too much be preserved?* The New York City Landmarks Preservation Commission was created two years after the much-lamented demolition of Pennsylvania Station in 1963. By 2003, the commission had designated 1,200 sites as landmarks and 79 neighborhoods as historic districts, bringing about 3 percent of the city's buildings under its domain. Many have accused the commission of being overzealous. See, e.g., David W. Dunlap, The City Casts Its Theaters in Stone, N.Y. Times, Nov. 22, 1987, §4, at 6 (of 46 Broadway theaters, 21 are landmarked, and more designations are in pipeline); Editorial, Preserving Balance on Landmarks, N.Y. Times, Dec. 26, 1987, at 14 (opposing reappointment of two commission members whose "zealotry has cost the commission its reputation and the city some useful development"). See also Catesby Leigh, Historic Preservation Goes Awry, Am. Prospect, July/Aug. 2001, at 40, 43:

> The truth is, a great many cherished "historic" districts across our land are just decent neighborhoods that happened to be built before World War II. Preservationists deserve our gratitude for rescuing any number of these places from destruction at the hands of urban renewers and highway engineers. The National Trust, moreover, deserves special recognition for helping revive hundreds of neglected Main Streets, while spreading the word about their economic potential.
>
> But when it comes to the ongoing dearth of satisfying new architecture, the preservation movement is part of the problem rather than the solution. . . .
>
> Deciding what to save in our built environment is important. But what we build from scratch is of infinitely greater importance. . . .

5. *Neighborhood preservation through voluntary cooperation?* Is governmental regulation of building alterations essential to conserve an historic district such as Raleigh's Oakwood neighborhood? See Daphna Lewinsohn-Zamir, The "Conservation Game": The Possibility of Voluntary Cooperation in Preserving Buildings of Cultural Importance, 20 Harv. J.L. & Pub. Pol'y 733 (1997) (invoking game theory to tout possibilities of voluntary coordination among neighbors).

In 1995, Oregon, in a break from its traditional activism in land use regulation, enacted a statute that authorized an owner of property unilaterally to free the property from any state or local historic-preservation designation. Or. Rev. Stat. §197.772 (2004). Oregon thus may serve as a laboratory for testing the potential of voluntary preservation.

D. Streamlining the Regulatory Process

As this chapter has demonstrated, many municipalities have an array of overlapping regulatory schemes. A homebuilder may have to apply for not only subdivision approval and building permits, but also zoning changes, design approvals, and the like. These necessitate dealings with a battery of different local departments and boards. In addition, in some instances, approvals from state and federal agencies may be required. A developer's costs and risks inevitably mount as hearings and permits multiply. The Report of the

Keane Commission, a panel appointed by President George H.W. Bush, quotes William Connolly, director of New Jersey's Division of Housing and Development:

> Here . . . in Mercer County, a major subdivision would receive . . . 11 different reviews from 9 different agencies. Seven of those reviews concern themselves with the adequacy of storm drainage. Jet fighter planes and moon rockets get by with triple redundant control systems. We need seven government agencies to look at whether the storm drainage will drain. It is an important concern, but it is probably not that important.

Advisory Commission on Regulatory Barriers to Affordable Housing, "Not in My Backyard": Removing Barriers to Affordable Housing 5 (1991). See also Michael I. Luger & Kenneth Temkin, Red Tape and Housing Costs 140 (2000) (estimating cost of excessive regulations in New Jersey at $10,000 to $20,000 per new housing unit).

Report of the President's Commission on Housing
208–09 (1982)

Wherever possible, procedures for obtaining permits for subdivision and construction should be reduced and consolidated to a single comprehensive permit to minimize the time between purchase of land and occupancy by homeowners and tenants.

The previously cited GAO report on housing costs[39] determined that the average time for review and approval is 7-1/2 months from the time a developer submits his preliminary plans to the day a building permit is issued. Extreme cases range from a month to two years or more. Generally, larger developments (250 or more units) in the high-growth areas experience longer review times. In any case, added development time means increased carrying costs for the developer, varying from 1 percent to 10 percent of the final selling price of a house. . . .

LOCAL INITIATIVES

The Commission realizes that it is not possible to achieve immediately a single consolidated local development permit, especially in view of the plethora of independent agencies in so many local governments. Short of this, however, local governments have taken steps to expedite the permit process, among them the following:[41]

Create a central authority that provides all permit applications required in the development process. . . .

Conduct pre-application conferences. Developers need the opportunity to discuss with experienced staff such matters as community opposition, probable conditions for approval, and how other projects have been decided in the past. . . .

Establish a joint review committee whenever several departments are involved in a project approval. . . .

Implement "fast tracking" procedures for projects with minor impacts. . . .

Institute the simultaneous review of multiple permits. Reviews must follow sequentially when one permit is made a prerequisite for the next. In many cases this is logical and

---

39. Why Are New House Prices So High? How Are They Influenced by Government Regulations and Can Prices Be Reduced? [General Accounting Office, 1978].

41. For a more extensive discussion, see American Planning Association (with assistance of the Urban Land Institute), Streamlining Local Use Regulation: A Guidebook for Local Governments (Washington, D.C.: U.S. Government Printing Office, 1980).

efficient for both developer and the review staff, but some applications lend themselves to simultaneous review.

Consolidate or eliminate multiple public hearings. . . .

Employ a hearing officer. A hearing official is an appointed officer who conducts quasi-judicial hearings on applications for parcel rezonings, special use permits, variances, and other such devices. . . .

Note on State-Mandated Reforms

Is it realistic to expect a local government to respond to the commission's urgings on its own initiative? Many observers assert that only state compulsion can reform a municipality rife with antidevelopment sentiment. A number of states have enacted legislation aimed at streamlining local processes across the board. These statutes direct local governments to consolidate hearings and permit reviews, and to act on an application within a specified deadline after its receipt. Other state statutes are narrower, perhaps governing only decisionmaking by state agencies, or local processing of favored uses such as affordable housing projects. See, for example, the references at pp. 786–87 to the "anti-snob zoning acts" of several New England states.

California's Permit Streamlining Act, Cal. Gov't Code §§65920–65957.5 (West 2004), enabled a developer to prevail in Palmer v. City of Ojai, 223 Cal. Rptr. 542 (Ct. App. 1986). In December 1980, Palmer filed an application for approval of a project involving the construction of a shopping center and 73 housing units on a 31-acre parcel located in the resort city of Ojai. The city strung out the approval process until 1983, when it denied the necessary permits. Palmer's attorney invoked a provision of the Permit Streamlining Act that required the city to approve or disapprove an application within one year of its receipt. Rebuffing the city's argument that Palmer's original application had been incomplete, the court of appeals held that the statute had been violated and that Palmer's application should be "deemed approved."

The "deemed approved" remedy commonly is available under more traditional land use statutes. See, e.g., Viking Construction Co. v. Town Planning Commission, 435 A.2d 29 (Conn. 1980) (holding that statute imposing 65-day deadline for municipal subdivision review entitled developer to proceed with subdivision that municipality had disapproved 91 days after application had been submitted); Gridco, Inc. v. Zoning Board, 400 A.2d 869 (N.J. 1979) (plaintiff had right to receive variance because board had failed to act on plaintiff's application within statutory deadline of 120 days). See generally Gregory G. Brooker & Karen R. Cole, Automatic Approval Statutes, 29 Urb. Law. 439 (1997). A statute that converts an excessive agency delay into an affirmative agency decision penalizes an applicant's neighbors rather than the agency that acted too slowly. Would it be better to impose civil penalties on either the miscreant agency or its officials as individuals?

General streamlining statutes include Wash. Rev. Code §§36.70B.010–.230 (2004), and the handful discussed in Tod Read, Environmental Permit Coordination in Florida, 3 J. Land Use & Envtl. L. 53 (1987). See also American Law Institute, Model Land Development Code §§2-401–2-403 (1976) (on "development requiring multiple permits"); Stephen R. Seidel, Housing Costs and Government Regulations: Confronting the Regulatory Maze (1978).

Municipalities themselves have initiated a variety of measures to expedite their own review processes. Some have adopted "Unified Development Ordinances" that combine subdivision and zoning rules into a single document. See Barry Hogue, Unified Development Ordinances, Zoning News, Dec. 2002, at 1. Some localities have created a "one-stop shopping" center that places the various local permitting bodies under a single roof. Over a four-year period, the City of San Diego's one-stop permit center reportedly saved developers $3.5 million and the city $10 million. National Conference of States on Building Codes and Standards, Streamlining the Nation's Building Regulatory Process 8 (2000).

Note on State and Federal Permit Requirements: The Regulation of Wetlands

State and federal regulation of land use has become more pervasive, especially since the rise of environmental movement in the late 1960s. For example, Lucas v. South Carolina Coastal Council, 505 U.S. 1003 (1992) (excerpted at pp. 169–77), and Palazzolo v. Rhode Island, 533 U.S. 606 (2001) (excerpted at p. 180), both illustrate the tightening during the 1970s of state rules on the filling of coastal wetlands. The impetus for these programs was the federal Coastal Zone Management Act of 1972, which provided funds for state coastal programs administered consistently with federal guidelines. See Linda A. Malone, The Coastal Zone Management Act and the Takings Clause in the 1990's: Making the Case for Federal Land Use to Preserve Coastal Areas, 62 U. Colo. L. Rev. 711 (1991).

Wetlands, both coastal and inland, nicely illustrate the evolving complexities of state and federal permitting. Wetlands are a fragile and valuable component of the nation's natural resources. In addition to providing habitat for threatened species, they control flooding, prevent erosion, and filter toxins from the water supply. Under §404 of the Clean Water Act, 33 U.S.C. §1344 (2004) (first enacted in 1972), a landowner who intends to dredge or fill a wetland that is adjacent to a navigable waterway, or a tributary thereto, must apply for a permit. The U.S. Army Corps of Engineers issues these permits, but the Environmental Protection Agency establishes permitting guidelines and maintains veto authority.

The Corps' regulations define *wetlands* broadly to include any areas "that are inundated or saturated by surface or ground water at a frequency and duration sufficient to support, and that under normal circumstances do support, a prevalence of vegetation typically adapted for life in saturated soil conditions." 40 C.F.R. §232.2 (2003). The reach of the Corps' jurisdiction under §404 has been a subject of controversy. In 1977, the Corps defined *navigable waters* to include "isolated wetlands and lakes, intermittent streams, prairie potholes, and other waters that are not part of a tributary system to interstate waters or to navigable waters of the United States, the degradation or destruction of which could affect interstate commerce." 33 C.F.R. §323.2(a)(5) (1978) (repealed). The Supreme Court limited the Corps' jurisdiction in Solid Waste Agency of Northern Cook County (SWANCC) v. United States Army Corps of Engineers, 531 U.S. 159 (2001), by finding the Corps lacked jurisdiction over abandoned gravel pits that had filled with water, providing a migratory bird habitat. Though the precise reach of SWANCC remains unclear, lower courts now generally require a federally regulated wetland to have some physical connection to navigable waters. See Michael P. Healy, Law, Policy, and the Clean Water Act: The Courts, the Bush Administration, and the Statute's Uncertain Reach, 55 Ala. L. Rev. 695 (2004).

Compliance with §404 permit requirements can be costly. The Corps will not issue a permit "if there is a practicable alternative . . . which would have less adverse impact" on the environment. 40 C.F.R. §230.10(a) (2003). Even when a project is as environmentally sensitive as possible, the Corps can require the owner to mitigate the loss of wetlands by restoring, preserving, or creating other wetlands. A study of residential property sale prices in East Baton Rouge Parish, Louisiana, found that prices in areas likely to be deemed wetlands were discounted by more than 10 percent. Randall S. Guttery et al., Federal Wetlands Regulation: Restrictions on the Nationwide Permit Program and the Implications for Residential Property Owners, 37 Am. Bus. L.J. 299 (2000). The Corps itself does not consider a permit application until a developer already has received all necessary state and local permits. Wrongful denial of a permit by the Corps can give rise to a successful takings claim. See Loveladies Harbor v. United States, 28 F.3d 1171 (Fed. Cir. 1994) (finding a total deprivation of property value).

Many states have separate, state-administered wetlands permit programs. See, e.g., Del. Code Ann. tit. 7, §6604 (2004); N.C. Gen. Stat. §113-229 (2004). Other states delegate wetlands permitting authority to local agencies. See, e.g., Mass. Gen. Laws ch. 40, §8C (2004) (delegating power to local conservation commissions). See generally Allan E. Korpela, Annotation, Conservation: Validity, Construction, and Application of Enactments Restricting Land Development by Dredging or Filling, 46 A.L.R.3d 1422 (1972). Subtle differences between federal and state regulatory standards can create confusion. As one commentator notes of the Massachusetts program:

> Although in some ways the Section 404 program seems to mirror the [state program], there are important differences besides the permitting entity. The definition of wetlands, scope of jurisdiction, and allowable exemptions are handled differently. This leads to inconveniences for property holders, for instance when a landowner is obliged to apply for permits from both the Corps and a conservation commission, or when the same piece of land is considered a wetland by one agency and not by the other.

Cymie Payne, Local Regulations of Natural Resources: Efficiency, Effectiveness, and Fairness of Wetlands Permitting in Massachusetts, 28 Envtl. L. 519, 541 (1998).

Municipalities, invoking their powers under zoning enabling acts or home rule, may adopt their own wetland restrictions. See, e.g., Holiday Point Marina Partners v. Anne Arundel County, 707 A.2d 829 (Md. 1998) (holding local ordinance that restricted construction near oyster beds was not preempted by the state wetlands permit system); Lovequist v. Conservation Commission of Dennis, 393 N.E.2d 858 (Mass. 1979) (upholding town's authority to adopt wetlands regulations despite existence of state program). Should a state, under the banner of simplification, preempt local regulations of this sort?

There have been a number of efforts to simplify wetland permitting. The Clean Water Act (at 33 U.S.C. §1344(g)-(h) (2004)), gives a state the option of assuming full regulatory responsibility for all nonnavigable waters (including wetlands). This system eliminates regulatory overlap, but may put additional burdens on a state's budget. In 1994, New Jersey joined Michigan in adopting this option. For a mixed review of the Michigan program, see Mary Goodenough, Public Participation in a State-Assumed Wetlands Permit Program: The Michigan Example, 10 J. Envtl. L. & Litig. 221 (1995).

Far more popular are "State Programmatic General Permits." By granting a general permit, the EPA hands off regulatory authority to a state agency for projects with minimal environmental impacts provided that the state regulations are at least as strong as the Clean Water Act's. See 33 U.S.C. §1344(e) (2004). The EPA has issued more than 50 such permits, some covering entire states, others covering discrete areas within states, for example, the reservoirs under control of the Tennessee Valley Authority. See Proposed Regulatory Guidance Letter on Programmatic General Permits, 61 Fed. Reg. 18575 (1996).

Why have many states declined the federal invitation to exercise more control of their wetlands? See Oliver A. Houck & Michael Rolland, Environmental Federalism: Federalism in Wetlands Regulation: A Consideration of Delegation of Clean Water Act Section 404 and Related Programs to the States, 54 Md. L. Rev. 1242 (1995) (suggesting states may be attempting to avoid takings liabilities).

Chapter Six

Alternatives to Public Regulation: Nuisance Law, Fees and Rewards, Covenants

Chapter 2 posed the central question of land use policy: What is the appropriate mix among top-down systems of government land use regulation and bottom-up systems of interneighbor coordination? The intervening chapters dealt with zoning and the other principal command-and-control systems. To complete the basic inquiry, this chapter explores a variety of market-oriented systems that provide landowners relative autonomy in resolving disputes.

In the absence of mandatory public regulations, what rules influence how private landowners interact? Some of the most powerful forces are social norms, such as those that may informally obligate homeowners to paint their houses and maintain their yards. Because this is a law book, however, the current chapter concentrates on rules potentially enforceable in court. The first two subchapters address nuisance law and its converse, beneficence law. These provide the default rules of private law that govern rights when disputes arise among neighbors. The materials also explore fees (an alternative to nuisance liability) and public rewards (an alternative to rights to restitution). The chapter then turns to the law of covenants — that is, interneighbor contracts that alter the default rules of private law. An entire subchapter is devoted to residential community associations, the contractually based "private governments" that are increasingly prevalent in the United States. To add concreteness, the final subchapter explores the functioning of these relatively decentralized systems of land use control in Houston and other cities without zoning ordinances.

Is the dichotomy between top-down and bottom-up systems of land use control overly stark? Does it ignore the dynamic of dealmaking in public law (see pp. 303–08)? How law undergirds culture and all systems of private ordering?

A. *The Common Law Rights of Neighbors: Nuisance Law*

Over the centuries, judges have developed an incredibly rich, if not completely coherent, body of common law applicable to private land use disputes between neighboring landowners. Special legal doctrines have evolved for encroaching buildings, overhanging vegetation, deprivation of lateral support, trespass by animals, alteration of the flow of surface water, and so on. First-year law school courses cover many of these doctrines. In Torts, for example, a student usually encounters Rylands v. Fletcher, L.R. 3, H.L. 330 (1868), which imposed strict liability for damage to neighboring land caused by the overflow of unnaturally gathered substances. In Property, one might encounter encroachment law, water rights, and other special doctrines.

It should not be surprising that courts facing discrete cases have tended to develop narrow doctrines to resolve them. However, all types of disputes between a landowner and an aggrieved neighbor present essentially the same fundamental issues: from what types of landowner activities should a neighbor be entitled to protection? Should liability be strict or should it be contingent on the landowner's negligence? Should there be defenses based on a plaintiff neighbor's special sensitivity to harm or failure to act to mitigate damages? If a neighbor is entitled to a remedy, should it be damages (if so, how measured?) or an injunction against the offending activity? Most of this subchapter's materials have been culled from the law of nuisance — the body of principles that addresses nontrespassory interferences with the enjoyment of land.

When delving into nuisance law, keep two fundamental questions in mind. First, what function does this hoary system have in today's land-planning circus of planned-unit developments, overlay zones, transferable development rights, and all the rest? Second, what shortcomings in nuisance law might have contributed to the rise of public land use regulation?

1. *Private Nuisance: The Prima Facie Case*

By Shakespearean times, English law had entitled a neighboring homeowner to recover damages from a landowner who maintained a stinking pigsty. Aldred's Case, 77 Eng. Rep. 816, 9 Co. Rep. 57(b) (K.B. 1611). Any activity that threatened the use and enjoyment of neighboring property — thus lowering its market value — became potentially challengeable as a nuisance. The subsequent evolution of nuisance doctrine is traced in Robert G. Bone, Normative Theory and Legal Doctrine in American Nuisance Law: 1850 to 1920, 59 S. Cal. L. Rev. 1101 (1986); Jeff L. Lewin, *Boomer* and the American Law of Nuisance: Past, Present and Future, 54 Alb. L. Rev. 189 (1990); and Christine Rosen, Differing Perceptions of the Value of Pollution Abatement Across Time and Space: Balancing Doctrine in Pollution Nuisance Law, 1840–1906, 11 Law & Hist. Rev. 303 (1993).

Middlesex Co. v. McCue
21 N.E. 230 (Mass. 1889)

HOLMES, J.

This is a bill brought to restrain the defendant from filling up the plaintiff's mill-pond. The master reports that the defendant's land is on the slope of a hill running down to the pond, and that the only acts of the defendant tending to fill the pond have been those of cultivating and manuring his own soil in the ordinary way for the purpose of raising garden vegetables. The question is whether the defendant has a right to do these acts notwithstanding their effects upon the plaintiff's land and water rights. The respective rights and liabilities of adjoining land-owners cannot be determined in advance by a mathematical line, or a general formula; certainly not by the simple test of whether the obvious and necessary consequence of a given act by one is to damage the other. The fact that the damage is foreseen, or even intended, has nothing to do with the matter apart from statute. Some damage a man must put up with, however plainly his neighbor foresees it before bringing it to pass. Rideout v. Knox, (Mass.) 19 N.E. Rep. 390. Liability depends upon the nature of the act, and the kind and degree of harm done, considered in the light of expediency and usage. For certain kinds there is no liability, no matter what the extent of the harm. A man may lose half the value of his house by the obstruction of his view, and yet be without remedy. In other cases his right depends upon the degree of the damage, or rather of its cause. He must endure a certain amount of noise, smells, shaking, percolation, surface drainage, and so forth. If the amount is greater, he may be able to stop it, and to recover compensation. As in other matters of degree, a case which was near the line might be sent to a jury to determine what was reasonable. In a clear case it is the duty of the court to rule upon the parties' rights. The present case presents one of these questions of degree. If the plaintiff were complaining of offensive drainage from a vault it would be entitled to recover upon proof of the fact. Ball v. Nye, 99 Mass. 582. If it complained that the surface drainage was made offensive by the nature of the substances spread by the defendant upon his land the case would be nearer the line, and the right to recover possibly might depend upon further circumstances, such as whether the substances were usual and reasonable fertilizers, or refuse, etc. See Brown v. Illius, 25 Conn. 583, 27 Conn. 84. In this case it complains, not that the substances brought down are offensive, but that the defendant caused any solid substance to be brought down at all. Practically it would forbid the defendant to dig his land, at least without putting up a guard, since the surface drainage necessarily carries more of the soil along if the earth is made friable by digging. This would cut down the defendant's right of surface drainage to a very small matter indeed. We are of the opinion that a man has a right to cultivate his land in the usual and reasonable way, as well upon a hill as in the plain, and that damage to the lower proprietor of the kind complained of is something that he must protect himself against as best he may. The plaintiff says that a wall would stop the trouble. If so, it can build one upon its own land. . . .

Bill dismissed.

Rose v. Chaikin
453 A.2d 1378 (N.J. Super. Ct. Ch. Div. 1982)

Gibson, J.S.C.
This action seeks to enjoin the operation of a privately owned windmill. . . .

All of the parties are residents and/or owners of single-family homes located in a contiguous residential neighborhood in Brigantine, New Jersey. On or about June 18, 1981, defendants, in an effort to save on electric bills and conserve energy, obtained a building permit for the construction of a windmill. Pursuant to that permit they erected a 60'-high tower on top of which was housed a windmill and motor. The unit is located ten feet from the property line of one of plaintiffs. Shortly after the windmill became operational it began to produce offensive noise levels, as a result of which plaintiffs experienced various forms of stress-related symptoms, together with a general inability to enjoy the peace of their homes.

Relief was initially sought through city council. Although certain orders were issued reducing the times when the windmill could operate, the problem continued more or less until an action was instituted in this court. Following an initial hearing here, there was a preliminary finding of a nuisance and a temporary restraining order was issued restricting the use of the machine except for a period of no more than two hours a day, that being the time claimed to be needed for maintenance purposes. By consent, those restraints were continued up through the time of trial and still continue.

Although the evidence was in sharp dispute concerning the impact of the noise levels existing when the windmill is operational, this court is satisfied that those levels are of such a nature that they would be offensive to people of normal sensibilities and, in fact, have unreasonably interfered with plaintiffs' use and enjoyment of their properties. Measurements at the site reveal that the sound levels produced by the windmill vary, depending on the location, but generally show a range of 56 to 61 decibels (dBA). In all instances those levels exceed the 50 dBA permissible under the controlling city ordinance. Ordinance 11-1981, §906.6.3, City of Brigantine. Although there are other sources of sounds in the area, for the most part they are natural to the site. These background (or ambient) sounds include the ocean, the sounds of sea gulls, the wind and the distant sounds of occasional boat traffic in the adjacent inlet. An exception to these "natural" sounds is the heat pump owned by plaintiffs Joel and Isadora Rose, of which more will be said later.

The sounds of the windmill have been variously described. Generally, however, they most resemble those produced by a large motor upon which there is superimposed the action of blades cutting through the air. The sounds are distinguishable not just by the level of the noise produced (noise being defined as unwanted sound) but because they are unnatural to the scene and are more or less constant. Although a reduction in the wind speed to below eight m.p.h. will automatically shut down the unit, the prevailing winds at this site are generally above that. Given the proximity of the homes involved, the net result is a noise which is both difficult to ignore and almost impossible to escape. . . .

The basic standards for determining what constitutes a private nuisance were set forth by our Supreme Court in Sans v. Ramsey Golf & Country Club, 149 A.2d 599 (N.J. 1959). The court made clear that a case-by-case inquiry, balancing competing interests in property, is required.

> The essence of a private nuisance is an unreasonable interference with the use and enjoyment of land. The elements are myriad. . . . The utility of the defendant's conduct must be weighed against the quantum of harm to the plaintiff. The question is not simply whether a person is annoyed or disturbed, but whether the annoyance or disturbance arises from an unreasonable use of the neighbor's land. . . . Id. at 605.

Unreasonableness is judged

> ". . . 'not according to exceptionally refined, uncommon or luxurious habits of living, but according to the simple tastes and unaffected notions generally prevailing among plain people.'" Id. at 606.

Defendants resist plaintiffs' claim by advancing three basic arguments: first, that noise, standing alone, cannot constitute a private nuisance; second, that even if noise can amount to a nuisance, the noise from their windmill does not exceed the applicable threshold, and third, that in any event the circumstances of this case do not warrant the "extraordinary relief" of an injunction.

The first argument is without merit. New Jersey case law makes it clear that noise may, under the principles of unreasonable use, constitute an actionable private nuisance. [Four citations omitted.] Noise is an actionable private nuisance if two elements are present: (1) injury to the health and comfort of ordinary people in the vicinity, and (2) unreasonableness of that injury under all the circumstances. . . .

Broadly stated, the noises which a court of equity normally enjoins are those which affect injuriously the health and comfort of ordinary people in the vicinity to an unreasonable extent. . . . *Thus, the character, volume, frequency, duration, time, and locality are relevant factors in determining whether the annoyance materially interferes with the ordinary comfort of human existence.* (Lieberman v. Saddle River Tp., 116 A.2d at 811–12 (N.J. Super. 1955), emphasis supplied.)

To the factors listed in *Lieberman* may be added several others gleaned from New Jersey cases and cases in other jurisdictions applying a "reasonableness under the circumstances" test. For example, the availability of alternative means of achieving the defendant's objective has been found to be relevant. See *Sans*, supra, 149 A.2d at 604 (change in location of golf tee feasible); Malhame v. Demarest, 392 A.2d 652, 660–61 (N.J. Law Div. 1978) (plaintiffs failed to prove that alternative fire-siren system would not just transfer nuisance elsewhere). So, also, might the social utility of defendant's conduct, judged in light of prevailing notions of progress and the demands of modern life, be relevant. See Protokowicz v. Lesofski, 174 A.2d 385, 388 (N.J. Ch. Div. 1961) (in light of scientific progress, noise from Diesel engine cannot be considered nuisance per se). Whether a given use complies with controlling governmental regulations, while not dispositive on the question of private nuisance, does impact on its reasonableness.

An application of these factors to the present case supports the conclusion that defendants' windmill constitutes an actionable nuisance. As indicated, the noise produced is offensive because of its character, volume and duration. . . . Sounds which are natural to this area — the sea, the shore birds, the ocean breeze — are soothing and welcome. The noise of the windmill, which would be unwelcome in most neighborhoods, is particularly alien here. . . .

When consideration is given to the social utility of the windmill and the availability of reasonable alternatives, the conclusion supporting an injunction is the same. Defendants' purpose in installing the windmill was to conserve energy and save on electric bills. Speaking to the latter goal first, clearly the court can take judicial notice that alternative devices are available which are significantly less intrusive. As to its social utility, a more careful analysis is required. Defendants argue that the windmill furthers the national need to conserve energy by the use of an alternate renewable source of power. See, generally, Wind Energy Systems Act of 1980, 42 U.S.C.A., §§9201–9213. The social utility of alternate energy sources cannot be denied; nor should the court ignore the proposition that scientific and social progress sometimes reasonably require a reduction in personal comfort. On the other hand, the fact that a device represents a scientific advance and has social utility does not mean that it is permissible at any cost. Such factors must be weighed against the quantum of harm the device brings to others.

. . . Here, the benefits are relatively small and the irritation is substantial. On balance, therefore, the social utility of this windmill is outweighed by the quantum of harm that it creates.

With respect to the counterclaim, defendants have failed to prove that plaintiffs' heat pump constitutes an actionable nuisance. While the noise of the pump may at times be as loud as that of the windmill, several factors distinguish it. The operation of the pump is limited in duration and frequency, as it is rarely used and then only for short periods; also, the sound is less alien. In addition, defendants' proofs have failed to clearly and convincingly prove that the pump "unreasonably affects their health and comfort." They complain only of minor disturbances and distractions, rather than nuisances. That is not to say that a heat pump can never be a nuisance, or even that, given more substantial evidence, this particular heat pump could not be deemed a nuisance.

It is only to say that in this case, given these proofs, defendants did not meet their burden. . . .

In conclusion, it is the view of this court that, for a variety of reasons, defendants' windmill constitutes an actionable nuisance. . . . An alternative basis for granting injunctive relief is defendants' violation of the municipal zoning ordinance. An order should be entered accordingly.

Robert C. Ellickson, Alternatives to Zoning: Covenants, Nuisance Rules, and Fines as Land Use Controls
40 U. Chi. L. Rev. 681, 728–31 (1973)

. . . A landowner can reduce the welfare of his neighbors either by undertaking harmful activities or by terminating beneficial conditions that had previously existed on his property. . . . A layman would regard a smokestack or a billboard as "theft" of neighborhood enjoyment that should be tagged with liability or proscribed. He would perceive quite differently, however, the demolition of an architectural landmark or the construction of a housing development on a beautiful vacant meadow. These latter acts would no doubt diminish neighboring property values, yet a layman would not characterize the acting landowner as a thief of neighborhood enjoyment, but perhaps as a former "Good Samaritan" who has understandably become tired of bestowing "windfalls" on his neighbors. Thieves, the layman would probably say, should be liable for the damage they cause, but lapsed Good Samaritans should not.

The wisdom of attaching any operational significance to this linguistic distinction has been a matter of considerable controversy. Some commentators have criticized the distinction on the ground that it cannot be determined which party is causing harm to the other. . . . In ordinary speech, however, people consistently distinguish "harms" from "benefits." . . . Evaluative terms like good, bad, beneficial, and harmful are easily used because people have remarkably consistent perceptions of normal conditions and thus can agree in characterizing deviations from normalcy. In any community, observers empirically establish standards of normal conduct for repetitive activities; people largely agree on normal clothes styles or normal behavior in public places. Similarly there is considerable agreement on the identification of normal land uses, a category virtually certain to include characteristics of modestly priced residential developments. A specific land use is characterized in ordinary speech as beneficial when it would have a more positive than usual impact, and harmful when it would have a more negative than usual impact, on the values of normal surrounding properties. . . .

. . . [N]ormalcy is often used as a legal standard because the concept promises substantial efficiencies. In order to promote economically productive behavior that cannot be easily achieved by bargaining and to satisfy community desires to reward virtuous activities, legal rules should seek to transfer wealth from those whose actions have unusually harmful external impacts and to those whose actions are unusually beneficial to others. That pattern of transfers is now accomplished through a tripartite set of rules incorporating the normalcy standard: meritorious behavior is sometimes rewarded through quasi-contract doctrines and other devices, normal behavior is treated neutrally, and substandard behavior is penalized through liability rules and other sanctions.

Distribution from the substandard and to the meritorious could also be achieved through a unitary approach that would not use the concept of normalcy. For example, a token liability to neighbors could be placed on the most meritorious conduct, with increasing penalties for less meritorious conduct; the standard of conduct toward others would thus be perfection rather than normal behavior. In this system a substandard landowner would suffer net losses since he would pay high penalties and recover lower ones from his normal neighbors. The most meritorious actors would pay small penalties and recover larger ones. The distributional result sought under the tripartite approach can thus also be achieved under a unitary approach. The legal system's adoption of the former must be attributed to a desire to save administrative expenditures. Normal actors in a tripartite system neither pay penalties nor receive rewards; if the range of normal conduct on the land use spectrum is broad, the administrative economies of that system are considerable. . . .

The distinction in economic theory between harmful and beneficial spillovers reflects an underlying notion of normalcy. Modern scholars may be surprised that Pigou thought the proper way to handle air pollution was to give bounties to factories that cleaned up emissions, rather than to tax polluters. In an era when it was normal to pollute with coal-burning fireplaces, Pigou was probably right in recognizing that rewards were the most efficient internalization system and in perceiving the rare nonpolluter as a producer of beneficial externalities. Further, this example shows that the proper tagging of an externality should change as normal conditions change. Automobiles when they first appeared were nuisances to horse travel; as cars began to swamp horse drawn vehicles in number, horses were properly perceived as the nuisance.

Note on the Basis of Nuisance Liability

1. *Five approaches.* The basis of nuisance liability remains much contested. There are at least five approaches to the issue.

a. *Balance of utilities test.* Section 826 of the first Restatement of Torts (1939) in effect required a plaintiff in a nuisance case to prove that the gravity of the harm stemming from the defendant's conduct exceeded the utility of that conduct. This is essentially Learned Hand's cost/benefit approach to the proof of negligence. See United States v. Carroll Towing Co., 159 F.2d 169, 173 (2d Cir. 1947). This test is in tension with the widely accepted doctrine that a plaintiff in a nuisance case does *not* have to prove negligence to prevail. See, e.g., Morgan v. High Penn Oil Co., 77 S.E.2d 682 (N.C. 1953); Lacy Feed Co. v. Parish, 517 S.W.2d 845 (Tex. Civ. App. 1974). If proof of negligence were to be required, a jury could find that the owner of a stinking and polluting cattle feedlot was not liable to neighboring homeowners for nuisance damages because the utility of the feedlot outweighed the external harms it was causing. See Carpenter v. Double R Cattle Co., 701 P.2d 222 (Idaho 1985) (reaching this result). For endorsement of the balance of utilities approach in the nuisance context, see William M. Landes & Richard A. Posner, The Economic Structure of Tort Law 49 (1987).

b. *Section 826(b): constrained strict liability.* When William Prosser, the Reporter of the Restatement (Second) of Torts, proposed the retention of the balance-of-utilities test in 1970, he was challenged by Professors Fleming James and Robert Keaton. Eventually the challengers succeeded in persuading the American Law Institute (ALI) to add §826(b) to the Restatement (Second) of Torts. Section 826(b) invites a court to hold that a party carrying out a cost-justified nuisance nevertheless is liable for damages when "the harm caused by the conduct is serious and the financial burden of compensating this and similar harm to others would not make the continuation of the conduct not feasible." Are these limitations on strict liability for damages imposed when, say, a court imposes strict liability in tort for ultrahazardous activities? Are the limitations defensible in the nuisance context? The machinations within the ALI are reviewed in Robert E. Keaton, Restating Strict

Liability and Nuisance, 48 Vand. L. Rev. 595 (1995); Jeff L. Lewin, *Boomer* and the American Law of Nuisance, 54 Alb. L. Rev. 189, 221–28 (1990).

c. *Strict liability for any subnormal use that damages neighbors.* A less limited approach, elements of which are implicit in Justice Holmes's opinion in *Middlesex*, holds that a land use is prima facie a nuisance when it is significantly more injurious to ordinary neighbors than a land use ordinary for that locality would be. See Robert C. Ellickson, Alternatives to Zoning, 40 U. Chi. L. Rev. 681, 719–48 (1973). See also Donald Wittman, Liability for Harm or Restitution for Benefit, 13 J. Legal Stud. 57 (1984). Under this unconstrained strict liability approach, a court might weigh the costs and benefits of the defendant's conduct when considering whether to issue an injunction, but would not do so when deciding whether to award damages. Compare Boomer v. Atlantic Cement Co., 257 N.E.2d 870 (N.Y. 1970), excerpted at p. 528 (restricting plaintiff who prevails against a cost-justified nuisance to an award of damages).

d. *Strict liability for any use that makes a neighbor worse off.* The approach just described would not lead to nuisance liability if a subdivision of ordinary houses were to be built on a beautiful meadow, even if neighbors who had previously enjoyed views of the meadow were to suffer diminutions in their property values. If the definition of a nuisance included, however, any conduct that diminished the value of neighboring property, the subdivider of the meadow could be held liable for a nuisance in such a situation. Is this test the only one consistent with the ancient maxim *sic utere tuo ut alienum non laedas* ("so use your own property as not to injure that of another")? Why did Holmes reject this approach?

e. *List of factors. Rose*, the windmill decision, lists various unweighted factors that help determine whether a nuisance exists. Compare §§827–828 of the Restatement (Second) of Torts (1979), which mention a total of eight unranked factors that are "important" in determining the utility of the defendant's conduct and the gravity of harm it imposes. Is the list-of-factors approach a sign of intellectual bankruptcy? A triumph of pragmatist jurisprudence?

2. *Relevance of nuisance law to takings law.* Lucas v. South Carolina Coastal Council, 505 U.S. 1003 (1992), excerpted at p. 169, holds that a government does not run afoul of the Takings Clause even when it adopts a regulation that makes land valueless if the regulation imposes limits that "inhere in the title itself, in the restrictions that background principles of the State's law of property and nuisance already place upon land ownership." Which approach to nuisance liability would lead to the soundest outcomes in the takings context? For criticism of Justice Scalia's resort to nuisance law, see Louise A. Halper, Why the Nuisance Knot Can't Undo the Takings Muddle, 28 Ind. L. Rev. 329 (1995).

3. *Commercial uses as nuisances.* During the 1920s and 1930s, the law reports were full of cases in which neighbors were challenging a nearby service station or funeral parlor on a nuisance theory. The more exclusively residential a neighborhood was, the more likely a court would grant relief. These nuisance actions are now less common as zoning increasingly has supplanted nuisance law. The most recent cases are collected in Annotations, 124 A.L.R. 383 (1940) and 8 A.L.R. 4th 324 (1981).

Judges generally were less likely to protect homeowners from more ordinary commercial uses, however. In Essick v. Shillam, 32 A.2d 416 (Pa. 1943), defendant had intended to lease her property located in a predominantly residential area to the A&P chain for the operation of a supermarket. Distinguishing such a store from uses such as service stations that more "deleteriously affect the health and comfort of the community," the Supreme Court of Pennsylvania ruled that the courts below had erred in enjoining construction of the store. It indicated, however, that the plaintiffs might become entitled to equitable relief in the future if the store were to be operated in an offensive manner. But cf. Diehl v.

Lockard, 385 A.2d 550 (Pa. 1978) (enjoining proposed construction of Pizza Hut restaurant in residential area as nuisance per se). See generally J.H. Beuscher & Jerry W. Morrison, Judicial Zoning Through Recent Nuisance Cases, 1955 Wis. L. Rev. 440.

4. *"Right-to-Farm" statutes.* In 1979, North Carolina enacted the following statutory provision, which quickly became a model for so-called right-to-farm legislation:

NORTH CAROLINA GEN. STAT. §106-701 (2004)

> (a) No agricultural or forestry operation or any of its appurtenances shall be or become a nuisance, private or public, by any changed conditions in or about the locality thereof after the same has been in operation for more than one year, when such operation was not a nuisance at the time the operation began; provided, that provisions of this subsection shall not apply whenever a nuisance results from the negligent or improper operation of such agricultural or forestry operation or its appurtenances. . . .

See Margaret Rosso Grossman & Thomas G. Fischer, Protecting the Right to Farm: Statutory Limits on Nuisance Actions Against the Farmer, 1983 Wis. L. Rev. 95. By 1998, every state had adopted some sort of right-to-farm act. See Alexander A. Reinert, Note, The Right to Farm: Hog-Tied and Nuisance-Bound, 73 N.Y.U. L. Rev. 1694, 1706 (1998). The provisions of many of these acts vary in important respects from the North Carolina approach. New Jersey's Right to Farm Act, for example, entitles county agricultural boards to preempt municipal regulation of commercial farms. See Township of Franklin v. Hollander, 796 A.2d 874 (N.J. 2002).

What justifications might there be for limiting the nuisance liabilities of certain enterprises? Are agricultural operations more deserving of favored treatment than, say, industrial or mining operations? Did North Carolina confer on its farmers and ranchers the right quantum of protection from nuisance litigation? Compare pp. 544–49, on the use of subsidies to preserve agricultural lands.

In Bormann v. Board of Supervisors, 584 N.W.2d 309 (Iowa 1998), cert. denied, 525 U.S. 1172 (1999), the Supreme Court of Iowa invalidated the protections against nuisance liability that the Iowa Right to Farm statute had conferred on farmers. According to the court, these immunity provisions would entitle a farm operator to impose an easement for nuisance activities on neighbors. The court held that the takings clauses of the United States and Iowa Constitutions did not permit this outcome. Should every relaxation of neighbors' private nuisance entitlements (e.g., *Boomer,* excerpted at p. 528) be deemed a taking of property?

5. *Natural conditions as nuisances.* To the distress of neighbors, a graduate student writing a doctoral thesis on Henry David Thoreau permitted the lawn in front of his house in a suburb of Buffalo to become a natural meadow of wildflowers and tall clover. See N.Y. Times, Sept. 16, 1984, at 50. Can a landowner who has not committed an affirmative act incur nuisance liability? See Lussier v. San Lorenzo Valley Water District, 253 Cal. Rptr. 470 (Ct. App. 1988) (holding that landowner may be liable in nuisance for losses caused by natural conditions). Cf. Howard v. City of Lincoln, 497 N.W.2d 53 (Neb. 1993) (holding city could cut weeds on recalcitrant homeowner's property at homeowner's expense); James T.R. Jones, Trains, Trucks, Trees and Shrubs: Vision-Blocking Natural Vegetation and a Landowner's Duty to Those Off Premises, 39 Vill. L. Rev. 1263 (1994) (supporting an affirmative duty to control vegetation).

6. *Aesthetic nuisances.* Traditional nuisance law did not protect aesthetic sensibilities. For example, Mathewson v. Primeau, 395 P.2d 183 (Wash. 1964), granted plaintiff injunctive relief against the odors from defendant's hogs, but refused to grant relief against defendant's unsightly junk pile. See also Oliver v. AT&T Wireless Services, 90 Cal. Rptr.

2d 491, 500 (Ct. App. 1999) (holding that the "displeasing height and shape" of a new 130-foot-tall cellular telephone transmission tower did not constitute a nuisance to neighbors); Richard A. Epstein, Nuisance Law, 8 J. Legal Stud. 49, 60–65 (1979) (supporting judges' traditional reluctance to find visual blight a nuisance).

Most commentators, however, have argued that nuisance law should provide a remedy against visual offenses. See, e.g., Raymond Robert Coletta, The Case for Aesthetic Nuisance, 48 Ohio St. L.J. 141 (1987); Dix W. Noel, Unaesthetic Sights as Nuisances, 25 Cornell L.Q. 1 (1939). And some courts have ventured in this direction. See, e.g., Foley v. Harris, 286 S.E.2d 186 (Va. 1982) (enjoining defendant from collecting unsightly junked vehicles on subdivision lot).

7. *Abandoned buildings.* The plaintiff in Puritan Holding Co. v. Holloschitz, 372 N.Y.S.2d 500 (Sup. Ct. 1975), owned a recently renovated apartment building on West 93rd Street in Manhattan. Almost directly across the street was an abandoned building owned by defendant. Defendant's building had "deteriorated, become unsightly and been taken over by derelicts." Defendant did not appear in the action. The trial court held an inquest, found defendant's building to be a nuisance, and awarded plaintiff a judgment of $30,000 — the court's estimate of the difference in market value of plaintiff's building before and after the nuisance.

How much was this judgment worth to plaintiff? Didn't the fact that defendant had failed to appear indicate that plaintiff would find few assets on which to levy execution? See Note, A Nuisance Law Approach to the Problems of Housing Abandonment, 85 Yale L.J. 1130, 1138–40 (1976) (discussing risk that nuisance defendants may be judgment-proof).

What if the defendant's building had been a dilapidated tenement occupied by impoverished tenants? Compare pp. 522–24.

Note on Rights to Light, Air, and View

1. *Rejection of the doctrine of "ancient lights."* American courts have refused to adopt the English doctrine that a landowner can acquire a prescriptive easement of light and air by open and uninterrupted use of a particular light corridor for the time period set out in the relevant statute of limitations. See, e.g., Fontainebleau Hotel Corp. v. Forty-Five Twenty-Five, Inc., 114 So. 2d 357 (Fla. Dist. Ct. App. 1959) (refusing to enjoin construction of hotel tower that would cast shadows on swimming pool of rival hotel); Rogers v. Sawin, 76 Mass. (10 Gray) 376 (1858) (denying any remedy to a plaintiff whose fourth-story lotline window had been walled over by defendant). See also Wolford v. Thomas, 235 Cal. Rptr. 422 (Ct. App. 1987) (declining to provide remedy against newly constructed penthouse that impaired neighbor's view from San Francisco's Russian Hill). Nineteenth-century American judges apparently believed that the ancient lights doctrine would impede the rapid development of cities. But the owner of an ancient light should be willing to sell that right at some price. When transaction costs are zero, the Coase Theorem asserts that inefficient ancient lights would be eliminated by market transactions. Given that transaction costs are not zero, were American judges justified in their refusal to recognize ancient lights?

2. *Spite fences.* Although American nuisance law generally does not protect interests in light, air, and view, a number of important exceptions have been carved out. The spite-fence doctrine was one of the earliest to evolve. It holds that a neighbor is entitled to relief from a fence or structure that a landowner built on account of malice toward the neighbor, provided that the structure is totally lacking in other utility to the builder. See, e.g., Burke v. Smith, 37 N.W. 838 (Mich. 1888).

This doctrine continues to have vitality. In Sundowner, Inc. v. King, 509 P.2d 785 (Idaho 1973), the defendant motel owner had built a fence 18 feet high and 85 feet long. The fence obscured plaintiff's rival motel located 2 feet away from the back side of the fence. The twin prerequisites for a spite fence were found to have been met. The trial court's decree that the fence be reduced to 6 feet in height therefore was affirmed.

In Wilson v. Handley, 119 Cal. Rptr. 2d 263 (Ct. App. 2002), the plaintiff had begun to build a two-story log cabin in anticipation of enjoying views of Mount Shasta. The defendant then planted a line of spruces and cypresses — both excellent screening trees — near the common property line at a location that threatened to interfere with plaintiff's views. Plaintiff invoked California's spite-fence statute, Cal. Civ. Code §841.4 (West 2004), which affords relief against a "fence or other structure . . . unnecessarily exceeding 10 feet in height maliciously erected." The California Court of Appeals held that the trees could be regarded as a "fence" within the meaning of the statute and remanded the case for determination of whether the defendant's dominant purpose in planting the trees had been to annoy the plaintiff.

Note on Solar Access

1. *Common law protection?* In Prah v. Maretti, 321 N.W.2d 182 (Wis. 1982), the defendant had begun to construct a single-family house that the trial court found to be in compliance with applicable covenants and zoning restrictions. The plaintiff, the neighbor immediately to the north, sought a temporary injunction on the ground that the house would constitute a nuisance because it would partially shade the solar collectors the plaintiff previously had installed on his roof to supply energy for heat and hot water. The Supreme Court of Wisconsin held that the complaint had stated a claim for relief based on the common law of private nuisance and remanded the case for trial. Was the court's decision consistent with Holmes's approach in Middlesex Co. v. McCue, excerpted at p. 512?

Compare Sher v. Liederman, 226 Cal. Rptr. 698 (Ct. App. 1986), in which the growth of defendant's trees had impaired the utility of passive-solar features of plaintiff's house. The California Court of Appeal explicitly rejected the Wisconsin Supreme Court's reasoning in *Prah* and held that the plaintiff's complaint did not state a cause of action for private nuisance. See also Note, *Prah v. Maretti*: Deficiencies of a Nuisance Law Cause of Action for Obstruction of Solar Access, 78 Nw. U. L. Rev. 861 (1983) (criticizing *Prah* on numerous grounds).

2. *Statutory protection.* Wisconsin has a solar-access statute, Wis. Stat. §700.41 (2004). This act entitles the owner of a previously installed solar collector to recover damages when a neighbor subsequently blocks solar access by building a structure that intrudes beyond the permissible building envelope identified by a local zoning ordinance in effect at the time the solar collector was installed. This statute went into effect too late to affect the *Prah* litigation. Identify two reasons why the statute, had it been in effect, would not have helped the plaintiff in *Prah* obtain the remedy that he was seeking. What is the likelihood that neighbors will either ignore or bargain around the provisions of a solar-access statute? See pp. 38–39.

3. *Land of the Rising Sun.* In Japan, a landowner whose sunlight is blocked may be entitled to recover damages and, occasionally, may even obtain injunctive relief. In one case, the city of Tokyo was held liable for $6,670 in damages to seven plaintiffs whose residences were shaded by the city's new nine-story office building. Wash. Post, June 22, 1976, at A2. See generally Michael K. Young, Judicial Review of Administrative Guidance: Governmentally Encouraged Dispute Resolution in Japan, 84 Colum. L. Rev. 923 (1984)

(reporting that local authorities commonly withhold permits until a developer has settled light and air issues with neighbors); Note, Let the Sunshine In: A Comparison of Japanese and American Solar Rights, 1 Harv. Envtl. L. Rev. 578 (1976).

Falloon v. Schilling
29 Kan. 292 (1883)

BREWER, J. . . .

. . . Stated briefly, [plaintiff's grievance] is that defendant, the owner of adjacent lands, provoked at plaintiff because of [plaintiff's] refusal to sell at [defendant's] terms, and for the sake of annoying plaintiff and his family, erected small tenement houses close to plaintiff's land, and rented them to negroes.

Do these facts entitle him to an injunction? Plaintiff invokes the familiar maxim, "*sic utere tuo ut alienum non laedas,*" and insists that under that he is entitled to the injunction prayed for. It will be perceived that plaintiff's complaint is twofold — *First*, as to the kind of buildings that defendant is erecting; and, *second*, the uses to which he intends putting them. He complains that defendant is erecting small shanties, and that he proposes filling them with worthless negroes. His testimony fails to fully sustain his allegations. It is true the building defendant has erected is a small tenement house of but two rooms, without cellar or foundation walls, and yet the plaintiff himself says the building looks neat. The building is rented to a negro family, but that family is the family of a preacher, and well behaved. It cannot, therefore, be said that defendant is filling his buildings with *worthless* negroes. Now, does the fact that defendant is improving his property with small tenement houses, — houses which do not compare favorably with plaintiff's homestead, — and that he is renting those houses to negro families, give plaintiff a right to interfere by an injunction simply on the ground that defendant is so acting for the purpose of annoying plaintiff? We think not. Doubtless a party may obtain an injunction to restrain a neighbor from erecting or continuing on his premises a nuisance; but that, as a general rule, is the limit of interference. A man has a right to improve his own property in any way he sees fit, providing the improvement is not such a one as the law will pronounce a nuisance; and this he may do although he make such improvement through spite. And it may be laid down as a universal rule, that the size and quality of the improvement never of themselves constitute it a nuisance. A land-owner may erect upon his land the smallest or most temporary kind of dwelling-house or store in close proximity to the finest mansion or block of buildings, and that for the mere sake of spiting the owner of such mansion or block of buildings by the contrast, without becoming subject to restraint at the hands of the courts. In other words, if the improvement itself is legitimate and lawful, — is not, per se, a nuisance, — the law will not inquire into the motives with which he acts. It is true the law will interfere to prevent the erection of a nuisance such as a stable, out-building, etc., but not to prevent the erection of a store, tenement, or anything of that nature. . . .

. . . [E]quity will not interfere simply because the occupants of such house are by reason of race, color, or habits, disagreeable or offensive. A negro family is not, per se, a nuisance; and a white man cannot prevent his neighbor from renting his home to a negro family any more than he can to a German, an Irish, or a French family. The law makes no distinction on account of race or color, and recognizes no prejudices arising therefrom. As long as that neighbor's family is well behaved, it matters not what the color, race, or habits may be, or how offensive personally or socially it may be to plaintiff; plaintiff has no cause of complaint in the courts.

[Judgment for defendant affirmed.]

Note on Disfavored People and Low-Cost Housing as Nuisances

1. *Modest dwellings*. Prior to the spread of zoning in the 1920s, courts generally would refuse to rule that a tenement situated in a better-to-do neighborhood was a nuisance. In White v. Bernhart, 241 P. 367 (Idaho 1925), defendant had intended to move a "dilapidated frame dwelling house" into a block of "neatly kept residences" in Pocatello, and to situate the house only 11 feet back from the sidewalk. All existing houses were set back 25 or 30 feet. A neighbor offered evidence that his own six-room modern brick dwelling would lose $1,500 in value if defendant were to carry out his plans. The Idaho Supreme Court held that a dilapidated building cannot be a nuisance merely because it is unsightly. Facing outcomes like these, cities turned to zoning to control the location of modest-quality residential uses. See pp. 74-76.

2. *Housing projects that breed crime*. In several instances in northern California, neighbors of a troubled housing complex have filed clusters of nuisance actions in small claims courts to recover damages from the owner of the offending property. Lew v. Superior Court, 25 Cal. Rptr. 2d 42 (Ct. App. 1993), affirmed the propriety of an award totaling $218,000 to 66 neighbors of a private Berkeley project, subsidized under the Section 8 program, that had become a center of drug dealing. The plaintiffs fared less well in Housing Authority v. Superior Court, 18 Cal. Rptr. 218 (Ct. App. 1993), depublished (Cal. 1993). In that instance, 25 occupants of an apartment building across the street from a San Francisco public housing project had sought to recover small claims awards on account of a high level of street crime that the project allegedly fostered. The appellate court denied recovery, finding that most of the crimes had been committed by unknown third parties whom the housing authority had no duty to control. Do public landlords warrant more protection than private ones? See generally B.A. Glesner, Landlords as Cops: Tort, Nuisance and Forfeiture Standards Imposing Liability on Landlords for Crime on the Premises, 42 Case W. Res. L. Rev. 679 (1992).

3. *Facilities for the homeless*. In Spring-Gar Community Civic Association v. Homes for the Homeless, Inc., 516 N.Y.S.2d 399 (Sup. Ct. 1987), a nonprofit organization had leased a former Holiday Inn to provide emergency housing for up to 200 homeless families. Invoking private nuisance doctrine, among other grounds, a community association representing homeowners sought to enjoin operation of the facility. The court declined to issue an injunction, stressing that the neighbors had not adduced any evidence that the residents of the shelter had annoyed anyone during the two months the facility had been open.

Evidence of annoyance was plentiful in Armory Park Neighborhood Association v. Episcopal Community Services, 712 P.2d 914 (Ariz. 1985), and the outcome was quite different. The defendant was a Tucson soup kitchen that provided free meals to indigents. Neighborhood residents testified that, because of the soup kitchen, "transients frequently trespassed onto residents' yards, sometimes urinating, defecating, drinking and littering on the residents' property." The Supreme Court of Arizona held that the soup kitchen was responsible for the acts of its patrons, and that the neighbors were entitled to relief on the basis of public nuisance, the legal theory advanced in the complaint. The case was remanded for appropriate equitable relief, which was not necessarily to include an order closing the facility. Under what circumstances would the statutory and constitutional rights of persons with disabilities insulate a facility that serves the homeless from a nuisance action? See Chapter 8D. What protections against nuisance liability might either the Free Exercise Clause or the Religious Land Use and Institutionalized Persons Act offer a religious organization that serves the homeless? See pp. 209-20. Compare Fifth Avenue Presbyterian Church v. City of New York, 293 F.3d 570 (2d Cir. 2002) (implying that a church that opens its grounds to homeless people for sleeping may be able to successfully invoke the Free Exercise Clause to resist city dispersal efforts).

Note on Governmental Activity as a Nuisance

1. *Special doctrines.* A nuisance action against a public entity often is treated differently than a nuisance action against a private defendant. In some instances, a plaintiff may fare better when suing a government. The plaintiff may be able to constitutionalize the claim by alleging inverse condemnation. See, e.g., Lee County v. Kiesel, 705 So. 2d 1013 (Fla. Dist. Ct. App. 1998), where the county was held liable for a taking when it built a bridge that blocked the view from plaintiff's lot. Many jurisdictions entitle a successful plaintiff in an inverse-condemnation action to recover reasonable attorney fees and other litigation costs. See, e.g., Cal. Civ. Proc. Code §1036 (West 2004). In Abbott v. City of Bristol, 355 A.2d 68 (Conn. 1974), the city had built a massive water tank 50 feet from the lot where plaintiffs maintained their 11-room colonial wood-frame house. The court construed Bristol's city charter to require compensation for the diminution in the value of plaintiffs' property, regardless of plaintiffs' rights under nuisance law. But cf. Pierce v. Northeast Lake Washington Sewer & Water District, 870 P.2d 305 (Wash. 1994), where, on similar facts, a homeowner lost a takings claim based on the state constitution.

On the other hand, a government defendant may be able to invoke defenses, such as sovereign immunity, that are not available to a private defendant. Judges also may adjust the remedies they provide. A court willing to enjoin a noisy private factory might not be willing to enjoin the operation of an equally noisy public highway — perhaps on the ground that a government has broad powers of eminent domain. Other special doctrines may protect a government agency from liability for nuisance damages. In Mark v. Oregon State Department of Fish & Wildlife, 974 P.2d 716 (Or. Ct. App. 1999), the court held that a neighbor had stated a prima facie nuisance claim against a state agency that had permitted nude bathing on a nearby Columbia River beach. (Sound? See John Copeland Nagle, Moral Nuisances, 50 Emory L.J. 265 (2001).) The court went on to hold, however, that, because the state's action had been discretionary, under Oregon law the neighbor could seek only injunctive relief, not damages.

2. *Airport noise.* Airplanes have spawned the richest body of judicial and academic writing on governmental liability for nuisance activities. The federal courts generally have limited recovery against a government airport operator to landowners who have suffered at least some direct overflights. See, e.g., Argent v. United States, 124 F.3d 1277 (Fed. Cir. 1997). Some state courts, however, have rejected the overflight requirement and have been willing to award compensation to any landowner who can show substantial damage from airport noise. See, e.g., Thornburg v. Port of Portland, 376 P.2d 100 (Or. 1962); Jackson v. Metropolitan Knoxville Airport Authority, 922 S.W.2d 860 (Tenn. 1996). A pioneering legal analysis of the issue is William F. Baxter & Lillian R. Altree, Legal Aspects of Airport Noise, 15 J.L. & Econ. 1 (1970). For an introduction to the empirical literature, see Daniel P. McMillen, Airport Expansions and Property Values: The Case of Chicago O'Hare Airport, 55 J. Urb. Econ. 627 (2004) (reporting that technological improvements have made aircraft quieter).

If a municipality were previously to have been held liable for damage from airport noise, would it be entitled to obtain indemnification from the airlines that had used the airport and from the companies that had manufactured the aircraft? See City of Los Angeles v. Japan Air Lines Co., 116 Cal. Rptr. 69 (Ct. App. 1974) (holding indemnification was barred by express language in airport leases).

2.   *Private Nuisance: Defenses*

Kellogg v. Village of Viola
227 N.W.2d 55 (Wis. 1975)

WILKIE, Chief Justice.

The Village of Viola operated a private nuisance where burning was done at the village dump. John Kellogg, the plaintiff-respondent, operated a mink ranch on land purchased in 1966 from the village and located directly adjacent to the village dump. The village appeals from a jury verdict awarding $10,153 to Kellogg for smoke-caused damage to his mink herd during 1970.[1] On this appeal the village claims that in this action by Kellogg for damages attributable to this private nuisance, the plaintiff is barred from recovery because (1) he came to the nuisance, (2) he made representations to the village board which rendered him equitably estopped from suing, and (3) the mink are abnormally sensitive animals. We reject all of these contentions and affirm.

The basic facts are not in dispute. In 1951 the Village of Viola purchased land in lot 27 near the Kickapoo River in Vernon county and began to operate a dump at the site. The operation included the open and often unsupervised burning of trash by private citizens as well as by village employees. In 1965, because of space limitations and Department of Natural Resources regulations, the village purchased all or a portion of lots 15 and 16, directly adjacent to lot 27 to the north, for the purpose of creating a new dump site. After this purchase, but before the dump operations were actually transferred to the new area, the village sold portions of lots 15 and 16 to the plaintiff, John Kellogg, for use as a mink ranch. The board had bought more land than it thought it could use. . . .

. . . At the special meeting in July of 1966 the board members voted to sell portions of lots 15 and 16 to plaintiff and further, to grant him a mink ranch permit if he could establish that the water well on the property would be sufficient to meet his needs. (Plaintiff was subsequently granted the permit.) The question of whether the proximity of the dump would be harmful to the mink was raised at the meeting, and plaintiff said he did not "think it was a problem." Members of the village board agreed that plaintiff had made such a statement.

Plaintiff started mink ranch operations on lots 15 and 16 in the fall of 1966. In the spring of 1967 the village moved the dump to lot 16 from the old site at lot 27. The dump and the mink ranch apparently peacefully coexisted until the summer of 1969 when smoke from the dump allegedly caused the loss of 600 mink kits. This incident is not involved in the instant action. Following the loss, plaintiff told several members of the board that he "had a problem" due to smoke from the dump and that "maybe next year we can work something out so we don't have this loss." In the spring of 1970, plaintiff made a verbal request followed by a written request on April 9th that the burning cease during the mink breeding season. The burning stopped for three days and "no burning" signs were placed at the dump. However, the moratorium was ended by an April 22nd decision of the board upon the recommendation of the village employee in charge of the dump. He stated: "I felt that if we wasn't going to burn it, we were going to be buried in it." . . .

On Sunday, May 10, 1970, the mink pens were filled with heavy smoke from the village dump, causing the mother mink to become so excited they began killing their young. Plaintiff lost 2,500 mink kits as a result. Another fire occurred lasting from June 8th to June 10th, also causing great excitement of the mother mink. They refused to eat and neglected their young during a critical growing period, resulting in stunting of growth of

---

[1] EDS.: Plaintiff had asked for a damage award in excess of $30,000.

approximately 3,000 mink. . . . There is no indication in the record who started the May and June fires.

COMING TO THE NUISANCE

There is no dispute that plaintiff came to the nuisance. The dump had been operating since 1931 and, although its exact location changed after the plaintiff purchased his property, he was aware of the impending change which involved only a short move. The first question on this appeal is whether the fact that plaintiff came to the nuisance bars this action in which plaintiff seeks damages for the operation of a private nuisance. It does not. While coming to the nuisance may properly be considered while weighing the equities in an abatement action, it is irrelevant in a damage suit.

Just because it happened that the village landowner arrived in the area first and maintained a nuisance on this property, this does not grant to the village a perpetual easement to pollute the air over all surrounding lands.

ESTOPPEL

Coming to the nuisance and estoppel are somewhat related as the trial judge concluded. The difference is that coming to the nuisance embraces action by only one party. Kellogg came to the burning dump nuisance as operated by the village. Estoppel involves the conduct on the part of at least two parties: the party asserting the operation of equitable estoppel, the village, and the party whose claim is sought to be estopped — the mink rancher. . . . "Three facts or factors must be present: (1) *Action or nonaction* which induces (2) *reliance* by another (3) to his *detriment*."

The elements making the defense of equitable estoppel available would be present in the instant case except for the important fact that the nuisance was obviously increased during 1969 and 1970. . . .

. . . [I]t is undisputed that while plaintiff bought the land and started the mink ranch in 1966, the dump caused no damage during 1966, 1967, and 1968. During 1969, smoke caused the death of some mink, and in May and June of 1970, substantial losses were incurred as the result of the smoke, giving rise to this suit. It must be noted, too, that prior to these latter losses, plaintiff, orally and in writing, put the board on notice that continued burning during the breeding season was endangering the mink. We therefore conclude that based on these facts — increased level of nuisance and notice of same to the board — the defendant is precluded from asserting estoppel. . . .

ABNORMAL SENSITIVITY

Defendant argues that because mink are abnormally sensitive animals plaintiff may not maintain this nuisance action.

There is no question that the sensitivity of the plaintiff is a factor to be considered in deciding whether a nuisance exists. In Bie v. Ingersoll, 135 N.W.2d 250 (Wis. 1965), this court said: ". . . The activity complained of must create more than an inconvenience, and must be offensive to the person of ordinary and normal sensibilities. The result is not to be measured by its effect upon those of extreme sensibilities." However, the question whether a nuisance exists must be determined by the trier of fact, in this case, the jury. . . . Defendant does not complain that [the jury] instruction was erroneous, or that it did not allow the jury to take account of the special sensitivities of plaintiff's business, or that a special instruction should have been given concerning mink. Defendant is really asking this court to hold, as a matter of law, that injury to mink does not give rise to an actionable nuisance.

[This the court refused to do. Affirmed.]

Note on Defenses

1. *Coming to the nuisance*. What if the mink rancher in *Kellogg* had brought in more mink the following year (1971) and the kits again were lost on account of the smoke? Should the mink rancher have been entitled to recover for those losses? Should the plaintiff have been required to bear the disastrous losses in 1970, on the ground that the less severe losses in 1969 should have induced him to move?

There is disagreement about the proper relief, if any, to be awarded a plaintiff who has initiated an incompatible use in the face of an ongoing nuisance. Section 840D of the Restatement (Second) of Torts (1977) declares: "The fact that the plaintiff has acquired or improved his land after a nuisance interfering with it has come into existence is not in itself sufficient to bar his action, but is a factor to be considered in determining whether the nuisance is actionable." Queries: How big a factor? What are the other factors?

The Restatement approach was applied in McQuade v. Tucson Tiller Apartments, Ltd., 543 P.2d 150 (Ariz. 1975). Defendant had opened a shopping center and used it periodically as a site for outdoor rock concerts that had attracted as many as 7,000 people. After the first concerts, plaintiff constructed an apartment building nearby. The court affirmed the trial court's issuance of an injunction against concerts involving loud music or attracting large crowds. Plaintiff's "coming to the nuisance" was regarded as only one factor to be considered.

Several commentators have argued that some variant of a defense of coming-to-the-nuisance should be recognized to induce the nuisance's neighbors to mitigate damages. See, e.g., William F. Baxter & Lillian R. Altree, Legal Aspects of Airport Noise, 15 J.L. & Econ. 1, 3-5 (1972). These commentators would deny recovery for damages to improvements neighbors install after the nuisance is ongoing. How easy is this rule to apply when the severity of the nuisance increases over time, as it did in *Kellogg*?

Restatement §840D characterizes someone who *acquires* land near an ongoing nuisance as having come to it. Critics of this position contend that the coming-to defense should be restricted to situations where the plaintiff has *improved* land in face of a nuisance. According to the critics, a doctrine barring a land purchaser from recovering for a preexisting nuisance would impair the free alienation of land because the cause of action would evaporate in the event of sale. In addition, the doctrine would mainly hurt land sellers, not purchasers, because a buyer who was aware of the coming-to defense would bid less. Cf. pp. 180-85 (on coming to a taking) and p. 293 (on coming to the hardship by a variance applicant).

Should the law confer superior rights on the first person to arrive in a neighborhood? See Rohan Pitchford & Christopher M. Snyder, Coming to the Nuisance, 19 J.L. Econ. & Org. 491 (2003) (anticipating that first arriver will overinvest in nuisance activity if defense is made available); Donald Wittman, First Come, First Served: An Economic Analysis of "Coming to the Nuisance," 9 J. Legal Stud. 557 (1980).

2. *Special sensitivity*. In Amphitheatres, Inc. v. Portland Meadows, 198 P.2d 847 (Or. 1948), plaintiff and defendant had simultaneously constructed a drive-in movie theater and a racetrack on adjacent parcels of land. When defendant conducted night horse races, the racetrack floodlights seriously diminished the quality of the pictures on plaintiff's movie screen. Plaintiff sought to recover damages on trespass and nuisance theories. The court held this was not an instance of trespass, and "that a man cannot increase the [nuisance] liabilities of his neighbor by applying his own property to special and delicate uses, whether for business or pleasure." Judgment was given to defendant.

How do courts determine what uses are specially sensitive? To what extent does this determination rest on notions of normal and ordinary usage? Suppose the mink rancher in *Kellogg* had been denied compensation for his loss of mink on the ground that they were unusually vulnerable to smoke. Should that have affected his entitlement to recover for smoke damage to other, normally sensitive, property?

3. *Permissive regulation.* Should a defendant be able to defend against a nuisance action by demonstrating that municipal authorities had approved the disputed activity — perhaps by licensing it or placing it in a permissive zoning classification?

The general rule is that permissive regulation does not bar a plaintiff's suit. See, e.g., Morgan County Concrete Co. v. Tanner, 374 So. 2d 1344 (Ala. 1979); Walsh v. Town of Stonington Water Pollution Control Authority, 736 A.2d 811, 822 (Conn. 1999). (There is an analogous rule in negligence law that compliance with a statute does not necessarily indicate lack of negligence.) It has been argued, on the other hand, that permissive legislation (if silent on the issue of the preemption of preexisting nuisance law) should be a defense against a private suit for injunctive relief, but not against an action for damages. See Note, Nuisance and Legislative Authorization, 52 Colum. L. Rev. 781 (1952).

4. *Prescription?* Courts occasionally hold that the right to maintain a nuisance can ripen by prescription — that is, open, adverse, and continuous noxious use for the period of the relevant statute of limitations (commonly 10 to 20 years). See, e.g., Anneburg v. Kurtz, 28 S.E.2d 769 (Ga. 1944) (dumping of vegetable refuse into creek); Hoffman v. United Iron & Metal Co., 671 A.2d 55 (Md. Ct. Spec. App. 1996) (noise, explosions, and air pollution). Compare the English doctrine of ancient lights, discussed at p. 520.

Should this defense be recognized? The ordinary prescription case involves a pattern of continuing physical invasions, for example, the repeated driving of vehicles across the land of another. In this sort of situation, the law of prescription shows little sympathy to a sole victim who has failed to act for many years. Many nuisances, by contrast, cause pervasive harm. When victims are many, they may prefer to sit back and free-ride on the enforcement efforts of others. Inaction in a large-number case, in short, might be regarded as less blameworthy than inaction in a small-number case. Perhaps for this reason, many authorities hold that a right to maintain a nuisance cannot be acquired by prescription. See, e.g., Hillman v. Town of Greenwich, 587 A.2d 99 (Conn. 1991); Restatement (Third) of Property — Servitudes, §2.17, cmt. d, illus. 7 (2000) (prescriptive right to create nuisance would violate public policy).

5. *Partial defenses.* Should any of the defenses just reviewed operate only to reduce the plaintiff's monetary award (or extent of injunctive relief), but not to eliminate it? The winner-take-all tradition in nuisance law may be eroding. See Tint v. Sanborn, 259 Cal. Rptr. 902 (Ct. App. 1989) (applying comparative negligence approach); Jeff L. Lewin, Comparative Nuisance, 50 U. Pitt. L. Rev. 1009 (1989) (proposing "comparative responsibility" system).

3.   *Private Nuisance: Remedies*

Boomer v. Atlantic Cement Co.
257 N.E.2d 870 (N.Y. 1970)

BERGAN, Judge.
Defendant operates a large cement plant near Albany. These are actions for injunction and damages by neighboring land owners alleging injury to property from dirt, smoke and vibration emanating from the plant. A nuisance has been found after trial, temporary damages have been allowed; but an injunction has been denied.

The public concern with air pollution arising from many sources in industry and in transportation is currently accorded ever wider recognition accompanied by a growing sense of responsibility in State and Federal Governments to control it. Cement plants are obvious sources of air pollution in the neighborhoods where they operate.

But there is now before the court private litigation in which individual property owners have sought specific relief from a single plant operation. The threshold question raised by the division of view on this appeal is whether the court should resolve the litigation between the parties now before it as equitably as seems possible; or whether, seeking promotion of the general public welfare, it should channel private litigation into broad public objectives.

A court performs its essential function when it decides the rights of parties before it. Its decision of private controversies may sometimes greatly affect public issues. Large questions of law are often resolved by the manner in which private litigation is decided. But this is normally an incident to the court's main function to settle controversy. It is a rare exercise of judicial power to use a decision in private litigation as a purposeful mechanism to achieve direct public objectives greatly beyond the rights and interests before the court.

Effective control of air pollution is a problem presently far from solution even with the full public and financial powers of government. In large measure adequate technical procedures are yet to be developed and some that appear possible may be economically impracticable.

It seems apparent that the amelioration of air pollution will depend on technical research in great depth; on a carefully balanced consideration of the economic impact of close regulation; and of the actual effect on public health. It is likely to require massive public expenditure and to demand more than any local community can accomplish and to depend on regional and interstate controls.

A court should not try to do this on its own as a by-product of private litigation and it seems manifest that the judicial establishment is neither equipped in the limited nature of any judgment it can pronounce nor prepared to lay down and implement an effective policy for the elimination of air pollution. This is an area beyond the circumference of one private lawsuit. It is a direct responsibility for government and should not thus be undertaken as an incident to solving a dispute between property owners and a single cement plant — one of many — in the Hudson River valley.

The cement making operations of defendant have been found by the court of Special Term to have damaged the nearby properties of [the eight] plaintiffs in these two actions. That court, as it has been noted, accordingly found defendant maintained a nuisance and this has been affirmed at the Appellate Division. The total damage to plaintiffs' properties is, however, relatively small in comparison with the value of defendant's operation and with the consequences of the injunction which plaintiffs seek.

The ground for the denial of injunction, notwithstanding the finding both that there is a nuisance and that plaintiffs have been damaged substantially, is the large disparity in economic consequences of the nuisance and of the injunction. This theory cannot, however, be sustained without overruling a doctrine which has been consistently reaffirmed in several leading cases in this court and which has never been disavowed here, namely that where a nuisance has been found and where there has been any substantial damage shown by the party complaining an injunction will be granted.

The rule in New York has been that such a nuisance will be enjoined although marked disparity be shown in economic consequence between the effect of the injunction and the effect of the nuisance.

The problem of disparity in economic consequence was sharply in focus in Whalen v. Union Bag & Paper Co., 101 N.E. 805 (N.Y. 1913). A pulp mill entailing an investment of more than a million dollars polluted a stream in which plaintiff, who owned a farm, was "a lower riparian owner." The economic loss to plaintiff from this pollution was small.

This court, reversing the Appellate Division, reinstated the injunction granted by the Special Term against the argument of the mill owner that in view of "the slight advantage to plaintiff and the great loss that will be inflicted on defendant" an injunction should not be granted. "Such a balancing of injuries cannot be justified by the circumstances of this case," Judge Werner noted. He continued: "Although the damage to the plaintiff may be slight as compared with the defendant's expense of abating the condition, that is not a good reason for refusing an injunction."

Thus the unconditional injunction granted at Special Term was reinstated. The rule laid down in that case, then, is that whenever the damage resulting from a nuisance is found not "unsubstantial," viz., $100 a year, injunction would follow. This states a rule that had been followed in this court with marked consistency (McCarty v. Natural Carbonic Gas Co., 81 N.E. 549 (N.Y. 1907); Strobel v. Kerr Salt Co., 58 N.E. 142 (N.Y. 1900); Campbell v. Seaman, 63 N.Y. 568 (1876)).

. . . Thus if, within Whalen v. Union Bag & Paper Co., supra, which authoritatively states the rule in New York, the damage to plaintiffs in these present cases from defendant's cement plant is "not unsubstantial," an injunction should follow.

Although the court at Special Term and the Appellate Division held that injunction should be denied, it was found that plaintiffs had been damaged in various specific amounts up to the time of the trial and damages to the respective plaintiffs were awarded for those amounts. The effect of this was, injunction having been denied, plaintiffs could maintain successive actions at law for damages thereafter as further damage was incurred.

The court at Special Term also found the amount of permanent damage attributable to each plaintiff, for the guidance of the parties in the event both sides stipulated to the payment and acceptance of such permanent damage as a settlement of all the controversies among the parties. The total of permanent damages to all plaintiffs thus found was $185,000. This basis of adjustment has not resulted in any stipulation by the parties.

This result at Special Term and at the Appellate Division is a departure from a rule that has become settled; but to follow the rule literally in these cases would be to close down the plant at once. This court is fully agreed to avoid that immediately drastic remedy; the difference in view is how best to avoid it.*

One alternative is to grant the injunction but postpone its effect to a specified future date to give opportunity for technical advances to permit defendant to eliminate the nuisance; another is to grant the injunction conditioned on the payment of permanent damages to plaintiffs which would compensate them for the total economic loss to their property present and future caused by defendant's operations. For reasons which will be developed the court chooses the latter alternative.

If the injunction were to be granted unless within a short period — e.g., 18 months — the nuisance be abated by improved methods, there would be no assurance that any significant technical improvement would occur.

The parties could settle this private litigation at any time if defendant paid enough money and the imminent threat of closing the plant would build up the pressure on defendant. If there were no improved techniques found, there would inevitably be applications to the court at Special Term for extensions of time to perform on showing of good faith efforts to find such techniques.

Moreover, techniques to eliminate dust and other annoying by-products of cement making are unlikely to be developed by any research the defendant can undertake within

---

*Respondent's investment in the plant is in excess of $45,000,000. There are over 300 people employed there. [EDS.: Footnote in original.]

any short period, but will depend on the total resources of the cement industry nationwide and throughout the world. The problem is universal wherever cement is made.

For obvious reasons the rate of the research is beyond control of defendant. If at the end of 18 months the whole industry has not found a technical solution a court would be hard put to close down this one cement plant if due regard be given to equitable principles.

On the other hand, to grant the injunction unless defendant pays plaintiffs such permanent damages as may be fixed by the court seems to do justice between the contending parties. All of the attributions of economic loss to the properties on which plaintiffs' complaints are based will have been redressed.

The nuisance complained of by these plaintiffs may have other public or private consequences, but these particular parties are the only ones who have sought remedies and the judgment proposed will fully redress them. The limitation of relief granted is a limitation only within the four corners of these actions and does not foreclose public health or other public agencies from seeking proper relief in a proper court.

It seems reasonable to think that the risk of being required to pay permanent damages to injured property owners by cement plant owners would itself be a reasonable effective spur to research for improved techniques to minimize nuisance. . . .

Thus it seems fair to both sides to grant permanent damages to plaintiffs which will terminate this private litigation. The theory of damage is the "servitude on land" of plaintiffs imposed by defendant's nuisance. (See United States v. Causby, 328 U.S. 256, 261, 262, 267 (1946), where the term "servitude" addressed to the land was used by Justice Douglas relating to the effect of airplane noise on property near an airport.)

The judgment, by allowance of permanent damages imposing a servitude on land, which is the basis of the actions, would preclude future recovery by plaintiffs or their grantees. . . .

The orders should be reversed, without costs, and the cases remitted to Supreme Court, Albany County to grant an injunction which shall be vacated upon payment by defendant of such amounts of permanent damage to the respective plaintiffs as shall for this purpose be determined by the court.

JASEN, J., dissenting.

I agree with the majority that a reversal is required here, but I do not subscribe to the newly enunciated doctrine of assessment of permanent damages, in lieu of an injunction, where substantial property rights have been impaired by the creation of a nuisance.

It has long been the rule in this State, as the majority acknowledges, that a nuisance which results in substantial continuing damage to neighbors must be enjoined. . . . To now change the rule to permit the cement company to continue polluting the air indefinitely upon the payment of permanent damages is, in my opinion, compounding the magnitude of a very serious problem in our State and Nation today. . . .

. . . In permitting the injunction to become inoperative upon the payment of permanent damages, the majority is, in effect, licensing a continuing wrong. It is the same as saying to the cement company, you may continue to do harm to your neighbors so long as you pay a fee for it. Furthermore, once such permanent damages are assessed and paid, the incentive to alleviate the wrong would be eliminated, thereby continuing air pollution of an area without abatement. . . .

This kind of inverse condemnation . . . may not be invoked by a private person or corporation for private gain or advantage. Inverse condemnation should only be permitted when the public is primarily served in the taking or impairment of property.

I would enjoin the defendant cement company from continuing the discharge of dust particles upon its neighbors' properties unless, within 18 months, the cement company abated this nuisance. . . .

I am aware that the trial court found that the most modern dust control devices available have been installed in defendant's plant, but, I submit, this does not mean that better and more effective dust control devices could not be developed within the time allowed to abate the pollution. . . .

Guido Calabresi & A. Douglas Melamed, Property Rules, Liability Rules, and Inalienability
85 Harv. L. Rev. 1089, 1092, 1115–19 (1972)

An entitlement is protected by a property rule to the extent that someone who wishes to remove the entitlement from its holder must buy it from him in a voluntary transaction in which the value of the entitlement is agreed upon by the seller. It is the form of entitlement which gives rise to the least amount of state intervention: once the original entitlement is decided upon, the state does not try to decide its value. It lets each of the parties say how much the entitlement is worth to him, and gives the seller a veto if the buyer does not offer enough. Property rules involve a collective decision as to who is to be given an initial entitlement but not as to the value of the entitlement.

Whenever someone may destroy the initial entitlement if he is willing to pay an objectively determined value for it, an entitlement is protected by a liability rule. This value may be what it is thought the original holder of the entitlement would have sold it for. But the holder's complaint that he would have demanded more will not avail him once the objectively determined value is set. Obviously, liability rules involve an additional stage of state intervention: not only are entitlements protected, but their transfer or destruction is allowed on the basis of a value determined by some organ of the state rather than by the parties themselves. . . .

Nuisance or pollution is one of the most interesting areas where the question of who will be given an entitlement, and how it will be protected, is in frequent issue. Traditionally, and very ably in the recent article by Professor Michelman, the nuisance-pollution problem is viewed in terms of three rules.[53] First, Taney may not pollute unless his neighbor (his only neighbor let us assume), Marshall, allows it (Marshall may enjoin Taney's nuisance). Second, Taney may pollute but must compensate Marshall for damages caused (nuisance is found but the remedy is limited to damages). Third, Taney may pollute at will and can only be stopped by Marshall if Marshall pays him off (Taney's pollution is not held to be a nuisance to Marshall). In our terminology rules one and two (nuisance with injunction, and with damages only) are entitlements to Marshall. The first is an entitlement to be free from pollution and is protected by a property rule; the second is also an entitlement to be free from pollution but is protected only by a liability rule. Rule three (no nuisance) is instead an entitlement to Taney protected by a property rule, for only by buying Taney out at Taney's price can Marshall end the pollution.

The very statement of these rules in the context of our framework suggests that something is missing. Missing is a fourth rule representing an entitlement in Taney to pollute, but an entitlement which is protected only by a liability rule. The fourth rule, really a kind

---

53. Michelman, Pollution as a Tort: A Non-Accidental Perspective on Calabresi's Costs, 80 Yale L.J. 647, 670 (1971).

of partial eminent domain coupled with a benefits tax, can be stated as follows: Marshall may stop Taney from polluting, but if he does he must compensate Taney.

As a practical matter it will be easy to see why even legal writers as astute as Professor Michelman have ignored this rule. Unlike the first three it does not often lend itself to judicial imposition for a number of good legal process reasons. For example, even if Taney's injuries could practically be measured, apportionment of the duty of compensation among many Marshalls would present problems for which courts are not well suited. If only those Marshalls who voluntarily asserted the right to enjoin Taney's pollution were required to pay the compensation, there would be insuperable freeloader problems. If, on the other hand, the liability rule entitled one of the Marshalls alone to enjoin the pollution and required all the benefited Marshalls to pay their share of the compensation, the courts would be faced with the immensely difficult task of determining who was benefited how much and imposing a benefits tax accordingly, all the while observing procedural limits within which courts are expected to function.

The fourth rule is thus not part of the cases legal scholars read when they study nuisance law, and is therefore easily ignored by them. But it is available, and may sometimes make more sense than any of the three competing approaches. Indeed, in one form or another, it may well be the most frequent device employed. To appreciate the utility of the fourth rule and to compare it with the other three rules, we will examine why we might choose any of the given rules.

We would employ rule one (entitlement to be free from pollution protected by a property rule) from an economic efficiency point of view if we believed that the polluter, Taney, could avoid or reduce the costs of pollution more cheaply than the pollutee, Marshall. Or to put it another way, Taney would be enjoinable if he were in a better position to balance the costs of polluting against the costs of not polluting. We would employ rule three (entitlement to pollute protected by a property rule) again solely from an economic efficiency standpoint, if we made the converse judgment on who could best balance the harm of pollution against its avoidance costs. If we were wrong in our judgments and if transactions between Marshall and Taney were costless or even very cheap, the entitlement under rules one or three would be traded and an economically efficient result would occur in either case. . . .

. . . Unfortunately, transaction costs are often high on both sides [especially when there are many affected parties] and an initial entitlement, though incorrect in terms of economic efficiency, will not be altered in the market place.

Under these circumstances — and they are normal ones in the pollution area — we are likely to turn to liability rules whenever we are uncertain whether the polluter or the pollutees can most cheaply avoid the cost of pollution. We are only likely to use liability rules where we are uncertain because, if we are certain, the costs of liability rules — essentially the costs of collectively valuing the damages to all concerned plus the cost in coercion to those who would not sell at the collectively determined figure — are unnecessary. They are unnecessary because transaction costs and bargaining barriers become irrelevant when we are certain who is the cheapest cost avoider; economic efficiency will be attained without transactions by making the correct initial entitlement.

Note on Remedial Options

1. *Big splash. Boomer* is one of the most famous common law decisions of its era. Many commentators, drawing on the Calabresi and Melamed analysis, endorse *Boomer's* denial of injunctive relief when a nuisance is causing widespread damage and thus transaction

costs of negotiations are high. See, e.g., Louis Kaplow & Steven Shavell, Property Rules Versus Liability Rules, 109 Harv. L. Rev. 713 (1996) (extending the Calabresi & Melamed analysis and urging imposition of pollution taxes in industrial pollution cases). Others, however, question the propriety of restricting victims to damages. See, e.g., Daniel Farber, Reassessing *Boomer, in* Property Law and Legal Education 7 (Peter Hay & Michael H. Hoeflich eds., 1988) (arguing for a strong presumption in favor of injunctive relief for egregious nuisances); A. Mitchell Polinsky, Resolving Nuisance Disputes, 32 Stan. L. Rev. 1075 (1980) (contending that case for damage remedies is not open and shut); Henry E. Smith, Exclusion and Property Rules in the Law of Nuisance, 90 Va. L. Rev. 965 (2004) (stressing the informational simplicity of strong exclusion rules).

2. *Realism about bargaining.* Calabresi and Melamed's analysis assumes that parties involved in a nuisance case would be interested in bargaining after judgment if a court were to have conferred property-rule protection on the party who valued that right less than the other side did. But do people actually behave as this analysis supposes? Professor Ward Farnsworth investigated the aftermaths of 20 appellate decisions in nuisance cases. No bargaining after judgment took place in any of them. The lawyers involved thought that the parties had declined to bargain not because the court had allocated the outcome to the party that valued it most highly, but because the parties harbored animosity toward one another and had a distaste for cash bargaining over the rights at issue. Ward Farnsworth, Do Parties to Nuisance Cases Bargain after Judgment? A Glimpse Inside the Cathedral, 66 U. Chi. L. Rev. 373 (1999).

Might Farnsworth's sample of interneighbor disputes have been unrepresentative? As he recognizes, antagonists who battle long and hard enough to generate a reported appellate court opinion tend to be unusually litigious and uncompromising. An observer of disputes in Japan over noise from karaoke establishments found that those involved typically succeed in resolving their differences without resort to litigation. See Mark D. West, The Resolution of Karaoke Disputes: The Calculus of Institutions and Social Capital, 28 J. Japanese Stud. 301 (2002). Do the rules of nuisance law matter at all when neighbors solve disputes on their own?

A leading study of a large-number nuisance dispute is Gideon Parchomovsky & Peter Siegelman, Selling Mayberry: Communities and Individuals in Law and Economics, 92 Cal. L. Rev. 75 (2004). The authors investigated events in Cheshire, Ohio, where a huge coal-fired power plant had been polluting the atmosphere of a town of 90 households. Because Ohio law (unlike New York law after *Boomer*) arguably entitled each of the victims to obtain some form of injunctive relief, some analysts might have predicted that the risk of holdouts would prevent the power company from bargaining its way to a compromise. Parchomovsky and Siegelman report, however, that the power company did succeed in buying up the entire town, a result they regard as efficient under the circumstances. They attribute this coordinated outcome to the strong community ties among Cheshire's residents.

What implications do these various empirical studies have for the choice of remedies in nuisance cases?

3. *Rule four applied.* A variant of Calabresi and Melamed's rule-four remedy was rendered in Spur Industries, Inc. v. Del E. Webb Development Co., 494 P.2d. 700 (Ariz. 1972). Defendant operated a massive cattle feedlot near Phoenix. Plaintiff later began developing a large retirement community named Sun City. As Sun City expanded toward the feedlot, its residents increasingly were bothered by the odor of manure. Plaintiff sought an injunction closing the feedlot. The Supreme Court of Arizona, noting that the developer had come to an existing nuisance, granted what it admitted was a "novel" remedy. It granted the injunction on the condition that the developer compensate the feedlot operators for

their costs "of moving or shutting down." Observe that in this case the free-rider problems that Calabresi and Melamed felt limited the feasibility of rule four were not present because one plaintiff owned most of the damaged land. In retrospect, would it have been wiser for the developer to have sued for damages? See generally Jeff L. Lewin, Compensated Injunctions and the Evolution of Nuisance Law, 75 Iowa L. Rev. 775 (1986).

4. *Injunction against an anticipatory nuisance?* Some courts assert that when a defendant's alleged nuisance activity is still in its planning stages, a plaintiff must prove that the activity will cause imminent irreparable injury to merit an injunction against consummation of the activity. (However, this doctrine does not apply to a nuisance per se — that is, a use such as a brothel that is regarded as being a nuisance regardless of how it is operated or the nature of its surroundings.) The asserted rationale for the doctrine is that a court should not speculate about future events but instead require a plaintiff to sustain actual injury before coming to court. See, e.g., Green v. Castle Concrete Co., 509 P.2d 588 (Colo. 1973) (refusing to grant anticipatory injunction against limestone quarry). The increasing sophistication of the environmental sciences should make it easier than it has been in the past to prove that irreparable injury is in the offing. See, e.g., Opal Lake Association v. Michaywe Ltd. Partnership, 209 N.W.2d 478 (Mich. 1973) (affirming injunction designed to prevent future muddying of lake waters). See generally Douglas Laycock, The Death of the Irreparable Injury Rule (1991).

Should someone who plans to open, say, a funeral home be entitled to seek a declaratory judgment that the use will not later be adjudged a nuisance?

5. *Calculating plaintiff's damages.* The usual measure of damages is the difference between (1) the market value the plaintiff's property would command without the nuisance, and (2) the market value it commands given the nuisance. This measure of damages does not fully compensate if the property is unique and the plaintiff values it at greater than market value. See pp. 859–60 (on measurement of compensation in eminent domain cases).

The plaintiffs in Greater Westchester Homeowners Association v. City of Los Angeles, 603 P.2d 1329 (Cal. 1979), were homeowners bothered by noise from the nearby Los Angeles International Airport. In prior litigation, they had been awarded damages for the diminution in the value of their homes. In the cited decision, the California Supreme Court held they were entitled also to recover damages for the emotional distress they had suffered. Would the emotional trauma that residents suffer from airport noise largely be capitalized into lower property values? Was the court silently recognizing the inadequacy of the usual formula for computing damages in nuisance cases?

6. *Punitive damages.* Neighbors thwarted Ramsey's efforts to obtain permits to build a large motel on an open tract in Stowe, Vermont. Ramsey retaliated by bringing onto the tract junked automobiles, piles of chicken manure, and 100 cows and pigs that were fed at a site near the neighbors' properties. In Coty v. Ramsey Associates, 546 A.2d 196 (Vt. 1988), the Supreme Court of Vermont affirmed the neighbors' entitlements to a prospective injunction, compensatory damages, and (in light of Ramsey's malicious intent) punitive damages.

7. *Self-help.* In Detroit, some residents of working-class neighborhoods have spontaneously taken to demolishing or burning down abandoned buildings that have become havens for prostitution and drug dealing. James Risen, Detroit Residents Abandon the Legalities in Trying to Save Decaying Neighborhood, L.A. Times, July 15, 1989, at 20 (reporting acquittal of two accused arsonists). What civil and criminal penalties, if any, should be imposed on arsonists in these instances?

Ill-considered self-help is legally risky. Lippert moved a modest single-family dwelling onto a lot in a fancy new subdivision in southern California. This house no doubt would have violated the neighborhood's private architectural controls, but the developer had neglected to record them in time to bind Lippert's lot. A neighborhood couple, the Grants, began a private campaign to have Lippert remove the house. Over the next two and one-half years, Lippert and his family were subjected to threats and slurs and the house was vandalized more than 50 times. Lippert won a $1.1 million judgment against the Grants, the developer, and the residential community association for their roles in creating an atmosphere conducive to malicious action. L.A. Times, Dec. 16, 1975, §II, at 1.

On the privilege to use self-help to abate a nuisance, see generally 1 Fowler V. Harper et al., The Law of Torts §1.18 (2d ed. 1986).

4.   *Public Nuisance*

People v. Mason
177 Cal. Rptr. 284 (Ct. App. 1981)

REYNOSO, Associate Justice. . . .

In May 1980, the People filed a complaint for injunctive relief, alleging defendants were conducting their restaurant and bar business (hereafter the Lodge) in a loud, noisy, and unreasonable manner so as to constitute a public nuisance. Specifically, the complaint alleged defendants were permitting the use of sound amplifying equipment in such a fashion as to disturb the residents living close to the Lodge, and that the noise created by music, hand clapping and foot stomping "has greatly impaired the enjoyment of these premises as dwelling houses and has caused great nervous distress and loss of sleep which endangers the health, comfort and peace of the residents in the area."

Evidence presented at trial indicated the Lodge is contiguous to a rural residential area known as the Paradise Estates, which consists of approximately 33 homes which were built around 1970. For more than 30 years, the Lodge has provided both live and juke-box music for its patrons. Depending on the time of year, the live music is played either inside the Lodge or outside on a deck.

. . . The testimony concerning the loud noise was corroborated by sheriffs' officers who, upon entering the residents' homes for the purpose of receiving complaints about the noise, were able to hear the noise coming from the Lodge. The music is apparently played every weekend, beginning around 9:00 P.M., and continuing as late as 1:30–2:00 A.M. Further testimony indicated the residents' complaints, relayed to defendants, were of no avail. . . .

The specific language of the judgment permanently enjoins defendants from: (1) "Amplifying musical instruments and vocal selections to the extent that the resulting music, singing and other noise so amplified can be audible anywhere in the neighborhood knows (sic) as Paradise Estates or in any other place beyond the boundaries of the property owned or operated by defendants, excepting only public streets and roads. . . ."

Defendants argue the People lack standing to bring the present action. As a basis for this assertion, defendants contend their conduct can in no manner be considered a public nuisance. We disagree. A public nuisance, for which a civil action to abate may be brought by the People, is one which affects at the same time an entire community or neighborhood, or any considerable number of persons, even though the extent of the annoyance or damage inflicted upon individuals may be unequal. . . . Civil Code §3480 provides a public nuisance is one which affects any considerable number of persons. Thus, the section is not nearly as concerned with the number of people who actually complain, but rather with those who are in some manner affected by the defendant's conduct.

Three of the residents who complained of the noise live approximately 600–800 feet away from the Lodge. Another resident who testified also lives about 600–800 feet away from the Lodge, but in the opposite direction. Based on the difference in location between the complaining residents, a reasonable inference can be drawn that other homes in the subdivision were also affected by the noise. The People thus have standing to bring the instant action.

Further, the evidence presented was sufficient to support the finding that a public nuisance was created. "Anything which is injurious to health, or is indecent or offensive to senses, or an obstruction to the free use of property, so as to interfere with the comfortable enjoyment of life or property . . . is a nuisance." (Civ. Code, §3479.) . . . The court's determination that the amplified music, foot stomping and hand clapping creates discomfort and obstructs the free use of property so as to interfere with the comfortable enjoyment of life and property is supported by the evidence.

. . . The respondents conceded at oral argument that an audible level of noise is not necessarily a nuisance. We conclude that the injunction should have been worded so as to permit some noise to be audible, save and except that which unreasonably interferes with the residents' use and enjoyment of their property. . . .

The judgment is reversed with directions to the trial court to modify the terms of the injunction consistent with the opinion we express herein.

Note on Public Nuisance Law

1. *Two forms of public nuisance actions.* Many public nuisance actions, such as People v. Mason, are initiated by public officials. Others are hybrid actions, in which a private plaintiff acting as a private attorney general seeks to remedy a broadly damaging activity. For example, when an oil spill from a tanker has damaged the livelihoods of members of a fishing association, the members cannot succeed in a private nuisance action because the damage was not to land. The members instead might seek to recover on a public nuisance theory. Judges have erected a number of doctrinal barriers to these private actions, ostensibly to protect defendants from a multitude of lawsuits and to enhance the bargaining position of government enforcers. The "special injury" rule, for example, requires a private plaintiff pursuing a public nuisance action to prove damages different in kind, not just in degree, from those suffered by the general public. See, e.g., Wheeler v. Lebanon Valley Auto Racing Corp., 755 N.Y.S.2d 763 (App. Div. 2003) (holding that neighbors bothered by noise from an auto racetrack had not suffered special injury). The Restatement (Second) of Torts §821(C) (1979) retained the special-injury requirement for a private plaintiff seeking damages on account of a public nuisance, but sought to eviscerate it for a private plaintiff seeking injunctive relief. For a comprehensive review of the conflicting authorities, see Denise E. Antolini, Modernizing Public Nuisance: Solving the Paradox of the Special Injury Rule, 28 Ecology L.Q. 755 (2001).

2. *Remedies exclusively available to public enforcers.* Courts sometimes have been willing to empower government officials to raze private buildings to abate a public nuisance. In City of Minot v. Friedlander, 426 N.W.2d 556 (N.D. 1988), an elderly woman allowed her lifelong home to become a stinkhole of garbage and cat excrement. After many lesser measures had proven to be fruitless, the city sought and won judicial permission to demolish the home. In such an instance, must the public authorities obtain a search warrant before entering the property? See Freeman v. City of Dallas, 242 F.3d 642 (5th Cir. 2001) (en banc) (no). If the owner had been disabled by senility or mental illness, would the federal antidiscrimination statutes discussed at pp. 722–30 have required the city to offer her some sort

538 Chapter Six. Alternatives to Public Regulation

of "reasonable accommodation"? See McGary v. City of Portland, 386 F.3d 1259 (9th Cir. 2004) (perhaps). When an injunction against continuation of the offensive use would suffice, courts may deny public enforcers more draconian remedies. See Becker v. State, 767 A.2d 816 (Md. 2001) (reversing lower court's order that owner demolish grocery store that had been used for drug dealing). On the takings issues that demolition or temporary-closure orders may pose, see Keshbro, Inc. v. City of Miami, 801 So. 2d 864 (Fla. 2001).

Suppose a landlord has committed a public nuisance by intentionally permitting a slum tenement to blight a neighborhood. In the event of public (or private?) nuisance prosecution, should a judge have the authority to order the offender to personally occupy the premises? See La. Rev. Stat. Ann. §14:107.3 (West 2004) (authorizing this sanction, among others); compare People v. Avol, 238 Cal. Rptr. 45 (App. Dept. Super. Ct. 1987) (upholding a sentence that required a recalcitrant slumlord to occupy one of his own apartments for 30 days).

3. *Interplay between zoning and public nuisance law.* Because a local government has broad powers to bring public nuisance actions, why should it also be empowered to regulate through zoning? Observe that zoning enables a local government to control the attributes of land uses that fall short of being nuisances, to provide prospective guidance to land developers, and to assume decisionmaking powers that nuisance law places in the courts. In addition, in some localities different agencies may be responsible for nuisance prosecutions and zoning enforcement actions. Compare p. 286, on interagency disputes within a local government.

4. *Nuisance law in eclipse?* Zoning has come to overshadow nuisance law, both public and private. West's Eleventh Decennial Digest (Part I) contains, under various topic headings, keynote entries for all cases appearing in the West Reporter system for the period 1996–2001. There are 46 pages of entries under "Nuisance," and 446 pages under "Zoning and Planning."

5. Government-Administered Externality Fees

Since the pioneering work of Pigou, many economists have recommended that a government counter the effects of negative externalities by imposing fees. See, e.g., Frederick H. Reuter & Phillip Kushner, Economic Incentives for Land Use Control 1.6–1.8 (1977) (for Environmental Protection Agency), where the authors urge experimentation with "a policy requiring the payment of annual 'externality' fees to the government by the owners of property upon which external effects are generated." See also sources cited in John E. Anderson, Land Development, Externalities, and Pigouvian Taxes, 33 J. Urb. Econ. 1 (1993); Robert C. Ellickson, Alternatives to Zoning: Covenants, Nuisance Rules, and Fines as Land Use Controls, 40 U. Chi. L. Rev. 681, 772–77 (1973).

Instead of banning industrial uses along Euclid Avenue, would the Village of Euclid have been wiser to levy fees on industrial uses to internalize their harmful spillovers? Why might Reuter and Kushner have recommended an annual fee, rather than a lump-sum fee for all future externalities (perhaps collected when the permit for the industrial use was initially granted)? Why any sort of fee, as opposed to liability to neighbors? Would a program of externality fees founder on account of high administrative costs or uncertainties on the part of project developers? In the absence of enabling legislation, does a city in a home-rule state possess the power to levy externality fees?

Although local governments virtually never impose externality fees, some federal and state programs to combat air and water pollution make use of both emission fees and tradable emission permits. See, e.g., James E. Krier, Marketable Pollution Allowances, 25 U. Tol. L. Rev. 449 (1994); Thomas W. Merrill, Explaining Market Mechanisms, 2000 U. Ill. L. Rev. 275. Do emission fees and tradable permits have less political appeal when negative externalities impinge on only a few neighbors, as is typical in the land use context, than when the externalities are widely dispersed, as is common in the pollution context?

B. Beneficence Law (the Converse of Nuisance Law)

In Middlesex Co. v. McCue, excerpted at p. 512, Justice Holmes asserted that a nuisance is a land use that is more harmful to neighbors than an ordinary land use in that setting would be. Because there is no generally accepted term for the converse of a nuisance, we coin the term *beneficence* to denote a land use that is unusually beautiful, pollution-free, or otherwise superior to the ordinary. Just as an unusually harmful land use is likely to warrant being tagged with liability for either nuisance damages or externality fees, a beneficence is a prime candidate for the conferral of entitlements to either rewards from neighbors or government subsidies.

If a municipality were to aim to foster the presence of scenic trees on private land, should it fine landowners who fell outstanding specimens or give subsidies to owners who plant and nurture them? Cf. Jerry Gray, Shade Tree Commissions Now Have Teeth Like Chainsaws, N.Y. Times, Jan. 19, 1992, §4, at 6, describing N.J. Stat. Ann. §40:64-12 (West 2004), which empowers a municipality to impose a fine of up to $1,500 on a landowner who fells a protected tree.

1. Common Law Rights to Restitution for Benefits Conferred on Neighbors

Campbell v. Mesier
74 Johns. Ch. 333 (N.Y. Ch. 1820)

The bill was filed in April, 1809. In 1803 the plaintiff and Peter Mesier, deceased, were respectively owners of two houses and lots adjoining each other in the city of New York. The houses were old, and the plaintiff determined to pull down his house and erect a new one on its site. There was a party wall, standing equally on each lot, which divided the two houses. The plaintiff employed the city surveyor and two master masons to examine the party wall, and to ascertain whether he could safely build a new house without pulling down the wall; and they certified their opinion that it would be impossible for the plaintiff to rebuild on his lot without taking down the party wall to its foundation, it being decayed and ruinous, and incapable of being partially removed and repaired. The plaintiff delivered the certificate to the defendant M., the son and agent of P.M., then the owner, and requested that his father would unite in the expense of rebuilding the wall. The defendant and P.M. refused to accede to the plaintiff's proposal, and forbade him to pull down or injure the wall, for, if he did, he should be made responsible as a trespasser. The plaintiff, notwithstanding, proceeded to pull down his house, and with it the party wall; and he built a new house on his lot, with a new party wall, sixteen inches thick, above the stone foundation, on the site of the old wall. He afterwards applied to the defendant, as son and agent of his father, to have the new party wall surveyed and appraised, and that P.M. should pay to the plaintiff the one half of the appraised value. The bill further stated that, after the plaintiff's house and new party wall were built, P.M. devised his house and lot to his son, the defendant, who afterwards sold the lot to the defendant D., and in the deed expressly conveyed the use of the party wall for building, etc., and covenanted to indemnify the defendant D. for so using it. That D. pulled down the house so purchased by him of M., and erected a new house on the lot, making use of the party wall built by the plaintiff, as the side or end wall of his new house, and made holes in the wall, in which the beams were put and fastened. That the house of D. is higher than the house of the plaintiff. That the plaintiff caused the party wall to be again surveyed and appraised, and the master masons declared the one half to be worth $353.20, which the plaintiff demanded of the defendant D., with half the expenses of the survey, etc., which the defendant D. refused to pay. . . .

> Chancellor [KENT]:
>   . . . [T]he question now is whether the defendant Mesier, as heir and devisee of the original owner, who sold the lot to the other defendant, after the new wall was erected, ought not to be held to contribution for a moiety of the expense.
>   I have not found any adjudged case in point, but it appears to me that this case falls within the reason and equity of the doctrine of contribution which exists in the common law, and is bottomed and fixed on general principles of justice. . . .
>   . . . In England, the Statute of 14 Geo. III., chap. 78, has made special and very ample provision on this subject, in respect to houses and partition walls in the city of London; but, in the absence of statute regulation, we are obliged to call up and apply the principles of the common law. . . .
>   Papinian (Dig. 17, 2, 52, 10) states it as a rule of the civil law, that if one part owner of a house in decay repairs it at his own expense, upon the refusal of the others to unite in the expense, he can compel them to contribute their proportion, with interest, or, upon their default, at the end of four months the house, at his election, becomes his sole property. This unreasonable penalty or forfeiture has, in modern times, gone into disuse, but the claim to contribution remains. . . .
>   [In France, if] the common wall be in a state of ruin, and requires to be rebuilt, one party can compel the other, by action, to contribute to the expense of rebuilding it; but the necessity of the reparation must be established by the judgment of men skilled in the business, and made on due previous notice; and if the new wall is made wider or higher, etc., the party building it must bear the extra expense. . . .
>   In the present case the defendant M. had no previous notice of the examination of the wall in April, 1803. It was altogether ex parte. But the defendant, in his answer, put himself upon the denial of the right of the plaintiff, and refuses absolutely to unite in a friendly arrangement. The ruinous state of the wall, and the necessity of taking it down, and the character of the wall as a common or party wall, depended, then, upon the proof to be exhibited in the cause; and, in all these respects, the plaintiff has supported the charges in his bill, and the defendants have failed in proof to the contrary. But the estimate of the expense furnished by the plaintiff does not discriminate between the expense of the wall up to the former height, and up to the height to which the new wall was carried by the plaintiff, and on this point a reference may be necessary.
>   The materials of the new wall were better than those of the former wall, but they were such as are usual, and proper, and beneficial, and they were of the same nature. If the new materials had been of a different and unusual kind, such as marble, for instance,

then undoubtedly the plaintiff ought to have borne the extra expense of the new and rare materials, and this, according to Pothier, is the rule in the French law.

I am very forcibly struck with the equity of the demand. The houses on each side of the lot were old and almost untenable; and it would be the height of injustice to deny to the plaintiff the right of pulling down such a common wall, and of erecting a new one suitable to the value of the lot, in the most crowded part of a commercial city. It would be equally unjust to oblige him to do it at his exclusive expense, when the lot of the defendant was equally benefited by the erection, and much enhanced in value. Persons who own lots in the midst of a populous city must and ought to submit to the law of vicinage which applies to such cases and flows from such relations.

I shall accordingly declare that the wall in question was a party wall; that it was ruinous, and that the plaintiff was in the exercise of a lawful right when he took it down and erected a new one; and that the defendant M., as heir and devisee of his father, P.M. (and it is admitted in the answer that, for the purpose of this case, he represents his father), ought to contribute ratably to the expense of the new wall, and that a reference be had to ascertain the amount. Decree accordingly.

Note on Party Walls

1. *Food for thought.* Message in a Chinese fortune cookie: "One family builds a wall, two families enjoy it."

2. *Party walls.* Chancellor Kent's sympathy for the benefactor has not been universally shared. By the turn of the century, many judges asserted that rights to contribution for party-wall costs could be created only by statute or by contract between the owners of the adjoining properties. However, implied contracts to reimburse sometimes were fabricated out of thin air. See, e.g., Day v. Caton, 119 Mass. 513 (1876), where the builder of a brick party wall was held entitled to recover half of its construction costs from the owner of a neighboring vacant lot. The court emphasized that the neighbor had reason to know the builder expected compensation, yet the neighbor had allowed the builder to proceed without objecting to the project.

3. *Coase revisited.* Because most party-wall conflicts involve two parties who can easily contact each other, does the rule to be applied have much importance? If neighbors typically can succeed in negotiating contracts to share party-wall costs even in the absence of a legal obligation to share costs, would there be any advantage in creating a duty to contribute as a matter of law?

4. *Boundary fences.* At the outset, suppose that Rose and Jack owned adjoining, unenclosed, rectangular farms. Rose then enclosed her farm within a perimeter fence, thereby creating a fence on one of the four sides of Jack's farm. Jack later erected fences on his farm's remaining three boundaries and began to pasture livestock within the new enclosure. Should Rose then be entitled to restitution from Jack for one-half the value of the fence that she built on their common boundary? See Cal. Civ. Code §841(2) (West 2004) (yes). Can a legislature force a landowner who has no livestock to bear one-half the costs of maintaining a boundary fence with another who pastures livestock? Compare Choquette v. Perrault, 569 A.2d 455 (Vt. 1989) (holding statute requiring such a contribution to be "arbitrary and confiscatory"), with Gravert v. Nebergall, 539 N.W.2d 184 (Iowa 1995) (judges should defer to legislature's decisions on how neighbors should split fencing costs). For an empirical study of how rural neighbors actually share the costs of boundary fencing, see Robert C. Ellickson, Order Without Law 65–81 (1991) (asserting that law is far less important than informal norms in this context).

Detroit Base-Ball Club v. Deppert
27 N.W. 856 (Mich. 1886)

SHERWOOD, J.

The complainant is a corporation, organized under the laws of this state . . . to promote and encourage playing the game of base-ball. The defendant lives in the city of Detroit, residing in a house upon a lot which he owns, and upon which he also has a barn, on Brady street, in the city. The complainant occupies under a lease a parcel of land adjoining that of the defendant, and which is inclosed by a high board fence. This place is called "Recreation Park," and is used by the plaintiff as its playgrounds, in which its games are played and sports conducted. The company is a member of the National Base Ball League, which consists of eight clubs, each of which plays a game against each of the others. At the games in the park a large number of persons are usually present, and an admittance fee of 50 cents is charged by the company to those who are not members of the club, and good accommodations have been provided, at large expense to the club, for the use of spectators.

The bill . . . alleges that the defendant, (using the language of the complaint,) "(11) one John Deppert, Jr., has constructed upon land occupied by him on the south side of Leland street, in close proximity to the grounds leased and occupied by your orator, a stand for the accommodation of persons who desire to see the games played on the grounds of your orator. (12) That said stand is erected upon the roof of a barn or other building, has steps leading up to it, so that spectators can readily have access thereto, and is of such a height as to overlook the grounds of your orator, and give the persons thereon an opportunity to witness the games played upon said grounds. . . . (14) That an admission fee is generally charged to such stand by the said defendant, but the fee so charged is much less than that charged by your orator, so that your orator is deprived of profits which would otherwise inure to it in the legitimate use of its property." . . . The bill prays that the defendant may be perpetually enjoined from making the use of his buildings and premises in the manner alleged by complainant to be injurious to its interest, and for general relief. [The trial judge dismissed the bill.]

We think the case was correctly decided, and the decree entered is right. It does not appear that the complainant enjoyed any exclusive franchises emanating from the legislature, or under any provision of the charter or bylaws of the city, or under any resolution or other action of the city counsel, in the use it made of the park, or that it had any right to control the use, in any manner, of the adjoining property. . . . It is difficult to see how the complainant has been pecuniarily injured, and this is the grievance of the complaint; but if it has, the remedy at law is entirely adequate. Courts cannot limit the extent, up or down, to which a man may enjoy his property; and if he goes higher than his neighbor, so long as he does not interfere with the rights of others, or injure his neighbor, he subjects himself to no liability.

The decree must be affirmed, with costs.

CAMPBELL, C.J. (dissenting).

I think that the case before us is one where the equitable remedy is the only adequate one, and that complainant should not be turned over to a multiplicity of suits at law. The action of the defendant amounts to a private nuisance, of a provoking as well as serious nature. Giving to every land-owner the largest liberty in the reasonable use of his own premises, there is no principle which will justify him in resorting to measures which are calculated and designed to annoy his neighbors, as well as to reap a profit from their property. . . .

Note on External Benefits

1. *Supporting the national pastime.* In 2002, the Chicago Cubs sued 13 businesses operating on rooftops of buildings overlooking Wrigley Field. The controversy erupted when the Cubs planned an expansion to Wrigley Field that would have blocked rooftop views. These proprietors had been selling tickets of admission during Cubs games, a tradition dating to 1914. The team alleged such action was a violation of copyright law and a misappropriation of Cubs property. Eventually, the parties reached a settlement under which the Cubs agreed not to block the rooftop views in exchange for 17 percent of the rooftop businesses' revenue over the next 20 years. See Richard Sandomir, To Raise Money, Baseball Tries New Squeeze Play, N.Y. Times, Apr. 16, 2004, at A1; Jodi Wilgoren, Cubs Sue Neighborhood Bars on Rooftop Use, N.Y. Times, Dec. 18, 2002, at D4.

2. *Restitution law.* Restatement (Third) of Restitution §2(4) (Discussion Draft 2000) provides:

> There is no liability in restitution in respect of a benefit intentionally conferred by the claimant on the recipient, unless the circumstances of the transaction are such as to excuse the claimant from the necessity of basing a claim to payment on a contract with the recipient.

See also Note, A Theory of Hypothetical Contract, 94 Yale L.J. 415 (1984) (arguing that restitution is warranted only in contexts where high transaction costs preclude express contracting).

In Dinosaur Development, Inc. v. White, 265 Cal. Rptr. 525 (Ct. App. 1989), the county had required, as a condition for approval of a subdivision map, that the developer construct a road that provided access to the Whites' previously landlocked parcel. The court rejected the developer's cause of action against the Whites for restitution. Should the developer have been required to contract in advance with the Whites?

In Ulmer v. Farnsworth, 15 A. 65 (Me. 1888), plaintiffs had used a pump to drain groundwater that had seeped into their lime quarry. Plaintiffs' pumping also served to empty out defendant's nearby quarry because groundwater flowed from the one to the other. Plaintiffs' suit to recover compensation for this service was unavailing. The court found no express or implied promise on which to base relief. It also rejected as legally insufficient plaintiffs' invocation of a local custom that compensation be given in these situations. "If this alleged usage is allowed to prevail in this case, it imposes a contract liability upon this defendant in direct opposition to the established principle of law requiring assent to a binding contract." Id. at 67.

See generally R. Lisle Baker, Recovering Privately and Publicly Conferred Windfalls, 13:2 Urb. Law. vii (1981); James E. Krier & Stewart J. Schwab, Property Rules and Liability Rules: The Cathedral in Another Light, 70 N.Y.U. L. Rev. 440, 471–77 (1995) (discussing relative advantages of restitution and public subsidies as rewards for beneficial acts); Note, Efficient Land Use and the Internalization of Beneficial Spillovers, 31 Stan. L. Rev. 457 (1979) (criticizing current common law of restitution as too stingy to benefactors).

3. *When government is a unilateral benefactor.* As Chapter 7A demonstrates, a government that installs streets, sidewalks, or other infrastructure commonly is entitled to collect special assessments from unconsenting owners of lands benefited by those improvements. Should a government's rights to restitution for benefits unilaterally conferred be more ample than a private actor's rights? See generally John Dawson, The Self-Serving Intermeddler, 87 Harv. L. Rev. 1409 (1974).

4. *Merger with adjoining parcels to internalize spillover benefits.* After Disneyland opened in Anaheim, California, opportunistic developers promptly encircled it with

hotels and other attractions catering to Disneyland traffic. For its encore (Disney World near Orlando, Florida), the Disney Corporation deliberately assembled a tract 100 times larger.

An anchor department store tends to attract shoppers who then also patronize nearby stores. Recognizing these external benefits, a mall developer generally provides a prime anchor a significant discount in rent. See B. Peter Pashigian & Eric D. Gould, Internalizing Externalities: The Pricing of Space in Shopping Malls, 41 J.L. & Econ. 115 (1998).

2. *Public Subsidization of Beneficial Uses*

American cities will be endowed with too few historic buildings, architectural masterpieces, front-yard gardens, and other beneficences in the absence of mechanisms that internalize external benefits. Although private bargaining and informal social practices may alleviate the problem, they do not eliminate it. As just noted, restitution law seldom rides to the rescue. In addition, a city regulation mandating an above-normal land use might constitute a taking of property, and, in any event, would likely be politically unpopular with those who would be disproportionately burdened. Many governments therefore turn to other legal devices to nurture unusually beneficial land uses. To preserve agricultural lands, for example, a government may reward farmers who refrain from urbanizing land. Among the more common reward systems are tax breaks, cash subsidies, compensated regulations, and land acquisitions.

Hoffmann v. Clark
372 N.E.2d 74 (Ill. 1977)

RYAN, Justice.

Plaintiffs, Paul W. Hoffmann and other owners of real property in Du Page County, filed an amended complaint for declaratory judgment and injunctive relief in the circuit court of Du Page County against certain county and State officials in which they alleged the unconstitutionality of §§20a-1 through 20a-3 of the Revenue Act of 1939 (Ill. Rev. Stat. 1973, ch. 120, §§501a-1 through 501a-3). In brief, those sections provide that upon application of the owner, and subject to certain conditions specified therein, real estate used for farming or agricultural purposes which has been so used for the three preceding years shall be valued for purposes of taxation on the basis of its use for farming or agriculture rather than its fair cash value, which is the basis upon which real estate is normally assessed under §20 (Ill. Rev. Stat. 1973, ch. 120, §501). When such use changes, the person liable for taxes on that real estate must pay the difference between the taxes actually paid in each of the three preceding years and the amount which the taxes for each of those years would have been had the real estate been assessed at its fair cash value, together with five percent interest on such difference. . . .

. . . [Plaintiffs] alleged that, in 1974, tax bills had been received indicating that additional taxes and interest thereon were due for 1972 and 1973 in accordance with the so-called "rollback" provisions of §20a-3 as a consequence of alleged changes of use from agricultural or farming purposes. Plaintiffs prayed that §§20a-1 through 20a-3 be held unconstitutional and void in that they violated the equal protection and due process clauses of the State and Federal constitutions and furthermore constituted a legislative classification of real estate for purposes of taxation in violation of §4(b) of article IX of the Illinois Constitution of 1970. [The trial court held that the state legislature could constitutionally grant agricultural lands a favorable property-tax classification but that the rollback provisions that recouped, after development, previously conferred tax benefits were unconstitutional.]

. . . Sections 4(a) and 4(b) of article IX of the 1970 Illinois Constitution . . . provide as follows:

> Section 4. Real Property Taxation. (a) Except as otherwise provided in this Section, taxes upon real property shall be levied uniformly by valuation ascertained as the General Assembly shall provide by law.
>
> (b) Subject to such limitations as the General Assembly may hereafter prescribe by law, counties with a population of more than 200,000 may classify or to continue to classify real property for purposes of taxation. Any such classification shall be reasonable and assessments shall be uniform within each class. . . .

Defendants rely upon §1 of article IX of the Constitution, which provides:

> The General Assembly has the exclusive power to raise revenue by law except as limited or otherwise provided in this Constitution. The power of taxation shall not be surrendered, suspended, or contracted away.

[Ryan, J., then described the debate over article IX at the convention that produced the 1970 Illinois Constitution.]

Although classification of real property was a very controversial subject at the convention, the Committee on Revenue and Finance recognized that the constitution which was being written should not prohibit the use of this means to cope with future problems which may be brought about by changing conditions. The committee stated in its report to the convention:

> Finally, the complexity of urban life and the rapid changes that occur in our society mean that a uniform property tax may have undesirable economic and social effects. For example, the property tax may discourage the maintenance of property. It often encourages the use of land in ways that are not in the best interests of society — creating urban sprawl and the development of urban and rural slums. (7 Proceedings 2114.)

It thus appears that the committee prophetically recognized the problem which the General Assembly attempted to resolve when it enacted the statute under consideration in this case. . . .

From these explanations there can be no doubt that it was intended that the power to raise revenue through taxation is firmly vested in the General Assembly both through the inherent power of that body, and by the specific grant of the Constitution. It is further clear that it was the intent of the committee that this power be subject to only such limitations as are expressly stated in the Constitution and that the express limitations are to be exclusive. It was further clearly a concern of the committee that through court construction "narrow" and "unintended" limits might be placed upon the General Assembly's power.

Absent an express and specific constitutional limitation upon the General Assembly's power to classify real property, which we do not find, we must conclude that that body possesses the power to classify. The presence of the uniformity requirement in section 4(a) of article IX cannot be said to constitute an express limitation. . . .

. . . The formation of tax policy, although it may be foolish and unwise, as long as it remains within constitutional limits, is peculiarly within the province of the elected representatives of the People.

Plaintiffs also contend that the rollback provision of §20a-3 constitutes an invalid classification under our constitution. What has been said concerning the authority of the General Assembly under §4(b) of article IX to classify real property for assessment purposes also applies to its authority to classify real property for the application of the rollback provision of the statute.

Plaintiffs argue that the rollback provision constitutes a denial of equal protection. Their argument is that the General Assembly has by virtue of §§20a-1 through 20a-3 classified real property used for agricultural purposes and any assessment in this class must be uniform. They contend that uniformity is violated when property previously used for agricultural purposes is subjected to a rollback of taxes for 3 years. Such property, they argued, has effectively been taxed at a higher rate than other property in its class for that 3-year period.

We do not agree with plaintiff's contention. All real property that no longer qualifies for the special treatment given to farmland under §§20a-1 through 20a-3 constitutes a separate and distinct class and all parcels within that class are treated uniformly. This court has held that the legislature has a wide discretion in classifying objects of its legislation and the exercise of that discretion will not be interfered with judicially unless clearly in violation of some constitutional limitation. . . .

The tax bills attached to the pleadings demonstrate that if the farmland involved in this case were assessed at the market value under §20 and not its market value as agricultural land under §20a-1, the taxes would far exceed the value of the agricultural products that could be produced on the land. There can be no serious question that these facts support the special consideration given to assessment of agricultural land by the statute. An allied problem concerns the fast disappearance of agricultural land and open space, especially near urban areas. The preservation of farmland and open space has been considered a serious problem warranting legislative action by more than half of the States. The problem and the various legislative efforts to resolve it have received widespread attention in the periodicals. Many legislative efforts to preserve agricultural land and open space, in addition to extending preferential tax treatment to land used for agricultural purposes, have attempted to discourage the discontinuance of that use through rollback provisions similar to the one challenged by plaintiffs. See Note, Property Taxation of Agricultural and Open Space Land, 8 Harv. J. on Legis. 158, 161 (1970).

The general recognition of the need for some special effort for the preservation of farmland and open space demonstrates that there exists a rational basis for the creation by the legislature of a class of taxpayers from whom an additional tax is required when the land no longer qualifies for the special treatment given to it under the provisions of §20a-1. . . .

. . . Accordingly, the judgment of the circuit court of Du Page County is reversed.

[UNDERWOOD, J., dissented, arguing that the majority had misconstrued article IX, §4, of the Illinois Constitution.]

Barry Currier, An Analysis of Differential Taxation as a Method of Maintaining Agricultural and Open Space Land Uses
30 U. Fla. L. Rev. 821, 824–29, 836–37 (1978)

All differential taxation programs include land used for agricultural purposes among those land uses eligible for special tax treatment. Twelve states also provide some coverage of undeveloped land of scenic, environmental or historical significance. . . .

A small number of states have authorized tax relief for land in certain recreational uses. This type of provision usually supplements the coverage of open space uses and will apply to land dedicated to boating, camping, swimming, horseback riding, or golfing uses. The primary beneficiary of these programs appears to have been the country club.

Once the decision is made regarding those land uses to be included in a differential tax scheme, policymakers must select an appropriate mechanism to provide relief. There are two significant objectives. First, the program should be structured to enroll as much of the targeted land as possible. Second, the program should preserve the land in its desired use, rather than just delay its development or facilitate the holding of land for development by giving a low tax bill to the owner who will sell or develop the property at the earliest opportunity. Arguably, these two goals are conflicting. To enroll the maximum amount of land, the program should have the fewest possible disincentives to participation. Requiring the land to remain in the qualifying use for a stated period of time or imposing a penalty when the owner desires to withdraw his land from the program could discourage many landowners from participating. Yet such measures are the surest way to keep land in the desired use.

Three distinct approaches to differential taxation have evolved: preferential assessment, deferred taxation and the restrictive agreement. They reflect different judgments regarding the proper mixture of incentives to enroll land and disincentives to withdraw land from a differential tax program. Each approach depends upon the assessment of the land in its qualifying use rather than upon the determination of the land's value for property tax purposes according to its fair market value.

Pure preferential assessment programs[31] provide tax benefits to owners of eligible land by computing the tax on the basis of the land's use value. Taxation on such a basis continues as long as the land remains in the qualifying use. The owner is not penalized if at any time the eligible land is converted into a non-qualifying land use. . . .

Deferred taxation programs also provide for the determination of a qualifying landowner's property tax bill on the basis of its value in the qualifying use.[37] These programs differ from pure preferential assessment schemes because upon a change to a non-qualifying use some recapture is made of the taxes the landowner has saved through the program. This additional feature is arguably justified on two counts. Recapture forces the landowner, upon sale or development of his property, to return to the community a portion of the benefits previously received due to preferred tax status. This may be particularly equitable because the earlier benefits were probably subsidized by higher taxes on non-qualifying property. Further, and probably erroneously, it is believed by some that the charge will deter those who have been receiving tax benefits from converting land to a non-qualifying use. . . .

From the standpoint of the landowner, the third differential tax scheme is the most burdensome. The restrictive agreement approach requires the owner to contract with the relevant governmental unit for a term, generally ten years, to keep his land in its qualifying use.[48] Changing the use of the land is a breach of that agreement and will lead to the

---

31. The following states' programs can be classified as representing the pure preferential assessment variety: Arizona, Arkansas, Colorado, Delaware, Florida (agricultural uses), Idaho, Indiana, Iowa, Missouri, New Mexico, North Dakota, Oklahoma, South Dakota, and Wyoming. . . .

37. These schemes are the most popular. Some 25 states have adopted deferred tax programs: Alaska, Connecticut, Hawaii, Illinois, Kentucky, Maine, Maryland, Massachusetts, Minnesota, Montana, Nevada, Nebraska, New Hampshire, New Jersey, New York, North Carolina, Ohio, Oregon, Pennsylvania, Rhode Island, South Carolina, Texas, Utah, Virginia and Washington. . . .

48. This approach has been the least popular. It is utilized in California, Florida (regarding outdoor recreational and park uses), Michigan, New Hampshire and Vermont. . . .

imposition of a stiff penalty.[49] Although the governmental unit may be empowered to bring an action to specifically enforce the contract, apparently this power is not utilized. Thus, as with deferred tax programs, the owner may be able to develop his property whenever he believes it makes economic sense, although he will be penalized for doing so. . . .

. . . [T]he characteristics of the land enrolled need to be scrutinized. Is such land the prime farmland or the land in or close to the fringe of development at which the program was directed from a land planning viewpoint? Although not encouraging, studies generally conclude that land removed from the fringe of development is more likely to be enrolled than land more proximate to land already developed. Further, differential tax programs are relatively unsuccessful in halting the conversion of prime land from open space and agricultural uses to suburban housing and commercial uses.

California's Williamson Act has been criticized because of the large percentage of enrolled land that is distant from areas that are ripe for development. At the beginning of this decade a legislative report noted that only 6.4 percent of the land in the program was within three miles of a city and less than 2 percent was within one mile of a city. Subsequent studies have not questioned the conclusion that the program has failed to enroll land on the fringe of development. In fact, Los Angeles County and San Francisco County have not even taken the necessary legislative steps under the California law to qualify for participation in the program. Other counties in developing areas have among the lowest rates of participation in the state. The data from other states is scanty. However, the results of studies in Virginia, Washington and New Jersey, indicate that California's experience is not unique.

Note on Government Subsidization of Beneficial Uses

1. *Preserving agricultural lands.* For yet more evidence that most enrolled land is located far from developing areas, see Sandra A. Hoffman, Note, Farmland and Open Space Preservation in Michigan: An Empirical Analysis, 10 Mich. J.L. Reform 1107 (1986).

Some state constitutions explicitly authorize preferential property tax assessment of agricultural lands. See, e.g., Cal. Const. art. XIII, §8. A provision of this sort obviously constrains legislative structuring of tax preferences. See Sierra Club v. City of Hayward, 623 P.2d 180 (Cal. 1981); Jeffrey P. Widman, The New Cancellation Rules Under the Williamson Act, 22 Santa Clara L. Rev. 589 (1982).

The debate over farmland preservation was enlivened in 1981 with the publication of the Final Report of the National Agricultural Lands Study (NALS), a project of the Carter Administration's Department of Agriculture and Council on Environmental Quality. NALS reported a sharp escalation in the rate at which agricultural land was being converted to urban uses. This trend, it concluded, ultimately posed a threat to national and world food supply. It therefore recommended, with some equivocation, that governments adopt comprehensive growth management policies to curb the rate of farmland conversion. This NALS recommendation prompted Congress to enact the Farmland Protection Policy Act of 1981, 7 U.S.C. §§4201-4209 (2004), which directs federal agencies to consider program alternatives that will minimize loss of agricultural lands.

---

49. In California the penalty is 12.5 percent of market value. . . . In Washington, a breach of the restrictive agreement triggers recapture of the tax benefit plus a 20 percent penalty. Wash. Rev. Code §84-34.080 (Supp. 1977). These programs provide various ways of terminating or ending the agreement. In California, for example, the agreement is automatically extended each year for an additional year. Upon notice of non-renewal, the property is assessed gradually closer and closer to fair market value. Thus, at the end of the tenth year the preferential assessment has disappeared. . . .

Critics immediately attacked both NALS's factual premises and its policy recommendations. They asserted that NALS had exaggerated the urbanization rate of agricultural land during the 1970s by a factor of at least two to three. See Julian L. Simon, Are We Losing Our Farmland?, Pub. Int., No. 67, at 49 (1982); William A. Fischel, The Urbanization of Agricultural Land: A Review of the National Agricultural Lands Study, 58 Land Econ. 236 (1982). Fischel also asserted that local antidevelopment interests were the main proponents of farmland preservation because they saw it as a tool for intervening in the land use decisions of pro-development communities in which they did not reside. In 1982, the Report of the President's Commission on Housing (a Reagan Administration task force) cited Fischel's study and vainly recommended that Congress repeal the Farmland Protection Policy Act of 1981 "because it could have a potentially serious and detrimental impact on the cost and availability of land for housing." Id. at 195.

For a variety of perspectives, see The Vanishing Farmland Crisis (John Baden ed., 1984); William L. Church, Farmland Conversion, 1986 U. Ill. L. Rev. 521 (providing overview of evidence). See also pp. 13–15 (on the rate of development of agricultural lands), p. 519 (on right-to-farm acts), and pp. 580–82 (on the use of conservation easements to preserve agricultural lands).

2. *Property tax policy.* What other land uses should be encouraged, or discouraged, through adjustment of property tax assessments? Several states have a comprehensive statutory system of assessment classes. Industrial or utility properties usually are assessed at the highest percentage of market value. The percentage drops as one progresses through commercial property, multifamily property, and single-family residences. In Arizona in tax year 1999, the highest statutory percentage (25 percent) was assigned to land used for mining and utility operations, and the lowest (1 percent), to noncommercial registered historic buildings. See Ariz. Rev. Stat. §§42-12001 to -12011, 42-15001 to -15011 (2004). Cf. Wash. Rev. Code §84.26.010 (2004) (entitling rehabilitator of historic building listed in national or local register to have value of rehabilitation work excluded from property tax assessment for ten-year period). Moreover, all states exempt some land users, such as religious institutions, from property taxation and may offer partial exemptions to homeowners or other preferred taxpayers.

On taxation as a land use control, see generally Curtis J. Berger, Controlling Urban Growth via Tax Policy, 2 Urb. L. & Pol'y 295 (1979); Barry A. Currier, Exploring the Role of Taxation in the Land Use Planning Process, 51 Ind. L.J. 27 (1975).

3. *Federal tax incentives.* The Internal Revenue Code influences most aspects of American life, including the landscape. For example, the failure of the Code to impute the rental value of an owner-occupied dwelling unit as income to the owner is thought to have greatly increased investment in owner-occupied dwellings. See p. 868 and Henry Aaron, Shelter and Subsidies 53–73 (1972).

Some portions of the Code overtly aim to promote land use goals. Since 1976, for example, the Code has provided incentives for the rehabilitation of historic structures. These carrots were pared back, but not eliminated, in 1986. See p. 497. In addition, the owner of a registered historic building may donate a facade easement to a government or preservation society and then succeed in claiming a charitable deduction. See I.R.C. §170(h) (2004); Hilborn v. Commissioner, 85 T.C. 677 (1985).

How might Congress employ the Internal Revenue Code to encourage outstanding landscape architecture? To discourage off-site billboards?

4. *Subsidies administered outside the tax system.* Many government grants and loans are designed in part to foster desired physical outcomes. Some cities pay a large fraction of the costs that owners of older commercial buildings incur to beautify facades. See also Chapter 10, which explores the tortuous history of federal, state, and local aids to

housing and redevelopment projects. Foundations and other private donors similarly may reward meritorious land uses. By offering to pay the fees of architects who designed public buildings in Columbus, Indiana, J. Irwin Miller and the Cummins Engine Company turned the small city into an architectural showcase. See Robert Campbell, Columbus, Ind. — Architectural Mecca, Wall St. J., Sept. 1, 2004, at D10.

5. *Problem: Brownfields.* A brownfield is an abandoned or underutilized urban tract that investors and lenders have been shunning for fear of incurring liability for cleanup costs under federal hazardous waste legislation. Suppose that the redevelopment of a brownfield located in a poor neighborhood of a Rust Belt city would generate significant environmental benefits for the immediate area and also major economic benefits for the local economy. Through what legal mechanisms, if any, should subsidies be extended to induce private redevelopment? See Hope Whitney, Cities and Superfund: Encouraging Brownfield Redevelopment, 30 Ecology L.Q. 59 (2003) (analyzing policies in California); Flannary P. Collins, Note, The Small Business Liability Relief and Brownfields Revitalization Act: A Critique, 13 Duke Envtl. L. & Pol'y F. 303 (2003) (assessing federal statute enacted in 2002 that reduces liability risks and provides grants and loans for remediation costs).

C.   Covenants Among Neighbors

Regardless of how property rights are originally allocated, adjoining landowners may be able to negotiate mutually advantageous contracts concerning land uses. A subdivider also can enhance the market value of unsold lots by imposing specially drafted covenants that bind and benefit both initial and subsequent purchasers.

Private land use controls designed to protect residential neighborhoods date back at least to the mid-nineteenth century. See Easterbrook v. Hebrew Ladies' Orphan Society, 82 A. 561 (Conn. 1912) (interpreting covenants imposed in 1834 on New Haven subdivision); David T. Beito & Bruce Smith, The Formation of Urban Infrastructure Through Nongovernmental Planning: The Private Places of St. Louis, 16 J. Urb. Hist. 263 (1990) (reporting that deed restrictions first appeared in St. Louis subdivisions in 1867). By the 1920s, many large-scale developers were routinely employing covenants. See Gerald Korngold, The Emergence of Private Land Use Controls in Large-Scale Subdivisions, 51 Case W. Res. L. Rev. 617 (2001) (describing development of Shaker Heights, Ohio).

On the relative advantages and disadvantages of this contractual system of land use regulation, especially compared to zoning, see Robert C. Ellickson, Alternatives to Zoning: Covenants, Nuisance Rules, and Fines as Land Use Controls, 40 U. Chi. L. Rev. 681 (1973) (noting that transaction costs commonly bar the retrofitting of a covenant scheme to an established neighborhood that lacks one); William T. Hughes, Jr. & Geoffrey K. Turnbull, Restrictive Land Covenants, 12 J. Real Est. Fin. & Econ. 9 (1996) (contending that covenants are less changeable than zoning restrictions).

There is widespread dissatisfaction with the complexity and arbitrary formalism of many of the legal doctrines that traditionally have applied to servitudes (the umbrella term for privately tailored land use restrictions). See especially Symposium, 55 S. Cal. L. Rev. 1177 (1982). Influenced by this discontent, in the latter part of the 1980s the American Law Institute embarked on the Restatement (Third) of Property — Servitudes, a project completed in 1998. In the next selection, Professor Susan French, the Reporter for this Restatement, describes the undertaking. Later portions of this subchapter treat some of the traditional doctrines to which she refers.

Susan F. French, Tradition and Innovation in the New Restatement of Servitudes: A Report from Midpoint

27 Conn. L. Rev. 119, 119–26 (1994)

The American Law Institute's current servitudes project began with a lofty mission — to simplify, clarify, and modernize the law — and a bold and sweeping design — to unify the heretofore separate bodies of law governing easements, profits, irrevocable licenses, equitable servitudes, and real covenants under the single conceptual heading of servitudes. . . .

I. The New Restatement Is Traditional at the Core

Reduced to its essence, servitudes law permits people to rearrange and reallocate land use entitlements provided by law and to impose obligations on land holders beyond those imposed by law. These rearrangements are accomplished by private agreements which can be made relatively permanent by tying the adjusted rights and obligations to ownership and occupancy of the land so that they pass automatically to successors. There are two highly significant features of servitudes: they permit individual tailoring of the incidents of land ownership by private transactions; and, the customized incidents of ownership persist beyond the lives and proprietorship of the parties who make the alterations. By permitting private reordering of the incidents of ownership, servitudes add an important element of flexibility to land ownership regimes based on exclusive private ownership of property. Speaking generally, servitudes are used to implement four distinct kinds of modifications to the underlying land law: (1) shared use arrangements in which users need not acquire an "ownership" interest in the land; (2) arrangements to limit development of land to increase land values; (3) arrangements to assure a flow of payments, goods, services, or other benefits from the owner or occupant of land; and (4) arrangements by which land is subjected to a local governance structure and provides the resources for governmental operations.

Easements and profits are used to implement shared use arrangements in which more stability is needed than a license will afford. Easements are often used to create transportation corridors and utility lines, and profits are used for exploitation of natural resources because these purposes can be accomplished without having to pay the price of an ownership interest in the land. The second type of modification, limiting development to enhance the amenity or social value of land, is accomplished by negative easements and covenants. Familiar examples include residential use restrictions, covenants to protect views, and conservation easements.

Assuring the flow of payments, goods, services, and other benefits from the owner or occupier of land can also be accomplished by servitudes. Covenants, the performance of which is often secured by a lien, are frequently used for this purpose today. Rent covenants, covenants to pay debts secured by mortgages, covenants to keep the lawn mowed and submit plans for external structural alterations to an architectural control committee are common features of modern life. Covenants to purchase supplies to be sold on the premises from particular sources or not to operate a competitive business on the premises are also common modern examples of this type of servitude use.

Use of servitudes to constitute and provide the resources for operation of governmental structures is also common in modern life. The owners and occupants of condominiums, cooperatives, and a wide variety of other residential developments are required by covenants to submit to the authority of other owners and the board of directors of the property owners' association to enforce and to modify the governing use restrictions, to make rules regulating use of common areas, and to levy assessments to pay for operations of the association.

All four of these types of servitude use are recognized and facilitated by the new Restatement; none of them is new. Roman law clearly recognized the first two. . . .

. . . [A]nother traditional and important aspect of Anglo-American servitudes law is that judges have exercised a pervasive supervisory role over servitudes, refusing enforcement to freely negotiated private arrangements on a variety of stated grounds, most of which apparently reflected a conclusion that enforcement of the servitude would be unfair or unreasonably restrain alienability or marketability of land. The new Restatement does not attempt to eliminate, or even significantly restrict, this traditional role of the judiciary, although it does try to clarify the terms of the discourse and sharpen the analysis of the reasons for invalidation or termination of servitudes. Although a radical simplification of servitudes law could have been achieved by adopting Richard Epstein's suggestion that the only grounds for refusing enforcement to a servitude should be illegality, or that the property has come into the hands of a bona fide purchaser without notice,[15] the potential negative impact of servitudes on patterns of land use and value seems too great to justify advocating that the judges abdicate their traditional role.

At its core, then, the new Restatement is traditional. It does not make radical, or even substantial, changes in the principle that introduces flexibility into the private property system by permitting private reordering of legally assigned entitlements, or in the principle that such arrangements will be subjected to careful judicial scrutiny to prevent serious interference with the social value of land.

II. Overview of the Innovations . . .

In determining whether to enforce servitudes, courts have traditionally asked whether the servitude was valid or whether the interest sought to be enforced ran with the land. Lack of horizontal privity, inclusion of benefits in gross or benefits to third parties, imposition of affirmative burdens, and failure to touch or concern were all given as grounds for concluding that no servitude was created or that a particular interest did not run with the land. Satisfactory explanations of the reasons why any of these requirements were imposed or why failure to meet them should lead to interference with freely negotiated arrangements have seldom, if ever, been given. The Restatement separates questions traditionally lumped under these doctrines into three discrete inquiries: creation, treated in Chapter 2; validity, treated in Chapter 3; and termination and enforcement, dealt with in Chapters 8 and 9.

. . . Answers that would yield a conclusion that the servitude should not be enforced under the three [inquiries] would include: (1) creation: the statute of frauds was not complied with; (2) validity: the servitude is illegal or violates public policy; and (3) termination and enforcement: the servitude is obsolete or unduly burdensome. . . . These changes are intended to encourage clearer focus on the questions that should be asked and articulation of the actual substantive reasons for refusing to enforce a particular servitude.

. . . As I said before this project began:

> Early law restricted the creation of running servitudes because it lacked the means to terminate them. Since modern law can terminate servitudes, it no longer needs to restrict their creation. This change makes possible a substantial simplification in the structure of modern servitudes law. Agreements creating servitudes can be treated like other agreements: if the agreement itself is valid, the law should give effect to the parties' intentions, enforcing the agreement until it becomes obsolete or unreasonably burdensome. At that point the law should terminate them.[17]

---

15. Richard A. Epstein, Notice and Freedom of Contract in the Law of Servitudes, 55 S. Cal. L. Rev. 1353 (1982).

17. Susan F. French, Toward a Modern Law of Servitudes, 55 S. Cal. L. Rev. 1261, 1305 (1982).

1. Validity Between the Contracting Parties

Humphrey, the owner of Rickacre, promises Ingrid that he will refrain from opening a bar on Rickacre, which abuts Ingrid's houselot. In the vocabulary of covenants, Humphrey is a covenantor (CR) and Ingrid, a covenantee (CE). In general, familiar contract doctrines — on capacity, fraud, unconscionability, and so on — determine whether Ingrid can enforce this promise against Humphrey. See, e.g., Villa Milano Homeowners Association v. Il Davorge, 102 Cal. Rptr. 2d 1 (Ct. App. 2000) (refusing to enforce clause that required purchaser to submit complaint against developer about construction defects to binding arbitration on ground that clause was both procedurally and substantively unconscionable). The Statute of Frauds normally applies to promises affecting the use of land, and therefore a covenant is unlikely to be enforceable unless it is in writing. See Annotation, 5 A.L.R.2d 1316 (1949).

a. Interpretation

If a covenant prohibits buildings other than a single-family dwelling, does it bar the construction of a children's playhouse? See Traylor v. Holloway, 142 S.E.2d 521 (Va. 1965) (yes). Of a concrete doghouse? See University Gardens Property Owners Association v. Solomon, 88 N.Y.S.2d 789 (Sup. Ct. 1946) (yes). Of a wire-mesh cage on a concrete floor, designed as a pen for two pet cougars? See Turudic v. Stephens, 31 P.3d 465 (Or. Ct. App. 2001) (no, because this is a permissible aspect of "residential" use). Of a parking lot and menu board for a drive-in Burger King restaurant? See 5011 Community Organization v. Harris, 548 A.2d 9 (Conn. App. Ct. 1988) (no, because these are not "buildings"). Of the use of a house as a group home, say for persons with disabilities? See pp. 561 and 729.
Consider the wisdom of the following constructional preference:

> Idaho recognizes the validity of covenants that restrict the use of private property. When interpreting such covenants, the Court generally applies the rules of contract construction. However, because restrictive covenants are in derogation of the common law right to use land for all lawful purposes, the Court will not extend by implication any restriction not clearly expressed. Further, all doubts are to be resolved in favor of free use of land.

Pinehaven Planning Board v. Brooks, 70 P.3d 664, 667 (Idaho 2003). Would Professor French endorse this formulation? In Hiner v. Hoffman, 977 P.2d 878 (Hawaii 1999), the court, over a spirited dissent, held that a covenant prohibiting dwellings over "two stories in height" was too vague to be enforced against a homeowner who had built a three-story house. Was this a proper occasion for judicial defense of the free use of land?

b. Remedies

A person enforcing a covenant is potentially entitled to an equitable remedy — namely, an injunction to prevent violation of a negative covenant, and specific performance to compel compliance with an affirmative one. In fact, these are the remedies most commonly granted, perhaps because courts recognize that land is unique and thus that damages may be inadequate. Equitable relief nevertheless is discretionary. Some courts have invoked the doctrine of relative hardship as the basis for denying injunctive relief when the damage from the violation appears to be less than the cost of undoing it. See, e.g., Gilpin v. Jacob Ellis

Realties, 135 A.2d 204 (N.J. Super. Ct. App. Div. 1957) (granting plaintiff damages, not injunction, because of disproportionate expense defendant would have to bear to remodel building to cure violation). But cf. Wright v. Cypress Shores Development Co., 461 So. 2d 1296 (Ala. 1984) (ordering demolition of convenience store); McDonough v. W.W. Snow Construction Co., 306 A.2d 119 (Vt. 1973) (requiring removal of second story of house that violated height restriction).

Recall Calabresi and Melamed's distinction between using property rules and liability rules to protect entitlements and those authors' discussion of the relative advantages of the various rules. See pp. 532–33. In what situations would their analysis support the denial of property rule protection for covenantees? Do the classical equitable defenses of unclean hands (misconduct by plaintiff) and laches (unreasonable delay in bringing suit) make sense under their system? Should a covenantee's remedies change as covenants age? See pp. 576–80.

Under a defeasible-fee arrangement, a defendant who violates a deed condition forfeits his ownership interest. Because forfeiture is a disfavored remedy (why?), courts are inclined to construe a private use restriction as a covenant rather than as a condition — at least when the language is at all ambiguous. A leading case for this proposition is W.F. White Land Co. v. Christenson, 14 S.W.2d 369 (Tex. Civ. App. 1928). Compare p. 598, on the power of a residential community association to force a member who has violated an association rule to sell and depart.

c. *Limitations on the Substance of Covenants*

Nahrstedt v. Lakeside Village Condominium Association
878 P.2d 1275 (Cal. 1994)

KENNARD, Justice.

A homeowner in a 530-unit condominium complex sued to prevent the homeowners association from enforcing a restriction against keeping cats, dogs, and other animals in the condominium development. The owner asserted that the restriction, which was contained in the project's declaration recorded by the condominium project's developer, was "unreasonable" as applied to her because she kept her three cats indoors and because her cats were "noiseless" and "created no nuisance." Agreeing with the premise underlying the owner's complaint, the Court of Appeal concluded that the homeowners association could enforce the restriction only upon proof that plaintiff's cats would be likely to interfere with the right of other homeowners "to the peaceful and quiet enjoyment of their property." . . .

[W]e reverse the judgment of the Court of Appeal and remand for further proceedings consistent with the views expressed in this opinion.

I

Lakeside Village is a large condominium development in Culver City, Los Angeles County. It consists of 530 units spread throughout 12 separate 3-story buildings. The residents share common lobbies and hallways, in addition to laundry and trash facilities.

The Lakeside Village project is subject to certain covenants, conditions and restrictions (hereafter CC&R's) that were included in the developer's declaration recorded with the Los Angeles County Recorder on April 17, 1978, at the inception of the development project. Ownership of a unit includes membership in the project's homeowners association, the Lakeside Village Condominium Association (hereafter Association), the body that enforces the project's CC&R's, including the pet restriction, which provides in relevant part: "No animals (which shall mean dogs and cats), livestock, reptiles or poultry shall be kept in any unit."

In January 1988, plaintiff Natore Nahrstedt purchased a Lakeside Village condominium and moved in with her three cats. When the Association learned of the cats' presence, it demanded their removal and assessed fines against Nahrstedt for each successive month that she remained in violation of the condominium project's pet restriction.

Nahrstedt then brought this lawsuit against the Association, its officers, and two of its employees, asking the trial court to invalidate the assessments, to enjoin future assessments, to award damages for violation of her privacy when the Association "peered" into her condominium unit, to award damages for infliction of emotional distress, and to declare the pet restriction "unreasonable" as applied to indoor cats (such as hers) that are not allowed free run of the project's common areas. Nahrstedt also alleged she did not know of the pet restriction when she bought her condominium. . . . [The trial court sustained the Association's demurrer as to each clause of action, but was reversed by the Court of Appeal.]

II

Today, condominiums, cooperatives, and planned-unit developments with homeowners associations have become a widely accepted form of real property ownership. These ownership arrangements are known as "common interest" developments. The owner not only enjoys many of the traditional advantages associated with individual ownership of real property, but also acquires an interest in common with others in the amenities and facilities included in the project. It is this hybrid nature of property rights that largely accounts for the popularity of these new and innovative forms of ownership in the 20th century. . . .

To divide a plot of land into interests severable by blocks or planes, the attorney for the land developer must prepare a declaration that must be recorded prior to the sale of any unit in the county where the land is located. . . . The declaration, which is the operative document for the creation of any common interest development, is a collection of covenants, conditions and servitudes that govern the project. . . .

The restrictions on the use of property in any common interest development may limit activities conducted in the common areas as well as in the confines of the home itself. Commonly, use restrictions preclude alteration of building exteriors, limit the number of persons that can occupy each unit, and place limitations on — or prohibit altogether — the keeping of pets. (Natelson, Consent, Coercion, and "Reasonableness," in Private Law, 51 Ohio St. L.J. 41, 48, n.28 (1990) (as of 1986, 58 percent of highrise developments and 39 percent of townhouse projects had some kind of pet restriction).) . . .

When restrictions limiting the use of property within a common interest development satisfy the requirements of covenants running with the land or of equitable servitudes, what standard or test governs their enforceability? In California, . . . our Legislature has made common interest development use restrictions contained in a project's recorded declaration "enforceable . . . *unless unreasonable*." (Cal. Civ. Code §1354(a), italics added.)

In states lacking such legislative guidance, some courts have adopted a standard under which a common interest development's recorded use restrictions will be enforced so long as they are "reasonable." (See Riley v. Stoves, 526 P.2d 747, 752 (Ariz. Ct. App. 1974) (asking whether the challenged restriction provided "a reasonable means to accomplish the private objective").) . . . Others would limit the "reasonableness" standard only to those restrictions adopted by majority vote of the homeowners or enacted under the rulemaking power of an association's governing board, and would not apply this test to restrictions included in a planned development project's recorded declaration or master deed. Because such restrictions are presumptively valid, these authorities would enforce them regardless of reasonableness. The first court to articulate this view was the Florida Fourth District Court of Appeal [in] Hidden Harbour Estates v. Basso, 393 So. 2d 637 (Fla. Dist. Ct. App. 1981). . . .

. . . The Florida court's decision was cited with approval recently by a Massachusetts appellate court in Noble v. Murphy, 612 N.E.2d 266 (Mass. App. Ct. 1993). . . .

In *Noble,* managers of a condominium development sought to enforce against the owners of one unit a pet restriction contained in the project's master deed. The Massachusetts court upheld the validity of the restriction. The court stated that "[a] condominium use restriction appearing in originating documents which predate the purchase of individual units" was entitled to greater judicial deference than restrictions "promulgated after units have been individually acquired." . . .

Indeed, giving deference to use restrictions contained in a condominium project's originating documents protects the general expectations of condominium owners "that restrictions in place at the time they purchase their units will be enforceable." (Note, Judicial Review of Condominium Rulemaking, 94 Harv. L. Rev. 647, 653 (1981).) . . . This in turn encourages the development of shared ownership housing — generally a less costly alternative to single-dwelling ownership — by attracting buyers who prefer a stable, planned environment. It also protects buyers who have paid a premium for condominium units in reliance on a particular restrictive scheme. . . .

III . . .

Under the law of equitable servitudes, courts may enforce a promise about the use of land even though the person who made the promise has transferred the land to another. . . .

In choosing equitable servitude law as the standard for enforcing CC&R's in common interest developments, the Legislature has manifested a preference in favor of their enforcement. This preference is underscored by the use of the word "shall" in the first phrase of §1354: "The covenants and restrictions shall be enforceable equitable servitudes. . . ." (See Common Cause v. Board of Supervisors, 777 P.2d 610 (Cal. 1989) ("shall" is ordinarily mandatory).)

The Legislature did, however, set a condition for the mandatory enforcement of a declaration's CC&R's: a covenant, condition or restriction is "enforceable . . . *unless unreasonable.*" (§1354(a), italics added.) The Legislature's use of the phrase "unless unreasonable" in §1354 was a marked change from the prior version of that statutory provision, which stated that "restrictions shall be enforceable equitable servitudes *where reasonable.*" . . . Under settled principles of statutory construction, such a material alteration of a statute's phrasing signals the Legislature's intent to give an enactment a new meaning. Here, the change in statutory language, from "where reasonable" to "unless unreasonable," cloaked use restrictions contained in a condominium development's recorded declaration with a presumption of reasonableness by shifting the burden of proving otherwise to the party challenging the use restriction.

How is that burden satisfied? To answer this question, we must examine the principles governing enforcement of equitable servitudes.

. . . [E]quitable servitudes permit courts to enforce promises restricting land use when there is no privity of contract between the party seeking to enforce the promise and the party resisting enforcement. Like any promise given in exchange for consideration, an agreement to refrain from a particular use of land is subject to contract principles, under which courts try "to effectuate the legitimate desires of the covenanting parties." (Hannula v. Hacienda Homes, 211 P.2d 302, 304 (Cal. 1949).) When landowners express the intention to limit land use, "that intention should be carried out." (Id. at 304; Epstein, Notice and Freedom of Contract in the Law of Servitudes, 55 S. Cal. L. Rev. 1353, 1359 (1982) ("We may not understand why property owners want certain obligations to run with the land, but as it is *their* land . . . some very strong reason should be advanced" before courts should override those obligations. (Original italics.)).)

Thus, when enforcing equitable servitudes, courts are generally disinclined to question the wisdom of agreed-to restrictions. . . . This rule does not apply, however, when the restriction does not comport with public policy. Equity will not enforce any restrictive covenant that violates public policy. (See Shelley v. Kraemer, 334 U.S. 1 (1948) (racial restriction unenforceable); Cal. Civ. Code §53(b) (voiding property use restrictions based on "sex, race, color, religion, ancestry, national origin, or disability").) Nor will courts enforce as equitable servitudes those restrictions that are arbitrary, that is, bearing no rational relationship to the protection, preservation, operation or purpose of the affected land. (See Laguna Royale Owners Ass'n v. Darger, 174 Cal. Rptr. 136, 145 (Cal. Ct. App. 1981).)

These limitations on the equitable enforcement of restrictive servitudes that are either arbitrary or violate fundamental public policy are specific applications of the general rule that courts will not enforce a restrictive covenant when "the harm caused by the restriction is so disproportionate to the benefit produced" by its enforcement that the restriction "ought not to be enforced." (Restatement of Property, §539, comment f, pp. 3229-3230). . . .

From the authorities discussed above, we distill these principles: An equitable servitude will be enforced unless it violates public policy; it bears no rational relationship to the protection, preservation, operation or purpose of the affected land; or it otherwise imposes burdens on the affected land that are so disproportionate to the restriction's beneficial effects that the restriction should not be enforced. . . .

When courts accord a presumption of validity to all such recorded use restrictions and measure them against deferential standards of equitable servitude law, it discourages lawsuits by owners of individual units seeking personal exemptions from the restrictions. This also promotes stability and predictability in two ways. It provides substantial assurance to prospective condominium purchasers that they may rely with confidence on the promises embodied in the project's recorded CC&R's. And it protects all owners in the planned development from unanticipated increases in association fees to fund the defense of legal challenges to recorded restrictions. . . .

There is an additional beneficiary of legal rules that are protective of recorded use restrictions: the judicial system. Fewer lawsuits challenging such restrictions will be brought, and those that are filed may be disposed of more expeditiously, if the rules courts use in evaluating such restrictions are clear, simple, and not subject to exceptions based on the peculiar circumstances or hardships of individual residents in condominiums and other shared-ownership developments. . . .

Refusing to enforce the CC&R's contained in a recorded declaration, or enforcing them only after protracted litigation that would require justification of their application on a case-by-case basis, would impose great strain on the social fabric of the common interest development. It would frustrate owners who had purchased their units in reliance on the CC&R's. It would put the owners and the homeowners association in the difficult and divisive position of deciding whether particular CC&R's should be applied to a particular owner. . . .

. . . [The Court of Appeal] relied on . . . Bernardo Villas Management Corp. v. Black, 235 Cal. Rptr. 509 (Cal. Ct. App. 1987), and Portola Hills Community Ass'n v.

James, 5 Cal. Rptr. 2d 580 (Cal. Ct. App. 1992), both of which had invalidated recorded restrictions covered by §1354.

In *Bernardo Villas*, the manager of a condominium project sued two condominium residents to enforce a restriction that prohibited them from keeping any "truck, camper, trailer, boat . . . or other form of recreational vehicle" in the carports. (235 Cal. Rptr. 509.) In holding that the restriction was unreasonable as applied to the clean new pickup truck with camper shell that the defendants used for personal transportation, the Court of Appeal observed that parking the truck in the development's carport would "not interfere with other owners' use or enjoyment of their property." (Id. at 510.)

Thereafter, a different division of the same district Court of Appeal used a similar analysis in *Portola Hills*. There, the court refused to enforce a planned community's landscape restriction banning satellite dishes against a homeowner who had installed a satellite dish in his backyard. After expressing the view that "[a] homeowner is allowed to prove a particular restriction is unreasonable as applied to his property," the court observed that the defendant's satellite dish was not visible to other project residents or the public, leading the court to conclude that the ban promoted no legitimate goal of the homeowners association.

At issue in both *Bernardo Villas* and *Portola Hills* were recorded use restrictions contained in a common interest development's declaration that had been recorded with the county recorder. Accordingly, the use restrictions involved in these two cases were covered by §1354, rendering them presumptively reasonable and enforceable under the rules governing equitable servitudes. . . . [T]o the extent they differ from the views expressed in this opinion, we disapprove *Bernardo Villas* and *Portola Hills*.

V

Under the holding we adopt today, the reasonableness or unreasonableness of a condominium use restriction that the Legislature has made subject to §1354 is to be determined not by reference to facts that are specific to the objecting homeowner, but by reference to the common interest development as a whole. As we have explained, when, as here, a restriction is contained in the declaration of the common interest development and is recorded with the county recorder, the restriction is presumed to be reasonable and will be enforced uniformly against all residents of the common interest development unless the restriction is arbitrary, imposes burdens on the use of lands it affects that substantially outweigh the restriction's benefits to the development's residents, or violates a fundamental public policy.

. . . For the reasons set forth below, Nahrstedt's complaint fails to adequately allege any of these three grounds of unreasonableness. [Discussion omitted.]

CONCLUSION . . .

In this case, the pet restriction was contained in the project's declaration or governing document, which was recorded with the county recorder before any of the 530 units was sold. For many owners, the pet restriction may have been an important inducement to purchase into the development. Because the homeowners collectively have the power to repeal the pet restriction, its continued existence reflects their desire to retain it. . . .

ARABIAN, Justice, dissenting. . . .
. . . I find the provision known as the "pet restriction" contained in the covenants, conditions, and restrictions (CC&R's) governing the Lakeside Village project patently arbitrary and unreasonable within the meaning of Cal. Civ. Code §1354. Beyond dispute,

human beings have long enjoyed an abiding and cherished association with their house-hold animals. Given the substantial benefits derived from pet ownership, the undue burden on the use of property imposed on condominium owners who can maintain pets within the confines of their units without creating a nuisance or disturbing the quiet enjoyment of others substantially outweighs whatever meager utility the restriction may serve in the abstract. It certainly does not promote "health, happiness [or] peace of mind" commensu-rate with its tariff on the quality of life for those who value the companionship of animals. Worse, it contributes to the fraying of our social fabric. . . .

Note on the Validity of Covenants

1. *The merits of* Nahrstedt. When reviewing the validity of an ordinary contract, courts are willing to search for unconscionability or violation of public policy, but are disinclined to apply a "reasonableness" test to the contract's substantive provisions. After *Nahrstedt*, does California law place covenants under stricter scrutiny than other sorts of contracts? Should it? See generally Restatement (Third) of Property — Servitudes ch. 3 (2000).

2. *Scope of* Nahrstedt. *Nahrstedt* deals with the validity of covenants contained in an association's initial declaration, not with the validity of subsequently adopted association rules. On the latter, see pp. 597–605.

Cal. Civ. Code §1354(a) (West 2004), construed in *Nahrstedt*, governs the validity of covenants only in "common interest communities." The statute defines these as real estate developments that either contain common areas or have an association empowered to levy assessments on the owners of separate interests. The statute therefore would not apply to the simplest sort of covenant scheme — for example, one that a subdivider of a dozen lots might impose to restrict the lots to single-family use. Should judges employ a different test to determine the validity of covenants in the absence of a "common interest community"?

3. *The merits of pet covenants*. What pet covenants appeal most to purchasers? See Roger E. Cannaday, Condominium Covenants: Cats, Yes; Dogs, No, 35 J. Urb. Econ. 71 (1994) (concluding, after study of Chicago condominium complexes, that covenants that permit cats but not dogs are value-maximizing).

Cal. Civ. Code §1360.5(a) (West 2004), enacted in 2000, states that "No govern-ing documents shall prohibit the owner of a separate interest within a common interest community development from keeping at least one pet within the common interest devel-opment, subject to reasonable rules and regulations of the association." This statute applies only to governing documents taking effect after 2000. Was the California legislature right to intervene on this issue?

Note on Racial Restrictions

In Gandolfo v. Hartman, 49 F. 181 (S.D. Cal. 1892), the court refused to enforce a covenant that prohibited the defendant from renting to "Chinamen":

> The federal courts have had frequent occasion to declare null and void hostile and dis-criminating state and municipal legislation aimed at Chinese residents of this country. But it is urged on behalf of the complainant that, as the [covenant] does not present a case of legislation at all, it is not reached by the decisions referred to, and that it does not come within any of the inhibitions of the fourteenth amendment to the constitution of the United States, which, among other things, declares that no state shall "deny to any person the equal protection of the laws." . . .

It would be a very narrow construction of the constitutional amendment in question and of the decisions based upon it, and a very restricted application of the broad principles upon which both the amendment and the decisions proceed, to hold that, while state and municipal legislatures are forbidden to discriminate against the Chinese in their legislation, a citizen of the state may lawfully do so by contract, which the courts may enforce. Such a view is, I think, entirely inadmissible. Any result inhibited by the constitution can no more be accomplished by contract of individual citizens than by legislation, and the courts should no more enforce the one than the other. This would seem to be very clear.

Soon, however, it was no longer so clear. A Caucasians-only restriction was enforced in L.A. Investment Co. v. Gary, 186 P. 596 (Cal. 1919), on the theory that the Fourteenth Amendment barred only discrimination resulting from "action by the state, and has no reference to action by individuals." This view also was apparently adopted in Corrigan v. Buckley, 271 U.S. 323 (1926). Racially restrictive covenants spread like wildfire over the next few decades. See U.S. Dep't of Justice, Prejudice and Property (1948).

Then, in 1948, the Supreme Court issued the key decisions that eviscerated racially restrictive covenants. Hurd v. Hodge, 334 U.S. 24 (1948), involved covenants in Washington, D.C. In that case, the Court, exercising its supervisory powers over the development of private law by the courts of the District of Columbia, declared that racial covenants violated public policy. It could not employ this same legal theory, however, in the companion case of Shelley v. Kraemer, 334 U.S. 1 (1948), which involved racially restrictive covenants placed on land in Missouri. The *Shelley* opinion finessed the state action limitation in the Fourteenth Amendment by holding that, while the covenants themselves did not violate the Equal Protection Clause, it would be a violation for courts to enforce them. On the history of this famous case, see Carol Rose, Property Stories: *Shelley v. Kraemer, in* Property Stories 169 (Gerald Korngold & Andrew P. Morriss eds., 2004).

The *Shelley* result has been approved by virtually all commentators, even those who are strong advocates of private ordering. See, e.g., Ralph K. Winter, Changing Concepts of Equality, 1979 Wash. U. L.Q. 741, 744-46. However, few analysts endorse the *Shelley* notion that judicial enforcement of a private agreement necessarily constitutes state action. See Shelley Ross Saxer, *Shelley v. Kraemer's* Fiftieth Birthday, 47 Kan. L. Rev. 61 (1998), and sources cited therein. The courts themselves have been chary of extending *Shelley* to nonracial discrimination by landowners. See, e.g., Girard v. 94th St. & Fifth Ave. Corp., 530 F.2d 66 (2d Cir. 1976) (holding judicial enforcement of cooperative housing owners association's alleged sex discrimination would not constitute state action). On the general issue of when a residential community association should be deemed a state actor, see p. 591.

Today a racially restrictive covenant commonly would run afoul of a federal, state, or local fair housing law. See, e.g., Sullivan v. Little Hunting Park, 396 U.S. 229 (1969) (holding that Civil Rights Act of 1866 prohibits homeowners association from limiting, on the basis of race, the transfer of rights to use its recreation facilities). See generally Chapter 8A.

In Mayers v. Ridley, 465 F.2d 630 (D.C. Cir. 1972), the court held that the Civil Rights Act of 1968 prevented the District of Columbia Recorder of Deeds from accepting for recordation any instruments containing racially restrictive covenants. The court also ordered the recorder to insert, in each existing book of deeds that might contain such covenants, a notice indicating that these covenants are null and void. While recognizing the administrative costs involved, the court viewed those costs as being outweighed by the danger that racially restrictive covenants contained in official records might achieve "a legitimacy and effectiveness in the eyes of laymen which they do not have in law." But cf. Woodward v. Bowers, 630 F. Supp. 1205 (M.D. Pa. 1986) (holding that a Recorder of Deeds who places in an official file a copy of a deed containing a racially restrictive covenant does not violate Civil Rights Act of 1968). Some title insurance companies refuse to include racial covenants in title reports. See Motoko Rich, Restrictive Covenants Stubbornly Stay on the Books, N.Y. Times, Apr. 21, 2005, at F1. If an attorney involved in the sale of a house were to discover that the property was burdened by a pre-*Shelley* racial restriction, should the attorney pass on that information to the buyer?

Note on Covenants Restricting Age and Household Composition

1. *The fiscal logic of retirement communities.* Developer Ross Cortese pioneered the creation of communities ("Leisure Worlds") where occupancy is restricted by covenant to the elderly. Many seniors apparently regard younger persons as threats to peace and quiet. More importantly, households with school-age children usually are a fiscal burden on a local government. See pp. 617–19. A developer who agrees to exclude children therefore is more likely to be granted a request for a rezoning. Is state action present when it can be shown that the developer had imposed age-restrictive covenants in order to obtain development approval? See Park Redlands Covenant Control Committee v. Simon, 226 Cal. Rptr. 199 (Ct. App. 1986) (yes).

2. *State civil rights statutes.* In O'Connor v. Village Green Owners Association, 662 P.2d 427 (Cal. 1983), the California Supreme Court held that the state's civil rights act generally prohibited the blanket exclusion of children from residence in a condominium association. The following year, the California legislature responded by enacting a narrow amendment that expressly permitted certain forms of senior citizen housing. See Cal. Civ. Code §51.3 (West 2004).

3. *Federal statutes.* The federal Fair Housing Act generally prohibits discrimination based on familial status, but exempts many senior citizen housing projects that existed prior to 1988, and prospectively exempts certain categories of new projects for the elderly. See 42 U.S.C. §3607(b) (2004). A multipronged constitutional challenge by elderly plaintiffs to these selective federal restrictions on their associational options was rebuffed in Seniors Civil Liberties Association v. Kemp, 965 F.2d 1030 (11th Cir. 1992). See also Taylor v. Rancho Santa Barbara, 206 F.3d 932 (9th Cir. 2000) (holding these special federal exemptions for the elderly do not deny the nonelderly equal protection). Was Congress wise to federalize this pocket of law?

4. *Group homes.* Social services agencies increasingly seek to supervise their clients in deinstitutionalized settings. See Chapter 8D. Can an agency use a house as a group home in the face of a covenant that permits only single-family residential use? In Crane Neck Association v. New York City/Long Island County Services Group, 460 N.E.2d 1336 (N.Y. 1984), the court held that a group home for eight profoundly retarded adults did not meet the covenant's definition of "single-family" use but that public policy prevented enforcement of the covenant against the facility. Compare Cal. Health & Safety Code §1566.5 (West 2004) (post-1978 covenants limiting land to single-family use shall be construed to permit a residential facility serving six or fewer persons). But compare Terrien v. Zwit, 648 N.W.2d 602 (Mich. 2002) (holding covenant that barred operation of day care business in home did not violate public policy). See generally Gerald Korngold, Single Family Use Covenants, 22 U.C. Davis L. Rev. 951 (1989).

5. *Cross-reference.* The legal limits on *municipal* restrictions on the characteristics of residents are explored in Chapter 8.

Note on Other Controversial Restrictions

1. *Religion.* In Taormina Theosophical Community, Inc. v. Silver, 190 Cal. Rptr. 38 (Ct. App. 1983), a nonprofit organization (Taormina) had acquired a tract of exurban land for the purpose of establishing a retirement community for Theosophists. Although Theosophists are not required to adhere to a particular religious creed, they are expected to study comparative religion and philosophy. Before subdividing the tract, Taormina recorded covenants that, among other things, restricted ownership and occupancy of lots to persons who were members of the Theosophical Society. Taormina brought this action to enforce these restrictions against the Silvers, a couple who had purchased a lot in violation of some of the covenants. (Some facts of the case suggest that this was a friendly lawsuit designed to free the tract from the burdens of these covenants.) The California Court of Appeal held that the restriction that limited *ownership* to Theosophists violated a state statute prohibiting unreasonable restraints on alienation. It found the quantum of the restraint to be "very great" because the Theosophical Society had only 6,000 members nationwide. "While the gathering of like minded people may be a laudable goal, such purpose is not sufficient to sustain the heavy burden on alienability." The court also held that the provision limiting *occupancy* to Theosophists violated another statute that prohibited covenants restricting occupancy on the basis of a person's religion. Although the court did not characterize Theosophy as a religion, it concluded that, in enacting this statute, "the Legislature indicated that it considered the manner in which a person approaches spiritual matters an improper and irrelevant criterion for denying access to land."

How might one advise Jesuits and Hare Krishnas, to pick two unrelated examples, to exclude nonbelievers from their communities?

2. *Speech.* On the permissibility of restrictions on the display of symbols and signs, see, e.g., Cal. Civ. Code §1353.6(a) (West 2004) (protecting right to fly flag of any sort); Mich. Comp. Laws Ann. §559.156a (West 2004) (covenants cannot bar owner of condominium unit from external display of U.S. flag of a size not greater than 3 by 5 feet); Cal. Civ. Code §712 (West 2004) (voiding restrictions on "For Sale" signs); Murphy v. Timber Trace Association, 779 S.W.2d 603 (Mo. Ct. App. 1989) (holding that covenant prohibiting the posting of "For Sale" signs except during weekend afternoons did not violate public policy).

A state court may interpret the free speech clause of its state constitution as more protective of speakers' rights than the First Amendment. Should an association be regarded as a "state actor" under a state free speech clause? Cf. Golden Gateway Center v. Golden Gateway Tenants Association, 29 P.3d 797 (Cal. 2001) (holding private landlord of huge apartment complex was not state actor when it constrained internal distribution of newsletter).

Section 207 of the federal Telecommunications Act of 1996 forbids the enforcement of any covenant (or zoning ordinance, for that matter) that would impair a television viewer's ability to receive video programming by way of either a conventional television antenna or a satellite dish less than one meter in diameter. See 47 C.F.R. §1.4000 (2004). In Daly v. River Oaks Place Council of Homeowners, 59 S.W.3d 416 (Tex. App. 2001), the court held this federal regulation did not prevent the association from barring a member from installing a satellite dish on roof of his unit (a common area). The court remanded, however, the issue of whether the regulation entitled the member to install a dish in his patio area. What considerations, if any, justify a federal override of private covenants to assure resident access to television signals?

3. *Restraints of trade.* In State v. Hossan-Maxwell, Inc., 436 A.2d 384 (Conn. 1980), Connecticut's Antitrust Act was held to bar enforcement of covenants that limited owners of 64 subdivision lots to use of a particular brokerage firm at time of resale.

2.   The Running of the Burdens and Benefits of Covenants to Succeeding Owners

Humphrey's promise not to open a bar would be more valuable to Ingrid if the promise also were to bind subsequent owners of Rickacre — that is, in the language of covenant law, if the *burden* of the covenantor's (CR's) promise were to run to CR's successors in interest (collectively referred to as CR*). Ingrid, the covenantee (CE), also might want her successors (CE*) to be able to enforce the restriction against a bar on Rickacre. For them to have that power, the *benefit* of the covenant would have to run to them.

No body of traditional common law is more exasperating than that dealing with the running of the benefits and burdens of private land use restrictions. This casebook's coverage of the cobwebbed history of these rules is brief, both because most introductory Property courses explore this material in detail and because the new Restatement's attack on traditional common law doctrine is likely to be increasingly successful.

Lewis v. Gollner
14 N.Y.S. 362 (City Ct. of Brooklyn 1891)

[Ervin Gollner contracted to purchase a lot on the south side of Union Street for the purpose of erecting flats, the nineteenth-century term for an inexpensive apartment building. Plaintiff owned an expensive residence in the immediate area. To prevent the construction of the flats, plaintiff and three of his neighbors purchased Ervin Gollner's contract on the south lot for $6,300, and also obtained Ervin's oral promise not to erect flats anywhere else in the immediate area. A few days later, Ervin Gollner acquired a lot on the north side of Union Street, diagonally across from the south lot. He immediately began to erect flats on the north lot. After about two months of construction, he sold the north lot to his wife, Ada Gollner, who continued the construction. "Mrs. Gollner took with full notice of the claim of plaintiff." Plaintiff sought an injunction to prevent both Gollners from erecting flats on the north lot.]

CLEMENT, C.J. . . .
. . . If there was any authority which was directly or indirectly in point in favor of the plaintiff, we would have no hesitation, on the facts, in rendering a decision in his favor and against the defendant. We have examined all the authorities cited, but it will suffice to refer to two only. In Tulk v. Moxhay, 2 Phil. Ch. 774, 41 Eng. Rep. 1143 (Ch. 1848), A., being seised of houses and a garden on Leicester square, conveyed the garden to B., and B. covenanted for himself and assigns not to build in the garden. Held, that purchaser from B. with notice of the covenant was bound by it in equity, although the covenant did not run with the land. This is the leading case in England, and has been repeatedly followed in that country. The second authority to which we shall refer is Hodge v. Sloan, 17 N.E. 335 (N.Y. 1887). In that case the facts were briefly as follows: N. was the owner of lands containing building sand, and the sale of the sand was his business. S. purchased a portion of the land, and covenanted in the deed not to sell sand from the parcel. S. subsequently conveyed to C., by warranty deed, and without covenants on the part of C., who, however, had notice of the covenant in the deed of N. to S. Held, that an action could be maintained by N. against C. to restrain the sale of sand by him. In each of the above cases the agreement related to a specific piece of land, and was to be found in a deed which would appear in the chain of title. The agreement was a covenant as to the use of the land which was made

on the sale, and was restrictive. The parties purchasing took with notice of the agreement, and an action would lie against them for a specific performance on the same principle that a party who purchases from one who had contracted to sell real property with notice of the contract can be compelled to carry out such contract, as in Duffy v. Donovan, 46 N.Y. 223. The question in equity is not whether the covenant runs with the land, but whether the party purchasing the land shall be allowed to use it in violation of the contract entered into by his grantor, and when the party purchased with full notice of the covenant. Hodge v. Sloan, supra. The agreement made by Gollner related to no specific piece of land, for he owned no land in the neighborhood when he made it. He agreed that he would not in the future buy any land in the neighborhood for the purpose of erecting flats thereon. This, in our opinion, was a personal agreement between the plaintiff and Gollner, and did not impose any covenant or equity upon any lands which he should buy which could be enforced against any subsequent grantee from him, even though the party who purchased had notice of the agreement. Courts should not spell out a restrictive covenant as to real property unless the agreement is clear, and for a defined purpose. It may be said that the distinction that Gollner did not own the lots on the north side of Union street when he made the agreement is finely drawn. The answer is that if he had owned the lots when he made the agreement it might be well claimed that he contracted as to the particular lots which he owned. His agreement was as to his future acts, and not to the restrictive use of land which he should purchase. Judgment [for defendants] should be affirmed with costs to the respondent Ada F.M. Gollner.

Note on the Core Requirements for the Running of Covenant Burdens and Benefits

1. *Subsequent history.* On appeal, the decision was reversed and a new trial ordered:

> But, if the contract remains technically a personal one, I think the reasonable and settled doctrine is that the contract equity is so attached to the use of the land which is its subject matter as to follow the land itself into the hands of a purchaser with full knowledge of all the facts, who buys with his eyes open to the existing equity, and more especially when he buys for the express purpose of defeating and evading that equity.

Lewis v. Gollner, 29 N.E. 81 (N.Y. 1891) (Finch, J.). Was Judge Finch's decision sound, given that Ervin Gollner's promise had been oral and that the original parties had not intended to impose burdens on any particular lot? Should the plaintiffs have been limited to the remedy of collecting damages from Ervin Gollner for breach of contract?

2. *The archaic distinction between covenants and equitable servitudes.* Tulk v. Moxhay, cited in the intermediate court's opinion in Lewis v. Gollner, is the foundational decision that supports the proposition that CR^* is bound by the burden of a promise if CR^* took with notice of the promise and if CR and CE intended CR^* to be bound. *Tulk* was decided in 1848 by the English Court of Chancery, a court of equity that was not required to honor the more arcane requirements for the running of covenants that the English law courts had developed over the centuries. Hence, it came to be said that although a covenant might not run with the land "at law," it would be enforced against a transferee by an equity court as an "equitable servitude" if the twin requirements of notice and intent had been met. One might have thought that the subsequent merger of law and equity courts would have led to the emergence of a single, unified set of requirements for the running of covenants. Nevertheless, some courts still maintain distinctions between the enforceability of land

restrictions in law and equity — a peculiar holdover from the era when law and equity courts were separate.

3. *The relevance of intent and notice. Tulk* identified two sensible prerequisites for the running of burdens of covenants. Courts hardly advance private ordering when they ignore the intent of contracting parties. For example, Ingrid and Humphrey might have intended that Humphrey's successors *not* be bound by the restriction against opening a bar. In *Tulk*, the court found an intent that the burden run with the land because the original instrument stated that the promise bound not only *CR*, but also *CR*'s "heirs, and assigns."

The requirement that *CR** take with notice is essential to protect bona fide purchasers from being held bound by restrictions they neither knew about, nor could have discovered by examining either public records or the premises conveyed. Suppose that *CE* conveys a parcel to *CR* (perhaps Ervin Gollner) by means of a deed, promptly recorded, that includes express covenants intended to bind *CR*'s successors. *CR* later conveys the same parcel to *CR** by means of a deed that not only fails to refer to the covenants but even fraudulently asserts that the parcel is not burdened by covenants. If *CE* were to seek to enforce the covenants against *CR**, should *CR** prevail on the ground of lack of notice? See Citizens for Covenant Compliance v. Anderson, 906 P.2d 1314 (Cal. 1995) (a transferee such as *CR** has constructive notice of all recorded documents in the transferee's chain of title). The rule that a purchaser has constructive notice of properly recorded and indexed documents greatly encourages both a covenant beneficiary to record the instrument that created the covenant, and also a land purchaser to arrange for a title search prior to closing.

4. *The running of benefits.* The first Restatement of Property, promulgated in 1944, incorporated a number of rules that allowed benefits to run with the land more easily than burdens. See, e.g., §§547-548. The Restatement (Third) of Property — Servitudes §§5.1–5.2 (2000) lessens the requirements for the running of burdens so that, in most contexts, the requirements for the running of burdens and benefits are identical.

To retain flexibility, an entrepreneur creating a large residential community customarily develops the project in sections. Each section is the subject of a separate subdivision map. The developer also records separately the covenants for each section before selling lots in it. The basic terms of these covenants, however, commonly do not vary from section to section. Assume Sections A and B are adjoining, and that the developer has attached identical sets of covenants to them. Is a homeowner in Section A entitled to enforce the covenants on adjoining land in Section B? The court in Speer v. Turner, 366 A.2d 93 (Md. Ct. Spec. App. 1976), considered the key question to be whom the developer intended to benefit when imposing the covenants. It concluded that the trial court had not been clearly erroneous in deciding that the benefits of Section B covenants had been intended to flow to Section A. But see Rooney v. Peoples Bank, 513 P.2d 1077 (Colo. Ct. App. 1973) (no "general plan" existed to authorize enforcement of covenants throughout tract developed in separate sections). See generally Note, The Existence of a Uniform Plan of Development Embracing Two Subdivisions, 52 Cornell L.Q. 611 (1967). See also pp. 585–87, on a developer's representations about community quality.

5. *Benefits in gross.* The landmark Neponsit Property Owners' Association v. Emigrant Industrial Savings Bank, 15 N.E.2d 793 (N.Y. 1938), held that a residential community association that owned no land was not as a consequence barred from collecting periodic assessments from subdivision homeowners and their successors. *Neponsit* therefore is cited for the proposition that the benefits of a covenant may be held in gross. On the history of *Neponsit*, see Stewart E. Sterk's contribution to Property Stories (Gerald Korngold & Andrew P. Morriss eds., 2004), at 301. See also B.C.E. Development, Inc. v. Smith, 264 Cal. Rptr. 55 (Ct. App. 1989) (holding that a subdivider's successor, which owned no land in the vicinity, had right to enforce subdivision covenants).

May a municipality enforce covenants burdening lands within it? Houston, Texas, the largest American city not to employ zoning, is empowered to seek mandatory enforcement of negative covenants. Tex. Loc. Gov't Code Ann. §§212.151–212.156 (Vernon Supp. 2004). In a three-year period, the city invoked this power to abate 2,300 violations. Bernard Siegan, Non-Zoning in Houston, 13 J.L. & Econ. 71, 77 (1970). See also City of Houston v. Klonis, 468 S.W.2d 182 (Tex. Civ. App. 1971) (upholding city's refusal to issue building permit for commercial structure that would violate covenant scheme); Comment, Municipal Enforcement of Private Restrictive Covenants, 44 Tex. L. Rev. 741 (1966). Municipal enforcement can overcome free-rider problems that might inhibit an individual homeowner from enforcing covenants. Where a residential community association exists, should it or the city be saddled with enforcement functions?

Note on Some Archaic(?) Requirements for the Running of Covenants

1. *Ancient precedent.* For more than four centuries, judges facing the issue of whether the burden of a promise made by CR runs to CR* have tended to apply tests that first appeared in Spencer's Case, 5 Co. Rep. 16a, 77 Eng. Rep. 72 (K.B. 1583). In particular, Spencer's Case states that a burden cannot run unless the burden "touches and concerns" the land and also unless the original covenanting parties were in "privity of estate." As the balance of this Note indicates, the authors of the Restatement (Third) of Property — Servitudes regarded both these requirements to be confusing and obsolete, and urged their replacement with better-tailored doctrines.

English judges had good reason to be chary of allowing covenant burdens to run with the land. Prior to the twentieth century, England lacked a public land records system that would have enabled a land purchaser to learn about existing encumbrances. In addition, legal doctrines that terminate covenants on grounds of obsolescence did not develop until long after Spencer's Case. Given these deficiencies in the English legal framework, the rules of Spencer's Case served, if crudely, to clear lands of unfair and inefficient covenant burdens. Because both these legal deficiencies are not present in the United States, however, the authors of the Restatement (Third) have (1) provided tests for judging the substantive validity of a covenant at the outset (see id. at §3.1 and pp. 554–62); (2) allowed the burdens of a valid covenant to run with the land provided only that the original parties so intended and that the successor in question took with actual or constructive notice of the burden (the *Tulk* requirements) (see id. at §§5.1–5.2); and (3) provided tests for the modification or termination of obsolete covenants (see id. at §§7.1–7.13 and pp. 572–80). Although this Restatement approach is becoming increasingly influential, many state court judges continue to reiterate the requirements set out in Spencer's Case. Why might judges be more hesitant to abandon long-standing doctrines in land law than in, say, tort law?

2. *Touch and concern.* Judicial interpretations of this phrase have been bewildering. Compare Neponsit Property Owners' Association v. Emigrant Industrial Savings Bank, 15 N.E.2d 793 (N.Y. 1938) (association's assessment charges touched and concerned land), with Eagle Enterprises v. Gross, 349 N.E.2d 816 (N.Y. 1976) (developer's charges for water services did not touch and concern land).

A court may hold that the touch-and-concern requirement has not been met in order to eviscerate a covenant that it would not want to enforce for other, unarticulated, reasons. For example, in Norcross v. James, 2 N.E. 946 (Mass. 1885), Justice Holmes held that grantee's promise not to compete with grantor's quarry could not be enforced against the grantee's successors. Although the parties intended that the burden of the restriction run to grantee's assigns, Holmes held it could not because it did not touch and concern the land:

> It does not in any way affect the use or occupation [of grantor's quarry]; it simply tends indirectly to increase its value, by excluding a competitor from the market for its products. . . . [I]t creates an easement of monopoly. . . . It is true that a man could accomplish the same results by buying the whole land and regulating production. But it does not follow because you can do a thing in one way that you can do it in all. . . .

Almost a century later, in Whitinsville Plaza, Inc. v. Kotseas, 390 N.E.2d 243 (Mass. 1979), Massachusetts's highest court overruled *Norcross*, saying in part:

> If free competition policies were indeed the basis for the *Norcross* decision, it would now seem preferable for us to deal with them explicitly rather than to condemn all anticompetitive covenants regardless of reasonableness.

The doctrinal drift in Massachusetts is consistent with Restatement (Third) of Property — Servitudes §§3.2, 3.6 (2000) (dismissing touch-and-concern requirement as obsolete, but asserting invalidity of covenant that unreasonably restrains competition). See also Davidson Bros., Inc. v. D. Katz & Sons, Inc., 579 A.2d 288 (N.J. 1990) (stopping just short of abandoning touch-and-concern requirement).

Were the authors of the Restatement (Third) too unappreciative of this ancient doctrine? Sophisticated defenses of the traditional touch-and-concern requirement include Jeffrey E. Stake, Toward an Economic Understanding of Touch and Concern, 1988 Duke L.J. 925; Stewart Sterk, Freedom from Freedom of Contract, 70 Iowa L. Rev. 615 (1985); and A. Dan Tarlock, Touch and Concern Is Dead, Long Live the Doctrine, 77 Neb. L. Rev. 804 (1998).

3. *Horizontal privity of estate.* According to the archaic requirement of horizontal privity, the burden of a promise could run with the land only if the original contracting parties, *CR* and *CE*, shared some specified special relationship at the time they created the covenant. The most restrictive of the traditional tests required that each of the parties already possessed some partial interest in the land to which the covenant's burden would attach — for example, to be involved in a landlord-tenant relationship. Section 534 of the Restatement of Property (1944) was somewhat more generous in that it recognized horizontal privity to exist when the covenant was contained in a conveyance from *CE* to *CR* or vice versa. Note, however, that a covenant between two neighbors who owned separate fee simple interests would not satisfy this horizontal privity test (unless they first went through a straw transaction that temporarily consolidated their parcels). Judge Clark was the leader of the fight for abolition of this mystical barrier to landowner contracting. Charles E. Clark, Real Covenants and Other Interests Which "Run with the Land," 111–43 (2d ed. 1947). Although many courts continue to state as dictum that "privity of estate" is a prerequisite for the running of covenants, only a few reported U.S. decisions in recent decades have in fact invoked the horizontal privity requirement to free a *CR** from a land use restriction. A dismaying example is Johnson v. Myers, 172 S.E.2d 421 (Ga. 1970), where a developer contracted to set aside a buffer strip if his neighbors would support his application for a rezoning. The Georgia Supreme Court held that this promise was not enforceable against the developer's successor in ownership (who apparently took with notice) because there had been no horizontal privity of estate.

Restatement (Third) of Property — Servitudes §2.4 (2000) seeks to eradicate all vestiges of the horizontal privity requirement from the common law. Unlike the touch-and-concern doctrine, horizontal privity appears to have no scholarly defenders.

4. *Vertical privity of estate.* In its second (vertical) sense, privity of estate rightly retains considerable legal relevance. Here the focus is on the relationship between *CR* and *CR** (or *CE* and *CE**). When *CR** is only a partial successor to *CR*'s ownership interest, a vertical privity issue arises. Suppose *CR* owns a unit in a conventional residential community association that imposes periodic assessments on members to defray its operating and maintenance costs. The burden of these assessments is intended to run to *CR*'s "heirs and assigns." Is the residential community association entitled to obtain a personal judgment for an unpaid assessment against college students who rent *CR*'s unit during the summer? Against a cable television company that recently bought from *CR* a right-of-way for its wires? Against Grantee, who acquired *CR*'s property in fee simple absolute, but subject to the college students' lease and the cable television company's easement? There are few cases on the issue. As a default rule, the Restatement (Third) of Property — Servitudes §§5.2–5.4 (2000) would make only Grantee liable for paying the assessment, on the ground that this result would most likely accord with the intent of all parties.

What if a *CR* were to subdivide the burdened lot into two smaller parcels and sell them? Should each of the grantees be liable for the full assessment? Or should the association's assessment be apportioned between the two lots? Or not be enforceable against either? See id. at §5.7 (calling for apportionment if the affirmative act is not one that need be performed on a specific part of the land).

Observe that a vertical privity requirement should be applied only when a *CR*'s *affirmative* obligations are at issue. *Negative* restrictions on *CR* should be enforceable against any of *CR*'s partial successors, as long as they took with notice and *CE* and *CR* intended that the burdens should run to them. For example, *CR*'s summer tenants no doubt should have to comply with any covenants restricting ownership of pets.

5. *Are affirmative covenants suspect?* Consistent with their general hostility to the running of covenant burdens, English courts declined to extend Tulk v. Moxhay to affirmative covenants. Haywood v. Brunswick Permanent Benefit Building Society, 8 Q.B. 403, 51 L.J.Q.B. 73 (1881) (refusing to enforce against *CR** a covenant to keep buildings in repair).

Because decrees directing future conduct are relatively intrusive, judges understandably were reluctant to order a succeeding owner to honor an affirmative covenant. Nevertheless, if affirmative obligations cannot run with the land, neighbors will not be able to make lasting agreements to maintain party walls or contribute to a homeowners association. American courts now are generally willing to enforce affirmative covenants that require *CR** to pay money or to provide impersonal services (like building maintenance) that can be delegated to independent contractors. See, e.g., Peterson v. Beekmere, Inc., 283 A.2d 911 (N.J. 1971) (distinction between affirmative and negative covenants is an "anachronism"). See generally Restatement (Third) of Property — Servitudes §4.7 (2000); Note, Affirmative Duties Running with the Land, 35 N.Y.U. L. Rev. 1344 (1960).

6. *Running of burdens to nonconsensual successors.* Assume that Humphrey's promise not to open a bar on Rickacre binds his "heirs and assigns." Should it also bind a party who succeeds to the ownership of Rickacre without Humphrey's consent — for example, an adverse possessor or foreclosing mortgagee? See Restatement (Third) of Property — Servitudes §5.2 (2000) (usually it should).

If the state were to acquire Rickacre through exercise of the power of eminent domain, Ingrid could not prevent the state from opening a bar because the state also could condemn the benefit of the covenant. But should the state have to compensate Ingrid if it were to violate the restriction? Courts in a majority of jurisdictions now hold that it should. For criticism of the majority approach, see Note, Nuisance Damages as an Alternative to Compensation of Land Use Restrictions in Eminent Domain, 47 S. Cal. L. Rev. 998 (1974).

Should compensation be awarded to benefited landowners who created the protective covenants *after* they learned of the condemnor's project? The Supreme Court of California has hinted that beneficiaries of bad faith restrictions should be denied recovery. Southern California Edison Co. v. Bourgerie, 507 P.2d 964, 968 (Cal. 1973).

7. *Liabilities of covenantors after they transfer their interests.* Suppose that Rachel owns a condominium unit in a development where all unit owners are obligated to comply with architectural controls and pay periodic assessments. Rachel later sells her entire interest to Ross. Is Rachel liable for the damage that results when Ross subsequently breaches these obligations? In general, the intent of the original parties to the covenant determines whether *CR* remains liable after *CR* transfers to *CR**. See In re Val Moritz Investment Group, Ltd., 116 B.R. 257 (D. Colo. 1990) (condominium owner's liability for assessments ceased when secured creditor obtained deed in lieu of foreclosure); Restatement (Third) of Property — Servitudes §4.4 (2000).

3.   *Tying Up a Subdivision with Covenants*

a.   *Doing It Right*

Homes Association Handbook
197–99 (Urb. Land Inst. Tech. Bull. No. 50, 1966)[2]

12.1 INTRODUCTION

Four steps are involved in establishing the legal foundation necessary to sustain a residential development with common properties maintained by a homes association: (1) preparation and recording of final subdivision plat of the development; (2) preparation and recording of a declaration of covenants and restrictions applicable to the land within the subdivision; (3) preparation of the articles and bylaws of a homes association and its incorporation; and (4) sale and conveyance of the homes by deed that confirms the rights and duties which are provided for in the first three steps.

We recommend . . . that the first three steps be taken concurrently before any lots are sold. . . .

12.2 LEGAL FUNCTION OF THE RECORDED PLAT AND DECLARATION OF COVENANTS AND RESTRICTIONS

12.21. FUNCTION OF THE RECORDED SUBDIVISION PLAT

In a residential development where common properties are planned to be deeded to homes association for use and maintenance by the home owners, rather than dedicated to a public agency for public use and maintenance, the recorded subdivision plan or plat plays a critical role with respect to the common properties. It must set certain legal rights and duties of the developer, the home purchaser, the association, and of the public.

The plat itself is in the nature of a deed. By well established doctrines of the common law, the sale of lots by reference to a recorded plan may constitute an implied dedication to the public of all community areas shown on it. The courts, on occasion, have given this effect to the plat notwithstanding that local practice may require a separate deed of

---

[2] EDS.: This excerpt is the work of Jan Z. Krasnowiecki.

dedication for streets and other areas which are to be accepted for public maintenance. The fact that the local public authority has accepted some community facilities such as streets for public maintenance does not militate against its right later to accept other community areas shown on the plat. It is well settled that an implied offer of dedication remains open for acceptance for a considerable period of time. Obviously, where common properties shown on the plat are to be conveyed to a homes association, the possibility that such properties have been impliedly dedicated to the public will cast a cloud on the association's title to such areas.

The courts have been solicitous of the rights of a purchaser who is led to believe that he will be entitled to continued enjoyment of the common areas shown on the plat. Even in the absence of any express provision on the plat or in the deeds of conveyance to each lot, they have held that the lot purchasers impliedly acquire easements of enjoyment over such common areas. These rights should not be left to implication but should be expressly confirmed on the face of the plat itself or in the text of a separate deed of dedication to the common use and enjoyment of the home owners. . . .

Along with the plat, the developer will, of course, prepare and record a declaration of covenants and restrictions applicable to the platted area. The full text of the provisions which are to govern the property rights in the common areas shown on the plat can most easily be set forth in the covenants. . . . We recommend, however, that the same provisions should be incorporated by reference on the face of the recorded plat so that the rights and duties involved will be controlled not only by the covenants, but also by the plat. . . .

12.22. FUNCTION OF A RECORDED DECLARATION OF COVENANTS AND RESTRICTIONS . . .

When a developer records a declaration of covenants and restrictions with respect to the land he then owns, he is the only party to the agreements expressed therein, and so these agreements do not become binding upon him or upon the land until another party to them is supplied. When he sells the first lot and makes the declaration a part of the deed of conveyance,[1] the covenants and restrictions expressed in the declaration attach to the lot sold and become binding upon the purchaser, and they will, subject to further discussion of this point, run with the land against all subsequent purchasers who take title to the lot with notice of the covenants and restrictions. Since the covenants and restrictions are recorded, the law presumes that subsequent purchasers have notice. . . .

The sale of the first lot subject to the declaration has a confirming effect upon the land use pattern within the area subject to the declaration. This is highly desirable. But the resulting right of individual purchasers to force strict adherence to the scheme without reference to its continued feasibility tends to discourage the developer from committing to it any more of his proposed development than he is assured of marketing over a short span of time. This presents the problem of the staged development, by sections. . . .

Note on Restrictions Created by Recorded Declaration

On the historical evolution of the declaration, see Robert Kratovil, The Declaration of Restrictions, Easements, Liens, and Covenants, 22 J. Marshall L. Rev. 69 (1988).

---

1. This is done by a clause in the deed of conveyance "subject to covenants and restrictions of record."

What if the developer's attorney were to omit the fourth step — that is, fail to include in the first (or any) deed to a lot the clause "subject to covenants and restrictions of record." See Citizens for Covenant Compliance v. Anderson, 906 P.2d 1314, 1316 (Cal. 1995):

> We . . . adopt the following rule: If a declaration establishing a common plan for the ownership of property in a subdivision and containing restrictions upon the use of the property as part of the common plan, is recorded before the execution of the contract of sale, describes the property it is to govern, and states that it is to bind all purchasers and their successors, subsequent purchasers who have constructive notice of the recorded declaration are deemed to intend and agree to be bound by, and to accept the benefits of, the common plan; the restrictions, therefore, are not unenforceable merely because they are not additionally cited in a deed or other document at the time of the sale.

b.   Doing It Sloppily: Judicial Rescue via the "General Plan" Doctrine

In Clancy v. Recker, 316 A.2d 898 (Pa. 1974), William Recker had owned a 155-acre tract of land in Union Township. Between 1956 and 1962, he made 11 separate conveyances, involving a total of 7 acres, of portions of the tract. Each of the 11 deeds included a covenant prohibiting the use of "trailers" on the conveyed lot. Partly because Recker had neglected to draft and record a uniform declaration of covenants at the outset, it was not clear who the beneficiaries of these covenants were nor whether the retained land was to be burdened by the same restriction. When William Recker, Sr., died in 1969, his will devised the remaining 148 acres to his son, William Recker, Jr. In 1971, the junior Recker received township approval to construct a trailer park on the site. The purchasers of the original lots brought an action to enjoin construction of the trailer park. Their attorneys asserted the existence of an implicit general plan, citing the leading case of Sanborn v. McLean, 206 N.W. 496 (Mich. 1925), which states in part:

> If the owner of two or more lots, so situated as to bear the relation, sells one with restrictions of benefit to the land retained, the servitude becomes mutual, and, during the period of restraint, the owner of the lot or lots retained can do nothing forbidden to the owner of the lot sold. For want of a better descriptive term this is styled a reciprocal negative easement. It runs with the land sold by virtue of express fastening and abides with the land retained until loosened by expiration of its period of service or by events working its destruction. It is not personal to owners, but operative upon use of the land by any owner having actual or constructive notice thereof.

The trial court nevertheless found that the plaintiffs had failed to prove that the senior Recker had implicitly promised a general scheme of development. The Supreme Court of Pennsylvania, however, reversed and remanded for further findings.

In Forster v. Hall, 576 S.E.2d 746 (Va. 2003), the court held that a general plan existed when 93 percent of the lots had been individually burdened by covenants prohibiting placement of mobile homes. The opinion noted that the original grantees of some of the excepted lots had affirmatively asked to be free of such covenants and thus were aware of the majority's expectations.

Two sorts of relatively innocent parties may suffer when a developer has been sloppy in establishing a scheme of covenants: (a) the (usually early) purchasers of restricted lots who naively thought the rest of the developer's subdivision would be subject to restrictions, and (b) the (usually late) purchasers of apparently unrestricted parts of the subdivision who may be surprised to find that their neighbors regard what they bought to be restricted. Which of these two parties, at time of purchase, is better able to recognize that they may be becoming embroiled in a messy legal situation? If courts systematically were to protect members of one of these groups, should the members of the other group be entitled to recover damages from the developer who created the mess? Deed covenants of title may provide a basis for a suit by a subsequent purchaser who is surprised to find that restrictions apply. Conversely, an early lot purchaser damaged by a developer's failure to insert restrictions in subsequent deeds may be able to make out a case of intentional misrepresentation. How valuable is a lawsuit against the derelict developer likely to be at the time the conflict is discovered?

How should one go about searching the title to a lot in a state that honors the general-plan doctrine? Houghton v. Rizzo, 281 N.E.2d 577 (Mass. 1972), remarks on the difficulty of the task:

> . . . [T]he proliferation of implied rights in or servitudes upon real estate, which cannot be readily ascertained by an examination of the records of the appropriate registry of deeds or of the Land Court, will serve only to further erode the integrity and reliability of such records and will be a subversion of the fundamental purpose for which such records are required to be made and maintained. A prospective purchaser of a lot on a plan from a developer who has not previously expressly subjected that lot to any restrictions of record should not be subjected to the nearly impossible burden and risk of deciding at his peril whether, by a series of restrictions imposed on lots previously conveyed, the developer has impliedly restricted his remaining land in the same way.

The general-plan doctrine receives a qualified endorsement in Restatement (Third) of Property — Servitudes §2.14 (2000). Illustration 5 reveals the authors' ambivalence:

> D subdivided a tract of land into 200 lots. Restrictions limiting use of the lots to residential purposes were included in deeds to 150 of the 200 lots. The original deeds to 50 lots, scattered randomly throughout the subdivision, contained no restrictions. In the absence of other evidence that the unrestricted lots were intended to be burdened by the restrictions, the conclusion would be justified that a general plan existed for the purpose of implying that all of the lots in the subdivision were intended beneficiaries of the restrictions expressly imposed on the 150 lots, but it would not be justified for the purpose of implying reciprocal servitudes burdening the 50 lots whose deeds included no restrictions.

The Reporter's Note that follows §2.14 comprehensively reviews the case law and observes that courts in some states (including Arizona, California, and Ohio) have been unwilling to employ the general-plan doctrine to impose servitude burdens.

4. Termination

To maximize profits, a subdivider has an interest in imposing covenants that most lot purchasers initially regard as more beneficial than burdensome. However, as time passes and conditions change, even the most brilliantly drafted restrictions are likely to become inefficient. What can the parties to a covenant scheme do to free themselves from the dead hand of the past? One possibility is for all beneficiaries to agree to modify or terminate the obsolete covenants. High transaction costs, however, are likely to make unanimous agreement impossible, at least in a large subdivision. Those who draft covenants therefore are wise either to limit the life of covenants by express provision or to authorize the group, after several decades have passed, to alter the covenants by less than unanimous vote.

Especially when covenants are not subject to express termination provisions, courts and legislatures can enhance the efficiency of land use by establishing rules that loosen the grip of inefficient covenants. This section explores a variety of termination rules that have been developed by private drafters, courts, and legislatures. Termination is already one of the most frequently litigated issues in covenant law and may become even more contested as the suburbs that mushroomed in the mid-twentieth century start showing their age.

Cordogan v. Union National Bank of Elgin
380 N.E.2d 1194 (Ill. App. Ct. 1978)

RECHENMACHER, Justice:

The defendant appeals from the order of the circuit court of Kane County which granted an injunction restraining the defendant from erecting a duplex apartment building in Riverside Manor No. 1, during the term of a restrictive covenant.

The defendant, Roy C. Wauchope, developed Riverside Manor No. 1 in 1957, and at that time set up certain restrictions running with the land as to the lots therein when the plat of subdivision was recorded. Among these restrictive covenants was the following:

> No lot shall be used except for residential purposes. No buildings shall be erected, altered, placed or permitted to remain on any lot other than one detached single family dwelling and a private garage for not more than three cars.
>
> These covenants are to run with the land and shall be binding on all parties and all persons claiming under them for a period of twenty-five years from the date these covenants are recorded, after which time said covenants shall be automatically extended for successive periods of ten years unless an instrument signed by a majority of the then owners of the lots has been recorded, agreeing to change said covenants in whole or in part.

During the years between 1957 and 1977 Wauchope had purchased farm property in the area immediately surrounding the subdivision, some of which was developed by him as Riverside Manor No. 2 and some of which was sold to other developers for commercial purposes. Sometime after Riverside Manor No. 1 was developed, State Route 31, which adjoins the western boundary of the subdivision, was changed from a two lane to a four lane highway and the Northwest Tollway was built, just to the north of the subdivision. A Ramada Inn was also built nearby on a tract of land between the subdivision and State Route 31, the northwest corner of Riverside Manor No. 1 being across the frontage road from the Ramada Inn. Lots 18, 19 and 20, still owned by Wauchope and undeveloped, lie in the northwest corner and run north and south and to the west of Lot 18. Across the frontage road is the service area or "backyard" of the Ramada Inn. Wauchope testified he had never been able to sell these 3 lots as single family residential lots. The land surrounding Riverside Manor No. 1, mostly owned at one time by Wauchope, not however including the Ramada Inn property, has been sold by Wauchope to other developers or commercial institutions. Surrounding the subdivision in various directions are located a trailer camp, a Holiday Inn, a McGraw Edison manufacturing building, the campus and dormitories of Judson College and a building housing the National Federation of High School Athletic Associations, all of these being commercially zoned and on land sold by the defendant, Wauchope, to others for development. The defendant conceded that these tracts were all sold without restrictions.

The plaintiffs testified that when they bought their lots in Riverside Manor they were informed of and relied on the single family restriction and it was an inducement for their purchases.

In the spring of 1977, the defendant began laying the foundation for a building on Lot 18 which, by a sign announced it would be a duplex apartment building. Previous to this the city council of Elgin had rezoned Lots 18, 19 and 20 to allow such occupancy, which change the plaintiffs had opposed. The plaintiffs then filed a complaint for injunction to enjoin the defendant from constructing the duplex apartment building in violation of the restrictive covenant set out above. After hearing testimony and viewing exhibits submitted in the case, the trial court granted a permanent injunction restraining the defendant from building any structure on Lots 18, 19 or 20, other than a one family residence. This appeal followed. . . .

We consider first the contention of the defendant that the character of the surrounding area has so changed as to render the restriction precluding the building of any structures, other than a single family residence, ineffective to accomplish its original aims. The defendant in his brief suggests that the "object" of this restriction was to promote peace, tranquility and a low volume of traffic and population density and to attract other single family home owners. This, the defendant argues, can no longer be accomplished by enforcing the restriction because it would merely result in the 3 lots in question remaining vacant, thus lacking the shield from surrounding commercial or higher density occupancies which might otherwise be provided by the duplex buildings. If, on the other hand, the duplexes were built, the defendant argues they would act as a shield or "buffer" zone from nearby, less pleasing prospects. . . .

. . . We do not think that the buffering effect of the proposed buildings would be of much consequence so far as the residents of Riverside Manor No. 1 are concerned, as compared with single family residences, or even leaving the lots vacant with the present poplar trees on them.

. . . [N]ot only would the proposed duplex buildings have little effect in diminishing the evidence of a commercial presence in other directions, but much of the land which these other enterprises are built on, was sold to the owner or developer by the defendant Wauchope, himself, without restrictions as to use or density. To the extent that enterprises occupying such land might be thought to encroach on the subdivision, the defendant is partly responsible for this change. . . .

The defendant also contends that the trial court erred in disregarding the principle that a court of equity will not generally restrain a use of property where to grant such a relief would be a great handicap on the property owner and of little or no benefit to the complainant.

This argument requires no extended comment. We are dealing here with a restrictive covenant originated by the defendant himself. A covenant such as this, running with the land, is not a matter which requires the nice balancing of the equities that might be required in an ordinary nuisance case or a request for rezoning or the enforcement of an ordinary business contract. Restrictive covenants concerning the use of land are in a somewhat different category and unless against public policy, or the principles of waiver of estoppel operate, their violation will generally be enjoined by a court of equity. . . .

The person in whose favor the restriction runs is . . . prima facie entitled to have it enforced by a court of equity. As was said by this court in Tones, Inc. v. LaSalle National Bank, 339 N.E.2d 3, 7 (Ill. App. Ct. 1975): "The burden of proving that there has been a change in circumstances affecting the validity of the restriction so that the object of the restriction can no longer be accomplished and therefore may be removed without unjustly injuring neighboring properties is on the party who seeks relief from the enforcement of the restriction."

In the case before us there was no showing of any change in the subdivision itself which would render the restriction ineffective and whatever the benefits of the restrictions were originally to the grantees who are the beneficiaries thereof, those benefits still apply. The defendant has not shown merely because his remaining lots would be more saleable with the restriction removed that the equities are with him in doing so. . . .

Judgment affirmed.

Note on the Doctrine of Changed Conditions

1. *Relevant factors.* Should the court in *Cordogan* have given weight to the fact that the City of Elgin had rezoned the defendant's land to allow construction of a duplex apartment building?

If covenants could expire solely on account of change outside the restricted area, restrictions in a residential subdivision could fall like dominos. In River Heights Associates Ltd. Partnership v. Batten, 591 S.E.2d 683 (Va. 2004), the Virginia Supreme Court refused to free four lots abutting U.S. Route 29 from residence-only restrictions even though the highway had evolved from a two-lane road to a bustling eight-lane commercial strip. The court stressed the lack of change within the subdivision itself. But see, e.g., Hecht v. Stephens, 464 P.2d 258 (Kan. 1970) (refusing to enforce, on grounds of external change, covenant prohibiting mobile homes).

In Explaining Contingent Rights: The Puzzle of "Obsolete" Covenants, 91 Colum. L. Rev. 546, 549 n.10 (1991), Glen O. Robinson tallied 65 state appellate cases decided between 1970 and 1990 on the topic of changed conditions. In 17 of the 65, the covenantor was excused from compliance; in the remaining 48, sufficient change was not found.

2. *Waiver and abandonment.* Courts usually give more weight to physical changes that have occurred within the restricted subdivision than to those that have occurred outside it. Is internal change more relevant because it is better evidence that the covenants are now inefficient, or because it enables those who propose to violate the restrictions to argue that the would-be enforcers have forfeited their rights on account of their past actions or inactions?

A residential community association's governing documents may authorize it to grant variances from design restrictions. See, e.g., Morris v. Kadrmas, 812 P.2d 549 (Wyo. 1991). If an association were to execute a written waiver of enforcement rights against homeowner A, should that waiver impair the association's enforcement rights against homeowner B? Should A's permitted departure from the covenants be counted as a change in neighborhood conditions?

In Prisco v. Forest Villas Condominium Apartments, 847 So. 2d 1012 (Fla. Dist. Ct. App. 2003), a unit owner complained to the condominium association of hearing a barking dog in Prisco's unit. The association's amended declaration of covenants forbade owners from harboring both dogs and cats. Prisco adduced evidence that the association previously had expressly permitted one owner to harbor a dog and had tolerated the presence of several cats. The appellate court held that the trial court had wrongly refused to permit Prisco to raise the affirmative defense of selective enforcement.

In Fink v. Miller, 896 P.2d 649 (Utah Ct. App. 1995), a subdivision covenant called for the roofs of all houses to be finished with wood shingles. In fact, 23 of the 81 subdivision houses violated this covenant. The court examined the number, nature, and severity of the violations, and held that the homeowners had abandoned the covenant governing shingling materials (although not necessarily covenants governing other architectural features).

3. *Express termination dates.* Should the doctrine of changed conditions be applied to cut short covenants already limited by an express termination date? In McClure v. Leaycraft, 75 N.E. 961 (N.Y. 1905), the court invalidated a 25-year restriction on apartment

construction that had been in effect for 19 years. In Norris v. Williams, 54 A.2d 3314 (Md. 1947), a restriction to residential uses with an express life of 50 years was terminated after 30 years. Are these results defensible on the ground that conditions might have changed more than the developer and original purchasers had anticipated?

The covenants at issue in *Cordogan* contained the express termination provision once advocated by the Federal Housing Administration (FHA). See FHA, Land Planning Bulletin No. 3, Part H (rev. Apr. 1959). Reread the quoted material in the second paragraph of *Cordogan*. To take effect, must an instrument that changes the covenants be signed by (a) the owners of a majority of the lots, or (b) a majority of the owners of lots? Why might the proper interpretation matter a great deal in the case of a failed subdivision? Suppose a properly executed instrument imposing a modification had been recorded in year 28. Would it become effective immediately under the FHA system? In year 35? In year 38?

The Homes Association Handbook 212 (1966) suggests:

> The best approach is to provide that, after the initial period, the covenants shall continue automatically for periods of ten years each unless the home owners alter or abrogate them by recording an instrument signed by two-thirds of the then owners. Very important in such a provision is a requirement that the covenants be reviewed by the home owners and changes determined upon well in advance (we suggest three years) of the end of any period of their existence — a precaution which will avoid the rancor and disappointment that can attend modifications that are made hastily at the very end of any such period.
>
> An alternative approach to the one that we suggest would terminate the covenants after the initial period unless reinstated by majority vote of the home owners; this is extremely undesirable. Although most home owners would rather see the covenants continue, a majority vote to reinstate them may be difficult to marshal; moreover this approach raises serious legal questions. A covenant, as we have seen, is an undertaking attached to the land by an agreement of each original purchaser. If by their terms the covenants cease to apply to each parcel of land in the development at a certain date, further serious legal objections can be raised to a provision which allows them to be reattached by the vote of less than all of the owners. . . .

What if developer Wauchope in *Cordogan* had *bought* the signatures necessary to free his lot from restrictions? Should a court throw out the modification as being tainted by procedural illegality? Or should it instead regard the payments as having internalized future externalities?

Blakeley v. Gorin
313 N.E.2d 903 (Mass. 1974)

[In the mid-nineteenth century, the Commonwealth of Massachusetts filled in the tidal flats located in the Back Bay area of Boston. Beginning in 1857, the Commonwealth subdivided the filled land into lots for dwelling units. In virtually all of the deeds to the lots it inserted restrictive covenants known as the Commonwealth Restrictions. One of these restrictions required "that a passageway, sixteen feet wide, is to be laid out in the rear of the premises . . . and to be kept open and maintained by the abutters in common. . . ."

Petitioners currently own the entire frontage of the block on Arlington Street between Newbury Street and Commonwealth Avenue, opposite the Boston Public Garden. The portion near Newbury Street is the site of the Ritz Carlton Hotel. The portion near Commonwealth Avenue is vacant. Petitioners desire to use the vacant portion for a new 28-story hotel-apartment building. This building would be connected to the existing hotel by a "bridge" over the alley protected by the covenants. The bridge would connect all floors between the second and thirteenth stories, and would in effect convert the alley into a tunnel. Respondents own an eight-story apartment building on adjoining land on Commonwealth Avenue. The proposed bridging structure over the alley would interfere with the light and air available to their apartment building. They assert the bridge would violate the covenant requiring that the alley be "kept open."

Petitioners sought a judicial declaration that the restrictions were obsolete and unenforceable. They relied on Mass. Gen. Laws ch. 184, §30 (2004), which provides that no restriction shall be enforceable unless it is determined that the restriction is, at the time of the proceeding, of actual and substantial benefit to a person claiming rights of enforcement. The statute further provides that even if a restriction is found to be of such benefit, it shall not be enforced except by an award of money damages if, among other things, an injunction would be "inequitable or not in the public interest."

The trial judge held that none of the restrictions should be enforced, either by injunction or money damages. On appeal, one of the respondents' arguments was that the statute permitted an unconstitutional taking of property for private purposes.]

HENNESSEY, J. . . .

To rule that Mass. Gen. Laws c. 184, §30, is unconstitutional would raise to a constitutional right the ordinary rule of equity that property interests may be enforced by a decree of specific performance. This result, by removing the discretion inherent in courts of equity to determine whether to grant specific performance, would reverse legal precedents even older than the Commonwealth Restrictions themselves. The Legislature has appropriately left the decision on specific enforcement of these rights where it has traditionally resided, in the sound discretion of a judge of a court of equity. It seems inappropriate to transform this discretionary remedy into a constitutional right. . . .

[We do not] believe that such changes as have occurred in the neighborhood make this restriction obsolete. While restrictions requiring setbacks or prohibiting mercantile uses clearly have reference to maintaining the overall character of a neighborhood and can thus become obsolete as that neighborhood changes, this restriction is intended to secure a specific benefit to each residence it affects. So long as any of those residences continues to exist it cannot be called obsolete. As this urban area has grown and become ever more congested in the century since this restriction was first imposed, light and air have become more, not less, valuable. The restriction securing the respondents' rights to them is certainly not obsolete. . . .

. . . [W]e observe that the evidence shows, inter alia, that the properties and the neighborhood have drastically changed. Single-family residences have been replaced by moderately high-rise buildings for apartments and institutional use. We have found that the passageway restriction is of an actual and substantial benefit in its effect on light and air, but the proposed bridge will have only a modest impact in view of the drastic changes which have already occurred. . . .

Further, since this restriction was first imposed, public controls have been imposed which tend to preempt the restriction in a manner contemplated by §30. At least three different public authorities have been given control over the basic design structure of buildings on premises subject to the restrictions. Also, a public commission of the city has been given authority, with the approval of the mayor, to permit bridging over public alleys. Additionally, at least three zoning variances will have to be procured before the entire structure can be completed.

The record also clearly supports a conclusion that continued enforcement of the restriction would tend to impede reasonable use of the land for purposes for which it is most suitable. The uncontradicted evidence was that a free standing tower is economically infeasible presumably because of the small size of the parcel, and that the plaintiffs' proposal for an apartment-hotel complex connected to the adjacent Ritz-Carlton is the most suitable use of the land. . . .

Weighing and comparing the interests of the parties and the public in accordance with the several provisions of §30 brings us almost inevitably to the conclusion that there should be no specific enforcement. In the words of provision (5) of the statute, which unquestionably confers the broadest discretion on the court, enforcement here would be inequitable and not in the public interest. The magnitude of the harm to the petitioners in specific enforcement of the restriction far exceeds that to the respondents in its denial. Moreover we are mandated by the statute to have due regard for the public interest in determining the manner of enforcement of a restriction. The land in question has been vacant for over a decade. We take judicial notice of the exceedingly high property tax rates current in the city of Boston and the beneficial effect on the tax base of the petitioners' plan to construct a multimillion dollar project of public usefulness on presently unutilized land. In the circumstances both the balance of equities between the parties and a consideration of the public interest require that the respondents accept money damages by way of enforcement of this restriction.

We consider it appropriate to comment on one statement in the dissenting opinion, viz., the statement of the two dissenting Justices that they "cannot be unmindful of the precedential effect which the court's decision of this case will have on a large part of the Back Bay of Boston, far beyond the several parcels of land owned by these particular litigants." We comment here that the statute, Mass. Gen. Laws c. 184, §30, as well as the reasoning of our opinion in this case makes it clear that each case is to be decided according to its own circumstances. The determination by the Superior Court in this case of the public interest and the equities between the parties will not be determinative of the rights of other parties to other petitions, concerning other parcels of real property, and this will be so even if the terms of the restrictive covenants are the same. Nor, in the consideration of the future welfare of the Back Bay area, should we overlook the comprehensive controls exerted by public laws concerning land use.

The final decree is reversed and the case is remanded to the Superior Court, where damages are to be assessed for the loss of benefit in light and air. . . . [T]he proposed construction may commence forthwith, before the issue of damages is resolved, with such provision for security for the respondents as the judge in his discretion deems appropriate. . . .

[Justice QUIRICO dissented, arguing that the covenantee could not be deprived of the benefits of the covenant except by "proper exercise of the power of eminent domain."]

Note on Statutory Limits on the Life of Covenants

1. *Questions about* Blakeley. Why did the developer seek a declaratory judgment? What risks would it (and its lenders) have run if it had simply started building the hotel annex, thereby forcing neighboring landowners to initiate legal action to enforce the covenants? (When a landowner brings a declaratory action to remove old covenants, one court has held that the Due Process Clause requires that the covenantees receive personal notice, not just notice by publication. Batinich v. Harvey, 277 N.W.2d 355 (Minn. 1979).)

Observe the statement in *Blakeley* that restrictions requiring setbacks and prohibiting mercantile uses are more vulnerable to evisceration by neighborhood change than are restrictions designed to protect light and air. Perhaps this distinction can be justified by the difference in transaction costs involved to reach bargained terminations. Bargaining to modify controls on neighborhood characteristics (including front-yard setbacks) is greatly hindered by the large number of concerned covenantees, any one of whom can scotch the modification by holding out. By contrast, only a few landowners are interested in any particular corridor of light and air along a side or rear yard. A court therefore has less reason to intervene in a dispute over one of these corridors because the parties are more likely to be able to bargain away an inefficient restriction. Cf. Waldrop v. Town of Brevard, 62 S.E.2d 512 (N.C. 1950) (doctrine of changed conditions does not apply to easements).

How is the problem in *Blakeley* similar to the problem of the appropriate remedy in a nuisance case? See pp. 528–36.

How should one construe the majority's statement that disputes over the termination of a covenant must be decided piecemeal — not only provision-by-provision, but also parcel-by-parcel? How many decisions would it take before a title insurer or mortgage lender would be confident that subdivision titles had been completely cleared?

The dissenting opinion implies that government agencies should eradicate obsolete covenants through exercise of the power of eminent domain. If that were done, landowners losing the benefit of covenants presumably would receive compensation from public coffers. The majority opinion, by contrast, calls for them to be compensated by neighbors who abridge the restrictions. Who should foot the bill — taxpayers or unshackled landowners?

2. *Modification and damages as remedies.* There is growing support for the Massachusetts approach reflected in *Blakeley*. In Professor Robinson's sample of 65 appellate cases, 9 mentioned damages as a possible remedy. Glen O. Robinson, Explaining Contingent Rights: The Puzzle of "Obsolete" Covenants, 91 Colum. L. Rev. 546, 549 n.10 (1991). Section 7.10 of the Restatement (Third) of Property — Servitudes (2000) calls for a court addressing an obsolete covenant to consider the possibilities of modification and award of damages to the covenantees. Would either of these remedies have been appropriate in *Cordogan*? On the merits of adjusting parties' remedies as conditions change, see Jay Weiser, The Real Estate Covenant as Commons: Incomplete Contract Remedies over Time, 13 S. Cal. Interdisc. L.J. 269 (2004); Abraham Bell & Gideon Parchomovsky, Pliability Rules, 101 Mich. L. Rev. 1 (2002).

3. *Statutes that address the issue of obsolete covenants.* Mass. Gen. Laws ch. 184, §27 (2004), enacted in 1961, provides that no restriction imposed after December 31, 1961, shall be enforceable after 30 years unless a notice of extension is recorded before the 30 years have expired; if a notice *is* recorded, there begins a new 20-year period, which in turn may be extended for additional 20-year periods. Compare La. Civ. Code Ann. art. 780 (West 2004), which, after a covenant scheme has been in effect for 15 years, empowers the owners of at least one-half of the burdened land area to record a document terminating the scheme.

A number of states have enacted statutes that either impose maximum limits on the duration of covenants or require a majority of beneficiaries to periodically record a reaffirmation to keep the covenants in force. By and large, these statutes have withstood constitutional challenge, including those based on an asserted impairment of the obligation of contracts. See, e.g., Amana Society v. Colony Inn, Inc., 315 N.W.2d 101 (Iowa 1982) (reviewing statute that limited enforcement of recorded use restrictions to maximum of 21 years); Manning v. New England Mutual Life Insurance Co., 506 N.E.2d 870 (Mass. 1987) (reviewing statute that required reaffirmation by beneficiaries).

Statutes that unconditionally limit the lives of covenants have fallen out of fashion. An old Georgia statute, now codified at Ga. Code Ann. §44-5-60(b) (2004), provides that "covenants restricting lands to certain uses shall not run for more than 20 years in municipalities [and counties] which have adopted zoning laws." The Georgia legislature has amended this section to exempt covenants in subdivisions of 15 or more lots.

See id. at §44-5-60(d). In 1982, Minnesota repealed a statute that had limited the lives of covenants to 20 years. See Haugen v. Peterson, 400 N.W.2d 723 (Minn. 1987) (on retrospective consequences of this repeal). Apparently, legislators increasingly embrace the view that covenants generally enhance, not impair, the value of land.

Consider the merits of a statute that, after 20 years, would limit the power to enforce a restrictive covenant to owners of lots located within 200 feet of the burdened lot. Cf. James L. Winokur, The Mixed Blessings of Promissory Servitudes, 1989 Wis. L. Rev. 1, 79–84 (proposing, after 20 years, devolution of enforcement to "pods" containing no more than 12 lots). See also Gerald Korngold, Resolving the Flaws of Residential Servitudes and Owners Associations, 1990 Wis. L. Rev. 513 (critiquing Winokur's proposal).

4. *Burying anachronisms?* Were the ancient barriers to the running of the burdens of covenants (principally the horizontal-privity-of-estate and touch-and-concern requirements) crude judicial attempts to limit the life of covenants? If so, can those old doctrines be regarded as obsolete now that termination systems have become better developed?

5.   *Conservation and Historic-Preservation Servitudes*

Prior to *Euclid*, some land use regulations provided for automatic landowner compensation for the costs of regulatory restrictions. See, e.g., Attorney General v. Williams, 55 N.E. 77 (Mass. 1899), which involved a Massachusetts statute that limited new buildings near Copley Square in Boston to a maximum height of 100 feet and required Boston to compensate any landowner damaged by the restriction. The early proponents of zoning were aware of the possibility of compensable regulation, but rejected it as impractical. See, e.g., Edward M. Bassett, Zoning 27 (1940):

> No effective zoning plan could be accomplished by the exercise of eminent domain. If there were some diminution of the full use of property, the city would need to pay the loss to the private owner. This would mean a laborious and expensive proceeding for almost every parcel of land.

See generally Donald G. Hagman, Compensable Regulation, 54 J. Urb. L. 45 (1976).

Nevertheless, governments and nonprofit organizations increasingly are acquiring in-gross covenants and easements that restrict activity on particularly prized lands such as farms (where they are scarce), forests, and historic structures. Why might a government make use of servitudes in these contexts, as opposed to the command-and-control regulations that Bassett favors? A regulation that compels above-normal conduct (such as the nondevelopment of agricultural land) is likely to be perceived as unfair. It thus can be expected to trigger strong political opposition and perhaps even a takings challenge. See pp. 134–97. A servitude arrangement, by contrast, typically provides some form of monetary relief to the burdened landowner. A farmer, for example, receives compensation when development rights are either purchased or condemned, but typically not when open-space zoning is imposed. In addition, a servitude arrangement can enable the precise tailoring of controls to a particular parcel and perhaps also the decentralization of enforcement responsibilities to a highly motivated nonprofit organization. On the other hand, as Bassett notes, a servitude arrangement may give rise to administrative costs greater than those associated with uncompensated regulation.

Since the early 1980s, most states have adopted detailed statutes governing conservation easements. About half of these are versions of the Uniform Conservation Easement

Act, approved in 1981 by the National Conference of Commissioners on Uniform State Laws.

1. *Creation*. The owner of the benefit of a conservation servitude usually acquires that interest either by purchase, gift, exercise of the power of eminent domain (assuming it possesses that power), or reservation of the interest at the time it conveys the underlying fee simple estate to the burdened transferee.

a. *Servitude acquisitions by governments*. A government may be able to acquire development rights through exercise of the power of eminent domain (a topic more fully covered in Chapter 10B). See, e.g., Kamrowski v. State, 142 N.W.2d 793 (Wis. 1966) (state acquisition of conservation easement was for public use). Some state statutes that authorize governmental purchase of scenic easements, however, decline to authorize the use of eminent domain for this purpose. See, e.g., Or. Rev. Stat. §271.725 (2004); Tenn. Code Ann. §11-15-103 (2004). Why might such a statute be politically popular?

In 1972, Suffolk County (on Long Island in New York State) initiated a well-publicized effort to preserve farmland by voluntarily purchasing development rights. For an overview, see Mark R. Rielly, Comment, Evaluating Farmland Protection Through Suffolk County, New York's Purchase of Development Rights Program, 18 Pace Envtl. L. Rev. 197 (2000). During the next decades, this government-purchase movement spread to other states, especially ones in the Northeast. See Thomas L. Daniels, The Purchase of Development Rights: Preserving Agricultural Land and Open Space, 57 J. Am. Plan. Ass'n 421 (1991). See also Chapter 10A (on state and local public lands). On the motivations that underlie these acquisition programs, see Jeffrey Kline & Dennis Wichelns, Using Referendum Data to Characterize Public Support for Purchasing Development Rights to Farmland, 70 Land Econ. 223 (1994). If a state has a purchase program, can the owner of a particular farm force the state to buy development rights? See Appeal of MacEachran, 438 A.2d 302 (N.H. 1981) (no).

A government also can reserve a servitude interest when it conveys land to a transferee. Professor Tondro regards disposition with restrictions as a promising tool for historic preservation. He recommends that, instead of directing reluctant owners to preserve aging structures, governments purchase historic buildings and then resell them subject to covenants assuring proper maintenance. See Terry Tondro, An Historic Preservation Approach to Municipal Rehabilitation of Older Neighborhoods, 8 Conn. L. Rev. 248 (1976).

During the mid-1970s, Wilmington, Delaware, developed a program of urban homesteading to dispose of some of the thousand abandoned houses with which it was saddled. After acquiring an abandoned house by tax sale, Wilmington offered to give it for free to anyone who would promise to renovate the building to code standards within 18 months and to stay in the house for at least three years. More than 20 other cities then adopted similar ordinances. Many urban homesteaders quickly found that the costs of rehabilitating an abandoned house exceeded the market value of the rehabilitated property. See generally Joshua A. Newberg, Anatomy of a Housing Program: Urban Homesteading in Theory and Practice, 8 J.L. & Pol'y 731 (1992); William A. Rohe, Expanding Urban Homesteading, 57 J. Am. Plan. Ass'n 444 (1991).

b. *Servitude acquisitions by private associations*. Some conservation organizations seek to purchase development rights. The Nature Conservancy, which strives to protect habitat on all continents, has been a leader in this effort. In 2001, the New England Forestry Foundation paid $28 million to acquire conservation easements burdening private forestland areas in northern Maine — huge tracts that together exceeded the area of Rhode Island. Carey Goldberg, Deal in Maine Prevents Development of Forestland, N.Y. Times, Mar. 21, 2001, at A12.

Land trusts, which now number more than 1,200 in North America, are nonprofit organizations whose main role is to accept donations of easements and other restrictions on development rights. See generally Richard Brower, Conservancy: The Land Trust Movement in America (2003). In return for a gift to a land trust, a landowner-donor can expect to reap a variety of tax benefits, including a charitable deduction and a reduction in property tax assessments. On the amount of the charitable deduction a taxpayer may take, see Browning v. Commissioner, 109 T.C. 303 (1997). Inflated appraisals, particularly of gifts of facade easements in tightly regulated historic districts, have been common and have begun to draw the wrath of federal lawmakers. See Josh Barbanel, Tax Breaks on Historic Houses Face Restrictions, N.Y. Times, Dec. 26, 2004, at §11, p.5.

2. *Scope and administration of servitudes.* Drafters of conservation servitudes confront complex issues. If a conservation organization desires to purchase a servitude restricting development on certain forestlands, for example, it could reduce its acquisition costs if the servitude were to expressly permit selective logging to continue. But how much logging, where, and in what manner? Should the servitude scheme also assure public access to some of the burdened land? If so, for what purposes? Particularly when an historic building is the subject of a servitude, a drafter may want to consider imposing affirmative covenants that obligate the fee owner to maintain the premises. For case studies of actual servitudes, see Protecting the Land: Conservation Easements Past, Present, and Future (Julie Ann Gustanski & Roderick H. Squires eds., 2000); James Boyd et al., The Law and Economics of Habitat Conservation: Lessons from an Analysis of Easement Acquisitions, 19 Stan. Envtl. L.J. 209 (2000).

What sort of organization is best qualified to monitor compliance by the owner-occupant of the burdened land? Will a nonprofit usually monitor more effectively than a government? A small organization more effectively than a large one?

3. *Termination.* Many conservation servitudes are expressly intended to last forever. Section §2(c) of Uniform Conservation Easement Act (1981) provides that unlimited duration is to be implied in the absence of an express provision to the contrary. Moreover, §§7.10–7.11 of the Restatement (Third) of Property — Servitudes (2000) exempt conservation servitudes from the usual changed-conditions doctrine. Section 7.11 authorizes their termination only in more limited circumstances, such as when "the servitude can no longer be used to accomplish any conservation purpose." In addition, the Restatement commonly calls for the owner of the burdened estate, after termination, to compensate the owner of the beneficial interest.

As decades pass, will today's conservation servitudes increasingly raise the specter of excessive dead-hand control? For the argument that they will, see Julia D. Mahoney, Perpetual Restrictions on Land and the Problem of the Future, 88 Va. L. Rev. 739 (2002). Mahoney stresses the limits of human foresight and contends that many observers exaggerate the irreversibility of development. Given that a government can exercise the power of eminent domain to acquire the rights of servitude enforcers, how serious are the rigidities that concern Mahoney?

D. Residential Community Associations

1. Functions and Structure

Note on Private Governments

1. *Functions performed.* Nahrstedt, excerpted at p. 554, introduced the residential community association, a private government that a developer may choose to create for

home purchasers. Such an association typically performs three major functions. First, its elected board of directors manages and maintains the common areas the developer has deeded to it — for example, streets, sidewalks, and parking areas; recreational facilities such as swimming pools and tennis courts; and open space. In carrying out this function, the board may delegate authority to association officers elected by the board, to various appointed committees, or (increasingly) to a property management firm hired to relieve association members of the headaches of day-to-day supervision.

Second, the association promulgates and enforces regulations on member behavior, such as the harboring of pets and the alteration of the exterior appearance of an individual unit.

Third, the association's board of directors is empowered to levy assessments enforceable by lien on a member's individual unit. Other income may be derived from user fees — perhaps from those who use recreational facilities — and from fines imposed on members. Association revenues are dispensed to defray the costs of maintaining and improving common areas, to compensate the property management firm, and to cover any other administrative costs of the association. The directors, officers, and committee members of a residential community association usually serve without pay. In many associations, volunteers to take on these roles are in short supply. See Edwin McDowell, Looking for a Few Good Board Members, N.Y. Times, Mar. 10, 2002, at §11, p.1.

2. *History*. Among the earliest common interest developments in the United States were New York's Gramercy Park (1831), Boston's Louisburg Square (1844), and San Francisco's South Park (1852). In 1960, there were fewer than 500 associations apart from New York co-ops. During the 1960s, all states enacted enabling legislation for condominium ownership. By 1970, there were 10,000 associations. See Common Interest Communities 7–11 (Stephen E. Barton & Carol J. Silverman eds., 1994). Growth was even more explosive thereafter. In California in the late 1980s, 40 percent of new for-sale housing units came coupled with a residential community association, with the proportion exceeding 80 percent in Orange County. Id. at 12. In 2003, the Community Associations Institute (CAI) estimated that there were 249,000 associations in the United States, containing an average of about 80 housing units each. Together these associations housed 50 million people. CAI estimated that 1.25 million Americans were serving on association boards. For an update, visit http://www.caionline.org/about/facts.cfm.

Residential associations vary greatly. Some are gated enclaves for the wealthy. In 2001, 7 million occupied American dwelling units were located in communities (including high-rise buildings) to which access was limited by walls or fences. Statistical Abstract 2003, at 629. These associations have drawn the wrath of the sharpest critics. See Edward J. Blakely & Mary Gail Snyder, Fortress America: Gated Communities in the United States (1997); Setha Low, Behind the Gates: Life, Security, and the Pursuit of Happiness in Fortress America (2003). Far more common are small condominium projects inhabited by residents of modest wealth. Idealistic innovators who wish to create new living environments also have tended to create associations. Developers of new towns and New Urbanist communities have done so. So have promoters of cohousing arrangements, which contemplate separate ownership of housing units but typically obligate members to contribute labor toward group meals in a common house. See Kathryn McCamant & Charles Durrett, Cohousing (2d ed. 1994); Mark Fenster, Community by Covenant, Process, and Design: Cohousing and the Contemporary Common Interest Community, 15 J. Land Use & Envtl. L. 3 (1999).

Robert Jay Dilger, Neighborhood Politics: Residential Community Associations in American Governance (1992), summarizes national evidence about the operations of homeowners associations. In 1990, over 90 percent of associations were caring for lawns and trees in common areas; about 50 percent were maintaining streets and sidewalks; and about 33 percent were providing recreational facilities. Id. at 20–27.

Barton and Silverman provide a profile of residential community associations in California as of 1987. They found that 92 percent of the associations provided open space or lawns; 58 percent, a swimming facility; and 15 percent, an entry guard or security patrol. The great majority of associations consisted of either townhouses or apartments. Most of these were organized as condominium associations; residential cooperative corporations, which are rare outside New York City, represented only 1 percent. Some 18 percent of the associations consisted entirely of detached houses; in most of these developments, members separately owned the houses and the association owned and managed the common areas. The median size of associations was 43 units, and over time, the trend in size has been downward. Barton and Silverman mention that some local governments in California require a developer to create an association. This municipal policy can benefit taxpayers in existing neighborhoods who enjoy, for example, city-financed recreation facilities or trash removal services, but don't have to help finance equivalent services in new developments. See generally Common Interest Communities, supra, at 3–12.

3. *Legal structure.* The sections Jan Krasnowiecki contributed to the Homes Association Handbook (1966) became a primary source for attorneys engaged in forming these entities. Krasnowiecki recommends that such associations (1) be incorporated, (2) be non-profit in character, and (3) issue memberships as opposed to stock. See Homes Association Handbook 338–41 (1966). What rules of corporate law might have induced Krasnowiecki to make these recommendations? (Consider the desirability of limitations on personal liability of association officials and the savings that would result from avoiding blue-sky laws governing the issuance of securities.)

Most states have enacted detailed statutes that govern the formation and structure of residential community associations. Many of these are patterned after the Uniform Common Interest Ownership Act (UCIOA), promulgated in 1982 and amended in 1994. See also Restatement (Third) of Property — Servitudes ch. 6 (2000) (addressing common interest communities).

4. *Communitywide associations.* Between roughly 1965 and 1975, there was great academic and entrepreneurial interest in so-called new towns — grandly scaled private developments designed to offer the entire range of urban land uses. The creators of the most celebrated of these towns — Reston, Virginia, and Columbia, Maryland — chose to establish complex systems of private government based on a federal model. Each homeowner was made a member of a local association that provided services to the immediate village or cluster. A homeowner also was automatically made a member of a larger (and distinct) association, whose jurisdiction encompassed the entire new town and which was responsible for communitywide services. In some instances, renters were eligible to become members of these associations. See generally Fred Foldvary, Public Goods and Private Communities 186–87 (1994); Note, Democracy in the New Towns: The Limits of Private Government, 36 U. Chi. L. Rev. 379 (1969).

5. *Shopping centers.* Common interest communities also appear in nonresidential contexts. For example, the developer of a shopping center may convey to major storeowners fee simple interests in not only their particular tracts but also in portions of adjoining parking areas. To create an institution to coordinate management of the center, the developer may record a declaration of covenants and also a reciprocal easement agreement (calling, for example, for shared use of the parking areas). These documents typically impose use restrictions, provide for architectural review by member stores, and authorize members to amend the rules and regulations. See generally Thomas J. Terkel, Reciprocal Agreements in Shopping Center Developments, 14 St. Mary's L.J. 541 (1983).

2.   *Developer-Homeowner Relations in a New Community*

Homebuyers in a new community commonly become angry with its creator. They may be disappointed by both the slowness of the developer's progress and the quality of previous and ongoing construction. Continuing developer domination of a private government can be another source of buyer resentment. Therefore, before turning to the role of residential community associations in implementing private land use controls, this subchapter treats the land use disputes that are likely to arise during the transition from developer to resident control.

Tobin v. Paparone Construction Co.

7349 A.2d 574 (N.J. Super. Ct. Law Div. 1975)

KING, J.S.C. . . .

Plaintiffs Leo Tobin and his wife (Tobin) seek equitable and legal relief from defendants, each of whom they allege are responsible for the construction and presence of a tennis court on their adjacent neighbor's property. The side fence of this 106' × 50' court comes to within one foot of plaintiffs' property line. The court is surrounded by a 10'-high chain link fence. . . .

On October 12, 1973, Tobin agreed in writing to buy a lot and new home for $54,000 in this affluent Cherry Hill development from defendant Paparone, the builder and developer. The agreement of sale was not recorded. Settlement on the Tobin property (1918 Country Club Drive) was concluded on March 25, 1974, and Tobin took immediate occupancy. By deed dated December 6, 1973, defendant Paparone had previously conveyed to defendants Shefter the adjoining lot and house (1916 Country Club Drive). Defendants Shefter, with defendant Paparone's encouragement and assistance, had their house constructed in a special position on the lot to allow room for the construction of a tennis court. The testimony indicates that Paparone used the tennis court feature as an inducement to Shefter in order to sell him the lot and house. However, Paparone never disclosed the plans for a tennis court to Tobin during his negotiations. The conveyances made by Paparone to Tobin and to Shefter were subject to several declarations of restrictions not recited in their deeds but properly recorded in prior deeds. Both residents deny knowledge of the restrictive covenants because they were not recited in the deed and no report of title was provided at settlement. Neither buyer was represented by counsel during the negotiations for purchase or at final settlement.

On March 22, 1974, three days before Tobin settled and took possession, defendant Shefter filed a petition with the zoning board of adjustment requesting a variance to permit construction of a tennis court to within one foot of the common boundary line, and also to obtain relief from fence height requirements (six feet maximum) to permit a ten-foot fence. Defendant Paparone was served with notice of the Shefter petition for variance on March 27, 1974, two days after closing on Tobin's property. The hearing was scheduled for April 9, 1974. The Tobins were never served with any notice as they were not record owners on March 22, 1974, the date the variance application was filed. Paparone did not notify Tobin of the notice of application for variance, nor did he oppose the application for variance. The unopposed application for variance was granted by the zoning board on the hearing date of April 9, 1974. . . .

During July 1974 defendant Shefter installed the tennis court and fence. Plaintiffs filed this suit on August 29, 1974, after the court was completed. . . .

Tobin properly relied on Paparone's representations as to the character of the surrounding neighborhood. Paparone's silence created a mistaken impression on the part of the purchaser which operated to induce the purchaser to buy. This silence was a fraudulent representation and a failure of an implicit condition of sale. . . .

The court finds that Tobin has a cause of action against Paparone. Tobin was damaged in his reasonable contractual expectations by Paparone's conduct in (1) encouraging Shefter in his desire to acquire a property particularly suitable for the installation of a tennis court, (2) failing to reveal Shefter's plans for the tennis court to Tobin, (3) failing to provide copies of the deed restrictions to either property owner at settlement and failing itself to enforce the covenants, and (4) failing to furnish Tobin with the notice of the application for variance which Paparone received two days after Tobin's settlement. We find no wrongdoing or inequitable conduct on Shefter's part and find that Tobin has no cause for action against him, either equitable or legal.

The question of remedy now arises. Tobin's prayer for rescission of the contract of sale has been abandoned. Equity cannot here require the removal of the tennis court. Shefter's conduct was wholly conscientious and he now has $16,000 invested in the tennis court. Upon inspection of the property, with the parties' permission, the court feels that an award of money damages in favor of Tobin and against Paparone is a suitable and adequate remedy. . . . Tobin is awarded damages of $5000 against Paparone, the sum of the cost of [landscaping to screen the court and] the residual loss of value. . . .

Note on Protecting Purchasers' Expectations About Community Quality

1. *A fiduciary duty?* See Uriel Reichman, Residential Private Governments, 43 U. Chi. L. Rev. 253, 291–300 (1976), for the recommendation that the developer of a new community be judged according to the fiduciary standards applicable to a trustee administering trust property. UCIOA §3-103(a) (1994) imposes this standard on an association's developer-appointed directors and officers. Did Paparone violate duties of care and loyalty to Tobin?

2. *Problem.* The Panglossian Development Company owns a tract of 3,000 acres outside a major city. It intends to build a major community to house a population of 15,000. Panglossian's planners envision a town center on a lake, a championship golf course, a regional shopping center, neighborhood day care centers, and so on. They have commissioned artistic renderings and scale models that suggest the beauty and vibrancy of the finished community. If all goes well, the planners believe this final stage will be achieved within ten years.

Panglossian's executives wish to use these renderings and models to help market the residential and commercial space in the first sections to be built. However, they are less optimistic than their planners that the original scheme will prove to be economically viable. The executives remember that the dreams of Robert E. Simon, the developer of Reston, Virginia, proved to be unrealistic, and that his financier and successor, the Gulf Oil Corporation, had to amend them. These executives want to retain the flexibility to change the mix of housing units, to use the golf course site for an industrial park, or, indeed, to cease development short of completion.

What legal risks would Panglossian run if it were to make use of the artists' renderings and scale models to promote its initial sales? Could it employ written disclaimers to minimize these risks? How should an attorney phrase a disclaimer? Consider the cases that follow.

In Ute Park Summer Homes Association v. Maxwell Land Grant Co., 494 P.2d 971 (N.M. 1972), the developer had prepared a plat map for a recreational subdivision. The map designated a certain area as "Golf Course, Tennis Court, and Club House." Although this map was never recorded (or referred to in purchasers' deeds), the developer's agents used the map to promote sales and said that the developer would devote the area to those uses. The developer later sought to sell the designated area without restrictions. The New Mexico Supreme Court affirmed the trial court's decree restricting the disputed area to recreational uses. Compare Cogburn v. Holness, 237 S.E.2d 905 (N.C. Ct. App. 1977) (holding that lot purchasers' rights are determined by recorded deeds and plats, not developer's advertising).

In White Cypress Lakes Development Corp. v. Hertz, 541 So. 2d 1031 (Miss. 1989), a large project had been developed in phases, each of which was burdened by covenants whose benefits did not expressly run to lands in the other phases. Promotional materials touted the entire development as a place of "quality." After many high-quality homes had been built, a successor to the original developer sought to use land in two of the remaining phases for a park for recreational vehicles. According to the Mississippi court:

> The more serious question is whether Plaintiff homeowners have a right to relief in the form of injunctive enforcement of the covenants in Mallard Point, Phases V and VI, when none of the plaintiffs own property in either of those two subdivisions. The development company's point . . . is that the entire White Cypress Lakes development has been divided into thirteen separate and legally distinct subdivisions and that no property owner has any right to enforce the covenants outside the particular subdivision where that person owns property. Immediately prior to trial, the development company did indeed own all lots in Mallard Point, Phases V and VI, and had then pending before the court a petition to vacate the plat in these two subdivisions.
>
> The record before us is replete with evidence that the development company and, more particularly, its predecessor in title, substantially induced purchasers including these Plaintiffs to believe that all lots in the entire White Cypress Lakes development area would be used solely for single family homes located upon lots of at least one acre in size. ". . . [Q]uality will surround [you]" [to quote from the promotional materials]. On these facts the development company is equitably estopped from using the lands in Mallard Point, Phases V and VI, in a manner inconsistent with the general representations it and its predecessors made in marketing the lots in the other phases of the White Cypress Lakes development.

Jan Z. Krasnowiecki, Townhouses with Homes Associations: A New Perspective
123 U. Pa. L. Rev. 711, 742-43 (1975)

The Homes Association Handbook proposed that the developer retain a 3 to 1 voting superiority over the residents until the total outstanding votes of the residents equal the total outstanding votes of the developer. Since the votes were based on the number of lots, the developer would lose control when seventy-five percent had been sold. To prevent the developer from using his voting control to make changes adverse to the interests of the residents, the Handbook proposed that the developer votes be placed in a separate class. This would enable the draftsman to specify in the covenants which issues would require the assent of the majority of both classes and which could be determined by a simple majority of the entire voting membership. In this way, some issues could not be decided by either the developer or the residents alone. On these issues, each class would, in effect, have a veto power over the proposed action of the other. The Handbook proposed that critical issues such as increases in the maximum assessment, diversion of any existing common areas or facilities to some other use, and additions that substantially depart from the "general plan" should require the assent of both classes of voters. On the other hand, election of directors and daily operations would remain subject to the voting superiority of the developer.

I hold no brief for the 3 to 1 formula. On the contrary, in larger projects where a two-tier association system should be employed, I believe that the developer should be allowed to retain control over the central association until he completes the entire project. On the other hand, in the neighborhood association the developer may have less at stake and an earlier relinquishment of control makes some sense.

Doesn't like

Note on the Transfer of Control of a Residential Community Association from the Developer to Unit Owners

1. *Troubled passage.* Consider this sentence from Wayne S. Hyatt & James B. Rhoads, Concepts of Liability in the Development and Administration of Condominium and Home Owners Associations, 12 Wake Forest L. Rev. 915, 916 (1976):

> A reflection of the wry humor that regrettably is part of current condominium developments is the statement that upon turnover of the association to the unit owners, the first three things they do are raise the assessment, fire the manager, and sue the developer.

2. *Stacking votes.* Like the Homes Association Handbook, UCIOA §3-103(d) (1994) endorses transfer of control to purchasers after three-quarters of the units have been sold, and in any event two years after the developer has ceased to offer units for sale in the ordinary course of business.

Why permit a developer to retain three votes for every unit not yet sold, when purchasers of units receive only one vote per unit? Consider the risk that purchasers will employ an association's rulemaking powers to unduly strengthen their bargaining position against the developer. Suppose, for example, that some purchasers are disgruntled about the quality of the developer's postclosing fix-up work on their houses. If purchasers could gain control of the association before the developer had completed all units in the development, they could threaten to regulate the permitted hours of construction activity. Does this scenario help explain why a developer is apt to divide a large project into sections in which votes are separately counted? See generally Roger D. Winston & Timothy P. Martin, Transition of Homeowners Association Control: The Developer's Perspective, 15 Prob. & Prop. 15 (Sept.-Oct. 2001).

3. *Abuse of the developer's voting power.* If permitted, a development company might misuse its early domination of a residential community association in countless ways. Among them:

(a)   Unfavorable long-term management contracts or leases that association officers (elected by developer votes) enter into with business entities in which the developer has a financial interest;

(b)   Decisions by a developer-controlled board of directors to waive possible claims arising from defects in the conditions of the common areas deeded to it; and

(c)   Manipulation of architectural controls to require use of materials manufactured by subsidiaries of the conglomerate corporation of which the developer is a part.

These sorts of developer abuses, common in the early days of condominium development, now are vulnerable to legal attack on many grounds. See, e.g., UCIOA §3-105 (1994) (on long-term and self-dealing contracts); Restatement (Third) of Property — Servitudes §§6.19–6.21 (2000) (and sources cited in notes following those sections).

Note on a Developer's Retention of Discretionary Powers

1. *Reasons for continuing developer involvement.* On occasion, a developer will draft covenants that vest powers of architectural review and covenant amendment not in the association but in the developer entity itself. This arrangement spares the expense of legal fees to set up an association and may safeguard neighboring lands that the developer retains.

2. *Architectural review by a developer.* Jones v. Northwest Real Estate Co., 131 A. 446 (Md. 1925), was the first in a line of cases to uphold the enforceability of architectural review by a developer entity. These cases uniformly require, however, that the developer exercise its power reasonably and in good faith. In Donoghue v. Prynnwood Corp., 255 N.E.2d 326 (Mass. 1970), the subdivider had refused to approve plans for a "one-story, modern-style, square-shaped, flat-roofed" house projected to cost at least $130,000. He claimed he had a personal dislike for flat roofs, but mainly noted that some neighbors, friends of his, had vehemently objected to the proposed structure. The court held his refusal to be unreasonable, especially since the trial court had found that the house would not be detrimental to the neighborhood. Should a court scrutinize architectural review by a developer more carefully than it does architectural review by a municipality or residential community association? Compare pp. 489–94 and 593–96.

3. *A developer's power to amend.* What if the development firm includes in the declaration a provision that entitles it to amend the covenants unilaterally? Some courts have held that if a developer retains the power to modify a restriction (e.g., on front-yard setbacks), there is no general scheme with regard to that restriction, and therefore the lot owners cannot enforce it among themselves, even if the developer has not exercised its power to modify. See, e.g., Suttle v. Bailey, 361 P.2d 325 (N.M. 1961).

This doctrine, which invites developer fraud, was explicitly rejected in Nelle v. Loch Haven Homeowners' Association, 413 So. 2d 28 (Fla. 1982). More recent authorities require that a developer exercise any retained right to amend only to advance the general purposes of the covenant scheme. See Wright v. Cypress Shores Development Co., 413 So. 2d 1115 (Ala. 1982); Flamingo Ranch Estates, Inc. v. Sunshine Ranches Homeowners, Inc., 303 So. 2d 665 (Fla. Dist. Ct. App. 1974). See also Restatement (Third) of Property — Servitudes §6.21 (2000) (stressing importance of whether purchasers were fairly apprised of risk of that particular amendment when they bought).

4. *A developer's power to veto amendments.* In the mid-1990s, the Disney Corporation started development of Celebration, Florida, a New Urbanist community located at the fringe of Disney World. Disney created a residential community association, but reserved to itself special powers to control the physical character of Celebration and to veto amendments members otherwise might make to the declaration and rules. According to one observer:

> . . . Disney seems to have set in motion two powerful forces that are bound sooner or later to collide. They have built a most impressive landscape of community — a place expressly designed to encourage neighbors to engage one another, to form associations and acquire the "civic virtues" — yet they have built it atop a subsoil of authoritarianism, which limits participation to only the most trivial matters of that community's business.

Michael Pollan, Town-Building Is No Mickey Mouse Operation, N.Y. Times Magazine, Dec. 14, 1997, at 56, 88. In 2004, Disney sold all its interests in Celebration to Lexin Capital, a real estate investment firm. Should implicit fiduciary obligations limit how Disney and its successors exercise veto powers? See also pp. 598–601.

3. *Judicial Review of Residential Community Associations*

Once the developer has left the scene, the functions of architectural review and management of common areas fall into the hands of unit owners. A variety of association actions may aggrieve a member who was content with the original declaration of covenants. There may be procedural controversies, perhaps stemming from high-handed tactics by incumbent members of the elected governing board. An adjudicative action, such as an architectural review committee's denial of a member's application for permission to alter, may raise hackles. A member may bridle at a new substantive rule that the governing board has adopted — for example, a ban on bringing liquor to the swimming pool. What prospect does a member have of obtaining judicial relief in any of these instances?

Basic contract law entitles a member to compel an association to adhere to a valid rule set out in the declaration and other governing documents. (See Nahrstedt v. Lakeside Village Condominium Association, 878 P.2d 1275 (Cal. 1994), excerpted at p. 554, on tests for the validity of declaration rules.) In Pertzsch v. Upper Oconomowoc Lake Association, 635 N.W.2d 829 (Wis. Ct. App. 2001), the association's covenants stated that "a boat house may be permitted with consent of the Architectural Control Committee." The court held that this language prevented the association from following a policy of refusing to allow the construction of *any* detached boathouse.

In addition, in many states a member can turn to one or more detailed statutes governing the structure and operation of associations. See, e.g., Cal. Civ. Code §§1350–1376 (West 2004) (applicable to a variety of common interest developments); Fla. Stat. §§718.101–718.618 (2004) (Florida Condominium Act). Some state statutes are patterned after UCIOA (1994), which addresses most of the pertinent issues. See also Restatement (Third) of Property — Servitudes ch. 6 (2000). For a comprehensive overview, see Stewart E. Sterk, Minority Protection in Residential Private Governments, 77 B.U. L. Rev. 273 (1997). For a superb account of how courts intervene in the affairs of all types of private associations, and how they try to rationalize their interventions, see Developments in the Law — Judicial Control of Actions of Private Associations, 76 Harv. L. Rev. 983 (1963).

a.   *Legal Constraints on Association Structure and Procedures*

Allocation of voting rights. The Supreme Court's voting-rights cases generally require a municipality to entitle each adult resident citizen to one vote. See Avery v. Midland County, 390 U.S. 474 (1968). Property owners associations seldom allocate votes in this fashion. Some state statutes compel an association to follow a specific ownership-based voting scheme, such as one vote per unit, one vote per square foot of floor area, or one vote per dollar of assessed valuation. See, e.g., Ky. Rev. Stat. Ann. §381.810(9) (West 2004) (owners of condominium units have votes in proportion to floor area). Most statutes, however, empower a developer drafting a declaration to choose a voting formula. See, e.g., Conn. Gen. Stat. §§47-74, 47-80(b) (2004) (condominium act). When given this power, developers almost invariably confer votes on the basis of unit ownership, an approach that fails to enfranchise tenants. In addition, like a shareholder in a corporation, an owner of multiple units in an association typically has multiple votes.

Why might a prospective purchaser balk at a scheme that enfranchised tenants? See Robert C. Ellickson, Cities and Homeowners Associations, 130 U. Pa. L. Rev. 1519, 1539–63 (1982) (comparing voting schemes in municipalities and associations). Can market forces be counted on to give rise to appropriate vote allocations? If the formula were to be one vote per unit, what should happen if a married couple were to own a unit concurrently and were to disagree on an issue?

Electoral and governance procedures. Courts and legislatures may seek to regulate an association's elections and internal procedures. One New York court, when asked to supervise an association's electoral process, prohibited electioneering near the polling place and decreed procedures for the preparation of voting lists, the appointment of election inspectors, and the opening of the ballot box. Patrick J. Rohan & Melvin A. Reskin, Condominium Law and Practice 48–49 (Supp. June 1976). What if a minority faction complains of majority shenanigans at meetings? See Cal. Civ. Code §1363(d) (West 2004): "Meetings of the membership of the association should be conducted in accordance with a recognized system of parliamentary procedure or any parliamentary procedures the association may adopt." UCIOA §3-108 (1994) requires a governing board to meet at least once a year and to publicize in advance the meeting time, place, and agenda.

Constitutional constraints. When an association's activities constitute "state action," it is constrained by the Fourteenth Amendment and perhaps other federal and state constitutional clauses. As explained in Katherine Rosenberry, The Application of the Federal and State Constitutions to Condominiums, Cooperatives, and Planned Developments, 19 Real Prop. Prob. & Tr. J. 1 (1984), the Supreme Court has developed two basic tests. First, state action is present when there is a symbiotic relationship between a nominally private entity and a government. See, e.g., Park Redlands Covenant Control Committee v. Simon, 226 Cal. Rptr. 199 (Ct. App. 1986) (covenant restricting age of occupants constituted state action because city had conditioned development approval on developer's imposition of this covenant). Second, state action is present when an association is serving a public function. Cf. Laguna Publishing Co. v. Golden-Rain Foundation, 182 Cal. Rptr. 813 (Ct. App. 1982) (holding that corporation owning common areas of walled and gated retirement community with population of 20,000 was a "state actor" for state constitutional purposes when it prohibited circulation of giveaway newspaper).

If a residential community association's activities are held to constitute state action, does it necessarily follow that

(a) Votes have to be allocated to members according to the "one-person, one-vote" principle (as noted, a system that virtually no association follows)?

(b) Outsiders have to be given access to common areas?

(c) Applicants for architectural review have the right to call witnesses, cross-examine opposing witnesses, and receive a written opinion?

(d) Substantive rules regarding behavior in common areas are subject to a substantive due process test?

Might a court find state action for some purposes but not for others?

Some scholars argue that public law standards are inherently ill suited for ordinary property owners associations. See, e.g., Robert G. Natelson, Consent, Coercion, and "Reasonableness" in Private Law, 51 Ohio St. L.J. 41, 49–50 (1990). But cf. David J. Kennedy, Note, Residential Associations as State Actors, 105 Yale L.J. 761 (1995) (arguing that case for finding state action is strong when *nonmembers* are challenging association policy).

b. Judicial Review of Association Decisions

Levandusky v. One Fifth Avenue Apartment Corp.
553 N.E.2d 1317 (N.Y. 1990)

KAYE, Judge.

[Levandusky, an ex-president of his residential cooperative's board of directors, desired to enlarge his kitchen. He informed the board that this renovation would require him to relocate by a slight distance one of the two-inch steam risers that served the building. Advised by an engineer that the relocation of old piping was risky, the board denied approval to carry out the project. Levandusky went ahead anyway and brought this action to prevent the board from interfering with the renovation.

It is apparent . . . that a standard for judicial review of the actions of a cooperative or condominium governing board must be sensitive to a variety of concerns — sometimes competing concerns. Even when the governing board acts within the scope of its authority, some check on its potential powers to regulate residents' conduct, life-style and property rights is necessary to protect individual residents from abusive exercise, notwithstanding that the residents have, to an extent, consented to be regulated and even selected their representatives (see Note, The Rule of Law in Residential Associations, 99 Harv. L. Rev. 472 (1985)). At the same time, the chosen standard of review should not undermine the purposes for which the residential community and its governing structure were formed: protection of the interest of the entire community of residents in an environment managed by the board for the common benefit.

We conclude that these goals are best served by a standard of review that is analogous to the business judgment rule applied by courts to determine challenges to decisions made by corporate directors. . . .

Developed in the context of commercial enterprises, the business judgment rule prohibits judicial inquiry into actions of corporate directors "taken in good faith and in the exercise of honest judgment in the lawful and legitimate furtherance of corporate purposes." Auerbach v. Bennett, 393 N.E.2d 994, 1000 (N.Y. 1979). So long as the corporation's directors have not breached their fiduciary obligation to the corporation, "the exercise of [their powers] for the common and general interests of the corporation may not be questioned, although the results show that what they did was unwise or inexpedient." Pollitz v. Wabash R.R., 100 N.E. 721, 724 (N.Y. 1912). . . .

In reaching this conclusion, we reject the test seemingly applied by the Appellate Division majority and explicitly applied by Supreme Court in its initial decision. That inquiry was directed at the reasonableness of the board's decision; having itself found that relocation of the riser posed no "dangerous aspect" to the building, the Appellate Division concluded that the renovation should remain. . . .

. . . The difference between the reasonableness test and the rule we adopt is twofold. First — unlike the business judgment rule, which places on the owner seeking review the burden to demonstrate a breach of the board's fiduciary duty — reasonableness review requires the board to demonstrate that its decision was reasonable. Second, although in practice a certain amount of deference appears to be accorded to board decisions, reasonableness review permits — indeed, in theory requires — the court itself to evaluate the merits or wisdom of the board's decision (see, e.g., Hidden Harbour Estates v. Basso, 393 So. 2d 637, 640 (Fla. Dist. Ct. App.)), just as the Appellate Division did in the present case.

The more limited judicial review embodied in the business judgment rule is preferable. In the context of the decisions of a for-profit corporation, "courts are ill equipped and infrequently called on to evaluate what are and must be essentially business judgments . . . by definition the responsibility for business judgments must rest with the corporate directors; their individual capabilities and experience peculiarly qualify them for the discharge of that responsibility." (Auerbach v. Bennett, 393 N.E.2d, supra, at 1000.) Even if decisions of a cooperative board do not generally involve expertise beyond the usual ken of the judiciary, at the least board members will possess experience of the peculiar needs of their building and its residents not shared by the court.

Several related concerns persuade us that such a rule should apply here. As this case exemplifies, board decisions concerning what residents may or may not do with their living space may be highly charged and emotional. A cooperative or condominium is by nature

handwritten margin note: A contrary rule would threaten the stability of the common living arrangement

a myriad of often competing views regarding personal living space, and decisions taken to benefit the collective interest may be unpalatable to one resident or another, creating the prospect that board decisions will be subjected to undue court involvement and judicial second-guessing. Allowing an owner who is simply dissatisfied with particular board action a second opportunity to reopen the matter completely before a court, which — generally without knowing the property — may or may not agree with the reasonableness of the board's determination, threatens the stability of the common living arrangement.

Moreover, the prospect that each board decision may be subjected to full judicial review hampers the effectiveness of the board's managing authority. The business judgment rule protects the board's business decisions and managerial authority from indiscriminate attack. At the same time, it permits review of improper decisions, as when the challenger demonstrates that the board's action has no legitimate relationship to the welfare of the cooperative, deliberately singles out individuals for harmful treatment, is taken without notice or consideration of the relevant facts, or is beyond the scope of the board's authority. . . .

[Applying the approach it had articulated, the court held that the trial judge properly had dismissed Levandusky's petition for relief.]

handwritten margin note: Dismiss suit.

Note on Judicial Review of Association Decisionmaking

1. *Standard of review.* The analysis in *Levandusky* is consistent with the position advocated in an influential student note, Jeffrey A. Goldberg, Note, Community Association Use Restrictions: Applying the Business Judgment Doctrine, 64 Chi.-Kent L. Rev. 653 (1988). See also Lamden v. La Jolla Shores Clubdominium Homeowners Association, 980 P.2d 940 (Cal. 1999) (holding association's decision on how to treat termite infestation should be reviewed deferentially, although not literally according to a "business judgment rule"). But see Restatement (Third) of Property — Servitudes §6.13(1)(c) (2000) (requiring an association to "act reasonably in the exercise of its discretionary powers including rulemaking, enforcement, and design-control powers").

2. *Decisions to alter a portion of the common area.* In Amoruso v. Board of Managers, 330 N.Y.S.2d 107 (App. Div. 1972), the plaintiffs were challenging a condominium board's approval of construction of a basketball court in the common area near their units. The court held that the board's decision had been reasonable and that the board was empowered to build the court without obtaining the consent of affected owners. Was it also reasonable for the board not to have compensated the immediate neighbors? See also Schaefer v. Eastman Community Association, 836 A.2d 752 (N.H. 2003) (holding that association's decision to close ski area at recreational community met reasonableness standard).

3. *Architectural review.* As *Levandusky* suggests, association decisions about individual members' proposed building projects are particularly likely to generate controversy. An association may appoint a special review committee to carry out this function. On the general topic of association design review, see the comments and notes following §6.9 of the Restatement (Third) of Property — Servitudes (2000).

Town & Country Estates Association v. Slater
740 P.2d 668 (Mont. 1987)

TURNAGE, Chief Justice. . . .
Town & Country Estates Association (TCE) is a subdivision in Billings, Montana. TCE contains sixteen single-family houses, one duplex, and several vacant lots. The deeds

to the TCE lots incorporate by reference a "Declaration of Covenants, Conditions and Restrictions," which was publicly recorded on December 20, 1973.

The Declaration, in Article V, grants architectural control to the DRC (Design Review Committee) and outlines relevant aesthetic factors.

> No residential . . . structure . . . shall be made . . . upon the Properties . . . until plans and specifications showing the nature, kind, shape, height, materials, colors and location of the same shall have been submitted to and approved in writing as to *harmony of external design*, location and relation to surrounding structures and topography, the construction, colors, and the materials to be used in the construction have been approved in writing by a Design Review Committee consisting of five members appointed by the Board of Directors of Town & Country Estates Association. (Emphasis added.)

Article V does not place a minimum value on TCE houses, which vary in size, shape, color, building materials, and architectural style. However, the TCE houses all have a minimum of 2,400 square feet and shake roofs.

Prior to 1986, all TCE houses had either been built or approved by the developer of the subdivision. In early 1986, the Slaters expressed an interest in a TCE lot. They were aware of the prior approval restriction of Article V. In April of 1986, they learned that the developer had left the area, and that a five-member DRC was being formed to review Slaters' house plan. The plan was the first to be reviewed by the newly-formed DRC. Slaters' proposed house had a shake roof, wood siding, and 2,600 square feet of living space.

On May 1, 1986, Slaters bought the TCE lot before receiving approval of their house plan. On May 19, 1986, Slaters received a letter from DRC rejecting Slaters' plan because the house did not "conform to the general tone of the area." The letter also stated, "We would suggest that the price of the lot commands a residence more near the size of houses in the surrounding area. As you know, the neighborhood consists of $200,000 plus homes, and this is the kind of conformity that you should look to." Without approval, Slaters began house construction on August 5, 1986.

On August 6, 1986, TCE obtained a temporary restraining order prohibiting the Slaters from building, alleging that Slaters' house violated the minimum size restrictions contained in the Declaration. Based on the court's order, Slaters resubmitted their plans to DRC. On August 26, 1986, the DRC again rejected the plan and stated, "we find that the structure is not in *harmony of external design* to surrounding structures and topography as specified in [the Declaration]." (Emphasis added.) On November 5, 1986, the District Court granted a permanent injunction against Slaters, until they complied with the TCE Declaration. . . .

The District Court based its permanent injunction on the fact that the Slaters had not complied with Article V. The court held that the restrictive covenant was enforceable, and that the committee's review was performed in good faith and not unreasonable.

Slaters contend that a prior approval covenant is not enforceable if it contains no specific objective standards. Slaters argue that the term "harmony of external design" is too vague and ambiguous to be enforceable. Slaters further argue that their house has major features found in existing TCE houses, and therefore their house would not differ in aesthetic merit from the other houses.

TCE contends that Article V is enforceable, even without express standards of application, because the DRC acted reasonably and in good faith. TCE admits that other TCE houses share some of the same physical characteristics and materials of the Slater house, but argues that Slaters' design is not as attractive and harmonious as the existing houses.

. . . We will closely review any enlargement of restrictions which conflict with reasonable land use, and which hinder substantive due process. As we held in State v. District

Ct., 609 P.2d 245, 248 (Mont. 1980), "Moreover, restrictive covenants are to be strictly construed; ambiguities therein are to be construed to allow free use of the property." However, the free use of the property must be balanced against the rights of the other purchasers in the subdivision. . . .

We recognize that aesthetic considerations have a place in prior approval covenants, and that there are no absolute standards to guide a committee's judgment and taste. Aesthetic terms must be sufficiently flexible to cover a variety of house designs. The term "harmony of external design" is not ambiguous per se. However, a restrictive covenant which fails to define the standard of approval is too vague to be enforceable.

The record reveals that every TCE house had a unique external design, in a cacophony of styles. The houses ranged from single and split-level to bi-level, the roofs from gable-end and hip to mansard, and the siding from stucco and wood to stone. The styles were a hybrid mix of traditional, Tudor, ranch, and contemporary. The only common design characteristics were a 2400 square foot minimum size and a shake roof. When questioned at the show cause hearing on August 29, 1986, DRC was unable to state any design standard for TCE.

If the subdivision itself lacks consonance, the Slaters' plan cannot lack harmony. In the context of TCE and Slaters' plan, the term "harmony of external design" lacks the mutuality of obligation central to the purpose of a restrictive covenant. In view of the wide variety of designs, no one seemed burdened by the covenant except the Slaters.

Slaters' plan was not discordant with others in the subdivision. The proposed house would be split-level contemporary, 2600 square feet, with a gable-end shake roof and wood siding. The single most distinguishing feature of the Slaters' house was its cost, which was not an express factor under Article V. The proposed house would be worth approximately $135,000. The other TCE houses appraised above $200,000. As revealed in its initial rejection letter, DRC seems more concerned with harmony of appraisal than harmony of design. However, DRC's review of external design was limited to the factors set forth in Article V, and to observable characteristics of all other houses in the subdivision.

. . . Applied to the TCE subdivision and Slaters' plan, we hold that Article V lacks sufficient objectivity, and is vague to a degree that denies substantive due process to the Slaters.

We therefore vacate the injunction based on this issue, and need not proceed to appellants' issues of notice and good faith.

Note on Architectural Control by Residential Community Associations

1. *Adequacy of standards.* But see Oakbrook Civic Association v. Sonnier, 481 So. 2d 1008 (La. 1986), which held that covenant language identical to that construed in *Slater* was not fatally vague. The Louisiana Supreme Court, asserting that it was following the approach of a majority of states, held that the pertinent issue is whether the review committee had exercised its broad authority reasonably and in good faith. If the Montana Supreme Court were to have adopted the Louisiana approach, how should it have decided *Slater*?

The Homes Association Handbook 209–10 (1966) argues that the drafter of a declaration should provide for architectural review under a general standard, and not articulate detailed design rules in the Conditions, Covenants, and Restrictions (CC&Rs):

> [A] provision for architectural control permits the draftsman of the protective covenants to avoid specificity on minor items such as fences, shrubbery, driveways, and the like. As fashions on these matters tend to change drastically, a specific provision as to height, type, and extent

of a fence, for example, far from adding to the value of the homes, can markedly detract from it. By leaving approval of such matters to an architectural control committee under a general standard, a desirable flexibility on such minor details can be achieved. . . .

Compare the judicial critique of amorphous municipal design standards in Anderson v. City of Issaquah, 851 P.2d 744 (Wash. Ct. App. 1993), excerpted at p. 489.

2. *The popularity of stringent controls.* CC&Rs governing design commonly are highly restrictive, apparently because developers anticipate that most homebuyers will pay a premium to live in a closely controlled environment. See, e.g., Connelly v. Schafer, 837 S.W.2d 344 (Mo. Ct. App. 1992) (enforcing covenant requiring wood-shingle roof against homeowner who had used high-quality asphalt shingles); Liebowitz v. Mandel, 494 N.Y.S.2d 404 (App. Div. 1985) (enforcing covenant that barred planting of hedge along property's boundary).

Many associations strive to keep basketball hoops and satellite dishes away from sites in easy view of neighbors. In Killearn Acres Homeowners Association v. Keever, 595 So. 2d 1019 (Fla. Dist. Ct. App. 1992), the architectural control committee won an injunction against installation of a dish for television reception in a side yard. The court held that the dish was a "structure" that the committee was empowered to review. When Keever pointed out that the committee had not challenged eight dishes that had been installed in the rear yards of other unit owners, the court concluded that the committee had not been arbitrary in its enforcement because those locations had been less conspicuous.

3. *Remedies for violations of design standards.* Courts do not hesitate to compel recalcitrant homeowners to comply with design restrictions and the process of architectural review. In Pelican Island Property Owners Association v. Murphy, 554 So. 2d 1179 (Fla. Dist. Ct. App. 1989), the court ordered the removal of a carport built without association approval. See also Seagrove Owners Association v. Smith, 834 P.2d 469 (Or. Ct. App. 1992) (ordering removal of garage at cost of $9,000).

May an association record in the official land records a notice of noncompliance with architectural review, a step that would tend to impair an owner's ability to sell or refinance? In Ward v. Superior Court, 63 Cal. Rptr. 2d 731 (Ct. App. 1997), the association had recorded such a notice after a unit owner had painted a house bright blue, allegedly without the association's approval. The court held that California statutes did not authorize a recorder's office to accept such an instrument.

4. *Remedies of an applicant wrongfully denied approval.* In Riss v. Angel, 934 P.2d 669 (Wash. 1997), the association had unreasonably denied architectural approval to a lot owner who had sought to replace an existing house. The court affirmed the trial court judgment that the applicant was entitled to $104,000 in delay damages and $102,000 in attorney fees. The members of the association who had participated in the unreasonable conduct were held jointly and severally liable for these sums. Should the Slaters have asked for damages?

5. *Neighbor challenges to design approvals.* What if the design review committee had approved the Slaters' plans and a neighbor had challenged that association action? See Cohen v. Kite Hill Community Association, 191 Cal. Rptr. 209 (Ct. App. 1983) (remanding case for determination of whether committee approval of construction of stone wall that blocked plaintiff's view had been in good faith and not arbitrary).

6. *Relationship to municipal architectural review.* Is the judicial role in supervising private architectural review identical to the judicial role in supervising public architectural review? Compare pp. 489–94. Would a municipality be wise to exempt construction that is subject to private architectural review from the public design review process? From local building codes and zoning ordinances?

c.   *Judicial Review of Board Rulemaking*

New rules as opposed to rules in the original documents. Judges generally are less deferential to a new rule or bylaw provision than they are to a provision that appeared in the original declaration of covenants. The full opinion in *Nahrstedt* (Cal. 1994), excerpted at p. 554, which involved a pet restriction included in the original declaration, approvingly cites a distinction articulated in Hidden Harbour Estates, Inc. v. Basso, 393 So. 2d 637, 640 (Fla. Dist. Ct. App. 1981): "[The original] restrictions are clothed with a very strong presumption of validity which arises from the fact that each individual unit owner purchases his unit knowing of and accepting the restrictions to be imposed. . . . Indeed, a use restriction *in a declaration of condominium* may have a certain degree of unreasonableness to it, and yet withstand attack in the courts." (Emphasis in original.)

By contrast, an association's subsequently enacted rules typically must pass a reasonableness test. See Note, Judicial Review of Condominium Rulemaking, 95 Harv. L. Rev. 647, 652 n.29 (1981) (listing ten statutes imposing reasonableness standard on association rulemaking). In Board of Directors v. Hinojosa, 679 N.E.2d 407 (Ill. App. Ct. 1997), the board of the condominium association governing floors 45 through 92 of Chicago's John Hancock building was seeking to enforce a no-dog rule. The association's original documents had been silent on the pet issue, but did authorize the board to promulgate rules regarding the use of units. After a number of years, the board had adopted a rule that prohibited owners from bringing new dogs onto the premises. Applying a reasonableness test, the court sustained the validity of this rule. What if the association had attempted to apply its rule retrospectively to evict dogs already in the building at the time the rule was adopted? See Winston Towers 200 Association v. Saverio, 360 So. 2d 470 (Fla. Dist. Ct. App. 1978) (holding retrospective application of pet rule to be invalid). Compare the legislative and judicial solicitude for nonconforming uses, discussed at pp. 197–202.

See also Hidden Harbour Estates, Inc. v. Norman, 309 So. 2d 180 (Fla. Dist. Ct. App. 1975) (sustaining the reasonableness of a new rule prohibiting the use of alcoholic beverages in the clubhouse and adjacent common areas); Holleman v. Mission Trace Homeowners Association, 556 S.W.2d 632 (Tex. Civ. App. 1977) (holding new board rule banning parking on common-area pavement met reasonableness test).

Lochnerian supervision of the private sector? Why should a court actively review the substance of association rulemaking rather than advise the aggrieved minority that its only recourse is to become more involved in the association's internal politics? If a court does appraise the reasonableness of a new association rule, should it judge the rule according to general societal standards or according to the particular collective purposes reflected in the association's declaration? Does *reasonable* have the same meaning in this context as it does in Due Process Clause litigation over the validity of public enactments, canvassed at pp. 76–117? See generally Paula A. Franzese, Common Interest Communities: Standards of Review and Review of Standards, 3 Wash. U. J.L. & Pol'y 663 (2000).

Association rules on remedies. Restatement (Third) of Property — Servitudes §6.8 (2000) provides: "In addition to seeking court enforcement [of governing documents and the obligation to pay assessments], the association may adopt reasonable rules and procedures to encourage compliance and deter violations, including the imposition of fines, penalties, late fees, and the withdrawal of privileges to use common recreational and social facilities." Courts have been receptive to member complaints about association enforcement actions that went beyond the letter of association rules. In Grenier v. Barclay Square Commercial Condominium Owners' Association, 834 A.2d 238 (N.H. 2003), a commercial condominium association's rules authorized it to enforce parking rules by means of fines and suspension of parking privileges. In light of the express mention of those two remedies, the court held that the association was not entitled to administer another — the towing away of a violator's vehicle. In The Glen, Section I Condominium Association v. June, 782 A.2d 430 (N.J. Super. Ct. App. Div. 2001), a residential association was held to have gone too far when it responded to a member's failure to pay the monthly assessment by obstructing the member's driveway with a column. See generally Amos B. Elberg, Note, Remedies for Common Interest Development Rule Violations, 101 Colum. L. Rev. 1958 (2001) (urging the limiting of association remedies to damages, as opposed to fines and specific performance, in order to enable efficient breach).

Can a residential community association order a member who has violated its rules to sell and depart? See 40 West 67th Street Corp. v. Pullman, 790 N.E.2d 1174 (N.Y. 2003) (according business-judgment deference to co-op association's decision to vote to oust member regarded as having engaged in "objectionable conduct" in violation of lease agreement); Michael C. Kim, Involuntary Sale: Banishing an Owner from the Condominium Community, 31 J. Marshall L. Rev. 429 (1998).

d. Limitations on Amendments to the Basic Governing Documents

An attorney who drafts documents creating a residential community association normally includes explicit procedures for amendment of the declaration of covenants, the articles of incorporation, and the bylaws. It is common to require that fundamental changes be approved by a two-thirds or three-fourths vote of the membership, and, during a development's embryonic stages, to give the developer a separate veto power over amendments. Should a court come to the aid of a lot owner who bought into a private residential government and then unsuccessfully opposed a change in the basic rules?

Harrison v. Air Park Estates Zoning Committee
533 S.W.2d 108 (Tex. Civ. App. 1976)

Akin, Justice.

This is an appeal from a temporary injunction against defendant Ivan Harrison, obtained by plaintiff Air Park Estates Zoning Committee, restraining defendant's completion of an aircraft hangar on property of which he is equitable owner. Plaintiff's property is a part of a larger tract originally owned by Milton J. Noell, which was subdivided into individual lots to provide "homesites for people who like airplanes." The development contemplated that persons buying lots would build both a hangar and a residence on each lot. In 1969, Harrison purchased one of the lots under a note and a contract for deed containing the following restrictions and provisions: "¶12b. . . . A *hangar may be built before the home is built. . . .* ¶16. These covenants . . . shall be binding . . . until revoked or *modified in whole or in part by a three-fourths majority vote of the then owners of real property therein,* said vote to be on the basis of one vote per lot therein." (Emphasis added.) Acting under ¶16, ¶12b was modified by written agreement of 76.4 percent of the equitable owners of lots in the development to read as follows: . . . *a home may be built with a hangar as a later addition but no hangar may be built before a home) . . ."* (Emphasis added.) The documents changing the restriction were filed of record on March 22, 1971, although the modification had been approved and executed on March 24, 1970. All equitable and legal lot owners were notified by plaintiff of this modification on February 19, 1971. Noell, the developer, owned equitably 42 percent of the lots which percentage he voted to change ¶12b.

On April 26, 1974, defendant Harrison submitted to plaintiffs a plan for the construction of a hangar on his lot without first building a house. This plan was disapproved on May 21st by plaintiffs because it violated restriction ¶12b as modified. Harrison, nevertheless, began construction of the hangar, and this action precipitated suit by the zoning committee to enjoin construction. The trial court issued its temporary injunction and Harrison appeals. We affirm.

Harrison contends that the trial court erred in granting the temporary injunction because: (1) The modification of ¶12b was not valid because it was approved by the various lot owners signing circulated documents rather than at a formal meeting, and (2) equity will not permit a grantor (Noell) to sell property under certain restrictions and to retain rights to impose further restrictions. . . .

. . . [E]arly in 1970 before execution of the document modifying the restrictions, notice was given of a meeting of equitable and legal owners of lots in the subdivision to discuss the modification of ¶12b. Although notice of the meeting was given to all owners, an insufficient number to modify the restriction attended. Although Harrison attended this meeting, he neither signed the petition nor voiced objection. After this meeting a petition to modify was hand circulated to other lot owners. By this effort the proponents of the modification were successful in securing sufficient votes to change the restriction. We see nothing unfair in obtaining the necessary vote by personal contact with the owners. We conclude, therefore, that this contention is without merit.

Harrison also argues that the modification is void because it is more restrictive than the original covenant. We cannot agree with this contention because, even though the modification was more restrictive, it was consistent with the overall plan of development and was neither unreasonable nor prohibited by law. Furthermore, ¶16 of the covenants gave the right to amend the restrictions to three-fourths of the owners of the property. Since the subdivision was designed to provide "homesites for people who like airplanes," the apparent purpose of the modification was to protect the rights of the property owners by insuring that both homes and hangars would be built. Because this modification enhanced, rather than abrogated, the original plan specified in the contracts between the developer and the various lot owners, we hold it to be reasonable. . . .

Note on Declaration Amendments

1. *A reasonableness test for declaration amendments?* A court concerned about majoritarian oppression understandably would review the merits of a declaration amendment somewhat more strictly than the merits of an original provision in a declaration. Like *Harrison*, some authorities indeed hold that an amendment should be subjected to a "reasonableness" test. See Mulligan v. Panther Valley Property Owners Association, 766 A.2d 1186 (N.J. Super. Ct. App. Div. 2001). But compare Villa De Las Palmas Homeowners Association v. Terifaj, 90 P.3d 1223 (Cal. 2004) (holding that association rule changes after creation are entitled to a *Nahrstedt*-style presumption of reasonableness). How great is the risk that active judicial review of the amendment process will place an association in a straitjacket? In Brier Lake, Inc. v. Jones, 710 So. 2d 1054 (La. 1998), the court interpreted Louisiana statutes to require *unanimous* member approval of any amendment that toughened association restrictions on building. The following year, the Louisiana legislature enacted La. Rev. Stat. Ann. §9:1141.1–.9 (West 2004), which "legislatively overruled" *Brier Lake*. When an association's declaration otherwise permits, the Louisiana statute authorizes a supermajority of members to impose a new building restriction, from which individual members have a limited right to opt out.

Should the Founders have included a "reasonableness" constraint on amendments to the U.S. Constitution? Is that analogy a good one?

2. *Amendments that affect only selected lots.* In Boyles v. Hausman, 517 N.W.2d 610 (Neb. 1994), the members had approved an amendment imposing a 120-foot building setback requirement, but only for lots fronting on a particular road. The Boyles, who owned one of the affected lots, asserted the amendment had made their lot unsuitable for building. Noting that the amendment applied only to a few lots, the Supreme Court of Nebraska invalidated it. But see Bay Island Towers, Inc. v. Bay Island-Siesta Association, 316 So. 2d 574 (Fla. Dist. Ct. App. 1975). In that instance, the original declaration of covenants had permitted the construction of multifamily structures on selected lots in the subdivision. Twenty-one years later, the association members (mostly owners of individual houses) approved an amendment restricting the use of those selected lots to single-family dwellings. The Florida appellate court refused to provide relief to the owners of the lots formerly designated for multifamily use. A modification will be upheld, the court said, if it is not unreasonable in light of the general scheme of development. It adjudged the amendment at issue to be a reasonable one. What if the owners, making an analogy to an unconstitutional regulatory taking, had sought to recover damages from the association?

Associations sometimes adopt amendments that ease, as opposed to toughen, restrictions on selected lots. In Ridge Park Home Owners v. Pena, 544 P.2d 278 (N.M. 1975), the members had voted to repeal prohibitions on commercial uses that had previously been applicable to certain subdivision lots that had since been zoned commercial by the City of Albuquerque:

> . . . The dissenting minority consisted mostly of the individuals living near and around the lots subject to the amendment.
>
> The issue is whether the majority (or whatever percentage is required by an agreement) can amend or delete restrictive covenants on fewer than all lots subject thereto. Absent a specific provision in the agreement stating otherwise, we hold that the requisite vote cannot change the applicability of restrictive covenants to a few of the lots; the change must apply to all lots. Montoya v. Barreras, 473 P.2d 363 (N.M. 1970). . . . The mutuality of restrictive covenants would be destroyed if we were to allow the majority of owners, who might not be adversely affected because of their insulated location in the subdivision, to authorize offensive consequences for the minority by removing or imposing restrictions only on certain lots within the minority's area. . . . No changes may be made with respect to any one lot without affecting all the others subject to the restrictions.

This ban on selective relaxation has wide support. See Licker v. Harkleroad, 558 S.E.2d 31 (Ga. Ct. App. 2001) (reviewing case law).

Restatement (Third) of Property — Servitudes §6.10(2) (2000) states, as a general rule: "[A]mendments that do not apply uniformly to similar lots or units . . . are not effective without the approval of members whose interests would be adversely affected unless the declaration fairly apprises purchasers that such amendments may be made." If the variance process brings a desirable flexibility to municipal zoning (see pp. 286–96), why shouldn't an association be entitled to engage in a similar process?

3. *Limits on declaration amendments that reshape common areas.* As a development matures, the bulk of an association's membership may desire to add new recreational facilities or to give away or sell parts of the common area. Can these sorts of steps be taken over minority objections?

In Downey v. Jungle Den Villas Recreation Association, 525 So. 2d 438 (Fla. Dist. Ct. App. 1988), a bare majority of unit owners had voted to install a swimming pool in the common area and to assess each unit owner $450 toward the cost of the project. At the behest of members of the outvoted minority, the court held that Florida statutes required unanimous consent in this instance. But compare Lincolnshire Civic Association v. Beach, 364 N.Y.S.2d 248 (App. Div. 1975) (dissenters can be compelled to contribute lump-sum assessment to defray cost of rebuilding damaged pool). Can these two holdings be reconciled?

The outvoted minority was protected in Kaplan v. Boudreaux, 573 N.E.2d 495 (Mass. 1991). There, 77 percent of the unit owners had ratified an amendment that granted the owners of a particular unit exclusive use of a walkway area that had no use other than as a means of access to their unit. The court held this alteration of ownership of a portion of the common area required unanimous consent of the membership. Why might a court be more suspicious of an association's decision to transfer part of the common area to a member than of a decision to sell a portion to outsiders?

4. *Termination procedures.* The dissolution of an association is governed not by the common law doctrine of changed conditions but by provisions in the declaration or applicable statutes. See 14859 Moorpark Homeowners Association v. VRT Corp., 74 Cal. Rptr. 2d 712 (Ct. App. 1998) (involving a condominium complex that had suffered earthquake damage); Uniform Common Interest Ownership Act §2-118 (1994) (requiring, in most instances, that at least 80 percent of votes be cast in favor of termination). For analysis of the internal political dynamics of associations in distress, see Mark D. West & Emily M. Morris, The Tragedy of the Condominiums: Legal Responses to Collective Action Problems After the Kobe Earthquake, 51 Am. J. Comp. L. 903 (2003) (an empirical study of association responses to earthquake damage in Kobe, Japan, and Northridge, California).

4.   Association Finances

A residential community association's assessments on members might be apportioned

(1)   equally per dwelling unit;
(2)   equally per square foot of lot (or dwelling) area; or
(3)   equally per dollar of unit value, as established by
    (a)   the original declaration of covenants;
    (b)   the property tax assessor; or
    (c)   an independent appraiser hired periodically by the association.

Which of these systems is to be preferred if the objective is to equate charges with benefits conferred by association activities? To ensure ease in administration? To redistribute wealth from rich to poor? Should the legislature dictate a particular system for apportioning assessments, or should a developer be allowed to choose among the various alternatives? Must votes be apportioned like assessments are? When might an association appropriately impose user fees or special assessments on members who enjoy special facilities?

Thiess v. Island House Association
311 So. 2d 142 (Fla. Dist. Ct. App. 1975)

PER CURIAM.
This is an appeal from a judgment upholding the validity of certain amendments to the Declaration of Condominium of Island House Association, Inc. (Association).

Island House is a beachfront residential condominium in Sarasota County. Thirty-eight of its seventy-three units are one-story villas; the remaining thirty-five are apartments grouped in four high-rise buildings. The Declaration of Condominium provided that the undivided share owned by each unit in the common elements appurtenant to each unit and the fraction of sharing common expenses and owning common surplus should be one-seventy-third each. The value of the apartment units was somewhat higher than the villa units. Thus were sown the seeds of the problem which later occurred.

By 1969 the Association, which is a non-profit corporation consisting of the property owners, had assumed the management of Island House from the developer. In that year numerous leaks occurred, particularly in the high-rise apartment buildings, which caused serious water damage. Repairs were urgently required, but in order to pay for the repairs the Association needed to obtain $50,000. Since there were more villa units than apartment units, where self interest was concerned, the villa units could out-vote the apartment units. The villa unit owners did not wish to carry the burden of paying an amount equal to that of the apartment owners to repair the apartment roofs, particularly where the value of the apartment units exceeded that of the villa units. On the other hand, in view of the condominium concept of sharing common expenses, the apartment owners were reluctant to pay the entire cost of the repairs. Several of the unit owners were threatening to sue the Association for failure to go forward with the repairs.

After failing to obtain a voluntary agreement, the Association proposed an amendment to the declaration whereby the share of the common expenses and the common surplus for each unit would be changed so as to reflect the pro rata portion of each unit's assessed value as compared to the total assessed value of all units. The amendment was approved by more than fifty-one percent of the unit owners, and the $50,000 assessment was made in the new proportions. Mr. and Mrs. Thiess (appellants), who were apartment owners, refused to pay the assessment. The Association brought suit to enforce the assessment pursuant to the authority of Fla. Stat. §711.15 (1969).

In addition to contesting the validity of the amendment, which modified the share of the common expenses, appellants also attacked a subsequent amendment relating to laundry machines. This problem was precipitated by the fact that the two apartments on each floor of the high-rise buildings were serviced by a washer and dryer located in an adjacent hallway; whereas, the thirty-eight villas shared a single washroom equipped with coin-operated machines. In 1971, the Association, by a majority vote of the unit owners, further amended the declaration to provide that the washers and dryers in the apartment buildings should be limited to the exclusive use of the apartment owners on the respective apartment floors served by such equipment and be maintained at the sole expense of such apartment owners. Thereafter, the Association refused to pay the expenses of maintaining the machines in the apartment buildings. Following the taking of testimony, the lower court ruled both amendments to be valid.

Those portions of the Condominium Act in 1969 pertinent to this appeal are as follows: . . .

711.04 *Condominium parcels; appurtenances; possession and enjoyment.* (1) A condominium parcel is a separate parcel of real property, the ownership of which may be in fee simple, or any other estate in real property recognized by law. (2) There shall pass with a unit as appurtenances thereto: (a) An undivided share in the common elements. (b) The exclusive right to use such portion of the common elements as may be provided by the declaration. . . . (d) An undivided share in the common surplus. . . .

711.06 *Common elements.* (1) Common elements includes within its meaning the following items: . . . (e) Installations for the furnishing of utility services to more than one unit or to the common elements or to a unit other than the unit containing the installation. (f) The property and installations in connection therewith required for the furnishing of services to more than one unit or to the common elements.

711.10 *Amendment of declaration*. . . . (3) Unless otherwise provided in the declaration as originally recorded, no amendment shall change any condominium parcel unless the record owner thereof and all record owners of liens thereon shall join in the execution of the amendment. . . .

. . . It is evident the common surplus of Island House is created by the extent that the assessments against the condominium owners have exceeded the costs of operating and maintaining the property. Therefore, if the share of the common surplus cannot be changed without the consent of the affected owner, [as §§711.04 and 711.10 together provide,] it follows that to change his share of common expenses should also require his consent.

. . . [T]he appellants had a right to rely on the fact that their proportionate obligation to share in the common expenses could not be altered unless they agreed to it. Since §711.15 provides that the Association may have a lien on each condominium parcel for any unpaid assessments, any other interpretation would place the minority of condominium owners at the mercy of the majority. The sharing of common expenses based upon a proportion of each unit's value may be advisable, but the original declaration specified otherwise. In this instance most of the money went to the upkeep of the apartments, but the next time it may be the villas which will need the repairs. Appellants did not join in the execution of the amendment; therefore, they may not be charged more than the share of common expenses allocated to them in the original declaration.

Our ruling on the first amendment necessarily disposes of the second. The washers and dryers in the apartments were common elements. The effect of the amendment was to place the entire expense of operating these machines upon the apartment owners rather than apportioning the expenses among all of the unit owners. Appellants' share of the common expenses with respect to these machines has been changed without their consent. The fact that they have been given exclusive use of the machines is irrelevant because they have not sought this. Presumably, the ready access to washers and dryers which would be maintained out of common expenses was a factor in determining the price for which appellants purchased their unit. . . .

Reversed.

Note on Association Fiscal Policies

1. *Current Florida law.* Fla. Stat. §711.10(3) has been superseded by Fla. Stat. §718.110(4) (2004), a section of the Florida Condominium Act. The new section reads:

> Unless otherwise provided in the declaration as originally recorded, no amendment may change the configuration or size of any unit in any material fashion, materially alter or modify the appurtenances to the unit, or change the proportion or percentage by which the owner shares the common expenses of the condominium and owns the common surplus of the condominium unless the record owner of the unit and all record owners of liens on the unit join in the execution of the amendment and unless all the record owners of all other units in the same condominium approve the amendment. . . .

Why is unanimity a prerequisite for one of these structural amendments but not for a covenant amendment that alters substantive land use controls?

2. *Inequalities in services provided.* Did the court in *Thiess* really do much to protect minority interests from financial exploitation? Even if the majority faction were to be

prohibited from changing the assessment formula, it could still attempt to reduce maintenance expenditures on common areas serving the minority faction. (Recall how this had
been done in *Thiess*.) Should the Florida courts or legislature do anything to prevent that?
Compare Chapter 7C (on a municipality's duties to provide services).

3. *Special fees and assessments.* Could the association in *Thiess* have levied special
charges against the owners of the units in the high-rise buildings whose roofs required
repairs? See Belson v. Thayer & Associates, Inc., 588 N.E.2d 695 (Mass. App. Ct. 1992)
(upholding assessment of most of costs of repairing roof patio decks to owners of adjacent
penthouse units). Given that the association in *Thiess* had declined to pursue that policy,
could the owners of the villas have refused to pay assessments to fund repairs in the high-
rises? See Workman v. Brighton Properties, Inc., 976 P.2d 1209 (Utah 1999) (lack of benefit
does not excuse member's nonpayment of assessment).

In Thanasoulis v. Winston Towers 200 Association, 542 A.2d 900 (N.J. 1988), the
association had adopted a rule that imposed on nonresident owners parking fees higher
than the parking fees imposed on resident owners. The majority opinion held that neither
the declaration nor the New Jersey condominium act authorized this sort of fee differential.
The dissenting judges would have been willing to sustain the differential under the business
judgment rule.

Courts review the fiscal decisions of private residential associations more strictly than
the fiscal decisions of municipalities. (See Chapter 7.) Why is this so?

4. *Priority of association liens for unpaid assessments.* Prudential Insurance Co. v.
Wetzel, 248 N.W. 791 (Wis. 1933), is a leading case on the priority of association assessment
liens. At Time 1, when the association's declaration of covenants had been recorded, the
declaration stated that assessments were to be enforceable by lien on a debtor's unit. At
Time 2, various mortgages on the debtor's lot were recorded. Debtor then defaulted on
assessment payments due at Time 3. The Wisconsin Supreme Court held the lien securing
the assessments to be senior to the mortgages.

Because the declaration of covenants for a subdivision normally would have been
recorded before any homeowner had purchased a lot, the *Wetzel* rule gives the lien securing
assessments priority over most mortgages. Many mortgage lenders, however, insist that their
mortgage be made senior to the lien. The Homes Association Handbook therefore suggests,
at page 391, that the following subordination agreement be included in the declaration of
covenants:

> The lien of the assessments provided for herein shall be subordinate to the lien of any mortgage
> or mortgages now or hereafter placed upon the properties subject to assessment. . . .

Is this more sweeping than necessary? Compare N.J. Stat. Ann. §46.8B-21 (West 2004)
(limiting priority of association's lien to six months of unpaid dues), and Thaler v. Household Finance Corp., 95 Cal. Rptr. 2d 779 (Ct. App. 2000) (construing California statute
to give seniority to a recorded mortgage over a subsequently recorded notice of delinquent
assessments).

5. *Implied powers to levy assessments.* Restatement (Third) of Property — Servitudes
§6.5 (2000) states that if the original declaration is silent on the issue of assessments,
an association nevertheless should be regarded as having the authority to levy them. See
Evergreen Highlands Association v. West, 73 P.3d 1 (Colo. 2003) (endorsing Restatement
approach).

6. *Tactical refusals to pay assessments.* When a residential tenant is suffering from a
landlord's breach of the implied warranty of habitability, most states entitle the tenant to
set off the ongoing damages against rent due. By analogy, in *Thiess*, could a unit owner

disgruntled about roof leaks have withheld a portion of the assessments due the association? See Rivers Edge Condominium Association v. Rere, Inc., 568 A.2d 261 (Pa. Super. Ct. 1990) (no, but the owner can complain to the association and ultimately bring a legal action against it).

7. *Tax considerations*. A member who pays an assessment cannot deduct that amount for federal income tax purposes. An assessment paid to a residential community association is regarded neither as a charitable contribution deductible under §170 of the Internal Revenue Code (see Rev. Rul. 68-485), nor as a municipal property tax deductible under §164. Because property taxes *are* deductible, community residents prefer (everything else being equal) to have services provided by a unit of local government rather than by a private homeowners association. Several municipalities in southern California — Palos Verdes Estates, Rolling Hills, Hidden Hills — were incorporated primarily so that their residents could transfer association functions to them and thereby qualify for tax deductions. Residents of the planned community of Columbia, Maryland, have pushed for cityhood to attain deductibility and the power to issue tax-exempt municipal bonds. See Michael Janofsky, Citizens Debate Change in a Maryland Suburb, N.Y. Times, Feb. 26, 1995, §1, at 26.

Less drastically, homeowners may attempt to transfer selected association facilities to an existing city or county. This stratagem, if successful, can free members of both main-tenance costs and liabilities for local property taxes on the facilities. See Michael M. Shultz III, Note, The Real Property Taxation of Common Areas in Planned Unit Devel-opments, 1983 Utah L. Rev. 825. Should federal and local tax systems create incentives for community management by municipalities as opposed to associations?

There also is the question of the federal tax status of an association itself. Section 528 of the Internal Revenue Code authorizes certain residential community associations to exclude from income "any amount received as membership dues, fees, or assessments" from unit owners. To qualify for the benefits of this section, the association must obtain 60 percent or more of its income from those sources, and spend 90 percent or more of its funds on maintenance, management, improvement, and acquisition of association property. Might these limitations deter an association from opening up its golf course to outsiders and charging them greens fees?

5. *The Merits of Residential Community Associations*

After visiting North America in 1831, the young Frenchman Alexis de Tocqueville applauded the inhabitants' propensity to join together in associations. See Democracy in America 513–24 (J.P. Mayer ed., 1969) (1835). At the start of the twenty-first century, some commentators assert that this spirit is waning. See, e.g., Robert D. Putnam, Bowling Alone: The Collapse and Revival of American Community (2000). Putnam emphasizes the importance of social capital, that is, interpersonal networks that involve trust and reci-procity. A residential community association, by knitting neighbors together in a collective endeavor, conceivably might promote what Putnam calls *bonding* social capital. Relations within an association, however, may be fractious. There may be dissidents at either extreme: sticklers inclined to be excessively intrusive in the lives of their neighbors, and individual-ists who resist any form of restraint. See Iver Peterson, When a Man's Condo Is Not His Castle, N.Y. Times, Feb. 11, 1990, §10, at 1. (Which sort of extremist is more likely to seek election to the board?) In addition, the presence of an association may cause members to

[handwritten margin note: Most think that spirit is waning]

be less involved with both outsiders and their local governments, thereby lessening what Putnam calls *bridging* social capital.

Given these complexities, commentators understandably dispute the merits of residential community associations. Some regard them as commendable ventures in private ordering in a massive and pluralistic society and urge lawmakers to give them wide berth. See, e.g., Fred Foldvary, Public Goods and Private Communities (1994); Robert C. Ellickson, Cities and Homeowners Associations, 130 U. Pa. L. Rev. 1519 (1982); Richard A. Epstein, Covenants and Constitutions, 73 Cornell L. Rev. 906 (1988). Others, however, assert that associations, by fostering reliance on formal rules rather than informal norms, may do more to weaken social connectedness among members than to build it. See Paula A. Franzese, Does It Take a Village? Privatization, Patterns of Restrictiveness and the Demise of Community, 47 Vill. L. Rev. 553 (2002). But compare Robert Jay Dilger, Neighborhood Politics: Residential Community Associations in American Governance 131–44 (1992) (suggesting how residential associations may enhance civic virtue). Does the fact that most developers of new communities continue to create associations indicate that most purchasers regard associations as advantageous on balance? For doubts about the efficiency of the market for association forms, see Lee Anne Fennell, Contracting Communities, 2004 U. Ill. L. Rev. 829.

The staunchest critics of residential community associations stress negative effects on outsiders. Associations are seen as inherently exclusionary and as fostering isolation among social subgroups. See, e.g., Gregory S. Alexander, Dilemmas of Group Autonomy, 75 Cornell L. Rev. 1 (1989). Gated communities trigger the greatest wrath. See sources cited at p. 583. Other skeptics assert that associations are insufficiently accountable to public authorities and undermine support for provision of public goods by local governments. See, e.g., Evan McKenzie, Privatopia (1994). More generally, the growth of associations is thought to have weakened involvement in public life. See, e.g., the essays that Stephen E. Barton and Carol J. Silverman contributed to Common Interest Communities (1994), a volume they edited.

Finally, there are centrist commentators who see complex tradeoffs of advantages and disadvantages. See, e.g., Clayton P. Gillette, Courts, Covenants, and Communities, 61 U. Chi. L. Rev. 1375 (1994); James L. Winokur, The Mixed Blessings of Promissory Servitudes, 1989 Wis. L. Rev. 1. Winokur marshals sources indicating that a unit purchaser is unlikely to read the CC&Rs carefully before buying, and that a majority of members rarely attend association meetings. See id. at 59–62. Cf. Dilger, supra, at 140 (reporting that attendance at general meetings typically ranges from 25 percent to 50 percent, and that candidates for board membership seldom outnumber board openings).

Critics of associations construe such findings as evidence that most associations are failures as participatory institutions. On the other hand, how likely is it that a homebuyer moving into a municipality will read its ordinances in advance or attend its public meetings? What are the comparative institutional advantages of associations and municipalities? Of what relevance is it that the typical association involves less than a few blocks of territory and fewer than 100 housing units, making it much smaller than the typical municipality?

One-volume works on residential community associations include Wayne S. Hyatt & Susan F. French, Community Association Law: Cases and Materials on Common Interest Communities (1998), and Robert G. Natelson, Law of Property Owners Associations (1989). For general perspectives on the appropriate role of associations of all types, see Henry B. Hansmann, The Role of Nonprofit Enterprise, 89 Yale L.J. 835 (1980), and Special Issue: Mediating Institutions: Beyond the Public/Private Distinction, 61 U. Chi. L. Rev. 1213 (1994).

615-638

6. *Retrofitting an Association onto a Previously Subdivided Territory*

A number of commentators speculate that mandatory-membership residential community associations could usefully provide local public goods in old neighborhoods. See Robert C. Ellickson, New Institutions for Old Neighborhoods, 48 Duke L.J. 75 (1998); George W. Liebmann, Devolution of Power to Community and Block Associations, 25 Urb. Law. 335 (1993); Robert H. Nelson, Privatizing the Neighborhood, 7 Geo. Mason U. L. Rev. 827 (1999).

but doesn't happen that often b/c of issue free-riding

How might such an association be created? The risk of free-riding normally prevents lot owners in an already subdivided territory from unanimously agreeing to form an association with power to levy assessments. The proponents of retrofitted associations therefore urge state legislatures to enact enabling statutes that would authorize the owners of a super-majority of the property value in an area of a few blocks to create an association and force any outvoted minority to join it. Compare compulsory unification systems such as Business Improvement Districts and land readjustment (discussed respectively at pp. 630–34 and 854). For doubts about the wisdom of any sort of compelled joinder, see Steven J. Eagle, Privatizing Urban Land Use Regulation: The Problem of Consent, 7 Geo. Mason L. Rev. 905 (1999).

Proponents of retrofitted associations differ on many details, including procedures for formation, the services an association would provide, whether the association should have the power to regulate (or waive municipal zoning regulations), the allocation of votes to resident tenants, and the power of a city to veto the creation of a retrofitted association.

E. *Land Use in the Absence of Zoning*

Especially since the advent of zoning in the early years of the twentieth century, government agencies have increasingly regulated the use of private land in the United States. Most commentators have regarded this overall trend as salutary. Since 1970, however, dissenters favoring substantial deregulation of land use have surfaced. The opening salvo was Siegan's empirical study of Houston, Texas, excerpted below. He concluded that privately arranged covenant schemes can coordinate land uses more efficiently than zoning can. See Bernard H. Siegan, Non-Zoning in Houston, 13 J.L. & Econ. 71 (1970), later expanded into a book, Land Use Without Zoning (1972). Ellickson also extols the advantages of regulation by covenant in a newly developed area, but thinks that the imposition of new covenants normally is infeasible in an older neighborhood; in lieu of public regulations, he proposes greater reliance on private nuisance actions for damages (when conflicts are localized) and on fines on unneighborly activities (when conflicts involve many parties). Robert C. Ellickson, Alternatives to Zoning: Covenants, Nuisance Rules, and Fines as Land Use Controls, 40 U. Chi. L. Rev. 681 (1973).

Krasnowiecki is wary of Ellickson's approach because a developer benefits greatly from knowing, before commencing construction, the magnitudes of future costs. Instead of current zoning, Krasnowiecki proposes a "statutory presumption that any housing project must be approved unless the approving agency gives persuasive reasons why it should not." Jan Z. Krasnowiecki, Abolish Zoning, 31 Syracuse L. Rev. 719, 750 (1980). Other works by skeptics of zoning include Robert H. Nelson, Zoning Myth and Practice, *in* Zoning and the

American Dream 299 (Charles M. Haar & Jerold S. Kayden eds., 1989) (providing concise comparison of policies that various critics of zoning have proposed); Orlando E. Delogu, Local Land Use Controls: An Idea Whose Time Has Passed, 36 Me. L. Rev. 261 (1984) (urging state-administered performance standards); Douglas W. Kmiec, Deregulating Land Use, 130 U. Pa. L. Rev. 28 (1981) (proposing local imposition of performance standards and exactions).

New Urbanists such as Peter Calthorpe and Andres Duany also have been highly critical of conventional zoning on the ground that, among other sins, it excessively segregates uses and bars the evolution of urbanistic settings. See sources cited at pp. 422–24 and 793–95. James Howard Kunstler, the New Urbanist author of The Geography of Nowhere: The Rise and Decline of America's Man-Made Landscape (1993), writes:

> Main Street is illegal in most of America today. You can't build it, even if you want to. You can't add to it or extend it where it already exists. The zoning codes tell you that any new building has to be set back from the road and from the side and rear property lines 75 feet. With those setbacks everything is so spread out there's no way you can walk it. Don't even bother putting sidewalks in.
>
> When people dream about the kind of ideal neighborhood they'd like to live in, they conjure up an image of tree-lined streets and woodframe houses with front porches. That's Elm Street, the classic American small town. You can't build it today under our laws, because of large-lot zoning, and because highway engineers have decided that trees on streets are a menace to motorists. . . .
>
> Planning today is administration: issuing permits, filling out forms, shuffling papers. At Harvard the planning department was kicked out of the architecture school and installed in the school of government.
>
> Meanwhile, Americans know what a good place feels like. We go to Charleston, South Carolina, and Beacon Hill in Boston, Savannah, Georgetown, and towns in Vermont. We like the intimacy of the streets, the mix of shops with the variety of people, the nearness of genuine countryside. Many Americans make the mistake of thinking they like these places simply because they're old and picturesque. But what they're really enjoying are physical relationships between structures — relationships that can no longer be built under our laws.

Quoted in Zoning Kills Community Life, Am. Enter., Nov./Dec. 1996, at 13–14. New Urbanists, however, tend to favor mandatory regulations that would advance their goals, not the deregulatory approach that Siegan and others have advocated. See Andres Duany, Elizabeth Plater-Zyberk & Jeff Speck, Suburban Nation: The Rise of Sprawl and the Decline of the American Dream 220–24 (2000) (discussing examples of New Urbanist ordinances).

For general defenses of traditional zoning practices, see Bradley C. Karkkainen, Zoning: A Reply to Critics, 10 J. Land Use & Envtl. L. 45 (1994); Eric H. Steele, Participation and Rules — The Functions of Zoning, 1986 Am. B. Found. Res. J. 709.

To assist appraisal of the positions espoused in this debate, this subchapter presents materials on how land use patterns evolve in urban areas that lack zoning. It is important to note that the two cities featured — San Francisco after the Gold Rush and modern-day Houston — both had other significant public regulations during the periods discussed. In addition, keep in mind the status of both nuisance and covenant law during the eras in question and ponder how those rules of private law might have affected patterns of development.

Roger W. Lotchin, San Francisco 1846–1856
vii, 11–13, 17–18, 23–24, 165 (1974)

"It's an odd place: unlike any other place in creation," wrote a San Franciscan in 1849, "and so should it be; for it is not created in the ordinary way, but hatched like chickens by artificial heat." In that year the California town had 1,000 people; ten years later the population exceeded 50,000. The nineteenth century had never seen anything quite like it. . . .

Enriched by the Gold Rush and nourished by its own and the world's husbandmen, San Francisco underwent extensive physical growth. Yet most of this development was anarchic. There was little government planning for the use of land, and much of what there was turned out badly. Most of the planning, therefore, was private, individual, and small rather than public, communitarian, and large-scale. The best, and biggest, example of these private efforts was undertaken toward the end of the period at the suburb of South Park, where the promoter banned all liquor saloons, required brick buildings in the area of most congestion, and laid out the plat in an oval form surrounding a park. South Park soon became a source of considerable local pride; but there were few other examples, public or private, to match it.

The council set apart the street plat and several plazas for public use instead of speculation; and, after the passage of the Van Ness Ordinance, it reserved certain western areas for schools and more squares. In addition, this body established a master plan to regulate all grades. As the metropolis became more complex, however, the public demanded segregation or prohibition of particular activities within given neighborhoods. Though the response to these requests was minimal, the demands were significant for the future.

At first, zoning efforts took the form of nuisance indictments. Slaughterhouses, chandleries, soap and acid factories, charcoal burners, and other petty manufacturers whose trades had offensive side effects, such as odor or waste, were constantly prosecuted as well as mauled in the press. Another deterrent was the purchase of land earmarked for some obnoxious use. When J. Wieland proposed to put a brewery at the corner of Folsom and Second, in an aristocratic area, the "indignant" residents "authorized fellow resident Milton S. Latham [a lawyer and politician] . . . to wait upon [Mr. Wieland] and make an offer of purchase for the property." Sometimes the transaction involved blackmail. In 1853 the Alta reported that a speculator had purchased a lot in a respectable section for the purpose of establishing a house of prostitution on it, knowing full well that the residents would buy him out at an inflated price.

This informal zoning soon graduated into legal banishment of distasteful practices from certain areas. In 1852 the fire danger led the city to the prohibition of tents and wooden buildings within the limits of Union, Powell, Post, Second, and Folsom streets. This ordinance also forbade or regulated the storage of combustibles and powder within the same section. The same year saw slaughterhouses excluded from the area east of Larkin and north of Market; and in 1854 they, along with stockyards, were driven from the city altogether. . . .

The most ambitious plan for controlling land use [was never adopted]. This was an effort by the manufacturers to protect themselves from prosecution by establishing a "haven" and shows very clearly the connection between zoning and annoyance prosecution. In 1855 various manufacturers, "having been driven from pillar to post" by their neighbors, proposed to the aldermen that a parcel of land be set aside south of Mission Creek where industry could locate with security. This section was to be situated "so remote from the inhabited part of the city that no legal question would likely arise as to what might constitute nuisances in the district, at least within the period named in the ordinances — January 1st, 1869."

Zoning was, therefore, an attempt at reconciling the homeowning and the manufacturing interests while preserving the community dedication to two ideals; but after passing one board of aldermen, the proposal lost in the other. However, the proposed regulations were in no way a new departure except as to means. The normal growth of the city had encouraged a natural segregation which sorted out retail from wholesale trades, residential from both, and one kind of residence from another. Zoning would have made formal legal provision for what had already been happening informally to freeze the separation, to substitute artificial for natural parceling, to supplant individual control over the evolution of land use patterns with community, and to replace transient and changing areas with relatively stable ones.

Historically, American cities have suffered from lack of planning; San Francisco was no exception. A more flexible street plat, wider thoroughfares, and a manufacturing zone all were promising ideas, and several other improvements could have been made. Yet if San Francisco had indulged in comprehensive planning, it would have been a disastrous mistake. Many of the most elementary necessities could not have been supplied. Most importantly, no one had anything close to an accurate notion of the city's rate of growth. Even the most optimistic boosters repeatedly underestimated its development. . . .

Accompanying decentralization of economic and residential patterns [by 1857] came considerable specialization of land use, and hand in hand with decentralization came greater concentration of the various categories within each. For example, commission merchants were congregated on the angle of Front and California; produce merchants were segregated together on Clay Street or close by; lumber dealers were in an odd-shaped linear district along Steuart, California, and Market; clothing and dry goods merchants were on Sacramento; the lawyers, on Montgomery or Merchant; and the large-scale manufacturing, south of Market. These segregated areas were often close to each other; and the differentiation was not complete, but it was present and growing. Many of the economic spatial relationships can be explained by reference to a number of urban frontiers which delineated the areas of relative safety from fire, of high rent and land prices, of minimum drayage rates, of planked streets, of newly made land, and of accessible water supply. . . .

[Lotchin then discusses where different social groups resided.] Numerically and proportionately, the middle-class lead was greatest in the area geographically farther from the center city, and the working-class predominance was just the reverse. The separation of classes was most evident where population was heavily concentrated. Dense settlement and segregation of social groups clearly went together. . . .

Whatever its defects, the mere existence of [an official street map] prior to the Gold Rush was a godsend. The gridiron pattern was one of the few elements of order in an initially anarchic situation. San Francisco had quite enough trouble over land titles; and if the O'Farrell survey [an 1847 street map issued by the alcalde (mayor)] had not reserved at least the streets from squatting, the confusion would have been much worse. . . .

Note on City Development in the Prezoning Era

The evolution of Boston, especially in the nineteenth century, is analyzed in Walter Firey, Land Use in Central Boston (1947). For a painstaking examination of evolving patterns of uses, setbacks, heights, and lot areas in a predominantly residential neighborhood elsewhere in New England, see Andrew J. Cappel, Note, A Walk Along Willow: Patterns of Land Use Coordination in Pre-Zoning New Haven (1870–1926), 101 Yale L.J. 617 (1991). Cappel concludes:

> . . . [T]his study of New Haven casts doubt upon the prevailing assumption that coherent land use cannot take place without the type of planned public regulation represented by zoning. . . .
>
> In addition, this study suggests that the introduction of zoning into New Haven was not necessitated by actual conditions of local land use, but rather was the work of certain

elites . . . who were influenced by theories developed as part of the national "City Beautiful" movement. Therefore, in contrast to the narrative traditionally advanced by supporters of zoning, the rapid spread of zoning in the 1920's may well have brought zoning to cities like New Haven where it was not really needed.

Id. at 636–37.

Bernard H. Siegan, Non-Zoning in Houston
13 J.L. & Econ. 71, 142–43 (1970)

[Houston never has had a zoning ordinance. During the period Siegan studied, however, Houston did have a subdivision ordinance that required a minimum lot size of 5,000 square feet and, for single-family dwellings, a minimum front-yard setback of 25 feet. The city also had adopted conventional building and housing codes. Because the location of activities in Houston is not controlled by ordinance, restrictive covenants are regarded as so important that the city itself began to enforce them in 1965. See p. 566. Siegan describes the various public and private controls, and compares them with the systems in force in zoned cities. He concludes with a list of "Lessons of Houston."]

1. Economic forces tend to make for a separation of uses even without zoning. Business uses will . . . tend to locate in certain areas, residential in others, and industrial in still others. Apartments, however, may be built in almost any area except within an industrial one. There is also a tendency for further separation within a category; light industrial uses do not want to adjoin heavy industrial uses, and vice versa. Different kinds of [businesses] require different locations. Expensive homes will separate from less expensive ones, townhouses, duplexes, etc. It is difficult to assess the effectiveness of zoning in furthering this process. It is highly successful in this respect in the "bedroom" suburbs, but much less so in the larger cities.

2. When these economic forces do not guarantee that there will be a separation, and separation is vital to maximize profits (or promote one's tastes and desires), property owners will enter into agreements to provide such protection. The restrictive covenants covering home and industrial subdivisions are the most prominent example of this. Adjoining property owners (such as those on a strip location) can also make agreements not to sell for a use that will be injurious to one or both.

3. Because many of the early restrictive covenants in Houston were (a) limited in duration, or (b) legally insufficient, or (c) not enforced by owners, zoning would have kept more areas as strictly single-family. The covenants created subsequent to 1950 were more durable and as a practical matter will remain in force for long periods. They may be as effective as zoning in maintaining single-family homogeneity.

4. When covenants expire, land and properties will be used as economic pressures dictate. Most business uses will not locate on interior streets because they require favorable traffic conditions available only on major thoroughfares. Within recent years, the most important factor influencing diversity in non-restricted interior areas is the strong demand for multiple-family accommodations. But this demand does not extend to all sections of the city. Accordingly, some areas fronting on interior streets will remain relatively free of diverse uses after their covenants expire.

5. A non-zoned city is a cosmopolitan collection of property uses. The standard is supply and demand, and if there is economic justification for the use, it is likely to be forthcoming. Zoning restricts the supply of some uses, and thereby prevents some demands from being satisfied. It may likewise impede innovation. However, in general, zoning

in the major cities, which contain diverse life styles, has responded and accommodated to most consumer demands. This has not occurred usually in the more homogeneous suburbs.

6. Zoning is a legislative function. As such, political, economic and social pressures of many, or even a relatively few, often influence or control zoning decisions. These pressures may even be more important than the provisions of the zoning ordinance. Such forces play no part in a non-zoned city.

7. The most measurable influence of zoning is its effect on multiple-family dwellings. If Houston had adopted zoning in 1962, this would probably have resulted in higher rents and a lesser number and variety of apartments and, in consequence, some tenants would have been priced out of the new apartment market. Most adversely affected would be tenants of average incomes.

8. The experience of the FHA [Federal Housing Administration] suggests that the appreciation over the years in values of new and existing single-family homes has not differed in Houston from those of zoned cities.

Note on Houston

1. *Legal update.* Houston imposed additional regulations after Siegan conducted his study. See generally Archie Henderson, Land Use Controls in Houston, 29 S. Tex. L. Rev. 131 (1987); Teddy M. Kapur, Land Use Regulation in Houston Contradicts the City's Free Market Reputation, 34 Envtl. L. Rep. 10045 (2004). A comprehensive billboard ordinance was adopted in 1980. See City of Houston v. Harris County Outdoor Advertising Association, 732 S.W.2d 42 (Tex. App. 1987) (sustaining ordinance against a variety of challenges). In 1982, the city approved a development ordinance that, among other things, extended the 25-foot setback requirement to certain commercial structures. In 2001, Houston authorized owners of at least 51 percent of the tracts in an uncovenanted neighborhood to petition the city to establish a "prevailing lot size" for the neighborhood to prevent excessive splitting of residential lots. See Kapur, supra, at 10055–56.

But Houston still has refused to adopt zoning. The city electorate rejected zoning by wide margins in 1948 and 1962. Proponents of zoning narrowly failed in 1993, when 52 percent of the electorate voted against it. In the 1993 referendum, opponents outspent proponents by a margin of three to one. Low-income blacks and Anglos were most likely to vote against zoning, and middle-income blacks and Anglos were most likely to favor it. See John F. McDonald, Houston Remains Unzoned, 71 Land Econ. 137 (1995). McDonald concludes that "The pattern of voting suggests that the demand for zoning stems from its use as a device for excluding lower-income people from certain areas."

Advocates of zoning in Houston are likely to be heard from again. Cf. John Mixon, Neighborhood Zoning for Houston, 31 S. Tex. L. Rev. 1 (1990) (offering proposal for zoning selected Houston neighborhoods).

Popular skepticism about zoning hardly is confined to Houston. For example, voters in fast-developing Lincoln County, Missouri, located less than an hour's drive west of St. Louis, have repeatedly repulsed proposed planning and zoning codes. Sherrie Voss Matthews, Missouri County Rejects Planning Again, Again, and Again, Planning, Aug./Sept. 2004, at 41.

2. *Zoning vs. covenants.* Janet Furman Speyrer studied determinants of house value in Houston and two zoned municipalities that Houston surrounds. She investigated whether buyers paid a premium to obtain housing protected by either zoning or covenants, as opposed to housing protected by neither. Controlling for other basic variables, Speyrer

found that buyers paid a 7.0 percent premium for zoning and an 8.7 percent premium for covenants. (No houses in her sample were protected by both sorts of controls.) Statistically, the effect of zoning was not significantly different from the effect of covenants, but the effect of each differed significantly from an environment in which both were absent. See Janet Furman Speyrer, The Effect of Land-Use Restrictions on Market Values of Single-Family Homes in Houston, 2 J. Real Est. Fin. & Econ. 117 (1989). What do Speyrer's results indicate about the effectiveness of nuisance law in Houston? About the magnitude of transaction costs involved in establishing covenants in an existing neighborhood? About the relative merits of covenants and zoning?

3. *The Houston scene.* With a population of 1.95 million in 2000, Houston ranked fourth among U.S. cities. Houston gained 0.99 million in population between 1960 to 2000, in part on account of annexations; the city contained 328 square miles in 1960, and 618 square miles 40 years later. Joel Kotkin attributes Houston's economic strength to its "maintaining the right entrepreneurial climate" and its attracting immigrants from abroad. Joel Kotkin, The Entrepreneurial City, Wall St. J., Aug. 12, 1997, at A14. Citing a Regional Financial Review survey, Kotkin asserts that business costs in Houston are "roughly 18% lower than in Los Angeles, almost 25% below San Francisco and Seattle, and roughly 35% lower than New York's."

In 2000, 5 percent of Houston's residents identified themselves as Asian, 26 percent as African American, and (a partially overlapping) 37 percent as Hispanic. In 2001, Black Enterprise magazine appraised ten large cities and ranked Houston the best in the group for African Americans. Among the reasons for Houston's top ranking were the city's relatively low level of housing segregation, the second-lowest cost-of-living index, the second-lowest housing prices, and the highest incidence of African American business enterprise. See Monique R. Brown & David A. Padgett, 10 Best Cities for African Americans, Black Enterprise, July 2001, at 74, 90.

Most observers assert that land use patterns in Houston are not greatly different from those in other American cities. See, e.g., Hearings Before the Subcomm. on Housing & Community Dev. of the House Comm. on Banking, Finance & Urb. Affairs, 95th Cong. (Jan. 24, 1978) (testimony of Roscoe H. Jones, Director of City Planning in Houston, and of John Mixon, Professor of Law, University of Houston). Downtown Houston includes a striking concentration of skyscrapers, many of them built in the 1970s. Houston has many detractors, however, who are quick to point out its relatively high levels of air pollution, traffic congestion, toxic-waste, and water and sewer problems. See generally Joe R. Feagin, Free Enterprise City: Houston in Political and Economic Perspectives (1988).

4. *Housing costs.* Houston long has been noted for low housing prices. According to 2000 Census data, of the 25 most populous U.S. metropolitan areas, Houston had the second-lowest median market value of owner-occupied houses. (Pittsburgh, a metropolitan area that has been losing population, had slightly lower figure.) Houston's median house value was $79,300, compared to $135,300 for the median top-25 area (Atlanta) and $353,500 for the most expensive area (San Francisco). Statistical Abstract 2003, at 625.

When differences in the quality of housing stocks in these metropolitan areas are taken into account, Houston's relative price advantage remains. In 1991, Houston's quality-adjusted house price was $54,800, compared to $88,600 for Chicago (the median area) and $224,800 for San Francisco (the most expensive). See Thomas G. Thibodeau, House Price Indices from the 1984–1992 MSA American Housing Surveys, 6 J. Housing Res. 439, 466–67 (1995). In 1991, quality-adjusted monthly rents also were relatively low in Houston ($284), compared with the median area (Baltimore, $381) and the most expensive (New York, $640). Id. at 463–64.

To what extent do Houston's relatively low prices stem from the absence of inefficient zoning constraints on housing supply? Or, conversely, from a lessening in the demand for housing when zoning is not present to regulate negative externalities? Recall that Speyrer's findings, reported supra Note 2, indicate that the presence of either zoning or covenants can be expected to boost house values by a bit less that 10 percent, a percentage much smaller that Houston's house-value advantage. See also sources cited at pp. 27–29 (studies indicating that intensive land use regulation contributes to higher housing prices).

Chapter Seven

Financing the Urban Infrastructure

Fiscal considerations deeply influence municipal land use policies. The construction of an improvement such as an apartment building, pizza parlor, or furniture factory typically not only enhances a city's property tax revenues, but also requires the provision of costly new city services. Municipal officials therefore typically are concerned about the net fiscal impact of a proposed new development. Current homeowners, to whom local politicians are likely to cater, generally prefer projects that are fiscal winners, that is, that more than *(pay for themselves.* As a result, in many suburbs, public land use regulation has evolved into a system of fiscal protection and fund-raising. These goals frequently dominate the original rationale for zoning, namely, the minimization of the nuisance effects of physically subnormal land uses.

This chapter begins with a descriptive overview of the system of local public finance. The first full subchapter addresses special assessments — devices local governments traditionally have used to obtain funds from benefited landowners to finance the construction of streets, sewers, and other infrastructure. An important contemporary variant of the special assessment is the business improvement district (BID), an institution that enables neighborhood property owners to arrange for the supply of supplementary urban services. The remaining subchapters turn to issues of central importance in land use law: the power of a local government to raise revenues from developers by either exacting physical improvements or imposing fees, and the duty of a local government to provide services to landowners it would rather leave unserved.

Note on the Fiscal Situation of Local Governments

The statistics reproduced below have been culled mainly from the Statistical Abstract of the United States 2003; Tax Foundation, Inc., Facts and Figures on Government Finance (38th ed. 2004); and prior editions of these two basic sources.

1. *The expanding niche of local government.* In 2001, local governments employed 13.3 million workers, of whom 54 percent were engaged in the provision of public education. In the same year, state governments employed 5.0 million workers, and the federal government, 2.7 million civilian employees. Statistical Abstract 2003, at 312. Thus in 2001, only 13 percent of all government civilian jobholders were working for the

615

federal government, the institution whose workings are the focus of (too?) much of legal education.

Expenditures by all governments in the United States increased from 10 percent of Gross Domestic Product (GDP) in 1929 to 32.4 percent in 2003 — a more than tripling of the governmental share. Local governments took part in this expansion. Local expenditures as a share of GDP rose from 5.9 percent to 10.1 percent between 1950 and 2000. Local governments now obtain about one-third of their funds not from their own sources, but rather from either federal or state subventions.

2. *The objects of local expenditures.* Local governments spend about 40 percent of their funds on primary and secondary education. Public schools have become increasingly costly to operate. Between 1960 and 2000, public school enrollment in grades K through 12 rose by less than a third (from 36.7 million to 47.2 million). At the same time, the cost of operating these schools (measured in constant (2000) dollars) more than quadrupled (from $91 billion to $382 billion). It is hardly surprising that municipal officials who weigh the fiscal impacts of a proposed development are likely to think first of impacts on school-district tax rates.

Table 7-1 provides a more detailed look at how local governments budgeted their spending in 2000. Because Table 7-1 presents aggregate figures, it obscures significant variations from locality to locality.

3. *Sources of local government revenue.* Local governments still obtain most of their funds through their own taxes and user charges. Nevertheless, as Table 7-2 demonstrates, transfer payments from federal and state government provide a major fraction of local wherewithal. In recent decades, state transfers to local units have stabilized at around 30 percent of total local revenue. The recent trend in federal grants to local governments has been more erratic. As Table 7-2 shows, the percentage of local revenue from direct federal grants peaked in the 1970s and since then has tailed off sharply. Table 7-2, however, somewhat understates federal contributions because it fails to itemize the amounts of federal grants to states that states in turn pass on to local governments.

State and federal transfer payments are especially significant in the field of education, where they cover about half the costs of operating local public elementary and secondary schools. The fiscal structure of education, however, varies greatly from state to state. In 2000, the states at the extremes were Vermont, where local taxpayers supported 74 percent of schooling costs, and Hawaii, where the figure was less than 1 percent. (State contributions

TABLE 7-1
Local General Expenditures by Function, Fiscal Year 2000

	($ billions)
Total Local Expenditures	$996.3
Selected Functions:	
Education	$383.3
Highways	39.4
Public Welfare	34.7
Health and Hospitals	67.8
Police and Fire Protection	71.3
Government Administration	47.2
Parks and Recreation	21.0
Sewerage and Solid Waste	42.0
Housing and Community Development	23.4

Source: Statistical Abstract 2003, at 304–05.

TABLE 7-2
Local Revenue and Percentage Distribution by Source
(Selected Fiscal Years)

Year	Total Local Revenue ($ billions)	Percent from Local Sources	Percent from States	Percent from Federal Government
1922	4.1	92.3%	7.5%	0.2%
1940	7.7	75.0	21.4	3.6
1960	37.3	72.9	25.5	1.6
1977	196.5	60.9	30.7	8.5
1985	402.5	65.7	28.9	5.4
1992	647.8	66.6	30.3	3.1
2000	1,013.8	65.5	31.3	3.2

Source: Tax Foundation, Inc., Facts and Figures on Government Finance 243 (1979); id. at 232, 233 (1995); Statistical Abstract 2003, at 302.

in Vermont are likely to increase as a result of Brigham v. State, 692 A.2d 384 (Vt. 1997), which held that the school finance system violated the state constitution.)

Federal transfer payments to local governments can be made in a variety of forms — for example, specific grants-in-aid (e.g., for sewer systems) and less narrowly targeted block-grant programs. Significant state transfer systems commonly include foundation grants in support of local public schools and the sharing of locally generated sales- or gasoline-tax revenues. The formulas by which these state and federal subventions are calculated may affect the fate of development proposals. For example, local officials would be more enthusiastic about a new shopping center if the local treasury would receive a share of the state sales taxes collected there. When state foundation grants and federal education funds are distributed to school districts according to student enrollment, there is less local opposition to proposed residential developments suitable for families with school-age children.

Although state and federal transfer payments can considerably cushion the fiscal burdens of new development, local governments still rely on their own sources for two-thirds of their aggregate revenue. These local sources are quite diverse, as Table 7-3 shows. While local dependence on the property tax has eased somewhat in recent decades, property taxes continue to be the prime source of local revenue (a tradition lauded in William A. Fischel, The Homevoter Hypothesis: How Home Values Influence Local Government Taxation, School Finance, and Land-Use Policies (2001)). Table 7-3 also indicates that nearly one-half of all locally raised revenue is derived from user fees of various kinds.

The history of California's Proposition 13 demonstrates the close linkage between fiscal systems and land use policy. Approved by California voters in 1977, Proposition 13 sharply reduced both property tax rates and future assessment increases. Faced with the prospect of lower property tax revenues, California localities now disfavor residential and industrial uses and favor shopping centers and other sales tax generating uses. See Jonathan Schwartz, Note, Prisoners of Proposition 13: Sales Taxes, Property Taxes, and the Fiscalization of Municipal Land Use Decisions, 71 S. Cal. L. Rev. 183 (1997).

Note on Fiscal-Impact Analysis of a Proposed Development

Because local politicians are loath to add to the tax burden, they may request an evaluation of the fiscal impact of a proposed development. As noted, to perform such a

TABLE 7-3
Local Sources of Local Revenue, Fiscal Year 2000

		($ billions)
Property Taxes		$238.2
General Sales Taxes		57.1
Income Taxes		20.6
Other Taxes		16.8
Charges and Miscellaneous		206.3
Selected Components:		
Special Assessments	3.7	
Solid Waste Management	15.6	
Parks and Recreation	36.0	
Sewerage	24.3	
Utility and Liquor Store Revenue		81.1
Insurance Trust Revenue		43.8
Total Revenue from Local Sources		$662.9

Source: Statistical Abstract 2003, at 302–03.

for study:

study, an investigator must calculate both the new revenue the project would generate to the various local governments within whose boundaries it falls, and also the incremental costs those governments would have to bear to provide services to the development.

There is a voluminous literature — both empirical and theoretical — on revenue/expenditure analysis. See, e.g., Robert W. Burchell et al., Development Impact Assessment Handbook (1994); Gene Bunnell, Fiscal Impact Studies as Advocacy and Story Telling, 12 J. Plan. Liter. 136 (1997). This literature suggests that, in the case of a residential development, the critical fiscal variable is the number of schoolchildren the development will bring in its train. This point is dramatically made by Table 7-4, which presents the results of a Milwaukee study.

As Table 7-4 indicates, most industrial and commercial establishments are fiscal winners. For environmental reasons, most local governments favor light industry (e.g., printing plants or research laboratories) over heavy industry (e.g., manufacture of chemicals or metals). Large shopping centers may be fiscally superior to strip commercial developments if

TABLE 7-4
Revenues and Costs by Land Use and Household Type as a Percent of
All Revenues and Costs, Milwaukee, Wisconsin, 1975*

Land Use or Household Type	Percent of Revenues	Percent of Costs
Industrial	16%	6%
Commercial/Service	16	8
Households with Adults Only	29	20
Households with Children Not in Public Schools	8	5
Households with Children in Public Schools	31	61
Total	100%	100%

*Note: Assumes allocation of all state school aids to households with children in the public schools.
Source: Arlyne S. Bernhard & Mary J. Stott, Milwaukee Revenue Cost Analysis, 36 Urb. Land 16, 18 (No. 11, Dec. 1977).

shopping center owners can be required to provide their own internal parking and police protection.

Dwelling units that contain many bedrooms are magnets for households with school-age children — the fiscal analyst's worst nightmare. According to Robert W. Burchell et al., The New Practitioner's Guide to Fiscal Impact Analysis 64–65, 69 (1985), a two-bedroom, single-family house generates an average of 0.256 school-age children; a three-bedroom house, 0.737; a four-bedroom house, 1.371; and a five-bedroom house, 2.007. In terms of generating school-age children, type of housing matters less than bedroom count. In fact, Burchell et al. report that a three-bedroom, single-family dwelling tends to house slightly *fewer* school-age children (0.737) than does a three-bedroom garden apartment (0.818) or a three-bedroom mobile home (0.937).

On balance, as a fiscal matter local officials are apt to prefer a project of small garden-apartment units to a subdivision of spacious single-family houses. But a generalization of this sort is hazardous. First, as noted, fiscal practices are not uniform throughout the United States. For example, the more a state government contributes to the costs of public schools, the less municipal officials are likely to concern themselves with preventing the entry of schoolchildren. Second, urban growth has numerous subtle secondary effects. The residents of a new housing tract are both consumers and workers, and their presence therefore may later attract fiscally advantageous stores and factories. As another possibility, the construction of a new residential development might cause a chain of moves in the local housing market that ultimately leads to the abandonment and demolition of some older, outmoded, housing units; in that case, the increase in local expenditures to serve the new subdivision would be partly offset by a decrease in expenditures in older neighborhoods. Lastly, analysts may have difficulty taking into account the effects of economies (or diseconomies) of scale in the provision of municipal services.

These complexities often provide a fiscal-impact analyst with enough leeway to reach whatever conclusions a particular patron favors. Hence, consultants to developers tend rosily to foresee favorable fiscal effects, while advisers to antidevelopment organizations gloomily predict net fiscal costs. In any case, local officials may be tempted to levy special assessments or exactions on new developments to improve fiscal outcomes for current residents.

A. *Special Assessments*

McNally v. Township of Teaneck
379 A.2d 446 (N.J. 1977)

SCHREIBER, J.

The Township of Teaneck, pursuant to N.J.S.A. §40:56-1, which authorizes a municipality to assess lands benefited by a local improvement, levied special assessments against 313 residential properties for reimbursement of the costs of paving streets and installing curbs. Owners of 74 properties appealed asserting that the criteria used in determining the amounts of the assessments were improper. . . .

The total project costs consisted of $331,280 for the street paving, $12,105 for the curbing, and 7% overhead. These costs were itemized by streets and were furnished to the commissioners by the Township Engineer, Milton Robbins. The respective street costs varied depending upon such factors as the soil condition and size of the street. The accuracy and reasonableness of these figures are not in dispute.

Proposed assessments were calculated on a front-foot basis, that is, the total cost on a particular street was divided by the total foot frontage and the resultant figure multiplied by the foot frontage of each property. Thereafter, each commissioner visually inspected the improvements and the properties. After having satisfied themselves that the improvements were properly installed, checking the layout of each property on the municipal tax map and considering whether any special circumstances existed, the commissioners compared the allocated cost per property with the increased value in the land. The commissioners met on numerous occasions and held two public meetings with the property owners, some of whom appeared and voiced their objections to the proposed assessments. The commissioners concluded that in each instance the cost of the improvement did not exceed the enhanced value of the property.

In September 1973 the commissioners submitted a report to the Township Council setting forth the proposed assessments and including a map showing the real estate benefited. After holding a hearing at which some property owners appeared, the Council confirmed the assessments with two modifications. The front footage on one property which had been miscalculated was corrected and a street paving cost on one street was adjusted.

In their complaint the landowners asserted that the assessments were improper because "there was no attempt made to assess for the peculiar benefits" to each property as a result of the improvement. They sought the return of any monies which had been paid and a restraint to enjoin the Township from assessing the plaintiffs on any basis other than the peculiar benefits or increased value received. . . .

Municipalities are authorized to undertake the paving or repaving of a street and the curbing of a sidewalk along a street as local improvements. By definition a local improvement is one the cost of which in whole or in part "may be assessed upon the lands in the vicinity thereof benefited thereby." N.J.S.A. §40:56-1. The governing body may in the ordinance authorizing a local improvement provide that a part of the costs be paid by the municipality. N.J.S.A. §40:56-12. Particular assessments may be made either by the tax assessor or board charged with the duty of making general assessments or by a board created for that purpose. N.J.S.A. §40:56-21. In the absence of a board, the governing body may appoint by resolution "three discreet freeholders, residents of the municipality, in no way interested in the improvement, as commissioners to make the assessments for benefits for such improvement." N.J.S.A. §40:56-22. [Commissioners had been appointed in this instance.]

Certain guidelines are statutorily mandated. The total amount of the assessment levied cannot exceed the total project cost less any municipal contribution. N.J.S.A. §40:56-24. Further, all assessments are to be "as nearly as may be in proportion to and not in excess of the peculiar benefit, advantage or increase in value which the respective lots and parcels of real estate shall be deemed to receive by reason of such improvement." N.J.S.A. §40:56-27. If the total cost exceeds the assessments, the municipality must pay the difference. N.J.S.A. §40:56-37.

The key issue in this case is whether utilization of cost per front-foot basis, when employed in conjunction with the judgment of commissioners based upon their visual observations and examinations of each property and their individual experiences, is appropriate in fixing assessments for paving streets and installing curbs in a residential neighborhood.

Use of the cost per foot frontage formula has been constitutionally sustained. Webster v. Fargo, 181 U.S. 394 (1901). It has long been embedded in our history as an appropriate tool for commissioners to use. . . . See Annot., "Assessments for improvements by the front-foot rule," 56 A.L.R. 941 (1928) (listing 23 states other than New Jersey which have upheld the validity of assessments in which the cost per foot frontage has been utilized).

Whether the property subject to assessment has been benefited and, if so, the extent thereof are factual issues. The ultimate test is, of course, the difference between the market value of the land before and after the improvement. . . .

The cost of the new pavement and curb is evidence of its value to the abutting property owner. In the absence of any proof to the contrary the enhancement in value presumably would be equated with that cost. That is comparable to the use of cost to ascertain increased market value for general tax assessments when an improvement is made to an existing structure. In that case, in the absence of other evidence, the value increase would usually be presumptively equivalent to the cost. . . .

Exaction of more than the special benefit to the property owner would constitute a taking of private property for public use without compensation. [Village of] Norwood v. Baker, 172 U.S. 269 (1898); The Tidewater Company v. Coster, 18 N.J. Eq. 518, 526–531 (N.J. 1866). So, if it is shown that the market value enhancement is less than cost, then the assessment must be reduced accordingly. . . .

The special assessment is not a tax which comes within the constitutional provision requiring that property be assessed for taxation under general laws and by uniform rules. N.J. Const. (1947), Art. VIII, §1, ¶1; 14 McQuillin, Municipal Corporations §38.01, at 10–11, §38.05, at 34 (3d ed. 1970). The purpose of a special assessment is to reimburse the municipality in whole or in part for a particular expenditure. The scheme of the local improvement law makes it abundantly clear that its function is not to raise funds for revenue purposes. . . .

The record reveals that the commissioners certified and reported that the assessments were as nearly as may be in proportion to and not in excess of the peculiar benefit, advantage or increase in value which the respective parcels of real estate received by reason of the improvements. The contents of the report are presumptively correct and the taxpayers had the burden of overcoming that presumption by clear and convincing evidence. . . .

[Plaintiffs'] expert Burek's testimony, accepted by the trial court, established that the enhancement in market value for certain properties was less than the assessed proportionate cost. We conclude that it therefore satisfied those taxpayers' burdens of overcoming the presumption. However, the presumption was not overcome as to the remaining properties. . . .

Accordingly, the matter is remanded to the trial court to enter appropriate judgments directing reduction of assessments in those cases where the total assessment exceeded the enhancement value. The remaining assessments shall be confirmed.

Note on Special Assessments

1. *Rules of thumb for assessments.* To reduce administrative costs, a local government is likely to apply a rough formula to estimate the benefits an improvement confers on particular landowners. The front-foot formula is one of the most common, especially for street improvements. How well does this formula work for flag lots that are connected to streets only by narrow rights-of-way? For corner lots? Cf. Palmer Township Municipal Sewer Authority v. Witty, 388 A.2d 306 (Pa. 1978) (owner of lot abutting two streets cannot be assessed for costs of sanitary sewer mains in both streets).

The *area* of the benefited parcel is often used as the basis for assessments for storm sewers. Is area or frontage the better formula for sanitary sewers? How about assessments based on the *value* of the property served? See City of Boca Raton v. State, 595 So. 2d 25 (Fla. 1992) (upholding formula that apportioned special assessments according to property value).

American-Hawaiian Steamship Co. v. Home Savings & Loan Association, 112 Cal. Rptr. 897 (Ct. App. 1974), addressed the issue of how the owners of five large tracts of land should split the costs of a water main servicing all five tracts:

> At trial the parties advocated three potential allocations:
>
> The *straight capacity* method (supported by Home and Calleguas) allocates a share of the cost of the whole water system to each landowner in direct proportion to his share of the whole capacity of the system. If the system has a total capacity of ten c.f.s. [cubic feet per second] and the landowner receives one c.f.s., he pays ten percent of the cost of the whole system. On the assumption that future land development will correspond to the amount of water delivered to the land, advocates of the straight capacity method argue that it spreads the cost and the savings of the entire system evenly among the ultimate consumers on a per capita basis.
>
> The *reaches* method (supported by Metropolitan) allocates cost to a landowner according to his proportionate share of the system, but only for the portions or "reaches" of the system which bring water to his land, not for reaches of the system "down-stream" from the last access on his property. The landowner at the end of the line pays a share of the cost of the whole line, but a landowner near the beginning of the line pays only as though the line ended at his land. Advocates of the reaches method argue that each landowner shares in the savings of the entire system but pays only for what he uses.
>
> The *alternative-facilities* method (supported by American-Hawaiian) allocates costs of the whole system to a landowner in proportion to the savings he incurs by participating in a joint system compared to the cost of building a separate system to deliver the same amount of water to his land. Advocates of the alternative facilities method argue that it spreads the savings incurred by construction of a joint system equitably among the individual landowners.

The court ruled in favor of the straight capacity method because the parties had previously agreed to use that system of allocation. Which of the three methods corresponds most closely to marginal-cost pricing?

2. *Inconsistent municipal use of special assessments.* What if the McNallys' main grievance was that the Township of Teaneck had made use of special assessments when paving the streets in their neighborhood, while spending general municipal revenues to financing similar paving projects elsewhere within the township? In many legal contexts, the victim of an arbitrary governmental classification primarily asserts an unconstitutional denial of equal protection. Special assessment law, however, developed earlier than equal protection law. It gave rise to two special (and implicitly constitutional) doctrines that serve to protect landowners from certain narrow forms of discrimination.

First, as *McNally* notes, a local government can impose a special assessment only for a *local* improvement, as opposed to a *general* improvement. For example, in Heavens v. King County Rural Library District, 404 P.2d 453 (Wash. 1965), the court held that construction of a rural library did not enhance the value of surrounding real estate, and therefore was a general improvement that, under the state constitution, could not be financed by means of special assessments. In that instance, the cost of constructing other rural libraries had been defrayed from general revenues. The local/general improvement distinction, however, is at best a limited tool for preventing discrimination among landowners. Suppose a municipality arbitrarily were to impose special assessments to finance a street repaving on Opposition Street, an exception to its usual policy of financing street repavings through general revenues. The homeowners on Opposition Street would get no benefit from the local/general improvement distinction because repavings undeniably are local improvements. Conversely, if a rural library district were to build an especially fine facility in a particular neighborhood, why shouldn't it be able to use special assessments to recoup those extra expenditures?

Second, a closely related tenet of special assessment law holds that a landowner may be assessed only for *special* benefits, not for *general* benefits that also accrue to others in the community. See, e.g., Blake v. City of Port Hueneme, 68 Cal. Rptr. 2d 627 (Ct. App. 1997) (holding that benefits from beach maintenance program were not special enough to sustain special assessment); City of North Lauderdale v. SMM Properties, Inc., 825 So. 2d 343 (Fla. 2002) (holding that emergency medical services, unlike fire protection services, were not special enough to be financed via special assessment). The following example may provide a fairness rationale for this distinction. A city completes a stunningly efficient public improvement. The project boosts land values within the special assessment district by $500 per acre and land values outside the district by $50 per acre (the amount of the general benefit). In this situation, if special assessments were to be limited to $450 per acre (the amount of the special benefit), all landowners would end up receiving net benefits of $50 per acre.

As the results in the cases cited in this note indicate, state judges in fact are willing to apply the doctrinal distinctions between both local and general improvements and special and general benefits to remedy arbitrary municipal financing practices. Is it likely that state judges would be as responsive if a complaining landowner instead were to invoke the state constitution's equal protection clause (assuming there is one)? Or the state constitution's takings clause (one of the grounds in *McNally*)?

Louisville & Nashville Railroad v. Barber Asphalt Paving Co.
197 U.S. 430 (1905)

Mr. Justice HOLMES delivered the opinion of the court.

This is a proceeding under the Kentucky Statutes, §2834, to enforce a lien upon a lot adjoining a part of Frankfort avenue, in Louisville, for grading, curbing and paving with asphalt the carriageway of that part of the avenue. The defendant, the plaintiff in error, pleaded that its only interest in the lot was a right of way for its main roadbed, and that neither the right of way nor the lot would or could get any benefit from the improvement, but on the contrary rather would be hurt by the increase of travel close to the defendant's tracks. On this ground it set up that any special assessment would deny to it the equal protection of the laws, contrary to the Fourteenth Amendment of the Constitution of the United States. . . .

. . . There is a look of logic when it is said that special assessments are founded on special benefits and that a law which makes it possible to assess beyond the amount of the special benefit attempts to rise above its source. But that mode of argument assumes an exactness in the premises which does not exist. The foundation of this familiar form of taxation is a question of theory. The amount of benefit which an improvement will confer upon particular land, indeed whether it is a benefit at all, is a matter of forecast and estimate. In its general aspects at least it is peculiarly a thing to be decided by those who make the law. The result of the supposed constitutional principle is simply to shift the burden to a somewhat large taxing district, the municipality, and to disguise rather than to answer the theoretic doubt. It is dangerous to tie down legislatures too closely by judicial constructions not necessarily arising from the words of the Constitution. . . .

A statute like the present manifestly might lead to the assessment of a particular lot for a sum larger than the value of the benefits to that lot. The whole cost of the improvement is distributed in proportion to area, and a particular area might receive no benefits at all, at least if its present and probable use be taken into account. If that possibility does not invalidate the act it would be surprising if the corresponding fact should invalidate an assessment. Upholding the act as embodying a principle generally fair and doing as nearly equal justice as can be expected seems to import that if a particular case of hardship arises under it in its natural and ordinary application, that hardship must be borne as one of the imperfections of human things. And this has been the implication of the cases.

     . . . We are not called on to say that we think the assessment fair. But we are compelled to declare that it does not go beyond the bounds set by the Fourteenth Amendment of the Constitution of the United States.

     Judgment affirmed.

     [Justices WHITE and PECKHAM dissented without opinion.]

Note on the Different Roles of Federal and State Courts in Special Assessment Cases

1. *The Supreme Court bows out.* The Supreme Court's decision in Village of Norwood v. Baker, 172 U.S. 269 (1898), federalized special assessment law by holding that a special assessment substantially in excess of special benefits was, to the extent of the excess, a taking of property in violation of the Fourteenth Amendment. This doctrine immediately flooded the federal courts with special assessment cases. As *Barber Asphalt* indicates, by 1905 the Supreme Court had backed away from the activist *Norwood* doctrine. In his opinion, Justice Holmes declines even to cite *Norwood*, perhaps because the Court had already begun its retreat from *Norwood* in French v. Barber Asphalt Paving Co., 181 U.S. 324 (1901). For an endorsement of the Supreme Court's implicit decision to relegate this area of constitutional law to the state courts, see Robert C. Ellickson, Suburban Growth Controls, 86 Yale L.J. 385, 469–73 (1977).

Harbours Pointe of Nashotah, LLC v. Town of Nashotah, 278 F.3d 701 (7th Cir. 2002), holds that Williamson County Regional Planning Commission v. Hamilton Bank, 473 U.S. 172 (1985), excerpted at p. 234, applies to a federal takings challenge to an allegedly excessive special assessment, and therefore that a complainant must exhaust state remedies before pursuing a claim in federal court.

2. *The wisdom of active judicial review of the fairness of special assessments.* Should state courts also defer to municipal assessment practices on the ground that local political processes can be expected to prevent most abuses and thus that judges are wise to devote their limited energies to other fronts? Would this argument be persuasive in a case such as *Barber Asphalt*, where the aggrieved landowner was an interstate railroad, a particularly inviting target for local taxation?

A variety of other standards of review lie between the active scrutiny of *McNally* and the extreme deference of *Barber Asphalt.* Although most courts presume the correctness of assessment amounts (see, e.g., City of Wasilla v. Wilsonoff, 698 P.2d 656 (Alaska 1985)), the presumption is rebuttable. Fluckey v. City of Plymouth, 100 N.W.2d 486 (Mich. 1960), invalidated the assessment of abutting homeowners for part of the costs of widening a "Class A road." The Supreme Court of Michigan implied that it might sometimes uphold assessments in excess of benefits, but concluded it would not permit the assessment of those — such as the plaintiff homeowners — who had received no benefits from "the conversion of a sleepy country road into a 4-lane thoroughfare for heavy traffic." Id. at 487.

Richard A. Musgrave & Peggy B. Musgrave, Public Finance in Theory and Practice
8–9, 43–44, 49 (5th ed. 1989)

We begin with . . . the proposition that certain goods — referred to here as *social*, or public, as distinct from *private* goods — cannot be provided for through the market system, i.e., by transactions between individual consumers and producers. In some cases the market fails entirely, while in others it can function only in an inefficient way. Why is this the case?

SOCIAL GOODS AND MARKET FAILURE

The basic reason for market failure in the provision of social goods is not that the need for such goods is felt collectively whereas that for private goods is felt individually. While peoples' preferences are influenced by their social environment, in the last resort wants and preferences are experienced by individuals and not by society as a whole. Moreover, both social and private goods are included in their preference maps. Just as I can rank my preferences among housing and backyard facilities, so I may also rank my preferences among my private yard and my use of public parks. Rather, the difference arises because the benefits to which social goods give rise are not limited to one particular consumer who purchases the good, as is the case for private goods, but become available to others as well.

If I consume a hamburger or wear a pair of shoes, these particular products will not be available to other individuals. My and their consumption stand in a rival relationship. But now consider measures to reduce air pollution. If a given improvement in air quality is obtained, the resulting gain will be available to all who breathe. In other words, consumption of such products by various individuals is "nonrival" in the sense that one person's partaking of benefits does not reduce the benefits available to others. This has important implications for how consumers behave and how the two types of goods are to be provided.

The market mechanism is well suited for the provision of private goods. It is based on exchange, and exchange can occur only where there is an exclusive title to the property which is to be exchanged. In fact, the market system may be viewed as a giant auction where consumers bid for products and producers sell to the highest bidders. Thus the market furnishes a signaling system whereby producers are guided by consumer demands. For goods such as hamburgers or pairs of shoes this is an efficient mechanism. Nothing is lost and much is gained when consumers are excluded unless they pay. Application of the exclusion principle tends to be an efficient solution.

But such is not the case with respect to social goods. Here it would be inefficient to exclude any one consumer from partaking in the benefits, since such participation does not reduce consumption by anyone else. The application of exclusion would thus be undesirable even if it were readily feasible. . . .

MARKET FAILURE DUE TO NONEXCLUDABILITY

A second instance of market failure arises where consumption is rival but exclusion though appropriate is not feasible. Whereas most goods which are rival in consumption also lend themselves to exclusion, some rival goods may not do so. Consider, for example, travel on a crowded cross-Manhattan street during rush hours. The use of the available space is distinctly rival and exclusion (the auctioning off or sale of the available space) would be efficient and should be applied. The reason is that use of crowded space would then go to those who value it most and who are willing to offer the highest price. But such exclusion would be impossible or too costly to be administered.[1] We are dealing with a situation in which exclusion should but cannot be applied. Here the difficulty of applying exclusion is *the* cause of market failure. Public provision is required until techniques can be found to apply exclusion. . . .

[margin handwritten note: ex - use of Manhattan street goto should go to the highest bidder (person who values it the most) → but . . . .]

[handwritten: ...ld be impossible or too costly to be administered.]

COMBINED CAUSES OF MARKET FAILURE

Although the features of nonrival consumption and nonexcludability need not go together, they frequently do. In these instances — for example, air purification, national defense, streetlights — exclusion both *cannot* and *should not* be applied. . . .

MIXED GOODS

Throughout the preceding discussion, a sharp distinction was drawn between private goods, such as hamburgers, the benefits of which are wholly internalized (rival), and others, such as air purification, the benefits of which are wholly external (nonrival). This polarized view is helpful for understanding the essential difference between private and social goods, but it is not realistic. In reality, mixed situations of various kinds arise.

EXTERNALITIES OF PRIVATE GOODS

Such is the case wherever private consumption or production activities generate externalities. Suppose, for instance, that A derives benefits from being inoculated against polio, but so do many others for whom the number of potential carriers, and hence the danger of infection, is reduced. Or by getting educated, A not only derives personal benefits but also makes it possible for others to enjoy association with a more educated community. Since large numbers of other consumers may be affected, bargaining does not work and a budgetary process will again be needed to secure preference revelation. But the correct budgetary intervention in this case will not involve full budgetary provision; rather, it will take the form of subsidy to private purchases. . . .

PUBLIC PROVISION FOR SOCIAL GOODS

The problem, then, is how the government should determine how much of such goods is to be provided. . . .

. . . Consumers have no reason to step forward and declare what the service is truly worth to them individually unless they are assured that others will do the same. Placing tax contributions on a voluntary basis would therefore be to no avail. People will prefer to enjoy as free riders what is provided by others. A different technique is needed by which the supply of social goods and the cost allocation thereof can be determined.

This is where the political process must enter the picture as a substitute for the market mechanism. Voting by ballot must be resorted to in place of voting by dollar bids. Since voters know that they will be subject to the voting decision (whether by simple majority or some other voting rule), they will find it in their interest to vote such that the outcome will fall closer to their own preferences. Decision making by voting becomes a substitute for

1. As suggested by Prof. William Vickrey of Columbia University, electronic devices may eventually be developed which record the passage of vehicles through intersections and permit the imposition of corresponding charges, adjusted to differ for rush hours and slack periods. Such charges may then be billed to the vehicle owner via a computer, and the costs of crowding city streets may thus be internalized.

preference revelation through the market, and the collection of cost shares thus decided upon must be implemented via the tax system. As shown later, taxation generates efficiency costs or deadweight losses which do not arise in a market for private goods. The result of the vote, moreover, will not please everyone but it can only hope to approximate an efficient solution. It will do so more or less perfectly, depending on the efficiency of the voting process and the homogeneity of the community's preferences in the matter. . . .

PUBLIC PROVISION VERSUS PUBLIC PRODUCTION ⟩   — *Different*

. . . [W]e must draw a clear distinction between public *provision* for social goods, as the term is used here, and public *production*. These are two distinct and indeed unrelated concepts which should not be confused with one another.

Private goods may be produced and sold to private buyers either by private firms, as is normally done, or by public enterprises, such as public power and transportation authorities or the nationalized British coal industry. Social goods, such as spaceships or military hardware, similarly may be produced by private firms and sold to government; or they may be produced directly under public management, as are services rendered by civil servants or municipal enterprises. If we say that social goods are *provided* publicly, we mean that they are financed through the budget and made available free of direct charge. How they are *produced* does not matter. . . .

Note on Special Assessments and Public Goods

1. *Rationales for municipal programs.* Is it appropriate for a municipality to *provide* streets? To *produce* them? Which of the following three rationales, all mentioned by Musgrave and Musgrave, best supports the use of local general revenues to defray some or all of street costs. (1) additional street users cause no congestion; (2) nonpaying street users cannot practically be excluded; and (3) street use generates positive externalities?

Should a local government provide (and produce?) fireworks displays on the Fourth of July? Nursery schools? Banks?

2. *Benefits charges vs. general taxes.* Special assessments, subdivision exactions, and other user fees are varieties of *benefits charges*, a category distinguishable from the *general taxes* on which local governments otherwise rely for revenue. In 1972, the Urban Institute published an important collection of essays discussing the potential use of benefits financing for a wide variety of municipal services, including schools, transportation, waste collection, fire protection, and recreation. In their introduction, the editors emphasize the possible efficiencies to be gained from pricing urban services:

> The economic case for the expansion and rationalization of pricing in the urban public sector rests essentially on the contribution it can make to allocative efficiency. Prices will provide correct signals to indicate the quantity and quality of things citizens desire and help bring about the proper balance between private and public production of these things. A properly designed price system can potentially serve this end whenever the public provision of a service, or the private use of a common property resource such as air or water, is accompanied by significant divisible or appropriable benefits accruing to identifiable individuals, provided the cost of its implementation and operation does not exceed the gains in terms of more efficient resource allocation. Many of the services provided by urban local governments appear to qualify by this criterion.
>
> In practice, of course, it may not be desirable to exclude people by imposing user charges even when it is technically possible to do so; for example, because an objective of policy is to

redistribute income in the form of a particular service, or because it is believed that individuals will, if faced with a money price, choose to consume less of certain services than is considered socially desirable. . . .

Selma J. Mushkin, Public Prices: An Overview, *in* Public Prices for Public Products 3, 11 (Selma J. Mushkin ed., 1972). See also Clayton P. Gillette & Thomas D. Hopkins, Federal User Fees: A Legal and Economic Analysis, 67 B.U. L. Rev. 795 (1987) (overview of the theory of user fees).

3. *An efficiency justification for simple (and inexact) formulas for special assessments.* Perhaps Justice Holmes's tolerance of the overcharging that had allegedly occurred in *Barber Asphalt* can be illuminated by Professor Michelman's fairness test for takings, excerpted at p. 147. The argument runs as follows. Municipal use of special assessments (and other benefits charges) promises to improve the efficiency of resource allocation because the organized beneficiaries of a project will not be able to externalize its cost to unorganized taxpayers. All citizens thus have an interest in more widespread employment of user charges. However, the administrative costs of precisely calculating individual benefits from specific projects far exceed the administrative costs of collecting most types of general taxes. An efficiency-minded citizen, therefore, should see the fairness of using a crude rule of thumb (such as the front-foot rule) to approximate benefits. Although this approach might occasionally result in the overassessment of some landowners, even those victims should be able to understand that precision in special assessments is not in their own long-term self-interest.

4. *Principles of tax equity.* Notions of fairness (perhaps unrelated to efficiency considerations) may affect politicians' and judges' assessments of municipal fiscal practices. In The Theory of Public Finance (1959), a pathbreaking work that was a predecessor of the book just excerpted, Richard Musgrave identifies two major schools of tax equity. Members of the first school espouse what Musgrave calls the *benefit approach* to taxation. Its adherents — who have included Grotius, Hobbes, Locke, and Bentham — believe that fair taxes are those scaled according to the governmental benefits received by a taxpayer. See id. at 61–64. If this principle were to be exclusively followed, government would be hard put to effect any major redistribution of wealth.

Musgrave identifies a second camp adhering to an *ability-to-pay approach* to taxation. Rousseau and John Stuart Mill are among those who have championed this principle. See id. at 90–92. If a government were to tax by ability to pay, but to distribute services equally to all constituents, it would redistribute wealth from rich to poor. How much a government should redistribute in this way is a question of *vertical equity*. Economists have yet to reach consensus on the optimal amount of redistribution, and voters also tend to hold divergent opinions on this issue.

Members of both the benefit and ability-to-pay schools tend to recognize the importance of a third principle of taxation: *horizontal equity* — that is, the equal treatment of equals. See id. at 160–61. For example, advocates of the benefit approach might not want some taxpayers to be charged for services they were receiving if similarly situated taxpayers were not being charged. By the same token, adherents of the ability-to-pay approach would not want some rich persons to be able to escape taxation or some poor persons to be ineligible for government benefits that similar poor persons were receiving.

Should all types of governments necessarily adopt the same principles of tax equity? Public finance economists traditionally have argued that local governments should mainly relegate ability-to-pay fiscal programs to the national government, partly on account of risks of strategic migration. See Kirk J. Stark, Fiscal Federalism and Tax Progressivity, 51 UCLA

L. Rev. 1389, 1408–10 (2004) (reviewing the debate over the issue). Does it follow that a local government should tax primarily according to benefits conferred?

Tax Foundation, Inc., Special Assessments and Service Charges in Municipal Finance
9–10, 19–20 (1970)

During the first three decades of the 20th century, special assessments played a key role in financing the development of public capital in American cities. In fact, at times the special assessment rivaled the general property tax as a source of revenue for some localities.

In 1913, cities over 100,000 population obtained about 12 percent of their revenue from this source. Four — Los Angeles, Kansas City, Portland, and Oakland — derived 20 percent of their revenue from this source, while only five cities out of 199 over 30,000 did not use it. . . . [S]pecial assessments as a percent of total general revenue for all municipalities have declined from 6.7 percent in 1930 to 1.5 percent in 1968 [and to 0.6 percent in 2000 — EDS.]. . . .

Today, the special assessment is playing a relatively minor role in municipal finance. For example, in 1962 New York City completely abandoned the use of special assessments as a financing instrument. All local improvements are now included in the capital budget and paid for by levying the cost by citywide assessment which is collectible with the real estate tax.

One explanation for the decreasing use of special assessment financing lies in the adoption of long-range city planning, including modern subdivision regulations where the subdivider is often required to install urban facilities before he can sell lots. Federal Housing Administration regulations require that facilities be available before mortgages will be insured. The subdivider customarily meets these requirements by installing the necessary improvements and including their cost in the sale price of the property, which in turn is financed by the buyer through regular payments on the mortgage.

Another factor accounting for the diminishing importance of special assessments, particularly in large cities, may be traceable to political maneuvering. Any fiscal device of this general character which attempts to recover from its direct beneficiaries the cost of a governmental expenditure will be subject to constant pressure and attrition. A politician who can secure the reduction or cancellation of special assessments may win the gratitude of many constituents of his district. There have been instances where elected officials have sought to demonstrate their competence and worthiness of support at the polls by citing the volume of special assessments they have diverted from their districts.

A third factor which helps explain the decline of special assessment financing, particularly in densely populated urban areas, is the increasing difficulty of separating private benefits from general public benefits. The improvement of a street or installation of a sewer in 1970 cannot always be viewed as an isolated project related solely to the adjacent property. The tremendous increase in automobile traffic has made the width and quality of many street improvements as much a matter of benefit and interest to the general public as a matter of convenience to adjacent property owners. Because of rising concern about environmental quality, the installation of storm and sanitary sewers has become a matter of regional as well as local importance. . . .

The fact that special assessments are not deductible for Federal income tax purposes reduces their popularity as a financing device. Property owners may also fear that their property taxes will be increased if properties are revalued for special assessment purposes.

Note on the Near Death and Eventual Transfiguration of Special Assessments

1. *History.* Special assessments appeared as early as 1250, when an English statute apportioned by acreage the costs of repairing a seawall around Romney Marsh. At the dawn of the nineteenth century, the City of New York began using the device to finance the opening and paving of streets. See generally Stephen Diamond, The Death and Transfiguration of Benefit Taxation: Special Assessments in Nineteenth-Century America, 12 J. Legal Stud. 201 (1983). On the major role of special assessments in the early years of Chicago, see Robin L. Einhorn, Property Rules: Political Economy in Chicago, 1833–1872 (1991). As the Tax Foundation study indicates, however, the importance of this financing tool generally declined over the course of the twentieth century.

2. *Federal income tax treatment of special assessments.* The advent of the income tax may partly explain the waning popularity of special assessments. Property taxes are deductible from income (I.R.C. §164(a)(1)), but special assessments for capital improvements are not and instead are added to the basis of the benefited property (I.R.C. §164(c)(1)). Therefore, if a small suburb were about to install streetlights on all its residential streets, its residents would emphatically prefer that the streetlights be financed by property taxes, not special assessments. What principles of tax policy, if any, support allowing nonbusiness taxpayers to deduct local general taxes, but not user charges? See Brookes Billman & Noel Cunningham, Nonbusiness State and Local Taxes: The Case for Deductibility, 28 Tax Notes 1107 (1985).

3. *Revival.* The business improvement district (BID), which relies on a variant of special assessment financing, was first invented in Canada. Beginning in the 1980s, BIDs burgeoned in the United States.

2nd Roc-Jersey Associates v. Town of Morristown
731 A.2d 1 (N.J. 1999)

HANDLER, Judge.

The principal issue raised in this appeal is whether assessments imposed on real property in a municipal Special Improvement District are unconstitutional because residential properties are excluded from the assessments. [Both the trial court and the intermediate appellate court had sustained the constitutionality of the assessments at issue.] . . .

I

In 1993, the Town of Morristown enacted Ordinance 0-42-93 . . . pursuant to N.J.S.A. §40:56-65 to -89, which authorized municipalities to establish Special Improvement Districts (SIDs).

The statute provided for the creation of a District Management Corporation empowered to fund, manage, acquire, and oversee the rehabilitation of properties in SID districts, and to attract new businesses. N.J.S.A. §40:56-83(b). The SID was created due to declining economic conditions in Morristown. . . .

. . . The overwhelming majority of [New Jersey] SIDs, like the Morristown SID, use real property value as the basis for determining SID special assessments. The Morristown ordinance specifically exempted residential property from the SID special assessment, *viz*:

(c) All properties within the [SID] that are used for residential purposes, and those portions of mixed use properties that are residential are deemed excluded from the assessing or taxing provisions of this ordinance and are expressly exempt from any tax or assessment made for Special Improvement District purposes. . . .

The annual budget for the SID in 1994 was $500,000. A special assessment was made on all subject property within the SID on the basis of .105% of the property's assessed value for local real property tax purposes. [All revenues from these assessments went exclusively to the SID.] Plaintiffs, . . . (collectively Roc-Jersey), the owners of Headquarters Plaza, a commercial office complex, were assessed $64,317.75. . .

Forty states, including New Jersey, have adopted legislation enabling the creation of SIDs, which various states also term Business Improvement Districts, Community Development Districts, Municipal Improvement Districts, and Economic Development Districts. See David J. Kennedy, Note, Restraining the Power of Business Improvement Districts: The Case of the Grand Central Partnership, 15 Yale L. & Pol'y Rev. 283, 290 (1996). Of these states, the vast majority have constitutional provisions requiring uniformity of taxation similar to New Jersey's, but they have yet to strike down SID legislation as unconstitutional. As of 1995, at least twenty-five other municipalities in New Jersey had established SIDs.

The urban setting in which SIDs are created is central to understanding the benefit offered by the Morristown SID. Urban sprawl, that is, a landscape dotted by planned office developments and malls connected by highways and thoroughfares, has resulted in the diminishing vitality of traditional city centers, such as Morristown's Green. Increasingly, office developments and shopping malls provide services associated with town centers, such as dry cleaning, pharmacies and food courts, while town centers, which already have such services as a result of being integrated communities, languish.

SIDs provide a quasi-public solution to this problem. . . . SIDs are organized and financed by property owners and merchants, operate on the basis of state and local laws, and use revenues garnered from self-taxation to finance various services and capital improvements not provided by the municipality. See John C. Bollens, Special District Governments in the United States 68 (1957).[1]

II

Plaintiffs focus their constitutional challenge on the 1995 amendment to N.J.S.A. §40:56-66(b), which allows municipalities to exclude residential properties from the SID assessment. That exclusion, according to plaintiffs, violates several constitutional principles. They contend foremost that the exclusion of residential property is unconstitutional because the SID special assessment is a tax, rather than a special assessment, and therefore violates the Uniformity Clause of the New Jersey Constitution, which requires real property taxes to be applied uniformly to all classes of real property. N.J. Const. art. VIII, §1, ¶1(a). Plaintiffs also contend that the exclusion of residential property from such a tax violates the constitutional provision that authorizes only general or special purpose exemptions from taxation. N.J. Const. art. VIII, §1, ¶2. Plaintiffs present the related claim that the factors that serve to invalidate the special assessments under the Uniformity Clause also invalidate the assessments as an unconstitutional taking without just compensation. N.J. Const. art. I, ¶20; U.S. Const. amend. v. . . .

It is well recognized that the Uniformity Clause of the Constitution is inapplicable to special assessments. McNally v. Township of Teaneck, 379 A.2d 446 ([N.J.] 1977). Assessments "are not such taxes as are referred to in the various clauses of the constitution

---

[1] [EDS: The prior three paragraphs were repositioned from later in Judge Handler's opinion.]

and they are neither embraced, nor intended to be embraced in them." 14 McQuillin, Municipal Corporations §38.05 at 44 (3d ed. 1987). . . .

Traditionally, the differences between an assessment and a tax include: an assessment supports local improvements, while a tax finances general operations; an assessment is a one-time charge, while a tax is annual; and an assessment requires that the benefit be direct, while a tax requires no such direct benefit. 5 Richard R. Powell, Powell on Real Property, §39.03[1] (1998). The improvement must benefit the assessed property, and that benefit must be special and local, that is, the benefit to the specific property must be substantially greater than to the public in general. Id. at §39.03[2]. The benefit can be measured by increased market value or by the overall economic effect of the improvement. Ibid. Lastly, the benefit must be certain rather than speculative, although it may arise in the future. Ibid. These salient features of the special assessment are codified by statute. . . .

The SID special assessment does not conform to the prototypical special assessment. Unlike N.J.S.A. §40:56-21, which authorizes special assessments for local improvements that are essentially identified with specific properties, the SID statute, N.J.S.A. §40:56-73, permits special assessments that bestow general benefits consisting of services and improvements on a class of properties within the SID. The underlying improvements that are funded by the SID assessments are not necessarily physical, concrete, or permanent, nor are they directly adherent to the specific commercial properties that are assessed. Further, the benefits to the commercial properties are derived from improvements that are generalized and relatively intangible; the benefits consist of the results of the provision of ongoing public activities and services, such as advertising campaigns, meter bagging, street sweeping, the encouragement of tourism, hospitality guides, and business recruitment, as well as physical improvements, such as streetscape enhancement, supplemental lighting, and other aesthetic measures. N.J.S.A. §40:56-83(b). These kinds of services supplement traditional municipal services, but they are specifically intended and designed to better commercial properties and promote economic growth in the business community. Further, while traditional special assessments are one-time payments for a specific improvement, the SID assessments are levied annually for continuing services and recurrent improvements and are collected to finance the SID's ongoing operations.

Governmental services in conjunction with physical improvements that are designed to enhance property use, function and value have been upheld as a benefit to specific property sufficient to support the imposition of a special assessment. In City of Seattle v. Rogers Clothing for Men, 787 P.2d 39 (Wash. 1990), the Supreme Court of Washington upheld SID special assessments used to support advertising, maintenance, flower planting, sidewalk cleaning, information and direction signs, and other services provided to businesses, because these constituted special benefits to commercial properties. . . . We are persuaded by the holding of *City of Seattle* that special assessments in a SID will not be deemed taxes for the purposes of the Uniformity Clause of the Washington Constitution and that such special assessments could be limited to commercial properties. That court determined that any spillover of benefits to the general public that might accrue from the services provided by the SID were insufficient to alter the calculus, nor did such spillover alter the essential purpose and effect of the SID to benefit primarily the commercial properties.

We conclude that the core of the definition of a special assessment [is met when a levy] is used to provide a combination of services and improvements that are intended and designed to benefit particular properties and demonstrably enhance the value and/or the use or function of the properties that are subject to the special assessment. . . .

Plaintiffs argue that even if the assessments are upheld as special assessments that confer benefits to the commercial properties, the method of assessment was overly broad and not sufficiently tailored to the benefit received by individual properties. For that reason, plaintiffs contend, the assessments are invalid.

A valid special assessment must be "as nearly as may be in proportion" to the benefit received. *McNally*, supra, 379 A.2d at 449. It must not be in "substantial excess" of the special benefits to the land. See [Village of] Norwood v. Baker, 172 U.S. 269, 279 (1898). Special assessments, however, need not be measured with mathematical precision. . . .

None of the benefits provided by the SID are aimed directly at residences and none of its budget is spent directly on residential properties. Although a portion of the SID budget is spent on beautification and street cleaning, services from which residents also benefit, a larger portion is spent on hospitality guards (who assist visitors to Morristown, not residents), business and retail recruitment, advertising campaigns and facade loans and grants to commercial and retail properties. In addition, the SID is responsible for aesthetic or cosmetic physical improvements that serve as part of a larger effort aimed exclusively at benefiting commercial properties. . . .

The Appellate Division was aware of the classical method to determine assessments strongly urged by plaintiffs, that is, "the difference between the market value of the land before and after the improvement." *McNally*, supra, 379 A.2d at 450. The Court found, however, that this method would be "overwhelming" to the SID, and would divert its existing resources to expert valuation of increased market value rather than to the services and improvements the SID was meant to provide. . . .

It is not unreasonable for Morristown to select one of the simpler methods of valuing benefits during the initial phase of the SID. The tax system offers several advantages in that it is updated periodically and provides property owners with a basis to challenge erroneous tax assessments and the derivative SID assessments. Although a more complex method might yield a fairer apportionment, it would be substantially more expensive and difficult to employ in the early stages of the SID. . . .

We conclude that the SID provides sufficiently identifiable benefits to the subject properties and that the special assessments are measured reasonably and fairly in proportion to the benefits conferred. Therefore, the enabling legislation and implementing ordinance have not created real property taxes and do not violate the tax clauses of the Constitution in allowing municipalities to exempt residential properties from the SID assessment. Further, because the benefits are substantial and the cost proportional to those benefits, the SID assessment is not an unconstitutional taking of property without compensation. . . .

[Affirmed.]

Note on Business Improvement Districts

1. *BIDs*. In 2005, New York City had 50 BIDs, and, according to some estimates, there are over 1,000 nationwide. For favorable descriptive assessments, see Lawrence Houstoun, Capitalist Tool, Planning, Jan. 2004, at 26; Heather MacDonald, BIDs Really Work, City J., Spring 1996, at 29. On the law of BIDs, see generally Richard Briffault, A Government for Our Time? The Business Improvement District and Urban Governance, 99 Colum. L. Rev. 365 (1999) (a superb overview); Mark S. Davies, Business Improvement Districts, 52 Wash. U. J. Urb. & Contemp. L. 187 (1997).

Many BIDs focus on services such as litter removal, security, business promotion, and prevention of graffiti and aggressive panhandling. Does the provision of *supplementary* police protection and trash collection confer a "special" and "local" benefit? Cf. McGowan v. Capital Center, Inc., 19 F. Supp. 2d 642 (S.D. Miss. 1998) (rebuffing equal protection challenge to BID assessment used in part to finance such supplementary services).

How should votes to elect members of a BID's board of directors be allocated? The statutes and ordinances that undergird these organizations commonly permit the conferral of significant voting power on the owners of the property assessed to finance BID operations. Should a BID instead have to comport with the one-person/one-vote electoral principle, whose application would shift political control from property owners to residents of the BID district? See Kessler v. Grand Central District Management Association, 960 F. Supp. 760 (S.D.N.Y. 1997) (finding one-person/one-vote principle inapplicable to the BID at hand). For contrasting views on this issue, compare David J. Kennedy, Restraining the Power of Business Improvement Districts: The Case of the Grand Central Partnership, 15 Yale L. & Pol'y Rev. 283 (1996) (urging application of one-person/one-vote principle to a BID that provides more than limited services), with Brian R. Hochleutner, Note, BIDs Fare Well: The Democratic Accountability of Business Improvement Districts, 78 N.Y.U. L. Rev. 374 (2003) (defending traditional BID governance structure that substantially empowers landowners). How, if at all, does a BID differ from a residential community association, which typically allocates votes according to property ownership, not residency? See p. 590.

2. *Exemptions from special assessments.* Is a charitable organization such as a religious organization that is exempt under state law from local property taxes also exempt from special assessments, including ones for BIDs? Many courts hold otherwise. See, e.g., German Evangelical Lutheran Church v. City of Charleston, 576 S.E.2d 150 (S.C. 2003) (holding that legislature did not intend to exempt charitable institutions from assessments). But see City of New Hope v. Catholic Cemeteries, 467 N.W.3d 336 (Minn. Ct. App. 1991) (holding that city could not impose on tax-exempt cemetery a special assessment for street improvements). Can government-owned lands be subjected to assessments? See Annot., Exemption of Public School Property from Assessments for Local Improvements, 15 A.L.R.3d 847 (1967).

3. *Judicial policing of assessment district boundaries.* In Snyder Realty Co. v. City of Overland Park, 492 P.2d 187 (Kan. 1971), the city had used special assessments to defray part of the costs of improving two major streets. The assessment district was defined to include all owners of abutting land and also one nonabutter (the plaintiff), whose 63-unit apartment development was about one-half mile from the improvements but connected to one of the improved streets by means of a private right-of-way. Plaintiff objected to being the only nonabutter subjected to an assessment. The Supreme Court of Kansas noted that challengers to assessment district boundaries "must shoulder a heavy burden." Nevertheless it found the plaintiff's inclusion to have been arbitrary and therefore quashed the assessment on plaintiff's property. Should courts be more active in policing district boundaries than in scrutinizing the accuracy of the formulas used to spread costs among assessed owners? Cf. A-S-P Associates v. City of Raleigh, 258 S.E.2d 444 (N.C. 1979), excerpted at p. 500 (unsuccessful challenge to how city had drawn boundary of historic district).

B.   Development Exactions

A land developer typically has to render many forms of tribute to obtain regulatory clearances. A local government may exact land, land improvements, and fees during the course of awarding a zoning change, subdivision map approval, site plan approval, or building permit. Municipal exactions from developers, whatever their drawbacks, plainly are administratively cheaper than a municipality's subsequent imposition on lot purchasers of special assessments to finance the same item of infrastructure.

The limit on municipal exactions is a central issue in land development law. The Calabresi-Melamed framework, excerpted at p. 532, helps place the issue in perspective. A municipality has "property rule" protection when it is entitled to forbid development outright. Partly because takings doctrines and related legal rules set a ceiling on a municipality's property rule protections, a municipality instead may seek to make a developer pay for certain costs associated with development — a form of "liability rule" protection for the municipality. If there were to be no limits on development charges, a municipality in practice could forbid all development by charging a sufficiently high price. Inevitably, then, a legal system that aspires to protect landowners from regulatory takings also must protect them from confiscatory development charges that would have the same consequences.

Vicki Been, "Exit" as a Constraint on Land Use Exactions: Rethinking the Unconstitutional Conditions Doctrine
91 Colum. L. Rev. 473, 474–83 (1991)

I. Land Use Exactions: A Brief Overview

Exactions require that developers provide, or pay for, some public facility or other amenity as a condition for receiving permission for a land use that the local government could otherwise prohibit. Exactions are an outgrowth of the centuries-old practice of levying "special assessments" upon real property to pay for public improvements, such as paved streets, that provide a direct and special benefit to the property. In the 1920s and 1930s, widespread bankruptcies and delinquencies on special assessments, which typically were levied after an improvement was installed, left many local governments unable to recoup the costs of public improvements. Communities then sought ways of shifting the initial costs of improvements, and hence the risk of failure, to the private subdivider. Initially, local governments required *on-site dedications*: the community demanded that a developer dedicate land within the subdivision on which the community could construct streets, sidewalks, utilities, and other such facilities. Alternatively, the local government required the developer to construct and dedicate these facilities to the community. Communities initially required dedications only for such basic facilities as streets and sidewalks, but many communities eventually demanded that developers dedicate land within the subdivision for schools, fire and police stations, and parks or open space.

Land or facilities within a subdivision were not always ideally suited to meet a particular need, so local governments began to impose *off-site dedications*, which required developers to dedicate land or facilities not located within the subdivision. They also began to charge *fees-in-lieu-of-dedication*, giving developers the option of contributing money to the community rather than dedicating land or facilities.

Because fees-in-lieu-of-dedication typically could be applied only to subdivisions, many local governments implemented broader *impact fees*, which assess developers for the costs that the development will impose upon the government's capital budget for public services. Impact fees can be levied upon apartment buildings or other residential dwellings that are not located in a subdivision, as well as upon office, commercial, and industrial developments.

Linkages are a hybrid of impact fees and off-site dedications. Linkage programs condition approval of certain central city developments (usually commercial or office space) upon the developer's provision of facilities or services for which the development will create a need, or that the development will displace. These programs have been adopted in a variety of cities for such needs as low-income housing, mass transit facilities, day care services, and job-training and employment opportunities. *Set-asides* or *inclusionary zoning programs* are similar in concept to linkages, but are addressed specifically to the need for low- and moderate-income housing. They require a developer to make a certain percentage of the units within a development available at prices affordable to residents with low and moderate incomes, or to pay in-lieu-of contributions to an affordable housing fund.

The practice of imposing exactions is fairly widespread, although exactions are most common in communities in growth areas.[42] Local governments impose exactions either according to a nondiscretionary, predetermined schedule, or through case-by-case negotiations.[43] Nondiscretionary exactions may be a set amount per square foot or per unit, or may be calculated based upon mathematical formulas that attempt to measure the precise impact that the development will have on particular public services. Studies of municipalities' exactions reveal a wide variation in prices. Recent nationwide surveys of recreational impact fees for parks and playgrounds, for example, indicated that the fees charged for a 1500 square foot single family house ranged from $25 to $1800. A 1981 survey of cities and counties in the San Francisco Bay region revealed that total impact fees ranged from $23 to $4287 for single-family homes, and from $300 to $18,371 for multifamily dwellings.

The main reason municipalities impose exactions upon development is, of course, to shift to the developer the costs of the public infrastructure that the development requires.[50] But exactions serve a variety of other purposes as well. First, by forcing the developer and its customers to assume or share in the costs of infrastructure, exactions induce a more efficient use of the infrastructure. Second, exactions serve to mitigate the negative effects a development may have on a neighborhood, such as increased traffic congestion, noise, and environmental degradation. In serving this purpose, exactions again encourage efficiency by forcing the developer and its customers to internalize the full costs of the harms that the development causes.

Third, exactions serve as growth enablers: in areas that are growing so rapidly that the government cannot provide public facilities fast enough, exactions allow growth that might otherwise be stalled by growth control measures. Or, in areas in which a particular development, or growth in general, is controversial, a local government that favors a project may use exactions to counter or "buy off" opposition. Fourth, a local government may use exactions to try to discourage all growth, or to prevent certain kinds of development, such as low and moderate-income housing, in order to preserve the exclusiveness of a community or to preserve its fiscal position.

Finally, exactions may be used either to redistribute wealth from the developer or its customers to others, or to prevent the developer from appropriating wealth created by the activities of the local government. A community may impose exactions as a means

42. A national survey of a random sample of cities and counties concluded that at least 89% of all communities in the United States impose some form of dedication requirement (either of land or of facilities), usually for roads, water and sewer lines, and drainage facilities. Fifty-eight percent require fees-in-lieu-of-dedications or impact fees. See Elizabeth D. Purdum & James E. Frank, Community Use of Exactions: Results of a National Survey, in Development Exactions 126–43 (James E. Frank & Robert M. Rhodes eds., 1987). For surveys with similar results, see Gus Bauman & William H. Ethier, Development Exactions and Impact Fees: A Survey of American Practices, 50 Law & Contemp. Probs. 51, 55–60 (1987). . . .

43. A survey of a random sample of cities and counties showed that 52% of communities with land dedication requirements determine the amount of land to be dedicated either by formula or by standards containing some flexibility, while 35.6% of communities negotiate the amount on a case-by-case basis. Approximately 34% of local governments imposing impact fees determine the amount by formula or by standards allowing some flexibility, while 17.4% use case-by-case negotiations. See Purdam & Frank, supra note 42, at 126, 128, 137, 141; see also Bauman & Ethier, supra note 42, at 57–59 (of communities responding to survey, 18.2% impose off-site exactions, and 9% impose impact fees, on the basis of project-by-project negotiations).

50. The increasing reluctance of municipalities to provide the facilities necessary to accommodate growth results from many factors: the taxpayer revolt; decreased federal and state funding of local facilities; disenchantment with the negative effects of growth on pollution, congestion, and general quality of life; and an increasing skepticism about the ability of growth to pay for itself. See Mark P. Barnebey et al., Paying for Growth: Community Approaches to Development Impact Fees, 54 J. Am. Plan. Assn. 18, 18–21 (1988). . . .

of capturing part of the developer's profit. Or, in some markets, a community may adopt exactions in order to inflate the price of existing housing and thereby allow the current residents to profit at the expense of newcomers. On the other hand, a community may use exactions to recapture from the developer part of the value added to land by improvements financed by the community.

Note on the Rise of Municipal Exactions

The history of exaction practices is reviewed in R. Marlin Smith, From Subdivision Improvement Requirements to Community Benefit Assessments and Linkage Payments, 50 Law & Contemp. Probs. 5 (1987). Smith asserts that through the 1930s, a developer typically could subdivide land on paper, sell off lots, and leave the provision of infrastructure to either the lot purchasers or the municipality. According to Smith, because subdividing was so easy, developers flooded urban-fringe markets with an oversupply of unimproved lots. During this era, municipalities commonly levied special assessments to finance the extension of services to these raw subdivisions. By the time of the Great Depression, however, delinquencies on special assessments were rampant, and many municipalities found that they could not recoup the costs of the services they had extended. As Professor Been describes, localities therefore increasingly imposed exactions on developers, an approach that exposed them to less financial risk.

Statistics on localities' exaction practices during the mid-twentieth century are presented in David Listokin & Carole Walker, The Subdivision and Site Plan Handbook 152–53, 158 (1989). The authors report a survey conducted in 1941 that found that less than a quarter of localities were requiring subdividers to pay for each of the following: surfacing interior streets, providing on-site water mains, and installing on-site sanitary sewers. Exactions for each of these purposes became more common during the suburban boom that followed World War II. A 1950 study found that developers were paying all costs of on-site paving in 71 percent of subdivisions, and of water supply in 40 percent. By 1979, both of these latter percentages had surpassed 90 percent.

For a general review of the surge in municipal use of exactions (especially impact fees) in the late twentieth century, see Alan A. Altshuler & José A. Gómez-Ibánez, Regulation for Revenue: The Political Economy of Land Use Exactions 34–41 (1993). They report that the number of Florida jurisdictions imposing impact fees rose from 5 in 1972 to more than 400 in 1991. A survey of 89 selected California cities in 2001 found that 99 percent were imposing impact fees for school construction; the average per-unit cost of impact fees for all purposes was $19,552, and ranged from a low of $6,783 to a high of $47,742 per home. Vicki Been, Impact Fees and Housing Affordability, 8 Cityscape 139, 141-42 (2005). (Exactions are exceptionally high in California, in part because Proposition 13 has forced municipalities to turn to sources of revenue other than the property tax. See p. 617.)

1.   *State Court Review of Exactions Prior to* Nollan

Exaction cases first surfaced in state courts, which adopted tests ranging from strict to deferential. The Supreme Court of Illinois was at the strict end of the spectrum. In Pioneer Trust & Savings Bank v. Mount Prospect, 176 N.E.2d 799, 802 (Ill. 1961), it held:

> If the requirement is within the statutory grant of power to the municipality and if the burden cast upon the subdivider is specifically and uniquely attributable to his activity, then the requirement

is permissible; if not, it is forbidden and amounts to a confiscation of private property in contravention of the constitutional prohibitions rather than reasonable regulation under the police power.

Although the *Pioneer Trust* test had considerable influence in the 1960s, most state courts came to require only a "reasonable relationship" (or "rational nexus") between an exaction and the impact of a proposed development. The following passage from a decision by the Missouri Supreme Court typifies this approach:

> We have concluded that the *Pioneer Trust* rule . . . is too restrictive and should be modified. The fact that a subdivision merely threatens to "contribute" to a community need for open space should not exempt it from bearing a fair share of the burden of meeting the need. We adopt the following rule in Missouri as to mandatory dedications for recreational purposes: If the requirement is within the statutory grant of power to the municipality and if the burden cast upon the subdivider is *reasonably* attributable to his activity, then the requirement is permissible; if not, it is forbidden and amounts to a confiscation of private property in contravention of the constitutional prohibitions rather than reasonable regulation under the police power. *Insofar as the establishment of a subdivision within a city increases the recreational needs of the city, then to that extent the cost of meeting that increase in needs may reasonably be required of the subdivider.* [Emphasis in original.]

Home Builders Association v. City of Kansas City, 555 S.W.2d 832, 835 (Mo. 1977).

As usual, the California courts placed themselves at the deferential end of the spectrum, far distant from the Illinois courts. (Compare pp. 104–10.) In Associated Home Builders v. City of Walnut Creek, 484 P.2d 606 (Cal. 1971), the state supreme court, citing the rapid disappearance of open land, upheld a scheme of land dedications and in-lieu fees for recreational purposes where the only connection shown was that the development would reduce open space and increase the need for parks. The court hinted broadly that an exaction aimed at any nongeneral need created by a development would satisfy its test. California's deferential approach eventually helped prompt the U.S. Supreme Court to consider the constitutional issues that development exactions pose. Compare pp. 98–112 and 619–24, which explore the varying roles of federal and state courts in reviewing landowner challenges to zoning regulations and special assessments.

2. *The Supreme Court Enters the Fray*

Nollan v. California Coastal Commission
483 U.S. 825 (1987)

Justice SCALIA delivered the opinion of the Court.

James and Marilyn Nollan appeal from a decision of the California Court of Appeal ruling that the California Coastal Commission could condition its grant of permission to rebuild their house on their transfer to the public of an easement across their beachfront property. The California Court rejected their claim that imposition of that condition violates the Takings Clause of the Fifth Amendment, as incorporated against the States by the Fourteenth Amendment.

Cal Ct said it's Not a taking

I

The Nollans own a beachfront lot in Ventura County, California. A quarter-mile north of their property is Faria County Park, an oceanside public park with a public beach and recreation area. Another public beach area, known locally as "the Cove," lies 1,800 feet south of their lot. A concrete seawall approximately eight feet high separates the beach portion of the Nollans' property from the rest of the lot. The historic mean high tide line determines the lot's oceanside boundary.

The Nollans originally leased their property with an option to buy. The building on the lot was a small bungalow, totaling 504 square feet, which for a time they rented to summer vacationers. After years of rental use, however, the building had fallen into disrepair, and could no longer be rented out.

The Nollans' option to purchase was conditioned on their promise to demolish the bungalow and replace it. In order to do so, under California Public Resources Code §§30106, 30212, and 30600 (West 1986), they were required to obtain a coastal development permit from the California Coastal Commission. On February 25, 1982, they submitted a permit application to the Commission in which they proposed to demolish the existing structure and replace it with a three-bedroom house in keeping with the rest of the neighborhood.

The Nollans were informed that their application had been placed on the administrative calendar, and that the Commission staff had recommended that the permit be granted subject to the condition that they allow the public an easement to pass across a portion of their property bounded by the mean high tide line on one side, and their seawall on the other side. This would make it easier for the public to get to Faria County Park and the Cove. The Nollans protested imposition of the condition, but the Commission overruled their objections and granted the permit subject to their recordation of a deed restriction granting the easement.

On June 3, 1982, the Nollans filed a petition for writ of administrative mandamus asking the Ventura County Superior Court to invalidate the access condition. [The record indicated that the Commission had "similarly conditioned 43 out of 60 coastal development permits along the same tract of land, and that of the 17 not so conditioned, 14 had been approved when the Commission did not have administrative regulations in place allowing imposition of the condition, and the remaining 3 had not involved shorefront property." The California Court of Appeal eventually rejected the Nollans' statutory and constitutional arguments.]

. . . The Nollans appealed to this Court, raising only the constitutional question.

II

. . . We think a "permanent physical occupation" has occurred . . . where individuals are given a permanent and continuous right to pass to and fro, so that the real property may continuously be traversed, even though no particular individual is permitted to station himself permanently upon the premises.[2] . . .

Given . . . that requiring uncompensated conveyance of the easement outright would violate [the *Loretto* interpretation of] the Fourteenth Amendment, the question becomes whether requiring it to be conveyed as a condition for issuing a land use permit alters the outcome. We have long recognized that land use regulation does not effect a taking if it "substantially advance[s] legitimate state interests" and does not "den[y] an owner economically viable use of his land." Agins v. Tiburon, 447 U.S. 255, 260 (1980). . . . Our cases have not elaborated on the standards for determining what constitutes a "legitimate state interest" or what type of connection between the regulation and the state interest

---

2. . . . Nor are the Nollans' rights altered because they acquired the land well after the Commission had begun to implement its policy. So long as the Commission could not have deprived the prior owners of the easement without compensating them, the prior owners must be understood to have transferred their full property rights in conveying the lot. [EDS.: Footnote repositioned.]

satisfies the requirement that the former "substantially advance" the latter.[3] The Commission argues that among these permissible purposes are protecting the public's ability to see the beach, assisting the public in overcoming the "psychological barrier" to using the beach created by a developed storefront, and preventing congestion on the public beaches. We assume, without deciding, that this is so — in which case the Commission unquestionably would be able to deny the Nollans their permit outright if their new house (alone, or by reason of the cumulative impact produced in conjunction with other construction) would substantially impede these purposes, unless the denial would interfere so drastically with the Nollans' use of their property as to constitute a taking. See Penn Central Transp. Co. v. New York City, [438 U.S. 104 (1978)].

The Commission argues that a permit condition that serves the same legitimate police-power purpose as a refusal to issue the permit should not be found to be a taking if the refusal to issue the permit would not constitute a taking. We agree. Thus, if the Commission attached to the permit some condition that would have protected the public's ability to see the beach notwithstanding construction of the new house — for example, a height limitation, a width restriction, or a ban on fences — so long as the Commission could have exercised its police power (as we have assumed it could) to forbid construction of the house altogether, imposition of the condition would also be constitutional. Moreover (and here we come closer to the facts of the present case), the condition would be constitutional even if it consisted of the requirement that the Nollans provide a viewing spot on their property for passersby with whose sighting of the ocean their new house would interfere. Although such a requirement, constituting a permanent grant of continuous access to the property, would have to be considered a taking if it were not attached to a development permit, the Commission's assumed power to forbid construction of the house in order to protect the public's view of the beach must surely include the power to condition construction upon some concession by the owner, even a concession of property rights, that serves the same end. If a prohibition designed to accomplish that purpose would be a legitimate exercise of the police power rather than a taking, it would be strange to conclude that providing the owner an alternative to that prohibition which accomplishes the same purpose is not. The evident constitutional propriety disappears, however, if the condition substituted for the prohibition utterly fails to further the end advanced as the justification for the prohibition. When that essential nexus is eliminated, the situation becomes the same as if California law forbade shouting fire in a crowded theater, but granted dispensations to those willing to contribute $100 to the state treasury. While a ban on shouting fire can be a core exercise of the State's police power to protect the public safety, and can thus meet even our stringent standards for regulation of speech, adding the unrelated condition alters the purpose to one which, while it may be legitimate, is inadequate to sustain the ban. Therefore, even though, in a sense, requiring a $100 tax contribution in order to shout

3. Contrary to Justice Brennan's claim, our opinions do not establish that these standards are the same as those applied to due process or equal-protection claims. To the contrary, our verbal formulations in the takings field have generally been quite different. We have required that the regulation "substantially advance" the "legitimate state interest" sought to be achieved, Agins v. Tiburon, 447 U.S. 255, 260 (1980), not that "the State 'could rationally have decided' the measure adopted might achieve the State's objective." . . . Justice Brennan relies principally on an equal protection case, Minnesota v. Clover Leaf Creamery Co., [449 U.S. 456 (1980),] and two substantive due process cases, Williamson v. Lee Optical of Oklahoma, Inc., 348 U.S. 483, 487–488 (1955) and Day-Brite Lighting, Inc. v. Missouri, 342 U.S. 421, 423 (1952), in support of the standards he would adopt. But there is no reason to believe (and the language of our cases gives some reason to disbelieve) that so long as the regulation of property is at issue the standards for taking challenges, due process challenges, and equal protection challenges are identical; any more than there is any reason to believe that so long as the regulation of speech is at issue the standards for due process challenges, equal protection changes, and First Amendment changes are identical. Goldblatt v. Hempstead, 369 U.S. 590 (1962), does appear to assume that the inquiries are the same, but that assumption is inconsistent with the formulations of our later cases.

fire is a lesser restriction on speech than an outright ban, it would not pass constitutional muster. Similarly here, the lack of nexus between the condition and the original purpose of the building restriction converts that purpose to something other than what it was. The purpose then becomes, quite simply, the obtaining of an easement to serve some valid governmental purpose, but without payment of compensation. Whatever may be the outer limits of "legitimate state interests" in the takings and land use context, this is not one of them. In short, unless the permit condition serves the same governmental purpose as the development ban, the building restriction is not a valid regulation of land use but "an out-and-out plan of extortion." J.E.D. Associates, Inc. v. Atkinson, 432 A.2d 12, 14–15 (N.H. 1981). . . .[5]

III

The Commission claims that it concedes as much, and that we may sustain the condition at issue here by finding that it is reasonably related to the public need or burden that the Nollans' new house creates or to which it contributes. We can accept, for purposes of discussion, the Commission's proposed test as to how close a "fit" between the condition and the burden is required, because we find that this case does not meet even the most untailored standards. The Commission's principal contention to the contrary essentially turns on a play on the word "access." The Nollans' new house, the Commission found, will interfere with "visual access" to the beach. That in turn (along with other shorefront development) will interfere with the desire of people who drive past the Nollans' house to use the beach, thus creating a "psychological barrier" to "access." The Nollans' new house will also, by a process not altogether clear from the Commission's opinion but presumably potent enough to more than offset the effects of the psychological barrier, increase the use of the public beaches, thus creating the need for more "access." These burdens on "access" would be alleviated by a requirement that the Nollans provide "lateral access" to the beach.

Rewriting the argument to eliminate the play on words makes clear that there is nothing to it. It is quite impossible to understand how a requirement that people already on the public beaches be able to walk across the Nollans' property reduces any obstacles to viewing the beach created by the new house. It is also impossible to understand how it lowers any "psychological barrier" to using the public beaches, or how it helps to remedy any additional congestion on them caused by construction of the Nollans' new house. We therefore find that the Commission's imposition of the permit condition cannot be treated as an exercise of its land use power for any of these purposes. Our conclusion on this point is consistent with the approach taken by every other court that has considered the question, with the exception of the California state courts. [Citations to 1 federal and 21 state court decisions omitted.]

Justice Brennan['s dissenting opinion] argues that imposition of the access requirement is not irrational. In his version of the Commission's argument, the reason for the requirement is that in its absence, a person looking toward the beach from the road will see a street of residential structures including the Nollans' new home and conclude that there is no public beach nearby. If, however, that person sees people passing and repassing

---

5. One would expect that a regime in which this kind of leveraging of the police power is allowed would produce stringent land-use regulation which the State then waives to accomplish other purposes, leading to lesser realization of the land-use goals purportedly sought to be served than would result from more lenient (but nontradeable) development restrictions. Thus, the importance of the purpose underlying the prohibition not only does not *justify* the imposition of unrelated conditions for eliminating the prohibition, but positively militates against the practice.

along the dry sand behind the Nollans' home, he will realize that there is a public beach somewhere in the vicinity. The Commission's action, however, was based on the opposite factual finding that the wall of houses completely blocked the view of the beach and that a person looking from the road would not be able to see it at all. . . .

We are left, then, with the Commission's justification for the access requirement unrelated to land use regulation:

> Finally, the Commission notes that there are several existing provisions of pass and repass lateral access benefits already given by past Faria Beach Tract applicants as a result of prior coastal permit decisions. The access required as a condition of this permit is part of a comprehensive program to provide continuous public access along Faria Beach as the lots undergo development or redevelopment.

That is simply an expression of the Commission's belief that the public interest will be served by a continuous strip of publicly accessible beach along the coast. The Commission may well be right that it is a good idea, but that does not establish that the Nollans (and other coastal residents) alone can be compelled to contribute to its realization. Rather, California is free to advance its "comprehensive program," if it wishes, by using its power of eminent domain for this "public purpose," see U.S. Const., Amdt. V; but if it wants an easement across the Nollans' property, it must pay for it.

Reversed.

Justice BRENNAN, with whom Justice MARSHALL joins, dissenting. . . .

The Court's conclusion that the permit condition imposed on appellants is unreasonable cannot withstand analysis. First, the Court demands a degree of exactitude that is inconsistent with our standard for reviewing the rationality of a state's exercise of its police power for the welfare of its citizens. Second, even if the nature of the public access condition imposed must be identical to the precise burden on access created by appellants, this requirement is plainly satisfied. . . .

Justice BLACKMUN, dissenting. . . .

Traditional takings analysis compels the conclusion that there is no taking here. The governmental action is a valid exercise of the police power, and, so far as the record reveals, has a nonexistent economic effect on the value of appellants' property. No investment-backed expectations were diminished. It is significant that the Nollans had notice of the easement before they purchased the property and that public use of the beach had been permitted for decades. . . .

[Justice STEVENS's dissenting opinion has been omitted.]

Note on *Nollan*'s "Essential Nexus"

1. *Applications.* Does *Nollan* permit a town to condition an applicant's connection to the public water supply on the deeding of a 15-foot-wide strip to accommodate a future road widening? See Walz v. Town of Smithtown, 46 F.3d 162 (2d Cir. 1995) (affirming, without mentioning *Nollan*, judgment that awarded §1983 damages to applicant on ground of violation of substantive due process). What if a developer complains of having been forced to provide an on-site road improvement that would primarily benefit a neighbor who had lobbied the local government to impose the exaction? See Paradyne Corp. v. State Department of Transportation, 528 So. 2d 921 (Fla. Dist. Ct. App. 1988) (construing *Nollan* to forbid forcing landowner to construct drive to provide access to neighbor's land).

2. *Mean-ends review in exaction cases.* Justice Scalia's opinion struck down the commission's exaction on the ground that the commission's regulatory purpose ("visual access") was utterly unrelated to the purpose the exaction served ("lateral access"). What if the commission were to have asserted that one of its aims was to use the permit process to obtain funds and land dedications that it could devote to enhancing public use of the coastal area? In his dissent, Justice Brennan in fact predicted that the commission, now alerted to the Court's apparently more demanding requirement, "should have little problem presenting its findings in a way that avoids a takings problem." 483 U.S. at 863. Justice Brennan's assertion prompted a sharp retort from Justice Scalia in the majority opinion: "We view the Fifth Amendment's property clause to be more than a pleading requirement, and compliance with it to be more than an exercise in cleverness and imagination." Id. at 841.

Lingle v. Chevron U.S.A., Inc., 125 S. Ct. 2074 (2005), excerpted at p. 193, involved a takings challenge to a state ceiling on rents owed by tenants of service stations. Writing for a unanimous Court, Justice O'Connor rejected interpreting the Takings Clause as a source of "heightened means-end review." She asserted that the Court's principal takings tests instead focus "directly upon the severity of the burden that government imposes upon private property rights." *Nollan* focuses on the means-end relationship, not on the landowner's burden. Aware of the tension between the two opinions, Justice O'Connor nevertheless states in *Lingle* that "our decision should not be read to disturb [*Nollan*]."

3. *Follow-up.* On the California Coastal Commission's response to *Nollan*, see Surfside Colony, Ltd. v. California Coastal Commission, 277 Cal. Rptr. 371 (Ct. App. 1991) (striking down another commission attempt to exact a beach easement); Bruce Goldstein & Sharon Buccino, Is the Bundle Bigger?, 8 Stan. Envtl. L.J. 46, 68–75 (1989) (focusing on the commission's unflagging determination to pursue beach access goals and its difficulties in creating sufficient documentation to satisfy the "essential nexus" requirement). Some permit applicants who ceded public easements to the commission later fought hard to prevent their use. See, e.g., Chris Dixon, Public to Get Beach Access by Geffen Home, N.Y. Times, Apr. 17, 2005, §1, at 29 (on a Hollywood mogul's ultimate defeat in a battle to prevent the public from using a beach accessway that he had dedicated 22 years before when receiving permission to build a Malibu mansion).

4. *Coming to an exaction.* Can a claimant who has acquired a parcel already encumbered by an onerous exaction policy prevail in a takings challenge to that policy? Compare how Justice Scalia treats the issue in footnote 2 of his opinion with how Justice Blackmun treats it in his dissent. See also pp. 180–85 (on Palazzolo v. Rhode Island, 533 U.S. 606 (2001), and the issue of coming to a regulatory taking).

5. *Commentary on* Nollan. Stewart Sterk contends that the standardlessness of exactions and their attendant inefficiencies in practice justify the *Nollan* majority's concerns about abuse. Stewart E. Sterk, *Nollan*, Henry George, and Exactions, 88 Colum. L. Rev. 1731 (1988). A student note, by contrast, counsels against the *Nollan* approach because, in the author's view, judicial competence in such cases is limited and fears about political-process failure are exaggerated. Note, Municipal Development Exactions, the Rational Nexus Test, and the Federal Constitution, 102 Harv. L. Rev. 92 (1989).

Dolan v. City of Tigard
512 U.S. 374 (1994)

Chief Justice REHNQUIST delivered the opinion of the Court.

Petitioner challenges the decision of the Oregon Supreme Court which held that the city of Tigard could condition the approval of her building permit on the dedication of a portion of her property for flood control and traffic improvements. 854 P.2d 437 (Ore. 1993). We granted certiorari to resolve a question left open by our decision in Nollan v. California Coastal Commission, 483 U.S. 825 (1987), of what is the required degree of connection between the exactions imposed by the city and the projected impacts of the proposed development.

I

The State of Oregon enacted a comprehensive land use management program in 1973. Ore. Rev. Stat. §§197.005–197.860 (1991). The program required all Oregon cities and counties to adopt new comprehensive land use plans that were consistent with the statewide planning goals. The plans are implemented by land use regulations which are part of an integrated hierarchy of legally binding goals, plans, and regulations. Pursuant to the State's requirements, the city of Tigard, a community of some 30,000 residents on the southwest edge of Portland, developed a comprehensive plan and codified it in its Community Development Code (CDC). The CDC requires property owners in the area zoned Central Business District to comply with a 15% open space and landscaping requirement, which limits total site coverage, including all structures and paved parking, to 85% of the parcel. CDC, ch. 18.66. After the completion of a transportation study that identified congestion in the Central Business District as a particular problem, the city adopted a plan for a pedestrian/bicycle pathway intended to encourage alternatives to automobile transportation for short trips. The CDC requires that new development facilitate this plan by dedicating land for pedestrian pathways where provided for in the pedestrian/bicycle pathway plan.

The city also adopted a Master Drainage Plan (Drainage Plan). The Drainage Plan noted that flooding occurred in several areas along Fanno Creek, including areas near petitioner's property. The Drainage Plan also established that the increase in impervious surfaces associated with continued urbanization would exacerbate these flooding problems. To combat these risks, the Drainage Plan suggested a series of improvements to the Fanno Creek Basin, including channel excavation in the area next to petitioner's property. Other recommendations included ensuring that the floodplain remains free of structures and that it be preserved as greenways to minimize flood damage to structures. The Drainage Plan concluded that the cost of these improvements should be shared based on both direct and indirect benefits, with property owners along the waterways paying more due to the direct benefit that they would receive. . . .

Petitioner Florence Dolan owns a plumbing and electric supply store located on Main Street in the Central Business District of the city. The store covers approximately 9,700 square feet on the eastern side of a 1.67-acre parcel, which includes a gravel parking lot. Fanno Creek flows through the southwestern corner of the lot and along its western boundary. [See Figure 7-1.] The year-round flow of the creek renders the area within the creek's 100-year floodplain virtually unusable for commercial development. The city's comprehensive plan includes the Fanno Creek floodplain as part of the city's greenway system.

Petitioner applied to the city for a permit to redevelop the site. Her proposed plans called for nearly doubling the size of the store to 17,600 square feet, and paving a 39-space parking lot. The existing store, located on the opposite side of the parcel, would be razed in sections as construction progressed on the new building. In the second phase of the project, petitioner proposed to build an additional structure on the northeast side of the site for complementary businesses, and to provide more parking. The proposed expansion

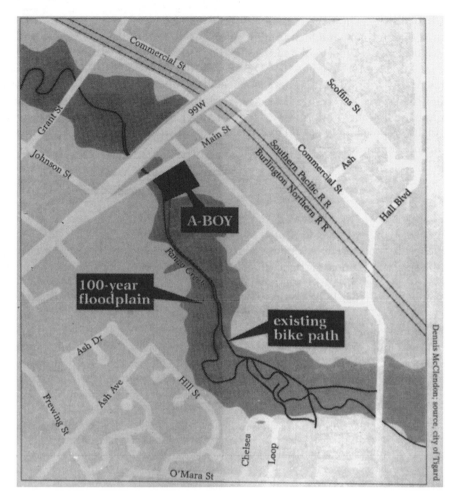

Source: John Tibbets, Everybody's Taking the Fifth, Planning, Jan. 1995, at 4, 8 (credited to Dennis McClendon; City of Tigard).

FIGURE 7-1
The Dolan Property (A-Boy) and Its Surroundings

and intensified use are consistent with the city's zoning scheme in the Central Business District.

The City Planning Commission granted petitioner's permit application subject to conditions imposed by the city's CDC. . . .

[Applying the CDC,] the Commission required that petitioner dedicate the portion of her property lying within the 100-year floodplain for improvement of a storm drainage system along Fanno Creek and that she dedicate an additional 15-foot strip of land adjacent to the floodplain as a pedestrian/bicycle pathway. The dedication required by that condition encompasses approximately 7,000 square feet, or roughly 10% of the property. In accordance with city practice, petitioner could rely on the dedicated property to meet the 15% open space and landscaping requirement mandated by the city's zoning scheme. The city would bear the cost of maintaining a landscaped buffer between the dedicated area and the new store.

[To obtain relief from these exactions, Petitioner vainly sought variances from the City Planning Commission, and then fruitlessly pursued appeals to the Tigard City Council, the Oregon Land Use Board of Appeals, and the Oregon Supreme Court.]

. . . The Oregon Supreme Court . . . read *Nollan* to mean that an "exaction is reasonably related to an impact if the exaction serves the same purpose that a denial of the permit would serve." 854 P.2d, at 443. The court decided that both the pedestrian/bicycle pathway condition and the storm drainage dedication had an essential nexus to the development of the proposed site.) . . . We granted certiorari because of an alleged conflict between the Oregon Supreme Court's decision and our decision in *Nollan*, supra.

II

. . . In *Nollan*, we held that governmental authority to exact such a condition was circumscribed by the Fifth and Fourteenth Amendments. Under the well-settled doctrine of "unconstitutional conditions," the government may not require a person to give up a constitutional right — here the right to receive just compensation when property is taken for a public use — in exchange for a discretionary benefit conferred by the government where the property sought has little or no relationship to the benefit. See Perry v. Sindermann, 408 U.S. 593 (1972). . . .

Petitioner contends that the city has forced her to choose between the building permit and her right under the Fifth Amendment to just compensation for the public easements. Petitioner does not quarrel with the city's authority to exact some forms of dedication as a condition for the grant of a building permit, but challenges the showing made by the city to justify these exactions. She argues that the city has identified "no special benefits" conferred on her, and has not identified any "special quantifiable burdens" created by her new store that would justify the particular dedications required from her which are not required from the public at large.

III

In evaluating petitioner's claim, we must first determine whether the "essential nexus" exists between the "legitimate state interest" and the permit condition exacted by the city. *Nollan*, 483 U.S. at 837. If we find that a nexus exists, we must then decide the required degree of connection between the exactions and the projected impact of the proposed development. We were not required to reach this question in *Nollan*, because we concluded that the connection did not meet even the loosest standard. 483 U.S., at 838. Here, however, we must decide this question.

A

We addressed the essential nexus question in *Nollan*. . . .

. . . [In contrast to the situation in *Nollan*, no] gimmicks are associated with the permit conditions imposed by the city in this case. Undoubtedly, the prevention of flooding along Fanno Creek and the reduction of traffic congestion in the Central Business District qualify as the type of legitimate public purposes we have upheld. It seems equally obvious that a nexus exists between preventing flooding along Fanno Creek and limiting development within the creek's 100-year floodplain. Petitioner proposes to double the size of her retail store and to pave her now-gravel parking lot, thereby expanding the impervious surface on the property and increasing the amount of stormwater run-off into Fanno Creek.

The same may be said for the city's attempt to reduce traffic congestion by providing for alternative means of transportation. In theory, a pedestrian/bicycle pathway provides a useful alternative means of transportation for workers and shoppers. . . .

B

The second part of our analysis requires us to determine whether the degree of the exactions demanded by the city's permit conditions bear the required relationship to the projected impact of petitioner's proposed development. . . .

. . . The city relies on the Commission's rather tentative findings that increased stormwater flow from petitioner's property "can only add to the public need to manage the [floodplain] for drainage purposes" to support its conclusion that the "requirement of dedication of the floodplain area on the site is related to the applicant's plan to intensify development on the site." City of Tigard Planning Commission Final Order No. 91-09 PC.

The city made the following specific findings relevant to the pedestrian/bicycle pathway:

> In addition, the proposed expanded use of this site is anticipated to generate additional vehicular traffic thereby increasing congestion on nearby collector and arterial streets. Creation of a convenient, safe pedestrian/bicycle pathway system as an alternative means of transportation could offset some of the traffic demand on these nearby streets and lessen the increase in traffic congestion.

The question for us is whether these findings are constitutionally sufficient to justify the conditions imposed by the city on petitioner's building permit. Since state courts have been dealing with this question a good deal longer than we have, we turn to representative decisions made by them.

In some States, very generalized statements as to the necessary connection between the required dedication and the proposed development seem to suffice. See, e.g., Billings Properties, Inc. v. Yellowstone County, 394 P.2d 182 (Mont. 1964); Jenad, Inc. v. Scarsdale, 218 N.E.2d 673 (N.Y. 1966). We think this standard is too lax to adequately protect petitioner's right to just compensation if her property is taken for a public purpose.

Other state courts require a very exacting correspondence, described as the "specific and uniquely attributable" test. The Supreme Court of Illinois first developed this test in Pioneer Trust & Savings Bank v. Mount Prospect, 176 N.E.2d 799, 802 (Ill. 1961). Under this standard, if the local government cannot demonstrate that its exaction is directly proportional to the specifically created need, the exaction becomes "a veiled exercise of the power of eminent domain and a confiscation of private property behind the defense of police regulations." Id. We do not think the Federal Constitution requires such exacting scrutiny, given the nature of the interests involved.

A number of state courts have taken an intermediate position, requiring the municipality to show a "reasonable relationship" between the required dedication and the impact of the proposed development. Typical is the Supreme Court of Nebraska's opinion in Simpson v. North Platte, 292 N.W.2d 297, 301 (Neb. 1980), where that court stated:

> The distinction, therefore, which must be made between an appropriate exercise of the police power and an improper exercise of eminent domain is whether the requirement has some reasonable relationship or nexus to the use to which the property is being made or is merely being used as an excuse for taking property simply because at that particular moment the landowner is asking the city for some license or permit.

Thus, the court held that a city may not require a property owner to dedicate private property for some future public use as a condition of obtaining a building permit when such future use is not "occasioned by the construction sought to be permitted." Id. at 302.

Some form of the reasonable relationship test has been adopted in many other jurisdictions. See, e.g., Jordan v. Menomonee Falls, 137 N.W.2d 442 (Wis. 1965); Collis v. Bloomington, 246 N.W.2d 19 (Minn. 1976) (requiring a showing of a reasonable relationship between the planned subdivision and the municipality's need for land); College Station v. Turtle Rock Corp., 680 S.W.2d 802, 807 (Tex. 1984); Call v. West Jordan, 606 P.2d 217, 220 (Utah 1979) (affirming use of the reasonable relation test). Despite any semantical differences, general agreement exists among the courts "that the dedication should have some reasonable relationship to the needs created by the [development]." Ibid.

We think the "reasonable relationship" test adopted by a majority of the state courts is closer to the federal constitutional norm than either of those previously discussed. But we do not adopt it as such, partly because the term "reasonable relationship" seems confusingly similar to the term "rational basis" which describes the minimal level of scrutiny under the Equal Protection Clause of the Fourteenth Amendment. We think a term such as "rough proportionality" best encapsulates what we hold to be the requirement of the Fifth Amendment. No precise mathematical calculation is required, but the city must make some sort of individualized determination that the required dedication is related both in nature and extent to the impact of the proposed development.[8]

Justice Stevens' dissent relies upon a law review article for the proposition that the city's conditional demands for part of petitioner's property are "a species of business regulation that heretofore warranted a strong presumption of constitutional validity." . . . We see no reason why the Takings Clause of the Fifth Amendment, as much a part of the Bill of Rights as the First Amendment or Fourth Amendment, should be relegated to the status of a poor relation. . . . We turn now to analysis of whether the findings relied upon by the city here, first with respect to the floodplain easement, and second with respect to the pedestrian/bicycle path, satisfied these requirements.

It is axiomatic that increasing the amount of impervious surface will increase the quantity and rate of storm-water flow from petitioner's property. Therefore, keeping the floodplain open and free from development would likely confine the pressures on Fanno Creek created by petitioner's development. In fact, because petitioner's property lies within the Central Business District, the Community Development Code already required that petitioner leave 15% of it as open space and the undeveloped floodplain would have nearly satisfied that requirement. But the city demanded more — it not only wanted petitioner not to build in the floodplain, but it also wanted petitioner's property along Fanno Creek for its Greenway system. The city has never said why a public greenway, as opposed to a private one, was required in the interest of flood control.

The difference to petitioner, of course, is the loss of her ability to exclude others. As we have noted, this right to exclude others is "one of the most essential sticks in the bundle of rights that are commonly characterized as property." Kaiser Aetna [v. United States, 444 U.S. 164, 176 (1979).] It is difficult to see why recreational visitors trampling along petitioner's floodplain easement are sufficiently related to the city's legitimate interest in

8. Justice Stevens' dissent takes us to task for placing the burden on the city to justify the required dedication. He is correct in arguing that in evaluating most generally applicable zoning regulations, the burden properly rests on the party challenging the regulation to prove that it constitutes an arbitrary regulation of property rights. See, e.g., Euclid v. Ambler Realty Co., 272 U.S. 365 (1926). Here, by contrast, the city made an adjudicative decision to condition petitioner's application for a building permit on an individual parcel. In this situation, the burden properly rests on the city. See *Nollan*, 483 U.S. at 836. . . .

reducing flooding problems along Fanno Creek, and the city has not attempted to make any individualized determination to support this part of its request. . . .

If petitioner's proposed development had somehow encroached on existing greenway space in the city, it would have been reasonable to require petitioner to provide some alternative greenway space for the public either on her property or elsewhere. See *Nollan*, 483 U.S. at 836. . . . But that is not the case here. We conclude that the findings upon which the city relies do not show the required reasonable relationship between the floodplain easement and the petitioner's proposed new building.

With respect to the pedestrian/bicycle pathway, we have no doubt that the city was correct in finding that the larger retail sales facility proposed by petitioner will increase traffic on the streets of the Central Business District. The city estimates that the proposed development would generate roughly 435 additional trips per day. Dedications for streets, sidewalks, and other public ways are generally reasonable exactions to avoid excessive congestion from a proposed property use. But on the record before us, the city has not met its burden of demonstrating that the additional number of vehicle and bicycle trips generated by the petitioner's development reasonably relate to the city's requirement for a dedication of the pedestrian/bicycle pathway easement. The city simply found that the creation of the pathway "could offset some of the traffic demand . . . and lessen the increase in traffic congestion."

As Justice Peterson of the Supreme Court of Oregon explained in his dissenting opinion, however, "the findings of fact that the bicycle pathway system '*could* offset some of the traffic demand' is a far cry from a finding that the bicycle pathway system *will*, or is *likely to*, offset some of the traffic demand." 84 P.2d, at 447 (emphasis in original). No precise mathematical calculation is required, but the city must make some effort to quantify its findings in support of the dedication for the pedestrian/bicycle pathway beyond the conclusory statement that it could offset some of the traffic demand generated. . . .

The judgment of the Supreme Court of Oregon is reversed, and the case is remanded for further proceedings consistent with this opinion. It is so ordered.

Justice STEVENS, with whom Justice BLACKMUN and Justice GINSBURG join, dissenting. . . .

The Court is correct in concluding that the city may not attach arbitrary conditions to a building permit or to a variance even when it can rightfully deny the application outright. I also agree that state court decisions dealing with ordinances that govern municipal development plans provide useful guidance in a case of this kind. Yet the Court's description of the doctrinal underpinnings of its decision, the phrasing of its fledgling test of "rough proportionality," and the application of that test to this case run contrary to the traditional treatment of these cases and break considerable and unpropitious new ground. . . .

First, although discussion of the state cases permeates the Court's analysis of the appropriate test to apply in this case, the test on which the Court settles is not naturally derived from those courts' decisions. . . . In addition to showing a rational nexus to a public purpose that would justify an outright denial of the permit, the city must also demonstrate "rough proportionality" between the harm caused by the new land use and the benefit obtained by the condition. The Court also decides for the first time that the city has the burden of establishing the constitutionality of its conditions by making an "individualized determination" that the condition in question satisfies the proportionality requirement. . . .

The Court's assurances that its "rough proportionality" test leaves ample room for cities to pursue the "commendable task of land use planning" — even twice avowing that "no precise mathematical calculation is required" — are wanting given the result that test compels here. Under the Court's approach, a city must not only "quantify its findings," and make "individualized determinations" with respect to the nature and the extent of the relationship between the conditions and the impact, but also demonstrate "proportionality." The correct inquiry should instead concentrate on whether the required nexus is present and venture beyond considerations of a condition's nature or germaneness only if the developer establishes that a concededly germane condition is so grossly disproportionate to the proposed development's adverse effects that it manifests motives other than land use regulation on the part of the city.[5] . . .

. . . If the Court proposes to have the federal judiciary micromanage state decisions of this kind, it is indeed extending its welcome mat to a significant new class of litigants. Although there is no reason to believe that state courts have failed to rise to the task, property owners have surely found a new friend today. . . .

Justice SOUTER, dissenting.

. . . *Nollan* . . . is satisfied, and . . . the city's conditions should not be held to fail a further rough proportionality test or any other that might be devised to give meaning to the constitutional limits. . . .

Note on *Dolan* and "Rough Proportionality"

1. *Subsequent history*. The parties eventually agreed to a settlement. In return for receipt of $1.5 million, Dolan dedicated the strips of land that the City of Tigard had sought and also relinquished all claims for interim damages for regulatory delays. See Richard H. Chused, Cases, Materials and Problems on Property 1039–40 (2d ed. 1999).

2. *Dolan's reception*. The decision has provoked dozens of articles. In praise, see, e.g., Richard A. Epstein, The Harms and Benefits of *Nollan* and *Dolan*, 15 N. Ill. U. L. Rev. 477 (1995); Thomas W. Merrill, *Dolan v. City of Tigard*: Constitutional Rights as Public Goods, 72 Denv. U. L. Rev. 859 (1995). For criticism, see, e.g., Julian Kossow, *Dolan v. City of Tigard*, Takings Law, and the Supreme Court, 14 Stan. Envtl. L.J. 215 (1995). Procedural effects are the focus of Marshall S. Sprung, Note, Taking Sides: The Burden of Proof Switch in *Dolan v. City of Tigard*, 71 N.Y.U. L. Rev. 1301 (1996). Sprung argues that *Dolan* properly shifts to the exacting government the burden of producing evidence, but wrongly shifts to it the risk of nonpersuasion.

3. *Problems that arise when limits on exactions exceed limits on regulations*. A municipality prohibited from imposing exactions might turn instead to techniques such as exclusionary zoning and growth controls, measures that, when legal, may have even worse consequences for landowners and housing consumers. See Chapters 8 and 9. This possibility has prompted many commentators to assert that exactions are not as bad as their most likely substitutes. See Alan A. Altshuler & José A. Gómez-Ibánez, Regulation for Revenue 134–39 (1993); Joseph Gyourko, Impact Fees, Exclusionary Zoning, and the Density of New Development, 30 J. Urb. Econ. 242 (1991). Would it be better to loosen legal limits on exactions or to tighten legal limits on exclusionary zoning and growth controls?

See also William A. Fischel, Regulatory Takings: Law, Economics, and Politics 348–51 (1995). Fischel gives *Dolan* a mixed review. He much prefers its rough-proportionality rule to the *Nollan* essential nexus test. The *Nollan* doctrine, he asserts, tends to block

---

5. Dolan's attorney overstated the danger when he suggested at oral argument that without some requirement for proportionality, "the City could have found that Mrs. Dolan's new store would have increased traffic by one additional vehicle trip per day [and] could have required her to dedicate 75, 95 percent of her land for a widening of Main Street."

desirable dealmaking between local governments and developers, partly because it may provide a basis for suits by third parties who object to a deal. While preferring *Dolan* to *Nollan*, Fischel worries that *Dolan* may flood the federal courts with cases, just as Village of Norwood v. Baker, 172 U.S. 269 (1898), inundated them with special-assessment cases a century earlier. See p. 624.

Like *Norwood*, *Dolan* eventually may come to be seen as an isolated shot across the bow of overly aggressive local government. Would the Supreme Court be wise to mimic its practice in the wake of *Norwood* and leave the further development of exaction law mostly to state courts and legislatures? See Stewart E. Sterk, The Federalist Dimension of Regulatory Takings Jurisprudence, 114 Yale L.J. 203, 244–47 (2004) (endorsing such an approach); Note, Municipal Development Exactions, the Rational Nexus Test, and the Federal Constitution, 102 Harv. L. Rev. 992 (1989) (favoring cabining of *Nollan* out of respect for federalism).

4. *Circumventing* Dolan. Other critics have echoed Fischel's concern that *Nollan* and *Dolan* may limit flexibility in bargaining between developers and local governments. See Mark Fenster, Takings Formalism and Regulatory Formulas: Exactions and the Consequences of Clarity, 92 Cal. L. Rev. 609 (2004); Lee Anne Fennell, Hard Bargains and Real Steals: Land Use Exactions Revisited, 86 Iowa L. Rev. 1 (2000).

To illustrate her critique, Professor Fennell poses the example of a landowner (Ambrose) who desires to construct a service station on residentially zoned land. See id. at 24–34. If the town were to entitle Ambrose to build this facility, he would gain $800,000, and, if the town loosened its zoning, its residents (other than Ambrose) would forgo $300,000 in environmental and other benefits. Under these circumstances, a mutually advantageous bargain could be struck. Suppose both sides would be willing to agree to a deal whereby the town would rezone to allow the service station and Ambrose would build and dedicate to the town a swimming pool that would cost him $400,000 to provide. Note that this deal fails the *Nollan* doctrine because the reason for the ban on service stations has no nexus with the town's desire for recreational facilities. The deal also flunks *Dolan* because construction of Ambrose's service station would have little or no effect on burdens on the town's recreational facilities. Nevertheless, because Ambrose is highly unlikely to prevail on a claim that the town's ban on service stations is a regulatory taking or otherwise illegal, he might be happy to agree to the deal. Especially if Ambrose also were to be a repeat player in town affairs, town officials could anticipate that he would be unlikely to invoke *Nollan-Dolan* rights to compensation after having provided the swimming pool (which the duress doctrine, pp. 674–75, might otherwise entitle him to do).

The upshot of the Ambrose example is that, in practice, developers and localities are likely to agree to many exactions that violate *Nollan-Dolan* standards. State judges who grasp the impulses behind these consensual efforts to evade the rules might in turn be reluctant to rigorously apply the *Nollan-Dolan* doctrines. Compare Lambert v. City & County of San Francisco, 529 U.S. 1045 (2000) (Scalia, J., dissenting from denial of certiorari) (lamenting the chilly reception of *Nollan-Dolan* in some state courts).

5. *Actual effects of the decisions.* For a valuable study of how local governments in California have responded, see Ann E. Carlson & Daniel Pollack, Takings on the Ground: How the Supreme Court's Takings Jurisprudence Affects Local Land Use Decisions, 35 U.C. Davis L. Rev. 103 (2001). Carlson and Pollack found that most planners endorse the rules that the Court has articulated. In growth areas with large amounts of developable land, *Dolan* prompted fiscal analyses that ultimately led to higher, not lower, charges on developers. The authors also found, however, that older, mostly built-out jurisdictions — the ones particularly tempted to impose excessive exactions — indeed have been constrained by *Nollan-Dolan*.

6. Dolan's *relevance to regulatory takings issues*. In City of Monterey v. Del Monte Dunes at Monterey, Ltd., 526 U.S. 687, 703 (1999), the Supreme Court attempted to clarify the reach of *Dolan*: "The rule applied in *Dolan* considers whether dedications demanded as conditions of development are proportional to the development's anticipated impacts. It was not designed to address, and is not readily applicable to, [a regulatory takings claim]."

3.   Who Ultimately Bears the Costs of Exactions?

Before canvassing legal developments in the wake of *Nollan* and *Dolan*, we turn to an issue highly relevant to this body of law: Who, in the end, bears the incidence of a development charge? The developer on whom it is imposed? Those who purchase or rent lots in the burdened development? Those who own undeveloped land within the jurisdiction that imposes the exactions? Others? Answering these questions requires a look at the economics of land taxes. We start with a classic source.

Henry George, Our Land and Land Policy
9 Works of Henry George 108–12 (1898)

The best tax by which public revenues can be raised is evidently that which will closest conform to the following conditions:

  (1)   That it bear as lightly as possible upon production — so as least to check the increase of the general fund from which taxes must be paid and the community maintained.
  (2)   That it be easily and cheaply collected, and fall as directly as may be upon the ultimate payers — so as to take from the people as little as possible in addition to what it yields the government.
  (3)   That it be certain — so as to give the least opportunity for tyranny or corruption on the part of officials, and the least temptation to lawbreaking and evasion on the part of the taxpayers.
  (4)   That it bear equally — so as to give no citizen an advantage or put any at a disadvantage, as compared with others.

Let us consider what form of taxation best accords with these conditions. Whatever it be, that evidently will be the best mode in which the public revenues can be raised.

I. The Effect of Taxes upon Production

All taxes must evidently come from the produce of land and labor, since there is no other source of wealth than the union of human exertion with the material and forces of nature. But the manner in which equal amounts of taxation may be imposed may very differently affect the production of wealth. Taxation which lessens the reward of the producer necessarily lessens the incentive to production; taxation which is conditioned upon the act of production, or the use of any of the three factors of production, necessarily discourages production. Thus taxation which diminishes the earnings of the laborer or the returns of the capitalist tends to render the one less industrious and intelligent, the other less disposed to save and invest. Taxation which falls upon the processes of production interposes an artificial obstacle to the creation of wealth. Taxation which falls upon labor as it is exerted, wealth as it is used as capital, and land as it is cultivated, will manifestly tend to discourage production much more powerfully than taxation to the same amount levied upon laborers, whether they work or play, upon wealth whether used productively or unproductively, or upon land whether cultivated or left waste.

The mode of taxation is, in fact, quite as important as the amount. As a small burden badly placed may distress a horse that could carry with ease a much larger one properly adjusted, so a people may be impoverished and their power of producing wealth destroyed by taxation which, if levied in another way, could be borne with ease. A tax on date trees, imposed by Mohammed Ali, caused the Egyptian fellahs to cut down their trees; but a tax of twice the amount imposed on the land produced no such result. The tax of ten per cent on all sales, imposed by the Duke of Alva in the Netherlands, would, had it been maintained, have all but stopped exchange while yielding but little revenue.

This checking of production is in greater or less degree characteristic of most of the taxes by which the revenues of modern governments are raised. All taxes upon manufactures, all taxes upon commerce, all taxes upon capital, all taxes upon improvements, are of this kind. Their tendency is the same as that of Mohammed Ali's tax on date trees, though their effect may not be so clearly seen.

All such taxes have a tendency to reduce the production of wealth, and should, therefore, never be resorted to when it is possible to raise money by taxes which do not check production. This becomes possible as society develops and wealth accumulates. Taxes which fall upon ostentation would simply turn into the public treasury what otherwise would be wasted in vain show for the sake of show; and taxes upon wills and devises of the rich would probably have little effect in checking the desire for accumulation, which, after it has fairly got hold of a man, becomes a blind passion. But the great class of taxes from which revenue may be derived without interference with production are taxes upon monopolies — for the profit of monopoly is in itself a tax levied upon production, and to tax it is simply to divert into the public coffers what production must in any event pay.

All other monopolies are trivial in extent as compared with the monopoly of land. And the value of land expressing a monopoly, pure and simple, is in every respect fitted for taxation. That is to say, while the value of a railroad or telegraph line, the price of gas or of a patent medicine, may express the price of monopoly, it also expresses the exertion of labor and capital; but the value of land, or economic rent . . . is in no part made up from these factors, and expresses nothing but the advantage of appropriation. Taxes levied upon the value of land cannot check production in the slightest degree, until they exceed rent, or the value of land taken annually, for unlike taxes upon commodities, or exchange, or capital, or any of the tools or processes of production, they do not bear upon production. The value of land does not express the reward of production as does the value of crops, of cattle, of buildings, or any of the things which are styled personal property and improvements. It expresses the exchange value of monopoly. It is not in any case the creation of the individual who owns the land; it is created by the growth of the community. Hence the community can take it all without in any way lessening the incentive to improvement or in the slightest degree lessening the production of wealth. Taxes may be imposed upon the value of land until all rent is taken by the State, without reducing the wages of labor or the reward of capital one iota, without increasing the price of a single commodity or making production in any way more difficult. . . .

II. As to Ease and Cheapness of Collection

With, perhaps, the exception of certain licenses and stamp duties, which may be made almost to collect themselves, but which can be relied on for only a trivial amount of revenue, a tax upon land values can, of all taxes, be most easily and cheaply collected.

For land cannot be hidden or carried off; its value can be readily ascertained, and the assessment once made, nothing but a receiver is required for collection.

A tax on land values does not add to prices, and is thus paid directly by the persons on whom it falls; whereas, all taxes upon things of unfixed quantity increase prices, and in the course of exchange are shifted from seller to buyer, increasing as they go. If we impose a tax upon money loaned, as has been often attempted, the lender will charge the tax to the borrower, and the borrower must pay it or not obtain the loan. If the borrower uses it in his business, he in his turn must get back the tax from his customers, or his business becomes unprofitable.

If we impose a tax upon buildings, the users of buildings must finally pay it, for the erection of buildings will cease until building rents become high enough to pay the regular profit and the tax besides. . . .

. . . Were all taxes placed upon land values, irrespective of improvements, the scheme of taxation would be so simple and clear, and public attention would be so directed to it, that the valuation for taxation could and would be made with the same certainty that a real estate agent can determine the price a seller can get for a lot. . . .

IV. As to Equality

Adam Smith's canon is, that "the subjects of every state ought to contribute toward the support of the government as nearly as possible in proportion to their respective abilities; that is, in proportion to the revenue which they respectively enjoy under the protection of the state." Every tax, he goes on to say, which falls only upon rent, or only upon wages, or only upon interest is necessarily unequal. In accordance with this is the common idea which our systems of taxing everything vainly attempt to carry out — that every one should pay taxes in proportion to his means, or in proportion to his income. . . .

Nature gives to labor, and to labor alone. In a very Garden of Eden a man would starve but for human exertion. Now, here are two men of equal incomes — that of the one derived from the exertion of his labor, that of the other from the rent of land. Is it just that they should equally contribute to the expenses of the State? Evidently not. The income of the one represents wealth he creates and adds to the general wealth of the State; the income of the other represents merely wealth that he takes from the general stock, returning nothing. The right of the one to the enjoyment of his income rests on the warrant of Nature, which returns wealth to labor; the right of the other to the enjoyment of his income is a mere fictitious right, the creation of municipal regulation, which is unknown and unrecognized by Nature. The father who is told that from his labor he must support his children must acquiesce, for such is the natural decree; but he may justly demand that from the income gained by his labor not one penny shall be taken, so long as a penny remains of incomes which are gained by a monopoly of the natural opportunities which Nature offers impartially to all, and in which his children have as their birthright an equal share. . . .

Note on the Economics of Land Taxes

1. *The ghost of Henry George.* A number of empirical studies support George's basic prediction. See Florenz Plassmann & T. Nicolaus Tideman, A Markov Chain Monte Carlo Analysis of the Effect of Two-Rate Property Taxes on Construction, 47 J. Urb. Econ. 216 (2000) (finding that cities that tax structures at a lower rate than land indeed experience higher levels of construction); Andrejs Skaburskis, The Consequence of Taxing Land

Value, 10 J. Plan. Liter. 3 (1995) (asserting that Pittsburgh and Melbourne witnessed more development activity after increasing property tax rates on site values and reducing them on land improvements). See generally Land Use and Taxation: Applying the Insights of Henry George (H. James Brown ed., 1997), a collection of essays by land economists.

Georgist taxes are criticized in Edwin S. Mills, Urban Economics 52–54 (1980):

> To levy the right tax, the assessor must know the best use and the resulting rent for each plot of land. If he levies an excessively high tax, resource misallocation results. Thus, the *single tax would assign to the tax assessor the task now assigned to real estate markets.* This is a serious matter, because urban land is a valuable resource and it is important that it be used efficiently. Whatever the deficiencies in the ways competitive markets allocate land, it is clear that the job should not be given to the tax assessor. Tax assessors are skilled at tax assessment, not at urban land allocation.

Starting in 1947, Great Britain intermittently imposed stiff taxes ("betterment charges") on site values. Unlike property taxes, these were collected not on an annual basis, but rather when a site was either transferred or developed. During periods when tax rates were relatively high, owners tended to withhold developable land from the market. Robin Goodchild & Richard Munton, Development and the Landowner: An Analysis of the British Experience 28–33, 125 (1985). To what extent, if at all, does the British experience undermine George's case for the taxation of site values?

2. *Net vs. gross exactions.* The incidence of an exaction may be relevant to a decision on its legality. The balance of this Note therefore analyzes who is likely to bear the burden of a development charge. The analysis addresses the incidence of the net amount of an exaction. When a landowner reaps special favors as a result of bearing an exaction, the net exaction equals the gross cost of the exaction to the landowner *less* the value of the special benefits that the landowner receives. A benefit is *special* when a municipality generally refuses to provide it except to those willing to pay a benefits charge for it. For example, suppose a suburb that otherwise finances its park system by means of general revenues were to require a subdivider to dedicate land for an especially good on-site park. In that case, the special benefit to the subdivision would be the value of the special park services (that is, the increment over ordinary park services). The net exaction would be the subdivider's cost of providing the park site, less that special benefit. In the paragraphs that follow, "tax" refers to the net amount of an exaction.

3. *The incidence of taxes on land itself.* Most economists subscribe to George's basic analysis of the economics of taxes on site values. The supply of land is essentially fixed — that is, to use the economic term, price-inelastic. A tax on land cannot reduce the amount of land potentially available on the market (unless the tax rate were to be set so high that a plot would have negative value to a private owner).

If a site-value tax were to be newly imposed on ownership of a particular plot, potential buyers who were aware of the tax would bid less for that plot. Thus the incidence of a tax on site values tends to be the one George predicted: It is *passed backward* to the persons who own land at the time the tax is imposed and is not passed on to subsequent purchasers (at least not to ones aware of the tax). See William A. Fischel, The Homevoter Hypothesis 39–71 (2001); Oded Palmon & Barton A. Smith, New Evidence of Property Tax Capitalization, 106 J. Pol. Econ. 1099 (1998).

4. *The incidence of taxes on construction and other land improvements.* Taxes on improvements — the main focus of this subchapter — are another matter. George asserts that these sorts of taxes reduce the quantity of building. He also asserts that they are ultimately *passed on* to purchasers of land improvements in the form of higher prices. Many courts and commentators have agreed that automatic passing on of a development charge

is to be expected. See, e.g., Colonial Oaks West, Inc. v. Township of East Brunswick, 296 A.2d 653 (N.J. 1972); John W. Reps & Jerry L. Smith, Control of Land Subdivision, 14 Syracuse L. Rev. 405, 409 (1963). Nevertheless, on this question, George is more vulnerable to criticism.

Three scenarios can illustrate the difficulty of unraveling the ultimate incidence of a development exaction. Who bears the cost mainly depends on price elasticities — that is, on how the quantities of development supplied and demanded within the taxing jurisdiction would vary with changes in the market price of developed property?

a. *Fungible suburb, unusual exaction.* In the first scenario, assume that a small, undistinguished suburb is the only government in its large metropolitan area to impose a tax on development. Assume its tax is $1,000 per new house built. George and many other commentators traditionally have asserted that the price of each new house would rise by $1,000 in this suburb. Economic theory predicts that in fact this would not occur. No consumer would be willing to buy at that higher price because the consumer could obtain an equivalent new house in another suburb, or even an equivalent used dwelling in the taxing suburb, for the pretax price. In more technical terms, where the demand for development is infinitely elastic, a tax on development is not passed on to consumers. Instead, because developers aware of the tax would bid less for land in the taxing jurisdiction, the tax would be passed backward and fall on owners of undeveloped land in that jurisdiction.

b. *Unique suburb, unusual exaction.* The second scenario, portrayed in Figure 7-2, retains the assumption that the tax is an unusual one but supposes that the taxing jurisdiction possesses a combination of features (topography, location, public services, and so on) unique enough that most consumers regard the locality as having no perfect substitute. Under this scenario, unlike the first one, the demand curve is not horizontal, but rather slopes downward to the right. The S1 and D curves in Figure 7-2 indicate, respectively, the supply and demand for improvements in the jurisdiction before the tax is imposed. These curves intersect at point A, the equilibrium for the pretax market. Before the tax, quantity q_a of improvements would be sold at price p_a per unit. Now suppose the locality were to levy a tax of T per unit of improvement. The supply curve would shift upward by distance T. The new supply curve would be S2 and the posttax market equilibrium would be B, the intersection of D and S2. The tax has caused the price of improvements to rise from p_a to p_b, and the quantity sold to drop from q_a to q_b.

These results partially vindicate Henry George. The tax has discouraged development and resulted in higher prices for consumers. However, the price increase is not as great as the tax, because T is greater than the difference between p_b and p_a. While part of the tax has been passed forward to consumers, the balance has been passed backward to owners of undeveloped land.

c. *Unique suburb, universal tax on capital.* Now consider a third scenario. Assume that all local governments in the United States were to tax *all* capital outlays at equal rates. Some theorists predict that in this situation, a portion of the taxes would fall ultimately on owners of capital. This unintuitive outcome rests on the assumption that, because all outlays would be taxed, developers would be less eager to develop and as a result lenders would have to charge lower interest rates to induce them to proceed. Cf. Louis Kaplow, Fiscal Federalism and the Deductibility of State and Local Taxes Under the Federal Income Tax, 82 Va. L. Rev. 413, 441–58 (1996); Peter Mieszkowski & George R. Zodrow, Taxation and the Tiebout Model: The Differential Effects of Head Taxes, Taxes on Land Rents, and Property Taxes, 27 J. Econ. Liter. 1098 (1989).

5. *Data on incidence.* A number of investigators have compiled empirical evidence on the incidence of development exactions. A study conducted in Loveland, Colorado, found that that city's adoption of impact fees in the short run increased the sale price of

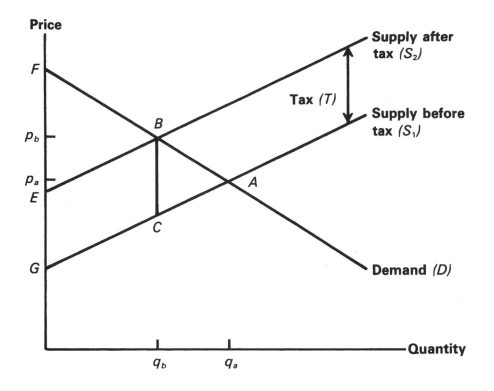

FIGURE 7-2
A Hypothetical Market for Land Improvements

both new and existing housing by *more* than the amount of the fees. Larry D. Singell &
Jane H. Lillydahl, An Empirical Examination of the Effect of Impact Fees on the Housing
Market, 66 Land Econ. 82 (1990). To reconcile this result with the standard economics of
tax incidence, one might hypothesize that participants in the Loveland market construed
the city's action as a signal that the city was likely to embrace other growth controls in
the future. A later study in Dade County, Florida, replicated the Singell-Lillydahl result.
Keith R. Ihlanfeldt & Timothy M. Shaughnessy, An Empirical Investigation of the Effects
of Impact Fees on Housing and Land Markets, 34 Reg'l Sci. & Urb. Econ. 639 (2004).
Ihlanfeldt and Shaughnessy also found empirical support for the theoretical prediction
that the costs of exactions commonly are passed backward to owners of undeveloped land.
For overviews of the various empirical studies, see Vicki Been, Impact Fees and Housing
Affordability, 8 Cityscape 139, 156–62 (2005); Jennifer S. Evans-Connolly & Larry L.
Lawhon, The Effects of Impact Fees on the Price of Housing and Land: A Literature
Review, 17 J. Plan. Liter. 351 (2003).

    6. *The legal relevance of the incidence of exactions.* The parties most likely to bear
the burden of a suburb's exactions — owners of undeveloped land and future house purchasers — commonly do not reside there. Current residents, the only persons entitled to
vote in a suburb's elections, are the primary beneficiaries of exactions. An overarching issue
in this subchapter therefore is when, if ever, the risk of failures in the political process warrants judicial or legislative efforts to protect landowners and consumers from majoritarian
abuse.

Some commentators on exactions law have focused on the degree of competition among municipalities and on the power of those who might bear the costs of an exaction to "exit" from the taxing jurisdiction. An early work in this vein is Vicki Been, Exit as a Constraint on Land Use Exactions, 91 Colum. L. Rev. 473 (1991), excerpted at p. 635. Been's analysis prompted a response, Stewart E. Sterk, Competition Among Municipalities as a Constraint on Land Use Exactions, 45 Vand. L. Rev. 831 (1992). Sterk asserts that, because real estate assets are immobile, competition among municipalities will not deter them from capturing economic rents associated with land and (when a locality faces a downwardly sloped demand curve) from pushing up the prices charged consumers. Sterk's conclusion: State courts (but not necessarily federal courts) should police exactions to curb inequitable "taxation without representation" and municipally created inefficiencies in land development markets.

4. A Necessary Aside: Equal Protection Issues Posed by Exactions

The analogy between takings law and strict equal protection analysis. A plaintiff who invokes the Takings Clause to seek relief from fiscal discrimination commonly is presenting a claim that could also be asserted under the Equal Protection Clause, which generally bans government employment of irrational or invidious classifications. See Note, The Principle of Equality in Takings Jurisprudence, 109 Harv. L. Rev. 1030 (1996), for a discussion of the relationship between these notions. When, if ever, would an exaction bear on a "fundamental right" or involve a "suspect classification" — two traditional triggers for strict equal protection scrutiny? When, if ever, are owners of developable land and housing consumers "discrete and insular minorities" of the sort that judges should protect from majoritarian exploitation? See United States v. Carolene Production Co., 304 U.S. 144, 152 n.4 (1938) (the origin of the quoted phrase).

Absent special circumstances, judges faced with an equal protection issue are apt to defer to the government's fiscal classification. In the course of rejecting casino developer Donald Trump's equal protection challenge to connection fees that were being imposed only on projects hooked up after a certain date, a New Jersey court quoted some standard equal protection doctrine:

> ". . . Equal protection does not require that all persons be dealt with identically. If there is some reasonable basis for the recognition of separate classes, and the disparate treatment of the classes has a rational relation to the object sought to be achieved by the lawmakers, the constitution is not offended. The transgression arises only when the classification rests upon grounds wholly irrelevant to achievement of the State's objective; the separate treatment must admit of but one conclusion beyond a rational doubt, i.e., that the basis therefor is arbitrary and unreasonable, and without relevance to the legislative goal."

Trump Plaza v. Atlantic City Municipal Utilities Authority, 470 A.2d 31, 35 (N.J. Super. Ct. Law Div. 1983) (quoting Airwick Industries v. Carlstadt Sewerage Authority, 270 A.2d 18, 23 (N.J. 1970)). But compare Tapalian v. Tusino, 377 F.3d 1 (1st Cir. 2004) (finding denial of equal protection when town official had vindictively imposed unusually stringent standards for improvement of access road to subdivision).

Discrimination against new neighborhoods? Responding to political pressure from existing homeowners, local officials may levy user fees to finance a service in developing neighborhoods that they simultaneously finance out of general revenues in existing neighborhoods. West Park Avenue, Inc. v. Township of Ocean, 224 A.2d 1 (N.J. 1966) (excerpted at p. 674 on another issue), pinpoints the possible inequities that may result. In the course of invalidating an ad hoc school exaction of $300 per new house, Weintraub, C.J., said in part:

> [T]here would be an imbalance if new construction alone were to bear the capital cost of new schools while being also charged with the capital costs of schools serving other portions of the school district. And if new construction were required in like manner to contribute specially to other programs supported by general taxation, for example, police and fire protection, then a municipality, if its hands were wholly unguided, could so deal with new housing as to burden, perhaps intolerably, the right of every citizen to seek a better home.

Id. at 4. Note that neither *Nollan* nor *Dolan* as such provide relief from this potential type of unfairness. If the Township of Ocean had stated that its land use controls were designed in part for fund-raising, its school charges might satisfy the need for an essential nexus with an articulated government purpose. The township's school fees also arguably were roughly proportional to the schooling needs created by the new subdivision. The fairness problem arose instead from another source — the township's deviation from its prior tradition of not levying user fees for schools.

An equal protection clause surely should not prevent a local government from ever switching from general financing to user fees for a specific service, such as construction of school facilities. As discussed at pp. 627–28, requiring the beneficiaries of a government service to pay for that service can have a variety of advantages. On the other hand, a locality may impose exactions solely to exploit the political weakness of future residents and owners of undeveloped land — the persons who would bear the costs of the charges. When, if ever, should a local government have to bear the burden of proving that it had imposed an impact fee for a legitimate public purpose, and not principally to enrich current residents at the expense of nonresidents?

Discrimination among developers. Should a court provide relief to a development firm that can prove that it had been asked to provide more physical exactions than others had? See Village of Willowbrook v. Olech, 528 U.S. 562 (2000), excerpted at p. 129 (holding Equal Protection Clause may protect a member of a "class of one"). Brown v. City of Joliet, 247 N.E.2d 47 (Ill. App. Ct. 1969), was decided in favor of a subdivider who had been the only one in his area required to install storm-drain trunklines. See also Johnson v. Reasor, 392 S.W.2d 54 (Ky. 1965) (utility connection fees imposed on subdividers but not on individual lot owners held discriminatory). But compare Miles v. Planning Board of Millbury, 536 N.E.2d 328 (Mass. 1989), excerpted at p. 418 (sustaining town's exaction of granite curbs in town where they were unusual).

Givings to favored developers. Just as an excessive exaction may pose a takings or equal protection issue, an overly light exaction may pose a givings issue. In C.I.V.I.C. Group v. City of Warren, 723 N.E.2d 106 (Ohio 2000), a civic association challenged the city's agreement to pay 20 percent of the costs of a developer's interior streets, sewers, and water lines. Asserting that in the usual course of business a developer pays for the entire cost of these improvements, the court held the city's subsidies violated the state constitutional provision against aid to a private corporation.

5.   *Physical Exactions After* Dolan

There are two general kinds of exactions. When a locality imposes a *physical exaction*, it is requiring a developer either to dedicate to it interests in land or to produce or pay for specific physical improvements located within or near the development. The easements at issue in both *Nollan* and *Dolan* are examples of physical exactions. When a locality insists on a contribution to a fund to be used to finance improvements or services at a more general set of locations, it is imposing a *monetary exaction*. We take up the evolving law of physical exactions first.

Goss v. City of Little Rock

151 F.3d 861 (8th Cir. 1998)

BOWMAN, Chief Judge.

Charles Goss owned 3.7 acres in the city of Little Rock, Arkansas. Little Rock's zoning laws classified Goss's property as residential. In 1993, Goss filed an application requesting that the city rezone his property as commercial. Little Rock's Planning Commission recommended that the City Board of Directors approve Goss's request only if Goss would dedicate to the city 22 percent of his property to be used for the expansion of an adjacent highway. Goss did not agree to this condition, and the City Board denied his application for rezoning.

Goss then sued Little Rock in the District Court, alleging that Little Rock's requirement that he dedicate to the city part of his property as a condition of the city's approving his rezoning application constituted a taking of private property without just compensation in violation of the Fifth and Fourteenth Amendments to the United States Constitution and Article Two, §22 of the Arkansas Constitution. . . . [A]fter trying the case the District Court held that the dedication requirement did constitute a taking, and the court therefore ordered Little Rock to rezone Goss's property without the dedication requirement. The District Court also held that Goss was not entitled to compensatory or punitive damages or attorney fees. Little Rock now appeals the District Court's judgment that the dedication requirement was a taking, and Goss appeals the denials of compensatory damages and attorney fees. . . .

Applying *Nollan* . . . , the District Court held that there was a nexus between the dedication and the city's interest in declining to rezone Goss's property — an interest in preventing increased traffic that could result from rezoning the property as commercial. The District Court's conclusion is correct: the dedication could alleviate the problems associated with increased traffic if it were used, as planned, to expand the highway adjacent to Goss's land. Applying *Dolan*, the District Court held that Little Rock had not met its burden of proving that the dedication was roughly proportionate to the impact that the proposed rezoning would have on traffic. The court found that Little Rock's assessment of the impact of rezoning was too speculative because that assessment was based on traffic that could, as said by the city's witness, "conceivably" be generated at some unknown point in the future if a strip mall were erected on Goss's land, although there are no plans to build a strip mall on the property and there is no reason to expect one to be built. The District Court concluded that Little Rock had failed to comply with *Dolan*'s requirement that the government make an "individualized determination that the required dedication is related both in nature and extent to the impact of the proposed development." *Dolan*, 512 U.S. at 391. . . .

. . . We . . . affirm the District Court's judgment that the dedication requirement constituted a taking.

Next we consider the question of remedy. The District Court ordered that, because the dedication requirement was a taking, Little Rock must rezone Goss's property without the requirement. We reverse this order. As discussed above, Little Rock has a legitimate

[handwritten: ∆ has legit.]

interest in declining to rezone Goss's property, and the city may pursue that interest by denying Goss's rezoning application outright, as opposed to denying it because of Goss's refusal to agree to an unconstitutional condition, as the city did here. See *Nollan*, 483 U.S. at 835-36 (stating that the government may deny the applicant's request outright if it has a legitimate interest in doing so). Since Little Rock may deny Goss's rezoning application outright, it may seem that we are awarding Goss a purely Pyrrhic victory. That, however, is not entirely so. Because Little Rock violated Goss's constitutional right, Goss is at least potentially eligible for damages and attorney fees, the issues to which we now turn.

[handwritten margin: but]

First Goss contends that the District Court erred in denying him compensatory damages. Goss argues that Little Rock's failure to rezone his property without the dedication requirement prevented him from selling the property, thereby costing him $265,000. As we just discussed, however, Little Rock was not legally required to rezone Goss's property. Accordingly, Goss is not entitled to damages on account of Little Rock's failure to do so. The District Court thus did not err in denying Goss compensatory damages. . . .

[handwritten margin: comp damages ? No b/c ∆ wasn't legally required to rezone π's property.]

Goss also argues that the District Court erred in denying him attorney fees. Under 42 U.S.C. §1988(b) (1994), district courts have discretion to award attorney fees to a prevailing party "in any action or proceeding to enforce a provision of [several civil rights statutes including 42 U.S.C. §1983 (1994)]." Section 1983 provides that a person who, acting under color of state law, violates another person's constitutional rights is liable to the person whose rights he violates. In this case Goss proved the elements of §1983: he proved that Little Rock, acting under color of state law, violated his constitutional right not to have his property taken without just compensation. Goss, however, did not cite §1983 in his complaint or in any argument before the District Court. Instead he cited the Constitution itself as the basis of his lawsuit. . . .

[handwritten margin: Atty fees? under 1983 - yes (but only partial atty fees)]

. . . We conclude that Goss's suit is a "proceeding to enforce" §1983 within the meaning of §1988(b). . . .

For the foregoing reasons, we conclude that the District Court erred in denying Goss attorney fees on account of his failure specifically to plead or argue §1983. This does not mean, however, that Goss is entitled to recover all his attorney fees. Because Goss did not prevail on his request that Little Rock be ordered to rezone his property without the dedication requirement or on his claims for monetary damages, he should receive only a partial award. We remand to the District Court for its determination of a reasonable award, taking into account the limited success Goss has achieved in the litigation. . . .

Note on the Exaction of Land and Physical Improvements

1. *Questions about* Goss. How Pyrrhic was Goss's victory? Should Goss instead have agreed to dedicate the 22 percent of his parcel that Little Rock coveted and later sued for compensation for an unconstitutional taking? (See pp. 674-75 on whether a complainant who pursues this strategy is barred by waiver.) To what extent does the *Goss* outcome support the argument, made by Fennell, Fischel, and others (see pp. 650-51), that *Nollan* and *Dolan* are likely to impede mutually advantageous dealmaking between localities and developers?

2. *On-site street dedications and improvements after* Dolan. Prior to *Dolan*, courts commonly allowed a municipality to exact on-site land for a street of regional benefit. See, e.g., Ayres v. City Council, 207 P.2d 1 (Cal. 1949) (sustaining exaction from subdivider of strip of land to be used to widen major thoroughfare). *Dolan*, however, seems to be altering outcomes in cases of this kind, particularly where the subdivision is small. In Schultz v. City of Grants Pass, 884 P.2d 569 (Or. Ct. App. 1994), the landowner had

applied to divide a 3.85-acre parcel into two lots. The city conditioned its approval on the dedication of 0.5-acre to provide land for the widening of two adjacent streets. The court, accepting the city's assertion that the land division would increase vehicle trips on these streets by about eight per day, held that the exaction failed the *Dolan* rough proportionality test. See also Town of Flower Mound v. Stafford Estates Ltd. Partnership, 71 S.W.3d 18 (Tex. App. 2002), affirmed, 135 S.W.3d 620 (Tex. 2004) (holding that town requirement that developer spend $484,000 to replace asphalt pavement on abutting road with concrete pavement to accommodate 750 additional trips per day was not roughly proportional when less expensive road improvements would suffice). But compare Sparks v. Douglas County, 904 P.2d 738 (Wash. 1995), where the majority of a divided court held that the exaction of strips to widen adjoining streets comported with *Dolan* in an instance where the proposed development would approximately double the amount of local street traffic.

3. *Neighbor suits protesting municipal accommodation of* Dolan. In Dudek v. Umatilla County, 69 P.3d 751 (Or. Ct. App. 2003), the road standards set out in a county ordinance required a subdivider to widen and improve a long roadway, much of it off-site. Deciding that imposition of this requirement might violate *Dolan*, the county waived it. Neighbors sought judicial invalidation of the county's waiver, but without success.

4. *Off-site road and utility linkups.* A municipality may attempt to compel the developer of a remote subdivision to bear part or all of its costs of extending the off-site umbilical cords that the subdivision needs. Suppose that a municipality would have to extend a water main one mile to reach the closest edge of a homebuilder's proposed development. Suppose also that none of the owners of the intermediate lands by which the main would run have any immediate interest in development, but that some of them are apt to change their minds in the near future. Suppose lastly that the water-main project would be cost-effective only if most intermediate lands actually were developed within a few years. In this instance, the risk of nondevelopment of the intermediate lands might be allocated in three basic ways.

a. If the city initially were to pay for most of the costs of the extension, with an eye to recouping those costs by imposing exactions when the intermediate lands were subdivided, the risk of nondevelopment would be borne by city taxpayers or water ratepayers. Cf. Baltica Construction Co. v. Planning Board, 537 A.2d 319 (N.J. Super. Ct. App. Div. 1988) (statute barred township from charging developer more than its pro rata share of costs of off-site water line).

b. If special assessments were levied to finance the entire cost of the extension at the time of its construction (cf. Cal. Gov't Code §§66485–66488 (West 2004)), the risk would be borne by the owners of the intermediate lands assessed to help finance the extension.

c. If the homebuilder were required to pay for the entire construction cost of the water main, but also were entitled to obtain reimbursement from owners of any intermediate lands who subsequently tapped into the main, the risk of nondevelopment would be borne by the homebuilder.

The third method, under which developers themselves bear the risks of overestimating the rate of urban expansion, is increasingly employed. Some statutes expressly authorize municipalities to reimburse developers from charges imposed on subsequent tappers. See, e.g., 65 Ill. Comp. Stat. 5/9-5-1 (2004). Even in the absence of a statute, this method has been held to be within the power of a chartered city. Long v. City of Fresno, 36 Cal. Rptr. 886 (Ct. App. 1964). Usually the city and the developer execute a written contract specifying the developer's rights to reimbursement. A scheme that entitles a developer to charge later connectors may trigger a due process challenge, especially if the affected third parties were not given an effective opportunity to influence the deal between the city and the pioneering developer. See Village Square No. 1, Inc. v. Crow-Frederick Retail Ltd. Partnership, 551 A.2d 471 (Md. App. 1989).

By imposing greater burdens on remote development, the third method of financing extensions promises to reduce the amount of urban sprawl, a pattern widely criticized. See sources cited at pp. 789–96. Is leap-frog development to be decried even when developers are bearing the financial risks of wasted infrastructure?

6. *Monetary Exactions after* Dolan

For a number of reasons, both developers and local governments may prefer monetary exactions to physical exactions. First, cash is fungible and therefore typically more valuable to a recipient than the transfer of an in-kind item costing the same amount. Second, cash transfers tend to be administratively cheaper, in part because the transferee need not inspect the quality of the good transferred. Third, the amount of a cash transfer can be scaled more precisely than an in-kind transfer, easing compliance with *Dolan*'s "rough proportionality" requirement. Indeed, for this last reason, *Dolan* appears to have spurred local officials to rely somewhat less on physical exactions and more on monetary exactions. See Ann E. Carlson & Daniel Pollak, Takings on the Ground, 35 U.C. Davis L. Rev. 103, 137–38 (2001).

Nevertheless, both *Nollan* and *Dolan* potentially limit monetary exactions. *Nollan* may be pertinent because the articulated goals of most land use regulations rarely include revenue-raising from applicants for permits, perhaps because this may be an impermissible reason for the exercise of regulatory power. See pp. 133–34 and 438. *Dolan*, moreover, may compel a local government to justify the amount that it is charging.

Ehrlich v. City of Culver City
911 P.2d 429 (Cal. 1996)

ARABIAN, Justice. . . .

I. FACTUAL AND PROCEDURAL BACKGROUND . . .

Between 1973 and 1975, plaintiff acquired a vacant 2.4-acre lot on Overland Avenue in Culver City and obtained city approval to develop the site as a private tennis club and recreational facility. At plaintiff's request, the city amended its zoning and general plan ordinances governing uses on the property from a split zone R-1 (single family residential) and C-2 (retail commercial) to C-3 (commercial). A specific plan was also adopted by the city providing for the development of a privately operated tennis club and recreational facility. . . . From 1975 to 1988, plaintiff, alone or through others, operated the sports complex — consisting by then of a swimming pool, five tennis courts, racquetball courts, and weight training and aerobic facilities — on the site.

In 1981, in response to financial losses, plaintiff applied to the city for a change in land use in order to construct an office building on the site; that application was abandoned after the city planning commission recommended against approval on the ground that the existing sports and tennis club provided a needed commercial recreational facility within the city. The club continued in operation under a series of managers until August 1988, when plaintiff closed it as a result of continuing financial losses. The following month, he again applied to the city for an amendment to the general plan, a zoning change and amendment of the specific plan to allow construction of a 30-unit condominium complex valued at $10 million.

Shortly after the submission of plaintiff's application, the city expressed an interest in acquiring the property for operation as a municipally owned sports facility and hired outside consultants to study the feasibility of the acquisition. The impetus behind the city's interest was a perceived deficiency in existing municipal recreational facilities. . . .

. . . In April 1989, the city decided not to purchase the property. At the same time, the city council disapproved plaintiff's application based on concerns over the loss of a recreational land use needed by the community. In the meantime, plaintiff obtained a demolition permit and tore down the existing site improvements. The still useful equipment, including the tennis court lights, nets, and lockers, he donated to the city.

Following the rejection of his application, plaintiff entered into discussions with members of the city council and city staff in an attempt to restructure the project. . . . [T]he city council voted to approve plaintiff's application conditioned upon the payment of certain monetary exactions. In lieu of the construction of four tennis courts as a condition of approval, the city required the payment of $280,000 "to be used" as stated in the ratifying ordinance, "for additional [public] recreational facilities as directed by the City Council." . . . The amount of the fee was based upon a city study which showed that the replacement costs for the recreational facilities "lost" as a result of amending the specific plan would be $250,000 to $280,000 for the pool, $135,000 to $150,000 for the paddle tennis courts, and $275,000 to $300,000 for the tennis courts.

In addition to the $280,000 recreation fee, the city also required plaintiff to pay an exaction under the city's "art in public places" program. By municipal ordinance, new residential development projects of more than four units, as well as all commercial, industrial, and public building projects with a building valuation exceeding $500,000, are required to provide "art work" (as defined by the ordinance) for the project in an amount equal to 1 percent of the total building valuation, or to pay an equal amount in cash to the city art fund. The city valued plaintiff's project at $3,200,000. He elected initially to pay the fee, which totaled $33,200, but his successor in interest apparently subsequently placed art of his own choosing on the site rather than pay the in-lieu fee.

Thereafter, plaintiff filed with the city formal written protests to the imposition of the $280,000 recreation fee and the $32,000 art in public places exaction, pursuant to Cal. Govt. Code §§66020 & 66021. The city rejected both protests. Plaintiff then amended his complaint to allege that imposition of the fees amounted to an unconstitutional taking without just compensation in violation of the Fifth and Fourteenth Amendments of the United States Constitution and article I, section 19 of the California Constitution. The parties later entered into an agreement whereby plaintiff agreed to pay the $280,000 recreation fee under protest in exchange for the necessary building and grading permits for the project. Plaintiff retained the right to proceed with his lawsuit, and agreed that the city would obtain a lien on the property as security for payment of the $280,000 fee. The site was subsequently developed and residential units were sold to the public. . . .

IV. Do NOLLAN AND DOLAN APPLY TO NONPOSSESSORY EXACTIONS?

Both *Nollan* and *Dolan* involved regulatory schemes under which the local government had required the possessory dedication of real property by the owner as a condition for issuing the necessary development permit. [The court summarized judicial decisions and commentary suggesting that a taking not involving a possessory dedication should be subjected to a lower standard of review.]

[Several of these decisions] dealt with . . . legislatively formulated development assessments imposed on a broad class of property owners. Fees of this nature may indeed be subject to a lesser standard of judicial scrutiny than that formulated by the court in *Nollan* and *Dolan* because the heightened risk of the "extortionate" use of the police power to exact unconstitutional conditions is not present. Nonetheless, we reject the proposition that *Nollan* and *Dolan* are entirely without application to monetary exactions. When such exactions are imposed — as in this case — neither generally nor ministerially, but on an individual and discretionary basis, we conclude that the heightened standard of judicial scrutiny of *Nollan* and *Dolan* is triggered. . . .

. . . [I]t matters little whether the local land use permit authority demands the actual *conveyance* of property or the *payment* of a monetary exaction. In a context in which the constraints imposed by legislative and political processes are absent or substantially reduced, the risk of too elastic or diluted a takings standard — the vice of distributive injustice in the allocation of civic costs — is heightened in either case. . . .

V. Applying the Heightened Standard in This Case . . .

. . . [T]he $280,000 fee, which the city has committed to the purchase of additional recreational facilities, will substantially advance its legitimate interest in correcting a demonstrated deficiency in municipal recreational resources. Unlike *Nollan*, where the high court found no logical connection between the commission's demand for a lateral easement across the owner's property and the purported governmental purpose of enhancing visual access, the "essential nexus" in this case is plain. . . .

We must next decide whether there is a "rough proportionality" between the public impact of the land use change and the recreational fee. . . .

. . . The city argues that its $280,000 recreation fee is warranted as partial compensation for the loss of some $800,000 in recreational improvements that were formerly located on plaintiff's property. But in this case it is error to measure the lost recreational benefits by the lost value of plaintiff's health club. The loss which the city seeks to mitigate by levying the contested recreational fee is not the loss of any particular recreational facility, but the loss of property reserved for private recreational use.

. . . The city may not constitutionally measure the magnitude of its loss, or of the recreational exaction, by the value of facilities it had no right to appropriate without payment.

This is not to say, however, that *some* type of recreational fee imposed by the city as a condition of the zoning and related changes cannot be justified. The amount of such a fee, however, must be tied more closely to the actual impact of the land use change the city granted plaintiff. Although we are unable to discern, on this record, the precise value or the economic cost of these impacts, several possibilities suggest themselves. One such possibility is likely to be the additional administrative expenses incurred in redesignating other property within Culver City for recreational use. The city's director of human services, who opposed the abandonment of a recreational use restriction on plaintiff's property, stated that to "permit this type of recreational development elsewhere would . . . involve arduous and costly rezoning and public hearings." It would be reasonable to require plaintiff to contribute toward defraying these anticipated rezoning costs, so that the city does not have to bear them itself or pass them along to future private developers seeking to construct recreational facilities.

More generally, the city's approval of plaintiff's condominium project may have given rise to public costs in the form of a diminished ability to attract private recreational development. If the city can show that it would have to incur greater costs to attract a developer of suitable private recreational facilities because plaintiff's parcel is no longer reserved for such a recreational use, it may consider these costs to be a part of the impact of plaintiff's project, and would be constitutionally permitted to impose such an exaction. Such a fee would enable the city to induce private health club development by offering monetary incentives roughly proportional to the land use incentive it relinquished when it removed the recreational use restriction from plaintiff's property.

Of course, the city could not constitutionally require plaintiff to dedicate the same amount of land for *public* recreational facilities. It could, however, require plaintiff to transfer, so to speak, the restricted land use designation at the Overland Avenue site to a comparable parcel plaintiff owns within the city, thus returning the city to the status quo as it existed prior to approval of the condominium project, that is, with a similar parcel of vacant land reserved for recreational use as an inducement to the development of private recreational facilities. If the city decides, however, that such a restricted land use transfer is impracticable, it may surely levy an in-lieu exaction to accomplish the same objective. . . .

. . . [T]he record suggests that some exaction may be warranted. It is thus appropriate to return the case to the city to reconsider its valuation of the fee in light of the principles we have articulated. . . . The determination of such a fee will, of course, require the city to make specific findings supported by substantial evidence. . . . (*Dolan*, supra, 512 U.S. at 391.)

VI. THE ART IN PUBLIC PLACES FEE . . .

Plaintiff contends that the required dedication of art or the cash equivalent thereof constitutes a taking under the *Nollan-Dolan* standards. This follows, he asserts, from the fact that the city made no individualized determination that the art mitigates a need generated by the project. . . .

. . . [W]e agree with the city that the art in public places fee is not a development exaction of the kind subject to the *Nollan-Dolan* takings analysis. As both the trial court and the Court of Appeal concluded, the requirement to provide either art or a cash equivalent thereof is more akin to traditional land use regulations imposing minimal building setbacks, parking and lighting conditions, landscaping requirements, and other *design* conditions such as color schemes, building materials and architectural amenities. Such aesthetic conditions have long been held to be valid exercises of the city's traditional police power, and do not amount to a taking merely because they might incidentally restrict a use, diminish the value, or impose a cost in connection with the property. . . .

CONCLUSION . . .

The judgment of the Court of Appeal is reversed; the cause is remanded to that court with directions to order the case returned to the City of Culver City.

KENNARD, Justice, concurring and dissenting.
I concur in the judgment insofar as it upholds the "art in public places" fee. . . .
I dissent from the judgment insofar as it concludes that a city may impose a mitigation fee for the "loss" of private recreation facilities when property on which such facilities were located is redeveloped for a different use. . . .
The fundamental flaw in the majority's reasoning is the assumption that the City, without violating the takings clause, could restrict Ehrlich's property to private recreational uses. . . . [S]uch a restriction might well deprive Ehrlich of economically viable use of his land and be invalid on that basis. But even if constitutionally valid on that basis, the restriction would be invalid because it impermissibly singled out Ehrlich's property for special restriction. This is akin to prohibited spot zoning. . . .

Here, Ehrlich initially voluntarily accepted the recreational use restriction in 1975 as a condition of approval of the specific plan for the property. So long as Ehrlich continued to accept the benefits of the specific plan, he might well have been estopped to challenge the validity of the restriction. But Ehrlich has now waived all benefits he received under the previous specific plan in order to redevelop the property for a different use. Having surrendered the benefits, he should no longer be required to bear the burden of the recreational use restriction. City should now permit Ehrlich to use his property in a manner consistent with the uses of surrounding parcels, without unfairly penalizing him for his unsuccessful attempt to operate a private recreational club.

Had Ehrlich applied in 1975 for approval to build townhouses rather than a private recreational club, City would have had no reason to impose a fee for the "loss" of a recreational land-use designation. Absent some evidence that Ehrlich gained some enduring advantage or City suffered some lasting detriment as a result of Ehrlich's unsuccessful efforts to operate a private recreational club on his land, the removal of the recreational use restriction imposed in 1975 will not support the imposition of any additional fee. (See Kmiec, At Last, the Supreme Court Solves the Takings Puzzle, 19 Harv. J.L. & Pub. Policy 147, 156 n.43 (1995) (characterizing as an "extraordinary notion" the assertion "that once a private landowner has undertaken a permitted common law use, like [construction of] a private swimming pool or tennis court, he either must continue that use or must pay to stop").)

Note on Impact Fees

1. *Questions about* Ehrlich. Justice Kennard's dissent assumes that Culver City could not have zoned Ehrlich's land so restrictively that it could be used only as a private recreational club. Do the materials on takings at pp. 134–97 support that conclusion?

In an omitted part of his plurality opinion, Justice Arabian interpreted a California statute that requires a "reasonable relationship" between the impact of development and the fee exacted to embody the later-minted *Dolan* "rough proportionality" test. Was this interpretive move defensible?

For stinging criticism of *Ehrlich*, see Gideon Kanner, Tennis Anyone? How California Judges Made Land Ransom and Art Censorship Legal, 25 Real Est. L.J. 214 (1997).

2. *The applicability of the Supreme Court rulings to monetary exactions. Ehrlich* holds that *Nollan* and *Dolan* apply to monetary exactions imposed on a discretionary basis. However, Justice O'Connor's opinion in Lingle v. Chevron U.S.A., Inc., 125 S. Ct. 2074 (2005) (excerpted at p. 193), emphasizes that *Nollan* and *Dolan* both involved physical exactions. Does this imply that the Takings Clause provides developers a lesser degree of protection against monetary exactions?

3. *The applicability of* Nollan *and* Dolan *to nondiscretionary exactions.* Rogers Machinery, Inc. v. Washington County, 45 P.3d 966 (Or. Ct. App. 2002), holds that *Dolan* does not apply to fees imposed on broad classes of property owners pursuant to a legislatively set formula. The California Supreme Court reached the same conclusion in San Remo Hotel, L.P. v. City & County of San Francisco, 41 P.3d 87 (Cal. 2002) (a case also discussed at pp. 245 and 672). Justice Brown dissented in *San Remo Hotel*, arguing:

> A public agency can just as easily extort unfair fees legislatively from a class of property owners as it can adjudicatively from a single property owner. The nature of the wrong is not different or less abusive to its victims, but the scope of the wrong is multiplied many times over. Therefore, I believe *Ehrlich* should apply whenever the risk is great that greed for public revenues has driven public regulatory policy. In other words, where a legislative scheme imposes a burdensome fee on a small class of property owners as a condition to buying relief from a regulation, I believe

careful judicial scrutiny is appropriate, including finding a close link between the fee and the purpose of the regulation. In light of the majority's decision, however, we can be sure that agencies will now act legislatively, rather than adjudicatively, and thereby insulate their actions from close judicial scrutiny.

Id. at 124. See also Town of Flower Mound v. Stafford Estates Ltd. Partnership, 135 S.W.3d 620 (Tex. 2004) (explicitly rejecting the position of the *San Remo* majority on this issue).

However, in *Lingle*, supra, Justice O'Connor repeatedly observes that *Nollan* and *Dolan* both involved "adjudicative" land-use exactions. Is this a correct characterization of the government actions in those two cases? Is it a hint that the two decisions apply only to discretionary exactions? For a review of the deeply contested case law on the reach of *Nollan* and *Dolan*, see J. David Breemer, The Evolution of the "Essential Nexus": How State Courts Have Applied *Nollan* and *Dolan* and Where They Should Go from Here, 59 Wash. & Lee L. Rev. 373 (2002).

4. *Varieties of impact fees.* In general, courts and state legislatures have been most accepting of impact fees levied to finance the sorts of local infrastructural improvements that municipalities traditionally could have financed by means of special assessments. When impact fees are levied to finance what traditionally would have been regarded as a general improvement, however, judicial suspicions are heightened. The following review of the evolving law on impact fees for physical infrastructure, schools and parks, and inclusionary housing units supports these assertions, although hardly perfectly.

a.   *Impact Fees Placed in Special Accounts to Finance Utility and Transportation Systems*

Impact fees for utility and transportation systems generally have been the easiest for municipalities to defend. When a municipality has commissioned an engineering study that indicated the infrastructure needed and has chosen a formula that plausibly apportions the cost of that infrastructure among developers, the municipality is likely to be on safe legal ground. For example, City of Dunedin v. Contractors & Builders Association, 312 So. 2d 763, 766 (Fla. Dist. Ct. App. 1975), holds "that where the growth patterns are such that an existing water or sewer system will have to be expanded in the near future, a municipality may properly charge for the privilege of connecting to the system a fee which is in excess of the physical cost of connection, if this fee does not exceed a proportionate part of the amount reasonably necessary to finance the expansion and is earmarked for that purpose." The court found that the fees before it passed this test.

Does a city's imposition of impact fees to finance utility systems in new neighborhoods satisfy principles of horizontal equity when the city finances utility system improvements in existing neighborhoods out of general revenues? In New Jersey Shore Builders Association v. Township of Marlboro, 591 A.2d 950 (N.J. Super. Ct. App. Div. 1991), the township had attempted to make subdividers pay for the first two years of electricity bills for street lighting in their subdivisions. This attempt was held to violate a New Jersey statute governing subdivision approvals. Compare Southern Nevada Homebuilders Association v. Las Vegas Valley Water District, 693 P.2d 1255 (Nev. 1985) (holding that water district exceeded its authority in attempting to charge new developments with entire capital cost of major water-system expansion that would benefit whole district).

Illinois law is particularly hostile to the imposition of impact fees for any purpose. See Northern Illinois Home Builders Association v. County of DuPage, 649 N.E.2d 384 (Ill. 1995) (holding impact fees must satisfy the "specifically and uniquely attributable" test set forth in *Pioneer Trust*, discussed at p. 637–38, thereby inhibiting municipal pooling of financial burdens among developers).

b.   Impact Fees for Schools and Parks

Perhaps because local governments traditionally have rarely levied special assessments or other sorts of benefits charges to finance schools and parks, developers frequently contest the legality of impact fees imposed for these purposes.

Volusia County v. Aberdeen at Ormond Beach
760 So. 2d 126 (Fla. 2000)

QUINCE, J.

. . . For the reasons discussed below, we affirm the trial court's decision finding the impact fee ordinance unconstitutional as applied to Aberdeen at Ormond Beach Manufactured Housing Community [Aberdeen].

Aberdeen [owns] a mobile home park in Ormond Beach that provides housing for persons at least 55 years of age or older. Aberdeen brought suit against Volusia County and the Volusia County School Board [Volusia County] to challenge the constitutionality of public school impact fees assessed on new homes constructed at Aberdeen.

. . . Aberdeen's Supplemental Declaration of Covenants, Conditions and Restrictions contains the following provisions:

> exceptions to the minimum age requirement are permitted under limited circumstances; persons under eighteen are prohibited from permanently residing in any dwelling unit; the developer reserves the absolute right to modify or revoke all other covenants; and restrictions are binding upon owners for thirty years from the date of recordation.

. . . As of July 1998, Aberdeen housed 142 people, 119 of whom were over 60. No children have ever lived in Aberdeen, and the youngest resident ever was 42.

Effective October 1, 1992, Volusia County enacted Ordinance No. 92-9, imposing countywide public school impact fees on new dwelling units constructed in Volusia County. . . .

The impact fee represents the cost per dwelling unit of providing new facilities. . . . In calculating the fee, the County utilized the student generation rate, which is the average number of public school students per dwelling unit. Pursuant to the Volusia County impact fee ordinances, Aberdeen has paid $86,984.07 under protest for 84 homes as of July 31, 1998.

Aberdeen filed suit against Volusia County, claiming, inter alia, that public school impact fees were unconstitutional as applied to Aberdeen because of the deed restrictions prohibiting minors from living on the property. In response, the County argued that exempting Aberdeen would convert the impact fee into a "user fee," thereby violating the state constitutional guarantee of a free public school system. Although both parties filed motions for summary judgment, the trial court denied Volusia County's motion and granted Aberdeen's motion. . . .

. . . St. Johns County [v. Northeastern Florida Builders Association, 583 So. 2d 635 (Fla. 1991)], does not preclude review of Aberdeen's claims. In *St. Johns County*, the plaintiffs attacked the impact fee ordinance as unconstitutional on its face. The ordinance allocated the cost of new schools to each new unit of residential development. . . . The

Court rejected the argument that dwelling units without children did not have an impact on the school system, noting that occupants would change and children would "come and go." . . . However, the Court ultimately found that the ordinance was defective because fee funds could be spent within municipalities whose residents were not subject to the fee. . . .

. . . In *St. Johns County*, the Court expressly adopted the dual rational nexus test for determining the constitutionality of impact fees: the local government must demonstrate reasonable connections between (1) "the need for additional capital facilities and the growth in population generated by the subdivision" and (2) "the expenditures of the funds collected and the benefits accruing to the subdivision." Volusia County argues that the test requires needs and benefits to be assessed based on countywide growth, and that the specific-need/special-benefit analysis is limited to the water and sewer line context. This argument, however, is without merit.

The language of the test itself belies the assertion that a countywide standard should be employed. The first prong of the test explicitly requires a nexus between the County's need and the "growth in population generated by the subdivision." 583 So. 2d at 637. Similarly, the test's second prong ensures that "benefits accrue to the subdivision." Id. Thus, the explicit references to subdivisions indicate that the standard is not tailored to countywide growth, but to growth of a particular subdivision. . . .

. . . [I]mposing a countywide standard would eviscerate the substantial nexus requirement. This nexus is significant because of the distinction between taxes and fees. As this Court noted in Collier County [v. State, 733 So. 2d 1012 (Fla. 1999)], "There is no requirement that taxes provide any specific benefit to the property; instead, they may be levied throughout the particular taxing unit for the general benefit of residents and property." Fees, by contrast, must confer a special benefit on feepayers "in a manner not shared by those not paying the fee." 733 So. 2d at 1019. . . . Thus, a liberal reading of the dual rational nexus test would obliterate the distinction between an unconstitutional tax and a valid fee. . . .

Volusia County also contends that Aberdeen contributes to the need for schools because the Volusia County School District is required to provide free schooling to all students with disabilities up to the age of twenty-one. Because Aberdeen's age restrictions only prohibit minors from living on the property, the County asserts that the potential to generate students still exists. . . . As the trial court correctly concluded, [however,] "The rational nexus test requires Aberdeen to have more than a possible or an incidental impact on the need for schools. In the final analysis, housing that allows children is the land use that creates the need for new school facilities."

Volusia County is also unable to satisfy the "benefits" prong of the dual rational nexus test. Because no children can live at Aberdeen, impact fees collected at Aberdeen will not be spent for Aberdeen's benefit, but for the benefit of children living in other developments. Volusia County contends that Aberdeen benefits from the construction of new schools because they also serve as emergency shelters and sites for adult education classes. However, the connection between the expenditure of impact fee funds for the construction of new schools and the tangential benefit of having places of refuge in natural disasters is too attenuated to demonstrate a substantial nexus. Put another way, the schools are built primarily for the educational benefit of school-age children and, to the extent that Aberdeen derives any incidental benefit from their construction, it is insufficient to satisfy the dual rational nexus test.

In sum, Aberdeen neither contributes to the need for additional schools nor benefits from their construction. Accordingly, the imposition of impact fees as applied to Aberdeen does not satisfy the dual rational nexus test.

Volusia County also argues that requiring an exemption for age-restricted communities converts the impact fees into user fees, thereby violating the constitutional guarantee of free public schools. [The court rejected this argument.] . . .

For the foregoing reasons, we hold that Volusia County's public school impact fees are unconstitutional as applied to Aberdeen. . . .

Note on Monetary Exactions for Schools and Parks

1. *Questions about* Volusia County. What if the complainant in *Volusia County* had been a developer who could convincingly prove that its development would generate only 10 percent of the number of schoolchildren that an ordinary residential development would generate? Is the Florida Supreme Court's all-or-nothing approach superior to *Dolan's* "rough proportionality" approach? Should counsel for Aberdeen have invoked *Dolan*?

2. *Impact fees for schools.* School impact fees have spread rapidly where state courts have given them a green light. Besides *St. Johns County* (Fla. 1991), see, e.g., Candid Enterprises, Inc. v. Grossmont Union High School District, 705 P.2d 876 (Cal. 1985) (holding neither state law nor Equal Protection Clause forbade use of school impact fees); Krughoff v. City of Naperville, 369 N.E.2d 892 (Ill. 1977) (similar). But compare Greater Franklin Developers Association v. Town of Franklin, 730 N.E.2d 900 (Mass. App. Ct. 2000) (holding that school impact fee was a tax that town was not empowered to levy).

3. *Impact fees for parks.* There is a voluminous body of case law on whether a municipality can compel a subdivider to either dedicate a park site or pay an in-lieu fee. Some outcomes have turned on statutory issues. Decisions sympathetic to municipal imposition of park exactions include Associated Home Builders v. City of Walnut Creek, 484 P.2d 606 (Cal. 1971) (expansively upholding in-lieu fees for parks), and Twin Lakes Development Corp. v. Town of Monroe, 801 N.E.2d 821 (N.Y. 2003) (holding that developer had not carried burden of proving that town's $1,500 per-lot park fee violated *Dolan*). But compare, e.g., Home Builders Association of Greater Des Moines v. City of West Des Moines, 644 N.W.2d 339 (Iowa 2002) (holding that city's home-rule powers did not authorize imposition of impact fees for parks); Berg Development Co. v. City of Missouri City, 603 S.W.2d 273 (Tex. Civ. App. 1980) (construing Texas's takings clause to forbid exaction of either land or in-lieu fees for park purposes).

c. *Exactions for Inclusionary Housing*

Countless suburbs engage in exclusionary zoning — that is, the use of regulatory powers to limit the development of modest-cost housing. This practice poses numerous legal issues, which are addressed in Chapters 8 and 9. Ostensibly to counter the effects of exclusionary practices, a government may seek to induce developers to contribute to the financing of housing programs for low- and moderate-income families. This policy, typically referred to as "inclusionary zoning" or a "housing linkage program," may entail exactions that are vulnerable to legal attack.

Basic varieties. An inclusionary program involves the exaction either of monetary fees (to be placed in a housing development fund) or of actual dwelling units (which the developer is required to sell or rent to a qualifying household at a below-market price). Particularly when dwellings are exacted in-kind, the program must specify (1) the households that qualify for the inclusionary units, (2) the procedures for choosing recipient households from among the larger pool of applicants, (3) the design and location of inclusionary units,

(4) the depth of the subsidy that a recipient receives, and (5) the restraints on a program-beneficiary's power to rent or sell a unit previously acquired at a below-market price. On the last of these issues, see City of Oceanside v. McKenna, 264 Cal. Rptr. 275 (Ct. App. 1989) (restriction on power of grantee of inclusionary condominium unit to lease unit did not constitute an illegal restraint on alienation). See generally Alan M. Mallach, Inclusionary Housing Programs (1984); Douglas R. Porter, Inclusionary Zoning for Affordable Housing (2004).

An inclusionary program automatically may entitle a developer who provides the desired units to receive a density bonus or some other special development privilege. A density bonus tends to offset the financial burdens the developer otherwise would bear. When the bonus is generous enough, inclusionary zoning — contrary to claims of some of its critics — may work to augment, not dampen, total housing production. The leading empirical study on this complex topic is Robert A. Johnston et al., Selling Zoning: Do Density Bonus Incentives for Moderate-Cost Housing Work?, 42 Land Use L. 3 (Aug. 1990). The net effects are particularly hard to divine when a municipality has offered a bonus only after *reducing* the densities its zoning ordinance previously had allowed. See id. at 6 ("One [Concord, California] official confidentially told us that permitted densities were lowered prior to the adoption of the density bonus program.").

History. The nation's first inclusionary ordinance, adopted in 1971 by Fairfax County, required a developer of 50 or more dwelling units to provide at least 15 percent of the units at below-market prices to low- and moderate-income families. The program was struck down in Board of Supervisors v. DeGroff Enterprises, Inc., 198 S.E.2d 600 (Va. 1973), in part for violating the Virginia Constitution's takings clause. Despite this early setback, over the course of the next decade, dozens of communities — mainly affluent ones such as Montgomery County, Maryland, and the California cities of Del Mar, Irvine, and Palo Alto — embraced the technique.

The Supreme Court of New Jersey then gave inclusionary zoning a major boost in Southern Burlington County NAACP v. Township of Mount Laurel, 456 A.2d 390 (N.J. 1983), further discussed at p. 773. This decision, usually called *Mount Laurel II*, strongly encouraged a municipality to require a developer to set aside at least 20 percent of the proposed housing units for inclusionary purposes. In most instances, the court opined, this sort of requirement would constitute neither a taking of property nor impermissible socioeconomic zoning. The Connecticut and Massachusetts anti-snob zoning acts (see pp. 786–87) also have served to stimulate inclusionary housing projects in those states.

In 1980, San Francisco pioneered a variant approach, sometimes referred to as a linkage program. It began requiring developers of new office buildings to pay fees to help finance the production of inclusionary housing. To receive approval to build a downtown skyscraper, one developer paid $2.4 million into the city's housing fund. S.F. Chron., June 12, 1982, at 2. On the spread of this program to other cities, see Jane E. Schukaske, Housing Linkage, 76 Iowa L. Rev. 1011 (1991).

According to a 2003 estimate, 107 cities and counties in California had some form of inclusionary housing program, and together they had created over 34,000 affordable units over the course of the prior 30 years. Daniel J. Curtin, Jr. & Nadia L. Costa, Inclusionary Zoning Update, 35 Urb. Law. 739–40 (2003). (For purposes of comparison, in 2003 alone there were 192,000 total housing starts in California. Statistical Abstract 2005, at 600.)

The unruly case law. In California, attacks on inclusionary housing initiatives have rarely succeeded. In San Remo Hotel, L.P. v. City & County of San Francisco, 41 P.3d 87 (Cal. 2002), cited on pp. 245 and 667, the owner of an old hotel had applied to convert all 61 of the hotel's units from long-term rentals to short-term rentals. A San Francisco ordinance required, as a precondition, that the owner either (1) replace the eliminated long-term rental units one-for-one; (2) provide other types of low-income housing; or (3) pay an in-lieu fee, which in this case amounted to a total of $567,000. The owner chose the third option and then sought refund of the fee, in part on the ground that it violated *Dolan*. The California Supreme Court first interpreted *Dolan* to apply only to individualized development fees, not to generally applicable ones. It then held that San Francisco's financing system was not individualized because the city had offered a number of formulaic options and the applicant had chosen one of them. Applying a less demanding standard of review, the court concluded that San Francisco's housing replacement fees bore a reasonable relationship to the threatened loss of housing. See also Home Builders Association v. City of Napa, 108 Cal. Rptr. 2d 60 (Ct. App. 2001) (upholding against a takings challenge a program of inclusionary housing exactions imposed on developers of new housing).

But see Sintra, Inc. v. City of Seattle, 829 P.2d 765 (Wash. 1992). In that instance, Seattle officials, applying the city's Housing Preservation Ordinance (HPO), had attempted to impose a fee of $220,000 on a developer who had sought to convert a vacant, dilapidated, three-story hotel into a ministorage warehouse. The revenue was to have been placed in a housing replacement fund. The Washington Supreme Court held that the fee constituted a taking of property:

> The regulatory scheme here goes beyond preventing harm. The HPO required that landowners who wished to alter the use of their property either replace the low-income housing or pay extremely high sums of money into a housing replacement fund. The harm sought to be prevented — people standing on the street corner with nowhere to go — was exceeded. The regulation required the improper additional step of providing new housing. Moreover, this burden was unfairly allocated to individual property owners, rather than equally distributed among all citizens.

Id. at 773. See also Seawall Associates v. City of New York, 543 N.E.2d 1059 (N.Y. 1989) (invalidating, as a taking of property, ordinance that in effect required the owner of a building with single-room occupancy units to pay $45,000 for every unit eliminated). Compare Town of Telluride v. Lot Thirty-Four Venture, LLC, 3 P.3d 30 (Colo. 2000) (holding that town's inclusionary zoning ordinance was invalid under state law prohibiting rent control).

Academic set-to. Inclusionary zoning has attracted both severe critics and staunch defenders. For criticism of suburban practices, see Robert C. Ellickson, The Irony of "Inclusionary Zoning," 54 S. Cal. L. Rev. 1167 (1981), arguing that an inclusionary program imposes a potentially counterproductive tax on housing construction and is a wasteful and unfair way to provide housing assistance. (See also pp. 869–78 on the demerits and merits of project-based housing subsidies.) But see Andrew G. Dietderich, An Egalitarian Market: The Economics of Inclusionary Zoning Reclaimed, 24 Fordham Urb. L.J. 23 (1996) (attacking Ellickson's economic analysis and concluding that all forms of inclusionary programs help low- and moderate-income families). On exactions from developers of office buildings, compare John A. Henning, Jr., Note, Mitigating Price Effects with a Housing Linkage Fee, 78 Cal. L. Rev. 721 (1990) (no police-power rationale supports making office developers pay for housing programs), with Jerold S. Kayden & Robert Pollard, Linkage Ordinances and Traditional Exactions Analysis, 50 Law & Contemp. Probs. 127 (1987) (defending Boston's linkage program). Most observers of the aftermath of *Mount Laurel II* have concluded that the inclusionary programs it spawned have contributed little to racial and social integration in New Jersey. Bernard K. Ham, Exclusionary Zoning and Racial Segregation: A Reconsideration of the *Mount Laurel* Doctrine, 7 Seton Hall Const. L.J. 577 (1997); John M. Payne, Norman Williams, Exclusionary Zoning, and the *Mount Laurel* Doctrine, 20 Vt. L. Rev. 665 (1996). See also p. 781. On experience further west, see Nico Calavita & Kenneth Grimes, Inclusionary Housing in California, 64 J. Am. Plan. Ass'n 150 (1998).

7.   Defenses and Remedies

West Park Avenue, Inc. v. Township of Ocean
224 A.2d 1 (N.J. 1966)

WEINTRAUB, C.J.

Plaintiff sued to recover $17,700 which it paid defendants, allegedly under duress.

. . . After completing a model home, plaintiff erected signs advertising its tract, whereupon plaintiff was told by municipal officials that it could not use a billboard or receive further building permits or certificates of occupancy unless it agreed to pay to the defendant Board of Education the sum of $300 per house.

. . . [T]he trial court found that plaintiff yielded unwillingly to this imposition. That finding, we think, was inescapably correct. Plaintiff feared it could not survive if its project stood still during a period of litigation. It also sensed a danger of hostile enforcement of ordinances bearing upon the construction of homes. This was especially understandable because of the boldness with which the dollar demand was made, for the municipality did not so much as adopt an ordinance to give color to the exaction. Rather the demand was made at the administrative level by minor officials, who, pursuant to instructions from above, simply refused to obey their duties of office. . . .

[The court held that the legislature had not authorized municipalities to impose this sort of charge on a developer.]

. . . [D]efendants say plaintiff's payments, although in fact made unwillingly, were nonetheless "voluntary" in law because plaintiff failed to resist the illegal demand by suit. This is the ground upon which defendants prevailed below.

It is usually said that payments are made under duress when (1) they are induced by the wrongful pressure of the payee and (2) the payor has no immediate and adequate remedy in the courts to resist them. Ross Systems v. Linden Dari-Delite, Inc., 173 A.2d 258 (N.J. 1961). Defendants rely upon the second component. . . .

In the case before us an unlawful demand was made with a consciousness of its unlawfulness. If it were crucial, we would not hesitate to say that plaintiff had no feasible remedy, both because of the pressure of its own financial picture and because of its fear of recrimination in other matters. But we prefer to say the wrong of the municipality was so palpable that it would be against good morals to permit defendants to complain that plaintiff was not valiant enough. Nor can we agree with defendants that they should be permitted so to say because they are governmental bodies. On the contrary, the wrong is the more grievous because the power of public office was put behind it. As was said in Robertson v. Frank Brothers Company, 132 U.S. 17, 23 (1889), "When the duress has been exerted by one clothed with official authority, or exercising a public employment, less evidence of compulsion or pressure is required; as where an officer exacts illegal fees. . . ." There should be every inducement to local government to stay within the law. Accountability for moneys so flagrantly obtained serves that end.

Finally, defendants say the action is barred by laches. The payments were made from July 1959 into October 1961. This suit was started August 1, 1963. Plaintiff explains that it still holds one of the 60 lots and that prior to suit it was also concerned about possible retaliation with respect to other properties it had in the municipality. We need not, however, weigh the sufficiency of this explanation because the defense of laches is unavailing for several reasons. . . . First, there is no proof that defendants in fact were prejudiced by plaintiff's failure to make an earlier demand. Second, laches is not available to a conscious wrongdoer. . . .

The judgment is reversed and the matter remanded to the trial court with directions to enter judgment in favor of plaintiff for $17,700 together with interest.

Note on Defenses and Remedies

1. *Duress as a counter to the defense of waiver.* Some states have enacted statutes that require a developer who objects to an exaction both to tender it and, within a short time period, to file a formal notice of protest with the exacting locality. See, e.g., Cal. Gov't Code §66020 (2004) (90-day time limit) (a procedure employed in Ehrlich v. City of Culver City, 911 P.2d 429 (Cal. 1996), excerpted at p. 663). See also Town of Flower Mound v. Stafford Estates Ltd. Partnership, 135 S.W.3d 620 (Tex. 2004) (holding for developer who made early protest).

In *West Park Avenue*, how might township officials have responded if the developer were to have announced that it was paying under protest? Could statutory restrictions on a developer's rights to restitution violate takings strictures? Should the continuing presence of duress toll the running of the statute of limitations on a developer's claims? If so, when would the duress end? Suppose that a development company were to have sold all the lots in the subdivision where it had suffered excessive exactions, but that it had an application for an unrelated rezoning pending before the same city council that had overcharged it before. Would it still be under duress?

A developer who voluntarily proposes a donation to help win municipal assent cannot expect later to succeed in reneging. See KMST, LLC v. County of Ada, 67 P.3d 56, 61 (Idaho 2003) (holding developer could not challenge street dedication as a taking when he "voluntarily decided to dedicate the road to the public in order to speed the approval of its development").

Can a third party object when a municipality has induced a competitor to waive rights to protest exactions? In United Artists Theatre Circuit, Inc. v. Township of Warrington, 316 F.3d 392 (3d Cir. 2003), two rival developers of movie theater complexes were competing for development approval in a township where the market would support only one complex. Regal Cinema won the race for the township's approval by agreeing to payment of annual impact fees of $100,000. United Artists had refused the township's demand that it pay these same fees because it deemed the fees illegal. Should United Artists have a remedy under §1983 against the township or its officials? The Third Circuit remanded the case for a determination of whether the officials' conduct "shocked the conscience." (This is one of several standards for finding a violation of substantive due process. See p. 102.) Would the commentators who want exaction law not to interfere with the dealmaking process (see sources cited at pp. 650–51) be sympathetic to a third-party challenge of this sort?

2. *The amount of a prevailing landowner's damage award.* Should a developer who has been overcharged necessarily receive a complete refund, the remedy granted in *West Park Avenue*? Not according to Town of Flower Mound v. Stafford Estates Ltd. Partnership, 71 S.W.3d 18 (Tex. App. 2002), affirmed, 135 S.W.3d 620 (Tex. 2004), which states that the local government should be able to deduct from the developer's payments both (1) an amount equal to the maximum exaction that *Dolan*'s "rough proportionality" test would have permitted, and (2) any special benefits (such as higher quality infrastructure) the developer received as a result of having made the excessive payments. The *Flower Mound* opinions also consider a successful claimant's entitlements to recover attorney fees, an

issue addressed in Goss v. City of Little Rock, 151 F.3d 861 (8th Cir. 1998), excerpted at p. 660.

3. *Punitive damages to deter municipal misconduct?* Does the return of the illegal portion of an exaction, even with interest and attorney fees, adequately deter municipal misconduct? Despite the holding in *West Park Avenue*, townships in New Jersey continued to impose illegal exactions for schools. See, e.g., Southern Burlington County NAACP v. Township of Mount Laurel, 336 A.2d 713, 721–22 (N.J. 1975). Chicago suburbs similarly evaded the constraints that Illinois courts had imposed on exactions. See Rutherford H. Platt & Jon Moloney-Merkel, Municipal Improvisation: Open Space Exactions in the Land of *Pioneer Trust*, 5 Urb. Law. 706 (1973).

Should a prevailing landowner be entitled to recover punitive damages? Unless a statute explicitly has made punitive damages available, most courts decline to allow this remedy against a municipal corporation. See City of Newport v. Fact Concerts, Inc., 453 U.S. 247 (1981) (holding that §1983 provides no basis for an award of punitive damages against a municipality). Even though the municipality may be immune, an official who had levied an illegal exaction conceivably could be held liable for punitive damages. For discussion of all these questions, see Sintra, Inc. v. City of Seattle, 935 P.2d 555 (Wash. 1997). In that instance, the jury had decided that the city's housing-replacement exactions had effected a taking, but then declined to hold the defendant officials liable for punitive damages. But compare Tapalian v. Tusino, 377 F.3d 1 (1st Cir. 2004). In that instance, the town's superintendent of public works asked a developer to set him up with two women. When the developer refused, the superintendent unilaterally imposed unusually stringent standards for the improvement of an access road to the developer's subdivision. The court, agreeing that the developer had been denied equal protection, affirmed judgments against the superintendent of $59,000 in compensatory damages and $150,000 in punitive damages.

8.   *State Statutes Governing Exactions from Developers*

1. *Pre*-Nollan *statutes.* Many long-standing subdivision-regulation statutes include provisions that could be construed to limit municipal exactions. See, for example, Mo. Rev. Stat. §89.410 (2004), which declares that local subdivision regulations

> . . . may provide for the dedication, reservation or acquisition of lands and open spaces necessary for public uses indicated on the city plan and for appropriate means of providing for the compensation, including reasonable charges against the subdivision, if any, and over a period of time and in a manner as is in the public interest.

2. *The explosion of detailed statutory provisions.* The law of exactions increasingly has become statutory. Between 1986 and 1993, at least 20 states enacted detailed statutes governing exactions, especially impact fees. See Martin L. Leitner & Susan P. Schoettle, A Survey of State Impact Fee Enabling Legislation, 25 Urb. Law. 491 (1993). These statutes typically emerge out of legislative battles between lobbyists for homebuilders and lobbyists for local governments. Perhaps as a result, in many states the enacted statutes are ambiguous, riddled with exceptions, and untidily integrated with one another.

The most far-reaching of the new exaction statutes aspire to:

a.   clarify local governmental powers to impose exactions;
b.   identify the infrastructural improvements for which exactions may be levied;

c.   place ceilings on the amounts of exactions;
d.   specify whether fee proceeds have to be placed in a separate fund and, if so, when and where the fund's assets must be spent;
e.   detail special procedures that a developer challenging an exaction must pursue; and
f.   address issues of remedy, such as the award of prejudgment interest.

A statutory ceiling on amounts may be set by dollar figure or mathematical formula. More commonly, however, legislators opt for a verbal test reminiscent of one of the constitutional tests that judges apply to exactions. See, e.g., Ga. Code Ann. §§36-71-2(15) & 36-71-4(a) (2004) (enacted 1990) (limiting a "development impact fee" to "that portion of the cost of system improvements which is reasonably related to the service demands and needs of the project"). This Georgia statute was construed in Cherokee County v. Greater Atlanta Homebuilders Association, 566 S.E.2d 470 (Ga. Ct. App. 2002), to permit, over due process and equal protection objections, impact fees for libraries and parks.

Wash. Rev. Code §82.02.050(3) (2004) (enacted 1990) provides that impact fees:

> (a) Shall only be imposed for system improvements that are reasonably related to the new development;
> (b) Shall not exceed a proportionate share of the costs of system improvements that are reasonably related to the new development; and
> (c) Shall be used for system improvements that will reasonably benefit the new development.

In City of Olympia v. Drebick, 83 P.3d 443 (Wash. Ct. App. 2004), the developer of an office building successfully invoked the statute to quash a traffic impact fee that had been calculated on the basis of the traffic impacts of average office space (per square foot), not on the basis of the projected impacts of his proposed building.

The California legislature, whose web of exaction statutes is perhaps the most tangled of any state's, in 1977 authorized imposition of development charges for interim school facilities. Cal. Gov't Code §65974 (West 2004). In 1986, a more precise statute limited school fees levied on new residential development to $1.50 per square foot (indexed for inflation). See Cal. Gov't Code §65995 (West 2004) (construed in Grupe Development Co. v. Superior Court, 844 P.2d 545 (Cal. 1993), as having preempted other local ordinances imposing development exactions for schools).

In Illinois and Texas, developers have succeeded in pushing through statutes that significantly limit local government discretion. See 605 Ill. Comp. Stat. 5/5-901 to -919 (2004) ("Road Improvement Impact Fee Law," enacted 1989); Tex. Loc. Gov't Code Ann. §§395.001–395.080 (2004) (enacted 1989). An Arizona statute strictly limits a municipality's power to exact *land* for parks, recreational facilities, school sites, and fire stations:

> The public agency for whose benefit an area has been reserved shall have a period of one year after recording the final subdivision plat to enter into an agreement to acquire such reserved land area. The purchase price shall be the fair market value thereof at the time of the filing of the preliminary subdivision plat plus the taxes against such reserved area from the date of the reservation and any other costs incurred by the subdivider in the maintenance of such reserved area, including the interest cost incurred in any loan covering such reserved area.

Ariz. Rev. Stat. §9-463.01(E) (2004) (enacted 1973). Should this statute be interpreted also to limit monetary exactions to finance acquisition of sites for these same facilities?

3. *The applicability of broader statutes.* Some states have general statutes that call for takings assessments, takings compensation, or both. See pp. 274–82. Do these have any relevance in exaction disputes?

9.   *General Taxes on Development*

Limits on subdivision exactions and other benefits charges do little to aid landowners and consumers in the absence of limits on general taxes on construction. In a leading case, Daniels v. Borough of Point Pleasant, 129 A.2d 265 (N.J. 1957), a homebuilder attacked a borough ordinance that had increased the building-permit fee for a single-family house from $18 to $262. The builder's houses sold for about $12,000. The New Jersey Supreme Court, in an opinion by Vanderbilt, C.J., struck down the ordinance on the ground that the state legislature had not plainly granted the borough the power to impose a tax of this sort:

> What the Borough of Point Pleasant is attempting to do here is to defray the general cost of government under the guise of reimbursement for the special services required by the regulation and control of new buildings.
>
> Here, the difference between the cost to the borough of regulating and controlling new construction bears no reasonable relation to the amount of revenue raised by the new amendatory ordinance. The record indicates that approximately the same services will now be rendered as were rendered in the prior years by the building inspector, and that the fees raised by the new ordinance exceed by more than 700% the cost of inspecting the buildings and regulating the construction. Admittedly, the purpose of the ordinance was to raise revenue to defray the increased cost of school and other government services. The philosophy of this ordinance is that the tax rate of the borough should remain the same and the new people coming into the municipality should bear the burden of the increased costs of their presence. This is so totally contrary to tax philosophy as to require it to be stricken down; see Gilbert v. Town of Irvington, 120 A.2d 114 (N.J. 1956). Admittedly, these fiscal problems confronting many of our rapidly growing municipalities are grave ones and would seem to call for legislative action; the remedy must come not from the municipalities nor from the courts but from the Legislature.

Id. at 267–68.

The *Daniels* rule that, in the absence of clear legislative authorization, building fees cannot exceed the cost of operating a building department has won the adherence of most courts that have faced the issue. See, e.g., Idaho Building Contractors Association v. City of Coeur D'Alene, 890 P.2d 326 (Idaho 1995), which considered a self-styled "impact fee" that the city had imposed on developers to fund general municipal services. The court stated, "The impact fee at issue here serves the purpose of providing funding for public services at large, and not to the individual assessed, and therefore is a tax." Id. at 330. Having characterized the fee as a tax, the court struck it down on the ground that it exceeded the city's delegated authority.

Daniels and *Idaho Building* were decided on statutory grounds. Compare Weber Basin Home Builders Association v. Roy City, 487 P.2d 866 (Utah 1971), which explicitly holds that excessive building-permit fees are unconstitutional. The Supreme Court of Utah concluded that they violate the Equal Protection Clause by placing a disproportionate fiscal burden on incoming households.

Recall the criticisms of taxes on construction in the work by Henry George excerpted at p. 652. General taxes on development typically benefit owners of developed land (e.g., homeowners) to the detriment of owners of undeveloped land. Is that pattern unfair? Even if it is, should judges nevertheless relegate correction of the problem to the local political process?

C.   Municipal Duties to Provide Services

A constituent may complain not only about how a local government raises its revenues, but also about how it distributes its favors. There is, invariably, some unevenness in the quality of roads, parks, drainage systems, and other types of municipal infrastructure.

1.   Municipal Obligations to Furnish Equal Services

Hawkins v. Town of Shaw
437 F.2d 1286 (5th Cir. 1971)

TUTTLE, Circuit Judge:

Referring to a portion of town or a segment of society as being "on the other side of the tracks" has for too long been a familiar expression to most Americans. Such a phrase immediately conjures up an area characterized by poor housing, overcrowded conditions and, in short, overall deterioration. While there may be many reasons why such areas exist in nearly all of our cities, one reason that cannot be accepted is the discriminatory provision of municipal services based on race. It is such a reason that is alleged as the basis of this action.[1]

The Town of Shaw, Mississippi, was incorporated in 1886 and is located in the Mississippi Delta. Its population, which has undergone little change since 1930, consists of about 2,500 people — 1,500 black and 1,000 white residents. Residential racial segregation is almost total. There are 451 dwelling units occupied by blacks in town, and, of these, 97% (439) are located in neighborhoods in which no whites reside. That the town's policies in administering various municipal services have led to substantially less attention being paid to the black portion of town is clear.

Nearly 98% of all homes that front on unpaved streets in Shaw are occupied by blacks. Ninety-seven percent of the homes not served by sanitary sewers are in black neighborhoods. Further, while the town has acquired a significant number of medium and high intensity mercury vapor street lighting fixtures, every one of them has been installed in white neighborhoods. . . .

Appellants are Negro citizens of the Town of Shaw, Mississippi. They alleged that the town has provided various municipal services including street paving and street lighting, sanitary sewers, surface water drainage as well as water mains and fire hydrants in a discriminatory manner based on race. Appellants brought a class action seeking injunctive relief under 42 U.S.C. §1983 against the town, the town's mayor, clerk and five aldermen. After a three-day trial, the trial court applied the traditional equal protection standard despite the presence of appellants' undisputed statistical evidence which we feel clearly showed a substantial qualitative and quantitative inequity in the level and nature of services accorded "white" and "black" neighborhoods in Shaw. The court stated:

---

1. Appellants also alleged the discriminatory provision of municipal services based on wealth. This claim was dropped on appeal. . . .

> If actions of public officials are shown to have rested upon rational considerations, irrespective of race or poverty, they are not within the condemnation of the Fourteenth Amendment, and may not be properly condemned upon judicial review. Persons or groups who are treated differently must be shown to be similarly situated and their unequal treatment demonstrated to be *without any rational basis* or based upon an invidious factor such as race.

303 F. Supp. 1162, 1168 (N.D. Miss. 1969). (Emphasis added.)

Because this court has long adhered to the theory that "figures speak and when they do, Courts listen," Brooks v. Beto, 366 F.2d 1, 9 (5th Cir. 1966), . . . we feel that appellants clearly made out a prima facie case of racial discrimination. The trial court thus erred in applying the traditional equal protection standard, for as this Court and the Supreme Court have held: "Where racial classifications are involved, the Equal Protection and Due Process Clauses of the Fourteenth Amendment 'command a more stringent standard' in reviewing discretionary acts of state or local officers. Jackson v. Godwin, 400 F.2d 529, 537 (5th Cir., 1968)." In applying this test, defendants' actions may be justified only if they show a compelling state interest. Loving v. Virginia, 388 U.S. 1 (1967). We have thoroughly examined the evidence and conclude that no such compelling interests could possibly justify the gross disparities in services between black and white areas of town that this record reveals. [Discussion omitted.]

We feel that issuing a specific order outlining exactly how the equalization of municipal services should occur is neither necessary nor proper in the context of this case. We do require, however, that the Town of Shaw, itself, submit a plan for the court's approval detailing how it proposes to cure the results of the long history of discrimination which the record reveals. We are confident that the municipal authorities can, particularly because they so staunchly deny any racial motivation, propose a program of improvements that will, within a reasonable time, remove the disparities that bear so heavily on the black citizens of Shaw.

The case is reversed and remanded for further proceedings not inconsistent with the above opinion.

BELL, Circuit Judge (specially concurring): . . .

We begin with the proposition that the Town of Shaw is unusual in the sense that paving, sewerage, and other city improvements are made without special assessments. The costs of such improvements are paid out of general funds derived from ad valorem taxes and revenues from the operation of municipal electrical and water systems. The town has a cash surplus and no bonded indebtedness. In that connection, it is very much unlike the City of Prattville with which Judge Johnson dealt in Hadnott v. City of Prattville, 309 F. Supp. 967 (M.D. Ala. 1970).

In that case the plaintiffs launched a wide ranging attack against the City of Prattville, Alabama on the basis of a disparity in services with respect to paving, sewerage, and water lines. Under the city charter it was necessary for property owners to pay a part of the cost of services of this type. The court rejected the claim of racial discrimination finding that the plaintiffs had failed to seek the services in question through the ordinary channels of initiating a request for such services as an incident to property ownership. It was also found that there was no discrimination in the furnishing of street lights, fire hydrants, and police and fire department protection. The Court did find a discriminatory policy in the operation and maintenance of parks and granted injunctive relief as to the parks.

Here the Town of Shaw furnishes services without regard to assessment or property ownership and there is no basis in the record for the failure to have equalized many of the services in question. . . .

[The panel decision excerpted above was reviewed en banc by the Fifth Circuit, which affirmed in a per curiam opinion. 461 F.2d 1171 (1972). In dissent, Judge RONEY said in part:]

At the outset it seems to me that we must recognize the inherent uniqueness, in the Equal Protection context, of cases involving those municipal services which require capital expenditures. The provision of municipal services to the property of residents is largely a question of priorities which our system of government conceives should be determined by elected officials responsive to the people. The daily news media well portray the difficulties every city is having in establishing such priorities. It is doubtful that any priority determination could ever be justified on the compelling interest standard as laid down by the cases which fathered the doctrine. In the provision of streets, sewers, lights, water and other facilities, given limited resources, the city simply has to start with something some place. As municipal improvements are originated, installed, repaired, improved and modernized, it is intrinsic to the process that at any given point of time services will be unequal, a condition which probably does not serve any compelling interest. While there could be no compelling state interest in starting with the provision of services in the white areas of a town with segregated neighborhoods, neither could there be a compelling state interest to start any other particular place. . . .

. . . The correct principle would appear to be that every citizen has a right not to be denied services because of race, and that any denial of services must have occurred only as a result of the nonracial resolution of all of the competing influences in the politics of self-government.

Note on Inequalities in Municipal Services

1. *Input vs. output equality.* In Beal v. Lindsay, 468 F.2d 287 (2d Cir. 1972), the plaintiffs were African Americans and Puerto Ricans living near Crotona Park in the Borough of the Bronx, New York City. Their complaint alleged that the city did not maintain Crotona Park as well as comparable parks in Bronx neighborhoods where white households were more numerous. The city's administrator of parks filed an affidavit stating that the city's efforts at Crotona were as good as or better than at other Bronx parks, but that its efforts were being undone by vandalism. Judge Friendly, in the process of affirming the district judge's order dismissing the complaint, said in part, "In a case like this, the City has satisfied its constitutional obligations by equal input even though, because of conditions for which it is not responsible, it has not achieved the equal results it desires." Id. at 290–91.

2. *Equal protection law in retreat.* A few years after these decisions, the Supreme Court expressly disapproved *Town of Shaw* to the extent that the decision holds that racially disparate *effects* of a policy are enough to trigger strict judicial scrutiny under the Equal Protection Clause; instead, some racially discriminatory *purpose* on the part of the governing officials must be proven. Washington v. Davis, 426 U.S. 229, 244–45 & n.12 (1976).

Although plaintiffs rarely meet this more onerous test, they did in Ammons v. Dade City, 783 F.2d 982 (11th Cir. 1986). In *Ammons*, 31.8 percent of residences in black neighborhoods were on unpaved streets, compared to 13.8 percent of residences in white neighborhoods. The court affirmed the district court's order that the city not spend funds on new street paving and storm sewers in white neighborhoods until those in black neighborhoods had reached a comparable level of quality.

3. *Nonracial discrimination.* Federal judges have shown little sympathy when the alleged municipal discrimination is not along racial or other constitutionally suspect lines.

See, for example, Mlikotin v. City of Los Angeles, 643 F.2d 652 (9th Cir. 1981), in which an owner of property situated in the Venice district of the City of Los Angeles brought a §1983 suit for damages. The plaintiff asserted that the city had been providing inadequate services in the Venice district and that as a result the plaintiff's property had a lower market value than it otherwise would have had. The Ninth Circuit affirmed the district court's decision to dismiss the suit for failing to state a claim for which relief can be granted.

A number of lawsuits have tested nonracial disparities in trash collection services. In the usual case, the defendant government has been providing full service to single-family homes but either no service or very limited service to multifamily structures or industrial plants. A number of state courts have held these practices to be illegally discriminatory. See, e.g., WHS Realty Co. v. Town of Morristown, 733 A.2d 1206 (N.J. Super. Ct. App. Div. 1999) (holding that town violated Equal Protection Clause when it provided free garbage collection to houses and condominium projects but not to multifamily apartment buildings). In the federal courts, however, municipalities usually survive similar challenges. See, e.g., Goldstein v. City of Chicago, 504 F.2d 989 (7th Cir. 1974). This pattern of outcomes again may reflect federal judges' reluctance to become involved with issues of municipal law.

4. *Statutory issues.* On the possible application of federal civil rights acts to cases of unfair governmental discrimination among neighborhoods, see pp. 754–60 (on environmental justice).

5. *Common law bases for attacks on unequal spending patterns.* Charles M. Haar & Daniel W. Fessler, The Wrong Side of the Tracks (1986), is a leading work on fiscal equity. The authors argue that state courts should assume primary responsibility for fiscal fairness and should base their decisions not on constitutional grounds but on the ancient common law principle that a private monopoly whose business is burdened with a "public interest" has a duty to serve all members of the community alike. Can a private monopoly withhold services from those unwilling to pay its fees?

6. *Defining fiscal equity.* Figure 7-3 shows the fiscal relationships between a municipality and its constituents. To determine whether an aggrieved constituent has been treated unfairly, one may have to attend to all four flows indicated by the arrows in the figure. Does a constituent have a viable constitutional claim to the equalization of total services — that is, the combination of the two right-hand arrows? Or just to equalization of services financed with general revenues?

In Hadnott v. City of Prattville, 309 F. Supp. 967 (M.D. Ala. 1970), discussed in Judge Bell's concurring opinion in *Town of Shaw*, the district court rebuffed an equal protection

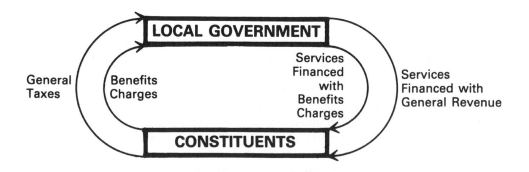

FIGURE 7-3

challenge to the use of special assessments to finance street paving and water and sewer lines. Because many public finance theorists regard the expansion of benefits financing as a major avenue for improving the efficiency of governmental operation, they probably would endorse *Hadnott*'s implicit subordination of the goal of equality to the goal of efficiency. See Note, Equalization of Municipal Services: The Economics of *Serrano* and *Shaw*, 82 Yale L.J. 89 (1972) (criticizing legal requirements for equalization of services). See also Robert P. Inman & Daniel L. Rubinfeld, The Judicial Pursuit of Fiscal Equity, 92 Harv. L. Rev. 1662 (1979).

7. *Source.* A venerable casebook, Frank I. Michelman & Terrance Sandalow, Government in Urban Areas 533–38 (1970), offers pioneering insights into issues of local fiscal equity.

2.   *Municipal Privileges to Deny Services*

Variations in the quality of utility services may raise hackles, especially when the utility is a monopoly provider. The legal rules governing a utility's duty to serve often vary according to whether the provider is a general-purpose government, special district, or private utility company. Most states have public utility commissions that regulate the pricing and service practices of private utility companies. When a municipality itself provides a utility service, state law may exempt it from regulation by the public utility commission on the theory that complainants can protect themselves through the political process. See, e.g., Pa. Stat. Ann. tit. 66, §1141 (West 2004) (municipality exempt unless operating beyond city limits). Each utility provider, regardless of type, has a designated service area. The public utility commission issues orders (often called "certificates of convenience") to define the service area of a private utility company. A municipality's service area normally includes its entire territory plus adjoining areas that it has customarily served.

a.   *The Costs of Extensions to Remote Areas*

Moore v. City of Harrodsburg [*Moore I*]
105 S.W. 925 (Ky. 1907)

HOBSON, J.

D.L. Moore filed in the Mercer circuit court his petition in equity against the city of Harrodsburg, in which he alleged these facts: He is the owner of 30 acres of farming land on which is located his dwelling house, about one mile from the courthouse in Harrodsburg. His property is assessed for municipal purposes at $12,000. It lies on the pike leading to Lexington; but is remote from the pavements of the city. It is entirely without a supply of water for the extinguishment of fire or other purposes. It is not supplied with light, the light system of the city and the water mains not extending out as far as his place, and no pavements have been constructed out that far. The city maintains a plant for lighting the streets of the city and furnishing light to the citizens. It also maintains a water plant to supply water to the citizens and for fire protection; but he gets no benefit from either of these plants because of his remoteness from the body of the city, although he is within the city boundary. The city has levied a tax amounting to $1.06 upon each $100 of property for city purposes, and to meet the indebtedness incurred in building the plants referred to, none of which are of any benefit to him. On these facts he prayed the court to enjoin the city from collecting on his property the taxes levied for the water and light plants until it furnished him the water and light as they were furnishing them to other citizens of the city living in the more central part of it. The circuit court sustained a demurrer to his petition. . . .

In a long line of cases it has been held by this court that under the present Constitution agricultural lands within the limits of a city are not exempt from municipal taxation, though they derive no benefit from the municipal government. [Citations omitted.] The question made has been decided so often that it is no longer open.

Judgment affirmed.

Moore v. City Council of Harrodsburg [*Moore II*]
105 S.W. 926 (Ky. 1907)

Hobson, J.

After the circuit court had decided against him in the case of Moore v. Harrodsburg, 105 S.W. 925 (Ky. 1907) (this day decided), D.L. Moore filed against the city council of Harrodsburg his petition, in which he alleged, in substance, the same facts as in the petition in that case, and prayed that the court compel the defendants, the city councilmen, to extend the water mains and electric light lines so as to give him relatively the same benefits from them as was afforded to other citizens and property owners of the city. The circuit court sustained a general demurrer to his petition, and, he failing to plead further, dismissed the action.

The city officials are charged with the administration of the affairs of the city. They must determine when and where water mains must be put in, and when and how an electric light line must be extended. The courts cannot undertake to manage the affairs of a city by injunction. Where a public duty is enjoined, the court may require the city authorities to act, but it cannot control their discretion as to how they shall act. The city authorities are on the ground. They live among the people who pay the taxes. They can judge much better than we can as to what the best interest of the city requires. In the absence of fraud, corruption, or arbitrary action, the judgment of the city officials as to the management of the affairs of the city is beyond judicial control. . . .

Judgment affirmed.

Crowell v. Hackensack Water Co.
73 Pub. U. Rep. (PUR) 3d 406 (N.J. Bd. Pub. Util. Comm'rs 1968)

By the Board:

On February 14, 1968, Harry L. Crowell (petitioner) filed a petition in letter form requesting the board to order the Hackensack Water Company (respondent) to extend service to the petitioner without cost to him pursuant to the provisions of N.J.S.A. §48:2-27.

On February 21, 1968, the respondent answered, denying the allegations of the petitioner, and alleging that the requested extension is unreasonable and impractical, that the financial condition of the respondent does not reasonably warrant the original expenditure required in making and operating the extension, and that the extension would be discriminatory against its other customers. . . .

[The petitioner is the owner of property on North avenue in the township of Montvale. At the hearing before the board,] he presented a map which shows his property with the proposed extension running from the respondent's nearest existing main in Summit avenue, along Spring Valley road to North avenue. The petitioner contends that there would be eleven potential customers who could be served from the extension as proposed. . . .

The petitioner, in an attempt to show that the respondent was financially able to provide the extension, read from a published report that the consolidated 1966 operating revenues of the respondent were $17,374,969, total assets were $113,474,407, and cited other data from which he concluded that the [$9,754] expenditure would not be a financial hardship on the company.

The respondent presented its vice president-treasurer, who testified that it was estimated that [1,334] feet of pipe would be required for the extension, and would require a deposit of [$9,754] from the petitioner. . . .

Under the formula for extension deposits, the petitioner would be required to pay the net estimated cost of the extension, less 5 times the estimated annual revenue including fire service revenue. (This was estimated at $80 per year for the petitioner's residence plus $135 per year for fire service.) He would receive credit on substantially the same basis for every connection made from the extension over a 10-year period from the date of installation. . . .

It was the vice president's opinion that most, if not all, of the potential customers proximate to the proposed extension now receive their water from wells, and that such individuals would not and do not connect to a public water supply until they experience a breakdown of their well, and then only if it is to their economic advantage. He said that the respondent would be gambling if they were to speculate on the future use of presently vacant land.

Assuming a 6 percent interest rate on money and a depreciation rate of 1.3 percent, he estimated that respondent would lose approximately $600 per year, indefinitely, if none other than the petitioner accepted service. . . .

In Langan v. West Keansburg Water Co., 143 A.2d 185 (N.J. Super. Ct. App. Div. 1958), the court held that a utility is not obligated to take a "speculative stake" in the success of a real-estate development. Here we do not have a real-estate developer, but an existing homeowner, some 1,300 feet from the nearest facilities of the respondent, located within its franchise area, who desires service; there is no "speculative risk" which the utility is being asked to underwrite. . . .

. . . [T]he petitioner's property is along natural lines of expansion, not located on an island from which further expansion is not possible. There is sufficient evidence to support the conclusion that further prospective users will be available by virtue of the proposed extension.

A public utility has a duty to serve within its franchise area where such duty can be reasonably performed. Each service extension need not by itself produce a profit; it must simply generate sufficient business. Piscataway Fire Commrs. v. Elizabethtown Water Co., [142 A.2d 85 (N.J. 1958)]. Here, the loss to the respondent in installing and operating this proposed extension, on the overall return to the utility, is negligible.

The board concludes that the extension is reasonable and practicable and will furnish sufficient business to justify its construction and maintenance, and that the financial condition of the public utility reasonably warrants the expenditure. . . .

Accordingly, the board hereby *orders* Hackensack Water Company to extend its facilities, at its own cost, to the property of Harry L. Crowell. . . .

Note on Refusal to Serve on Grounds of Unjustifiably High Costs of Service

1. *Remedial options.* Once again Calabresi and Melamed's four rules for protecting entitlements, introduced at p. 532, help clarify the legal options available. From the perspective of a landowner seeking utility service, the four possible rules are these:

Rule 1: The landowner can compel that the service be freely provided (the result in *Crowell*).

Rule 2: The landowner can recover interim damages for losses sustained during the period when the utility was failing to provide the service (a remedy sought but denied in Front Royal & Warren County Industrial Park Corp. v. Town of Front Royal, 135 F.3d 275 (4th Cir. 1998)).

Rule 3: The provider of the utility can deny service without being liable for damages (the result in *Moore II*).

Rule 4: The landowner can compel that the service be extended, but only if the landowner pays any special costs of service (cf. the water company's position in *Crowell*).

Rules 2 and 4 (the liability rules) commonly provide more room for compromise because they readily enable an adjudicator to award something to both sides.

In AvalonBay Communities, Inc. v. Sewer Commission, 853 A.2d 497 (Conn. 2004), the developer of a multifamily project including affordable housing components had offered to pay the costs of extending the city's sewer system to service the project. When the city stalled, the developer brought a mandamus action to force the extension. Regarding mandamus as extraordinary, the court declined to grant that remedy. What if the developer instead had sought an award of damages?

2. *The relevant legal variables.* To what extent, if any, should the remedy available to a remotely located landowner vary according to (a) the identity of the landowner (e.g., developer or homeowner) or (b) the identity of the provider (e.g., municipality or utility company)? In considering the latter question, be aware that private utility companies provide less than 15 percent of public water nationwide. Craig Anthony (Tony) Arnold, Privatization of Public Water Service, 32 Pepp. L. Rev. 561, 562 (2005).

b.   Lack of Service Capacity

Could the Hackensack Water Company have refused to extend service to Crowell on the ground that it lacked an adequate supply of water? Traditionally, the statutes and charters governing utility companies were interpreted to require them to anticipate future demand for their services. See, e.g., Lukrawka v. Spring Valley Water Co., 146 P. 640 (Cal. 1915). Should a duty of this sort attach to a municipal utility as well as a private one? Can a municipality ration utility connections to slow its pace of development?

First Peoples Bank of New Jersey v. Township of Medford
599 A.2d 1248 (N.J. 1991)

POLLACK, J.

[In the mid-1970s, rapid development within the Township of Medford had begun to overburden the municipal sanitary sewer system. In 1983, to finance additional sewer capacity, the township began selling sewer-connection permits that a property owner could purchase even before having obtained development approval. These permits apparently were not transferable. In 1988, the bank was unable to purchase any connection permits because the township had no more to sell. The frustrated bank sought judicial relief. In the first part of its opinion, the court refused to order the township to repurchase some permits for subsequent resale to applicants such as the bank.]

The final question is whether this Court should order the Township to expand the sewer plant to provide sufficient capacity for the Bank's development. The lower courts refused to issue such an order, characterizing the matter as a nonjusticiable political question. We need not go so far as to say that courts may never order an expansion of sewer capacity. It suffices to hold that the facts of this case do not justify such an intrusion in municipal affairs. . . .

. . . As with decisions to extend water lines, municipalities enjoy broad discretion when deciding to expand sewer plants. 11 E. McQuillin, Municipal Corporations §31.17 at 229. The critical question for a reviewing court is whether the municipality has exercised its discretion in an arbitrary or discriminatory manner. See Deerfield Estates, Inc. v. Township of East Brunswick, 286 A.2d 498 (N.J. 1972) (municipality obliged to serve impartially all similarly situated applicants); Reid Development Corp. v. Township of Parsippany-Troy Hills, 89 A.2d 667 (N.J. 1952) ("The utility is under a duty to serve all within the area who comply with fair and just rules and regulations applicable to all alike.").

Here, Medford has not been arbitrary or unreasonable in implementing the ordinance. All developers enjoyed equal access to the limited supply of sewer permits. The challenged ordinance is a reasonable, if homespun, attempt to meet the sewage treatment needs of a developing community.

This is not a case in which a municipality has rigidly refused to construct needed sewer capacity. The record does not support an inference that Medford's refusal "is the result of a determination not to discharge a plain duty. . . ." 13 McQuillin, supra, §37.27 at 101. Because of a municipality's greater familiarity with local conditions and expertise in constructing sewer capacity, a court should supplant the exercise of municipal discretion only in a compelling case. This is not such a case. . . .

Note on Lack of Service Capacity

Gilbert v. State, 266 Cal. Rptr. 891 (Ct. App. 1990), is one of several reported cases stemming from a highly publicized water-hookup moratorium that government agencies imposed in the unincorporated Bolinas area of Marin County. The Bolinas District first imposed the moratorium in 1971 on account of a water shortage. In 1982, the California Department of Health Services ordered the district to continue the moratorium until the department was satisfied that the water supply was adequate. Unable to improve their property because of the long-enduring moratorium, in 1987 the plaintiff landowners filed a broad-gauge complaint against both the district and the department. The California Court of Appeals declined to order these government agencies to develop new service capacity, and also rejected the landowners' claim for damages premised on a regulatory taking in violation of the California Constitution.

See also Charles v. Diamond, 360 N.E.2d 1295 (N.Y. 1977) (holding landowner was not entitled to recover damages for losses stemming from a municipal failure to expand service capacity). But see Dennis J. Herman, Note, Sometimes There's Nothing Left to Give: The Justification for Denying Water Service to New Consumers to Control Growth, 44 Stan. L. Rev. 429 (1992) (favoring municipal duty to augment water supply and arguing that remedy of compensation is appropriate in some cases). For more on the use of utility-service policies to control growth, see pp. 809-13.

3.   *Rights of Outsiders to Demand the Extension of Municipal Services*

Yakima County (West Valley) Fire Protection District No. 12 v. City of Yakima
858 P.2d 245 (Wash. 1993)

BRACHTENBACH, Justice.

In this declaratory judgment action, appellants challenge the validity of Outside Utility Agreements (OUA's) signed by appellant landowners as a condition of receiving sewer service from the City of Yakima (City), which required appellant landowners to sign a future petition for annexation when annexation of their property should become feasible. . . . We hold that the OUA's are valid. . . .

The [central] issue in this case is whether the City had a duty to provide sewer service to appellant landowners. Under Rev. Code Wash. §35.67.310, which provides that a city *"may* permit connections with any of its sewers . . . from property beyond its limits,"the City has authority to provide service outside its borders. (Italics ours.) The use of "may" in RCW §35.67.310 supports the City's argument that the power granted by RCW §35.67.310 is discretionary and that the City is not bound to provide sewer service to persons residing outside its boundaries. . . . Further support for the argument that a city has no duty to extend sewer service beyond its borders can be found in cases from this state. See . . . Brookens v. Yakima, 550 P.2d 30 (Wash. Ct. App. 1976); see also 11 E. McQuillin, Municipal Corporations §31.16 at 226–27 (3d ed. 1991).

However, there are several cases recognizing an exception to this "no duty" rule in circumstances where a city "holds itself out" as willing to supply sewer or water service to an area or where a city is the exclusive supplier of sewer or water service in a region extending beyond the borders of the city. See Barbaccia v. County of Santa Clara, 451 F. Supp. 260, 264 n.2 (N.D. Cal. 1978) (commenting that "several state courts have recently held that a city holding itself out as the sole provider of sewer services in a given locale will be considered a public utility and allowed to deny sewer hook-ups to property within its 'service area' only for such utility-related reasons as lack of capacity") (citing Robinson v. Boulder, 547 P.2d 228 (Colo. 1976), overruled by Board of County Comm'rs v. Denver Bd. of Water Comm'rs, 718 P.2d 235, 244 (Colo. 1986); Mayor & Council v. Delmarva Enters., Inc., 301 A.2d 276 (Del. 1973)). . . . The Court of Appeals in *Brookens* recognized a similar exception. "A contract to supply water may also be found by implication, as where a municipality holds itself out as a public utility willing to supply all those who request service in a general area." *Brookens*, 550 P.2d 30.

By entering the four-party agreement and adopting the Yakima urban area comprehensive plan, which effectively established the City as the sole provider of sewer collection services to areas within the Yakima urban area not already served by Union Gap or the Terrace Heights Sewer District, the City did hold itself out as willing to provide service to the Yakima urban area. However, there is one fact present in this case that was not present in the cases cited above. The agreement that made the City the exclusive supplier of sewage treatment services, the 1976 four-party agreement, also set forth the City's policy of requiring present or future annexation as a condition of receiving service. Thus, to the extent that the City held itself out as willing to provide service, it made clear that it was willing to do so only if the landowner accepted its future annexation condition. . . . The City has no duty to provide service absent the future annexation condition, and the inclusion of this condition does not render the OUA's improper or invalid.

Alternatively, appellants argue that the City had a duty to provide sewer service to appellant landowners because the primary source of funding for the upgrade of the City's treatment plant was the federal government. However, appellants cite no legal authority to support this proposition. . . .

[The trial court's judgment in favor of the city is affirmed.]

Note on Annexations and Extraterritorial Utility Service

1. *Annexations.* A municipality generally cannot be compelled to annex land. See, e.g., Wilkerson v. City of Coralville, 478 F.2d 709 (8th Cir. 1973) (Equal Protection Clause does not require city to annex unincorporated area inhabited by poor households). Because annexation is discretionary, there are few limits on what a city may exact as a condition for annexation. See, e.g., Mayor & Council of Rockville v. Brookeville Turnpike Construction Co., 228 A.2d 263 (Md. 1967). Certainly the constitutional limitations on subdivision exactions do not apply. Developers with land in unincorporated areas therefore have little bargaining power unless the nearby city previously had committed itself to a practice of unconditional service. However, if municipal authorities and the owner of land to be annexed have agreed to a contract that limits the municipality's power to raise permit fees and impose new zoning restrictions, that contract normally will be enforced. See, e.g., 65 Ill. Comp. Stat. 5/11-15.1-1 to -5 (2004) (authorizing such contracts as long as they are not binding for more than 20 years). On annexation and de-annexation generally, see Richard Briffault & Laurie Reynolds, State and Local Government Law 180–227 (6th ed. 2004).

2. *Discrimination in fees charged outsiders.* Perhaps because outsiders who desire services cannot vote in city elections, many municipalities attempt to charge them higher tap-in fees and flow charges. If outsiders attack this sort of practice as discriminatory, a city's best defense is that the outsiders have not been paying the city property tax, revenues from which have been used to help finance the city's utility facilities. As any calloused law student might predict, courts apply a "reasonableness" test when judging differentials of this sort. Because the facts of these disputes tend to be bewilderingly complex and because the external ratepayers have the burden of showing unreasonableness, the cities win almost every time. See Joseph L. Sax, Municipal Water Supply for Nonresidents, 5 Nat. Resources J. 54 (1965).

D. *Easing the Fiscal Pressure on Municipalities*

What reforms would reduce the dominance of fiscal considerations in local land use planning? Both taxing and spending policies could be adjusted. On the taxation side, to dim the fiscal allure of light industrial facilities and shopping centers, property tax revenues from such improvements might be pooled on a regional or metropolitan basis and then distributed to local governing units according to population (or some other formula). Programs of this sort have been upheld against a variety of legal challenges. See Village of Burnsville v. Onischuk, 222 N.W.2d 523 (Minn. 1974) (pooling of 40 percent of the increase in revenues from taxes on commercial and industrial property in Twin Cities area); Meadowlands Regional Redevelopment Agency v. State, 304 A.2d 545 (N.J. 1973) (tax-sharing scheme for municipalities in Meadowlands area). See also Note, Making Mixed-Income Communities Possible: Tax-Base Sharing and Class Desegregation, 114 Harv. L. Rev. 1575 (2001) (arguing that regional tax sharing would reduce municipalities' incentives to avoid attracting low income housing and lead eventually to deconcentration of poverty). But compare William A. Fischel, The Homevoter Hypothesis 178–79 (2001) (questioning the wisdom of regionalizing the tax revenues from a facility that causes localized environmental harm).

On the expenditure side, to make fiscal losers such as modest-cost or subsidized housing more advantageous to suburbs, higher-level governments could provide compensatory payments to municipalities that accept such developments. See Ronald H. Silverman, Subsidizing Tolerance for Open Communities, 1977 Wis. L. Rev. 375. More fundamentally, a state can shift responsibilities for selected spending programs away from local governments. The most prominent candidate, of course, is primary and secondary education. In a state like Hawaii, where almost all schooling costs are borne by state government, local officials need not worry much about a potential influx of youngsters. Many state supreme courts have abetted greater state involvement in the financing of public schools by holding that reliance on local property tax revenues to finance education is a violation of a state constitutional guarantee. See, e.g., Serrano v. Priest, 487 P.2d 1241 (Cal. 1971); Rose v. Council for Better Education, Inc., 790 S.W.2d 186 (Ky. 1989). See generally Symposium, School Finance Litigation, 22 Yale L. & Pol'y Rev. 463 (2004). But compare San Antonio Independent School District v. Rodriguez, 411 U.S. 1 (1973) (federal Equal Protection Clause is not violated by such a financing system). Similarly, a state-funded school-voucher system would reduce a local government's inclinations toward fiscal parochialism.

Do the advantages of any of these proposed reforms outweigh the disadvantages, such as the lessening of local autonomy?

Chapter Eight

Discriminatory Land
Use Controls

In formulating their land use policies, local governments may ignore, or actively seek to harm, the interests of various groups. In jurisdictions characterized by majoritarian politics, groups that have a minority of votes will be disfavored unless they can form coalitions with other groups to augment their power. In jurisdictions characterized by influence politics, a group will be disfavored if its organizational abilities (including its ability to form coalitions) and its access to resources to contribute to local politicians' election campaigns fall short of those of other groups. See pp. 304–08. In either type of jurisdiction, someone inevitably will be a loser in the process. The courts typically provide no solace for the losers; instead, the losers' remedy is to forge new alliances, try to improve their organizational and fund-raising abilities, and then attempt to recoup their losses on some later day or on some other issue.

The courts may show more concern for the losing group, however, when the losers are the victims of racial or other discrimination. Land use regulation provides ample opportunity for discrimination. Local officials can largely control the composition of a city's housing stock through general plans, zoning ordinances, housing codes, and so on. Because city officials can predict that certain types of households are likely to choose to live in certain types of housing units, they can use land use regulations as an effective — if indirect — mechanism for excluding certain groups from the city's resident population. If local governments believe, for example, that occupants of single-family houses on one-acre lots are likely to be wealthier than occupants of mobile-home parks, they can attempt to influence the socioeconomic status of residents by zoning out mobile homes. Indeed, local officials can directly specify the types of households that may reside in various neighborhoods. They may, for instance, attempt to bar school-age children — either for fiscal reasons or to combat noise, delinquency, or other problems children sometimes are perceived to cause.

This chapter explores the kinds of discrimination that several groups — racial and ethnic minorities, the poor, unconventional households, and people with disabilities — have faced (and continue to face) in the housing market and in state and local land use regulation. It examines the efforts of each group to secure constitutional protection against discrimination. Where applicable, it also explores prohibitions against discrimination that Congress and some state legislatures have adopted over the past several decades.

In studying these materials on discriminatory restrictions imposed by local governments, consider whether private landowners could impose similar restrictions by contract, in light of the materials at pp. 554–62.

A.   *Discrimination Against Racial and Ethnic Minorities*

Between the Civil War and the end of the nineteenth century, blacks and whites "lived side by side" in American cities both in the North and the South. In the North, the black population was small but "scattered widely throughout white neighborhoods." In the South, "black servants and laborers lived on alleys and side streets near the mansions of their employers." One could identify neighborhoods in most cities in which blacks lived, but "before 1900 those areas were not predominantly black, and most blacks didn't live in them." Douglas S. Massey & Nancy A. Denton, American Apartheid: Segregation and the Making of the Underclass 17 (1993).

The increasing industrialization of America, and the accompanying migration of African Americans from the farms to the cities, brought increasing racial tension and put an end to residential integration:

> As the tide of violence rose in northern cities, blacks were increasingly divided from whites by a hardening color line in employment, education, and especially housing. Whites became increasingly intolerant of black neighbors and fear of racial turnover and black "invasion" spread. Those blacks living away from recognized Negro areas were forced to move into expanding "black belts," "darkytowns," "Bronzevilles," or "Niggertowns." Well-educated, middle-class blacks of the old elite found themselves increasingly lumped together with poorly educated, impoverished migrants from the rural south; and well-to-do African Americans were progressively less able to find housing commensurate with their social status. In white eyes, black people belonged in black neighborhoods no matter what their social or economic standing; the color line grew increasingly impermeable.

Id. at 30.

Whites turned to the law to enforce the "color line," even though earlier efforts to segregate Asian Americans by law had failed judicial scrutiny. See In re Lee Sing, 43 F. 359 (N.D. Cal. 1890) (San Francisco's Bingham Ordinance, which gave all Chinese inhabitants of the city 60 days to leave town or to move to a designated city neighborhood, found to violate the Fourteenth Amendment, the Civil Rights Acts, and treaties with China). In 1910, Baltimore passed an ordinance establishing separate neighborhoods for whites and blacks. See Garrett Power, Apartheid Baltimore Style: The Residential Segregation Ordinances of 1910–1913, 42 Md. L. Rev. 289 (1983). Similar ordinances were adopted in Alabama, Georgia, Indiana, Kentucky, Louisiana, Missouri, North Carolina, Oklahoma, South Carolina, Texas, and Virginia. Roger L. Rice, Residential Segregation by Law, 1910–1917, 34 J.S. Hist. 179 (1968). See generally Stephen Grant Meyer, As Long as They Don't Move Next Door: Segregation and Racial Conflict in American Neighborhoods (2000); A. Leon Higginbotham, Jr. et al., *De Jure* Housing Segregation in the United States and South Africa: The Difficult Pursuit for Racial Justice, 1990 U. Ill. L. Rev. 763, 807–62; James A. Kushner, Apartheid in America: An Historical and Legal Analysis of Contemporary Racial Residential Segregation in the United States, 22 How. L.J. 547 (1979).

In 1916, however, the National Association for the Advancement of Colored People (NAACP) engineered a challenge to a Louisville, Kentucky, ordinance that prohibited blacks from moving to city blocks that had white majorities, and whites from moving to city blocks that had black majorities. The president of the NAACP's Louisville branch, William Warley, contracted with a white realtor friendly to the NAACP, Charles Buchanan, to buy a corner lot in a white area. The sales contract provided that Warley would not have to pay the balance due under the contract unless he was able to use the property for his residence. Warley breached the contract, Buchanan sued for specific performance, and Warley defended by invoking the ordinance to excuse his nonperformance. Buchanan asserted that the ordinance violated his rights under the Due Process Clause to be free from unreasonable restraints on selling his property. After two rounds of oral argument, a unanimous Supreme Court agreed and held the ordinance unconstitutional. Buchanan v. Warley, 245 U.S. 60 (1917). Justice Day's opinion struggled to distinguish prior Supreme Court decisions that had sustained the segregation of schools and public transportation by race so long as equal accommodations were provided to each race. For fascinating descriptions of the litigation, see Benno C. Schmidt, Jr., Principle and Prejudice: The Supreme Court and Race in the Progressive Era, Part 1: The Heyday of Jim Crow, 82 Colum. L. Rev. 444, 498–523 (1982); Colloquium: Rethinking Buchanan v. Warley, 51 Vand. L. Rev. 787 (1998).

In theory, then, after Buchanan, zoning ordinances could not explicitly segregate by race. Some cities ignored Buchanan, and even as late as 1949, courts were still confronted with explicitly racial zoning ordinances. See, e.g., Monk v. City of Birmingham, 87 F. Supp. 538 (N.D. Ala. 1949), aff'd, 185 F.2d 859 (5th Cir. 1950) (invalidating ordinance Birmingham passed in 1949 to implement racial zoning statutes enacted in 1926). See also Baker v. City of Kissimmee, 645 F. Supp. 571, 579 (M.D. Fla. 1986) (noting that Kissimmee's racial zoning was enforced well into the 1940s); State v. Wilson, 25 So. 2d 860 (Fla. 1946) (invalidating racial zoning ordinance adopted by Dade County in 1945). Other cities, however, developed more indirect land use controls to confine African Americans and other racial and ethnic minorities to certain areas of town.

Those controls (combined with private covenants, see pp. 559–61, the siting and management of public housing, transportation policies, mortgage insurance requirements, "ethical" constraints on real estate brokers not to sell property in white areas to blacks, and a myriad of other factors) were highly effective in perpetuating segregation. See Reynolds Farley et al., "Chocolate City, Vanilla Suburbs": Will the Trend Toward Racially Separate Communities Continue?, 7 Soc. Sci. Res. 319 (1978). For discussions of the multitude of factors that have contributed to residential segregation, see, e.g., Kenneth T. Jackson, Crabgrass Frontier: The Suburbanization of the United States (1985); Meyer, supra; John Yinger, Closed Doors, Opportunities Lost: The Continuing Costs of Housing Discrimination (1995); David M. Cutler et al., The Rise and Decline of the American Ghetto, 107 J. Pol. Econ. 455, 495 (1999).

The following excerpt summarizes the state of residential segregation in the 1990s.

Nancy A. Denton, Half Empty or Half Full: Segregation and Segregated Neighborhoods 30 Years After the Fair Housing Act
4 Cityscape 107, 108-10, 112-14, 116 (1999)

The year 1998 marks the 30th anniversary of the passage of the Fair Housing Act, the last major civil rights law passed during the 1960s. It is also the 30th anniversary of the publication of the Kerner Report[1] on the violence that erupted in our cities in the same decade. In my mind the two are closely linked because residential segregation so dramatically embodies the Report's most famous words: "This is our basic conclusion: Our Nation is moving toward two societies, one Black, one White — separate and unequal." . . .

One of the many items offered in support of that conclusion was data on residential segregation from the 1960 census of population and housing. Segregation is measured

---

[1] EDS.: Kerner Commission, The Kerner Report: The 1968 Report of the National Advisory Commission on Civil Disorders (1988).

with the Index of Dissimilarity, which varies from 0 (no segregation) to 100 (complete segregation).[2]

The index showed that the average segregation of Blacks from Whites in the Nation's largest cities was 86.2 in 1960 and had been relatively stable over time, averaging 85.2 in 1940 and 87.3 in 1960. These numbers can be interpreted as the percent of either group that would have to change neighborhoods to be evenly distributed across the neighborhoods of a city; in other words, for every neighborhood to have the same percent Black or White as the city as a whole. . . .

What happens if we update these numbers to the present? Studies of segregation were done using data from each of the decennial censuses following the passage of the Fair Housing Act: 1970, 1980, and 1990. [The studies] extend the series of segregation indices in the Commission's report to the 1990 census. . . . The newer numbers are taken from a recent book[2] and refer to the 30 metropolitan areas with the largest Black populations. Roughly two-thirds of the metropolitan African-American population live in these areas.

. . . [The numbers show that] Black-White segregation remains at a very high level and is changing only modestly. . . . In the Northern metropolitan areas, Black-White segregation averaged 85.5 in 1970, 80.1 in 1980, and 77.8 in 1990. The comparable figures for Southern metropolitan areas were 75.3, 68.3, and 66.5. During the past 20 years, segregation in these large metropolitan areas has declined only 8 points in the North and 9 in the South. The largest declines have been in newer metropolitan areas in the South and West, which tend to have small Black populations. African-American segregation remains extremely high in those U.S. metropolitan areas with the largest Black populations.

The pattern shown here is the same as that reported by other researchers who have looked at more metropolitan areas. . . .

What all these researchers agree on is that the segregation of African-Americans is higher than that for any other group. On average, the segregation of African-Americans is about 65 percent greater than that of Asians and about 35 percent greater than that of Hispanics. . . . Both the Hispanic and Asian populations saw their segregation increase between 1980 and 1990, especially in the gateway areas where new immigrants first locate, but in other areas they saw declines in their segregation. As a result, it is unlikely that they will ever reach the uniformly high levels of segregation of African-Americans, a pattern that was described as *hypersegregation* in 1980 and persisted in 1990 as well.

Focusing on segregation by race ignores another little known fact: Segregation by race for African-Americans is higher than segregation by any other characteristic in United States cities and metropolitan areas. This statement is true in the present, but also in the past: Lieberson[3] has shown that in the early decades of this century, the segregation levels of European immigrants, at their highest, seldom reached that of African-Americans today. To put the current segregation of people by race and ethnicity into context, we can look at segregation by other demographic characteristics. Using the same index as above, segregation of the poor from the nonpoor averages around 36 in 1990 while that of employed from the unemployed, single parents from married couple families, high

2. [Eds.: footnote relocated] . . . These numbers are the Index of Dissimilarity, a commonly used measure that compares, for two groups, each neighborhood's proportion of a group to that group's proportion of the city or metropolitan area. It varies from 1 (total segregation) to 0 (each neighborhood has the same proportion of each group as the city or metropolitan area as a whole). The resulting index shows how far away from a pattern of evenness the groups are and can be interpreted as the proportion of either group that would have to change neighborhoods to be evenly distributed. Neighborhoods are approximated by census tracts, small nonoverlapping geographic areas that average about 5,000–7,000 people.

[2] Eds.: Douglas S. Massey & Nancy A. Denton, American Apartheid: Segregation and the Making of the Underclass (1993).

[3] Eds.: Stanley Lieberson, A Piece of the Pie: Blacks and White Immigrants Since 1880 (1980).

school versus nonhigh school graduates, or welfare versus non-welfare recipients is even lower. Indices of poverty concentration, defined as the percentage of all the poor who live in census tracts with more than 40 percent of their residents poor, are frequently under 10. Put in this light, the emphasis placed on residential segregation by race, and that of African-Americans in particular, is more understandable.

Thus far, it is clear that much of the racial residential segregation used by the Kerner Commission to justify its famous two societies quote is still with us today. Despite the desire of some researchers to focus more on Black progress and attribute the remaining segregation to voluntary causes . . . segregation remains high. Though there is clear evidence of declines, they are small and their pace slow. Much of the progress in lowering segregation has been made in places where African-Americans do not live in large numbers. Segregation remains at very high levels for African-Americans, particularly so in places where the riots of the 1960s took place and where there are large absolute and proportionate African-American populations. . . .

Further progress toward fair housing will take place in a world quite different from that in which the law was originally passed. The most obvious change is the increasing diversity of the U.S. population. As of 1998, the United States is home to just over 270 million people. In proportional terms, non-Hispanic Whites make up 72.3 percent and non-Hispanic Blacks 12.1 percent, with Hispanics and Asians at 11.3 and 3.6 percent respectively. Since the passage of the Fair Housing Act, the White population has declined more than 11.2 percentage points, while all other groups have increased their shares. . . .

The increased diversity comes from immigrants and their children. The 1965 changes in immigration law have meant that millions of new immigrants are now coming to the United States, mainly from Central and South America and Asia. It is no longer correct to think of housing integration between just two groups — Blacks and Whites. . . .

A second aspect of the changing context of fair housing efforts has to do with the current nature of discrimination in the housing market. There is no doubt that housing discrimination has declined substantially since 1968. To a certain extent, in that year, it was a virtual certainty: Newspapers advertised housing by race, and there were few who objected to statements about not wanting Blacks to live near them or real estate agents saying they did not rent or sell to Blacks. It is equally certain that there is still an enormous amount of discrimination in today's housing market. When HUD did its first nationally representative housing audit study in 1978, it found that discrimination against Blacks was widespread, a finding reconfirmed by the latest National study, almost 10 years ago, which found Blacks and Hispanics likely to be discriminated against roughly 50 percent of the time on a single visit to a real estate agent. Since the acquisition of housing normally requires several visits to an agent, the probability of experiencing differential treatment quickly approaches 90 percent once one factors in these multiple visits. In 1998 Housing Secretary Cuomo announced plans for a new national study that will update our information on this important topic.

But what is most different about today's discrimination compared with that of the past is not its level but its subtlety. Even victims of discrimination find it hard to know if they have been mistreated without the results of audits, when matched pairs of homeseekers report the treatment they receive and the results are compared across races. Because discrimination is so subtle and pernicious, it is seldom seen by Whites. It has been incorporated into the structure of how business is done and is treated as normal. But it is by no means costless. In a recent article, John Yinger[4] estimates that discrimination costs Black and Hispanic households a "tax" of $4,000, on average, every time they search for a house to buy.

---

[4] EDS.: John Yinger, Cash in Your Face: The Cost of Racial and Ethnic Discrimination in Housing, 42 J. Urb. Econ. 339 (1997).

Housing discrimination today promotes and reinforces the effects of historical segregation in housing in U.S. cities. The effects of segregation — and by analogy the effects of vigorous pursuit of fair housing — operate at two different levels: individual and structural. These are conceptually distinct but very intertwined in reality. George Galster[5] calls this the vicious circle of inequality: Housing discrimination operates at an individual level to deny persons of color the opportunity to live wherever they want and can afford and to maintain and reinforce prejudice — the stereotypes that Whites hold of people of color. Through these individual processes, housing discrimination's effects then move to the structural level to maintain the socioeconomic inequalities between Blacks and Whites, between Whites and persons of color, and to deny persons of color the wealth accumulation that comes from rising property values. This last is a particularly salient point because rising housing value has been the primary route for middle-class families to acquire some wealth. But it is unearned income related to the location of the house. Melvin L. Oliver and Thomas M. Shapiro[6] estimate that the current generation of Blacks have missed out on $82 billion this way — $58 billion through the lack of housing appreciation with another $10.5 billion due to paying higher mortgage rates, and $13.5 billion from the denial of mortgages. . . .

The final change in the context in which future fair housing efforts will take place occurs at the neighborhood level. My work with my Albany colleagues, Richard Alba[7] and Bridget Anderson[8] shows that the number of all-White (more than 98 percent or 95 percent) neighborhoods is declining rather quickly — declining both in cities and suburbs. Though 95 percent White neighborhoods still represented around one-half of all suburban neighborhoods in the Midwest and one-third in the Northeast in 1990, they were less than 20 percent in the South and about 10 percent in the West. It is safe to conclude that Americans are currently living in neighborhoods that have some degree of racial or ethnic integration. While this may seem surprising in light of the segregation figures discussed above, the mathematical fact is that high segregation can persist with many, if not nearly all, individual neighborhoods being minimally integrated. One statistic is from the neighborhood's point of view, while the other is from the population's point of view. . . .

These neighborhood-level changes have two important implications for continued work toward the promotion of fair housing. First, individual people will be able to say that their neighborhood is integrated and segregation statistics will not be backed up by their personal experience. Second, as a result, it will become easier for them to think that segregation is no longer a problem. The decrease in the number of all-White neighborhoods is certainly progress, especially because it decreases the number of all-White neighborhoods to which Whites can flee. The decrease is also a point of concern if it leads us into complacency before the job is really done, while discrimination is still high and the vicious circle of inequality persists. . . .

---

[5] EDS.: George Galster, The Case for Residential Integration, *in* The Metropolis in Black and White (George C. Galster & E. W. Hill, 1992).

[6] EDS.: Melvin L. Oliver & Thomas M. Shapiro, Black Wealth/White Wealth: A New Perspective on Racial Inequality (1995).

[7] EDS.: Nancy A. Denton & Richard D. Alba, The Decline of the All-White Neighborhood and the Growth of Suburban Diversity (unpublished paper prepared for the Suburban Racial Change Conference, Harvard University, March 28, 1998).

[8] EDS.: Nancy A. Denton & Bridget J. Anderson, A Tale of Five Cities: Neighborhood Change in Philadelphia, Chicago, Miami, Houston and Los Angeles, 1970–1990 (unpublished paper presented at the annual meetings of the Population Association of America, San Francisco, April 6–8, 1995).

As we previewed at pp. 11–13, the trends Denton describes continued between 1990 and 2000. Some analysts find more reason for optimism in those trends than Denton sees. See, e.g., Edward L. Glaeser & Jacob L. Vigdor, Racial Segregation in the 2000 Census: Promising News, *in* Redefining Urban and Suburban America: Evidence from Census 2000, at 211 (Bruce Katz & Robert E. Lang eds., 2003). Using data from the 2000 census, researchers have shown that the index of dissimilarity fell by an average of 5.5 percent during the 1990s in 291 metropolitan areas (a broader group than that examined by the studies Denton references). Again, the declines were most pronounced in rapidly growing areas such as metropolitan areas of the West, in those areas in which the percentage of African Americans was relatively small, and in the South. The declines resulted from the integration of formerly all-white areas, rather than the desegregation of the overwhelmingly African American areas. See, e.g., Glaeser & Vigdor, supra; John Iceland et al., Racial and Ethnic Residential Segregation in the United States: 1980–2000 (U.S. Census Bureau, Series CENSR-3, 2002).

There is increasing evidence that reductions in the gap between the education, income and wealth of blacks and whites do not lead to a decrease in residential segregation. Indeed, Professor Bayer and his colleagues have shown that as the proportion of highly educated blacks in a metropolitan area increases, the segregation of highly edu cated blacks, and all blacks more generally, goes up. Patrick Bayer et al., Separate When Equal? Racial Inequality and Residential Segregation (2005) (unpublished manuscript). That increase in segregation stems in large part from the emergence of middle class black suburbs. See Sheryll D. Cashin, The Failures of Integration: How Race and Class are Undermining the American Dream (2004). For other helpful overviews of the current state of residential segregation, see, e.g., Desegregating the City (David P. Varady ed., 2005), and the sources cited at pp. 12–13.

The updated study of discrimination by HUD that Denton mentions revealed that in 2000, African Americans and Hispanics continued to experience "significant levels of adverse treatment, relative to comparable white homeseekers" in both rental and sales markets of metropolitan areas nationwide. Levels of discrimination against both African Americans and Hispanics purchasing a home had decreased markedly since 1989, but discrimination against African Americans in the rental market had decreased only slightly, and discrimination against Hispanic renters had increased. Margery Austin Turner et al., Discrimination in Metropolitan Housing Markets: National Results from Phase I HDS 2000 (Nov. 2002), available at http://www.urban.org/url.cfm?ID=410821.

Why hasn't the law been more successful in changing patterns of residential segregation? The next sections discuss the tools available to lawyers who challenge land use controls that have the intent or effect of creating or maintaining racially segregated neighborhoods.

1. Constitutional Challenges

Although *Buchanan* was decided under the Fourteenth Amendment's Due Process Clause, such an explicit racial zoning classification would be struck down today as a violation of the Equal Protection Clause. Because race is a suspect classification, under modern law an explicit racial classification is invalid unless it furthers a compelling state interest.

Today, however, few local governments are so bold (or so unrestrained by their legal counsel) to include explicit racial classifications in land use ordinances. Instead, attempts to create or maintain racial segregation take the form of facially neutral ordinances that have a racially disparate effect. In the early 1970s, several federal courts applied the Equal

Protection Clause to exclusionary zoning practices that stopped short of drawing explicitly racial classifications. See, e.g., Kennedy Park Homes Association v. City of Lackawanna, 436 F.2d 108 (2d Cir. 1970) (rezoning land and preventing sewer access to block low-income housing development in white neighborhood constituted racial discrimination); Dailey v. City of Lawton, 425 F.2d 1037 (10th Cir. 1970) (upholding finding of discrimination where city officials refused to allow construction of low-income housing project in response to racially motivated opposition by neighboring white property owners); Crow v. Brown, 332 F. Supp. 382 (N.D. Ga. 1971) (county's denial of building permits for public housing project on land zoned for apartments violated Equal Protection Clause), aff'd per curiam, 457 F.2d 788 (5th Cir. 1972). Soon thereafter, however, the Equal Protection Clause ceased to be a viable weapon against exclusionary, but not explicitly racial, land use controls.

Village of Arlington Heights v. Metropolitan Housing Development Corp. [*Arlington Heights I*]
429 U.S. 252 (1977)

Mr. Justice POWELL delivered the opinion of the Court.

In 1971 respondent Metropolitan Housing Development Corporation (MHDC) applied to petitioner, the Village of Arlington Heights, Ill., for the rezoning of a 15-acre parcel from single-family to multiple-family classification. Using federal financial assistance, MHDC planned to build 190 clustered townhouse units for low- and moderate-income tenants. The Village denied the rezoning request. MHDC . . . brought suit in the United States District Court for the Northern District of Illinois. They alleged that the denial was racially discriminatory and that it violated, inter alia, the Fourteenth Amendment and the Fair Housing Act of 1968, 82 Stat. 81, 42 U.S.C. §3601 et seq. Following a bench trial, the District Court entered judgment for the Village, 373 F. Supp. 208 (1974). . . . The Court of Appeals for the Seventh Circuit reversed, finding that the "ultimate effect" of the denial was racially discriminatory, and that the refusal to rezone therefore violated the Fourteenth Amendment. 517 F.2d 409 (1975). We . . . reverse.

I

Arlington Heights is a suburb of Chicago, located about 26 miles northwest of the downtown Loop area. Most of the land in Arlington Heights is zoned for detached single-family homes, and this is in fact the prevailing land use. The Village experienced substantial growth during the 1960's, but, like other communities in northwest Cook County, its population of racial minority groups remained quite low. According to the 1970 census, only 27 of the Village's 64,000 residents were black.

The Clerics of St. Viator, a religious order (Order), own an 80-acre parcel just east of the center of Arlington Heights. Part of the site is occupied by the Viatorian high school, and part by the Order's three-story novitiate building, which houses dormitories and a Montessori school. Much of the site, however, remains vacant. Since 1959, when the Village first adopted a zoning ordinance, all the land surrounding the Viatorian property has been zoned R-3, a single-family specification with relatively small minimum lot-size requirements. On three sides of the Viatorian land there are single-family homes just across a street; to the east the Viatorian property directly adjoins the backyards of other single-family homes.

The Order decided in 1970 to devote some of its land to low- and moderate-income housing. Investigation revealed that the most expeditious way to build such housing was to work through a nonprofit developer experienced in the use of federal housing subsidies under §236 of the National Housing Act, 48 Stat. 1246, as added and amended, 12 U.S.C. §1715z-1.

MHDC is such a developer. . . .

MHDC engaged an architect and proceeded with the project, to be known as Lincoln Green. The plans called for 20 two-story buildings with a total of 190 units, each unit having its own private entrance from outside. One hundred of the units would have a single bedroom, thought likely to attract elderly citizens. The remainder would have two, three, or four bedrooms. A large portion of the site would remain open, with shrubs and trees to screen the homes abutting the property to the east.

The planned development did not conform to the Village's zoning ordinance and could not be built unless Arlington Heights rezoned the parcel to R-5, its multiple-family housing classification. Accordingly, MHDC filed with the Village Plan Commission a petition for rezoning. . . .

During the spring of 1971, the Plan Commission considered the proposal at a series of three public meetings, which drew large crowds. Although many of those attending were quite vocal and demonstrative in opposition to Lincoln Green, a number of individuals and representatives of community groups spoke in support of rezoning. Some of the comments, both from opponents and supporters, addressed what was referred to as the "social issue" — the desirability or undesirability of introducing at this location in Arlington Heights low- and moderate-income housing, housing that would probably be racially integrated.

Many of the opponents, however, focused on the zoning aspects of the petition, stressing two arguments. First, the area always had been zoned single-family, and the neighboring citizens had built or purchased there in reliance on that classification. Rezoning threatened to cause a measurable drop in property value for neighboring sites. Second, the Village's apartment policy, adopted by the Village Board in 1962 and amended in 1970, called for R-5 zoning primarily to serve as a buffer between single-family development and land uses thought incompatible, such as commercial or manufacturing districts. Lincoln Green did not meet this requirement, as it adjoined no commercial or manufacturing district.

At the close of the third meeting, the Plan Commission adopted a motion to recommend to the Village's Board of Trustees that it deny the request. The motion stated: "While the need for low and moderate income housing may exist in Arlington Heights or its environs, the Plan Commission would be derelict in recommending it at the proposed location." Two members voted against the motion and submitted a minority report, stressing that in their view the change to accommodate Lincoln Green represented "good zoning." . . . After a public hearing, the Board [of Trustees] denied the rezoning by a 6–1 vote.

The following June MHDC and three Negro individuals filed this lawsuit against the Village, seeking declaratory and injunctive relief. . . .

III

Our decision last Term in Washington v. Davis, 426 U.S. 229 (1976), made it clear that official action will not be held unconstitutional solely because it results in a racially disproportionate impact. "Disproportionate impact is not irrelevant, but it is not the sole touchstone of an invidious racial discrimination." Id. at 242. Proof of racially discriminatory intent or purpose is required to show a violation of the Equal Protection Clause. . . .

Davis does not require a plaintiff to prove that the challenged action rested solely on racially discriminatory purposes. Rarely can it be said that a legislature or administrative body operating under a broad mandate made a decision motivated solely by a single concern, or even that a particular purpose was the "dominant" or "primary" one. In fact, it is because legislators and administrators are properly concerned with balancing numerous competing considerations that courts refrain from reviewing the merits of their decisions, absent a showing of arbitrariness or irrationality. But racial discrimination is not just another competing consideration. When there is a proof that a discriminatory purpose has been a motivating factor in the decision, this judicial deference is no longer justified.

Determining whether invidious discriminatory purpose was a motivating factor demands a sensitive inquiry into such circumstantial and direct evidence of intent as may be available. The impact of the official action — whether it "bears more heavily on one race than another," Washington v. Davis, supra, 426 U.S. at 242 — may provide an important starting point. Sometimes a clear pattern, unexplainable on grounds other than race, emerges from the effect of the state action even when the governing legislation appears neutral on its face. Yick Wo v. Hopkins, 118 U.S. 356 (1886); . . . Gomillion v. Lightfoot, 364 U.S. 339 (1960). The evidentiary inquiry is then relatively easy. But such cases are rare. Absent a pattern as stark as that in *Gomillion* or *Yick Wo*, impact alone is not determinative, and the Court must look to other evidence.

The historical background of the decision is one evidentiary source, particularly if it reveals a series of official actions taken for invidious purposes. . . . The specific sequence of events leading up to the challenged decision also may shed some light on the decision-maker's purposes. . . . For example, if the property involved here always had been zoned R-5 but suddenly was changed to R-3 when the town learned of MHDC's plans to erect integrated housing,[16] we would have a far different case. Departures from the normal procedural sequence also might afford evidence that improper purposes are playing a role. Substantive departures too may be relevant, particularly if the factors usually considered important by the decisionmaker strongly favor a decision contrary to the one reached.[17]

The legislative or administrative history may be highly relevant, especially where there are contemporary statements by members of the decisionmaking body, minutes of its meetings, or reports. In some extraordinary instances the members might be called to the stand at trial to testify concerning the purpose of the official action, although even then such testimony frequently will be barred by privilege. . . .

The foregoing summary identifies, without purporting to be exhaustive, subjects of proper inquiry in determining whether racially discriminatory intent existed. With these in mind, we now address the case before us.

IV . . .

. . . The impact of the Village's decision does arguably bear more heavily on racial minorities. Minorities constitute 18 percent of the Chicago area population, and 40 percent of the income groups said to be eligible for Lincoln Green. But there is little about the

---

16. See, e.g., Progress Dev. Corp. v. Mitchell, 286 F.2d 222 (7th Cir. 1961) (park board allegedly condemned plaintiffs' land for a park upon learning that the homes plaintiffs were erecting there would be sold under a marketing plan designed to assure integration); Kennedy Park Homes Ass'n v. City of Lackawanna, 436 F.2d 108 (2d Cir. 1970) (town declared moratorium on new subdivisions and rezoned area for parkland shortly after learning of plaintiffs' plans to build low income housing).

17. See Dailey v. City of Lawton, 425 F.2d 1037 (10th Cir. 1970). The plaintiffs in *Dailey* planned to build low-income housing on the site of a former school that they had purchased. The city refused to rezone the land from PF, its public facilities classification, to R-4, high-density residential. All the surrounding area was zoned R-4, and both the present and the former planning director for the city testified that there was no reason "from a zoning standpoint" why the land should not be classified R-4. Based on this and other evidence, the Court of Appeals ruled that "the record sustains the [District Court's] holding of racial motivation and of arbitrary and unreasonable action." Id. at 1040.

sequence of events leading up to the decision that would spark suspicion. The area around the Viatorian property has been zoned R-3 since 1959, the year when Arlington Heights first adopted a zoning map. Single-family homes surround the 80-acre site, and the Village is undeniably committed to single-family homes as its dominant residential land use. The rezoning request progressed according to the usual procedures. The Plan Commission even scheduled two additional hearings, at least in part to accommodate MHDC and permit it to supplement its presentation with answers to questions generated at the first hearing.

The statements by the Plan Commission and Village Board members, as reflected in the official minutes, focused almost exclusively on the zoning aspects of the MHDC petition, and the zoning factors on which they relied are not novel criteria in the Village's rezoning decisions. There is no reason to doubt that there has been reliance by some neighboring property owners on the maintenance of single-family zoning in the vicinity. The Village originally adopted its buffer policy long before MHDC entered the picture and has applied the policy too consistently for us to infer discriminatory purpose from its application in this case. Finally, MHDC called one member of the Village Board to the stand at trial. Nothing in her testimony supports an inference of invidious purpose.

In sum, the evidence does not warrant overturning the concurrent findings of both courts below [that the Village had not acted with a discriminatory purpose]. Respondents simply failed to carry their burden of proving that discriminatory purpose was a motivating factor in the Village's decision.[21] This conclusion ends the constitutional inquiry. The Court of Appeals' further finding that the Village's decision carried a discriminatory "ultimate effect" is without independent constitutional significance.

V

Respondents' complaint also alleged that the refusal to rezone violated the Fair Housing Act of 1968, 12 U.S.C. §3601 et seq. . . . The Court of Appeals, however, proceeding in a somewhat unorthodox fashion, did not decide the statutory question. We remand the case for further consideration of respondents' statutory claims.

Reversed and remanded.

Mr. Justice MARSHALL, with whom Mr. Justice BRENNAN joins, concurring in part and dissenting in part. . . .

Note on Racial Motivation

1. *The demise of equal protection challenges.* After *Arlington Heights I*, only a few litigants have been able to prove discriminatory intent. See, e.g., United States v. Yonkers Board of Education, 837 F.2d 1181, 1222 (2d Cir. 1987) (intent to discriminate in the siting of public housing found where city constructed more units of low-income housing in black neighborhoods than planning board recommended, rejected board's site recommendations, rezoned available sites to make them unavailable, and refused to rezone other sites to allow their use for low-income housing); Dews v. Town of Sunnyvale, 109 F. Supp. 2d 526, 570–73 (N.D. Tex. 2000) (discriminatory intent proven where Texas town's zoning laws, including ban on apartments and one-acre lot requirement for residential development,

---

21. Proof that the decision by the Village was motivated in part by a racially discriminatory purpose would not necessarily have required invalidation of the challenged decision. Such proof would, however, have shifted to the Village the burden of establishing that the same decision would have resulted even had the impermissible purpose not been considered. . . .

disproportionately affected African Americans and plaintiff demonstrated that the town had a history of discouraging African Americans from moving to the town, had departed from normal procedures in rejecting developer's rezoning application for multifamily housing, and had adopted zoning laws that were ineffective in achieving their alleged purpose); Atkins v. Robinson, 545 F. Supp. 852, 874–75, 878 (E.D. Va. 1982) (discriminatory intent found in county board of supervisors' veto of low-income housing project when two voting officials made "veiled racial expressions"), aff'd, 733 F.2d 318 (4th Cir. 1984). For an empirical evaluation of the cases, see Theodore Eisenberg & Sheri Lynn Johnson, The Effects of Intent: Do We Know How Legal Standards Work?, 76 Cornell L. Rev. 1151 (1991).

2. *The fickle fortunes of motive inquiry.* Recall from the discussions at pp. 112–17 and pp. 220–29 that the courts are hesitant to inquire into decisionmakers' motives when developers challenge anticompetitive zoning or zoning decisions alleged to violate the First Amendment's Free Speech Clause. For an analysis of whether the requirement that plaintiffs challenging exclusionary zoning must prove intent can be reconciled with those rules, see Alan E. Brownstein, Illicit Legislative Motive in the Municipal Land Use Regulation Process, 57 U. Cin. L. Rev. 1 (1988).

3. *The difficulty of proving intent.* The small number of plaintiffs who successfully prove discriminatory intent might suggest that the problems of proof *Arlington Heights I* poses are virtually insurmountable. For debate about whether that is accurate, see sources cited at pp. 116–17.

4. *Would an effects test have made a difference?* On remand in a decision excerpted in the next subsection, the lower court held that the Fair Housing Act claim in *Arlington Heights I* should be subject to an effects test. The parties eventually settled, however, so we will never know whether plaintiffs would have prevailed under the effects test. For an argument that the Supreme Court's inability to see subtle discrimination will lead it to accept most justifications defendants offer, thereby rendering the effects test no more likely to result in a judgment for the plaintiff than the intent requirement, see Michael Selmi, Proving Intentional Discrimination: The Reality of Supreme Court Rhetoric, 86 Geo. L.J. 279 (1997).

Note on Expulsive Zoning

Some jurisdictions have not been content with efforts to keep racial minorities from moving in; they have tried as well to drive out any minorities already there:

> Apart from land use controls that placed blacks in residentially inferior environments, governments have also engaged in practices that diminish the quality of life for the residents within African-American communities. These practices include the provision of inferior municipal services, selective use of annexation and boundary line changes to disenfranchise and deny services to black residents, inequitable relocation or non-location of important public institutions, regressive and disparate property tax assessments, encouragement of mortgage and insurance redlining, and the disproportionate displacement of African-American families through urban renewal, highway, and local redevelopment projects.

Jon C. Dubin, From Junkyards to Gentrification: Explicating a Right to Protective Zoning in Low-Income Communities of Color, 77 Minn. L. Rev. 739, 760 (1993). See also Yale Rabin, Expulsive Zoning: The Inequitable Legacy of *Euclid, in* Zoning and the American Dream 101 (Charles M. Haar & Jerold S. Kayden eds., 1989); Craig Anthony (Tony) Arnold, Planning Milagros: Environmental Justice and Land Use Regulation, 76 Denv.

U. L. Rev. 1 (1998); Mary Jo Wiggins, Race, Class, and Suburbia: The Modern Black Suburb as a "Race-Making Situation," 35 U. Mich. J.L. Reform 749 (2002).

Recent challenges to such practices have not fared well under *Arlington Heights I*. See, e.g., R.I.S.E., Inc. v. Kay, 768 F. Supp. 1144 (E.D. Va. 1991) (plaintiff failed to prove that county intended to discriminate in siting landfill in predominantly black neighborhood), aff'd, 977 F.2d 573 (4th Cir. 1992). See also pp. 754–60 for a discussion of "environmental justice" challenges to siting decisions. Challenges to municipal service disparities, discussed at pp. 679–83, do however occasionally survive *Arlington Heights I*. See, e.g., Miller v. City of Dallas, 2002 WL 230834 (N.D. Tex. Feb. 14, 2002) (rejecting city's motion for summary judgment on a claim of expulsive zoning and municipal service disparities after analyzing the *Arlington Heights I* factors).

Note on Standing and the Role of Federal Courts in Discriminatory Zoning Cases

1. *Federal law of standing.* Warth v. Seldin, 422 U.S. 490 (1975), invoked in *Arlington Heights I*, was a broad constitutional and statutory attack on the zoning practices of the town of Penfield, an elite suburb of the city of Rochester, New York. The plaintiffs included (1) not-for-profit organizations interested in alleviating housing problems of low-income families, (2) Rochester taxpayers, (3) low-income minority residents living in the Rochester area, and (4) the Rochester Home Builders Association. In a five-to-four decision, the Supreme Court held that none of these parties had standing to bring the action. Justice Powell, writing for the majority, emphasized that neither the consumers nor builders had interests in specific projects that Penfield had frustrated. The low-income minorities who claimed to have been excluded from Penfield had not "allege[d] facts from which it reasonably could be inferred that, absent the respondents' restrictive zoning practices, there is a substantial probability that they would have been able to purchase or lease in Penfield. . . ." Id. at 504. The Court reasoned that the petitioner's allegations suggested that their inability to live in Penfield resulted from the economics of the housing market, rather than the allegedly exclusionary zoning, and faulted the petitioners for failing to show "more than the remote possibility" that "their situation . . . might improve were the court to afford relief." Id. at 507.

Similarly, the Court held that the builders association had failed to point to any specific project that one of its members was precluded from building by the city's alleged exclusionary zoning. The Court held that the taxpayer plaintiffs and fair housing associations were seeking to raise the rights of third parties, but fell "squarely within the prudential standing rule that normally bars litigants from asserting the rights or legal interests of others in order to obtain relief from injury to themselves." Id. at 509.

In *Arlington Heights I*, the Court held that MHDC had standing because the village's denial of the requested rezoning was "an absolute barrier to constructing the housing MHDC had contracted to place on the Viatorian site." In addition, one individual plaintiff, an African American, had testified that he would qualify for the housing MHDC sought to build and would probably move there if it were built. The Court held that the individual had standing because he had presented more than a "generalized grievance" and had shown a "substantial probability" that if the relief sought were awarded, the housing opportunity he desired would materialize.

Arlington Heights I shows, then, that *Warth* does not pose an insurmountable barrier to federal litigation against exclusionary zoning. But *Warth*'s requirements do impose substantial upfront costs on civil rights organizations planning to undertake federal court challenges to a particular jurisdiction's land use regulations. Indeed, in 1992, the Court made even clearer its insistence that plaintiffs allege a "concrete and particularized" injury and show that it is "'likely,' as opposed to merely 'speculative,' that the injury will be redressed by a favorable decision" in order to meet the constitutional requirements for standing. Lujan v. Defenders of Wildlife, 504 U.S. 555, 561 (1992). At what point will the costs of showing such an injury serve as an inappropriate deterrent to litigation?

The impact of *Warth* and *Lujan* on exclusionary zoning litigation is somewhat softened by the fact that the Court's prudential (as opposed to constitutional) standing limitations, such as the rule against assertion of the rights of third parties, do not apply where plaintiffs sue under the Fair Housing Act. See Havens Realty Corp. v. Coleman, 455 U.S. 363 (1982); Gladstone, Realtors v. Village of Bellwood, 441 U.S. 91 (1979); Trafficante v. Metropolitan Life Insurance Co., 409 U.S. 205 (1972). See also Dash T. Douglas, Standing on Shaky Ground: Standing Under the Fair Housing Act, 34 Akron L. Rev. 613 (2001).

2. *State law of standing*. Standing is more liberally granted in most state courts. For example, in Southern Burlington County NAACP v. Township of Mount Laurel, 336 A.2d 713 (N.J. 1975), excerpted at p. 763, the New Jersey Supreme Court conferred standing on nonresident housing consumers who lacked an interest in any specific project. New York courts applied even more relaxed standing rules in Suffolk Housing Services v. Town of Brookhaven, 397 N.Y.S.2d 302 (Sup. Ct. 1977), which held that resident housing consumers, nonresident housing consumers, various nonprofit housing organizations, and the local branch of the NAACP all had standing to mount a general assault on the town's land use practices. On appeal, resident taxpayers also were held to have standing. 405 N.Y.S.2d 302 (App. Div. 1978). While the New York Court of Appeals has not directly cabined those liberal standing rules, when confronted with an appeal of the case on the merits, it lamented the "abstract" nature of the plaintiffs' claims and noted "the desirability of a more particularized claim directed at a specific parcel of land or project or plan for housing." Suffolk Housing Services v. Town of Brookhaven, 511 N.E.2d 67 (N.Y. 1987).

Note that many of the state court cases involving exactions that were discussed at pp. 637–38 and 659–76 were brought by homebuilders associations. Builders groups are sensible plaintiffs to initiate litigation against measures that broadly injure landowner and developer interests because these groups can spread litigation costs among their members. By the same token, why shouldn't consumer and civil rights organizations be consistently granted standing in land use litigation in state courts?

3. *The role of federal courts in exclusionary zoning cases. Warth* and *Arlington Heights I* may signify that federal judges regard exclusionary zoning as a problem ill suited for resolution in the federal courts (or through the use of federal law). After all, state court judges tend to be more expert than federal judges in matters of land use and local government. See also pp. 250–51 (discussing whether takings cases should be heard by federal courts). Moreover, relegation of these disputes to state legislatures and judges would produce a more diverse set of legal results, perhaps better tailored to local economic and political conditions.

The generally passive role the federal courts have played is endorsed, at least for cases in which the government policy at issue has few interstate consequences, in Robert C. Ellickson, Suburban Growth Controls: An Economic and Legal Analysis, 86 Yale L.J. 385, 472 (1977). But see Lawrence G. Sager, Insular Majorities Unabated: *Warth v. Seldin* and *City of Eastlake v. Forest City Enterprises, Inc.*, 91 Harv. L. Rev. 1373, 1390–92 (1978) (contending that the practices of elite suburbs often jeopardize important federal constitutional values).

2.   *The Fair Housing Act*

Metropolitan Housing Development Corp. v. Village of Arlington Heights [*Arlington Heights II*]
558 F.2d 1283 (7th Cir. 1977), cert. denied, 434 U.S. 1025 (1978)

SWYGERT, Circuit Judge. . . .

The Fair Housing Act, 42 U.S.C. §§3601 et seq., was enacted as Title VIII of the Civil Rights Act of 1968. Plaintiffs contend that the Village's refusal to rezone violated . . . 42 U.S.C. §3604(a), which provides in part that "it shall be unlawful . . . [t]o make unavailable or deny . . . a dwelling to any person because of race, color, religion, . . . or national origin." . . .

We reaffirm our earlier holding that the Village's refusal to rezone had a discriminatory effect. The construction of Lincoln Green would create a substantial number of federally subsidized low-cost housing units which are not presently available in Arlington Heights. Because a greater number of black people than white people in the Chicago metropolitan area satisfy the income requirements for federally subsidized housing, the Village's refusal to permit MHDC to construct the project had a greater impact on black people than on white people. Moreover, Arlington Heights remains almost totally white in a metropolitan area with a significant percentage of black people. Since Lincoln Green would have to be racially integrated in order to qualify for federal subsidization, the Village's action in preventing the project from being built had the effect of perpetuating segregation in Arlington Heights.

The basic question we must answer is whether the Village's action violated section[] 3604(a) . . . because it had discriminatory effects when that action was taken without discriminatory intent. . . .

The major obstacle to concluding that action taken without discriminatory intent can violate section 3604(a) is the phrase "because of race" contained in the statutory provision. The narrow view of the phrase is that a party cannot commit an act "because of race" unless he intends to discriminate between races. . . . The broad view is that a party commits an act "because of race" whenever the natural and foreseeable consequence of that act is to discriminate between races, regardless of his intent. Under this statistical, effect-oriented view of causality, the Village could be liable since the natural and foreseeable consequence of its failure to rezone was to adversely affect black people seeking low-cost housing and to perpetuate segregation in Arlington Heights.

The Supreme Court adopted the narrow view for equal protection purposes in Washington v. Davis, and defendant argues that that decision should bind us in this case as well. However, *Washington* undercuts more than it supports defendant's position. In that case, the Court created a dichotomy between the Equal Protection Clause and Title VII of the Civil Rights Act of 1964, 42 U.S.C. §§2000e et seq. Although the Court announced its new intent requirement for equal protection cases, it reaffirmed the viability of Griggs v. Duke Power Co., 401 U.S. 424 (1971), in which it had previously held that an employment practice that produced a racially discriminatory effect was invalid under Title VII unless it was shown to be job-related. Washington v. Davis, 426 U.S. 229, 238–39, 246–48 (1976). Thus, a prima facie case of employment discrimination can still be established under Title VII by statistical evidence of discriminatory impact, without a showing of discriminatory intent. . . .

Defendant asserts that Title VII is distinguishable from the Fair Housing Act because Congress in Title VII mandated a more probing standard of review than it did under the Fair Housing Act. An examination of the two statutes, however, does not indicate Congress intended that proof of discriminatory intent was unnecessary under one but necessary under the other. . . .

. . . A strict focus on intent permits racial discrimination to go unpunished in the absence of evidence of overt bigotry. As overtly bigoted behavior has become more unfashionable, evidence of intent has become harder to find. But this does not mean that racial discrimination has disappeared. We cannot agree that Congress in enacting the Fair Housing Act intended to permit municipalities to systematically deprive minorities of housing opportunities simply because those municipalities act discreetly. See Paul Brest, The Supreme Court, 1975 Term — Foreword: In Defense of the Antidiscrimination Principle, 90 Harv. L. Rev. 1, 28–29 (1976).

We therefore hold that at least under some circumstances a violation of section 3604(a) can be established by a showing of discriminatory effect without a showing of discriminatory intent. A number of courts have agreed. . . .

We turn now to determining under what circumstances conduct that produces a discriminatory impact but which was taken without discriminatory intent will violate section 3604(a). Four critical factors are discernible from previous cases. They are: (1) how strong is the plaintiff's showing of discriminatory effect; (2) is there some evidence of discriminatory intent, though not enough to satisfy the constitutional standard of Washington v. Davis; (3) what is the defendant's interest in taking the action complained of; and (4) does the plaintiff seek to compel the defendant to affirmatively provide housing for members of minority groups or merely to restrain the defendant from interfering with individual property owners who wish to provide such housing. . . .

Analysis of the four factors that we have enumerated reveals that this is a close case. The Village is acting pursuant to a legitimate grant of authority and there is no evidence that its refusal to rezone was the result of intentional racial discrimination. On the other hand, plaintiffs are seeking to effectuate the national goal of integrated housing within Arlington Heights and are asking nothing more of the Village than that they be allowed to pursue that objective. Whether the Village's refusal to rezone has a strong discriminatory impact because it effectively assures that Arlington Heights will remain a segregated community is unclear from the record.

In our judgment the resolution of this case turns on clarification of the discriminatory effect of the Village's zoning decision. We hold that, if there is no land other than plaintiffs' property within Arlington Heights which is both properly zoned and suitable for federally subsidized low-cost housing, the Village's refusal to rezone constituted a violation of section 3604(a). Accordingly, we remand the case to the district court for a determination of this question. . . .

Note on the Fair Housing Act

1. *Arlington Heights III.* The district court ultimately approved a settlement hammered out by MHDC and the Village of Arlington Heights. Arlington Heights agreed to annex some then unincorporated land (presumably controlled by MHDC) abutting the nearby Village of Mount Prospect. Arlington Heights also pledged that for at least five years it would zone this land to permit multifamily and commercial uses and that it would exempt the tract from most subdivision exactions. MHDC in turn promised to build 190 units of

subsidized rental housing on the tract and to give residents of Arlington Heights priority in occupying these units (to the extent permitted by federal law). Both the Village of Mount Prospect and owners of land near the site to be annexed intervened and objected to this arrangement, but the district judge approved the settlement. Metropolitan Housing Development Corp. v. Village of Arlington Heights, 469 F. Supp. 836 (N.D. Ill. 1979), aff'd, 616 F.2d 1006 (7th Cir. 1980).

The development, called Linden Place, was built. In addition, Arlington Heights now hosts two federally subsidized housing projects for senior citizens and 316 units for moderate-income residents. The village also contributed $100,000 towards the renovation of a 12-unit apartment building that provides temporary housing for low-income tenants. Karen Cullotta Krause, Town's Turnaround Builds 1st-Place Honor: Arlington Heights' Affordable-Housing Effort Wins Accolade, Chi. Trib., June 19, 1995, Metro Northwest, at 1; Curtis Lawrence, Housing Gains in the Suburbs Earning Praise, Chi. Trib., Feb. 18, 1993, Metro Northwest, at 1; Teresa Wiltz, Stop Here for a Real "Hometown Downtown," Chi. Trib., Feb. 27, 1993, Home Guide, at 1. Nevertheless, as of the 2000 census, Arlington Heights was almost 91 percent white.

2. *Evaluation of the Fair Housing Act.* The FHA has been roundly criticized as failing to make much headway against residential segregation. For a sampling of the criticisms, as well as some attempts to understand how the FHA could be improved, see, e.g., the articles collected in Symposium: The 30th Anniversary of the Fair Housing Act, 4 Cityscape 1 (1999). See also Charles E. Daye, Whither Fair Housing: Meditations on Wrong Paradigms, Ambivalent Answers, and a Legislative Proposal, 3 Wash. U. J.L. & Pol'y 241 (2000); Wendell E. Pritchett, Where Shall We Live? Class and the Limitations of Fair Housing Law, 35 Urb. Law. 399 (2003).

3. *Disparate impact.* The lower federal courts have agreed with *Arlington Heights II* that plaintiffs can establish a prima facie case under the FHA by showing that the challenged practice has a disparate impact on classes protected by the FHA. See, e.g., Fair Housing in Huntington Committee Inc. v. Town of Huntington, 316 F.3d 357 (2d Cir. 2003). The Supreme Court has not reached the question. See City of Cuyahoga Falls v. Buckeye Community Hope Foundation, 538 U.S. 188 (2003) (vacating the Sixth Circuit's decision that plaintiffs had stated an FHA claim by alleging a disparate impact, after the plaintiffs abandoned the claim following the Supreme Court's grant of certiorari); Town of Huntington v. Huntington Branch, NAACP, 488 U.S. 15, 18 (1988) (not reaching the issue because the parties agreed that the impact standard was appropriate).

Arlington Heights II has created confusion, however, because it considered whether plaintiffs had introduced evidence of intentional discrimination to be relevant to the analysis of whether the plaintiffs had proved a violation of the FHA under a disparate impact standard. The courts are divided over whether proof of disparate impact therefore must be accompanied by at least some evidence of discriminatory intent. Compare Brown v. Artery Organization, 654 F. Supp. 1106, 1116 (D.D.C. 1987) (evidence of intent is required, but "the more devastating to minorities the effect or impact of the [defendant's] actions, the less evidence will be required of his actual intentions"), with Huntington Branch, NAACP v. Town of Huntington, 844 F.2d 926, 934–36 (2d Cir.), aff'd in part, 488 U.S. 15 (1988) (per curiam) (no evidence of intent required). See generally Kristopher E. Ahrend, Effect, or No Effect: A Comparison of Prima Facie Standards Applied in "Disparate Impact" Cases Brought Under the Fair Housing Act (Title VIII), 2 Race & Ethnic Ancestry L. Dig. 64 (1996). For a useful discussion of the theoretical difficulties of using disparate impact as an "evidentiary dragnet," see Richard Primus, Equal Protection and Disparate Impact: Round Three, 117 Harv. L. Rev. 493, 518–23 (2003).

4. *Numbers or proportions?* Can plaintiffs establish a prima facie case of disparate impact if the challenged practice primarily affects whites? Compare *Huntington Branch, NAACP*, supra, 844 F.2d at 937–38 (plaintiffs established a prima facie case of discriminatory effect by showing that even though more whites than blacks would be denied low-income housing because of the town's zoning policies, the proportion of the town's black population hurt by the policies was higher than the proportion of whites hurt), with Summerchase Ltd. Partnership I v. City of Gonzales, 970 F. Supp. 522 (M.D. La. 1997) (refusal to allow apartment complex for which larger numbers of whites than blacks would be eligible did not have a disparate impact on blacks, even though the percentage of all blacks who would be eligible for the housing was almost twice as high as the percentage of all whites who would be eligible).

5. *General policies versus individual decisions.* Can plaintiffs establish a prima facie case of disparate impact when challenging a local government's refusal to grant a rezoning, special use permit, or variance? Several courts have suggested that disparate impact analysis applies only to challenges to facially neutral policies, not to individual permitting decisions, because no comparison of the permitting decision's impact on groups other than the applicant is possible. Regional Economic Community Action Program, Inc. v. City of Middletown, 294 F.3d 35 (2d Cir. 2002); Ventura Village, Inc. v. City of Minneapolis, 318 F. Supp. 2d 822 (D. Minn. 2004).

6. *The defendant's rebuttal.* If plaintiffs establish a prima facie case under the FHA, the defendant "must prove that its actions furthered, in theory and in practice, a legitimate, bona fide governmental interest and that no alternative would serve that interest with less discriminatory effect." *Huntington Branch, NAACP*, supra, 844 F.2d at 936. *Huntington Branch, NAACP* rejected the lower court's holding that if defendants articulated a legitimate, nondiscriminatory reason for their conduct, the plaintiffs then bore the burden of proving that the reason was a "pretext." The court of appeals reasoned that pretext analysis applies only in cases of intentional discrimination. Id. at 939.

The courts have refused to require the defendant to prove that its actions furthered a compelling state interest, again reasoning that compelling interest analysis should be reserved for cases of intentional discrimination. See Resident Advisory Board v. Rizzo, 564 F.2d 126 (3d Cir. 1977). Should defendants be required to prove that the challenged practice is a "business necessity" like employers are required to do under Title VII (forbidding discrimination in employment)? See Betsey v. Turtle Creek Associates, 736 F.2d 983 (4th Cir. 1984) (requiring landlord to show that conversion of the development to an all-adult residence, which had a racially disparate effect, was justified by business necessity). What would constitute the equivalent of a "business necessity" for local governments? See Christopher P. McCormack, Note, Business Necessity in Title VIII: Importing an Employment Discrimination Doctrine into the Fair Housing Act, 54 Fordham L. Rev. 563 (1986).

Once the defendant has proved that the challenged policy serves a legitimate, bona fide interest, and that no less discriminatory alternative is available to serve that purpose, the court is not at liberty to "balance" the discriminatory impact against the importance of the government's rationale. See, e.g., Langlois v. Abington Housing Authority, 207 F.3d 43 (1st Cir. 2000).

7. *"Affirmative action."* Racial segregation of neighborhoods can result even if all governments and housing suppliers are completely race-blind in their decisions because the prejudices of housing consumers are sufficient to produce segregation. See Thomas C. Schelling, Micromotives and Macrobehavior 140–55 (1978); William A.V. Clark, Residential Preferences and Neighborhood Racial Segregation: A Test of the Schelling Segregation Model, 28 Demography 1 (1991). Can a government seek to prevent "white flight" by

guarantying property values in transitional neighborhoods? See, e.g., Home Equity Assurance Act, 65 Ill. Comp. Stat. 95/1–20 (2004) (establishing a homeowner's equity insurance program in Chicago in 1988). See also Abraham Bell & Gideon Parchomovsky, The Integration Game, 100 Colum. L. Rev. 1965 (2000); Maureen A. McNamara, Comment, The Legality and Efficacy of Homeowner's Equity Assurance: A Study of Oak Park, Illinois, 78 Nw. U. L. Rev. 1463 (1984). Can a local government try to prevent segregation by advertising to encourage blacks to move to or remain in mostly white neighborhoods, or vice versa? By paying them to do so? For discussions of such "affirmative action" strategies, see, e.g., W. Dennis Keating, The Suburban Racial Dilemma 202–20 (1994); George C. Galster, Neighborhood Racial Change, Segregationist Sentiments, and Affirmative Marketing Policies, 27 J. Urb. Econ. 344 (1990). Two early, but still valuable, sources that discuss affirmative action in the housing context are Boris I. Bittker, The Case of the Checker-Board Ordinance: An Experiment in Race Relations, 71 Yale L.J. 1387 (1962), and Bruce L. Ackerman, Integration for Subsidized Housing and the Question of Racial Occupancy Controls, 26 Stan. L. Rev. 245 (1974).

B. Discrimination Against the Poor

Municipal policies sometimes explicitly seek to exclude residents on the basis of wealth. See, e.g., Morales v. Haines, 349 F. Supp. 684 (N.D. Ill. 1972), modified, 486 F.2d 880 (7th Cir. 1973) (challenging town's prohibition on the grant of building permits for any home financed in part through federal housing subsidy programs). More often, municipal policies that bar construction of least-cost housing impede entry by lower-income families. Challenges to either de jure or de facto discrimination on the basis of wealth face two major obstacles. First, *Arlington Heights I* probably signals that plaintiffs would have to prove that the motive of excluding poor families was a but-for cause of the adoption of the municipal policy. As in challenges to alleged racial discrimination, proving intent to discriminate will be difficult. Second, the Supreme Court held that wealth is not necessarily a suspect classification in San Antonio Independent School District v. Rodriguez, 411 U.S. 1 (1973). There, the Court refused to apply strict scrutiny to plaintiffs' allegation that the Texas system of financing public education through property taxes discriminated against the poor because of "the absence of any evidence that the financing system discriminates against any definable category of 'poor' people or that it results in the absolute deprivation of education." Id. at 25. If poverty is not a suspect classification, even if municipal discrimination on the basis of wealth were proved, the defendant government would not necessarily have to show a compelling interest to justify it.

Local governments often are not explicit about their desire to exclude the poor; instead they seek to ensure the financial wherewithal of residents by imposing regulations that drive the price of housing beyond the reach of those the government deems too poor. The issue of de facto wealth discrimination through zoning was raised in pure form in Ybarra v. Town of Los Altos Hills, 503 F.2d 250 (9th Cir. 1974). The town, an exclusive suburb south of San Francisco in Santa Clara County, required a one-acre lot for each single-family unit. Two Mexican Americans and a Mexican American organization that wished to build subsidized multifamily housing obtained an option on a site in the town, and then challenged the one-acre zoning as discrimination on the basis of wealth. The Ninth Circuit cited *Rodriguez* as establishing that wealth is a suspect classification only when the plaintiffs' poverty made them "completely unable to pay for some desired benefit, and, as a consequence, they sustained an absolute deprivation of a meaningful opportunity to enjoy that benefit." The court held that the first prong of this test had been met because the town's ordinance in effect completely barred the poor. But the second requirement had not been met because the plaintiffs did not show that poor people had no other housing opportunities in the Santa Clara County area. (Observe, however, that there would be an absolute deprivation if one defined the benefit at issue to be housing in Los Altos Hills, not housing in Santa Clara County.) Because the court concluded that wealth was not a suspect classification under these circumstances, the town needed to show only that the ordinance bore a rational relationship to a legitimate government interest. The court found the ordinance to be rationally related to the goal of preserving the town's environment.

The poor do not enjoy protections such as those the Fair Housing Act gives racial or ethnic minorities. Title VIII does not explicitly reach discrimination against the poor, although the relationship between race and poverty means that Title VIII's prohibitions against racial discrimination may sometimes be useful in indirectly challenging wealth discrimination. See, e.g., Williams v. 5300 Columbia Pike Corp., 891 F. Supp. 1169 (E.D. Va. 1995) (plaintiff's proof of statistical disparity makes out a prima facie case of discrimination, even without proof as to whether the disparity is attributable to race rather than class; that proof can wait until the burden has shifted back to the plaintiff).

The federal courts and many state courts accordingly are, for all practical purposes, closed to those who wish to challenge a land use regulation as discriminatory against the poor. Some state courts have been sympathetic, however, to claims that the poor have suffered from "exclusionary zoning." We will defer that discussion until Chapter 9C because the state court cases primarily rest on theories about municipal obligations for regional needs, rather than on theories of discrimination.

C.   Discrimination Against Unconventional Households

Village of Belle Terre v. Boraas
416 U.S. 1 (1974)

Mr. Justice DOUGLAS delivered the opinion of the Court.

Belle Terre is a village on Long Island's north shore of about 220 homes inhabited by 700 people. Its total land area is less than one square mile. It has restricted land use to one-family dwellings excluding lodging houses, boarding houses, fraternity houses, or multiple-dwelling houses. The word "family" as used in the ordinance means, "[o]ne or more persons related by blood, adoption, or marriage, living and cooking together as a single housekeeping unit, exclusive of household servants. A number of persons but not exceeding two (2) living and cooking together as a single housekeeping unit though not related by blood, adoption, or marriage shall be deemed to constitute a family."

Appellees, the Dickmans, are owners of a house in the village and leased it in December 1971 . . . [to six college students, none of whom] is related to the other by blood, adoption, or marriage. When the village served the Dickmans with an "Order to Remedy Violations" of the ordinance, the owners plus three tenants thereupon brought this action under 42 U.S.C. §1983 for an injunction and a judgment declaring the ordinance unconstitutional. The District Court held the ordinance constitutional, 367 F. Supp. 136, and the Court of Appeals reversed, one judge dissenting. 476 F.2d 806.

The present ordinance is challenged on several grounds: that it interferes with a person's right to travel; that it interferes with the right to migrate to and settle within a

State; that it bars people who are uncongenial to the present residents; that it expresses the social preferences of the residents for groups that will be congenial to them; that social homogeneity is not a legitimate interest of government; that the restriction of those whom the neighbors do not like trenches on the newcomers' rights of privacy; that it is of no rightful concern to villagers whether the residents are married or unmarried; that the ordinance is antithetical to the Nation's experience, ideology, and self-perception as an open, egalitarian, and integrated society.

We find none of these reasons in the record before us. It is not aimed at transients. Cf. Shapiro v. Thompson, 394 U.S. 618 (1966). It involves no procedural disparity inflicted on some but not on others such as was presented by Griffin v. Illinois, 351 U.S. 12 (1956). It involves no "fundamental" right guaranteed by the Constitution, such as voting, Harper v. Virginia State Bd. of Elections, 383 U.S. 663 (1966); the right of association, NAACP v. Alabama ex rel. Patterson, 357 U.S. 449 (1958); the right of access to the courts, NAACP v. Button, 371 U.S. 415 (1962); or any rights of privacy, cf. Griswold v. Connecticut, 381 U.S. 479 (1965); Eisenstadt v. Baird, 405 U.S. 438, 453–54 (1972). We deal with economic and social legislation where legislatures have historically drawn lines which we respect against the charge of violation of the Equal Protection Clause if the law be "'reasonable, not arbitrary'" (quoting F.S. Royster Guano Co. v. Virginia, 253 U.S. 412, 415 (1920)) and bears "a rational relationship to a [permissible] state objective." Reed v. Reed, 404 U.S. 71, 76 (1971).

It is said, however, that if two unmarried people can constitute a "family," there is no reason why three or four may not. But every line drawn by a legislature leaves some out that might well have been included. That exercise of discretion, however, is a legislative, not a judicial, function.

It is said that the Belle Terre ordinance reeks with an animosity to unmarried couples who live together. There is no evidence to support it; and the provision of the ordinance bringing within the definition of a "family" two unmarried people belies the charge.

The ordinance places no ban on other forms of association, for a "family" may, so far as the ordinance is concerned, entertain whomever it likes.

The regimes of boarding houses, fraternity houses, and the like present urban problems. More people occupy a given space; more cars rather continuously pass by; more cars are parked; noise travels with crowds.

A quiet place where yards are wide, people few, and motor vehicles restricted are legitimate guidelines in a land-use project addressed to family needs. This goal is a permissible one within Berman v. Parker, 348 U.S. 26 (1954). The police power is not confined to elimination of filth, stench, and unhealthy places. It is ample to lay out zones where family values, youth values, and the blessings of quiet seclusion and clean air make the area a sanctuary for people. . . .

Reversed.

Mr. Justice MARSHALL, dissenting. . . .

. . . It is inconceivable to me that we would allow the exercise of the zoning power to burden First Amendment freedoms, as by ordinances that restrict occupancy to individuals adhering to particular religious, political, or scientific beliefs. Zoning officials properly concern themselves with the uses of land — with, for example, the number and kind of dwellings to be constructed in a certain neighborhood or the number of persons who can reside in those dwellings. But zoning authorities cannot validly consider who those persons are, what they believe, or how they choose to live, whether they are Negro or white, Catholic or Jew, Republican or Democrat, married or unmarried.

My disagreement with the Court today is based upon my view that the ordinance in this case unnecessarily burdens appellees' First Amendment freedom of association and their constitutionally guaranteed right to privacy. . . .

Moore v. City of East Cleveland
431 U.S. 494 (1977)

Mr. Justice POWELL announced the judgment of the Court, and delivered an opinion in which Mr. Justice BRENNAN, Mr. Justice MARSHALL, and Mr. Justice BLACKMUN joined.

East Cleveland's housing ordinance, like many throughout the country, limits occupancy of a dwelling unit to members of a single family. §1351.02.[1] But the ordinance contains an unusual and complicated definitional section that recognizes as a "family" only a few categories of related individuals. §1341.08.[2] Because her family, living together in her home, fits none of those categories, appellant stands convicted of a criminal offense. The question in this case is whether the ordinance violates the Due Process Clause of the Fourteenth Amendment.

I

Appellant, Mrs. Inez Moore, lives in her East Cleveland home together with her son, Dale Moore Sr., and her two grandsons, Dale, Jr., and John Moore, Jr. The two boys are first cousins rather than brothers; we are told that John came to live with his grandmother and with the elder and younger Dale Moores after his mother's death.

In early 1973, Mrs. Moore received a notice of violation from the city, stating that John was an "illegal occupant" and directing her to comply with the ordinance. When she failed to remove him from her home, the city filed a criminal charge. Mrs. Moore moved to dismiss, claiming that the ordinance was constitutionally invalid on its face. Her motion was overruled, and upon conviction she was sentenced to five days in jail and a $25 fine. The Ohio Court of Appeals affirmed after giving full consideration to her constitutional claims,[5] and the Ohio Supreme Court denied review. . . .

---

1. All citations by section number refer to the Housing Code of the city of East Cleveland, Ohio.
2. Section 1341.08 (1966) provides:

"Family" means a number of individuals related to the nominal head of the household or to the spouse of the nominal head of the household living as a single housekeeping unit in a single dwelling unit, but limited to the following:

    (a)   Husband or wife of the nominal head of the household.

    (b)   Unmarried children of the nominal head of the household or of the spouse of the nominal head of the household, provided, however, that such unmarried children have no children residing with them.

    (c)   Father or mother of the nominal head of the household or of the spouse of the nominal head of the household.

    (d)   Notwithstanding the provisions of subsection (b) hereof, a family may include not more than one dependent married or unmarried child of the nominal head of the household or of the spouse of the nominal head of the household and the spouse and dependent children of such dependent child. For the purpose of this subsection, a dependent person is one who has more than fifty percent of his total support furnished for him by the nominal head of the household and the spouse of the nominal head of the household.

    (e)   A family may consist of one individual.

5. The dissenting opinion of the Chief Justice suggests that Mrs. Moore should be denied a hearing in this Court because she failed to seek discretionary administrative relief in the form of a variance, relief that is no

II

The city argues that our decision in Village of Belle Terre v. Boraas, 416 U.S. 1 (1974), requires us to sustain the ordinance attacked here. . . .

But one overriding factor sets this case apart from *Belle Terre*. The ordinance there affected only unrelated individuals. It expressly allowed all who were related by "blood, adoption, or marriage" to live together, and in sustaining the ordinance we were careful to note that it promoted "family needs" and "family values." . . . East Cleveland, in contrast, has chosen to regulate the occupancy of its housing by slicing deeply into the family itself. This is no mere incidental result of the ordinance. On its face it selects certain categories of relatives who may live together and declares that others may not. In particular, it makes a crime of a grandmother's choice to live with her grandson in circumstances like those presented here.

When a city undertakes such intrusive regulation of the family, neither *Belle Terre* nor *Euclid* governs; the usual judicial deference to the legislature is inappropriate. "This Court has long recognized that freedom of personal choice in matters of marriage and family life is one of the liberties protected by the Due Process Clause of the Fourteenth Amendment." Cleveland Board of Education v. LaFleur, 414 U.S. 632 (1974). . . . [W]hen the government intrudes on choices concerning family living arrangements, this Court must examine carefully the importance of the governmental interests advanced and the extent to which they are served by the challenged regulation. . . .

When thus examined, this ordinance cannot survive. The city seeks to justify it as a means of preventing overcrowding, minimizing traffic and parking congestion, and avoiding an undue financial burden on East Cleveland's school system. Although these are legitimate goals, the ordinance before us serves them marginally, at best.[7] For example, the ordinance permits any family consisting only of husband, wife, and unmarried children to live together, even if the family contains a half dozen licensed drivers, each with his or her own car. At the same time it forbids an adult brother and sister to share a household, even if both faithfully use public transportation. The ordinance would permit a grandmother to live with a single dependent son and children, even if his school-age children number a dozen, yet it forces Mrs. Moore to find another dwelling for her grandson John, simply because of the presence of his uncle and cousin in the same household. We need not labor the point. Section 1341.08 has but a tenuous relation to alleviation of the conditions mentioned by the city.

III

The city . . . suggests that any constitutional right to live together as a family extends only to the nuclear family — essentially a couple and their dependent children. . . .

Ours is by no means a tradition limited to respect for the bonds uniting the members of the nuclear family. The tradition of uncles, aunts, cousins, and especially grandparents sharing a household along with parents and children has roots equally venerable and equally deserving of constitutional recognition. Over the years millions of our citizens have grown up in just such an environment, and most, surely, have profited from it. Even if conditions of modern society have brought about a decline in extended family

---

longer available. There are sound reasons for requiring exhaustion of administrative remedies in some situations, but such a requirement is wholly inappropriate where the party is a criminal defendant in circumstances like those present here. . . .

7. It is significant that East Cleveland has another ordinance specifically addressed to the problem of overcrowding. . . . Section 1351.03 limits population density directly, tying the maximum permissible occupancy of a dwelling to the habitable floor area. Even if John Jr. and his father both remain in Mrs. Moore's household, the family stays in these limits.

households, they have not erased the accumulated wisdom of civilization, gained over the centuries and honored throughout our history, that supports a larger conception of the family. Out of choice, necessity, or a sense of family responsibility, it has been common for close relatives to draw together and participate in the duties and the satisfactions of a common home. . . . Especially in times of adversity, such as the death of a spouse or economic need, the broader family has tended to come together for mutual sustenance and to maintain or rebuild a secure home life. This is apparently what happened here.[16]

Whether or not such a household is established because of personal tragedy, the choice of relatives in this degree of kinship to live together may not lightly be denied by the State. Pierce v. Society of Sisters, 268 U.S. 510 (1925), struck down an Oregon law requiring all children to attend the State's public schools, holding that the Constitution "excludes any general power of the State to standardize its children by forcing them to accept instruction from public teachers only." 268 U.S. at 535. By the same token the Constitution prevents East Cleveland from standardizing its children — and its adults — by forcing all to live in certain narrowly defined family patterns.

Reversed.

Mr. Justice BRENNAN, with whom Mr. Justice MARSHALL joins, concurring. . . .

. . . Even in husband and wife households, 13% of black families compared with 3% of white families include relatives under 18 years old, in addition to the couple's own children.[8] In black households whose head is an elderly woman, as in this case, the contrast is even more striking: 48% of such black households, compared with 10% of counterpart white households, include related minor children not offspring of the head of the household.[9]

I do not wish to be understood as implying that East Cleveland's enforcement of its ordinance is motivated by a racially discriminatory purpose: The record of this case would not support that implication. But the prominence of other than nuclear families among ethnic and racial minority groups, including our black citizens, surely demonstrates that the "extended family" pattern remains a vital tenet of our society. It suffices that in prohibiting this pattern of family living as a means of achieving its objectives, appellee city has chosen a device that deeply intrudes into family associational rights that historically have been central, and today remain central, to a large proportion of our population. . . .

Mr. Justice STEVENS, concurring in the judgment. . . .

Mr. Chief Justice BURGER, dissenting. . . .

Mr. Justice STEWARD, with whom Mr. Justice Rehnquist joins, dissenting. . . .

Note on Untraditional Families and Households

1. *Background of* Moore. Informed sources[9] report that East Cleveland employed its controversial ordinance in part to prevent freeloading on East Cleveland schools. Families living in Cleveland and other nearby areas apparently had been sending their children to live with relatives in East Cleveland to take advantage of the superior East Cleveland

16. We are told that the mother of John Moore, Jr., died when he was less than one year old. He, like uncounted others who have suffered a similar tragedy, then came to live with the grandmother to provide the infant with a substitute for his mother's care and to establish a more normal home environment. Brief for Appellant 25.

8. R. Hill, The Strengths of Black Families 5 (1972).

9. Id. at 5–6. . . .

[9] This information was provided by Cleveland attorneys Harold Babbit and Henry Fischer. Mr. Fischer was Law Director of the City of East Cleveland during the *Moore* litigation.

public school system. Because Mrs. Moore's family members were not participating in any such ploy, East Cleveland officials informed her that it was likely that she could obtain a variance from the ordinance. But the Legal Aid Society lawyers representing Mrs. Moore wished to test the constitutional issues at stake and advised her not to apply for a variance. Assuming Mrs. Moore agreed with this strategy, did her attorneys violate legal ethics? Is this an appropriate case to impose a finality requirement like that discussed at pp. 234–51?

2. *Critiques.* For critical analysis of *Belle Terre* and *Moore*, see Frank I. Michelman, Political Markets and Community Self-Determination: Competing Judicial Models of Local Government Legitimacy, 53 Ind. L.J. 145, 187–99 (1977–1978); Lawrence G. Sager, Questions I Wish I Had Never Asked: The Burger Court on Exclusionary Zoning, 11 Sw. U. L. Rev. 510 (1979); Lawrence G. Sager, Tight Little Islands: Exclusionary Zoning, Equal Protection, and the Indigent, 21 Stan. L. Rev. 767 (1969).

3. *Prohibitions on "living in sin."* Do zoning restrictions prohibiting unmarried, heterosexual couples from living together fall under *Belle Terre* or *Moore?* See Zavala v. City & County of Denver, 759 P.2d 664 (Colo. 1988) (trial court's dismissal of challenge to Denver zoning ordinance that restricted single-family residential zones to people related by blood or marriage reversed; case remanded for further fact-finding about the extent to which the ordinance limited unmarried couples' rights to own or occupy property within Denver, and about the purposes of the ordinances). See also City of Ladue v. Horn, 720 S.W.2d 745 (Mo. App. 1986) (upholding ordinance prohibiting unmarried men and women from living together).

4. *Dissension among the states. Belle Terre* failed to convince some of the state courts. See, e.g., City of Santa Barbara v. Adamson, 610 P.2d 436 (Cal. 1980) (en banc); Charter Township of Delta v. Dinolfo, 351 N.W.2d 831 (Mich. 1984), State v. Baker, 405 A.2d 368 (N.J. 1979); Baer v. Town of Brookhaven, 537 N.E.2d 619 (N.Y. 1989) (all striking down restrictive definitions of "family"). For analysis of those decisions, see Katia Brener, Note, *Belle Terre* and Single-Family Home Ordinances: Judicial Perceptions of Local Government and the Presumption of Validity, 71 N.Y.U. L. Rev. 447 (1999), Rebecca Ginzburg, Note, Altering "Family": Another Look at the Supreme Court's Narrow Protection of Family in *Belle Terre*, 83 B.U. L. Rev. 875 (2003). The majority of the cases, however, including several of the most recent cases, have followed the reasoning of *Belle Terre* in upholding zoning ordinances with restrictive definitions of family. See, e.g., Dinan v. Board of Zoning Appeals, 595 A.2d 864 (Conn. 1991); State v. Champoux, 566 N.W.2d 763 (Neb. 1997); City of Brookings v. Winker, 554 N.W.2d 827 (S.D. 1996).

5. *Other grounds for attack.* In 1988, the FHA was amended to prohibit discrimination in the provision of housing on the basis of "familial status," which is defined to protect pregnant women and children living with a parent or custodian. 42 U.S.C. §3602(k) (2005). Would the FHA prohibit the ordinance at issue in *Moore?*

As was discussed at p. 128, efforts to control "mini-dorms" and other student housing sometimes have been invalidated under the Equal Protection Clause. Local governments' attempts to limit religious communes may raise the Free Exercise Clause issues discussed at pp. 209–20.

6. *Enforcement.* What mechanisms might local officials use to determine who is actually occupying a dwelling unit? Inspections triggered by neighbors' complaints are probably the most common enforcement device. University City, Missouri (a St. Louis suburb), pioneered a more systematic control system in 1967. The city requires new renters and owner-occupants of residential units to obtain occupancy permits before moving in. An applicant for a permit must describe the number, age, and family relationships of all occupants. City officials then inspect the dwelling unit involved to determine whether the applicant household qualifies for it under the city's occupancy restrictions, and to identify

any outstanding violations of the city's housing code. To foster compliance, the local public schools require new students to show valid occupancy permits before enrolling. See generally Bryan T. Downes et al., Occupancy Permits Provide an Older Suburb with an Anti-Blight Tool, 32 J. Housing 506 (1975). The program can be evaded, however, when additional people move into the house after the permit is granted. See Cynthia Todd, Fatal Fire Unraveled History of Crowding: Family Grew Beyond Limits of University City's Housing Code, St. Louis Post-Dispatch, Jan. 24, 1995, at 1C.

D.   Discrimination Against People with Disabilities

Until the late 1960s, most people with disabilities, especially the mentally retarded and mentally ill, were housed in institutions or lived with their families. A better understanding of the potential promised by individuals with disabilities, growing respect for their individuality and dignity, and increasing horror at the abuses many suffered in institutions led scores of parents and advocacy groups to resort to the courts to seek alternatives to institutions. Many of the lawsuits were successful. David Braddock, Deinstitutionalization of the Retarded: Trends in Public Policy, 32 Hosp. & Community Psychiatry 607 (1981). Congress passed the Developmental Disabilities Act in 1984, see 42 U.S.C. §6000 et seq. (2000), and in 2000, replaced that with the Developmental Disabilities Assistance and Bill of Rights Act, 42 U.S.C. §15001 et seq. (2005), mandating that the disabled receive individualized treatment in the least restrictive setting. Many states followed suit. See, e.g., N.J. Stat. Ann. §§30:6D-1 to -12 (West 2005).

The result has been a sweeping deinstitutionalization of people with disabilities over the past few decades, and a concomitant rise in the use of community residential treatment centers. One of the most commonly used facilities is a group home, "where typically four to eight individuals reside in a house or apartment with a live-in or shift staff that provides training in the fundamentals of daily living. . . . The group home constitutes a family, a single housekeeping unit where residents share responsibilities, meals and recreational activities as in any family." Daniel Lauber, A Real LULU: Zoning for Group Homes and Halfway Houses Under the Fair Housing Amendments Act of 1988, 29 J. Marshall L. Rev. 369, 373, 384 (1996).

Group homes have met enormous resistance from communities and their zoning officials:

> One of the most common exclusionary tools is to simply not mention community residences at all in the zoning ordinance and then prevent the development of proposed community residences by enforcing a restrictive definition of "family." . . . [Most zoning ordinances] place a cap on the number of unrelated people in a dwelling unit. Most set the limit at three, four or five unrelated individuals. . . . The U.S. Supreme Court upheld these restrictive definitions in *Village of Belle Terre v. Boraas.* Since most community residences need six or more residents to succeed therapeutically and financially, this restriction effectively blocked them from locating in the residential areas where they need to locate. . . . A second common exclusionary technique is to require a special use permit to establish a community residence in residential districts. . . .

Lauber, supra, at 387–88. Restrictive covenants limiting a building's use to single-family residences or explicitly forbidding group homes, discussed at p. 561, are a third serious impediment for group homes.

The following sections explore the constitutional and statutory tools group home developers currently use to overcome local opposition. In reviewing these tools, keep in mind that studies of the property value effects of group homes have produced mixed results, as discussed at p. 44.

1. Constitutional Challenges

City of Cleburne v. Cleburne Living Center
473 U.S. 432 (1985)

Justice WHITE delivered the opinion of the Court.

A Texas city denied a special use permit for the operation of a group home for the mentally retarded, acting pursuant to a municipal zoning ordinance requiring permits for such homes. The Court of Appeals for the Fifth Circuit held that mental retardation is a "quasi-suspect" classification and that the ordinance violated the Equal Protection Clause because it did not substantially further an important governmental purpose. We hold that a lesser standard of scrutiny is appropriate, but conclude that under that standard the ordinance is invalid as applied in this case.

I

In July 1980, respondent Jan Hannah purchased a building at 201 Featherston Street in the city of Cleburne, Texas, with the intention of leasing it to Cleburne Living Center, Inc. (CLC), for the operation of a group home for the mentally retarded. It was anticipated that the home would house 13 retarded men and women, who would be under the constant supervision of CLC staff members. The house had four bedrooms and two baths, with a half bath to be added. CLC planned to comply with all applicable state and federal regulations.

The city informed CLC that a special use permit would be required for the operation of a group home at the site, and CLC accordingly submitted a permit application. In response to a subsequent inquiry from CLC, the city explained that under the zoning regulations applicable to the site, a special use permit, renewable annually, was required for the construction of "[h]ospitals for the insane or feeble-minded, or alcoholic [sic] or drug addicts, or penal or correctional institutions."[3] The city had determined that the proposed

---

3. The site of the home is in an area zoned "R-3," an "Apartment House District." Section 8 of the Cleburne zoning ordinance, in pertinent part, allows the following uses in an R-3 district:

1. Any use permitted in District R-2.
2. Apartment houses, or multiple dwellings.
3. Boarding and lodging houses.
4. Fraternity or sorority houses and dormitories.
5. Apartment hotels.
6. Hospitals, sanitariums, nursing homes or homes for convalescents or aged, other than for the insane or feeble-minded or alcoholics or drug addicts.
7. Private clubs or fraternal orders, except those whose chief activity is carried on as a business.
8. Philanthropic or eleemosynary institutions, other than penal institutions.
9. Accessory uses customarily incident to any of the above uses.

Section 16 of the ordinance specifies the uses for which a special use permit is required. These include "[h]ospitals for the insane or feebleminded, or alcoholic [sic] or drug addicts, or penal or correctional institutions." Section 16 provides that a permit for such a use may be issued by "the Governing Body, after public hearing, and after recommendation of the Planning Commission." All special use permits are limited to one year, and each applicant is required "to obtain the signatures of the property owners within two hundred (200) feet of the property to be used."

group home should be classified as a "hospital for the feebleminded." After holding a public hearing on CLC's application, the city council voted 3 to 1 to deny a special use permit.

CLC then filed suit in Federal District Court against the city and a number of its officials, alleging, inter alia, that the zoning ordinance was invalid on its face and as applied because it discriminated against the mentally retarded in violation of the equal protection rights of CLC and its potential residents. The District Court found that "[i]f the potential residents of the Featherston Street home were not mentally retarded, but the home was the same in all other respects, its use would be permitted under the city's zoning ordinance," and that the city council's decision "was motivated primarily by the fact that the residents of the home would be persons who are mentally retarded." Even so, the District Court held the ordinance and its application constitutional. Concluding that no fundamental right was implicated and that mental retardation was neither a suspect nor a quasi-suspect classification, the court employed the minimum level of judicial scrutiny applicable to equal protection claims. The court deemed the ordinance, as written and applied, to be rationally related to the city's legitimate interests in "the legal responsibility of CLC and its residents, . . . the safety and fears of residents in the adjoining neighborhood," and the number of people to be housed in the home.

The Court of Appeals for the Fifth Circuit reversed, determining that mental retardation was a quasi-suspect classification and that it should assess the validity of the ordinance under intermediate-level scrutiny. . . . Applying the test that it considered appropriate, the court held that the ordinance was invalid on its face because it did not substantially further any important governmental interests. . . .

III

Against this background, we conclude for several reasons that the Court of Appeals erred in holding mental retardation a quasi-suspect classification calling for a more exacting standard of judicial review than is normally accorded economic and social legislation. First, it is undeniable, and it is not argued otherwise here, that those who are mentally retarded have a reduced ability to cope with and function in the everyday world. Nor are they all cut from the same pattern: as the testimony in this record indicates, they range from those whose disability is not immediately evident to those who must be constantly cared for. They are thus different, immutably so, in relevant respects, and the states' interest in dealing with and providing for them is plainly a legitimate one. How this large and diversified group is to be treated under the law is a difficult and often a technical matter, very much a task for legislators guided by qualified professionals and not by the perhaps ill-informed opinions of the judiciary. Heightened scrutiny inevitably involves substantive judgments about legislative decisions, and we doubt that the predicate for such judicial oversight is present where the classification deals with mental retardation.

Second, the distinctive legislative response, both national and state, to the plight of those who are mentally retarded demonstrates not only that they have unique problems, but also that the lawmakers have been addressing their difficulties in a manner that belies a continuing antipathy or prejudice and a corresponding need for more intrusive oversight by the judiciary. Thus, the federal government has not only outlawed discrimination against the mentally retarded in federally funded programs, see §504 of the Rehabilitation Act of 1973, 29 U.S.C. §794, but it has also provided the retarded with the right to receive "appropriate treatment, services, and habilitation" in a setting that is "least restrictive of [their] personal liberty." Development Disabilities Assistance and Bill of Rights Act, 42 U.S.C. §§6010(1), (2).

Third, the legislative response, which could hardly have occurred and survived without public support, negates any claim that the mentally retarded are politically powerless in the sense that they have no ability to attract the attention of the lawmakers. . . .

Fourth, if the large and amorphous class of the mentally retarded were deemed quasi-suspect . . . , it would be difficult to find a principled way to distinguish a variety of other groups who have perhaps immutable disabilities setting them off from others. . . . One need mention in this respect only the aging, the disabled, the mentally ill, and the infirm. We are reluctant to set out on that course, and we decline to do so.

Doubtless, there have been and there will continue to be instances of discrimination against the retarded that are in fact invidious, and that are properly subject to judicial correction under constitutional norms. But the appropriate method of reaching such instances is not to create a new quasi-suspect classification and subject all governmental action based on that classification to more searching evaluation. . . .

Our refusal to recognize the retarded as a quasi-suspect class does not leave them entirely unprotected from invidious discrimination. To withstand equal protection review, legislation that distinguishes between the mentally retarded and others must be rationally related to a legitimate governmental purpose. This standard, we believe, affords government the latitude necessary both to pursue policies designed to assist the retarded in realizing their full potential, and to freely and efficiently engage in activities that burden the retarded in what is essentially an incidental manner. The State may not rely on a classification whose relationship to an asserted goal is so attenuated as to render the distinction arbitrary or irrational. See Zobel v. Williams, 457 U.S. 55, 61–63 (1982); United States Dep't of Agric. v. Moreno, 413 U.S. 528, 535 (1973). Furthermore, some objectives — such as "a bare . . . desire to harm a politically unpopular group," id. at 534 — are not legitimate state interests. Beyond that, the mentally retarded, like others, have and retain their substantive constitutional rights in addition to the right to be treated equally by the law.

IV

We turn to the issue of the validity of the zoning ordinance insofar as it requires a special use permit for homes for the mentally retarded. We inquire first whether requiring a special use permit for the Featherston home in the circumstances here deprives respondents of the equal protection of the laws. . . .

The constitutional issue is clearly posed. The city does not require a special use permit in an R-3 zone for apartment houses, multiple dwellings, boarding and lodging houses, fraternity or sorority houses, dormitories, apartment hotels, hospitals, sanitariums, nursing homes for convalescents or the aged (other than for the insane or feebleminded or alcoholics or drug addicts), private clubs or fraternal orders, and other specified uses. It does, however, insist on a special permit for the Featherston home, and it does so, as the District Court found, because it would be a facility for the mentally retarded. May the city require the permit for this facility when other care and multiple-dwelling facilities are freely permitted?

It is true, as already pointed out, that the mentally retarded as a group are indeed different from others not sharing their misfortune, and in this respect they may be different from those who would occupy other facilities that would be permitted in an R-3 zone without a special permit. But this difference is largely irrelevant unless the Featherston home and those who would occupy it would threaten legitimate interests of the city in a way that other permitted uses such as boarding houses and hospitals would not. Because in our view the record does not reveal any rational basis for believing that the Featherston home would pose any special threat to the city's legitimate interests, we affirm the judgment below insofar as it holds the ordinance invalid as applied in this case.

The District Court found that the City Council's insistence on the permit rested on several factors. First, the Council was concerned with the negative attitude of the majority of property owners located within 200 feet of the Featherston facility, as well as with the fears of elderly residents of the neighborhood. But mere negative attitudes, or fear, unsubstantiated by factors which are properly cognizable in a zoning proceeding, are not permissible bases for treating a home for the mentally retarded differently from apartment houses, multiple dwellings, and the like. It is plain that the electorate as a whole, whether by referendum or otherwise, could not order city action violative of the Equal Protection Clause, Lucas v. Forty-Fourth General Assembly of Colorado, 377 U.S. 713, 736–37 (1964), and the City may not avoid the strictures of that Clause by deferring to the wishes or objections of some fraction of the body politic. "Private biases may be outside the reach of the law, but the law cannot, directly or indirectly, give them effect." Palmore v. Sidoti, 466 U.S. 429, 433 (1984).

Second, the Council had two objections to the location of the facility. It was concerned that the facility was across the street from a junior high school, and it feared that the students might harass the occupants of the Featherston home. But the school itself is attended by about 30 mentally retarded students, and denying a permit based on such vague, undifferentiated fears is again permitting some portion of the community to validate what would otherwise be an equal protection violation. The other objection to the home's location was that it was located on "a five hundred year flood plain." This concern with the possibility of a flood, however, can hardly be based on a distinction between the Featherston home and, for example, nursing homes, homes for convalescents or the aged, or sanitariums or hospitals, any of which could be located on the Featherston site without obtaining a special use permit. The same may be said of another concern of the Council — doubts about the legal responsibility for actions which the mentally retarded might take. If there is no concern about legal responsibility with respect to other uses that would be permitted in the area, such as boarding and fraternity houses, it is difficult to believe that the groups of mildly or moderately mentally retarded individuals who would live at 201 Featherston would present any different or special hazard.

Fourth, the Council was concerned with the size of the home and the number of people that would occupy it. The District Court found, and the Court of Appeals repeated, that "[i]f the potential residents of the Featherston Street home were not mentally retarded, but the home was the same in all other respects, its use would be permitted under the city's zoning ordinance." . . . In the words of the Court of Appeals, "[t]he City never justifies its apparent view that other people can live under such 'crowded' conditions when mentally retarded persons cannot." 726 F.2d at 202.

In the courts below the city also urged that the ordinance is aimed at avoiding concentration of population and at lessening congestion of the streets. These concerns obviously fail to explain why apartment houses, fraternity and sorority houses, hospitals and the like, may freely locate in the area without a permit. So, too, the expressed worry about fire hazards, the serenity of the neighborhood, and the avoidance of danger to other residents fail rationally to justify singling out a home such as 201 Featherston for the special use permit, yet imposing no such restrictions on the many other uses freely permitted in the neighborhood.

The short of it is that requiring the permit in this case appears to us to rest on an irrational prejudice against the mentally retarded, including those who would occupy the Featherston facility and who would live under the closely supervised and highly regulated conditions expressly provided for by state and federal law.

The judgment of the Court of Appeals is affirmed insofar as it invalidates the zoning ordinance as applied to the Featherston home. The judgment is otherwise vacated, and the case is remanded.

Justice STEVENS, with whom The CHIEF JUSTICE joins, concurring. . . .

Justice MARSHALL, with whom Justice BRENNAN and Justice BLACKMUN join, concurring in the judgment in part and dissenting in part. . . .

I cannot agree . . . with the way in which the Court reaches its result or with the narrow, as-applied remedy it provides for the City of Cleburne's equal protection violation. The Court holds the ordinance invalid on rational-basis grounds and disclaims that anything special, in the form of heightened scrutiny, is taking place. Yet Cleburne's ordinance surely would be valid under the traditional rational-basis test applicable to economic and commercial regulation. In my view, it is important to articulate, as the Court does not, the facts and principles that justify subjecting this zoning ordinance to the searching review — the heightened scrutiny — that actually leads to its invalidation. . . .

Note on *Cleburne*

1. *Rational basis with teeth?* Is Justice Marshall correct that the majority applies something other than the usual rational basis scrutiny? Many commentators initially thought *Cleburne* required more. See, e.g., Martha Minow, When Difference Has Its Home: Group Homes for the Mentally Retarded, Equal Protection and Legal Treatment of Difference, 22 Harv. C.R.-C.L. L. Rev. 111 (1987); Cass R. Sunstein, Foreword: Leaving Things Undecided, 110 Harv. L. Rev. 4, 60–64 (1996). The Supreme Court has insisted, however, that *Cleburne* imposes "only the minimum 'rational-basis' review applicable to general social and economic legislation." University of Alabama v. Garrett, 531 U.S. 356, 357 (2001).

2. *The special use permit requirement.* The *Cleburne* Court refused to address plaintiff's facial challenge to the very existence of the special use requirement, arguing that addressing the claim instead on an as-applied basis would allow the Court to avoid making unnecessarily broad constitutional arguments. Lower courts have followed that tack, with the result that successful individual plaintiffs secure their special use permits, but are unable to clear an easier path for themselves or other social service providers seeking to locate facilities in the future. See, e.g., Open Homes Fellowship, Inc. v. Orange County, Florida, 325 F. Supp. 2d 1349 (M.D. Fla. 2004). Even if special use permits eventually will be granted to those applicants who legitimately meet the standards for the permit, should the courts be concerned about the chilling effect the requirement may have on those seeking to locate group homes? Daniel Lauber, a planner and an attorney who specializes in zoning for group homes, notes:

> When cities require a special use permit, buyers usually include a clause in the purchase and sale agreement that makes the sale contingent on receiving the special use permit. While these clauses are quite common in commercial property sales, they are extremely rare in sales of owner-occupied residential property. . . . Most home owners need the proceeds from the sale of their current house to buy a new one. Consequently, few home owners are willing to sell to a group home operator who insists on this kind of contingency clause and few group home operators can afford to risk that the city will deny their special use permit application. . . .

Daniel Lauber, A Real LULU: Zoning for Group Homes and Halfway Houses Under the Fair Housing Amendments Act of 1988, 29 J. Marshall L. Rev. 369, 388 (1996).

2.   *Statutory Protections*

Smith & Lee Associates v. City of Taylor
102 F.3d 781 (6th Cir. 1996)

KENNEDY, Circuit Judge. . . .

Smith & Lee Associates, Inc. ("Smith & Lee") is a for-profit Michigan corporation that owns and operates Adult Foster Care ("AFC") homes in the State of Michigan. AFC homes provide twenty-four hour supervised care to dependent adults who require ongoing supervision but not continuous nursing care. Smith & Lee was organized for the purpose of purchasing the residential home at dispute in this case, Mortenview Manor ("Mortenview"), in Taylor, Michigan ("the City" or "Taylor").

Mortenview specializes in care for the elderly disabled. It houses six elderly disabled residents who suffer from Alzheimer's disease and other forms of dementia, organic brain syndrome, and other ailments. Whereas other AFCs, known as "contract" homes, which house persons with other types of disabilities, receive subsidies from state or community social service agencies, homes for the elderly disabled like Mortenview must rely solely on payments from their residents to cover operating costs. Mortenview is a one-story dwelling that includes a kitchen, living room, dining room, six bedrooms, two full baths, and a small office; its circular driveway provides parking for visitors and staff.

Mortenview is located in a residential neighborhood in Taylor that is zoned for single-family use. Smith & Lee has authority to house six unrelated disabled adults in Mortenview by virtue of Mich. Comp. Laws Ann. §125.583b(2) (West 1986),[1] which permits AFC homes for six or fewer residents to operate in all residential zones, including single-family neighborhoods. . . .

From the time it purchased Mortenview, Smith & Lee sought to house twelve residents. Michael Manore, then Director of Taylor's Office of Development Services, informed Smith & Lee that the home could not operate with twelve residents unless the City rezoned the property from R-1A, which is the City's designation for single-family use, to RM-1, which is its designation for multiple-family use. . . .

In January of 1990, Smith & Lee petitioned the City to rezone Mortenview from R-1A to RM-1. Taylor officials referred the petition to the City's planning consultant, Wade/Trim Impact, which recommended that Smith & Lee's petition be denied for three reasons: (1) RM-1 zoning would be inconsistent with the established zoning pattern of the neighborhood; (2) RM-1 zoning would allow for land uses that are incompatible with the established single-family residential character of the neighborhood; and (3) the request was inconsistent with the City's Master Land Use Plan 2000.

On February 21, 1990, the City's Planning Commission held a public hearing on Smith & Lee's zoning proposal. No residents voiced objections to Smith & Lee's rezoning petition. The Commission voted to recommend that the City Council deny Smith & Lee's petition. . . . At its March 6, 1990 meeting, the Council denied the zoning request, citing

---

1. That section provides:

> In order to implement the policy of this state that persons in need of community residential care shall not be excluded by zoning from the benefits of normal residential surroundings, a state licensed residential facility providing supervision or care, or both, to 6 or less persons shall be considered a residential use of property for the purpose of zoning and a permitted use in all residential zones, including those zoned for single-family dwellings, and shall not be subject to a special use or conditional use permit or procedure different from those required for other dwellings of similar density in the same zone.

Mich. Comp. Laws Ann. §125.583b(2) (West 1986).

spot zoning concerns and the proposal's incompatibility with the City's master development plan. . . .

II

On May 10, 1991, Smith & Lee brought suit alleging that the City had violated Section Six of the Fair Housing Amendments Act of 1988 ("FHAA"), 42 U.S.C. §3604(f)(1)(B) & (3)(B), by intentionally discriminating against and failing to make reasonable accommodations for the handicapped. . . .

[The District Court held that Taylor intentionally discriminated and failed to make reasonable accommodations.]

The District Court based its finding that the City intentionally discriminated against the handicapped on four considerations: that the City characterized AFC homes as a multiple-family use without inquiring into such homes' similarity to families; that the City enforced the ban on for-profit uses against Mortenview even though it tolerated other home businesses in the immediate area; that City officials' comments reflected a paternalistic and discriminatory attitude toward the handicapped; and that the City's 1981 declaratory judgment suit to prevent another AFC home from operating was historical evidence of the City's discriminatory animus — evidence that was not rebutted by the City's willingness to rezone another twelve-resident AFC facility from single-family to multiple-family use.

The Court also held that the City had failed to make reasonable accommodations. The Court found that "AFC homes are often the only means by which disabled adults are able to live in single-family type homes in residential communities." . . .

The Court found a shortage of AFC homes for the elderly disabled in the Taylor area. It found that there were only three AFC homes serving the elderly disabled and that only one of them, Mortenview, was located in a single-family neighborhood. It also found that Mortenview has a waiting list of elderly disabled individuals who desire to live there. . . .

The Court found that "the shortage of AFC homes for elderly disabled residents in the City of Taylor is caused, at least in part, by the fact that such homes are not economically viable with only six residents." . . . The Court relied on expert testimony offered by William F. Lasky, President and CEO of Alternative Living Services, a national provider of elderly assisted living facilities. . . . [Mr. Lasky] testified that it is no longer economically feasible for AFC homes for the elderly disabled to operate with fewer than nine residents.

The Court then considered whether it would be reasonable to require Taylor to allow AFC homes for the elderly disabled to operate with twelve residents in areas zoned R-1A. The Court found that Taylor faced no significant financial or administrative burdens in accommodating Smith & Lee. It also found that such an accommodation would not fundamentally alter the residential nature of areas zoned for single-family use because the residents at Mortenview live as a family. . . . For these reasons, the Court concluded that the requested accommodation was reasonable. . . .

III . . .

Section Six of the Fair Housing Amendments Act of 1988, P.L. 100–430, 102 Stat. 1620, 42 U.S.C. §3604(f)(1) makes it unlawful

> to discriminate in the sale or rental, or to otherwise make unavailable or deny, a dwelling to any buyer or renter because of a handicap of —
>   (A) that buyer or renter,
>   (B) a person residing in or intending to reside in that dwelling after it is so sold, rented, or made available; or
>   (C) any person associated with that buyer or renter.

Moreover, it defines discrimination to include

> a refusal to make reasonable accommodations in rules, policies, practices, or services, when such accommodations may be necessary to afford such person equal opportunity to use and enjoy a dwelling.

42 U.S.C. §3604(f)(3)(B).

Plaintiffs who allege a violation of 42 U.S.C. §3604(f) may proceed under any or all of three theories: disparate treatment, disparate impact, and failure to make reasonable accommodations. . . . Smith & Lee and the United States have alleged claims under the first and third theories.

A

We begin by considering the District Court's finding that Taylor intentionally discriminated against the handicapped. In this case, plaintiffs may show disparate treatment by proving that the City would have approved Smith & Lee's rezoning petition but for discriminatory animus toward the handicapped. . . . See Village of Arlington Heights v. Metropolitan Hous. Dev. Corp., 429 U.S. 252, 270 (1977). . . .

[The Court rejected the trial court's finding of intentional discrimination. The City's classification of the home as a multifamily use was a reasonable interpretation of the zoning ordinance, which was not alleged to have been passed specifically to exclude handicapped residents from single-family areas. The City's differential treatment of home businesses was reasonable because a 12-person AFC is not comparable to single-family homes whose owners run a home business. Comments of only one member of the City Council did not constitute proof of discrimination. Further, that individual's fears that the AFC would reduce neighboring property values does not necessarily show animus toward the handicapped. The fact that the City had sued to prevent a group home from operating in 1981 did not support an inference that the City's decision roughly ten years later to deny Smith & Lee's rezoning petition was motivated in part by discriminatory animus.]

. . . [Further], it is abundantly clear that the City Council would have denied the petition even if it had not been motivated by an unlawful purpose. . . . The City Council members all testified that they were opposed to Smith & Lee's petition because, as a rule, they are opposed to spot zoning. According to the District Court,

> [e]ach [City official] who testified voiced a fundamental opposition to "spot zoning." They explained that even if Smith & Lee's use of the Mortenview property was not inconsistent with the surrounding property uses, a rezoning of the land could result in future inconsistent uses over which the City would have no control. All witnesses viewed this inability to control the future use of the rezoned property as a burden to the City and a significant interference with its zoning powers.

See City of Taylor, 872 F. Supp. at 441. Significantly, the District "Court accept[ed] the City's objections to 'spot zoning.' . . ." Id. Since Smith & Lee's rezoning petition required that the Mortenview parcel be spot zoned, and since the City Council members were strongly opposed to spot zoning, the evidence is clear that the City Council would have voted to deny Smith & Lee's petition even if it lacked discriminatory animus toward the handicapped.

In sum, we believe the District Court's finding that the City's decision to deny Smith & Lee's zoning petition was motivated by discriminatory animus is erroneous. Moreover, we find that even if the Court's finding were not erroneous, plaintiffs' intentional discrimination claim fails because the City would have taken the same action in the absence of discriminatory animus.

B

Next, we consider the District Court's finding that Taylor violated the FHAA by failing to make reasonable accommodations. We begin by defining the three operative elements of 42 U.S.C. §3604(f)(3)(B): "equal opportunity," "necessary," and "reasonable."

. . . We find persuasive the analysis of courts that define equal opportunity under the FHAA as giving handicapped individuals the right to choose to live in single-family neighborhoods, for that right serves to end the exclusion of handicapped individuals from the American mainstream. . . .

The statute links the term "necessary" to the goal of equal opportunity. See 42 U.S.C. §3604(f)(3)(B) ("accommodation . . . necessary to afford . . . equal opportunity"). Plaintiffs must show that, but for the accommodation, they likely will be denied an equal opportunity to enjoy the housing of their choice. . . .

Finally, with respect to what constitutes "reasonable," the House Report . . . cites Southeastern Community College v. Davis, 442 U.S. 397 (1979), which interpreted Section 504 of the Rehabilitation Act. . . . Under Davis, an accommodation is reasonable unless it requires "a fundamental alteration in the nature of a program" or imposes "undue financial and administrative burdens." 442 U.S. at 410, 412. As the Seventh Circuit has noted, "cost (to the defendant) and benefit (to the plaintiff) merit consideration as well." Bronk v. Ineichen, 54 F.3d 425, 429 (7th Cir. 1995). . . .

. . . Because the elderly disabled can no longer live independently, AFC homes often provide the only means by which this population can continue to live in residential neighborhoods. AFC homes for the elderly disabled in Taylor are in insufficient supply, in part, because, unlike contract AFC homes, which receive state subsidies, AFCs for the elderly disabled must rely solely on residents' payments to meet operating costs. Evidence at trial established that, in Taylor, Michigan, a six-person occupancy limit on for-profit AFCs serving the elderly disabled guarantees a negligible or negative rate of return for investors. . . .

[A]llowing AFCs housing nine elderly disabled residents to operate in Taylor's single-family neighborhoods is reasonable. Michigan already permits AFC homes to operate with six or fewer residents in areas zoned for single-family use. See Mich. Comp. Laws Ann. §125.583b(2) (West 1986). We are not convinced that an additional three residents will fundamentally alter the nature of single-family neighborhoods. The residents of AFC homes live like most of the other families in their neighborhoods. They eat together, and they rely on each other for social activities and succor. Moreover, as none of Mortenview's elderly disabled residents drive, traffic and parking problems should not significantly increase with three more residents. Weighing the benefits to the elderly disabled against the cost to Taylor, we conclude that permitting AFC homes for the elderly disabled to operate with nine residents in neighborhoods zoned for single-family use is a reasonable accommodation.

Nevertheless, Taylor argues that since other AFC homes operate profitably with six or fewer residents, Taylor should not be required to allow more than six residents to occupy an AFC in a single-family neighborhood. . . .

We do not believe the District Court erred. Mortenview does not receive the kinds of government subsidies and insurance payments that other AFC homes serving different populations receive. Accordingly, the District Court concluded that "the economic viability of 'non-contract' homes like Mortenview Manor cannot be fairly compared to that of 'contract' AFC homes receiving external financial support." . . .

For these reasons, we reverse the District Court's finding that the City intentionally discriminated against the elderly disabled when it denied Smith & Lee's rezoning petition. We affirm the Court's judgment that the City must allow AFC homes for the elderly disabled to operate in single-family neighborhoods, but we reverse to the extent the Court required Taylor to allow such homes to operate with more than nine residents. . . .

Note on the Fair Housing Act's Accommodation Requirement

1. *Accommodation by spot zoning.* How would you advise the city to implement the court's order? Must the city rezone the property and bear the risk that the owner will convert it to multifamily use in the future? If the city's concern about spot zoning is enough to overcome evidence of discriminatory intent, won't savvy officials almost always be able to invoke that defense?

2. *The contract/noncontract distinction.* If it is unreasonable for a city to limit for-profit noncontract AFCs to six residents, why is it reasonable to limit the contract homes to six? Presumably, the contract homes would be able to provide more homes if they could operate the homes they run more cost-effectively and make the subsidies they receive from governmental or charitable agencies stretch further. If the need for accommodation arises from the shortage of homes, then what justifies different treatment of the contract homes? If a shortage is the problem, would allowing ten residents be more likely to induce others to enter the field than just allowing the nine necessary to make the homes "economically feasible"? See also Douglas E. Miller, Note, The Fair Housing Act, Oxford House, and the Limits of Local Control over the Regulation of Group Homes for Recovering Addicts, 36 Wm. & Mary L. Rev. 1467 (1995) (analyzing economic viability argument).

Does accommodation become unnecessary under the court's rationale when there is a surfeit of AFC homes? Cf. Bryant Woods Inn, Inc. v. Howard County, Maryland, 124 F.3d 597 (4th Cir. 1997) (denial of variance to group home to expand from 8 to 15 residents not a failure to reasonably accommodate when vacancy rate at other group homes in the county was 18 to 23 percent).

3. *Available where?* What if the city had proved that although there was a waiting list for group homes within Taylor, adjacent towns had surplus capacity? Does the FHAA require every city to make accommodations for group homes if persons protected by the FHAA desire to live in that city? The issue was raised but not resolved in Erdman v. City of Fort Atkinson, 84 F.3d 960 (7th Cir. 1996), in which a developer sued the municipality for refusing to allow a group home for 24 elderly handicapped individuals on a 9-acre plot within Fort Atkinson, even though the adjacent town would allow the home on the adjoining 13-acre plot the developer owned within its borders. Recall the discussion of this issue, in the context of adult use zoning, at pp. 229–30. The most recent cases suggest that the availability of alternative sites, even in the same neighborhood, is not determinative. See, e.g., Dr. Gertrude A. Barber Center, Inc. v. Peters Township, 273 F. Supp. 2d 643, 655 (W.D. Pa. 2003) (issue is whether municipality has failed to reasonably accommodate the right of the plaintiff to operate the group home in the home and neighborhood of plaintiff's choice); United States v. City of Chicago Heights, 161 F. Supp. 2d 819, 836 (N.D. Ill. 2001) (the FHAA "speaks to the denial of the opportunity to live in particular dwellings, not the denial of housing all together").

4. *Burden of persuasion.* Who should bear the burden of persuasion on the issue of whether six residents are too few to be profitable, or whether ten would "fundamentally alter" the nature of the neighborhood? The majority of circuits require a plaintiff to make an initial showing that the accommodation plaintiff requests is necessary and reasonable on its face, at which point the burden shifts to the defendant to show that the accommodation is in fact unreasonable. See Oconomowoc Residential Programs v. City of Milwaukee, 300 F.3d 775, 783 (7th Cir. 2002) (surveying cases).

5. *Defining "reasonable."* Should the determination whether a requested accommodation is reasonable be an explicit cost/benefit calculation, assessing the benefits of the accommodation to the plaintiff (or the plaintiff's clients) versus the costs the accommodation imposes on the municipality (and the neighbors for which the municipality may be acting)? See, e.g., *Oconomowoc*, supra, 300 F.3d at 784 (accommodation must be "both efficacious and proportional to the costs to implement it"). But see Hemisphere Building Co. v. Village of Richton Park, 171 F.3d 437, 439–40 (7th Cir. 1999) (balancing "the interests of [the municipality] in adhering to its zoning ordinance . . . against the interest of handicapped people in being able to obtain housing suitable for their special needs at the lowest possible price . . . would be an unwieldy analytical task for a court to undertake").

When is the departure from the local government's regulatory scheme just too much to ask? See, e.g., Lapid-Laurel, L.L.C. v. Zoning Board of Adjustment, 284 F.3d 442, 457 (3d Cir. 2002) (municipality met burden of proving that traffic safety concerns rendered the proposed accommodation unreasonable); Dadian v. Village of Wilmette, 269 F.3d 831, 838–39 (7th Cir. 2001) (test is whether accommodation is so "at odds with the purposes behind the rule that it would be a fundamental and unreasonable change"); Forest City Daly Housing, Inc. v. Town of North Hempstead, 175 F.3d 144, 152 (2d Cir. 1999) ("if a building permit would not be granted even for comparable 'traditional' residences (that is, residences where persons without disabilities can live) in the relevant area, a municipality is not required to make accommodations that would facilitate a building permit for housing designed for the disabled").

6. *Defining "necessary."* If an accommodation is needed to make the housing more affordable to the disabled, is the accommodation "necessary"? Compare *Hemisphere*, supra, 171 F.3d at 440 (the duty of reasonable accommodation applies only to "rules, policies, etc. that hurt handicapped people by reason of their handicap, rather than that hurt them solely by virtue of what they have in common with other people, such as a limited amount of money to spend on housing"), with Giebeler v. M & B Associates, 343 F.3d 1143, 1153–54 (9th Cir. 2003) (rejecting that reasoning and holding that the FHAA may require accommodations necessitated by the inability of the disabled to generate income by working).

7. *Overriding local definitions of family.* Like the Michigan statute referred to in *Smith & Lee*, many states have attempted to ease the siting problems of group homes by mandating that they be considered single-family residential uses. Such statutes often cap the number of residents, however, at between six and eight. See Lester D. Steinman, The Effect of Land-Use Restrictions on the Establishment of Community Residences for the Disabled: A National Study, 19 Urb. Law. 1 (1987). What weight should the *Smith & Lee* court have given the state's determination that group homes with more than six residents should not qualify as a single-family residential use?

For an overview of state legislation overriding or preempting local zoning that excludes group homes, see Arlene S. Kanter, A Home of One's Own: The Fair Housing Amendments Act of 1988 and Housing Discrimination Against People with Mental Disabilities, 43 Am. U. L. Rev. 925, 974–79 (1994). See also Chapter 9B for discussion of legislative and judicial attempts to overcome the difficulty of siting locally undesirable land uses.

Note on the Fair Housing Act Amendments

1. *Disparate treatment claims.* Most courts have adapted the analytical framework used in Title VII (employment-related) disparate treatment claims for fair housing claims.

The Ninth Circuit, for example, has held that a plaintiff challenging the denial of a permit can make out a prima facie case of disparate treatment only by showing that:

1) plaintiff is a member of a protected class;
2) plaintiff applied for a permit and was qualified to receive it;
3) the permit was denied despite plaintiff having been qualified; and
4) defendant approved a permit for a similarly situated party at a time relatively near the time plaintiff was denied its conditional use permit.

Gamble v. City of Escondido, 104 F.3d 300 (9th Cir. 1997). Cf. Regional Economic Community Action Program, Inc. v. City of Middletown 294 F.3d 35, 49 (2d Cir. 2002) (to make out a prima facie case, plaintiffs must present evidence that "animus against the protected group was a significant factor in the position taken by the municipal decision-makers themselves or by those to whom the decision-makers were knowingly responsive"). If the plaintiff makes out a prima facie case of disparate treatment, the burden shifts to the defendant to set forth a legitimate, nondiscriminatory reason for the disparate treatment. Sanghvi v. City of Claremont, 328 F.3d 532, 536 (9th Cir. 2003).

2. *Disparate impact claims.* Alternatively, plaintiffs invoking the FHAA may proceed under a disparate impact claim that a land use regulation has a disproportionate effect on people with disabilities. Most courts adopt the Title VIII framework discussed at pp. 705–08. See, e.g., Tsombanidis v. West Haven Fire Department, 352 F.3d 565, 575 (2d Cir. 2003).

3. *Requiring conditional use permits.* Under the FHAA, can cities require that group homes or other facilities for people with disabilities obtain conditional use permits (or other permits) if similar facilities for people without disabilities are not required to obtain a permit? See Community Housing Trust v. Department of Consumer & Regulatory Affairs, 257 F. Supp. 2d 208 (D.D.C. 2003) (granting plaintiff's motion for summary judgment on claim that requirement that group home for mentally disabled receive a certificate of occupancy violated FHAA). But cf. United States v. Village of Palatine, 37 F.3d 1230 (7th Cir. 1994) (requirement that group homes obtain a special use permit and submit to a public hearing was not a failure to make a reasonable accommodation, because the burden of applying for the permit did not outweigh the village's interest in public participation and because the village had an "exemplary" record of responding to the needs of the handicapped).

4. *Occupancy limits.* The FHAA exempts from its proscriptions "any reasonable local, State or Federal restrictions regarding the maximum number of occupants permitted to occupy a dwelling." 42 U.S.C. §3607(b)(1) (2005). The Supreme Court ruled in City of Edmonds v. Oxford House, Inc., 514 U.S. 725 (1995), that the exemption does not extend to an ordinance defining "family" as "persons [without regard to number] related by genetics, adoption, or marriage, or a group of five or fewer [unrelated] persons." The Court held that the occupancy exemption applies only to "total occupancy limits, i.e., numerical ceilings that serve to prevent overcrowding in living quarters." Id. at 728. For analysis of the case, see The Supreme Court, 1994 Term: Fair Housing Act: Zoning Law-Occupancy Limits on Group Homes, 109 Harv. L. Rev. 309 (1995).

5. *Safety requirements.* The courts have routinely struck down safety requirements for group homes that are stricter than those imposed on single-family homes of similar density. While the FHAA does not prohibit special safety standards for the protection of people with disabilities, that protection must be "warranted by the unique and specific needs and abilities of those handicapped persons." Marbrunak, Inc. v. City of Stow, 974 F.2d 43, 47 (6th Cir. 1992) (extensive fire safety requirements not shown to be necessary to protect mentally retarded residents); Bangerter v. Orem City Corp., 46 F.3d

1491, 1503–04 (10th Cir. 1995) ("restrictions that are narrowly tailored to the particular individuals affected could be acceptable . . . if the benefit to the handicapped . . . clearly outweigh[s] whatever burden may result to them").

If the safety requirements imposed for people with disabilities are no greater than those imposed for all other people, could refusal to waive the requirements for a group home constitute a failure to accommodate?

6. *Dispersion ordinances.* Communities sometimes oppose group homes in part because they fear that allowing one will open the floodgates and that the neighborhood will then become a group home "ghetto." To prevent clustering of group homes and to ensure that no neighborhood bears an unfair share of the burdens, some local governments and some states have passed dispersion ordinances, prohibiting various community residential treatment facilities from locating within a specified distance of similar facilities. See, e.g., Mich. Comp. Laws §125.286g (2005) (1,500 feet). See also Wis. Stat. §62.23(7)(i) (2005) (allowing cities to limit the population in community-based residential facilities to 1 percent of a city's population or 25, whichever is greater). Challenges to dispersion ordinances under the Equal Protection Clause were not successful, even after *Cleburne*. See, e.g., Shannon & Riordan v. Board of Zoning Appeals, 451 N.W.2d 479 (Wis. Ct. App. 1989). Initially, challenges under the FHAA were unsuccessful as well. FamilyStyle of St. Paul, Inc. v. City of St. Paul, 923 F.2d 91 (8th Cir. 1991). Subsequent courts, however, have uniformly held that spacing requirements violate the FHAA. See, e.g., Oconomowoc Residential Programs v. City of Milwaukee, 300 F.3d 775 (7th Cir. 2002). For analyses of dispersion requirements, see Brian E. Davis, Comment, The State Giveth and the Court Taketh Away: Preserving the Municipality's Ability to Zone for Group Homes Under the Fair Housing Amendments Act of 1988, 59 U. Pitt. L. Rev. 193 (1997); Kevin J. Zanner, Comment, Dispersion Requirements for the Siting of Group Homes: Reconciling New York's Padavan Law with the Fair Housing Amendments Act of 1988, 44 Buff. L. Rev. 249 (1996). See also pp. 754–60 for a discussion of fairness in the siting of locally undesirable land uses.

7. *The FHAA and private covenants.* HUD's regulations state that the FHAA prohibits "enforcing covenants . . . which preclude the sale or rental of a dwelling to any person because of . . . handicap." 24 C.F.R. §100.80(b)(3) (2005). See, e.g., Hill v. Community of Damien, 911 P.2d 861 (N.M. 1996) (group home qualified as a single-family use for purposes of restrictive covenant; if covenant were interpreted to exclude the group home, it would violate the FHAA). Pages 554–62 discuss public policy limits on the substance of private covenants.

8. *Neighbors' liability.* Can neighbors be liable under the FHAA for opposing the siting of a group home? A few courts have found such liability. See, e.g., Advocacy Center for Persons with Disabilities, Inc. v. Woodlands Estates Association, 192 F. Supp. 2d 1344 (M.D. Fla. 2002). The Eastern District of Michigan was sharply critical of applying the FHAA to average citizens, however, reasoning that protesting neighbors had a First Amendment right to express their concerns. Michigan Protection & Advocacy Service, Inc. v. Babin, 799 F. Supp. 695 (E.D. Mich. 1992), aff'd on other grounds, 18 F.3d 337 (6th Cir. 1994). See also Gourlay v. Forest Lake Estates Civic Association of Port Richey, Inc., 276 F. Supp. 2d 1222, 1231 (M.D. Fla. 2003) (expressing concern about First Amendment rights of neighbors). Cf. White v. Lee, 227 F.3d 1214, 1232–37 (9th Cir. 2000) (HUD investigation of neighbors who opposed conversion of a motel into a facility that might house mentally disabled violated the neighbors' First Amendment rights). See generally David Franklin, Comment, Civil Rights v. Civil Liberties? The Legality of State Court Lawsuits Under the Fair Housing Act, 63 U. Chi. L. Rev. 1607 (1996).

Note on the Rehabilitation Act of 1973 and the Americans with Disabilities Act of 1990

Providers of facilities for people with disabilities sometimes are precluded from using the FHAA because they seek to site nonresidential facilities. Courts have allowed such providers to invoke the Americans with Disabilities Act of 1990 (ADA), 42 U.S.C. §12101 et seq. (2005), or the Rehabilitation Act of 1973, 29 U.S.C. §794 (2005). The ADA provides that "no qualified individual with a disability shall, by reason of such disability, be excluded from participation in or be denied the benefits of the services, programs, or activities of a public entity, or be subjected to discrimination by any such entity." 42 U.S.C. §12132 (2005). The Rehabilitation Act provides that "[n]o otherwise qualified individual with a disability . . . shall, solely by reason of her or his disability, be excluded from the participation in, be denied the benefits of, or be subjected to discrimination under any program or activity receiving Federal financial assistance." 29 U.S.C. §794(a) (2005). The access requirements imposed by the ADA are discussed at pp. 450–52.

Local governments, of course, are public entities, and many have received federal financial assistance, so both protections may be triggered. The issue is whether land use regulation is a "benefit" under the Rehabilitation Act or a "service, program or activity" under the ADA. Bay Area Addiction Research & Treatment, Inc. v. City of Antioch, 179 F.3d 725 (9th Cir. 1999), surveys the cases and concludes that both acts apply to zoning. See also Regional Economic Community Action Program, Inc. v. City of Middletown, 294 F.3d 35, 46 (2d Cir. 2002) (ADA and Rehabilitation Act apply to zoning decisions); MX Group, Inc. v. City of Covington, 293 F.3d 326, 332 (6th Cir. 2002) (applying the ADA to denial of a zoning permit, and amendment to zoning ordinance that foreclosed opportunity of methadone clinic to locate within town). In general, the courts have regarded the elements and burden of proof in ADA and Rehabilitation Act claims as parallel to those in FHAA litigation. See, e.g. Regional Economic Community Action Program, supra.

Chapter Nine

The Regional Obligations of Municipalities

When a proposed land use would have no significant impact beyond local boundaries, most observers agree that government planning decisions should be left entirely to local officials. The advantages of local control are summarized in Robert G. Healy & John S. Rosenberg, Land Use and the States 6–7 (2d ed. 1979):

> Our working presumption here will be that local control of land use is, other things equal, the most desirable arrangement. In judging the merits of most land use changes, local authorities are not only better informed about the facts of the situation, but are also (at least ideally) more responsive to the interests affected. When higher levels of government deal with such problems, they typically must create layers of bureaucracy simply to channel the appropriate information to decision makers. The decision makers, moreover, are responsible to a constituency which is probably far larger than the group of citizens affected by most land use decisions. Thus, by virtue not only of tradition, but of efficiency and political responsiveness, there is a strong case for local control of land use.

Local control becomes problematic, however, when a proposed land use would affect the welfare of persons living beyond local boundaries. For example, suppose the owner of land situated at site X in Figure 9-1 is proposing an activity that would affect the utility of all land located within the dotted circle. Site X is located within City A, a municipality of State S. Some of the land that would be affected by the proposed activity at site X lies in City B and some in an unincorporated area of County C.

Locally based land use regulation can result in inefficient decisions when the net spillover effects of an activity are harmful. A billboard or garbage dump near municipal boundaries might harm outsiders in ways local officials would be likely to ignore. Because the municipality reaps all the benefits of the land use (such as tax revenue, employment for residents, and the political support of the property owner) but is able to externalize some of the costs to nearby municipalities and property owners, the risk is that local officials will be too quick to grant a permit.

When a proposed activity would have net extraterritorial benefits — by creating new opportunities for outsiders to shop, work, or reside in City A — City A's officials might ignore those benefits and refuse to permit the landowner's activity even when it would be efficient from a regional standpoint. This is the problem of locally undesirable land uses (LULUs): Communities are reluctant to host facilities, such as group homes, low- and

731

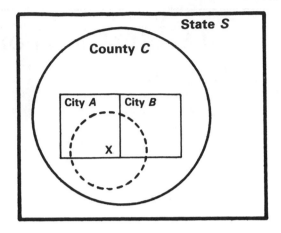

FIGURE 9-1

moderate-income housing, prisons, or waste management facilities, that impose (or are perceived to impose) concentrated local costs, even when the more diffuse regional benefits outweigh those costs. The market failure here is one of positive, rather than negative, externalities. Because the benefits of the facility are spread over the entire region while the costs are concentrated on the host municipality, that community is likely to be too slow to allow development.

This chapter addresses both the *private* rights that landowners and housing consumers may have against parochial government decisionmaking and possible *intergovernmental* solutions to the same problem. Intergovernmental solutions may involve the creation of rights between governments or the reassignment of governmental functions to different government units. For example, if the land use at site X would impose costs outside City A, State S might: (a) entitle City B and County C to enjoin that use (or to recover damages from City A); (b) compensate B and C from state funds; or (c) confer regulatory control over the activity in controversy to County C, or to the state itself.

When a higher-level government adopts land use regulations, they may take either of two dramatically different forms. Assume State S becomes involved in regulating the activity proposed for site X. How might its controls relate to those of City A? First, State S might *preempt* City A's controls. This seems to be the correct strategy when the extraterritorial impacts of an activity are on balance beneficial, as in the case of the regionally beneficial prison. In other words, efficiency will generally be enhanced if local governments are unable to veto development that has regional benefits. Alternatively, the state controls could simply *supplement* the local ones; a developer would then have to pass muster twice, with both the state and municipality having independent veto power. A "double veto" system of this sort is theoretically defensible only for an activity that would have net external costs, for instance, a garbage dump at the edge of a city.

The next section addresses the situation in which local governments fail to take into account the negative externalities that land uses at their borders may impose on neighboring jurisdictions and property owners. The chapter then turns to the problem of positive externalities, in which the host community fails to adequately consider the benefits a land use within its borders will bring to the region as a whole. The discussion first focuses on the siting of LULUs, such as waste management facilities. The chapter then moves to two especially common problems: municipalities' attempts to exclude low- and moderate-income housing, and municipal growth management.

As you review these materials, keep in mind that traditional land use litigation only requires the courts to adjust the rights and duties between a municipality and a property owner or among property owners. Challenges to parochial land use policies require the courts to decide if diffuse groups, such as housing consumers in a large region, have rights against a municipality, and, if so, what their remedies should be. Although the cases in this chapter show that courts indeed can intervene to curb local abuses, the cases also suggest that there are limits to judicial capacities to achieve regional coordination of land use controls.

A.   *Obligations to Consider the Negative Spillover Effects of Uses Located Near Municipal Borders*

Borough of Cresskill v. Borough of Dumont
104 A.2d 441 (N.J. 1954)

[Dumont rezoned a one-block parcel of land in the extreme northeast corner of the borough from a residential classification to a classification that would permit the development of a shopping center. Directly across the street from this block were residential areas of three other boroughs. Those three boroughs, as well as several landowners within and without Dumont, successfully challenged the validity of the rezoning in the trial court.]

VANDERBILT, C.J. . .
. . . The appellant . . . [argues that the language of the zoning enabling act mandates] that the responsibility of a municipality for zoning halts at the municipal boundary lines without regard to the effect of its zoning ordinances on adjoining and nearby land outside the municipality. Such a view might prevail where there are large undeveloped areas at the borders of two contiguous towns, but it cannot be tolerated where, as here, the area is built up and one cannot tell when one is passing from one borough to another. Knickerbocker Road and Massachusetts Avenue are not Chinese walls separating Dumont from the adjoining boroughs. At the very least Dumont owes a duty to hear any residents and taxpayers of adjoining municipalities who may be adversely affected by proposed zoning changes and to give as much consideration to their rights as [it] would to those of residents and taxpayers of Dumont. To do less would be to make a fetish out of invisible municipal boundary lines and a mockery of the principles of zoning. There is no merit to the defendant's contention. The views set forth in Duffcon Concrete Prod. v. Borough of Cresskill, 64 A.2d 347, 349–50 (N.J. 1949), apply here with equal force:

> What may be the most appropriate use of any particular property depends not only on all the conditions, physical, economic and social, prevailing within the municipality and its needs, present and reasonably prospective, but also on the nature of the entire region in which the municipality is located and the use to which the land in that region has been or may be put most advantageously. The effective development of a region should not and cannot be made to depend upon the adventitious location of municipal boundaries, often prescribed decades or even centuries ago, and based in many instances on considerations of geography, of commerce, or of politics that are no longer significant with respect to zoning. The direction of growth of residential areas on the one hand and of industrial concentration on the other refuses to be governed by such artificial lines. Changes in methods of transportation as well as in living

conditions have served only to accentuate the unreality in dealing with zoning problems on the basis of the territorial limits of a municipality. . . .

[The court then held that Dumont's map amendment constituted illegal spot zoning.]

Note on Private Challenges to Parochial Decisions

1. *The political influence of nonvoters.* Will local politicians necessarily ignore the interests of nonresident individuals or neighboring governments? How might individual outsiders bring political pressure to bear on the deciding government? Through campaign contributions? By inducing *their own* local officials to protest and to threaten retaliation? By seeking to have higher levels of government (county or state agencies or legislatures) intervene?

2. *Notice and opportunity to be heard.* Does *Dumont's* mandate that the deciding municipality take into account the interests of nearby nonresidents mean that municipalities must give such nonresidents notice of any pending land use matters that might affect their interests? See, e.g., Scott v. City of Indian Wells, 492 P.2d 1137 (Cal. 1972) (en banc) (imposing duty to give adjoining nonresident landowners "notice to the extent given similarly situated city residents" and imposing "duty to hear their views"). Many state zoning enabling acts now require such notice. See, e.g., R.I. Gen. Laws §45-24-53(c)(2) (2004) (requiring notice to adjoining property owners regardless of whether the property is within the jurisdiction).

Must nonresidents be given the same rights to *participate* in hearings and other procedures as residents? See, e.g., Smagula v. Town of Hooksett, 834 A.2d 333, 337 (N.H. 2003) (owners of property in neighboring municipality may participate in a protest petition against the decision of a municipality's zoning board of adjustment or planning board so long as they have a "sufficient interest" in the outcome). How valuable are these procedural rights if the deciding municipality has no specific duty to weigh the adjoining municipalities' concerns equally with its own residents' interests?

3. *Duty to consider.* Which of the following interpretations should be given to the court's admonition that Dumont must "give as much consideration to [the nonresidents'] rights as [it] would to those of residents and taxpayers of Dumont"?

a. The contents of planning-staff reports, environmental impact statements, and other relevant inputs must include discussion of any external effects. As long as this is done, courts will review the final decision in the usual way. See, e.g., City of Rye v. Korff, 671 N.Y.S.2d 526 (App. Div. 1998) (municipality had adequately considered effects on adjoining municipality in its environmental impact review, even if the adjacent municipality would have required additional mitigation measures if it had been the lead agency).

b. *Dumont* affects the standard of judicial review. When a local policy affects outsiders, a reviewing court is required (pick one or more):

(1)   to drop any presumption of validity for the city's decision;
(2)   to place on the local government the burden of proving the "reasonableness," "rational basis," or what-have-you, of its policy;
(3)   to insist that the local government have a rational basis for believing that the policy reasonably relates to the *regional*, as opposed to the *local*, welfare;
(4)   to undertake a de novo cost/benefit analysis of the local policy, and strike it down if the court decides the policy is inefficient from a regional standpoint; or
(5)   to invalidate the policy if the court concludes that the policy would not have been adopted if the affected outsiders had been entitled to vote in local elections.

4. *Consistency with a neighboring jurisdiction's comprehensive plan?* In Ferraro v. Zoning Board of Adjustment, 574 A.2d 38 (N.J. 1990), the plaintiff owned a plot of land that was divided by the line separating Holmdel from Hazlet. The portion in Hazlet was zoned "business highway," while the portion in Holmdel was zoned for residential use. The owner wanted to build a car wash, and applied to Holmdel for a use variance, which Holmdel denied. When the property owner appealed, the trial court held that Holmdel had ceded its jurisdiction over the parcel's land use to Hazlet in a joint resolution between the two townships regarding taxes on the land. The Supreme Court refused to read the agreement to divest Holmdel of its zoning power over the parcel, but warned that "in exercising its own zoning responsibilities, Holmdel is obligated to give significant weight to the zoning ordinance and plan of the adjacent municipality, Hazlet, as well as to the character and uses of surrounding property . . . " Id. at 44. How ought a court reviewing any subsequent action on the variance request evaluate whether Holmdel has given due regard to Hazlet's plan?

5. *Damages as a remedy available to outsiders.* Should local governments be liable in damages for nuisance spillovers (assuming that the liable local government would be entitled to indemnity from the private developer whose project caused the external damage)? Would current nuisance law, discussed in Chapter 6A, give the *Dumont* plaintiffs any private remedies against the development they oppose?

City of Del Mar v. City of San Diego
183 Cal. Rptr. 898 (Ct. App. 1982)

WIENER, Associate Justice.

This appeal by the City of Del Mar (Del Mar) describes the negative, almost frightening, physical, social and financial costs imposed upon society by the further urbanization of the City of San Diego (San Diego) in its creation of the new community called North City West. Del Mar's emotionally compelling narrative challenges San Diego's willingness to extend its megalopolis northward changing the sparse development of approximately 4,286 acres of agricultural land located 20 miles from downtown San Diego to a bustling urban enclave consisting at completion of about 40,000 people from the upper and middle classes living in expensive homes. . . . The trial court [held that San Diego acted properly in giving threshold approval for the first phase of North City West]. . . . As we shall explain, although it is undisputed the project will have numerous adverse environmental impacts on the region, we nevertheless conclude that San Diego did not abuse its discretion in approving the steps at issue here as a rational accommodation of the social, economic and environmental interests with which the city must concern itself. We will, therefore, affirm the trial court's decision. . . .

FACTUAL AND PROCEDURAL BACKGROUND

. . . Although primarily residential, North City West, located near the northern boundary of the City of San Diego is designed to incorporate many self-contained community concepts; one of the nine development phases is scheduled to be an employment center and commercial service centers will be located at various points in the project. . . .

Carmel Valley is the first of the nine phases scheduled for development. Situated on 358 acres, it will contain 2,065 units of various types including single family, duplex, cluster and garden apartments. Population for the phase is projected at approximately 5,000 persons.

In 1979, the San Diego City Council approved the North City West Planned District Ordinance . . . which provide[s] the necessary zoning, regulations and procedures for the submission of subdivision maps and development plans of the Carmel Valley phase. . . .

Within weeks of San Diego's action, Del Mar sought a writ of mandate and declaratory relief challenging San Diego's approval of the North City West Planned District Ordinance. . . . It claimed . . . [that] San Diego's approval of the project failed to adequately consider the welfare of the entire San Diego region as required by Associated Home Builders v. City of Livermore, 557 P.2d 473 (Cal. 1976) (en banc). . . .

DISCUSSION . . .

. . . Recognizing that any zoning decision involves a cost-benefit accommodation of competing interests, Del Mar's attack is two-pronged. On the cost side, Del Mar points to the substantial adverse environmental impacts on the San Diego region which will result from the North City West development. . . . On the benefits side, Del Mar contends that North City West is an ineffective contribution to solution of the regional housing need because attempts to provide low and moderate income housing opportunities within the development are inadequate. Thus, by focusing upon the regional cost and questioning the regional benefit, Del Mar argues that the North City West approvals are unreasonable.

A . . .

In *Livermore*, the California Supreme Court reviewed the validity of a municipal . . . [growth management] ordinance which had significant spillover effects on the entire San Francisco Bay region. . . . [T]he court noted, "[M]unicipalities are not isolated islands remote from the needs and problems of the area in which they are located; thus an ordinance, superficially reasonable from the limited viewpoint of the municipality, may be disclosed as unreasonable when viewed from a larger perspective." Although rejecting an argument that spillover ordinances should be subject to strict scrutiny — invalid unless necessary to achieve a compelling state interest — the court nonetheless required municipalities to evaluate more than their local self-interest in enacting such land use regulations. . . .

> These considerations impel us to the conclusion that the proper constitutional test is one which inquires whether the ordinance reasonably relates to the welfare of those whom it significantly affects. If its impact is limited to the city boundaries, the inquiry may be limited accordingly; if, as alleged here, the ordinance may strongly influence the supply and distribution of housing for an entire metropolitan region, judicial inquiry must consider the welfare of that region.[4]

Id.

---

4. Although *Livermore*'s statement of the proper considerations is undoubtedly correct, inherent in the statement is something of a theoretical inconsistency. The concept of judicial deference to legislative determinations is based, at least in part, on the assumption that legislative abuse is constrained by the political process. One can normally assume that a city council will accurately assess the best interests of the city's residents; if it does not, the residents may express their dissatisfaction in the next election. But when a city council is asked to consider and evaluate the interests of non-residents (i.e., inhabitants of the region surrounding the municipality), there would appear to be a latent predisposition toward undervaluation of these interests even in the most well-meaning of municipal governing bodies. See Willemsen & Phillips, Down-Zoning and Exclusionary Zoning in California Law, 31 Hastings L.J. 103, 136 (1979).

Del Mar suggests what may be a solution to this dilemma when it argues that once a plaintiff has presented evidence sufficient to demonstrate the existence of significant regional spillover, the burden should shift to the enacting city to demonstrate the regional reasonableness of the land use regulation. Of course, the city need only prove it was "'fairly debatable,' Village of Euclid v. Ambler Realty Co., 272 U.S. 365, 388 (1926), that the ordinance reasonably relates to the regional welfare. . . ." *Livermore*, 557 P.2d 473. We need not decide the issue here, however, since we conclude that even if San Diego were to bear the burden of proof, it has carried that burden in this case.

Although *Livermore* and the instant case are similar in that both involve significant regional spillovers, it is also important to recognize some relevant distinctions. The Livermore ordinance was exclusionary in character. . . .

By contrast, the North City West approvals are inclusionary in nature. San Diego has attempted to provide for its share of regional new housing need. Although Del Mar argues that substantial adverse environmental impacts will beset the region as a result of the construction of North City West, San Diego is in no way shielded from these impacts. There are clearly regional spillovers which San Diego must take into account, but unlike Livermore, San Diego is not able to shift the entire burden of its zoning decision to other municipalities in the region. In that sense, the San Diego action is considerably less suspect.

B

The trial court found and San Diego does not dispute that the construction of North City West will cause at least some significant adverse regional impacts. *Livermore* thus provides the applicable legal standard against which the reasonableness of San Diego's actions must be measured. The trial court correctly applied this standard in developing findings of fact and conclusions of law. Included among them were Finding of Fact No. 26 and Conclusion of Law No. 1:

> 26. The approvals by the City of San Diego of the Carmel Valley Precise Plan, the Carmel Valley Design Element and the Planned District Ordinance whether viewed alone, or in conjunction with City of San Diego land use policies, promote the general welfare of the region significantly affected thereby in that:
>
>   a.   They provide needed housing in the region and in the north San Diego area and serve to satisfy housing demand in those areas;
>   b.   They aid in the reasonable distribution of new development along major transportation corridors and from a geographical standpoint within San Diego and the region;
>   c.   They provide for residences near employment centers;
>   d.   They will provide employment opportunities in the region and generally benefit the economy of the region;
>   e.   The north city and north county areas will probably experience substantial population growth without the approvals and may undergo incremental growth of negative patterns without an overall plan; and
>   f.   They provide relief from growth pressures for development in the north city and county areas. . . .
>
>   1.   The approvals . . . relating to . . . North City West represent a reasonable accommodation of the competing interests of the region affected thereby.

In addition, the trial court addressed each of Del Mar's arguments dealing with specific regional impacts (e.g., air quality, water supply, sewage treatment, etc.), the sum total of which Del Mar asserted made the North City West approvals unreasonable. The trial court found otherwise. Accordingly, since the correct standard was applied, we must determine whether the trial court's findings are supported by substantial evidence. . . .

Foundationally, it should be recognized that the parties make profoundly contradictory assumptions which affect the presentation of the issue in all its aspects. Del Mar proceeds on the premise that North City West will cause all the various regional impacts which it documents, or that in other words, but for North City West, the articulated impacts would not occur. San Diego, on the other hand, views itself as merely planning for the inevitable population growth of the north city region. . . .

... [T]he evidence includes the County of San Diego's estimate that north county population in the year 2000 will be 26,000 persons less if North City West is built. This constitutes more than substantial evidence to support the trial court's finding that "[i]f the North City West community planning area were not built as planned, residents would still come to live in the areas of the north county and north City. ..." Moreover, the addition of 26,000 additional persons to north county would create many if not most of the same adverse regional impacts which North City West's 40,000 residents will. ...

D

In conclusion, applying the standard enunciated in *Livermore*, we conclude that San Diego's approval of the North City West Planned District Ordinance ... bears a real and substantial relationship to the general welfare of the entire San Diego region. Specifically, San Diego has adequately researched and considered the numerous competing interests in the region, and in view of the demonstrated need for new housing, the North City West approvals at this stage constitute a reasonable accommodation of these interests. ...

Note on Local Governments Litigating Against Other Local Governments

1. *Statutory rights to receive notice and to participate.* Cal. Gov't Code §66453 (West 2005) establishes a procedure whereby municipalities may make recommendations about a proposed subdivision in an adjoining municipality, if the subdivision is within three miles of the commenting municipality's border, and directs that the municipality with jurisdiction over the subdivision "shall consider these recommendations." Should California courts interpret this statute as requiring that such subdivision decisions be measured by the *Livermore* standard? By some higher standard?

N.Y. Town Law §264 (McKinney 2005) requires towns considering zoning ordinances or amendments affecting property within 500 feet of another jurisdiction's borders to notify the adjacent jurisdiction of the proposal. In addition, N.Y. Gen. Mun. Law §239-m (McKinney 2005) provides that if a municipality wants to change the zoning classification of land within 500 feet of the boundary of another municipality, it must refer the matter to the *county* planning agency for evaluation. If the county agency recommends modification or disapproval of a proposed action, the municipal agency having jurisdiction "shall not act contrary to such recommendation except by a vote of a majority plus one of all the members thereof" and must "set forth the reasons for the contrary action" in a report. Greater deference therefore is given to the county planning agency's comments than to the adjoining municipality's comments. Is that appropriate? Are the supermajority and "reasons" requirements preferable to the California courts' approach?

Rather than rely on distance alone as a proxy for potential externalities, Conn. Gen. Stat. §8-7d(f) (2005) requires a municipality to notify adjoining municipalities of any proposed zoning matter affecting property within 500 feet of the adjoining municipality or involving a project in which a significant amount of traffic, sewage or water drainage, or water runoff will enter the adjoining municipality. What are the risks of trying to specify the impacts that might trigger a neighboring municipality's concern rather than using an objective measure such as distance as the trigger? See Lauer v. Zoning Commission, 600 A.2d 310 (Conn. 1991) (because complex factual inquiries required under the statute are difficult to make within the time allowed, the requirement should not be construed as jurisdictional).

2. *The standing of municipalities to sue their neighbors.* Many courts have held that municipalities have standing to challenge a neighboring jurisdiction's zoning decisions in court, if the municipality can demonstrate that it would be "substantially, directly and adversely affected in its corporate capacity." Village of Barrington Hills v. Village of Hoffman Estates, 410 N.E.2d 37 (Ill. 1980). See also, e.g., City of Brentwood v. Metropolitan Board of Zoning Appeals, 149 S.W.3d 49, 58 (Tenn. Ct. App. 2004) (collecting cases and concluding that the courts have granted standing "when the actions of one local government cause (1) reduction in another local government's revenue due to decreased property values, (2) depreciation in the value of another local government's property, (3) interference with another local government's ability to provide police and fire protection, (4) increased safety hazards on roads, (5) interference with another local government's construction of court-ordered improvements to a sewer and water system, (6) interference with another local government's urban development plan, (7) use of property inconsistent with the character of the adjoining area, and (8) general impairment to the health, safety, or welfare of the residents of another local government").

But some courts refuse to grant standing on the basis of such concerns. See, e.g., D & R Properties v. Newbury Township, 2004 WL 2941267 (Ohio App. Dec. 2004) (adjoining municipality's assertion that a proposed asphalt plant would have a negative impact on its road traffic, air quality, and safety was insufficient to give it standing to intervene in applicant's appeal from denial of a variance). Even courts that typically recognize the standing of jurisdictions to challenge a neighboring jurisdiction's decisions may deny such standing when it would interfere with statewide interests. See, e.g., City of Elgin v. County of Cook, 660 N.E.2d 875, 884, (Ill. 1995) (municipality would not be given standing to challenge a neighboring jurisdiction's decision to allow a landfill because if such standing were granted "it is unlikely that any significant landfill, regardless of how necessary and environmentally sound, [would] ever again be developed in Illinois").

A government that lacks standing in its "governmental" capacity nevertheless may have standing in its capacity as an owner of affected lands. See, e.g., Town of Pleasant Valley v. Town of Poughkeepsie Planning Board, 736 N.Y.S.2d 70 (App. Div. 2001). See generally John J. Michalik, Annotation, Standing of Municipal Corporation or Other Governmental Body to Attack Zoning of Land Lying Outside Its Borders, 49 A.L.R.3d 1126 (1973 & Supp. 2004).

3. *A municipality's substantive rights. City of Del Mar* applies the *Livermore* test in a dispute between neighboring municipalities, even though *Livermore* involved a challenge by private plaintiffs. Should the standard of review (or the allocation of the burdens of production or persuasion) vary when the plaintiff is a co-equal government? Should the presumption of rationality usually given to a local government's decisions apply when two municipalities (both entitled to the presumption) are at war? See, e.g., Borough of Allendale v. Township Committee, 404 A.2d 50 (N.J. Super. Ct. Law Div. 1979) (suggesting that presumption should drop out in such a case), aff'd on other grounds, 426 A.2d 73 (N.J. Super. Ct. App. Div. 1981).

What if the fight is between the deciding government and a "higher" level of government such as a county? See, e.g., Mayor & Board of Aldermen of Town of Prentiss v. Jefferson Davis County, 874 So. 2d 962 (Miss. 2004) (court correctly required county to prove need for a special permit from town by clear and convincing evidence).

Should the presumption be different if the fight is between a deciding government and a special purpose government? In Corona-Norco Unified School District v. City of Corona, 21 Cal. Rptr. 2d 803 (Ct. App. 1993), for example, the court rejected the school district's challenge to the city's approval of a development the district believed would overtax the school system, after applying the same substantive law and allocation of proof that would have applied if the challenger were a private citizen. Given the school district's expertise, should the district's conclusion that the proposed development would unduly strain the school system receive more deference than the city's contrary conclusion? In *Corona-Norco*, the district initially had not opposed approval of the development, but had asked the city to condition approval on the developer's agreement to provide funds for school construction beyond the impact fees allowed by state law. When the city did not exact that concession from the developer, the school district sued. If special districts and other specialized local governments (or subunits of a municipal government, such as community boards or neighborhood councils) are given procedural or substantive rights to protest a municipality's land use decisions, won't each such entity want a piece of the exactions pie?

4. *Remedies.* If a local government has the right to receive some consideration from neighboring or overlapping governments, what remedies should it have when its rights are violated? The courts might invalidate the deciding government's selfish zoning decision, or might instead restrict the injured government to the remedy of damages. How would damages have worked as a remedy in *City of Del Mar*?

5. *Alternatives.* Is a system of judge-made intermunicipal rights preferable to state legislation creating state or regional agencies to resolve conflicts between neighboring municipalities? Or state legislation granting municipalities substantive rights against their neighbors — the right to recover damages on behalf of their residents, for example, or the right to veto development projects within a specified distance of municipal borders? To legislation granting municipalities the authority to enter into compacts with their neighbors? How about to legislation establishing a system of arbitration and mediation? See Shelley Ross Saxer, Local Autonomy or Regionalism? Sharing the Benefits and Burdens of Suburban Commercial Development, 30 Ind. L. Rev. 659 (1997) (exploring the use of compacts and alternative dispute resolution). See generally Robert C. Ellickson, Public Property Rights: A Government's Rights and Duties When Its Landowners Come into Conflict with Outsiders, 52 S. Cal. L. Rev. 1627 (1979) (discussing intergovernmental environmental rights at the interlocal, interstate, and international levels).

B. *Obligations to Consider Regional Needs for Locally Undesirable Land Uses*

Many land uses provide benefits to a relatively large and diffuse group of consumers, clients, or citizens, but impose significant burdens on a much smaller group — their immediate neighbors. Such "locally undesirable land uses" (LULUs) generate a "not in my backyard" (NIMBY) reaction that makes them extremely difficult to site. Neighbors of the land selected for a LULU have considerable incentives to fight the siting, while each individual beneficiary of the project is likely to have little at stake in the project and will find it costly to join with other beneficiaries to support the proposal. The siting of LULUs accordingly has become a difficult public policy challenge. Industries and social service agencies claim that problems in siting facilities have made it increasingly difficult to manufacture their products or to deliver their services. Dissatisfaction over the disparate abilities of communities to block the siting of LULUs has contributed to the rise of the environmental justice movement. In short, siting has become a major source of frustration for local governments, industries, and social service agencies, on the one hand, and for the communities targeted for facilities, on the other. For discussions of the difficulty of siting LULUs, see, e.g., Daniel Mazmanian & David Morell, The "NIMBY" Syndrome: Facility Siting and the Failure of Democratic Discourse, *in* Environmental Policy in the 1990s, at 125, 137–38 (Norman J. Vig & Michael E. Kraft eds., 1990); Michael Dear, Understanding and Overcoming the NIMBY Syndrome, 58 J. Am. Plan. Ass'n 288 (1992); Herbert Inhaber, Of LULUs, NIM-BYs, and NIMTOOs, 107 Pub. Int. 52 (1992); Jane Chuang, Note, Who Should Win The Garbage Wars? Lessons from the Low-Level Radioactive Waste Policy Act, 72 Fordham L. Rev. 2403 (2004).

This section explores various approaches state and regional governments have adopted to try to ensure that local governments accept facilities the state or region needs, even when the costs the land use imposes on the host community outweigh the benefits to that community. The section concludes with a discussion of challenges to the fairness of the distribution of LULUs.

1.   Siting LULUs

Don Munton, Introduction: The NIMBY Phenomenon and Approaches to Facility Siting

in Hazardous Waste Siting and Democratic Choice 10–23 (Don Munton ed., 1996)

. . . A brief review of some of the more prominent strategies [for siting facilities] follows.

DECIDE, ANNOUNCE, DEFEND APPROACH

What can be fairly termed the first generation of siting efforts is characterized by a "top-down" approach. They featured decisions, often unilateral, by facility proponents or governments to construct a facility in a chosen location. Most siting decisions until the 1980s or so were of this kind and met with little or no opposition. One variant was what could be called the "low-profile" approach. Essentially, and not to put too fine a gloss on it, the strategy was to slip quietly into a community and build a facility before potential critics, even neighbors, noticed. . . .

The most common top-down process is known as the DAD approach (Decide, Announce, Defend). It can be distinguished by a nonpublic process of choosing a particular site, announcing this choice publicly, and then mounting whatever effort seems necessary to defend and secure approval of, or at least acquiescence to, this choice. . . .

A sophisticated version of the DAD approach . . . is a "centralized planning process," in which a blue ribbon panel, applying largely engineering criteria, identifies a short list of "best sites" and holds hearings on these, and then prospective firms bid on specific sites. New Jersey developed and then utilized this process in the early to mid-1980s to choose a site for a major hazardous waste incinerator. . . .

The DAD strategy for siting assumes, first, that the establishment of facilities is largely a technical issue, to be planned and decided by experts and on the basis of technical knowledge and objective standards. It also assumes that people living in the locale of these planned facilities either will not have any serious objections to them or can and will be convinced, after the fact, that the decision is a good or reasonable one. The bias of the former assumption is given little credence today. And clearly, given the regular emergence of determined local opposition, the second assumption is equally invalid. . . .

Preemption

Trying to stem a tide of NIMBY movements, some governments moved to preempt local authority in siting matters. Eliminating local authority's power to make land use decisions regarding the siting of facilities or to adopt local environmental laws that might restrict such siting, it was thought, would make it possible to force "needed" facilities on reluctant localities. One assumption here, as in the DAD approach, was that senior governments had the technical and policy expertise to decide what was best for all concerned. In any case, the strategy of preemption had a fatal flaw. . . . [Even stripped of their permitting power,] [l]ocal governments proved quite resourceful in thinking up novel and semi-legal ways to halt projects they opposed. One American town, for example, dug a substantial trench across the only access road into an unwanted facility, as part of so-called flood control measures. . . .

Public Education

Another response to growing local resistance was to try to engage in public education. . . . Given the difficulties facing, and the limited success of, public-education campaigns in general, it is questionable whether these efforts had much impact. (They may, in fact, have been counterproductive; some research suggests knowledge and opposition are positively related.) A related tendency was to see siting and risk management as communications problems and to think that the secret to success lay in the way siting proponents communicate with the public.

Public Participation

Yet another response to NIMBY movements was to recognize the important and legitimate role of local citizens in these decisions and to allow for that, if not encourage it. This was also a response to the conflict engendered by DAD and preemptive processes and to the acceptance of the right of local veto. The aim of the public-participation approach, of course, was to facilitate cooperation rather than engender opposition. . . . The fear of siting proponents here, of course, is that more active public participation may increase the likelihood of rejection. . . .

Override

A less accommodating strategy advanced and adopted to overcome local opposition and counter the local veto problem is that of the legislated override. If, after becoming involved, local residents insisted on refusing a facility under the offered conditions, governments, it was argued, should then override that opposition. The underlying assumption was that the greater and broader public good, represented, of course, by senior governments, should prevail in the end over narrow local self-interest and emotionalism, represented, of course, by local councils. . . . By the 1990s, at least twenty-four American states had assumed some override powers in the siting of hazardous waste facilities.

Override has fared little better than earlier approaches, which is to say, not well at all. When applied, it probably seemed to those affected no different from the preemption approach. The difference was merely one of timing, of when the local community lost control. And like preemption, it failed to address the essential political problem of local opposition. There were also political pressures in many jurisdictions against adopting override laws and against utilizing those that existed. . . .

NEGOTIATION

Negotiation is . . . not so much a specific alternative strategy, like the others discussed above, as it is a generic process. It became particularly popular in American states that had tried and failed with preemptive strategies. . . .

In contrast to the preemption and override strategies, negotiation assumes that interests are not permanently fixed and necessarily irreconcilable. While often held to be an alternative to more coercive techniques such as preemption or override, it can, at the same time, also be a complement to them. In some jurisdictions the override option was seen not as an alternative to negotiation but as a measure of last resort after negotiation had failed. . . .

Negotiation has few critics but some fairly obvious weaknesses. Wherever it is prescribed and at whatever issues it may be aimed, negotiation assumes that the (usually two) opposing sides each have at least some common interests to discuss and a degree of shared interest in working toward some sort of an agreement, albeit perhaps a minimal degree. For negotiation to succeed, there must be a mutual willingness to reach a compromise solution. These assumptions are often not met. . . . Siting proponents clearly want a particular solution and are usually willing to compromise on compensation packages, benefits, and the like. The opponents' ultimate objective, on the other hand, is usually to prevent the siting. Often that objective is one on which compromise is unthinkable. The "solution" preferred is for the proponents to abandon their siting effort. . . . This weakness is more than evident in the experience of Massachusetts, which pioneered negotiation processes and where siting efforts have still run into continual failure.

COMPENSATION AND INCENTIVES

For many who advocate negotiation over siting, a key issue to be discussed and agreed upon is compensation of those affected by a facility. . . . It is also asserted, not unreasonably, that offering incentives is more conducive to reaching agreement than is threatening coercion. Compensation can take a variety of forms. Governments or potential waste facility developers might offer guarantees that individuals' property values will not decline, or offer direct monetary payments to affected residents on an individual basis. Either operators or governments might agree to provide affected communities with desired infrastructure (e.g., new highway access), social services (e.g., a new hospital), or amenities (e.g., new parks). . . . Facility operators might agree to pay special taxes or a share of the facility's profits to the affected municipality. There are two underlying assumptions in strategies that depend on compensation packages. The first is that individuals in a potential host community are essentially — and mainly — rational economic actors. The second is that the disparity between the diffuse social benefits from a facility and the disproportionate individual costs borne by those living close by is the basic problem in a siting controversy, and that compensation can close this gap. . . . Both assumptions are highly questionable. The lack of compensation for economic costs imposed by a nearby facility is seldom the underlying cause of local opposition, and virtually never the only cause. . . . There are some experts who argue, sometimes flatly, that compensation cannot and does not work, that is, it is not at all an effective measure in siting facilities. Indeed, offering it may be counterproductive if people perceive the compensation offers by a facility's proponents as attempts to buy them off or bribe them. This perception can be heightened if compensation is being offered by a facility proponent but other concerns, for example, about health risks, are not being addressed.

To say economic costs are neither the most important nor the only underlying cause of local opposition is not to say that individuals' or a local community's perceptions about an unfair distribution of costs is of no importance to whether they accept or oppose a facility. Some evidence suggests that compensation may in fact have a role to play in reaching an agreement on siting. It has been a part, and perhaps an important part, of some successful siting cases. These packages almost always deal with more than the financial and economic concerns of those affected, however. . . .

COST AND RISK SHARING

Yet another strategy involves sharing widely the social costs of waste treatment, rather than concentrating treatment facilities, and thus these costs, in one location. This has been labeled the YIMBY (Yes in Many Backyards) approach. The YIMBY philosophy, as employed in California, "asked each county to take responsibility for its fair share of the waste problem, though not necessarily to manage all of its own wastes. . . . [Thus] waste management problems are addressed at a comprehensive regional level." This approach might involve various treatment options, including dispersing the facilities or the transportable hazardous waste treatment equipment. More grandly, YIMBY might underlie a national strategy. Each state or province might be allocated in some sense an equitable share of the overall treatment and disposal responsibilities. . . .

Various assumptions underlie cost and risk sharing. One is that if the costs and risks are divided somewhat equitably, and are seen to be divided equitably, there will be greater public support for accepting some of this overall burden. Another assumption seems to be that the approach will encourage a sense that everyone is involved in the problem and everyone needs to be involved in the solution. While the experience with this strategy is too limited to judge its results, it is clear from the California experience that it can easily be undermined by governmental missteps.

THE VOLUNTARY-CHOICE PROCESS

Where most of the other strategies take as a given a prior decision to site in a particular locale, the voluntary approach does not. It assumes that this decision will be made only after invitations have been issued to potential host communities, after the expressions of interest by volunteer communities have been considered, after the communities have had the opportunity to study the proposal in depth and secure expert advice, and after key provisions of the arrangements for the siting and operation of the facility have been negotiated between its proponents and one or more communities. Rather than aim to secure local approval for a particular site chosen by a private developer or government agency or panel, it seeks first to identify potentially interested communities. Rather than keeping the local community at arm's length, it seeks to involve them directly and intimately, not only in the siting decision itself but also in the management and operation of the facility. . . . At the outset, potential communities must choose to opt in. At every stage, from exploration of possible physical allocations through community acceptance (for example, by means of a referendum), communities can drop out of the siting process. And prior to acceptance, they can negotiate with the facility proponent the terms of both the siting and the operation of the facility, and do so from a position of some strength.

Chief among the advantages of the voluntary-choice approach is that it is nonthreatening. . . . The distinction between being presented with what appears to be a fait accompli and voluntarily accepting certain risks is a crucial one. There is convincing evidence that people perceive risks as lower, or are often more willing to accept risks, if the risks are assumed voluntarily. . . .

Quite apart from the potential for facilitating agreement of host communities through perceived-risk reduction, a voluntary process also seems ethically preferable. . . . Assuming that risks are minimized and that there is no manipulation or coercion behind the choice, it is surely preferable to an imposed solution, no matter how well considered that solution. . . .

Another advantage is that a voluntary-choice process is usually seen to be legitimate. It affords local control and respects local decisions. . . .

A third advantage of the voluntary-choice approach is the efficiency of its self-selection process. Those communities more inclined to assume what others regard as the substantial risks of facilities select themselves. . . . And despite the considerable consultative effort required in dealing with prospective communities, voluntary approaches may save time. They may identify interested communities more easily and more quickly than would be possible in a more top-down process. . . .

There are some close links between the voluntary-choice approach and some of the auction-based ideas that have been developed by advocates of compensation strategies. Howard Kunreuther and colleagues proposed in 1987 the notion of a "low-bid auction," in which communities would submit a sealed bid indicating the minimum amount they would need to host a facility. . . . Inherent in all these proposals is the notion that communities would volunteer to host a waste site, for a price, of course. The emphasis here is more on costs and compensation and less on a negotiation process than in the case of the voluntary-choice approach, but there are some important parallels in the underlying structure. . . .

Note on Siting Strategies

1. *Implicit preemption.* In some cases, states are quite explicit about preempting local land use regulations. In many instances, however, state legislators who are wary of making any highly visible incursions on local powers enact regulatory measures that do not explicitly address the preemption issue. Developers facing local opposition for their facilities then argue that local regulation has been implicitly preempted. In trying to decipher legislative intent, courts look to whether the state regulatory scheme is comprehensive, whether the subject area inherently requires uniform regulation, and whether the continuation of local regulation would impair achievement of explicit statutory objectives.

In Incorporated Village of Nyack v. Daytop Village, Inc., 583 N.E.2d 928 (N.Y. 1991), for example, the operator of a residential substance abuse facility argued that New York's extensive state regulation and permitting of such facilities evidenced the state's intent to preempt local land use regulation. New York's highest court rejected the argument, despite sweeping language in the state's Mental Hygiene Law about the state's interest in "develop[ing] a comprehensive system of services to serve the full range of needs of . . . substance abusers and substance dependent persons." The court reasoned that another portion of the Mental Hygiene Law explicitly preempted local control over facilities for the mentally retarded, so the absence of explicit preemption language as to facilities for substance abusers was telling. In addition, the court found that the interests of the state and local governments were not necessarily contradictory.

In contrast, the Supreme Court of Illinois held that the state's scheme for licensing day care homes implicitly preempted a "home occupations" provision of the local zoning ordinance because the local ordinance would render the state licensing scheme "a nullity." Hawthorne v. Village of Olympia Fields, 790 N.E.2d 832, 836 (Ill. 2003). See also Charter Township of Northville v. Northville Public Schools, 666 N.W.2d 213, 220 (Mich. 2003) (statute vesting "sole and exclusive jurisdiction" over school construction and site plans in the state superintendent of public instruction immunized schools from the application of local zoning and site plan ordinances).

Local land use regulation related to environmental concerns has been particularly prone to preemption challenges. Compare, e.g., Envirosafe Services v. County of Owyhee, 735 P.2d 998, 1002 (Idaho 1987) (a state regulatory and permitting scheme for hazardous waste facilities implicitly preempted local land use regulations, given the comprehensiveness of the scheme, and the fact that "the field of hazardous waste disposal is fraught with such unique concerns and dangers . . . that its regulation demands a statewide, rather than local, approach"), with, e.g., Thayer v. Town of Tilton, 861 A.2d 800 (N.H. 2004) (state law did not preempt local adoption of an ordinance regulating sludge facilities).

When the land use activity in controversy would generate spillover benefits beyond the municipality, should the legislature be presumed to have intended preemption because preemption would be the efficiency-maximizing approach?

2. *Consideration of local concerns.* Some state laws that explicitly preempt local control over the siting of hazardous waste facilities require the state to take into account the local government's regulations (at least those in effect prior to the siting controversy). When an explicit preemption statute does not include that requirement (or when a court finds that a state implicitly preempted local regulation), should the courts require similar accommodation for local governments? See, e.g., Township of Franklin v. Hollander, 796 A.2d 874 (N.J. 2002) (although state's Right to Farm Act preempts municipal land use authority over commercial farms, the county and state agricultural boards must give appropriate consideration to local ordinances and concerns in regulating the farms).

3. *Semi-successful preemptive approaches.* Munton is dismissive of state preemption of the siting of hazardous waste facilities. As discussed at p. 727, many states have preempted some local zoning regulations to allow the siting of group homes. While those efforts have not smoothed the waters entirely, as *Cleburne*, excerpted at p. 717, and *Smith & Lee Associates*, excerpted at p. 722, illustrate, they are not considered failures. Is the different rate of "success" just a matter of the degree or type of threat posed by the facility, or is there more at work than the special noxiousness of hazardous waste?

4. *Federal preemption.* Federal law may explicitly or impliedly preempt local zoning or land use controls in areas in which the federal government has a special interest. See, e.g., United States v. City & County of Denver, 100 F.3d 1509 (10th Cir. 1996) (federal laws regarding the clean-up of hazardous waste preempted zoning ordinance which precluded the method of remediation the federal Environmental Protection Agency had ordered for a Denver Superfund site).

5. *State overrides.* Where the state has the authority to override local exclusion on a case-by-case basis, what criteria should the state use to decide when to exercise its authority? If the local government can show that it considered all the benefits, even those it could not capture, but nevertheless (rationally) concluded that the proposed siting was not efficient or was less efficient than alternatives, should the state be able to override the decision?

6. *Negotiation.* Munton cites the Massachusetts Hazardous Waste Facility Siting Act, Mass. Gen. Laws ch. 21D, §§1–19 (2005), as a telling example of the failure of negotiated processes to overcome siting opposition. For analyses of the Massachusetts experiment, see Vicki Been, Compensated Siting Proposals: Is It Time to Pay Attention?, 21 Fordham Urb. L.J. 787, 811–19 (1994); Barak D. Richman, Mandating Negotiations to Solve the NIMBY Problem: A Creative Regulatory Response, 20 UCLA J. Envtl. L. & Pol'y 223 (2001/2002). For a much more optimistic account of the role of negotiation in resolving land use and environmental disputes generally, see Lawrence Susskind & Jeffrey Cruikshank, Breaking the Impasse: Consensual Approaches to Resolving Public Disputes (1987). But see Luke W. Cole, The Theory and Reality of Community-Based Environmental Decisionmaking: The Failure of California's Tanner Act and Its Implications for Environmental Justice,

25 Ecology L.Q. 733 (1999); David Schoenbrod, Limits and Dangers of Environmental Mediation: A Review Essay, 58 N.Y.U. L. Rev. 1453 (1983).

7. *Compensation.* For research on whether offers of compensation increase a community's willingness to accept a facility, see Been, supra (surveying literature). For an argument that offering compensation *decreases* support for a siting, see Bruno S. Frey & Felix Oberholzer-Gee, The Cost of Price Incentives: An Empirical Analysis of Motivation Crowding Out, 87 Am. Econ. Rev. 746 (1997); Bruno S. Frey et al., The Old Lady Visits Your Backyard: A Tale of Morals and Markets, 104 J. Pol. Econ. 1297 (1996). If a state is tempted to require compensation in order to facilitate siting, how ought it to structure the requirement? Should the state dictate the compensation or specify a minimum and allow the proposed host community to bargain for more? Should compensation be tied to nuisance and tort damages as determined by an administrative agency or court?

Should the state provide funding to the proposed host government to allow it to hire experts to assess the likely impact of the facility, or lawyers to bargain with the developer? For a discussion of how communities fare in the bargaining process, see Been, supra, at 819–25.

8. *Reverse auctions.* Under the "auction-based" ideas Munton discusses, local governments that might have some interest in hosting the proposed facility would specify their asking price — the amount their residents would have to be compensated to accept the project. The project developer (whether a private firm or a public entity) would be obligated to pay the asking price of the local government where the facility was ultimately located. The developer would thus consider those potential costs in making the siting decision. The schemes typically contemplate that the developer's payments would go directly to the citizens of the community and not to the local treasury. See Michael O'Hare, "Not on My Block You Don't": Facility Siting and the Strategic Importance of Compensation, 25 Pub. Pol'y 407 (1977). Who ought to decide how the compensation is distributed? See Bradford C. Mank, Environmental Justice and Discriminatory Siting: Risk-Based Representation and Equitable Compensation, 56 Ohio St. L.J. 329, 363 (1995).

When local governments impose the exactions discussed at pp. 634–78, are they essentially participating in a reverse auction for the development? Should *Nollan* and *Dolan*, excerpted at pp. 638 and 643, apply to reverse auctions for LULUs? See also p. 778 for a discussion of a similar concept for low- and moderate-income housing.

Would the reverse auction system of compensation be superior to a system of private nuisance suits for damages?

9. *Further reading.* For additional views on the merits and failures of the various siting strategies, see, e.g., Richard N.L. Andrews, Hazardous Waste Facility Siting: State Approaches, *in* Dimensions of Hazardous Waste Politics and Policy (Charles E. Davis & James P. Lester eds., 1988); Mary R. English, Siting Low-Level Radioactive Waste Disposal Facilities: The Public Policy Dilemma (1992); Michael B. Gerrard, Whose Backyard, Whose Risk: Fear and Fairness in Toxic and Nuclear Waste Siting (1994).

10. *Judicial "solutions."* The siting strategies Munton discusses are legislative in nature. The following case illustrates one court's attempt to resolve the problem of siting LULUs.

Beaver Gasoline Co. v. Zoning Hearing Board of the Borough of Osborne
285 A.2d 501 (Pa. 1971)

O'BRIEN, Justice. . . .
     . . . [I]t is undisputed that the zoning ordinance of the Borough of Osborne prohibits gasoline service stations within the territorial limits of the borough. Beaver applied for a

permit to erect a gasoline service station, and the permit was refused on the basis of the prohibition against gasoline service stations. . . . We allowed an appeal and specifically directed the parties "to brief and argue the question of whether a municipality should bear the initial burden of demonstrating the constitutionality of a zoning ordinance which completely prohibits an otherwise legitimate business operation in the municipality." . . .

We are not prepared to, nor do we, abandon our established policy that the validity of a zoning ordinance is presumed and that the burden of establishing its invalidity is upon the party who seeks to have it declared invalid. However, requiring an applicant for a building permit to establish by affirmative evidence the nonexistence of a proper zoning purpose in the total prohibition of an otherwise legitimate business activity would be to place upon him an unrealistic and insurmountable burden. It is always difficult to prove a negative — to require a party to prove a negative such as the nonexistence of a proper zoning purpose is to raise difficulty to virtual impossibility. Common knowledge indicates that certain types of business activities, by reason of the particularly objectionable quality of those activities, are undesirable land uses and total prohibition would appear prima facie to be designed to protect those public interests which zoning statutes permit municipalities to protect. In the instant case, we are not dealing with such an activity. Were this ordinance to ban from the borough an activity generally known to give off noxious odors, disturb the tranquility of a large area by making loud noises, have the obvious potential of poisoning the air or the water of the area, or similarly have clearly deleterious effects upon the general public, the situation would be entirely different from that in the instant case.

Here, the applicant can do no more, realistically, than show that the zoning ordinance has banned from the borough in its entirety a type of business activity which, in our society, is conducted without hindrance, it seems, almost everywhere. What more can the applicant do to meet his burden? We believe that at least in those circumstances where a total municipality-wide prohibition of an activity which, on its face, does not give rise to an indication of the protection of a legitimate public interest controllable by zoning laws, the applicant has met his burden by showing the total prohibition and the municipality must then establish the legitimacy of the prohibition by evidence establishing what public interest is sought to be protected. . . .

JONES, Justice (concurring). . . .

Note on Municipal Duties to Allow the Full Spectrum of Nonresidential Uses

1. *The merits of land use diversity?* Who is the Pennsylvania Supreme Court trying to help by easing the burden for those challenging totally excluded land uses? The landowners who are proposing those uses? The households who will live, shop, or work at the site where local officials are compelled to allow a formerly excluded use? The owners and occupants of neighboring land who are thereby saved from bland environs? Might the pro-diversity courts be trying to assure that a mix of interest groups will be active in local politics in order to prevent small suburbs from being dominated by any single "faction"?

If diversity is indeed worthy of judicial support, should a court focus on the spectrum of uses represented throughout (but within) a municipality, or should it instead examine diversity in uses: (1) at the (usually broader) regional level; or (2) at the (usually narrower) neighborhood or block level? Put another way, doesn't the Pennsylvania Supreme Court's approach give much more leeway to a large city like Philadelphia than it gives to a small suburb?

Is there something to be said in favor of permitting local governments to specialize? See p. 771 for discussion of the Tiebout Hypothesis that municipal specialization enhances efficiency.

2. *What if other siting strategies are in place?* Where a state has adopted one or more of the siting strategies described above, should the courts nevertheless insist on a *Beaver Gasoline* type rule? See Hudachek v. Zoning Hearing Board, 608 A.2d 652 (Pa. Commw. Ct. 1992) (rejecting *Beaver Gasoline* claims where municipality had contracted with other jurisdictions, through a "joint municipal zoning ordinance," to provide for the prohibited use in another area of the region). Cf. Petition of Dolington Land Group & Toll Bros., Inc., 839 A.2d 1021 (2003) (declining to reach question whether court should subject a municipality that had entered into such an agreement to the stricter requirements applicable to some its contracting municipal partners).

3. *Uses too objectionable to merit protection under* Beaver Gasoline. What uses might fall outside the *Beaver Gasoline* rule because they are "particularly objectionable"? See, e.g., Centre Lime & Stone Co., Inc. v. Spring Township Board of Supervisors, 787 A.2d 1105 (Pa. Commw. Ct. 2001) (quarrying protected); H & R Builders, Inc. v. Borough Council, 555 A.2d 948 (Pa. Commw. Ct. 1989) (junkyards protected); WMI Properties, Inc. v. Falls Township Zoning Hearing Board, 517 A.2d 1378 (Pa. Commw. Ct. 1986) (landfills protected). But see South Whitford Associates v. Zoning Hearing Board, 630 A.2d 903 (Pa. Commw. Ct. 1993) (heliports are particularly objectionable, and not entitled to protection).

How does one classify land uses to decide which are represented and which missing? For example, are self-service gasoline stations to be distinguished from full-service stations? Service stations from truck stops?

4. *Remedy.* If Pennsylvania municipalities must presumptively allow a diversity of land uses, does it follow that the proponent of a missing activity is entitled to conduct it on the proponent's particular piece of land? By what standard should a court decide when to grant site-specific relief?

5. *Partial exclusions.* Should plaintiffs be able to invoke *Beaver Gasoline* even when the use is not totally excluded, but plaintiffs claim that not enough land is set aside for the use? See, e.g., Macioce v. Zoning Hearing Board of Borough of Baldwin, 850 A.2d 882, 889 (Pa. Commw. Ct. 2004) (cellular provider failed to prove a violation of *Beaver Gasoline* where less than 1 percent of the jurisdiction's acreage because "it is not sufficient for a developer to merely point out that a relatively small area of the municipality is zoned for commercial use without any proof that the needs of the community's residents are not being adequately served"); Centre Lime & Stone Co., Inc. v. Spring Township Board of Supervisors, 787 A.2d 1105, 1111 (Pa. Commw. Ct. 2001) ("If the zoning exclusion is partial, the percentage of community land available under the ordinance for the proposed use . . . must be considered in light of the total amount of undeveloped land in the community. Where the amount of land zoned for the proposed use is disproportionately small in relation to the total amount of undeveloped land in the community, the ordinance will be held to be exclusionary."). Pennsylvania's approach to partial exclusions is discussed more fully at p. 783.

Can a municipality escape *Beaver Gasoline* by showing that it already has the use, albeit on a nonconforming basis? See, e.g., WMI Properties, Inc. v. Falls Township Zoning Hearing Board, 517 A.2d 1378 (Pa. Commw. Ct. 1986) (no).

2. *The Special Problems Posed by Government Facilities*

City of Crown Point v. Lake County
510 N.E.2d 684 (Ind. 1987)

SHEPARD, Chief Justice.

This case requires us to decide whether a county government's property is subject to the zoning authority of the city within which it is located. We conclude that it is.

In 1972, the City of Crown Point annexed territory which encompassed the Lake County Government Center, bringing the Government Center within the boundaries of that county seat. At the time, the City's zoning ordinance declared that all annexed property would be zoned R-1, residential, and that public buildings were not a permitted use in such a zone. However, the public buildings of the Government Center continued to operate on the annexed property as a pre-existing nonconforming use.

The Government Center . . . include[s] a house which had once been used as a residence for the administrator of the hospital located on the grounds and more recently as a residence for the County Sheriff and his family. . . .

. . . The County intends to use [the house] for the Community Corrections Program, making improvements to the house as necessary and housing up to fifteen class D felons. Such a use is not permitted on property zoned R-1, though apparently a special use permit would allow it.

The County did not apply for re-zoning or a special permit, and the City sought an injunction. Following a hearing, the trial court denied the injunction. . . . We granted the City's petition for transfer . . . [in order to determine] [w]hether the County is immune or exempt from the City's zoning code. . . .

While this Court has not encountered this dilemma before, courts in other jurisdictions have relied primarily on three different tests to resolve a conflict between a local zoning authority and an intruding government entity which seeks to avoid zoning regulation. First, the traditional governmental-proprietary test has been applied to give governmental entities pursuing government functions immunity from local zoning laws, while requiring compliance of those entities performing merely proprietary functions. Second, the superior sovereign rule recognizes immunity for those governmental entities with a superior position in the governmental hierarchy. Finally, the eminent domain test grants immunity to any government unit which has the power to take property by condemnation. 5 Rohan, Zoning and Land Use Controls §35.05 (1987).

These traditional tests have encountered a great deal of criticism. The application of the governmental-proprietary test has led to inconsistent results. Because the definitions of governmental and proprietary vary, the same function may be classified differently depending on the jurisdiction, or may vary even within the same jurisdiction. The governmental-proprietary distinction arose in the context of governmental immunity from tort claims and is not related to the central question of land use control.

The eminent domain test has likewise been developed for a different though related purpose, namely, deciding whether a public body may acquire ownership of private property.

> Cases which have applied this test generally take the position that where a political unit is authorized to condemn, it is automatically immune from local zoning regulations when it acts in furtherance of its designated public function. Yet, the power to condemn simply provides a method whereby property can be acquired. Such power has nothing to do with the use of the property.

City of Temple Terrace v. Hillsborough Ass'n for Retarded Citizens, Inc., 322 So. 2d 571, 578 (Fla. Dist. Ct. App. 1975).

The superior sovereign test presents the difficulty of attempting to establish a meaningful hierarchical ranking. Marco Adelfio, Note, Governmental Immunity from Zoning, 22 B.C. L. Rev. 783, 790 (1981). "Since a municipal corporation is an agent of the state whose zoning power is governed by the legislature, its interest in enforcing this power is equal to the state agency's interest in performing those functions for which it was formed." 8 McQuillan, Municipal Corporations §25.15, at 20 (3d ed. 1983). Attempting to label one government entity "superior" merely begs the question of which agent of the sovereign should prevail on the issue of land use. Note, Government Immunity from Land Zoning Ordinances, 84 Harv. L. Rev. [869,] 877 [(1971)]. Though we find the notion of sovereign immunity unhelpful in resolving disputes between local governments, a case in which the state government itself is involved might well be resolved on this basis.

These traditional tests attempt to resolve zoning conflicts by applying labels which bear little, if any, relationship to the underlying concerns of land use control. "More generally, all three traditional tests share a common flaw; they are overly simplistic and often lead to resolution of a multifaceted zoning-conflicts issue through the use of conclusive labels rather than through perceptive adjudication." Blackstone Park [Improvement Ass'n v. Board of Standards & Appeals,] 448 A.2d [1233,] 1238 [(R.I. 1982)]. Moreover, use of these three tests has invariably led to the same result: government entities are immune from zoning ordinances. Note, Government Immunity from Zoning, 22 B.C. L. Rev. at 785. . . .

The modern trend in resolving governmental zoning conflicts is to apply the balancing of interests test. See 5 Rohan, Zoning and Land Use Controls §35.05 (listing those jurisdictions which have adopted such a test). The balancing of interests has generally consisted of a two-tiered analysis. The first step is to determine whether the intruding authority is immune from the local zoning authority. If the intruding entity is immune, it may make the initial land use decision without complying with local zoning. If not immune, the intruding entity must attempt compliance with local zoning, thus giving the local zoning authority the initial land use decision. The second tier of the balancing test requires a determination of the reasonableness of the initial land use decision. . . .

. . . [A]n intruding entity must be allowed to seek relief under some circumstances. It must, however, bear the burden to show that immunity is necessary to advance the governmental ends it seeks. The essential purpose of zoning, "to rationally coordinate land use planning to promote orderly development and preservation of property values," City of Fargo [v. Harwood Township], 256 N.W.2d [694,] 697 [(N.D. 1977)], generally can best be furthered by local zoning authorities which have been established to accomplish that very purpose. Local zoning proceedings also provide for public debate in an administrative hearing which can address the interests of all parties.

However, there will be occasions when the land use plan of a community must fall before other critical government objectives. . . . Local land use decisions must be evaluated not only in terms of local need and benefit, but in light of community, area or state-wide interests as well.

When a zoning authority has denied an intruding government's request for approval of a given land use, an appeal can lie to the courts, which will balance the interests to determine which must prevail. Factors to be considered include the propriety of the land use, such as the economic and environmental impact on the area, the kind of function or land use involved, the availability of alternative locations, and any attempts to minimize detriments to adjacent landowners, as well as a consideration of competing interests, such as the nature and scope of the intruding government unit, the essential use to the local community and the broader community, the need for the specific site as compared to the adverse impact, the social utility of the proposed use, and the possible frustration of a government function. These are the sort of decisions assigned to local executive and legislative bodies. Where their determinations are irreconcilable, the legislature has provided for a review of the zoning decision by the judiciary.

Here, the County never sought re-zoning or a special use permit. . . . Whether injunctive relief is appropriate pending an application by Lake County for rezoning or a special use permit, we leave to the discretion of the trial court. The cause is remanded for that purpose.

Note on Governmental Immunities from Municipal Land-Use Regulation

1. *The dangers of balancing.* Professor Laurie Reynolds argues that the balancing test is inappropriate because it fails to encourage cooperation between governments, is so indeterminate that it leads to increased litigation and inconsistent decisions, involves the courts in land use questions beyond their expertise, and polarizes the issue too starkly.

> Finally, and perhaps most importantly, a balancing test is an inadequate tool for allocating legal rights between two governmental units, each of which is attempting to exercise properly delegated state power and each of which is furthering an express state policy. Although balancing may be appropriate or even required when a court assumes, for instance, the task of protecting individual rights from the excesses of government, judicial balancing in the case of intergovernmental conflict requires a court to make the legislative decision of choosing one public policy over another equally valid public policy. In practice, such judicial balancing has frequently resulted in a decision in favor of the governmental unit with a larger constituency, thus recalling the superior sovereign test's assumption that the project of a superior governmental unit furthers a broader public interest. It is not for courts, however, to pick and choose between valid public purposes.

Laurie Reynolds, The Judicial Role in Intergovernmental Land Use Disputes: The Case Against Balancing, 71 Minn. L. Rev. 611, 640 (1987).

Reynolds suggests that "intruder governments" should always be forced to submit to the host government's siting processes, and that the right to decide whether to allow another government's land use should be allocated to the government that has the greatest incentive to accommodate the other's concerns. Thus, if the intruder embraces the proposed host, the intruder should enjoy immunity, but if the intruder is part of the host government, the host government should have the right to stop the project. Does Reynolds's proposal improve on the "superior sovereign" test that some courts apply?

2. *Can private parties piggyback on a government's immunity?* In Crown Communication New York, Inc. v. Department of Transportation, 824 N.E.2d 934 (N.Y. 2005), New York's highest court held that commercial telecommunications providers seeking to install their private antennas on two state-owned telecommunications towers were exempt from local zoning regulation, just as the state had been in building the towers, because "the public and private uses of the towers are sufficiently intertwined to justify exemption of the wireless providers from local zoning regulations." If the state has not preempted local control over cellular providers, why should the commercial providers be exempt from local regulations? If private providers are piggybacking on the state's exemption, how should the balancing of interests approach be modified to take into account the private interests at issue? Should the public interest have to predominate over the private interest? See, e.g., pp. 112–17.

If services once provided by the government are privatized, should the private entity enjoy the same immunity from zoning as the government did? Cf. City of Louisville Board of Zoning Adjustment v. Gailor, 920 S.W.2d 887 (Ky. Ct. App. 1996) (county jail operated by private corporation under contract with fiscal court was not subject to local zoning regulations).

3. *Legislative intent.* Some courts have eschewed the three tests described in *City of Crown Point* and instead have focused on discerning whether the legislature intended to exempt a particular government from the zoning authority of another. See, e.g., Pitts-field Charter Township v. Washtenaw County, 664 N.W.2d 193 (Mich. 2003). Michigan's Court of Appeals has described the exercise, however, as akin to a "Hegelian dialetic." Capital Region Airport Authority v. DeWitt Charter Township, 601 N.W.2d 141 (Mich. Ct. App. 1999). For a description of which states use which approaches, see Elaine Marie Tomko-DeLuca, Annotation, Applicability of Zoning Regulations to Governmental Projects or Activities, 53 A.L.R.5th 1 (1997 & Supp. 2004).

4. *When the shoe is on the other foot.* Municipalities themselves may argue for immu-nity when they purchase or condemn land outside their boundaries for airports, sewage treatment plants, and the like. See, e.g., City of Bridgeton v. City of St. Louis, 18 S.W.3d 107 (Mo. Ct. App. 2000) (city owning airport held immune from zoning ordinances of city in which airport was located); City of Everett v. Snohomish County, 772 P.2d 992 (Wash. 1989) (en banc) (city trying to site sludge and solid waste disposal facility in unincorporated area of county held subject to county's zoning code). A leading case granting immunity in this situation is City of Scottsdale v. Municipal Court, 368 P.2d 637 (Ariz. 1962). The dissent in that case argued in part:

> Conceivably, under the majority opinion, a situation may develop where City A will locate a sewage disposal plant within the limits of City B, which in turn will retaliate by locating its sewage disposal plant within City A's borders, and so ad infinitum. That Scottsdale urgently needs a sewage disposal plant is undenied; that it may locate it with impunity within another city's borders without regard to a proper restriction in the interest of the general welfare of the latter establishes a principle fraught with danger and confusion.

Id. at 644.

5. *A government's own projects.* Should a local government be immune from its own land use regulations when it seeks to site governmental facilities? See, e.g., Morrison v. City of East Lansing, 660 N.W.2d 395, 401 (Mich. Ct. App. 2003) (city was immune from its own zoning in building a community center because a government "must have freedom to make its projects work in an environment confined within its borders").

6. *Liability schemes.* Would liability rules help resolve these disputes? For example, should the Indiana Supreme Court immunize Lake County from the City of Crown Point's zoning regulations if the county compensates the city (or perhaps the immediate neighbors of the proposed facility)?

7. *Federal and Native American lands.* The doctrine of federal supremacy generally immunizes federal lands from local land use regulation. See, e.g., United States Postal Service v. Town of Greenwich, 901 F. Supp. 500 (D. Conn. 1995) (state building code could not be applied to post office).

The tangled question of state and local regulation of lands within Native Amer-ican reservations is explored in Brendale v. Confederated Tribes & Bands of Yakima Indian Nation, 492 U.S. 408 (1989). See also Pamela R. Logsdon, Jurisdiction to Reg-ulate Land Uses in Indian Country: Basic Concepts and Recent Developments, 33 Urb. Law. 765 (2001); Rebecca Tsosie, Land, Culture, and Community: Reflections on Native Sovereignty and Property in America, 34 Ind. L. Rev. 1291 (2001).

8. *Statutory resolutions.* Evaluate California's approach to the problem:

[T]he governing board of a school district, . . . by a vote of two-thirds of its members, may render a city or county zoning ordinance inapplicable to a proposed use of property by the school district. The governing board of the school district may not take this action when the proposed use of the property by the school district is for nonclassroom facilities, including, but not limited to, warehouses, administrative buildings, and automotive storage and repair buildings. . . . [T]he city or county may commence an action in . . . superior court . . . seeking a review of such action of the governing board of the school district. . . . If the court determines that such action was arbitrary and capricious, it shall declare it to be of no force and effect, and the zoning ordinance in question shall be applicable. . . .

Cal. Gov't Code §53094 (West 2005).

9. *Priorities in the exercise of eminent domain — who is king of the mountain?* When can one government compel another government to transfer land to it? Is a state entitled to force its highways through a federal military base? A school district to condemn a city park as the site for a new high school? Some system of priorities must be established to prevent eminent-domain wars. A first rule, derived from the principle of federal supremacy, is that lands of the United States (including Native American lands) may not be condemned by a state or local government without authorization from Congress. Minnesota v. United States, 305 U.S. 382, 386-87 (1939). The federal government may, however, acquire state lands by eminent domain. See Stockton v. Baltimore & New York Railroad Co., 32 F. 9, 19 (D.N.J. 1887).

If state statutes establish eminent-domain priorities among a state and its political subdivisions, those statutes are controlling. Rarely will a state authorize a local unit to condemn state lands. By contrast, some state agencies are typically empowered by statute to condemn land owned by local governments. Where statutory priorities have not been set, courts often apply a first-in-time rule: The turf of a current public owner is protected from the claims of would-be usurpers who lack clear legislative backing. This seniority rule has been applied to protect local governmental units from state agencies.

When one unit of government takes the land of another, should it pay just compensation? See Michael H. Schill, Intergovernmental Takings and Just Compensation: A Question of Federalism, 137 U. Pa. L. Rev. 829 (1989).

3. *Environmental Justice and Other Objections to the Siting of LULUs*

Controversies over the siting of LULUs increasingly include charges that the proposed siting violates principles of "environmental justice." Advocates for environmental justice argue that people of color and the poor are exposed to greater environmental risks and burdens than are whites and wealthier individuals as a result of racism and classism in the siting of LULUs, the promulgation and enforcement of environmental and land use regulations, and the effort spent cleaning polluted areas. One of the environmental justice movement's concerns has been the siting of undesirable land uses. According to environmental justice advocates, undesirable facilities either are placed deliberately in minority neighborhoods or are sited in a manner that results in minority neighborhoods hosting a disproportionate share of the facilities. See, e.g., Robert D. Bullard, Dumping in Dixie: Race, Class, and Environmental Quality (1990); Kenneth A. Manaster, Environmental

Protection and Justice — Readings and Commentary on Environmental Law and Practice (1995); Clifford Rechtschaffen & Eileen Guana, Environmental Justice: Law, Policy and Regulation (2002).

The environmental justice movement has had a significant impact on individual siting processes. The charge that a proposed siting is discriminatory is politically explosive, giving siting opponents a powerful public relations weapon. In the courts, however, siting opponents have fared poorly. Early environmental justice cases, brought under the Equal Protection Clause, floundered under the *Arlington Heights* intent requirement discussed at pp. 698–702. Environmental justice advocates then turned to Title VI of the Civil Rights Act of 1964, 42 U.S.C. §2000d (2005), which provides that "no person in the United States shall, on the ground of race, color, or national origin, be excluded from participation in, be denied the benefits of, or be subjected to discrimination under any program or activity receiving Federal financial assistance." Title VI does not require proof of discriminatory intent as long as the federal agency providing the financial assistance has promulgated regulations to implement Title VI that define discrimination to include disparate impact. The implementing regulations of the U.S. Environmental Protection Agency (EPA) do define discrimination that broadly.

The promise of Title VI litigation proved short-lived. In Chester Residents Concerned for Quality Living v. Seif, 132 F.3d 925 (3d Cir. 1997), a community group alleged that the Pennsylvania Department of Environmental Protection had violated Title VI by issuing a permit to a waste handler to operate a facility in a predominantly black community. The Court of Appeals held that the group had a private right of action to enforce the regulations the EPA had promulgated to enforce Title VI. The Supreme Court granted certiorari to hear the issue, but the case became moot when the permit was revoked for other reasons. 524 U.S. 974 (1998). The Supreme Court then reached the issue in a case that did not involve environmental justice, holding that Title VI did not provide a private right of action. Alexander v. Sandoval, 532 U.S. 275 (2000). The *Chester Residents* plaintiffs tried again, asserting a right to enforce the EPA's regulations implementing Title VI through 42 U.S.C. §1983. The Court of Appeals rejected that move as well, holding that an administrative regulation cannot create an interest enforceable under §1983 unless the interest is implicit in the statute authorizing the regulation. Because Title VI itself proscribes only intentional discrimination, the Court of Appeals reasoned, plaintiffs do not have a right enforceable through a §1983 action under the EPA's disparate impact discrimination regulations. South Camden Citizens in Action v. New Jersey Department of Environmental Protection, 274 F.3d 771, 774 (3d Cir. 2001). The Supreme Court later also closed the door on such §1983 challenges. Gonzaga University v. Doe, 536 U.S. 273, 286–87 (2002).

Federal legal challenges based on environmental justice theories accordingly are, at least for now, effectively limited to administrative complaints filed with the EPA's Office of Civil Rights under the EPA's regulations implementing Title VI. See Kyle W. La Londe, Who Wants to Be an Environmental Justice Advocate?: Options for Bringing an Environmental Justice Complaint in the Wake of *Alexander v. Sandoval*, 31 B.C. Envtl. Aff. L. Rev. 27 (2004). The EPA's draft "guidance" for investigating those complaints, as well as its guidance for the state permitting agencies trying to comply with the implementing regulations, see Draft Title VI Guidance for EPA Assistance Recipients Administering Environmental Permitting Programs (Draft Recipient Guidance) and Draft Revised Guidance for Investigating Title VI Administrative Complaints Challenging Permits (Draft Revised Investigation Guidance), 65 Fed. Reg. 39,650 (June 27, 2000), have yet to be formally adopted and appear to be in bureaucratic limbo. The "guidance" documents are widely criticized as ill-conceived and inadequate. See, e.g., Eileen Guana, EPA at 30: Fairness in Environmental Protection, 31 Envtl. L. Rep. 10528, 10540–41 (2001); Bradford C. Mank,

The Draft Title VI Recipient and Revised Investigation Guidances: Too Much Discretion for EPA and a More Difficult Standard for Complainants?, 30 Envtl. L. Rep. 11144, 11146 (2000); Tseming Yang, The Form and Substance of Environmental Justice: The Challenge of Title VI of the Civil Rights Act of 1964 for Environmental Regulation, 29 B.C. Envtl. Aff. L. Rev. 143, 156 (2002); E. Andrew Long, Comment, Protection of Minority Environmental Interests in the Administrative Process: A Critical Analysis of the EPA's Guidance for Complaints Under Title VI, 39 Willamette L. Rev. 1163 (2003). In any event, of the 156 administrative complaints filed with the Office of Civil Rights by December 2004, the vast majority were dismissed as not warranting further investigation. Of the very few that were decided on the merits, none were decided in favor of the complainant. See http://www.epa.gov/civilrights/docs/t6stdec012004.pdf.

Note on Environmental Justice

1. *The evidence of disproportionate siting.* The charge that LULUs are disproportionately sited in minority or poor communities is based on dozens of studies that analyze the correlation between the location of LULUs and the demographics of the neighborhoods. The foundational studies are reviewed in Vicki Been, Environmental Justice and Equity Issues, *in* 4 Zoning and Land Use Controls §25D.06 (Patrick J. Rohan ed., 1995); Benjamin Goldman, Not Just Prosperity: Achieving Sustainability with Environmental Justice (1993). Recent work is reviewed in Luke Cole & Sheila Foster, From the Ground Up — Environmental Racism and the Rise of the Environmental Justice Movement 167–83 (2001); James P. Lester et al., Environmental Injustice in the United States: Myths and Realities 9–20 (2001); Clifford Rechtschaffen & Eileen Gauna, Environmental Justice: Law, Policy and Regulation (2002).

The most prominent research remains a nationwide analysis of the demographic characteristics of areas surrounding commercial hazardous waste facilities. United Church of Christ Commission for Racial Justice, Toxic Wastes and Race in the United States 13–14 (1987). The Commission for Racial Justice (CRJ) found a significant correlation between the number of commercial hazardous waste facilities in a zip code and the percentage of minorities in the zip code's population. The percentage of minorities in areas with one operating facility was almost twice that of areas without facilities. As the number or noxiousness of facilities in a neighborhood increased, so did the percentage of minorities in that neighborhood. In 1994, the CRJ updated its study using 1990 census data, and again found that zip codes hosting one facility had more than twice the percentage of minorities as zip codes hosting no facilities. Benjamin A. Goldman & Laura Fitton, Toxic Wastes and Race Revisited 3 (1994).

The CRJ's findings have been sharply contested. In 1994, researchers at the Social and Demographic Research Institute (SADRI) of the University of Massachusetts examined the demographics of the *census tracts* hosting commercial hazardous waste facilities and reached quite different conclusions from the CRJ's study of the zip codes hosting those same facilities. SADRI found that, as of the 1990 census, there was no statistically significant difference in the percentages of the population that were African American or Hispanic in host and nonhost tracts. Andy B. Anderson et al., Environmental Equity: Evaluating TSDF Siting over the Past Two Decades, Waste Age, July 1994, at 83. Professor Been then examined the same facilities, also focusing on census tracts rather than zip codes, and found that the areas surrounding the facilities *were* disproportionately populated by African Americans and Hispanics in 1990. Vicki Been with Francis Gupta, Coming to the Nuisance or Going to the Barrios? A Longitudinal Analysis of Environmental Justice Claims, 24 Ecology L.Q. 1 (1997). For Been's explanation of how the three research teams reached such different results, see Vicki Been, Analyzing Evidence of Environmental Justice, 11 J. Land Use & Envtl. L. 1 (1995).

2. *Which came first?* The CRJ study examined the demographics of communities surrounding LULUs as of the most recent census. If the host community is currently disproportionately poor or minority, does that necessarily mean that the siting had a discriminatory purpose or effect? Might the minorities or poor have "come to the nuisance," attracted by the lower housing values or driven by segregation in other parts of the housing market? Why would it matter which came first? See Vicki Been, Locally Undesirable Land Uses in Minority Neighborhoods: Disproportionate Siting or Market Dynamics? 103 Yale L.J. 1383 (1994). For empirical studies trying to disentangle the "which came first" problem, see Been & Gupta, supra; Christopher Boerner & Thomas Lambert, Environmental Inequity: Economic Causes, Economic Solutions, 14 Yale J. on Reg. 195 (1997); John Michael Oakes et al., A Longitudinal Analysis of Environmental Equity in Communities with Hazardous Waste Facilities, 25 Soc. Sci. Res. 125, 144–46 (1996); Manuel Pastor, Jr., et al., Which Came First? Toxic Facilities, Minority Move-In, and Environmental Justice, 23 J. Urb. Aff. 1, 18 (2001).

3. *Fairness and the market.* Should the benefit of living far from LULUs be allocated through the free market, just as the benefit of living near pristine mountain lakes or beautiful city parks is allocated? Compare, e.g., Lynn E. Blais, Environmental Racism Reconsidered, 75 N.C. L. Rev. 75 (1996), with Kristin Shrader-Frechette, Environmental Justice: Creating Equality, Reclaiming Democracy 33 (2002); Rachel D. Godsil, Viewing the Cathedral from Behind the Color Line: Property Rules, Liability Rules, and Environmental Racism, 53 Emory L.J. 1807, 1838–57 (2004); Alice Kaswan, Distributive Justice and the Environment, 81 N.C. L. Rev. 1031, 1053–55 (2003).

4. *"Environmental" justice?* The environmental justice movement has focused on environmentally undesirable land uses. But evidence suggests that social service LULUs like group homes also are more likely to be located in poor and minority neighborhoods. See, e.g., Susan Chira, New York's Poorest Neighborhoods Bear the Brunt of Social Programs, N.Y. Times, July 16, 1989, at 1, col. 1. Is the problem of how to fairly site environmental LULUs different from the problem of siting other forms of LULUs?

Is the fairness of the distribution of undesirable land uses conceptually different from the question raised by Hawkins v. Town of Shaw, excerpted at p. 679?

5. *Cost/benefit analysis?* Many undesirable land uses bring some benefits to a community, either in the form of jobs or in taxes. Should those benefits be considered in assessing whether a siting is unjust? What if the benefits and the burdens accrue to different groups? Does environmental justice require a strict nexus requirement, modeled after *Nollan*, excerpted at p. 638, to ensure that any exactions a town collects from an undesirable land use be used to mitigate the harms it causes or be distributed to those who bear its harms? See generally Tara R. Kebodeaux & Danielle M. Brock, Environmental Justice: A Choice Between Social Justice and Economic Development?, 28 S.U. L. Rev. 123 (2001); Rhoda J. Yen, Green Versus Green: When the Economic Needs of Minority Communities Clash with Environmental Justice Concerns, 17 J. Nat. Resources & Envtl. L. 109 (2002–2003).

6. *What to do?* What can local governments, state legislatures, the EPA, Congress, or the courts do to ensure that siting processes distribute the benefits and burdens of LULUs fairly, or at least are perceived to do so?

Vicki Been, Conceptions of Fairness in Proposals for Facility Siting
5 Md. J. Contemp. Legal Issues 13, 13–17 (1993/1994)

Five major legislative strategies for preventing discriminatory siting of various kinds of LULUs either have been adopted by state or local governments, or proposed for federal legislation. The first, . . . the dispersion strategy . . . is most commonly associated with group homes for the mentally disabled, but has been used for a variety of LULUs, including hazardous waste facilities.

Dispersion statutes prohibit "undue" or "excessive" concentration of a particular kind of LULU, or mandate rather arbitrary distance limits between LULUs. For example, a Wisconsin statute specifies that no group home shall be located within 2,500 feet of another. Some statutes tie the dispersion requirement to political jurisdictions — no county shall have more than one facility until all counties have at least one, for example. . . .

The second approach to the disproportionate siting problem, followed in a few states, is the impact statement approach. One version of the approach requires that the agencies responsible for proposing or approving facility sites maintain statistics regarding the number and location of existing facilities within a neighborhood, and take the concentration of uses into account in making their decisions.

A more general version of the impact statement approach requires that decision-makers consider the impact a siting will have on the "quality of life" in the community. An example is the legislation introduced by Congressmen Mike Synar (D-Okla.) and William Clinger (R-Pa.) and Senator John Glenn (D-Ohio) which would require that the process for permitting any new off-site solid waste treatment or disposal facilities include consideration of a "community information statement."[12] The statement would . . . [assess] the demographic characteristics of the host community and the presence of other solid waste treatment and disposal facilities or hazardous waste sites within the community.

A third technique the states have used to ensure that the burden of a particular land use is spread over all communities is . . . the fair share approach. The New Jersey Supreme Court's *Mount Laurel* decisions, in which the court attempted to force exclusive suburbs to bear their fair share of the burden of providing low- and moderate-income housing, are the best known examples of this technique. Basically, the approach uses mathematical models to quantify how a particular LULU should be allocated throughout a region.

The fourth approach, represented by the New York City Fair Share requirements, is a hybrid between the fair share and impact statement approaches. In brief, New York's fair share program requires the mayor to publish an annual "citywide statement of needs" that identifies all new facilities or expansions that the mayor intends to propose in the subsequent two fiscal years, and specifies the borough, and if possible, the community, in which the mayor proposes to site the use.[17] The mayor also is required to provide an "Atlas of City Property" — a map revealing all existing city-owned property and its current use, as well as all state and federal social service land uses.

The sites proposed by the mayor must conform with what have become known as "fair share criteria." Those criteria require city agencies deciding where to site facilities to take into account such factors as the facility's compatibility with the neighborhood's existing facilities and the extent to which the neighborhood's character will be adversely

---

12. H.R. 495, 103d Cong., 1st Sess. (1993). . . .

17. N.Y. City Charter, §§203–204 (1989); City Planning Comm'n, Criteria for the Location of City Facilities (Dec. 3, 1990). For an overview of the fair share criteria, see William Valletta, Siting Public Facilities on a Fair Share Basis in New York City, 25 Urb. Law. 1, 8–20 (1993); Barbara Weisberg, One City's Approach to NIMBY, 59 J. Am. Plan. Ass'n 93 (1993). . . .

affected by a further concentration of such facilities. The New York City program thus adopts a basic "impact statement" approach by requiring that neighborhoods be provided with information they can use to evaluate the distribution of burdens within the city, and by requiring that siting decisions take into account the existing distribution. However, the New York City program reinforces the impact statement approach with additional features borrowed from the formulaic fair share approach. The City Planning Commission's fair share criteria establish separate criteria for siting facilities such as "local or neighborhood facilities" and "regional or citywide facilities," in much the same way that formulaic plans carefully define their allocation regions.

5)   The fifth approach, . . . the "suspect class" approach . . . identifies certain communities in which any siting attempt will receive special scrutiny. The proposed Environmental Equal Rights Act, for example, protects "environmentally disadvantaged" communities — those communities with disproportionate percentages of people of color, people living below the poverty line, or people whose income falls below the national average, and which already have a solid or hazardous waste facility. . . . [24] Proposed sitings in those communities will be prohibited if the facility would be likely to adversely affect health, environmental quality, or economic well-being, unless no nonsuspect alternatives exist.

Note on Fair Siting Proposals

1. *State environmental justice initiatives.* Several states have adopted substantial programs to address concerns about environmental justice. See National Academy of Public Administration, Models for Change: Efforts by Four States to Address Environmental Justice (2002); Chuck D. Barlow, State Environmental Justice Programs and Related Authorities, *in* The Law of Environmental Justice: Theories and Procedures to Address Disproportionate Risks 140 (Michael B. Gerrard ed., 1999) (see also the monthly updates at http://www.abanet.org./environ/committees/envtab/ejupdates.html); Hillary Gross et al., Environmental Justice: A Review of State Responses, 8 Hastings W.-Nw. J. Envtl. L. & Pol'y 41 (2001). In New York, for example, the Department of Environmental Conservation has adopted regulations that increase opportunities for public participation in permitting processes, require scrutiny to identify permit applications that may affect low-income or minority communities, and enhance the opportunities for considering environmental justice concerns in the environmental impact review process. See http://www.dec.state.ny.us/website/ej/ejpolicy.html. Most state programs recognize the critical role that local land use procedures play in the distribution of undesirable land uses. Efforts to address environmental justice concerns accordingly focus on local and regional planning and zoning processes, in addition to state environmental impact review and facility permitting procedures. See, e.g., Clifford Rechtschaffen, Advancing Environmental Justice Norms, 37 U.C. Davis L. Rev. 95 (2003).

2. *Is fairness always the paramount concern?* Should fair siting concerns always trump other goals? If a facility will be safer at site A than at site B, but site B is a disproportionately minority community, what should the siting decisionmaker do? What if site A is much cheaper than site B? What if more of the facility's clients live near site B? See, e.g., Sheila Foster, Impact Assessment, *in* The Law of Environmental Justice, supra, at 287–89.

3. *Rating LULUs.* Several of the approaches require implicit assessments and comparisons of the burdensomeness of various LULUs. If community A has a prison and a homeless shelter, and community B has a landfill, have the LULUs been distributed fairly?

---

24. H.R. 1924, 103d Cong., 1st Sess. (1993). . . .

4. *Where's the 'hood?* In deciding whether neighborhood A has been treated fairly in the siting process, how should we define the neighborhood? Who should do the defining? Is the "community" measured by the reach of the facility's effects? By the residents' understanding of boundaries? For a look at the myriad of problems raised by the quest for fairness in siting, see Vicki Been, "What's Fairness Got to Do with It?" Environmental Justice and the Siting of Locally Undesirable Land Uses, 78 Cornell L. Rev. 1001 (1993); Bradford C. Mank, Proving an Environmental Justice Case: Determining an Appropriate Comparison Population, 20 Va. Envtl. L.J. 365, 379 (2001).

5. *When is a host neighborhood disproportionately minority?* How should one measure whether a proposed host community is "environmentally disadvantaged," to use the language of the Environmental Equal Rights Act? Is any community that has a higher percentage of racial or ethnic minorities than the city (county, state, or nation) as a whole "disadvantaged"? Given the patterns of racial and class segregation, discussed at pp. 10–12 and 692–97, how likely is it that a community will contain the same percentage of any group as the city or nation as a whole?

6. *Hold the award?* New York City's Fair Share Criteria received a special award from the American Planning Association in 1992. Many residents of the city were less enthralled, especially after then-Mayor Dinkins announced where 24 homeless shelters would be sited under the criteria. Public outcry forced Dinkins to withdraw the siting proposals. One of the most outspoken critics of the Fair Share Criteria, Joseph Rose, was later appointed director of the city's Department of City Planning. See Joseph B. Rose, A Critical Assessment of New York City's Fair Share Criteria, 59 J. Am. Plan. Ass'n 97 (1993). Under his direction, the department issued a report on the program in 1995, finding "little evidence that fair share has promoted wider dispersion of unpopular city facilities" but concluding nonetheless that it was "a significant step in the right direction." New York City Department of City Planning, Fair Share: An Assessment of New York City's Facility Siting Process 18 (1995). The report noted that "it would be helpful to discontinue use of the term 'fair share' since it generates so many unrealistic expectations. The . . . notion of fair *share* implies more than the process can deliver." Id. at 26 (emphasis in original). Since that report was issued, the Fair Share Criteria have largely become a dead letter. Michael B. Gerrard, Environmental Justice and Local Land Use Decisionmaking, *in* Trends in Land Use Law from A to Z 135–36 (Patricia E. Salkin ed., 2001).

C.   Obligations to Allow (or Provide) Low- and Moderate-Income Housing

This section tackles the most troublesome example of local government parochialism — the desire of local governments to exclude the poor from their jurisdictions. In 1973, Anthony Downs, a leading critic of American housing and land use policy, issued a call for America to "open up the suburbs." He argued that removing the barriers keeping low- and moderate-income households out of the suburbs would:

- give lower income workers access to expanding suburban job opportunities;
- allow lower-income households to "upgrade themselves" by moving to middle-income neighborhoods;
- give low-income children access to better schools;
- make it more likely that housing quality will be improved;

[handwritten margin note: give better access to jobs, schools, better quality of housing]

- result in a fairer geographic distribution of the fiscal and social costs of poverty;
- reduce the possibility of "confrontations between two spatially separate and unequal societies"; and
- afford better possibilities for improving the adverse conditions of the ghetto without displacing those problems to adjacent neighborhoods.

Anthony Downs, Opening Up the Suburbs (1973). See also Anthony Downs, New Visions for Metropolitan America (1994).

Downs's analysis of the consequences caused by segregating the poor in inner cities has been confirmed by many studies of the "geography of opportunity." The link between housing and such critical determinants of individual achievement as educational opportunities, access to health care, employment opportunities, access to information and mentoring networks, and the availability of financial capital means that where one lives can have a significant role in determining one's life chances. Sociologist Nancy Denton summarizes the literature about how residential segregation limits one's opportunities to acquire and accumulate wealth, for example:

[handwritten margin note: residential segregation limits opps for college, accumulating wealth, etc.]

> Research . . . shows that living in segregated neighborhoods negatively affects student performance. For example, Yongmin Sun found measures of community socioeconomic status to be associated with eighth grade performance in a variety of subjects.[31] . . . April Pattavina found similar effects for children in all grades, while controlling for community socio-economic status and school violence.[33] In addition to its effects on educational performance and the school environment, segregation also negatively affects the chances of completing a college education because it limits home value, the asset that has the largest positive impact on college completion rates.[34] To the extent that people with more and higher quality education have better paying jobs, segregation limits earning opportunities.[35] In addition, segregated neighborhoods often lack access to job networks[36] and transportation to available jobs.[37] Conley concludes that "the value of a family's home positively affects how much offspring work when they become adults, suggesting support for spatial (neighborhood) dynamics."[38] By preventing residents of segregated neighborhoods from obtaining high quality educations and jobs, segregation imposes limits on how much wealth and property they can amass as a result of their own efforts, a facet overlooked in a focus on "endowments" and "returns to endowments."[39]
>
> Segregation also works to limit people's accumulation of wealth through asset appreciation, particularly that of houses and businesses. Especially for the middle and lower middle classes, home appreciation is a large component of wealth.[40] Of course, to realize gains from housing appreciation, one must first own a house. Though home ownership rates are at an all

31. See [Yongmin Sun, The Contextual Effects of Community Social Capital on Academic Performance, 28 Soc. Sci. Res. 403, 403–26 (1999).]

33. See April Pattavina, The Influence of Community Violence on Child Development in an Urban Setting, 7 Res. Pol. & Soc. 163, 163–82 (1999).

34. See Dalton Conley, Being Black, Living in the Red: Race, Wealth and Social Policy in America 74 (1999).

35. See Douglas S. Massey & Kumiko Shibuya, Unraveling the Tangle of Pathology: The Effect of Spatially Concentrated Joblessness on the Well-Being of African Americans, 24 Soc. Sci. Res. 352, 352–66 (1995).

36. See James R. Elliot, Social Isolation and Labor Market Insulation: Network and Neighborhood Effects on Less-Educated Urban Workers, 40 Soc. Q. 199, 199–216 (1999).

37. See Stuart A. Gabriel & Stuart S. Rosenthal, Commutes, Neighborhood Effects, and Earnings: An Analysis of Racial Discrimination and Compensating Differentials, 40 J. Urb. Econ. 61, 61–83 (1996).

38. Conley, supra, note 34, at 102 fig. 4.5 (alteration in original).

39. Thomas A. DiPrete, Discrimination, Choice, and Group Inequality: A Discussion of How Allocative and Choice-Based Processes Complicate the Standard Decomposition, 22 Soc. Sci. Res. 415, 415–40 (1993).

40. See Thomas M. Holloway, The Role of Homeownership and Home Price Appreciation in the Accumulation and Distribution of Household Sector Wealth, 26 Bus. Econ. 38 (1991); Oliver and Shapiro estimate that homes account for about forty-three percent of whites' assets and sixty-three percent of blacks' assets. See Melvin L. Oliver & Thomas M. Shapiro, Black Wealth/White Wealth: A New Perspective on Racial Inequity 106 (1997); see also Miriam Wasserman, Appreciating the House, 8 Reg. Rev. 20 (1998).

time high, whites are still far more likely to be homeowners than other groups. In 1998, 72.6% of whites owned their own homes, as compared to only 46.1% of blacks and 44.7% of Hispanics. . . . [41] Even among homeowners, however, African Americans consistently own homes of lower value, regardless of their socioeconomic status and household structure.[42] . . .

Another way to accumulate wealth is through self employment and business ownership. A recent article by Douglas Massey and Mary Fischer documents the effects of segregation on the probability of business ownership.[48] . . . When considered in conjunction with the lower disposable income of many non-white groups, it is hardly surprising that segregation limits the ability to establish businesses and accumulate wealth through business ownership.

Finally, segregation limits people's ability to acquire wealth and property via inheritance and inter-vivos transfers. Research shows that whites are much more likely to receive parental help with the down payment on a home than blacks.[50] To the extent that segregation blocks pathways to human capital accumulation and appreciation of assets, logic dictates that there are fewer assets to be inherited by the next generation. . . .

Nancy A. Denton, The Role of Residential Segregation in Promoting and Maintaining Inequality in Wealth and Property, 34 Ind. L. Rev. 1199, 1205–07 (2001). See also, e.g., Choosing a Better Life? Evaluating the Moving to Opportunity Social Experiment (John Goering & Judith D. Feins eds., 2003); David M. Cutler & Edward L. Glaeser, Are Ghettos Good or Bad?, 112 Q.J. Econ. 827, 865 (1997) (estimating that a 13 percent decrease in residential segregation would eliminate approximately one-third of the gap between whites and blacks in schooling, employment, earning, and out-of-wedlock pregnancies).

Not only does residential segregation limit access to opportunities; it generates what William Julius Wilson has called "concentration effects." William J. Wilson, The Truly Disadvantaged: The Inner City, the Underclass and Public Policy 58 (1987). Michael H. Schill has summarized those effects as follows:

> Concentrated inner city poverty generates problems that are different both in kind and in magnitude from those experienced by poor people in less isolated settings. Specifically, children growing up in neighborhoods with few employed role models may develop weak attachments to the labor force. Lacking employment opportunities and the appropriate socialization to seek work, youths will frequently engage in deviant or illegal activities to earn income and gain status, thereby further distancing themselves from middle class norms. These behaviors are reinforced by local peer groups. Activities that are likely to assist young people in obtaining employment and social mobility, such as graduating from high school, are stigmatized rather than valued.

Michael H. Schill, Assessing the Role of Community Development Corporations in Inner City Economic Development, 22 N.Y.U. Rev. L. & Soc. Change 753, 758 (1996–1997).

What legal tools can reformers use to "open up the suburbs" to expand the geography of opportunity for racial minorities and the poor? In the period around 1970, reformers harbored considerable hope that the Supreme Court's interpretation of the U.S. Constitution would lead to the demise of exclusionary zoning. The chief constitutional theory then in vogue was that such zoning effectively discriminates against poor and minority housing

---

41. See George S. Masnick et al., A Critical Look at Rising Home Ownership Rates in the United States Since 1994 (unpublished working paper). . . .

42. Hayward Derrick Horton & Melvin E. Thomas, Race, Class, and Family Structure: Differences in Housing Values for Black and White Homeowners, 68 Soc. Inq. 114, 114–36 (1998).

48. Mary J. Fischer & Douglas S. Massey, Residential Segregation and Ethnic Enterprise in U.S. Metropolitan Areas, 47 Soc. Probs. 408, 408–24 (2000).

50. See Paul L. Menchik & Nancy Ammon Jianakoplos, Black-White Wealth Inequality: Is Inheritance the Reason?, 35 Econ. Inq. 428, 428–42 (1997); Moira Munro, Housing Wealth and Inheritance, 17 J. Soc. Pol'y 417 (1988).

consumers, and should be construed to violate the Equal Protection Clause. See especially Lawrence G. Sager, Tight Little Islands: Exclusionary Zoning, Equal Protection, and the Indigent, 21 Stan. L. Rev. 767 (1969). It also was suggested that exclusionary zoning was a violation of the voting rights of prospective entrants into the community, Note, The Constitutionality of Local Zoning, 79 Yale L.J. 896 (1970), and of their freedom of travel, Note, The Right to Travel: Another Constitutional Standard for Local Land Use Regulations? 39 U. Chi. L. Rev. 612 (1972).

Subsequent Supreme Court decisions undermined all these theories. In Lindsey v. Normet, 405 U.S. 56 (1972), the Court held that housing is not a fundamental right; and, in San Antonio Independent School District v. Rodriguez, 411 U.S. 1 (1973), that wealth is not necessarily a suspect classification. See pp. 709-10. The idea that zoning restrictions threaten freedom of travel was brushed aside in *Village of Belle Terre*, excerpted at p. 710. The protections of the Equal Protection Clause were seriously weakened by *Arlington Heights*, excerpted at p. 698, which held that a plaintiff could trigger strict judicial scrutiny only by proving that the defendant intended to discriminate.

The states, however, read their constitutions more broadly.

Southern Burlington County NAACP v. Township of Mount Laurel [*Mount Laurel I*]

336 A.2d 713 (N.J.), appeal dismissed and cert. denied, 423 U.S. 808 (1975)

HALL, J.

This case attacks the system of land use regulation by defendant Township of Mount Laurel on the ground that low and moderate income families are thereby unlawfully excluded from the municipality. The trial court so found, 290 A.2d 465 (N.J. Law Div. 1972), and declared the township zoning ordinance totally invalid. . . .

Plaintiffs represent the minority group poor (black and Hispanic)[3] seeking such quarters. But they are not the only category of persons barred from so many municipalities by reason of restrictive land use regulations. We have reference to young and elderly couples, single persons and large, growing families not in the poverty class, but who still cannot afford the only kinds of housing realistically permitted in most places — relatively high-priced, single-family detached dwellings on sizeable lots and, in some municipalities, expensive apartments. We will, therefore, consider the case from the wider viewpoint that the effect of Mount Laurel's land use regulation has been to prevent various categories of persons from living in the township because of the limited extent of their income and resources. In this connection, we accept the representation of the municipality's counsel at oral argument that the regulatory scheme was not adopted with any desire or intent to exclude prospective residents on the obviously illegal bases of race, origin or believed social incompatibility.

. . . The . . . [township's] candid position is that, conceding its land use regulation was intended to result and has resulted in economic discrimination and exclusion of substantial segments of the area population, its policies and practices are in the best present

---

3. Plaintiffs fall into four categories: (1) present residents of the township residing in dilapidated or substandard housing; (2) former residents who were forced to move elsewhere because of the absence of suitable housing; (3) nonresidents living in central city substandard housing in the region who desire to secure decent housing and accompanying advantages within their means elsewhere; (4) three organizations representing the housing and other interests of racial minorities. The township originally challenged plaintiffs' standing to bring this action. The trial court properly held that the resident plaintiffs had adequate standing to ground the entire action and found it unnecessary to pass on that of the other plaintiffs. The issue has not been raised on appeal. We merely add that both categories of nonresident individuals likewise have standing. . . . No opinion is expressed as to the standing of the organizations.

and future fiscal interest of the municipality and its inhabitants and are legally permissible and justified. . . .

THE FACTS

Mount Laurel is a flat, sprawling township, 22 square miles, or about 14,000 acres, in area, on the west central edge of Burlington County. . . .

. . . [The southerly] section of the township is about seven miles from the boundary line of the city of Camden and not more than 10 miles from the Benjamin Franklin Bridge crossing the river to Philadelphia.

In 1950, the township had a population of 2,817. . . . It was then, as it had been for decades, primarily a rural agricultural area with no sizeable settlements or commercial or industrial enterprises. . . . By 1960 the population had almost doubled to 5,249 and by 1970 had more than doubled again to 11,221. These new residents were, of course, "outsiders" from the nearby central cities and older suburbs or from more distant places drawn here by reason of employment in the region. The township is now definitely a part of the outer ring of the South Jersey metropolitan area. . . . [Sixty-five] percent of the township is still vacant land or in agricultural use. . . .

The location and nature of development has been, as usual, controlled by the local zoning enactments. The general ordinance presently in force . . . was adopted in 1964. . . . The growth pattern dictated by the ordinance is typical.

Under the present ordinance, 29.2 percent of all the land in the township, or 4,121 acres, is zoned for industry. . . .

. . . At the time of trial no more than 100 acres . . . were actually occupied by industrial uses. . . . [I]t appeared clear that, as happens in the case of so many municipalities, much more land has been so zoned than the reasonable potential for industrial movement or expansion warrants. At the same time, however, the land cannot be used for residential development under the general ordinance.

The amount of land zoned for retail business use under the general ordinance is relatively small — 169 acres, or 1.2 percent of the total. . . .

The balance of the land area, almost 10,000 acres, has been developed until recently in the conventional form of major subdivisions. The general ordinance provides for four residential zones, designated R-1, R-1D, R-2 and R-3. All permit only single-family, detached dwellings, one house per lot — the usual form of grid development. Attached townhouses, apartments (except on farms for agricultural workers) and mobile homes are not allowed anywhere in the township under the general ordinance. . . .

[The R-1 and R-2 districts have only a few hundred acres remaining to be developed.]

[The other major residential zone, R-3,] comprises over 7,000 acres — slightly more than half of the total municipal area. . . . The testimony was that about 4,600 acres of it then remained available for housing development. Ordinance requirements are substantially higher, however, . . . [than in the R-1 and R-2 districts, with large minimum lot size, lot width and minimum floor area requirements]. Presently this section is primarily in agricultural use; it contains as well most of the municipality's substandard housing. . . .

[Between 1967 and 1971, Mount Laurel approved four PUD projects.] These projects, . . . are very substantial and involve at least 10,000 sale and rental housing units of various types to be erected over a period of years. Their bounds were created by agreement rather than legislative specification on the zoning map, invading industrial, R-1, R-1D, R-3 and even flood plain zones. If completed as planned, they will in themselves ultimately quadruple the 1970 township population, but still leave a good part of the township undeveloped. (The record does not indicate how far development in each of the projects has progressed.) While multi-family housing in the form of rental garden, medium rise and high rise apartments and attached townhouses is for the first time provided for, as well as single-family detached dwellings for sale, it is not designed to accommodate and is beyond the financial reach of low and moderate income families, especially those with young children. The aim is quite the contrary; as with the single-family homes in the older conventional subdivisions, only persons of medium and upper income are sought as residents.

A few details will furnish sufficient documentation. Each of the resolutions of tentative approval of the projects contains a similar fact finding to the effect that the development will attract a highly educated and trained population base to support the nearby industrial parks in the township as well as the business and commercial facilities. The approvals also sharply limit the number of apartments having more than one bedroom. Further, they require that the developer must provide in its leases that no school-age children shall be permitted to occupy any one-bedroom apartment and that no more than two such children shall reside in any two-bedroom unit. The developer is also required, prior to the issuance of the first building permit, to record a covenant, running with all land on which multi-family housing is to be constructed, providing that in the event more than .3 school children per multi-family unit shall attend the township school system in any one year, the developer will pay the cost of tuition and other school expenses of all such excess numbers of children. In addition, low density, required amenities, such as central air conditioning, and specified developer contributions help to push rents and sales prices to high levels. These contributions include fire apparatus, ambulances, fire houses, and very large sums of money for educational facilities, a cultural center and the township library. . . .

[Approval of these PUD projects] . . . for the benefit of certain segments of the population is in sharp contrast to the lack of action, and indeed hostility, with respect to affording any opportunity for decent housing for the township's own poor living in substandard accommodations, found largely in the section known as Springville (R-3 zone). . . .

In 1968 a private non-profit association sought to build subsidized, multi-family housing in the Springville section with funds to be granted by a higher level governmental agency. Advance municipal approval of the project was required. The Township Committee responded with a purportedly approving resolution, which found a need for "moderate" income housing in the area, but went on to specify that such housing must be constructed subject to all zoning, planning, building and other applicable ordinances and codes. This meant single-family detached dwellings on 20,000 square foot lots. (Fear was also expressed that such housing would attract low income families from outside the township.) Needless to say, such requirements killed realistic housing for this group of low and moderate income families. . . .

The record thoroughly substantiates the findings of the trial court that over the years Mount Laurel "has acted affirmatively to control development and to attract a selective type of growth" and that "through its zoning ordinances has exhibited economic discrimination in that the poor have been deprived of adequate housing and the opportunity to secure the construction of subsidized housing, and has used federal, state, county and local finances and resources solely for the betterment of middle and upper-income persons."

There cannot be the slightest doubt that the reason for this course of conduct has been to keep down local taxes on *property* (Mount Laurel is not a high tax municipality) and that the policy was carried out without regard for non-fiscal considerations with respect to *people*, either within or without its boundaries. . . .

This policy of land use regulation for a fiscal end derives from New Jersey's tax structure, which has imposed on local real estate most of the cost of municipal and county government and of the primary and secondary education of the municipality's children.

Want to keep kids out b/c the fewer school kids, the lower the tax rate

The latter expense is much the largest, so, basically, the fewer the school children, the lower the tax rate. Sizeable industrial and commercial ratables are eagerly sought and homes and the lots on which they are situated are required to be large enough, through minimum lot sizes and minimum floor areas, to have substantial value in order to produce greater tax revenues to meet school costs. Large families who cannot afford to buy large houses and must live in cheaper rental accommodations are definitely not wanted, so we find drastic bedroom restrictions for, or complete prohibition of, multi-family or other feasible housing for those of lesser income.

This pattern of land use regulation has been adopted for the same purpose in developing municipality after developing municipality. Almost every one acts solely in its own selfish and parochial interest and in effect builds a wall around itself to keep out those people or entities not adding favorably to the tax base, despite the location of the municipality or the demand for varied kinds of housing. There has been no effective intermunicipal or area planning or land use regulation. . . .

THE LEGAL ISSUE

The legal question before us, as earlier indicated, is whether a developing municipality like Mount Laurel may validly, by a system of land use regulation, make it physically and economically impossible to provide low and moderate income housing in the municipality for the various categories of persons who need and want it and thereby, as Mount Laurel has, exclude such people from living within its confines because of the limited extent of their income and resources. Necessarily implicated are the broader questions of the right of such municipalities to limit the kinds of available housing and of any obligation to make possible a variety and choice of types of living accommodations.

We conclude that every such municipality must, by its land use regulations, presumptively make realistically possible an appropriate variety and choice of housing. More specifically, presumptively it cannot foreclose the opportunity of the classes of people mentioned for low and moderate income housing and in its regulations must affirmatively afford that opportunity, at least to the extent of the municipality's fair share of the present and prospective regional need therefor. These obligations must be met unless the particular municipality can sustain the heavy burden of demonstrating peculiar circumstances which dictate that it should not be required to do so.

We reach this conclusion under state law and so do not find it necessary to consider federal constitutional grounds urged by plaintiffs. . . .

under state law, Not fed const — even for state

It is elementary theory that all police power enactments, no matter at what level of government, must conform to the basic state constitutional requirements of substantive due process and equal protection of the laws. These are inherent in Art. I, par. 1 of our Constitution,[11] the requirements of which may be more demanding than those of the federal Constitution. It is required that, affirmatively, a zoning regulation, like any police power enactment, must promote public health, safety, morals or the general welfare. . . .

. . . Frequently the decisions in this state, . . . have spoken only in terms of the interest of the enacting municipality, so that it has been thought, at least in some quarters, that such was the only welfare requiring consideration. It is, of course, true that many cases have dealt only with regulations having little, if any, outside impact where the local decision is ordinarily entitled to prevail. However, it is fundamental and not to be forgotten that the

---

11. The paragraph reads: "All persons are by nature free and independent, and have certain natural and unalienable rights, among which are those of enjoying and defending life and liberty, of acquiring, possessing, and protecting property, and of pursuing and obtaining safety and happiness."

zoning power is a police power of the state and the local authority is acting only as a delegate of that power and is restricted in the same manner as is the state. So, when regulation does have a substantial external impact, the welfare of the state's citizens beyond the borders of the particular municipality cannot be disregarded and must be recognized and served. . . .

It is plain beyond dispute that proper provision for adequate housing of all categories of people is certainly an absolute essential in promotion of the general welfare required in all local land use regulation. Further the universal and constant need for such housing is so important and of such broad public interest that the general welfare which developing municipalities like Mount Laurel must consider extends beyond their boundaries and cannot be parochially confined to the claimed good of the particular municipality. . . .

. . . [O]ur opinion is that Mount Laurel's zoning ordinance is presumptively contrary to the general welfare and outside the intended scope of the zoning power in the particulars mentioned. A facial showing of invalidity is thus established, shifting to the municipality the burden of establishing valid superseding reasons for its action and non-action. We now examine the reasons it advances.

The township's principal reason in support of its zoning plan and ordinance housing provisions, advanced especially strongly at oral argument, is the fiscal one previously adverted to, i.e., that by reason of New Jersey's tax structure which substantially finances municipal governmental and educational costs from taxes on local real property, every municipality may, by the exercise of the zoning power, allow only such uses and to such extent as will be beneficial to the local tax rate. . . .

. . . We have no hesitancy in now saying, and do so emphatically, that, considering the basic importance of the opportunity for appropriate housing for all classes of our citizenry, no municipality may exclude or limit categories of housing for that reason or purpose. While we fully recognize the increasingly heavy burden of local taxes for municipal governmental and school costs on homeowners, relief from the consequences of this tax system will have to be furnished by other branches of government. It cannot legitimately be accomplished by restricting types of housing through the zoning process in developing municipalities. . . .

By way of summary, what we have said comes down to this. As a developing municipality, Mount Laurel must, by its land use regulations, make realistically possible the opportunity for an appropriate variety and choice of housing for all categories of people who may desire to live there, of course including those of low and moderate income. It must permit multi-family housing, without bedroom or similar restrictions, as well as small dwellings on very small lots, low cost housing of other types and, in general, high density zoning, without artificial and unjustifiable minimum requirements as to lot size, building size and the like, to meet the full panoply of these needs. Certainly when a municipality zones for industry and commerce for local tax benefit purposes, it without question must zone to permit adequate housing within the means of the employees involved in such uses. . . . The amount of land removed from residential use by allocation to industrial and commercial purposes must be reasonably related to the present and future potential for such purposes. In other words, such municipalities must zone primarily for the living welfare of people and not for the benefit of the local tax rate. . . .

. . . [W]e feel that every municipality therein must bear its fair share of the regional burden. . . .

The composition of the applicable "region" will necessarily vary from situation to situation and probably no hard and fast rule will serve to furnish the answer in every case. . . . Here we have already defined the region at present as "those portions of Camden, Burlington and Gloucester Counties within a semicircle having a radius of 20 miles or so from the heart of Camden City." The concept of "fair share" is coming into more general use and, through the expertise of the municipal planning adviser, the county planning boards and the state planning agency, a reasonable figure for Mount Laurel can be determined, which can then be translated to the allocation of sufficient land therefor on the zoning map. . . .

The Remedy

[T]he trial court invalidated the zoning ordinance in toto and ordered the township to make certain studies and investigations and to present to the court a plan of affirmative public action designed "to enable and encourage the satisfaction of the indicated needs" for township related low and moderate income housing. . . .

We are of the view that the trial court's judgment should be modified in certain respects. We see no reason why the entire zoning ordinance should be nullified. Therefore we declare it to be invalid only to the extent and in the particulars set forth in this opinion. The township is granted 90 days from the date hereof, or such additional time as the trial court may find it reasonable and necessary to allow, to adopt amendments to correct the deficiencies herein specified. It is the local function and responsibility, in the first instance at least, rather than the court's, to decide on the details of the same within the guidelines we have laid down. If plaintiffs desire to attack such amendments, they may do so by supplemental complaint. . . .

. . . Courts do not build housing nor do municipalities. That function is performed by private builders, various kinds of associations, or, for public housing, by special agencies created for that purpose at various levels of government. The municipal function is initially to provide the opportunity through appropriate land use regulations and we have spelled out what Mount Laurel must do in that regard. . . . The municipality should first have full opportunity to itself act without judicial supervision. We trust it will do so in the spirit we have suggested, both by appropriate zoning ordinance amendments and whatever additional action encouraging the fulfillment of its fair share of the regional need for low and moderate income housing may be indicated as necessary and advisable. . . . Should Mount Laurel not perform as we expect, further judicial action may be sought by supplemental pleading in this cause.

The judgment of the Law Division is modified as set forth herein. . . .

[Two concurring opinions have been omitted.]

Note on the Motivations for Exclusionary Zoning

1. *Fiscal zoning. Mt. Laurel I* assumed that the motivation behind Mt. Laurel's hostility to low- and moderate-income housing was the desire to keep taxes low. Professors Inman and Rubinfeld explain that phenomenon:

> The economic forces which give rise to exclusionary zoning are easily described. The residents of the high income suburbs have an incentive to protect their favorable tax base, since a large tax base per family means low tax rates for any chosen spending level. Admitting families into the community who purchase homes with a value below the community average will lower the tax base per family. Thus, if the community wishes to maintain current spending levels, it will be forced to raise tax rates. This increase in tax rates will make the suburb less attractive to future residents and hence lower the resale value of the remaining residents' properties. While existing residents wish to exclude, private developers have a strong incentive to build high density housing for lower income families in these communities. They can offer an attractive price for a residential site within a rich community and then earn sizeable profits by subdividing

the lot into many smaller plots and selling them to lower income families. Furthermore, current residents of the suburb planning to move to another region for nonfiscal reasons will have a strong incentive to sell to these high-bid developers. Thus, working through a developer, a "coalition" of low income families can, in effect, pool their resources and outbid one high income family for a residential plot in the high tax base suburb.

Of course, current residents are not powerless in this situation. They could pool their own resources and outbid the low income families for available property. If such a strategy were adopted, the existing residents would bear the costs of preserving the community's high tax base. A far more appealing alternative — since it shifts the burden to the nonresident low income families, developers, and resident families who would otherwise sell to low income families — is the enactment of exclusionary zoning controls. . . .

Robert Inman & Daniel Rubinfeld, The Judicial Pursuit of Local Fiscal Equity, 92 Harv. L. Rev. 1662, 1685–89 (1979). See also, e.g., Myron Orfield, Metropolitics 5–6 (1997).

Why shouldn't municipalities protect themselves from "free-riding" by those who want to enjoy the community's services while paying less in taxes than the higher-value homes? Jeffrey Lehmann argues that fiscal zoning is inefficient because it imposes costs on developers, landowners, and the potential consumers of housing; leads to a spatial mismatch between the demand for and supply of labor; and increases the consumption of land and its attendant environmental harms. Jeffrey M. Lehmann, Reversing Judicial Deference Toward Exclusionary Zoning: A Suggested Approach, 12 J. Affordable Housing & Community Dev. L. 229, 231–34 (2003). Richard Briffault argues that it is simply unfair:

> With property wealth and service needs unevenly distributed throughout the region and greater property wealth per household generally concentrated in areas of lower need, there are profound interlocal taxing and spending inequalities. More affluent localities do very well under this system, but poorer localities do not. The localities whose people are in greatest need are simply unable to meet the needs of their residents or to compete for the tax base that would enhance their fiscal capacity.

Richard Briffault, Localism and Regionalism, 48 Buff. L. Rev. 1, 25–26 (2000). See also Sheryll D. Cashin, Essay, Drifting Apart: How Wealth and Race Segregation Are Reshaping the American Dream, 47 Vill. L. Rev. 595 (2002). Does either Briffault's or Lehmann's argument suggest that municipalities should not be allowed to engage in fiscal zoning, or that the fiscal burdens poorer families impose on communities should be shared on a regional, state, or federal basis? See, e.g., Dmitri Evseev, Note, Making Mixed-Income Communities Possible: Tax Base Sharing and Class Desegregation, 114 Harv. L. Rev. 1575 (2001). Are local governments appropriate vehicles for implementing the wealth-redistribution policy inherent in a decision to prohibit local governments from engaging in fiscal zoning?

2. *Racism and classism.* Another (not necessarily conflicting) theory is that exclusionary zoning is driven by the desire to keep people of different races and social classes out of the community. See Peter H. Schuck, Diversity in America 207, 258 (2003) (discussing the "ubiquitous classism [that] rejects the idea that people should have a right to live in a neighborhood they cannot afford"); Richard Thompson Ford, The Boundaries of Race: Political Geography in Legal Analysis, 107 Harv. L. Rev. 1843 (1994); Jerry Frug, The Geography of Community, 48 Stan. L. Rev. 1047, 1081–89 (1996). Even if it could be proved that racial bias did not motivate exclusionary zoning today, given the history of racial discrimination and residential segregation, see pp. 692–97, might exclusionary zoning for non-racial reasons nevertheless work to "lock in" segregation? See Daria Roithmayr, Locked In Segregation, 12 Va. J. Soc. Pol'y & L. 197 (2004).

For evidence that low-density zoning, whatever its motivations, does indeed lead to fewer racial minorities in a jurisdiction, see Rolf Pendall, Local Land Use Regulation and the Chain of Exclusion, 66 J. Am. Plan. Ass'n 125 (2000).

3. *Empirical evidence of the motivations behind exclusionary zoning.* A few empiricists have tried to sort out what motivates jurisdictions, or their voters, to engage in exclusionary zoning. One of the studies finds support for both the fiscal zoning thesis and the racism thesis: The restrictiveness of zoning was positively correlated with fiscal measures such as the proportion of the local tax base derived from nonresidential property and was positively correlated with the extent to which communities had smaller percentages of racial minorities than surrounding communities. Barbara Sherman Rolleston, Determinants of Restrictive Suburban Zoning: An Empirical Analysis, 21 J. Urb. Econ. 1 (1987). See also Eric J. Branfman et al., Measuring the Invisible Wall: Land Use Controls and the Residential Patterns of the Poor, 82 Yale L.J. 483 (1973) (finding no substantial relationship between clustering of the poor and fiscal incentives for exclusionary controls, such as local property tax rates as a percentage of local revenues, but finding that clustering increased as the number of zoning authorities increased, and as the proportion of African Americans and Latinos increased); James C. Clingermayer, Quasi-Judicial Decision Making and Exclusionary Zoning, 31 Urb. Aff. Rev. 544 (1996) (finding correlation between level of exclusionary zoning and levels of home ownership, thereby supporting the fiscal zoning theory). Cf. William T. Bogart, "What Big Teeth You Have!": Identifying the Motivations for Exclusionary Zoning, 30 Urb. Stud. 1669 (1993) (discussing flaws in the models for identifying motivations for exclusionary zoning). For helpful literature reviews, see Melvyn R. Durchslag, *Village of Euclid v. Ambler Realty Co.*, Seventy-Five Years Later: This Is Not Your Father's Zoning Ordinance, 51 Case W. Res. L. Rev. 645, 657–60 (2001); Keith R. Ihlanfeldt, Exclusionary Land Use Regulations within Suburban Communities: A Review of the Evidence and Policy Prescriptions, 41 Urb. Stud. 261, 272–75 (2004).

4. *Is economic integration possible? Necessarily desirable?* Professor Schuck sees little reason to believe that efforts to end segregation by class will be successful because "almost all" Americans "endorse classism — the notion that one may properly choose to live with others of one's wealth or income level but has no moral claim to live in a community one cannot afford." Peter H. Schuck, Diversity in America 319 (2003). See also Paul Boudreaux, Vouchers, Buses, and Flats: The Persistence of Social Segregation, 49 Vill. L. Rev. 55, 55 (2004) (efforts at residential integration fail in part "because of a taboo against social integration of poor persons into middle-class society").

Other commentators have found cause for limited optimism about the prospects for economic integration in various efforts to "deconcentrate" the inner city poor, such as the Illinois Gautreaux program, which relocated about 7,000 poor black families from Chicago to wealthier suburbs over a 22-year period; "inclusionary zoning" programs created in many California municipalities; and the national "Moving to Opportunity" program, which provided selected poor families with housing vouchers redeemable only in higher-income neighborhoods. One study of such mobility programs concludes that they "demonstrate that low-income families can make moves that facilitate racial or economic integration." Leonard S. Rubinowitz & James E. Rosenbaum, Crossing the Class and Color Lines: From Public Housing to White Suburbia 92 (2000). See also Choosing a Better Life: Evaluating the Moving to Opportunity Social Experiment (John Goering & Judith D. Feins eds., 2003); Nico Calavita & Kenneth Grimes, Inclusionary Housing in California: The Experience of Two Decades, 64 J. Am. Plan. Ass'n 150 (1998) (discussing the effectiveness and stability of the California inclusionary housing initiatives).

If economic integration is possible, is it necessarily desirable? See, e.g., Henry A. Span, How the Courts Should Fight Exclusionary Zoning, 32 Seton Hall L. Rev. 1 (2001) (noting that studies show that even when controlling for income, race, and population density, economic homogeneity is correlated with lower rates of both property and violent crime, better academic performance by school students, and greater "social capital," and observing that community self-determination is valuable in itself).

If economic integration is both possible and desirable, should courts prevent local governments from trying to segregate *communities* by wealth? What about *neighborhoods? Individual blocks?*

5. *The Tiebout Hypothesis.* A number of urban economists have suggested that specialization among suburbs is efficiency-enhancing. The leading article is by Professor Charles Tiebout, A Pure Theory of Local Expenditures, 64 J. Pol. Econ. 416 (1956). The Tiebout Hypothesis (developed with the aid of several simplifying assumptions) is that consumers benefit from being able to "vote with their feet" among municipalities offering varying packages of spending and taxing policies. Families with young children might settle in jurisdictions with excellent schools, for example, while elderly individuals worried about public safety might pick locations with excellent police services. According to Tiebout, the specialization of municipalities and the competition among them will enhance the efficiency of metropolitan organization because people will congregate with others of similar tastes and therefore be more likely to get the public goods they most prefer.

The Tiebout Hypothesis may be contrasted with what might be called a "Waring Blender model," which would call for all land uses and all types of households to be represented in each neighborhood in proportion to their representation in the entire metropolitan area. (Does the *Mount Laurel I* court endorse a pure Waring Blender approach?) Note that the Waring Blender model produces great diversity *within* neighborhoods, but no diversity *between* neighborhoods, and thus may limit the variety of residential choices available to households.

One of Tiebout's key assumptions was that there are no cost or benefit spillovers between communities. What cost spillovers does the geography of opportunity literature, discussed at pp. 761–62, suggest might be created by the concentration of, say, wealthy whites in exclusive suburbs? How might one investigate the magnitude of these cost spillovers to determine whether they exceed the benefits arising from diversification among communities?

There is a rich literature regarding the Tiebout Hypothesis and the implications of specialization among suburbs. See, e.g., William A. Fischel, The Homevoter Hypothesis (2001); Gerald Frug, City Making: Building Communities Without Building Walls (1999); William T. Bogart, "Trading Places": The Role of Zoning in Promoting and Discouraging Intrametropolitan Trade, 51 Case W. Res. L. Rev. 697, 707–10 (2001); William W. Bratton & Joseph A. McCahery, The New Economics of Jurisdictional Competition: Devolutionary Federalism in a Second-Best World, 86 Geo. L.J. 201 (1997); Richard Briffault, Localism and Regionalism, 48 Buff. L. Rev. 1 (2000); Todd E. Pettys, The Mobility Paradox, 92 Geo. L.J. 481 (2004).

Note on *Mount Laurel I*

1. *The doctrinal footing.* Professor Charles Haar, an ardent supporter of the *Mount Laurel* cases, described Justice Hall's reasoning as "a doctrinal free-for-all with minimal linkage to prior case law." Charles M. Haar, Suburbs Under Siege: Race, Space, and Audacious Judges 19 (1996). Is that accurate?

At times, *Mount Laurel I* verges on a declaration that exclusionary zoning discriminates against the poor. For the reasons explored at pp. 709–10, that would be problematic if the opinion were based on the federal Constitution. But the New Jersey Supreme Court was careful to rest the opinion on state constitutional grounds. What exactly does *Mount Laurel I* read the New Jersey Constitution to require or forbid? See, e.g., Haar, supra, at 23 (describing the opinion as establishing that "economic discrimination could be invoked as an inherently suspect basis of classification not only by those of low- and moderate-incomes excluded from a community by virtue of local zoning regulations but also by all those who were poor in the sense that they paid too large a proportion of their incomes for shelter").

Was the tactical judgment to avoid resting the holding on constitutional prohibitions against racial discrimination sound? See, e.g., John M. Payne, Lawyers, Judges, and the Public Interest, 96 Mich. L. Rev. 1685, 1706, 1709 (1998) (reviewing Haar, supra) ("By glossing over race . . . the New Jersey Supreme Court lost the opportunity to draw the clearest of moral lines, and hence to defend the legitimacy of its intervention. . . . The morality of a constitutional rule requiring municipalities to exercise their land-use power in a racially fair way would command broad, if sometimes grudging, respect as a legitimate exercise of judicial power. Such a rule therefore would achieve greater and better results than has the complex, hard-to-explain *Mount Laurel* doctrine.").

2. *Leave it to the market.* If Mount Laurel were to respond to the decision by deregulating altogether — scrapping its zoning ordinance and disbanding its planning department — would it satisfy the court's mandates? Would low- and moderate-income housing then necessarily be built in Mount Laurel? To what extent did *Mount Laurel I* rest on the notion that if government would just get out of the way, the market would provide low- and moderate-income housing?

3. *What's a responsible municipality to do?* After *Mount Laurel I*, what would you have advised Mount Laurel's planning commission and city council to do, short of getting out of the zoning business? What does it mean to make the opportunity for low- and moderate-income housing "realistically possible"? What qualifies as "low- and moderate-income" or "affordable" housing? Obviously, the municipality must permit multifamily housing, but how much, and where? What is Mount Laurel's "fair share" of the region's burden for low- and moderate-income housing? Who does the housing have to accommodate — can the municipality provide housing for the poor elderly, rather than more generally? Who decides all these issues? How?

4. *What's a recalcitrant municipality to do?* Consider Mount Laurel's response. Following the court's remand in *Mount Laurel I*, the town zoned three plots of land, totaling less than one-quarter of 1 percent of the township's area, for multifamily housing. One plot, a wetland behind an industrial park, had no access to other parts of the community, was far from water or sewer connections, and was in the path of a proposed high-speed railroad line. Another was too small to support more than about 30 homes and had such serious drainage problems that it would be quite costly to develop. It could not be developed for at least five years because sewer and water connections would not be available before then. The third was an established PUD district, in which the town agreed to allow up to 10 percent of the homes to be affordable housing. The developer of the project had shown no interest in providing such housing, however, and the town had offered no incentives for doing so. See David L. Kirp et al., Our Town: Race, Housing, and the Soul of Suburbia 85–92 (1995).

5. *"Least cost" housing, "numberless" obligations, and "developing" communities.* The New Jersey Supreme Court seemed to equivocate in its next two exclusionary zoning cases. In Oakwood at Madison, Inc. v. Township of Madison, 371 A.2d 1192 (N.J. 1977), a majority of the court reframed the *Mount Laurel I* mandate as requiring only that municipalities adjust their land use regulations to permit construction of "the 'least cost'

housing, consistent with minimum standards of health and safety, which private industry will undertake," reasoning that such housing would help low- and moderate-income housing consumers indirectly through the "filtering down" process of the housing market. The court also adopted a "numberless" approach, holding that a trial court that finds a municipality in violation of *Mount Laurel* need not precisely demarcate the municipality's "region" nor fix a specific number of lower-cost housing units as the municipality's "fair share" of the regional need. In Pascack Associates v. Mayor & Council of Township of Washington, 379 A.2d 6 (N.J. 1977), the court further waffled by holding that the obligations of *Mount Laurel I* were limited to "developing" municipalities.

6. *Back to the Supreme Court for a "legislative" hearing.* Not surprisingly, municipalities seized on the hesitancy shown in *Madison* and *Pascack*, and the ensuing chaos eventually forced the New Jersey Supreme Court to revisit the issues. The court consolidated six cases to allow comprehensive review of the issues raised by *Mount Laurel I*. The procedures the *Mount Laurel II* court followed to hear the cases were unusual, to say the least. Before the argument, the court sent the parties a list of 24 questions it wanted addressed. The list included such questions as: "Is the underlying goal of *Mount Laurel* economically feasible?" The "argument" took three days. John M. Payne, Housing Rights and Remedies: A "Legislative" History of *Mount Laurel II*, 14 Seton Hall L. Rev. 889 (1984). See also Kirp et al., supra, at 95–100; Henry A. Span, How the Courts Should Fight Exclusionary Zoning, 32 Seton Hall L. Rev. 1, 50 (2001). The court then took more than two years to issue an opinion.

[handwritten margin note: Btwn MT I and II NJ SC waivered, then got II.]

Southern Burlington County NAACP v. Township of Mount Laurel [*Mount Laurel II*]
456 A.2d 390 (N.J. 1983)

[The opinion takes up 120 pages of the Atlantic Reporter. This excerpt deletes all discussion except what appears in the introduction and the Court's own "Summary of Rulings."]

WILENTZ, C.J.

This is the return, eight years later, of . . . *Mount Laurel I*. We set forth in that case, for the first time, the doctrine requiring that municipalities' land use regulations provide a realistic opportunity for low and moderate income housing. The doctrine has become famous. The *Mount Laurel* case itself threatens to become infamous. After all this time, ten years after the trial court's initial order invalidating its zoning ordinance, Mount Laurel remains afflicted with a blatantly exclusionary ordinance. Papered over with studies, rationalized by hired experts, the ordinance at its core is true to nothing but Mount Laurel's determination to exclude the poor. Mount Laurel is not alone; we believe that there is widespread non-compliance with the constitutional mandate of our original opinion in this case.

To the best of our ability, we shall not allow it to continue. This Court is more firmly committed to the original *Mount Laurel* doctrine than ever, and we are determined, within appropriate judicial bounds, to make it work. The obligation is to provide a realistic opportunity for housing, not litigation. We have learned from experience, however, that unless a strong judicial hand is used, *Mount Laurel* will not result in housing, but in paper, process, witnesses, trials and appeals. We intend by this decision to strengthen it, clarify it, and make it easier for public officials, including judges, to apply it. . . .

[handwritten margin note: Ct firmly committed to MT doctrine]

. . . The basis for the constitutional obligation is simple: the State controls the use of land, all of the land. In exercising that control it cannot favor rich over poor. It cannot legislatively set aside dilapidated housing in urban ghettos for the poor and decent housing elsewhere for everyone else. The government that controls this land represents everyone. While the State may not have the ability to eliminate poverty, it cannot use that condition as the basis for imposing further disadvantages. And the same applies to the municipality, to which this control over land has been constitutionally delegated. . . .

. . . We act first and foremost because the Constitution of our State requires protection of the interests involved and because the Legislature has not protected them. We recognize the social and economic controversy (and its political consequences) that has resulted in relatively little legislative action in this field. We understand the enormous difficulty of achieving a political consensus that might lead to significant legislation enforcing the constitutional mandate better than we can, legislation that might completely remove this Court from those controversies. But enforcement of constitutional rights cannot await a supporting political consensus. So while we have always preferred legislative to judicial action in this field, we shall continue — until the Legislature acts — to do our best to uphold the constitutional obligation that underlies the *Mount Laurel* doctrine. That is our duty. We may not build houses, but we do enforce the Constitution. . . .

C. Summary of Rulings . . .

The following is a summary of the more significant rulings of these cases:

(1) *Every* municipality's land use regulations should provide a realistic opportunity for decent housing for at least some part of its resident poor who now occupy dilapidated housing. . . .

(2) The existence of a municipal obligation to provide a realistic opportunity for a fair share of the region's present and prospective low and moderate income housing need will no longer be determined by whether or not a municipality is "developing." The obligation extends, instead, to every municipality, any portion of which is designated by the State, through the SDGP [State Development Guide Plan] as a "growth area." This obligation, imposed as a remedial measure, does not extend to those areas where the SDGP discourages growth — namely, open space, rural areas, prime farmland, conservation areas, limited growth areas, parts of the Pinelands and certain Coastal Zone areas. . . .

(3) *Mount Laurel* litigation will ordinarily include proof of the municipality's fair share of low and moderate income housing in terms of the number of units needed immediately, as well as the number needed for a reasonable period of time in the future. "Numberless" resolution of the issue based upon a conclusion that the ordinance provides a realistic opportunity for *some* low and moderate income housing will be insufficient. Plaintiffs, however, will still be able to prove a prima facie case, without proving the precise fair share of the municipality, by proving that the zoning ordinance is substantially affected by restrictive devices, that proof creating a presumption that the ordinance is invalid.

The municipal obligation to provide a realistic opportunity for low and moderate income housing is not satisfied by a good faith attempt. The housing opportunity provided must, in fact, be the substantial equivalent of the fair share.

(4) Any future *Mount Laurel* litigation shall be assigned only to those judges selected by the Chief Justice with the approval of the Supreme Court. The initial group shall consist of three judges, the number to be increased or decreased hereafter by the Chief Justice with the Court's approval. The Chief Justice shall define the area of the State for which each of the three judges is responsible: any *Mount Laurel* case challenging the land use ordinance or a municipality included in that area shall be assigned to that judge. . . .

(5) The municipal obligation to provide a realistic opportunity for the construction of its fair share of low and moderate income housing may require more than the elimination of unnecessary cost-producing requirements and restrictions. Affirmative governmental

devices should be used to make that opportunity realistic, including lower-income density bonuses and mandatory set-asides. Furthermore the municipality should cooperate with the developer's attempts to obtain federal subsidies. For instance, where federal subsidies depend on the municipality providing certain municipal tax treatment allowed by state statutes for lower income housing, the municipality should make a good faith effort to provide it. Mobile homes may not be prohibited, unless there is solid proof that sound planning in a particular municipality requires such prohibition. . . .

(8) Builder's remedies will be afforded to plaintiffs in *Mount Laurel* litigation where appropriate, on a case-by-case basis. Where the plaintiff has acted in good faith, attempted to obtain relief without litigation, and thereafter vindicates the constitutional obligation in *Mount Laurel*-type litigation, ordinarily a builder's remedy will be granted, provided that the proposed project includes an appropriate portion of low and moderate income housing, and provided further that it is located and designed in accordance with sound zoning and planning concepts, including its environmental impact. . . .

We reassure all concerned that *Mount Laurel* is not designed to sweep away all land use restrictions or leave our open spaces and natural resources prey to speculators. Municipalities consisting largely of conservation, agricultural, or environmentally sensitive areas will not be required to grow because of *Mount Laurel*. No forests or small towns need be paved over and covered with high-rise apartments as a result of today's decision.

As for those municipalities that may have to make adjustments in their lifestyles to provide for their fair share of low and moderate income housing, they should remember that they are not being required to provide more than their *fair* share. No one community need be concerned that it will be radically transformed by a deluge of low and moderate income developments. Nor should any community conclude that its residents will move to other suburbs as a result of this decision, for those "other suburbs" may very well be required to do their part to provide the same housing. Finally, once a community has satisfied its fair share obligation, the *Mount Laurel* doctrine will not restrict other measures, including large-lot and open area zoning, that would maintain its beauty and communal character.

. . . Our scenic and rural areas will remain essentially scenic and rural, and our suburban communities will retain their basic suburban character. But there will be some change, as there must be if the constitutional rights of our lower income citizens are ever to be protected. That change will be much less painful for us than the status quo has been for them. . . .

[The unanimous Court then remanded the case to the trial court for proceedings to determine Mount Laurel's fair share, and "upon such determination to require further actions by the municipality to assure the expeditious revision of Mount Laurel's land use regulations (and other actions) all in accordance with this opinion." The Court suggested that the evidence of bad faith by the township should lead the trial court to appoint a special master to monitor compliance.]

Note on *Mount Laurel II*

1. *From deregulation to regulation.* Mount Laurel *I* seemed to require only deregulation, but Mount Laurel *II* requires municipalities to do much more than just get out of the way of the market. Do the doctrinal underpinnings of *Mount Laurel I* stretch far enough to cover *Mount Laurel II*'s view that local government must act affirmatively to provide incentives to the market, or is *Mount Laurel II* essentially a "gut rehab" of *Mount Laurel I*? See Peter H. Schuck, Diversity in America 221 (2003) (reporting Professor John Payne's use of the "gut rehab" analogy); J. Peter Byrne, Are Suburbs Unconstitutional?, 85 Geo.

L.J. 2265 (1997) (book review) (*Mount Laurel II* loses touch with the constitutional wrong that set the court's remedial power in motion).

2. *Why not redistribute income instead?* In a forum on *Mount Laurel*, Professor Peter Van Doren suggests: "The problem is that poor people don't have much money, so if you care about housing market outcomes, my advice to you is not to worry so much about housing markets, and to redistribute wealth to the poor people." Symposium, *Mount Laurel and the Fair Housing Act: Success or Failure,* 19 Fordham. Urb. L.J. 59, 81 (1991). How would you respond? Does *Mount Laurel II*'s emphasis on inclusionary zoning measures essentially order a redistribution from developers (or their buyers) to poor people? Why should the burden of redistribution fall there, rather than more broadly?

3. *Developer/municipal collusion.* Armed with the weapon of a builder's remedy if they include low- and moderate-income housing in their proposals, developers have an effective tool to convince local governments to approve even middle- and higher-income housing that local governments might not want. See, e.g., Charles M. Haar, Suburbs Under Siege: Race, Space, and Audacious Judges 63 (1996); Symposium, *Mount Laurel* and the Fair Housing Act: Success or Failure, 19 Fordham Urb. L.J. 59, 74 (1991) (Art Bernard, deputy executive director of the Council of Affordable Housing, notes that "developers and municipalities have become more adept at negotiating deals that avoid litigation, but do not benefit the poor"). If a developer sues a municipality, the judge, of course, can determine the appropriateness of the builder's remedy after hearing from all parties, including representatives of low- and moderate-income housing consumers. But if no litigation is pending, how can abuse of the threat of the builder's remedy be controlled? See John M. Payne, Lawyers, Judges, and the Public Interest, 96 Mich. L. Rev. 1685, 1691–1702 (1998) (reviewing Haar, supra) (offering a scathing indictment of the role of the builder's remedy); John M. Payne, Norman Williams, Exclusionary Zoning, and the *Mount Laurel* Doctrine: Making the Theory Fit the Facts, 20 Vt. L. Rev. 665, 677–79 (1996).

Despite such criticisms of the builder's remedy, the New Jersey Supreme Court reaffirmed the availability of the remedy in Toll Bros., Inc. v. Township of West Windsor, 803 A.2d 53 (N.J. 2002).

Note on the Fair Housing Act

1. *Legislative response.* *Mount Laurel II* evoked a furious reaction from the executive and legislative branches. Then-Governor Thomas Kean likened the decision to communism: "I don't believe that every municipality has got to be a carbon copy of another. That's a socialist country, a communistic country, a dictatorship." Robert Hanley, Some Jersey Towns, Giving into Courts, Let in Modest Homes, N.Y. Times, Feb. 29, 1984, at B5. Many state legislators also were sharply critical of the decision. Local government officials threatened noncompliance, and 100 municipalities held advisory referendums asking the state legislature to adopt a constitutional amendment essentially overturning the *Mount Laurel* holdings. See Richard F. Babcock & Charles L. Siemon, The Zoning Game Revisited 211–19 (1985); Update on *Mount Laurel*, Zoning News, Nov. 1986, at 1.

The state legislature responded by passing the Fair Housing Act of 1985, N.J. Stat. Ann. §§52:27D-301 et seq. (West 2005). That act created an administrative agency, the Council on Affordable Housing (COAH), and assigned it the responsibility for defining housing regions within the state, determining the regional need for low- and moderate-income housing, and specifying the criteria by which that need should be allocated among municipalities within each region. Further, the act gave the council jurisdiction over litigation under the *Mt. Laurel* decisions, empowered the council to determine whether a municipality was satisfying its obligation to provide its fair share of the regional need, and prohibited the courts from setting aside that determination except upon "clear and convincing evidence." The act also allowed municipalities to transfer to other "receiving" municipalities up to 50 percent of their fair share obligation under so-called regional contribution agreements (RCAs). Finally, the act limited the use of the builder's remedy.

2. Mount Laurel III: *A Retreat?* The New Jersey Supreme Court upheld the Fair Housing Act in Hills Development Co. v. Township of Bernards, 510 A.2d 621 (N.J. 1986), but declared:

> No one should assume that our exercise of comity today signals a weakening of our resolve to enforce the constitutional rights of New Jersey's lower income citizens. The constitutional obligation has not changed; the judiciary's ultimate duty to enforce it has not changed; our determination to perform that duty has not changed. What has changed is that we are no longer alone in this field. The other branches of government have fashioned a comprehensive statewide response to the *Mount Laurel* obligation. This kind of response, one that would permit us to withdraw from this field, is what this Court has always wanted and sought. It is potentially far better for the State and for its lower income citizens. . . .

Id. at 655.

Many observers view the Fair Housing Act of 1985 as "diluting" the *Mount Laurel* doctrine and are disappointed by the court's response to the act. See, e.g., Charles M. Haar, Suburbs Under Siege: Race, Space, and Audacious Judges 93, 108–10 (1996); David L. Kirp et al., Our Town: Race, Housing, and the Soul of Suburbia 147 (1995); Wynona M. Lipman, The "Fair" Housing Act?, 9 Seton Hall Legis. J. 569 (1986). Cf. John M. Payne, Lawyers, Judges, and the Public Interest, 96 Mich. L. Rev. 1685, 1688, 1690 (1998) (reviewing Haar, supra) (the Fair Housing Act was "arguably the most progressive piece of state housing legislation anywhere in the country" and "codified the core, although not always the details, of the *Mount Laurel* doctrine"). Would continued judicial oversight have been preferable? See J. Peter Byrne, Are Suburbs Unconstitutional?, 85 Geo. L.J. 2265, 2280 (1997) (book review); Jerome G. Rose, New Jersey Enacts a Fair Housing Law, 14 Real Est. L.J. 195 (1986).

3. *Post* Mount Laurel III *litigation.* For the first few years after the Fair Housing Act of 1985 was passed, the courts showed considerable deference to COAH. See James E. McGuire, Essay, The Judiciary's Role in Implementing the *Mount Laurel* Doctrine: Deference or Activism?, 23 Seton Hall L. Rev. 1276 (1993) (reviewing the cases). In Carlton Homes, Inc. v. COAH, 582 A.2d 1024 (N.J. Super. Ct. App. Div. 1990), however, the lower court struck down COAH's 1,000 unit cap on any municipality's fair share obligation, holding that such a cap was unreasonable because it "substantially exacerbates disparity in the obligation imposed on various municipalities in the same region." Id. at 1033. Then in 1993, the New Jersey Supreme Court stepped back into the fray by invalidating a COAH regulation that allowed a municipality to give preference to its own residents or workers in filling up to 50 percent of its low- and moderate-income housing, finding no evidence that the occupancy preference served any legitimate governmental policy. In re Township of Warren, 622 A.2d 1257 (N.J. 1993). Most recently, the supreme court reaffirmed the continued validity of the builder's remedy against municipalities failing to meet their fair share obligations. Toll Bros., Inc. v. Township of West Windsor, 803 A.2d 53, 90 (N.J. 2002).

4. *From the incredible shrinking need to growth shares.* One of the three specialized judges established under *Mount Laurel II* determined that the statewide housing need was 243,736 units. In its "first-round" certification in 1986, COAH determined that 145,707

units would be needed between 1987 to 1993. It lowered that number in its "second-round" certification in 1993 to 86,000 units needed between 1993 and 1999. John M. Payne, Norman Williams, Exclusionary Zoning, and the *Mount Laurel* Doctrine: Making the Theory Fit the Facts, 20 Vt. L. Rev. 665, 674 (1996). Although its "third-round" certification was due in 1999, COAH failed to issue that certification, until finally, late in 2004, it announced it was abandoning the effort to specify the need, or each municipality's fair share of that need, and substituting instead a "growth share" approach. N.J. Admin. Code tit. 5, §94 (2004). Under that approach, for every eight market-rate residential units, and for every 25 new jobs created by nonresidential development, a municipality will be obligated to provide one unit of affordable housing. In addition, municipalities will have to satisfy any unmet obligations from prior certification "rounds" and will have to satisfy a "rehabilitation share" based on the number of existing units in the municipality found to be both deficient and occupied by households of low or moderate income. Id. at App. A.

Litigation challenging the new growth share approach was filed within days of COAH's announcement. Nina Rizzo, Affordable Housing Lawsuit: Coalition Faults New Methodology, Asbury Park Press, Dec. 22, 2004, at 3.

5. *Regional contribution agreements.* The RCAs allowed under the act have engendered enormous controversy. Some argue that they simply allow the rich to get away with exclusionary zoning. See, e.g., Cynthia N. McKee, Resurrecting *Mount Laurel*: Using Title VIII Litigation to Achieve the Ultimate *Mount Laurel* Goal of Integration, 27 Seton Hall L. Rev. 1338 (1997) (RCAs "encourage and ratify segregation" and therefore violate the Federal Fair Housing Act). Others see some advantages to the agreements. See, e.g., Byrne, supra, at 2281; Richard Thompson Ford, The Boundaries of Race: Political Geography in Legal Analysis, 107 Harv. L. Rev. 1841 (1994); Harold A. McDougall, Regional Contribution Agreements: Compensation for Exclusionary Zoning, 60 Temp. L.Q. 665 (1987); Georgette C. Poindexter, Towards a Legal Framework for Regional Redistribution of Poverty-Related Expenses, 47 Wash. U. J. Urb. & Contemp. L. 3 (1995). Cf. Ronald H. Silverman, Subsidizing Tolerance for Open Communities, 1977 Wis. L. Rev. 375 (urging use of government subsidies to encourage suburbs to accept low-income families).

How well are cities like Trenton or Camden likely to do in bargaining with suburbs over RCAs? Will there be a "race to the bottom" among communities competing to serve as receiving municipalities? COAH's regulations require that RCAs be reviewed by the county planning board of the receiving municipality and then by the council itself. COAH's regulations also require the receiving municipality to charge at least $35,000 per unit, as of late 2004. N.J. Admin. Code tit. 5, §94-5.1(a) (2004). Are those "protections" appropriate? For studies of the characteristics of sending and receiving communities, as well as analysis of the bargaining that takes place between them, see Patrick Field et al., Trading the Poor: Intermunicipal Housing Negotiation in New Jersey, 2 Harv. Negot. L. Rev. 1 (1997); Mark Alan Hughes & Therese J. McGuire, A Market for Exclusion: Trading Low-Income Housing Obligations under *Mount Laurel III*, 29 J. Urb. Econ. 207 (1991).

Should a developer who builds market rate units, but who pays an inclusionary zoning fee to fund the provision of affordable housing elsewhere, qualify for special benefits given to affordable housing development? See Bi-County Developers of Clinton, Inc. v. Borough of High Bridge, 805 A.2d 433 (N.J. 2002) (developer could not take advantage of the right of affordable housing projects to compel an adjoining municipality to allow it to connect into its municipal sewer system, even though the developer paid money into the township's affordable housing fund). See Thomas A. Brown, Democratizing the American Dream: The Role of a Regional Housing Legislature in the Production of Affordable Housing, 37 U. Mich. J.L. Reform 599, 678 (2004) (reading the opinion as creating second-class status for payments to fund off-site provision of affordable housing); Note, Refining

Municipal Obligations Under *Mount Laurel*, the New Jersey Supreme Court Hints at a New Conception of Regional Responsibility, 116 Harv. L. Rev. 1541 (2003).

6. *COAH enforcement actions.* What recourse should COAH have if a municipality shirks its fair share obligations? Should it prevent noncomplying municipalities from engaging in development that does not contribute to its fair share obligations? See, e.g., COAH Orders Denville to Sell Tract to Public Housing Authority, Housing N.J., Mar./Apr. 1994, at 12 (COAH ordered the township to sell a tract of land to the Morris County Housing Authority, which planned to build public housing on the site, and barred the township from allocating sewer capacity to any other project).

David L. Kirp et al., Our Town: Race, Housing, and the Soul of Suburbia
186-87 (1995)

In 1984 in Mount Laurel, a year after the New Jersey Supreme Court's decision in *Mount Laurel II*, developer Roger Davis finally got to build Tricia Meadows, the manufactured homes that were supposed to provide affordable housing. And in Rancocas Woods . . . one apartment building dedicated specifically to affordable housing was opened.

On the surface, it seemed as though the town had turned around — that the idea of fair share had come to life — but the reality was otherwise. . . . In fact, the 460-unit development, a fifth of which was designated for poor and moderate-income families, proved not to be the trailer park eyesore that fretful town-council members had expected. The trailers are double-width, about the size of a normal home, and they have been dressed up in all sorts of ways, including a faux log cabin. Homes in Tricia Meadows designated as "affordable" sell for upwards of forty thousand dollars, and rentals there run five hundred dollars a month. This is within reach for families with moderate incomes, but not for the poor.

In Renaissance Homes, located in Rancocas Woods, all the condominiums in Building 15 are designated for low- and moderate-income households. Yet while everyone who lives in that building may technically qualify, they certainly aren't the people whom housing activists had in mind. Like the rest of the Renaissance Homes residents, they are at least fifty-five years old — "safe seniors," as they are called, no drain on township resources and no threat to anyone. Most are widows living on fixed pensions, who sold their bigger family homes, paying the below-market price for their apartments in cash. All are white. . . .

This is how matters stand, not only in the township but also in most New Jersey communities where affordable housing has been built to satisfy a judge or COAH. Developers and town officials tacitly agree to make what amounts to a gift to the kinds of families who will blend in nicely, rather than inviting the poor, black families of Camden — inviting "them" — into "our town." The beneficiaries of this largesse have mainly been retirees with modest paper income but significant assets and young families who can rely on their parents for help with the down payment on their first home. The forty-something generation, which predominates in these suburbs, has been able to use *Mount Laurel* to underwrite housing for its grown-up children as well as for its aging parents. . . .

Note on the *Mount Laurel* Trilogy

1. *Happy ending?* In addition to the two projects Kirp describes, in 1997, 25 years after the trial court's decision in *Mt. Laurel I*, Mount Laurel officials approved a rental complex of 140 townhouses for low- and moderate-income families. The vote was unanimous,

despite angry protests from more than 200 opponents. Ronald Smothers, Ending Battle, Suburb Allows Homes for Poor, N.Y. Times, Apr. 12, 1997, at A21. Named for the original plaintiff, who died in 1994, the Ethel R. Lawrence Homes opened for tenants in 2001. The units are administered by the plaintiff's daughter, Ethel Lawrence-Halley, and house mostly single mothers and their children. Councilman Peter McCaffrey, who has lived in Mount Laurel since 1972 and served as mayor five times, says that the town "is happy with its new neighbors" and attributes all the controversy to "fear of the unknown, fear of people you didn't know." Josh Getlin, Finally, Housing for Poor in Upscale Suburb, L.A. Times, Nov. 25, 2004, at E10.

2. *How many houses have been built?* In the ten years between *Mount Laurel I* and the enactment of the Fair Housing Act of 1985, more than 100 exclusionary zoning lawsuits were filed against 68 suburbs. After the Fair Housing Act went into effect, COAH reviewed the housing plans of more than 200 municipalities. As a result of the litigation and COAH review, it is estimated that between 1980 and June 2001, at least 28,855 affordable housing units have been constructed, compared with approximately 450,000 market rate units during those same decades. Toll Bros., Inc. v. Township of West Windsor, 803 A.2d 53, 91 (N.J. 2002). An additional 13,231 homes have been zoned for or approved; 11,246 more have been created through rehabilitation; and 7,396 units have been built in the cities through regional contribution agreements. COAH 2001 Annual Report; David N. Kinsey, Reaffirm Mount Laurel, N.J.L.J., Aug. 13, 2001, at 619. See also Naomi Bailin Wish & Stephen Eisdorfer, The Impact of *Mount Laurel* Initiatives: An Analysis of the Characteristics of Applicants and Occupants, 27 Seton Hall L. Rev. 1268, 1270–71 (1997).

Source: Sian DeLuca

FIGURE 9-2
The Ethel R. Lawrence Homes, Finally!

Although the number of affordable units is small compared to the number of market rate units, consider that since the federal Housing Act of 1937, which inaugurated federal subsidies for low- and moderate-income housing, an average of 2,400 federally subsidized units have been produced each year, while approximately 1,350 Mount Laurel units have been produced each year since *Mount Laurel II* was decided. John M. Payne, Norman Williams, Exclusionary Zoning, and the *Mount Laurel* Doctrine: Making the Theory Fit the Facts, 20 Vt. L. Rev. 665, 674 (1996).

Professor Payne suggests that analysis of the "success" of *Mount Laurel* ought to take into account that many of the market rate housing units built under *Mount Laurel* settlements or builder's remedies were themselves more affordable than noninclusionary projects would have been. Id. at 681–82.

3. *Who lives in those houses?* A study of the characteristics of occupants of low- and moderate-income housing in New Jersey (not all of which is necessarily attributable to *Mount Laurel* or the Fair Housing Act) concluded that *Mount Laurel* and the Fair Housing Act "have resulted in very few urban residents moving to suburban areas." Wish & Eisdorfer, supra, at 1302. Of those who did move to suburbia, the vast majority were white; black and Latino applicants for affordable housing were much less successful than whites. The principal beneficiaries of the housing were white elderly women. Id. at 1303–05. See also Martha Lamar et al., *Mount Laurel* at Work: Affordable Housing in New Jersey, 1983–88, 41 Rutgers L. Rev. 1197 (1989) (also finding that many *Mount Laurel* developments have very small minority populations, with especially low numbers of African Americans).

That raises again the question whether *Mount Laurel I* or the Fair Housing Act of 1985 should have been aimed more directly at the racial implications of exclusionary zoning. What might have been (or now should be) done to ensure that *Mount Laurel* housing effects racial integration in the suburbs? For suggestions, see, e.g., John Charles Boger, *Mount Laurel* at 21 Years: Reflections on the Power of Courts and Legislatures to Shape Social Change, 27 Seton Hall L. Rev. 1450, 1459–60 (1997); Justin D. Cummins, Recasting Fair Share: Toward Effective Housing Law and Principled Social Policy, 14 Law & Ineq. J. 339 (1996); Robert C. Holmes, A Black Perspective on *Mount Laurel II*: Toward a Black Fair Share, 14 Seton Hall L. Rev. 944 (1984); Florence Wagman Roisman, The Role of the State, the Necessity of Race-Conscious Remedies, and Other Lessons from the *Mount Laurel* Study, 27 Seton Hall L. Rev. 1386 (1997).

4. *Destabilization?* Consider the arguments of Professor John Payne, who has been involved in the *Mount Laurel* litigations for decades:

> One of the great achievements of the *Mount Laurel* cases was that they forced the legislature to consider the consequences of exclusionary zoning, even though the interest group that benefited — poor people — was relatively powerless and the interest group that was burdened — suburbanites — was the dominant political voice in statewide politics. . . .
>
> The constitutional right that is implicated in this approach to the problem of exclusionary zoning is the right to have fair participation in the political process. . . . The remedy for such a reformulated right is much more straightforward than the substantive implementation of "fair share" rules that has preoccupied the *Mount Laurel* process for the last twenty years. All that is required is that the court order the state to reclaim the delegated zoning power from the gaggle of fragmented, parochial municipalities and either exercise the power itself, redelegate it to new state or regional planning agencies, or redelegate it to municipalities subject to tighter standards that protect the interests of prospective as well as present residents of the decisionmaking community. . . .
>
> Arguably, the representation approach that I am suggesting can be teased out of the history of the *Mount Laurel* doctrine. . . . The New Jersey Supreme Court and its three designated trial judges, after the requisite period of Sturm und Drang, convinced the politicians of New Jersey that the *Mount Laurel* decision would be enforced vigorously. In the face of judicial

orders rezoning specific towns, the legislature put aside traditional home rule concerns and created a state-level decisionmaking institution, the Council on Affordable Housing, which brings together — imperfectly — municipal and housing advocates to hash out ground rules within which municipalities must then act in the exercise of their delegated zoning powers, though compliance with the Act is voluntary. As a housing advocate, I now have a political forum within which to lobby, scheme, and intrigue, just as any other interest group does, with recourse to the cabinet officer who oversees COAH and, on those occasions when the stakes are high enough — usually just before an election — to the office of the governor herself.

John M. Payne, Lawyers, Judges, and the Public Interest, 96 Mich. L. Rev. 1685, 1711–12 (1998) (reviewing Charles Haar, Suburbs Under Siege: Race, Space, and Audacious Judges). See also Charles F. Sabel & William H. Simon, Destabilization Rights: How Public Law Litigation Succeeds, 117 Harv. L. Rev. 1015, 1016 (2004) (describing *Mount Laurel* as an example of litigation over "destabilization rights — rights to disentrench an institution that has systematically failed to meet its obligations and remained immune to traditional forces of political correction," and asserting that it can "plausibly be seen as a 'marginal success'").

5. *Alternative approaches.* Consider the alternative Professor Peter Byrne offers:

[A]n interesting alternate approach might have been to change the structure of local government land use planning more radically — by combining the local governments of Camden and Mount Laurel or by shifting the land use planning authority to the state, for example. Either approach would give poor people in cities some political say over the entirety of land use on the fringe of cities and, perhaps, the tax revenues stemming from such land.

J. Peter Byrne, Are Suburbs Unconstitutional?, 85 Geo. L.J. 2265, 2278 (1997) (book review).

Professor John Boger advocates a national fair share program, which would disperse new federal housing funds to municipalities that shoulder their fair share of housing obligations and would disallow property tax deductions from federal income taxes to residents of municipalities who do not. John Charles Boger, *Mount Laurel* at 21 Years: Reflections on the Power of Courts and Legislatures to Shape Social Change, 27 Seton Hall L. Rev. 1450, 1459–60 (1997); John Charles Boger, Toward Ending Residential Segregation: A Fair Share Proposal for the Next Reconstruction, 71 N.C. L. Rev. 1573 (1993).

Which of these, or which other, directions should reform take?

6. *Exclusionary zoning in other courts.* Although the federal courts have not been sympathetic to constitutional theories for attacking exclusionary zoning, the Federal Fair Housing Act, discussed at pp. 705–09, is currently interpreted to reach land use regulations that have the effect of excluding racial or ethnic minorities from a municipality. Federal courts therefore are not totally out of the exclusionary zoning picture.

Most state courts continue to attach a presumption of validity even to admittedly exclusionary municipal land use controls (absent evidence of a racially discriminatory purpose), and merely require that the controls be rationally related to some permissible governmental objective. Several state courts — New Hampshire, Pennsylvania and New York — have broken rank, at least by a few steps. In other states, such as Michigan, California, and Massachusetts, any judicial inclination to enter the exclusionary zoning fray was largely suppressed by the state legislature's attention to the problem. Those programs are addressed in the next note.

In New Hampshire, Britton v. Town of Chester, 595 A.2d 492 (N.H. 1991), adopted an approach similar to the *Livermore* rule discussed at pp. 735–40 and 797–800, but there has been very little litigation under *Chester*. New York's Berenson v. Town of New Castle,

341 N.E.2d 236 (N.Y. 1975) (decided eight months after *Mount Laurel I*), held that a zoning ordinance should "provide for the development of a balanced, cohesive community which will make efficient use of the town's available land." In Robert E. Kurzius, Inc. v. Incorporated Village of Upper Brookville, 414 N.E.2d 680 (N.Y. 1980), a challenge to the village's 5-acre minimum zoning, the court interpreted *Berenson* to require a zoning ordinance to be invalidated if it was enacted with an exclusionary purpose or if it ignored regional needs and had an unjustifiably exclusionary effect. The court held, however, that even large lot zoning ordinances were entitled to a presumption of validity, and the plaintiffs had not overcome that presumption because the "record shows clearly that the purpose of the ordinance was to preserve the open-space areas of the village" and because "[t]here was no proof that persons of low or moderate incomes were foreclosed from housing in the general region because of an unavailability of properly zoned land." Id. at 684. That requirement has rendered *Berenson* unhelpful for most low- and moderate-income housing consumers. See also Suffolk Housing Services v. Town of Brookhaven, 511 N.E.2d 67 (N.Y. 1987).

Pennsylvania's approach has involved numerous twists and turns too complicated to detail here. Like *Beaver Gasoline*, excerpted at p. 747, the cases generally have emphasized the property owner's right to be free of unreasonable regulation, rather than focusing on the rights of the housing consumers excluded from the jurisdiction. Because of their concern for landowners' rights, Pennsylvania courts have limited patience for total prohibitions of particular land uses and do not hesitate to use a builder's remedy when confronted with such prohibitions. But once a municipality provides some opportunity for multifamily housing or other specific land uses, the Pennsylvania courts are skeptical of demands for more, unless the local government's justifications fail a reasonableness test applied with considerable sympathy to the landowner. The main cases are C & M Developers, Inc. v. Bedminster Township Zoning Hearing Board, 820 A.2d 143 (Pa. 2002); BAC, Inc. v. Board of Supervisors, 633 A.2d 144 (Pa. 1993); Fernley v. Board of Supervisors, 502 A.2d 585 (Pa. 1985); Appeal of M.A. Kravitz Co. v. Board of Supervisors, 460 A.2d 1075 (Pa. 1983), Surrick v. Zoning Hearing Board, 382 A.2d 105 (Pa. 1977); Township of Willistown v. Chesterdale Farms, Inc., 341 A.2d 466 (Pa. 1975); and Appeal of Girsh, 263 A.2d 395 (Pa. 1970).

For one recent analysis of the shortcomings of the various approaches, see, e.g., Henry A. Span, How the Courts Should Fight Exclusionary Zoning, 32 Seton Hall L. Rev. 1, 48 (2001).

Note on Legislative Attempts to Curb Exclusionary Zoning

State legislatures, spurred no doubt in part by the threat of judicial rulings on exclusionary zoning, have adopted a variety of techniques to encourage local governments to provide opportunities for affordable housing within their borders. See Harold A. McDougall, From Litigation to Legislation in Exclusionary Zoning Law, 22 Harv. C.R.-C.L. L. Rev. 623 (1987). As illustrated by the state statutes regarding the siting of group homes, discussed at p. 727, one obvious legislative approach is to preempt or override local zoning on certain kinds of affordable housing, such as mobile homes. See pp. 732 and 742–46. Other models are explored in the following notes. For other overviews of various approaches, see, e.g., Stuart Meck et al., Regional Approaches to Affordable Housing 2, 5–8 (2003).

1. *The comprehensive plan model: California.* In 1980, California enacted a requirement that every locality "adopt a comprehensive, long-term general plan for the physical

development of the county or city." Cal. Gov't Code §65300 (West 2005). The plan must include a "housing element," which must contain:

(a) An assessment of housing needs and an inventory of resources and constraints . . . [which shall include the following]:

(1) An analysis of population and employment trends and . . . a quantification of the locality's existing and projected housing needs for all income levels. These existing and projected needs shall include the locality's share of the regional housing need. . . .

(3) An inventory of land suitable for residential development, . . . and an analysis of the relationship of zoning and public facilities and services to these sites.

(4) An analysis of potential and actual governmental constraints upon the maintenance, improvement, or development of housing for all income levels. . . .

(5) An analysis of potential and actual nongovernmental constraints upon the maintenance, improvement, or development of housing for all income levels, including the availability of financing, the price of land, and the cost of construction.

(6) An analysis of any special housing needs, such as those of the elderly, persons with disabilities, large families, farmworkers, families with female heads of households, and families and persons in need of emergency shelter. . . .

(b)(1) A statement of the community's goals, quantified objectives, and policies relative to the maintenance, preservation, improvement, and development of housing. . . .

(c) A program which sets forth a five-year schedule of actions the local government is undertaking or intends to undertake to implement the policies and achieve the goals and objectives of the housing element. . . . [T]he program shall do all of the following:

(1) Identify actions that will be taken to make sites available during the planning period of the general plan with appropriate zoning and development standards and with services and facilities to accommodate that portion of the city's or county's share of the regional housing need for each income level that could not be accommodated on sites identified in the inventory completed pursuant to paragraph (3) of subdivision (a) without rezoning. . . .

(3) Address and, where appropriate and legally possible, remove governmental constraints to the maintenance, improvement, and development of housing. . . .

Id. at §65583. The regional need the planning requirement refers to is established by regional "council[s] of governments," which allocate the need among municipalities within the region. Id. at §65584.

California's comprehensive planning requirement is reinforced by a mandate in the state's zoning enabling act that local governments consider the effect of their zoning ordinances and other regulatory activities on the housing needs of the region. See, e.g., id. at §66412.3. The planning scheme is supplemented substantively by various state overrides of local government control over specific types of housing. See, e.g., id. at §65852.7 (requiring mobile home parks to be permitted in any area zoned residential, but allowing local government to subject such parks to a special use permit requirement). It also is reinforced by California's "least cost zoning law," which requires local governments to "zone sufficient vacant land for residential use with appropriate standards . . . to meet housing needs for all income categories as identified in the housing element of the general plan." Id. at §65913.1.

California's comprehensive plan approach to ensuring affordable housing has been severely criticized as ineffectual. As of the beginning of 1996, only 58 percent of the local governments required to adopt housing elements had done so. Nico Calavita et al., Inclusionary Housing in California and New Jersey: A Comparative Analysis, 8 Housing Pol'y Debate 109, 118 (1997). Although at least one court took tough measures against a recalcitrant community, enjoining it from approving any subdivision maps or rezonings until it had complied with the requirements, Camp v. Board of Supervisors, 176 Cal. Rptr. 620 (Ct. App. 1981), critics argue that there have been relatively few challenges to the plans, and most courts have been more deferential than the *Camp* court. See Ben Field, Why Our

Fair Share Housing Laws Fail, 34 Santa Clara L. Rev. 35 (1993) (blaming failure on obstacles to litigation, limits of judicial expertise, and a judicial reluctance to intervene in local land use matters). For further analysis of California's approach, see Jeffrey M. Lehmann, Reversing Judicial Deference Toward Exclusionary Zoning: A Suggested Approach, 12 J. Affordable Housing & Community Dev. L. 229, 237 (2003); Thomas A. Brown, Note, Democratizing the American Dream: The Role of a Regional Housing Legislature in the Production of Affordable Housing, 37 U. Mich. J.L. Reform 599, 637-41 (2004).

Florida and Washington have adopted planning requirements similar to California's. See Fla. Stat. ch. 163.3177(6)(f)(1)(d) (2005); Wash. Rev. Code §36.70A.070 (2005).

2. *The state goals approach*: *Oregon*. In contrast to California's "bottom up" specific planning approach, Oregon has instituted a "top down" system of promoting affordable housing. Oregon has established 19 statewide land use goals and requires its communities to develop comprehensive plans that are in accord with those goals. Goal 10, Housing, requires local plans to "encourage the availability of adequate numbers of needed housing units at price ranges and rent levels which are commensurate with the financial capabilities of Oregon households and allow for flexibility of housing location, type and density." See Planning the Oregon Way: A Twenty Year Evaluation 301 (Carl Abbott et al. eds., 1994).

Local governments' plans must be "acknowledged" by a state administrative agency, the Oregon Land Conservation & Development Commission (LCDC). Soon after local governments began to submit their plans for approval, LCDC signaled its view of Goal 10 in reviewing an amendment to the City of Durham's comprehensive plan that reduced permitted densities in the town by one-half:

> The housing goal clearly says that municipalities are not going to be able to do what they have done in metropolitan areas in the rest of the country. They are not going to be able to pass the housing buck to their neighbors on the assumption that some other community will open wide its doors and take in the teachers, police, firemen, clerks, secretaries and other ordinary folk who can't afford homes in the towns where they work. . . .
>
> Goal 10 speaks of the housing needs of Oregon households, not the housing needs of Durham's households. Its meaning is clear: planning for housing must not be parochial. Planning jurisdictions must consider the needs of the relevant region in arriving at a fair allocation of housing types. . . .

Seaman v. City of Durham, Or. LCDC, No. 77-0925 (1978).

The LCDC went on to rule that because the amendment reduced, rather than increased, housing opportunity, the burden of proof was on the town to show "by compelling reasons" how the amendment complied with Goal 10. The city failed to carry that burden, and the amendment therefore was invalid. Id. The LCDC's strict view of Goal 10 is reflected in the fact that of the 53 comprehensive plans submitted by cities with populations over 5,000, LCDC rejected 52 of them as not in compliance with Goal 10. Gerrit Knaap & Arthur C. Nelson, The Regulated Landscape: Lessons on State Land Use Planning from Oregon 80 (1992).

The Oregon courts also have interpreted Goal 10 strictly. In City of Hillsboro v. Housing Development Corp., 657 P.2d 726 (Or. Ct. App. 1983), for example, the court struck down a local government's attempt to subject migrant farmworker housing to a conditional use permit procedure. Although the court rested its decision on the language of the city's zoning ordinance, it "noted in passing" that the city's requirement would be inconsistent with Goal 10. LCDC reinforced that by applying what became known as the "St. Helens policy": requiring municipalities that submitted plans classifying multifamily and mobile home uses as conditional uses to specify clearly the criteria by which the permit application would be judged.

The legislature also put more substance into the goal by adopting a *Beaver Gaso-line*-type rule barring any local government from prohibiting "attached or detached single-family housing, multiple-family housing for both owner and renter occupancy or manufactured homes" in residential zones. Or. Rev. Stat. §197.312 (2005).

Finally, Goal 10 must be read in conjunction with Goal 14, Urbanization, which requires cities to establish "urban growth boundaries" (UGBs) that seek to contain growth compactly. Goal 14 is discussed at pp. 813–17. Because the goals obviously may conflict, the LCDC adopted a special "Metropolitan Housing Rule" to apply to the state's largest population center, the Portland UGB. The rule requires that jurisdictions within that UGB designate sufficient buildable land to allow at least 50 percent of new residential units to be attached single-family housing or multifamily housing. Or. Admin. R. 660-07-035 (2005). It specifies that the smaller cities with growth potential in the region must provide for an overall density of at least six units per acre, that medium-sized cities provide for at least eight units per acre, and that the larger urbanized areas provide for at least ten units per acre. Id. In addition, it requires that local land use procedures and standards "must be clear and objective, and must not have the effect, either of themselves or cumulatively, of discouraging needed housing through unreasonable cost or delay." Id. at 660-07-015.

Whether Oregon's requirements have increased density, increased the number of affordable housing units available, or changed median housing prices or rents is the subject of considerable debate. See p. 816. See also, e.g., Paul Ketcham & Scott Siegel, Managing Growth to Promote Affordable Housing: Revisiting Oregon's Goal 10 (1991); Robert L. Liberty, Abolishing Exclusionary Zoning: A Natural Policy Alliance for Environmentalists and Affordable Housing Advocates, 30 B.C. Envtl. Aff. L. Rev. 581, 592–600 (2003); Rusty Russell, Equity in Eden: Can Environmental Protection and Affordable Housing Comfortably Cohabit in Suburbia?, 30 B.C. Envtl. Aff. L. Rev. 437, 476–81 (2003).

3. *The procedural approach*: Connecticut. In 1990, Connecticut enacted the Affordable Housing Land Use Appeals Act, Conn. Gen. Stat. §8-30G (2005), to allow developers whose proposed affordable housing projects are denied or substantially restricted by local zoning or planning officials to appeal to specially designated judges, who must hear the appeal as soon as practicable. In the appeal, the burden is shifted to the municipality to prove that the denial or restriction is supported by substantial evidence and is necessary to protect substantial public interests, and that those public interests clearly outweigh the need for affordable housing and cannot be protected by reasonable changes to the proposed project. If the local government does not satisfy its burden of proof, the court may reverse, remand, or modify the local government's decision. The special appeals procedure is limited to proposals for housing that will receive financial assistance under government programs for low- and moderate-income housing, and housing in which at least 30 percent of the units will be reserved, for at least 40 years, for sale or rent at or below prices affordable to persons whose income is 80 percent or less of the area's or state's median income.

The special-appeals procedure cannot be invoked against a municipality in which at least 10 percent of the municipality's dwelling units are affordable housing. Municipalities that have received a certified affordable housing project completion within the past year also are exempt.

The special-appeals procedure has been invoked by dozens of developers and have survived both challenges to their validity and attempts to narrow their availability. See, e.g., Wisniowski v. Planning Commission, 655 A.2d 1146 (Conn. 1995); West Hartford

Interfaith Coalition, Inc. v. Town Council, 636 A.2d 1342 (Conn. 1994). See generally Terry J. Tondro, Connecticut's Affordable Housing Appeals Statute: After Ten Years, Why Only Middling Results?, 23 W. New Eng. L. Rev. 115 (2001); Robert D. Carroll, Note, Connecticut Retrenches: A Proposal to Save the Affordable Housing Appeals Procedure, 110 Yale L.J. 1247 (2001).

Connecticut's appeals procedure is modeled after the Massachusetts Low and Moderate Income Housing Act, Mass. Gen. Laws ch. 40B, §§20–23 (2005), colloquially known as the "anti-snob zoning act," which was enacted in 1969. For favorable appraisals of that act, see Sharon Perlman Krefetz, The Impact and Evolution of the Massachusetts Comprehensive Permit and Zoning Appeals Act: Thirty Years of Experience with a State Legislative Effort to Overcome Exclusive Zoning, 22 W. New Eng. L. Rev. 381 (2001); Paul K. Stockman, Note, Anti-Snob Zoning in Massachusetts: Assessing One Attempt at Opening the Suburbs to Affordable Housing, 78 Va. L. Rev. 535 (1992). For estimates of the housing it has produced, see Citizens Housing and Planning Association, The Record on 40B: The Effectiveness of the Massachusetts Affordable Housing Zoning Law (2003), available at http://www.chapa.org/TheRecordon40B.pdf. For more critical reviews, see Mark Bobrowski, Affordable Housing v. Open Space: A Proposal for Reconciliation, 30 B.C. Envtl. Aff. L. Rev. 487 (2003); Jonathan Douglas Witten, The Cost of Developing Affordable Housing: At What Price?, 30 B.C. Envtl. Aff. L. Rev. 509 (2003); Christophe Courchesne, Note, What Regional Agenda?: Reconciling Massachusetts's Affordable Housing Law and Environmental Protection, 28 Harv. Envtl. L. Rev. 215 (2004). The act remains so controversial that in the 2003 legislative session, more than 60 bills were introduced to refine, revise, or abolish its requirements. Anthony Flint, Zoning at Issue in Affordable Housing, Boston Globe, Mar. 31, 2003, at B2.

One particularly interesting feature of Massachusetts's efforts to counter exclusionary zoning is its use of financial incentives. In 1982, Governor King issued an executive order directing all state agencies to withhold "discretionary development-related financial assistance" to communities that are "unreasonably restrictive of new housing growth." See id. See also Peter S. Canellos, After 20 Years, Anti-Snob Zoning Found Ineffective, Boston Globe, Jan. 1, 1989, at 1, 16 (reporting that 5 wealthy Boston suburbs had been declared ineligible for state funding under the executive order, and 50 others had received a warning).

4. *More radical approaches.* What other approaches might be preferable to the programs just outlined? Many affordable housing advocates place their faith in the inclusionary zoning programs described at pp. 671–73. See, e.g., California Inclusionary Housing Reader (Bill Higgins ed., 2003), available at http://www.cacities.org/resource_files/20276.California%20Inclusionary%20Housing%20Reader.pdf; Barbara Ehrlich Kautz, Comment, In Defense of Inclusionary Zoning: Successfully Creating Affordable Housing, 36 U.S.F. L. Rev. 971 (2002); Cecily T. Talbert & Nadia L. Costa, Current Issues in Inclusionary Zoning, 36 Urb. Law. 557 (2004). Others prefer solutions based upon regional governments or governance. See, e.g., Reflections on Regionalism (Bruce Katz ed., 2000); John A. Powell, Opportunity-Based Housing, 12 J. Affordable Housing & Community Dev. L. 188 (2003). For other proposals, see, e.g., Tim Iglesias, Housing Impact Assessments: Opening New Doors for State Housing Regulation While Localism Persists, 82 Or. L. Rev. 433 (2003) (proposing housing impact assessments, modeled after environmental impact reviews, for local discretionary actions that may affect housing, such as infrastructure planning and financing decisions, adoption and amendment of general (or comprehensive) plans, approval of development agreements, zoning and rezoning, subdivision approvals, variance, special use permits, and building permits).

Note on Challenges to Specific Types of Exclusionary Measures

1. *Minimum lot sizes.* In no state can one identify a threshold (e.g., 3 acres) at which a lot-size requirement *always* will be declared invalid. For example, in *Mount Laurel I*, Justice Hall explicitly stated that developing municipalities in New Jersey could use land use controls to foster development of exclusive housing in *some* neighborhoods. Moreover, *Madison*, discussed at pp. 772–73, held that environmental considerations may justify large-lot requirements. Nor are the Pennsylvania decisions hostile to all lot-size minima. So long as a township zones some land for apartments, townhouses, and so on, it can zone the balance of its acreage rather restrictively, provided that it meets the substantive due process requirement of achieving a reasonable balance between legitimate interests of the public and the landowner's rights. C & M Developers, Inc. v. Bedminster Township Zoning Hearing Board, 820 A.2d 143 (Pa. 2002).

In fact, outside New Jersey and Pennsylvania (and a few other activist states such as Illinois and Virginia), local governments have beaten back most constitutional challenges to large-lot zoning. See, e.g., Johnson v. Town of Edgartown, 680 N.E.2d 37 (Mass. 1997) (3-acre minimum area requirement for residential lots in town on Martha's Vineyard upheld because large lots were needed to protect ecology of nearby lake and to protect "the amenities and character of a rural resort").

2. *Restrictions on mobile homes.* Mobile home parks generate an enormous amount of litigation. They promise large profits to developers, but pose fiscal risks to local officials and undesirable side effects to neighboring landowners. Some states prohibit local governments from excluding from the community mobile homes that meet building code standards. See, e.g., Colo. Rev. Stat. §31-23-301 (2005). Others prohibit local governments from treating manufactured homes any differently from conventional "stick built" homes. See, e.g., Iowa Code §414.28 (2005).

The courts are split on the reasonableness of various restrictions on mobile homes. Compare, e.g., Carpenter v. City of Petal, 699 So. 2d 928 (Miss. 1997) (city has no valid reason for excluding mobile homes from Rural Fringe District or any other zoning district), with Mack T. Anderson Insurance Agency v. City of Belgrade, 803 P.2d 648 (Mont. 1990) (reasonable to confine mobile homes to parks, excluding them from residential districts). See also N.M. Stat. Ann. §3-21A-4 (Michie 2005) (allowing local governments to restrict mobile homes to parks). See generally Howard J. Barewin, Note, Rescuing Manufactured Housing from the Perils of Municipal Zoning Laws, 37 Wash. U. J. Urb. & Contemp. L. 189 (1990).

D. Municipal Obligations to Accommodate Pressures for Regional Growth

Chapter 8 and the prior subchapter dealt with municipal mechanisms to discourage immigration by *particular types of newcomers*, such as poor people, or to forestall development of *particular types of buildings*, such as mobile home parks or least-cost single-family housing. This subchapter turns to the issues raised when a local government tries to stop, slow or channel all types of development (or at least all types of residential development). It explores conflicts arising from state, regional, and municipal regulations that affect the *supply side* of the land development market.

The terminology used to describe efforts to address problems created by growth is imprecise and (frankly) political. For our purposes, *growth control* will be used to describe regulatory practices aimed at slowing or halting growth within a particular jurisdiction or region. *Growth management* refers to policies that seek to accommodate growth but to ensure that it occurs in the most rational and efficient manner. *Smart growth* refers to policies to limit sprawl by, among other things, encouraging contiguous and infill development, encouraging mixed use zoning instead of segregated land uses, encouraging higher density, and reducing travel by private automobile. All three types of programs take many forms. This subchapter focuses on four of the most common techniques:

1. *moratoria*, which stop all or most development for some limited period of time that the jurisdiction claims it needs to respond to a planning or infrastructure crisis;

2. *rate of growth programs*, or growth caps, which limit the number of building permits issued each year, the rate of change in the jurisdiction's population, or some other indicator of growth; and

3. *growth phasing programs*, which tie the location and timing of new development to the adequacy of the community's infrastructure and other public facilities or to the community's plans for providing adequate facilities in the future;

4. *urban growth boundaries*, which draw lines around the jurisdiction to contain urban growth and prevent the spread of development into the surrounding farms or countryside.

As you study the legal implications of these techniques, however, keep in mind that the principal tools many communities use to limit or manage growth or fight sprawl are the traditional land use controls: comprehensive plans, zoning ordinances, subdivision regulations, and exactions. Keep in mind also that the techniques studied here are only a fraction of the increasingly sophisticated weapons state and local governments have at their disposal. Although this subchapter focuses on the sticks governments use to address growth issues, some states are beginning to use carrots. The smart growth program introduced in Maryland in 1996 by then-Governor Glendening, for example, featured a variety of tax credits and other incentives to encourage redevelopment or infill development. See James R. Cohen, Maryland's "Smart Growth": Using Incentives to Combat Sprawl *in* Urban Sprawl: Causes, Consequences and Policy Responses 3 (Gregory D. Squires ed., 2002). For comprehensive descriptions of the variety of tools state and local governments use to address growth and sprawl issues, see, e.g., Arthur C. Nelson & James B. Duncan, Growth Management Principles and Practices (1995); Robert H. Freilich, From Sprawl to Smart Growth: Successful Legal, Planning, and Environmental Systems (1999); Douglas R. Porter, Making Smart Growth Work (2002); John R. Nolon, Local Land Use Controls That Achieve Smart Growth, 31 Envtl. L. Rep. 11025 (2001).

Growth management techniques may be imposed by a single jurisdiction or by state or regional authorities. Growth management programs increasingly are adopted at the state or regional level. For a comparison of the programs, see, e.g., American Planning Association, Planning for "Smart Growth": 2002 State of the States (2002); David Rusk, Growth Management: The Core Regional Issue *in* Reflections on Regionalism 78 (Bruce Katz ed., 2000); Patricia E. Salkin, Smart Growth at Century's End: The State of the States, 31 Urb. Law. 601 (1999).

1.   *Justifications for Growth Management*

Growth management programs may address either or both of two distinct issues: the population growth within the jurisdiction, and the physical form development to accommodate that growth takes. The first issue is a question of optimal city size; the second is a question of the optimal pattern of development — compact versus sprawling, high- versus low-density, contiguous versus scattered, and so on.

The growth of a metropolitan area's population has obvious costs, such as increased traffic congestion and air pollution. But growth also produces benefits by helping achieve the critical mass necessary to support, for example, a daily newspaper or a children's theater. At what point does growth become inefficient, so that the costs of growth outweigh its benefits?

Before tackling that question, it is useful to ask why governments should care about city size. After all, as the discussion of Tiebout's theory at p. 771 revealed, people can (within certain constraints) "vote with their feet" in choosing where to live, so if a city is too big, people will stop moving there. Voluntary market transactions do not necessarily produce cities of optimal population, however, because an immigrant to a city considers only the average congestion costs — not the marginal congestion costs — his or her entry will cause. See George S. Tolley, The Welfare Economics of City Bigness, 1 J. Urb. Econ. 324 (1974).

Empirical studies of city size usually examine differences in wage rates between various metropolitan areas. They assume that in a competitive labor market, wage rates reflect environmental amenities and disamenities. For reviews of the literature, see Masahisa Fujita, Urban Economic Theory: Land Use and City Size (1989); Richard Arnott, Does the Henry George Theorem Provide a Practical Guide to Optimal City Size?, 63 Am. J. Econ. Soc. 1057 (2004). Suffice it to say that the studies produce no consistent measurement of optimal city size.

That is hardly surprising. The optimal size to support a daily newspaper is unlikely to be optimal for supporting a children's theater. Different groups are unlikely to have the same preferences for amenities, so the optimal city size for one group is unlikely to be optimal for another. In addition, preferences for the social goods that cities can provide, as well as preferences regarding crowding and density, may be culturally influenced. A typical U.S. suburb contains 5,000 to 10,000 people per square mile, and the densest section of Manhattan has about 140,000 people per square mile. For fascinating comparisons of the densities of various cities around the world, see Alain Bertaud, Clearing the Air in Atlanta: Transit and Smart Growth or Conventional Economics? 54 J. Urb. Econ. 379 (2003). The inability of economists (or sociologists) to specify exactly what size is optimal for a city convinces some that controls on urban size are inappropriate. A leading urban economics textbook, for example, argues that "if an activity [such as pollution] distorts urban sizes, the activity should be controlled directly. Urban size distortions are no more than symptoms of resource misallocation. To attack the urban size distribution directly is to attack the wrong variable." Edwin S. Mills & Bruce W. Hamilton, Urban Economics 405–06 (5th ed. 1994).

If size alone is the "wrong variable," what about the form that size takes?

Robert W. Burchell et al., The Costs of Sprawl – 2000, Transit Cooperative Research Program Rep. 74
Preface, Executive Summary at 9-17 (2002)

. . . The purpose of this volume is to project historic national development patterns (sprawl, or uncontrolled growth) into the future and measure the impacts of such development compared to . . . more contained development (compact or "smart" growth), which has its own impacts. The two sets of impacts are then compared to derive the costs of sprawl, which essentially are the savings incurred due to the differences between compact and sprawl growth. The costs of sprawl are calculated from 25-year growth projections. . . .

costs + benefits of sprawl

. . . This report looks very carefully at the many costs and benefits of sprawl and concludes that there is clearly evidence of each.

Costs and benefits are not weighed on a balanced scale, however. There appear to be more costs than benefits, even though the magnitude of these costs to the general public is not nearly what has been chronicled in the popular press. On the other hand, the level of resource consumption resulting from development is increasing in the United States, and this increase is not related to need. There is no reason to support two underutilized systems of infrastructure when one fully subscribed system will do. Growth need not "skip" to the farthest and least-expensive location in the metropolitan area, with the expectation that infrastructure will be put in place, if adequate undeveloped space exists closer in. Thus, while sprawl is not the villain it has been portrayed to be, it is without question an unnecessary and increasing drain on natural resources. More-compact development patterns produce savings that are both profound and measurable. It makes sense to pursue these development savings. . . .

— More costs than benefits

LAND CONVERSION

. . . [According to our] projections using the uncontrolled-growth scenario, over the next 25 years, the United States will convert 18.8 million acres of land . . . to build 26.5 million new housing units and 26.5 billion square feet of new nonresidential space, the latter to accommodate a growth of 49.4 million jobs. Land will be converted at a rate of approximately 0.6 acres per residential unit and 0.2 acres per 1,000 square feet of nonresidential space. . . .

Almost one-quarter of this land conversion could be avoided through simple growth control measures without compromising growth or altering housing markets. Nearly 2.5 million acres could be saved by employing the equivalent of an urban growth boundary . . . to direct growth away from rural and undeveloped counties to the more-developed urban and suburban counties. . . . An additional 1.6 million acres could be saved through the use of an urban service area within a county to direct development away from undeveloped areas to developed areas in the same county. Included in the overall land savings are approximately 1.5 million acres of agricultural land, 1.5 million acres of environmentally fragile land, and 1.0 million other lands (e.g., barren, etc.). . . .

WATER AND SEWER INFRASTRUCTURE

During the period from 2000 to 2025, under traditional development or uncontrolled growth, developers and local governments in the United States will expend more than $190 billion to provide necessary water and sewer infrastructure. . . .

With both intercounty and intracounty growth-control measures in place, more than 150 million gallons of water and sewer demand per day can be saved without depriving residential or nonresidential users of this fundamental utility. . . . The combined cost saving . . . amounts to infrastructure savings of $12.6 billion over the projection period. . . .

a lot of $
con save water

LOCAL ROAD INFRASTRUCTURE . . .

— again controlled growth

For the projection period 2000 to 2025, under traditional or uncontrolled growth, the United States will spend more than $927 billion to provide necessary road infrastructure amounting to an additional 2.0 million lane-miles of local roads . . . Under controlled growth, 1.9 million lane-miles of local roads will be required, amounting to $817 billion in local road costs. Overall, a saving of 188,300 lane-miles of local roads and $110 billion can be achieved with more-compact growth patterns. This is a saving of 9.2 percent in local lane-miles and 11.8 percent in local road costs. . . .

LOCAL PUBLIC-SERVICE COSTS . . .

During the period 2000 to 2025, under traditional or uncontrolled-growth development, the nation will expend $143.2 billion annually for public services. . . . Under controlled-growth development, for the same projection period, the nation will expend annually $139.2 billion in local public-service costs—a decrease of $4 billion. . . .

TRAVEL MILES AND COSTS . . .

The controlled-growth scenario decreases overall daily travel miles by 4 percent and daily travel costs by 2.4 percent. In the process of achieving these savings, miles traveled daily in privately operated vehicles (POVs) are decreased by 4.7 percent and miles traveled in transit are increased by 19 percent. . . .

THE BENEFITS OF SPRAWL . . .

. . . The three potential benefits that clearly have merit are (1) larger average lot sizes at a distance from the center of a metropolitan area; (2) reflection of consumer preferences for low-density living; and (3) the provision of consumer households with more combinations of tax levels and social services than would occur under nonsprawl development. The two that are probably beneficial are (1) lower land and housing costs obtained when moving farther from each region's center, and (2) stronger citizen participation and influence in small, fragmented local governments rather than large, single political jurisdictions. . . .

[Another] three benefits of sprawl are not unequivocally beneficial to society because they have seriously negative side effects or consequences: access to better-quality schools and access to neighborhoods with lower crime rates in peripheral areas distant from regional centers, and creation of relatively homogeneous neighborhoods. These conditions are surely perceived as benefits by the residents of those peripheral areas, but such neighborhoods achieve these benefits by engaging in economically and socially exclusionary practices that accentuate the consequent concentration of very poor households in inner-core, high-poverty neighborhoods. Therefore, the conditions that the residents of these outlying areas perceive as benefiting them cannot be considered unequivocally good for society.

The same criticism might be made about two other benefits of sprawl, both of which are based on the fragmentation of governance powers over land uses among many relatively small municipalities or towns. These are (1) a wider range of choices about combinations of tax and public-service levels and (2) greater citizen participation and influence in local government decision making. Neither wider choice of tax and public-service combinations nor greater citizen influence is inherently harmful to low-income households, though the outcomes of both benefits can produce such harm to poor households in inner-core, high-poverty neighborhoods. Moreover, both these conditions are widespread and highly valued by millions of Americans—enough so that they are regarded in this study as net benefits to society.

Surveying the results of the analysis of sprawl's benefits, is it possible to arrive at an overall conclusion concerning whether sprawl's "true" benefits—and others that surely contribute some positive results to many households—make sprawl an acceptable development form? Sprawl has benefits that can be measured, and these are reasonably significant. It has more costs that can be measured, and these are more significant. Sprawl has some benefits that cannot be measured empirically; these may be significant. Overall, from what can be measured, sprawl has more costs than benefits. . . .

[handwritten: sprawl = low density vs compact, higher density]

Note on Sprawl

1. *Will you know it when you see it?* Exactly what constitutes sprawl? For a review of the many different ways to define sprawl, see Gerrit-Jan Knaap et al., Seeing the Elephant: Multi-disciplinary Measures of Urban Sprawl (National Center for Smart Growth Research and Education Working Paper 2005), available at http://www.smartgrowth.umd.edu/research/pdf/KnaapSongEwingEtAl_Elephant_022305.doc.

The best attempts to measure sprawl are Reid Ewing et al., Measuring Sprawl and Its Impact: The Character and Consequences of Metropolitan Expansion (2002); George Galster et al., Wrestling Sprawl to the Ground: Defining and Measuring an Elusive Concept, 12 Housing Pol'y Debate 681 (2001). Dolores Hayden's delightful A Field Guide to Sprawl (2004) provides colorful slang such as "ozoner" and "zoomburb," as well as photos, to define different types of sprawl.

2. *New Urbanism.* What's the alternative to sprawl? The leading contender is "New Urbanism," a movement discussed at pp. 424–24. One of the leading proponents of New Urbanism describes its principles as follows:

> The alternative to sprawl is simple and timely: neighborhoods of housing, parks, and schools placed within walking distance of shops, civic services, jobs, and transit — a modern version of the traditional town. The convenience of the car and the opportunity to walk or use transit can be blended in an environment with local access for all the daily needs of a diverse community. It is a strategy which could preserve open space, support transit, reduce auto traffic, and create affordable neighborhoods. Applied at a regional scale, a network of such mixed-use neighborhoods could create order in our balkanized metropolis. It could balance inner-city development with suburban investment by organizing growth around an expanding transit system and setting defensible urban limit lines and greenbelts. The increments of growth in each neighborhood would be small, but the aggregate could accommodate regional growth with minimal environmental impacts; less land consumed, less traffic generated, less pollution produced.
>
> Such neighborhoods, called Pedestrian Pockets or Transit-Oriented Developments, ultimately could be more affordable for working families, environmentally responsible, and cost-effective for business and government. But, such a growth strategy will mean fundamentally changing our preconceptions and local regulatory priorities, as well as redesigning the federal programs that shape our cities.

Peter Calthorpe, The Next American Metropolis: Ecology, Community, and the American Dream (1993). See also Andres Duany, et al., Suburban Nation: The Rise of Sprawl and the Decline of the American Dream (2000); New Urbanism and Traditional Neighborhood Development: Comprehensive Report & Best Practices Guide (2000). Figure 9-3 illustrates the differences between traditional suburban style and New Urbanism. For analysis of how well New Urbanism does as an antidote to sprawl, see, e.g., Jeremy R. Meredith, Note, Sprawl and the New Urbanist Solution, 89 Va. L. Rev. 447, 487–95 (2003).

3. *If you build it, will they come?* New age planners may prefer compact, higher-density urban forms to low-density "sprawl," but will consumers? Many argue that Americans

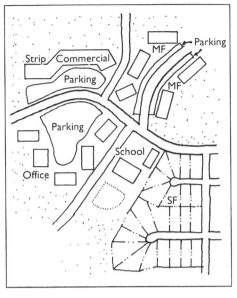

CONVENTIONAL SUBURBAN
DEVELOPMENT

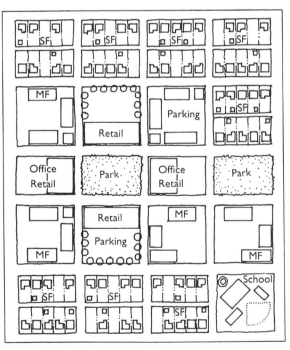

TRADITIONAL NEIGHBORHOOD DEVELOPMENT

Source: Peter Calthorpe, The Next American Metropolis: Ecology, Community, and the American Dream (1993).

FIGURE 9-3
Conventional Versus New Urbanist Development

will not give up their single-family detached houses. See, e.g., Anthony Downs, New Visions for a Metropolitan America 3–16 (1994). The empirical evidence, discussed at pp. 423–24, is mixed. If consumer preferences do run counter to solutions to sprawl, should consumer preferences control? For a good review of the debate about consumers' preferences for sprawl or smart growth, see Todd Litman, Evaluating Criticism of Smart Growth (Victoria Transport Policy Institute Working Paper, 2004), available at http://www.vtpi.org/sgcritics.pdf. For explorations of the cultural forces behind Americans' love for low-density single-family homes, see, e.g., Douglas Kelbaugh, Common Place: Toward Neighborhood and Regional Design 26–28 (1997); Constance Perin, Everything in Its Place; Social Order and Land Use in America (1977).

4. *The personal costs of sprawl.* For detailed explorations of some of the personal costs, such as health effects, for which sprawl is blamed, see, e.g. Reid Ewing et al., Relationship Between Urban Sprawl and Physical Activity, Obesity, and Morbidity, 5 Am. J. Health Promotion 1 (2003); Lance Freeman, The Effect of Sprawl on Neighborhood Social Ties: An Exploratory Analysis, 67 J. Am. Plan. Ass'n 69 (2001).

5. *The environmental costs of sprawl.* For arguments and evidence about the impacts sprawl has on the environment, see, e.g., U.S. Environmental Protection Agency, Our Built and Natural Environments, A Technical Review of the Interactions between Land Use, Transportation, and Environmental Quality (2001); Reid Ewing et al., Measuring Sprawl and Its Transportation Impacts, *in* Transportation Research Board, Transportation Research Record No. 1831, at 175 (2003); Patrick Gallagher, The Environmental, Social, and Cultural Impacts of Sprawl, 15 Nat. Resources & Env't 219 (2001).

6. *What causes sprawl?* We began to look at this issue in Chapter 1, at pp. 5–9, in our discussion of the forces behind suburbanization. It's fair to say that there are many culprits behind urban sprawl, and little agreement on which are most to blame. Government subsidies, such as the federal mortgage interest deduction and FHA loan guarantees, allowed suburban land and homes to be underpriced; the federal road building program and energy subsidies led to artificially low prices for commuting and other operating costs of suburban living; federal grants to allow construction of sewers and other subsidies for infrastructure resulted in underpricing of land and utility services. National transportation policy tended to support construction of new roads instead of mass transit systems. Racial and fiscal exclusionary zoning encouraged large-lot zoning, and restrictive land use policies often drove developers further out on the urban fringe. Higher-quality schools and other public services in the suburbs drew many people out of the cities. The classic exploration of the causes of sprawl is Kenneth T. Jackson, Crabgrass Frontier: The Suburbanization of the United States (1985). See also Duany, supra; Larry Keating, Atlanta: Race, Class, and Urban Expansion 34 (2001); Edward H. Ziegler, Urban Sprawl, Growth Management and Sustainable Development in the United States: Thoughts on the Sentimental Quest for a New Middle Landscape, 11 Va. J. Soc. Pol'y & L. 26 (2003). For a review of the literature attempting to quantify the extent to which various policies contribute to sprawl, see General Accounting Office, Community Development: Extent of Federal Influence on "Urban Sprawl" Is Unclear (1999).

Professor William Fischel argues that *growth controls* cause sprawl by causing developers to go even further out into exurban and rural areas to find communities that do not impose such restrictions. William A. Fischel, Do Growth Controls Matter? 55–56 (Lincoln Institute of Land Policy Working Paper, 1990). Might a developer forced to "go to other communities" choose to "infill" land within already built-up areas rather than move to exurbia? Could growth management programs encourage that adaptation? If a developer does go to exurban or rural areas, does it necessarily follow that energy costs and pollution are thereby increased because of additional commuting? Compare Benjamin Chinitz, Growth Management: Good for the Town, Bad for the Nation?, 56 J. Am. Plan. Ass'n 3, 7

(1990), with William A. Fischel, Growth Management Reconsidered: Good for the Town, Bad for the Nation? A Comment, 57 J. Am. Plan. Ass'n 341 (1991).

Note on the Danger of Monopolistic Control of City Size

Even if planners, economists, and the like could agree on a city's optimal size and form, how likely is it that government regulators would impose the efficient level of control? A number of commentators predict that if political, economic, and legal conditions permit, current owners of housing units will induce their local officials to prevent construction of new housing in order to drive up the market price of their own units.

Robert C. Ellickson, Suburban Growth Controls:
An Economic and Legal Analysis
86 Yale L.J. 385, 400–02, 430–32 (1977)

Antigrowth measures have one premier class of beneficiaries: those who already own residential structures in the municipality doing the excluding. If consumer demand for residency in a suburb is not completely elastic, its housing owners can employ growth controls to cartelize housing supply. Current landlords obviously have an interest in barring the entry of competitors. Upon reflection, one can see that suburban homeowners also should be tempted to exert monopoly power. The owner-occupant of a single-family house at some point will sell or rent his house to a third party. The owner-occupant's gains from that transfer will be increased if construction of new housing units is limited, since the price of all used housing will be raised. The more unique a suburb (i.e., the more sloped its demand curve), the more lucrative the monopoly possibilities for its homeowners. . . .

When a suburb has close substitutes, its current housing owners will not be particularly successful in using antigrowth measures to raise the market values of their buildings. Consumers will respond to exclusionary practices not by bidding up home values but by settling elsewhere. . . .

. . . Demand for housing is apt to be downwardly sloped (not perfectly elastic) in suburbs that have unique topographic or cultural features, that offer unusual public services, or that have special locational advantages. For example, Baltimore County and Prince Georges County, Maryland, are both so large in area that no other suburb can compete perfectly with them. These counties may be able to adopt policies that raise housing prices above competitive levels. . . .

If a unique suburb under the political control of a homeowner cartel were conceded unfettered discretion, it could be expected to behave like any other entrepreneur with monopoly power. The profit-maximizing strategy of any monopolist is to raise price by restricting output. . . . A homeowner cartel can profit from two basic types of housing transactions in this market: the sale of used housing units (which its members own) and the collection of development charges from suppliers of new units. If a suburb captures all available producers' surplus through variable charges, it, in effect, has commandeered all developers as wholly-owned subsidiaries. . . . The simplest way to collect those charges would be to impose quotas, moratoria, and wasteful development standards, and then sell relief from those ordinances for variable prices. . . .

Note on Monopolistic Homeowners

1. *Homeownership and support for growth control.* If existing homeowners are likely to benefit from the imposition of growth controls, support for growth management programs

should be correlated with levels of homeownership. Several studies have found such a relationship. See Mark Baldassare, Trouble in Paradise: The Suburban Transformation in America 95 (1986) (finding strong correlation between home ownership and support for controls on apartments); Alan Gin & Jonathan Sandy, Evaluating the Demand for Residential Growth Controls, 3 J. Housing Econ. 109 (1994) (higher rates of homeownership increase the demand for growth controls). But others have found no such correlation. Mark Baldassare & Georjeanna Wilson, Changing Sources of Suburban Support for Local Growths, 33 Urb. Stud. 3 (1996) (finding a correlation between rates of homeownership and support for growth controls in only one of three periods studied); Todd Donovan & Max Neiman, Community Social Status, Suburban Growth, and Local Government Restrictions on Residential Development, 28 Urb. Aff. Q. 323, 332 (1992) (finding no correlation). See also Keith R. Ihlanfeldt, Exclusionary Land Use Regulations within Suburban Communities: A Review of the Evidence and Policy Prescriptions, 41 Urb. Stud. 261, 272–75 (2004); Arthur C. Nelson et al., The Link between Growth Management and Housing Affordability: The Academic Evidence in Growth Management and Affordable Housing: Do They Conflict? 117, 150–53 (Anthony Downs ed., 2004).

2. *Evidence of monopolistic behavior.* Another test of the monopoly zoning theory is whether property values are higher in jurisdictions that have more monopoly power, either because there are relatively few neighboring jurisdictions or because the community has some unique feature. The evidence is mixed. See, e.g., William A. Fischel, Zoning and the Exercise of Monopoly Power: A Reevaluation, 8 J. Urb. Econ. 283 (1980); Bruce W. Hamilton, Zoning and the Exercise of Monopoly Power, 5 J. Urb. Econ. 116 (1978); Louis A. Rose, Urban Land Supply: Natural and Contrived Restrictions, 25 J. Urb. Econ. 325 (1989); James A. Thorson, An Examination of the Monopoly Zoning Hypothesis, 72 Land Econ. 43 (1996).

3. *Beggar thy neighbor.* Homeowners may use growth controls to drive up the prices of their homes by limiting supply, as Ellickson explains. To the extent growth controls improve the quality of life in the community relative to other communities, that too should increase housing values. Might sophisticated homeowners try to exclude growth not only to prevent its ill effects within their community, but also to foist those effects on nearby municipalities, making them relatively less desirable places to live and thereby eliminating housing in those municipalities as competitors for homebuyers' attention? See Jan K. Brueckner, Growth Controls and Land Values in an Open City, 66 Land Econ. 237 (1990); Robert W. Helsley & William C. Strange, Strategic Growth Controls, 25 Reg. Sci & Urb. Econ. 435 (1995); Susan M. Wachter & Man Cho, Interjurisdictional Price Effects of Land Use Controls, 40 Wash. U. J. Urb. & Contemp. L. 49 (1994). Might they also seek to limit growth to reduce business competition? See Phillip Longman, Growthbusters, Fla. Trend, June 1990, at 34 (supporters of growth control group "see a building moratorium as a way to get their cake and eat it too — as a way to escape higher taxes, boost their property values and escape new business competition, all the while enjoying less traffic, cheaper water and a cleaner environment").

2. *Moratoria*

Associated Home Builders, Inc. v. City of Livermore
557 P.2d 473 (Cal. 1976)

TOBRINER, Justice. . . .

The initiative ordinance in question was enacted by a majority of the voters at the Livermore municipal election of April 11, 1972, and became effective on April 28, 1972.

The ordinance . . . states that it was enacted to further the health, safety, and welfare of the citizens of Livermore and to contribute to the solution of air pollution. Finding that excessive issuance of residential building permits has caused school overcrowding, sewage pollution, and water rationing, the ordinance prohibits issuance of further permits until three standards are met: 1. EDUCATIONAL FACILITIES — No double sessions in the schools nor overcrowded classrooms as determined by the California Education Code. 2. SEWAGE — The sewage treatment facilities and capacities meet the standards set by the Regional Water Quality Control Board. 3. WATER SUPPLY — No rationing of water with respect to human consumption or irrigation and adequate water reserves for fire protection exist."

Plaintiff association filed suit to enjoin enforcement of the ordinance and for declaratory relief. . . .

. . . Plaintiff contends that the ordinance proposes, and will cause, the prevention of nonresidents from migrating to Livermore, and that the ordinance therefore attempts an unconstitutional exercise of the police power, both because no compelling state interest justifies its infringement upon the migrant's constitutionally protected right to travel, and because it exceeds the police power of the municipality.[18] . . .

Many writers have contended that exclusionary land use ordinances tend primarily to exclude racial minorities and the poor, and on that account should be subject to strict judicial scrutiny. See e.g., Paul Davidoff & Linda Davidoff, Opening the Suburbs: Toward Inclusionary Land Use Controls, 22 Syracuse L. Rev. 509 (1971); Lawrence G. Sager, Tight Little Islands: Exclusionary Zoning, Equal Protection, and the Indigent, 21 Stan. L. Rev. 767 (1969). . . . These writers, however, are concerned primarily with ordinances which ban or limit less expensive forms of housing while permitting expensive single-family residences on large lots. The Livermore ordinance is not made from this mold; it impartially bans all residential construction, expensive or inexpensive. Consequently plaintiff at bar has eschewed reliance upon any claim that the ordinance discriminates on a basis of race or wealth.

Plaintiff's contention that the Livermore ordinance must be tested by a standard of strict scrutiny, and can be sustained only upon a showing of a compelling state interest, thus rests solely on plaintiff's assertion that the ordinance abridges a constitutionally protected right to travel. . . .

In asserting that legislation which burdens a right to travel requires strict scrutiny, and can be sustained only upon proof of compelling need, plaintiff relies on . . . Memorial Hospital v. Maricopa County, 415 U.S. 250 (1974); Dunn v. Blumstein, 405 U.S. 330 (1972); Shapiro v. Thompson, 394 U.S. 618 (1969). The legislation held invalid by those decisions, however, directly burdened the right to travel by distinguishing between nonresidents or newly arrived residents on the one hand and established residents on the other, and imposing penalties or disabilities on the former group.

Both the United States Supreme Court and this court have refused to apply the strict constitutional test to legislation, such as the present ordinance, which does not penalize travel and resettlement but merely makes it more difficult for the outsider to establish his residence in the place of his choosing. See Village of Belle Terre v. Boraas, 416 U.S. 1, 7 (1973). . . .

---

18. Plaintiff does not contend that the ordinance constitutes an inverse condemnation of property, compare Associated Home Builders, Inc. v. City of Walnut Creek, 484 P.2d 606 (Cal. 1971), that it unreasonably burdens interstate commerce, compare Construction Indus. Ass'n. Sonoma County. v. City of Petaluma, 522 F.2d 897, 909 (9th Cir. 1975), or that it denies the equal protection of the laws either to landowners, compare Town of Los Altos Hills v. Adobe Creek Properties, Inc., 108 Cal. Rptr. 271 (Ct. App. 1973), or to migrants, compare Ybarra v. Town of Los Altos Hills, 503 F.2d 250 (9th Cir. 1974).

→ No strict scrutiny

We conclude that the indirect burden upon the right to travel imposed by the Livermore ordinance does not call for strict judicial scrutiny. The validity of the challenged ordinance must be measured by the more liberal standards that have traditionally tested the validity of land use restrictions enacted under the municipal police power. . . .

. . . A number of recent decisions from courts of other states, however, have declined to accord the traditional deference to legislative judgment in the review of exclusionary ordinances, and ruled that communities lacked authority to adopt such ordinances. Plaintiff urges that we apply the standards of review employed in those decisions in passing upon the instant ordinance.

The cases cited by plaintiff, however, cannot serve as a guide to resolution of the present controversy. Not only do those decisions rest, for the most part, upon principles of state law inapplicable in California, but, unlike the present case, all involve ordinances which impede the ability of low or moderate income persons to immigrate to a community but permit largely unimpeded entry by wealthier persons.

We therefore reaffirm the established constitutional principle that a local land use ordinance falls within the authority of the police power if it is reasonably related to the public welfare. Most previous decisions applying this test, however, have involved ordinances without substantial effect beyond the municipal boundaries. The present ordinance, *Here,* in contrast, significantly affects the interests of nonresidents who are not represented in the city legislative body and cannot vote on a city initiative. We therefore believe *So ct will clarify to* it desirable for the guidance of the trial court to clarify the application of the tradi- *make it easier* tional police power test to an ordinance which significantly affects nonresidents of the *for trial ct.* municipality.

When we inquire whether an ordinance reasonably relates to the public welfare, inquiry should begin by asking *whose* welfare must the ordinance serve. In past cases, when discussing ordinances without significant effect beyond the municipal boundaries, we have been content to assume that the ordinance need only reasonably relate to the welfare of the enacting municipality and its residents. But municipalities are not isolated islands remote from the needs and problems of the area in which they are located; thus an ordinance, superficially reasonable from the limited viewpoint of the municipality, may be disclosed as unreasonable when viewed from a larger perspective.

These considerations impel us to the conclusion that the proper constitutional test is one which inquires whether the ordinance reasonably relates to the welfare of those whom it significantly affects. If its impact is limited to the city boundaries, the inquiry may be limited accordingly; if, as alleged here, the ordinance may strongly influence the supply and distribution of housing for an entire metropolitan region, judicial inquiry must consider the welfare of that region.[24] . . .

trial ct analysis:
We explain the process by which a trial court may determine whether a challenged restriction reasonably relates to the regional welfare. The first step in that analysis is to *1)* forecast the probable effect and duration of the restriction. In the instant case the Livermore *here* ordinance posits a total ban on residential construction, but one which terminates as soon as *so* public facilities reach specified standards. Thus to evaluate the impact of the restriction, the court must ascertain the extent to which public facilities currently fall short of the specified standards, must inquire whether the city or appropriate regional agencies have undertaken to construct needed improvements, and must determine when the improvements are likely to be completed.

---

24. In ascertaining whether a challenged ordinance reasonably relates to the regional welfare, the extent and bounds of the region significantly affected by the ordinance should be determined as a question of fact by the trial court.

The second step is to identify the competing interests affected by the restriction. We touch in this area deep social antagonisms. We allude to the conflict between the environmental protectionists and the egalitarian humanists; a collision between the forces that would save the benefits of nature and those that would preserve the opportunity of people in general to settle. Suburban residents who seek to overcome problems of inadequate schools and public facilities to secure "the blessing of quiet seclusion and clean air" and to "make the area a sanctuary for people," Village of Belle Terre v. Boraas, 416 U.S. 1, 9 (1973), may assert a vital interest in limiting immigration to their community. Outsiders searching for a place to live in the face of a growing shortage of adequate housing, and hoping to share in the perceived benefits of suburban life, may present a countervailing interest opposing barriers to immigration.

Having identified and weighed the competing interests, the final step is to determine whether the ordinance, in light of its probable impact, represents a reasonable accommodation of the competing interests. We do not hold that a court in inquiring whether an ordinance reasonably relates to the regional welfare, cannot defer to the judgment of the municipality's legislative body. But judicial deference is not judicial abdication. The ordinance must have a *real and substantial* relation to the public welfare. . . .

The burden rests with the party challenging the constitutionality of an ordinance to present the evidence and documentation which the court will require in undertaking this constitutional analysis. Plaintiff in the present case has not yet attempted to shoulder that burden. . . . Consequently we cannot determine the impact upon either Livermore or the surrounding region of the ordinance's restriction on the issuance of building permits pending achievement of its goals.

. . . Without an evidentiary record to demonstrate the validity and significance of the asserted interests, we cannot determine whether the instant ordinance attempts a reasonable accommodation of those interests.

. . . That issue can only be resolved by a trial at which evidence is presented to document the probable impact of the ordinance upon the municipality and the surrounding region.

The judgment of the superior court is reversed, and the cause remanded for further proceedings consistent with the views expressed herein.

Mosk, Justice (dissenting). . . .

. . . Accommodation between environmental preservation and satisfaction of housing needs can be reached through rational guidelines for land use decision-making. Ours, of course, is not the legislative function. But two legal inhibitions must be the benchmark of any such guidelines. First, any absolute prohibition on housing development is presumptively invalid. And second, local regulations, based on parochialism, that limit population densities in growing suburban areas may be found invalid unless the community is absorbing a reasonable share of the region's population pressures.

Under the foregoing test, the Livermore ordinance is fatally flawed. . . .

Note on Moratoria and Interim Zoning

1. *Costs and benefits of moratoria.* Moratoria were described in an amicus brief filed by the Council of State Governments and other government associations in *Tahoe-Sierra*, excerpted at p. 185, as "an essential and well-accepted part of land use planning":

> . . . [G]ood land-use planning takes time. Absent a temporary delay in issuing new permits, planning could be undermined by new development. Courts long have recognized

that planning efforts often trigger a rush to the permit office by developers hoping to obtain vested rights before new controls are implemented. Without moratoria, new construction could undercut planning measures before they see the light of day.

Development moratoria also promote public participation in planning. Where moratoria authority is lacking, municipalities sometimes adopt hastily prepared, permanent controls insensitive to the needs of certain landowners. "[W]ith the adoption of an interim provision [the landowner] is made aware that a new plan is in the offing and is thus able to participate in the debate over what that new plan should contain." Collura v. Town of Arlington, 329 N.E.2d 733, 737 (Mass. 1975). . . .

. . . Development moratoria . . . assist municipalities in addressing overburdened public services such as schools, roads, and sewers. . . .

Development moratoria also are used to address imminent threats to public health and safety [such as floods or unstable slopes].

Brief of the Council of State Governments at 4–6, Tahoe-Sierra Preservation Council, Inc. v. Tahoe Regional Planning Agency, 535 U.S. 302 (2002).

Others see moratoria not as a necessary tool of planning, but as "a symptom of failed planning." Critics argue that moratoria

- disrupt the economic base of the development industry and the community, and impose inequitable burdens on small builders who are less able to withstand the economic strain;
- generate a "panic" atmosphere that increases land speculation and inflation;
- increase building activity in the short term as builders try to beat a rumored moratorium deadline, or to vest rights in the prior regulatory scheme;
- promote urban sprawl by forcing development out to more remote jurisdictions.

John J. Delaney, Coping with Moratoria in the Aftermath of Tahoe-Sierra — A Landowner's Guide, SJ015 ALI-ABA 889, 893–94 (2003).

Who has the better of the argument?

2. Public activities frozen. The Livermore moratorium curtailed the granting of residential building permits. Why didn't the sponsors of the initiative measure seek a moratorium on all building permits (including those for commercial and office development)? Other types of moratorium measures may freeze municipal action on rezonings, subdivision approvals, or utility hookups. Which of these types of moratoria can be expected to stop growth the fastest?

Note on Other Legal Challenges to Moratoria

1. Authority challenges. Several states specifically forbid local governments from enacting moratoria, at least under certain circumstances. See, e.g., N.J. Stat. Ann. §40:55D-90(a) (West 2005) (prohibiting moratoria on development "in order to prepare a master plan and development regulations"); N.M. Stat. Ann. §5-8-42 (Michie 2005) (prohibiting moratoria for purpose of allowing local government time to adopt or update impact fees). As discussed subsequently in this note, some states explicitly authorize moratoria. In the more common situation in which states do not forbid but also do not specifically permit moratoria, municipalities must argue that moratoria or interim zoning measures are authorized by the general language of the zoning enabling act. Liberal construction of local governmental powers is common. For instance, in Brazos Land, Inc. v. Board of County Commissioners of Rio Arriba County, 848 P.2d 1095 (N.M. Ct. App. 1993), the state's general zoning enabling

act was interpreted to authorize a moratorium on subdivision approvals to allow the county to draft more restrictive regulations to address groundwater contamination problems. But see Naylor v. Township of Hellam, 773 A.2d 770, 776 (Pa. 2001) (Municipalities Planning Code did not implicitly authorize local governments to impose moratoria because the "power to 'halt' development is not an extension of or incidental to any power to regulate land use or development").

2. *Compliance with statutory mandates.* Statutes in about a dozen states expressly authorize local governments to adopt emergency measures to control development on specific tracts while permanent regulations are being prepared. Such statutes may impose severe constraints on the use of moratoria, see, e.g., Ariz. Rev. Stat. §9-463.06 (2005) (a moratorium necessitated by shortage of such public services as police and fire facilities must be based on findings that application of existing regulations is inadequate to prevent "irrevocable public harm," moratorium is sufficiently limited to ensure that a needed supply of housing is not unreasonably restricted, alternative methods of achieving the objectives of the moratorium are unsatisfactory, and the public harm caused by the failure to impose a moratorium outweighs the adverse effects of the moratorium on other affected local governments).

Such statutes frequently impose time limits on interim measures. See, e.g., Mont. Code Ann. §76-2-306 (2005) (authorizing municipalities to adopt interim zoning limited to six months, plus no more than two one-year extensions). Some require extraordinary majorities for adoption. See, e.g., Cal. Gov't Code §65858 (West 2005) (four-fifths of local legislative body). If statutes set out specific procedures or substantive constraints on the adoption of interim measures, these statutory restrictions are likely to be strictly enforced by the courts. See, e.g., New Jersey Shore Builders Association v. Mayor & Township Committee, 561 A.2d 319 (N.J. Super. Ct. Law. Div. 1989) (moratoria failed to comply with New Jersey statute requiring a municipality enacting a moratoria to demonstrate "on the basis of a written opinion by a qualified health professional . . . a clear imminent danger to the health of the inhabitants").

Because of the emergency alleged to justify a moratorium, a local government may be authorized either by the enabling act or by common law to adopt interim measures without following the procedural requirements — e.g., notice and hearing — which normally apply to adoption of zoning controls. See, e.g., Duncanson v. Board of Supervisors, 551 N.W.2d 248 (Minn. Ct. App. 1996). But cf. Wash. Rev. Code §35.63.200 (2005) (requiring body adopting a moratorium or interim zoning control to hold a public hearing within 60 days of the adoption). Some courts, however, have required that moratoria be enacted with the same procedural safeguards as any other zoning matter, at least where there is no life-threatening emergency justifying the moratoria. See, e.g., Sandy Mush Properties, Inc. v. Rutherford County, 595 S.E.2d 233, 236 (N.C. Ct. App. 2004) (invalidating moratorium because county had not published notice of the public for two successive weeks as required by statute governing zoning ordinances).

Should moratoria have to comply with laws requiring jurisdictions to plan before they zone? See Pro-Eco, Inc. v. Board of Commissioners, 956 F.2d 635 (7th Cir. 1992) (moratoria governed by Illinois law prohibiting jurisdictions from adopting zoning ordinances unless they have approved a comprehensive plan).

3. *Due process.* Even if a local government has acted within its power and has followed the correct adoption procedures, its interim controls may nevertheless be deemed to violate the substantive due process rights of landowners. Most courts are influenced by the temporary character of the controls and thus tend to allow local governments to impose harsher short-term, than long-term, restrictions. But a court may find a violation of due process if the evidence does not support the local government's assertions that an emergency exists.

See, e.g., Cellular Telephone Co. v. Village of Tarrytown, 624 N.Y.S.2d 170 (App. Div. 1995) (moratorium on cellular telephone antennas was unreasonable where there was "not a scintilla of evidence" in the record to support village's acceptance of "community perception" that emissions from the antennas might be dangerous and that siting of antennas should await long-term health studies).

In addition, most courts insist that the municipality make good faith progress in ending the "emergency" situation — for example, by completing a long-awaited comprehensive plan. See, e.g., Q.C. Construction Co. v. Gallo, 649 F. Supp. 1331 (D.R.I. 1986) (moratorium unreasonable where town has taken no actions to correct problems in the town's sewer system in the three years since the moratorium was enacted). Of course, a "temporary" moratorium may become unreasonable if left in place too long. See, e.g., Mitchell v. Kemp, 575 N.Y.S.2d 337 (App. Div. 1991) (fifth renewal of a one-year planning moratorium unreasonable where city offered no explanation for the delay in enacting a zoning ordinance).

4. *Takings*. *Tahoe-Sierra*, excerpted at p. 185, made clear that moratoria do not effect a per se taking under *Lucas*. Instead, whether a particular moratorium effects a taking must be determined under *Penn Central*'s multifactored analysis. For a review of post–*Tahoe-Sierra* decisions, which generally have rejected takings claims involving moratoria, see Matthew G. St. Amand & Dwight H. Merriam, Defensible Moratoria: The Law Before and After the *Tahoe-Sierra* Decision, 43 Nat. Resources J. 703 (2003).

5. *Equal protection*. Should courts be more suspicious of moratoria that seem aimed at particular development proposals? See, e.g., Medical Services, Inc., v. City of Savage, 487 N.W.2d 263 (Minn. Ct. App. 1992) (invalidating moratorium affecting only one pending proposal, where proposal had been pending for several years but city had done nothing to study the impact of such facilities during that time and the moratorium was passed a few weeks after the developer sued the city). But see Haberman v. City of Long Beach, 748 N.Y.S.2d 397 (App. Div. 2002) (no equal protection violation when city lifted moratorium for surrounding properties, but not for plaintiff's property).

6. *Vested rights, variances, and other exceptions to moratoria*. Few moratoria are ironclad. Moratoria often are imposed at the building permit stage, and therefore may affect developments that already received rezonings, subdivision approvals, or other early approvals. Developers that have made significant investments in site improvements on the basis of those approvals often have vested rights to proceed (or at least to be compensated), as discussed at pp. 202–09. In addition, some moratoria provide for exceptions and include explicit variance procedures. The lack of a variance provision may trouble reviewing courts, see, e.g., Innkeepers Motor Lodge, Inc. v. City of New Smyrna Beach, 460 So. 2d 379 (Fla. Dist. Ct. App. 1984) (absence of variance procedure renders moratorium unconstitutionally arbitrary). On the other hand, a porous variance procedure also may doom a moratorium. See Davidson Mineral Properties, Inc. v. Monroe County, 357 S.E.2d 95 (Ga. 1987) (where 23 of 24 variance requests from moratorium had been granted, the unsuccessful applicant's argument that the variance procedure was too vague to satisfy due process requirements was correct).

Note on "Ballot Box" Growth Management

Many jurisdictions adopt growth management measures through initiatives. While many courts allow such initiatives, see, e.g., Garvin v. Ninth Judicial District Court, 59 P.3d 1180 (Nev. 2002) (overruling precedent to hold that growth control measure was legislative, rather than administrative in nature, and therefore could be adopted by initiative), some courts have refused to allow growth control plans to be initiated by the voters or submitted to the voters in a referendum. See Whatcom County v. Brisbane, 884 P.2d 1326 (Wash. 1994) (growth management by initiative or referendum conflicts with state growth management legislation, which delegated power to manage growth to county legislative bodies; further, growth management by local initiative and referendum would frustrate the purposes of the state legislation). Some courts reject growth management plans passed by initiative on the ground that they fail the consistency with the comprehensive plan requirements discussed at pp. 336–41. See, e.g., Building Industry Association v. City of Oceanside, 33 Cal. Rptr. 2d 137 (Ct. App. 1994) (initiative measure adopting an annual quota inconsistent with the comprehensive plan, which included a policy of avoiding "direct controls on the number or location" of housing).

3. Rate of Growth or Quota Programs

Construction Industry Association v. City of Petaluma

522 F.2d 897 (9th Cir. 1975), cert. denied, 424 U.S. 934 (1976)

Choy, Circuit Judge:

The City of Petaluma (the City) appeals from a district court decision voiding as unconstitutional certain aspects of its five-year housing and zoning plan. We reverse.

The City is located in southern Sonoma County, about 40 miles north of San Francisco. . . . It experienced a steady population growth from 10,315 in 1950 to 24,870 in 1970. Eventually, the City was drawn into the Bay Area metropolitan housing market as people working in San Francisco and San Rafael became willing to commute longer distances to secure relatively inexpensive housing available there. By November 1972, according to unofficial figures, Petaluma's population was at 30,500, a dramatic increase of almost 25 percent in little over two years. . . . Alarmed by the accelerated rate of growth in 1970 and 1971, the demand for even more housing, and the sprawl of the City eastward, the City adopted a temporary freeze on development in early 1971. The construction and zoning change moratorium was intended to give the City Council and the City planners an opportunity to study the housing and zoning situation and to develop short and long range plans. The Council made specific findings with respect to housing patterns and availability in Petaluma, including the following: . . . that in 1970, 83 percent of Petaluma's housing was single-family dwellings; that the bulk of recent development (largely single-family homes) occurred in the eastern portion of the City, causing a large deficiency in moderately priced multi-family and apartment units on the east side.

To correct the imbalance between single-family and multi-family dwellings, curb the sprawl of the City on the east, and retard the accelerating growth of the City, the Council in 1972 adopted several resolutions, which collectively are called the "Petaluma Plan" (the Plan).

The Plan, on its face limited to a five-year period (1972–1977), fixes a housing development growth rate not to exceed 500 dwelling units per year. . . . The 500-unit figure is somewhat misleading, however, because it applies only to housing units (hereinafter referred to as "development-units") that are part of projects involving five units or more. Thus, the 500-unit figure does not reflect any housing and population growth due to construction of single-family homes or even four-unit apartment buildings not part of any larger project.

. . . One of the most innovative features of the Plan is the Residential Development Control System which provides procedures and criteria for the award of the annual 500 development-unit permits. At the heart of the allocation procedure is an intricate point system, whereby a builder accumulates points for conformity by his projects with the City's general plan and environmental design plans, for good architectural design, and for providing low and moderate income dwelling units and various recreational facilities. The Plan further directs that allocations of building permits are to be divided as evenly as feasible between the west and east sections of the City and between single-family dwellings and multiple residential units (including rental units), that the sections of the City closest to the center are to be developed first in order to cause "infilling" of vacant area, and that 8 to 12 percent of the housing units approved be for low and moderate income persons. . . .

For purposes of this decision, . . . we will assume that the 500 development-unit growth rate is in fact below the reasonably anticipated market demand for such units and that absent the Petaluma Plan, the City would grow at a faster rate.

According to undisputed expert testimony at trial, if the Plan (limiting housing starts to approximately 6 percent of existing housing stock each year) were to be adopted by municipalities throughout the region, the impact on the housing market would be substantial. For the decade 1970 to 1980, the shortfall in needed housing in the region would be about 105,000 units (or 25 percent of the units needed). Further, the aggregate effect of a proliferation of the Plan throughout the San Francisco region would be a decline in regional housing stock quality, a loss of the mobility of current and prospective residents and a deterioration in the quality and choice of housing available to income earners with real incomes of $14,000 per year or less. If, however, the Plan were considered by itself and with respect to Petaluma only, there is no evidence to suggest that there would be a deterioration in the quality and choice of housing available there to persons in the lower and middle income brackets. Actually, the Plan increases the availability of multi-family units (owner-occupied and rental units) and low-income units which were rarely constructed in the pre-Plan days.

. . . The district court ruled that certain aspects of the Plan unconstitutionally denied the right to travel insofar as they tended "to limit the natural population growth of the area." 375 F. Supp. [574], at 588. The court enjoined the City and its agents from implementing the unconstitutional elements of the Plan, but the order was stayed by Justice Douglas pending this appeal. . . .

[The Court found that the plaintiffs did not have standing to raise the right-to-travel claim on behalf of unknown third parties allegedly excluded from living in Petaluma. The plaintiffs did have standing to challenge the Petaluma Plan as arbitrary and thus a violation of the Fourteenth Amendment, and as an unreasonable burden on interstate commerce.]

SUBSTANTIVE DUE PROCESS . . .

In attacking the validity of the Plan, appellees rely heavily on the district court's finding that the express purpose and the actual effect of the Plan is to exclude substantial numbers of people who would otherwise elect to move to the City. 375 F. Supp. at 581. The existence of an exclusionary purpose and effect reflects, however, only *one* side of the zoning regulation. Practically all zoning restrictions have as a purpose and effect the *exclusion* of some activity or type of structure or a certain density of inhabitants. And in reviewing the reasonableness of a zoning ordinance, our inquiry does not terminate with a finding that it is for an exclusionary purpose. We must determine further whether the *exclusion* bears any rational relationship to a *legitimate state interest.* If it does not, then the zoning regulation is invalid. If, on the other hand, a legitimate state interest is furthered by the zoning regulation, we must defer to the legislative act. Being neither a super legislature nor a zoning board of appeal, a federal court is without authority to weigh and reappraise the factors considered or ignored by the legislative body in passing the challenged zoning regulation. The reasonableness, not the wisdom, of the Petaluma Plan is at issue in this suit.

Although we assume that some persons desirous of living in Petaluma will be excluded under the housing permit limitation and that, thus, the Plan may frustrate some legitimate regional housing needs, the Plan is not arbitrary or unreasonable. . . . If the present system of delegated zoning power does not effectively serve the state interest in furthering the general welfare of the region or entire state, it is the state legislature's and not the federal courts' role to intervene and adjust the system. . . .

[handwritten margin note: only the reasonableness is at issue]

[handwritten note: state leg is free to get involved if plan is not effectively serving the state interest]

COMMERCE CLAUSE . . .

It is well settled that a state regulation validly based on the police power does not impermissibly burden interstate commerce where the regulation neither discriminates against interstate commerce nor operates to disrupt its required uniformity. Huron Cement Co. v. Detroit, 362 U.S. 440, 448 (1960). As stated by the Supreme Court almost 25 years ago: "When there is a reasonable basis for legislation to protect the social, as distinguished from the economic, welfare of a community, it is not for this Court because of the Commerce Clause to deny the exercise locally of the sovereign power of the [state]." Breard v. Alexandria, 341 U.S. 622, 640 (1951). . . .

Consequently, since the local regulation here is rationally related to the social and environmental welfare of the community and does not discriminate against interstate commerce or operate to disrupt its required uniformity, appellees' claim that the Plan unreasonably burdens commerce must fail.

[handwritten note: commerce claim / argument fails]

Reversed.

Note on Quotas

1. *Comparison with* Livermore. In *Livermore*, excerpted at p. 797, decided shortly after *Petaluma*, the California Supreme Court held that municipal growth controls must be reasonably related to the *regional* welfare. Would the Petaluma Plan pass that test?

2. *Copycats.* In the few years following the *Petaluma* decision, voters in many California cities approved initiative measures mimicking Petaluma's quota system. State of California, Office of Planning & Research, The Growth Revolt (1980). In 1980, the California legislature shifted the burden and standard of proof on challenges to such quotas:

> [T]he city . . . enacting [any ordinance which "(1) directly limits, by number, the building permits that may be issued for residential constructions or the buildable lots which may be developed for residential purposes"] shall bear the burden of proof that the ordinance is necessary for the protection of the public health, safety, or welfare of the population of the city. . . .

Cal. Evid. Code §669.5 (West 2005). Nevertheless, many California cities continue to use quota systems. Indeed, as of 1989, more than 10 percent of California residents lived in a city or county that had adopted some form of growth cap. John D. Landis, Do Growth Controls Work? A New Assessment, 58 J. Am. Plan. Ass'n 489, 490 (1992).

3. *Epilogue on the Petaluma Plan.* Between 1972 and 1977, Petaluma fell far short of filling its quota of 500 "development-units" per year. In 1978, it dropped the 500-unit quota and instead capped annual new construction at 5 percent of the existing housing stock. In 1987, the city reverted to the annual 500-unit cap. In the two decades following

enactment of the program, however, the actual growth in Petaluma was less than the growth "limited" by the program. See Eric Damian Kelly, Managing Community Growth: Policies, Techniques, and Impacts 55 (2d ed. 2004). Regional downturns in the housing market were, no doubt, partly responsible for the lower-than-expected growth rates. But problems plagued the program:

> Developers had difficulty understanding the complex point system. City staff had difficulty administering it despite a computer program designed to compute points. Projects which met minimum standards eventually obtained approvals. The time-consuming and costly ranking process had little impact on actual approval or denial of projects. In order to achieve minimum numbers of points, developers included in their projects some expensive features, probably not wanted by occupants or really needed by the city. As a few large developers came to dominate homebuilding in Petaluma, and as the pattern of approvals became clear, developers submitted projects which were adequate, but not excellent. In addition, it was difficult to get a majority of the evaluation committee to meet. Finally, one member could unduly skew the total points awarded and complicate the approval process by ranking a project very low or very high.

Richard T. LeGates, The Emergence of Flexible Growth Management Systems in the San Francisco Bay Area, 24 Loy. L.A. L. Rev. 1035, 1060 (1991) (citing interviews with Petaluma planning officials).

In 1987, Petaluma abandoned its point system and adopted a system of "development objectives." Each year, the city council must adopt development objectives to indicate the "City's expectations" on such issues as "housing mix (types and affordability); East/West development ratio; needed public facilities; infrastructure improvements; and infill areas where development might be encouraged." Petaluma Municipal Code ch. 17.26.050. If the applications for development allocation exceed the quota, the city council "shall use the Development Objectives in addition to General Plan policy as criteria for distributing allocations to individual projects." Id. at 17.26.030(E) & 17.25.060.

Boulder, Colorado, is often cited as another leading example of rate-of-growth programs, but Boulder too has moved from a "merit" point system to a less complicated and more flexible system. Boulder Streamlines Growth Management, Zoning News, Mar. 1985, at 3 (change was intended to reduce paperwork because developers were submitting volumes of documentation to prove that their projects should be awarded the maximum points, and to make the process fairer because the point system favored larger developers). For a thoughtful perspective on Boulder's point system, see James Leach, A Homebuilder Looks at Boulder's Controls: Stonewalling Growth, in Growth Management: Keeping on Target (Douglas R. Porter ed., 1986).

4. *Allocation systems.* The allocation of development permits within a quota system is subject to a number of familiar challenges. See, e.g., Schenck v. City of Hudson Village, 114 F.3d 590 (6th Cir. 1997) (property owners were unlikely to succeed in proving a claim that distribution of permits by lottery was irrational); Wilkinson v. Board of County Commissioners, 872 P.2d 1269 (Colo. Ct. App. 1993) (guidelines used to allocate permits under quota system were sufficiently definite to withstand vagueness challenge). Should the application of point systems to specific property be considered a legislative or adjudicative decision?

5. *Rate-of-growth caps.* When jurisdictions impose limits on the percentage rate of growth, how should courts evaluate the percentage rate chosen? In Rancourt v. Town of Barnstead, 523 A.2d 55 (N.H. 1986), the town refused to approve a subdivision because it would cause the town to exceed the 3 percent annual growth rate the town's comprehensive plan stated as a goal. The town defended the percentage with estimates by the Office of State Planning that the town would grow only 2.3 percent over the following decade,

and by evidence that town residents responding to a questionnaire most often chose 3 percent as an "ideal" growth rate. The Supreme Court of New Hampshire overturned the denial because (among other problems) the state's figures appeared unrealistic in light of the town's historic 10 percent growth rate and therefore there was no "solid, scientific, statistical basis" for the 3 percent goal. Id. at 59. See also Cal. Evid. Code §669.5(d) (West 2005) (shifting burden of proof to city to defend validity of certain growth control ordinances, but making an exception for certain measures that set a growth rate "of no more than the average population growth rate experienced by the state as a whole").

Consider the proposal advanced by Professor Delogu and his colleagues, which would require a jurisdiction imposing a growth cap to demonstrate a need for the cap by showing that "the average rate of growth for the two preceding calendar years exceeds by more than 50% the average rate of growth for the five calendar years proceeding these two years" or by showing "(by compelling evidence) that some element of essential public infrastructure, e.g., roads, water supply, waste water treatment plant capacity, school space, etc., is in such short supply that continued growth at the rate of the average of the two preceding calendar years poses a health or safety risk." If either of those showings were made, the jurisdiction would be allowed to set "the annual number of building permits that issue in a calendar year, at a level no lower than either: 50% of the average number of building permits issued during the preceding two calendar years; or at the average number of building permits issued during the preceding seven calendar years." The rate of growth cap could not be in effect for more than two years, or three years in the case of an infrastructure deficit, and the municipality would not be allowed to use growth caps for more than three years in any seven-year period. Orlando E. Delogu et al., Some Model Amendments to Maine (and Other States') Land Use Control Legislation, 56 Me. L. Rev. 323, 335 (2004).

6. *Takings claims.* Landowners' allegations that the development delays imposed by quota systems effect a taking did not meet with much success before *Tahoe-Sierra*, excerpted at p. 185, and are even less likely to succeed given that decision. See Del Oro Hills v. City of Oceanside, 37 Cal. Rptr. 2d 677 (Ct. App. 1995) (rejecting claim that delay caused by growth management plan resulted in $2 million in lost profits and therefore effected a taking, reasoning that "[m]ere fluctuations in value during the process of governmental decision making, absent extraordinary delay, are 'incidents of ownership'" (quoting Agins v. Tiburon, 447 U.S. 255, 263 n.9 (1980))). If a developer does not receive an allocation one year but is free to apply again in the future, is the takings challenge ripe under *Williamson County*? See Katherine E. Stone & Philip A. Seymour, Regulating the Timing of Development: Takings Clause and Substantive Due Process Challenges to Growth Control Regulations, 24 Loy. L.A. L. Rev. 1205, 1238–39 (1991).

4. *Growth Phasing and Concurrency Programs*

Golden v. Planning Board of Town of Ramapo
285 N.E.2d 291 (N.Y.), appeal dismissed, 409 U.S. 1003 (1972)

[The following statement of facts was taken from Judge Breitel's dissenting opinion.]
The Town of Ramapo, following an intensive study by highly-competent experts, amended its zoning ordinance by adding to it section 46-13.1. . . . It broadly defines a developer as any landowner who proposes to erect and sell a dwelling or dwellings for residential use. Regardless of the district zone, any proposed development, as so broadly defined, is forbidden unless a special permit is obtained. Permits will be granted only if the land qualifies for enough assigned points under some five categories of available municipal

facilities, namely, sewerage, drainage, park-recreation-public school facilities, roads, and firehouses. The purpose is to prohibit development until an acceptable level of supporting facilities exists. The town has committed itself, it is said, by its capital budget and capital improvement plans to insure eventual availability of supporting facilities. But in some areas this eventuality will not be realized for 18 years. To prevent undue delay, the town allows for a crediting of points based on the scheduled improvements even if the town program should not be realized as planned, because of fiscal, economic, or political impediments. Because the effect of the ordinance is to freeze an owner's use for varying periods of time, up to 18 years, the town also allows the owner to apply for a reduction in tax assessments.

[The town planning board denied Golden's application for permission to undertake a residential subdivision because she had failed to obtain the special permit required under section 46-13.1. She sought judicial review of this denial.]

SCILEPPI, Judge. . . .

The undisputed effect of these integrated efforts in land use planning and development is to provide an over-all program of orderly growth and adequate facilities through a sequential development policy commensurate with progressing availability and capacity of public facilities. While its goals are clear and its purposes undisputably laudatory, serious questions are raised as to the manner in which these ends are to be effected, not the least of which relates to their legal viability under present zoning enabling legislation. . . .

[Although the zoning enabling act contained no specific authorization for the "sequential" and "timing" controls challenged here, the court held that the controls nevertheless find their basis within the perimeters of the devices authorized and purposes sanctioned under current enabling legislation. The court therefore rejected the authority challenge.]

What we will not countenance, . . . under any guise, is community efforts at immunization or exclusion. But, far from being exclusionary, the present amendments merely seek, by the implementation of sequential development and timed growth, to provide a balanced cohesive community dedicated to the efficient utilization of land. The restrictions conform to the community's considered land use policies as expressed in its comprehensive plan and represent a bona fide effort to maximize population density consistent with orderly growth. . . .

. . . Ramapo asks not that it be left alone, but only that it be allowed to prevent the kind of deterioration that has transformed well-ordered and thriving residential communities into blighted ghettos with attendant hazards to health, security and social stability — a danger not without substantial basis in fact. . . .

The proposed amendments have the effect of restricting development for onwards to 18 years in certain areas. Whether the subject parcels will be so restricted for the full term is not clear, for it is equally probable that the proposed facilities will be brought into these areas well before that time. Assuming, however, that the restrictions will remain outstanding for the life of the program, they still fall short of a confiscation within the meaning of the Constitution.

An ordinance which seeks to permanently restrict the use of property so that it may not be used for any reasonable purpose must be recognized as a taking: The only difference between the restriction and an outright taking in such a case "is that the restriction leaves the owner subject to the burden of payment of taxation, while outright confiscation would relieve him of that burden." (Arverne Bay Constr. Co. v. Thatcher, 15 N.E.2d 587, 592 (N.Y. 1938).) An appreciably different situation obtains where the restriction constitutes a temporary restriction, promising that the property may be put to a profitable use within a reasonable time. The hardship of holding unproductive property for some time might be compensated for by the ultimate benefit inuring to the individual owner in the form of a substantial increase in valuation; or, for that matter, the landowner, might be compelled to chafe under the temporary restriction, without the benefit of such compensation, when that burden serves to promote the public good. . . .

. . . [P]roperty owners under the terms of the amendments may elect to accelerate the date of development by installing, at their own expense, the necessary public services to bring the parcel within the required number of development points. While even the best of plans may not always be realized, in the absence of proof to the contrary, we must assume the Town will put its best effort forward in implementing the physical and fiscal timetable outlined under the plan. Should subsequent events prove this assumption unwarranted, or should the Town because of some unforeseen event fail in its primary obligation to these landowners, there will be ample opportunity to undo the restrictions upon default. . . .

In sum, where it is clear that the existing physical and financial resources of the community are inadequate to furnish the essential services and facilities which a substantial increase in population requires, there is a rational basis for "phased growth" and hence, the challenged ordinance is not violative of the Federal and State Constitutions. Accordingly, the order appealed from should be reversed and the actions remitted to Special Term for entry of a judgment declaring section 46-13.1 of the Town Ordinance constitutional.

BREITEL, Judge (dissenting). . . .

. . . Existing enabling legislation does not grant the power upon which the Ramapo ordinance rests. And for policy reasons, one should not strain the reading of the enabling acts, even if straining would avail, to distort them, beyond any meaning ever attributed to them, except by the ingenious draftsmen of the Ramapo ordinance. . . .

. . . [A]lthough the town had no power under the enabling act to adopt the ordinance in question, this does not mean that the town is not faced with a grave problem. It is. So are the many towns and villages in the State, and elsewhere in the country. But there is no doubt that the Ramapos, in isolation, cannot solve their problems alone, legally, under existing laws, or socially, politically, or economically. For the time being, the Ramapos must do what they can with district zoning and subdivision platting control. They may not declare moratoria on growth and development for as much as a generation. They may not separately or in concert impair the freedom of movement or residence of those outside their borders, even by ingenious schemes. Nor is it important whether their intention is to exclude, if that is the effect of their arrogated powers. . . .

. . . Ramapo would preserve its nature, delightful as that may be, but the supervening question is whether it alone may decide this or whether it must be decided by the larger community represented by the Legislature. Legally, politically, economically, and sociologically, the base for determination must be larger than that provided by the town fathers. . . .

Note on Phasing Controls

1. *A success story?* The Ramapo plan won initial praise from many commentators. See, e.g., Note, 47 N.Y.U. L. Rev. 723 (1972). Ramapo repealed the program in 1983, however, 13 years into the 18-year plan. Eric Damian Kelly, citing an unpublished study of the program, describes the reasons for the repeal:

Of the facilities used by the town as the basis for the program, the town of Ramapo controlled only parks, sewage collection (not treatment), drainage, and some roads. Many roads, the proposed regional sewer system, schools, and fire protection were the responsibilities of other entities, meaning that Ramapo's "plans" for construction of such facilities were more like wish lists than plans. The second problem was that the town never really followed the system, awarding unearned points because of a planning problem and approving nearly as many lots that did not meet the standards of the ordinance as it approved because they complied with it. Further, the impact of the program was probably just to reduce Ramapo's share of regional growth, not to change the growth patterns. Like most economic trends, the growth pressures that temporarily overwhelmed . . . Ramapo and Rockland County had waned by the 1980s . . .

Eric Damian Kelly, Managing Community Growth: Policies, Techniques, and Impacts 30 (2d ed. 2004) (citing Hammer, Siler, George Associates, Impact on Ramapo Fiscal and Economic Conditions of the Town's Growth Control Ordinance (1977) (unpublished draft prepared for the National Association of Homebuilders)). See also Robert H. Freilich, From Sprawl to Smart Growth: Successful Legal, Planning, and Environmental Systems 55 (1999) (Republicans gained control over the town board and dropped the program); Robert Geneslaw & George Raymond, Ramapo Dropping Its Famed Point System, Planning, June 1983, at 8, 9 (program was dropped because it discouraged needed growth and deterred economic development). Professor John Nolon argues, however, that the limited effect of Ramapo's program may be attributable to the fact that the town was unable to prevent communities within the town from seceding, incorporating separately, and adopting their own land use controls. By 2002, Ramapo had been split into twelve villages, leaving "very little contiguous land left in Ramapo for the town's comprehensive plan and inventive zoning controls to regulate." John R. Nolon, *Golden* and Its Emanations: The Surprising Origins of Smart Growth, 35 Urb. Law. 15, 56–57 (2003).

2. *Takings challenges*. Presumably takings challenges to growth phasing programs, like those challenging moratoria, will be measured under the *Penn Central* analysis, given the Supreme Court's decision in *Tahoe-Sierra*, excerpted at p. 185. If a growth phasing program puts a developer to the choice of waiting for the local government to provide services or constructing the facilities at the developer's own expense, do the *Nollan* nexus test and the *Dolan* proportionality requirement discussed at pp. 638–52 apply?

3. *Exclusionary zoning?* A leading zoning practitioner has argued that the net effect of the Ramapo scheme was to increase housing costs (and thereby decrease the supply of affordable housing) by forcing development further into the rural-urban fringe. Fred P. Bosselman, Can the Town of Ramapo Pass a Law to Bind the Rights of the Whole World?, 1 Fla. St. L. Rev. 234 (1973). See also Stephen R. Seidel, Housing Costs and Government Regulations: Confronting the Regulatory Maze 218–22 (1978). Others also have criticized the Ramapo program for failing to include multifamily housing or public housing. See Herbert M. Franklin, Controlling Urban Growth — But for Whom? (1973). Again, Professor Nolon disagrees, arguing that Ramapo "balanced the effects of growth control on affordable housing by taking direct action to produce over 800 units of public and subsidized housing." Nolon, supra, at 29. See also Freilich, supra, at 44.

4. *Fiscal impact requirements*. Instead of focusing on the availability of public facilities as Ramapo did, could a city simply condition permits on a showing that the tax dollars the development would generate would be higher than the local government's cost of providing and maintaining services?

5. *Duty to serve*. Can timing controls be reconciled with the traditional rule, discussed at pp. 683–89, that municipalities acting as public utilities have a duty to serve new customers?

6. *A moratorium in disguise?* Where a state has prohibited or limited moratoria, must phasing programs comply with those limits? See Toll Bros., Inc., v. West Windsor Township,

712 A.2d 266 (N.J. Super. Ct. App. Div. 1998) (phased growth program is a moratorium, which state law prohibits because it imposes a "period of permissive or obligatory delay").

Note on Concurrency, or Adequacy of Public Facilities, Requirements

The phased-growth plan in *Ramapo* was inexact, to say the least; points were assigned on the basis of distance from existing facilities, even though distance is only one of the determinants of whether the facilities would be adequate to serve the project. A project could amass enough points on one criterion to balance out few or no points on another facility, so that a project near a school might be approved even if it was far from sewage facilities. Even second-generation phased-growth programs paint with a fairly broad brush in linking development to the availability of facilities. If a city's goal is to limit growth, that broad-brush approach may be appropriate, but if the goal is to channel growth, a finer-grained approach may be required.

Adequacy of public facilities (APF) programs typically specify detailed standards for determining whether facilities are adequate to support a proposed development. To secure approval for a project, the developer must show that the impacts of the proposed project will not violate the level-of-service (LOS) standards for each of the facilities covered in the APF. If the project would cause the quantity or quality of service to fall below the standard, the developer must either finance the infrastructure improvements personally or postpone development until government provides additional facilities. APF requirements are increasingly common; a 1991 survey showed that almost one-third of California communities have APF requirements, for example. Douglas R. Porter, Managing Growth in America's Communities 123 (1997).

Florida adopted a statewide APF program, which it calls a concurrency requirement, in 1986 as part of its Local Government Comprehensive Planning and Land Development Regulation Act, Fla. Stat. ch. 163.3161–163.3243 (2005). The act, as amended in 1993, requires all local governments to prepare a comprehensive plan that includes a "capital improvements element" addressing (among other things) "standards to ensure the availability of public facilities and the adequacy of those facilities including acceptable levels of service." Id. at ch. 163.3177(10)(h). The act then prohibits a local government from permitting any new development "which results in a reduction in the level of services for the affected public facilities below the level of services provided in the comprehensive plan." Id. at ch. 163.3202(2)(g). Public facilities and services are defined to include roads, sewers, solid waste, drainage, potable water, parks and recreation, and in certain jurisdictions, mass transit. Local governments may extend the concurrency requirement to other public facilities, and some are considering doing so for schools.

Concurrency is defined differently for the various services: sewer, solid waste, drainage, and drinking water services must be available at the time the new development would be issued its certificate of occupancy or comparable permit. In contrast, parks and recreational facilities must be available within one year of the occupancy permit. Roads and mass transit facilities must be under construction no later than the end of the third year after occupancy. "Available" means either in place or under construction at the time the development permit is issued, or guaranteed in an enforceable development agreement.

Under certain circumstances, developers stymied by the unavailability of parks and recreation facilities or roads are allowed to proceed if they make a binding commitment to pay the development's fair share of the cost of the facility.

Florida's growth management system, including its concurrency requirement, has been a disappointment to many stakeholders and currently is under review by the governor and legislature. See, e.g., A Liveable Florida for Today and Tomorrow, Florida's Growth Management Study Commission Final Report 13 (2001) (concluding that despite the growth management program, "the quality of growth has not met our expectations, the strains on infrastructure have been only marginally reduced and, in essence, . . . a more complicated, more costly process [has not delivered] the expected corresponding benefits"). See also Thomas G. Pelham, Restructuring Florida's Growth Management System: Alternative Approaches to Plan Implementation and Concurrency, 12 J. Law & Pub. Pol'y 299 (2001); J. Celeste Sakowicz, Urban Sprawl: Florida's and Maryland's Approaches, 19 J. Land Use & Envtl. L. 377 (2004); Ruth L. Steiner, Florida's Transportation Concurrency: Are the Current Tools Adequate to Meet the Need for Coordinated Land Use and Transportation Planning?, 12. J.L. & Pub. Pol'y 269, 270–71 (2001).

5. *Urban Expansion Limits*   OR's history

In 1973, Oregon adopted a sweeping land use program that required local governments to plan in a manner consistent with state land use goals. See pp. 785–86. This program ultimately included a system of urban growth boundaries around cities and metropolitan areas. In 2004, however, Oregon voters approved Measure 37, the property-rights initiative excerpted at p. 278. Measure 37 creates great uncertainty about the future directions of land use regulation in the state, and indeed about the future of urban expansion limits around the nation. This tumultuous history makes Oregon's efforts to control urban expansion particularly worthy of examination.

The 1973 legislation created the Land Conservation and Development Commission (LCDC) and charged it with establishing the state's land use goals. After extensive public hearings, LCDC adopted 19 statewide planning goals. Goal 14, entitled "Urbanization," reads:

> *To provide for an orderly and efficient transition from rural to urban land use.*
> Urban growth boundaries shall be established to identify and separate urbanizable land from rural land. Establishment and change of the boundaries shall be based upon considerations of the following factors:
>
> 1) demonstrated need to accommodate long-range urban population growth requirements consistent with LCDC goals;
> 2) need for housing, employment opportunities, and livability;
> 3) orderly and economic provision for public facilities and services;
> 4) maximum efficiency of land uses within and on the fringe of the existing urban areas;
> 5) environmental, energy, economic and social consequences;
> 6) retention of agricultural land . . . ;
> 7) compatibility of the proposed urban uses with nearby agricultural activities.

LCDC, Oregon's Statewide Planning Goals, *in* Planning the Oregon Way: A Twenty Year Evaluation (Carl Abbott et al. eds., 1994).

Once the LCDC had established the statewide goals, all cities and counties were required to adopt comprehensive land use plans that would implement the state's goals. As part of their plans, they were required to establish the urban growth boundaries (UGBs) called for by Goal 14. If a proposed UGB would affect more than one local government, all those affected had to agree on the placement of the boundary.

then had to submit plan + receive acknowledgment from LCDC

Each local government then had to submit its plan for "acknowledgment" by the LCDC. Interested individuals, developers, state agencies, and interest groups were allowed an opportunity to object to the plans. Many local governments had to revise and resubmit their plans several times before receiving acknowledgment. The LCDC's decision whether to acknowledge a local plan could be appealed to the Oregon Court of Appeals, and the court overturned a significant number. By 1986, however, all Oregon cities had adopted comprehensive plans containing UGBs.

Portland's UGB is shown in Figure 9-4. It is administered by METRO, an elected regional government, and incorporates parts of 3 counties, 24 cities, and 60 special districts. Cities within the UGB plan for the land within their borders; counties plan for the unincorporated areas between the cities and the UGB. See V. Gail Easley, Staying Inside the Lines: Urban Growth Boundaries, APA Plan. Adv. Serv. Rep. No. 440, at 18 (1992). Within the UGB, there are two classes of land: "urban" land, in which most existing development is located, and "urbanizable" land, which is available for development once necessary infrastructure has been provided. Outside the UGB, the land is "rural" and is to be preserved for agricultural and forest uses.

A local government can permit nonagricultural or nonforest uses on rural land only if they establish an "exception," which essentially is a variance from the goal. The standards for granting an exception are stringent, see Or. Rev. Stat. §197.732(1)(c) (2005), and a local government's designation of "exception" land in its comprehensive plan will be reviewed by the LCDC when it acknowledges the plan. A local government is free to amend its comprehensive plan; however, if the amendment would create an exception, there must be a public hearing on the exception, and the local government must set forth findings of fact and a statement of reasons for adopting the exception. Recall Oregon's *Fasano* decision, discussed at pp. 341–52. What level of deference ought to be afforded the local government's decision that it has met the criteria for an exception? For a discussion of the exceptions process, see 1000 Friends of Oregon v. Land Conservation & Development Commission, 724 P.2d 268 (Or. 1986) (en banc).

To further constrain the ability of local governments to approve development outside the UGB, Goal 11 prohibits local governments from building new sewer systems or extending old ones outside UGBs, or from relying on the establishment of a new water system, or the extension of a water system, outside a UGB to permit more intensive use than would be allowed without that water system. See Department of Land Conservation & Development v. Lincoln County, 925 P.2d 135 (Or. Ct. App. 1996). More generally, Goal 11 requires that public facilities and services for rural areas be provided at levels appropriate for rural use only and not support urban uses.

When local governments seek to deviate from their UGBs or their comprehensive plans, they must use the exceptions process, *essentially a variance* and the courts reviewing exceptions test their validity directly against the statewide goals. When local governments grant or deny rezonings, subdivision approvals, variances, or conditional use permits, however, the courts generally review such actions only for consistency with the comprehensive plans. Because the comprehensive plans have been acknowledged as consistent with the statewide goals, as long as the challenged decision is consistent with the plan, the courts assume that it is consistent with the statewide goals. Friends of Neabeack Hill v. City of Philomath, 911 P.2d 350 (Or. Ct. App. 1996).

For further descriptions of the Oregon program, see, e.g., Gerrit Knaap, Land Use Politics in Oregon, *in* Planning the Oregon Way, supra; Robert L. Liberty, Oregon's Comprehensive Growth Management Program: An Implementation Review and Lessons for Other States, 22 Envtl. L. Rep. 10367 (1992). Keep in mind, however, that Measure 37, excerpted at p. 278, may result in substantial changes to the program.

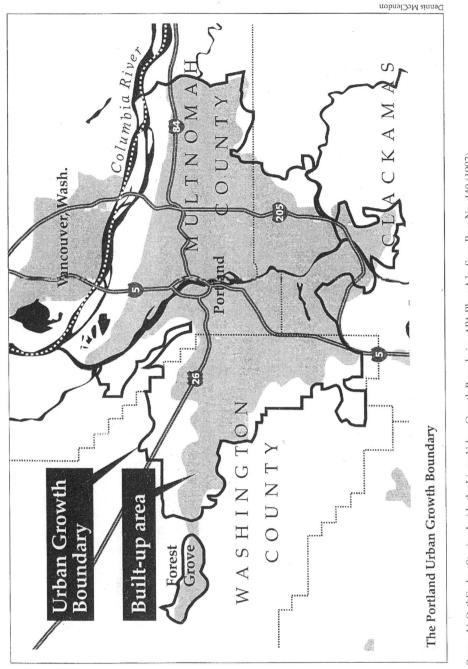

The Portland Urban Growth Boundary

Source: V. Gail Easley, Staying Inside the Lines: Urban Growth Boundaries, APA Plan. Adv. Serv. Rep. No. 440 (1992).

FIGURE 9-4

Portland's Urban Growth Boundary (as of 1992)

Note on Urban Growth Boundaries

1. *Price effects.* Studies of land values in the Portland area show significant differences between the value of *land* within the UGB and that outside the boundary. Gerrit Knaap & Arthur C. Nelson, The Regulated Landscape: Lessons on State Land Use Planning from Oregon 51–58 (1992). The UGB's effect on *housing* prices in Portland, however, is contested. For a review of the research, see Arthur C. Nelson et al., The Link between Growth Management and Housing Affordability: The Academic Evidence *in* Growth Management and Affordable Housing: Do They Conflict? 117, 144–49 (Anthony Downs ed., 2004); Forum, Have Housing Prices Risen Faster in Portland Than Elsewhere?, 13 Housing Pol'y Debate 7 (2002) (contributions by Anthony Downs, Arthur C. Nelson, and William Fischel). Cf. Clint Bolick, Subverting the American Dream: Government Dictated "Smart Growth" Is Unwise and Unconstitutional, 148 U. Pa. L. Rev. 859 (2000) (asserting price effects on the basis of non-academic studies).

The price effects of the UGB may be offset by the requirements of Goal 10, Housing, which requires local governments within the Portland UGB to zone for an overall density of six to ten units per acre of vacant residential land and to allow multifamily housing on at least half of all land zoned residential. See Arthur C. Nelson, Oregon's Urban Growth Boundary Policy as a Landmark Planning Tool, *in* Planning the Oregon Way, supra, at 25, 31–32. That relaxation of prior zoning constraints may have offset the inflationary pressures of the UGB limits. Henry R. Richmond, Comment on Carl Abbott's "The Portland Region: Where City and Suburbs Talk to Each Other — And Often Agree," 8 Housing Pol'y Debate 53 (1997).

Potential price effects of the UGB also may be offset because the UGB originally adopted left plenty of room for growth by including a 15 percent "market factor" to account for error, and the UGB was expanded somewhat in 1999. In addition, the UGB may have diverted growth from Portland to nearby Clark County, Washington. That "safety valve" closed when Washington adopted a state growth management program modeled after Oregon's. Carl Abbott, The Portland Region: Where City and Suburbs Talk to Each Other — and Often Agree, 8 Housing Pol'y Debate 11, 36–37 (1997); William A. Fischel, Comment on Carl Abbott's "The Portland Region," 8 Housing Pol'y Debate 65 (1997).

2. *Effects on urban form?* Several studies have found that development within Portland's UGB has become denser, more internally connected and friendlier to pedestrians since the UGB was drawn. See Carl Abbott, Planning a Sustainable City: The Promise and Performance of Portland's Urban Growth Boundary *in* Urban Sprawl: Causes, Consequences and Policy Responses 207, 221 (Gregory D. Squires ed., 2002); Yan Song & Gerrit-Jan Knaap, Measuring Urban Form: Is Portland Winning the War on Sprawl, 70 J. Am. Plan. Ass'n 210 (2004); Robert Stacey, Urban Growth Boundaries: Saying "Yes" to Strengthening Communities, 34 Conn. L. Rev. 597, 602-03 (2002). Others point out, however, that Portland is less dense than many cities without UGBs. Russ Lopez & H. Patricia Hynes, Sprawl in the 1990s: Measurement, Distribution and Trends, 38 Urb. Aff. Rev. 325, 342 (2003).

3. *Sprawl within the UGB.* Although UGBs generally seek to steer development back toward the center city to fill in underdeveloped properties and make efficient use of existing infrastructure, cities have found that the neighborhoods surrounding those parcels are not enthused about high-density development and often prevent exactly the kind of development the growth management plan envisions. See, e.g., Douglas R. Porter, San Diego's Brand of Growth Management: A for Effort, C for Accomplishment, Urb. Land, May 1989, at 21, 25, 27. That may account for reports that new development within the Portland UGB has been at lower densities than zoning allows. Or developers may be building

at lower-than-allowable densities on the basis of their perceptions of market demand. See Deborah A. Howe, Growth Management in Oregon, *in* Growth Management: The Planning Challenge of the 1990s, at 61, 70 (Jay M. Stein ed., 1993). Should cities prescribe minimum densities within UGBs?

4. *Other UGB programs.* For discussions of other growth management programs that rely substantially on urban containment strategies, see Rolf Pendall & Jonathan Martin, Holding The Line: Urban Containment in the United States (Brookings Discussion Paper 2002), available at http://www.brookings.edu/es/urban/publications/pendallfultoncontainment.pdf. A fascinating review of more than 150 urban containment programs is contained in Arthur C. Nelson & Casey J. Dawkins, Urban Containment in the US, APA Plan. Adv. Serv. Rep. No. 520 (2004).

Note on the Effects of Growth Controls and Growth Management Programs

1. *Are growth controls effective?* Professor John D. Landis compared seven representative cities in California that had adopted population or housing permit caps, moratoria, or annexation limits in the late 1970s or early 1980s with similar communities that had no growth controls. He found that the growth control measures had "only slightly restrained population growth and housing development" between 1980 and 1989. He attributed the limited effectiveness of the growth controls to two factors. First, caps often were set at rates that appeared stringent in comparison to the few years of atypical growth that preceded their adoption, but that in fact were not significantly different from historic growth rates. Controls therefore served primarily to "regularize the development cycle by smoothing out the normal peaks and valleys that characterize real estate development." Second, growth controls often are full of loopholes. John D. Landis, Do Growth Controls Work? A New Assessment, 58 J. Am. Plan. Ass'n 489, 494, 498 (1992). See also John R. Logan & Min Zhou, Do Suburban Growth Controls Control Growth?, 54 Am. Soc. Rev. 461 (1989) (finding little effect on population growth).

But Professor Shen compared projections based on historical trends with the actual distribution of population in California and concluded that local growth control policies had a significant impact on the distribution of population in California. The study found that approximately 150,000 people who would have chosen to live in growth-controlled cities moved instead to other areas between 1980 and 1990. Q. Shen, Spatial Impacts of Locally Enacted Growth Controls: The San Francisco Bay Region in the 1980s, 23 Env't & Plan. B: Plan. & Design 61 (1996).

2. *At what cost?* Many empirical studies have sought to identify whether and how much growth controls or growth management raises the price of housing. According to recent surveys of the literature, most studies conclude that such programs raise housing prices. Arthur C. Nelson et al., The Link between Growth Management and Housing Affordability: The Academic Evidence *in* Growth Management and Affordable Housing: Do They Conflict? 117 (Anthony Downs ed., 2004); William A. Fischel, Do Growth Controls Matter? (Lincoln Institute of Land Policy Working Paper, 1990).

If regulations aimed at controlling or channeling growth raise housing prices, is that necessarily an indication that the programs are inefficient? Might the increase reflect the value to consumers of the amenities created or disamenities prevented by growth management? Might differences between cities that impose growth management programs and those that don't (such as differences in demand caused by the availability of different amenities) account for the price disparities? For a good discussion of those issues, see Fischel, supra, at 33.

3. *To whom?* Opponents of growth management programs allege that the programs have a regressive effect by raising the price of housing generally, but to the particular detriment of the poor, and by excluding the poor from certain communities. The evidence about the effect such programs have on the affordability of housing is mixed and inconclusive. See, e.g., Jerry Anthony, The Effects of Florida's Growth Management Act on Housing Affordability, 69 J. Am. Plan. Ass'n 282 (2003) (finding that housing in Florida has become less affordable since the implementation of Florida's growth management programs). How could a growth management program have an effect on housing prices but not necessarily have an effect on housing affordability? See Vicki Been, Impact Fees and Housing Affordability, 8 Cityscape 139, 164–68 (2005).

For an excellent discussion of the effects of growth controls and growth management on residential segregation, see Rolf Pendall, Local Land Use Regulation and the Chain of Exclusion, 66 J. Am. Plan. Ass'n 125 (2000). See also Robert D. Bullard, Sprawl City: Race, Politics and Planning in Atlanta (Robert D. Bullard et al. eds., 2000).

Some communities with growth management programs have attempted to soften the programs' impacts on lower-income renters and purchasers by setting aside a percentage of their development quota for affordable units, for example, or by exempting affordable housing from moratoria or quotas. See Taming the Exclusionary Effects of Growth Controls, Zoning News, Sept. 1989, at 1, 2 (concluding that the most successful efforts are inclusionary housing requirements coupled with state and local programs to provide housing subsidies). Inclusionary zoning is discussed further at pp. 671–73.

Chapter Ten

Government as Landowner, Developer, and Financier

Individuals, households, and firms initiate most land development projects. This casebook therefore has emphasized legal regulation of these private land users. But a government can involve itself more actively in the development process — for example, by acquiring and managing land; lending money; or designing, constructing, and managing real estate complexes. This chapter deals with legal and policy issues that arise when a government carries out one of these proprietary or spending functions.

An overarching issue is the relative competence of public and private agencies to accomplish a particular task. Would patterns of metropolitan development be better if governments (not farmers, homebuilders, and speculators) were to own much of the undeveloped land at the urban fringe? Can public redevelopment agencies bring back declining urban neighborhoods faster and at lower cost than market forces can? Was the federal government justified in building "new towns" during the New Deal? Wise to sell them off at the beginning of the Truman Administration? Should public housing authorities compete with private firms in developing and managing subsidized housing projects? When might targeted government loans to homebuyers or businesses usefully supplement private capital markets?

Whether government should participate in these sorts of proprietary activities is an issue much beclouded by ideology. Many economists assume that the private firms that survive in a competitive market are likely to be most efficient agents of production, especially in a context where externalities are absent. Both theory and evidence support the notion that market forces tend to weed out inefficient firms faster than voters weed out inefficient government agencies. However, almost all important markets (and certainly the land market) are neither perfectly competitive nor free from externalities. The identification of a "market imperfection," of course, rarely clinches the case for government takeover of an activity. Government itself hardly is error-free. The quandary, as usual, is how much to rely on imperfect markets and how much on imperfect governments. See generally Neil K. Komesar, Imperfect Alternatives: Choosing Institutions in Law, Economics, and Public Policy (1994).

A.   *Government as Landowner*

Governments own about one-third of the land area of the United States. Even in central cities, governments own over one-third of the land area, primarily in the form of rights-of-way for streets and highways. See p. 15.

A government's powers as an owner of land are greater than its powers as a regulator of private landowners. First, by acquiring ownership, a government frees itself from legal constraints, such as takings clauses, on the scope of regulation. Second, while a regulator can merely veto private owners' land use decisions, a government that owns can affirmatively decide the nature and timing of land uses. A government's land management decisions, however, may be constrained by special procedural requirements (such as preparation of an environmental impact report) and are subject to the complexities of ordinary legislative and administrative processes.

1.   *Federal Exurban Lands*

Federal holdings and dispositions. Throughout U.S. history, the federal government has had extensive land holdings, especially outside the original 13 colonies. It acquired most of these lands by treaty, purchase, or conquest. Prior to the twentieth century, the national government sought to transfer most of its newly acquired lands to private owners. Although some federal lands were auctioned off to highest bidders, Congress offered a variety of special deals to favored transferees such as war veterans, railroad companies, mining interests, and homesteaders. See, e.g., the Homestead Act of 1862, 12 Stat. 392. Federal disposition was headlong during its heyday. By 1993, federal lands constituted only 2.3 percent of the area of the Northeast states, 3.8 percent of the South, and 4.9 percent of the Midwest.

The situation in the West is different. By the mid-1920s, before much of the West had been settled, privatization of the federal domain had slowed to a trickle. Congress halted the general policy of disposal with enactment of the Taylor Grazing Act of 1934, 48 Stat. 1269. As a result, in 1993 the United States still owned 53 percent of the land area in the West (which, partly because it includes Alaska, constitutes almost half of the nation's territory). Statistical Abstract 1996, at 228. Much of this residual federal land is managed by specialized agencies. In general, the Bureau of Land Management (BLM) administers the vast tracts of relatively infertile grazing lands, the U.S. Forest Service manages forested areas of ordinary aesthetic value, and the National Park Service supervises the areas of greatest scenic splendor. The federal government continues to dispose of selected surplus lands, if at much a slower pace than in the nineteenth century. It also makes selected purchases. For example, the Land and Water Conservation Fund, 16 U.S.C. §§4601-4 to -11 (2000), provides monies to fund acquisitions for recreational and environmental purposes.

The standard history of the disposition of federal exurban lands is Paul Gates, History of Public Land Law Development (1968). On legal issues, see George Cameron Coggins et al., Federal Public Land and Resources Law (5th ed. 2002); Christine A. Klein et al., Natural Resources Law (2005).

How much federal land ownership is desirable? The sharpest debate over the relative merits of public and private land management has arisen in the context of federal exurban lands. Scholars associated with the Political Economy Research Center (PERC), headquartered in Bozeman, Montana, have roundly criticized the performance of federal land agencies and urged the privatization of most federal exurban lands. See Terry L. Anderson &

Donald Leal, Free Market Environmentalism (rev. ed. 2001); Richard L. Stroup & John A. Baden, Natural Resources: Bureaucratic Myths and Environmental Management (1983). Critics regard the case for privatization as particularly strong for the federal lands best allocated to commodity-based uses such as grazing, mining, and timber. See, e.g., Gary D. Libecap, Locking Up the Range (1981) (calling for privatization of BLM lands).

On the other hand, numerous commentators vigorously defend continued federal ownership of most of these rural and wilderness lands. See, e.g., Scott Lehmann, Privatizing Public Lands (1995); Joseph L. Sax, Why We Will Not (Should Not) Sell the Public Lands, 1983 Utah L. Rev. 313.

Marion Clawson, The Federal Lands Revisited 123–69 (1983), provides a handy summary of arguments for and against government ownership of exurban lands. The issues are similar to those that arise in the debate over whether government planners or private landowners are likely to be superior at choosing land uses. See Chapter 2.

Advocates of privatization assert that a private landowner is apt to have better localized knowledge and sharper incentives to economize than a government official does. In response, advocates of public ownership assert that government agents can better handle externalities that arise from land allocations when the agents act in a proprietary as opposed to regulatory capacity. See Joseph L. Sax, The Legitimacy of Collective Values: The Case of Public Lands, 56 U. Colo. L. Rev. 537 (1985).

Some observers identify pertinent social interests other than ordinary externalities that market participants such as private landowners might not take into account. The existence of these separate "option values," "existence values," and distinct "citizen preferences" is much contested. Compare, e.g., David A. Dana, Existence Value and Federal Preservation Regulation, 28 Harv. Envtl. L. Rev. 343 (2004), with Donald J. Boudreaux et al., Talk Is Cheap: The Existence Value Fallacy, 29 Envtl. L. 765 (1999). See also Daphna Lewinsohn-Zamir, Consumer Preferences, Citizen Preferences, and Provision of Public Goods, 108 Yale L.J. 377 (1998). If additional values of these sorts indeed are at stake, does it necessarily follow that government agents are especially likely to take them into account?

Are private or public landowners more likely to appropriately weigh the interests of future generations? Advocates of privatization note that a private landowner with a fee-simple interest has an infinite time horizon, and thus the incentive to consider the long-term value of the resource. See Richard Stroup & John Baden, Externality, Property Rights, and the Management of Our National Forests, 16 J.L. & Econ. 303 (1973). By contrast, a politician, instead of being farsighted, may focus too much on the near future, particularly as an election approaches. Which sort of owner is more apt to discount the value of future land uses at the proper interest rate? See Stephen F. Williams, Running Out: The Problem of Exhaustible Resources, 7 J. Legal Stud. 165 (1975) (discussing private and social discount rates). On whether the discounting of future benefits is appropriate at all, compare Douglas A. Kysar, Climate Change, Cultural Transmission, and Comprehensive Rationality, 31 B.C. Envtl. Aff. L. Rev. 555, 578–85 (2004), with John J. Donohue III, Why We Should Discount the Views of Those Who Discount Discounting, 108 Yale L.J. 1901 (1999).

The political feasibility of privatization. In 1982, Secretary of the Interior James Watt announced that he was considering the sale of 5 percent of the Interior Department's acreage. This aroused great opposition from environmentalists, federal lessees, and localists, who worried that outside investors would be the highest bidders at auctions. Secretary Watt soon dropped the idea. For an overview of this episode, see Richard H. Cowart & Sally K. Fairfax, Public Lands Federalism, 15 Ecology L.Q. 375 (1988). See generally James L. Huffman, The Inevitability of Private Rights in Public Lands, 65 U. Colo. L. Rev. 241

(1994) (on ideological and interest-group obstacles to federal sales of marginal exurban lands).

2.   *Federal Urban Lands*

In urban areas the federal government owns widely scattered military facilities, veterans' hospitals, post offices, and other miscellaneous holdings. According to one estimate, in 1981 the value of federal urban land was almost double the value of federal rural land. Michael J. Boskin et al., New Estimates of the Value of Federal Mineral Rights and Land, 75 Am. Econ. Rev. 923, 933 (1985).

Many federal military facilities, particularly the most outdated ones, are sited at urban locations that are prime for redevelopment. The disposition of these lands is both politically and legally complex. See Natalie Hanlon, Military Base Closings, 62 U. Colo. L. Rev. 331 (1991); Dale Pennys Levy, Military Base Closures, 8 Prob. & Prop. 32 (Nov./Dec. 1994). In general, when disposing of surplus land, a military department must first offer the land to other military departments and then to other federal agencies. If there have been no takers, next in line are state and local governments asserting "public benefit" purposes such as education, public health (including shelter for the homeless), recreational facilities, and prisons. Last in line are private bidders. In light of the relevant competencies of different transferees, has Congress gotten its priorities right?

3.   *State Lands*

Scholars and journalists have tended to pay less attention to state lands than to federal lands. State holdings include parks, highways, and university campuses; the ocean foreshore (from the mean high-tide line out to the three-mile limit); and the beds of navigable waterways. There is an unusually large amount of state land in Texas, a formerly independent republic that successfully bargained to retain its lands when it joined the Union. Especially after 1980, many states increased their spending on land purchases for recreational and conservation purposes. See Richard J. Fink, Public Land Acquisition for Environmental Protection, 18 Ecology L. Rev. 485, 486–90 (1991); pp. 580–82 (on state and local programs to acquire either conservation easements or fee simple interests).

Many states other than the original 13 still retain some of the lands that the United States transferred to them in the nineteenth century. For example, the Northwest Ordinances of 1785 and 1787 established the precedent for federal lands to be surveyed into townships containing 36 sections, each a mile square. During subsequent dispositions, Congress commonly transferred into state ownership one or more sections in each township to help finance public education. See generally Sally K. Fairfax et al., The School Trust Lands, 22 Envt'l L. 797 (1992).

Should the federal government transfer ownership of parts of its vast holdings of Western lands to the states? For an affirmative answer, see Robert H. Nelson, Public Lands and Private Rights: The Failure of Scientific Management (1995) (recommending transfer of many federal lands to state and local governments, subject to de jure recognition of existing de facto private entitlements in use of those lands). Gifts of these lands to Western states might not be popular in nonwestern states. Should Congress instead consider entitling a Western state to buy marginal federal lands within it at, say, 90 percent of market value?

4.   Local Lands

A local government may acquire a site by purchase, gift, or dedication, or through exercise of the power of eminent domain. Particularly in the Northeast, localities increasingly have been acquiring undeveloped farms, pastures, and forests in order to better control future development. For example, the island town of Nantucket, Massachusetts, has imposed a 2 percent tax on property sales to generate funds to finance town purchases of land. By 1986, Nantucket already owned one-third of its territory and had set its sights on owning one-half. See Charles M. Haar & Michael Allan Wolf, Land-Use Planning 826–30 (4th ed. 1989). Following the nearby Nantucket example, residents of Cape Cod towns now pay a 3 percent surcharge on property tax bills to help fund town land acquisitions. See Patricia Daley, Preserving Open Space on Cape Cod, 73 St. John's L. Rev. 1091 (1999).

A town that actively engages in this sort of land banking is likely to make buildable lots scarcer and more expensive. How great is the risk that local land acquisitions will be used for exclusionary purposes? Under what circumstances and subject to what conditions should a locality sell banked land to a developer? See generally Ann L. Strong, Land Banking (1979); William B. Stoebuck, Suburban Land Banking, 1986 U. Ill. L. Rev. 581.

A local government also can have land thrust upon it. For example, the abandonment of central-city buildings typically is accompanied by widespread defaults on property tax obligations. Cities, when they foreclose their tax liens, may assume ownership of these distressed properties. Should a city prepare its own development plans for sites acquired in this manner? Auction off the foreclosed lands to highest bidders? Make the lands available on favorable terms to preferred transferees such as nonprofit housing developers, sponsors of community gardens, or owners of abutting lands? (These latter options may be subject to legal constraints on gifts of public assets.) For detailed description of New York City's tortured efforts to deal with its "in rem" housing, see David Reiss, Housing Abandonment and New York City's Response, 22 N.Y.U. Rev. L. & Soc. Change 783 (1996–1997). When should a city that transfers land impose covenants restricting its use? See p. 581.

B.   Government as Land Assembler: Eminent Domain

In many contexts, a government can compel an owner to transfer land to it in return for just compensation. Resort to the power of eminent domain is thought to be particularly necessary when many parcels must be assembled to complete a highway, airport, convention center, or other large project. If a private firm were to attempt such an assemblage, some owners might recognize the advantages of strategically holding out for an exorbitant price. A would-be land assembler that lacked the power of eminent domain therefore might be discouraged from pursuing a socially worthwhile land consolidation. According to this analysis, governments, public utilities, and the other entities that possess the power of eminent domain should play a special role in land assembly. This subchapter explores both the legal limitations on the exercise of eminent domain powers and the soundness of the theory just presented.

The power of eminent domain has long been a central instrument of land use policy. For an excellent account of the early history of its use, see Tony Freyer, Reassessing the Impact of Eminent Domain in Early American Economic Development, 1981 Wis. L. Rev. 1263. In 1970, a time of significant road building in California, 8 percent of the civil jury trials in the state's Superior Courts involved eminent domain issues. County of San Luis Obispo v. Bailey, 87 Cal. Rptr. 802, 807 (Ct. App. 1970).

1.   The Public Use Issue

Both constitutional and statutory provisions limit governmental exercise of the power of eminent domain. The most-cited precedents are federal court decisions construing "public use," a phrase that appears in the Takings Clause of the Fifth Amendment ("nor shall private property be taken for public use, without just compensation"). The Due Process Clause of the Fourteenth Amendment makes this public use limitation applicable to the states. Missouri Pacific Railway v. Nebraska, 164 U.S. 403 (1896).

Kelo v. City of New London
125 S. Ct. 2655

Justice STEVENS delivered the opinion of the Court.

In 2000, the city of New London approved a development plan that, in the words of the Supreme Court of Connecticut, was "projected to create in excess of 1,000 jobs, to increase tax and other revenues, and to revitalize an economically distressed city, including its downtown and waterfront areas." 843 A.2d 500, 507 (2004). In assembling the land needed for this project, the city's development agent has purchased property from willing sellers and proposes to use the power of eminent domain to acquire the remainder of the property from unwilling owners in exchange for just compensation. The question presented is whether the city's proposed disposition of this property qualifies as a "public use" within the meaning of the Takings Clause of the Fifth Amendment to the Constitution.

I

The city of New London (hereinafter City) sits at the junction of the Thames River and the Long Island Sound in southeastern Connecticut. Decades of economic decline led a state agency in 1990 to designate the City a "distressed municipality." In 1996, the Federal Government closed the Naval Undersea Warfare Center, which had been located in the Fort Trumbull area of the City and had employed over 1,500 people. In 1998, the City's unemployment rate was nearly double that of the State, and its population of just under 24,000 residents was at its lowest since 1920.

These conditions prompted state and local officials to target New London, and particularly its Fort Trumbull area, for economic revitalization. To this end, respondent New London Development Corporation (NLDC), a private nonprofit entity established some years earlier to assist the City in planning economic development, was reactivated. In January 1998, the State authorized a $5.35 million bond issue to support the NLDC's planning activities and a $10 million bond issue toward the creation of a Fort Trumbull State Park. In February, the pharmaceutical company Pfizer Inc. announced that it would build a $300 million research facility on a site immediately adjacent to Fort Trumbull; local planners hoped that Pfizer would draw new business to the area, thereby serving as a catalyst to the area's rejuvenation. After receiving initial approval from the city council, the NLDC continued its planning activities and held a series of neighborhood meetings to educate the public about the process. In May, the city council authorized the NLDC to formally submit its plans to the relevant state agencies for review. Upon obtaining state-level approval, the NLDC finalized an integrated development plan focused on 90 acres of the Fort Trumbull area.

The Fort Trumbull area is situated on a peninsula that juts into the Thames River. The area comprises approximately 115 privately owned properties . . . . The development plan encompasses seven parcels. [Parcels 1 and 2 are designated for a waterfront conference hotel, recreational and commercial uses, 80 new residences, and a space reserved for a new U.S. Coast Guard Museum.] Parcel 3, which is located immediately north of the Pfizer facility, will contain at least 90,000 square feet of research and development office space. Parcel 4A is a 2.4-acre site that will be used either to support the adjacent state park, by providing parking or retail services for visitors, or to support the nearby marina. [Parcels 4B, 5, 6, and 7 will include a renovated marina, office and retail space, and parking.]

The NLDC intended the development plan to capitalize on the arrival of the Pfizer facility and the new commerce it was expected to attract. In addition to creating jobs, generating tax revenue, and helping to "build momentum for the revitalization of downtown New London," the plan was also designed to make the City more attractive and to create leisure and recreational opportunities on the waterfront and in the park.

The city council approved the plan in January 2000, and designated the NLDC as its development agent in charge of implementation. The city council also authorized the NLDC to purchase property or to acquire property by exercising eminent domain in the City's name. See Conn. Gen. Stat. §8-193 (2005). The NLDC successfully negotiated the purchase of most of the real estate in the 90-acre area, but its negotiations with petitioners failed. As a consequence, in November 2000, the NLDC initiated the condemnation proceedings that gave rise to this case.

II

Petitioner Susette Kelo has lived in the Fort Trumbull area since 1997. She has made extensive improvements to her house, which she prizes for its water view. Petitioner Wilhelmina Dery was born in her Fort Trumbull house in 1918 and has lived there her entire life. . . . In all, the nine petitioners own 15 properties in Fort Trumbull — 4 in parcel 3 of the development plan and 11 in parcel 4A. Ten of the parcels are occupied by the owner or a family member. . . . There is no allegation that any of these properties is blighted or otherwise in poor condition; rather, they were condemned only because they happen to be located in the development area.

In December 2000, petitioners brought this action in the New London Superior Court. . . . After a 7-day bench trial, the Superior Court granted a permanent restraining order prohibiting the taking of the properties located in parcel 4A (park or marina support). It, however, denied petitioners relief as to the properties located in parcel 3 (office space).[4] [On appeal, the Supreme Court of Connecticut held, in a 4–3 decision, that all of the City's proposed takings were valid.]

III

Two polar propositions are perfectly clear. On the one hand, it has long been accepted that the sovereign may not take the property of A for the sole purpose of transferring it to another private party B, even though A is paid just compensation. On the other hand, it is

---

4. While this litigation was pending before the Superior Court, the NLDC announced that it would lease some of the parcels to private developers in exchange for their agreement to develop the land according to the terms of the development plan. Specifically, the NLDC was negotiating a 99-year ground lease with Corcoran Jennison, a developer selected from a group of applicants. The negotiations contemplated a nominal rent of $1 per year, but no agreement had yet been signed.

equally clear that a State may transfer property from one private party to another if future "use by the public" is the purpose of the taking; the condemnation of land for a railroad with common-carrier duties is a familiar example. Neither of these propositions, however, determines the disposition of this case.

As for the first proposition, the City would no doubt be forbidden from taking petitioners' land for the purpose of conferring a private benefit on a particular private party. . . . Nor would the City be allowed to take property under the mere pretext of a public purpose, when its actual purpose was to bestow a private benefit. . . . The trial judge and all the members of the Supreme Court of Connecticut agreed that there was no evidence of an illegitimate purpose in this case. Therefore, as was true of the statute challenged in Hawaii Housing Authority v. Midkiff, 467 U.S. 229, 245 (1984), the City's development plan was not adopted "to benefit a particular class of identifiable individuals."

On the other hand, this is not a case in which the City is planning to open the condemned land — at least not in its entirety — to use by the general public. Nor will the private lessees of the land in any sense be required to operate like common carriers, making their services available to all comers. . . . [However,] when this Court began applying the Fifth Amendment to the States at the close of the 19th century, it embraced the broader and more natural interpretation of public use as "public purpose." See, e.g., Fallbrook Irrigation Dist. v. Bradley, 164 U.S. 112, 158–164 (1896). . . .

The disposition of this case therefore turns on the question whether the City's development plan serves a "public purpose." Without exception, our cases have defined that concept broadly, reflecting our longstanding policy of deference to legislative judgments in this field.

In Berman v. Parker, 348 U.S. 26 (1954), this Court upheld a redevelopment plan targeting a blighted area of Washington, D.C., in which most of the housing for the area's 5,000 inhabitants was beyond repair. Under the plan, the area would be condemned and part of it utilized for the construction of streets, schools, and other public facilities. The remainder of the land would be leased or sold to private parties for the purpose of redevelopment, including the construction of low-cost housing.

The owner of a department store located in the area challenged the condemnation, pointing out that his store was not itself blighted and arguing that the creation of a "better balanced, more attractive community" was not a valid public use. Writing for a unanimous Court, Justice Douglas refused to evaluate this claim in isolation, deferring instead to the legislative and agency judgment that the area "must be planned as a whole" for the plan to be successful. The Court explained that "community redevelopment programs need not, by force of the Constitution, be on a piecemeal basis — lot by lot, building by building." Id. at 35. The public use underlying the taking was unequivocally affirmed:

> We do not sit to determine whether a particular housing project is or is not desirable. The concept of the public welfare is broad and inclusive. . . . The values it represents are spiritual as well as physical, aesthetic as well as monetary. It is within the power of the legislature to determine that the community should be beautiful as well as healthy, spacious as well as clean, well-balanced as well as carefully patrolled. In the present case, the Congress and its authorized agencies have made determinations that take into account a wide variety of values. It is not for us to reappraise them. If those who govern the District of Columbia decide that the Nation's Capital should be beautiful as well as sanitary, there is nothing in the Fifth Amendment that stands in the way. Id. at 33.

In Hawaii Housing Authority v. Midkiff, 467 U.S. 229 (1984), the Court considered a Hawaii statute whereby fee title was taken from lessors and transferred to lessees (for just compensation) in order to reduce the concentration of land ownership. We unanimously upheld the statute and rejected the Ninth Circuit's view that it was "a naked attempt on the part of the state of Hawaii to take the property of A and transfer it to B solely for B's private use and benefit." Id. at 235. Reaffirming *Berman*'s deferential approach to legislative judgments in this field, we concluded that the State's purpose of eliminating the "social and economic evils of a land oligopoly" qualified as a valid public use. Our opinion also rejected the contention that the mere fact that the State immediately transferred the properties to private individuals upon condemnation somehow diminished the public character of the taking. "[I]t is only the taking's purpose, and not its mechanics," we explained, that matters in determining public use. Id. at 244. . . .

Viewed as a whole, our jurisprudence has recognized that the needs of society have varied between different parts of the Nation, just as they have evolved over time in response to changed circumstances. Our earliest cases in particular embodied a strong theme of federalism, emphasizing the "great respect" that we owe to state legislatures and state courts in discerning local public needs. See Hairston v. Danville & Western R. Co., 208 U.S. 598, 606–607 (1908). . . .

IV

Those who govern the City were not confronted with the need to remove blight in the Fort Trumbull area, but their determination that the area was sufficiently distressed to justify a program of economic rejuvenation is entitled to our deference. . . . [T]he City is endeavoring to coordinate a variety of commercial, residential, and recreational uses of land, with the hope that they will form a whole greater than the sum of its parts. . . . Given the comprehensive character of the plan, the thorough deliberation that preceded its adoption, and the limited scope of our review, it is appropriate for us, as it was in *Berman*, to resolve the challenges of the individual owners, not on a piecemeal basis, but rather in light of the entire plan. Because that plan unquestionably serves a public purpose, the takings challenged here satisfy the public use requirement of the Fifth Amendment.

To avoid this result, petitioners urge us to adopt a new bright-line rule that economic development does not qualify as a public use. Promoting economic development is a traditional and long accepted function of government[, however]. There is, moreover, no principled way of distinguishing economic development from the other public purposes that we have recognized [in decisions such as *Berman* and *Midkiff*]. . . .

It is further argued that without a bright-line rule nothing would stop a city from transferring citizen A's property to citizen B for the sole reason that citizen B will put the property to a more productive use and thus pay more taxes. Such a one-to-one transfer of property, executed outside the confines of an integrated development plan, is not presented in this case. While such an unusual exercise of government power would certainly raise a suspicion that a private purpose was afoot,[17] the hypothetical cases posited by petitioners can be confronted if and when they arise. . . .

Alternatively, petitioners maintain that for takings of this kind we should require a "reasonable certainty" that the expected public benefits will actually accrue. Such a rule, however, would represent an even greater departure from [*Midkiff* and other prior decisions]. . . .

Just as we decline to second-guess the City's considered judgments about the efficacy of its development plan, we also decline to second-guess the City's determinations as to what lands it needs to acquire in order to effectuate the project. . . . *Berman*, 348 U.S. at 35–36.

---

17. Courts have viewed such aberrations with a skeptical eye. See, e.g., 99 Cents Only Stores v. Lancaster Redevelopment Agency, 237 F. Supp. 2d 1123 (C.D. Cal. 2001). . . . These types of takings may also implicate other constitutional guarantees. See Village of Willowbrook v. Olech, 528 U.S. 562 (2000) (per curiam).

In affirming the City's authority to take petitioners' properties, we do not minimize the hardship that condemnations may entail, notwithstanding the payment of just compensation.[21] We emphasize that nothing in our opinion precludes any State from placing further restrictions on its exercise of the takings power. Indeed, many States already impose "public use" requirements that are stricter than the federal baseline. Some of these requirements have been established as a matter of state constitutional law,[22] while others are expressed in state eminent domain statutes that carefully limit the grounds upon which takings may be exercised. As the submissions of the parties and their *amici* make clear, the necessity and wisdom of using eminent domain to promote economic development are certainly matters of legitimate public debate. This Court's authority, however, extends only to determining whether the City's proposed condemnations are for a "public use" within the meaning of the Fifth Amendment to the Federal Constitution. Because over a century of our case law interpreting that provision dictates an affirmative answer to that question, we may not grant petitioners the relief that they seek.

The judgment of the Supreme Court of Connecticut is affirmed.

Justice KENNEDY, concurring. . . .

A court applying rational-basis review under the Public Use Clause should strike down a taking that, by a clear showing, is intended to favor a particular private party, with only incidental or pretextual public benefits. . . .

A court confronted with a plausible accusation of impermissible favoritism to private parties should treat the objection as a serious one and review the record to see if it has merit, though with the presumption that the government's actions were reasonable and intended to serve a public purpose. Here, the trial court conducted a careful and extensive inquiry into "whether, in fact, the development plan is of primary benefit to . . . the developer (i.e., Corcoran Jennison), and private businesses which may eventually locate in the plan area (e.g., Pfizer), and in that regard, only of incidental benefit to the city." . . . The trial court considered [various items of evidence, including] the substantial commitment of public funds by the State to the development project before most of the private beneficiaries were known; [and] evidence that respondents reviewed a variety of development plans and chose a private developer from a group of applicants rather than picking out a particular transferee beforehand. . . .

The trial court concluded, based on these findings, that benefiting Pfizer was not "the primary motivation or effect of this development plan"; instead, "the primary motivation for [respondents] was to take advantage of Pfizer's presence." . . . Even the dissenting justices on the Connecticut Supreme Court agreed that respondents' development plan was intended to revitalize the local economy, not to serve the interests of Pfizer, Corcoran Jennison, or any other private party. 843 A.2d 500, 595 (2004) (Zarella, J., concurring in part and dissenting in part). This case, then, survives the meaningful rational basis review that in my view is required under the Public Use Clause. . . .

. . . This taking occurred in the context of a comprehensive development plan meant to address a serious city-wide depression, and the projected economic benefits of the project cannot be characterized as de minimus. The identity of most of the private beneficiaries were unknown at the time the city formulated its plans. The city complied with elaborate procedural requirements that facilitate review of the record and inquiry into the city's purposes. In sum, while there may be categories of cases in which the transfers are so

---

21. The amici raise questions about the fairness of the measure of just compensation. While important, these questions are not before us in this litigation.

22. See, e.g., County of Wayne v. Hathcock, 684 N.W.2d 765 (Mich. 2004).

suspicious, or the procedures employed so prone to abuse, or the purported benefits are so trivial or implausible, that courts should presume an impermissible private purpose, no such circumstances are present in this case. . . .

Justice O'CONNOR, with whom THE CHIEF JUSTICE, Justice SCALIA, and Justice THOMAS join, dissenting. . .

. . . [W]ere the political branches the sole arbiters of the public-private distinction, the Public Use Clause would amount to little more than hortatory fluff. An external, judicial check on how the public use requirement is interpreted, however limited, is necessary if this constraint on government power is to retain any meaning. . . .

Are economic development takings constitutional? I would hold that they are not. We are guided by two precedents about the taking of real property by eminent domain. In *Berman*, we upheld takings within a blighted neighborhood of Washington, D.C. The neighborhood had so deteriorated that, for example, 64.3% of its dwellings were beyond repair. It had become burdened with "overcrowding of dwellings," "lack of adequate streets and alleys," and "lack of light and air." . . .

In *Midkiff*, we upheld a land condemnation scheme in Hawaii whereby title in real property was taken from lessors and transferred to lessees. At that time, the State and Federal Governments owned nearly 49% of the State's land, and another 47% was in the hands of only 72 private landowners. Concentration of land ownership was so dramatic that on the State's most urbanized island, Oahu, 22 landowners owned 72.5% of the fee simple titles. . . .

The Court's holdings in *Berman* and *Midkiff* were true to the principle underlying the Public Use Clause. In both those cases, the extraordinary, precondemnation use of the targeted property inflicted affirmative harm on society — in *Berman* through blight resulting from extreme poverty and in *Midkiff* through oligopoly resulting from extreme wealth. And in both cases, the relevant legislative body had found that eliminating the existing property use was necessary to remedy the harm. Thus a public purpose was realized when the harmful use was eliminated. Because each taking *directly* achieved a public benefit, it did not matter that the property was turned over to private use. Here, in contrast, New London does not claim that Susette Kelo's and Wilhelmina Dery's well-maintained homes are the source of any social harm. Indeed, it could not so claim without adopting the absurd argument that any single-family home that might be razed to make way for an apartment building, or any church that might be replaced with a retail store, or any small business that might be more lucrative if it were instead part of a national franchise, is inherently harmful to society and thus within the government's power to condemn.

In moving away from our decisions sanctioning the condemnation of harmful property use, the Court today significantly expands the meaning of public use. It holds that the sovereign may take private property currently put to ordinary private use, and give it over for new, ordinary private use, so long as the new use is predicted to generate some secondary benefit for the public — such as increased tax revenue, more jobs, maybe even aesthetic pleasure. But nearly any lawful use of real private property can be said to generate some incidental benefit to the public. Thus, if predicted (or even guaranteed) positive side-effects are enough to render transfer from one private party to another constitutional, then the words "for public use" do not realistically exclude *any* takings, and thus do not exert any constraint on the eminent domain power. . . .

The specter of condemnation hangs over all property. Nothing is to prevent the State from replacing any Motel 6 with a Ritz-Carlton, any home with a shopping mall, or any farm with a factory. . . .

. . . [I]n a coda, the Court suggests that property owners should turn to the States, who may or may not choose to impose appropriate limits on economic development takings. This is an abdication of our responsibility. States play many important functions in our system of dual sovereignty, but compensating for our refusal to enforce properly the Federal Constitution (and a provision meant to curtail state action, no less) is not among them. . . .

Any property may now be taken for the benefit of another private party, but the fallout from this decision will not be random. The beneficiaries are likely to be those citizens with disproportionate influence and power in the political process, including large corporations and development firms. As for the victims, the government now has license to transfer property from those with fewer resources to those with more. The Founders cannot have intended this perverse result. "[T]hat alone is a *just* government," wrote James Madison, "which *impartially* secures to every man, whatever is his *own*." For the National Gazette, Property, (Mar. 29, 1792). . . .

I would hold that the takings in both Parcel 3 and Parcel 4A are unconstitutional, reverse the judgment of the Supreme Court of Connecticut, and remand for further proceedings.

Justice THOMAS, dissenting. . . .

Tellingly, the phrase "public use" contrasts with the very different phrase "general Welfare" used elsewhere in the Constitution. See Article I, §8 ("Congress shall have Power To . . . provide for the common Defence and general Welfare of the United States"); preamble (Constitution established "to promote the general Welfare"). The Framers would have used some such broader term if they had meant the Public Use Clause to have a similarly sweeping scope. . . .

. . . [I]t is most implausible that the Framers intended to defer to legislatures as to what satisfies the Public Use Clause, uniquely among all the express provisions of the Bill of Rights. We would not defer to a legislature's determination of the various circumstances that establish, for example, when a search of a home would be reasonable, see, e.g., Payton v. New York, 445 U.S. 573, 589–590 (1980). . . .

. . . Yet today the Court tells us that we are not to "second-guess the City's considered judgments," when the issue is, instead, whether the government may take the infinitely more intrusive step of tearing down petitioners' homes. . . .

. . . I would revisit our Public Use Clause cases and consider returning to the original meaning of the Public Use Clause: that the government may take property only if it actually uses or gives the public a legal right to use the property. . . .

. . . In the 1950's, no doubt emboldened in part by the expansive understanding of "public use" this Court adopted in *Berman,* cities [undertook urban renewal projects that mostly displaced residents who were nonwhite and poor]. Regrettably, the predictable consequence of the Court's decision will be to exacerbate these effects.

Note on the Federal Public Use Requirement

1. *The Court's deferential approach in* Berman *and* Midkiff. As the opinions in *Kelo* indicate, in its two most pertinent prior precedents on the public use issue, the Court had been extraordinarily respectful of legislative decisions authorizing use of eminent domain powers. The redevelopment project unanimously approved in Berman v. Parker, 348 U.S. 26 (1954), cleared much of the southwest section of Washington, D.C. This District of Columbia effort served as the model for the national urban renewal program initiated by Title I of the Housing Act of 1949, 63 Stat. 414.

In *Berman*, Justice Douglas said in part:

> Subject to specific constitutional limitations, when the legislature has spoken, the public interest has been declared in terms well-nigh conclusive. In such cases the legislature, not the judiciary, is the main guardian of the public needs to be served by social legislation. . . . This principle admits of no exception merely because the power of eminent domain is involved. The role of the judiciary in determining whether that power is being exercised for a public purpose is an extremely narrow one.

Id. at 32. *Berman* ushered in a period of great federal court deference to government use of the power of eminent domain. See Wendell E. Pritchett, The "Public Menace" of Blight: Urban Renewal and the Private Uses of Eminent Domain, 21 Yale L. & Pol'y Rev. 1 (2003).

Prior to the clearance of the *Berman* project area, over 97 percent of its residents were black (348 U.S. at 30) and most were poor. By the 1960s, after the area had been redeveloped, most residents were both white and middle class (although some poor African Americans then were residing in public housing projects, largely in the southern portion of the project area). Decades after their forced dislocation, some of the 20,000 residents of southwest Washington who had lost their homes were still reminiscing about their former neighborhood and what might have come of it if it had not been razed. Linda Wheeler, Broken Ground, Broken Hearts, Wash. Post, June 21, 1999, at A1. See generally Howard Gillette, Jr., Between Justice and Beauty: Race, Planning and the Failure of Urban Policy in Washington, D.C. (1995). Urban renewal, the national program that *Berman* enabled, gradually encountered increasing opposition and eventually lost federal support. See pp. 840–42. As it happens, in the late 1960s the headquarters building of the newly created U.S. Department of Housing and Urban Development (HUD), the agency charged with providing urban renewal grants, was constructed within the *Berman* redevelopment area.

The Hawaii statute at issue in Hawaii Housing Authority v. Midkiff, 467 U.S. 229 (1984), entitled a residential lessee, in some situations, to arrange for the state to exercise its eminent domain powers to acquire the landlord's interest. The state then would sell the interest to the lessee for an amount equal to the state's acquisition cost, thereby elevating the homeowner's ownership interest to a fee simple. Justice O'Connor, writing for a unanimous court, said in part:

> . . . [W]here the exercise of the eminent domain power is rationally related to a conceivable public purpose, the Court has never held a compensated taking to be proscribed by the Public Use Clause. . . .
>
> Nor can we condemn as irrational the Act's approach to correcting [Hawaii's] land oligopoly problem. . . .
>
> . . . When the legislature's purpose is legitimate and its means are not irrational, our cases make clear that empirical debates over the wisdom of takings — no less than debates over the wisdom of other kinds of socioeconomic legislation — are not to be carried out in the federal courts.

Id. at 241–43.

2. *The cool reception, prior to* Kelo, *of public use claims in the lower federal courts.* In many areas of land use law — zoning changes, special assessments, subdivision exactions, exclusionary zoning — state courts typically have been more aggressive than federal courts in policing against abuses by local policymakers. At least prior to *Kelo*, the public use issue provided yet another illustration. Thomas Merrill examined 308 reported appellate decisions on the public use issue decided between 1954 and 1986:

> . . . [O]f the 308 opinions in the sample, 261, or 84.7%, held that the proposed taking served a public use; conversely, 47, or 15.3%, held that it did not. Given *Berman*'s and *Midkiff*'s

assertion that a legislative public use determination is virtually dispositive of the issue, the relatively high number of cases finding no public use is somewhat surprising. The apparent anomaly disappears, however, once we separate federal decisions from state decisions. Although the survey contained only 17 federal cases, each upheld a legislative public use determination, suggesting that lower federal courts have been faithful to *Berman*'s deferential standard of review. State courts, on the other hand, seem more willing to depart from *Berman*'s virtual abandonment of judicial review. Looking at the state appellate decisions alone, we find that 16.2%, roughly one in six, held that a proposed taking did not serve a public use.

Thomas W. Merrill, The Economics of Public Use, 72 Cornell L. Rev. 61, 96 (1986). For data from the ensuing 17-year period, see Corey J. Wilk, The Struggle over the Public Use Clause: Survey of Holdings and Trends, 1986–2003, 39 Real Prop. Prob. & Tr. J. 251 (2004). Wilk found a continuation of the pattern of relative federal court passivity. During the years he studied, the landowner lost on the public use issue in 13 out of the 14 federal court cases, but prevailed in 17.4 percent of the state court cases. (If the percentage of landowner successes on the public use issue in reported decisions were to increase over time, would that necessarily indicate that judges were becoming stricter? What about the alternative possibility that condemning governments increasingly were playing close to the constitutional edge?)

3. *Mill Acts as a test of the various Justices' positions in* Kelo. Mill Acts, an early form of state legislation aimed at promoting economic development, triggered many of the formative judicial decisions on the public use issue. These statutes authorized the owners of mills operated by water power to erect dams that flooded upstream lands, on the condition that the owners pay compensation to the upstream landowners. In Head v. Amoskeag Manufacturing Co., 113 U.S. 9 (1885), the Supreme Court unanimously upheld, against a public use challenge, a large manufacturer's right to proceed in this fashion. During the same era, however, a number of state courts ruled that state law prohibited takings of this sort. For extended discussion of this rich history, see Justice Thomas's full dissent in *Kelo*. Under what circumstances, if any, would Justice Kennedy regard a Mill Act as an instance of impermissible favoritism to private parties? Would Justice O'Connor regard Mill Acts as endeavors to eliminate affirmative harms to society? Could a Mill Act provide members of the public with sufficient use-rights to mill facilities to satisfy the legal standard that Justice Thomas would like the Court to consider?

4. *Kelo's likely effects.* All four opinions in *Kelo* break from the *Berman-Midkiff* tradition of extreme deference. Justice O'Connor, the author of *Midkiff*, wrote the principal dissent in *Kelo*. Justice Kennedy's concurring opinion implies that he would not countenance government use of eminent domain for the benefit of, for example, a single predetermined private actor. And even Justice Stevens's majority opinion signals reservations about the use of eminent domain to help a political favorite. Is *Kelo* likely to induce federal judges to be more sympathetic to public use claims? Should ongoing legal developments in the state courts, discussed below, influence how federal judges react to *Kelo*?

Southwestern Illinois Development Authority v. National City Environmental, L.L.C.

768 N.E.2d 1 (Ill.), *cert. denied*, 537 U.S. 880 (2002)

Justice GARMAN delivered the opinion of the court:

The issue in this case is whether the Southwestern Illinois Development Authority (SWIDA) properly exercised the power of eminent domain to take property owned by

National City Environmental, L.L.C. (NCE), and convey that property to Gateway International Motorsports Corporation (Gateway). The circuit court of St. Clair County ruled that SWIDA had properly exercised its authority to take the land in question. The appellate court reversed[, holding that SWIDA's proposed taking would violate the public use clause of the Illinois Constitution]. . . . We now affirm the decision of the appellate court.

BACKGROUND

SWIDA was created in 1987 by the Illinois General Assembly through passage of the Southwestern Illinois Development Authority Act, 70 Ill. Comp. Stat. 520/1. SWIDA is a political entity and municipal corporation whose stated purpose is to "promote industrial, commercial, residential, service, transportation and recreational activities and facilities, thereby reducing the evils attendant upon unemployment and enhancing the public health, safety, morals, happiness and general welfare of this State."

The Act mandates that SWIDA "promote development within the geographic confines of Madison and St. Clair counties." It is the duty of SWIDA to assist in the development, construction, and acquisition of industrial, commercial, housing or residential projects within these counties. A "commercial project" is defined as "any cultural facilities of a for-profit or not-for-profit type including . . . racetracks . . . [and] parking facilities." . . .

In June 1996, SWIDA issued $21.5 million in taxable sports facility revenue bonds. The proceeds of the bonds were lent to Gateway to finance the development of a multipurpose automotive sports and training facility in the region (the racetrack). Gateway signed a loan agreement and a note to evince its obligation to repay the loan. . . . [T]he bonds constitute a moral obligation of the state.

The racetrack was developed and has flourished. In 1997, the racetrack had a total attendance of 400,000 at various large and small events. Seating included 25,000 grandstand seats and 25,000 portable seats. In 1998, Gateway increased its seating capacity and desired to increase its parking capacity as well. It called upon SWIDA to use its quick-take eminent domain powers to acquire land to the west of the racetrack for the purposes of expanded parking facilities. The adjacent 148.5 acre tract of land sought was owned by NCE.

NCE operates a metal recycling center. . . . NCE employs 80 to 100 persons full time and has been at its present location since 1975. NCE shreds cars and appliances and separates the reusable metals. . . .

In early 1998, Gateway attempted to discuss the purchase of NCE's land with NCE's owner. NCE would not discuss the matter and, initially, Gateway made no offer to purchase the land. Instead, Gateway asked SWIDA to exercise its quick-take eminent domain powers to take the 148.5 acres of land and transfer it to Gateway.

Gateway completed a "Quick-Take Application Packet" and stated that it wanted to use the land as a parking lot for the purpose of increasing the value of Gateway's racetrack. Gateway paid SWIDA an application fee of $2,500, and the sum of $10,000 to be applied toward SWIDA's sliding scale fee of 6% to 10% of the acquisition price of property being condemned. In addition, Gateway agreed to pay SWIDA's expenses, including the acquisition price of the property, and other costs associated with the quick-take process. . . .

On March 5, 1998, SWIDA . . . adopted a resolution manifesting an intent to assist Gateway with racetrack expansion through the acquisition of NCE's property, [recounting] the numerous benefits that could be created for the region. SWIDA found that the acquisition of NCE's property was essential to the success of the proposed expansion and further development of the racetrack, and authorized its executive director, Alan Ortbals, to acquire title to the property by all necessary and appropriate means.

then IT made offer to purchase for 1mil

In an effort to acquire the property through a negotiated sale, Ortbals attended a meeting on March 17, 1998, at which he delivered to NCE a written offer to purchase the property for $1 million. By letter dated March 19, 1998, NCE rejected the $1 million offer but indicated its willingness to meet with SWIDA the week of March 30, 1998, following an expected appraisal of the property. On March 20, 1998, SWIDA made another written offer to NCE to purchase the property for $1 million and advised NCE that SWIDA would initiate proceedings to condemn the property if NCE did not accept the offer by 5 p.m. on March 30, 1998 . . . NCE indicated that it was again rejecting the offer of $1 million for the sale of its property.

then IT Sought condemnation

Meanwhile, on March 31, 1998, SWIDA filed a complaint in the circuit court of St. Clair County seeking condemnation of, and acquisition of fee simple title to, the property. . . .

The circuit court held a quick-take hearing and on April 27, 1998, ruled in SWIDA's favor. Relying on testimony from Mike Pritchett of the Illinois Department of Transportation (the Department), the circuit court found that the taking was for a public purpose as there were serious public safety issues involved. . . . According to traffic pattern data studied by the Department, significant traffic congestion occurred on Interstate 55–70 when major events were held at the racetrack. According to Pritchett, a safety hazard was created because drivers do not normally anticipate stopped traffic on the interstate. Pritchett further testified that pedestrians often crossed Illinois Route 203 from the parking areas east of the highway to the racetrack. A traffic signal was in place to allow patrons to cross Route 203. However, the signals created even more automobile traffic delays. . . . Pritchett testified that construction of a parking lot on NCE's property [would] alleviate traffic problems when major events were taking place at the racetrack.

. . . In addition, Ortbals testified that development of a parking facility on the property was necessary to promote economic development, as the number of spectators, development and expansion of neighboring businesses, and other economic spin-off, all had exceeded initial expectations. . . .

On April 28, 1998, the circuit court made a preliminary finding that $900,000 was just compensation for the property. On April 30, 1998, the circuit court entered an order of taking, vesting SWIDA with title to the property in fee simple and granting it the right to immediate possession of the property. On the same day, SWIDA conveyed title to the property to Gateway by way of a quit-claim deed. . . .

NCE filed an interlocutory appeal arguing in part that SWIDA lacked constitutional authority to take the property and convey it to Gateway. NCE also filed an emergency motion for a stay of the condemnation, which was granted. . . .

ANALYSIS

The State of Illinois, as a sovereign, has the inherent right to condemn property, subject to the state constitutional mandate that private property shall not be taken or damaged for public use without just compensation to its owner. The fifth amendment to the United States Constitution, made applicable to the states through the fourteenth amendment, also provides that private property shall not be taken for public use without just compensation.

In this case, we determine whether this taking achieves a legitimate public use pursuant to the constitutionally exercised police power of the government (Berman v. Parker, 348 U.S. 26 (1954)). . . .

The right of a sovereign to condemn private property is limited to takings for a public use. Clearly, private persons may ultimately acquire ownership of property arising out of a

Private persons may ultimately acquire the prop

taking and the subsequent transfer to private ownership does not by itself defeat the public purpose. Hawaii Housing Authority v. Midkiff, 467 U.S. 229, 243-44 (1984). However, that principle alone cannot adequately resolve the issues presented in this case. "Before the right of eminent domain may be exercised, the law, beyond a doubt, requires that the use for which the land is taken shall be public as distinguished from a private use." People ex rel. Tuohy v. City of Chicago, 68 N.E.2d 761 ([Ill.] 1946).

SWIDA's action in taking NCE's property and transferring it to Gateway for Gateway's private use presents fundamental constitutional issues that are essential to resolving this dispute. The essence of this case relates not to the ultimate transfer of property to a private party. Rather, the controlling issue is whether SWIDA exceeded the boundaries of constitutional principles and its authority by transferring the property to a private party for a profit when the property is not put to a public use.

It may be impossible to clearly delineate the boundary between what constitutes a legitimate public purpose and a private benefit with no sufficient, legitimate public purpose to support it. . . . Great deference should be afforded the legislature and its granting of eminent domain authority. However, the exercise of that power is not entirely beyond judicial scrutiny (see *Hawaii Housing Authority*, 467 U.S. at 241 (and cases cited therein)), and it is incumbent upon the judiciary to ensure that the power of eminent domain is used in a manner contemplated by the framers of the constitutions and by the legislature that granted the specific power in question. . . .

SWIDA contends that the condemnation and taking of NCE's property is sustainable because a public purpose will be served through (1) the fostering of economic development, (2) the promotion of public safety, and (3) the prevention or elimination of blight. . . .

We have . . . recognized that economic development is an important public purpose. SWIDA presented extensive testimony that expanding Gateway's facilities through the taking of NCE's property would allow it to grow and prosper and contribute to positive economic growth in the region. However, "incidentally, every lawful business does this." Gaylord [v. Sanitary District, 68 N.E. 522 (Ill. 1903)]. Moreover, nearly a century ago, *Gaylord* expressed the long-standing rule that "to constitute a public use, something more than a mere benefit to the public must flow from the contemplated improvement."

Ct: This was an indep. legit gov't'al decision

While the activities here were undertaken in the guise of carrying out its legislated mission, SWIDA's true intentions were not clothed in an independent, legitimate governmental decision to further a planned public use. SWIDA did not conduct or commission a thorough study of the parking situation at Gateway. Nor did it formulate any economic plan requiring additional parking at the racetrack. SWIDA advertised that, for a fee, it would condemn land at the request of "private developers" for the "private use" of developers. In addition, SWIDA entered into a contract with Gateway to condemn whatever land "may be desired . . . by Gateway." Clearly, the foundation of this taking is rooted not in the economic and planning process with which SWIDA has been charged. Rather, this action was undertaken solely in response to Gateway's expansion goals and its failure to accomplish those goals through purchasing NCE's land at an acceptable negotiated price. It appears SWIDA's true intentions were to act as a default broker of land for Gateway's proposed parking plan.

π was acting as default broker of land for G

This point is further emphasized by the fact that other options were available to Gateway that could have addressed many of the problems testified to by Pritchett, Ortbals and others. Gateway could have built a parking garage structure on its existing property rather than develop the land owned by NCE. However, when Gateway discovered that the cost of constructing a garage on land it already owned was substantially higher than using SWIDA as its agent to take NCE's property for open-field parking, Gateway chose the easier and less expensive avenue.

G had alts available to π but chose the easiest/ least expensive

As a result of the acquisition of NCE's property, Gateway could realize an estimated increase of $13 to $14 million in projected revenue per year. While we do not deny that this expansion in revenue could potentially trickle down and bring corresponding revenue increases to the region, revenue expansion alone does not justify an improper and unacceptable expansion of the eminent domain power of the government. Using the power of the government for purely private purposes to allow Gateway to avoid the open real estate market and expand its facilities in a more cost-efficient manner, and thus maximizing corporate profits, is a misuse of the power entrusted by the public.

The legislature intended that SWIDA actively foster economic development and expansion in Madison and St. Clair Counties. However, the actions of SWIDA in this case blur the lines between a public use and a private purpose. A highway toll authority may justify the use of eminent domain to ensure that motorists have reasonable access to gas stations. Does the highway authority's power include the ability to use eminent domain authority to take additional land for a car wash, and then a lube shop? Could the authority then use its power to facilitate additional expansions for a motel, small retail shops, and entertainment centers? The initial, legitimate development of a public project does not justify condemnation for any and all related business expansions. . . .

. . . The power of eminent domain is to be exercised with restraint, not abandon.

. . . [W]e agree with the appellate court's finding that, in this case, SWIDA exceeded its constitutional authority in taking NCE's land by eminent domain.

Justice Freeman, dissenting: . . .

In the present case, the majority cannot dispute the legislative findings regarding the need to alleviate certain economic, housing and other conditions in the southwestern part of this state. Nor can the majority dispute that alleviation of these conditions furthers certain public purposes. . . .

Applying the holdings of *Hawaii Housing Authority* and *Berman*, this court should defer to the legislative determination of the public use. Although the majority acknowledges that great deference is due the legislative determination, the majority does not act in accordance with such deference. Indeed, the majority does not afford any measure of deference to the legislative determination. . . .

Justice McMorrow joins in this dissent.

Note on the Public Use Issue in the State Courts

1. *State constitutional provisions.* All state constitutions, except North Carolina's, also contain public use clauses, many of them worded somewhat differently than the clause in the Fifth Amendment. For example:

> Arizona Const. art. 2, §17: " . . . No private property shall be taken or damaged for public or private use without just compensation having first been made. . . . Whenever an attempt is made to take private property for a use alleged to be public, the question whether the contemplated use be really public shall be a judicial question, and determined as such without regard to any legislative assertion that the use is public."

> Minnesota Const. art. I, §13: "Private property shall not be taken, destroyed or damaged for public use without just compensation therefor, first paid or secured."

> Ohio Const. art. I, §19: "Private property shall ever be held inviolate, but subservient to the public welfare. . . . [W]here private property shall be taken for public use, a compensation therefore shall first be made in money, or first secured by a deposit of money, and such compensation shall be assessed by a jury, without deduction for benefits to any property of the owner."

South Carolina Const. art. I, §13: " . . . [P]rivate property shall not be taken for private use without the consent of the owner, nor for public use without just compensation being first made therefor."

2. *Michigan's about face on the use of eminent domain for economic development.* As *SWIDA* exemplifies, even prior to the Supreme Court's decision in *Kelo*, some state courts were shifting away from *Berman*-style deference to economic development projects. In a highly controversial decision, Poletown Neighborhood Council v. City of Detroit, 304 N.W.2d 455 (Mich. 1981), the Michigan Supreme Court had sustained Detroit's use of eminent domain powers to raze a majority white ethnic neighborhood to provide a cleared site for a large General Motors assembly plant. On *Poletown*, compare Jeanie Wylie, Poletown: Community Betrayed (1989) (whose title reveals its point of view), with Bryan D. Jones et al., The Sustaining Hand: Community Leadership and Corporate Power (1986) (reporting that most Detroit voters and interest groups favored the project).

Two decades later, however, in County of Wayne v. Hathcock, 684 N.W.2d 765 (Mich. 2004) (a decision cited in *Kelo*), the Michigan Supreme Court unanimously over-ruled *Poletown*. In *Hathcock*, the county aspired to develop a 1,300-acre business park near the Detroit Metropolitan Airport for the announced purpose of strengthening the local economy. When the owners of 19 parcels refused to sell voluntarily, the county sought to condemn their lands. A majority of the court held that the county's plan to take the condemned properties and eventually transfer them to private entities violated the Michigan Constitution's public use clause: "[T]he landscape of our country is flecked with shopping centers, office parks, clusters of hotels, and centers of entertainment and commerce. We do not believe . . . that these constellations required the exercise of eminent domain or any other form of collective public action for their formation." Id. at 783–84. The majority indicated that it would have held otherwise if the condemned lands had been blighted or if the eventual private transferees would have been subject to continuing public oversight. What if the County of Wayne had intended to retain ownership of all the land within the business park and, on particular sites, to enter into long-term leases with private firms? See generally Symposium, The Death of *Poletown*: The Future of Eminent Domain and Urban Development After *County of Wayne v. Hathcock*, 2004 Mich. St. L. Rev. 837.

3. *The relevance of the number of parcels acquired.* In *Hathcock*, *Berman*, and *Kelo*, the redevelopment agencies were using eminent domain to assemble a large number of tracts held by different owners. In *SWIDA*, the agency was seeking to acquire only one parcel. When the targeted owners are few, government has more difficulty persuading a court that its resort to eminent domain is necessary to overcome multiperson holdout dynamics. Should the *SWIDA* court have stressed this feature of the case?

4. *When a "giving" taints a taking.* Or was the *SWIDA* court mainly bothered by condemning authority's generosity to Gateway? In his concurrence in *Kelo*, Justice Kennedy stresses the problem of "impermissible favoritism to private parties." This sort of favoritism can be thought of as an aspect of the givings problem — the takings problem turned on its head. See pp. 150–51. In what ways, if any, did Gateway receive more favorable treatment than General Motors did in *Poletown*? Than Pfizer did in *Kelo*?

In Port Authority v. Groppoli, 202 N.W.2d 371 (Minn. 1972), the Port Authority had attempted to condemn a private warehouse to subsequently lease it "as is" to another private party. The Minnesota Supreme Court held that this was not a "public purpose." See also Wilmington Parking Authority v. Land With Improvements, 521 A.2d 227 (Del. 1986) (squelching, on statutory grounds, city's use of eminent domain powers for benefit of major corporate citizen).

5. *Additional compensation when public use is doubtful?* In footnote 21 of his opinion, Justice Stevens states that questions regarding the measure of compensation, "while

important," were not before the Court in *Kelo*. Could the landowner in *SWIDA* have acquiesced in the taking but then sued for extraordinary compensation on account of the lack of a valid public use? See James E. Krier & Christopher Serkin, Public Ruses, 2004 Mich. St. L. Rev. 859 (urging augmentation of compensation as skepticism about the public nature and benefits of government action grows); Recent Case, Eleventh Circuit Finds Public Purpose Determination Irrelevant to Damages Calculation, 115 Harv. L. Rev. 899 (2002) (arguing that compensation for improper takings should be higher for deterrence and justice purposes).

6. *Federalism issues*. In *Kelo*, Justice Stevens notes the existence of state constitutional and statutory constraints on the exercise of eminent domain powers and implies that these constraints justify federal courts distancing themselves from the task of supervising state and local condemnations. Was Justice O'Connor right in her dissent to criticize Justice Stevens's position on this issue? In the five decades prior to *Kelo*, landowners raising the public use issue prevailed in the federal courts in only one reported case, but were considerably more successful in the state courts. See pp. 831–32. Is this difference likely to narrow after *Kelo*? Given the reluctance of federal judges to involve themselves in local land use issues of all sorts, under what circumstances should an attorney for a condemnee prefer to litigate a public use case in a federal court?

7. *Scholarly perspectives*. Thomas W. Merrill, The Economics of Public Use, 72 Cornell L. Rev. 61, 96 (1986), an article cited on p. 832, is a leading work on the public use issue. Merrill articulates and then critiques the case for virtually total judicial deference to governmental decisions to employ the power of eminent domain. Because eminent domain procedures entail additional administrative costs for governments, Merrill supposes that an agency typically would not invoke the power unless it faced a seller that had a degree of monopoly power. It follows that a government would seldom resort to a coerced exchange when a consensual exchange would be possible. Merrill nonetheless identifies three ways in which a government might abuse the power of eminent domain. First, because market values generally are used to calculate the just compensation that a government must pay, a condemnor might deliberately use eminent domain to avoid having to pay a condemnee for the "subjective value" (or "owner's surplus") that the condemnee attaches to unique property. (See pp. 859–60.) Second, Merrill notes that because a condemnor obtains all the surplus value generated by a land assemblage, private interests might jockey to have a government do their assemblages for them. Because competitive lobbying for government favors (so-called rent-seeking activity) itself consumes resources, courts have some reason to wield the public use doctrine to limit politicians' temptations to "lend" eminent domain powers to private interests. Third, Merrill argues that a court might hesitate to allow a government to use eminent domain at Time 2 to defuse a seller's monopoly power when the government had deliberately chosen at Time 1 to get itself into a bilateral monopoly situation; otherwise, a government would not have the proper incentives at Time 1. Applying this analytical approach, Merrill concludes that in *Poletown* the first two of these rationales would have justified heightened judicial scrutiny.

For a spectrum of commentary on the public use issue, see Richard A. Epstein, Takings 161–81 (1985) (sharply criticizing the Supreme Court's deferential approach in *Berman* and *Midkiff*); Nicole Stelle Garnett, The Public Use Question as a Takings Problem, 71 Geo. Wash. L. Rev. 934 (2003) (arguing that courts should require a taking government to demonstrate that its exercise of eminent domain is reasonably necessary to advance the public purpose it is invoking); Matthew P. Harrington, "Public Use" and the Original Understanding of the So-Called "Takings" Clause, 53 Hastings L.J. 1245 (2002) (arguing that the drafters of the Fifth Amendment did not intend the amendment's "public use" prong to be a substantive limitation on eminent domain); Ralph Nader &

Alan Hirsch, Making Eminent Domain Humane, 49 Vill. L. Rev. 207 (2004) (advocating strict judicial scrutiny in some contexts, especially when targeted landowners lack political power).

Note on Other Legal Limits on the Use of Eminent Domain

Notes
RLUIPA
May be a
limit on
use of
eminent
domain?

1. *When eminent domain threatens civil liberties.* Just as enforcement of a regulation can infringe on the exercise of civil liberties (see Chapter 3D), so can a condemnation action. For example, in Pillar of Fire v. Denver Urban Renewal Authority, 509 P.2d 1250 (Colo. 1973), a redevelopment authority undertaking an ambitious program of downtown renewal sought to force the sale of the original church building of an evangelistic offshoot of Methodism. The court deemed *Berman*-style deference to be inappropriate and remanded for determination of whether acquisition of the site was "vital" to the achievement of the authority's plans. In an instance of this sort, should an attorney for a religious institution rely on the Public Use Clause, the Free Exercise Clause, or both? A state court, of course, may construe state constitutional protections of religious exercise to be more expansive than the protections of the First Amendment. See City Chapel Evangelical Free Inc. v. City of South Bend, 744 N.E.2d 443 (Ind. 2001) (reviewing proposed condemnation of church building).

The Religious Land Use and Institutionalized Persons Act (RLUIPA), enacted in 2000, may provide a basis for a religious institution's challenge to a condemnation proceeding. See, e.g., Cottonwood Christian Center v. Cypress Redevelopment Agency, 218 F. Supp. 2d 1203 (C.D. Cal. 2002) (granting preliminary injunction against city's taking of site of planned religious facility). On RLUIPA and state RFRAs, see pp. 210–20.

What if a city planned to use eminent domain to acquire the editorial offices of a newspaper that had been critical of local politicians? Or of all adult movie houses located within its boundaries? Should an opponent of these condemnations rely on the Public Use Clause, the First Amendment, or both? Cf. pp. 220–31. See generally Shelley Ross Saxer, Eminent Domain Actions Targeting First Amendment Land Uses, 69 Mo. L. Rev. 653 (2004) (urging heightened scrutiny). Under what circumstances would a municipal program to condemn an abortion clinic violate Roe v. Wade, 410 U.S. 113 (1973), and its progeny? Cf. pp. 231–32.

2. *When government targets a small, politically weak minority.* The dissenting justices in *Kelo* assert that those with fewer resources are likely to be particularly popular targets of takings. In Borough of Essex Falls v. Kessler Institute for Rehabilitation, Inc., 673 A.2d 856 (N.J. Super. Ct. Law Div. 1995), the institute owned a 12-acre parcel on which it proposed to build a facility that would accommodate 20 adults receiving rehabilitative services to break habits of substance abuse. The proposal triggered active opposition from neighbors, who foresaw both traffic congestion and an influx of undesirable people. The borough's leaders responded by offering to buy the site. When the institute refused to sell, the borough sought to condemn the property for the announced purpose of using it as a park. The court held that this purpose was a pretext and dismissed the borough's complaint to condemn on the ground that it had been initiated in bad faith. Did the borough's misstep lie in its misrepresentation of its true purposes or in the illegitimacy of its underlying aim of discriminating against substance abusers? Could the institute have successfully invoked the provisions of the Fair Housing Amendments Act of 1988 that pertain to discrimination against the handicapped? See pp. 722–29.

Developers of controversial subsidized housing projects have similarly found themselves to be targets of eminent domain. In Pheasant Ridge Associates Ltd. Partnership v.

Town of Burlington, 506 N.E.2d 1152 (Mass. 1987), a developer with a 14-acre site had invoked the Massachusetts Anti-Snob Zoning Act, cited at p. 787, to obtain zoning approval for a project of 202 apartment units, 20 percent of which were to be rented to low- and moderate-income families. To thwart the project, the town initiated a condemnation action to acquire the site for a park and an affordable housing project that the town itself would manage. The court quashed the condemnation action on the ground that the town had acted in bad faith. Under what circumstances would a fair housing act or other antidiscrimination statute provide a basis for quashing a condemnation action of this sort? Should the U.S. Supreme Court hold (as it never has) that the federal Public Use Clause prevents a condemnor from acting in bad faith?

3. *Additional statutory constraints.* The state statutes that authorize local use of eminent power commonly place restrictions on its exercise, thereby providing ammunition to opponents of condemnations. See, e.g., Beach-Courchesne v. City of Diamond Bar, 95 Cal. Rptr. 2d 265 (Ct. App. 2000) (rejecting city redevelopment plan that failed to provide adequate evidence of "blight" as required by California's Community Redevelopment Law); Aposporos v. Urban Redevelopment Commission, 790 A.2d 1167 (Conn. 2002) (holding city violated statutorily mandated procedures when it amended redevelopment plan). For an argument that the California legislature, responding to decades of overreaching by redevelopment agencies, now imposes an overly strict definition of blight, see George Lefcoe, Finding the Blight That's Right for California Redevelopment Law, 52 Hastings L.J. 991 (2001). See generally Colin Gordon, Blighting the Way: Urban Renewal, Economic Development, and the Elusive Definition of Blight, 31 Fordham Urb. L.J. 305 (2004).

Opponents of the Yerba Buena Center urban renewal project in San Francisco invoked a wide array of legal authorities and succeeded both in tying up the project for years and in increasing its emphasis on low-income housing. In four different lawsuits, the opponents relied on the federal statute on relocation assistance, the California Environmental Quality Act, the National Environmental Policy Act, and state constitutional requirements governing general-obligation bond issues. See Chester Hartman, Yerba Buena: Land Grab and Community Resistance in San Francisco 23–27 (1974), updated in Chester Hartman, The Transformation of San Francisco (1984).

Judges seem to be particularly willing to find violations of statutory constraints when a local government is seeking to condemn a small area for a use that many other available sites could satisfy. See, e.g., City of Los Angeles v. Chadwick, 285 Cal. Rptr. 191 (Ct. App. 1991) (quashing forced assemblage of three lots for fire station); Board of Commissioners v. Intermountain Rural Electric Association, 655 P.2d 831 (Colo. 1982) (holding county could not exercise eminent domain power to acquire finished office space for district attorney and his staff).

2.   *The Metamorphosis of Urban Renewal: Tax-Increment Financing*

Bernard J. Frieden & Marshall Kaplan, The Politics of Neglect 24–25 (1975)[*]

Because urban renewal projects cleared blighted neighborhoods and rebuilt them with middle- and upper-income housing the program inevitably took more low-income housing off the market than it replaced. Further, because long delays were typical of the renewal process, many cleared sites remained vacant for years. As a result, the total impact was to reduce the housing supply in cities making use of the program. From 1949 through 1963, urban renewal demolished the housing of 177,000 families and another 66,000 single individuals, most of them poor and most of them black. During this period only 48,000 new housing units were completed in renewal projects, and another 18,000 were under construction; of this total, some 20,000 were low-rent public housing. Scott Greer summarized the results aptly in the opening sentence of his book on urban renewal "At a cost of more than three billion dollars the Urban Renewal Agency ... has succeeded in materially reducing the supply of low-cost housing in American cities."

. . . Social psychologist Marc Fried studied the aftermath of a 1958 clearance project in Boston's West End and found that half the displaced residents suffered from serious grief reactions and depression as much as two years later. Fried's research team also discovered that the city authorities covered their tracks: they reported to Washington that only 2 percent of the families had been relocated in physically substandard housing; yet Fried's independent survey revealed a figure of 25 percent. . . .

Note on the Demise of the Federal Urban Renewal Program

1. *Critics of urban renewal.* Urban renewal of the wholesale-clearance variety has been criticized on numerous grounds. Many detractors, like Frieden and Kaplan, deplore its usual distributive consequence: helping the rich at the expense of the poor, and whites at the expense of blacks. In her highly influential book, The Death and Life of Great American Cities (1961), Jane Jacobs emphasizes the inefficiency of tearing down fine-grained neighborhoods and replacing them with the coarse-grained conceptions of master planners. Other critics noted that, in many cities, urban renewal land tended to lie vacant for many years. See Jon C. Teaford, Urban Renewal and Its Aftermath, 11 Housing Pol'y Debate 443, 448–49 (2000) (citing examples in Buffalo, Los Angeles, St. Louis, and elsewhere). For assessments of the efficiency of urban renewal, compare Martin Anderson, The Federal Bulldozer (1964) (scathingly negative), with Jerome Rothenberg, Economic Evaluation of Urban Renewal (1967) (generally upbeat).

2. *The transfiguration of federal support for urban renewal.* During the 1960s, the federal urban renewal program was reshaped to deemphasize large-scale clearance and to put more stress on rehabilitation, citizen participation, and the construction of subsidized housing. Although these changes helped allay neighborhood opposition to urban renewal, they also tended to further prolong the time needed to produce results. The original 1949 version of urban renewal had required a city redevelopment agency to prepare a comprehensive plan for each redevelopment area and to submit it for detailed review by federal administrators. This format had proved unworkable by the late 1960s. The snail's pace at which renewal projects proceeded made comprehensive planning an exercise in frustration. In 1968, Congress recognized the rigidity of the comprehensive plan approach and authorized instead a system of "neighborhood development program" grants. Thereafter, to obtain federal funds, a renewal agency needed only to propose what it would do for the next year or two in a given renewal area, not what its detailed grand scheme was.

Eventually, even this amount of federal scrutiny over local decisions was deemed excessive. In 1974, with little fanfare, Congress terminated federal funding of future urban renewal projects. The 25-year-old program was folded into a special revenue-sharing program of "community development block grants" (described at p. 888). See John C. Weicher, The Fiscal Profitability of Urban Renewal under Matching Grants and Revenue Sharing,

3 J. Urb. Econ. 193 (1976) (concluding that cities will regard the typical urban renewal project of the past to be "a very poor investment" of block-grant funds).

The demise of the federal urban renewal program prompted many cities to turn to tax-increment financed (TIF) redevelopment, a technique that Minnesota had pioneered in 1947.

Wolper v. City Council of the City of Charleston
336 S.E.2d 871 (S.C. 1985)

NESS, Chief Justice:

Appellant Wolper brought this declaratory judgment action challenging the constitutionality of an ordinance enacted by the respondent City which authorizes a tax increment financing plan for the redevelopment of waterfront property within the City. The trial judge upheld the ordinance. We affirm.

Article X, §14(10) of the South Carolina Constitution authorizes municipalities to incur indebtedness for redevelopment within an incorporated municipality, with debt service to be provided from the increased increments of property tax revenue which result from the redevelopment project. The legislature subsequently enacted the Tax Increment Financing Law (the act), codified at S.C. Code Ann. §§31-6-10 to -120 (Supp. 1984), to establish authorization for municipalities to incur indebtedness to revitalize blighted and deteriorating areas within the municipalities.

Pursuant to the act, the City of Charleston enacted an ordinance authorizing a tax increment financing plan for the redevelopment of an area designated as the Cooper River Waterfront Redevelopment Project Area. The ordinance authorized redevelopment bonds to raise $4.6 million dollars, approximately fifteen percent of the total cost of the redevelopment project. Wolper raises [several] constitutional issues.

IMPAIRMENT OF CONTRACT RIGHTS

Article I, §4 of the South Carolina Constitution prohibits the enactment of any law which impairs the obligation of contract rights. Wolper asserts that the City has a contractual obligation to its general obligation bondholders to retire the general obligation bonds with the proceeds of ad valorem taxes. The redevelopment bonds are to be repaid from a special fund created by pooling the added increments of tax revenues which result from the increased property values in the redevelopment area. Wolper argues that the rights of the general obligation bondholders are impaired by the redevelopment bonds, since the increased revenue diverted for the repayment of the redevelopment bonds would have been available for the retirement of the general obligation bonds.

Before a tax increment redevelopment bond issue may be undertaken, there must be a finding that the property values in the targeted area are either static or in decline. S.C. Code Ann. §31-6-80(g)(iii) (Supp. 1984). The tax value of the property in the redevelopment area is frozen at a rate determined at the initiation of the bond issue. As redevelopment occurs, and property taxes in the area increase, the incremental increase in property tax is diverted to a special fund from which the redevelopment bonds will be retired. The frozen base portion of tax revenue on the redeveloped property is paid into the general fund for retirement of existing general obligation debt. Thus the same tax base is available for retirement of general obligation bonds during the redevelopment project as was available before the redevelopment bonds were issued.

The tax revenues from the redevelopment area would not have increased at all in the absence of the redevelopment project. The incremental increases which are diverted to the special fund have not affected the base ad valorem revenue, and consequently no impairment of contract rights has occurred. . . .

GENERAL OBLIGATION V. REVENUE BONDS

Municipalities are subject to a constitutional debt limitation for general obligation bonds which is based upon the assessed value of taxable property within the municipality. Article X, §14(7), South Carolina Constitution. Wolper argues the act contravenes this constitutional ceiling on general obligation debt. The trial judge held that redevelopment bonds issued pursuant to the act were not general obligation bonds, and therefore were not subject to the constitutional debt limitation. We agree.

Municipalities may incur two types of bonded indebtedness: (1) general obligation bonds, secured by the full faith, credit and taxing power of the municipality; and (2) indebtedness payable from a particular revenue-producing project or a special source. . . .

Tax increment redevelopment funding is expressly authorized by Article X, §14(10) of the South Carolina Constitution. The redevelopment debt is to be retired from a special source, i.e., the incremental increase of ad valorem taxes on property within the redevelopment area. In the event the property values in the redeveloped area do not increase, or increase at a slower rate than anticipated, the repayment of the redevelopment debt is negatively affected. The redevelopment bondholders may not look beyond the special fund for retirement of the debt. The bonds are not secured by the full faith, credit and taxing power of the municipality, and therefore cannot be classified as a general obligation debt. The debt limitation of Article X, §14(7) does not apply.

PUBLIC PURPOSE

The parties and the amicus curiae have strenuously argued whether the act, and the City's application of the act, contravene the constitutional requirements regarding public purpose. . . .

Article I, §3 requires that all legislation, including that authorizing the issuance of revenue bonds, serve a public purpose. Wolper argues the act, as applied by the City, is invalid in that the City's redevelopment plan is designed for the benefit of only private interests. . . .

By creating the act, the legislature declared the revitalization of blighted and deteriorating areas within the municipalities to be a public purpose. A determination of public purpose is primarily a question for the legislature. This Court will not interfere with that finding unless it is clearly wrong. State ex rel. McLeod v. Riley, 278 S.E.2d 612 (S.C. 1981).

We have recognized that the term public purpose is a fluid concept which eludes a precise definition. However, it includes the promotion of the "public health, safety, morals, general welfare, security, prosperity, and contentment" of our citizens. . . .

The elimination of decaying and unhealthy areas within a city directly benefits the public. The private parties who will eventually develop sites within the redevelopment area may benefit incidentally from the revitalization. However, an incidental benefit to private individuals is not fatal to a finding of public purpose. Johnson v. Piedmont Mun. Power Agency, 287 S.E.2d 476 (S.C. 1982). We have little hesitation in concluding that the public purpose declared by the act is a proper one.

The City's application of the act is directed toward revitalizing the waterfront area of downtown Charleston. Prior to the project, the area was characterized by rotted pilings, foundations of demolished buildings, and rubble-filled marsh areas. Much of the land was unusable and many of the structures that existed in the area were infested by rodents and other pests. Flooding was not uncommon. The City proposes to, among other things, build streets, sidewalks, utility lines, a drainage system, a public waterfront park and a marketplace. It is anticipated that the revitalization of the area will encourage private investment in an area that has been ignored and even avoided for many years by private investors. Not only will the redevelopment eliminate a health and safety threat to the City, it will significantly increase the tax base within the area. It is expected to stimulate growth and development in the areas immediately adjacent to the redevelopment area. We agree with the trial judge that the City's proposed plan envisions a public purpose.

CONCLUSION

Tax increment financing acts have been established and upheld by many states. See, e.g., People v. Crouch, 403 N.E.2d 242 (Ill. 1980). They allow local government officials to administer development without the restrictions which often accompany federal and state grants. See, Huddleston, A Comparison of State Tax Increment Financing Laws, 55 St. Gov't 1 (1982). South Carolina's Tax Increment Financing Act, as presently drawn, is constitutionally sound. The order of the trial judge is affirmed.

Note on Tax-Increment Financed Urban Renewal

1. *Popularity*. At least 47 states authorize municipalities to divert increments in property tax revenues in a defined area to finance improvements made there. See Colin Gordon, Blighting the Way, 31 Fordham Urb. L.J. 305, 314 (2004). Use of the TIF technique is particularly popular in California and the northern Midwest. See Richard Briffault, The Rise of Sublocal Structures in Urban Governance, 82 Minn. L. Rev. 503, 512–14 (1997).

2. *The mathematics of tax-increment financing*. A hypothetical example can clarify how tax-increment financing works. Suppose that in 1990, City were to have designated Area X for a tax-increment redevelopment project. Area X then contained real property assessed at $10 million on the property tax rolls. This $10 million would be the Area's "frozen" value. In 1990, City's annual property tax rate was 1 percent of assessed value. The County in which City was situated also imposed a 1 percent tax, and the School District (the only other local government taxing property in Area X) imposed a 2 percent tax. In 1990, owners of property in Area X thus would have paid a total of $400,000 ($10 million × 4 percent) in property taxes, of which City would have received $100,000, or one-quarter of the total.

Suppose by 2005 the assessed value of property in Area X had risen to $25 million — that is, $15 million above its frozen level. For simplicity, assume that the tax rates of the three taxing agencies were the same in 2005 as they had been in 1990. In 2005, Area X would be generating $1 million in property tax revenue ($25 million × 4 percent), up from $400,000 in 1990. A typical tax-increment statute would authorize City to devote the entire 2005 revenue increment of $600,000 to satisfy the claims of the investors who had purchased the bonds City had issued to finance improvements in Area X. Thus, in 2005, all local taxing authorities would continue to be receiving the revenues derived from their taxes on the frozen value, but revenues from *all* governments' taxes on the incremental value would be flowing entirely to City until its TIF bonds had been retired. This formula produces some rather odd results. For example, if County were to raise its tax rate, its new rate would be applied to both the frozen value (increasing County's revenues) and also to the increment (increasing City's urban renewal funds).

Tax-increment financing appears to rest on the assumption that the renewal project creates the entire increment in the area's land value. If that were true, one could justify a city's being able to capture all the benefits of its redevelopment efforts. But the assumption commonly is partly, if not entirely, false. In an inflationary economy, land values tend to rise in all urban renewal areas — even in those where public redevelopment programs were utterly misconceived. In light of the powerful impact of inflation, tax-increment financing can provide a city an almost surefire way to drain the treasuries of overlapping governments. For example, even if inflation alone had pushed the assessed value of Area X up to $25 million in 2005, the tax-increment device would have increased City's share of property tax revenues raised there from 25 percent in 1990 ($100,000 ÷ $400,000) to 70 percent in 2005 ($700,000 ÷ $1,000,000). The losers would be the taxpayers of County lying outside City. The availability of tax-increment financing thus may create a Prisoners' Dilemma (see p. 37, note 14): Cities are pushed by immediate self-interest to use the program, but each city's residents might be better off if no city were to use it.

3. *Judicial reception.* As *Wolper* indicates, tax-increment projects generally have enjoyed smooth legal sailing. See, e.g., In re Bunker Hill Urban Renewal Project 1B, 389 P.2d 538 (Cal. 1964) (consent of other taxing agencies that lose revenue on account of tax-increment project is not required); Princeton City School District Board of Education v. Zaino, 760 N.E.2d 375 (Ohio 2002) (rejecting multiple challenges to tax increment financing scheme). Cases of this sort sometimes are friendly lawsuits initiated by the redevelopment agencies themselves to clear up legal ambiguities and thus enhance market demand for tax-increment bonds. But see, e.g., Boone County v. Cooke, 475 S.E.2d 483 (W. Va. 1996) (holding TIF statute violated state constitutional restriction on debt).

4. *Source of popularity.* Central-city politicians, downtown commercial interests, and construction industry lobbyists generally support urban redevelopment projects. See John H. Mollenkopf, The Contested City (1983) (on the "pro-growth coalitions" that backed renewal efforts in Boston, San Francisco, and elsewhere). Many renewal projects, however, are not cost-justified. See Richard F. Dye & David F. Merriman, The Effects of Tax Increment Financing on Economic Development, 47 J. Urb. Econ. 306 (2000) (finding that cities that adopt TIF grow more slowly than those that do not). Supporters of a wasteful public project may benefit from using financing methods that are opaque and relatively immune from legislative oversight. To what extent does the stealth of tax increment financing explain its popularity?

3.   *Land Assembly by Private Firms*

b/c of risk of holdouts

It is widely thought that the risk of holdouts is likely to frustrate an entrepreneur who seeks to assemble many separately owned parcels without aid of eminent domain. The authors of the Model Land Development Code §§5-201 to -202 (1976) therefore favored authorizing a state agency to condemn outparcels at the request of a private developer who already owned 60 percent of a qualifying development site. (Constitutional, in light of *Kelo*?) The remarkable article that follows sheds light on the wisdom of this recommendation.

See article.

Peter Hellman, How They Assembled the Most Expensive Block in New York's History
New York, Feb. 25, 1974, at 31

One Saturday morning in September, 1968, two well-tailored men got out of a cab at the southeast corner of Lexington Avenue and 54th Street in front of the old St. Peter's Lutheran Church. They walked slowly south, out of step with the heavy pedestrian traffic, past Save-Mor Drugs, Anthony's Restaurant, Lexington Sandwich Shoppe, the American and Foreign Magazine Center, Pizza Plaza, Carroll's Pub, Trefner's, and the Howard Johnson's snack counter on the corner. In front of each, they took notes.

Turning east at 53rd, they did the same in front of the liquor shop, the Blarney Stone bar, and the seedy building next door on whose first floor was the superb Café Chauveron. Where they could, they took down names on lobby mailboxes. At Third Avenue they turned north, walking more quickly, then headed back toward Lexington on 54th Street. Again they took notes in front of each building. They stopped for a long time in front of the Medical Chambers, the handsome but dowdy doctors' building in the middle of the block. They continued past pleasant brownstones until they were back in front of three-spired, Gothic St. Peter's. They looked at it the longest of all.

[St. Peter's had hired] the real estate brokerage and consultation firm of Julien J. Studley, Inc., . . . to analyze the value of their property. Studley had a reputation for thorough and often imaginative research and its monthly report on office rentals in major cities was studied for trends by brokers and builders. Two polished young brokers, Don Schnabel and his associate, Charles McArthur, worked on the St. Peter's project. They had a pretty good idea of what the church property would fetch in the hot market of 1968. But the best guess was no substitute for a parcel-by-parcel analysis of the block. That was what Schnabel and McArthur began that September morning.

[The church was not] tempted by what Schnabel felt was the realistic selling price of $300 per square foot, or $4.5 million for its 15,000-foot plot. But Schnabel was thinking one step further. Suppose he could assemble all the Lexington Avenue frontage on the block and also get some depth on 53rd and 54th Streets? To the developer of a mighty office tower, each parcel in an assemblage might be worth twice what a single parcel was worth by itself.

Land assemblage, though, was perilous. No matter how quietly parcels were picked up, no matter how many dummy buyers fronted for the real interests, word would soon leak out. Then the remaining owners would dig in. Knowing it would be costly for the assembler to give up midway, they would make him pay dearly for the right to finish the job. Even the secret purchasers of the tract for Disney World had run into this problem in the Florida swampland. Here in Manhattan, it could get far more brutal. If an assemblage could be completed on a prime midtown block it would be fabulously profitable for the developer, for the broker, who stood to make whopping commissions, and most of all, for a keystone seller like St. Peter's.

Only the church was not yet a seller. But Schnabel thought that if St. Peter's were offered, say, double $300 per square foot, or $9 million for its property, it might reconsider.

So far as Schnabel knew, this block was as good as any to try to assemble. Of 31 parcels, most had not changed hands in twenty years. If someone else was thinking about an assemblage here, he had not yet started. But the Studley firm could not handle such a project itself. That was for Tishman, Uris, Fisher Brothers, or any of the other giants that had the resources to buy costly parcels one by one and to hold on for years until they were ready to build. If Schnabel was going to try to assemble the block, his firm needed a client.

Schnabel posed the problem late one evening to his partner, Julien Studley, an easy-going, superbly cultured man, fluent in six languages, whose family had fled the Nazis from Belgium to Havana, then brought him to New York as a teenager.

"Who could we approach on this assemblage?" Schnabel asked.

"Who's across the street?" asked Studley.

"Headquarters of First National City Bank."

"Let's ask them."

Schnabel and McArthur went to the bank cold. They were passed to a senior vice-president named Bob Graham. Would the bank be interested in the block across the street? After months of meetings, the answer was a cautious yes. As for why it wanted the block, the bank admitted to needing more space. But a more accurate explanation was left unspoken. In recent years, F.N.C.B. had begun to challenge the Chase Manhattan Bank in size, profits, and general oomph. Yet Citicorp had no architectural showplace to rival the Chase Manhattan Plaza downtown.

In June, 1969, what Studley describes as a "straightforward, almost primitive" contract was drawn up. It provided that the firm would attempt to assemble the block for the bank, and it would be paid a standard commission on each parcel. If the initial spadework indicated the assemblage was not feasible, the bank would pay Studley a research fee for his trouble.

It all had to be done in total secrecy, of course. A big developer could always go somewhere else if an assemblage got bogged down, but the bank wanted to be right across the street. Both Studley and the bank agreed to keep to a minimum the number who would know of the project. That was easy at Studley's main office on Madison Avenue. With a staff of 60, the firm had short and informal decision lines. But, astonishingly, at the bank, a publicly owned organization of 40,000 employees, not more than a half-dozen people would ever hear about this project.

Schnabel now set up a company called Lexman Realty. He was vice-president; Studley, president. That was public record. The name of its sole stockholder, the bank, was not. Now Schnabel was ready to make his first probe on the block. Where should it be? Getting the Lexington Avenue frontage was a must. But land cost would also be highest on the avenue. Why gamble high so soon? Besides, it was also too obvious, right across the street from the bank. The probe would best be made on 53rd or 54th Streets. [See Figure 10-1.]

Schnabel's eye settled on 139 East 53rd Street, a four-story walk-up whose ground floor Roger Chauveron had elevated to what some followers of haute cuisine called glory. It had not been easy. Most of the city's great French restaurants were located between Park and Madison. Here, east of Lexington, the Blarney Stone next door hardly helped. By hard work alone Roger Chauveron had made his restaurant a success. He would not give it up easily. But as it happened, it took only one meeting with Chauveron and his accountant partner Albert Kaiser to determine that the Café Chauveron's lease could be bought out. Now Schnabel went to the owner of the building, a broker named Vitagliano.

"Sorry," Vitagliano said, shaking his head. "I just made a contract to sell."

"May I ask with whom?"

"A fellow named Manny Duell."

Schnabel went up to Duell's tiny office on Park Avenue. A paunchy man with thinning black hair, Duell smiled at Schnabel with an old-country sharpness.

"Not only do I hold a contract to buy Chauveron," he said, "I also hold contracts to buy the buildings on each side."

Schnabel was not about to take Duell's word for it, of course. Getting the first whiff of an assemblage, Duell might be planning to tie up those very properties he claimed he already held as soon as Schnabel left his office. To check it out, Schnabel decided to

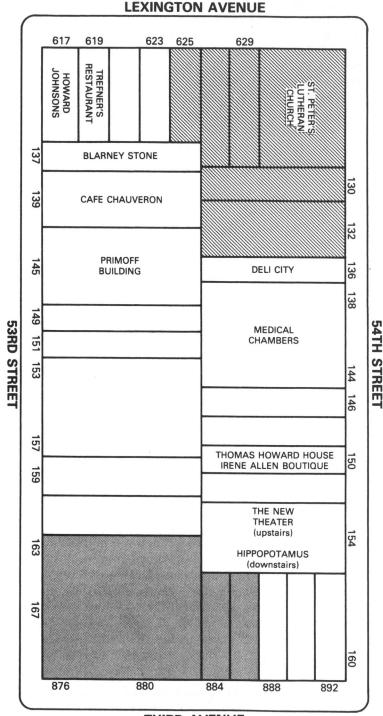

LEXINGTON AVENUE

THIRD AVENUE

FIGURE 10-1
"The Most Expensive Block in New York's History"

[The property originally owned by St. Peter's Lutheran Church is indicated by ▨▨▨. The parcels not acquired in the assemblage are indicated by ▓▓▓. — Eds.]

848

quietly ask the owner of the small apartment house at No. 145, sharing the east wall of Café Chauveron, if his building was for sale. The owner was an accountant named Morris Primoff.

"Gee," said Primoff, "I just made a deal."

Schnabel did not bother to ask the owner of the Blarney Stone if he too had sold a contract. Duell appeared to check out on two out of three. He probably did have three out of three. Schnabel was depressed. His careful research had shown no turnovers in decades. Now, on his very first probe, he was smack up against a smart fellow who, one step ahead, had carried off a mini-assemblage of his own.

Schnabel went back to the bank to see if it wanted him to dicker with Duell. It did. They parried through the summer.

"Who is this Lexman," Duell kept asking. "Is it Uris . . . Fisher Brothers . . . maybe Tishman? . . ."

"Manny," intoned Schnabel, "all you have to know is that my money is green."

His money was green. On August 13, 1969, Schnabel and Duell sat down with their lawyers to sign a deal. To be exact, Lexman was buying the purchase agreements that Duell had himself signed with the owners of the three buildings. Under standard real estate procedure, months or even a year may go by between the signing of this contract and the actual conveying of the deed. The buyer uses this time to "search" the title to be sure the seller in fact owns the property he is selling. For his part, the seller can check out the credit of the buyer. In the Lexman account at the F.N.C.B. branch at 42nd Street and Madison Avenue, Duell found a balance in excess of $2 million.

Schnabel was sure Duell would clear a handsome profit on the three contracts. Just how handsome, he did not realize until they sat down at the table. Duell had bought the Primoff property for $1.25 million. He was selling to Lexman for $2.28 million. What really surprised Schnabel, though, was the date Duell had signed with Primoff: July 25. That was almost a month after Primoff said he had "made a deal." He would be sorry now. By turning away Schnabel so quickly, he had cleared the way for Duell to make $1 million on a contract which Duell had held for exactly nineteen days.

Across the table now, Duell was beaming. In front of Schnabel, he could see a Lexman check filled in with a number ending in many zeros.

"Manny," said Schnabel, "just one thing. If you want me to take over these contracts, I need to know you are going to stay off the block from this point on. I don't want you popping up on the other side with more contracts. I want this to be good-by, Manny."

"Don't you worry, Don. I'll be off the block."

"And I want your partners, your cousins, and anyone else fronting for your interests to stay off, too."

"I promise," said Duell.

"I believe you Manny," said Schnabel. "As a token of your good faith, I'm sure you won't mind signing over to me a $300,000 mortgage on one of the buildings you own. Maybe that nice one at 530 Sixth Avenue. We'll put it in escrow. If you stay off the block for eighteen months, it reverts to you."

Manny Duell blanched. He jumped up and shook his fists. He swore he would never, never do such a thing. But Schnabel could see that even as Manny was leaping about and ranting, his eyes were fixed on the check with all the zeros. Schnabel waited. When Duell calmed down, the mortgage belonged to Lexman.

From the dates on the contract for the Chauveron parcel, Schnabel could see that Duell actually had signed that deal when he said he had. But the deal for the Blarney Stone property, like Primoff's, was contracted well after Duell said it was. Just the same, Schnabel felt Duell had earned that one. The seller had been the partnership of Sol Goldman and

Alex DiLorenzo, the toughest dealers in town. Predictably, Duell had not cleared nearly as much on the resale of that contract as he had on Primoff's. . . .

Schnabel now had to move fast. The first title would be conveyed to Lexman in six months. It would be recorded then at the registrar's office. Brokers who regularly check those title transfers would see that action was beginning on the block. From the tax stamps affixed to the deed, they would also know what Lexman had paid. In the interim, Schnabel would have to nail down as many parcels as he could. The bank agreed that the next beach-head should be established on Lexington Avenue. The spot they picked was a restaurant named Trefner's. Eva Trefner had run it for over twenty years. They felt she would be ready to give it up. She was. But she was also hesitant.

"If I go, what will happen to my people?" she asked, motioning at the scurrying waiters and busboys. "They have families to support."

"If you go," said Schnabel, "I promise we'll operate the place for at least a year with the same staff."

Reassured, Eva Trefner sold her restaurant. Before she left for Florida, she divided a portion of the proceeds among her most faithful employees. The checks were not tokens. They went as high as $25,000. Trefner's did not close up for eighteen more months. Around the corner, Roger Chauveron hung on for almost as long after Lexman bought out his lease for $300,000. Soon after, he reopened in Miami Beach.

With his beachheads secure on 53rd Street and on Lexington, Schnabel now focused on the 54th Street flank. It was lined mostly with brownstones, except for the Medical Chambers, jointly owned by 40 doctors. Prosperous and secure, they would be hell to buy out. [Schnabel therefore first bought a brownstone next door.]

Now it was fall. The time had come for Schnabel to see if St. Peter's could be induced to sell its property.

"All I can reveal about my client," he told Dr. Peterson [the pastor], "is that it is listed on the N.Y.S.E., it has assets in excess of $500 million, and it is not, I believe, in a business objectionable to you, like liquor or war munitions."

Dr. Peterson was charming and shrewd, but terrestrial real estate was not his line. So the church hired John White, president of the real estate consulting firm of James D. Landauer Associates, to negotiate for it. White was made to understand that the church was committed to staying at the center of the city. Yet it also needed a better facility for the new demands on it.

Was it possible for the church and Lexman's client to be satisfied all around? The answer slid over White like a lover: make the office tower a condominium. On the plaza in front, sell the church back its own corner. It would get a deed to its part of the whole just like an apartment owner in a residential condominium. If St. Peter's wanted to be "more human in skyscrapers," and if Lexman's client wanted a distinction shared by no other office tower in town, this was their chance. . . .

In February, 1970, St. Peter's signed a "letter of intent" to sell its church to Lexman's unnamed client for $9 million. It would get a new, bigger church of its own design on the same corner. At least 66 percent of the structure was to be free standing, with nothing but sky overhead. The projected cost of the church was $5.5 million. With interest on the original $9 million, that would leave over $4 million for St. Peter's expanding programs. All this was possible only through the condominium arrangement.

Besides not wanting to sell to an objectionable company, St. Peter's was also concerned, obviously, that no horrors be perpetrated on residential tenants who were being forced off the block. The bank was possibly even more concerned on that point. It had built a reputation as the most progressive big bank in town. It would hardly do for it to be associated with the image of palsied old ladies being hurled out of their homes.

handled residential tenants w/ care

The problem was real. As on almost any busy midtown block, residential tenants went unnoticed in the commercial crush. Many were poor and old. They usually did not come out ahead when the wreckers showed up. But in this case, they moved out with possibly less unpleasantness than in any similar project in the city's history of site clearings. This success owed more to psychology than money. Rather than send a terse notice to a pair of frail octogenarian sisters named Julia and Alyce Belora, for example, McArthur visited them personally to ask whether they had someplace to go.

"If we moved, it would be to our sister's place in California," said Alyce.

McArthur nodded. He ordered the best moving service he could find to follow their packing instructions exactly. He sent them two first-class airline tickets to Los Angeles. He sent a limousine to take them to the airport. The sisters loved it. They left without asking for a cash buy-out, and they sent a thank-you note from California.

An odd challenge was presented by a man who lived in a rooming house on 54th Street just off Third Avenue. He was paying $6.90 a week for a small room, linens included. He was a devout member of the Church of the Living God. Following Biblical examples, he walked to the East River each evening so that he could pray by the water.

"I'll never move," he said. "Not until God tells me."

Schnabel sent a $500 donation to his church in the man's name. God told him to move.

It was not as easy to deal with Thomas Howard, a middle-aged bachelor who had lived for 22 years in the town house he owned at 150 East 54th Street.

"They'll carry me out of here in a pine box," he told Charles McArthur.

Howard was not in good health. He had no dependents. He hardly ever left the house. When he did, he usually rented a limousine. He apparently had enough money to take care of his wants. Why should he sell? But McArthur gently persisted. He often visited Howard as he lay in bed in his purple bedroom, the walls covered with old paintings, the floor crawling with small asthmatic dogs. One evening McArthur brought over slides from his vacation in Portugal. Howard was a lonely man.

"Come often, Charlie," he said, "as long as it's only social. Because I'm never going to sell."

. . . A year, then two, went by. Finally, Studley felt the time had come to make a deal now or never.

"We'll draw up a contract," McArthur told Howard. "It'll be good for 48 hours. The line for the purchase price will be blank. Fill it in with a number you think is right. We'll say yes or no in those 48 hours. If we say no, Tom, I promise you'll never be bothered by us again."

Howard inserted the figure $815,000 in the blank. The bank took it. Howard now lives in a brownstone on East 35th Street.

Two doors down from Howard, at No. 154, Schnabel got into a nasty situation. Upstairs was the "New Theater." Downstairs, marked only by a small brass plaque, was Olivier Coquelin's trendy night spot, Hippopotamus. Both leases specified that the tenants had to get out within six months if the building was sold. Schnabel had no trouble buying the building. He was in no hurry to get either tenant out.

"You can keep on doing business for at least a year," he explained. "But you must agree to get out on 30 days' notice when my client is ready to demolish."

"Fair enough," said the owners of the New Theater.

"Go to hell," said Olivier Coquelin.

It took a team of marshals under court order to finally padlock Hippopotamus, which continued to ignore its new landlord. The theater owners, who had been cooperative, continued to operate for another season.

The big prize on 54th Street, of course, was the Medical Chambers. But the prospects for making a deal with its 40 prosperous doctor-owners did not look promising at first. Late in 1969, knowing that in their tax brackets a cash offer would not be especially tempting, Schnabel had proposed to the doctors' board of directors that they swap their building for a bigger, nicer one renovated to their specifications. The doctors responded by firing their board for even discussing the matter.

The next board was authorized to talk with Schnabel to the extent of rejecting an offer of $4 million for their building. On behalf of his client, Schnabel then offered to build a brand-new Medical Chambers building at the corner of 54th Street and Third Avenue. They could stay in their old place until it was ready. The doctors said no.

As the negotiations dragged into a third year, the doctors learned that their suitor was the bank. Despairing of ever making a deal with them, the bank suggested they hire John White to represent them as well as St. Peter's. An easily bored man, White sat through many meetings with the doctors, trying not to look numb as they lectured him in detail on real estate strategy. He understood that they were not interested in selling out for cash. Unlike the church, they would lose most of their profits to taxes. Was there a way for them to make big money and keep it?

Suddenly, the solution occurred to him. Citicorp was a stock company. So was the Medical Chambers. Why not merge them? In an exchange of stock, the doctors would get Citicorp shares which would not be taxed until they were sold. Even then, they or their children would pay no more than the maximum capital gains tax of 25 percent. On June 12, 1973, three and a half years after the doctors first said no, the S.E.C.-registered merger of the 3,000-share Medical Chambers and the 120-million-share Citicorp was consummated. For each dollar of their stock, the doctors got at current market value $24 in Citicorp shares. Over the summer, those shares performed strongly. By October 1, the day they had agreed to vacate, the doctors' $24 had turned into almost $30.

Cantankerous as they were, the doctors were not the most difficult owners on the block. That honor went to two children, heirs to an estate, who owned the shoddy building at the corner of Lexington and 53rd. It was leased to a liquor store, an optometrist, and Howard Johnson's snack counter.

The children were represented by a lawyer named Gloria Del Vecchio. She soon became known simply as the "Executrix." In the fall of 1969, she explained to Schnabel that her wards had secured a steady income from the busy stores. Why should she sell on their behalf? To invest in stocks or bonds? The best of them would not yield a rate of return as high as the children got from the commercial leases. Why indeed should she sell? They both knew the answer. She would sell as soon as the price was high enough to give the children more income than they were getting then.

Six months after bargaining began, Schnabel and the Executrix finally met to sign a purchase agreement on April 23, 1970. She had been tough. The price per square foot was the highest they had yet paid. But at least, Schnabel thought, the leases will all soon run out. I won't have to buy any tenant out for huge sums. But at the signing, the Executrix had a surprise for him.

"By the way, Don," she said casually. "Last fall, before I ever thought I'd be selling, the fellow from the liquor store and the optometrist came to ask me for a lease extension on their stores. I gave it to them."

"How long do the leases run?" Schnabel asked evenly.

"Twelve years."

"Oh," said Schnabel. He was furious. If the lease extension had been for as much as two years, it would have been barely tolerable. But twelve years? He was trapped; the assemblage was too far along now to stop, and the Executrix knew it.

Schnabel was not any happier to learn, a few days later, that it was not the optometrist and liquor store owner who had asked for twelve-year leases, as the Executrix had claimed. Instead, a totally new master lease had been given to a chunky, smiling man named Sam Salerno, operating as P.F.A. Enterprises, Inc. Every few days, he came to stand in front of the building and look benignly across the way at the current Citicorp headquarters. He also watched as, one by one, the wrecker's ball took down the buildings on the block. He did not look like a man in a hurry to sell out his lease. The bank was in no hurry, either. If necessary, it could build around Sam Salerno.   *bank to build*

On July 24, 1973, the bank formally announced it would build Citicorp Center, a 46-story tower on ten-story stilts. St. Peter's would occupy 45,000 square feet of the front plaza. Of shining aluminum and dark glass, the center would be topped off by a thrusting plane at a 45-degree angle. It would be every bit as impressive as the Chase Manhattan Plaza, maybe more so. . . .

. . . [Sam Salerno] knew the bank wasn't kidding when it said it would build around him. But he also knew they didn't want to. As a street-wise man, it must have amazed him that this mighty bank, which after all owned the building, did not simply order a bulldozer to flatten it one night. But he knew they did not operate by that code. At the end of the year, the bank bought out P.F.A.'s lease for $385,000. It had now paid a total of $40 million, the highest ever for one block of city land.

Now, five and a half years after Schnabel and McArthur first walked the block, its sixteen owners are gone. The ground has been paved over for temporary parking. Any day, the excavation for the unique venture of bank tower and church will begin. The city of dreams and deals renews itself.

Note on Land Assembly Without Eminent Domain

1. *Postscript.* St. Peter's new church and Citicorp's office tower opened in late 1977 to good notices from architecture critics. See, e.g., N.Y. Times, Oct. 12, 1977, at 39.

2. *Holdouts.* How great was the risk that the Citicorp assemblage would be thwarted? See generally Andrew Alpern & Seymour Durst, Holdouts! (1984). Assembling land certainly calls for patience. In one extreme case, Seymour Durst and his son Douglas spent 36 years acquiring all 32 parcels of a Manhattan block at 42nd Street and Broadway. In 2003, Douglas bought the final two parcels for approximately $380 per square foot, thought to be a record high price. Charles V. Bagli, Durst Gets Land to Build Tower Near Times Square, N.Y. Times, Dec. 19, 2003, at B3.

Other assemblages move much faster. In 1976, New Jersey legalized casino gambling in Atlantic City, but only in hotels offering at least 500 rooms and full convention facilities. Although casino developers needed large sites, ownership of land was highly fractionated in the small district that Atlantic City had zoned for casinos. Developers nevertheless had assembled a number of appropriate sites by 1978. In several instances, assemblers balked at meeting the asking prices of owners of key parcels and started construction around those holdouts. See, e.g., L.A. Times, Nov. 17, 1979, §1-A, at 4 (describing how the owner of a boardinghouse on a 2,000-square-foot lot had turned down an offer of $1.5 million).

In U.S. Journal: Atlantic City, N.J., New Yorker, Jan. 8, 1979, at 44, Calvin Trillin describes a creative effort by a real estate firm to assemble 72 residential lots on a beachfront block in Atlantic City. The assembler publicly offered to pay the owner of each house $100,000, provided that the owners of all 72 agreed to sell. Because the houses would have sold for no more than $15,000 five years earlier, most owners were tempted by the $100,000 offer. Neighborhood pressure on holdouts increased as the developer's deadline approached. At the time of Trillin's report, three holdouts remained — all of them absentee owners, whose unavailability would make them relatively immune to neighborhood pressure.

Examples of ambitious and largely successful private assemblages of exurban lands include Disney World (west of Orlando) and Columbia (a "new town" that the Rouse Company starting developing in the 1960s south of Baltimore).

3. *Voluntary coordination among homeowners to abet land assembly.* Owners of houses in a subdivision situated near a new expressway interchange or rapid transit station occasionally initiate their own assemblages. Homeowners are likely to be better able than a developer both to bring informal pressure to bear on holdouts and to lobby the municipality to rezone the assembled land for denser development. See Thomas A. Clary & Paul W. Rasmussen, The Buyout Phenomenon, Planning, Oct. 1985, at 18, an article featuring a homeowner-initiated sale of 22 houses in Arlington, Virginia, for a total of about $10 million; William E. Schmidt, Homeowners Unite in Selling to Developers, N.Y. Times, Jan. 16, 1985, at 1, which describes an assemblage and sale of 144 homes north of Atlanta for $35 million. In the latter instance, the neighborhood took nearly two years to reach consensus. Said one participant, "The real story is how you manage to get 144 people to agree to let three of their neighbors negotiate the sale of their homes."

4. *Land readjustment by supermajority?* As the drafters of the Model Land Development Code have suggested (see p. 845), to overcome the holdout problem, a legislature could authorize the owners of a supermajority of the land in a given area to force holdouts to join in a common endeavor to consolidate the territory. There are numerous historical precedents for powers of this sort. In England, for example, enclosure statutes enacted beginning in 1545 helped enable landowners to assemble the tiny planting strips of a traditional open-field village and then to resubdivide the whole into larger farms accessible via new roadways. See Frank A. Sharman, An Introduction to the Enclosure Acts, 10 J. Legal Hist. 45 (1989). A number of nations, notably Germany, Japan, and South Korea, currently authorize analogous land-readjustment procedures that are used primarily in cities and at the urban fringe. Advocates of importing the technique include George W. Liebmann, Land Readjustment for America: A Proposal for a Statute, 32 Urb. Law. 1 (2000), and Michael M. Shultz & Frank Schnidman, The Potential of Land Readjustment in the United States, 22 Urb. Law. 197 (1990). How would such a statute have to be drafted to survive challenges based on the state and federal public use clauses?

5. *Is condemnation ever advisable?* Patricia Munch, An Economic Analysis of Eminent Domain, 84 J. Pol. Econ. 473 (1976), concludes that forced sales probably are less efficient than consensual sales in the assembly of sites for urban redevelopment.

Could a government assemble through consensual transactions a site for a major airport, limited-access highway, or lake behind a dam? Political opponents of the development of Narita Airport, Tokyo's main international terminal, forced the Airport Authority to acquire the farmlands at the site solely by means of consensual sales. The authority began planning its purchases in 1965 and, by 1997, had acquired over 99 percent of the relevant land area. Because of strategically located holdout parcels, however, it was then operating just one runway. See Sheryl WuDunn, Airfield Swallowing Potato Fields, in Tiny Bites, N.Y. Times, Aug. 26, 1997, at A4. After further acquisitions, in 2002, the authority opened a second runway at Narita, but one barely more than half the length of the first and inadequate for accommodation of jumbo jets. To what extent does this tale support Calabresi & Melamed's analysis of when a landowner merits only liability-rule protection? See pp. 532–33.

4. *Just Compensation*

O'Donnell v. State
370 A.2d 233 (R.I. 1977)

KELLEHER, Justice.

On May 13, 1971, the plaintiffs, Eleanor and James O'Donnell, owned a farm called "Ye Homestead" consisting of 34.69 acres of land, a 10-room typical New England farmhouse, a two-car garage, a cement block structure, several outbuildings, and a well that produced 30 gallons of water per minute. The farm was situated in the town of North Smithfield and fronted on the northern side of Pound Hill Road for a distance of 690 feet. Mr. O'Donnell used a portion of the land as experimental turf plots, on which he tested various fertilizer compounds derived from sewer sludge. He hoped that his research efforts would reach the point where some governmental agency would approve O'Donnell's final product as a new marketable fertilizer. The cement block structure was a converted barn, which he called a "pilot plant." There Mr. O'Donnell produced small quantities of compounds that he was applying to the turf plots. Hopefully, the "pilot plant" was to be a prototype of the fertilizer production facility of the future.

Unfortunately for the O'Donnells, the Director of Public Works had other plans for their grassy fields, and on May 13, he took appropriate steps to condemn approximately 2.3 acres of the O'Donnell farm. This acreage, which is now part of a state highway called North Smithfield Industrial Drive, was situated at the southwest corner of their land, and it included a substantial portion of the frontage, the well, and about 75 percent of the turf plots. In November 1974 a nonjury trial on the question of damages was held before a justice of the Superior Court, who in due course awarded the O'Donnells $101,100 in damages. Both parties have appealed.

Mr. O'Donnell is a chemist who has long been engaged in fertilizer research. From 1953 to 1960 he conducted fertilizer experiments on the turf plots at Ye Homestead. Having received numerous patents for a marketable product, he terminated the project and joined Hercules, Inc. After a brief sojourn with Hercules, Mr. O'Donnell returned to Rhode Island to begin anew.

Back at Ye Homestead Mr. O'Donnell began to prepare his turf plots for sewer sludge experimentation. During his time with Hercules, the plots had been "dormant," growing only ornamental shrubbery. In 1963 and 1964 various plantings were made, and the crops were plowed under. In the fall of 1964 Mr. O'Donnell seeded the experimental design. From 1964 to 1967 the plots were further treated to establish a "mature stand," a uniform turf grass plot suitable for experimentation. Mr. O'Donnell testified that this process was designed to "bleed-out" of the soil the excess nitrogen which had accumulated during the nitroform experiments and that "bleeding-out" had to be completed in order for the turf plots to have any further experimental use. In 1967 the land had reached the maturation point and was finally ready for the sewer sludge experiment. . . .

The experiment was in full swing from 1967 to 1971. During that period Mr. O'Donnell manufactured various sewer sludge compounds and applied these organic nitrogen fertilizers to the turf plots in varying degrees and patterns. For 4 years data was duly accumulated. A real estate appraiser who testified for the O'Donnells estimated the value of the data at the time of the completion of the experiment to be approximately 5 million dollars. However, at the time of condemnation Mr. O'Donnell was still experimenting with the soil. He had not reached the point where he had developed an environmentally compatible fertilizer. Such an accomplishment was years away. . . .

On the whole, the trial justice, in adopting most of the estimates presented by the O'Donnells' expert, concluded that the turf plots, the pilot plant, and fixtures therein had great value.

The director, on the other hand, had little regard for the plots, the pilot plant, or its fixtures. His real estate expert saw the turf plots when covered with snow and never even went inside the pilot building. The expert ignored the turf plots and the pilot building because, in his opinion, they were part of a business venture of an experimental nature for which no compensation should be paid.

It is well-established that in a condemnation proceeding a property owner is entitled to just compensation for the fair market value of the property as of the date of taking. . . . While the preferred method of determining fair market value is the comparable sales approach, it is within the trial justice's discretion to depart from this method where he finds that the subject property is unique or has a special purpose.

The director has argued at great length that because Mr. O'Donnell was conducting a business, he should not be compensated. We agree wholeheartedly that Mr. O'Donnell . . . was conducting a business. But this does not dispose of the issue. While there can be no compensation for the intangibles of business, for loss of good will or future profits, 4 Nichols, Eminent Domain §13.3 at 13-148.2, 13-161 (3d ed. 1976), there is compensation for land which has a special function. Thus, a gravel pit may in fact be a business, but the land is nonetheless assessed as property adapted for a special use. See Bruce v. State of Rhode Island Dept. of Pub. Works, 177 A.2d 630 (R.I. 1962). It does not appear to us that the trial justice awarded damages for lost profits or good will; nor do we have trouble in theory with his granting damages for property developed as a turf research and design area (i.e., unique or special-purpose property).

We say "in theory" because it is clear that the trial justice misconceived or overlooked material evidence. He compensated the O'Donnells for the value of their turf plots as of 1967, the point at which they became mature stands, i.e., ripe for experimentation. He reasoned that the ". . . amount that the turf plots separate from the data would add to the fair market value of the land would seem to be fully established when the plots reach maturity." He further determined that based on the record as a whole the plots would not depreciate; nor would they appreciate apart from their value in yielding data. Thus, the 1967 value was key.

It may well be that such property would be unique, special-purpose, premium land for someone wanting to conduct turf research. However, there is no evidence that those plots still possessed that attribute on May 13, 1971, the day the condemnation plat was filed in the North Smithfield Town Hall. A purchaser at that point would be purchasing turf plots already subjected to 4 years of sewer sludge applications. Mr. O'Donnell testified at great length to the process of and necessity for bleeding-out the soil prior to any new experiment. He later testified that there would be nitrogen residue in the soil from this experiment. Indeed, he had intended to conduct a corollary experiment to determine just how great the nitrogen buildup would be. We fail to see how a 1971 purchaser could escape the need to bleed-out the soil before using these turf plots, just as Mr. O'Donnell had done in the 1960's. Thus, in May 1971 the turf plots no longer existed in their pristine 1967 state. By misinterpreting the nature of this evidence, the trial justice granted compensation based on value other than that of the condemnation date. This is clearly wrong. . . .

The trial justice also erred in his calculation of [severance] damages relating to the pilot plant and fixtures. His award is based on the premise that the plant would no longer function in its present use, that "[a]fter the taking . . . . structural changes . . . would be needed to fit it for other uses. . . ." Mr. O'Donnell testified that a great deal of his remaining property was not suited to turf research. However, he also testified that he was actively proposing a regional treatment plant in northern Rhode Island which would "encompass obtaining new turf plots." There was also testimony that the University of Rhode Island conducted various forms of turf research. The trial justice erred in assuming that the pilot plant could have no further use. Mr. O'Donnell could still use his laboratory for turf analysis and could produce sludge compounds for application to other turf plots. Once he established new turf plots or contracted for the use of other plots, his plant would be as useful as ever. Granted, the facility might stand unused for awhile, but we fail to see that Mr. O'Donnell met his burden of showing that the plant and fixtures were consequentially damaged. His problem was primarily one of relocating the turf plots. Long ago we said that when a business has to be moved and conducted at another location, any incidental loss or inconvenience to the business must be borne by the owner in the interest of the general public.

... [T]he case is remitted to the Superior Court for a new trial.[1]

APPENDIX

The O'Donnells' real estate expert, in estimating the severance damages suffered by his clients, gave an appraisal of each of the following items which, when totaled, gave a before-and-after condemnation value to Ye Homestead. He used the reproduction cost less depreciation approach in establishing the fair market value of the pilot plant and of the turf plots. [See Table 10-1 on p. 858.]

State v. Caoili
639 A.2d 275 (N.J. 1994)

HANDLER, J. . . .
Estrella and Frederico Caoili owned nearly an acre of land located near a highway in Dover Township. On July 15, 1989, the State of New Jersey, Commissioner of Transportation, filed a complaint to condemn the property for the purpose of constructing a "jug-handle" turn for a nearby highway. At that time the property was zoned for residential use. . . . A 262-foot border of the property ran along a highway on which were located a number of nearby commercial establishments, including a gas station, bank, and bus garage. . . .

At trial, the State moved to exclude the appraisal report of the owners' experts, Jon Brody and William Steinhart, on the ground that the evidence was insufficient to support their conclusion that a reasonable probability existed that the property would receive a zoning variance for commercial development. In their report, Brody and Steinhart valued the property at $445,000. They arrived at that figure by comparing the property to allegedly similar properties and estimating the value of the property based on the recent sale prices of those properties. The properties used for comparison in the Brody/Steinhart Report were all zoned for commercial use at the time of their sale. Brody and Steinhart justified the use of commercially-zoned property in their appraisal by claiming that a reasonable probability existed that the property would receive a use variance, which would allow the property to be used for a specific nonresidential purpose. In valuing the property, the experts discounted the sale prices of the comparison properties by ten percent to account for the fact that the

---

[1] EDS.: The new trial resulted in an award of $125,600, a judgment later affirmed on appeal. O'Donnell v. State, 474 A.2d 1244 (R.I. 1984).

TABLE 10-1

(1) Land without improvements		
Valuation before (34.69 acres)	$138,500	
Valuation after (32.39 acres)	127,000	
Damages (2.3 acres at $5,000/acre)		$11,500
(2) Dwelling, garage, driveway		
Valuation before	30,000	
Valuation after	29,000	
Damages		1,000
(3) Pilot Plant		
(a) *Building*		
Valuation before	30,000	
Valuation after	20,000	
Damages[1]		10,000
(b) *Fixtures*		
Valuation before	66,000	
Valuation after	13,000	
Damages[2]		53,000
(4) Well		
Valuation before	5,000	
Valuation after	3,000	
Damages		2,000
(5) Turf plots		
Valuation before[3]	154,000	
Valuation after	15,500	
Damages		138,500
Total Damages Sustained by the O'Donnells		$216,000

1. The expert felt that the inflationary trend since 1967 offset any depreciation.
2. No depreciation was applied because the expert felt that without the turf plots, the fixtures were only useful for salvage.
3. This figure represents the costs of developing and maintaining the turf plots from 1963 to 1971. Cost items included labor and materials. The expert emphasized that this appraisal represented the value of the plots as a special use property and did not represent the value of any possible data.

property had not yet obtained a zoning variance. [The trial judge denied the State's motion to exclude the Brody/Steinhart Report.]

At trial, Brody testified that "based on analyzing and looking at close to fifteen years worth of variances that had taken place in Dover Township," the property had a "very strong probability of obtaining a variance to utilize that parcel of land for something other than what it's presently zoned for."

One of the State's three witnesses, William Burke, testified that in his opinion the property had a fair market value at the time of the taking of $232,500. Burke arrived at that figure by comparing the property to allegedly similar properties, but the comparison properties used in Burke's appraisal were residential properties because he believed that a reasonable probability existed that the zoning for the property would remain residential. . . .

When the State exercises its power to take private property under the Eminent Domain Act, N.J.S.A. §§20:3-1 to -50, the State must pay the property owner just compensation for the property taken. N.J. Const. art. I, ¶20. Just compensation is "the fair market value of the property as of the date of the taking, determined by what a willing buyer and a willing seller would agree to, neither being under any compulsion to act." State v. Silver, 457 A.2d 463 (N.J. 1983). It is the "value that would be assigned to the acquired property by knowledgeable parties freely negotiating for its sale under normal market conditions based on all surrounding circumstances at the time of the taking." Id. at 463.

... The reasonableness of a use of condemned property, including its highest and best use, must be considered in light of any zoning restrictions that apply to the property. Hence, the zoning restrictions that govern the use of the property are material factors in determining its fair market value.

[The court then approvingly discussed prior case law.]

We remain convinced ... that allowing a factfinder to consider evidence of a zoning change that indicates at most that a change was not probable or only possible could lead to "unbridled speculation" regarding the fair market value of such property. . . . That risk can be reduced substantially if the determination of fair market value is based on more cogent evidence indicating beyond a mere possibility that a change of use is likely and, further, that such a change would be an important factor in the valuation of the property. . . .

In conclusion, we now hold ... that in determining the fair market value of condemned property as a basis for just compensation, the jury may consider a potential zoning change affecting the use of the property provided the court is satisfied that the evidence is sufficient to warrant a determination that such a change is reasonably probable. If evidence meets that level of proof, it may be considered in fixing just compensation in light of the weight and effect that reasonable buyers and sellers would give to such evidence in their determination of the fair market value of the property. . . .

We are satisfied that the methodology used by the owners' experts was reasonable. [The judgment of $351,000 in favor of the owners is affirmed.]

Note on Just Compensation

1. *Determining market value.* The Just Compensation Clause is construed to entitle a condemnee to recover the market value of property that the condemning government has taken. When possible, market value is estimated by examining sale prices of comparable property recently transferred between willing sellers and willing buyers. When like-sales data are difficult to obtain, as in the case of the O'Donnells' turf plots, market value is estimated either by capitalizing net income from the property in question or, in the case of land improvements, by using reproduction cost less depreciation. (Why might these two methods produce quite different results in *O'Donnell*?) Litigation over the size of a condemnation award typically ends up as a battle between expert witnesses.

2. *Some shortcomings of using loss of market value as a measure of compensation.* The legal system understandably rejects using the owner's subjective valuation of the condemned property as the standard for compensation because an owner might be tempted to exaggerate. However, the prevailing legal standard — market value — also has its shortcomings, at least when the loss of unique property is at issue. If transaction costs were zero, the owner of a unique piece of property would be the person who valued the property the most highly. To acquire the property, however, that person might be able to bid as little as the *value to the second highest user* plus a peppercorn. See James G. Durham, Efficient Just Compensation as a Limit on Eminent Domain, 69 Minn. L. Rev. 1277 (1985); Jack L. Knetsch & Thomas E. Borcherding, Expropriation of Private Property and the Basis for Compensation, 29 U. Toronto L.J. 237 (1979). In addition, cognitive psychologists have documented that, all else equal, an owner is likely to demand a higher price to be bought

out than a bidder is to offer to acquire something not owned. For a review of the literature, see Elizabeth Hoffman & Matthew L. Spitzer, Willingness to Pay vs. Willingness to Accept: Legal and Economic Implications, 71 Wash. U. L.Q. 59 (1993). One reason for this disparity is that a current owner, if forced to move, might lose site-specific good will or site-specific social capital. A condemnee also may incur consequential damages, such as moving expenses, that the standard formula for just compensation fails to include. Finally, a condemnee suffers a loss of autonomy — namely, the power to control *when* to sell. See Lee Anne Fennell, Taking Eminent Domain Apart, 2004 Michigan St. L. Rev. 957, 966–67. For all these reasons, equating landowner compensation with the market value of the acquired property results in less-than-full redress. See also pp. 837–38 (on proposals to augment compensation when a condemnor's public-use claim is doubtful).

Professor Merrill nevertheless suggests three possible rationales for incomplete compensation: reducing the costs of calculating awards, deterring landowners from making improvident investments, and subsidizing public actions. Thomas W. Merrill, Incomplete Compensation for Takings, 11 N.Y.U. Envtl. L.J. 110, 128–34 (2002). See generally Christopher Serkin, The Meaning of Value: Assessing Just Compensation for Regulatory Takings, 99 Nw. U. L. Rev. 677 (2005) (urging that compensation rules be shaped to advance the substantive purposes of takings law).

Should an owner of land be authorized to self-assess its value for purposes of both eminent domain compensation and property tax liability, provided that the owner also is willing to sell the property to any buyer who tenders the value the owner has set? For proposals in this vein, see Lee Anne Fennell, Revealing Options, 118 Harv. L. Rev. 1399 (2005); Saul Levmore, Self-Assessed Valuation Systems for Tort and Other Law, 68 Va. L. Rev. 771 (1982).

3. *Legislatures speak.* Persistent complaints about the inadequacy of compensation in eminent domain cases led to passage of the Uniform Relocation and Real Property Acquisition Policies Act of 1970, 42 U.S.C. §§4601–4655 (2004). The Act applies when the federal government takes land. It also set standards for compensation that state and local agencies must meet to be eligible for certain federal grants-in-aid. The Act has spurred the states to enact statutes meeting the federal requirements. See, e.g., Colo. Rev. Stat. §24-56-101 to -113 (2004). To comply with the Act, a state must reimburse a condemnee for reasonable moving expenses. In addition, the Act seeks to provide condemnees with certain bonus payments over the market value of the condemned property. In 2004, a displaced homeowner was eligible to receive up to $22,500 (and a tenant, up to $5,250) above market value to pay the costs of obtaining a "comparable" replacement dwelling. 42 U.S.C. §§4623–4624 (2004). (Is this formula self-contradictory? Defensible in light of owner's surplus?) When its programs are involved, the federal government reimburses state and local governments for most of these additional outlays. One analyst has concluded that, after the passage of the Act, displaced renters commonly are overcompensated. See Joseph J. Cordes, Compensation Through Relocation Assistance, 55 Land Econ. 486 (1979).

A statutory formula of course may not be ample enough to comport with the constitutional mandate of just compensation. See, e.g., Redevelopment Agency v. Gilmore, 214 Cal. Rptr. 904 (Cal. 1985) (condemnee is entitled to earn interest on precompensation value of taken property at market rate of interest, as opposed to lower statutory rate).

4. *Effects of governmental policy on market value.* In *Caoili*, the landowners were granted greater compensation on account of a probable future relaxation of zoning restrictions. In other contexts, however, a condemning government may succeed in introducing evidence that value of the claimant's land is lower than previous sales transactions might indicate because current buyers are anticipating that stricter regulations are in the offing. See, e.g., People v. Talleur, 145 Cal. Rptr. 150 (Ct. App. 1978) (holding trial court should

have admitted evidence of negative effects of California Coastal Commission's evolving policies on market value of undeveloped coastal land). On the other hand, a government cannot deliberately adopt an onerous regulation to reduce its subsequent costs of acquiring land. See p. 133.

Should a court accept evidence that a condemnee's parcel is worth less because it is vulnerable to a city's future exactions? In City of Porterville v. Young, 241 Cal. Rptr. 349 (Ct. App. 1987), the city was condemning a 12-foot-wide strip along the edge of the landowner's 5-acre agricultural property in order to widen a roadway. The city's attorney noted that the city's general plan would require the city to exact the same 12-foot strip without compensation should the landowner ever seek to obtain a building permit. Held: because the landowner realistically never could develop the strip, the trial court should have valued it as if it were permanently in agricultural use.

5. *Other complications*. Valuation in eminent domain can be intricate. When only a portion of an owner's land is being taken, as in *O'Donnell*, the issue of severance damages (i.e., damages to the property not taken) arises. If the condemnor's project will confer some benefits on the owner's remnant (for example, by improving access to it), the legal system must determine the extent to which those benefits should be set off against the condemnee's award.

When ownership of a condemned tract is divided among several claimants (e.g., landlord and tenant or mortgagor and mortgagee), there must be rules on how the award is to be apportioned among them. When a superior government condemns an inferior government's land, valuation may be difficult if the land had been devoted to a nonproprietary function, such as a street, for which comparable sales are not available.

These and the other knotty questions of eminent domain valuation are considered in a long-lived treatise: Julius L. Sackman, Nichols on Eminent Domain (rev. 3d ed. 2003).

6. *Procedure*. Eminent domain procedure is primarily statutory, although limited by constitutional constraints of due process. Most states authorize a "quick take" method that enables a government to acquire title rapidly provided that it deposits an estimated award in court. See, e.g., 735 Ill. Comp. Stat. 5/7-103 to -105 (2004) (involved in *SWIDA*, at p. 832); Tex. Prop. Code Ann. §21.021 (Vernon 2004).

C.   *Government as Developer*

The urban renewal program of the 1950s and 1960s induced municipal agencies to prepare comprehensive plans for large tracts and to design and install the infrastructure needed to carry out their plans. In most renewal projects, however, the agency itself did not act as a developer. Instead, it typically would sell a cleared parcel to a private firm, subject to covenants designed to achieve plan objectives. The transferee developer (and its successors) then would be responsible for designing, constructing, marketing, and managing any buildings placed on the parcel. Law permitting, however, a municipality may opt to act as the developer and building owner. When it does, it plays the most active role it can in the land development process.

In what situations should a government, instead of leasing space in private buildings, develop and manage the structures it needs for its proprietary programs? Is leasing a viable option for federal post offices? Military bases? Dormitories for state university students? Neighborhood police stations? To what degree might a government's access to tax-exempt bond financing and exemption from property taxation skew the incentives of the heads of public agencies toward public production and ownership of buildings?

Should governments ever compete with private firms in producing housing, retail space, or factories? Many theorists of public finance doubt whether a government can produce and manage private goods as efficiently as can a private firm, primarily because a government is less subject to competitive pressures. Some analysts, however, believe that in some contexts a public agency can serve as a useful yardstick for assessing the relative competence of private firms. (On the theory of public finance, see Musgrave & Musgrave, excerpted at p. 625.) Experience sheds light on these issues. This subchapter reviews the disheartening history in the United States of governmental forays into direct land development, particularly in the field of housing. Although local governments have been at the forefront of these efforts, states and the federal government also have tried their hands at it.

1.   Federal and State Homebuilding

a.   Early Federal Endeavors

During World War I, Congress created and funded two corporations to construct housing that would aid the military effort. The most significant undertaking was Yorkship Village, a residential community of 1,578 houses built on 225 acres in Camden, New Jersey, to help house the workforce of a shipbuilder. Originally occupied as rental units, in 1921 the Yorkship Village houses were auctioned off, mostly to their occupants.

Several New Deal agencies were similarly involved in designing and building housing projects. The Public Works Administration financed and built approximately 21,000 units of public housing between 1933 and 1937. See Elizabeth Wood, The Beautiful Beginnings, The Failure to Learn: Fifty Years of Public Housing in America 2–7 (1982). In 1936, the Resettlement Administration started work on three greenbelt towns: Greenhills, Ohio; Greendale, Wisconsin; and Greenbelt, Maryland. Each town originally consisted of a school, a shopping-community area, and fewer than 1,000 houses. These greenbelt communities were not particularly innovative in design.

Prior to 1937, there were a number of successful constitutional attacks on these New Deal programs. See Franklin Township v. Tugwell, 85 F.2d 208 (D.C. Cir. 1936) (holding that statute establishing Resettlement Administration unconstitutionally delegated legislative power to agency and that federal government lacked power to resettle population); United States v. Certain Lands in Louisville, 78 F.2d 684 (6th Cir. 1935) (holding exercise of eminent domain to acquire land for low-cost housing project was not a public use). Shortly after these decisions, the Supreme Court began to interpret federal powers much more expansively. Nevertheless, political support for direct federal development of housing eventually waned. In 1949, Congress followed the Yorkship Village precedent and enacted 63 Stat. 68, according to whose mandate all three of the greenbelt towns were sold at market value to private purchasers. See generally K.C. Parsons, Clarence Stein and the Greenbelt Towns, 56 J. Am. Plan. Ass'n 161 (1990).

b.   State Homebuilding: The Saga of the New York State Urban Development Corporation

In 1968, the New York legislature established a state Urban Development Corporation and endowed it with expansive powers of eminent domain and also, for a time, immunity from some local zoning and building code provisions. Governor Nelson Rockefeller appointed

Edward Logue to direct the UDC. Logue, an energetic and aggressive administrator, previously had directed urban renewal efforts in New Haven and Boston. At first, the UDC obtained its financing through the New York State Housing Finance Agency, which issued special revenue bonds tied to particular projects. Finding this too constraining, the UDC soon obtained the power to issue its own general revenue bonds secured only by its "full faith and credit." By the end of 1972, 30,000 UDC housing units were under construction throughout the state, a majority of them on a fast track based on a UDC gamble that they later would qualify for federal housing subsidies. A 1973 federal moratorium on approvals of Section 236 subsidies (see p. 875) placed the UDC in great jeopardy. After several years of financial distress, in 1975, the UDC defaulted on a portion of its debt, precipitating a financial crisis. New York eventually chose not to abolish the agency but to reorganize and recapitalize it on a much smaller scale. A state commission established to study the collapse of the UDC pinpointed as sources of failure (among others): (1) the undertaking of too many expensive projects in marginal areas, (2) the elimination of separate lender scrutiny, and (3) the presence on the UDC board of too many directors with conflicts of interest. See Mendes Hershman, What Went Wrong with UDC?, Urb. Land, Apr. 1977, at 3.

The statute establishing the UDC is codified at N.Y. Unconsol. Laws §§6251–6285 (2004). Reviews of the agency's performance include Louis K. Lowenstein, The New York State Urban Development Corporation, 44 J. Am. Inst. Planners 261 (1978); John E. Osborn, New York's Urban Development Corporation, 43 Brook. L. Rev. 237 (1977).

2. *Local Homebuilding: The Public Housing Program of 1937*

The federal public housing program dates from the Great Depression, when a coalition of housing reformers, labor unions, and central-city mayors helped push through the United States Housing Act of 1937, codified as amended at 42 U.S.C. §§1437 et seq. (2004). At that time, voters had relatively little faith in the private entrepreneurs who traditionally had developed the nation's housing and managed its rental units. Embracing the faith in government enterprise that characterized much of the New Deal, the public housing program provided deep federal subsidies to local governments that set up special agencies ("public housing authorities" [PHAs]) to develop, own, and manage rental housing complexes. Local governments provided an additional subsidy by exempting public housing projects from some or all property taxes. The public housing program initially was aimed at creating jobs, providing housing to working-class families, and replacing existing slum buildings on fine-grained lots with modernist projects on megablocks — urban designs favored by Lewis Mumford and many other planning theorists of the era.

Senator Robert Wagner of New York, a leading proponent of the 1937 Act, patterned the program after one that New York City had established in 1934. Professor Schill explains that New Dealers chose to funnel public housing aid through special-purpose PHAs because:

> earlier efforts by the federal government itself to acquire land for subsidized housing had been thwarted by federal courts on the ground that housing was not a public purpose under the Takings Clause. See United States v. Certain Lands in Louisville, 78 F.2d 684, 687 (6th Cir. 1935) (federal government cannot use power of eminent domain to assemble sites for public housing because the provision of housing to low-salaried workers and residents of slum districts is not a public purpose). State courts had already decided that states and localities

could constitutionally use their powers of eminent domain to provide low-cost housing. See, for example, New York City Housing Authority v. Muller, 1 N.E.2d 153, 156 (N.Y. 1936) (upholding the creation of a housing authority because the legislation aimed to protect and safeguard the entire public from the menace of the slums). Specially formed authorities were used instead of general purpose municipal governments, so as to insulate the public housing program from politics and to avoid statutory borrowing limits.

Michael H. Schill, Distressed Public Housing: Where Do We Go from Here?, 60 U. Chi. L. Rev. 497, 499 n.12 (1993). On the intellectual roots of the public housing movement, see Gail Radford, Modern Housing for America (1996). Radford states that prominent public housing advocates such as Edith Wood and Catherine Bauer admired what Frankfurt, Germany, had accomplished in the 1920s and sought to replicate it.

In 1949, Congress greatly boosted funding, spurring a burst of construction of high-rise projects for families. This proved to be a high-water mark of the public housing movement. By the mid-1960s, public housing projects were disproportionately serving households receiving public assistance, many of whom were members of racial minorities. In many a city, the most notorious slums were public housing projects themselves. The public housing movement suffered a public relations disaster when the high-rise Pruitt-Igoe project in St. Louis, which had won a prize when first built in the early 1950s, was demolished as uninhabitable in 1976. Political support for building additional projects for families, especially outside of poor, minority neighborhoods, evaporated. Recognizing this reality, from the mid-1960s to the mid-1990s, central-city PHAs tended to devote their capital outlays either to renovating decaying projects or to building new projects set aside for occupation by the elderly or disabled.

On the history of public housing, see Kenneth T. Jackson, Crabgrass Frontier 223–29 (1985); Lawrence J. Vale, From the Puritans to the Projects (2000) (on the Boston experience).

Stephen B. Kinnaird, Note, Public Housing: Abandon HOPE, But Not Privatization
103 Yale L.J. 961, 966–73, 984–85 (1994)

Public housing is far more diverse than the crime-ridden, deteriorating, urban high-rise projects that haunt the popular imagination. The 3,253 Public Housing Authorities (PHAs) differ greatly in terms of size, markets served, and performance. While some PHAs are colossal (the New York Housing Authority manages nearly 180,000 units), 87% of the PHAs operate fewer than 500 units. PHAs house 1.4 million households in 13,200 developments of highly variegated structures. Fewer than half of public housing units are in high-rises, and federal law now bars the construction of high-rise projects to house families with children if there are feasible alternatives. Public housing developments are not all concentrated in areas of urban decay, nor are they all dens of despair. Some PHAs run quite efficiently; 500 of them require no federal operating subsidy.

Defenders of public housing often emphasize this alternative vision. Two cautions are in order, however. First, the success of some PHAs in implementing public housing within the terms of the program does not mean that public housing is justified vis-à-vis competing housing policies, including privatization. Second, the alternative image of public housing should not distract us from the reality underlying the popular image. The small clutch of suburban garden apartments is not the problem; rather, the distressed and wasteful projects in our central cities should command our attention. It is true that in 1992 HUD designated only twenty-one PHAs — a fraction of 1% of the PHAs — as "troubled"; however, these

PHAs alone managed 18% of the nation's public housing units and consumed one-quarter of federal public housing subsidies. The well-known scourges of urban public housing — crime, drug trafficking, vandalism, and concentrated poverty — show no signs of relenting in these or other PHAs, and the evidence now points to a costly crisis in the mismanagement and deterioration of the stock itself.

Vacancies have been growing at an alarming rate. Nearly 8% of all public housing units were vacant in 1991, a total of almost 104,000 units. That is nearly double the number of vacancies that existed in 1986. In troubled housing authorities, vacancy rates reached a staggering 14% of units in 1991. Detroit topped the league with a vacancy rate of 44%, while East St. Louis and Newark weighed in at 38% and 32% respectively. Often, such high vacancy rates signal irresponsible management. None of Detroit's units were deemed uninhabitable in 1990, and a HUD official estimated in 1991 that 2,500 of Detroit's 3,500 vacant units could have been relet with minimal work like painting and plastering. Perversely, these high vacancies coexist with total PHA waiting lists of nearly one million households.

The stock has been not only underutilized but also neglected. Now the bill is due. In 1992, the Commission on Severely Distressed Public Housing concluded that the total cost of fully modernizing public housing could run as high as $29.2 billion . . .

Many factors contribute to the high costs of modernizing public housing — notably the age of the stock and the scheme by which public housing has been financed — but mis-management is surely prominent among them. . . . In Washington, the average uncollected rents from 1989–1991 were four times (396%) the total monthly rents due the PHA. . . .

Defenders of public housing contend that problems of mismanagement are cor-rectable, at least if funding levels are increased. However, the waste and abuses seem endemic to public housing, and support the theory that bureaucratic management of housing will lead to rentseeking and inefficiency. . . .

The most egregious rentseeking by public housing officials is outright corruption. The HUD Inspector General reported eleven instances of corruption involving bid-rigging, bribery, embezzlement, or ethics violations, at least nine of which resulted in suspension or criminal sentences for PHA officials between 1988 and 1990. Political corruption drove the Philadelphia PHA into receivership in 1992. A similar fate has befallen five other PHAs since 1989. Fraud and theft have loomed large in recent scandals at PHAs in Washington, D.C. and Boston. . . .

. . . The multilevel structure of the public housing system — Congress, HUD (national and regional), PHAs — makes monitoring difficult and further exacerbates the agency problem. . . .

If [privatization] theory is correct, one would expect PHAs to incur substantially higher costs than private housing suppliers. The empirical evidence is unambiguous: a 1982 study done for HUD found that it cost 40% more per-unit to build conventional public housing than unsubsidized FHA housing. Most of the cost differential was owing to inefficiency in production, and not to inherent cost differences in the types of projects built.

PHAs also fare poorly in controlling operating costs. Another 1982 study found that PHA per-unit operating costs were 61% higher than costs in the private sector in 1980. . . . From 1989 to 1991, all but one of the twenty-three PHAs designated as "troubled" in January 1992 had excess administrative staff by HUD standards, and all but three had excess maintenance staff. Generally, these high costs buy precious little service. The notorious District of Columbia Department of Public and Assisted Housing (DPAH) has consistently failed to fix the heating or roofs at its projects despite having 168 excess maintenance workers; Philadelphia's 627 maintenance workers had roused themselves to repair only 25 vacant units per year prior to HUD's seizure of the PHA in 1992. . . .

The last fifteen years have seen a shift into more efficient demand-side programs like Section 8 existing-housing certificates and vouchers. . . .

Demand-side programs like vouchers not only have more beneficial market effects, but also are more cost-effective for government. In 1992, HUD estimated that, over a twenty-year period, building a new public housing unit is 36% more expensive than providing the same subsidy via a rental voucher or certificate. Voucher programs also deliver far superior value to low-income households. In the Housing Supply Experiment, 85% of program dollars in housing were found to serve low-income recipients, versus just 34% of public housing dollars. Builders and administrators captured 60% of the spending on public housing.

Note on Public Housing

1. *Alternative methods of housing assistance to poor tenants.* Kinnaird touches on the use of vouchers to help tenants pay rent in private housing units. This and other forms of housing assistance are taken up at pp. 870–80. In other portions of his Note, Kinnaird critiques one-time HUD Secretary Jack Kemp's proposal to sell units in public housing projects to their resident tenants. Kinnaird instead advocates converting existing public housing subsidies to portable tenant vouchers and authorizing a PHA to auction off its existing projects.

2. *Defenders of traditional public housing.* Many observers, especially those who do not share Kinnaird's relative confidence in the private sector, have championed the record of public housing. See, e.g., Mary K. Nenno, Ending the Stalemate 97–129 (1996) (generally sympathetic account of public housing); Michael A. Stegman, The Role of Public Housing in a Revitalized National Housing Policy, *in* Building Foundations 333 (Denise DiPasquale & Langley C. Keyes eds., 1990) (similar).

3. *Particular criticisms of public housing.* It is almost universally agreed that the construction, especially during the 1950s, of massive high-rise housing projects for families proved to be a disastrous urban policy. Evaluate the relative cogency of the following explanations for why these projects failed:

a. The site plans and architectural designs were unsound (cf. Oscar Newman, Defensible Space (1972)).

b. Admissions policies, many of them stemming from federal statutory requirements, led to excessive concentrations of households vulnerable to social pathologies such as persistent unemployment, welfare dependency, crime, and drug abuse (cf. Michael H. Schill & Susan M. Wachter, The Spatial Bias of Federal Housing Law and Policy: Concentrated Poverty in Urban America, 143 U. Pa. L. Rev. 1285 (1995) (advocating overhaul of federal admissions requirements)).

c. Because public housing subsidies are project-based, PHAs lack adequate incentives to please their tenants (as argued by Weicher, at pp. 871–72).

d. Because voters cannot monitor a government as readily as owners can monitor a firm, a government is inherently less efficient at producing a private good such as housing.

4. *The future of public housing.* When it became clear that the major rehabilitation of the most troubled projects was overly costly, the federal government had two basic options. It could encourage PHAs either to raze and then to build new and better projects on the same sites, or to provide the current tenants with transportable vouchers and then sell off the projects. PHAs have explored both avenues. In 1992, Congress approved the HOPE VI program, which invited PHAs to compete for federal funds to be used to demolish

existing structures and replace them with higher-quality, lower-density units intended for occupancy by households from a mix of income groups. Yet more significant was the Quality Housing and Work Responsibility Act of 1998, Pub. L. No. 105-276. Prior to 1998, Congress had required a PHA to replace, in some fashion, each demolished unit of public housing on a one-for-one basis. The 1998 Act eliminated this requirement. It also gave PHAs more flexibility in establishing admission preferences, set rent levels according to a formula designed to help enable a PHA to retain tenants who are prospering, and established procedures to govern conversions of public housing projects to vouchers.

Given this additional room to maneuver, many PHAs began to raze some of their most troubled projects for families. By 2003, a total of 140,000 public housing units had either been demolished or scheduled for demolition. Particularly notable was the decision of the Chicago Housing Authority (CHA) to redevelop the notorious Robert Taylor Homes project on the South Side into a mixed-income community. Opened in 1962, the Robert Taylor Homes consisted of 28 high-rise buildings containing 4,500 units for families — the largest public housing project in the United States. On the decline of this project, see Sudhir Alladi Venkatesh, American Project: The Rise and Fall of a Modern Ghetto (2000). By early 2003 the CHA had razed 23 of the Robert Taylor high-rises and had plans for the prompt demolition of the remaining five.

For a mix of assessments, see Ngai Pindell, Is There Hope for Hope VI?, 35 Conn. L. Rev. 385 (2003); Note, When Hope Falls Short: HOPE VI, Accountability, and the Privatization of Public Housing, 116 Harv. L. Rev. 1477 (2003).

As mentioned, instead of building anew, a PHA could pursue a dispersal strategy. The CHA's Gautreaux program, an outgrowth of successful lawsuits against CHA and HUD to remedy racially concentrated public housing, exemplifies two dispersal options. Under the first, *scattered-site public housing*, a PHA acquires (or builds) small residential buildings at multiple locations within its jurisdiction, especially outside mostly minority neighborhoods. This has proved to be politically difficult in Chicago. The second, *vouchering out*, is the solution that Kinnaird endorses. The PHA provides current residents of public housing projects with housing vouchers that they can apply toward renting private dwelling units of their own choosing. Under the Gautreaux program, 6,000 low-income black households who previously had been living in projects such as the Robert Taylor Homes were selected through a screening process and enabled through vouchers to move elsewhere, including to Chicago suburbs. Most parents who did relocate to the suburbs later reported that their children had benefited from the move. On the Gautreaux program's dispersal policies, see Leonard S. Rabinowitz & James E. Rosenbaum, Crossing the Class and Color Lines: From Public Housing to White Suburbia (2000). For an assessment of the Gautreaux litigation, beginning with Gautreaux v. Chicago Housing Authority, 296 F. Supp. 907 (N.D. Ill. 1969), see Joseph Seliga, Comment, *Gautreaux* a Generation Later: Remedying the Second Ghetto or Creating a Third?, 94 Nw. U. L. Rev. 1049 (2000).

On events in other metropolitan areas, see Thompson v. United States Department of Housing & Urban Development, 348 F. Supp. 2d 398 (D. Md. 2005) (holding HUD had violated Fair Housing Act of 1968 by failing to consider regionally-oriented housing desegregation policies in Baltimore area); Edward G. Goetz, Desegregation Lawsuits and Public Housing Dispersal: The Case of *Hollman v. Cisneros* in Minneapolis, 70 J. Am. Plan. Ass'n 282 (2004). See generally Peter H. Schuck, Judging Remedies: Judicial Approaches to Housing Segregation, 37 Harv. C.R.-C.L. L. Rev. 289 (2002); and sources cited at pp. 876-77 (on the use of vouchers to reduce racial and class segregation).

D.   Government as Financier

Instead of itself acting as an entrepreneur, a government can seek to influence urban patterns by providing financial support to selected beneficiaries. The instruments of aid are many: grants, direct loans (perhaps at below-market rates), insurance of others' mortgage loans, tax breaks, operating subsidies, seed capital, and so on. The topic of government aid to housing and community development is too complex to receive detailed treatment here. Countless federal and state aid programs have been enacted, each with its own statute and implementing regulations. Because many urban problems have proved to be intractable, legislatures tend to churn their policy instruments. Instead of presenting details of the current state of a constantly changing legal framework, this subchapter is organized around three principal objectives that policymakers articulate in this context: (1) aiding housing consumers (especially poor ones), (2) promoting economic and community development, and (3) nurturing innovations in the design of urban spaces and institutions.

1.   Government Assistance to Housing Consumers

The federal Department of Housing and Urban Development and its state and local counterparts devote much of their efforts to helping buyers and renters obtain housing at lower cost. Among the basic issues of housing policy are: Whom should a government aid? Should aid be given as an entitlement to all who meet the categorical criteria for eligibility, or rationed by queue or otherwise (as is common in the housing context)? Should aid be provided to firms on the supply side (on condition that they lower the prices they charge housing consumers), or on the demand side (to consumers themselves)? If a household does receive aid, should it take the form of cash benefits that the household can spend as it chooses, or of in-kind benefits the household must spend on designated goods such as housing?

a.   Federal Assistance to Homebuyers

Federal tax concessions to homeowners. The Internal Revenue Code makes homeowner-ship highly advantageous, particularly for high-income households that face the highest marginal income tax rates. Major tax benefits include: (1) the failure to impute the rental value of owner-occupied housing as income; (2) the deductibility, within limits, by an item-izing taxpayer of interest paid on a home mortgage; and (3) generous exclusions for capital gains accruing from sale of a home (I.R.C. §121). See generally Steven C. Bourassa & William G. Grigsby, Income Tax Concessions for Owner-Occupied Housing, 11 Housing Pol'y Debate 521 (2000). Many contend that these income tax preferences have caused too much of the nation's capital to be invested in housing, thereby exacerbating sprawl. See, e.g., Roberta F. Mann, The (Not So) Little House on the Prairie: The Hidden Costs of the Home Mortgage Interest Deduction, 32 Ariz. St. L.J. 1347 (2000). Analysts who subscribe to the notion of a neutral tax base estimate the annual "tax expenditure" resulting from the home mortgage interest deduction alone at over $50 billion. Id. at 1353. This figure far exceeds annual federal outlays for low-income housing. Other commentators defend at least some of these federal tax policies, however, on grounds of economic efficiency and the social benefits of homeownership (see p. 25). See, e.g., John C. Weicher, Comment on Bourassa and Grigsby, 11 Housing Pol'y Debate 547 (2000).

Federal mortgage insurance. Since the creation of the Federal Housing Administration (FHA) in 1934, 48 Stat. 1246, the federal government has been heavily involved in the supply of mortgage money to owners of residential property. Between 1935 and 1969, 19 percent of all privately financed nonfarm dwelling units were built to qualify for FHA aid. FHA itself does not lend money, but rather insures certain loans to protect private lenders from the losses they would suffer if borrowers were to default on their obligations. By providing this insurance, FHA has induced many lenders to raise loan-to-value ratios (thereby reducing down payments) and to extend mortgage lives (thereby lowering monthly payments). FHA charges the borrower (not the lender) a mortgage insurance premium. Because of its potential financial exposure, FHA reviews the borrower's credit; the design, condition, and neighborhood of the insured structure; and all relevant legal documents.

After 1970, the FHA share of the single-family market began to decline, largely on account of the rise of private mortgage insurance companies. Of residential mortgages originated in 2002, private companies insured 2.3 million, compared to 1.6 million for FHA and VA (Veterans Administration) combined. See Quintin Johnstone, Private Mortgage Insurance, 39 Wake Forest L. Rev. 783, 787 n.17 (2004).

The basic FHA single-family program, Section 203(b), amassed large reserves until the 1980s, when it began to suffer major outflows and had to be shored up. See Patric H. Hendershott & James A. Waddell, The Changing Fortunes of FHA's Mutual Mortgage Insurance Fund and the Legislative Response, 5 J. Real Est. Fin. & Econ. 119 (1992). FHA's multifamily and subsidized housing programs always have been actuarially precarious. See John C. Weicher, Comment on Kerry D. Vandell's "FHA Restructuring Proposals," 6 Housing Pol'y Debate 417 (1995). Especially during the 1998–2000 period, shady operators learned how to bilk FHA by "flipping" property in poor neighborhoods. The co-conspirators would buy a distressed property for a low price, make cosmetic improvements, and obtain an inflated appraisal from a cooperating appraiser. The property then would be sold at an inflated price, with most of the purchase financed by means of an FHA-insured mortgage. When the buyer defaulted on payments, FHA risked bearing the loss. See Terry Pristin, Official Says Deal Is Near on Housing Scandal, N.Y. Times, Sept. 11, 2001, at B7. These practices prompted numerous criminal prosecutions and eventual FHA reforms to deter flipping.

Other federal home-loan programs run by the Veterans Administration and the Farmer's Home Administration (FmHA) enable eligible borrowers to obtain mortgage financing on better-than-market terms. On these and other forms of mortgage insurance, see generally Grant S. Nelson & Dale A. Whitman, Real Estate Finance Law 848–64 (4th ed. 2001).

Federal aid to secondary mortgage markets. Mortgage money is more cheaply available when a lender who originates a mortgage loan can sell it readily in a secondary market to other investors. Beginning in the New Deal and especially in the years 1968–1970, the federal government helped create three institutions that are still prominent in secondary mortgage markets. The Government National Mortgage Association (Ginnie Mae) concentrates on creating markets for the riskiest FHA and VA loans. The Federal National Mortgage Association (Fannie Mae) and the Federal Home Loan Mortgage Corporation (Freddie Mac) mostly deal with less risky mortgages. Both are for-profit, shareholder-owned, and exempt by act of Congress from most securities laws and state and local income taxes. In addition, both Fannie Mae and Freddie Mac have had a $2.25 billion line of credit with the U.S. Treasury. As in the case of mortgage insurance, however, private competitors offering a wide variety of mortgage-backed securities have begun to enter the field.

Some observers urge greater privatization of these federal institutions. See, e.g., W. Scott Frame & Lawrence J. White, Fussing and Fuming over Fannie and Freddie: How Much Smoke, How Much Fire?, 19 J. Econ. Persp. 159 (2003). For an accessible introduction to secondary mortgage markets of all types, see Nelson & Whitman, supra, at 864–78.

b.   Federal Assistance to Tenants

John C. Weicher, Privatizing Subsidized Housing
3–12, 43–44 (1997)

A BRIEF TAXONOMY OF SUBSIDIZED HOUSING

To understand the issues, it is necessary first to understand the three major categories of subsidized housing programs: public housing, privately owned projects, and vouchers and certificates for use in privately owned housing. Each is now about one-third of the subsidized rental housing stock, as Table 10-2 shows.

Public housing is the oldest subsidy program, dating back to the U.S. Housing Act of 1937. There are now about 1.4 million public housing units. Most of the units (over 850,000) were built between 1950 and 1975; in the past ten years, about 100,000 units have been built. . . .

In 1961, the federal government began to subsidize the construction of privately owned subsidized housing projects. The projects were financed by mortgages obtained from private lenders, but the government paid part of the cost of the mortgage. In addition, for well over half of the projects, the government insured the mortgages through the Federal Housing Administration (FHA). There was a series of these programs, each terminated within a few years: Section 221(d)(3) BMIR (below-market interest rate), enacted in 1961, terminated in 1968; Section 236, enacted in 1968, terminated in 1974; and Section 8 new construction, enacted in 1974, terminated in 1983. There are now about 1.7 million subsidized units in these programs. The projects built under these programs are commonly and conveniently divided into the older and newer inventory: those built under the first two programs and those built under Section 8, respectively. This distinction corresponds to the most important difference between the programs: subsidies for the older projects typically were much lower. In many cases, the original subsidy has not been enough to cover operations and pay for renovation, and HUD now also provides subsidies for these purposes. Some of these projects have received additional subsidies under Section 8 and therefore are treated for policy purposes as part of the newer inventory.

Despite the differences in ownership, public housing and the privately owned projects have a fundamentally similar subsidy mechanism. In both, the federal subsidy is *project-based*: the federal government makes a commitment to subsidize the housing unit, and the subsidies are given to the owner of the housing. Residents receive the benefit of the subsidy as long as they live in the housing unit. If they move out, they no longer receive a subsidy; it goes instead to the next occupant of the unit. Because both programs have project-based subsidies, they have substantially the same problems. Because the privately owned projects combine FHA insurance with federal subsidy, they pose the more complicated policy issues.

Housing certificates and vouchers are the third type of subsidy program, with a basic subsidy mechanism very different from the project-based subsidies described above. These subsidies are given directly to low-income families and individuals in the form of commitments by the federal government to pay part of the rent in housing selected by the family.

TABLE 10-2
Housing Subsidy Programs, 1997

Program		Number of Subsidized Households or Units
Project-based assistance		3,100,000
Public housing		1,400,000
Privately owned projects		1,700,000
Older programs	600,000	
Section 8	1,100,000	
Tenant-based assistance		1,500,000
Certificates		1,100,000
Vouchers		400,000
Total		4,600,000

Source: Weicher Table 2-1, drawn from HUD program data.

The federal government establishes a maximum rent that it will pay, based on the cost of modest, decent private housing in the local market (technically known as the fair market rent, or FMR). The recipients search for acceptable housing in the private market and negotiate directly with the property owner; once they reach an agreement and the unit and lease are approved by the local PHA (which administers the programs), the PHA pays part of the rent directly to the owner, using funds provided by the federal government. [Since 1981, the tenant's monthly share of rent has been 30 percent of the tenant's monthly cash income. The PHA's share typically is larger — in 2000, a average of more than $400 per month. Statistical Abstract 2003, at 360. — EDS.] The tenants choose their own housing. If they choose to move, they can take the subsidy with them to a new unit. Because the subsidy commitment is given to the family, certificates and vouchers are termed *tenant-based* assistance.

Certificates were enacted in 1974, and vouchers, in 1983. Together, they now serve about 1.5 million households: 1.1 million receive certificates, and 400,000 receive vouchers. The role of the FMR differs between the programs. In the certificate program, the family cannot live in a housing unit that rents for more than the FMR, while, in the voucher program, the family can live in a more expensive unit if willing to spend a larger share of the voucher to do so. Thus, the family in the voucher program has a wider range of options. In addition, if the family finds a unit renting for less than the FMR, it can keep all the savings in the voucher program (the shopping incentive), but in the certificate program it cannot keep any.

The important distinction among the three housing program categories is not ownership but the basis of the assistance — between housing that is subsidized because the federal government has made a commitment to subsidize it (as long as an eligible family lives in it) and housing that is subsidized because, and as long as, a low-income family chooses to live in it.

Project-based and tenant-based assistance confront both property owners and low-income households — and the federal government, for that matter — with very different incentives. These result partly because of program design and partly because housing assistance is not an entitlement. It is the only major low-income benefit program that is not. Assistance is provided to about one-third of eligible households. There are long waiting lists in many metropolitan areas for all types of subsidized housing.

In the project-based programs, PHAs and project owners must satisfy HUD, not their tenants. As long as HUD is satisfied, the project will be assured a steady stream of subsidized tenants; if one moves out, another is in line to take its place and move into the vacant apartment. There is no market discipline in this process. Poorly maintained projects continue to be occupied and continue to receive subsidies, except in extreme cases. HUD does not serve as a proxy for the market. In the case of public housing, ultimately its only recourse is to replace or take over the management of a PHA. The department has done this on several occasions, most recently and most spectacularly in Chicago, but it does not really want the direct responsibility for managing public housing. In the case of the privately owned projects, HUD can pressure the owner to maintain or improve the quality of the housing, and it can threaten to withhold subsidies or can actually withhold them. But then the owner can always default on the mortgage and walk away from the property, leaving HUD to own and manage it. Again, HUD does not want this responsibility if it can avoid it, and it also does not want to pay the insurance claim on a defaulted mortgage.

This similarity in subsidy mechanisms seems to be more or less generally recognized, if somewhat vaguely and in an odd way. The term *public housing* is often used to describe both types of programs. Thus, a 1995 story in the Wall Street Journal describing two privately owned projects was headlined, "A Tale of Contrasts: Two Buildings Show How *Public Housing* Slid into Such a Mess" (italics added).

In the certificate and voucher programs, the property owner faces a different situation. To keep a subsidized tenant, he must satisfy that tenant. The owner is subject to the discipline of the housing market and must compete with other owners of rental housing for subsidized tenants, just as he must compete with them for unsubsidized tenants. The owner must continue to satisfy the PHA that the unit meets program quality standards, although this criterion is secondary; it is a necessary but not a sufficient condition for the owner to receive a subsidy.

The household also faces different constraints and incentives in the different programs, beginning when the household comes to the top of the waiting list. In the project-based programs, a household is offered the next unit that becomes available for occupancy. The choice is that particular unit in that specific project — or nothing. If the household rejects that unit, it drops to the bottom of the waiting list and may wait years for another opportunity. In the tenant-based programs, the household is offered the chance to rent any privately owned unit it chooses, including the unit currently occupied. The property owner must be willing to rent the unit to this household, and the unit must meet the program quality standards, which are established by the federal government and administered by the PHA. If the household receives a certificate instead of a voucher, the selected unit must rent for less than the federally established maximum, though exceptions are permitted. Apart from these constraints, the household is free to choose where to live.

Once the household starts receiving the subsidy, its choices also differ by program. In the project-based programs, a household loses the subsidy if it chooses to move out of the unit. At best, it goes back on the waiting list. In the tenant-based programs, a household can move to any other privately owned housing that it chooses, subject to the same conditions that apply to the original unit.

WHY PRIVATIZE?

There are several reasons for the recent bipartisan interest in privatizing project-based housing. First, public housing has not worked, in the sense that it has not achieved its original purpose and, indeed, is widely considered to be counterproductive. The original purpose of public housing was to improve the social, economic, and even the medical well-being of the poor. To the urban reformers of the 1930s and earlier, urban social problems were largely caused by poor housing. At least as far back as the turn of the century, reformers were pointing out that the slums were the home of all the ills of urban society and arguing that they were the breeding ground for crime, delinquency, disease, mental illness, and even death. Living in the slums kept people from realizing their full potential ability to become productive members of society. The reformers felt that if the slums were razed and replaced with decent housing, the social and medical problems of their poor residents would be solved or at least greatly ameliorated. These views were buttressed by a large body of research showing that medical problems and social pathologies were much more common in the slums than elsewhere. The concerns that the federal government sought to address in the 1930s were largely the concerns of these urban reformers. Housing mattered not so much for its own sake as for its effect on social welfare and economic well-being in general. It is not too much to say that housing was seen as a war on poverty all by itself.

No one now claims that public housing has met these objectives. Its failure in this sense has been recognized since the 1950s and is the most basic reason why housing policy and programs have changed so frequently over the past thirty-five years.

Second, some subsidized housing projects — both public and privately owned — do not achieve even the more limited objective of providing decent housing. Most projects do, but in nearly every large city some are clearly not fit to live in. These projects are noticeable — some are notorious, locally and even nationally. The magnitude of the problem is always open to debate. For public housing, there is at least a clear lower bound: HUD has proposed to demolish 84,000 public housing units for this reason, about 6 percent of the stock. For the privately owned projects, a 1992 HUD study found that 42,000 units in 510 insured subsidized projects in the older programs needed at least $6,000 per unit worth of renovation, without having the funds to pay for it. That is also about 6 percent of the total in the older insured assisted inventory. In the Section 8 program, some 9,000 units, or 3 percent of the total, had $6,000 worth of unfunded renovation needs, even though these projects were no more than fifteen years old and had been receiving large subsidies. At least some of these privately owned projects probably should be razed.

These numbers are likely to increase over time. In both types of programs, the projects are aging. The median construction year is 1964 for public housing and 1974 for the privately owned projects. . . .

Third, and related, is the large and growing cost of subsidizing the projects in these programs. . . .

To this list of problems economists would add the previously mentioned concerns about freedom of choice for tenants and market discipline for providers of subsidized housing, and they would stress the well-documented inefficiency of project-based assistance.

VOUCHERING OUT

Conceptually, privatizing subsidized housing projects is not difficult. There have been three proposals to do so within the past two years. They differ in detail, but all take the same approach: they would *voucher out* subsidized housing. Project-based assistance could be converted to housing vouchers. The vouchers would be given to the tenants of the subsidized projects. The money that now goes from HUD to private project owners and PHAs would go instead to the tenants. These households would be given the opportunity to choose their own housing — to stay where they are, or to move wherever they want to, and wherever a property owner is willing to rent to them. This is exactly the way the 30 million unsubsidized renters and 1.5 million current recipients of tenant-based assistance find their housing. . . .

WHY IS PROGRESS SO SLOW?

The problems of project-based assistance have been recognized for many years. The programs do not appear to have much general public support. As a result, the programs for privately owned projects have been terminated, one after another. Yet policy makers, particularly in Congress, are unwilling to trust the housing market to serve low-income renters. They continue to enact new programs with the potential for the same problems as the old ones, and they have not reacted positively to the vouchering-out proposals.

The policy concerns [of skeptics of the wisdom of vouchering out] are essentially . . . : whether housing is available; whether tenants will be able to afford it or, alternatively, whether landlords will simply raise rents; whether members of minority groups will be able to find housing; whether, on the contrary, tenant-based assistance will succeed too well and destabilize neighborhoods with a flood of low-income renters. After twenty years of experience with, and extensive study of, tenant-based assistance as an operating program, the evidence strongly indicates that these concerns are unfounded. The voucher and certificate programs work better and are less expensive than public housing and other forms of project-based assistance. The stated concerns, however, remain in the minds of policy makers.

Policy differences seem to be institutional as much as ideological. Five of the last six administrations have favored tenant-based assistance as the main housing program for the poor, and the exception — the Carter administration — largely reversed itself by the end of its term. But successive Congresses have regularly insisted on continued funding for new public housing projects (sometimes in the form of funds for replacement of projects that have become slums or uninhabitable). They have also nearly always cut administration proposals for incremental tenant-based assistance.

The institutional differences may arise because the different branches of government respond to different pressures. The high cost of project-based assistance becomes a budget issue within the executive branch. Decisions in favor of one type of expenditure imply less funding for other desirable programs or a bigger deficit. At the other end of Pennsylvania Avenue, cost is certainly a concern, but policy decisions are made on a smaller scale, and lobbying is more intense. Builders, owners, and managers of subsidized projects argue strongly and persistently for continuing the current programs: they have much at stake. Advocates for vouchering out or other reforms are less evident; they are mostly independent academic or policy analysts, who do not devote as much time to the policy process. Those who would directly benefit from vouchering out — the tenants in subsidized projects — are rarely heard. Spokespersons for tenant groups tend to favor the status quo; they have established their positions within the system of project-based assistance. Those who might benefit financially from vouchering out — owners of lower-cost private rental housing — are not as concerned with the issue as those who would lose from it. There is thus no strong constituency for tenant-based assistance, despite the systematic evidence of its advantages, while there are several constituencies in favor of project-based assistance.

Note on Federal Financial Assistance to Tenants

1. *Subsidization of private rental projects.* Weicher mentions a variety of federal programs to subsidize rents in privately developed and owned housing projects. (For legal materials on these and other housing assistance programs, see Charles Daye et al., Housing and Community Development (3d ed. 1999).) Subsidies for private rental projects first took wing in the 1960s, a time of growing disenchantment with the traditional public

housing program. Under most programs, a for-profit, nonprofit, or cooperative housing organization could qualify as a developer. A developer whose project won approval would be awarded a significant subsidy (such as a low-interest mortgage loan or a continuing flow of assistance payments), and in return the federal government would regulate the rents in the development so as to limit profit margins.

Annual production under these project-based subsidy programs peaked in the early 1970s, when Section 236 and its companion homeownership assistance program (Section 235) were generating hundreds of thousands of housing starts annually. On the collapse of the Section 235 and Section 236 programs, see Pennsylvania v. Lynn, 501 F.2d 848 (D.C. Cir. 1974) (affirming HUD's power to impose a moratorium on project approvals); R. Allen Hays, The Federal Government and Urban Housing 113-38 (2d ed. 1995).

As their short life spans imply, most of these private project-based programs have been beset with troubles. The ratio of tenant benefits to subsidy costs, although perhaps superior to that of public housing, has tended to be on the order of 50 cents per dollar of subsidy. See Stephen K. Mayo, Sources of Inefficiency in Subsidized Housing Programs, 20 J. Urb. Econ. 229 (1986). Defaults by developers have been common. For example, in the case of newly constructed Section 236 projects, 7.1 percent of for-profit developers and 32.6 percent of nonprofit developers lost their projects (often eventually back to HUD) for failure to keep up with mortgage payments. Hays, supra, at 128. On HUD's attempts to deal with its troubled private-project inventory, see James R. Barth & Robert E. Litan, Uncle Sam in the Housing Market: The Section 8 Rental Subsidy Disaster, 14 Brookings Rev. 22 (Fall 1996) (on project-based Section 8 projects, a successor to Section 236).

Because politicians are tempted to channel benefits to developers who have been campaign contributors, these programs frequently have been rocked by scandal. Neither major party has a clean record. See, e.g., Albert R. Hunt, In Washington, the Spoils Go to the Big Contributors, Wall St. J., Dec. 18, 1997, at A23 (describing contributions to federal legislators of both parties by A. Bruce Rozet, the largest developer of project-based Section 8 housing, called by some the "poster child for bad landlords"); Edward T. Pound & Kenneth H. Bacon, Housing Subsidy Plan for the Poor Helped Contributors to GOP, Wall St. J., May 25, 1989, at A1; How Clintonites Built Fund-Raising Machine of Breadth and Power, Wall St. J., Feb. 7, 1997, at A1. See generally Irving Welfeld, HUD Scandals (1992).

By the turn of the twenty-first century, significant federal project-based subsidies still were being awarded to private developers through the HOME program (enacted in 1990) and the Low-Income Housing Tax Credit program (enacted in 1986 and described at pp. 878-79). In a notable structural change, both these programs shifted from HUD to state and local agencies much of the power to select winners from the pool of developers who apply for subsidies. Is that innovation likely to decrease (or increase) the incidence of corruption?

2. *Disposition of the aging stock of private project-based subsidized housing.* The federal contracts governing a Section 221(d)(3) project or Section 236 project seemingly entitled the project owner to prepay the mortgage and exit from the program after 20 years had elapsed. Because a prepayment of this sort would terminate tenants' subsidy benefits, project residents typically oppose these opt-outs. In 1990, Congress enacted a statute that permitted prepayment only under stringent conditions. Dozens of project owners who lost this option challenged the statute, primarily on a takings theory. See, e.g., Cienega Gardens v. United States, 331 F.3d 1319 (Fed. Cir. 2003) (holding some owners had suffered compensable takings and remanding for further proceedings).

3. *The shift toward tenant-based housing assistance.* As a result of these sorts of travails with project-based housing subsidies, there has been a pronounced shift toward tenant-based housing aid, both in the United States and other nations. See generally Edgar O.

Olsen, Housing Programs for Low-Income Households, *in* Means-Tested Transfer Programs in the United States 365 (Robert A. Moffitt ed., 2003); George E. Peterson, Housing Vouchers: The U.S. Experience, *in* Vouchers and the Provision of Public Services 139 (C. Eugene Steurle et al. eds., 2000); Hugo Priemus, Housing Vouchers: A Contribution from Abroad, *in* id. at 176.

Following a recommendation made by the President's Committee on Urban Housing (Kaiser Committee) in 1969, the Housing and Urban Development Act of 1970 authorized HUD to conduct an experiment with portable housing allowances. HUD hired the Rand Corporation to carry out a full-scale field testing in the counties containing Green Bay, Wisconsin, and South Bend, Indiana. Initiated in 1974, the experiment evolved into one of the largest social science experiments ever conducted. Rand's key finding was that housing allowances did not measurably inflate the price of housing in either Green Bay or South Bend. This may have resulted in part because less than half of the eligible households received allowances and because most recipients diverted over two-thirds of their benefits to increased nonhousing consumption. See generally Joseph Friedman & Daniel L. Weinberg, The Great Housing Experiment (1983).

In 1974, before waiting for complete results from Rand's ongoing experiment, Congress enacted Section 8, the first nationwide housing-allowance program. See 88 Stat. 662, 42 U.S.C. §1437f (2004). Local housing authorities — the ones that operate public housing projects — are the primary administrators of Section 8 tenant-based aid. A household that applies to a PHA usually must wait for a year or more before receiving benefits. Because the receipt of a flow of Section 8 aid has a discounted present value in the tens of thousands of dollars, the program has been vulnerable to corruption. See, e.g., Cindy Loose, Five D.C. Housing Employees Charged; Only 10 of 400 New Rent Vouchers Issued Since 1990 Didn't Involve Bribery, Probe Finds, Wash. Post, Apr. 13, 1994, at A1.

The Quality Housing and Work Responsibility Act of 1998, cited at p. 867, merged the Section 8 certificate and voucher programs. Under the Act's revised formula, a tenant must pay at least 30 percent of income toward rent. If the tenant selects a housing unit whose rent is greater than the "payment standard" set by the PHA, the assistance payment is capped at an amount equal to the payment standard less 30 percent of the tenant's income. This formula creates what Weicher calls a "shopping incentive" whenever a tenant is evaluating housing units that rent for more than the payment standard.

A tenant granted a Section 8 voucher has the burden of finding a qualifying unit and a landlord willing to participate. A tenant frustrated in this quest eventually loses the voucher. Many landlords decline to participate in Section 8, perhaps to avoid both red tape and the risk of adverse reactions by unsubsidized tenants. Federal law never has compelled a landlord to accept a Section 8 tenant. See Salute v. Stratford Greens Garden Apartments, 136 F.3d 293 (2d Cir. 1998). See also Carol Rickert & Associates v. Law, 54 P.3d 91 (N.M. Ct. App. 2002) (entitling landlord to terminate Section 8 tenant at end of lease). Congress once imposed a "take-one, take-all" requirement that barred a landlord already participating in Section 8 from turning down a prospective tenant on the ground that the tenant was receiving Section 8 benefits. In 1996, Congress repealed the take-one, take-all provision on the ground that it had deterred landlords from entering the program.

A New Jersey statute prohibits a landlord of a multidwelling structure from refusing to rent to an individual because of the source of any lawful rent payment. In Franklin Tower One, L.L.C. v. N.M., 725 A.2d 1104 (N.J. 1999), the Supreme Court of New Jersey held that the federal statute that governs Section 8 did not preempt this state statutory provision and therefore that the defendant landlord could not refuse to participate in Section 8.

4. *The effect of housing-assistance policies on segregation.* The construction of traditional subsidized housing projects, particularly public housing, tended to heighten racial

and class segregation. See Michael H. Schill & Susan M. Wachter, The Spatial Bias of Federal Housing Law and Policy: Concentrated Poverty in Urban America, 143 U. Pa. L. Rev. 1285 (1995) (arguing against housing policies that concentrate the poor in high-poverty areas). Because Section 8 housing vouchers are portable, even across state lines, they tend to be better at promoting racial and class integration. See Mark A. Malaspina, Demanding the Best: How to Restructure the Section 8 Household-Based Rental Assistance Program, 14 Yale L. & Pol'y Rev. 287 (1996); Olsen, supra, at 407–11. Beginning in 1994, HUD experimented with a Moving to Opportunity Demonstration Program in which some central-city households receiving vouchers could use them only in nonpoor neighborhoods. Compared to members of control groups, adults in the households complying with this requirement were less likely to become dependent on welfare, and their young children had greater educational attainments. See Olsen, supra, at 423–24. To access the full array of Moving to Opportunity research results, visit http://www.wws.Princeton.EDU/~kling/mto/.

When vouchers contribute to class integration of a neighborhood, how do longtime residents react? Sometimes negatively. Critics indeed argue that Section 8 has promoted too much class integration. See, e.g., Howard Husock, Let's End Housing Vouchers, City J., Autumn 2000, at 84 (asserting, based on study of south suburban Chicago, that Section 8 wrongly rewards poor tenants to the detriment of working-class and middle-class households struggling to establish themselves). Other observers doubt if these negative effects are significant as long as the new entrants are small in number. See George C. Galster et al., Why Not in My Backyard? Neighborhood Impacts of Deconcentrating Assisted Housing 173–74 (2003) (reporting results of study conducted in Baltimore County). On racial and class segregation, see also pp. 11–13 and 692–710.

5. *The effect of housing vouchers on the housing stock.* Critics of tenant-based housing aid advance a number of arguments. Self-styled progressive housing analysts generally favor increasing the amount of housing provided by nonprofit and governmental organizations. Essentially, they disapprove of housing allowances because those transfers tend to perpetuate profit-oriented housing supply. See Rachel G. Bratt, Rebuilding a Low-Income Housing Policy 10–15 (1989); Chester Hartman, Housing Allowances: A Critical Look, 5 J. Urb. Aff. 41 (1983). But see Barbara Sard, The Massachusetts Experience with Targeted Tenant-Based Rental Assistance for the Homeless, Pts. I, II & III, 1 Geo. J. on Fighting Poverty 16, 182, 216 (1994) (legal-services lawyer's praise of voucher approach).

Another criticism of tenant-based subsidies is that project-based subsidies may be more successful than vouchers at increasing the stock of affordable housing units. See Mary K. Nenno, Ending the Stalemate 136–61 (1996); William C. Apgar, Jr., Which Housing Policy Is Best?, 1 Housing Pol'y Debate 1 (1990). Advocates of a shift to vouchers respond that the construction of subsidized projects tends to substitute for, not augment, the supply of unsubsidized housing units. See John C. Weicher, The Voucher/Production Debate, *in* Building Foundations 263 (Denise DiPasquale & Langley C. Keyes eds., 1990) (reviewing econometric studies). In addition, housing economists argue that demand expressed through vouchers itself can prompt a favorable supply-side response. See Jerome Rothenberg et al., The Maze of Urban Housing Markets 355 (1991).

6. *Relative cost.* A leading study by Mayo, cited at p. 875, found that project-based subsidies tend to be almost twice as expensive as tenant-based subsidies. Because of administrative complexities, government inefficiency, and the in-kind nature of the transfers, project-based subsidies deliver around 40 to 50 cents worth of tenant benefits per dollar of outlays, whereas tenant-based subsidies deliver 65 to 94 cents of benefits per dollar. Most housing economists agree that vouchers are far more cost-effective. See, e.g., Olsen, supra, at 394–99, 437 (reviewing various studies). But compare Denise DiPasquale et al., Comparing the Costs of Federal Housing Assistance Programs, 9 Econ. Pol'y Rev., June 2003, at 147

(finding vouchers to be cheaper but noting some advantages of production programs); Amy Ellen Schwartz et al., The External Effects of Placed-Based Subsidized Housing (Furman Center Working Paper, 2005) (finding that subsidized projects can generate significant positive neighborhood externalities).

7. *Housing vouchers vs. unrestricted cash transfers.* Consider the merits of the following three arguments (and counterarguments) for government provision of in-kind housing subsidies of any type:

(a) *Positive externalities*: Bad housing may endanger neighbors with fire, infectious disease, and other harmful effects. See Jerome Rothenberg, Economic Evaluation of Urban Renewal 54–60, 160–75 (1967) (reviewing literature on this topic). Counterargument: Housing code enforcement is the tailored response to housing conditions that threaten outsiders.

(b) *Child welfare*: Housing subsidies are more likely than cash to be passed through to benefit children in a recipient household. Counterargument: Child welfare agencies can intervene in cases where parents or guardians neglect children.

(c) *Preferences of taxpayers*: Those who pay for income transfers desire to place constraints on how transferees spend the money. Counterargument: Why should middle-class taxpayers be entitled to impose their values on others?

For fuller discussion, see Olsen, supra, at 368–70; Michael H. Schill, Privatizing Federal Low Income Housing Assistance, 75 Cornell L. Rev. 878, 890–93 (1990). As noted above, housing assistance programs are not entitlement programs, available to all who satisfy categorical eligibility criteria; instead, benefits typically are allotted by queue. On the potential inefficiencies of this approach, see David A. Super, The Political Economy of Entitlement, 104 Colum. L. Rev. 633, 672–77 (2004).

c.   *Federal Low-Income Housing Tax Credits*

The Tax Reform Act of 1986 eliminated many tax benefits that real estate investors previously had enjoyed, but at the same time created a major new "tax expenditure" — the low-income housing tax credit (LIHTC). See I.R.C. §42. The LIHTC quickly became the most significant federal program providing new project-based housing subsidies. Between 1987 and 2001, an estimated 28 percent of the multifamily housing units built in the United States benefited from LIHTC assistance. Megan J. Ballard, Profiting from Poverty: The Competition Between For-Profit and Non-Profit Developers for Low-Income Housing Tax Credits, 55 Hastings L.J. 211, 214 (2003). Project developers who seek these tax credits commonly also look for other housing subsidies, such as loans from state housing finance agencies and tenant-based Section 8 vouchers. See generally Jean L. Cummings & Denise DiPasquale, The Low-Income Housing Tax Credit: An Analysis of the First Ten Years, 10 Housing Pol'y Debate 251 (1999).

The aggregate LIHTCs for projects in a particular state generally are limited by an annual ceiling per state resident. This ceiling has limited the maximum federal revenue loss from the LIHTC to about $5 billion per year. In a display of cooperative federalism, the Internal Revenue Code authorizes each state (or chartered city) to determine which developers are to receive a portion of the state's share of the tax credits. To be eligible, a project must involve either new construction or substantial rehabilitation, and, for at least 15 years, offer at least 20 percent of units at reduced rents to households whose incomes are significantly below the median for the relevant geographic area. If a state receives more applications than it can accept, how should it select the winning projects? See Karl E. Case, Investors, Developers, and Supply-Side Subsidies, 2 Housing Pol'y Debate 341

(1991) (proposing that states auction off credits to developers rather than allocating them through political decisions).

The maximum tax credit has a present value equal to 70 percent of the construction costs of the affordable units provided. A taxpayer who holds a credit apportions it evenly on tax returns submitted over a ten-year period to offset income taxes otherwise due. On the legal complexities, see Tracy A. Kaye, Sheltering Social Policy in the Tax Code, 38 Vill. L. Rev. 871 (1993). In practice, a developer who has successfully applied for a credit is likely to sell the credits to investors to raise equity capital. Firms prominently involved in syndicating tax credits to investors include the Local Initiatives Support Corporation (LISC) (which specializes in corporate investors) and Boston Capital (which specializes in individual investors, who face ceilings on credits allowed).

Critics of the LIHTC point to a variety of shortcomings. Some are concerned about who benefits from the program. See Ballard, supra (program is tilted in favor of for-profit developers); Janet Stearns, The Low-Income Housing Tax Credit: A Poor Solution to the Housing Crisis, 6 Yale L. & Pol'y Rev. 203 (1988) (LIHTC is not sufficiently aimed at helping the truly needy). Other critics stress various inefficiencies. First, the program is seen as excessively complex. See Michael A. Stegman, The Excessive Cost of Creative Finance: Growing Inefficiencies in the Production of Low-Income Housing, 2 Housing Pol'y Debate 357 (1991). In the early years, the costs of marketing credits commonly equaled 15 percent of their sale price. By 2000, however, when market participants had become more familiar with the program, this cost had fallen to 10 percent or less. Kirk McClure, The Low-Income Housing Tax Credit as an Aid to Housing Finance, 11 Housing Pol'y Debate 91 (2000). Second, the LIHTC program involves project-based subsidies, a form inherently less efficient than tenant-based subsidies. See Congressional Budget Office, The Cost-Effectiveness of the Low-Income Housing Tax Credits Compared with Housing Vouchers, Tax Notes, July 27, 1992, at 493; pp. 877–78. Third, there is some evidence that the LIHTC units fail to increase the size of the housing stock, but instead only substitute for unassisted production. Stephen Malpezzi & Kerry Vandell, Does the Low-Income Housing Tax Credit Increase the Supply of Housing?, 11 J. Housing Econ. 360 (2002).

But compare William Farina, One-Third of the Deal, Urb. Land, Oct. 1992, at 29 (defending credits as an effective way to achieve housing goals).

The political coalition favoring the LIHTC includes the developers who use them to raise capital, the syndicators who market them, and the state officials who allocate them. When the Treasury Department in 1989 opposed extension of the LIHTC, this coalition was able to keep the program alive. More significantly, in 1993, the program's proponents succeeded in removing the sunset provisions that previously had threatened the continued existence of the LIHTC.

d.   State and Local Housing Programs

As in other areas of welfare spending, the federal government has borne most of the expense of subsidizing low-income housing. Over the years, however, numerous states and localities have pursued initiatives of their own. A notable instance, mentioned at pp. 863–64, was New York City's embrace of public housing in 1934, three years before enactment of the federal counterpart. On state and local housing programs generally, see Charles E. Daye et al., Housing and Community Development 257–59 (3d ed. 1999); Mary K. Nenno, Ending the Stalemate 169–248 (1996).

State housing finance agencies. States and localities are able to borrow funds at below-market interest rates when interest paid to bondholders is excluded from federal and state income taxation. To exploit this advantage, all states except Arizona and Kansas have created a housing finance agency. Between 1960 and 1990, these agencies floated special-obligation bonds to raise over $50 billion in mortgage money for subsequent loans at below-market rates to targeted borrowers. Peter W. Salsich, Jr., Urban Housing: A Strategic Role for the States, 12 Yale L. & Pol'y Rev. 93, 103 (1994).

To cap the potential loss of federal tax revenue, in 1980, Congress placed ceilings on the aggregate amount of tax-exempt housing bonds that state and local governments can issue and, among other things, prohibited them from using bond revenues to help families purchase expensive single-family houses. See I.R.C. §§103, 142–43; Grant S. Nelson & Dale A. Whitman, Real Estate Finance Law 878–81 (4th ed. 2001). Despite this federal tightening, in 1990, state housing finance agencies made more than $6 billion in loans, supporting over 100,000 housing units. Salsich, supra, at 103.

Default rates on state housing finance agency loans have tended to be higher than on private loans. See Christopher Hoffman, Subsidizing High Rents, New Haven Reg., Sept. 11, 1994, at A1 (on high rates of default on Connecticut Housing Finance Authority loans); George Sternlieb et al., Tax Subsidies and Housing Investment 16–17 (1976) (on default rates by owners of New York Mitchell-Lama projects). In a notable instance, the New York Housing Finance Agency, to enable repairs at the huge Co-Op City complex in the Bronx, offered to reduce its claim for mortgage arrears from $154 million to $57 million. Alan Feuer, Albany Pact Would Refinance Co-Op City, N.Y. Times, Jan. 30, 2004, at B3.

Undue incentives for state involvement? The costs of the typical state mortgage bond program are entirely shifted to the federal treasury, which receives less revenue on account of the exclusion of bond interest. According to one estimate by the General Accounting Office, the federal revenue loss is almost four times the gain that mortgage borrowers receive. N.Y. Times, Aug. 15, 1983, at 16. Is the universal involvement of the states in mortgage lending another example of a counterproductive "race to the bottom"?

Direct state subsidies. A number of states — notably Maryland, Massachusetts, Minnesota, and Virginia — dip into their own revenues to finance grants or credit subsidies to low-income housing developers. Massachusetts also has adopted a low-income housing tax credit. Although patterned after the federal credit, Massachusetts's version enables reduction of state income-tax liabilities. Mass. Gen. Laws ch. 62, §61 (2004).

Local housing subsidies. Some local governments impose impact fees or other exactions to raise funds for affordable housing programs. See pp. 671–74 (on inclusionary zoning). These revenues commonly are placed in a housing trust fund that can be devoted to various forms of project-based and tenant-based assistance.

New York City's project-subsidy programs have been far more ambitious than those of any other U.S. locality. Although the city also has used devices such as land sales at below-market prices, it has relied heavily on property tax exemptions. Its two major exemption programs resulted in its forgoing $2.2 billion in tax revenue from 1990 to 1996. See Dennis Hevesi, A Pillar of City Housing: Tax Relief, N.Y. Times, Feb. 16, 1997, §9, at 1. For the argument that the city should aim its housing programs at correcting externalities and not at redistributing income, see Ingrid Gould Ellen et al., The Role of Cities in Providing Housing Assistance: A New York Perspective, *in* City Taxes, City Spending 101 (Amy Ellen Schwartz ed., 2004).

2.   *Government Aid to Urban Places*

Governments housing assistance programs have a narrowly targeted set of primary beneficiaries, namely the households that receive aid. Other urban programs have far more diffuse aims. This section first examines programs intended to reinvigorate the local economy generally, and then those intended to improve conditions in particular low-income neighborhoods.

a. Subsidization of Economic Development

Maready v. City of Winston-Salem
467 S.E.2d 615 (N.C. 1996)

WHICHARD, Justice.

[Maready, a taxpayer, instituted this action against the City of Winston-Salem and Forsyth County. He contended that N.C. Gen. Stat. §158-7.1, which authorizes local governments to make economic development incentive grants to private corporations, violated the public purpose clause of the North Carolina Constitution.]

[Invoking the statute, the City and County had invested approximately $13,200,000, primarily from their own funds, in 24 projects.] City and County officials estimate an increase in the local tax base of $238,593,000 and a projected creation of over 5,500 new jobs as a result of these economic development incentive programs. They expect to recoup the full amount of their investment within three to seven years. The source of the return will be revenues generated by the additional property taxes paid by participating corporations. To date, all but one project has met or exceeded its goal.

Officials . . . apply a formula set out in written guidelines to determine the maximum amount of assistance that can be given to the receiving corporation. . . . The expenditures are in the form of reimbursement to the recipient for purposes such as on-the-job training, site preparation, facility upgrading, and parking. If a proposal satisfies the guidelines as well as community needs, it is submitted to the appropriate governing body for final approval at a regularly scheduled public meeting. . . .

Article V, §2(1) of the North Carolina Constitution provides that "[t]he power of taxation shall be exercised in a just and equitable manner, for public purposes only.". . .

Plaintiff . . . argues, and the trial court apparently agreed, that this question falls squarely within the purview of [Mitchell v. North Carolina Indus. Dev. Fin. Auth., 159 S.E.2d 745 (N.C. 1968)]. There we held unconstitutional the Industrial Facilities Financing Act, a statute that authorized issuance of industrial revenue bonds to finance the construction and equipping of facilities for private corporations. . . . We find *Mitchell* distinguishable.

One of the bases for the *Mitchell* decision was that the General Assembly had unenthusiastically passed the enacting legislation, declaring it to be bad policy. The opinion stated:

> At the time the General Assembly passed the Act, it declared in Resolution No. 52 that it considered the Act bad public policy. It explained that it felt compelled to authorize industrial revenue bonds in order to compete for industry with neighboring states which use them. As proof of its reluctance to join the industry-subsidizing group of states, the General Assembly requested the President and the other forty-nine states to petition Congress to make the interest on all such bonds thereafter issued subject to all applicable income-tax laws.

Mitchell, 159 S.E.2d at 751. . . . The converse is true here in that the Assembly [in the course of enacting N.C. Gen. Stat. §158-7.1] unequivocally embraced expenditures of public funds for the promotion of local economic development as advancing a public purpose.

Further, and more importantly, the holding in *Mitchell* clearly indicates that the Court considered private industry to be the primary benefactor of the legislation and considered any benefit to the public purely incidental. . . . In reiterating that it is not the function of the government to engage in private business, the opinion quoted with approval the following language from the Supreme Court of Idaho:

> An exemption which arbitrarily prefers one private enterprise operating by means of facilities provided by a municipality, over another engaged, or desiring to engage, in the same business in the same locality, is neither necessary nor just. . . . It is obvious that private enterprise, not so favored, could not compete with industries operating thereunder. If the state-favored industries were successfully managed, private enterprise would of necessity be forced out, and the state, through its municipalities, would increasingly become involved in promoting, sponsoring, regulating and controlling private business, and our free private enterprise economy would be replaced by socialism. The constitutions of both state and nation were founded upon a capitalistic private enterprise economy and were designed to protect and foster private property and private initiative.

Id. at 756 (quoting Village of Moyie Springs v. Aurora Mfg. Co., 353 P.2d 767, 775 (Idaho 1960)). Thus, the Court implicitly rejected the act because its primary object was private gain and its nature and purpose did not tend to yield public benefit. . . .

. . . In 1973 Article V, §2(7) was added to the North Carolina Constitution, specifically allowing direct appropriation to private entities for public purposes. This section provides:

> The General Assembly may enact laws whereby the State, any county, city or town, and any other public corporation may contract with and appropriate money to any person, association, or corporation for the accomplishment of public purposes only.

N.C. Const. art. V, §2(7). "[U]nder subsection (7) *direct disbursement* of public funds to private entities is a constitutionally permissible *means* of accomplishing a public purpose provided there is statutory authority to make such appropriation." Hughey v. Cloninger, 253 S.E.2d 898, 904 (N.C. 1979). Hence, the constitutional problem under the public purpose doctrine that the Court perceived in *Mitchell* . . . no longer exists. . . .

This Court is no stranger to the question of what activities are and are not for a public purpose. The following cases demonstrate the great variety of facilities, authorities, and activities which have been deemed to be public purposes. [The court then cited 29 of its prior decisions.] While these cases are not necessarily consistent and may not have involved industrial development as the challenged project, they reflect a trend toward broadening the scope of what constitutes a valid public purpose that permits the expenditure of public revenues. The General Assembly may provide for, inter alia, roads, schools, housing, health care, transportation, and occupational training. It would be anomalous to now hold that a government which expends large sums to alleviate the problems of its citizens through multiple humanitarian and social programs is proscribed from promoting the provision of jobs for the unemployed, an increase in the tax base, and the prevention of economic stagnation. . . .

. . . While private actors will necessarily benefit from the expenditures authorized, such benefit is merely incidental. . . .

Finally, while this Court does not pass upon the wisdom or propriety of legislation in determining the primary motivation behind a statute, it may consider the circumstances surrounding its enactment. In that regard, a Legislative Research Commission committee made a report to the 1989 General Assembly, warning that:

> The traditional foundations of North Carolina's economy — agriculture and manufacturing — are in decline. And, the traditional economic development tool — industrial recruitment —

has proven inadequate for many of North Carolina's communities. Low wages and low taxes are no longer sufficient incentives to entice new industry to our State, especially to our most remote, most distressed areas.

N.C. Legislative Research Commission, Committee on Economic Development and Recruiting, Report to the 1989 N.C. General Assembly, at 15. In the economic climate thus depicted, the pressure to induce responsible corporate citizens to relocate to or expand in North Carolina is not internal only, but results from the actions of other states as well. To date, courts in forty-six states have upheld the constitutionality of governmental expenditures and related assistance for economic development incentives. [The court then inserted a footnote citing judicial opinions in these 46 states, and noted that another 3 states had statutes authorizing such expenditures.] Thus, by virtue of the trial court's ruling, North Carolina currently stands alone in so holding. Considered in this light, it would be unrealistic to assume that the State will not suffer economically in the future if the incentive programs created pursuant to N.C.G.S. §158-7.1 are discontinued....

... Accordingly, the decision of the trial court ... is reversed....

ORR, Justice, dissenting.

... Because I believe that the majority's holding in this case is (1) based on a theory unsupported by the evidence, and (2) contrary to established precedent interpreting the intent of the North Carolina Constitution, I respectfully dissent....

... [P]laintiff and those supporting his point of view argue that direct grants to specific, selected businesses go beyond the acceptable bounds of public purpose expenditures for economic development. Instead, they say that this is selected corporate welfare to some of the largest and most prosperous companies in our State and in the country. Moreover, these opponents contend that the grants are not equitably applied because they generally favor the larger companies and projects and, in this case, under the County's Economic Incentives Program Guidelines, completely eliminate retail operations from being considered. In challenging the actual public benefit, a question also is raised about the economic loss and devastation to smaller North Carolina communities that lose valued industry to larger, wealthier areas. For example, the move of Southern National Bank headquarters from Lumberton to Winston-Salem undoubtedly adversely affected Lumberton.

Also troubling is the question of limits under the majority's theory. If it is an acceptable public purpose to spend tax dollars specifically for relocation expenses to benefit the spouses of corporate executives moving to the community in finding new jobs or for parking decks that benefit only the employees of the favored company, then what can a government not do if the end result will entice a company to produce new jobs and raise the tax base? If a potential corporate entity is considering a move to Winston-Salem but will only come if country club memberships are provided for its executives, do we sanction the use of tax revenue to facilitate the move? I would hope not, but under the holding of the majority opinion, I see no grounds for challenging such an expenditure provided that, as a result of such a grant, the company promises to create new jobs, and an increased tax base is projected....

LAKE, J., joins in this dissenting opinion.

Note on Legal Constraints on Municipal Economic Development Activity

1. *State constitutional constraints.* As *Maready* indicates, state constitutions typically contain clauses that limit expenditure of municipal tax and bond revenues to "public purposes." After *Maready*, to what extent do these clauses in fact constrain North Carolina

governments? A state constitution may contain other pertinent provisions. For example, there may be a limitation on the total amount of a government's general obligation debt. In addition, following scandals involving the lending of government credit to railroad corporations in the late nineteenth century, a majority of state constitutions prohibit gifts or loans of credit to private entities. On the increasing porosity of both these constraints, see Richard Briffault, The Disfavored Constitution: State Fiscal Limits and State Constitutional Law, 34 Rutgers L.J. 907 (2003); David M. Lawrence, Constitutional Limitations on Governmental Participation in Downtown Development Projects, 35 Vand. L. Rev. 277 (1982).

2. *Federal constitutional constraints. Maready* indicates that competition from other states helped induce North Carolina to join the economic-development parade. Many observers conclude that competition among states and localities for migratory businesses is a negative-sum game — a "race to the bottom." See, e.g., Peter D. Enrich, Saving the States from Themselves: Commerce Clause Constraints on State Tax Incentives for Business, 110 Harv. L. Rev. 377 (1996). Some commentators have urged enactment of federal legislation to curb the practice and rescue the states from their dilemma. See, e.g., Mark Taylor, Note, A Proposal to Prohibit Industrial Relocation Subsidies, 72 Tex. L. Rev. 669 (1994). Enrich concludes, however, that federal legislation is politically unlikely. He argues instead that the dormant Commerce Clause prohibits a state from adopting fiscal practices that distort firms' decisions about where to locate their activities. This argument met with some success in Cuno v. DaimlerChrysler, Inc., 386 F.3d 738 (6th Cir. 2004). In that instance, the City of Toledo, pursuant to a state program, had granted an auto manufacturer an estimated $280 million in credits against the state corporation franchise tax to help induce it to expand its local plant. The court held that this credit discriminated in favor of Ohio-based firms, which were more likely to value the credit, and thus violated the Commerce Clause.

But cf. Clayton P. Gillette, Business Incentives, Interstate Competition, and the Commerce Clause, 82 Minn. L. Rev. 447 (1997) (stressing advantages of competition among states). What relevance does the Enrich-Gillette debate have to the wisdom and legality of *substate* business incentives, such as the subsidies that Winston-Salem and Forsyth County provided out of their own funds?

3. *Internal Revenue Code restrictions on "private activity" bonds.* State and local development agencies have sought to enable business firms to take advantage of the federal income tax exclusion of interest on state and local bonds. One device is the industrial revenue bond, which is issued by a government but secured solely by a stream of payments that the benefited firm owes. Since the 1970s, a major fraction of new state and local debt has been devoted to arrangements of this sort. To stem this tide, in the 1980s, Congress began to impose restrictions (of increasing complexity) on the power of state and local governments to issue tax-exempt "private activity" bonds. See I.R.C. §§103, 141–150.

William J. Stern, State Capitalism, New York Style
City J., Summer 1994, at 70–75

In February 1994, New York City and State and the Disney Corporation announced a "public-private partnership" in which the city and state will lend Disney $21 million at 3 percent interest, which Disney will use to rehabilitate and reopen the landmark New Amsterdam theater on West 42nd Street. The agreement is an attempt to give the 12-year-old state-and city-sponsored 42nd Street Redevelopment Project a much-needed push.

It may seem odd that New York City and State, both of which are facing serious fiscal problems, are lending money at bargain rates to a highly profitable corporation whose chairman earned $200 million in 1993. In fact, it is perfectly in keeping with the economic development philosophy that New York officials have pursued for the past three decades — a philosophy I call "state capitalism." It is a philosophy based on the idea that these governments can act as all-knowing capitalists, allocating capital in a way that will maximize the creation of wealth, jobs, and tax revenues for New York.

State capitalism favors older industries over newer ones, established companies over up-and-coming ones, and the politically connected over ordinary citizens. It is a strategy that has failed, as evidenced by a variety of economic data. Forbes reported in January 1994 that one-third of Americans who lost their jobs during the recent recession lived in New York State, and that the state lost almost 10 percent of its private-sector jobs over four years.

State capitalism takes three basic forms: tax breaks for specific corporations to keep them from leaving New York; public-private partnerships, or subsidies for favored developments; and developments that are built, owned, and operated by the government.

TAX BREAKS FOR CORPORATIONS

In the first type of state capitalist venture, the state and city act as bureaucratic deal-makers. In order to prevent certain businesses from leaving the city, the governments award them a variety of tax breaks, cheaper energy costs, and other concessions. The businesses receiving these dispensations are almost always large, high-profile enterprises whose departure from the city would not only cost jobs and tax revenues but also cause embarrassment to New York's political leadership.

Consider the deal the city cut in 1987 with NBC. The network was supposedly evaluating whether to relocate its headquarters from 30 Rockefeller Plaza either to New Jersey or to a proposed Donald Trump development on the west side, which the developer was calling "Television City." . . .

. . . [T]he city . . . reassessed the entire Rockefeller Center complex, lowering the tax rate until 2006, when the city is to begin phasing in a higher rate over 17 years. The city projected this agreement would save NBC $73 million in taxes. Moreover, the city would become the temporary owner of the network's expanded Rockefeller Center space, entitling NBC to hundreds of millions of dollars in city industrial bond financing, as well as a full sales tax exemption. Adding up all the advantages of the deal they were offering, city officials estimated it would reduce NBC's anticipated Rockefeller Center costs by half a billion dollars.

Other examples of this practice are numerous. . . . It is understandable that the city would wish to persuade a large employer to remain in the city. But the practice of ad hoc deal-making to induce particular companies to stay is misguided. For one thing, it creates an incentive for businesses to threaten to leave, even if they have no intention of doing so. . . .

. . . If even some of the city's largest corporations find taxes and energy costs so burdensome that they consider leaving, the effect of these same costs is at least as great on small and mid-size businesses and on entrepreneurs deciding where to locate a new venture. But because the thousands of little decisions made by entrepreneurs garner no publicity, the city offers few incentives for small firms to stay or start in New York.

The city and state's deal-making is driven by politics, not economics. Its primary virtue is that it avoids the embarrassment that New York's political establishment suffers when a big company leaves the city. Keeping a firm in the city by offering it tax breaks and subsidies serves only to disguise the essential truth that in the highly competitive global marketplace, the cost of doing business in New York is too high for everyone.

PUBLIC-PRIVATE PARTNERSHIPS

The second economic development method used by New York's state capitalists is the "public-private partnership," in which the government subsidizes selected corporations in order to induce them to make their own investments in New York City. . . .

Battery Park City, a lower Manhattan development consisting of luxury apartments and offices, has been loudly proclaimed as a government success story. It was initially financed in 1972 with $200 million of moral obligation bonds issued by the state; the Battery Park City Authority has paid approximately $14 million a year in debt service since then. There has been much talk of expanding the activities of this "profitable" authority, northward on the Hudson as well as within the present project area.

Battery Park City is indeed an impressive development. But how much sense does it make for the government to have subsidized it? There was no shortage of office and luxury apartment development by the private sector in New York City during the 1980s. In fact, with hindsight, we can say there was a sizable overexpansion in lower and midtown Manhattan, which market forces have been correcting since 1988. In other words, the state government subsidized exactly the kind of development that went on all over the city without government subsidy.

Of course, at the time the project was initiated, officials did not know that this kind of expansion was going to take place. But that is precisely the point: How could they have known? How can they ever know? Even if individuals in state and city government could allocate capital with a kind of divine wisdom, these state capitalist projects take so long from inception to completion that all the assumptions that justify the initiation of a project no longer hold true by the time it is completed. The accelerating speed of change in the global market economy is simply not compatible with the slow pace that characterizes all state capitalist endeavors.

The Battery Park City "success story," then, is actually an excellent example of the inefficiency of state capitalism. Battery Park subsidized office space and luxury apartments, goods that were widely available, at a time when there was a severe shortage of low and moderately priced housing in New York City. It is rather like the government-run department stores of communist Bulgaria, which would often have a wide variety of socks available even though no shoes could be purchased anywhere.

Yet another example is the South Street Seaport, a city, state, and federally financed shopping complex on an East River pier and nearby Fulton Street. Today many of the restaurants and shops that comprise the Seaport complex are in financial difficulty, squeezed by high rents and the city's recession. Surveys have shown that the patrons of the area are people who, if they were not shopping and eating at the Seaport, would be frequenting establishments in other parts of Manhattan. Government has subsidized yet another zero-sum activity that merely alters who gets what slice of the economic pie and contributes nothing to the making of a bigger pie.

GOVERNMENT DEVELOPMENTS

In the third type of state capitalist project, the state or city dispenses with subsidies, deals, and partnerships, and enters a business itself. . . .

The Javits Convention Center is [an] example. . . . As is typical in state capitalist projects, the [agency sponsoring the convention center] had prepared detailed statistics purporting to show what is called the "multiplier effect." These reports estimated the amount of money that the convention center's visitors and construction would add to the city's economy. Extrapolating from these data, the reports estimated the number of permanent and temporary jobs that would be created, the amount of taxes collected by the city and state, revenue generated for the city's hotel, restaurant, and entertainment industries, and so forth. Based on these estimates, the project was pronounced economically sound, financially viable, and "profitable" for the city.

[The trouble with this kind of analysis is that] it does not calculate the "demultiplier" effect of such a project. It fails to ask: What if the tax money spent on building and managing a convention center had been left in the pockets of the citizens and businesses of the state, to be employed in the normal market economy? We will never know the answer to this question. But it requires an enormous leap of faith and ignorance of economic history to reject the principle that if individuals and businesses are allowed to make their own investment decisions in a market economy, the results are generally far superior than if the government makes those decisions for them.

A NEW STRATEGY

State capitalism has been New York's dominant economic development philosophy for three decades. During that time, New York's economy has steadily declined. Using figures provided by the U.S. Bureau of Economic Analysis, the Empire Foundation estimates that between 1963 and 1992 New York's Gross State Product grew only about half as much as the nation's Gross Domestic Product. New York's personal income growth during the same period lagged behind that of the nation as a whole by almost 30 percent, and the state's job creation rate was less than one-fifth of the national rate.

State capitalism has, however, enabled a group of political insiders to enrich themselves at taxpayer expense. New York's economic development policies have produced what Eastern Europeans call a *nomenklatura* — a privileged class of people who benefit handsomely from government involvement in the economy, at public expense. New York's *nomenklatura* includes politicians, public finance specialists on Wall Street, politically connected lawyers, public relations people, and lobbyists.

New York should abandon state capitalism in favor of a new economic development strategy based on the principle that the market can allocate capital far more productively than government. . . .

Note on the Merits of Economic Development Programs

1. *Do the programs work?* For a review of the profuse literature on the effectiveness of government economic development efforts, see Alan Peters & Peter Fisher, The Failures of Economic Development Incentives, 70 J. Am. Plan. Ass'n 27 (2004). Peters and Fisher estimate that governments expend about $50 billion per year on these programs, much of it in vain. They urge instead that governments concentrate on "providing the foundations for growth through sound fiscal practices, quality public infrastructure, and good education systems — and then letting the economy take care of itself." Id. at 36.

Works that are more upbeat about government aid to enterprise include Timothy J. Bartik, Who Benefits from State and Local Economic Development Policies? (1991); Peter K. Eisinger, The Rise of the Entrepreneurial State (1988); and Charles A.M. de Bartolome & Mark M. Spiegel, Does State Economic Development Spending Increase Manufacturing Employment?, 41 J. Urb. Econ. 153 (1997) (finding significant positive results). See generally Dilemmas of Urban Economic Development (Richard D. Bingham & Robert Mier eds., 1997).

For even sharper counterpoint to William Stern's perspective, see Buffalo Change and Community: A Symposium, 39 Buff. L. Rev. 313 (1991). While Stern urges cities to embrace market-oriented approaches, most contributors to the Buffalo symposium seek to mobilize labor unions, city agencies, religious institutions, and other nonprofits into a coalition to carry out community economic development. See also pp. 890–92 (on community development corporations).

2. *Sports venues*. There has been a particularly lively debate about the wisdom of city subsidization of venues for professional sports franchises. In recent years, public funds have defrayed about two-thirds of the costs of building new and renovated stadiums and arenas. Most commentators have been critical of these subsidies. See, e.g., Roger G. Noll & Andrew Zimbalist, Sports, Jobs, and Taxes (1997) (challenging argument that heavy subsidies to sports teams and facilities benefit a local economy). What positive externalities, if any, might a professional sports franchise generate?

3. *Government as equity investor*. Cities have begun to bargain for ownership shares in major development projects. See City Deal Making (Terry Jill Lassar ed., 1990) (marshaling examples). A study of 15 projects with profit-sharing arrangements found that three were generating a cash return for the participating city. Lynne B. Sagalyn, Public Profit Sharing: Symbol or Substance?, *in* City Deal Making, supra (arguing city politicians use profit-sharing to allay voters' anxieties about proposed projects). Does a city have an insuperable conflict of interest when it seeks to regulate the land uses entailed in a project in which it is an equity investor?

b.   *Assistance Targeted at Poor Cities and Neighborhoods*

After the demise of traditional urban renewal, both the federal government and most states created other aid programs for distressed neighborhoods, especially those in central cities.

Community Development Block Grants. In 1974, Congress consolidated ten major categorical grants into a Community Development Block Grant (CDBG). See Housing and Community Development Act of 1974, Pub. Law 93-383, 88 Stat. 633. These grants are allocated to cities and urban counties according to a formula that accords some weight to neediness. After 1981, a local government was directed to use a majority of the funds to benefit low- and moderate-income persons. At the turn of the century, Congress was providing almost $5 billion for CDBGs per fiscal year. Local officials mainly have used CDBG funds to finance housing programs, service providers, and public improvements in scattered locations, although rarely in the most distressed neighborhoods. On CDBGs, see R. Allen Hays, The Federal Government and Urban Housing 199–232 (2d ed. 1995); Louise A. Howells, Looking for the Butterfly Effect: An Analysis of Urban Economic Development Under the Community Development Block Grant Program, 16 St. Louis U. Pub. L. Rev. 383 (1997); Steven Malanga, America's Worst Urban Program, City J., Spring 2005, at 48. In early 2005, the Bush Administration proposed consolidating CDBGs with other local aids, shifting the consolidated program to the Commerce Department, and reducing the combined funding by over one-third. National organizations of local officials immediately mobilized to oppose the change.

Enterprise and empowerment zones. Drawing on a British model, the Reagan Administration advocated the conferral of substantial federal tax breaks (and possibly regulatory exemptions) on industrial firms that sited new facilities in poor urban neighborhoods. See Stuart Butler, Enterprise Zones (1981). Although Congress declined to approve enabling legislation during the Reagan years, the idea won many converts in statehouses. During the 1980s, a large majority of states authorized the creation of enterprise zones where favorable state tax treatment would be available.

In 1993, during the Clinton Administration, Congress enacted the Empowerment Zone and Enterprise Communities Act, 26 U.S.C. §§1391–1397D (2004), a variant designed to compensate firms through financial incentives, not regulatory concessions. The act provides significant tax benefits to eligible employers with facilities in designated "empowerment zones." These tax breaks include special depreciation deductions for new investment, a credit of up to $3,000 per year for each employee who both lives and works in the zone, and special deductions for the cost of environmental cleanups. In contrast to the Reagan Administration conception, an outside employer who moves a facility to a zone in order to receive these tax advantages is not eligible for empowerment zone subsidies. Since 1994, HUD has designated zones (under a bewildering variety of labels) in over 100 communities and also provided many zone agencies with grants. On the various federal and state programs, see generally Nicole Stelle Garnett, Ordering (and Order in) the City, 57 Stan. L. Rev. 1, 26–31 (2004); Audrey G. McFarlane, Race, Space and Place: The Geography of Economic Development, 36 San Diego L. Rev. 295 (1999).

On the effectiveness of the enterprise and empowerment zones, compare Leslie E. Papke, Tax Policy and Urban Development, 54 J. Pub. Econ. 37 (1994) (finding Indiana's state program to be effective in fostering economic development), with Alan H. Peters & Peter S. Fisher, State Enterprise Zone Programs: Have They Worked? (2002) (concluding that programs are ineffective). See generally E. Douglass Williams & Richard H. Sander, The Prospects for "Putting America Back to Work" in the Inner City, 81 Geo. L.J. 2003 (1993).

The merits of aiding neighborhoods as opposed to aiding people. When, if ever, should a government seek to help a spatially defined neighborhood as such, instead of (for example) providing transportable aid to the individuals and households currently living in that neighborhood? See Jeffrey S. Lehman, Updating Urban Policy, *in* Confronting Poverty: Prescriptions for Change 226, 228–35 (Sheldon H. Danziger et al. eds., 1994); Louis Winnick, Place Prosperity vs. People Prosperity, *in* Essays in Urban Land Economics 273 (1966) (pioneering economic critique of place-based aid).

3.   *Government Financial Support to Urban Innovators*

Intellectual property rights generally are not attainable in fresh urban designs and institutions. As a result, there tends to be too little research and development in the urban sector. This provides a rationale for federal funding.

The federal executive branch has tended to look more favorably than Congress on urban research-and-development initiatives. For example, the presidential task force that proposed the Model Cities program enacted in 1966 sought to focus outlays on only a few city neighborhoods. This targeting approach was not acceptable to members of relevant appropriations committees, who wanted to funnel benefits to their own districts. Congress eventually spread funds so diffusely that the experimental thrust of the Model Cities program was lost. See Charles M. Haar, Between the Idea and the Reality: A Study in the Origin, Fate and Legacy of the Model Cities Program (1975). What political minefields might have surrounded the federal programs to support new towns and community development corporations, the primary subjects of the materials that follow?

a.   *Experimental Urban Designs: The Example of New Towns*

During the mid-1960s, when riots rocked many central cities, there was an outburst of interest in "new towns" — economically independent planned communities on exurban sites. See, e.g., Wolf Von Eckardt, The Case for Building 350 New Towns, Harper's Mag.,

Dec. 1965, at 88. The seed of this idea usually is attributed to the English writer Ebenezer Howard, who had pushed the creation of analogous Garden Cities at the outset of the twentieth century. The plausibility of the new-town concept was enhanced when the private developers of Reston, Virginia, and Columbia, Maryland, two large communities then in the distant suburbs of Washington, D.C., latched onto the notion in their promotional materials. Responding to this upsurge of popular interest, in 1968 and 1970, Congress authorized a variety of grants and loan subsidies to qualifying developers of new towns. The program soon turned into a fiasco and had to be terminated. By 1979, at least 8 of the 13 private new towns that HUD had assisted under the program had been written off at a public loss of close to $200 million. See Robert C. Ellickson & A. Dan Tarlock, Land-Use Controls 1042–48 (1st ed. 1981); Hugh Evans & Lloyd Rodwin, The New Towns Program and Why It Failed, Pub. Interest, No. 56, at 90 (Summer 1979). The most successful of the projects, The Woodlands located north of Houston, went to the edge of bankruptcy. See George T. Morgan, Jr. & John O. King, The Woodlands (1987).

In The Mirage of New Towns, Pub. Interest, No. 19, at 3 (Spring 1970), William Alonso, while criticizing the escapist motivations of most new town proposals, endorses government support of developments that would test or exhibit innovations that others could mimic. The 1990s witnessed innovative New Urbanist developments such as Seaside, Florida, and Celebration at Disney World. Is there a case for federal support of research and development in town design? Planners associated with the New Urbanist movement advocate legal innovations in land use regulations. See, e.g., Andres Duany & Elizabeth Plater-Zyberk, New Town Ordinances and Codes, 59 Arch. Design 71 (1989). Should Congress authorize HUD to help fund experiments with these? To what extent does the new towns program fiasco of the 1970s demonstrate that federal funding tends to attract not the most talented developers and designers but rather the marginally qualified?

b.   New Urban Institutions: Community Development Corporations and Community Banks

The federal government has had some success in refining and propagating new institutional forms. Examples include the Department of Commerce's promotion of the Standard State Zoning Enabling Act in the early 1920s and FHA's support of the fully amortized mortgage in the 1930s. See pp. 74–76 and 869. Other federal progeny have fared less well — for example, local urban renewal agencies and (according to many observers) public housing authorities. To assess the merits of federal support for new urban institutions, consider these more contemporary examples:

Community development corporations (CDCs). A CDC is a neighborhood-based non-profit association, typically governed by a board consisting of local business and institutional leaders, neighborhood activists, and donor representatives. Although a CDC may undertake a broad range of revitalization activities, including business development and the provision of social services, most concentrate on the production and management of affordable housing projects. See generally William H. Simon, The Community Economic Development Movement (2001).

The number of CDCs in the United States rose from about 200 in 1980 to over 2,000 in 1994. In 1991, CDCs owned 0.3 percent of the total U.S. housing stock and produced 29,000 new units, almost 3 percent of the total national output in that year. Michael H. Schill, The Role of the Nonprofit Sector in Low-Income Housing Production: A Comparative Perspective, 30 Urb. Aff. Q. 74, 76 (1994). CDCs are increasingly prominent in the production of subsidized housing, particularly in metropolitan areas such as

Boston, the Twin Cities, and San Francisco. Indeed, one study estimates that community development corporations built 90 percent of the affordable housing produced in the city of Boston during the 1980s. Langley Keyes et al., Networks and Non-Profits: Opportunities and Challenges in an Era of Federal Devolution, 7 Housing Pol'y Debate 201, 205 (1996).

Throughout their existence, CDCs have relied heavily on both government aid and foundation support. The Economic Opportunity Act of 1964 helped give the CDC movement its start. In 1979, the Ford Foundation, a longtime booster, provided seed money for the founding of the Local Initiatives Support Corporation. LISC is an umbrella organization that provides CDCs with technical assistance, access to capital, and lobbying support. The Enterprise Foundation, founded by James Rouse in 1982, fills a similar niche. In what contexts can the federal government rely entirely on foundations to sponsor institutional innovations?

Current federal aids to CDCs take many forms, most of them indirect. Several federal programs include set-asides that favor nonprofit housing developers such as CDCs. See Schill, supra, at 85–87. CDCs commonly succeed in securing benefits from federal block grants to cities (particularly under CDBG and HOME), and raise funds for affordable housing projects through the use of federal Low-Income Housing Tax Credits. The New Markets Tax Credits program begun in 2000 (see infra p. 892) is designed to help organizations such as CDCs raise equity capital.

The merits of the CDC movement are contested. For praise, see Paul S. Grogan, Proof Positive: A Community-Based Solution to America's Affordable Housing Crisis, 7 Stan. L. & Pol'y Rev. 159 (1996); Benjamin B. Quinones, Redevelopment Redefined, 27 U. Mich. J.L. Reform 689 (1994). CDCs have special appeal to commentators who wish to expand the "social housing sector," in which housing "is neither resold as a commodity for speculation nor managed for profit taking." See Edward G. Goetz, Shelter Burden: Local Politics and Progressive Housing Policy 114 (1993). Compare Scott Cummings, Community Economic Development as Progressive Politics: Toward a Grassroots Movement for Economic Justice, 54 Stan. L. Rev. 399 (2001) (urging advocates to redirect their efforts from market-based activity to the building of progressive political coalitions).

Others are skeptical that nonprofit organizations have comparative advantages in developing and owning housing. See Robert C. Ellickson, New Institutions for Old Neighborhoods, 48 Duke L.J. 75, 86–87 (1998) (contending that CDCs primarily produce private goods that for-profit firms generally can provide more efficiently); Schill, supra, at 94 (doubting whether a nonprofit's advantages in obtaining grants would outweigh its inferior access to capital and its weak incentives to minimize costs). See generally Henry B. Hansmann, The Role of Nonprofit Enterprise, 89 Yale L.J. 835 (1980); Michael E. Porter, The Competitive Advantage of the Central City, Harv. Bus. Rev., May-June 1995, at 55 (stressing the advantages of self-supporting institutions).

How well CDCs have worked is far from clear. See Michael H. Schill, Assessing the Role of Community Development Corporations in Inner City Economic Development, 22 N.Y.U. Rev. L. & Soc. Change 753 (1997) (lamenting shortage of careful studies). The most thorough survey, funded by the Ford Foundation, is Avis C. Vidal, Rebuilding Communities: A National Study of Urban Community Development Corporations (1992). Vidal is generally positive. Some of the CDC's once singled out as national models, however, have foundered with age. See, e.g., Terry Pristin, In Bedford-Stuyvesant, The Boom Remains a Bust, N.Y. Times, May 29, 2000, at B1 (reporting that "the organization that was intended to help bring prosperity to central Brooklyn — the Bedford-Stuyvesant Restoration Corporation — has served as an impediment to progress, an entrenched and sluggish bureaucracy"); Amy Waldman, A Dream Foreclosed, N.Y. Times, June 27, 2000, at A1 (describing disarray at the Bronx's once-lauded Banana Kelly Improvement Association).

On the tendency of CDCs to become involved in machine politics, see Nicole P. Marwell, Privatizing the Welfare State: Non-Profit Community-Based Organizations as Political Actors, 69 Am. Soc. Rev. 265 (2004).

Community development banks. Governments and foundations have also fostered the creation of institutions devoted to lending and investing in distressed communities. The first and still most notable of these is ShoreBank, mainly active on the South Side of Chicago. Federal aid is provided mainly through the Community Development Financial Institutions Act of 1994, 12 U.S.C. §§4701–4718 (2004), amended in 2000 to include New Markets Tax Credits. The latter program provides several billion dollars a year in federal tax credits to investors in entities that in turn invest or lend in distressed urban and rural communities. See Susan R. Jones, Will New Markets Tax Credits Enhance Community Economic Development?, 8 J. Small & Emerging Bus. L. 229 (2004).

Do these financial institutions warrant federal aid? For an affirmative answer, see Rochelle E. Lento, Community Development Banking Strategy for Revitalizing Our Communities, 27 U. Mich. J.L. Reform 773 (1994). For a downbeat case study, see James Sterngold, A Grand Idea That Went Awry, N.Y. Times, Nov. 14, 1999, §3, at 1 (on the Los Angeles Community Development Bank). See generally Michael S. Barr, Banking the Poor, 21 Yale J. on Reg. 121 (2004); Michael Klausner, Market Failure and Community Investment, 143 U. Pa. L. Rev. 1561 (1995); Anthony D. Taibi, Banking, Finance, and Community Economic Empowerment, 107 Harv. L. Rev. 1463 (1994).

Table of Cases

Principal cases are in italics.

2nd Roc-Jersey Assocs. v. Town of Morristown, 630
40 West 67th St. Corp. v. Pullman, 598
1000 Friends of Oregon v. Land Conservation & Dev. Comm'n (Or. Ct. App. 1979), 341, 814
1000 Friends of Oregon v. Land Conservation & Dev. Comm'n (Or. 1986), 814
1000 Friends of Oregon v. Wasco County Ct., 360
14859 Moorpark Homeowners Ass'n v. VRT Corp., 601
Abbott v. City of Bristol, 524
Ackerley Communications of Northwest, Inc. v. Krochalis, 483
Adkins v. Children's Hosp., 85
Adolphson v. Zoning Bd. of Appeals, 202
Advocacy Center for Persons with Disabilities, Inc. v. Woodlands Estates Ass'n, 729
Agins v. City of Tiburon, 179, 239, 256, 808
Agripost, Inc. v. Metropolitan Miami-Dade County, 328
Aiken, City of, v. Cole, 94
Alderman v. Shanks, 446
Aldred's Case, 512
Aldrich v. ADD Inc., 445
Alexander v. Sandoval, 755
Ali v. City of Los Angeles, 457
Allendale, Borough of, v. Township Comm., 739
Allied Tube & Conduit Corp. v. Indian Head, Inc., 459
Allred v. City of Raleigh, 319
Amana Soc'y v. Colony Inn, Inc., 579
Ambler Realty Co. v. Village of Euclid, 81
American-Hawaiian Steamship Co. v. Home Sav. & Loan Ass'n, 622
American Pelagic Fishing Co. v. United States, 178
AMG Assocs. v. Township of Springfield, 256
Ammons v. Dade City, 681
Amoruso v. Board of Managers, 593
Amphitheatres, Inc. v. Portland Meadows, 527
Anderson v. City of Issaquah, 489, 596

Anderson v. Old King's Highway Regional Historic Dist. Comm'n, 504
Anneburg v. Kurtz, 528
Anthony v. Snyder, 440
Aposporos v. Urban Redev. Comm'n, 840
Appolo Fuels, Inc. v. United States, 265
Argent v. United States, 524
Arlington Heights, Village of, v. Metropolitan Hous. Dev. Corp., 116, 698, 755, 763
Armory Park Neighborhood Ass'n v. Episcopal Community Servs., 523
Armstrong v. United States, 145
Arnold v. Prince George's County, 415
Arundel, Town of, v. Swaim, 441
A-S-P Assocs. v. City of Raleigh, 500, 634
Associated Home Bldrs. v. City of Livermore, 405, 782, 797, 806
Associated Home Bldrs. v. City of Walnut Creek, 638, 671
Atkins v. Robinson, 702
Attorney Gen. v. Williams, 580
AvalonBay Communities, Inc. v. Sewer Comm'n, 686
Avalon Home & Land Owner's Ass'n v. Avalon, 201
Avery v. Midland County, 590
AWL Power, Inc. v. City of Rochester, 433
Ayres v. City Council, 30, 661
Azul-Pacifico, Inc. v. City of Los Angeles, 233

BAC, Inc. v. Board of Supervisors, 783
Baer v. Town of Brookhaven, 715
Baker v. Chartiers Township Zoning Hearing Bd., 316
Baker v. City of Kissimmee, 693
Baker v. City of Milwaukie, 336
Baker v. Coxe, 102
Baltica Constr. Co. v. Planning Bd., 662
Baltimore Scrap Corp. v. David J. Joseph Co., 119
Bangerter v. Orem City Corp., 728
Barancik v. County of Marin, 167
Barrett v. Union Township Comm., 364

Barrington Hills, Village of, v. Village of Hoffman Estates, 739

Bass Enters. Prod. Co. v. United States, 267, 272

Bateman v. City of West Bountiful, 103

Batinich v. Harvey, 578

Bay Area Addiction Research & Treatment, Inc. v. City of Antioch, 730

Bay Island Towers, Inc. v. Bay Island-Siesta Ass'n, 600

Bayou Landing, Ltd. v. Watts, 231

B.C.E. Dev., Inc. v. Smith, 565

Beach v. Planning & Zoning Comm'n, 438

Beach-Courchesne v. City of Diamond Bar, 840

Beal v. Lindsay, 681

Beaver Gasoline Co. v. Zoning Hearing Bd. of the Borough of Osborne, 747, 783, 786

Beck v. Bel Air Props., Inc., 440

Becker v. State, 538

Bell v. Duperrault, 131

Belle Terre, Village of, v. Boraas, 115, 710, 763

Belson v. Thayer & Assocs., Inc., 604

Berberian v. Housing Auth., 472

Berenson v. Town of New Castle, 782

Berg Dev. Co. v. City of Missouri City, 671

Berkeley Keep Jets Over the Bay Comm. v. Board of Port Comm'rs, 386

Berman v. Parker, 115, 830

Betsey v. Turtle Creek Assocs., 708

Bevan v. Brandon Township, 420

Bi-County Devs. of Clinton Inc. v. High Bridge, 778

Bituminous Mat'ls v. Rice County, 103

Blake v. City of Port Hueneme, 623

Blakeley v. Gorin, 576

Board Mach., Inc. v. United States, 265

Board of Aldermen v. Conerly, 318

Board of Comm'rs v. Intermountain Rural Elec. Ass'n, 840

Board of County Comm'rs v. H. Manny Holtz, Inc., 320

Board of County Comm'rs v. Snyder, 339, 346, 364, 379, 404

Board of Directors v. Hinojosa, 597

Board of Supervisors v. Board of Zoning Appeals, 286

Board of Supervisors v. Countryside Inv. Co., 437

Board of Supervisors v. DeGroff Enters., Inc., 672

Board of Supervisors v. McDonald's Corp., 302

Board of Supervisors v. Medical Structures, Inc., 434

Board of Supervisors v. Reed's Landing Corp., 328

Board of Supervisors v. Rowe, 256, 477

Board of Supervisors v. Stickley, 110

Board of Trustees of Univ. of Ala. v. Garrett, 132

Boca Raton, City of, v. State, 621

Boerne, City of, v. Flores, 210, 499

Boise Cascade Corp. v. Gwinnett County, 461

Boomer v. Atlantic Cement Co., 518, 528

Boone County v. Cooke, 845

Boos v. Barry, 231

Bormann v. Board of Supervisors, 519

Borough of: *see* name of borough

Bourque v. Dettore, 398

Bowers v. City of Flint, 102

Boyd v. Board of Councilmen, 463

Boyles v. Hausman, 600

Braden Trust v. County of Yuma, 448

Bradler v. Craig, 446

Brazos Land, Inc. v. Board of County Comm'rs of Rio Arriba County, 801

Breakzone Billiards v. City of Torrance, 286

Brendale v. Confederated Tribes & Bands of the Yakima Indian Nation, 753

Breneric Assocs. v. City of Del Mar, 493

Brentwood, City of, v. Metropolitan Bd. of Zoning Appeals, 739

Bridgeton, City of, v. City of St. Louis, 753

Brier Lake, Inc. v. Jones, 599

Brigham v. State, 617

Briseno v. City of Santa Ana, 469

Britton v. Town of Chester, 782

Brookings, City of, v. Winker, 715

Brooklyn-Queens Connecting Highway (Furman St.), In re, 415

Brown v. Artery Org., 707

Brown v. City of Joliet, 659

Brown v. Legal Found. of Wash., 168, 169

Browning v. Commissioner, 582

Bryant Woods Inn, Inc. v. Howard County, Md., 726

Buchanan v. Warley, 84, 693

Buckeye Community Hope Found. v. City of Cuyahoga Falls, 401

Buena Vista Gardens Apts. Ass'n v. City of San Diego, 60

Building Indus. Ass'n v. City of Oceanside, 804

Bunker Hill Urban Renewal Project 1B, In re, 845

Burford v. Sun Oil Co., 254

Burke v. Smith, 520

Burns v. City Council, 457

Burnsville, Village of, v. Onischuk, 689

Butler v. Bruno, 440

Camp v. Board of Supervisors, 784

Campbell v. Mesier, 539

Campion v. Board of Aldermen, 320

Candid Enters., Inc. v. Grossmont Union High Sch. Dist., 671

Capital Region Airport Auth. v. DeWitt Charter Township, 753

Carey v. Town of Westmoreland, 463

Carlton Homes, Inc. v. COAH, 777

Carol Rickert & Assocs. v. Law, 876

Carpenter v. City of Petal, 788

Carpenter v. Double R Cattle Co., 517

Carson Harbor Village, Ltd. v. City of Carson, 244

Carter v. City of Porterville, 273

Caruso v. Planning Bd., 440

Cary v. City of Rapid City, 396

Caspersen v. Town of Lyme, 125

Cederberg v. City of Rockford, 321

Cell South of N.J., Inc. v. Zoning Bd. of Adjustment, 293

Cellular Tel. Co. v. Village of Tarrytown, 803

Centre Lime & Stone Co., Inc. v. Spring Township Bd. of Supervisors, 749

Century Elec. Serv. & Repair, Inc. v. Stone, 465

Chapel Rd. Assocs., L.L.C. v. Town of Wells, 437

Chapman v. Montgomery County Council, 318

Charles v. Diamond, 256, 687

Charter Township of Delta v. Dinolfo, 715

Charter Township of Northville v. Northville Public Schs., 745

Chartiers, Township of, v. William H. Martin, Inc., 201

Cheney v. Village 2 at New Hope, Inc., 331

Cherokee County v. Greater Atlanta Homebuilders Ass'n, 677

Chesterfield Dev. Corp. v. City of Chesterfield, 102

Chester Residents Concerned for Quality Living v. Seif, 755

Chicago, City of, v. International College of Surgeons, 245

Chicago, City of, v. Stratton, 393

Chinese Staff & Workers Ass'n v. City of New York, 370

Choquette v. Perrault, 541

Chrinko v. South Brunswick Township Planning Bd., 331

Chrismon v. Guilford County, 322, 331, 335

Christopher Lake Dev. Co. v. St. Louis County, 240

Chung v. Sarasota County, 320

Church of the Lukumi Babalu Aye, Inc. v. City of Hialeah, 220

Ciampitti v. United States, 193

Cienega Gardens v. United States, 164, 875

Citizens for Covenant Compliance v. Anderson, 565, 571

Citizens of Goleta Valley v. Board of Supervisors, 386

City of: *see* name of city

City Council v. Naturile, 465

C.I.V.I.C. Group v. City of Warren, 659

Clancy v. Recker, 571

Clark v. City of Boulder, 316

Clear Channel Outdoor, Inc. v. City of Los Angeles, 483

Cleburne, City of, v. Cleburne Living Center, 228, 717

C & M Devs., Inc. v. Bedminster Township Zoning Hearing Bd., 783, 788

Cobert v. Home Owners Warranty Corp., 446

Cogburn v. Holness, 587

Cohen v. Kite Hill Community Ass'n, 596

Collard v. Incorporated Village of Flower Hill, 327

College Area Renters & Landlord Ass'n v. City of San Diego, 128

Collura v. Town of Arlington, 801

Colonial Oaks West, Inc. v. Township of East Brunswick, 656

Colorado River Water Conservation Dist. v. United States, 254

Colorado Springs, City of, v. Securcare Self Storage, Inc., 438

Columbia, City of, v. Omni Outdoor Advertising, Inc., 119, 484

Commercial Realty & Res. Corp. v. First Atlantic Props. Co., 289

Committee for Responsible Planning v. City of Indian Wells, 59

Committee to Preserve Brighton Beach v. Council of City of N.Y., 387

Commonwealth v. City of Pittsburgh, 301

Commonwealth v. Collins, 456

Communications Comm'n v. Florida Power Corp., 169

Communities for a Better Environment v. California Res. Agency, 376

Community Communications Co. v. City of Boulder, 124

Community Hous. Trust v. Department of Consumer & Regulatory Affairs, 728

Community Org. v. Harris, 553

Congregation Kol Ami v. Abington Township, 210

Coniston Corp. v. Village of Hoffman Estates, 99, 128, 131, 245, 251, 256

Connecticut Gen. Life Ins. Co. v. Department of Rev., 360

Connelly v. Schafer, 596

Consolidated Edison Co. v. Hoffman, 292

Construction Indus. Ass'n v. City of Petaluma, 804

Cook, County of, v. World Wide News Agency, 231

Cooley v. United States, 265, 269

Cooper v. Board of County Comm'rs, 359

Cordogan v. Union Nat'l Bank of Elgin, 573

Cormier v. County of San Luis Obispo, 107

Corn v. City of Lauderdale Lakes, 269

Cornell Univ. v. Bagnardi, 209

Coronadans Organized for Retail Enhancement v. City of Coronado, 117

Corona-Norco Unified Sch. Dist. v. City of Corona, 739

Corrigan v. Buckley, 560

Corrigan v. City of Scottsdale, 272

Cottonwood Christian Center v. Cypress Redev. Agency, 220, 839

Coty v. Ramsey Assocs., 535

County of: *see* name of county

Coventry Zoning Bd. of Review, Town of, v. Omni Dev. Corp., 421

Cowboy Country Estates v. Ellis County, 441

Crane Neck Ass'n v. New York City/Long Island County Servs. Group, 561

Cresskill, Borough of, v. Borough of Dumont, 733

Crider v. Board of County Comm'rs of County of Boulder, 104, 133

Croaff v. Evans, 368

Cromwell v. Ferrier, 477

Cronin v. People, 75

Crow v. Brown, 698

Crowell v. Hackensack Water Co., 684

Crown Communication N.Y., Inc. v. Department of Transp., 752

Crown Point, City of, v. Lake County, 750

Cruz v. Town of Cicero, 455

Cummings v. Town Bd., 301

Cuno v. DaimlerChrysler, 884

Cutter v. Wilkinson, 218

Cuyahoga Falls, City of, v. Buckeye Community Hope Found., 102, 403-04, 707

Dacy v. Village of Ruidoso, 319

Dadian v. Village of Wilmette, 727

Dailey v. City of Lawton, 698

Daly v. River Oaks Place Council of Homeowners, 562

Dangerfield Island Protective Soc'y v. Babbitt, 497

Daniels v. Borough of Point Pleasant, 678

Davidson Bros., Inc. v. D. Katz & Sons, Inc., 567

Davidson Mineral Props., Inc. v. Monroe County, 803

Davis v. City of Albuquerque, 318

Davis v. Passman, 233

Davis Enters. v. Karpf, 294

Day v. Caton, 541

DeBlasio v. Zoning Bd. of Adjustment, 103

Defreestville Area Neighborhoods Ass'n v. Town Bd. of North Greenbush, 387
Del Mar, City of, v. City of San Diego, 735
Del Monte Dunes at Monterey, Ltd. v. City of Monterey, 242
Del Oro Hills v. City of Oceanside, 808
Denny's, Inc. v. City of Agoura Hills, 484
Department of Land Conservation & Dev. v. Lincoln County, 814
Detroit Base-Ball Club v. Deppert, 542
Devines v. Maier, 468
Dews v. Town of Sunnyvale, 701
Dexter v. Town Bd., 437
D.I.A.L. v. Department of Consumer Affairs, 450
Diehl v. Lockard, 518
Diller & Fisher Co. v. Architectural Review Bd., 286
Dinan v. Board of Zoning Appeals, 715
Dinosaur Dev., Inc. v. White, 543
Dinsky v. Town of Framingham, 457
Dinsmore Dev. Co. v. Cherokee County, 300
Diocese of Rochester v. Planning Bd., 209
Dist. Intown Props. Ltd. Partnership v. District of Columbia, 500
District of Columbia Ct. of App. v. Feldman, 255
Dittmer v. County of Suffolk, 255
DLX, Inc. v. Kentucky, 251
Dolan v. City of Tigard, 228, 415, 643, 747, 811
Donoghue v. Prynnwood Corp., 589
Dougherty v. Town of North Hempstead Bd. of Zoning, 240
Dover Historical Soc'y v. City of Dover Planning Comm'n, 497
Downey v. Jungle Den Villas Recreation Ass'n, 600
Dr. Gertrude A. Barber Center, Inc. v. Peters Township, 726
D & R Props. v. Newbury Township, 739
Dudek v. Umatilla County, 662
Duncan v. Village of Middlefield, 291
Duncanson v. Board of Supervisors, 802
Dunedin, City of, v. Contractors & Bldrs. Ass'n, 668
Durand v. IDC Bellingham, LLC, 328, 335

Eagle Enters. v. Gross, 566
Earthburners, Inc. v. County of Carlton, 302
East Bay Asian Local Dev. Corp. v. State, 500
Easterbrook v. Hebrew Ladies' Orphan Soc'y, 550
Eastern Enters. v. Apfel, 164, 196
Eastlake, City of, v. Forest City Enters., Inc., 403
Edmonds, City of, v. Oxford House, Inc., 728
Edward Kraemer & Sons v. Sauk County Bd. of Adjustment, 300
Ehrlich v. City of Culver City, 663, 675
E.J. Bach v. County of St. Clair, 463
Elgin, City of, v. County of Cook, 739
Elysian Heights Residents Ass'n v. Los Angeles, 338
Employment Div., Dep't of Human Res. v. Smith, 209, 499
Encore Videos, Inc. v. City of San Antonio, 228
England v. Louisiana State Bd. of Med. Examiners, 251, 254
Ensign Bickford Realty Corp. v. City Council, 116
Enterprise Citizens Action Comm'n v. Clark County Bd. of Comm'rs, 338
Envirosafe Servs. v. County of Owyhee, 746
Episcopal Student Found. v. City of Ann Arbor, 500

Erdman v. City of Fort Atkinson, 726
Essex Falls, Borough of, v. Kessler Inst. for Rehabilitation, 839
Essick v. Shillam, 518
Eubank v. City of Richmond, 395
Euclid, Village of, v. Ambler Realty Co., 74, 76
Everett, City of, v. Snohomish County, 753
Evergreen Highlands Ass'n v. West, 604
Eves v. Zoning Bd. of Adjustment, 331
Ex parte Quong Wo, 75
Ex parte White, 118
Exxon Co. U.S.A. v. Township of Livingston, 118
Exxon Mobil Corp. v. Saudi Basic Indus. Corp., 255
Fair Hous. in Huntington Comm. Inc. v. Town of Huntington, 707

Falloon v. Schilling, 522
FamilyStyle of St. Paul, Inc. v. City of St. Paul, 729
Fasano v. Board of County Comm'rs, 350
Fernley v. Board of Supervisors, 783
Ferraro v. Zoning Bd. of Adjustment, 735
Ferris v. City of Alhambra, 303
Fifth Ave. Presbyterian Church v. City of New York, 523
Fink v. Miller, 575
First English Evangelical Lutheran Church of Glendale v. County of Los Angeles, 244-45, 258, 272, 274, 438, 457
First Peoples Bank of N.J. v. Township of Medford, 686
Fisher v. Giuliani, 167
Flamingo Ranch Estates, Inc. v. Sunshine Ranches Homeowners, 589
Fleming v. City of Tacoma, 365
Flower Mound, Town of, v. Stafford Estates Ltd. Partnership, 662, 668, 675
Fluckey v. City of Plymouth, 624
Foley v. Harris, 520
Fontainebleau Hotel Corp. v. Forty-Five Twenty-Five, Inc., 520
Forest City Daly Hous., Inc. v. Town of North Hempstead, 727
Forman v. Trustees of State Univ. of N.Y., 378
Forseth v. Village of Sussex, 103, 240
Forster v. Hall, 571
Forsyth County v. Nationalist Movement, 484
Foundation for the Preservation of Georgetown v. Arnold, 498
France Stone Co., Inc. v. Charter Township of Monroe, 273
Frankland v. City of Lake Oswego, 93
Franklin, Township of, v. Hollander, 519, 746
Franklin Township v. Tugwell, 862
Franklin Tower One, L.L.C. v. N.M, 876
Freeman v. City of Dallas, 537
French v. Barber Asphalt Paving Co., 624
Frey v. Panza, 455
Frickel v. Sunnyside Enters., Inc., 445
Friends of Davis v. City of Davis, 493
Friends of Mammoth v. Board of Supervisors, 28, 374
Friends of Neabeack Hill v. City of Philomath, 814
Friends of Sierra Madre v. City of Sierra Madre, 375, 407
Front Royal & Warren County Indus. Park Corp. v. Town of Front Royal, 686

Fry v. City of Hayward, 408
Furman St., In re, 412
Futernick v. Sumpter Township, 132
FW/PBS, Inc. v. City of Dallas, 231

Gage v. Town of Egremont, 302
Gamble v. City of Escondido, 728
Gandolfi v. Town of Hammonton, 319
Gandolfo v. Hartman, 559
Gardine, Town of, v. Stanley Orchards, Inc., 399
Gardner v. Baltimore, 103
Gardner v. County of Sonoma, 416
Garvin v. Ninth Judicial Dist. Ct., 404, 803
Gascoe, Ltd. v. Newtown Township, 231
Gautreaux v. Chicago Hous. Auth., 867
Gavlak v. Town of Somers, 240
George Washington Univ. v. District of Columbia, 102
Gerard v. San Juan County, 442
German Evangelical Lutheran Church v. City of Charleston, 634
Giebeler v. M & B Assocs., 727
Gifford v. Planning Bd. of Nantucket, 442, 443
Giger v. City of Omaha, 320, 328
Gilbert v. City of Cambridge, 240, 241
Gilbert v. State, 687
Gilpin v. Jacob Ellis Realties, 554
Giordano v. City of New York, 132
Girard v. 94th St. & Fifth Ave. Corp., 560
Gladden v. District of Columbia Bd. of Zoning Adjustment, 296
Gladstone Realtors v. Village of Bellwood, 704
Golden v. Planning Bd. of Town of Ramapo, 29, 808
Golden Gateway Center v. Golden Gateway Tenants Ass'n, 562
Goldstein v. City of Chicago, 682
Gonzaga Univ. v. Doe, 755
Goss v. City of Little Rock, 660, 676
Gourlay v. Forest Lake Estates Civic Ass'n of Port Richey, Inc., 729
Gravert v. Nebergall, 541
Great Atlantic & Pacific Tea Co. v. Borough of Point Pleasant, 405
Greater Atlanta Homebuilders Ass'n v. DeKalb County, 472
Greater Franklin Devs. Ass'n v. Town of Franklin, 671
Greater Westchester Homeowners Ass'n v. City of Los Angeles, 535
Green v. Castle Concrete Co., 535
Greenbriar, Ltd. v. City of Alabaster, 241
Green Meadows at Montville, L.L.C. v. Planning Bd., 437
Grenier v. Barclay Square Commercial Condominium Owners' Ass'n, 597
Gridco, Inc. v. Zoning Bd., 507
Griswold v. City of Homer (Alaska 1996), 309, 367
Griswold v. City of Homer (Alaska 2002), 360
Grupe Dev. Co. v. Superior Ct., 677
Gupta v. Ritter Homes, 446

Haberman v. City of Long Beach, 803
Hadacheck v. Sebastian, 138
Hadnott v. City of Prattville, 682
Haines v. City of Phoenix, 337

Hakim v. Board of Comm'rs, 433
Hall v. City of Santa Barbara, 169
Hallie, Town of, v. City of Eau Claire, 124
Handelsman v. Town of Palm Beach, 118
Hang Kie, In re, 75
Harbison v. City of Buffalo, 200
Harbours Pointe of Nashotah, LLC v. Town of Nashotah, 624
Hardin County v. Jost, 302
Harnish v. Manatee County, 482
Harrison v. Air Park Estates Zoning Comm., 598
Hartley v. City of Colorado Springs, 202
Hartsell v. Town of Talty, 434
Haugen v. Peterson, 580
Havens Realty Corp. v. Coleman, 704
Hawaii Hous. Auth. v. Midkiff, 831
Hawkins v. County of Marin, 338
Hawkins v. Town of Shaw, 679, 757
Hawthorne v. Village of Olympia Fields, 745
Hayes v. City of Seattle, 328
Hayssen v. Sonoma County Bd. of Zoning Adjustments, 359
Haywood v. Brunswick Permanent Benefit Bldg. Soc'y, 568
Head v. Amoskeag Mfg. Co., 832
Heavens v. King County Rural Library Dist., 622
Hecht v. Stephens, 575
Heine Farms v. Yankton County, 336
Hemisphere Bldg. Co. v. Village of Richton Park, 727
Heninger v. Board of Supervisors, 376
Henrietta, Town of, v. Department of Envtl. Conservation, 387
Henry v. Jefferson County Planning, 302
Hernandez v. City of Lafayette, 273
Herrington v. County of Peoria, 400
Herrington v. County of Sonoma, 270
Hidden Harbour Estates, Inc. v. Basso, 597
Hidden Harbour Estates, Inc. v. Norman, 597
Hilborn v. Commissioner, 549
Hill v. Community of Damien, 729
Hillman v. Town of Greenwich, 528
Hillsboro, City of, v. Housing Dev. Corp., 785
Hills Dev. Co. v. Township of Bernards, 777
Hiner v. Hoffman, 553
Hodel v. Irving, 164
Hodge v. Sloan, 563
Hoffmann v. Kinealy, 200
Hoffman v. United Iron & Metal Co., 528
Hoffmann v. Clark, 544
Hoffmeister v. City of San Diego, 59
Holbrook, Inc. v. Clark County, 358
Holiday Point Marina Partners v. Anne Arundel County, 509
Holleman v. Mission Trace Homeowners Ass'n, 597
Holt Civic Club v. City of Tuscaloosa, 30
Home Bldrs. Ass'n v. City of Kansas City, 638
Home Bldrs. Ass'n v. City of Napa, 673
Home Bldrs. Ass'n of Greater Des Moines v. City of West Des Moines, 671
Homer, City of, v. Campbell, 328
Horn v. County of Ventura, 359, 437
Horn v. International Bus. Mach. Corp., 386
Hornstein v. Barry, 399
Houghton v. Rizzo, 572
Housing Auth. v. Superior Ct., 523
Houston v. Klonis, 566

Houston, City of, v. Harris County Outdoor Adver. Ass'n, 612
Houston, City of, v. Kolb, 415
Howard v. City of Lincoln, 519
H & R Bldrs., Inc. v. Borough Council, 749
H.R.D.E., Inc. v. Zoning Officer, 207
Hudachek v. Zoning Hearing Bd., 749
Hudson, Village of, v. Albrecht, Inc., 477
Huffman v. Pursue, 255
Hull v. Hunt, 207
Humber v. Morton, 445
Hunter v. Erickson, 408
Huntington, Town of, v. Huntington Branch, NAACP, 707
Huntington Branch, NAACP v. Town of Huntington, 707, 708
Hurd v. Hodge, 560
Hutchinson v. City of Valdosta, 468
Hutchinson v. Damin Corp., 441
Hyson v. Montgomery County Council, 358

Idaho Bldg. Contractiors Ass'n v. City of Coeur D'Alene, 678
Idaho Springs, City of, v. Blackwell, 404
In re: see name of party
Incorporated Village of Atlantic Beach v. Gavalas, 375
Incorporated Village of Nyack v. Daytop Village, 745
Indio, City of, v. Arroyo, 488
Innkeepers Motor Lodge, Inc. v. City of New Smyrna Beach, 803
Innovations v. Traditions in Community Dev., 422
Instructional Sys., Inc. v. Computer Curriculum Corp., 254
International College of Surgeons v. City of Chicago, 255
International Paper Co. v. Town of Jay, 116
I'On, L.L.C. v. Town of Mt. Pleasant, 404
Iowa Coal Mining Co. v. Monroe County, 336
Islamic Center v. City of Starkville, 220
Islip, Town of, v. Caviglia, 200

Jackson v. Metropolitan Knoxville Airport Auth., 524
Jacobs, Visconsi & Jacobs Co. v. City of Lawrence, 103
Jake's, Ltd., Inc. v. City of Coates, 230
James v. Valtierra, 408
Jerozal v. South Carolina Dep't of Health & Envtl. Control, 177
Jewish Reconstructionist Synagogue v. Incorporated Village of Roslyn Harbor, 209
John Corp. v. City of Houston, 244
Johnson v. City of Shorewood, 255
Johnson v. Myers, 567
Johnson v. Reasor, 659
Johnson v. Town of Edgartown, 788
Joint Anti-Fascist Refugee Comm. v. McGrath, 353
Joint Ventures, Inc. v. Department of Transp., 415
Jones v. Northwest Real Estate Co., 589
Josephine County v. Garnier, 448

Kaiser Hawaii Kai Dev. Co. v. City of Honolulu, 404
Kamrowski v. State, 581
Kaplan v. Boudreaux, 601

Karlson v. City of Camarillo, 341
Kellogg v. Village of Viola, 525
Kelo v. City of New London, 824
Kenai Peninsula Borough v. Kenai Peninsula Bd. of Realtors, 441
Kennedy Park Homes Ass'n v. City of Lackawanna, 698
Keshbro, Inc. v. City of Miami, 265, 538
Kessler v. Grand Central Dist. Mgmt. Ass'n, 634
Key West, City of, v. R.L.J.S. Corp., 433
Keystone Bituminous Coal Ass'n v. DeBenedictis, 145, 164, 239
Killearn Acres Homeowners Ass'n v. Keever, 596
Kimball Laundry Co. v. United States, 271
King v. Caddo Parish Comm'n, 286
King v. City of Bainbridge, 449
King County v. Washington State Boundary Review Bd., 376
King's Mill Homeowners Ass'n v. City of Westminster, 318
Kinzli v. City of Santa Cruz, 241
Kirsch v. Prince George's County, 128
Klaeren v. Village of Lisle, 358
KMST, LLC v. County of Ada, 675
Knight v. Amelkin, 302
Knoxville, City of, v. Ambrister, 320, 321
Konkel v. Common Council, 329
Korean Buddhist Dae Won Sa Temple of Haw. v. Sullivan, 353
Kosalka v. Town of Georgetown, 300
Kosciusko County Bd. of Zoning Appeals v. Wygant, 92
Kottschade v. City of Rochester, 245
Kozesnik v. Township of Montgomery, 336
Krughoff v. City of Naperville, 671

LaBranche v. A.J. Lane & Co., 405
Lacy Feed Co. v. Parish, 517
Lacy Street Hospitality Serv., Inc. v. City of Los Angeles, 366
Ladue, City of, v. Gilleo, 484
Ladue, City of, v. Horn, 715
Laguna Publishing Co. v. Golden-Rain Found., 591
L.A. Inv. Co. v. Gary, 560
Lake Country Estates, Inc. v. Tahoe Regional Planning Agency, 233
Lakeside Bldrs., Inc. v. Planning Bd. of Town of Franklin, 132
Lambert v. City & County of San Francisco, 651
Lamden v. La Jolla Shores Clubdominium Homeowners Ass'n, 593
Landgate, Inc. v. California Coastal Comm'n, 266
Langlois v. Abington Hous. Auth., 708
Lapid-Laurel, L.L.C. v. Zoning Bd. of Adjustment, 727
Largo, Town of, v. Imperial Homes Corp., 208
Larkin v. Grendel's Den, Inc., 399
LaSalle Nat'l Bank v. City of Chicago, 428
Lauer v. Zoning Comm'n, 738
Laurel Heights Improvement Ass'n v. Regents of the Univ. of Cal., 380
Layne v. Zoning Bd. of Adjustment (Pa. 1983), 126
Layne v. Zoning Bd. of Adjustment (Pa. Commonw. Ct. 1982), 128
Lee County v. Kiesel, 524

Lee Sing, In re, 692
Lemke v. Cass County, 102
Lemon v. Kurtzman, 399
Leonard v. City of Bothell, 404
Lesher Communications, Inc. v. City of Walnut
     Creek, 339
Levandusky v. One Fifth Ave. Apt. Corp., 591
Levitt & Sons, Inc. v. Young, 463
Levy v. Alfano, 448
Lew v. Superior Ct., 523
Lewis v. Department of Natural Res., 290
Lewis v. Gollner (City Ct. of Brooklyn 1891), 563
Lewis v. Gollner (N.Y. 1891), 564
Licker v. Harkleroad, 600
Liebowitz v. Mandel, 596
Lincolnshire Civic Ass'n v. Beach, 601
Lincoln Trust Co. v. Williams Bldg. Corp., 90
Lindsey v. Normet, 763
Lingle v. Chevron U.S.A., Inc., 95, 193, 254, 643,
     667-68
Linmark Assocs. v. Willingboro Township, 483
Lisa's Party City, Inc. v. Town of Henrietta, 483
Lochner v. New York, 85, 143
Lombardo v. Warner, 488
Lonberg v. Sanborn Theaters, Inc., 450
Lone v. Montgomery County, 200
Long v. City of Fresno, 662
Long Island Bd. of Realtors, Inc. v. Incorporated
     Village of Massapequa Park, 483
Long Island Pine Barrens Soc'y v. Planning Bd., 378
Loretto v. Group W. Cable, 168
Loretto v. Teleprompter Manhattan CATV Corp.,
     164, 167, 168, 415
Lorillard Tobacco Co. v. Reilly, 483
Los Angeles, City of, v. Alameda Books, Inc., 222
Los Angeles, City of, v. Chadwick, 840
Los Angeles, City of, v. Japan Air Lines Co., 524
Louisville Bd. of Zoning Adjustment, City of, v.
     Gailor, 753
Louisville & Jefferson County Planning Comm'n v.
     Schmidt, 331
*Louisville & Nashville R.R. v. Barber Asphalt Paving
     Co.*, 623
Love v. Board of County Comm'rs of Bingham
     County, 339
Loveladies Harbor v. United States, 509
Lovequist v. Conservation Comm'n of Dennis, 509
Lucas v. South Carolina Coastal Council, 138, 139,
     163, 164, *169*, 273, 508, 518
Lucky Stores, Inc. v. Board of Appeals, 118
Lui v. Commission on Adult Entertainment
     Establishments, 255
Lujan v. Defenders of Wildlife, 704
Lukrawka v. Spring Valley Water Co., 686
Lum Yip Kee, Ltd. v. City of Honolulu, 318
Lussier v. San Lorenzo Valley Water Dist., 519
Lyman v. Planning Bd. of Winchester, 438

MacDonald, Sommer & Frates v. County of Yolo,
     240
MacEachran, Appeal of, 581
Macioce v. Zoning Hearing Bd. of Borough of
     Baldwin, 749
Mack T. Anderson Ins. Agency v. City of Belgrade,
     788

Madison v. Graham, 103
Madison River R.V. Ltd. v. Town of Ennis, 366
Main San Gabriel Basin Watermaster v. State Water
     Res. Control Bd., 378
M.A. Kravitz Co., Appeal of, v. Board of Supervisors,
     783
Manalapan Realty, L.P. v. Township Comm., 339
Manning v. New England Mutual Life Ins. Co., 579
Marbrunak, Inc. v. City of Stow, 728
Marchese v. Umstead, 132
Maready v. City of Winston-Salem, 881
Margolis v. District Ct., 404, 405
Mark v. Oregon State Dep't of Fish & Wildlife, 524
Marracci v. City of Scappoose, 339
Marriott Corp. v. Concord Hotel Mgmt., 291
Martin County v. Section 28 Partnership, Ltd., 243
Martin County v. Yusem, 351
Massey v. City of Charlotte, 327
Mathewson v. Primeau, 519
Matthew v. Smith, 286, 299
Mayers v. Ridley, 560
Mayor & Bd. of Aldermen of Town of Prentiss v.
     Jefferson Davis County, 739
Mayor & City Council of Baltimore v. Mano Swartz,
     Inc., 477
Mayor & Council of Rockville v. Brookeville
     Turnpike Constr. Co., 689
McClure v. Leaycraft, 575
McDonald v. Mianecki, 445
McDonough v. W.W. Snow Constr. Co., 554
McGary v. City of Portland, 538
McGowan v. Capital Center, Inc., 633
McKinley v. United States, 275
McNally v. Township of Teaneck, 619
McQuade v. Tucson Tiller Apts., 527
Meadowlands Regional Redev. Agency v. State, 689
Medical Servs., Inc., v. City of Savage, 803
Merson v. McNally, 378
Meszaros v. Planning Bd., 300
Metro 500, Inc. v. City of Brooklyn Park, 118
Metromedia, Inc. v. City of San Diego (Cal. 1980),
     472
Metromedia, Inc. v. City of San Diego (U.S. 1981),
     478
Metromedia, Inc. v. City of San Diego (Cal. 1982),
     482
*Metropolitan Hous. Dev. Corp. v. Village of Arlington
     Heights* (7th Cir. 1977), 705
Metropolitan Hous. Dev. Corp. v. Village of
     Arlington Heights (N.D. Ill. 1979), 705
Michigan Protection & Advocacy Serv., Inc. v. Babin,
     729
Middlesex Co. v. McCue, 512, 521, 539
Midtown Props., Inc. v. Madison Township, 320
Miles v. Planning Bd. of Millbury, 418, 659
Miller v. City of Dallas, 703
Miller v. City of Hermosa Beach, 375
Miller v. Schoene, 138
Miller & Son Paving, Inc., v. Plumstead Township,
     274
Mill Realty Assocs. v. Zoning Bd. of Review, 437
Mindel v. Township Council, 133
Minnaugh v. County Comm'n of Broward County,
     351
Minnesota v. United States, 754
Minot, City of, v. Friedlander, 537

Minton v. City of Fort Worth Planning Comm'n, 398
Mission Springs, Inc. v. City of Spokane, 103, 457
Missouri ex rel. Chiavola v. Village of Oakwood, 118
Missouri Pac. Ry. v. Nebraska, 824
Mitchell v. Kemp, 803
Mlikotin v. City of Los Angeles, 682
Mobil Oil Co. v. Township of Westtown, 118
Monk v. City of Birmingham, 693
Monterey, City of, v. Del Monte Dunes at Monterey, Ltd., 274
Montgomery County v. Woodward & Lothrop, Inc., 358
Moore v. City Council of Harrodsburg [Moore II], 684
Moore v. City of East Cleveland, 712
Moore v. City of Harrodsburg [Moore I], 683
Morales v. Haines, 709
Morgan v. High Penn Oil Co., 517
Morgan County Concrete Co. v. Tanner, 528
Morris v. Kadrmas, 575
Morrison v. City of East Lansing, 753
Mossburg v. Montgomery County, 301
M&T Chem., Inc. v. Westrick, 456
Mt. Healthy City Sch. Dist. Bd. of Educ. v. Doyle, 115
Mugler v. Kansas, 136, 142-44, 200, 264
Mulligan v. Panther Valley Prop. Owners Ass'n, 599
Municipal Art Soc'y v. City of New York, 332
Murphy v. Timber Trace Ass'n, 562
MX Group, Inc. v. City of Covington, 730

Nahrstedt v. Lakeside Village Condominium Ass'n, 554, 582, 590, 597, 599
Nasierowski Bros. Inv. Co. v. City of Sterling Heights, 240
Natale v. Town of Ridgefield, 457
National Bank & Trust Co. v. Village of Skokie, 285
Nautilus of Exeter, Inc. v. Town of Exeter, 119
Naylor v. Township of Hellam, 802
Nectow v. City of Cambridge, 96
Nelle v. Loch Haven Homeowners' Ass'n, 589
Nemmers v. City of Dubuque, 270
Neponsit Prop. Owners' Ass'n v. Emigrant Indus. Sav. Bank, 565, 566
Nestor Colon Medina & Sucesores, Inc. v. Custodio, 103
Neuberger v. City of Portland, 351
Neuzil v. City of Iowa City, 318
Nevel v. Village of Schaumburg, 504
New Hope, City of, v. Catholic Cemeteries, 634
New Jersey Shore Bldrs. Ass'n v. Mayor & Township Comm., 802
New Jersey Shore Bldrs. Ass'n v. Township of Marlboro, 668
New Jersey State League of Municipalities v. Department of Community Affairs, 421
New Orleans Pub. Serv., Inc. v. Council of New Orleans, 254
Newport, City of, v. Fact Concerts, Inc., 676
New York City Coalition to End Lead Poisoning, Inc. v. Vallone, 375
New York SMSA v. Board of Adjustment, 292
Nigro v. Planning Bd., 415
Noble Manor Co. v. Pierce County, 433
Nollan v. California Coastal Comm'n, 196-97, 638, 747

Norcross v. James, 566
Norris v. Williams, 576
Northern Ill. Home Bldrs. Ass'n v. County of DuPage, 668
North Fork Props. v. Bath Township, 290
North Lauderdale, City of, v. SMM Props., Inc., 623
Norton v. City of Danville, 504
Norway Hill Preservation & Protection Ass'n v. King County Council, 376
Norwood, Village of, v. Baker, 624, 651
Nottingham, Town of, v. Bonser, 92

Oakbrook Civic Ass'n v. Sonnier, 595
Oakwood at Madison, Inc. v. Township of Madison, 772
Oceanside, City of, v. McKenna, 672
O'Connor v. Village Green Owners Ass'n, 561
Oconomowoc Residential Programs v. City of Milwaukee, 726, 729
O'Donnell v. State, 855
Ohio Congregation of Jehovah's Witnesses, Inc. v. City of Lakewood, 209
Old Town Neighborhood Ass'n v. Kauffman, 497
Olech v. Village of Willowbrook, 131
Oliver v. AT&T Wireless Servs., 519
Oliver v. Superior Ct., 445
Olympia, City of, v. Drebick, 677
Opal Lake Ass'n v. Michaywe Ltd. Partnership, 535
Open Homes Fellowship, Inc. v. Orange County, Fla., 721
Orange Beach, City of, v. Perdido Pass Devs., 328
Orangetown, Town of, v. Magee, 457
Oregon City v. Hartke, 477
Osprey Pac. Corp. v. United States, 265

Painesville Bldg. Dep't, City of, v. Dworken & Bernstein Co., 488
Palazzolo v. Rhode Island, 178, *180*, 193, 241-44, 293, 508, 643
Palermo Land Co. v. Planning Comm'n, 318
Palmer Township Municipal Sewer Auth. v. Witty, 621
Palmer v. City of Ojai, 507
PA Northwestern Distribs., Inc. v. Zoning Hearing Bd., 199-200
Paquette v. Zoning Bd. of Review, 359
Paradyne Corp. v. State Dep't of Transp., 642
Parking Ass'n of Ga., Inc. v. City of Atlanta, 493
Park Redlands Covenant Control Comm. v. Simon, 561, 591
Parkridge v. City of Seattle, 318
Pascack Assocs. v. Mayor & Council of Township of Washington, 773
Passaic, City of, v. Paterson Bill Posting, Adver. & Sign Painting Co., 470
Patterson v. County of Tehama, 58, 408
Peabody v. Town of Windham, 202
Pearl Inv. Co. v. City & County of San Francisco, 253
Pearson v. City of Grand Blanc, 95, 104
Pecoraro v. Board of Appeals, 293
Peek-A-Boo Lounge of Bradenton, Inc. v. Manatee County, Fla., 228
Pelican Island Prop. Owners Ass'n v. Murphy, 596

Penn Central Transp. Co. v. City of New York, 138, 158, 167-68, 179, 184, 196, 197, 228, 265, 497, 500, 811
Pennell v. City of San Jose, 149
Pennobscot, Inc. v. Board of Comm'rs, 442
Pennsylvania v. Lynn, 875
Pennsylvania Coal Co. v. Mahon, 140, 164
People v. Adco Advers., 478
People v. Avol, 538
People v. Byers, 442
People v. Jack Resnick & Sons, Inc., 472
People v. Mason, 536
People v. Multari, 94
People v. Talleur, 860
People v. Tolman, 472
People v. Wheeler, 468
People's Counsel for Baltimore County v. Beachwood 1 Ltd. Partnership, 317, 327
People Tags, Inc. v. Jackson County Legislature, 230
Perry-Worth Concerned Citizens v. Board of Comm'rs, 365
Pertzsch v. Upper Oconomowoc Lake Ass'n, 590
Peters v. Environmental Protection Bd., 359
Peterson v. Beekmere, Inc., 568
Petrowski v. Norwich Free Academy, 364
Pheasant Ridge Assocs. Ltd. Partnership v. Town of Burlington, 840
Pierce v. Northeast Lake Washington Sewer & Water Dist., 524
Pinecrest Lakes, Inc. v. Shidel, 93
Pinehaven Planning Bd. v. Brooks, 553
Pinnock v. International House of Pancakes Franchisee, 450
Pioneer Trust & Sav. Bank v. Mount Prospect, 637
Pittsfield Charter Township v. Washtenaw County, 753
Planning Bd. v. Michaud, 441
Pleasant Valley, Town of, v. Town of Poughkeepsie Planning Bd., 739
Plymouth Coal Co. v. Pennsylvania, 141
Poirier v. Grand Blanc Township, 273
Poletown Neighborhood Council v. City of Detroit, 837
Pomponio v. Fauquier County Bd. of Supervisors, 254
Ponderosa Home Site Lot Owners v. Garfield Bay Resort, Inc., 428
Port Auth. v. Groppoli, 837
Porterville, City of, v. Young, 861
Prah v. Maretti, 521
Pratt v. Adams, 442
PRB Enters., Inc. v. South Brunswick Planning Bd., 286
Price v. Payette County Bd. of County Comm'rs, 340
Prin v. Council of Monroeville, 286
Princeton City Sch. Dist. Bd. of Educ. v. Zaino, 845
Prisco v. Forest Villas Condominium Apts., 575
Prock v. Town of Danville, 321
Pro-Eco, Inc. v. Board of Comm'rs, 802
Prudential Ins. Co. of Am. v. Board of Appeals, 438
Prudential Ins. Co. v. Wetzel, 604
Puritan Holding Co. v. Holloschitz, 520

Q.C. Constr. Co. v. Gallo, 803
Quackenbush v. Allstate Ins. Co., 254
Queenside Hills Realty Co. v. Saxl, 468

Raben-Pastel v. City of Coconut Creek, 457
Rancourt v. Town of Barnstead, 807
Rando v. Town of North Attleborough, 316
Raynes v. City of Leavenworth, 365
Realen Valley Forge Greenes Assocs., In re, 317
Rector of St. Bartholomew's Church v. City of New York, 498
Red Roof Inns, Inc. v. City of Ridgeland, 200
Redevelopment Agency v. Gilmore, 860
Redmond, City of, v. Central Puget Sound Growth Mgmt. Hearings Bd., 208
Regional Economic Community Action Program, Inc. v. City of Middletown, 708, 728, 730
Relosky v. Sacco, 358
Renton, City of, v. Playtime Theatres, Inc., 220
Reserve Mining Co. v. Herbst, 390
Resident Advisory Bd. v. Rizzo, 708
Restigouche, Inc. v. Town of Jupiter, 240
R.G. Moore Bldg. Corp. v. Committee for Repeal, 405
Richard Roeser Prof'l Bldr., Inc. v. Anne Arundel County, 293
Richardson v. City of Little Rock Planning Comm'n, 435
Ridge Park Home Owners v. Pena, 600
Riggs v. Township of Long Beach, 133
R.I.S.E., Inc. v. Kay, 703
Riss v. Angel, 596
River Heights Assocs. Ltd. Partnership v. Batten, 575
River Park, Inc. v. City of Highland Park, 103
Rivers Edge Condominium Ass'n v. Rere, Inc., 605
Robert E. Kurzius, Inc. v. Incorporated Village of Upper Brookville, 783
Robertson v. Methow Valley Citizens Council, 387, 390
Robinson v. City of Bloomfield Hills, 128
Rodgers v. Village of Tarrytown, 331
Roe v. Wade, 231, 839
Rogers Machinery, Inc. v. Washington County, 667
Rogers v. Sawin, 520
Rolling Pines Ltd. Partnership v. City of Little Rock, 493
Rooker v. Fidelity Trust Co., 255
Rooney v. Peoples Bank, 565
Rose v. Chaikin, 513
Rose v. Council for Better Educ., Inc., 690
Ross v. City of Yorba Linda, 129
Ross v. Goshi, 488
Rotter v. Coconino County, 202
RRI Realty Corp. v. Incorporated Village of Southampton, 103
Ruby v. Carlisle Zoning Hearing Bd., 202
Rural Area Concerned Citizens, Inc. v. Fayette County Zoning Hearing Bd., 367
Rye, City of, v. Korff, 734
Rylands v. Fletcher, 512

Sabo v. Township of Monroe, 50
Sacramento v. Lewis, 102
Salute v. Stratford Greens Garden Apts., 876
Samaritan Inns, Inc. v. District of Columbia, 457
Sameric Corp. of Del. v. City of Philadelphia, 239
San Antonio Indep. Sch. Dist. v. Rodriguez, 690, 709
Sanborn v. McLean, 571
Sander v. Planning Bd., 286

San Diego Gas & Elec. Co. v. City of San Diego, 256
Sandy Creek Invs., Ltd. v. City of Jonestown, Tex., 245
Sandy Mush Props., Inc. v. Rutherford County, 802
San Francisco, City & County of, v. Sainez, 468
Sanghvi v. City of Claremont, 728
San Joaquin Motel & Hotel Prop. Owners Ass'n v. City of Stockton, 469
San Luis Obispo, County of, v. Bailey, 824
San Remo Hotel, L.P. v. City & County of San Francisco (Cal. 2002), 667-68, 672
San Remo Hotel, L.P. v. City & County of San Francisco (U.S. 2005), 239, 243, 245, 254-56
Santa Barbara, City of. v. Adamson, 715
Santini v. Connecticut Hazardous Waste Mgmt. Serv., 251
Sasso v. Osgood, 291
Save Centennial Valley Ass'n v. Schultz, 440
Save Sunset Beach Coalition v. City & County of Honolulu, 315
Sawyer v. Town of Cape Elizabeth, 440
Schad v. Borough of Mount Ephraim, 230
Schaefer v. Eastman Community Ass'n, 593
Schauer v. City of Miami Beach, 364
Schenck v. City of Hudson Village, 807
Schipper v. Levitt & Sons, 445
Schoen v. Township of Hillside, 483
Schultz v. City of Grants Pass, 661
Schultz v. Pritts, 301
Schwarz v. City of Glendale, 400
Sciacca v. Caruso, 293
Scott v. City of Indian Wells, 734
Scottsdale v. Municipal Ct., 753
Scurlock v. City of Lynn Haven, 449
SDDS, Inc. v. South Dakota, 272
Seabrooke Partners v. City of Chesapeake, 318
Seagrove Owners Ass'n v. Smith, 596
Seaman v. City of Durham, 785
Seawall Assocs. v. City of New York, 169, 469, 673
Seiber v. United States, 264
Selby Realty Co. v. City of San Buenaventura, 415
Seniors Civil Liberties Ass'n v. Kemp, 561
Serrano v. Priest, 690
Shannon & Riordan v. Board of Zoning Appeals, 729
Sharp v. Zoning Hearing Bd., 315
Shea v. City of Muncie, 75
Sheerr v. Township of Evesham, 272
Shelley v. Kraemer, 560
Sher v. Liederman, 521
Sherbert v. Verner, 210
Shors v. Johnson, 458
Sica v. Board of Adjustment, 292
Sierra Club v. City of Hayward, 548
Sills v. Walworth County Land Mgmt. Comm., 367
Silveira v. Las Gallinas Valley Sanitary Dist., 376
Simplex Techs. v. Town of Newington, 290
Sinclair Oil Corp. v. County of Santa Barbara, 251
Sintra, Inc. v. City of Seattle, 673, 676
Slagle Constr. Co. v. County of Contra Costa, 434
Smagula v. Town of Hookset, 734
Smith v. Skagit County, 365
Smith v. Zoning Hearing Bd., 201
Smith & Lee Assocs. v. City of Taylor, 722, 746
Snohomish County Improvement Alliance v. Snohomish County, 366
Snyder v. Board of County Comm'rs, 341

Snyder Realty Co. v. City of Overland Park, 634
SOB, Inc. v. County of Benton, 229
Solid Waste Agency of Northern Cook County (SWANCC) v. United States Army Corps of Eng'rs, 508
South Camden Citizens in Action v. New Jersey Dep't of Envtl. Protection, 755
South County Sand & Gravel Co., Inc. v. Town of South Kingstown, 103
Southern Burlington County NAACP v. Township of Mount Laurel [Mount Laurel II], 773
Southern Burlington County NAACP v. Township of Mount Laurel [Mount Laurel I], 111, 134, 438, 672, 676, 704, 763
Southern Cal. Edison Co. v. Bourgerie, 569
Southern Nev. Homebldrs. Ass'n v. Las Vegas Valley Water Dist., 668
Southern Pac. Transp. Co. v. City of Los Angeles, 240
South of Sunnyside Neighborhood League v. Board of Comm'rs, 341
Southwestern Ill. Dev. Auth. v. National City Envtl., L.L.C., 832
South Whitford Assocs. v. Zoning Hearing Bd., 749
Sparks v. Douglas County, 662
Sparta, Township of, v. Spillane, 404
Speer v. Turner, 565
Spence v. Zimmerman, 103
Spencer's Case, 566
Sprenger, Grubb & Assocs., Inc. v. City of Hailey (Idaho 1995), *112*
Sprenger, Grubb & Assocs., Inc. v. City of Hailey (Idaho 1999), 59
Spring-Gar Community Civic Ass'n v. Homes for the Homeless, Inc., 523
Spur Indus., Inc. v. Del E. Webb Dev. Co., 138, 534-35
State v. Baker, 715
State v. Bates, 199
State v. Caoili, 857
State v. Champoux, 715
State v. Cook, 463
State v. Dahl, 482
State v. Gingerich, 463
State v. Hossan-Maxwell, Inc., 562
State v. Waushara County Bd. of Adjustment, 291
State v. Wilson, 693
State by Powderly v. Erickson, 494
State by Rochester Ass'n of Neighborhoods v. City of Rochester, 337
State ex rel. Battershell v. City of Albuquerque, 358
State ex rel. Foster v. City of Morgantown, 405
State ex rel. Stoyanoff v. Berkeley, 489
State ex rel. Zupancic v. Schimenz, 327
Steinbergh v. City of Cambridge, 265
Stepanov v. Gavrilovich, 444
Stern v. Halligan, 468
Stevens v. Cannon Beach, 178
St. Johns County v. Northeastern Fla. Bldrs. Ass'n, 671
St. Louis, City of, v. Brune, 465
St. Louis Gunning Adver. Co. v. City of St. Louis, 114
Stockton v. Baltimore & N.Y.R.R., 754
Stowe Club Highlands, In re, 202
Strand v. Planning Bd., 440

Stringfellow's of New York, Ltd. v. City of New York, 228

Strycker's Bay Neighborhood Council, Inc. v. Karlen, 390

Stuart v. Crestview Mutual Water Co., 445

Suffolk Hous. Servs. v. Town of Brookhaven, 704, 783

Suitum v. Tahoe Regional Planning Agency, 166, 239

Sullivan v. Little Hunting Park, 560

Summerchase Ltd. Partnership I v. City of Gonzales, 708

Sundowner, Inc. v. King, 521

Superior Uptown, Inc. v. City of Cleveland, 256

Super Wash, Inc. v. City of White Settlement, 326, 328

Surfside Colony, Ltd. v. California Coastal Comm'n, 643

Surrick v. Zoning Hearing Bd., 783

Suttle v. Bailey, 589

Tahoe-Sierra Preservation Council, Inc. v. Tahoe Regional Planning Agency (9th Cir. 1990), 242-43

Tahoe-Sierra Preservation Council, Inc. v. Tahoe Regional Planning Agency (9th Cir. 1991), 243

Tahoe-Sierra Preservation Council, Inc. v. Tahoe Regional Planning Agency (U.S. 2002), 185, 193, 264-66, 800-01, 803, 808, 811

Tampa-Hillsborough County Expressway Auth. v. A.G.W.S. Corp., 415

Taormina Theosophical Community, Inc. v. Silver, 562

Tapalian v. Tusino, 658, 676

Taylor v. Rancho Santa Barbara, 561

Teachers Ins. & Annuity Ass'n v. City of New York, 498

Telluride, Town of, v. Lot Thirty-Four Venture, LLC, 673

Temple Baptist Church, Inc. v. City of Albuquerque, 477

Terrien v. Zwit, 561

Texas Dep't of Transp. v. Barber, 488

Thaler v. Household Fin. Corp., 604

Thanasoulis v. Winston Towers 200 Ass'n, 604

Thayer v. Town of Tilton, 746

The Glen, Section I Condominium Ass'n v. June, 598

The President & Directors of Georgetown Coll. v. District of Columbia Bd. of Zoning Adjustment, 302

The Tidewater Co. v. Coster, 621

Thiess v. Island House Ass'n, 601

Thomas Cusack Co. v. City of Chicago, 396

Thompson v. United States Dep't of Hous. & Urban Dev., 867

Thornburg v. Port of Portland, 524

Tierney v. Duris, 340

Tint v. Sanborn, 528

Tippitt v. City of Hernando, 368

Tobin v. Paparone Constr. Co., 585

Toll Bros., Inc. v. Township of West Windsor, 776, 777, 780

Toll Bros., Inc, v. West Windsor Township, 811-12

Topanga Ass'n for a Scenic Community v. County of Los Angeles, 291

Topanga Press, Inc. v. City of Los Angeles, 229

Town & Country Estates Ass'n v. Slater, 593

Town or Township of: *see* name of town

Trafficante v. Metropolitan Life Ins. Co., 704

Transamerica Title Ins. Co. v. City of Tucson, 405

Traylor v. Holloway, 553

Trenkamp v. Township of Burlington, 458

Trump Plaza v. Atlantic City Municipal Utils. Auth., 658

Tsombanidis v. West Haven Fire Dep't, 728

Tulk v. Moxhay, 563, 564

Turudic v. Stephens, 553

Twigg v. County of Will, 104, 316

Twigg v. Town of Kennebunk, 293

Twin Lakes Dev. Corp. v. Town of Monroe, 671

Ulmer v. Farnsworth, 543

United Artists Theater Circuit, Inc. v. City of Philadelphia, 498

United Artists Theatre Circuit, Inc. v. Township of Warrington, 102, 675

United States v. Carolene Prod. Co., 658

United States v. Carroll Towing Co., 517

United States v. Certain Lands in Louisville, 862

United States v. City & County of Denver, 746

United States v. City of Chicago Heights, 726

United States v. Croft, 360

United States v. Ellerbe Becket, Inc., 450

United States v. Village of Palatine, 728

United States v. Yonkers Bd. of Educ., 701

United States Postal Serv. v. Town of Greenwich, 753

Unity Ventures v. County of Lake, 123

University Gardens Prop. Owners Ass'n v. Solomon, 553

University of Ala. v. Garrett, 721

Urrutia v. Blaine County, 440

U.S. Partners Fin. Corp. v. Kansas City, 230

Ute Park Summer Homes Ass'n v. Maxwell Land Grant Co., 587

Valatie, Village of, v. Smith, 197

Valley View Indus. Park v. City of Redmond, 202

Val Moritz Inv. Group, Ltd., In re, 569

Ventura Village, Inc. v. City of Minneapolis, 708

Vermont Nat'l Bank, In re, 496

Vermont Yankee Nuclear Power Corp. v. Natural Res. Defense Council, Inc., 390

Viking Constr. Co. v. Town Planning Comm'n, 507

Villa De Las Palmas Homeowners Ass'n v. Terifaj, 599

Villa Milano Homeowners Ass'n v. Il Davorge, 553

Village of: *see* name of village

Village Square No. 1, Inc. v. Crow-Frederick Retail Ltd. Partnership, 662

Villas of Lake Jackson, Ltd. v. Leon County, 95

Visionquest Nat'l, Ltd. v. Board of Supervisors, 301

Volusia County v. Aberdeen at Ormond Beach, 669

Vulcan Mat'ls Co. v. City of Tehuacana, 193, 245

Wakefield v. Kraft, 317

Wakelin v. Town of Yarmouth, 300

Walcek v. United States, 164

Waldrop v. Town of Brevard, 579

Wallace v. Brown County Area Plan Comm'n, 482

WalMart Stores, Inc., In re, 118

Walnut Props., Inc. v. City of Whittier, 230
Walsh v. Town of Stonington Water Pollution Control Auth., 528
Walz v. Town of Smithtown, 642
Ward v. Superior Ct., 596
Warner Co. v. Sutton, 319
Warren, In re Township of, 777
Warth v. Seldin, 703
Washington v. Davis, 681
Washington Arcade Assocs. v. Zoning Bd. of Review, 202
Washington ex rel. Seattle Title Trust Co. v. Roberge, 396
Wasilla, City of v. Wilsonoff, 624
Wayne, County of, v. Hathcock, 837
Weber Basin Home Bldrs. Ass'n v. Roy City, 678
Webster Assocs. v. Town of Webster, 285
Wesley Chapel Bluemount Ass'n v. Baltimore County, 360
Westborough Mall, Inc. v. City of Cape Girardeau, 124
West Hartford Interfaith Coalition, Inc. v. Town Council, 787
West Hollywood, City of, v. Beverly Towers, Inc., 430
West Main Assocs. v. City of Bellevue, 208
West Park Ave., Inc. v. Township of Ocean, 659, 674
West Side Women's Servs., Inc. v. City of Cleveland, 231
W.F. White Land Co. v. Christenson, 554
Whatcom County v. Brisbane, 804
Wheeler v. City of Pleasant Grove (11th Cir. 1987), 267
Wheeler v. City of Pleasant Grove (11th Cir. 1990), 269
Wheeler v. Lebanon Valley Auto Racing Corp., 537
White v. Bernhart, 523
White v. City of Dallas, 30
White v. Lee, 729
White Cypress Lakes Dev. Corp. v. Hertz, 587
Whitinsville Plaza, Inc. v. Kotseas, 567
WHS Realty Co. v. Town of Morristown, 682
Wilkerson v. City of Coralville, 689

Wilkinson v. Board of County Comm'rs, 807
Williams v. 5300 Columbia Pike Corp., 710
Williamson County Regional Planning Comm'n v. Hamilton Bank, 234, 266, 281, 624, 808
Willistown, Township of, v. Chesterdale Farms, Inc., 783
Willowbrook, Village of, v. Olech, 129, 659
Wilmington Parking Auth. v. Land With Improvements, 837
Wilson v. Handley, 521
Winston Towers 200 Ass'n v. Saverio, 597
Wisniowski v. Planning Comm'n, 786
WMI Props., Inc. v. Falls Township Zoning Hearing Bd., 749
Wolford v. Thomas, 20
Wolper v. City Council of the City of Charleston, 842
Wood v. Milin, 457
Woodland Hills Residents Ass'n v. City Council, 366
Woodward v. Bowers, 561
Workman v. Brighton Props., Inc., 604
World Wide Video of Wash., Inc. v. City of Spokane, 230
Wright v. Cypress Shores Dev. Co., 554, 589
Wyatt v. United States, 267

Yakima County (West Valley) Fire Protection Dist. No. 12 v. City of Yakima, 688
Yale Auto Parts, Inc. v. Johnson, 103
Ybarra v. Town of Los Altos Hills, 709
Yee v. City of Escondido, 169, 239
Young v. City of Simi Valley, 399
Younger v. Harris, 255
Yuba Nat. Res., Inc. v. United States, 271

Zaruta v. Zoning Hearing Bd., 293
Zavala v. City & County of Denver, 715
Z.J. Gifts, L.L.C. v. City of Aurora, 228
Zoning Bd. of Appeals v. Planning & Zoning Comm'n, 286
Zylka v. City of Crystal, 299

Author Index

Authors excerpted are in italics.

Aaron, Henry, 549
Abbott, Carl, 785, 813, 816
Abraham, Stephen E., 240
Abrams, Charles, 15
Ackerman, Bruce A., 39, 469
Ackerman, Bruce L., 709
Ackman, Daniel, 392
Adams, Rick, 59
Advisory Commission on Regulatory Barriers to
    Affordable Housing, 460, 506
Ahrend, Kristopher E., 707
Albaugh, Lyle D., 275
Albert, Craig J., 478
Alexander, Gregory S., 606
Allee, Benjamin, 193
Alley, Nathan G., 378
Alonso, William, 57, 890
Alpern, Andrew, 853
Altree, Lillian R., 524, 527
Altshuler, Alan A., 52, 637, 650
American Law Institute, 62, 69
American Planning Association, 53, 789
American Society of Civil Engineering., 420
Amick, George, 308
Anderson, Andy B., 756
Anderson, Jerry L., 365
Anderson, John E., 538
Anderson, Martin, 841
Anderson, Terry L., 820
Andres, Duany., 91, 422
Andrews, Richard N.L., 747
Angel, Shlomo, 25
Anthony, Jerry, 818
Antolini, Denise E., 537
Apgar, Robert C., 340
Apgar, William C., Jr., 877
Arnold, Craig Anthony, 142, 686, 703
Arnott, Richard, 790
Arrensen, David A., 273
Arthur Anderson Real Estate Servs. Group, 15
Asabere, Paul K., 422, 494, 504

Ashbrook, Robert, 103
Axelrad, Tina R., 103
Ayres, Ian, 306
Babcock, Richard F., 117, 294, 305, 347, 776
Bacon, Kenneth H., 875
Baden, John A., 549, 821
Bagby, D. Gordon, 422
Bagli, Charles V., 853
Bailey, Bruce R., 320
Bair, Frederick Haigh, 68
Baker, Lynn A., 30, 408
Baker, R. Lisle, 543
Baldassare, Mark, 797
Ballard, Megan J., 878, 879
Banfield, Edward C., 51
Barbanel, Josh, 582
Barewin, Howard J., 788
Barlow, Chuck D., 759
Barnes, Cynthia J., 273
Barnhizer, Daniel D., 150
Barr, Michael S., 892
Barros, D. Benjamin, 143
Barth, James R., 875
Barth, Scott J., 458
Bartik, Timothy J., 887
Bartlett, Sarah, 455
Barton, Stephen E., 583, 606
Bassett, Edward M., 580
Bauman, Gus, 340
Baumgartner, M.P., 39
Baxter, William F., 524, 527
Bayer, Patrick, 697
Beauvais, Joel C., 150, 153, 267
Becker, Kathleen, 387
Bederman, David J., 178
Been, Vicki, 150, 153, 177, 178, 179, 242, 243, 267,
    635, 637, 657, 658, 746, 747, 756, 757, 758, 760,
    818
Beito, David T., 550
Bell, Abraham, 150, 579, 709
Bell, Derrick A., Jr., 408
Ben-Joseph, Eran, 423, 424
Berens, Gayle, 57

Berger, Curtis J., 549
Berger, Lawrence, 138
Berger, Michael M., 242, 245, 250, 256, 265
Berkowitz, Harry, 166
Bernstein, Richard, 504
Berry, Brian J.L., 9
Bertaud, Alain, 790
Bettman, Alfred, 76
Beuscher, J.H., 519
Billman, Brookes, 630
Bingham, Richard D., 887
Bittker, Boris I., 709
Blaesser, Brian W., 250, 256
Blais, Lynn E., 178, 757
Blakely, Edward J., 583
Bley, Kenneth B., 103, 234
Blume, Lawrence, 151, 153
Blumm, Michael, 393
Bobrowski, Mark, 787
Boehm, Thomas P., 45
Boerner, Christopher, 757
Bogart, William T., 770, 771
Boger, John Charles, 781, 782
Bolick, Clint, 816
Bond, R. Douglass, 483
Bone, Robert G., 512
Borcherding, Thomas E., 859
Bornong, Joseph H., 295
Boskin, Michael J., 822
Bosselman, Fred P., 110, 395, 811
Boudreaux, Donald J., 821
Boudreaux, Paul, 770
Bourassa, Steven C., 868
Boyd, James, 582
Braddock, David, 716
Braithwaite, John, 306
Branch, Melville C., 52
Branfman, Eric J., 770
Bratt, Rachel G., 877
Bratton, William W., 771
Brauneis, Robert, 143
Breedlove, Scott W., 116
Breemer, J. David, 244, 668
Brener, Katia, 715
Brenner, Marie, 499
Bressi, Todd W., 93
Brest, Paul, 117, 702
Briffault, Richard, 30, 50, 407, 633, 689, 769, 771, 844, 884
Brock, Danielle M., 757
Broder, David S., 407
Bromley, Daniel W., 179
Brooker, Gregory G., 507
Brooks, Arthur V.N., 81
Brower, Richard, 582
Brown, Barbara B., 424
Brown, Carol Necole, 185
Brown, H. James, 15, 655
Brown, Jennifer G., 321, 327
Brown, Monique R., 613
Brown, Patricia Leigh, 472
Brown, Steve, 393
Brown, Thomas A., 778, 785
Brownstein, Alan E., 117, 702
Brueckner, Jan K., 797
Bryden, David P., 294

Bryden, Roderick M., 295
Buccino, Sharon, 643
Buchanan, James M., 139
Buchsbaum, Peter A., 243
Bufford, Samuel, 477
Bullard, Robert D., 754, 818
Bunnell, Gene, 618
Burby, Raymond J., 58, 460
Burcat, Joel R., 193
Burchell, Robert W., 55, 420, 618, 619, 790
Burke, Barlow, Jr., 318
Burling, James S., 242
Burnham, Daniel, 52
Butler, Stuart, 888
Byrne, J. Peter, 10, 775, 777, 782
Caffry, John W., 378
Calabresi, Guido, 331, 532
Calandrillo, Steve P., 153
Calavita, Nico, 57, 674, 770, 784
Caldwell, Lynton Keith, 392
Callies, David L., 84, 408, 434
Calthorpe, Peter, 422, 608, 793, 794
Calvert, Clay, 228
Campbell, Jay, 200
Campbell, Robert, 550
Canellos, Peter S., 787
Cannaday, Roger E., 559
Cappel, Andrew J., 416, 610
Carbonell, A., 406
Cardwell, Diane, 335
Carlson, Ann E., 267, 651, 663
Carroll, Robert D., 787
Case, Karl E., 878
Cashin, Sheryll D., 11, 697, 769
Cassedy, Melissa, 446
Catanese, Anthony J., 55
Caves, Roger, 57
Chapin, F. Stuart, 62
Charlow, Robin, 408
Chaves, Mark, 219
Chemerinsky, Erwin, 131
Cheshire, Paul, 41
Chinitz, Benjamin, 795
Chira, Susan, 757
Cho, Man, 797
Chuang, Jane, 741
Church, William L., 549
Chused, Richard H., 74, 84, 650
Claeys, Eric R., 137
Clark, Charles E., 567
Clark, William A.V., 708
Clary, Thomas A., 854
Clavel, Pierre, 55
Clawson, Marion, 15, 821
Clingermayer, James C., 770
Coase, Ronald, 34, 139
Coggins, George Cameron, 820
Cohen, Richard S., 319
Cohen, James R., 789
Cole, Karen R., 507
Cole, Luke W., 746, 756
Coleman, James S., 496
Coletta, Raymond Robert, 520
Coller, Craig, 351
Collins, Flannary P., 550
Collins, Margaret, 200

Collins, Richard B., 409
Colwell, Peter F., 44, 446
Congressional Budget Office, 879
Cook, Andrew, 445
Cooley, Thomas M., 140
Cooperstein, Theodore M., 267
Cooter, Robert, 40
Cordes, Joseph J., 860
Cordes, Mark W., 276, 280, 365, 368, 488
Correll, Mark R., 44
Costa, Nadia L., 672, 787
Costonis, John J., 471, 496
Cottman, Michael H., 166
Coulson, N. Edward, 25, 500
Council on Environmental Quality, 392
Courchesne, Christophe, 787
Coursen, David, 276
Cowart, Richard H., 821
Coyle, Dennis J., 110
Craswell, Richard, 153
Crecine, John P., 43
Crocker, Karen L., 207
Crone, Theodore M., 40
Cronin, Thomas E., 406
Cropper, Vivian L., 424
Cruikshank, Jeffrey, 746
Cullotta Krause, Karen, 707
Culpepper, Michael A., 280
Cummings, Jean L., 878
Cummings, Scott, 891
Cummins, Justin D., 781
Cunningham, Noel, 630
Currier, Barry A., 546, 549
Curtin, Daniel J., Jr., 672
Cushman, Barry, 85
Cutler, David M., 693, 762
Czarnezki, Jason J., 386
Dagan, Hanoch, 153
Dahlin, Doug, 65
Daley, Patricia, 823
Dana, David A., 821
Daniels, Thomas L., 581
Davies, Mark S., 633
Davis, Brian E., 729
Davis, Otto A., 34
Davis, Paul E., 446
Davis, R.P., 209
Dawkins, Casey J., 817
Dawson, John, 543
Daye, Charles E., 707, 874, 879
Dear, Michael, 741
de Bartolome, Charles A.M., 887
Delaney, John J., 110, 207, 433, 801
De Leon, Peter, 309
Delogu, Orlando E., 300, 608, 808
De Lucca, Sian, 780
Demsetz, Harold, 38
Dennis, Sharon, 196
Denton, Nancy A., 692, 693, 761-62
DeSalvo, Joseph S., 45
Deyle, Robert E., 58
Diamond, Douglas B., Jr., 44
Diamond, Stephen, 630
Dietderich, Andrew G., 673
Dietz, Robert D., 25
Dilger, Robert Jay, 583, 606

Di Mento, Joseph F., 340
DiPasquale, Denise, 25, 877-78
Diskin, Barry A., 281
Dixon, Chris, 643
Do, A. Quang, 44-45
Donohue, John J., III, 821
Donovan, Todd, 797
Doremus, Holly, 140, 185
Douglas, Dash T., 704
Douglass, Thomas G., Jr., 281
Downes, Bryan T., 716
Downs, Anthony, 760, 761, 795, 797, 816, 817
Drees, Marilyn F., 276
Dreyfus, Daniel A., 369
Duany, Andres, 10, 422, 608, 793, 890
Dubin, Jon C., 703
Dudek, Daniel J., 167
Duerksen, Christopher J., 117, 270
Duncan, James B., 789
Dunlap, David W., 93, 166, 498, 505
Durchslag, Melvyn R., 50, 770
Durham, James G., 859
Durkee, Michael, 407
Durrett, Charles, 583
Durst, Seymour, 853
Dworkin, Andrea, 231
Dye, Richard F., 845
Eagle, Steven J., 164, 184, 196, 265, 275, 607
Easley, V. Gail, 814, 815
Easterbrook, Frank, 124
Eby, Raymond B., 275
Echeverria, John D., 196, 266, 275
Eckardt, Wolf Von, 889
Egan, Timothy, 494
Ehrlich Kautz, Barbara, 787
Eichler, Ned, 19
Einhorn, Robin L., 630
Eisdorfer, Stephen, 780, 781
Eisenberg, Theodore, 702
Eisenstadt, Melvin M., 39
Eisgruber, Christopher L., 218
Eisinger, Peter K., 887
Elberg, Amos B., 598
Elhauge, Einer R., 306
Ellen, Ingrid Gould, 12, 880
Ellickson, Robert C., 39, 50, 139, 280, 305, 321, 516, 518, 538, 541, 550, 590, 606, 607, 624, 673, 704, 740, 796, 890, 891
Ells Cheverine, Carolyn, 497
Ely, James W., Jr., 137
Ely, John Hart, 117, 702
Emerson, Kirk, 275
English, Mary R., 747
Enrich, Peter D., 884
Epstein, Richard A., 85, 138, 139, 143, 144, 145, 148, 154, 178, 520, 606, 650, 838
Espeland, Wendy, 393
Eule, Julian N., 407, 408
Evans, Hugh, 890
Evans-Connolly, Jennifer S., 657
Evseev, Dmitri, 769
Ewing, Reid, 793, 795
Fairfax, Sally K., 821, 822
Fallon, Richard H., Jr., 50, 124
Farber, Daniel A., 50, 157, 305, 534
Farina, William, 879

Farley, Reynolds, 693
Farmer, W. Paul, 55
Farnsworth, Ward, 534
Farrell, Robert C., 131
Feagin, Joe R., 613
Fedun, Michael, 331
Fee, John E., 157, 193, 266
Fein, David B., 505
Feins, Judith D., 762, 770
Fennell, Lee Anne, 305, 321, 606, 651, 860
Fenster, Mark, 583, 651
Ferester, Philip Michael, 392
Fessler, Daniel W., 682
Feuer, Alan, 880
Field, Ben, 784
Field, Charles G., 460, 463
Field, Patrick, 778
Fink, Richard J., 822
Firey, Walter, 610
Fischel, William A., 13, 28, *41, 46*, 49, 139, 143, 149,
    151, 153, 154, 157, 178, 185, 305, 321, 415, 549,
    617, 650, 655, 690, 771, 795, 796, 797, 816, 817
Fischer, Thomas G., 519
Fischler, Raphaël, 75
Fisher, Peter S., 887, 889
Fisher, William W., III, 148, 179
Fitton, Laura, 756
Fleischmann, Arnold, 307
Flint, Anthony, 787
Floyd, Charles F., 478
Fluck, Timothy Alan, 81, 82
Foderaro, Lisa W., 463
Foglesong, Richard E., 448
Foldvary, Fred, 584, 606
Fondo, Grant P., 452
Ford, Richard Thompson, 769, 778
Forrest, Clyde W., 331
Foster, Sheila, 756, 759
Fountaine, Cynthia L., 407
Frame, W. Scott, 870
France, Thomas, 392
Franklin, David, 729
Franklin, Herbert M., 811
Franzese, Paula A., 597, 606
Frech, H.E., 43
Freeman, Lance, 795
Freilich, Robert H., 409, 416, 789, 811
French, Susan F., *551*, 606
Freund, Ernst, 138
Frey, Bruno S., 747
Frey, William H., 12
Freyer, Tony, 823
Freyfogle, Eric T., 179
Frickey, Philip P., 50, 305
Frieden, Bernard J., 307, *840*
Frieden, Jeffry A., 157
Friedman, Barry, 251
Friedman, Joseph, 876
Friedman, Lawrence M., 143
Frug, Gerald, 50, 769, 771
Fujita, Masahisa, 790
Fuller, Lon L., 65
Fulton, William, 407
Furman Speyrer, Janet, 613
Gallagher, Patrick, 795
Galster, George C., 44, 709, 793, 877

Gardiner, James A., 448
Gardiner, John A., 308
Gardner, Elliot, 299
Garnett, Nicole Stelle, 469, 838, 889
Garvey, Matthew C., 167
Garvin, Alexander, 51, 330
Gates, Paul, 820
Gavin, Robert, 445
Gehan, Shaun M., 133
General Accounting Office, 478, 795
Geneslaw, Robert, 811
George, Henry, 652
Gerard, Jules B., 231
Gerber, Elisabeth R., 407
Gerckens, Laurence C., 81
Gerrard, Michael B., 370, 747, 759, 760
Getlin, Josh, 780
Gibbons, Max, 184
Gillette, Clayton P., 30, 407, 606, 628, 884
Gillette, Howard, Jr., 831
Gilmartin, Gregory F., 75
Gin, Alan, 797
Ginzburg, Rebecca, 715
Givens, Ann, 308
Glaeser, Edward L., 2, 9, 12, 25, 28, 697, 762
Glancy, Dorothy J., 167, 498
Glencer, Julia M., 193
Glenn, Peter G., 404, 405
Glesner, B.A., 523
Godschalk, David R., 55, 63
Godsil, Rachel D., 757
Goering, John, 762, 770
Goetz, Edward G., 867, 891
Goetz, Jon E., 404
Gold, Andrew, 137
Gold, Seymour M., 15
Goldberg, Arthur Abba, 50
Goldberg, Carey, 581
Goldberg, Jeffrey A., 593
Goldberger, Paul, 93
Goldman, Benjamin A., 756
Goldstein, Bruce, 643
Gómez-Ibánez, Jose A., 637, 650
Gonzalez, David, 294
Goodchild, Robin, 655
Goodenough, Mary, 509
Gordon, Colin, 840, 844
Gottlieb, Martin, 166
Gould, Eric D., 544
Gray, Christopher, 477
Gray, Jerry, 539
Gray, Kevin R., 391
Grebler, Leo, 19
Green, Richard K., 25
Gregory, Robin, 386
Grether, David M., 45
Grieson, Ronald E., 43
Grigsby, William G., 868
Grimes, George E., Jr., 280
Grimes, Kenneth, 674, 770
Grogan, Paul S., 891
Gross, Hillary, 759
Grove, Jesse B., III, 271
Groves, Jeremy R., 41
Groy, Jeffrey B., 442
Grudnitski, Gary, 45

Guana, Eileen, 755
Gudis, Catherine, 477
Guemmer, Derek B., 409
Guenther, Robert, 500
Gupta, Francis, 756
Gustanski, Julie Ann, 582
Guttery, Randall S., 509
Guy, Donald C., 45, 167, 184
Gwyn, Allen Holt, 446
Gyourko, Joseph, 19, 28, 650
Haar, Charles M., 58, 81, 85, 682, 771, 776, 777, 823, 889
Hagman, Donald G., 272, 374, 580
Hall, Peter, 55
Halper, Louise A., 518
Ham, Bernard K., 673
Hamilton, Bruce W., 40, 790, 797
Hamilton, Marci A., 219
Hamilton, Stanley W., 44
Hammer, Thomas R., 45
Hanke, Steven H., 406
Hanley, Robert, 776
Hanlon, Natalie, 822
Hansmann, Henry B., 606, 891
Hanson, James A., 219
Hardin, Russell, 306
Harnik, Peter, 15
Harper, Fowler V., 536
Harrington, Matthew P., 838
Hart, John F., 137
Hartman, Chester, 810, 877
Hartog, Hendrik, 412
Hattis, David, 449
Haurin, Donald R., 25
Hayden, Dolores, 793
Hayek, Friedrich A., 68
Hays, R. Allen, 875, 888
Healy, Michael P., 508
Healy, Robert G., 15, 731
Hearle, Edward F.R., 15
Hedman, Richard, 68
Helland, Eric, 41
Heller, Michael A., 142, 149, 151
Hellman, Peter, 846
Helsley, Robert W., 797
Helvarg, David, 275
Hendershott, Patric H., 869
Henderson, Archie, 612
Henderson, Sally, 477
Hendon, William S., 44
Henning, John A., Jr., 673
Hentrich, Michele A., 359
Herman, Dennis J., 687
Herrman, Cyril, 471
Hershman, Mendes, 863
Herz, Michael, 392
Hetzel, Otto J., 468
Hevesi, Dennis, 455, 880
Heyman, Ira Michael, 86, 347
Higginbotham, A. Leon, Jr., 692
Higgins, Bill, 787
Hirokawa, Keith H., 378
Hirsch, Alan, 839
Hirshleifer, Jack, 32
Hochleutner, Brian R., 634
Hodas, David R., 392

Hoffman, Christopher, 880
Hoffman, Elizabeth, 860
Hoffman, Sandra A., 548
Hogue, Barry, 507
Holloway, James E., 167, 184
Holmes, Robert C., 781
Holt, Nancy D., 497
Homes Association, 584, 595, 604
Hopkins, Thomas D., 628
Hopperton, Robert J., 111, 197
Horwitz, Morton J., 137
Houck, Oliver A., 391, 509
Hough, Douglas E., 494
Housing Research News, 25
Houstoun, Lawrence, 633
Hovenkamp, Herbert, 124
Howard, Philip, 461
Howe, Deborah A., 817
Howe, Elizabeth, 57
Howells, Louise A., 888
Huffman, James L., 821
Hughes, James W., 25
Hughes, Mark Alan, 778
Hughes, William T., Jr., 550
Huhn, Wilson R., 228
Humstone, Elizabeth, 118
Hunt, Albert R., 875
Husock, Howard, 877
Hwang, Sean-Shong, 12
Hyatt, Wayne S., 588, 606
Hylton, Joseph Gordon, 85
Hynes, H. Patricia, 816
Iceland, John, 697
Iglesias, Tim, 391, 787
Ihlanfeldt, Keith R., 45, 657, 770, 797
Ingram, Helen M., 369
Inhaber, Herbert, 741
Inman, Robert P., 683, 769
Jackson, Jerry, 275
Jackson, Kenneth T., 9, 422, 693, 795, 864
Jacobs, Jane, 841
Janofsky, Michael, 605
Japenga, Ann, 455
Jargowsky, Paul A., 13
Johnson, Corwin W., 273
Johnson, Sheri Lynn, 702
Johnston, Robert A., 672
Johnstone, Quintin, 869
Joint Center for Housing Studies, 25, 29
Jolls, Christine, 32
Jones, Bryan D., 837
Jones, James T.R., 519
Jones, Susan R., 892
Jorden, Douglas A., 359
Juergensmeyer, Conrad, 167
Kades, Eric, 150, 153
Kain, John K., 44
Kaiser, Edward J., 55, 63
Kanner, Gideon, 243, 245, 256, 667
Kanter, Arlene S., 727
Kaplan, Marshall, 840
Kaplow, Louis, 153, 185, 534, 656
Kapur, Teddy M., 612
Karkkainen, Bradley C., 370, 379, 392, 393, 608
Kasarda, John D., 9
Kassouni, Timothy V., 243

Kaswan, Alice, 757
Katyal, Neal Kumar, 452
Katz, Lawrence F., 20
Kau, James B., 446
Kaufman, Jerome L., 57
Kaufman, Michael T., 504
Kayden, Jerold S., 81, 333, 335, 673
Kaye, Tracy A., 879
Keane Commission, 506
Keating, Larry, 795
Keating, W. Dennis, 709
Keaton, Robert E., 517
Kebodeaux, Tara R., 757
Kelbaugh, Douglas, 795
Kelley, Richard, 428
Kelly, Barbara M., 10
Kelly, Eric Damian, 93, 461, 807, 810, 811
Kelman, Mark, 38
Kennedy, David J., 591, 634
Kennedy, Nolan M., Jr., 321
Kennedy, Shawn G., 500
Kent, David L., 293, 294
Kessler, Daniel P., 20
Keyes, Langley, 891
Kim, Michael C., 598
King, Andrew J., 395
King, John O., 890
Kinnaird, Stephen B., 864
Kinsey, David N., 780
Kirchheim, Diana M., 207
Kirp, David L., 772, 773, 777, 779
Klausner, Michael, 892
Klein, Christine A., 820
Kleiner, Morris M., 465
Kline, Jeffrey, 581
Kmiec, Douglas W., 139, 145, 273, 449, 608
Knaap, Gerrit, 423, 785, 793, 814, 816
Knetsch, Jack L., 859
Knowles, C.C., 447
Kobach, Kris W., 137
Kolodney, Lawrence K., 10
Kolson, Kenneth L., 51
Komesar, Neil K., 34, 819
Korngold, Gerald, 85, 550, 561, 580
Korpela, Allan E., 509
Kossow, Julian, 650
Kotkin, Joel, 613
Kowaloff, Steven D., 166
Kramer, Bruce, 327
Krane, Dale., 30
Krasnowiecki, Jan Z., 347, 437, 587, 607
Kratovil, Robert, 570
Kratz, Charles G., 494
Krier, James E., 149, 151, 158, 539, 543, 838
Krotoszynski, Ronald J., Jr., 196
Krueckeberg, Donald A., 81
Krumholz, Norman, 55
Kublicki, Nicolas M., 404
Kunstler, James Howard, 608
Kushner, James A., 692
Kushner, Phillip, 538
Kysar, Douglas A., 821
La Londe, Kyle W., 755
Lafferty, Ronald N., 43
Laitos, Jan G., 165
Lamar, Martha, 781

Lambert, Thomas, 757
Landau, Robert, 477
Landes, William M., 517
Landis, John D., 19, 806, 817
Lang, Robert E., 9
Larson, Jane E., 417
LaRusso, Joseph, 270
Lassar, Terry Jill, 334, 888
Lauber, Daniel, 716, 721
Lawhon, Larry L., 657
Lawlor, James, 58
Lawrence, Charles R., III, 117, 702
Lawrence, Curtis, 707
Lawrence, David M., 884
Lawrence, Nathaniel S., 197
Laycock, Douglas, 219, 535
Lazos, Sylvia R., 281
Leach, James, 807
Leal, Donald, 821
LeDuff, Charlie, 493
Lee, Chang-Moo, 45
Lees, Martha A., 84
Lefcoe, George, 340, 840
Leffler, Keith B., 484
LeGates, Richard T., 807
Lehman, H. Jane, 177
Lehman, Jeffrey S., 889
Lehmann, Jeffrey M., 769, 785
Lehmann, Scott, 821
Leichenko, Robin M., 500, 504
Leigh, Catesby, 505
Leitner, Martin L., 676
Lento, Rochelle E., 892
Lester, James P., 756
Levin, Murray S., 117
Levinson, Daryl J, 149
Levmore, Saul, 157, 185, 860
Levy, Dale Pennys, 822
Lewin, Jeff L., 512, 518, 528, 535
Lewinsohn-Zamir, Daphna, 505, 821
Libecap, Gary D., 821
Liberty, Robert L., 786, 814
Liebmann, George W., 29, 607, 854
Lillydahl, Jane H., 657
Lindblom, Charles E., 32, 67
Linde, Hans A., 407
Linz, Daniel, 228
Lipman, Wynona M., 777
Listokin, David, 416, 420, 449, 637
Litan, Robert E., 875
Litman, Todd, 795
Logan, John R., 12, 306, 817
Logan, Thomas H., 75
Logsdon, Pamela R., 753
Long, E. Andrew, 756
Longman, Phillip, 797
Loose, Cindy, 876
Lopez, Russ, 816
Lotchin, Roger W., 608
Low, Setha, 583
Lowenstein, Louis K., 863
Lubove, Roy, 91
Lucy, William H., 10
Lueck, Thomas J., 93, 335
Luger, Michael I., 506
Lunney, Glynn S., Jr., 139, 148

Lyman, R. Jeffrey, 243
Lyman, Theodore R., 308, 448
MacDonald, Heather, 633
MacKerron, John A., III, 124
MacKinnon, Catharine A., 231
Magarian, Gregory P., 218
Magleby, David B., 407
Mahan, Brent L., 45
Mahoney, Julia D., 582
Maisel, Sherman J., 20
Maker, Elizabeth, 489
Malanga, Steven, 888
Malaspina, Mark A., 877
Mallach, Alan M., 672
Mallor, Jane P., 445
Malone, Linda A., 508
Malpezzi, Stephen, 28, 879
Manaster, Kenneth A., 754
Mandelker, Daniel R., 30, 58, 103, 111, 165, 184, 207, 340, 359, 386
Mank, Bradford C., 747, 755, 760
Mann, Roberta F., 497, 868
Maraist, Patrick W., 281
Marcellino, Carl P., 276
Mariah Hays, Charlotte, 497
Marini, N.J., 465
Markovits, Richard, 469
Marsh, Lindell L., 434
Martin, Jonathan, 817
Martin, Timothy P., 588
Marwell, Nicole P., 892
Maser, S. M., 43
Mashaw, Jerry L., 50
Massey, Douglas S., 692
Mattes, Philip V., 145
Mattix, Carla, 387
Mayer, J.P., 605
Mayo, Stephen K., 875
Mazmanian, Daniel, 741
McCahery, Joseph A., 771
McCamant, Kathryn, 583
McCarthy, Claire, 200
McClure, Kirk, 879
McCormack, Christopher P., 708
McCracken, Gregory W., 219
McDonald, John F., 12, 612
McDougall, Harold A., 778, 783
McDowell, Edwin, 583
McElyea, William D., 117
McFarlane, Audrey G., 889
McGuire, James E., 777
McGuire, Therese J., 778
McKee, Cynthia N., 778
McKenzie, Evan, 606
McMillen, Daniel P., 524
McMurry, Robert I., 219
McNamara, Maureen A., 709
McQuillan, Eugene, 30
Meck, Stuart, 59, 339, 783
Melamed, A. Douglas, 331, 532
Melli, Marygold S., 416
Meltz, Robert, 165, 233, 270, 275
Mendel, David S., 240
Meredith, Jeremy R., 424, 793
Merriam, Dwight H., 193, 803

Merrill, Thomas W., 139, 149, 539, 650, 832, 838, 860
Merriman, David F., 845
Meyer, Elizabeth B., 232
Meyer, Stephen Grant, 692
Meyerson, Martin, 51, 52
Miceli, Thomas J., 149
Michalik, John J., 739
Michel, Matthew J., 337
Michelman, Frank I., 47, 124, 145, 146, 179, 197, 265, 275, 400, 471, 683, 715
Mier, Robert, 887
Mieszkowski, Peter, 6, 45, 656
Mikitish, Joseph P., 273
Milani, Adam A., 450, 452
Miller, Andrew J., 167
Miller, Bill, 452
Miller, Douglas E., 726
Mills, Edwin S., 6, 655, 790
Minow, Martha, 721
Mirsky, Chester L., 118, 392
Mixon, John, 612
Mollenkopf, John H., 845
Moloney-Merkel, Jon, 676
Molotch, Harvey L., 24, 306
Monaghan, Henry Paul, 243
Montgomery, Lori, 449
Moore, Brenda, 308
Morell, David, 741
Morgan, George T., Jr., 890
Morgan, Terry D., 208
Morris, Emily M., 601
Morrison, Jerry W., 519
Morrow-Jones, Hazel A., 424
Mueller, Dennis C., 50, 306
Munch, Patricia, 854
Municipal Art Society, 294
Munton, Don, 741
Munton, Richard, 655
Murdock, Steve H., 12
Musgrave, Peggy B., 625, 862
Musgrave, Richard A., 625, 628, 862
Mushkin, Selma J., 628
Muth, Richard F., 12, 460
Myers, Caitlin Knowles, 12
Nader, Ralph, 838
Nagle, John Copeland, 524
Natelson, Robert G., 591, 606
National Academy of Public Administration, 759
National Commission on Urban Problems, 348, 460
National Conference of States on Building Codes and Standards, 508
Nedelsky, Jennifer, 142
Neiman, Max, 797
Nelson, Arthur C., 44, 785, 789, 797, 816, 817
Nelson, Grant S., 869, 870, 880
Nelson, Robert H., 395, 607, 822
Nenno, Mary K., 866, 877, 879
Netsch, Dawn Clark, 30
New York City Department of Buildings, 452
New York City Department of City Planning, 760
New York State Organized Crime Task Force, 455
Newberg, Joshua A., 581
Newman, Oscar, 866
Newville, Jack, 421
Niedercorn, John H., 15

Nieves, Evelyn, 496
Nitikman, Mark August, 407
Nivala, John, 493
Noam, Eli, 461
Noel, Dix W., 520
Noll, Roger G., 888
Nolon, John R., 789, 811
Novak, Jan Ryan, 232
Novak, William J., 137, 140, 447
Oakes, John Michael, 757
Oberholzer-Gee, Felix, 747
Oesterle, Dale, 409
O'Hare, Michael, 393, 747
Olsen, Edgar O., 876, 877, 878
Olson, Mancur, 306
Olson, Walter, 452
Orfield, Myron, 769
Ortiz, Daniel R., 158
Ortiz, Francesca, 229
Ortolano, Leonard, 393
Orts, Eric W., 392
Osborn, John E., 863
Oswald, Lynda J., 139, 165
Overstreet, Gregory, 207, 241, 243
Owens, David W., 290, 294
Pace, Stephen J.L., 493
Padgett, David A., 613
Painter, Gary et al., 25
Pak, Mihui, 408
Palmer, J. Jioni, 308
Palmon, Oded, 655
Papke, Leslie E., 889
Parchomovsky, Gideon, 39, 150, 534, 579, 709
Paris, Jonathan S., 407
Parsons, K.C., 862
Paschal, Joel F., 85
Pashigian, B. Peter, 544
Pastor, Manuel, 757
Paul, Bryant, 228
Paul, Jeremy, 139, 149, 251
Payne, Cymie, 509
Payne, John M., 673, 772, 773, 776, 777, 778, 781, 782
Pelham, Thomas G., 336, 351, 813
Pendall, Rolf, 770, 817, 818
Penn, Graham C., 352
Percival, Robert V., 124
Perin, Constance, 795
Perlman Krefetz, Sharon, 787
Peters, Alan H., 887, 889
Peterson, Andrea L., 139
Peterson, Craig A., 200
Peterson, George E., 876
Peterson, Iver, 405, 605
Peterson, Jon A., 51
Peterson, Paul E., 307
Pettys, Todd E., 771
Peyton, Bradley R., 295
Phillips, Ashley C., 230
Phillips, David L., 10
Picarello, Anthony R., Jr., 218
Pierannunzi, Carol A., 307
Pigou, A.C., 34
Pindell, Ngai, 867
Piorkowski, Jeff, 86
Pitchford, Rohan, 527

Pitt, P.H., 447
Plassmann, Florenz, 654
Plater-Zyberk, Elizabeth, 608, 890
Platt, Rutherford H., 676
Pogrund Stark, Debra, 445
Poindexter, Georgette C., 494, 778
Poirier, Marc, 179
Polinsky, A. Mitchell, 534
Pollak, Daniel, 267, 651
Pollan, Michael, 589
Pollard, Robert, 673
Porter, David, 118, 392
Porter, Douglas R., 171, 434, 672, 789, 807, 812, 816
Porter, Michael E., 891
Portnoy, Paul R., 49
Posner, Richard A., 149, 306, 469, 517
Poulton, Michael C., 424
Pound, Edward T., 875
Powell, Frona M., 445
Powell, John A., 10, 787
Power, Garrett, 81, 85, 271, 692
Powers, Kevin M., 218
Prall, Todd W., 351
President's Committee on Urban Housing, 16, 446
Priemus, Hugo, 876
Primus, Richard, 707
Pristin, Terry, 869, 891
Pritchett, Wendell E., 707, 831
Putnam, Robert D., 496, 605
Quigley, John M., 25, 29, 44
Quinones, Benjamin B., 891
Rabin, Jay Harris, 272
Rabin, Yale, 703
Rabinowitz, Leonard S., 867
Radford, Gail, 864
Radford, R.S., 196
Radin, Margaret Jane, 193, 201
Rahenkamp, John, 66, 421
Ramsey, Sarah H., 469
Randle, William M., 81, 84
Raphael, Steven, 25, 29
Rasmussen, Paul W., 854
Rather, John, 10
Raymond, George, 811
Read, Tod, 507
Rechtschaffen, Clifford, 755, 756, 759
Reichman, Uriel, 586
Reinert, Alexander A., 519
Reiss, David, 823
Remy, Michael H., 370
Report of the President's Commission on Housing, 460, 506
Reps, John W., 51, 411, 656
Reskin, Melvin A., 591
Reuter, Frederick H., 538
Reynolds, Laurie, 437, 689, 752
Reynolds, Osborne M., Jr., 293, 316
Rhoads, James B., 588
Rice, Roger L., 692
Rich, Motoko, 561
Richards, Joseph D., 102
Richards, Robert D., 228
Richman, Barak D., 746
Richman, Jack, 452
Richmond, Henry R., 816
Ricks, Thomas E., 19

Rielly, Mark R., 581
Risen, James, 535
Rivkin, Steven R., 460
Rizzo, Nina, 778
Roberts, Thomas E., 243, 244, 265
Robichaux, Mark, 442
Robinson, Glen O., 360, 575, 579
Roddewig, Richard J., 270
Rodgers, William H., Jr., 391
Rodwin, Lloyd, 57, 890
Rohan, Patrick J., 369, 591
Rohe, William A., 581
Roithmayr, Daria, 769
Rolland, Michael, 509
Roper, William E., 118
Rose, Carol M., 39, 49, 142, 144, 275, 295, 349, 350, 496, 560
Rose, Jerome G., 777
Rose, Joseph, 760
Rose, Louis A., 797
Rose-Ackerman, Susan, 150, 153, 179, 193
Rosen, Christine, 512
Rosenbaum, James E., 770, 867
Rosenberg, John S., 731
Rosenberry, Katherine, 591
Rosener, Judy B., 307
Rosenthal Kwall, Roberta, 483
Ross, Andrew, 422
Ross, H. Laurence, 469
Rossi, Jim, 153
Rosso Grossman, Margaret, 519
Roth, Martha T., 444
Rothenberg, Jerome, 9, 841, 877, 878
Rubenfeld, Jed, 154
Rubin, Peter J., 103
Rubinfeld, Daniel L., 151, 769, 683
Rubinowitz, Leonard S., 770
Rudel, Thomas K., 24
Ruge, Alyssa A., 102
Rusk, David, 789
Russell, David, 477
Russell, Rusty, 786
Rybczynski, Witold, 34
Sabel, Charles F., 782
Sackman, Julius L., 861
Sagalyn, Lynne B., 888
Sager, Lawrence G., 218, 407, 408, 704, 715, 763, 798
Sagoff, Mark, 179
Saiz, Albert, 19
Sakowicz, J. Celeste, 813
Salama, Jerry J., 378, 455, 460
Salkin, Patricia E., 58, 760, 789
Salsich, Peter W., Jr., 880
Saltman, Alan I., 266
Salzberg, Kenneth, 179, 196
Salzmann, Victoria S., 116
Sandalow, Terrance, 683
Sandel, Michael J., 49, 50
Sander, Richard H., 889
Sandomir, Richard, 543
Sandy, Jonathan, 797
Sanyal, Bishwapriya, 57
Sard, Barbara, 877
Sarratt, W. David, 178
Sass, Erin, 365

Sax, Joseph L., 139, 369, 392, 689, 821
Saxer, Shelley Ross, 560, 740, 839
Sayfie, Nicole S., 282
Schacter, Jane S., 408
Schalow, Thomas, 446
Schelling, Thomas C., 12, 708
Schiffer, Lois J., 275
Schill, Michael H., 45, 754, 762, 864, 866, 877, 878, 890, 891
Schmidt, Benno C., Jr., 693
Schmidt, William E., 854
Schnidman, Frank, 854
Schoenbrod, David, 747
Schoettle, Susan P., 676
Schragger, Richard C., 218
Schuck, Peter H., 769, 770, 775, 867
Schukaske, Jane E., 672
Schulze, William D., 452
Schwab, Stewart J., 543
Schwann, Gregory M., 44
Schwartz, Amy Ellen, 45, 878
Schwartz, Jonathan, 617
Scott, James C., 70
Scott, Paul R., 274
Segerson, Kathleen, 149
Seidel, Stephen R., 444, 454, 458, 507, 811
Seliga, Joseph, 867
Selmi, Daniel P., 404, 405
Selmi, Michael, 702
Seneker, Carl J., 374
Serkin, Christopher, 270, 274, 838, 860
Seymour, Philip A., 808
Shapiro, Jesse M., 2
Shapiro, Perry, 149, 153, 154, 185, 415
Sharman, Frank A., 854
Shattuck, Kathryn, 493
Shaughnessy, Timothy M., 657
Shavell, Steven, 534
Shen, Q., 817
Sheppard, Stephen, 41
Sherman Rolleston, Barbara, 770
Shleifer, Andrei, 309
Short, James L., 15
Shrader-Frechette, Kristin, 757
Shultz, Michael M., 416, 442, 605, 854
Siegan, Bernard H., 85, 154, 566, 607, 611
Siegel, Scott, 786
Siegelman, Peter, 39, 534
Siemon, Charles L., 305, 347, 776
Silverman, Carol J., 583, 606
Silverman, Ronald H., 690, 778
Silversmith, Jed Michael, 266
Simon, Julian L., 549
Simon, William H., 782, 890
Singell, Larry D., 657
Skaburskis, Andrejs, 654
Smith, Barton A., 655
Smith, Bruce, 550
Smith, Henry E., 139, 534
Smith, Jerry L., 656
Smith, R. Marlin, 117, 637
Smith, Richard A., 58
Smothers, Ronald, 780
Snyder, Christopher M., 527
Snyder, Mary Gail, 583
Sohmer, Rebecca R., 9

Soiffer, Bill, 496
Song, Yan, 423, 816
Sonstelie, Jon C., 49
Southworth, Michael, 423, 424
Span, Henry A., 157, 770, 773, 783
Speck, Jeff, 608
Spencer, Marguerite L., 10
Spiegel, Mark M., 887
Spitzer, Matthew L., 860
Spokes, Susan E., 300
Sprung, Marshall S., 650
Squires, Roderick H., 582
Stacey, Robert, 816
Stake, Jeffrey E., 567
St. Amand, Matthew G., 803
Stark, Kirk J., 628
Staszewski, Glen, 407
Statistical Abstract 2003, 613
Stearns, Janet, 879
Steele, Eric H., 295, 307, 608
Stegman, Michael A., 866, 879
Stein, Gregory M., 185, 242, 266
Steiner, Ruth L., 813
Steinman, Lester D., 727
Stephan, Paul B., 178
Sterk, Stewart E., 179, 370, 393, 565, 567, 590, 643, 651, 658
Stern, William J., 884
Sterngold, James, 892
Sternlieb, George, 55, 880
Stevenson, George E., 144
Stewart, Richard B., 392
Stockman, Paul K., 787
Stoebuck, William B., 137, 823
Stone, Katherine E., 808
Storzer, Roman P., 218
Strange, William C., 797
Strong, Ann L., 823
Strossen, Nadine, 231
Stroup, Richard L., 821
Stull, William J., 43
Sullivan, E. Thomas, 123
Sullivan, Edward J., 196, 281, 336, 337
Sunstein, Cass R., 32, 50, 387, 721
Super, David A., 878
Susskind, Lawrence, 58, 746
Sutcliffe, Anthony, 75
Taibi, Anthony D., 892
Talbert, Cecily T., 787
Talen, Emily, 63
Tappendorf, Julie A., 434
Taranto, James, 452
Tarlock, A. Dan, 111, 340, 395, 567, 890
Tax Foundation, Inc., 629
Taylor, Jeffrey M., 351
Taylor, John M., 97, 110, 202, 318
Taylor, Mark, 884
Taylor, Samuel, 185
Taylor, Serge, 392
Taylor, William David, III, 266
Teaford, Jon C., 447, 841
Temkin, Kenneth, 506
Terkel, Thomas J., 584
Thaler, Richard, 32
Theebe, Marcel A. J., 44
Thibodeau, Thomas G., 44, 613

Thomas, David A., 137, 275
Thompson, Barton H., Jr., 178, 179, 280
Thorson, James A., 797
Tibbets, John, 645
Tideman, T. Nicolaus, 654
Tiebout, Charles, 771
Todd, Cynthia, 716
Toll, Seymour I., 75
Tolley, George S., 44, 790
Tomko-DeLuca, Elaine Marie, 753
Tondro, Terry J., 581, 787
Treanor, William Michael, 134, 143, *154*, 280
Trefzger, Joseph W., 178
Tretbar, J. Margaret, 272
Trevarthen, Susan L., 282
Tribe, Laurence H., 158
Trillin, Calvin, 493, 853
Tripp, James B., 167, 378
Tsitsos, William, 219
Tsosie, Rebecca, 753
Tunick, Mark, 179, 196
Turnbull, Geoffrey K., 550
Turner, Margery Austin, 9, 697
Turner, Michael D., 452
Tushnet, Mark, 218
Ulen, Thomas, 40
Underkuffler-Freund, Laura S., 143
Urofsky, Melvin I., 145
U.S. Department of Justice, 309, 560
U.S. Environmental Protection Agency, 795
Utton, Albert E., 39
Vaias, Emily J., 207
Vale, Lawrence J., 864
Van Alstine, Michael P., 185
Vandell, Kerry, 879
Vandervelden, Mark, 393
Van Doren, Peter, 776
Van Noy, Carolyn M., 365
Varadarajan, Deepa, 478
Varady, David P., 697
Varner, Sean Stuart, 376
Venkatesh, Sudhir Alladi, 867
Venturi, Robert, 471
Vickory, Frank A., 281
Vidal, Avis C., 891
Vigdor, Jacob L., 12, 697
Vishny, Robert W., 309
Voss Matthews, Sherrie, 612
Wachter, Susan M., 797, 866, 877
Waddell, James A., 869
Wagman Roisman, Florence, 781
Walden, Michael L., 469
Waldman, Amy, 891
Waldron, Jeremy, 142
Walker, Carole, 416, 637
Wang, Ko, 45
Warley, William, 692
Washburn, Robert M., 165
Waters, M. Dane, 401
Watterson, W.T., 365
Weaver, Clifford L., 117, 294
Weaver, Ronald L., 282
Webber, Melvin, 63
Wegner, Judith Welch, 318, 320, 434
Weicher, John C., 25, 841, 866, 869, 870, 877
Weinberg, Daniel L., 876

Weinberg, Philip, 393
Weinstein, Alan C., 75, 220
Weiser, Jay, 579
Weiss, Marc A., 416
Welfeld, Irving, 875
West, Mark D., 39, 534, 601
Wetzler, Elliot, 460
Wheeler, Linda, 831
White, James R., 43
White, Lawrence J., 870
White, Michelle J., 25
White, Stacey S., 282
Whitman, Dale A., 869, 870, 880
Whitney, Hope, 550
Whyte, William H., 422
Wichelns, Dennis, 581
Wickersham, Jay, 91
Widman, Jeffrey P., 548
Wiggins, Mary Jo, 703
Wiley, John Shepard, Jr., 124
Wilgoren, Jodi, 543
Wilk, Corey J., 832
Williams, E. Douglass, 889
Williams, Norman, Jr., 97, 110, 202, 318, 673, 776, 778, 781
Williams, Robert A., 85
Williams, Stephen F., 39, 470, 821
Wilson, Georjeanna, 797
Wilson, Paul D., 328
Wilson, William Julius, 13, 762
Wiltz, Teresa, 707
Winerip, Michael, 440

Winnick, Louis, 889
Winokur, James L., 580, 606
Winston, Roger D., 588
Winter, Ralph K., 560
Wise, Charles R., 275
Wish, Naomi Bailin, 780, 781
Witten, Jonathan Douglas, 787
Wittman, Donald, 518, 527
Wolf, Michael Allan, 85, 86, 823
Wood, Elizabeth, 862
Wright, Danaya C., 193
WuDunn, Sheryl, 854
Wylie, Jeanie, 837
Wynne, Roger D., 207
Yandle, Bruce, 275
Yang, Tseming, 756
Yen, Rhoda J., 757
Yinger, John, 693
Yost, Nicholas C., 392
Young, Kenneth H., 110, 115, 209, 329
Young, Michael K., 521
Zanner, Kevin J., 729
Zhou, Min, 817
Zick, Timothy, 131
Ziegler, Edward H., 434, 795
Zimbalist, Andrew, 888
Zinn, Matthew D., 266
Zipzer, Dean J., 446
Zitter, Jay M., 200
Zodrow, George R., 656
Zolna, Fredrick, 469

Subject Index

A

Abandoned buildings
  converted to urban homesteads, 581
  disposition of, 581, 823
  as nuisances, 520, 535–536
Abortion clinics, 231–232, 839
Abstention by federal courts, 251–256
Adjudicative actions, 338, 341–352, 358–368. *See also* Administrative actions; Legislative actions
  architectural reviews as, 493–494
  initiatives or referenda used for, 404
  subdivision approvals as, 437
Administrative actions, 284–302, 341–352. *See also* Adjudicative actions
  flexibility devices used in, 461
  judicial review of, 104, 291–292, 294–295
Adult entertainment, 220–232
Aesthetic regulation, 469–505
  adequacy of standards for, 470–472, 489–493, 500–504
  architectural review. *See* Architectural review
  Due Process Clause and, 470–477
  First Amendment and, 478–489
  merits of, 470–472, 476–477, 484
  to preserve historic sites. *See* Historic
  purposes of, 496
  of signs, 469–489
  through nuisance law, 519–520
  vagueness issue in, 470–471, 489–493, 593–596
Affirmative action against racial segregation, 708–709
Age discrimination, 561
Agricultural land
  amount of, 13–15, 548–549
  easements to preserve, 581–582
  as nuisance, 519
  owners of, 14–15
  property taxation of, 544–549
Airports as nuisances, 524
Americans with Disabilities Act, 450–452, 730
Amortization of nonconforming uses. *See* Nonconforming uses, amortization of
Ancient lights, doctrine of, 520

Annexations by municipalities, 688–689
Anti-snob zoning acts, 787, 840
Antitrust laws, application of. *See also* Competition
  to building codes, 459–460
  to land use controls, 119–124
Appearance-of-fairness doctrine, 360–368
Architectural review. *See also* Aesthetic regulation
  by developer, 589
  and freedom of speech, 493
  by government, 489–494, 596
  merits of, 493–494
  by residential community association, 593–596
Associations, residential community. *See* Residential community associations
Attorney fees, 524, 596, 660–661, 675–676
Auctions, reverse, 747

B

Bargaining. *See* Dealmaking between governments and landowners; Neighbors, bargaining among
Beneficence (the converse of nuisance), 539–550
Benefits charges, 627–628, 682–683
Billboards, 119–123, 472–484, 496. *See also* Aesthetic regulation; Signs
Board of Adjustment, 284–289
Bonds
  to assure building quality, 446–447
  for completion of subdivision improvements, 429
  municipal, 842–845, 881–884
  private-activity, 884
  state, 863, 879–880, 886
Bonus zoning, 331–336
Brasilia, 70
Brokers' signs, 483
Brownfields, 550
Builders, 16–20
Building and housing codes, 444–469. *See also* Building permits
  administration of, 447–448, 452–458
  to aid the disabled, 450–452
  alternatives to, 444–447, 468–469

criticism of, 450–452, 458–461, 469
evasions of, 455
federal, 449–452, 460–461
free exercise limitations, 463
history of, 444, 447
housing codes, 448, 465–469
licensing of contractors under, 463–465
for mobile homes, 449–450, 788
rationales for, 444–445, 469
state, 449, 452
statutory innovations, 448–452
and substantive due process, 461–463
varieties of, 447–452
Building permits, 448, 456–458
fees for, 678–679
illegal construction without, 455
moratorium on, 186–192, 797–800
and vesting of rights, 433
wrongly denied, 456–457
wrongly granted, 458
Burden of proof in case involving
exaction from developer, 643–652
exclusionary zoning, 763–768, 783, 785–787
fair housing laws, 727–728
quota program, 806–807
racial discrimination in zoning, 698–704, 705–708
rezoning, 110–111
special exception, 301
Business improvement districts (BIDs), 607, 630, 633–634

C

Calabresi and Melamed, 532–533. *See also* Injunctions
California
housing prices in, 28
Proposition 13 in, 617, 637
Campaign contributions, 366
CC&Rs. *See* Covenants
Certificate of occupancy, 454, 455
Change or mistake doctrine, 317–318
Chain stores, 117–118
Cities. *See* Local governments
City size and form, theory of, 789–796
Civic republicanism
compared to public choice theory, 47–50
and neighbors' consent procedure, 400
and residential community associations, 605–606
and zoning, 295–296
Civil liberties. *See also* First Amendment; Voting rights
freedom of travel, 763
right of privacy, 231–232
Civil rights acts. *See* Fair housing laws
Clean Water Act, 508–509
Cluster zoning, 329–331, 335
Coase Theorem, 34–39. *See also* Economics
Coastal Zone Management Act, 508
Columbus, Indiana, 550
Coming to the
hardship, in variance cases, 293
LULU, 757
nuisance, 525–527
taking, 165, 185, 643
Commercial speech. *See* Signs

Commercial uses
exclusion of, 117–124
external effects of, 43–44
Common interest communities. *See* Residential community associations
Community development banks, 892
Community Development Block Grants, 841–842, 888, 891
Community development corporations (CDCs), 890–892
Compensation. *See* Just Compensation Clause
Compensation statutes, 274–282, 860
Competition. *See also* Antitrust laws
among states, 881–884
covenants restraining, 562, 566–567
effects of growth controls on, 796–797
impaired by building regulation, 458–465
zoning to suppress, 112–124
Comprehensive plans, 58–65. *See also* Official maps; Planning
adequacy of, 59
amendments to, 340–341, 350–351, 803–804
consistency with, 58–59, 312–313, 336–341, 346–347
criticism of, 65–71
elements of, 59–64
housing elements of, 783–786
names for, 50
of neighboring government, 734–735
politics of, 65
samples of, 62–65
state requirement of, 58–59, 783–786, 802, 812–813
for urban renewal areas, 841
Conditional uses. *See* Special exceptions
Conflict of interest, 360–368
Consent of neighbors required, 231, 393–400
Conservation servitudes, 581–582
Consistency with comprehensive plan, 58–59, 312–313, 336–341, 346–347
Construction statistics, 26–28
Contract zoning, 318–329
Corruption of public officials administering
building codes, 454
housing subsidies, 865, 875–876
zoning, 304, 308–309, 320, 360–368
Counties, 731–733, 738–739, 750–754. *See also* Local governments
Covenants, 550–607. *See also* Residential community associations
affirmative, 568, 582
amendments to, 589, 598–603
changed conditions as affecting, 573–579
city enforcement of, 566
compared to zoning, 611–613
conservation servitudes, 581–582
declaration of, 569–571
"General Plan" doctrine, 571–572
history of, 550, 566–567
intended to run with the land, 564
interpretation of, 553
merits of, 550–552, 580
notice of, 565
privity-of-estate requirement, 566–568
racially restrictive, 559–561
remedies for breach of, 553–554, 576–579

in restraint of trade, 562, 566–567
restricting age and household composition, 561
restricting architectural designs, 593–596
restricting religion, 562
restricting speech, 562
running of, 551–552, 563–569
statutes addressing obsolete, 579
statutes limiting lives of, 576–580
termination of, 572–580
touch-and-concern requirement, 566–567, 580
validity of, 553–562

D

Damages. *See* Remedies of landowners
Davis-Bacon Act, 19–20
Dealmaking between governments and landowners,
        283–284, 303–309, 320–321. *See also*
        Neighbors, bargaining among; Zoning
        amendments
    evolution of, 86–90
    over proposed subdivision, 435–438
Declaration of covenants, 569–571
Dedication of land by developer, 429–430, 569–570.
        See also Exactions from developers
"Deemed approved" statutes, 429, 507–508
Defeasible fees, compared to covenants, 554
Delays, regulatory, 505–509
Deregulation of land use, advocates of, 607–614
Developers, 18–19, 73–74. *See also* Landowners
    with bad track records, 437–438
    exactions from. *See* Exactions from developers
    governments as, 861–867, 886–887
    nonprofit, 875, 890–892
    relations of, with homebuyers, 585–587
Development agreements, 209, 432–433
Development rights, government purchase of,
        585–587
Dillon's Rule, 29
Direct democracy. *See* Initiatives and referenda
Disabilities, people with
    building codes to aid, 450–452
    discrimination against, 716–730
Discount rates, 821
Discrimination. *See also* Equal Protection Clause;
        Exclusionary zoning; Fair housing laws
    by age, 561
    initiative or referendum as means of, 408
    against people with disabilities, 716–730
    against the poor, 522–524, 709–710, 754–788
    racial. *See* Racial discrimination
    by religion, 562
    in siting of facilities, 754–760
    against unconventional households, 561, 710–716
    against users of housing vouchers, 876
    zoning as means of, 691–730
Distributive justice, 41, 144, 628
Due Process Clause. *See also* Procedural, due process
    architectural review as violation of, 489–493
    building code as violation of, 461–463
    exclusionary zoning as violation of, 782–783
    historic districting as violation of, 500–504
    housing code as violation of, 465–468
    landowners' rights under, 73–119, 352–368,
        393–409, 465–468

legitimate governmental objective required by,
        114–117
    moratorium as violation of, 797–803
    neighbors' rights under, 352–368
    quota as violation of, 804–813
    racial zoning as violation of, 692–693
    sign regulations as violation of, 470–477
    as source of regional obligations, 734–739, 747–748
    Takings Clause, compared to, 102–103, 142,
        196–197, 640n
    text of, 94
    zoning as violation of, 73–119
Duress, exaction given under, 674–675

E

Earthquake safety, 452
Easements, 519, 551–552, 581–582. *See also*
        Covenants
    conservation, 580–582
    historic-preservation, 497–498, 580–582
    in shopping centers, 584
Economic development programs, 842–845, 880–889
    aid to poor neighborhoods, 888–889
    enterprise and empowerment zones, 888–889
Economics. *See also* Externalities
    of city form, 789–796
    of city size, 790
    definitions of efficiency in, 96
    of eminent domain, 754
    of exactions and land taxes, 652–658
    of growth management, 795–797, 817–818
    of housing subsidies, 877–878
    of just compensation, 859–861
    of land use conflicts, 32–45
    of property taxation, 652–658
    of public finance. *See* Public finance, theory of
    of Takings Clause, 145–154
    of urban growth boundaries, 814, 817–818
Education. *See* Schools
Eminent domain, 823–864
    conservation easements acquired by, 580–581
    by higher-level government, 754
    history of, 823–824
    just compensation issue. *See* Just Compensation
        Clause
    justifications for, 823, 854
    procedure for, 861
    public use issue. *See* Public Use Clause
    takings issue. *See* Takings Clause
Empowerment zones, 888–889
Energy conservation, 450
Engineers, civil, 412, 420–421
Enterprise zones, 888–889
Environmental impact statements, 368–393
    adequacy of, 380–387
    conditioned negative declarations, 378–380
    criticism of, 391–393
    justifications for, 369–370
    weight to be given to, 387–391
    when required, 370–380, 426
Environmental justice, 754–760

Equal Protection Clause. *See also* Discrimination
  applied to discriminatory zoning, 697–721
  and delivery of municipal services, 679–683
  and exactions from developers, 658–659
  and exclusionary zoning, 762–763
  landowners' rights under, 125, 126–129, 156–157,
      504
  moratorium as violation of, 803
  and siting of facilities, 755
  state action, requirement of, 559–561, 591
  Takings Clause, compared to, 156–157, 640n
  text of, 94
  and variances, 302
Equitable servitudes, 563–565. *See also* Covenants
Equity, horizontal and vertical, 628. *See also*
      Distributive justice
Estoppel. *See also* Vested rights of landowners
  as bar to enforcing covenant, 574
  of government, 208
  of nuisance plaintiffs, 525–526
Euclid, Ohio, 76–92
Exactions from developers, 634–679
  burden of proof in case involving, 643–652
  compared to exclusionary zoning, 650
  compared to reverse auctions, 747
  compared to special assessments, 634–635
  defenses of local governments, 674–675
  discriminatory imposition, 658–659
  economics of, 652–658
  effect of prospect of, on eminent domain award,
      861
  Equal Protection Clause and, 658–659
  given under duress, 674–675
  history of, 637
  impact fees, 667–674
  incidence of, 652–658
  for inclusionary housing units. *See* Inclusionary
      zoning
  merits of, 661–663, 671–674, 658
  monetary exactions, 663–674
  municipal evasion of legal limits, 651
  off-site, 662–663
  on-site, 661–662
  physical exactions, 659–663
  politics of, 657–658
  remedies for illegal, 674–676
  for schools, 658–659, 671
  statutes limiting, 663–667
  Supreme Court review of, 638–652
  types of, 635–637
  as violations of Takings Clause, 637–678
Exclusionary zoning, 760–788. *See also*
      Discrimination; Inclusionary zoning
  alleged presence of, in *Euclid*, 81–84
  builder's remedy in case of, 773–776, 782–783
  compared to exactions from developers, 650
  environmental justifications for, 788
  motivations for, 40, 763–770
  phasing controls as method of, 811
  regional contribution agreements, 776–779
  statutes addressing, 776–788
  through nuisance law, 522–524
Exhaustion of remedies in zoning litigation, 85–86,
      715
  in federal courts, 234–251
"Exit," 658

Externalities
  bounties to internalize, 539–550
  evidence of, 41–45, 878
  extramunicipal, 731–818
  fees to internalize, 538–539
  nuisance law to internalize. *See* Nuisance
  of substandard housing, 878
  theory of, 34–45, 626

F

Fair Housing Act, 776–778, 780–782
Fair housing laws. *See also* Discrimination; Racial
      discrimination
  applied to discriminatory zoning, 705–710,
      715–730
  applied to siting of facilities, 755
  in New Jersey, 776–782
Fair share
  of low- and moderate-income housing, 763–788
  of LULUs, 758–760
Families. *See* Household composition, controls on
Federal
  aid to innovators, 889–892
  aid to poor neighborhoods and cities, 888–889
  building codes, 450–452, 449–450
  courts. *See* Federal courts
  Greenbelt towns, 862
  homebuilding, 861–862
  housing subsidies. *See* Housing subsidy programs
  income taxation. *See* Federal income taxation
  land holdings, 754, 820–823
  Model Cities program, 889
  revenue sharing programs, 841–842
  urban renewal program. *See* Urban renewal
Federal courts
  abstention by, 251–256
  jurisdiction of, in takings cases, 233–240
  preclusion of claims in, 245–251, 254
  removal of cases to, 245
  ripeness of landowner claims in, 234–251
  role of, in discriminatory zoning cases, 704–705
  role of, in eminent domain cases, 824–832
  role of, in exaction cases, 638–652
  role of, in exclusionary zoning cases, 782
  role of, in special assessment cases, 624
  role of, in zoning cases, 96–104, 233–256
Federal Housing Administration (FHA), 576, 612,
      869–870, 890
Federal income taxation
  breaks for homeowners, 868–869
  caps on housing bonds, 880
  credits for low-income housing, 878–879
  of land sales, 23–24
  of owners of historic landmarks, 497, 549
  as policy instrument, 549
  of private-activity bonds, 884
  and residential community associations, 605
  and special assessments, 630
Fees as land use controls, 538–539
Fences, 472, 520–521, 541
Fertility rates, 1–2
FHA (Federal Housing Administration), 576, 612,
      869–870, 890

Filtering in housing markets, 6, 9, 619, 772–773
Financing
　of community development, 890–892
　of developers, 20–24
　of house purchasers, 868–870
　liability for house defects of those engaged in,
　　445–446
　of local governments, 615–679
　provided by governments, 868–892
Findings requirements, 291–292, 302
First Amendment, 209–231
　as bar to eminent domain, 839
　Due Process Clause, compared to, 103
　freedom of speech, 220–231, 474, 478–489, 493,
　　729
Free Exercise Clause, 209–220, 498–500, 838–839
Fiscal-impact analysis, 617–619
Fiscal motives of local governments, 125–126,
　　615–619, 654–658, 689–690. *See also*
　　Legislative motivation; Local governments,
　　permissible goals of
　as basis for exclusionary zoning, 40, 763–771
　to phase growth, 808–811
　to prevent sprawl, 790–796
　in rejecting proposed subdivision, 438
Floating zones, 331
Freedom of travel, 763

G

Gated communities, 583, 606
Gautreaux program, 867
General plans. *See* Comprehensive plans
Gentrification of central cities, 9–10, 505
George, Henry, 15, 652–657, 678
Givings, 273, 281, 837
Government. *See* Federal; Landowners, governments
　　as; Local governments; Public facilities; State
Greenbelt towns, federal, 862
Group homes
　covenants restricting, 561, 729
　siting of, 757
　zoning restricting, 296–299, 716–730
Growth management, 788–818. *See also*
　　Exclusionary zoning
　adequacy of public facilities programs, 812–813
　by ballot box, 339, 797–800, 803–804
　cap on total housing units, 807–808
　economic effects of, 796–797, 817–818
　justifications for, 789–797
　moratoria, 186–192, 797–803
　of nonresidential uses, 807–808
　phasing controls, 808–813
　quota programs, 804–808
　rate of growth caps, 807–808
　state programs of, 788–789, 812–813
　techniques of, 789

H

Hammurabi, Code of, 444, 446
Handicapped. *See* Disabilities, people with
Highway Beautification Act, 475, 478, 488

Historic
　building interiors, preservation of, 498
　districts, preservation of, 500–505
　landmarks, preservation of, 158–167, 494–500,
　　549, 580–582
　properties, taxation of, 497, 549
Holdouts from land assemblages, 845–854
Homebuilders, 16–19
Homeless, facilities for the
　as nuisances, 523
　siting of, 760
　variances for, 293
Homeowners associations. *See* Residential
　　community associations
HOME program, 875
Home rule, 29–30, 465, 509
Homestead Act of 1862, 820
Homevoter Hypothesis, 46–47
Household composition, controls on, 128, 561,
　　710–730
Housing, 16–29
　affordable. *See* Exclusionary zoning; Inclusionary
　　zoning
　codes, 448, 465–469
　demand for, 793–794
　filtering of, 6, 9, 619, 772–773
　industry, 16–24
　linkage program. *See* Inclusionary zoning
　manufactured. *See* Mobile homes
　multifamily. *See* Multifamily housing
　owners of, 25–26
　prices. *See* Housing prices
　production of, 16–20, 26–27
　quality of, 25–26
　stock of, 24–26
　stock of, effect of vouchers on, 877
　subsidies. *See* Housing subsidy programs
Housing prices, 27–29
　in California, 27–28
　effects of growth controls on, 796–797, 816–818
　effects of land use controls on, 28
　effects of neighboring uses on, 41–45
　in Houston, 27–28, 613–614
　race and, 12–13
Housing subsidy programs, 862–880
　bounties for localities that use, 690
　compared to cash transfers, 776, 878
　effects of projects on neighbors, 45
　federal tax credits, 878–879
　during New Deal, 862
　for privately owned projects, 870–872, 875,
　　878–879
　production in New Jersey under, 780–781
　public housing, 862–867
　state and local, 879–880
　types of, 870–872
　vouchers, 866–867, 870–878
Houston, absence of zoning in, 28, 611–614
HOW program, 446–447

I

Immunities, governmental
　from another government's zoning, 750–754
　in nuisance cases, 524

Immunities, of private parties, 752–753
Impact fees, 635–637, 656–657, 667–671, 675–677.
        See also Exactions from developers
Incentive zoning, 331–336
Inclusionary zoning, 335, 635–636, 671–674,
        786–787, 818. *See also* Exclusionary zoning
    in California, 672
    in New Jersey, 773–782
Information, availability of
    to planners, 65–69
    to voters, 407
Initiatives and referenda, 401–409
    criticism of, 405–409
    growth management by, 339, 797–800, 803–804
Injunctions. *See also* Remedies of landowners
    to enforce covenants, 553–554, 576–578, 596
    in nuisance cases, 528–535
Interim zoning, 800–801

J

Jacobs, Jane, 51–52, 70, 841
Judicial actions. *See* Adjudicative actions
Jurisdiction of federal courts, 233–240. *See also*
        Federal courts
Jury, role of, 274
Just Compensation Clause, 166–167, 168, 256–274,
        754, 838, 855–861
    text of, 94

K

Kaldor-Hicks test for efficiency, 96

L

Land
    agricultural. *See* Agricultural land
    assembly, 823–861
    banking, 823
    ownership of. *See* Landowners
    readjustment, 607, 854
    trusts, 581–582
    uses of, 13–15
Landowners, 14–15, 73–74, 304. *See also* Developers
    constitutional rights of, 73–282
    governments as, 15, 820–823, 888
    remedies of. *See* Remedies of landowners
    statutory rights of, 274–282
Legislative actions, 284–286, 300–303, 341–352, 358,
        364–368. *See also* Adjudicative actions;
        Administrative actions
Legislative motivation, 114–117, 316, 701–702. *See
        also* Fiscal motives of local governments;
        Local governments, permissible goals of
L'Enfant plan for Washington, D.C., 412
Levittown, New York, 10, 496
Licensing of contractors, 463–465
Linkage program to provide housing. *See*
        Inclusionary zoning

Local governments
    activities of, as nuisances, 524
    conceptions of, 47–50
    counties. *See* Counties
    delegation by, 286
    discrimination by. *See* Discrimination
    duties of, to provide services, 679–689
    economic development programs of, 842–845,
        880–888
    employees of, 615–616
    expenditures of, 616
    finances of, 615–679
    fiscal motives of. *See* Fiscal motives of local
        governments
    functions of, 625–627
    immunities of, from zoning, 750–754
    as landowners, 820–823, 888
    liability of, for lax code enforcement, 457–458
    liability of, to outsiders, 735, 740
    number of, 29
    organization of, 284–289
    permissible goals of, 114–117, 125–126, 316,
        470–474, 477, 763–770
    politics of. *See* Politics of, local governments. *See
        also* Public choice theory
    powers of, 29–30, 465, 801–802
    regional obligations of, 731–818
    standing of, to sue neighboring government,
        738–739
Local Initiatives Support Corp. (LISC), 879, 891
Logue, Edward, 862–863
Low- and moderate-income housing. *See*
        Exclusionary zoning; Housing subsidy
        programs; Inclusionary zoning
Low-Income Housing Tax Credits, 878–879, 891
LULUs (locally undesirable land uses), 731–733,
        733–760
    discrimination in siting of, 754–760

M

Manufactured housing. *See* Mobile homes
Master plans. *See* Comprehensive plans
Military facilities, obsolete, 822
Mill Acts, 832
Mitigation of damages by takings claimant, 274
Mobile homes, 17, 24, 27, 449–450
    exclusion of, 197–199, 764, 775, 783–785, 788
Model Cities program, 889
Moral hazard, 152–153, 415
Moratoria, 186–193, 797–803, 811–812
Mortgage assistance programs, 868–870
Moving to Opportunity Demonstration Program, 762,
        770, 877
Muddling through, 67
Multifamily housing. *See also* Housing
    exclusion of, 763–769, 783, 786–787
    external effects of, 45
Municipalities. *See* Local governments

N

National Environmental Policy Act (NEPA),
        368–370, 379–380, 386–393

Neighborhoods
    definitions of, 760
    evolution of, 9, 12–13
    government aid to, 881, 888–889
Neighbors. *See also* Neighbors' rights
    bargaining among, 34–41, 144, 294, 399, 532–534,
        539–543, 572–573, 607–613
    consent required of, 231, 393–400
    interests of, 73–74, 304
    liability of, for discriminatory lawsuits, 729
    norms among. *See* Norms among neighbors
Neighbors' rights, 283–409. *See also* Neighbors
    under building codes, 458
    in exaction cases, 642, 662
    to consent to proposed land use, 231, 393–400
    to enforce public regulations, 93
    to protest group home, 729
    against subdivider of nearby land, 438–441
New Deal housing programs, 862–864, 869
New Markets Tax Credits, 891–892
New towns, 584, 890
New Urbanism, 49, 422–424, 583, 589, 608,
        793–794, 890
NIMBY (Not In My Backyard). *See* LULUs
Nonconforming uses, 197–202, 230–231, 290, 749.
        See also Vested rights of landowners
    amortization of, 197–201, 230, 475–478
    zoning enforcement to eliminate, 92–94
Nonconvexities, 40
Nonprofit developers, 875, 877, 890–892
Norms among neighbors, 31, 39, 471, 494, 511, 541
Northwest Ordinances, 822
Notice, rights to receive
    developer's, 405
    neighboring government's, 734, 738
    neighbors', 358–359
    when moratorium is adopted, 802
Nuisance, 511–539
    aesthetic, 519–520
    anticipatory, 535
    coming to the, 525–526
    comparative, 528
    defenses to, 525–528
    government activity as, 524
    harm/benefit distinction in, 516–518, 538–539
    housing as, 520, 522–524, 535–536
    law, history of, 512, 538
    law, limitations of, 395, 538, 607–608
    natural condition as, 519
    negligence compared to, 517–518
    people as, 522–524
    prescriptive, 528
    prima facie case for, 512–524
    public, 524, 536–538
    relevance to takings issue, 138–140, 169–179, 200,
        518
    remedies for, 528–536
    solar, 39, 521–522
    without physical invasion, 519–524
    zoning's effect on law of, 528, 538

O

Occupancy controls. *See* Household composition,
        controls on

Official maps, 411–416, 610. *See also*
        Comprehensive plans
Oregon Land Conservation & Development
        Commission (LCDC), 785–786, 813–818

P

Pareto principle, 96
Parks
    city land-area devoted to, 15
    exactions for, 671. *See also* Exactions from
        developers
    external effects of, 44–45
Party walls, 539–541
Planned-unit development (PUD), 92, 329–331
Planners. *See* Planning profession
Planning, 50–71. *See also* Comprehensive plans;
        Official maps; Planning profession
    definitions of, 51, 53
    land use in absence of, 607–614
    local resistance to, 58–59, 303
    moratorium to allow for, 186–192, 800–801, 803
    skeptics of, 65–71
    state, 785–786, 813–818
    subsidies for, 52, 59
    theory of, 51–55
    transportation, 52, 59
Planning Commission, 285–286
Planning profession, 51–57, 284–285
    incentives of, 69
    politicization of, 55–57
    rivalry of, with engineering profession, 421
Politics of. *See also* Public choice theory
    billboards, 119–123, 478, 484
    building codes, 446–447, 458–461
    comprehensive plans, 65, 69–71
    exactions from developers, 637–638, 658
    initiatives and referenda, 401–409
    intermunicipal disputes, 733–734
    local governments, 24, 37, 46–50, 124, 303–309,
        348–349, 360–366
    neighborhood voting, 400
    property rights protection acts, 281–282
    residential community associations, 590–606
    subdivider's timing, 433–434
    zoning. *See* Politics of, local governments
Population
    metropolitan trends in, 1–9
    national trends in, 1–2
Pornography, 220–231
Poverty. *See also* Housing subsidy programs
    discrimination on basis of, 522–524, 709–710,
        754–760
    in public housing projects, 864, 866
    stricken neighborhoods, aid to, 888–889
Preemption
    federal, 449–450, 562, 746
    by state and federal billboard acts, 475, 478
    by state and federal building codes, 449–452
    by state subdivision acts, 442
    by states, to allow LULUs, 732, 740–748
    by states, to reduce regulatory delay, 507–508
Presumption of constitutionality, 110, 783
Prisoners' Dilemma, 37n, 845
Privacy, right of, 231–232

Procedural. *See also* Due Process Clause
    due process, 319–320, 352–368, 393–409, 437, 458
    errors in rezoning, 316
Products liability. *See* Warranties of fitness of
Property rights protection statutes, 274–282
Property taxation
    of agricultural lands, 544–549
    amount of revenue from, 617
    economics of, 652–658
    effects of, on residential community associations, 605
    exemptions for economic development, 885
    exemptions to subsidize housing, 863, 880
    as policy instrument, 544–550
    regional pooling of revenues from, 689–690
    use of, to finance urban renewal, 841–845
Proposition 13, California's, 617, 637
Public choice theory, 47–50, 348–349. *See also* Civic
        republicanism; Politics of
    applied to neighbors' consent procedure, 400
    applied to plebiscites, 406–408
    applied to public use issue, 838–840
    applied to Takings Clause, 155–158
    applied to zoning, 34–37, 303–309, 348–349
    compared to civic republicanism, 47–50
Public facilities. *See also* Exactions from developers
    costs of new. *See* Urban sprawl
    limited by urban growth boundary, 813–817
    programs to ensure adequacy of, 812–813
    siting of, 750–754
Public finance, theory of, 49, 625–629, 819–820, 862, 887–888
Public goods. *See* Public finance, theory of
Public housing, 862–867, 870–874. *See also* Housing
        subsidy programs
    privatization of, 866–867, 872–874
    project, as nuisance, 523
Public lands. *See* Landowners, governments as
Public-private partnerships, 880–888
Public purpose, needed for municipal outlay, 842–845, 880–884
Public Use Clause, 824–840, 854, 862–864
    relative state court activism, 831–40
    relative federal court deference, 824–832
Public utilities. *See* Utilities
PUD (planned-unit development), 92, 329–331
Punitive damages
    in exaction cases, 660–661, 676
    in nuisance cases, 535

Q

Quasi-judicial. *See* Adjudicative actions
Quorum of zoning body, 368
Quota
    on commercial uses, 117
    to manage growth, 803–808

R

Racial discrimination. *See also* Discrimination;
        Segregation, residential, by race
    covenants as means of, 559–561
    in delivery of municipal services, 679–683
    and Euclid ordinance, 84–85

fair housing laws and. *See* Fair housing laws
    in housing markets, 11–13, 559–561, 692–697
    nuisance law as means of, 522
    in siting of facilities, 754–760
    zoning as means of, 84–85, 692–709, 763–770
Referendum. *See* Initiatives and referenda
Regional. *See also* State
    contribution agreements, 776–779
    facilities. *See* LULUs
    governments, 740
    growth, municipal duties to accommodate, 788–818
    obligations of local governments, 731–818
    welfare, 736n, 799–800, 806
Regulatory delays, 505–509
Regulatory takings. *See* Takings Clause
Religious institutions
    consent of, to liquor license, 399
    external effects of, 44
    First Amendment protection of, 209–220, 498–500, 839
    property taxation of, 549
    statutory protections of, 94, 210–220, 499–500
    vulnerability of, to eminent domain, 839
Religious Land Use and Institutionalized Persons Act
        (RLUIPA), 210–220, 463, 500, 839
Remedies of landowners. *See also* Injunctions
    enforcing covenants, 553–554, 576–579
    against governments, 256–274. *See also* Just
        Compensation Clause
    in nuisance cases, 528–536
Residential community associations, 582–607. *See
        also* Covenants
    amendments to declarations of, 598–603
    architectural review by, 589, 591, 593–596
    assessments by, 583, 587–588, 601–605
    common areas of, 593, 600–601
    compared to municipalities, 591, 596, 606
    dissolution of, 601
    federal income taxation and, 605
    finances of, 601–605
    functions and structure of, 582–584
    gated, 583, 606
    history of, 583–584
    judicial review of, 590–605
    merits of, 605–606
    powers and duties of developers of, 585–589
    property taxation and, 605
    retrofitted, 607
    rules of, changes in, 597
    voting rights in, 587–588, 590–591
Restitution for conferral of benefits, 539–544
Revenue sharing programs, 841–842
"Right to Farm" statutes, 519
Ripeness of claims
    in federal courts, 234–251
    against mapped street, 415
    against plan amendment, 341
    in state courts, 243–244, 281
RLUIPA (Religious Land Use and Institutionalized
        Persons Act), 210–220, 463, 500, 839
Roads. *See* Streets

S

Schools
  expenditures on, 615–617
  external effects of, 44
  fiscal impacts of, 617–619, 690
  impact fees for, 669–671
  land use lawsuits brought by, 739–740
  racial segregation and, 693–697
Search warrant, 455
Section 8
  housing assistance, 870–878
  project, as nuisance, 523
Section 236 housing projects, 863, 870, 874–875. *See also* Housing subsidy programs
Section 1983
  landowners' rights under, 233–251
  text of, 233
Segregation, residential. *See also* Discrimination; Exclusionary zoning; Racial discrimination
  consequences of, 760–763
  housing vouchers to combat, 866–867, 876–877
  by race, 11–13, 692–697, 706–709, 780–781
  by social class, 9–10, 768–771
Servitudes. *See* Covenants
Sherman Act. *See* Antitrust laws
Shopping centers
  servitudes in, 584
  suppression of suburban, 117
Signs, 470–489. *See also* Aesthetic regulation
  amortization of, 475–478
  anticompetitive exclusion of, 119–123
  brokers', 483
  commercial, 469–484
  covenants restricting, 562
  historic, 496
  political, 484–489
  state regulation of, 484
Simplification of regulatory maze, 505–509
Site plan reviews, 99–102, 202–206, 411, 417–418, 434, 438
Siting of regional facilities. *See* LULUs
Social capital, 496, 605–606
Solar rights, 39, 521–522
Sovereign immunity. *See* Immunities, governmental
Special assessments, 619–634
  compared to exactions from developers, 634–635
  efficiency justification for, 628
  exemptions from, 634
  federal income taxation and, 630
  formulas for, 619–622
  history of, 629–630
  inconsistent municipal use of, 622–623
  "local improvement" needed for, 622
  popularity of, 629–630
  roles of state and federal courts, 624
  Takings Clause and, 619–624
Special exceptions (conditional uses), 296–303, 728
  compared to variances, 299
  SZEA authorization of, 284
Spite fences, 520–521
Spontaneous order, 31–40, 68–71, 607–614
Spot zoning, 309–317, 338, 726
Sprawl. *See* Urban sprawl

Standard State Zoning Enabling Act (SZEA), 29, 74–76, 81, 91–92, 114, 284–285, 289, 320, 336, 400, 416, 890
Standing to sue
  competitor's, 119
  local government's, 739
  of plaintiff alleging racial discrimination in zoning, 703–704
State. *See also* Regional
  action, 560, 591
  building code, 449–450
  constitutions, 544–546, 763–781, 836–837, 842–845, 881–884
  courts, role of, in zoning cases, 104–112. *See also* Federal courts, role of
  delegations of power to local governments, 29–30
  growth management programs, 812–813
  homebuilding, 862
  housing subsidy programs, 879–880
  land holdings, 822
  planning goals, in Oregon, 785–786, 813–818
  preemption by. *See* Preemption
  zoning, 782
Statute of Frauds, 552, 553
Statute of limitations applicable to suit for defective construction, 446
Streets
  city land-area devoted to, 15
  design standards for, 418–430
  eminent domain awards in event of widening of, 857–861
  exactions for, 662–663
  layouts of, 411–416, 421–428
  naming of, 429
Subdivided Lands Act, 430–431, 442
Subdividers, liability of
  to lot purchasers, 444
  to neighbors, 440–441
Subdivision maps
  examples of, 424–428
  vesting of, 430–435
Subdivision regulations, 411–444
  administration of, 424–430, 435–438
  attempts to evade, 442–444
  bonds required under, 429
  exactions under. *See* Exactions from developers
  exemptions from, 441–444
  interest of neighboring governments in, 738
  neighbors' rights under, 438–441
  rationales for, 416–417
  remedies of developers, 438
  standards imposed by, 416–424
  statutes authorizing, 416–418
  waiver of standards, 437
Subsidies
  for beneficial uses, 539–550
  for economic development, 880–889
  for housing. *See* Housing subsidy programs
  to induce urban innovations, 889–892
  for local planning, 52, 59
  for urban renewal. *See* Urban renewal
Suburbanization. *See also* Urban sprawl
  causes of, 6–10, 795–796
  process of, 9, 13–15, 24
  rate of, 6–10, 13–15
Suburban sprawl. *See* Suburbanization; Urban sprawl

Sunshine laws, 360
SZEA. *See* Standard State Zoning Enabling Act

T

Takings Clause, 134–209
adequate public facilities requirements, applied to, 811
balancing test, 143, 158–164, 179, 477
coming-to defense, 165, 180–185, 643
denominator issue, 145, 185–193, 280–281
diminution-in-value test, 163–164
Due Process Clause, compared to, 102–103, 142, 193–197, 640n
economics of, 145–154
Equal Protection Clause, compared to, 156–157, 640n, 658–659
exactions from developers as violation of, 637–678
harm/benefit distinction, 138–139, 518
historic landmarking as violation of, 158–167, 498–504
history of, 154–156
justifications for, 145–158
mapping of street as violation of, 411–415
means-end analysis, relevance of, 193–197
money, applicability to, 143, 196, 663–674
moratorium as violation of, 185–193, 808
nuisance exception, 138–140, 169–179, 200, 518
phasing controls as violation of, 808–811
physical appropriations, applied to, 134–138, 157, 164, 167–169, 537–538
public choice theories of, 155–158
regulatory actions, applied to, 136–209, 652
remedies available under. *See* Just Compensation Clause
special assessments as violations of, 619–624
state constitutional, 134–136, 836–837
taxation, applied to, 143, 196, 663–674
temporary regulation as violation of, 185–193, 258–274
text of, 94, 824, 836–837
total elimination of value, applied to case involving, 169–179
vested rights under. *See* Vested rights of landowners
Takings impact assessments, 274–282
Takings legislation, 274–282
Taxation
federal income. *See* Federal income taxation
of land improvements, 652–658, 678–679
as policy instrument, 544–549
property. *See* Property taxation
revenues of local governments, 616–619
of signs, 483–484
as taking, 143
theories of, 625–628, 628–629, 652–658
Tax-increment-financed urban renewal, 842–845
Taylor Grazing Act, 820
TDRs. *See* Transferable development rights
Television signals, reception of, 562, 596
Tiebout Hypothesis, 749, 771, 790
Trademarks, regulation of, on signs, 482–483
Transcripts of hearings, 359–360
Transferable development rights (TDRs), 92, 165–167, 243
Travel, right to, 763
Tucker Act, 233, 239

U

Uniform Relocation and Real Property Acquisition Policies Act of 1970, 860
Unions, 19–20, 460
Urban growth boundaries, 786, 813–818
Urban homesteading, 581
Urban renewal, 581, 826, 830–831, 840–845, 861–862
programs that supplanted, 840–845, 888–892
Urban sprawl, 790–796. *See also* Suburbanization
affected by urban growth boundary, 813–818
causes of, 795–796
exactions and, 662–663
Utilities
duties of, to expand capacity, 686–687
duties of, to provide services, 683–689
energy-saving programs of, 450
exactions for, 662–663
extraterritorial service by, 688–689
regulation of, 683
variances for, 292

V

Vagueness of aesthetic standards, 470–471, 489–493, 593–596. *See also* Due Process Clause
Variances, 284–296
area, 289–291
compared to special exceptions, 299
local legislative body's review of, 286
to moratoria, 803
SZEA authorization of, 284–285
use, 286–290
Vested rights of landowners. *See also* Estoppel; Nonconforming uses; Takings Clause
to build, 202–209, 433–434, 457
to ignore moratorium, 803
to ignore zoning amendment, 202–209
to maintain subcode conditions, 465–469, 493
to subdivide, 430–435
Voting rights
in business improvement districts, 634
of outsiders, 30
in residential community associations, 587–588, 590–591
when neighbors' consent is required, 400
Vouchers, housing, 866–867, 870–878

W

Warranties of fitness of
lots, 444
new housing, 445–447
Witnesses
at public hearings, 353–358
in zoning litigation, 111

Z

Zoning, 73–409, 691–788. *See also* Standard State Zoning Enabling Act (SZEA)

absence of, 607–614
administration of, 283–289
amendments. *See* Zoning amendments
Board of Adjustment, 284–289
bonus, 331–336
civic republicanism and, 295–296
cluster, 329–331, 335
compared to covenants, 611–613
with compensation, 580–582
comprehensive plan, relationship of, to, 75–76,
    336–341
conditional, 322–329
constitutionality of, in principle, 76–86
contract, 318–329
corrupt, 304, 308–309, 320
cumulative, 90
discriminatory. *See* Discrimination; Racial
    discrimination
effect of, on eminent domain award, 857–861
enforcement of, 92–94
Euclidian, 76–92
exclusionary. *See* Exclusionary zoning
expulsive, 702–703
for fiscal purposes. *See* Fiscal motives of local
    governments
flexibility devices used in, 91–92, 283–284,
    294–302
floating, 331
of government-owned land, 750–754
history of, 74–92, 608–612
incentive, 332–336
inclusionary. *See* Inclusionary zoning
inspections, 93

interim, 800–803
map, example of, 87
merits of, 34–41, 294–296, 607–614
minimum lot size, 788. *See also* Exclusionary
    zoning
nonconforming uses arising under. *See*
    Nonconforming uses
noncumulative, 90–91
ordinance, modern, 86–94
overlay, 91–92
permissible goals in, 114–117, 125–126. *See also*
    Local governments, permissible goals of
politics of. *See* Politics of, local governments
procedural errors in, 316
public choice theory and, 34–36, 303–308,
    348–349
PUD allowed by. *See* Planned-unit development
    (PUD)
racial, 692–693. *See also* Racial discrimination
special exceptions to. *See* Special exceptions
    (conditional uses)
spot, 309–317, 338, 726
state, 782
that limits competition, 112–124
totally prohibiting certain uses, 747–749
variances. *See* Variances
wait-and-see, 283–284, 347–348. *See also*
    Dealmaking between governments and
    landowners
Zoning amendments, 283–285. *See also* Dealmaking
    between governments and landowners
initiatives or referenda used for, 401–409
judicial review of, 125–233, 302–352

.